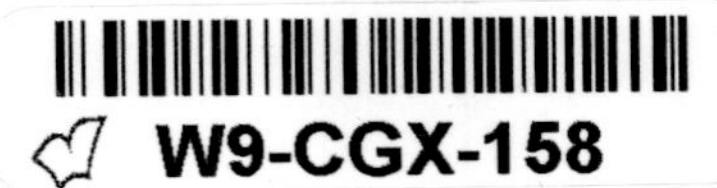

CRIMINAL PROCEDURE
Cases, Notes & Materials

Second Edition

CRIMINAL PROCEDURE
Cases, Notes & Materials

Second Edition

Fern M. Weinper
Mark Sandler

Criminal Procedure: Cases, Notes & Materials, Second Edition

December 2003

Members of the LexisNexis Group worldwide

Canada	LexisNexis Canada Inc, 75 Clegg Road, MARKHAM, Ontario
Argentina	Abeledo Perrot, Jurisprudencia Argentina and Depalma, BUENOS AIRES
Australia	Butterworths, a Division of Reed International Books Australia Pty Ltd, CHATSWOOD, New South Wales
Austria	ARD Betriebsdienst and Verlag Orac, VIENNA
Chile	Publitecsa and Conosur Ltda, SANTIAGO DE CHILE
Czech Republic	Orac sro, PRAGUE
France	Éditions du Juris-Classeur SA, PARIS
Hong Kong	Butterworths Asia (Hong Kong), HONG KONG
Hungary	Hvg Orac, BUDAPEST
India	Butterworths India, NEW DELHI
Ireland	Butterworths (Ireland) Ltd, DUBLIN
Italy	Giuffré, MILAN
Malaysia	Malayan Law Journal Sdn Bhd, KUALA LUMPUR
New Zealand	Butterworths of New Zealand, WELLINGTON
Poland	Wydawnictwa Prawnicze PWN, WARSAW
Singapore	Butterworths Asia, SINGAPORE
South Africa	Butterworth Publishers (Pty) Ltd, DURBAN
Switzerland	Stämpfli Verlag AG, BERNE
United Kingdom	Butterworths Tolley, a Division of Reed Elsevier (UK), LONDON, WC2A
USA	LexisNexis, DAYTON, Ohio

National Library of Canada Cataloguing in Publication

Weinper, Fern
Criminal procedure : cases, notes & materials / Fern Weinper and Mark Sandler. — 2nd ed.

Includes index.
ISBN 0-433-43078-8

1. Criminal procedure — Canada — Cases. I. Sandler, Mark II. Title

KE9260.A7W44 2003 345.71'05 C2003-906964-8
KF9620.ZA2W45 2003

Printed and bound in Canada.

ABOUT THE AUTHORS

Fern M. Weinper is a Justice of the Ontario Court of Justice currently sitting in Newmarket, Ontario. Justice Weinper received her B.A. from York University, her LL.B. from the University of Windsor Law School and her LL.M. from the London School of Economics and Political Science. She is currently an editor of the *Annotated Youth Criminal Justice Service*, published by LexisNexis Canada Inc.

Mark Sandler is a partner at Cooper, Sandler & West, Toronto, Ontario. He is Adjunct Professor at Osgoode Hall Law School and teaches criminal procedure. Mr. Sandler has lectured and written extensively on criminal law, evidence, procedure and advocacy. He has served as counsel to a number of inquiries, and was Associate Commission Counsel for the Commission of Inquiry on Proceedings Involving Guy Paul Morin.

PREFACE

Criminal Procedure: Cases, Notes & Materials, Second Edition, is intended to provide students and practitioners with an introduction to the important rules of criminal procedure and their strategic use by Crown and defence counsel. Accordingly, all of the cases reproduced or cited have current relevance to the practitioner; those cases or former statutory provisions which are solely of historical interest are not referenced. Frankly, there are enough challenging and sometimes unanswerable issues relating to the present rules of criminal procedure to consume all of us indefinitely.

Similarly, issues are prioritized to reflect their importance to the practice of criminal law. For example, the conduct of bail and sentencing hearings, recurring trial issues, and the considerations that prompt specific elections and re-elections as to the mode of trial receive greater attention than *autrefois acquit* or *convict, certiorari* applications or even the form and content of informations and indictments, though the reader will be familiarized with them all.

Criminal procedure interplays with substantive criminal law issues, criminal evidence and the *Charter*. However, these are not the prime focus of this book. Indeed, it is often counterproductive for students, who take these courses separate and apart from criminal procedure, to be constantly revisiting the same issues. Accordingly, the authors attempt to strike a balance. For example, the reader will learn enough about the "defence" of entrapment to understand the very different procedures that regulate its injection into the trial. The reader will learn only enough about wiretap law to understand the many difficult procedural issues that arise when counsel seeks access to sealed documents and moves to attack the validity of intercepted communications. More emphasis is necessarily placed upon *Charter* issues because *Charter*-based motions have significantly affected the conduct of criminal proceedings and also because the *Charter* has dramatically modified the pre-trial procedures employed by the authorities.

The authors' commentary, which is set in bold type to distinguish it from those cases which have been reproduced, is intended to place the reproduced cases in context, to explain difficult procedural points or to outline the "typical" proceeding. Sometimes, a summary of relevant principles is culled from the jurisprudence as a handy guide for students and practitioners. Many questions are posed which are intended to challenge the reader. All of these questions may well arise in the life of a criminal law practitioner.

The authors practice in Ontario, one as a defence counsel and the other as a judge of the Ontario Court of Justice. Nonetheless, they recognize that the sun does not rise and set in Ontario alone. The cases reproduced draw upon the entire Canadian experience. Pursuant to s. 482 of the *Criminal Code*, various Ontario courts have made rules governing certain aspects of criminal proceedings. These detailed rules, which apply only to Ontario but often parallel the practice in other jurisdictions, are sometimes noted where they may be particularly helpful.

Many statutory changes, as well as developments in the jurisprudence since the first edition, have been incorporated into this text. The text includes those amendments to the *Criminal Code* contained in Bill C-15A (S.C. 2002, c. 13) that have been proclaimed, but, by order-in-council, are not in force at the time of writing. These are presently scheduled to come into force on June 1, 2004. There are additional amendments to the *Criminal Code* contained in Bill C-32 (clarifying, *inter alia*, that the need to request a preliminary inquiry extends to section 469 offences such as murder). However, Bill C-32 was not passed when Parliament was prorogued in late 2003.

The authors wish to express their gratitude to LexisNexis Butterworths, in particular to Rose Knecht and Anand Ablack for their assistance throughout the publishing process.

Finally, the authors would like to thank their children, Julia, Jordan and Chelsea, for their love and support, their respective colleagues at the Ontario Court of Justice and at Cooper, Sandler & West, and, importantly, Ngai On Young, their research assistant for this latest edition, and Vincent Paris, their first research assistant, for their indispensable assistance.

Fern M. Weinper
Mark J. Sandler
December 1, 2003

TABLE OF CONTENTS

TABLE OF CASES

Cases are listed under the name of the accused whenever the usual method of citation would cause them to be preceded by the abbreviation "R. v." signifying that the prosecution was undertaken by the Crown.

E

F

G

H

J

K

L

M

N

O

P

Q

R

S

CHAPTER 1

INTRODUCTION TO THE CRIMINAL PROCESS

A. OVERVIEW

A person can be charged with offences enacted by the Parliament of Canada, such as those listed in the *Criminal Code*, R.S.C. 1985, c. C-46, or in the *Controlled Drugs and Substances Act*, S.C. 1996, c. 19, or with offences enacted by provincial legislatures (such as those contained in highway traffic or securities legislation). This manual and casebook is largely devoted to the criminal process for offences enacted by the Parliament of Canada, and most particularly, to the *Criminal Code*, where most crimes which are of greatest interest to criminal law practitioners are contained.

The *Criminal Code* defines many crimes and the penalties attached to them. As well, it codifies much of the criminal procedure that governs the prosecution and defence of those crimes. Other federal statutes, such as the *Controlled Drugs and Substances Act*, may incorporate, by reference, selected parts of the procedures as set out in the *Criminal Code*, as well as create their own procedures. Persons who are accused of committing offences as young offenders are subject to special procedures, which are reflected in the *Youth Criminal Justice Act*, S.C. 2002, c. 1 (in force as of April 2003), and which are separately addressed in Chapter 12.

B. CLASSIFICATION OF OFFENCES

All offences created by federal statutes, including the *Criminal Code*, are classified as:

(a) indictable;
(b) summary conviction; or,
(c) dual procedure (hybrid).

In Canada, the distinction between felonies and misdemeanours was abolished in 1892. These terms have no place in Canadian law. Indictable offences are more serious offences, most closely analogous to felonies. Summary conviction offences are less serious offences, most closely analogous to misdemeanours.

Hybrid offences are those which provide the prosecution with the option or election as to whether they will be proceeded with summarily or by indictment. Section 34(1)(*a*) of the *Interpretation Act*, R.S.C. 1985, c. I-21, deems hybrid offences to be indictable until the Crown elects to

proceed summarily. Sexual assault under s. 271 of the *Criminal Code* is an example of a hybrid offence. Possession of cocaine under s. 4(3) of the *Controlled Drugs and Substances Act* is another example of a hybrid offence. All provincially enacted offences are summary conviction offences.

C. INDICTABLE OFFENCES

The mode of procedure in circumstances where an offence is purely indictable or is a hybrid offence where the prosecution has elected to prosecute by indictment is described in Parts XVIII, XIX and XX of the *Criminal Code*. Each indictable offence carries with it a penalty provision. Indictable offences carry maximum terms of imprisonment of two, five, ten or 14 years, or life. Each indictable offence falls into one of three categories: offences within the exclusive trial jurisdiction of the superior court of criminal jurisdiction, offences within the absolute jurisdiction of the provincial court, and offences where the accused may elect a mode of trial.

1. Offences Within the Exclusive Trial Jurisdiction of the Superior Court of Criminal Jurisdiction

These are the most serious offences and can be tried only in the superior court of criminal jurisdiction, that is, the highest trial court of each province or territory. Section 469 of the *Criminal Code* sets out these offences, which include murder, conspiracy to commit murder and accessory after the fact to murder. A number of rarely prosecuted offences, such as piracy, are also listed in s. 469.

Section 2 of the *Criminal Code* defines the superior court of criminal jurisdiction to mean: in Ontario, the Superior Court of Justice (formerly the Ontario Court (General Division)); in Manitoba, New Brunswick, Saskatchewan and Alberta, the Court of Queen's Bench; in Quebec, the Superior Court; in Nunavut, the Nunavut Court of Justice; and elsewhere, the Supreme Court of the relevant province or territory qualifies as the superior court. Superior court judges are federally appointed.

Offences within the exclusive jurisdiction of the superior court must be tried by a court composed of a judge of that court together with a jury, unless, as stated under s. 473(1) of the *Criminal Code*, both the accused and the prosecution consent to a trial by a judge of that court without a jury. The consent, once given, cannot be withdrawn by one party without the other's consent (s. 473(2) of the *Criminal Code*).

Under s. 522 of the *Criminal Code,* only a judge of the superior court may grant bail pending trial to an accused charged with an offence listed under s. 469 of the *Criminal Code*.

QUESTIONS

1. **Why is attempted murder not included as an offence within the exclusive jurisdiction of the superior court?**

2. The accused is charged with murder. Several weeks before trial, the pretrial publicity associated with the case prompts the accused's counsel to indicate her desire to re-elect to be tried by judge without a jury. Crown counsel defers judgment on whether she will consent to the re-election until the identity of the presiding judge is known. In the local jurisdiction, a judge is assigned only several days before the trial. Two days before trial, Justice Softtouch is assigned. Crown counsel indicates that consent will be withheld. Can the Crown's decision to withhold consent be dispensed with or overridden by the court? Would your answer be different if the accused's counsel only expressed her desire to re-elect after she learned the judge's identity? Consider, in this regard, *R. v. Bird* (1996), 107 C.C.C. (3d) 186 (Alta. Q.B.). Is Crown counsel required to provide reasons for withholding consent to a re-election? Consider *R. v. Ng,* [2003] A.J. No. 489 (C.A.), which is substantially reproduced at p. 11.

---

2. Offences Within the Absolute Jurisdiction of the Provincial Court

A provincial court judge has absolute jurisdiction to try offences listed in s. 553 of the *Criminal Code*. These offences are generally the least serious indictable offences and include various property offences (such as theft, false pretences, possession of property obtained by crime, fraud, and mischief), where the subject matter is not a testamentary instrument and its value does not exceed $5,000, and, breach of recognizance.

Section 2 of the *Criminal Code* defines "provincial court judge". The nomenclature used to describe the provincial court differs in each province and territory. For example, in Ontario, provincial court judges are members of the Ontario Court of Justice, in Alberta, provincial court judges are members of the Alberta Provincial Court (Criminal Division), and in New Brunswick, they are members of the New Brunswick Provincial Court. Trials by provincial court judges are always conducted without a jury. These judges are provincially appointed.

The jurisdiction under s. 553, though absolute in the sense that it does not depend upon the election or consent of the accused, is not exclusive. For example, under s. 468 of the *Criminal Code*, a superior court of criminal jurisdiction may also try these offences (see *R. v. Holliday* (1973), 12 C.C.C. (2d) 56 (Alta. C.A.)).

Some of the offences set out in s. 553 are hybrid or dual procedure offences. Where the Crown elects to proceed by indictment, a provincial court judge will try the case, and the accused has no election. Where the Crown elects to proceed summarily, a provincial court judge will nonetheless try the case. However, the Crown's election has other implications. For example, the range of penalties are greater for indictable offences, and the appellate procedures which may follow are very different.

QUESTION

3. What circumstances might prompt the Crown to elect to proceed by indictment for these offences even where it is seeking no greater penalty by

reason of the election? Consider, in this regard, an accused charged with multiple offences, some of which are purely indictable.

---

3. OFFENCES RESPECTING WHICH THE ACCUSED MAY ELECT A MODE OF TRIAL[1]

Where an offence is not within the absolute jurisdiction of a provincial court judge (s. 553 of the *Criminal Code*) and is not an offence within the exclusive jurisdiction of the superior court of criminal jurisdiction (s. 469 of the *Criminal Code*), s. 536 allows the accused to elect any one of the following modes of trial:

(a) a provincial court judge without a jury and without a preliminary inquiry;
(b) a judge without a jury and with a preliminary inquiry, if the latter is requested by the accused or the prosecutor; or
(c) a judge with a jury and with a preliminary inquiry, if the latter is requested by the accused or the prosecutor.

Very often, the document charging the accused (the *information*) contains several counts. The accused has *one* election in respect of all the counts on the information which are elective indictable offences (see *R. v. Puric* (1990), 54 C.C.C. (3d) 373 (Sask. Q.B.)).

A "judge", for the purposes of this election, includes a judge of a court of criminal jurisdiction (not a provincial court judge) and a judge of a superior court of criminal jurisdiction, as those terms are defined in s. 2 and s. 552 of the *Criminal Code*. For example, in Ontario, a judge of the Superior Court of Justice, with or without a jury, hears all trials of indictable offences which are not tried by a provincial court judge.

Where the accused is to be tried either by a judge (other than a provincial court judge) alone or by judge and jury, a preliminary inquiry can be requested by the accused under s. 536(4)[2] and will generally be conducted by a provincial court judge.[3] If the provincial court judge determines that the evidence presented by the prosecution is sufficient to send the matter to trial, the accused is *committed* to stand trial on the relevant offences. Under ss. 535 and 548(1) of the *Criminal Code*, the provincial court judge is entitled to commit the accused to stand trial on the offences charged and any other indictable offences, disclosed by the evidence, in respect of the same transaction. If the provincial court judge determines that the evidence on some or all of the charges contained in the information is insufficient, the accused is *discharged* on those charges (s. 548(1)(*b*) of the *Criminal Code*). The provincial court judge may also, at any stage of the preliminary inquiry, with the consent of the accused and the Crown, commit the accused to stand trial, without receiving further, or indeed, any evidence (s. 549 of the *Code*). This is

---

1 The commentary in this chapter incorporates recent *Criminal Code* amendments to the preliminary inquiry that have been proclaimed but are not in force at time of writing.

2 See section 536.1(3) for the procedure in Nunavut.

3 The *Criminal Code* actually permits "justices", defined to include not only provincial court judges but justices of the peace, to conduct preliminary inquiries. However, the practice is generally as described above (s. 2 and s. 535 of the *Criminal Code*).

commonly referred to as the accused's *waiver* of the preliminary inquiry, since the accused is waiving the requirement that the Crown tender sufficient evidence to justify committal. Under s. 536.5 of the *Code* (not yet in force at time of writing), the accused and the Crown may agree to limit the scope of the preliminary inquiry to specific issues, and the provincial court judge may order the accused to stand trial, without recording evidence on other issues, under s. 549(1.1) of the *Code* (not yet in force at time of writing). The test for committal at a preliminary inquiry is addressed in Chapter 7.

QUESTION

4. Under what circumstances would defence counsel waive a preliminary inquiry? Under what limited circumstances would Crown counsel refuse to consent to a waiver and insist upon tendering evidence at a preliminary inquiry? Under what circumstances will defence counsel seek a limited scope preliminary inquiry?

Where a provincial court judge is conducting a trial for an offence within his or her absolute jurisdiction, and the evidence establishes that the subject matter of the offence is, in fact, a testamentary instrument or has a value in excess of $5,000, then, under s. 555(2) of the *Criminal Code*, the provincial court judge must, at that point, put the accused to an election as to the mode of trial. Of course, the accused may elect to continue the trial before that judge. Alternatively, if the accused elects trial by judge and jury or by judge without a jury, the proceedings continue before the provincial court judge as a preliminary inquiry only and, if committed to stand trial, the accused will be tried in the higher court.

Section 555(1) of the *Criminal Code* allows a provincial court judge to refuse to try a matter within his or her absolute jurisdiction and decide, on his or her own initiative, to continue the proceedings as a preliminary inquiry. The accused is deemed to have elected to be tried by judge and jury and has no election (s. 565(1)(*a*) of the *Criminal Code*).

QUESTION

5. Under what circumstances might a provincial court judge refuse to try a matter within his or her absolute jurisdiction pursuant to s. 555(1) of the *Criminal Code*?

D. OVERRIDING THE ACCUSED'S ELECTION

Notwithstanding any other provisions relating to elections or re-elections, where multiple accused are charged with the same offence, unless *all of them* elect, re-elect or are deemed to elect the same mode of trial, the court may decline to record the election, re-election or deemed election for trial by provincial court judge or judge without a jury (s. 567 of the *Criminal Code*).

QUESTIONS

6. **Can the court combine a preliminary inquiry respecting one accused with a trial respecting another accused, if both accused consent? Consider, in this regard, *R. v. Niedzwieki and Tribe* (1980), 57 C.C.C. (2d) 184 (B.C.S.C.).**

7. **Four accused are jointly charged with fraud. Three accused elect trial by judge and jury. The fourth accused wishes to be tried by provincial court judge but it is clear that the election will be declined by the presiding judge to avoid duplication of proceedings. Is there any tactical reason why the fourth accused should nonetheless formally make an election which will be declined? Consider, in this regard, potential trial motions which may be affected. What if three accused elect trial by judge without a jury and the fourth elects to be tried by a provincial court judge?**

As well, under s. 568 of the *Criminal Code*, the Attorney General is entitled to *override* an accused's election or re-election to be tried by judge without a jury or provincial court judge and insist upon a jury trial, unless the offence is punishable by five years or less.

The s. 2 definition of "Attorney General" under the *Criminal Code* applies to either a provincial Attorney General or to the federal Attorney General. For the purposes of this book, it is unnecessary to discuss the constitutional dimensions of the jurisdiction to prosecute. Simply put, counsel for the provincial Attorney General generally prosecutes most *Criminal Code* offences. Counsel for the federal Attorney General generally prosecutes offences under other federal statutes such as the *Income Tax Act*, R.S.C. 1985, c. 1 (5th Supp.), and the *Controlled Drugs and Substances Act*, as well as instances of conspiracy, or attempts to contravene or counsel the contravention of those statutes.

QUESTIONS

8. **The accused is charged with possession of stolen property and possession of heroin, all of which was found in the glove compartment of the accused's car during one search. Who will prosecute these charges?**

9. **Under what circumstances might the Attorney General require a jury trial, notwithstanding the accused's election?**

Section 11(*f*) of the *Canadian Charter of Rights and Freedoms* provides that there is a constitutional right to a jury trial for any accused charged with offences punishable by five years or more. However, there is no constitutional right to be tried by judge alone (see *R. v. Turpin* (1989), 48 C.C.C. (3d) 8 (S.C.C.)).

E. THE TIMING AND STRATEGIC EXERCISE OF THE ACCUSED'S ELECTION

Practices vary between jurisdictions as to when the accused is invited to make his or her election. In many jurisdictions, initial court appearances are before a justice of the peace who presides over various remands while counsel is formally retained, legal aid is sought, disclosure is ordered from the Crown and obtained and ultimately before whom a date is set for preliminary inquiry or trial. In other jurisdictions, these earlier court appearances are before a provincial court judge, who will not necessarily be the one who conducts the trial or preliminary inquiry (see, for example, s. 536 of the *Criminal Code*; *R. v. Gillis*, [1967] 1 C.C.C. 266 (Sask. C.A.); *R. v. Wiseberg* (1973), 15 C.C.C. (2d) 26 (Ont. C.A.)). In some jurisdictions, the accused is put to his or her election before a date is set for preliminary inquiry or trial. In this way, the parties and the court know whether they are booking a date for a preliminary inquiry or for a trial. In some jurisdictions, the accused is not put to his or her election until the date actually arrives for preliminary inquiry or trial. Those jurisdictions may have already inquired informally as to the accused's intended election. The different practices may have significant implications. For example, if defence counsel is permitted to reserve election until the date actually set for preliminary inquiry or trial, the election made may be heavily dependent upon the identity of the provincial court judge actually presiding that day. This practice is likely to change, given recent amendments to the *Criminal Code* requiring that a preliminary inquiry be requested within certain time frames (not in force at time of writing).

Whenever the election is formally made, the law is clear that the accused should not be put to his or her election until the Crown has provided appropriate disclosure to the defence; otherwise, the election is not a fully informed one (see *R. v. Stinchcombe* (1991), 68 C.C.C. (3d) 1 (S.C.C.), substantially reproduced at p. 313).

QUESTIONS

10. One of the most difficult issues for defence counsel is assessing the most appropriate mode of trial. Consider how the following factors might affect that assessment:
    (a) the accused is a police officer;
    (b) the accused has a substantial criminal record, which the defence may seek to exclude in a "Corbett" application;
    (c) the prosecution's case is dependent upon eyewitness identification;
    (d) the accused killed an abusive spouse in circumstances which may not strictly fall within the defence of self-defence;
    (e) the accused confessed to police but the statement is likely to be excluded as a violation of the *Charter*;
    (f) the credibility of one or more of the Crown witnesses is very much in issue;
    (g) the police are continuing their investigation and may uncover more evidence in time;
    (h) there are "legalistic" defences available;

(i) counsel is in a jurisdiction where the identity of the provincial court judge who would handle the preliminary inquiry or trial is known prior to the election;
(j) the defence case is patently weak but the accused insists on a trial;
(k) the outstanding charges are exacting a great emotional toll on the accused and the accused's family;
(l) a Crown witness may be available when the matter proceeds before the provincial court but is expected to return to the witness's own country immediately thereafter;
(m) the accused is likely to plead guilty but wishes time to collect restitution for the fraud perpetrated;
(n) no one will be assigned to prosecute the case until a day or two before the matter proceeds before the provincial court;
(o) the police have failed to charge the accused with all of the offences disclosed by their witnesses who are available to testify at a preliminary inquiry, should it be held.

You may wish to revisit these factors after later gaining some familiarity with the preliminary inquiry and pre-trial motions.

11. The accused is charged with an indictable offence for which the maximum sentence is ten years imprisonment. At the time he was charged, he would have been entitled to a jury trial, pursuant to the *Criminal Code* and s. 11(*f*) of the *Charter*. Amendments to the *Criminal Code* then make the offence a hybrid offence, which, when prosecuted by way of summary conviction, carries a maximum sentence of 18 months. At trial, the Crown elects summarily. The accused, who wants a jury trial and a preliminary inquiry, objects. Do the amendments apply to his trial? Consider *R. v. Hafeez* (1996), 27 O.R. (3d) 799 (C.A.).

F. THE INFORMATION AND PREFERRING THE INDICTMENT

Where an accused elects to be tried by provincial court judge, or the offence is within the absolute jurisdiction of the provincial court, the case proceeds upon an *information*, a document in accordance with Form 2 contained in the *Criminal Code*, which is generally sworn before a justice of the peace by the informant. The informant, usually a police officer, swears that he or she has reasonable grounds to believe and does believe that the named accused (one or more of them) committed the named offence(s). Summary conviction offences also proceed upon an information. Where the accused is charged with an offence within the exclusive jurisdiction of the superior court or elects to be tried by judge alone or by judge and jury, the case also commences with and initially proceeds upon the information. However, once proceedings such as the preliminary inquiry, are completed in the provincial court, the accused is remanded to next appear in the higher court and the Crown prepares an *indictment*, a document in accordance with Form 4 contained in the *Criminal Code*. This document replaces the information. Where a provincial court judge presides over the trial of an indictable offence, either because the accused has so elected or because the offence is within the absolute jurisdiction of the provincial court, it is still said that the accused is tried by indictment, though a Form 4 indictment has no place in these proceedings.

The Crown is said to *prefer the indictment* before the court, generally meaning that the Crown places the indictment before the court, which is prepared to try the accused with or without a jury. This most often occurs after the accused has been committed for trial by a provincial court judge after a preliminary inquiry or after the inquiry has been waived by the accused. Section 574(1) permits the Crown to "prefer an indictment against any person who has been ordered to stand trial in respect of (*a*) any charge on which that person was ordered to stand trial, or, (*b*) any charge founded on the facts disclosed by the evidence taken on the preliminary inquiry, in addition to or in substitution for any charge on which that person was ordered to stand trial," or, certain other charges, where the accused consents.

QUESTION

12. Under what circumstances would the accused consent to the preferral of charges, not otherwise available to the Crown?

Section 577 of the *Criminal Code* also allows the Crown, with the personal consent of the Attorney General (meaning the Attorney General or Deputy Attorney General), to prefer an indictment even if the accused has not been given the opportunity to request a preliminary inquiry, a preliminary inquiry has been commenced but not concluded, or a preliminary inquiry has been held and the accused has been discharged. This is referred to as a *direct indictment*, a *direct line indictment* or a *preferred indictment*. The latter usage creates some confusion, since all indictments are preferred.

QUESTIONS

13. Under what circumstances would the Attorney General prefer a direct indictment?

14. Can a direct indictment be preferred for an accused who is already committed for trial? Why would the Crown choose this course of action? Consider where there are two co-accused, and the Crown chooses to proceed with a preliminary inquiry with one of the accused due to unavailability of the other. This accused is subsequently committed for trial, and the previously unavailable accused is now available. What steps does the Crown now have to take to try the two co-accused together? Consider, in this regard, *R. v. Benji* (2002), 161 C.C.C. (3d) 479 (S.C.C.).

This issue will be revisited in Chapter 7.

G. RE-ELECTIONS

An accused who has elected a mode of trial may later wish to change that election to secure another mode of trial. In some situations, an accused can re-elect as of right. In other situations, an accused can only re-elect with the consent of the Crown. The rights of re-election are summarized below:

ORIGINAL ELECTION	DESIRED RE-ELECTION	RULE
Provincial court judge	**Judge with or without jury**	**As of right not later than 14 days before the trial date. Otherwise, only with Crown's written consent (s. 561(2), *Criminal Code*) procedures for re-election (ss. 561(4),(6),(7), 562(2)).**
Judge with or without jury	**Provincial court judge**	**At any time, before or after the preliminary inquiry is completed, only with Crown's written consent (s. 561(1)(*a*), *Criminal Code*); procedures for re-election (ss. 561(3)(*b*),(5),(6), 562(1),(2)).**
Judge with or without a jury	**Judge with or without a jury**	**As of right not later than 14 days before the trial date, if no preliminary inquiry has been requested. Otherwise, only with Crown's written consent (s. 561(2), *Criminal Code*); procedures for re-election (ss. 561(4),(6),(7), 562(2)).** **As of right, before the completion of the preliminary inquiry (s. 561(1)(*b*), *Criminal Code*); procedures for re-election (ss. 561(3)(*a*), 562(2)).** **or** **As of right, within 15 days of the completion of the preliminary inquiry (s. 561(1)(*b*), *Criminal Code*); procedures for re-election (s. 561(5),(6)).** **or**

		On or after 15 days following the completion of the preliminary inquiry, only with Crown's written consent (s. 561(1)(*c*), *Criminal Code*); procedures for re-election (s. 561(5),(6),(7)).
Provincial court judge or judge without a jury	**Judge with a jury**	**As of right, after a successful conviction appeal, if the re-election request is made in the notice of appeal or notice of application for leave to appeal (s. 686(5), *Criminal Code*).**
Judge and jury	**Judge without a jury or provincial court judge**	**At any time, after a new trial is ordered on appeal, only with the Crown's written consent (s. 686 (5.1), *Criminal Code*).**

Where a *direct* indictment has been preferred against an accused (s. 577 of the *Code*), the accused is deemed both to have elected to be tried by court composed of judge and jury and not to have requested a preliminary inquiry. However, the accused may re-elect to be tried by a judge without a jury and without a preliminary inquiry, with the written consent of the Crown (s. 565(2) of the *Criminal Code*). Procedures for re-election are contained in s. 565(3) and (4) of the *Criminal Code*.

Various cases examine when the Crown's refusal to consent to a re-election can be overridden by the court. The following case contains a good discussion of the exercise of Crown discretion and the court's power to review this discretion.

R. v. NG

[2003] A.J. No. 489 (C.A.)

[The accused respondent was charged with two counts of first degree murder, three counts of attempted murder, and one count of a weapons charge. On September 1, 1998, the respondent elected trial by judge and jury. At a pre-trial conference on May 12, 2000, the respondent did not attempt to re-elect trial by judge alone. His counsel indicated that he might do so and asked the Crown whether he would consent to such a re-election. The prosecutor indicated he would not consent and refused to give reasons. On June 14, 2000, the parties were given the name of the trial judge appointed to the case. On the following day at jury selection, the respondent told the court he wished to re-elect. The respondent had sought consent from the prosecutor earlier that morning, but the Crown again refused to consent and refused to give reasons. On June 16, 2000, the trial judge heard the respondent's application for re-election and to dispense with the Crown's consent. The prosecutor once again refused to consent to re-election, and the trial judge asked the prosecutor if he would give reasons for his refusal. The prosecutor declined to give reasons. The trial judge directed that the trial proceed by judge alone. The accused was acquitted of all charges except the weapons charge. The Crown's appeal was based on the judge's decision to proceed without a jury.]

Wittmann J.A. [Kenny J. and Fraser C.J.A concurring]: —

.....

RELEVANT LEGISLATION AND ITS HISTORY

Section 473 of the *Criminal Code* is specific to the murder charges and allows for a trial without a jury when both the accused and Attorney General consent. Section 561 governs re-elections and applies to the non-murder charges.

.....

Prosecutorial Discretion

.....

The Supreme Court of Canada has discussed and affirmed the existence of prosecutorial discretion in several decisions. In *R. v. Beare* (1988), 45 C.C.C. (3d) 57 at 76, La Forest. J., writing for the court, discussed the importance of discretion as a feature of our criminal justice system:

> The existence of the discretion conferred by the statutory provisions does not, in my view, offend principles of fundamental justice. Discretion is an essential feature of the criminal justice system. A system that attempted to eliminate discretion would be unworkably complex and rigid. Police necessarily exercise discretion in deciding when to lay charges, to arrest and to conduct incidental searches, as prosecutors do in deciding whether or not to withdraw a charge, enter a stay, consent to an adjournment, proceed by way of indictment or summary conviction, launch an appeal and so on.
>
> The *Criminal Code* provides no guidelines for the exercise of discretion in any of these areas. The day-to-day operation of law enforcement and the criminal justice system none the less depends upon the exercise of that discretion.

La Forest, J. also acknowledged the constitutionality of a prosecutor's discretionary powers at 76:

> This court has already recognized that the existence of prosecutorial discretion does not offend the principles of fundamental justice: see *R. v. Lyons* [(1987), 37 C.C.C. (3d) 1, [1987] 2 S.C.R. 309] at p. 36 C.C.C., p. 348 S.C.R.; see also *Jones v. The Queen*, [1986] 2 S.C.R. 284 at 303-304, 28 C.C.C. (3d) 513 at 540-1.

.....

More recently, in *R. v. Regan* (2002), 209 D.L.R. (4th) 41, [2002] S.C.J. No. 14, 2002 SCC 12 Binnie, J., dissenting on a different point, said of prosecutorial discretion at paras. 166-68:

> The trial judge in this case was careful not to understate or diminish the broad scope traditionally and properly afforded to prosecutorial discretion. Courts are very slow to second-guess the exercise of that discretion and do so only in narrow circumstances.

In the same vein, in *Krieger v. Law Society of Alberta* (2002), 217 D.L.R. (4th) 513, [2002] S.C.J. No. 45, 2002 SCC 65, Iacobucci, and Major, JJ., for the court, re-iterated the reasons of L'Heureux-Dubé [J.] in *Power* [(1994), 89 C.C.C. (3d) 1 (S.C.C.)] that, as a matter of principle and policy, courts should not interfere with prosecutorial discretion out of respect for the separation of powers and the rule of law. "Subject to the abuse of process doctrine," they stated at para. 32, "supervising one litigant's decision-making process — rather than the conduct of litigants before the court — is beyond the legitimate reach of the court."

In *Regan*, LeBel, J., writing for the majority, reviewed the principles governing abuse of process on the part of the Crown in the *Charter* era. Since *O'Connor* [(1995), 103 C.C.C. (3d) 1 (S.C.C.)], the common law doctrine of abuse of process has been subsumed into the principles of the *Charter*, but *O'Connor* also recognized a residual category of abuse of process in which the individual's right to a fair trial is not implicated. LeBel, J. characterized abuse of process in terms quoted from McLachlin, J. (as she then was) in *R. v. Scott*, [1990] 3 S.C.R. 979 at 1007:

> ... abuse of process may be established where: (1) the proceedings are oppressive or vexatious; and, (2) violate the fundamental principles of justice underlying the community's sense of fair play and decency. The concepts of oppressiveness and vexatiousness underline the interest of the accused in a fair trial. But the doctrine evokes as well the public interest in a fair and just trial process and the proper administration of justice. I add that I would read these criteria cumulatively.

In *Cook* [(1997), 114 C.C.C. (3d) 481 (S.C.C.)], L'Heureux-Dubé J. also discussed early authorities stating that a court can interfere with Crown discretion where the discretion is exercised for an "oblique motive". In her view, that term, which has garnered a prominent place in the jurisprudence, would seem to have much in common with the doctrine of abuse of process. She continued at 1139:

> Indeed, given that the finding of an "oblique motive" by its very name implies improper conduct on the part of the Crown, I feel it is unlikely that such a finding could arise without there being a legitimate claim of an abuse of process.

The basis for a court to probe into prosecutorial discretion, therefore, arises in the limited case of an abuse of the court's process where the prosecutor's misconduct threatens either the accused's *Charter* right to a fair trial or the public interest in a fair and just trial process.

Onus and Standard of Proof

The accused, who is making the allegation, bears the onus of proof that the Crown's exercise of discretion amounts to, or would amount to, an abuse of process but for the intervention by the trial judge. The standard of proof is on the balance of probabilities: *Cook* at para. 60.

In *R. v. E.(L.)* [(1994), 94 C.C.C. (3d) 228 (Ont. C.A.)], Finlayson, J.A. said at 241-3, "there would have to be some showing before the trial judge that the Crown had exercised its discretion arbitrarily, capriciously or for some improper motive", which required a finding that the conduct of the Crown amounted to an abuse of process. He also noted that the standard for establishing an abuse of process is very onerous.

The case authorities confirm that a trial judge may review a prosecutor's discretionary decision where the accused has proven on a balance of probabilities that the prosecutor exercised his discretion abusively, capriciously, or for improper motive such that the court may examine whether there was an abuse of process. The court may intervene if it finds it is necessary to prevent the prosecutor's conduct from resulting in oppressive or vexatious proceedings that would have violated the fundamental principles of justice underlying the community's sense of fair play and decency.

2. Refusal to Give Reasons

Can the Prosecution be Required to Provide Reasons for its Exercise of Discretion?

The trial judge in this case did not specifically find an abuse of process or arbitrary, capricious or improper conduct in the prosecution's exercise of discretion. She held that because the prosecutor refused to give reasons for the discretionary decision, she was unable to determine whether an abuse of process had occurred or may occur. In these circumstances, she noted the accused was unable to challenge the substance of the decision.

Since the only recognized standard for interfering with prosecutorial discretion is misconduct amounting to an abuse of process, the trial judge, in effect, decided the refusal to provide reasons was sufficient to find arbitrary or capricious conduct or improper motive amounting to an abuse of process. Put another way, she drew an adverse inference based on the refusal of the prosecutor to give reasons for withholding consent.

As the trial judge noted, the jurisprudence in Alberta and elsewhere has not set out a consistent answer to this issue. Neither s. 473 or s. 561 requires a prosecutor to give reasons for withholding consent.

.....

One of the cases relied on by the trial judge was *R. v. Oommen*, (14 February 1992), Fort McMurray (Alta. Q.B.). There, the court considered the Crown's decision to withhold consent under s. 473 and at 2-3 interpreted s. 473(1) as "not the intention of Parliament that the Crown ... would withhold its consent except for clear and obvious reasons". The court continued at 3 to hold there must be "a palpable reason for the Crown to withhold its consent if the trial process under the present legislation is to be perceived in a given case as being fair and in accordance with the principle of fundamental justice". The Crown had not given reasons for its refusal to consent. The trial judge concluded that the reason for refusal was simply that the Crown wanted a jury trial. This, he held, was an arbitrary reason and the refusal was a violation of the accused's s. 7 *Charter* rights. He ordered trial by judge alone.

With respect, the approach of the trial judge in *Oommen* neglected to consider the fundamental place of prosecutorial discretion in the criminal law process, the established constitutionality of this discretion, and the principle that an accused has no constitutional right to trial by judge alone: *R. v. Turpin* (1989), 48 C.C.C. (3d) 8 at 26-28 (S.C.C.).

The Supreme Court of Canada in *Turpin* held that s. 11(*f*) of the *Charter* accords to individuals charged with an offence the right to the benefit of a trial by jury in certain prescribed circumstances. The section was read as permitting an accused to waive the benefit if in fact he or she viewed it as in his or her best interests. However, *Turpin* did not hold there is a corresponding right or benefit to a trial by judge alone. That decision has not been challenged.

.....

In *R. v. Cardinal* [(1996), 105 C.C.C. (3d) 163 (Alta. Q.B.)], two accused were charged with second degree murder and sought the Crown's consent under s. 473 to a trial by judge alone. The Crown refused and offered no reasons for its refusal. The accused argued the Crown's decision was arbitrary and capricious. During argument on the issue, the court invited the Crown to articulate reasons. The Crown declined to do so. The Crown argued it was not required to justify its exercise of discretion; rather, the onus was on the accused to show an abuse of process or a *Charter* breach. However, the Crown added that the nature of the offence deserves a trial involving the community unless there is some reason that this position should be overridden.

On the basis of the Crown's statement, the trial judge said, at 185-6, that it did not seem to be "a reason that involves legitimate exercise of discretion" as discretion "requires a consideration of the articulation of the reasoning behind the decision to consent or the refusal of consent". The trial judge stated that he could not determine on the material before him whether the Crown had engaged in any meaningful reasoning. On this basis, he concluded at 186 that the Crown's exercise of discretion "was capricious and arbitrary as being without any kind of articulable reason for the making of the decision to refuse to give consent to these two applicants to be tried by judge alone". The reasoning applied in *Cardinal* was similar to that adopted by the trial judge in the present case.

.....

In *R. v. Tonner (No. 2)*, [2001] A.J. No. 60 (23 January 2001), Edmonton 9803 2119 C5 (Alta. Q.B.), decided after the trial proceedings in this appeal, the trial judge stated in *obiter* that if the Crown chooses to withhold consent, it should give reasons for that decision. If it does not do so, it faces an adverse finding about its exercise of discretion. The Crown gave reasons in that case, but the trial judge found them insufficient.

The trial judge in this case chose not to follow *R. v. Tonner (No. 1),* [(18 June 1999), Edmonton 9803 2119 C5 (Alta. Q.B.)]. The Crown in *Tonner (No. 1)* withheld its consent to a re-election under s. 561 and gave no reasons. The court agreed that the Crown was not required to give reasons for its decision and stated that the onus rests on the accused to make out an abuse of process in the exercise of discretion. The trial judge in *Tonner (No. 1)* stated at para. 20:

> The Crown has given no reasons nor does it have to. The onus rests upon the accused to establish that there has been an abuse of process by the Crown and, as noted, that is very onerous. This hurdle must be achieved before a consideration of s. 7 is triggered. I would think that if that onus of proof is discharged a violation of s. 7 would in all likelihood follow and the relief sought by the accused as in this case would be granted unless the facts were unique.

The trial judge further concluded that the Crown's refusal to give reasons did not itself constitute an abuse of process.

Outside Alberta, the issue of inquiry into the Crown's reasons for its exercise of discretion arose in *R. v. Durette* (1992), 72 C.C.C. (3d) 421 (Ont. C.A.); reversed on other grounds at (1994), 88 C.C.C. (3d) 1 (S.C.C.). That decision supports the line of reasoning in *Tonner (No. 1).* Alleging *Charter* violations, the accused in *Durette* wanted to call evidence on the reasons for the Crown's decisions about conduct of the prosecution. The trial judge refused. On appeal, Finlayson J.A., for the majority, discussed the issue of justiciability of prosecutorial discretion, and held that to simply point out that discretion could have been exercised differently could not justify an evidentiary hearing into the Crown's reasons. At 437-438, Finlayson, J.A. wrote:

> ... there must be some basis for suspecting the Crown's choice of conduct. In order to ask the court to delve into the circumstances surrounding the exercise of the Crown's discretion, or to inquire into the motivation of the Crown officers responsible for advising the Attorney-General, the accused bears the burden of making a tenable allegation of *mala fides* on the part of the Crown. Such an allegation must be supportable by the record before the court, or if the record is lacking or insufficient, by an offer of proof. Without such an allegation, the court is entitled to assume what is inherent in the process, that the Crown exercised its discretion properly, and not for improper or arbitrary motives.

Similarly, in *E.(L.),* the Ontario Court of Appeal considered the court's residual discretion to review a refusal to consent to a late re-election. After the jury panel had been summoned and trial was otherwise ready to begin, the two accuseds sought to re-elect to trial by judge alone. The Crown refused to consent and argued the accuseds were motivated by judge-shopping. The trial judge refused to examine the motives of defence counsel, overrode the Crown's refusal, and the trial proceeded. It resulted in convictions and acquittals. The Crown appealed.

On appeal, Finlayson, J.A. agreed that counsel's motives should not be examined but this approach had not been sufficiently extended to Crown counsel. He held that a trial judge can review prosecutorial discretion only on the basis of abuse of process or an unfair trial. He connected the power of review with the onus which rests on the accused, stating at 241, there must be something on the record indicating an abuse of process before the court can act:

> While I do not believe that the Crown has an unfettered right to withhold consent to a re-election under s. 561(1)(*c*), the court cannot review this exercise of statutory discretion relating to the mode of trial unless it has been demonstrated on the record that there has been an abuse of the court's process through oppressive proceedings on the part of the Crown. I would think that there would have to be some showing before the trial judge that the Crown had exercised its discretion arbitrarily, capriciously or for some improper motive so as to invite an examination as to whether there was an abuse of process under s. 7 of the *Charter*.

At 243 he concluded that the trial judge erred:

> I reject the concept that the trial judge can substitute his discretion for that of the Crown and consent to a late re-election under s. 561(1)(*c*) of the *Code*. In my opinion, based on the authority of *Turpin*, a trial judge can only supplant or ignore the clear language of the *Code* when constitutional considerations are engaged. The level of intervention in this case required a finding that the conduct of the Crown amounted to an abuse of process.

.....

In *R. v. Cook, supra*, the court considered the exercise of prosecutorial discretion where the Crown chose not to call witnesses, including one of the complainants. One argument advanced on behalf of the defence, and accepted by the majority of the appellate court, was that the Crown did not offer any reasons for its decision not to call the complainant, and that the trial judge did not seek any.

For the Supreme Court of Canada, L'Heureux-Dubé J. summarized the majority of the provincial appellate court as holding there is a duty on the trial judge to inquire why the complainant is not being called, and a corresponding duty on the prosecutor to satisfy the judge that his reason was not "oblique". L'Heureux-Dubé J. further summarized the majority's view at 1141:

> In essence, Ryan J.A. felt a mandatory inquiry on the part of the trial judge was necessary for two reasons: (1) to determine whether or not the Crown possesses an "oblique motive", and (2) to get a full appreciation of whether he or she should exercise the discretion to call the witness.

She held neither of these reasons was supportable. An oblique motive referred to whether there had been an abuse of process by the Crown. This is a finding for which the accused bears the onus of proof on a balance of probabilities. Even if an oblique motive differs from an abuse of process, there is no conceptual basis for reversing the onus of proof. The discretion to call witnesses should be left to each prosecutor with consideration of certain guiding principles and under the overarching principle that it is essential to do justice in the particular case. To mandate a judge inquire into the Crown's reasons for not calling a witness is inconsistent with this discretionary exercise.

A caution expressed by L'Heureux-Dubé J. in *Power* also implied that a requirement to give reasons would not be supported. Judicial review would lead to a reviewing court embarking upon an evaluation of the rationales advanced by prosecutors for their discretionary decisions, as well as the legitimacy of those rationales. She warned at 18:

> Moreover, should judicial review of prosecutorial discretion be allowed courts would also be asked to consider the validity of various rationales advanced for each and every decision, involving the analysis of policies, practices and procedure of the Attorney-General. The court would then have to "second-guess" the prosecutor's judgment in a variety of cases to determine whether the reasons advanced for the exercise of his or her judgment are a subterfuge.

This is precisely what occurred in *Delorey*, *Cardinal*, and *Tonner (No. 2)*. The courts had to second guess the prosecutor's judgment. In *Bird* and *Oommen*, the courts embarked upon an evaluation of unarticulated rationales which they deemed to be motivating. In none of those cases did the accused establish a proper basis for the court to review prosecutorial discretion.

Here, the exercise of prosecutorial discretion was not shown to be arbitrary, capricious or motivated by an improper consideration. The absence of reasons does not make it so. I adopt the reasoning in *Tonner (No. 1)* and the Ontario Court of Appeal decisions discussed above and find that they represent the law in Alberta. I do not agree with the line of authorities preferred by the trial judge. The inquiry by a court into the exercise of prosecutorial discretion is premised upon the need to determine whether there was an abuse of process. The standard for establishing an abuse of process is very onerous, the court having discretion to remedy abuse only in the clearest of cases. It is inconsistent with this very high standard to permit a court to conclude an abuse of process has occurred when a prosecutor declines to give reasons for an exercise of discretion, particularly, in this case, where the requirement for Crown consent is conferred by the *Criminal Code* without obligation to give reasons.

.....

CONCLUSION

The trial judge erred in overriding the Crown's discretionary decision to refuse to consent to a trial by judge alone. That exercise of discretion was not shown to be arbitrary, capricious, or for improper motive such that it would be an abuse of process. That basis is the only one upon which a court can interfere with prosecutorial discretion to withhold consent to re-election. The prosecutor's refusal to articulate reasons for his lack of consent does not make the exercise of discretion an abuse of process.

A court ought not to embark upon a review of the exercise of prosecutorial discretion refusing consent to re-elect unless there is an admission, or evidence, or an allegation supported by an offer of proof. Until then, the threshold for judicial scrutiny is not engaged, including asking a prosecutor for the reasons for his decision.

Wrongfully overriding the requirement for the consent of the Crown to a re-election results in a loss of jurisdiction not curable on appeal from acquittal. There is no justification for a judicial stay in the circumstances of this case.

The appeal is allowed. The trial proceeded without jurisdiction and the acquittals and convictions are set aside and a new trial is ordered.

QUESTION

15. You are defending a case of sexual assault. The Crown proceeded by indictment and the accused elected judge and jury. A preliminary inquiry was conducted. The complainant was cross-examined about her initial complaint about the accused's conduct and why she had failed to disclose until much later all of the particulars of the complaint now being made. Several months after the preliminary inquiry, you advise the Crown that the accused wishes to re-elect to be tried by judge without a jury. The Crown will not consent to the re-election. One month later, the Crown indicates that, upon review of the preliminary inquiry transcript, she has determined that an expert will be called by the Crown to address untimely and incremental disclosure by *bona fide* victims of sexual assault. You are convinced, rightly or wrongly, that such expert evidence is less likely to be persuasive to a judge than to a jury. Can you successfully move the court to dispense with the Crown's consent?

H. SUMMARY CONVICTION OFFENCES

The *Criminal Code* creates offences that are purely summary conviction offences. As well, it creates hybrid offences which permit the Crown to elect to proceed summarily. The mode of procedure for summary conviction offences of either kind is described in Part XXVII of the *Criminal Code*. Summary conviction offences are tried by a provincial court judge on an information. The party charged is described as the *defendant*, rather than the *accused*. Section 787(1) of the *Criminal Code* states that, "[e]xcept where otherwise provided by law, every one who is convicted of an offence punishable on summary conviction is liable to a fine of not more than two thousand dollars or to imprisonment for six months or to both." This general provision governs most summary conviction offences. However, amendments to the *Criminal Code* since 1995 have created hybrid offences which are punishable, if proceeded with summarily, by up to 18 months imprisonment. These offences are: sexual exploitation of person with disability (s. 153.1(1)), uttering threats to cause death or bodily harm (s. 264.1(1)(*a*)), assault with a weapon (s. 267(*a*)), assault causing bodily harm (s. 267(*b*)), unlawfully causing bodily harm (s. 269), disarming a peace officer (s. 270.1(1)), sexual assault (s. 271), forcible confinement (s. 279(2)), mischief relating to religious property (s. 430(4.1)) and failure to comply with probation order (s. 733.1(1)). Many federal statutes other than the *Criminal Code* also create summary conviction or hybrid offences, drawing upon the procedural provisions contained in Part XXVII, with or without some variations. Provincial statutes enact only summary conviction offences. Provincial legislation should be consulted for the governing procedural codes. See, for example, the Ontario *Provincial Offences Act*, R.S.O. 1990, c. P.33.

QUESTION

16. You are Crown counsel reviewing a charge of uttering death threats. Consider what factors would affect your decision as to whether to elect to proceed summarily or by indictment.

CHAPTER 2

TERRITORIAL JURISDICTION

A. GENERAL RULE: OFFENCES COMMITTED WITHIN CANADA

Section 6(2) of the *Criminal Code*, R.S.C. 1985, c. C-46, provides that no person shall be convicted or found guilty of an offence committed outside Canada.[1] There are numerous statutory exceptions to this rule (see ss. 7, 46(3), 57, 58, 74(2), 75, 77, 78, 290(1)(*b*), 465(1)(*a*), 465(3) and 465(4)). Section 465 relating to conspiracy deserves particular attention.

QUESTION

1. Several accused in Canada agreed to sell cocaine to a purchaser in Texas. The planning and preparation took place in Canada. One accused was to receive his share of the proceeds in Canada. The accused anticipated that the purchaser would be returning to Canada from Texas with the drugs. Can the accused be tried in Canada for conspiracy to traffic? Need the Crown prove that trafficking is an offence under Texan law? Consider, in this regard, *R. v. Rowbotham* (1992), 76 C.C.C. (3d) 542 (Ont. C.A.); affd (1993), 85 C.C.C. (3d) 575 (S.C.C.).

B. GENERAL RULE: OFFENCES COMMITTED WITHIN THE PROVINCE

Section 478(1) of the *Criminal Code* provides that "a court in a province shall not try an offence committed entirely in another province."

A notable exception to this rule is found in s. 478(3), which provides that an accused charged with an offence alleged to have been committed in a different province from where the accused is, may, provided the offence is not one listed in s. 469, plead guilty and be sentenced in the province where the accused is. The consent of the relevant Attorney General must be obtained.

This section is often utilized where an accused faces outstanding charges in several provinces and wishes to dispose of all of the charges at the same time.

---

1 An accused may be found guilty, but no conviction registered under s. 730 of the *Criminal Code*. An absolute or conditional discharge is granted.

QUESTION

2. The accused faces charges in Toronto and 15 assorted counts in Vancouver involving property offences. He wishes to plea negotiate the Vancouver and Toronto charges. This ideally might involve a plea to five or six of the charges he faces in Vancouver. It would be advantageous if sentencing occurred exclusively before one judge in Toronto. He hopes to work out the charges to which he will plead guilty with Crown counsel in Toronto. The accused cannot employ s. 478(3). Why? Assuming that Crown counsel in Vancouver is content with the suggested plea negotiation and content that the sentencing will occur in Toronto, how might the accused's wishes be accommodated?

C. GENERAL RULE: OFFENCES COMMITTED WITHIN THE TERRITORIAL DIVISION

As a general rule, an offence is to be tried in the territorial division in which it allegedly occurred. "Territorial division" is defined in s. 2 of the *Criminal Code*. However, s. 2 of the *Criminal Code* is not terribly helpful since it provides a range of meanings, depending upon the context. Usually, the venue in criminal matters is determined by the county, district or region within which the offence allegedly occurred. Special statutory rules address situations where an offence is committed in several territorial divisions or where there is some nexus between the offence and several territorial divisions (see s. 476 of the *Criminal Code*). An application may be brought by the Crown or defence to change the venue of trial from the territorial division in which it would normally take place (see s. 599 of the *Criminal Code*).

D. APPLICATION FOR CHANGE OF VENUE

Section 599(1)(*a*) of the *Criminal Code* permits the court, upon the application of the Crown or the defence, to "order the trial to be held in a territorial division in the same province other than that in which the offence would otherwise be tried *if it appears expedient to the ends of justice*" (emphasis added).[2] The most common ground for such an application is that the pre-trial publicity surrounding the case prevents a fair and impartial trial in the original venue. It is clear that the remedy is an exceptional one, since there is a policy interest in having trials dealt with in the communities to which they relate.

---

[2] The italicized portion outlines the prime ground for seeking a change of venue. The unavailability of a jury in the division where the trial would otherwise be held is the other ground listed.

R. v. CHAREST

(1990), 57 C.C.C. (3d) 312 (Que. C.A.)

[The accused was convicted of the first degree murder of an 11-year-old boy. Defences included insanity, lack of intent, and intoxication. The defence unsuccessfully applied for a change of the trial venue due to pre-trial publicity. Various grounds of appeal were argued, including the failure to change the trial venue and the inflammatory character of the Crown's closing address to the jury.]

The judgment of the court was delivered by

Fish J.A.: —

.....

Charest's strongest complaint is that he did not have a fair trial. The Crown's address, he says, was inflammatory and violated well-established rules laid down by the courts. With respect, I agree. Charest says as well that the trial judge did not put his defence properly to the jury. Again, with respect, I agree.

A fresh trial should therefore be had and, for reasons later explained, I would direct a change of venue.

.....

[The court then directs itself to the various grounds of appeal, unrelated to change of venue.]

The appellant raises as an additional ground the dismissal before trial of his motion for a change of venue.

It is well established that the matter of a change of venue is one of discretion, which must of course be exercised in a principled manner. [text from footnote 10 within the judgment: See *R. v. Collins* (1989), 48 C.C.C. (3d) 343, 69 C.R. (3d) 235, 41 C.R.R. 193 (Ont. C.A.); *R. v. Beaudry*, [1966] 3 C.C.C. 51 (B.C.S.C.); *R. v. Turvey* (1970), 1 C.C.C. (2d) 90, 12 C.R.N.S. 329, 2 N.S.R. (2d) 12 (S.C.); *R. v. Kully* (1973), 15 C.C.C. (2d) 488, 44 D.L.R. (3d) 401, 2 O.R. (2d) 463 (H.C.J.); *R. v. Talbot* (1977), 38 C.C.C. (2d) 555 (Ont. H.C.J.); *Simard v. The Queen*, [1978] S.C. 819 (Que. S.C.), and the authorities to which they refer.] The relevant statutory test is, accordingly, framed in broad language by s. 599(1)(*a*) of the *Criminal Code* (s. 527(1)(*a*) at the time of the appellant's conviction), which empowers a court to change the venue of a trial whenever "it appears expedient to the ends of justice".

Trial courts, generally speaking, have interpreted these words conservatively. They have sometimes substituted for the broad language of the *Code* a narrower jurisprudential formula, contemplating a change of venue only where the accused has "made out a probable cause that a jury sworn and properly instructed would not render a true verdict according to the evidence, free of any bias or partiality", *per* Aikins J. in the off-cited case of *Beaudry*, *supra*, at p. 57... How, in truth, could an accused *ever* prove that a properly instructed jury would not render a true verdict? How could he or she prove that 12 impartial jurors cannot — or probably will not — be found in the entire judicial district?

In *Collins, supra*, ... the accused — charged with first degree murder of a police officer — had sought a change of venue primarily on the grounds of (1) adverse publicity at the time of his arrest; (2) widespread media coverage of the killing of two other police officers in the Toronto area, and (3) publicity relating to the shooting, a few days before his trial commenced, of two more constables in the same mall where the victim in his case had been shot and killed. The material relied on in support of the motion did not, for the most part, specifically relate to the accused — he was mentioned in only four of the 24 articles produced as exhibits. The trial judge dismissed the motion, finding that the initial adverse publicity had occurred almost one year before the trial, that the other shootings were clearly unconnected with the accused and that there was a large panel from which to select an impartial jury.

Delivering the judgment of the Ontario Court of Appeal, Goodman J.A. stated that the "fundamental consideration is whether a change of venue is necessary in order to ensure that an accused has a *fair trial with an impartial jury*" (at pp. 241-2, my emphasis). Noting that a change of venue was within the trial judge's discretion, the court held that the trial judge had not erred in refusing to adjourn the trial or grant a change of venue on the facts of that case, "particularly so having regard to the fact that he acceded to the request of trial counsel for the appellant to question prospective jurors by way of challenge for cause without placing any restriction upon him as to the questions to be asked" (at p. 242).

With respect, I prefer the test formulated in *Collins* to the narrower one laid down by Aikins J. in *Beaudry*. It adds to the "impartial jury" standard the additional and broader concept of a *fair trial*. In my view, a fair trial can be conducted only in a reasonably serene environment. Extensive prejudicial publicity shortly before the trial, pronounced hostility toward the accused, widespread sympathy for the victim, and a frightened or enraged community, surely create — especially in a small judicial district — the kind of emotionally charged atmosphere in which the ends of justice may be best served by removal of the trial to another venue.

Appellant's motion before trial

On the appellant's motion prior to trial, the applicable test was framed as follows by Cliche J. (appellant's factum, p. 275) [translation]:

> The applicant must demonstrate that a fair and impartial trial cannot be held. It is not a question of determining whether there is a possibility of a partial and unfair trial, but rather whether there is a probability of such a trial.

The evidence before him, in the view of Cliche J., did not meet this test. Another judge might well have decided otherwise, but that does not mean Cliche J. committed a reversible error. The law provides that an accused ought in principle to be tried where he is alleged to have committed a crime. That principle is subject to s. 599(1)(*a*) of the *Code*, which vests in the trial court a discretion to change the venue. The appellant has not satisfied me that Cliche J., in refusing to grant the motion, did not exercise his discretion judicially. The appellant's ground fails for that reason.

The trial judge in this case, unlike that of *Collins*, did not permit the appellant's counsel much latitude in questioning prospective jurors. In the circumstances of this case, a change of venue having been refused, it would have been preferable to err on the side of caution, prohibiting only those questions which were abusive, vexatious or clearly irrelevant. In view of the other conclusions I have reached, however, it is unnecessary to decide whether the trial judge's restrictive approach would provide a sufficient basis for a new trial.

Venue of new trial

A new trial should in my view proceed in a different district. This appears to me, in the language of the *Code*, "expedient to the ends of justice".

My conclusion is not at odds with any finding of fact by Cliche J. In support of the motion before him, serious evidence was presented to indicate intense local hostility toward the appellant and understandable outrage at his crime. This evidence was not disbelieved or rejected. One witness, a reporter who by then had covered sensational criminal trials throughout Quebec for nearly a quarter-century, said he had rarely encountered an atmosphere as "aggressive" as the one greeting the appellant outside the court-house on his first court appearance (p. 390). He heard shouts from the crowd such as, "Kill him, cut off his balls" and so forth (p. 389). Several other journalists testified that, on the same occasion, they heard threats and shouts. Crown counsel himself, not on the motion but in cross-examination of a defence witness during the trial, referred to the crime as one that had aroused "the ire of the population" (at p. 742). It was committed in Contrecoeur, a small municipality in a rural or semi-rural judicial district with a total population, in 1984, of 87,000.

Since the hearing before Cliche J., apart from the trial and its attendant publicity, there have been other material developments. The day after the verdict, the municipal arena in Contrecoeur was renamed "Aréna Steve Mandeville" to honour the victim's memory. We are told approximately 1,000 people — most presumably from the area — attended the ceremony: compare *Talbot, supra* ...

In these circumstances, it is my opinion that any further trial should be held in a district other than Richelieu.

QUESTIONS

3. **The accused is a police officer charged with manslaughter arising from the death of a suspect whom he had arrested. It is alleged that he used excessive force to effect the arrest and thereby caused the suspect's death. In 1993, the accused was convicted after a jury trial and sentenced to three years imprisonment. The trial was prominently reported in the local and regional news media. After the verdict, many community members wrote letters to the editor suggesting that the sentence was too light. Many community members expressed public indignation when the accused was released on bail and then reinstated as a police officer, pending the appeal. An opinion poll commissioned by a local newspaper reflected that**

550 citizens were outraged at the favouritism shown to the police officer. 540 citizens suggested that the deceased was the author of his own misfortune and the city should rally behind the police. The deceased's family and its views were prominently featured in the media. Then, several years passed while the case awaited disposition in the court of appeal. There was no publicity during this time frame. In 1995, the court of appeal ordered a new trial and in late 1995, the Supreme Court refused leave to the Crown to appeal. The media reported these appellate proceedings factually, revisiting the facts of the case, the accused's prior conviction, sentence and the community polarization over his reinstatement. It also reported on the accused's application for a change of venue at the new trial. What factors would be relevant to the disposition of this application? What submissions would you make as defence and Crown counsel? What materials would you file to support the respective positions? What would you like to know as trial judge before deciding the application that has not been noted above? What, if any, safeguards are available to you to ensure a fair trial if you refuse to grant the application? Consider, in this regard, *R. v. Tricker* (June 28, 1996) (Ont. Gen. Div.).

4. **Whether the application for a change of venue is or is not granted, can the court hearing the application order that the fact of the application itself not be published until the trial is completed? Consider, in this regard, *Re Southam Inc. and The Queen* (1982), 70 C.C.C. (2d) 264 (Ont. H.C.J.).**

CHAPTER 3

TEMPORAL AND OTHER LIMITATIONS UPON JURISDICTION

A. LIMITATION PERIODS

Under s. 786(2) of the *Criminal Code*, no summary conviction proceedings shall be instituted more than six months after the time when the subject matter of the proceedings arose, unless the prosecutor and the defendant so agree. This applies whether or not the offence is a pure summary conviction offence or a hybrid offence where the Crown elects to proceed summarily. A charge involving a *continuing offence* may not be invalidated by the limitation period, even though part of the offence occurred outside the limitation period. Generally, limitation periods have no application to indictable offences. Treason is an exception (s. 48(1) of the *Criminal Code*).

QUESTIONS

1. **The accused is charged with sexual assault on September 1, 2002 for assaulting his younger cousin from September 2001 to April 2002. The alleged victim is emotionally distraught and the Crown would like to avoid subjecting her to cross-examination at both a preliminary inquiry and at a trial. The Crown, therefore, elects to proceed summarily. Can the Crown do so?**

2. **The accused is charged with a hybrid offence. The Crown elects to proceed summarily. On the day of trial, the Crown notes that the offence was committed one year prior to the information being sworn. Can the Crown change its election over the objection of the defence? Alternatively, can the Crown withdraw the charge and instruct the police to relay the same charge to be prosecuted by indictment? What if the trial has already commenced? Consider, in this regard, the conflicting authorities on this issue: *R. v. Kelly* (1998), 128 C.C.C. (3d) 206 (Ont. C.A.), *Re Parkin and the Queen* (1986), 28 C.C.C. (3d) 252 (Ont. C.A.); *R. v. Quinn* (1989), 54 C.C.C. (3d) 157 (Que. C.A.); *R. v. Belair* (1988), 41 C.C.C. (3d) 329 (Ont. C.A.); *R. v. Jans* (1990), 59 C.C.C. (3d) 398 (Alta C.A.); *R. v. Maramba* (1995), 104 C.C.C. (3d) 85 (Ont. C.A.); *R. v. Boutilier* (1995), 104 C.C.C. (3d) 327 (N.S.C.A.). The resolution of this issue is clear if the Crown attempts to reproceed after the charge has been *dismissed* by the court after arraignment.**

3. **Under what circumstances would the defendant agree to an information alleging a summary conviction offence being laid outside of the six month limitation period?**

B. CHARTER DELAY: SECTION 11(*b*)

Section 11(*b*) of the *Charter* provides that "[a]ny person charged with an offence has the right to be tried within a reasonable time". If the accused demonstrates to the trial judge that his or her right under s. 11(*b*) has been violated, a judicial stay of the proceedings may be entered pursuant to s. 24(1) of the *Charter*. Accordingly, numerous judgments have addressed the meaning of a trial "within a reasonable time".

R. v. ASKOV

(1990), 59 C.C.C. (3d) 449 (S.C.C.)

[Extortion, weapons and assault charges against the accused had taken three years to come to trial. The court found that the one-year delay prior to the preliminary inquiry was largely attributable to the defence, but that the two-year delay between the preliminary inquiry and the trial resulted from a lack of resources in that particular jurisdiction.]

Cory J. [Dickson C.J.C., La Forest, L'Heureux-Dubé and Gonthier JJ. concurring]: — Section 11(*b*) of the *Canadian Charter of Rights and Freedoms* provides that any person charged with an offence has the right to be tried within a reasonable time. What constitutes an unreasonable delay of a trial must be determined on this appeal. In order to reach a conclusion it will be necessary to consider and apply criteria or factors which should be used to ascertain if a delay is unreasonable and in particular, to consider the consequences of so-called institutional delays.

.....

The United States

In the United States the Sixth Amendment ensures that "[i]n all criminal prosecutions, the accused shall enjoy the right to a speedy and public trial". The United States Supreme Court considered the issue in *Barker v. Wingo*, 407 U.S. 514 (1972). In that case Barker, who was charged with murder, was brought to trial five years after the murder was committed. The delay was caused by the necessity of trying an accomplice beforehand. This prerequisite trial was extremely complicated; the accomplice was tried no less than six times. During this ongoing process, Barker initially had agreed to continuances or adjournments. He only began to assert his right to a speedy trial three and one-half years after the charges were laid.

The court held that a flexible approach should be taken to cases involving delay and that the multiple purposes or aims of the Sixth Amendment must be appreciated. Powell J., giving the reasons for the court, recognized the general concern that all persons accused of crimes should be treated according to fair and decent procedures. He particularly noted that there were three individual interests which the right was designed to protect. They were:

(i) to prevent oppressive pre-trial incarceration;
(ii) to minimize the anxiety and concern of the accused, and
(iii) to limit the possibility that the defence will be impaired or prejudiced.

However, Powell J. went on to observe that unlike other constitutional rights which only have an individual interest, the right to a speedy trial involved the added dimension of a societal interest. He found that a delay could result in increased financial cost to society and as well, could have a negative effect upon the credibility of the justice system. Further, it was noted that a delay could work to the advantage of the accused. For example, the fostering of a delay could become a defence tactic designed to take advantage of failing memories or missing witnesses or could permit the accused to manipulate the system in order to bargain for a lesser sentence. Specifically, he stated at p. 521 that the right to a speedy trial was:

> a more vague concept than other procedural rights. It is, for example, impossible to determine with precision when the right has been denied. We cannot definitely say how long is too long in a system where justice is supposed to be swift but deliberate. As a consequence, there is no fixed point in the criminal process when the State can put the defendant to the choice of either exercising or waiving the right to a speedy trial.

In order to balance the individual right and the communal aspect of the Sixth Amendment, the U.S. Supreme Court adopted an approach of *ad hoc* balancing "in which the conduct of both the prosecution and the defendant are weighed" (p. 530). The balancing is undertaken by reference to four factors identified by Powell J. as the test for infringement of the right to a "speedy trial". They are as follows:

(i) the length of the delay;
(ii) the reason for the delay;
(iii) the accused's assertion of the right, and
(iv) prejudice to the accused.

The first factor is the triggering mechanism or threshold determination of the excessiveness of the delay. If that delay appears *prima facie* excessive, the court must then consider the three remaining factors to determine whether the accused has been deprived of the Sixth Amendment right.

[Cory J. then reviewed the Supreme Court of Canada decisions on s. 11(*b*) of the *Charter: R. v. Mills* (1986), 26 C.C.C. (3d) 481; *R. v. Rahey* (1987), 33 C.C.C. (3d) 289; *R. v. Conway* (1989), 49 C.C.C. (3d) 289; and *R. v. Smith* (1989), 52 C.C.C. (3d) 97.]

Purpose of s. 11(b)

I agree with the position taken by Lamer J. that s. 11(*b*) explicitly focuses upon the individual interest of liberty and security of the person. Like other specific guarantees provided by s. 11, this paragraph is primarily concerned with an aspect of fundamental justice guaranteed by s. 7 of the

Charter. There could be no greater frustration imaginable for innocent persons charged with an offence than to be denied the opportunity of demonstrating their innocence for an unconscionable time as a result of unreasonable delays in their trial. The time awaiting trial must be exquisite agony for accused persons and their immediate family. It is a fundamental precept of our criminal law that every individual is presumed to be innocent until proven guilty. It follows that on the same fundamental level of importance, all accused persons, each one of whom is presumed to be innocent, should be given the opportunity to defend themselves against the charges they face and to have their name cleared and reputation re-established at the earliest possible time.

Although the primary aim of s. 11(*b*) is the protection of the individual's rights and the provision of fundamental justice for the accused, none the less there is, in my view, at least by inference, a community or societal interest implicit in s. 11(*b*). That community interest has a dual dimension. First, there is a collective interest in ensuring that those who transgress the law are brought to trial and dealt with according to the law. Secondly, those individuals on trial must be treated fairly and justly. Speedy trials strengthen both those aspects of the community interest. A trial held within a reasonable time must benefit the individual accused as the prejudice which results from criminal proceedings is bound to be minimized. If the accused is in custody, the custodial time awaiting trial will be kept to a minimum. If the accused is at liberty on bail and subject to conditions, then the curtailments on the liberty of the accused will be kept to a minimum. From the point of view of the community interest, in those cases where the accused is detained in custody awaiting trial, society will benefit by the quick resolution of the case either by reintegrating into society the accused found to be innocent or if found guilty by dealing with the accused according to the law. If the accused is released on bail and subsequently found guilty, the frustration felt by the community on seeing an unpunished wrongdoer in their midst for an extended period of time will be relieved.

There are as well important practical benefits which flow from a quick resolution of the charges. There can be no doubt that memories fade with time. Witnesses are likely to be more reliable testifying to events in the immediate past as opposed to events that transpired many months or even years before the trial. Not only is there an erosion of the witnesses' memory with the passage of time, but there is bound to be an erosion of the witnesses themselves. Witnesses are people; they are moved out of the country by their employer, or for reasons related to family or work they move from the east coast to the west coast; they become sick and unable to testify in court; they are involved in debilitating accidents; they die and their testimony is forever lost. Witnesses too are concerned that their evidence be taken as quickly as possible. Testifying is often thought to be an ordeal. It is something that weighs on the minds of witnesses and is a source of worry and frustration for them until they have given their testimony.

It can never be forgotten that the victims may be devastated by criminal acts. They have a special interest and good reason to expect that criminal trials take place within a reasonable time. From a wider point of view, it is fair to say that all crime disturbs the community and that serious crime alarms the community. All members of the community are thus entitled to see that the justice system works fairly, efficiently and with reasonable dispatch. The very reasonable concern and alarm of the community which naturally arises from acts of crime cannot be assuaged until the trial has taken place. The trial not only resolves the guilt or innocence of the individual, but acts as a reassurance to the community that serious crimes are investigated and that those implicated are brought to trial and dealt with according to the law.

The failure of the justice system to deal fairly, quickly and efficiently with criminal trials inevitably leads to the community's frustration with the judicial system and eventually to a feeling of contempt for court procedures. When a trial takes place without unreasonable delay, with all witnesses available and memories fresh, it is far more certain that the guilty parties who committed the crimes will be convicted and punished and those that did not, will be acquitted and vindicated. It is no exaggeration to say that a fair and balanced criminal justice system simply cannot exist without the support of the community. Continued community support for our system will not endure in the face of lengthy and unreasonable delays.

Further, implicit support for the concept that there is a societal aspect to s. 11(*b*) can be derived from the observation that the last thing that some wish for is a speedy trial. There is no doubt that many accused earnestly hope that the memory of a witness will fail and that other witnesses will become unavailable. This factor was noted by T.G. Zuber in his *Report of the Ontario Courts Inquiry* (1987), p. 73:

> It is, however, the observation of this Inquiry that those accused of crime and their counsel are often disinterested in trial within a reasonable time. Delay is perceived not as a factor which will impair the ability of the accused to present a defence but rather a factor which will erode the case for the prosecution.

Doherty J. wrote to the same effect in a paper delivered to the National Criminal Law Programme in July, 1989. He wrote:

> Many accused do not want to be tried at all, and many embrace any opportunity to delay judgment day. This reluctance to go to trial is no doubt a very human reaction to judgment days of any sort; as well as a reflection of the fact that in many cases delay inures to the benefit of the accused. An accused is often not interested in exercising the right bestowed on him by s. 11(*b*). His interest lies in having the right infringed by the prosecution so that he can escape a trial on the merits. This view may seem harsh but experience supports its validity.
>
> This unique attitude on the part of the accused toward his right often puts a court in a position where it perceives itself as being asked to dismiss a charge, not because the accused was denied something which he wanted, and which could have assisted him, but rather, because he got exactly what he wanted, or at least was happy to have — delay. A dismissal of the charge, the only remedy available when s. 11(*b*) is found to have been violated sticks in the judicial craw when everyone in the courtroom knows that the last thing the accused wanted was a speedy trial. It hardly enhances the reputation of the administration of justice when an accused escapes a trial on the merits, not because he was wronged in any real sense, but rather because he successfully played the waiting game.

As these comments from distinguished jurists indicate, the s. 11(*b*) right is one which can often be transformed from a protective shield to an offensive weapon in the hands of the accused.

.....

Although it must be recognized that the primary goal of s. 11(*b*) is the protection of the individual's interest in fundamental justice, nevertheless that same section contains a secondary and inferred societal interest that should not be ignored. If the recognition of both the primary individual interest and the inferred society interest is accepted as the true aim of s. 11(*b*), then I think the various factors which should be taken into consideration in determining whether there has been an unreasonable delay, can be clarified and set forth in a consistent test.

Factors to be taken into account in determining whether or not there has been an infringement of s. 11(b)

(i) The length of the delay

It is clear that the longer the delay, the more difficult it should be for a court to excuse it. This is not a threshold requirement as in the United States, but rather is a factor to be balanced along with the others. However, very lengthy delays may be such that they cannot be justified for any reason.

(ii) Explanation for the delay

This category referred to by Sopinka J. in *Smith, supra,* may be usefully subdivided with the aspects of systemic delay and conduct of the accused amplified.

(a) The conduct of the Crown (or delay attributable to the Crown)

Generally speaking, this category will comprise all of the potential factors causing delay which flow from the nature of the case, the conduct of the Crown, including officers of the State, and the inherent time requirements of the case. Delays attributable to the actions of the Crown or its officers will weigh in favour of the accused. For example, the 19 adjournments initiated by the trial judge in *Rahey* or the unavailability of judges because of holidays in *Smith* are examples where the actions or the lack of actions of Crown officers weighed against the State in the assessment of the reasonableness of the delay.

It is under this heading that the complexity of the case should be taken into account. Complex cases which require longer time for preparation, a greater expenditure of resources by Crown officers and the longer use of institutional facilities will justify delays longer than those that would be acceptable in simple cases.

(b) Systemic or institutional delays

On a more specific level, the question of delays caused by systemic or institutional limitations should also be discussed under the heading of delays attributable to the Crown. This factor will often be the most difficult to assess. A careful and sensitive balancing will be required in order to properly assess the significance of this aspect of delay. First, let us consider the problem from the point of view of society. Section 11(*b*) applies to all Canadians in every part of our land. In a country as vast and diverse as ours, the institutional problems are bound to differ greatly from province to province and from district to district within each province. Differences of climate, terrain, population and financial resources will require different solutions for the problem of providing adequate facilities and personnel. Lack of financial resources may require imaginative answers to difficult problems, including the provision of temporary facilities. The problems presented and the solutions required will vary between heavily populated centres such as Toronto and Montreal and the sparsely populated districts bordering on Hudson Bay.

Wise political decisions will be required with regard to the allocation of scarce funds. Due deference will have to be given to those political decisions as the provisions of court-room facilities and Crown Attorneys must, for example, be balanced against the provision of health care and highways. Yet solutions must be found as indeed they have been in many jurisdictions outside Ontario. Similarly situated communities can provide a rough comparison and some guidance as to what time period constitutes an unreasonable delay of the trial of an accused person. That comparison should always be made with the more efficient of the comparable jurisdictions.

The right guaranteed by s. 11(*b*) is of such fundamental importance to the individual and of such significance to the community as a whole that the lack of institutional resources cannot be employed to justify a continuing unreasonable postponement of trials.

.....

However, the lack of institutional facilities can never be used as a basis for rendering the s. 11(*b*) guarantee meaningless. In the same case, Lamer J. gave clear warning of the dangers that would ensue from permitting the lack of institutional resources to constitute an acceptable excuse for unreasonable delays. At p. 550 C.C.C., p. 230 D.L.R., he stated:

> It is imperative, however, that in recognizing the need for such a criterion we do not simply legitimate current and future delays resulting from inadequate institutional resources. *For the criterion of institutional resources, more than any other, threatens to become a source of justification for prolonged and unacceptable delay*. There must, therefore, be some limit to which inadequate resources can be used to excuse delay and impair the interests of the individual.

(Emphasis added.)

It must be remembered that it is the duty of the Crown to bring the accused to trial. It is the Crown which is responsible for the provision of facilities and staff to see that accused persons are tried in a reasonable time.

.....

Where inordinate delays do occur, it is those who are responsible for the lack of facilities who should bear the public criticism that is bound to arise as a result of the staying of proceedings which must be the inevitable consequence of unreasonable delays. Members of the community will not and should not condone or accept a situation where those alleged to have committed serious crimes are never brought to trial solely as a result of unduly long delays. It is a serious consequence with potentially dangerous overtones for the community. It is right and proper that there be criticism of the situation when it occurs.

.....

... when considering delays occasioned by inadequate institutional resources, the question of how long a delay is too long may be resolved by comparing the questioned jurisdiction to the standard maintained by the best comparable jurisdiction in the country. The comparison need not be too precise or exact. Rather, it should look to the appropriate ranges of delay to determine what is a reasonable limit. In all cases it will be incumbent upon the Crown to show that the institutional delay in question is justifiable.

(c) The conduct of the accused (or delay attributable to the accused)

As Lamer J. so cogently observed in *Mills*, it is a fundamental precept of our criminal justice system that it is the responsibility of the Crown to bring the accused to trial. Further, the right to be tried within a reasonable time is an aspect of fundamental justice protected by s. 7 of the *Charter*. It follows that any inquiry into the conduct of the accused should in no way absolve the Crown from its responsibility to bring the accused to trial. None the less, there is a societal interest in preventing an accused from using the guarantee as a means of escaping trial. It should be emphasized that an inquiry into the actions of the accused should be restricted to discovering those situations where the accused's acts either directly caused the delay (as in *Conway*), or the acts of the accused are shown to be a deliberate and calculated tactic employed to delay the trial. These direct acts on the part of the accused, such as seeking an adjournment to retain new counsel, must of course be distinguished from those situations where the delay was caused by factors beyond the control of the accused, or a situation where the accused did nothing to prevent a delay caused by the Crown.

In addition, since the protection of the right of the individual is the primary aim of s. 11(*b*), the burden of proving that the direct acts of the accused caused the delay must fall upon the Crown. This would be true except in those cases where the effects of the accused's action are so clear and readily apparent that the intent of the accused to cause a delay is the inference that must be drawn from the record of his or her actions.

(iii) Waiver

.....

The accused should not be required to assert the explicitly protected individual right to trial within a reasonable time. It is now well established that any waiver of a *Charter* right must be "clear and unequivocal ... with full knowledge of the rights the procedure was enacted to protect and of the effect the waiver will have on those rights in the process": see *Korponey v. A.-G. Can.* (1982), 65 C.C.C. (2d) 65 at p. 74, 132 D.L.R. (3d) 354 at p. 363, [1982] 1 S.C.R. 41 *sub nom. Korponay v. A.-G. Can.* The failure of an accused to assert the right does not give the Crown licence to proceed with an unfair trial. Failure to assert the right would be insufficient in itself to impugn the motives of the accused as might be the case with regard to other s. 11 rights. Rather there must be something in the conduct of the accused that is sufficient to give rise to an inference that the accused has understood that he or she had a s. 11(*b*) guarantee, understood its nature and has waived the right provided by that guarantee. Although no particular magical incantation of words is required to waive a right, nevertheless the waiver must be expressed in some manner. Silence or lack of objection cannot constitute a lawful waiver. The matter was put in these words by Dickson J., as he then was, in *Park v. The Queen* (1981), 59 C.C.C. (2d) 385 at pp. 392-3, 122 D.L.R. (3d) 1 at pp. 8-9, [1981] 2 S.C.R. 64:

> No particular words or formula need be uttered by defence counsel to express the waiver and admission. All that is necessary is that the trial Judge be satisfied that counsel understands the matter and has made an informed decision to waive ... Although no particular form of words is necessary the waiver must be express. Silence or mere lack of objection does not constitute a lawful waiver.

If the Crown is relying upon actions of the accused to demonstrate waiver, then the onus will lie upon the Crown to prove that a specific waiver can be inferred. It may well be that the setting of trial dates and the agreement to those dates by counsel for the accused may be sufficient to constitute waiver.

.....

In sum, the burden always rests with the Crown to bring the case to trial. Further, the mere silence of the accused is not sufficient to indicate a waiver of a *Charter* right; rather, the accused must undertake some direct action from which a consent to delay can be properly inferred. The onus rests upon the Crown to establish on a balance of probabilities that the actions of the accused constitute a waiver of his or her rights.

(iv) Prejudice to the accused

The different positions taken by members of the court with regard to the prejudice suffered by an accused as a result of a delayed trial are set forth in *Mills* and *Rahey*. Perhaps the differences can be resolved in this manner. It should be inferred that a very long and unreasonable delay has prejudiced the accused. As Sopinka J. put it in *Smith, supra*, at p. 111:

> Having found that the delay is substantially longer than can be justified on any acceptable basis, it would be difficult indeed to conclude that the appellant's s. 11(*b*) rights have not been violated because the appellant has suffered no prejudice. In this particular context, the inference of prejudice is so strong that it would be difficult to disagree with the view of Lamer J. in *Mills* and *Rahey* that it is virtually irrebuttable.

Nevertheless, it will be open to the Crown to attempt to demonstrate that the accused has not been prejudiced. This would preserve the societal interest by providing that a trial would proceed in those cases where despite a long delay no resulting damage had been suffered by the accused. Yet, the existence of the inference of prejudice drawn from a very long delay will safely preserve the pre-eminent right of the individual. Obviously, the difficulty of overcoming the inference will of necessity become more difficult with the passage of time and at some point will become irrebuttable. None the less, the factual situation presented in *Conway* serves as an example of an extremely lengthy delay which did not prejudice the accused. However, in most situations, as Sopinka J. pointed out in *Smith*, the presumption will be "virtually irrebuttable".

Furthermore, the option left open by Sopinka J. in the *Smith* case whereby accused persons who have suffered some additional form of prejudice are permitted to adduce evidence of prejudice on their own initiative in order to strengthen their position in seeking a remedy under s. 24(1) of the *Charter* is consistent with the primary concern of protecting the individual's right under s. 11(*b*).

Application of the principles to the case at bar

As the disposition of this case will ultimately turn on the factors headed (ii) Explanation for the delay, particularly (b) Systemic or institutional delay and (c) Delays attributable to the accused, and (iii) Waiver, I need but briefly deal with the factors titled (i) The length of the delay and (iv) Prejudice to the accused.

(i) The length of the delay

No matter what standard of measure is used or what test is applied, the trial in this case has been inordinately delayed. Even when the first period of delay of approximately one year prior to the preliminary hearing is discounted as being in large part attributable to the request for adjournments by the appellants, there remains a delay period of almost two years. The experienced trial judge who has presided for many years in Peel District described the delay as "clearly excessive and unreasonable". It is interesting to note that the delay at issue in *Mills* was 19 months, in *Rahey* 11 months, and in *Smith* one year. Although the period of delay in *Conway* is comparable to that of this case, it must be remembered that in that case the delay was directly attributable to the actions of Conway.

.....

(iv) Prejudice to the accused

The trial judge found that the appellants had been prejudiced by the delay. In support, he noted the lengthy period of incarceration for three of the appellants and the restrictions contained in the bail terms. Those conditions of bail included curfews, a direction not to associate with the co-accused and a system of regular reporting to the police. There has been no attack on these findings. Consequently, it is impossible to say that the Crown discharged the burden that rested upon it to show that the delay caused no prejudice to the appellants. As a result, the prejudice suffered by the appellants weighs against the Crown and cannot be used to excuse the length of delay.

(ii) Explanation for the delay

(a) Delays attributable to the Crown

It is clear that delays cannot be attributable to any action of the Crown. At no time did the Crown make any requests for adjournments or take any step that delayed the trial of the action in any way.

There is nothing in the case that is so complex or inherently difficult that it would justify a lengthy delay. It is true that the case involves a charge of conspiracy. However, the proof would consist of what was seen and heard by the witnesses, particularly the undercover officer. It is reasonable to assume that the victim and the police officers were ready and capable of testifying on relatively short notice. There was no need for any lengthy investigation or the retention of and discussions with expert witnesses. There was not any aspect of this case that could even remotely be considered to be an exceptional circumstance that would justify a lengthy delay.

(b) Systemic or institutional delay

This trial was to be heard in Brampton, in the District of Peel in Ontario. This district has long been notorious for the inordinate length of time required to obtain a trial date. The delays are said to be caused by lack of facilities. The evidence submitted contains a study done by Professor Carl Baar, Director of the Judicial Administration Programme at Brock University. From the research and comparative studies that he has undertaken, Professor Baar has concluded that the Peel District (referred to as Brampton by Professor Baar) experiences extremely long delays that are out of the ordinary compared to the rest of Ontario, the rest of Canada or the United States. He notes that the situation has arisen partly as a result of rapid urban growth and the presence of a very large international airport which generates a great many drug-related offences. He also finds that a shortage of court space and judges are significant factors which contribute to the lengthy delays. His research indicates that comparatively speaking it is without doubt one of the worst districts in Canada, if not the worst, in terms of delays between committal and trial. Ontario can take no pride in this situation and must indeed bear the responsibility for it.

.....

The extent and gravity of the problem in Peel is brought home by reference to the comparative study done in 1987 by Professor Baar. The study illustrated that in Canada, New Brunswick and Quebec were best able to bring their cases to trial within the 30 to 90-day range. In terms of the time taken to completely dispose of a case from committal to disposition, the median total time in New Brunswick's lower courts (Provincial Courts) was 152 days. The median total time in upper courts (s. 96 courts) was 72 days. By comparison, in Ontario the best district was London with a median total time of 239 days and the median upper court time of 105 days. Toronto,

Ottawa and St. Catharines were all close together with median total times of between 315 and 349 days, and upper court times between 133 and 144 days.

Professor Baar wrote that "[b]y all measures used in the study, Brampton District Court was significantly slower than any other location studied: median total time was 607 days and median upper court time was 423 days". Nor can any comfort be drawn by comparison to the United States. Professor Baar concluded that the Peel District is generally substantially slower than the slowest United States jurisdictions. Further, he noted that the delay in the present case was longer than 90% of all cases in terms of median total time among those heard even in Peel District. This case therefore represents one of the worst from the point of view of delay in the worst district not only in Canada, but so far as the studies indicate, anywhere north of the Rio Grande.

.....

Making a very rough comparison and more than doubling the longest waiting period to make every allowance for the special circumstances in Peel would indicate a period of delay in a range of some six to eight months between committal and trial might be deemed to be the outside limit of what is reasonable. The usual delays in Peel are more than four times as long as those of busy metropolitan districts in the Province of Quebec and the delay in this case is more than eight times as long. The figures from the comparable districts demonstrate that the Peel District situation is unreasonable and intolerable.

The delay in this case is such that it is impossible to come to any other conclusion than that the s. 11(*b*) *Charter* rights guaranteed to the individual accused have been infringed. As well, the societal interest in ensuring that these accused be brought to trial within a reasonable time has been grossly offended and denigrated. Indeed, the delay is of such an inordinate length that public confidence in the administration of justice must be shaken. Justice so delayed is an affront to the individual, to the community and to the very administration of justice. The lack of institutional facilities cannot in this case be accepted as a basis for justifying the delay.

I am well aware that as a consequence of this decision, a stay of proceedings must be directed. This is, to say the least, most unfortunate and regrettable. It is obvious that the charges against the appellants are serious. Extortion and threatened armed violence tears at the basic fabric of society. To accede to such conduct would constitute a denial of the rule of law and an acceptance of a rule that unlawful might makes right. The community has good reason to be alarmed by the commission of serious crimes. There can be no doubt that it would be in the best interest of society to proceed with the trial of those who are charged with posing such a serious threat to the community. Yet, that trial can only be undertaken if the *Charter* right to trial within a reasonable time has not been infringed. In this case that right has been grievously infringed and the sad result is that a stay of proceedings must be entered. To conclude otherwise would render meaningless a right enshrined in the *Charter* as the supreme law of the land.

.....

[Cory J. conducted a review of the transcript of the proceedings and concluded that, apart from delay which occurred prior to the preliminary inquiry, there was no delay attributable to the accused nor did the accused waive their s. 11(*b*) *Charter* rights.]

Conclusion

The foregoing review indicates that there is no basis upon which this delay can be justified and as a result, a stay of proceedings must be directed.

Soon after *Askov*'s impact was felt throughout Canada, and most particularly in Ontario, the Supreme Court of Canada reconsidered its earlier judgment.

R. v. MORIN

(1992), 71 C.C.C. (3d) 1 (S.C.C.)

[The accused was charged with impaired driving and "over 80" on January 9, 1988. The Crown proceeded summarily. At the defendant's first appearance in court, counsel requested "the earliest possible trial date". On March 28, 1989, the trial date, the defence unsuccessfully brought a motion for a stay of proceedings on the grounds that the 14 and a half month delay to trial violated the defendant's s. 11(*b*) *Charter* rights. The defendant was convicted. The defendant successfully appealed to the summary conviction appeal court and a stay was granted. The Ontario Court of Appeal allowed the appeal and restored the conviction. The defendant appealed to the Supreme Court of Canada.]

Sopinka J. [La Forest, Stevenson, Iacobucci JJ. concurring]: — The issue in this appeal concerns the right of an accused to be tried within a reasonable time. This right is enshrined in s. 11(*b*) of the *Canadian Charter of Rights and Freedoms* ...

.....

Though beguiling in its simplicity, [the language in s. 11(*b*)] has presented the court with one of its most difficult challenges in search of an interpretation that respects the right of the individual in an era in which the administration of justice is faced both with dwindling resources and a burgeoning case-load. We are asked in this appeal to re-examine the problem in light of the effect on the administration of justice of our decision in *R. v. Askov* (1990), 59 C.C.C. (3d) 449, 74 D.L.R. (4th) 355, [1990] 2 S.C.R. 1199. Evidence presented to us indicates that between October 22, 1990, and September 6, 1991, over 47,000 charges have been stayed or withdrawn in Ontario alone. The reaction to this has been mixed. On the one hand, many applaud the result which has in their view unclogged the system of much dead wood in the form of charges that should not have been laid or, having been laid, ought to have been dropped. This, they say, will enable the system to more quickly accommodate cases that are more pressing and lessen the period during which alleged criminals are free to roam the streets while awaiting trial. On the other hand, many others deprecate what in their opinion amounts to an amnesty for criminals, some of whom were charged with very serious crimes. They assert that accused persons are discharged when they have suffered no prejudice to the complete dismay of victims who have suffered, in some cases, tragic losses.

.....

Points in issue

The major issue to be determined in this appeal is whether the accused's right to a trial within a reasonable time as guaranteed by s. 11(*b*) of the *Charter* has been infringed by the delay experienced in this case. A subsidiary issue arises if the answer to the above question is in the affirmative. That subsidiary question is whether the delay can be excused as a result of the need for a transitional period to allow the government to discharge its burden of providing trials within a reasonable time.

Jurisprudential development of s. 11(b)

The development of the jurisprudence relating to s. 11(*b*) is instructive in that it underscores the importance of avoiding rigidity in the interpretation of new constitutional rights early in the life of a constitutional document. The court could have simply adopted the American approach articulated in *Barker v. Wingo*, 407 U.S. 514 (1972), which has resulted in only the most egregious delays being proscribed. Instead, in accordance with the intent of the *Charter*, this court has attempted to develop a Canadian approach with due regard for the American experience. Embarking as we did on uncharted waters, it is not surprising that the course we steered has required, and may require in the future, some alteration in its direction to accord with experience.

.....

Finally, in *Askov* [(1990), 59 C.C.C. (3d) 449 (S.C.C.)] we dealt with a case which came to us from the Court of Appeal for Ontario and originated in Brampton, Ontario, a notorious sore spot in relation to unreasonable delay. Applying the basic criteria in *Smith*, the court was unanimous that the delay was unreasonable. The court went on to suggest that "a period of delay in a range of some six to eight months between committal and trial might be deemed to be the outside limit of what is reasonable" (p. 490). It is the interpretation and application of this statement that resulted in the large number of stays and withdrawals to which I have referred.

This appeal came before the Court of Appeal for Ontario after the release of our judgments in *Smith* and *Stensrud* but before *Askov*. I have already indicated that the court invited the parties to provide additional evidence with respect to the situation in the District of Durham relating to institutional limitations and resources. It was in this jurisprudential and evidentiary setting that the Court of Appeal reached its decision.

The purpose of s. 11(b)

The primary purpose of s. 11(*b*) is the protection of the individual rights of accused. A secondary interest of society as a whole has, however, been recognized by this court. I will address each of these interests and their interaction.

The individual rights which the section seeks to protect are: (1) the right to security of the person; (2) the right to liberty, and (3) the right to a fair trial.

The right to security of the person is protected in s. 11(*b*) by seeking to minimize the anxiety, concern and stigma of exposure to criminal proceedings. The right to liberty is protected by seeking to minimize exposure to the restrictions on liberty which result from pre-trial incarceration and restrictive bail conditions. The right to a fair trial is protected by attempting to ensure that proceedings take place while evidence is available and fresh.

The secondary societal interest is most obvious when it parallels that of the accused. Society as a whole has an interest in seeing that the least fortunate of its citizens who are accused of crimes are treated humanely and fairly. In this respect trials held promptly enjoy the confidence of the public. As observed by Martin J.A. in *R. v. Beason* (1983), 7 C.C.C. (3d) 20, 1 D.L.R. (4th) 218, 36 C.R. (3d) 73 (Ont. C.A.): "Trials held within a reasonable time have an intrinsic value. The constitutional guarantee enures to the benefit of society as a whole and, indeed, to the ultimate benefit of the accused..." (p. 41). In some cases, however, the accused has no interest in an early trial and society's interest will not parallel that of the accused.

There is, as well, a societal interest that is by its very nature adverse to the interests of the accused. In *Conway*, a majority of this court recognized that the interests of the accused must be balanced by the interests of society in law enforcement. This theme was picked up in *Askov* in the reasons of Cory J. who referred to "a collective interest in ensuring that those who transgress the law are brought to trial and dealt with according to the law" (p. 474). As the seriousness of the offence increases so does the societal demand that the accused be brought to trial. The role of this interest is most evident and its influence most apparent when it is sought to absolve persons accused of serious crimes simply to clean up the docket.

The approach to unreasonable delay — the factors

The general approach to a determination as to whether the right has been denied is not by the application of a mathematical or administrative formula but rather by a judicial determination balancing the interests which the section is designed to protect against factors which either inevitably lead to delay or are otherwise the cause of delay. As I noted in *Smith, supra*, "[i]t is axiomatic that some delay is inevitable. The question is, at what point does the delay become unreasonable?" (p. 105). While the court has at times indicated otherwise, it is now accepted that the factors to be considered in analyzing how long is too long may be listed as follows:

1. the length of the delay;
2. waiver of time periods;

3. the reasons for the delay, including
   (a) inherent time requirements of the case;
   (b) actions of the accused;
   (c) actions of the Crown;
   (d) limits on institutional resources, and
   (e) other reasons for delay, and
4. prejudice to the accused.

.....

The judicial process referred to as "balancing" requires an examination of the length of the delay and its evaluation in light of the other factors. A judicial determination is then made as to whether the period of delay is unreasonable. In coming to this conclusion, account must be taken of the interests which s. 11(*b*) is designed to protect. Leaving aside the question of delay on appeal, the period to be scrutinized is the time elapsed from the date of the charge to the end of the trial: see *R. v. Kalanj* (1989), 48 C.C.C. (3d) 459, [1989] 1 S.C.R. 1594, 70 C.R. (3d) 260. The length of this period may be shortened by subtracting periods of delay that have been waived. It must then be determined whether this period is unreasonable having regard to the interests s. 11(*b*) seeks to protect, the explanation for the delay and the prejudice to the accused.

.....

The role of the burden of proof in this balancing process was set out in the unanimous judgment of this court in *Smith* [(1989), 52 C.C.C. (3d) 97], as follows (at pp. 106-7):

> I accept that the accused has the ultimate or legal burden of proof throughout. A case will only be decided by reference to the burden of proof if the court cannot come to a determinate conclusion on the facts presented to it. Although the accused may have the ultimate or legal burden, a secondary or evidentiary burden of putting forth evidence or argument may shift depending on the circumstances of each case. For example, a long period of delay occasioned by a request of the Crown for an adjournment would ordinarily call for an explanation from the Crown as to the necessity for the adjournment. In the absence of such an explanation, the court would be entitled to infer that the delay is unjustified. It would be appropriate to speak of the Crown having a secondary or evidentiary burden under these circumstances. In all cases, the court should be mindful that it is seldom necessary or desirable to decide this question on the basis of burden of proof and that it is preferable to evaluate the reasonableness of the over-all lapse of time, having regard to the factors referred to above.

I do not read the *Askov* decision as having departed from this statement although portions of the reasons of Cory J. emphasized certain aspects of the evidentiary burden on the Crown.

A definition of each of these factors and their interaction follows. I will deal with them in the order that they should be considered by a trial court.

1. The length of the delay

As I have indicated, this factor requires the court to examine the period from the charge to the end of the trial. "Charge" means the date on which an information is sworn or an indictment is preferred: see *Kalanj, supra*, at p. 469. Pre-charge delay may in certain circumstances have an influence on the over-all determination as to whether post-charge delay is unreasonable but of itself it is not counted in determining the length of the delay.

An inquiry into unreasonable delay is triggered by an application under s. 24(1) of the *Charter*. The applicant has the legal burden of establishing a *Charter* violation. The inquiry, which can be complex ... should only be undertaken if the period is of sufficient length to raise an issue as to its reasonableness. If the length of the delay is unexceptional, no inquiry is warranted and no explanation for the delay is called for unless the applicant is able to raise the issue of reasonableness of the period by reference to other factors such as prejudice. If, for example, the applicant is in custody, a shorter period of delay will raise the issue.

2. Waiver of time periods

If the length of the delay warrants an inquiry into the reasons for delay, it appears logical to deal with any allegation of waiver before embarking on the more detailed examination of the reasons for delay. If by agreement or other conduct the accused has waived in whole or in part his or her rights to complain of delay, then this will either dispose of the matter or allow the period waived to be deducted.

This court has clearly stated that in order for an accused to waive his or her rights under s. 11(*b*), such waiver must be clear and unequivocal, with full knowledge of the rights the procedure was enacted to protect and of the effect that waiver will have on those rights: *Korponey v. A.-G. Can.* (1982), 65 C.C.C. (2d) 65 at p. 74, 132 D.L.R. (3d) 354, [1982] 1 S.C.R. 41; *R. v. Clarkson* (1986), 25 C.C.C. (3d) 207 at pp. 217-9, 26 D.L.R. (4th) 493, [1986] 1 S.C.R. 383; *Askov, supra*, at pp. 481-2). Waiver can be explicit or implicit. If the waiver is said to be implicit, the conduct of the accused must comply with the stringent test for waiver set out above.

.....

Waiver requires advertence to the act of release rather than mere inadvertence. If the mind of the accused or his or her counsel is not turned to the issue of waiver and is not aware of what his or her conduct signifies, then this conduct does not constitute waiver. Such conduct may be taken into account under the factor "actions of the accused" but it is not waiver. As I stated in *Smith, supra*, which was adopted in *Askov, supra*, consent to a trial date can give rise to an inference of waiver. This will not be so if consent to a date amounts to mere acquiescence in the inevitable.

.....

3. The reasons for the delay

If the application by an accused is not resolved by reason of the principles of waiver, the court will have to consider the other explanations for delay. Some delay is inevitable. Courts are not in session day and night. Time will be taken up in processing the charge, retention of counsel, applications for bail and other pre-trial procedures. Time is required for counsel to prepare. Over and above these inherent time requirements of a case, time may be consumed to accommodate the prosecution or defence. Neither side, however, can rely on their own delay to support their respective positions. When a case is ready for trial a judge, court-room or essential court staff may not be available and so the case cannot go on. This latter type of delay is referred to as institutional or systemic delay. I now turn to a closer examination of each of these reasons and the role each plays in determining what delay is unreasonable.

(a) Inherent time requirements

All offences have certain inherent time requirements which inevitably lead to delay. Just as the fire-truck must get to the fire, so must a case be prepared. The complexity of the trial is one requirement which has often been mentioned. All other factors being equal, the more complicated a case, the longer it will take counsel to prepare for trial and for the trial to be conducted once it begins. For example, a fraud case may involve the analysis of many documents, some conspiracies may involve a large number of witnesses and other cases may involve numerous intercepted communications which all must be transcribed and analyzed. The inherent requirements of such cases will serve to excuse longer periods of delay than for cases which are less complex. Each case will bring its own set of facts which must be evaluated. Account must also be taken of the fact that counsel for the prosecution and the defence cannot be expected to devote their time exclusively to one case. The amount of time that should be allowed counsel is well within the field of expertise of trial judges.

As well as the complexity of a case, there are inherent requirements which are common to almost all cases. The respondent has described such activities as "intake requirements". Whatever one wishes to call these requirements, they consist of activities such as retention of counsel, bail hearings, police and administration paperwork, disclosure, etc. All of these activities may or may not be necessary in a particular case but each takes some amount of time. As the number and complexity of these activities increase, so does the amount of delay that is reasonable. Equally, the fewer the activities which are necessary and the simpler the form each activity takes, the shorter should be the delay. The respondent suggests that this court should set an administrative guideline for such an "intake period". We decline to do so on the basis of the record that is before us. The length of time necessary will be influenced by local practices and conditions and should reflect that fact.

.....

Another inherent delay that must be taken into account is whether a case must proceed through a preliminary inquiry. Clearly a longer time must be allowed for cases that must proceed through a "two-stage" trial process than for cases which do not require a preliminary hearing. Equally, a two-stage process will involve additional inherent delays such as further pre-trial meetings and added court dates. An additional period for inherent time requirements must be allowed for this second stage. This period will be shorter than in the case of the one-stage trial process because many of the intake procedures will not have to be duplicated.

(b) Actions of the accused

This aspect of the reasons for the delay should not be read as putting the "blame" on the accused for certain portions of delay. There is no necessity to impute improper motives to the accused in considering this factor. Included under this heading are all actions taken by the accused which may have caused delay. In this section I am concerned with actions of the accused which are voluntarily undertaken. Actions which could be included in this category include change of venue motions, attacks on wiretap packets, adjournments which do not amount to waiver, attacks on search warrants, etc. I do not wish to be interpreted as advocating that the accused sacrifice all preliminary procedures and strategy, but simply point out that if the accused chooses to take such action, this will be taken into account in determining what length of delay is reasonable.

.....

(c) Actions of the Crown

As with the conduct of the accused, this factor does not serve to assign blame. This factor simply serves as a means whereby actions of the Crown which delay the trial may be investigated. Such actions include adjournments requested by the Crown, failure or delay in disclosure, change of venue motions, etc.

.....

(d) Limits on institutional resources

Institutional delay is the most common source of delay and the most difficult to reconcile with the dictates of s. 11(*b*) of the *Charter*. It was the major source of the delay in *Askov*. As I have stated, this is the period that starts to run when the parties are ready for trial but the system cannot accommodate them.

.....

How are we to reconcile the demand that trials are to be held within a reasonable time in the imperfect world of scarce resources? While account must be taken of the fact that the state does not have unlimited funds and other government programs compete for the available resources, this consideration cannot be used to render s. 11(*b*) meaningless. The court cannot simply accede to the government's allocation of resources and tailor the period of permissible delay accordingly. The weight to be given to resource limitations must be assessed in light of the fact that the government has a constitutional obligation to commit sufficient resources to prevent unreasonable delay which distinguishes this obligation from many others that compete for funds with the administration of justice. There is a point in time at which the court will no longer tolerate delay based on the plea of inadequate resources. This period of time may be referred to as an administrative guideline. I hasten to add that this guideline is neither a limitation period nor a fixed ceiling on delay. Such a guideline was suggested in *Askov* and was treated by some courts as a limitation period. I propose therefore to examine in some detail the purpose of a guideline commencing with an examination of its role in *Askov*.

In *Askov* we were dealing with a period of delay of approximately two years subsequent to committal for trial. All of this delay was institutional or systemic delay. Applying the factors that had crystallized in *Smith, supra*, we concluded that the delay was clearly unreasonable. In his reasons, which in this respect were unanimous, Cory J. did go on to state (at p. 490): "...a period of delay in a range of some six to eight months between committal and trial might be deemed to be the outside limit of what is reasonable". With respect to institutional factors, he stated (at p. 479): "The question must be answered in light of the particular facts of each case. There can be no certain standard of a fixed time which will be applicable in every region of the country."

.....

The purpose of the suggested period was not therefore that it was to be treated as a limitation period and inflexible. The purpose in expressing a guideline is twofold. First, as I have already indicated, it is to recognize that there is a limit to the delay that can be tolerated on account of resource limitations. Secondly, it is to avoid each application pursuant to s. 11(*b*) being turned into a trial of the budgetary policy of the government as it relates to the administration of justice. The flavour of such a proceeding can be appreciated by a perusal of the voluminous record before the court in this case.

A number of considerations enter into the adoption of a guideline and its application by trial courts. A guideline is not intended to be applied in a purely mechanical fashion. It must lend itself and yield to other factors. This premise enters into its formulation. The court must acknowledge that a guideline is not the result of any precise legal or scientific formula. It is the result of the exercise of a judicial discretion based on experience and taking into account the evidence of the limitations on resources, the strain imposed on them, statistics from other comparable jurisdictions and the opinions of other courts and judges, as well as any expert opinion. ... Comparison with other jurisdictions is ... to be applied with caution and only as a rough guide. These then are the factors which enter into the formulation by an appellate court of a guideline with respect to administrative delay. I now turn to its application in the trial courts.

I have already stressed that a guideline is not to be treated as a fixed limitation period. It will yield to other factors. Rapidly changing conditions may place a sudden and temporary strain on resources. This was the situation in the District of Durham in which this case arose. Such changing conditions should not result in an amnesty for persons charged in that region. Rather, this fact should be taken into account in applying the guideline. On the other hand, when the case-load has been constant over a substantial period of time the delay envisaged by the guideline may be regarded as excessive.

.....

The application of a guideline will also be influenced by the presence or absence of prejudice. If an accused is in custody or, while not in custody, subject to restrictive bail terms or conditions or otherwise experiences substantial prejudice, the period of acceptable institutional delay may be shortened to reflect the court's concern. On the other hand, in a case in which there is no prejudice or prejudice is slight, the guideline may be applied to reflect this fact.

.....

In *Askov*, Cory J., after reviewing comparative statistics suggested that a period in the range of six to eight months between committal and trial would not be unreasonable. Based on the foregoing, it is appropriate for this court to suggest a period of institutional delay of between eight and 10 months as a guide to Provincial Courts. With respect to institutional delay after committal for trial, I would not depart from the range of six to eight months that was suggested in *Askov*. In such a case this institutional delay would be in addition to the delay prior to committal. This reflects the fact that after committal the system must cope with a different court with its special resource problems. It is therefore essential to take into account the inevitability of this additional institutional delay.

A longer period of institutional delay for Provincial Courts is justified on the basis that not only do these courts dispose of the vast majority of cases, but that on average it takes more time to dispose of cases by reason of the demands placed on these courts.

.....

The application of these guidelines under the supervision of the Court of Appeal is subject to the review of this court to ensure that the right to trial within a reasonable time is being respected.

.....

(e) Other reasons for delay

There may be reasons for delay other than those mentioned above, each of which should be taken into consideration. As I have been at pains to emphasize, an investigation of unreasonable delay must take into account all reasons for the delay in an attempt to delineate what is truly reasonable for the case before the court. One such factor which does not fit particularly well into any other category of delay is that of actions by trial judges. An extreme example is provided by *Rahey, supra*. In that case it was the trial court judge who caused a substantial amount of the delay. Nineteen adjournments over the course of 11 months were instigated by the judge during the course of the trial. Such delay is not institutional in the strict sense. Nevertheless, such delay cannot be relied upon by the Crown to justify the period under consideration.

Other delays that have not been mentioned may weigh against the accused, but in most cases delays will weigh against the Crown for the same reason as was discussed in the above example.

4. Prejudice to the accused

Section 11(*b*) protects the individual from impairment of the right to liberty, security of the person, and the ability to make full answer and defence resulting from unreasonable delay in bringing criminal trials to a conclusion. We have decided in several judgments, including the unanimous judgment in *Smith, supra*, that the right protected by s. 11(*b*) is not restricted to those who demonstrate that they desire a speedy resolution of their case by asserting the right to a trial within a reasonable time. Implicit in this finding is that prejudice to the accused can be inferred from prolonged delay. In the American concept of this principle, expounded in *Barker v. Wingo*, the inference is that no prejudice has been suffered by the accused unless he or she asserts the right. While the observation of Dubin C.J.O. in *Bennett* that many, perhaps most, accused are not anxious to have an early trial may no doubt be accurate, s. 11(*b*) was designed to protect the individual, whose rights are not to be determined on the basis of the desires or practices of the majority. Accordingly, in an individual case, prejudice may be inferred from the length of the delay. The longer the delay the more likely that such an inference will be drawn. In circumstances in which prejudice is not inferred and is not otherwise proved, the basis for the enforcement of the individual right is seriously undermined.

This court has made clear in previous decisions that it is the duty of the Crown to bring the accused to trial: see *Askov, supra*, at pp. 478, 480-2. While it was not necessary for the accused to assert her right to be tried within a reasonable time, strong views have been expressed that in many cases an accused person is not interested in a speedy trial and that delay works to the advantage of the accused. This view is summed up by Doherty J. (as he then was) in a paper given to the National Criminal Law Programme in July, 1989, which was referred to with approval by Dubin C.J.O. in *Bennett* (at p. 458), and echoes what has been noted by numerous commentators:

> An accused is often not interested in exercising the right bestowed on him by s. 11(*b*). His interest lies in having the right infringed by the prosecution so that he can escape a trial on the merits. This view may seem harsh but experience supports its validity.

As also noted by Cory J. in *Askov, supra*, "the s. 11(*b*) right is one which can often be transformed from a protective shield to an offensive weapon in the hands of the accused" (p. 476). This right must be interpreted in a manner which recognizes the abuse which may be invoked by some accused. The purpose of s. 11(*b*) is to expedite trials and minimize prejudice and not to avoid trials on the merits. Action or non-action by the accused which is inconsistent with a desire for a timely trial is something that the court must consider. This position is consistent with decisions of this court in regard to other *Charter* provisions. For example, this court has held that an accused must be reasonably diligent in contacting counsel under *Charter* s. 10(*b*): *R. v. Tremblay* (1987), 37 C.C.C. (3d) 565, 45 D.L.R. (4th) 445, [1987] 2 S.C.R. 435; *R. v. Smith* (1989), 50 C.C.C. (3d) 308, 6 D.L.R. (4th) 462, [1989] 2 S.C.R. 368. If this requirement is not enforced, the right to counsel could be used to frustrate police investigation and in certain cases prevent essential evidence from being obtained. None the less, in taking into account inaction by the accused, the court must be careful not to subvert the principle that there is no legal obligation on the accused to assert the right. Inaction may, however, be relevant in assessing the degree of prejudice, if any, that an accused has suffered as a result of delay.

Apart, however, from inferred prejudice, either party may rely on evidence to either show prejudice or dispel such a finding. For example, the accused may rely on evidence tending to show prejudice to his or her liberty interest as a result of pre-tria incarceration or restrictive bail conditions. Prejudice to the accused's security interest can be shown by evidence of the ongoing stress or damage to reputation as a result of overlong exposure to "the vexations and vicissitudes of a pending criminal accusation", to use the words adopted by Lamer J. in *Mills, supra,* at p. 538. The fact that the accused sought an early trial date will also be relevant. Evidence may also be adduced to show that delay has prejudiced the accused's ability to make full answer and defence.

Conversely, the prosecution may establish by evidence that the accused is in the majority group who do not want an early trial and that the delay benefited rather than prejudiced the accused. Conduct of the accused falling short of waiver may be relied upon to negative prejudice. As discussed previously, the degree of prejudice or absence thereof is also an important factor in determining the length of institutional delay that will be tolerated. The application of any guideline will be influenced by this factor.

Application to this case

1. The length of the delay

The accused was charged on January 9, 1988, and her trial was completed on March 28, 1989. The total period of time between charge and trial was therefore approximately 14½ months. For reasons which I will explain later in these reasons, the accused at no time waived her right to a trial within a reasonable time nor did she waive her right in regard to any particular time periods. The length of delay therefore totalled just over 14½ months.

A delay of 14½ months in bringing a case to trial can hardly be described as a model of dispatch. On the other hand, 14½ months is a time period which may be excused in suitable circumstances. The length of the delay is sufficient to raise the issue of reasonableness and the inquiry must turn to the reason why it took 14½ months to bring Ms. Morin to trial.

2. Waiver of time periods

Waiver must be clear and unequivocal and with full knowledge of the right one is waiving. In the circumstances of this case, it cannot be said that the accused waived any of her rights at any time. She neither explicitly waived her rights nor can one infer from her actions an intent to waive her rights. I am in agreement with the lower courts which concluded that there was no waiver in this case.

3. The reasons for the delay

(a) Inherent time requirements

The accused was charged with what is commonly referred to as "over 80" and impaired. These charges resulted from a roadside stop followed by a breathalyzer test taken at the police station. Subject to certain paperwork, the preparation of the case for the prosecution was essentially complete by the time the accused was released from custody shortly after her breathalyzer test. This was therefore not a complicated case from the perspective of the prosecution. All prosecution witnesses were police officers and all relevant testing and investigation were completed on the day of the arrest of Ms. Morin.

Although the investigation by the Crown may have been completed on the day of arrest, the case for the defence was merely beginning. This is most easily exemplified by the fact that Ms. Morin could hardly have been expected to be ready for trial, for example, the next day. She required a certain amount of time to complete preliminary matters such as consulting and retaining counsel. Additionally, counsel would have needed some time to consider and prepare her case. Equally, certain time would have been required by the prosecution to finish the required paperwork and by the judicial administration to bring the case into the system. All of these activities take time and all legitimize some delay.

Ms. Morin was before the court for her first appearance on February 23, 1988, six weeks after her arrest. At this time she had retained counsel and requested "the earliest date" for trial. By this date, it appears that most of the preliminary matters of both the prosecution and the defence had been completed. As counsel for the defence did not indicate a readiness for trial but merely a request for the earliest trial date, it is somewhat unclear whether the case for the defence was as yet ready for trial. It may be inferred, however, that both parties were ready for trial within a few weeks of the first appearance. Accordingly, the inherent time requirements for this case were about two months.

(b) Actions of the accused

At her first court appearance, the accused requested the earliest date for trial. In response to her request, she was given a trial date of March 28, 1989, fully 13 months in the future. The accused inquired as to whether this was actually "the earliest date" available and the presiding judge indicated a simple "yes". Other than this court appearance there is no action on record taken by the accused from the point of her charge until her date of trial. The inaction on the part of the accused will be considered further in assessing prejudice.

(c) Actions of the Crown

The appellant admits that there is nothing in the record to suggest that the Crown was in any way dilatory in proceeding in this matter. In fact, the appellant concedes that the Crown was anxious to get the case to trial. As discussed later in these reasons, counsel for the Crown sent a "form" letter to all defence counsel in the Durham region suggesting that earlier dates might be available for accused who were anxious for trial. While it is alleged that this letter may have been sent too late to help Ms. Morin, it does show some positive action by the Crown to expedite trial. None of the delay is therefore attributable to the action of the Crown.

(d) Limits on institutional resources

Perhaps the single most important factor in this case is the limit on institutional resources. It appears that from some time in March, 1988, until March, 1989, the parties were prepared for trial but the judicial system could not accommodate them. It is somewhat unclear whether a date in early 1989 could have been made available as a result of the letter from the Crown's office but I am prepared to infer from the totality of the facts that an institutional delay of about 12 months was involved. This time period is the time from which the parties were ready for trial until the point at which the courts were able to accommodate this case.

In considering the reasonableness of this delay, the court must consider the facts surrounding this institutional delay. It must be remembered that this appeal arises from Ontario Provincial Court and arises from a region which has experienced significant growth in recent years.

I will deal first with the consideration which must be given to the fact that we are dealing with a Provincial Court. The Ontario Provincial Court disposes of approximately 95% of criminal cases in Ontario. Evidence led by the Crown in this appeal shows that the case-load of this Provincial Court increased more than 125% from 1985/86 to 1989/90. After several years in which the case-load was stable at 80,000 cases, the case-load of the Provincial Court in Ontario increased from 80,000 to 180,000 from 1985/86 to 1989/90. This rapid increase in case-load cannot, of course, always be predicted, nor can the government respond immediately to the inevitable strain on resources. While this court has made it clear that there is no longer any general transitional period in which to allow the government to comply with its constitutional obligations to provide sufficient facilities, this does not remove the issue of changing local circumstances from consideration.

In the jurisdiction in which this case arose, the District of Durham, the increase in case-load from 1985/86 to 1990/91 was approximately 70% in adult court and an astounding 143% in youth court. This was only partially caused by a population increase of 40% during the previous decade. Thus it is not surprising that the provision of institutional resources may have lagged somewhat behind the demand. Since some time in July, 1990, however, it appears that the Durham Provincial Court has been able to dispose of cases at a more rapid rate than it has received new cases. While one cannot use institutional resources to nullify the right to be tried within a reasonable time, one also cannot use rapidly changing local conditions to compel a general amnesty. Based on the above factors, I would allow a period for systemic delay which is in the upper range of the guideline. In my view, a period in the order of 10 months would not be unreasonable. While I have suggested that a guideline of eight to 10 months be used by courts to assess institutional delay in Provincial Courts, deviations of several months in either direction can be justified by the presence or absence of prejudice.

(e) Other reasons for delay

There do not appear to be any other reasons for delay in this case beyond those already considered in these reasons.

4. Prejudice to the accused

The accused led no evidence of prejudice. The court must still consider what, if any, prejudice is to be inferred from the delay. In this regard the Crown relies on the fact that several months prior to trial, counsel in the Durham region received a letter dated January 16, 1989, from the Crown Attorney's office which stated in part (C.O.A., at p. 38):

> [i]f you wish to move any of your cases up or *feel that any clients are suffering prejudice as a result of delay please give Audrey or I a shout and we'll try to locate an earlier date*. Thank you for your co-operation.

[Emphasis added.] It may be unrealistic to suggest that a trial set for approximately two months from the date of this letter could have been significantly moved up but we will never know what would have happened as the accused did not request any action. While the accused was not *required* to do anything to expedite her trial, her inaction can be taken into account in assessing prejudice. I conclude for this reason that the accused was content with the pace with which things were proceeding and that therefore there was little or no prejudice occasioned by the delay.

Disposition

Applying the guideline to which I have referred and taking into account the strain on institutional resources, the reasons of the Court of Appeal in regard thereto and the absence of any significant prejudice, I am of the opinion that the delay in this case was not unreasonable. I have come to this conclusion without the necessity of resorting to the burden of proof.

.....

I would accordingly dismiss the appeal.

[Lamer C.J.C. dissented.]

QUESTION

4. How has the test articulated in *Askov* been modified in *Morin*?

In the following cases, the Supreme Court of Canada considered the relevance of pre-charge delay and post-conviction appellate delay.

R. v. KALANJ

(1989), 48 C.C.C. (3d) 459 (S.C.C.)

[In May, 1982, the accused were arrested and released by the police who advised that charges would be laid and a summons would be issued. More than eight and a half months after the arrests, an information was sworn alleging theft and conspiracy to commit theft. The trial commenced two years after the information was sworn. Before plea, the defence brought a successful motion to quash the indictment on the grounds that the accused's *Charter* s. 11(*b*) rights had been infringed. The trial judge found that the time from the swearing of the information to the trial date did not constitute unreasonable delay, but that the delay of eight and a half months between arrest and the swearing of the information was unreasonable. The British Columbia Court of Appeal vacated the order quashing the indictment, and directed a trial on the merits. The accused appealed to the Supreme Court of Canada.]

McIntyre J. [La Forest and L'Heureux-Dubé JJ. concurring]: —

[After reviewing the facts and the judgments below, McIntyre J. noted that the trial judge should have imposed a stay rather than making an order quashing the indictment where there had been a finding that an accused's s. 11(*b*) rights had been violated. Nevertheless, McIntyre J. concluded that the court had jurisdiction to hear the appeals.]

.....

The word "charged" or "charge" is not one of fixed or unvarying meaning at law. It may be and is used in a variety of ways to describe a variety of events. A person is clearly charged with an offence when a charge is read out to him in court and he is called upon to plead. Many authorities support this view if authority is necessary: see *R. v. Chabot* (1980), 55 C.C.C. (2d) 385, 117 D.L.R. (3d) 527, [1980] 2 S.C.R. 985 (S.C.C.), and the cases cited therein. A person could be considered in a general or popular sense to be charged with an offence when informed by one in authority that "you will be summoned to court" or upon an arrest when in answer to a demand to know what all this is about an officer replies: "You are arrested for murder." There are many other occasions when in the popular mind a person may be said to be charged for, according to Professor Mewett in *An Introduction to the Criminal Process in Canada* (1988), the word "charge" has no precise meaning at law but merely means that steps are being taken which in the normal course will lead to a criminal prosecution. However, despite what may be termed the imprecision of the word "charge" or the phrase "a person charged", the courts are faced with the task of developing a meaning of the word as used in s. 11 of the *Charter*.

In addressing this task, the courts have generally avoided the definite but restricted definition to be found in *Chabot, supra*, and have generally concluded that a person is charged with an offence within the meaning of s. 11 of the *Charter* when an information has been sworn which constitutes an initiating step in court proceedings. In *R. v. Boron* (1983), 8 C.C.C. (3d) 25, 3 D.L.R. (4th) 238, 43 O.R. (2d) 623 (Ont. H.C.J.), Ewaschuk J. considered what he saw as three possible interpretations of the word "charged", and he concluded, at p. 31, that:

> In conclusion, I adopt the more prevalent view that the word "charged" in s. 11 of the *Charter* refers to the laying of an information, or the preferment of a direct indictment where no information has been laid. In consequence, the time-frame to be considered in computing trial within a reasonable time only runs from the laying of a charge. This general rule may have certain exceptions which I deal with later. Accordingly, the trial judge erred in holding that the *Charter* guarantees the right of a person to have proceedings promptly instituted against a person charged with an offence.

.....

In dealing with s. 11, it must first be recognized that it is limited in its terms to a special group of persons, those "charged with an offence". It deals primarily with matters relating to the trial. It is to be noted that s. 11 is distinct from s. 10 and serves a different purpose: the two sections must not be equated. The framers of the *Charter* made a clear distinction between the rights guaranteed to a person arrested and those of a person upon charge. Sections 8 and 9, as well, guarantee essential rights ordinarily of significance in the investigatory period, separate and distinct from those covered in s. 11. It has been said that the purpose of s. 11 should be considered in deciding upon the extent of its application. This purpose, it has been said, is to afford protection for the liberty and security interests of persons accused of crime. While it is true that s. 11 operates for this purpose, I emphasize that it does so within its own sphere. It is not, nor was it intended to be, the sole guarantor and protector of such rights. As stated above, s. 7 affords broad protection for liberty and security, while the other sections, particularly those dealing with legal rights, apply to protect those rights in certain stated circumstances. Section 11 affords its protection after an accused is charged with an offence. The specific language of s. 11 should not be ignored and the meaning of the word "charged" should not be twisted in an attempt to extend the operation of the section into the pre-charge period. The purpose of s. 11(*b*) is clear. It is concerned with the period between the laying of the charge and the conclusion of the trial and it provides that a person charged with an offence will be promptly dealt with.

The length of the pre-information or investigatory period is wholly unpredictable. No reasonable assessment of what is, or is not, a reasonable time can be readily made. Circumstances will differ from case to case and much information gathered in an investigation must, by, its very nature, be confidential. A court will rarely, if ever, be able to fix in any realistic manner a time limit for the investigation of a given offence. It is notable that the law — save for some limited statutory exceptions — has never recognized a time limitation for the institution of criminal proceedings. Where, however, the investigation reveals evidence which would justify the swearing of an information, then for the first time the assessment of a reasonable period for the conclusion of the matter by trial becomes possible. It is for that reason that s. 11 limits its operation to the post-information period. Prior to the charge, the rights of the accused are protected by general law and guaranteed by ss. 7, 8, 9 and 10 of the *Charter*.

I acknowledge that in taking this position it may be said that I am departing from the earlier judgments of this court which have said that there will be exceptional cases where pre-charge delays will be relevant under s. 11(b). In my view, however, the departure is more apparent than real. The exception referred to by Lamer J. in *Carter* [(1986), 26 C.C.C. (3d) 572 (S.C.C.)] — where two indictments are preferred because of successful appeals after a first trial — has been dealt with in *R. v. Antoine* (1983), 5 C.C.C. (3d) 97, 148 D.L.R. (3d) 149, 41 O.R. (2d) 607 (Ont. C.A.), and *Re Garton and Whelan* (1984), 14 C.C.C. (3d) 449, 47 O.R. (2d) 672 (Ont. H.C.J.). These cases support the proposition that pre-charge delay is not relevant under s. 11(*b*), by holding that the time commences to run from the date the original information was sworn.

It has been considered that special circumstances could arise which, in the interests of justice, would require some consideration of pre-charge delay because of prejudice which could result from its occurrence. In my view, however, the exceptional cases should be dealt with by reliance on the general rules of law and, where necessary, the other sections of the *Charter*.

This approach would take account of and meet the concerns caused by the possibility of pre-charge delays. Delays which occur at the pre-charge stage are not immune from the law outside the scope of s. 11(*b*). The *Criminal Code* itself in ss. 577(3) [now s. 650(3)] and 737(1) [now s. 802(1)] protects the right to make full answer and defence should it be prejudiced by pre-charge delay. Section 455.1 [now s. 505] provides for a prompt swearing of an information where an appearance notice has been issued or an accused has been released from custody under ss. 452 [now s. 497] or 453 [now s. 498]. As well, the doctrine of abuse of process may be called in aid and as early as 1844 the common law demonstrated that it was capable of dealing with pre-information delays. Baron Alderson in *R. v. Robins* (1844), 1 Cox C.C. 114, in a case where nearly two years had elapsed from the alleged commission of an offence before a complaint was made to the justices, said:

> I ought not to allow this case to go further. It is monstrous to put a man on his trial after such a lapse of time. How can he account for his conduct so far back? If you accuse a man of a crime the next day, he may be enabled to bring forward his servants and family to say where he was and what he was about at the time; but if the charge be not preferred for a year or more, how can he clear himself? No man's life would be safe if such a prosecution were permitted. It would be very unjust to put him on his trial.

His Lordship then directed the jury to acquit the prisoner. In addition, given the broad wording of s. 7 and the other *Charter* provisions referred to above, it is not, in my view, necessary to distort the words of s. 11(*b*) in order to guard against a pre-charge delay. In my view, the concerns which have moved the court to recognize the possibility of special circumstances which would justify a consideration of pre-charge delay under s. 11(*b*) will thus be met.

In the case at bar, both the courts below considered that the post-charge delays were not such that they could be said to deprive the appellants of trial within a reasonable time. I am in agreement with this finding. The trial judge, however, considered the pre-charge delay of some eight months and concluded that it was unreasonable and upon that conclusion found that s. 11(*b*) had been infringed. In this, I, in agreement with the Court of Appeal, consider that he was in error. I would accordingly dismiss the appeals.

[Lamer and Wilson JJ. dissented.]

R. v. POTVIN

(1993), 83 C.C.C. (3d) 97 (S.C.C.)

[A s. 11(*b*) stay application was successful at trial. The stay was set aside on appeal to the Ontario Court of Appeal. The Supreme Court of Canada adopted the reasons of the Court of Appeal in finding no pre-trial unreasonable delay but went on to consider the applicability of s. 11(*b*) to appellate delay.]

Sopinka J. [L'Heureux-Dubé, Gonthier, Cory and Iacobucci JJ. concurring]: —

.....

Appellate delay

This issue was raised in the Court of Appeal but was not dealt with. I have concluded that s. 11(*b*) does not apply to delay in respect of an appeal from conviction by the accused nor an appeal from an acquittal by the Crown. Moreover, in my opinion, there is no distinction in this regard between an acquittal after trial and a judicial stay.

.....

Many of the rights found in s. 11 cannot apply to appeals and are restricted to the pre-trial or trial process. If "[a] person charged" in s. 11(*b*) necessarily includes the accused as a party to an appeal, then the same conclusion would have to apply to the other paragraphs of the section. An examination of the various paragraphs shows s. 11(*a*), (*c*), (*f*) and (*i*) clearly do not apply to appeals. Section 11(*e*) could not apply to an appellant who has been acquitted and other paragraphs are primarily concerned with what occurs at trial, although exceptionally they might have some application on appeal.

I conclude from the foregoing that as a general rule "a person charged" under s. 11 does not include an accused person who is party to an appeal. A particular paragraph may apply to appeal proceedings as an exception to the general rule if its purpose and language support this conclusion. After considering the purpose and language of s. 11(*b*), I have concluded that the interpretation that gives effect to both of these elements and best harmonizes the other paragraphs is that the paragraph applies to the pre-trial period and the trial process but not to appellate proceedings. While I am uncomfortably aware that I expressed a different view in my dissenting reasons in *R. v. Conway* (1989), 49 C.C.C. (3d) 289, [1989] 1 S.C.R. 1659, 70 C.R. (3d) 209 (S.C.C.), I have come to this conclusion in light of the considerable additional judicial experience of this court in the application of s. 11(*b*) since the judgment in *Conway*. In particular, I refer to the judgment in *R. v. Kalanj* (1989), 48 C.C.C. (3d) 459, [1989] 1 S.C.R. 1594, 70 C.R. (3d) 260 (S.C.C.), and cases that followed it as to the purpose of s. 11(*b*).

.....

Clearly, during the period after an acquittal and the service of a notice of appeal, the person acquitted is not a person charged. No proceeding is on foot which seeks to charge the person acquitted. Upon the appeal's being filed there is a possibility, the strength of which will vary with each case, that the acquittal will be set aside and the charge will be revived. The plight of the acquitted person is that of one against whom governmental action is directed which may result in a charge. In this respect the former accused is like the suspect against whom an investigation has been completed and charges are contemplated awaiting a decision by the prosecutor. Indeed, the acquitted accused is somewhat more removed from the prospect of being subject to a charge than the suspect. In the former case, no charge can be revived until the acquittal is set aside by reason of an error of law that a court determines with a reasonable degree of certainty affected the decision at trial. In the latter case, all that stands between the suspect and a charge is the *ex parte* decision of the prosecutor. It would be incongruous to extend protection to the acquitted accused pending appeal and not to the suspect awaiting a charge who knows he or she is awaiting the decision of the prosecutor.

There is even less reason to extend the protection of s. 11(b) to a convicted person who appeals. The appeal itself is not governmental action. In *R. v. C.I.P. Inc.* (1992), 71 C.C.C. (3d) 129, [1992] 1 S.C.R. 843, 12 C.R. (4th) 237 (S.C.C.), Stevenson J. stated for the court, at p. 145:

> We are reviewing the decision that was made on November 1, 1988. The delay after that motion was granted is appellate delay. The bulk of that delay is attributable to the appellant's decision to pursue appeals. The appellant invoked the processes of which it now complains and must accept the burdens inherent in full appellate review. There is no evidence or argument to support a finding that some extraordinary factor lengthened that review process.

The delay due to some extraordinary factor referred to by Stevenson J. would not be attributed to the fact that the accused was a person charged but rather to the conviction. A convicted person is not a person charged: see *Lyons* [(1987), 37 C.C.C. (3d) 1 (S.C.C.)], at p. 40. The effect of such an extraordinary factor would fall to be assessed under s. 7 in light of its impact on the fairness of the proceedings.

This discussion has focused on the interpretation of the words "[a] person charged" in s. 11(*b*) in the context of the purpose of the paragraph. The conclusion that those words limit the operation of the paragraph to the trial process is supported by the use of the word "tried". It would seem that if it was intended that the paragraph apply not only to the trial but also to final adjudication, more apt wording would have been employed. This is illustrated by the decision of The European Court of Human Rights, *"Wemhoff" Case*, judgment of June 27, 1968, 1 E.H.R.R. 55. The court dealt with two sections of the Convention: s. 5(3) and s. 6(1). The former provided that "everyone ... shall be entitled to trial within a reasonable time ..." while the latter provided that "[i]n the determination ... of any criminal charge against him everyone is entitled to a fair and public hearing ...". The court held that the former section extended only to the trial while the latter extended to the final determination even if this was on appeal. No doubt this language was before the framers of the *Charter* and the selection of the more limiting term is significant.

This does not mean that when there is an adjudication relating to a charge which is appealed, s. 11(*b*) is spent. If on the appeal the judgment is set aside and the matter is remitted for trial, the accused reverts to the status of a person charged. As stated by D.H. Doherty (now a justice of the Court of Appeal for Ontario) in "More Flesh on the Bones: The Continued Judicial Interpretation of s. 11(*b*) of the Canadian Charter of Rights and Freedoms" (1984), Canadian Bar Association — Ontario; Annual Institute on Continuing Legal Education, at p. 9:

> Section 11(*b*) does not appear to operate at the appellate stage. Section 11(*b*) guarantees a trial within a reasonable time, not a final determination of the matter at an appellate level within that time. If, however, a new trial is ordered on appeal, or some other order is made directing the continuation of the trial proceedings, the constitutional clock should be rewound at the time of the order by the appellate court.

.....

The conclusion I have reached applies to appeals from acquittals and convictions. Furthermore, I see no valid reason to distinguish between an acquittal on the merits and a judicial stay. In light of the interest protected under s. 11(*b*), the differences between an acquittal and a judicial stay are purely technical. In both cases the accused can plead *autrefois acquit* and no proceedings may be brought in respect of the same charge unless the acquittal or stay is set aside on appeal. No restraints can be placed on the liberty of the former accused pending appeal. There is no basis on which to assume that the theoretical existence of a charge that has been stayed carries any greater stigma or causes greater anxiety to the respondent in an appeal from a judicial stay than an appeal from acquittal. Certainly there is no evidence on this point. I doubt that the public understands the difference. An unpopular acquittal generates as much public indignation as a stay. The degree of anxiety is dictated more by the strength of the grounds of appeal than by the form of the verdict. These observations were neatly summed up by Estey J. in *Amato v. The Queen* (1982), 69 C.C.C. (2d) 31 at p. 70, 140 D.L.R. (3d) 405, [1982] 2 S.C.R. 418 (S.C.C.): "While the charge may be said to hang over the head of the accused, this is a wholly theoretical observation because there is no forum for its further processing."

The application of s. 7

This conclusion does not leave the criminal appellant or respondent without a remedy when delay of appeal proceedings affects the fairness of the trial. While s. 11(*b*) does not apply, s. 7 may in appropriate circumstances afford a remedy. In *R. v. L.(W.K.)* [(1991), 64 C.C.C. (3d) 321 (S.C.C.)], this court held that, in respect of pre-charge delay, if the particular circumstances of the case indicated that the fairness of the trial had been affected by the delay, s. 7 can be resorted to. This is simply the application to delay of the court's power to remedy an abuse of process which is enshrined in s. 7 as a principle of fundamental justice. The general principle was expressed in *R. v. Jewitt* (1985), 21 C.C.C. (3d) 7 at p. 14, 20 D.L.R. (4th) 651, [1985] 2 S.C.R. 128 (S.C.C.). Dickson C.J.C. adopted the following passage from the judgment of Dubin J.A. (as he then was) in *R. v. Young* (1984), 13 C.C.C. (3d) 1 at p. 31, 40 C.R. (3d) 289, 10 C.R.R. 307 (Ont. C.A.):

> ... there is a residual discretion in a trial court judge to stay proceedings where compelling an accused to stand trial would violate those fundamental principles of justice which underlie the community's sense of fair play and decency and to prevent the abuse of a court's process through oppressive or vexatious proceedings.

This test has been reaffirmed in *R. v. Keyowski* (1988), 40 C.C.C. (3d) 481, [1988] 1 S.C.R. 657, 62 C.R. (3d) 349 (S.C.C.).

In addition to s. 7, the criminal appeal rules and provisions of the *Criminal Code* afford a litigant in a criminal appeal a range of remedies at virtually every stage of the appellate proceeding. This enables a party interested in a timely disposition of the appeal to eliminate any substantial delay on the part of the adversary. As for systemic delay, resort can be had to s. 7 in the cases in which real prejudice is occasioned.

This raises the issue of the appropriate forum for a remedy pursuant to s. 7 with respect to appellate delay. ... I am of the opinion that the appropriate forum is the court in which the delay occurred. That court is in the best position to assess the consequences of delay. Moreover, this approach avoids the necessity of a referral back of the issue to a trial court whenever a serious case of delay is made out. In addition, it avoids the awkwardness inherent in a lower court's passing upon proceedings in a higher court which the latter must then review. While, generally matters of first instance are not decided in an appellate court the nature of the issues and the material in support would not be radically different from the issues and material in other motions which an appellate court is called upon to decide. If a further appeal lies from the first appellate court, the issue of delay can be reviewed in the second appellate court along with the consequences of additional delay resulting from the second appeal. As with other issues in appeal, this court does not favour issues being raised for the first time in an appeal to this court.

Application to this case

No evidence was offered nor was any attempt made in this appeal to show that any real prejudice resulted from the appellate delay. Counsel for the appellant quite properly conceded that no breach of s. 7 could be made out and I find none. The appeal is therefore dismissed.

[La Forest J. concurred in the result.]

QUESTIONS

5. The accused had been a suspect in the murder of a prison guard while the accused was a prison inmate 30 years ago. An information was sworn 30 years ago in the course of a pre-enquete hearing[1] before a justice of the peace to determine if process should issue. At the time, the Crown decided not to proceed with the case. Now, 30 years later, the Crown is attempting to prosecute the accused for this murder. Witnesses have died and evidence has been lost. What submissions would you make as Crown or defence counsel on the s. 11(*b*) motion? Consider, in this regard, *R. v. Cochrane* (1995), 30 C.R.R. (2d) D-8 (Ont. Gen. Div.).

6. A corporation is charged with an offence under provincial occupational health and safety legislation in connection with the death of an employee on the job. The allegations are that the employer corporation failed to ensure that heavy machinery was in proper working order. The matter could not proceed on two trial dates because of lack of court space. The time between the laying of the charges and the third trial date was 19 months. Is a corporation included as "any person charged with an offence" within the meaning of s. 11(*b*) of the *Charter*? What must the corporation establish in order to be successful on an application for a stay on the grounds of unreasonable delay? Consider, in this regard, *R. v. C.I.P. Inc.* (1992), 71 C.C.C. (3d) 129 (S.C.C.).

7. The accused was charged with 36 counts of fraud, and uttering forged documents in connection with the sale of American securities in Canada. The case required the forensic analysis of hundreds of documents and the interview of witnesses in Canada, the United States and the Bahamas. At the pre-trial conference, it was estimated that the Crown's case would take four months. The Crown sought an adjournment of the first trial date as soon as it became apparent that the case could not proceed on that date. On the second trial date, 23 months after the charges were laid, defence counsel sought a stay of proceedings on the grounds that the client's right to be tried within a reasonable time had been infringed. What submissions would you make as Crown or defence counsel on the s. 11(*b*) motion? Consider, in this regard, *R. v. Atkinson* (1991), 68 C.C.C. (3d) 109 (Ont. C.A.).

8. What if defence counsel fails to move for a stay of proceedings pursuant to s. 11(*b*) of the *Charter* at trial? Can this issue be raised for the first time on appeal? Consider, in this regard, *R. v. Rabba* (1991), 64 C.C.C. (3d) 445 (Ont. C.A.).

The Ontario Court of Justice Criminal Proceedings Rules, SI/92-99, were enacted by the court pursuant to s. 482(1) of the *Criminal Code*. Rule 27 in particular regulates the content of materials filed in support of an application to stay proceedings, and the time frame within which such materials must be served and filed. Absent some agreement as to the material facts, many courts will insist that transcripts of prior court appearances be produced on the application. This is to enable an accu-

---

[1] See Chapter 9 (Summary Conviction Proceedings).

rate determination of the cause for the various delays, the positions of the parties when those delays occurred, including any waiver, and the extent to which earlier dates were available to the court, but not to counsel. Accordingly, counsel must order these transcripts well in advance of the application date. As well, the defence must ensure that its position is fully and fairly articulated on the record at the various court appearances. For example: "we are in agreement that January 5, 2004 be set for trial, as I understand that this is the earliest date available to the court for the matter to be heard. I should indicate that I have earlier dates available commencing in September 2003."

C. ATTORNEY GENERAL'S CONSENT

Certain proceedings cannot be instituted without the consent of the Attorney General ("Attorney General" is defined in s. 2 of the *Criminal Code*). Examples of proceedings include hate propaganda (ss. 319(6) and 320(7)) and public nudity charges (s. 174(3)).

D. CHARTER JURISDICTION

1. Overview

The *Canadian Charter of Rights and Freedoms*, constitutionally entrenched in 1981, impacts upon criminal proceedings in at least four significant ways:

(a) it guarantees a series of rights and freedoms that regulate and, to a great extent, have modified, pre-trial and trial proceedings. For example, the s. 10(*b*) right, upon arrest or detention, to retain and instruct counsel without delay and to be informed of that right, as interpreted by the courts, has significantly altered pre-trial investigative procedures employed by the police.

(b) to the extent to which evidence has been obtained in a manner that infringed or denied any such rights or freedoms, the court is empowered under s. 24(2) of the *Charter* to exclude such evidence.

(c) to the extent to which any such rights or freedoms of the accused have been infringed or denied, the court is empowered under s. 24(1) of the *Charter* to grant an appropriate and just remedy, other than the exclusion of evidence: for example, a judicial stay of the proceedings against the accused.

(d) because the *Charter* is part of the *Canadian Constitution Act, 1982*, s. 52(1) of the Constitution empowers the court to declare that a statutory provision which is inconsistent with the *Charter* is, to the extent of the inconsistency, of no force or effect. Accordingly, an offence section, a statutory police power, a statutory restriction on evidence tendered by the accused, and a statutory burden of proof resting on the accused may all be struck down, in whole or in part, as inconsistent with the *Charter*.

This chapter addresses the narrow issue of which courts have jurisdiction to entertain *Charter*-related applications. Later chapters explore the impact of the *Charter* on pre-trial practices and the procedures which govern *Charter* related applications.

2. JURISDICTION UNDER SECTION 24 OF THE CHARTER

Section 24 of the *Charter* reads:

> **24. (1) Anyone whose rights or freedoms, as guaranteed by this *Charter*, have been infringed or denied may apply to a *court of competent jurisdiction* to obtain such remedy as the court considers appropriate and just in the circumstances.**
>
> **(2) Where, in proceedings under subsection (1), a court concludes that evidence was obtained in a manner that infringed or denied any rights or freedoms guaranteed by this *Charter*, the evidence shall be excluded if it is established that, having regard to all the circumstances, the admission of it in the proceedings would bring the administration of justice into disrepute.**

(Emphasis added.)

R. v. 974649 ONTARIO INC.

(2001), 159 C.C.C. (3d) 321 (S.C.C.)

[The respondents were charged under the *Occupational Health and Safety Act*, R.S.O. 1990, c. O.1, with failing to comply with safety requirements on a construction project. The respondents requested that the Crown disclose, among other items, a copy of the Prosecution Approval Form. This form is routinely prepared by Ministry of Labour inspectors when deciding whether to lay charges under the Act. The Crown twice refused to disclose the form on the ground that it was protected by solicitor-client privilege. A justice of the peace acting as a trial justice held that the Crown's failure to disclose this form amounted to a violation of the respondents' rights under the *Charter*. The justice of the peace ordered the Crown to disclose the form and to pay the costs of the respondents' disclosure motion. The Crown disclosed the form, but successfully applied to have the order for costs quashed on the basis that a provincial offences court is not a "court of competent jurisdiction" to direct such an order under s. 24(1) of the *Charter*. The Ontario Court of Appeal upheld the trial justice's holding. The Crown appealed that order to the Supreme Court of Canada. At issue was whether a provincial offences court is a court of competent jurisdiction for purposes of s. 24(1) of the *Charter*.]

The judgment of the court was delivered by

McLachlin C.J.C.: —

.....

V. ANALYSIS

The *Charter* guarantees the fundamental rights and freedoms of all Canadians. It does this through two kinds of provisions. The first are provisions describing the rights and freedoms guaranteed. The second are provisions providing remedies or sanctions for breaches of these rights. If a *law* is inconsistent with the *Charter*, s. 52 of the *Constitution Act, 1982* provides that it is invalid to the extent of the inconsistency. On the other hand, if a *government action* is inconsistent with the *Charter*, s. 24 provides remedies for the inconsistency. If the violation produced evidence that the Crown seeks to use against the accused, s. 24(2) provides that the court must exclude the evidence if its admission would bring the administration of justice into disrepute. In other cases, s. 24(1) permits a "court of competent jurisdiction" to provide "such remedy as the court considers appropriate and just in the circumstances". If a remedy is to be had in the instant case, it must issue under s. 24(1).

The essential issue is whether the trial justice who ordered the Crown to pay costs is "a court of competent jurisdiction" under s. 24(1) to make such an award. This Court has considered the attributes of a "court of competent jurisdiction" on a number of occasions, commencing with its seminal decision in *Mills* [(1986), 26 C.C.C. (3d) 481 (S.C.C.)]. In that case, Lamer J. (as he then was), with whom all agreed on this point, defined a "court of competent jurisdiction" as one that possesses (1) jurisdiction over the person; (2) jurisdiction over the subject matter; and (3) jurisdiction to grant the remedy (p. 890). Subsequent decisions of this Court have affirmed this three-tiered test for identifying the courts and tribunals competent to issue *Charter* remedies under s. 24: *Weber v. Ontario Hydro*, [1995] 2 S.C.R. 929, 125 D.L.R. (4th) 583; *Mooring v. Canada (National Parole Board),* [1996] 1 S.C.R. 75, 104 C.C.C. (3d) 97, 132 D.L.R. (4th) 56. Only where a court or tribunal possesses all three attributes is it considered a "court of competent jurisdiction" for the purpose of ordering the desired *Charter* relief under s. 24.

In the present case, the jurisdiction of the provincial offences court over the parties and the subject matter is uncontested. The dispute between the parties centres on the third and final attribute of a court of competent jurisdiction: the power to grant the remedy sought. In determining whether the *POA* justice in this case possessed the "power to grant the remedy sought", namely legal costs, we are guided by the principles set out in previous decisions, and the approach these decisions mandate to interpreting s. 24 of the *Charter*.

A. Section 24: Principles of Interpretation

In interpreting the phrase "court of competent jurisdiction", we must keep in mind four related propositions. These propositions have informed the Court's approach to s. 24 since it first considered this provision in *Mills*.

First, s. 24(1), like all *Charter* provisions, commands a broad and purposive interpretation. This section forms a vital part of the *Charter*, and must be construed generously, in a manner that best ensures the attainment of its objects: *R. v. Big M Drug Mart Ltd.*, [1985] 1 S.C.R. 295 at p. 344, 18 C.C.C.

(3d) 385, 18 D.L.R. (4th) 321; *Hunter v. Southam Inc.*, [1984] 2 S.C.R. 145 at p. 155, 14 C.C.C. (3d) 97, 11 D.L.R. (4th) 641; *Canadian National Railway Co. v. Canada (Canadian Human Rights Commission)*, [1987] 1 S.C.R. 1114, at p. 1134, 40 D.L.R. (4th) 193 (*sub nom. Action Travail des Femmes v. Canadian National Railway Co.*). Moreover, it is remedial, and hence benefits from the general rule of statutory interpretation that accords remedial statutes a "large and liberal" interpretation: *British Columbia Development Corp. v. Friedmann*, [1984] 2 S.C.R. 447 at p. 458, 14 D.L.R. (4th) 129; *Toronto Area Transit Operating Authority v. Dell Holdings Ltd.*, [1997] 1 S.C.R. 32, at para. 21, 142 D.L.R. (4th) 206. Finally, and most importantly, the language of this provision appears to confer the widest possible discretion on a court to craft remedies for violations of *Charter* rights. In *Mills*, McIntyre J. observed at p. 965 that "[i]t is difficult to imagine language which could give the court a wider and less fettered discretion". This broad remedial mandate for s. 24(1) should not be frustrated by a "narrow and formalist" reading of the provision (see: *Law Society of Upper Canada v. Skapinker*, [1984] 1 S.C.R. 357 at p. 366, 11 C.C.C. (3d) 481, 9 D.L.R. (4th) 161).

The second proposition flows from the first: s. 24 must be interpreted in a way that achieves its purpose of upholding *Charter* rights by providing effective remedies for their breach. If the Court's past decisions concerning s. 24(1) can be reduced to a single theme, it is that s. 24(1) must be interpreted in a manner that provides a full, effective and meaningful remedy for *Charter* violations: *Mills, supra*, at pp. 881-82 (*per* Lamer J.), p. 953 (*per* McIntyre J.); *Mooring, supra*, at paras. 50-52 (*per* Major J.). As Lamer J. observed in *Mills*, s. 24(1) "establishes the right to a remedy as the foundation stone for the effective enforcement of *Charter* rights" (p. 881). Through the provision of an enforcement mechanism, s. 24(1) "above all else ensures that the *Charter* will be a vibrant and vigorous instrument for the protection of the rights and freedoms of Canadians" (p. 881).

Section 24(1)'s interpretation necessarily resonates across *all Charter* rights, since a right, no matter how expansive in theory, is only as meaningful as the remedy provided for its breach. From the outset, this Court has characterized the purpose of s. 24(1) as the provision of a "direct remedy" (*Mills, supra*, p. 953, *per* McIntyre J.). As Lamer J. stated in *Mills*, "[a] remedy must be easily available and constitutional rights should not be 'smothered in procedural delays and difficulties'" (p. 882). Anything less would undermine the role of s. 24(1) as a cornerstone upon which the rights and freedoms guaranteed by the *Charter* are founded, and a critical means by which they are realized and preserved.

The third proposition guiding the interpretation of s. 24 is that subsections (1) and (2) must be read together to create a harmonious interpretation. The conjunction of the two subsections, one dealing with remedies in general and the other dealing with exclusion of evidence that would bring the administration of justice into disrepute, suggests that both are concerned with providing remedies for *Charter* breaches. Moreover, the remedies under each of the two subsections are confined to "court[s] of competent jurisdiction". Thus this phrase must be interpreted in a way that produces just and workable results for both the grant of general remedies and the exclusion of evidence in particular.

The final proposition is that s. 24 should not be read so broadly that it endows courts and tribunals with powers that they were never intended to exercise. The jurisdictions of Canada's various courts and tribunals are fixed by Parliament and the legislatures, not by judges: *Mills, supra*, at p. 952 (*per* McIntyre J.). It is Parliament or the legislature that determines if a court or tribunal is a "court of competent jurisdiction": *Weber, supra*, at para. 65. Legislative intention is the guiding light in identifying courts of competent jurisdiction.

As McIntyre J. cautioned in *Mills, supra*, at p. 953, the *Charter* was not intended to "turn the Canadian legal system upside down". The task facing the court is to interpret s. 24(1) in a manner that provides direct access to *Charter* remedies while respecting, so far as possible, "the existing jurisdictional scheme of the courts": *Mills, supra*, at p. 953 (*per* McIntyre J.); see also the comments of La Forest J. (at p. 971) and Lamer J. (at p. 882) in the same case; and *Weber, supra*, at para. 63. The framers of the *Charter* did not intend to erase the constitutional distinctions between different types of courts, nor to intrude on legislative powers more than necessary to achieve the aims of the *Charter*.

In summary, the task of the court in interpreting s. 24 of the *Charter* is to achieve a broad, purposive interpretation that facilitates direct access to appropriate and just *Charter* remedies under s. 24(1) and (2), while respecting the structure and practice of the existing court system and the exclusive role of Parliament and the legislatures in prescribing the jurisdiction of courts and tribunals. With these guiding principles in mind, I return to the question at the heart of this appeal: when does a court or tribunal possess "power to grant the remedy sought", such that it satisfies the final branch of the *Mills* test of a court of competent jurisdiction?

.....

[The Chief Justice reviewed different approaches to determining jurisdiction for remedies and held that the functional and structural approach is the most appropriate.]

In my view, the "functional and structural" approach is more consistent with the original intention of Parliament or the legislature in establishing the tribunal (albeit interpreted in light of the *Charter*'s enactment) and the aspirations of the *Charter* itself. Where the *Charter*'s enactment implicated a court or tribunal in new constitutional issues, it should be presumed that the legislature intended the court or tribunal to resolve these issues where it is suited to do so by virtue of its function and structure. It is only in this manner that the purpose of the *Charter* — and the mandates of those courts and tribunals that predate its enactment — can be meaningfully realized.

The content of the "functional and structural" approach may also require elaboration. Framed broadly, this test asks whether the court or tribunal in question is suited to grant the remedy sought under s. 24 in light of its *function* and *structure*. The assessment is contextual. The factors relevant to the inquiry and the weight they carry will vary with the particular circumstances at hand. Nonetheless, it is possible to catalogue some of the considerations captured under the general headings of "function" and "structure".

The *function* of the court or tribunal is an expression of its purpose or mandate. As such, it must be assessed in relation to both the legislative scheme and the broader legal system. First, what is the court or tribunal's function within the legislative scheme? Would jurisdiction to order the remedy sought under s. 24(1) frustrate or enhance this role? How essential is the power to grant the remedy sought to the effective and efficient functioning of the court or tribunal? Second, what is the function of the court or tribunal in the broader legal system? Is it more appropriate that a different forum redress the violation of *Charter* rights?

The inquiry into the *structure* of the court or tribunal relates to the compatibility of the institution and its processes with the remedy sought under s. 24. Depending on the particular remedy in issue, any or all of the following factors may be salient: whether the proceedings are judicial or quasi-judicial; the role of counsel; the applicability or otherwise of traditional rules of proof and evidence; whether the court or tribunal can issue subpoenas; whether evidence is offered under oath; the expertise and training of the decision-maker; and the institutional experience of the court or tribunal with the remedy in question: see *Mooring, supra*, at paras. 25-26. Other relevant considerations may include the workload of the court or tribunal, the time constraints it operates under, its ability to compile an adequate record for a reviewing court, and other such operational factors. The question, in essence, is whether the legislature or Parliament has furnished the court or tribunal with the tools necessary to fashion the remedy sought under s. 24 in a just, fair and consistent manner without impeding its ability to perform its intended function.

.....

In *Mills*, the Court considered whether a preliminary inquiry judge or justice is a court of competent jurisdiction for the purposes of entering a stay of proceedings as a remedy for the violation of an accused's right under s. 11(*b*) of the *Charter* to trial within a reasonable time. McIntyre J., speaking for a unanimous Court on this point, held that a preliminary inquiry judge or justice is not a court of competent jurisdiction for this purpose. In reaching this conclusion, he emphasized the specialized function performed by the preliminary inquiry judge in the criminal process, and the incompatibility of this function with the remedy sought (at pp. 954-55):

> After all the evidence has been taken, he may commit the accused for trial if, in his opinion, the evidence is sufficient, or discharge the accused if, in his opinion, upon the whole of the evidence no sufficient case is made out to put the accused on trial. He has no jurisdiction to acquit or convict, nor to impose a penalty, nor to give a remedy. He is given no jurisdiction which would permit him to hear and determine the question of whether or not a *Charter* right has been infringed or denied. He is, therefore, not a court of competent jurisdiction under s. 24(1) of the *Charter* ... . I might add at this stage that it would be a strange result indeed if the preliminary hearing magistrate could be said to have the jurisdiction to give a remedy, such as a stay under s. 24(1), and thus bring the proceedings to a halt before they have started and this in a process from which there is no appeal.

Although this holding disposed of the specific issue on appeal in *Mills*, McIntyre, Lamer and La Forest JJ. proceeded to consider the availability of *Charter* remedies in the criminal process more generally, both at the preliminary inquiry and at trial. Here functional and structural concerns dominated. McIntyre, Lamer and La Forest JJ., in defining the remedial jurisdiction of criminal courts under s. 24(1), were predominantly concerned with identifying the arsenal of remedies that would best fulfil the function of the provincial criminal court, as a court of first instance, without straining its competence as an institution.

In this regard, the function of statutory criminal courts in the broader criminal justice system was a paramount consideration. As McIntyre J. observed, "most of the criminal work at first instance is done in these courts, therefore most of the applications for a remedy under s. 24(1) of the *Charter* will be made to them" (p. 955). He emphasized the need for complete resolution, wherever possible, at the trial level, where the court is best situated to rule on *Charter* issues arising before it and to fashion appropriate and just remedies. This role, in his opinion, demanded an expansive remedial jurisdiction for statutory criminal courts under s. 24(1), unconstrained by the lesser array of remedies they might enjoy under statute. In his words, "[a] claim for a remedy under s. 24(1) arising in the course of the trial will fall within the jurisdiction of these courts as a necessary incident of the trial process" (p. 955). He contemplated resort to the superior court of the province for a *Charter* remedy only where prerogative relief is sought.

The only limit McIntyre J. placed on a statutory criminal court's "power to grant the remedy sought" under s. 24(1) was that imposed by the constitutional division of powers: "[s]uch remedies must remain ... within the ambit of criminal powers" (p. 955). One finds no requirement in McIntyre J.'s reasons that the statute under which the court is acting expressly authorize the remedy sought, or empower the court to order remedies of the same "type". Rather, the emphasis is on creative and complete resolution at the trial level. To this end, he contemplated the widest possible discretion in provincial trial judges to fashion appropriate and just remedies, circumscribed only by the requirement that these remedies fall within the criminal sphere. It is in this manner that the function of the court, as a criminal court of first instance, is best fulfilled.

Lamer J. arrived at the same conclusion. In his view, a criminal trial court, whether of statutory or inherent jurisdiction, is empowered to grant *any* criminal law remedy under s. 24(1). He expressly rejected the proposition that statutory trial courts are confined to the remedies assigned to them by statute, at least in the absence of clear legislative intent (at pp. 886-87):

> I do not see the need, once the distinction between criminal and other remedies is made, for making a further distinction within the criminal law system between trial judges dependent upon the trial court in which they sit. Since they already have the jurisdiction to make a final complete determination of the trial, they already have a plenitude of criminal law remedies available, such as adjournment, bail, ordering disclosure, excluding evidence, entering stays.

Again, the emphasis is not on the remedies that criminal courts "already have ... available", but rather on the remedies that will best promote the function of the criminal trial court in our system of criminal justice.

In determining the range of remedies available to criminal trial courts under s. 24(1), Lamer J. was motivated primarily by the concern that these courts not venture into the types of remedies which by their own process (or structure) they are not properly equipped to fashion. He considered two opposing interpretations of s. 24(1) in the heart of his argument. The first is the proposition that a criminal court with jurisdiction over both the subject matter and the parties enjoys full jurisdiction to grant *any* appropriate and just remedy, including "civil remedies in addition to those remedies that are traditionally within their jurisdiction" (p. 885). The second proposition would "extend to any judge having jurisdiction over the person and the subject matter jurisdiction to grant *any criminal law remedy*" (p. 886 (emphasis added)).

Lamer J. approached this matter as a choice between alternatives — permitting criminal trial judges to draw from the full range of remedies, including civil remedies, in addressing *Charter* violations or, alternatively, restricting the scope of available remedies to the criminal domain. Neither approach evinces concern with whether the court has a particular remedial power under statute, or pursuant to its inherent jurisdiction.

Lamer J. endorsed the second approach for criminal trial judges; that is, he concluded that once jurisdiction over the person and subject matter is established, a criminal court is empowered to grant any criminal law remedy. This conclusion was compelled by the structural limitations of the criminal trial process (at p. 886):

> [D]esirable as might be a system whereby a person could get from the judge he or she is before a plenitude of remedies [*i.e.* including civil remedies], this approach has to be defeated by the fundamental differences as between the civil and criminal process .... [I]t will be difficult to afford the alleged violators, susceptible to pay damages or to be the object of some injunction, a fair hearing within the criminal justice process, whilst guaranteeing the accused all traditional safeguards. Furthermore, the criminal courts are not staffed and equipped to cope with such types of determinations.

Thus, Lamer J. concluded that the function performed by criminal trial courts mandates an expansive remedial jurisdiction under the *Charter*, circumscribed only by the boundaries of the court's expertise and procedures, which coincided with the boundaries of the criminal law.

La Forest J.'s reasons in *Mills* are also consistent with the functional and structural approach to defining "power to grant the remedy sought". Like Lamer and McIntyre JJ., he expressed a preference for complete resolution of *Charter* issues at the trial level, stating, at p. 972, that the "trial court will ordinarily be the appropriate court to grant the remedy". He contemplated an exception to this general principle only for exigent circumstances, such as where a trial court has not been set at the time the remedy is required, or where the trial court itself is implicated in the breach of the *Charter* right. This language suggests that apart from such exceptional circumstances, provincially appointed criminal courts are courts of competent jurisdiction to issue remedies under s. 24. He imposes only one limitation on this remedial jurisdiction: "civil remedies should await action in a civil court" (p. 971).

Functional and structural considerations also dominated the Court's comments on the powers of preliminary inquiry judges to exclude evidence on *Charter* grounds. A minority, led by Lamer J., would have recognized this power, on the basis that excluding inadmissible evidence, including on *Charter* grounds, is central to the preliminary inquiry's function: determining whether there is sufficient admissible evidence to put the accused on trial. McIntyre and La Forest JJ., writing for the majority view, held that preliminary inquiry judges cannot exclude evidence under s. 24(2). In arriving at this result, they emphasized the limited screening function of the preliminary inquiry and the difficulty of making, at a preliminary stage, the s. 24(2) determination of whether in "all the circumstances" admission of evidence obtained in breach of the *Charter* would bring the administration of justice into disrepute (at pp. 970-71, *per* La Forest J.).

In summary, the reasons of McIntyre, Lamer and La Forest JJ. in *Mills* were unanimous in emphasizing that the power of courts to issue *Charter* remedies turns on the function and structure of these courts. In effect, a judge sitting on a criminal trial, by reason of the function he or she is discharging, has the power to grant *Charter* remedies incidental to that trial. To this end, the judge may draw from the full ambit of criminal law remedies in fashioning an appropriate and just response to a *Charter* violation. This approach facilitates the function of the trial court, by promoting complete resolution of *Charter* issues at the trial level and allowing the court significant flexibility in fashioning remedies to meet the precise circumstances of the case at bar. At the same time, it heeds the structural limits of the criminal trial process, by confining the courts' remedial powers to the criminal sphere.

Subsequent jurisprudence affirms this functional and structural approach. Since *Mills*, two judgments of this Court have dealt with "court of competent jurisdiction" under s. 24: *Weber*, *supra*, and *Mooring*, *supra*. Both cases focused on the remedial jurisdiction of administrative tribunals under s. 24. In *Weber*, the Court addressed the question of whether a labour arbitrator is a court of competent jurisdiction under s. 24(1) for the purposes of awarding damages for a *Charter* breach. In *Mooring*, the Court considered whether the National Parole Board could exclude *Charter*-offending evidence as a court of competent jurisdiction under s. 24. In both cases, the jurisdiction of the tribunal over the person and subject matter was established; the critical issue was whether the tribunal enjoyed the power to grant the remedy sought. This jurisdiction was found in the labour arbitrator in *Weber*, but not in the Parole Board in *Mooring*.

.....

(1) The Function of the Provincial Offences Court

The function of a provincial court operating under the *POA* is to try provincial offences. While the majority of these offences involve minor regulatory infractions, they also concern important matters like environmental protection and, as here, workplace health and safety. These offences carry penalties ranging from significant fines to terms of imprisonment. The public and penal nature of such prosecutions suggests they are more criminal than civil in nature: see W.D. Drinkwalter and J.D. Ewart, *Ontario Provincial Offences Procedure* (1980), at pp. 4-7. Provincial offences courts are, for practical purposes, quasi-criminal courts, determining guilt and innocence and imposing commensurate criminal penalties.

This brings the provincial offences court within the ambit of *Mills*. As discussed, this Court in *Mills* envisioned a front-line role for statutory criminal courts in dispensing *Charter* remedies, with the superior courts occupying a complete and concurrent, but primarily *residual* role in proceedings not originating before them. Indeed, a superior court is compelled to decline jurisdiction to issue *Charter* relief, unless "it is more suited than the trial court to assess and grant the remedy that is just and appropriate": *R. v. Rahey*, [1987] 1 S.C.R. 588 at p. 603, 33 C.C.C. (3d) 289, 39 D.L.R. (4th) 481; P. Hogg, *Constitutional Law of Canada*, (looseleaf ed.), vol. 2, at p. 37-24. Provincial offences courts, like other criminal trial courts, are the preferred forum for issuing *Charter* remedies in the cases originating before them, where they will have the "fullest account of the facts available" (*Mills, supra,* at p. 971, *per* La Forest J.). This is particularly true where the *Charter* violation relates to the conduct of the trial: *R. v. O'Connor*, [1995] 4 S.C.R. 411, 103 C.C.C. (3d) 1, 130 D.L.R. (4th) 235. This role commends a full complement of criminal law remedies at the disposal of provincial offences courts. This broad remedial jurisdiction is necessary to prevent frequent resort to superior courts to fill gaps in statutory jurisdiction, and to ensure that the remedy that ultimately flows is in fact both appropriate and just.

Costs awards to discipline untimely disclosure are integrally connected to the function of the provincial offences court as a quasi-criminal trial court. Costs awards have a long history as a traditional criminal law remedy. Although sparingly used prior to the advent of the *Charter*, superior courts have always possessed the inherent jurisdiction to award costs against the Crown: *R. v. Ouellette*, [1980] 1 S.C.R. 568, 52 C.C.C. (2d) 336, 111 D.L.R. (3d) 216; *R. v. Pawlowski* (1993), 12 O.R. (3d) 709 at p. 712, 79 C.C.C. (3d) 353, 101 D.L.R. (4th) 267 (C.A.). In recent years, costs awards have attained more prominence as an effective remedy in criminal cases; in particular, they have assumed a vital role in enforcing the standards of disclosure established by this Court in *R. v. Stinchcombe*, [1991] 3 S.C.R. 326, 68 C.C.C. (3d) 1. See, for example: *Pawlowski, supra*; *Pang, supra*; *R. v. Regan* (1999), 137 C.C.C. (3d) 449 (N.S.C.A.).

Such awards, while not without a compensatory element, are integrally connected to the court's control of its trial process, and intended as a means of disciplining and discouraging flagrant and unjustified incidents of non-disclosure. Deprived of this remedy, a provincial offences court may be confined to two extreme options for relief — a stay of proceedings or a mere adjournment — neither of which may be appropriate and just in the circumstances. Since untimely pre-trial disclosure will rarely merit a stay of proceedings when the court can protect the fairness of the trial with a disclosure order (*O'Connor, supra*, at paras. 75-83; *Canada (Minister of Citizenship and Immigration) v. Tobiass*, [1997] 3 S.C.R. 391, 118 C.C.C. (3d) 443, 151 D.L.R. (4th) 119, at paras. 90-92), denying the provincial offences court the jurisdiction to issue a costs award may deprive it of the only effective remedy to control its process and recognize the harm incurred, even in cases involving unjustified and flagrant disregard for the accused's rights. In these circumstances, the issuance of a costs award is a quintessential example of "the development of imaginative and innovative remedies when just and appropriate" that Lamer J. identified as essential to the meaningful enforcement of *Charter* rights through the s. 24 guarantee (*Mills, supra*, at p. 887).

.....

It is true that the provincial offences court performs a specialized function that is distinct, in some respects, from that of a traditional criminal court. The purpose of the *POA*, as set out in s. 2(1), is to establish a procedure for the prosecution of provincial offences "that reflects the distinction between provincial offences and criminal offences". However, as discussed, this distinction is not between criminal and *non-criminal* offences, but rather between criminal and *quasi-criminal* offences. The proceedings remain penal in nature. And while many of the prosecutions under the *POA* may indeed involve minor regulatory infractions, claims for *Charter* relief will generally arise from prosecutions that involve significant fines and the possibility of imprisonment. In these cases, the distinction between provincial courts operating under the *Criminal Code* and the *POA* is far less material. The maximum sentence faced by the individual respondent in the instant case — a $25,000 fine and/or 12 months' imprisonment — exceeds the penalties generally levied for a number of summary conviction offences.

Further, the Crown concedes that legal costs in criminal and regulatory matters are an exceptional or remarkable event. It is consequently difficult to see how empowering the provincial offences court to order this remedy as an exceptional tool, in the comparatively few instances when *Charter* breaches would arise before it, imperils the expedient operation of these courts.

Nor will recognizing the jurisdiction in provincial offences courts to issue costs awards as a *Charter* remedy risk turning the Canadian legal system "upside down". By ensuring that the remedies available to the provincial offences court fall within its competency as an institution to issue, meaningful access to *Charter* relief is promoted with minimal disruption to the existing jurisdictional scheme. There is little reason to believe that awarding costs will strain the work habits, resources or expertise of provincial offences courts; in fact, experience to this point suggests otherwise.

Neither is there any indication that the Crown will be subjected to such awards unfairly or arbitrarily. Crown counsel is not held to a standard of perfection, and costs awards will not flow from every failure to disclose in a timely fashion. Rather, the developing jurisprudence uniformly restricts such awards, at a minimum, to circumstances of a marked and unacceptable departure from the reasonable standards expected of the prosecution. I fail to see how the provision of an expedient remedy in such cases, from a trial court that is not only competent but also ideally situated to make such an assessment, risks disrupting the existing system of justice.

Indeed, a failure to recognize this jurisdiction may arguably result in far more disruption of the administration of justice, by requiring resort to another forum to obtain an appropriate and just remedy, with all the attendant delays, expense and inconvenience. Most importantly, it may, as a matter of practical reality, deprive an accused of an appropriate and just remedy for even flagrant violations of his or her *Charter* rights, and thus render illusory both these guaranteed protections and the promise of their enforcement.

In summary, the provincial offences court's role as a quasi-criminal court of first instance weighs strongly in favour of an expansive remedial jurisdiction under s. 24 to promote complete resolution of *Charter* issues in the forum best situated to resolve them. In this light, authority to discipline egregious incidents of non-disclosure through awards of legal costs is consistent with — and would enhance — the role performed by these courts in the administration of criminal justice.

(2) The Structure of the Provincial Offences Court

The same features that characterize the provincial offences court as a quasi-criminal court also commend it as an appropriate forum for assessing costs awards for *Charter* breaches arising from non-disclosure. There is no appreciable difference between criminal and quasi-criminal courts in terms of the structural limits of their proceedings. A court in which a justice presides over the trial of a provincial offence under the *POA* is clearly structured as a traditional "court". Iacobucci J., dissenting in *Weber*, noted, at p. 942, the salient characteristics of a "court": "the rules of procedure and evidence, the independence and legal training of its judges, the possibility of hearing from a third party intervener such as an Attorney General or an *amicus curiae*". A provincial offences court trying an offence under the *POA* satisfies this description. It has its own detailed procedural rules (*Rules of the Ontario Court (Provincial Division) in Provincial Offences Proceedings*, R.R.O. 1990, Reg. 200), and abides by the standard rules of evidence. Judicial independence is required of justices of the peace. They receive legal training. The court's rulings are subject to appellate review, and there can be interveners on this appeal (*Rules of the Court of Appeal in Appeals Under the Provincial Offences Act*, Reg. 721/94, Rule 21(1)). In sum, it is a judicial process in an adversarial forum governed by the traditional rules of evidence.

The Crown alleges that a number of structural deficiencies in *POA* proceedings impair the ability of provincial offences courts to justly and fairly order costs awards under s. 24(1). It notes that the *POA* lacks a formal method of tariff calculation and makes no provision for the enforcement of costs orders once levied. In sum, the Crown argues that recognizing a jurisdiction in provincial offences courts to order payment of legal costs under s. 24(1) would cast these courts into waters in which they are not properly equipped to tread.

I do not share this concern. Issues of notice and computation of costs have not proven unmanageable for provincial courts. Further, trial and appellate courts are developing guidelines to govern when such awards are appropriate and just, curbing the potential for arbitrary or unfair awards: *Pawlowski, supra*; *Pang, supra*; *R. v. Jedynack* (1994), 16 O.R. (3d) 612 (Gen. Div.); *R. v. Dodson* (2000), 70 C.R.R. (2d) 65 at p. 73, 142 C.C.C. (3d) 134, (Ont. C.A.); *R. v. Robinson* (1999), 142 C.C.C. (3d) 303 (Alta. C.A.). Finally, since costs awards are only issued against the Crown, complex collection mechanisms and contempt procedures are unnecessary. These considerations suggest that the fashioning of costs orders as a *Charter* remedy may be safely entrusted to provincial offences courts.

(3) Conclusions on Power to Grant the Remedy Sought in the Instant Case

As a quasi-criminal trial court, *POA* justices may be assumed, absent a contrary indication, to possess the power to order payment of legal costs by the Crown as a remedy for *Charter* violations arising from untimely disclosure. This power may be inferred from their quasi-criminal function and structure. As with other criminal trial courts, the role of the provincial offences court in the broader legal system, and particularly its role as a court of first instance, provide the most valuable insight into the powers the legislature intended it to exercise. It is not necessary to engage in a searching examination of the constituent statute to issue the same "type of" remedy in the non-*Charter* context.

The language of the *POA*, however, cannot be ignored. If it indicates that the legislature did *not* intend the provincial offences courts to issue costs orders as a *Charter* remedy, then these courts are not so empowered. This brings us to the Crown's argument that the legislature confined the power of *POA* justices to grant costs (and, even then, only witness costs) to specific procedural breaches and that this indicates an intention not to permit them to grant *Charter* remedies for costs in matters other than those prescribed by the *POA*.

I cannot accept this argument. Given all the elements in this case that point to the power to make the order sought under s. 24, I find it difficult to infer a contrary intention from the fact that the statute does not confer on the court a general right to award legal costs. The legislature gave the court functions destined to attract *Charter* issues. These functions by their nature are likely to bring the tribunal into the domain of *Charter* rights. They necessarily implicate matters covered by the *Charter*, including fair trial rights and remedies for violations of these rights. It is therefore reasonable to assume that the legislature intended the *POA* court to deal with those *Charter* issues incidental to its process that it is suited to resolve, by virtue of its function and structure.

In criminal proceedings, incidental *Charter* issues are routinely resolved at the trial stage without recourse to other proceedings, a procedure repeatedly endorsed by this Court as desirable: *Mills*, *supra*; *Rahey*, *supra*; *R. v. Garofoli*, [1990] 2 S.C.R. 1421, 60 C.C.C. (3d) 161; *Kourtessis v. M.N.R.*, [1993] 2 S.C.R. 53, 81 C.C.C. (3d) 286, 102 D.L.R. (4th) 456. It is logical to assume that the Ontario Legislature intended the *POA* to operate in tandem with the *Charter*, rather than to negate the *Charter*'s application. Rather than inferring that the legislature intended to narrow the operation of the *Charter* with its silence on the issue of the provincial offences court's jurisdiction under s. 24, the more reasonable inference is that it intended to supplement the court's work with the incidental *Charter* remedies that it is suited to issue.

Consequently, I conclude that the provincial offences court enjoys the necessary power to grant the remedy sought in the present case, and is thus a "court of competent jurisdiction" within the meaning of s. 24(1). In my opinion, this result represents an appropriate and principled integration of the procedural regime established by the legislature and the constitutional regime established by the *Charter*.

VI. Conclusion

I would dismiss the appeal and remit the matter to the Superior Court of Justice for determination of whether the trial justice erred in finding the conduct of the prosecution warranted an order for legal costs on the facts of the case. The respondents should have their costs here and below.

In the following case, the Supreme Court of Canada was invited to reconsider whether a preliminary inquiry justice is a "court of competent

jurisdiction" for the purpose of excluding evidence under s. 24(2) of the *Charter*.

R. v. HYNES

(2001), 159 C.C.C. (3d) 359 (S.C.C.)

McLachlin C.J.C. [L'Heureux-Dubé, Gonthier, Bastarache and LeBel JJ. concurring]: —

.....

B. Application of the Functional and Structural Test

The issue before the Court is whether a preliminary inquiry justice is a "court of competent jurisdiction" under s. 24(2) for the purpose of excluding evidence, in particular confessions, on grounds that they were obtained in breach of the *Charter* and that their admission would bring the administration of justice into disrepute.

.....

The primary function of a preliminary inquiry justice is to determine whether the Crown has sufficient evidence to warrant committing the accused to trial: *Criminal Code*, s. 548(1); *Caccamo v. The Queen*, [1976] 1 S.C.R. 786, 21 C.C.C. (2d) 257, 54 D.L.R. (3d) 685. The preliminary inquiry is not a trial. It is rather a pre-trial screening procedure aimed at filtering out weak cases that do not merit trial. Its paramount purpose is to "protect the accused from a needless, and indeed, improper, exposure to public trial where the enforcement agency is not in possession of evidence to warrant the continuation of the process": *Skogman v. The Queen*, [1984] 2 S.C.R. 93 at p. 105, 13 C.C.C. (3d) 161, 11 D.L.R. (4th) 161. The justice evaluates the admissible evidence to determine whether it is sufficient to justify requiring the accused to stand trial. (The trial judge cannot, with due respect to the contrary suggestion of Gushue and Green JJ.A., simply "choose not to" rely on offered evidence without first making a positive ruling against its admissibility.)

Over time, the preliminary inquiry has assumed an ancillary role as a discovery mechanism, providing the accused with an early opportunity to discover the Crown's case against him or her: *Skogman, supra*, at pp. 105-6. Nonetheless, this discovery element remains incidental to the central mandate of the preliminary inquiry as clearly prescribed by the *Criminal Code*; that is, the determination of whether "there is sufficient evidence to put the accused on trial" (s. 548(1)(*a*)).

In support of this function, Parliament equipped the preliminary inquiry with a structure that shares broad similarities with that of the trial court. It is conducted like a trial with regard to the presentation of evidence. Further, the preliminary inquiry is a court of record, and evidence is taken under oath in the presence of the accused. The accused has the right to cross-examine witnesses and respond to the Crown's case. The preliminary inquiry justice, in assessing the sufficiency of the Crown's case, may rule on the admissibility of evidence. Section 542(1) of the *Code* expressly includes statements made by the accused in the evidence that the Crown may call at a preliminary inquiry. The traditional rules governing the admissibility of evidence apply. Most notably, the preliminary inquiry justice may refuse to admit statements of the accused to persons in authority if they were not made voluntarily.

The preliminary inquiry is not a trial, however, and this distinction is reflected in the powers and procedure. Significantly, the preliminary inquiry justice has no authority to grant remedies. The justice cannot, for example, order the Crown to provide particulars or disclosure to the defence, stay proceedings for abuse of process, compel the production of third party records, or grant relief against informer privilege by recourse to the innocence at stake exception: *R. v. O'Connor*, [1995] 4 S.C.R. 411, 103 C.C.C. (3d) 1, 130 D.L.R. (4th) 235; *R. v. Chew*, [1968] 2 C.C.C. 127 (Ont. C.A.); *R. v. Girimonte* (1997), 121 C.C.C. (3d) 33 (Ont. C.A.); *R. v. Richards* (1997), 115 C.C.C. (3d) 377 (Ont. C.A.). These powers are reserved for the trial judge. The Crown also has a discretion to lead only a *prima facie* case at the preliminary inquiry and rarely calls all the evidence it plans to lead at trial: *Caccamo, supra*, at pp. 809-10.

The appellant argues that recognizing the power to exclude *Charter*-offending evidence at the preliminary inquiry would bolster its function as a screening mechanism. He relies in substance on the reasoning of Green J.A. (in dissent) in the Court of Appeal. Green J.A. emphasized that the preliminary inquiry justice is directed under the *Code* to inquire into whether sufficient evidence exists to commit the accused to trial. Pursuant to *United States of America v. Shephard*, [1977] 2 S.C.R. 1067, 30 C.C.C. (2d) 424, 70 D.L.R. (3d) 136, "sufficient evidence" under s. 548(1) of the *Code* means "sufficient *admissible* evidence". Further, the preliminary inquiry justice is granted the discretion to receive evidence tendered by the prosecutor or the accused, including admissions, confession or statements that are "by law ... *admissible* against [the accused]": s. 542(1) (emphasis added). This evidence-screening function, in Green J.A.'s view, requires the justice to examine *all* the evidence to determine whether it is relevant and, if so, whether it would be admissible against the accused at trial. Thus, the exclusion of evidence "whether based on a *Charter* breach or not, falls squarely within the basic purpose and function of a preliminary inquiry of screening evidence" (para. 51).

.....

On its face, this argument is strong. Yet against it may be put the fact that the preliminary inquiry, as mandated by Parliament, is in essence a screening process — its primary purpose is neither to determine rights, nor to grant remedies for their breach. It is quite plausible to infer that while Parliament intended preliminary inquiry justices to have the power to determine the admissibility of evidence in aid of their screening function, this power stops short of permitting them to enter on *Charter* questions. In fact, preliminary inquiry justices have for almost two decades performed their screening functions without apparent difficulty, absent any power to exclude evidence on grounds of *Charter* breach. The possibility that some cases may pass the screening stage which might be dismissed, were *Charter* exclusion possible, is not cause for serious concern, it is argued, since the offending evidence can be excluded at trial. This possibility may be less disadvantageous than allowing preliminary inquiring justices general powers to exclude evidence for *Charter* breaches.

The disadvantages of the latter course are manifest. First, recognizing a remedial jurisdiction in preliminary inquiry justices has the potential to transform the role Parliament intended this process to perform in the criminal justice system. Instead of performing a preliminary screening function, the preliminary inquiry might become a forum for trying *Charter* breaches and awarding remedies. This function seems remote from that envisaged by Parliament for preliminary inquiries.

Second, assigning this new role to preliminary inquiry justices might undermine the expeditious nature of the preliminary inquiry. As discussed, the preliminary inquiry "is not a trial and should not be allowed to become a trial": *Patterson v. The Queen*, [1970] S.C.R. 409 at p. 412, 2 C.C.C. (2d) 227, 9 D.L.R. (3d) 398. Yet s. 24(2) frequently involves an extensive and comprehensive inquiry. It requires the judge to determine the extent of *Charter* protections, whether they were breached, and finally whether, in "all the circumstances" it is necessary to exclude evidence to preserve the repute of the administration of justice. It seems reasonable to conclude that the Crown might be compelled to present a much fuller case — perhaps its entire case — in order to place "all the circumstances" before the court. The accused might also present more evidence than is generally the case, since it is the accused who bears the burden of establishing a *Charter* breach and showing that the threshold for exclusion is satisfied.

Without seeking to overdramatize the matter, experience and common sense suggest that preliminary inquiries would become longer and more complex if applications to exclude evidence on *Charter* grounds were part of their daily fare. This in turn would increase the degree to which preliminary inquiry justices and trial judges are doing the same work, resulting in additional cost and delay. In all probability, the preliminary inquiry would become less preliminary and more like a trial.

Third, trial courts are better situated than preliminary inquiry justices to engage in s. 24(2) determinations. This Court has repeatedly identified the trial court as the preferred forum for resolving *Charter* issues: *Mills* [(1986), 26 C.C.C. (3d) 481 (S.C.C.)]; *R. v. Rahey*, [1987] 1 S.C.R. 588, 33 C.C.C. (3d) 289, 39 D.L.R. (4th) 481; *R. v. Garofoli*, [1990] 2 S.C.R. 1421, 60 C.C.C. (3d) 161; *Kourtessis v. M.N.R.*, [1993] 2 S.C.R. 53, 81 C.C.C. (3d) 286, 102 D.L.R. (4th) 456; *O'Connor, supra*. This principle holds particularly true for s. 24(2) determinations. The inquiry is potentially wide-ranging, sometimes complex. Preliminary inquiry justices usually possess the expertise necessary to deal with *Charter* issues; indeed sitting as trial judges they do so routinely. However, it is the trial judge that will generally enjoy the fullest appreciation of "all the circumstances" relevant to a s. 24(2) determination. At the preliminary inquiry, where evidence may be incomplete and the full circumstances unknown, this assessment may be difficult, or worse, erroneous. The result may be to exclude evidence that would have been admitted in the light of the fuller picture presented at trial. This in turn may lead to the premature dismissal of cases warranting prosecution at the preliminary stage.

The question is at what stage of the proceedings it is best to assess whether "the admission of it in the proceedings would bring the administration of justice into disrepute". Clearly, there is much to be said in favour of leaving this assessment to the trial. As L'Heureux-Dubé J. observed in *R. v. Power*, [1994] 1 S.C.R. 601 at p. 630, 89 C.C.C. (3d) 1:

> It should also be underlined that evidence adduced at a preliminary inquiry is incomplete. Indeed, a number of witnesses, who will be called to testify at trial, are not called at the preliminary inquiry and vice versa. In my view, therefore, the evidence adduced at a preliminary inquiry does not properly reflect the whole of the evidence that will be presented at trial on the merits, nor does it give sufficient indication of the strength of the evidence that will be presented at trial.

The very nature of the preliminary inquiry suggests that the justice will have access to only a portion of the evidence that will be led at trial. Consequently, the preliminary inquiry may provide an insufficient vantage from which to assess "all the circumstances" that must inform the s. 24(2) analysis.

Moreover, whether the admission of evidence will bring the administration of justice into disrepute is not a matter of scientific precision so much as an informed judgment based on the entire context of the trial. While *R. v. Collins*, [1987] 1 S.C.R. 265, 33 C.C.C. (3d) 1, 38 D.L.R. (4th) 508, and subsequent cases, established the factors that must guide this determination, the ultimate decision depends to some degree on the judge's assessment of their relative significance in the case at hand. The trial judge evaluates these factors in the context of the trial as a whole and the requirements of essential fairness. This endeavour may involve the weighing of evidence, assessments of credibility, and other such determinations that fall outside the narrow mandate and powers of a preliminary inquiry justice. Justices at a further remove are also less likely to be able to evaluate the situation as well as the trial judge. Thus appellate courts accord considerable deference to the trial judge's conclusion on whether admission of a particular piece of evidence would bring the administration of justice into disrepute: *R. v. Duguay*, [1989] 1 S.C.R. 93, 46 C.C.C. (3d) 1, 56 D.L.R. (4th) 46; *R. v. Stillman*, [1997] 1 S.C.R. 607, 113 C.C.C. (3d) 321, 144 D.L.R. (4th) 193; *R. v. Belnavis*, [1997] 3 S.C.R. 341, 118 C.C.C. (3d) 405, 151 D.L.R. (4th) 443. The same reasoning suggests that justices at the stage of preliminary screening may be similarly disadvantaged.

Finally, *Charter* litigation at the preliminary stage may ultimately have no practical effect beyond increasing the costs and delays associated with this process. If the preliminary inquiry justice excludes evidence under s. 24(2), but still commits the accused to trial, his or her conclusion on this issue does not bind the trial judge. When the Crown seeks to introduce the evidence at trial, the exact same matter will require litigation again. Conversely, if the accused is discharged as the result of excluded evidence under s. 24(2), the Crown may still prefer a direct indictment against the accused pursuant to s. 577 of the *Criminal Code* and proceed to trial regardless.

Several of the intervening Attorneys General cautioned that the discretion of the Crown to prefer a direct indictment, now used sparingly, might be exercised routinely in situations where the preliminary inquiry justice's decision to exclude evidence under s. 24(2) curtailed a prosecution before it reached trial. Indeed, the Crown may have no other available option, since no right of appeal lies from the order made at the preliminary inquiry. Consequently, regardless of the finding at the preliminary stage on the s. 24(2) issue, its effect in practice might often prove negligible.

The lack of a statutory right of appeal from the ruling of a preliminary inquiry justice is particularly telling. The majority of the Court in *Mills, per* McIntyre J., clearly stated that decisions respecting a *Charter* remedy should be subject to review (at pp. 958-59):

> [T]he *Charter* is silent on the question of appeals and the conclusion must therefore be that the existing appeal structure must be employed in the resolution of s. 24(1) claims. *Since the Charter has conferred a right to seek a remedy under the provisions of s. 24(1) and since claims for remedy will involve claims alleging the infringement of basic rights and fundamental freedoms, it is essential that an appellate procedure exist.* There is no provision in the *Code* which provides a specific right to appeal against the granting, or the refusal, of a *Charter* remedy under s. 24(1), but appeals are provided for which involve questions of law and fact. *The Charter, forming part of the fundamental law of Canada, is therefore covered and the refusal of a claim for Charter relief will be appealable by a person aggrieved as a question of law, as will be the granting of such relief by the Crown.* The appeal will follow the normal, established procedure. [Emphasis added.]

Contrary to this principle, the Crown would lack a right of appeal from the decision of a preliminary inquiry justice excluding evidence under s. 24(2) and discharging the accused as a result. Such a decision would amount to a final determination in favour of the accused. The Crown's power to proceed by preferred indictment in such circumstances cannot be accepted as a proper substitute for a statutory appeal mechanism. This power is, and should be, exercised sparingly. Its routine exercise by the Crown to nullify rulings by a preliminary inquiry justice on *Charter* issues may carry serious ramifications. As Marshall J.A. emphasized in the court below, resort by the Crown to its discretion under s. 577 as a matter of course "would be calculated to engender impressions that there were no teeth in the recourse given to individuals" (para. 101) to enforce their *Charter* rights. It would certainly do little to preserve the repute of the administration of justice in the eyes of the public it serves. I have difficulty accepting that Parliament intended this result. The more compelling conclusion is that Parliament intended *Charter* issues to be resolved in a forum equipped with established and well understood avenues of appeal. The trial court is the obvious choice for this task.

The appellant argues that deferring s. 24(2) issues to trial creates anomalies in the operation of preliminary inquiries, particularly in relation to statements of the accused. Preliminary inquiry justices can generally exclude admissions, confessions or statements made by an accused on the grounds of inadmissibility at common law. Indeed, Parliament directly alludes to this power in s. 542(1) of the *Code*. This produces the apparent anomaly of a preliminary inquiry justice being empowered to exclude statements made by an accused because they are not voluntary (and thus inadmissible at common law) but not because they were obtained in breach of the *Charter*. This anomaly, the appellant contends, is exacerbated by the fact that the same circumstances may be relevant to both the voluntariness of a statement and the alleged breach of the *Charter*. Nonetheless, the preliminary inquiry justice, pursuant to the current rule, may consider the admissibility of the statement based on the former concern (voluntariness), but not the latter (*Charter* violations).

However, the fact that exclusion of evidence is involved should not blind us to the fundamental distinctions that exist between excluding evidence under the common law, on one hand, and excluding evidence under s. 24(2) of the *Charter* on the other. Although these powers appear similar, only the latter involves an exercise of *remedial* authority — an authority with which a preliminary inquiry justice is not cloaked: *Mills, supra,* at pp. 970-71 (*per* La Forest J.). Further, the common law confessions rule always results in the exclusion of offending evidence. As such, it involves a relatively focussed inquiry into the immediate circumstances surrounding the alleged statements of the accused. By contrast, the s. 24(2) inquiry transcends the immediate facts of the *Charter* breach and embraces a much more comprehensive appraisal of the impact of the evidence on the fairness of the trial and the repute of the justice system: see *R. v. Oickle,* [2000] 2 S.C.R. 3, 2000 SCC 38, 147 C.C.C. (3d) 321, 190 D.L.R. (4th) 257, at para. 30. As discussed, imposing this task on the preliminary inquiry may hamper or distort its intended function as an expeditious charge-screening mechanism. At any rate, given the non-binding nature of evidentiary rulings at the preliminary inquiry, and the power of the Crown to prefer a direct indictment, the perceived benefits of litigating s. 24(2) issues at the preliminary stage may prove more illusory than real.

The specialized and limited function of the preliminary inquiry leads me to conclude that Parliament, while furnishing this process with trial-like features, did not intend for it to engage in s. 24(2) considerations. These issues are best reserved for the trial judge, who "is likely to have a more complete picture of the evidence and its significance in the context of the case and is thus better situated to decide such questions": *Seaboyer,* [(1991), 66 C.C.C. (3d) 321 (S.C.C.)], at p. 638. Consequently, I see little reason to depart from the clear precedent to this effect established in *Mills* and *Seaboyer*.

VI. Conclusion

The preliminary inquiry justice, the reviewing judge and the Court of Appeal did not err in holding that the preliminary inquiry justice had no power to enter into the question of whether the statements taken from the appellant had been obtained as a result of *Charter* breach and, if so, whether they should be excluded on this ground. I would dismiss the appeal and remand the case for continuation of the preliminary inquiry.

[Major, Iacobucci, Binnie and Arbour JJ. dissented]

3. JURISDICTION UNDER SECTION 52 OF THE CONSTITUTION

Section 52(1) of the *Constitution Act, 1982* (being Schedule B of the *Canada Act 1982* (U.K.), 1982, c. 11), provides that "[t]he Constitution of Canada [which includes the *Charter*] is the supreme law of Canada, and any law that is inconsistent with the provisions of the Constitution is, to the extent of the inconsistency, of no force or effect."

QUESTION

9. Assume that the statutory power that permitted the police to seize the critical evidence in a case is inconsistent with the *Charter* and therefore of no force or effect. It seems clear that a provincial court judge presiding at a preliminary inquiry has no power to exclude evidence under s. 24(2) of the *Charter*, on the basis that it was obtained by means of a statute which should be declared of no force or effect. Now assume that the very offence with which the accused is charged is arguably inconsistent with the *Charter*. Can the preliminary inquiry judge address that argument? To put the question in its starkest form, what can be done if the accused appears at the preliminary inquiry charged with being redheaded, contrary to the fictitious *Need for Dominant Features Act of Canada*? Consider, in this regard, *R. v. Big M. Drug Mart* (1985), 18 C.C.C. (3d) 385 (S.C.C.).

CHAPTER 4

PRE-TRIAL INVESTIGATIVE PROCEDURES

A. SEARCHES OR SEIZURES

1. Overview

Government agencies, most particularly the police, are empowered by statute or at common law to search and or seize. Their statutory powers may be found in the *Criminal Code*, R.S.C. 1985, c. C-46, in other federal statutes, such as the *Controlled Drugs and Substances Act*, S.C. 1996, c. 19, or indeed, in provincial statutes. All of these powers are now regulated by the *Canadian Charter of Rights and Freedoms* (being Part I of the *Constitution Act, 1982*, being Schedule B of the *Canada Act 1982* (U.K.), 1982, c. 11), most particularly s. 8, which provides that everyone has the right to be secure against unreasonable search or seizure. Section 8 has been given a broad and liberal interpretation so as to protect one's reasonable expectation of privacy, thereby extending to government conduct far beyond the conventional "search" or "seizure" of one's premises or property (see *Hunter et al. v. Southam Inc.* (1984), 14 C.C.C. (3d) 97 (S.C.C.)). For example, s. 8 extends to the interception of private communications or video surveillance of individuals (see *R. v. Wong* (1990), 60 C.C.C. (3d) 460 (S.C.C.)), though this conduct would not, in common parlance, be described as search or seizure.

An appreciation of the investigative powers of the authorities and the impact of the *Charter* upon them is essential for Crown and defence counsel who may be called upon to advise the police or a suspect at the pre-trial investigative stage and who may later be initiating or responding to a *Charter*-based attack on the investigative procedures employed.

2. Impact of the Charter Generally

HUNTER ET AL. v. SOUTHAM INC.

(1984), 14 C.C.C. (3d) 97 (S.C.C.)

[Pursuant to s. 10(1) of the *Combines Investigation Act*, R.S.C. 1970, c. C-23, the Director of Investigation and Research of the Combines Investigation Branch authorized several Combines Investigation officers to enter and examine documents and other things at the respondent's business premises in Edmonton and elsewhere in Canada. The authorization was certified by a member of the Restrictive Trade Practices Commission pursuant to s. 10(3) of the Act. The appellants appealed from the holding of the Alberta Court of Appeal that s. 10(3), and, by implication, s. 10(1) of the Act were inconsistent with the *Charter* and, therefore, of no force or effect.]

The judgment of the court was delivered by

Dickson J.: — The Constitution of Canada, which includes the *Canadian Charter of Rights and Freedoms*, is the supreme law of Canada. Any law inconsistent with the provisions of the Constitution is, to the extent of the inconsistency, of no force or effect. Section 52(1) of the *Constitution Act, 1982* so mandates. The constitutional question posed in this appeal is whether s. 10(3), and by implication s. 10(1), of the *Combines Investigation Act*, R.S.C. 1970, c. C-23, (the "Act") are inconsistent with s. 8 of the *Charter* by reason of authorizing unreasonable searches and seizures and are therefore of no force and effect.

.....

Sections 10(1) and 10(3) of the *Combines Investigation Act* provide:

> 10(1) Subject to subsection (3), in any inquiry under this Act the Director [of Investigation and Research of the Combines Investigation Branch] or any representative authorized by him may enter any premises on which the Director believes there may be evidence relevant to the matters being inquired into and may examine any thing on the premises and may copy or take away for further examination or copying any book, paper, record or other document that in the opinion of the Director or his authorized representative, as the case may be, may afford such evidence.
>
> .....
>
> (3) Before exercising the power conferred by subsection (1), the Director or his representative shall produce a certificate from a member of the [Restrictive Trade Practices] Commission, which may be granted on the *ex parte* application of the Director, authorizing the exercise of such power.

.....

At the outset it is important to note that the issue in this appeal concerns the constitutional validity of a statute authorizing a search and seizure. It does not concern the reasonableness or otherwise of the manner in which the appellants carried out their statutory authority. It is not the conduct of the appellants, but rather the legislation under which they acted, to which attention must be directed.

.....

I begin with the obvious. The *Canadian Charter of Rights and Freedoms* is a purposive document. Its purpose is to guarantee and to protect, within the limits of reason, the enjoyment of the rights and freedoms it enshrines. It is intended to constrain governmental action inconsistent with those rights and freedoms; it is not in itself an authorization for governmental action. In the present case this means, as Prowse J.A. pointed out, that in guaranteeing the right to be secure from unreasonable searches and seizures, s. 8 acts as a limitation on whatever powers of search and seizure the federal or provincial governments already and otherwise possess. It does not in itself confer any powers, even of "reasonable" search and seizure, on these governments. This leads, in my view, to the further conclusion that an assessment of the constitutionality of a search and seizure, or of a statute authorizing a search or seizure, must focus on its "reasonable" or "unreasonable" impact on the subject of the search or the seizure, and not simply on its rationality in furthering some valid government objective.

Since the proper approach to the interpretation of the *Charter of Rights and Freedoms* is a purposive one, before it is possible to assess the reasonableness or unreasonableness of the impact of search or of a statute authorizing a search, it is first necessary to specify the purpose underlying s. 8: in other words, to delineate the nature of the interests it is meant to protect.

Historically, the common law protections with regard to governmental searches and seizures were based on the right to enjoy property and were linked to the law of trespass.

.....

In my view the interests protected by s. 8 are of a wider ambit...

.....

Like the Supreme Court of the United States, I would be wary of foreclosing the possibility that the right to be secure against unreasonable search and seizure might protect interests beyond the right of privacy, but for purposes of the present appeal I am satisfied that its protections go at least that far. The guarantee of security from *unreasonable* search and seizure only protects a *reasonable* expectation. This limitation on the right guaranteed by s. 8, whether it is expressed negatively as freedom from "unreasonable" search and seizure, or positively as an entitlement to a "reasonable" expectation of privacy, indicates that an assessment must be made as to whether in a particular situation the public's interest in being left alone by government must give way to the government's interest in intruding on the individual's privacy in order to advance its goals, notably those of law enforcement.

The question that remains, and the one upon which the present appeal hinges, is how this assessment is to be made. When is it to be made, by whom and on what basis? Here again, I think the proper approach is a purposive one.

A) When is the balance of interests to be assessed?

If the issue to be resolved in assessing the constitutionality of searches under s. 10 were *in fact* the governmental interest in carrying out a given search outweighed that of the individual in resisting the governmental intrusion upon his privacy, then it would be appropriate to determine the balance of the competing interests *after* the search had been conducted. Such a *post facto* analysis would, however, be seriously at odds with the purpose of s. 8. That purpose is, as I have said, to protect individuals from unjustified state intrusions upon their privacy. That purpose requires a means of *preventing* unjustified searches before they happen, not simply of determining, after the fact, whether they ought to have occurred in the first place. This, in my view, can only be accomplished by a system of prior authorization, not one of subsequent validation.

A requirement of *prior authorization*, usually in the form of a valid warrant, has been a consistent prerequisite for a valid search and seizure both at common law and under most statutes. Such a requirement puts the onus on the state to demonstrate the superiority of its interest to that of the individual. As such it accords with the apparent intention of the *Charter* to prefer, where feasible, the right of the individual to be free from state interference to the interests of the state in advancing its purposes through such interference.

I recognize that it may not be reasonable in every instance to insist on prior authorization in order to validate governmental intrusions upon individuals' expectations of privacy. Nevertheless where it is feasible to obtain prior authorization, I would hold that such authorization is a precondition for a valid search and seizure.

Here also, the decision in *Katz* [(1967), 389 U.S. 347 (U.S.S.C.)] is relevant. In *United States v. Rabinowitz* (1950), 339 U.S. 56, the Supreme Court of the United States had held that a search without warrant was not *ipso facto* unreasonable. Seventeen years later however, in *Katz*, Stewart J. concluded that warrantless search was *prima facie* "unreasonable" under the Fourth Amendment. The terms of the Fourth Amendment are not identical to those of s. 8 and American decisions can be transplanted to the Canadian context only with the greatest caution. Nevertheless, I would in the present instance respectfully adopt Stewart J.'s formulation as equally applicable to the concept of "unreasonableness" under s. 8, and would require the party seeking to justify a warrantless search rebut this presumption of unreasonableness.

...[Section]10(3) *does* purport to establish a requirement for prior authorization, specifying, as it does, that searches and seizures conducted under s. 10(1) must be authorized by a member of the [Restrictive Trade Practices Commission, the "R.T.P.C."]. The question then becomes whether s. 10(3) provides for an acceptable prior authorization procedure.

B) Who must grant the authorization?

The purpose of a requirement of prior authorization is to provide an opportunity, before the event, for the conflicting interests of the state and the individual to be assessed, so that the individual's right to privacy will be breached only where the appropriate standard has been met, and the interests of the state are thus demonstrably superior. For such an authorization procedure to be meaningful it is necessary for the person authorizing the search to be able to assess the evidence as to whether that standard has been met, in an entirely neutral and impartial manner... The person performing this function need not be a judge, but he must at a minimum be capable of acting judicially.

.....

In my view, investing the commission or its members with significant investigatory functions has the result of vitiating the ability of a member of the commission to act in a judicial capacity when authorizing a search or seizure under s. 10(3).

.....

On this basis alone I would conclude that the prior authorization mandated by s. 10(3) of the *Combines Investigation Act* is inadequate to satisfy the requirement of s. 8 of the *Charter* and consequently a search carried out under the authority of subss. 10(1) and 10(3) is an unreasonable one. Since, however, the Alberta Court of Appeal found other, perhaps even more serious defects in these provisions I pass on to consider whether even if s. 10(3) did specify a truly neutral and detached arbiter to authorize searches it would nevertheless remain inconsistent with s. 8 of the *Charter*.

C) On what basis must the balance of interests be assessed?

Section 10 is terse in the extreme on the subject of criteria for issuing an authorization for entry, search and seizure. Section 10(3) merely states that an R.T.P.C. member may grant an authorization *ex parte*. The only explicit criteria for granting such an authorization are those mentioned in s. 10(1), namely: (1) that an inquiry under the Act must be in progress, and (2) that the Director must believe that the premises may contain relevant evidence.

.....

The purpose of an objective criterion for granting prior authorization to conduct a search or seizure is to provide a consistent standard for identifying the point at which the interests of the state in such intrusions come to prevail over the interests of the individual in resisting them. To associate it with an applicant's reasonable belief that relevant evidence *may* be uncovered by the search, would be to define the proper standard as the *possibility* of finding evidence. This is a very low standard which would validate intrusion on the basis of suspicion, and authorize fishing expeditions of considerable latitude. It would tip the balance strongly in favour of the state and limit the right of the individual to resist, to only the most egregious intrusions. I do not believe that this is a proper standard for securing the right to be free from unreasonable search and seizure.

.....

The State's interest in detecting and preventing crime begins to prevail over the individual's interest in being left alone at the point where credibly-based probability replaces suspicion. History has confirmed the appropriateness of this requirement as the threshold for subordinating the expectation of privacy to the needs of law enforcement. Where the State's interest is not simply law enforcement as, for instance, where State security is involved, or where the individual's interest is not simply his expectation of privacy as, for instance, when the search threatens his bodily integrity, the relevant standard might well be a different one. That is not the situation in the present case. In cases like the present, reasonable and probable grounds, established upon oath, to believe that an offence has been committed and that there is evidence to be found at the place of the search, constitutes the minimum standard, consistent with s. 8 of the *Charter*, for authorizing search and seizure. In so far as s. 10(1) and (3) of the *Combines Investigation Act* do not embody such a requirement, I would hold them to be further inconsistent with s. 8.

D) Reading in and reading down

The appellants submit that even if s. 10(1) and (3) do not specify a standard consistent with s. 8 for authorizing entry, search and seizure, they should not be struck down as inconsistent with the *Charter*, but rather that the appropriate standard should be read into these provisions. ... In the present case, the overt inconsistency with s. 8 manifested by the lack of a neutral and detached arbiter renders the appellants' submissions on reading in appropriate standards for issuing a warrant purely academic. Even if this were not the case, however, I would be disinclined to give effect to these submissions. While the courts are guardians of the Constitution and of individuals' rights under it, it is the legislature's responsibility to enact legislation that embodies appropriate safeguards to comply with the Constitution's requirements. It should not fall to the courts to fill in the details that will render legislative lacunae constitutional. Without appropriate safeguards legislation authorizing search and seizure is inconsistent with s. 8 of the *Charter*. As I have said, any law inconsistent with the provisions of the Constitution is, to the extent of the inconsistency, of no force or effect. I would hold s. 10(1) and (3) of the *Combines Investigation Act* to be inconsistent with the *Charter* and of no force and effect, as much for their failure to specify an appropriate standard for the issuance of warrants as for their designation of an improper arbiter to issue them.

Section 1

Section 1 of the *Charter* provides:

> 1. The *Canadian Charter of Rights and Freedoms* guarantees the rights and freedoms set out in it subject only to such reasonable limits prescribed by law as can be demonstrably justified in a free and democratic society.

The phrase "demonstrably justified" puts the onus of justifying a limitation on a right or freedom set out in the *Charter* on the party seeking to limit. In the present case the appellants have made no submissions capable of supporting a claim that even if searches under subss. 10(1) and (3) are "unreasonable" within the meaning of s. 8, they are nevertheless a reasonable limit, demonstrably justified in a free and democratic society, on the right set out in s. 8. It is, therefore, not necessary in this case to consider the relationship between s. 8 and s. 1. I leave to another day the difficult question of the relationship between those two sections and, more particularly, what further balancing of interests, if any, may be contemplated by s. 1, beyond that envisaged by s. 8.

It follows from this judgment that a search or seizure will be presumptively unreasonable (and therefore violative of the *Charter*) unless it is conducted pursuant to prior authorization; obtained from an independent arbiter acting judicially; and based upon evidence under oath establishing that there are reasonable grounds to believe that an offence has been committed, and, that there is evidence to be found at the location to be searched.

The presumption of unreasonableness may be rebutted by the lack of feasibility of prior authorization, the statutory context within which the

searches or seizures are empowered (for example, regulatory rather than criminal legislation) or the lessened privacy interests involved (for example, border searches of luggage).

The following case addresses issues arising out of a "bedpan vigil" conducted by customs officials at an airport.

R. v. MONNEY

(1999), 133 C.C.C. (3d) 129 (S.C.C.)

[Prior to his arrival at Toronto airport, Monney had ingested 84 pellets, each containing approximately five grams of heroin. The customs inspector became suspicious about certain details of Monney's travel arrangements, decided he had sufficient grounds to detain Monney as a suspected drug courier, and informed him of his right to counsel. Officers from a special customs unit arrived some two hours later; they placed Monney under detention, informed him of his right to counsel, and took him to the "drug loo facility". When Monney refused to consent to a urine test, he was informed that he would remain in detention until either a negative urine test or clear bowel movement satisfied the officers that he had not ingested narcotics. Following a telephone conversation with his lawyer, Monney provided a urine sample, which confirmed the presence of heroin. Monney was arrested, and he confessed to ingesting the heroin pellets. Following a second telephone call to his lawyer, he began to excrete the pellets. None of the various customs officers who dealt with Monney was aware of the written protocol contained in the enforcement manual, which provides that travellers suspected of ingesting narcotics are to be detained in the presence of qualified medical personnel. Instead, the officers followed the conflicting port policy whereby a detained traveller is not taken to a medical facility unless the traveller makes such a request or appears to be in physical distress. Monney was convicted of importing narcotics. The Ontario Court of Appeal, in a majority decision, held that his rights under s. 8 of the *Charter* had been infringed, and that the evidence concerning the narcotics should be excluded pursuant to s. 24(2) of the *Charter*. The Crown appealed the acquittal to the Supreme Court of Canada.]

The judgment of the court was delivered by

Iacobucci J.: — This appeal deals with the authority of customs officers to detain and search travellers suspected of having swallowed narcotics.

.....

II. Relevant Constitutional and Statutory Provisions

.....

Customs Act

98 (1) An officer may search

(*a*) any person who has arrived in Canada, within a reasonable time after his arrival in Canada,

(*b*) any person who is about to leave Canada, at any time prior to his departure, or

(*c*) any person who has had access to an area designated for use by persons about to leave Canada and who leaves the area but does not leave Canada, within a reasonable time after he leaves the area,

if the officer suspects on reasonable grounds that the person has secreted on or about his person anything in respect of which this Act has been or might be contravened, anything that would afford evidence with respect to a contravention of this Act or any goods the importation or exportation of which is prohibited, controlled or regulated under this or any other Act of Parliament.

(2) An officer who is about to search a person under this section shall, on the request of that person, forthwith take him before the senior officer at the place where the search is to take place.

(3) A senior officer before whom a person is taken pursuant to subsection (2) shall, if he sees no reasonable grounds for the search, discharge the person or, if he believes otherwise, direct that the person be searched.

.....

V. Analysis

A. Were the actions of the customs officers authorized by s. 98 of the Customs Act?

1. Does the phrase "secreted on or about his person" in s. 98 of the Customs Act authorize customs officers to search for narcotics which they suspect a traveller has ingested?

In order to assess whether the search conducted by the customs officials on the respondent was authorized by s. 98 of the *Customs Act*, it is necessary first to determine whether the phrase "on or about his person" in s. 98(1) refers not only to contraband which is concealed by a traveller in luggage, under clothes or in some other manner external to the traveller's body, but includes as well contraband which the traveller has ingested. The respondent argues that as a matter of common parlance, standard dictionary definitions of the words "on" and "about" do not support an interpretation of the phrase "on or about his person" which is sufficiently broad to include items which a traveller has ingested and which are subsequently located internally within the traveller's digestive system. Further, s. 98 requires a customs official to conduct the search "within a reasonable time". The respondent argues that the inclusion of a time restriction within s. 98 necessarily leads to the conclusion that the phrase "on or about his person" is not meant to apply to ingested narcotics. A passive "bedpan vigil" such as was necessary to confirm the presence of heroin pellets within the respondent's digestive tract at the time he attempted to cross the Canadian border involves a lengthy detention process and therefore cannot be conducted "within a reasonable time".

.....

The respondent's suggested interpretation of s. 98 is unnecessarily restrictive, in terms of both the literal text and Parliamentary intent. The provision does not refer to a traveller who has "placed" items on or about his or her person, in which case a more compelling argument could be made that the legislative intent was to restrict the authority of customs officers to searches of a person's exterior physical body and associated personal effects. Instead, the English version of the provision refers to material which the traveller has "secreted" on or about his or her person. The verb "secrete" refers to the act of placing material into a concealed location: *Concise Oxford Dictionary* (9th ed. 1995). The French text confirms this interpretation, as the verb "dissimuler" refers to the act of hiding (*cacher*) or concealing (*celer*): *Le Nouveau Petit Robert 1* (1996). The concept of concealment, rather than the distinction between the interior or exterior of the traveller's physical body, is the fulcrum of the search power in s. 98 of the Act.

Parliament's intent in extending the authority of customs officers to search for any concealed material, whether located internal or external to the traveller's physical body, is further supported by the illogical outcome that would ensue if the Court were to adopt a more restrictive interpretation. A traveller intent on smuggling narcotics across the Canadian border would be able to defeat the purpose of the provision simply by concealing contraband inside his or her mouth rather than under his or her clothing or elsewhere on his or her body. Interpreting s. 98 in light of the provision's purpose, which is to restrict the entry of contraband material into Canada, the phrase "secreted on or about his person" cannot have been intended to permit such an absurd result.

2. *Does s. 98 of the Customs Act authorize a search in the manner conducted by the customs officers whereby a traveller is detained in a "drug loo facility" until a suspicion of ingesting narcotics is confirmed or dispelled?*

The actions of the customs officers in detaining the respondent in a "drug loo facility" and collecting the pellets which passed through his system amounted to a search and seizure for the purposes of s. 8 of the *Charter*. Pursuant to the Court's decision in *Hunter v. Southam Inc.*, [1984] 2 S.C.R. 145, 14 C.C.C. (3d) 97, 11 D.L.R. (4th) 641, prior authorization is a necessary precondition for a constitutionally valid search and seizure. A warrantless search or seizure is therefore *prima facie* unreasonable under s. 8, and the Crown bears the onus of rebutting the presumption of unreasonableness by demonstrating that its actions were authorized by law, that the law itself was reasonable and that the search was carried out in a reasonable manner: *Collins* [(1987), 33 C.C.C. (3d) 1 (S.C.C.)].

The Crown submits that the actions of the customs officers were reasonable in that they were authorized by s. 98 of the *Customs Act*. Section 98 permits customs officers to search a traveller provided there exists a reasonable suspicion that contraband has been "secreted on or about his person" and that the search occurs "within a reasonable time" of the traveller's arrival in Canada. The constitutionality of s. 98 itself is not in issue in this appeal. The relevant question for determination instead is whether the actions of the customs officers in detaining the respondent in a "drug loo facility" are within the scope of permissible activities authorized by s. 98. The respondent contends that s. 98 is meant to apply only to brief, non-intrusive searches such as a pat-down or at most a strip search, and cannot be read as authorization for the ostensibly lengthy detention and intrusive procedures carried out by the customs officers in this situation.

Section 98 of the *Customs Act* provides customs officers with the necessary authority to search travellers suspected of transporting narcotics across the border, but does not define the manner in which a search may be carried out. Nonetheless, as the following passage from the reasons of Lamer J. (as he was then) in *Slaight Communications Inc. v. Davidson*, [1989] 1 S.C.R. 1038 at p. 1078, 59 D.L.R. (4th) 416, indicates, statutory provisions are to be interpreted in a manner which is consistent with the *Charter*:

> Although this Court must not add anything to legislation or delete anything from it in order to make it consistent with the *Charter*, there is no doubt in my mind that it should also not interpret legislation that is open to more than one interpretation so as to make it inconsistent with the *Charter* and hence of no force or effect.

Accordingly, the alternatives available for customs officials in attempting to ascertain whether a traveller has indeed ingested narcotics are subject to constitutional limitations. Section 98 should not be interpreted, so far as is possible, in a manner which would permit customs officers to violate a traveller's rights under s. 8 of the *Charter*. The task of the Court in the present appeal is to determine whether the manner of search carried out against the respondent comes within these limitations.

In *Simmons*, [[1988] 2 S.C.R. 495], the Court considered the constitutional requirements of searches conducted at the Canadian border by customs officers. The accused had submitted that her rights under s. 8 of the *Charter* were violated when she was subjected to a strip search based on the customs officer's reasonable suspicion that she was attempting to smuggle narcotics into Canada. The relevant statutory provisions were ss. 143 and 144 of the former *Customs Act*, R.S.C. 1970, c. C-40, which permitted customs officers to conduct personal searches absent prior judicial authorization and to initiate such searches on the basis of a standard falling short of reasonable and probable grounds. At issue in particular was whether these provisions were constitutionally valid given that they did not meet the three criteria of a reasonable search and seizure articulated in *Hunter, supra*: (a) where possible, the search must be approved by prior authorization; (b) the person authorizing the search need not be a judge, but must be in a position to act in a judicial manner, i.e. the person must be able to assess in a neutral and impartial fashion whether on the evidence available a search is appropriate; and (c) there must be reasonable and probable grounds, established upon oath, to believe that an offence has been committed and that evidence of the offence is to be found at the location to be searched.

The Court concluded in *Simmons* that, although the constitutional safeguards articulated by the *Hunter* standard should not be rejected lightly, the framework established in *Hunter* for analysing the reasonableness of a search for the purposes of s. 8 was inapplicable to border searches. Dickson C.J.

accepted the proposition established in United States jurisprudence that border searches should be distinguished from searches occurring in other circumstances in which the security of Canada's interior is not engaged. He expressed his agreement with this distinction as follows, at pp. 527-28:

> The dominant theme uniting these cases is that border searches lacking prior authorization and based on a standard lower than probable cause are justified by the national interests of sovereign states in preventing the entry of undesirable persons and prohibited goods, and in protecting tariff revenue. These important state interests, combined with the individual's lowered expectation of privacy at an international border render border searches reasonable under the Fourth Amendment. In my view, the state interests enunciated throughout the American jurisprudence that are deemed to make border searches reasonable, are no different in principle from the state interests which are at stake in a Canadian customs search for illegal narcotics. National self-protection becomes a compelling component in the calculus.

Dickson C.J. also referred to the caveat expressed in the reasons in *Hunter* that the reasonableness of a search must be assessed in context. The relevant qualification of the reasonableness standard as stated in *Hunter* is that the standard of reasonableness is subject to change "[w]here the state's interest is not simply law enforcement as, for instance, where state security is involved, or where the individual's interest is not simply [an] expectation of privacy as, for instance, when the search threatens ... bodily integrity" (p. 168). Adopting a contextual approach to the assessment of reasonableness for the purposes of s. 8, the Court concluded in *Simmons* that the degree of personal privacy reasonably expected at border crossings is lower than would otherwise be available in a wholly domestic setting.

In *Simmons*, Dickson C.J. summarized the balance between a state's interest in preventing the flow of contraband across its borders and the individual's privacy interests as protected by s. 8 of the *Charter* as follows, at p. 528:

> I accept the proposition advanced by the Crown that the degree of personal privacy reasonably expected at customs is lower than in most other situations. People do not expect to be able to cross international borders free from scrutiny. It is commonly accepted that sovereign states have the right to control both who and what enters their boundaries. For the general welfare of the nation the state is expected to perform this role. Without the ability to establish that all persons who seek to cross its borders and their goods are legally entitled to enter the country, the state would be precluded from performing this crucially important function. Consequently, travellers seeking to cross national boundaries fully expect to be subject to a screening process. This process will typically require the production of proper identification and travel documentation and involve a search process beginning with completion of a declaration of all goods being brought into the country. Physical searches of luggage and of the person are accepted aspects of the search process where there are grounds for suspecting that a person has made a false declaration and is transporting prohibited goods.

In my opinion, the decision of the Court in *Simmons* governs the issue raised in the present appeal. Whereas s. 143 of the previous Act referred to whether a customs officer has "reasonable cause to suppose" that a traveller has prohibited material "secreted about his person", and s. 98 of the current Act refers instead to whether a customs officer "suspects on reasonable grounds" that the person has prohibited material "secreted on or about his person", these provisions are sufficiently similar to apply the analytical framework from *Simmons* to determine the outcome of this appeal. I say this notwithstanding the assertion made by Dickson C.J. in *Simmons* that s. 98 of the current Act changed the standard from one of suspicion in the former to reasonable grounds in the present Act, an assertion with which I do not agree.

In assessing the constitutionality of a strip search conducted on a person travelling through Canada Customs, Dickson C.J. in *Simmons* correlated three categories of border searches, based on the degree of intrusion into personal privacy and bodily integrity, with an increasing threshold of constitutional justification. In other words, the more intrusive the search, the greater the degree of constitutional protection required in terms of the standard of suspicion or belief which must be met prior to subjecting a traveller to a search by customs officers. Dickson C.J. articulated the necessary correlation as follows, at pp. 516-17:

> It is, I think, of importance that the cases and the literature seem to recognize three distinct types of border search. First is the routine of questioning which every traveller undergoes at a port of entry, accompanied in some cases by a search of baggage and perhaps a pat or frisk of outer clothing. No stigma is attached to being one of the thousands of travellers who are daily routinely checked in that manner upon entry to Canada and no constitutional issues are raised. It would be absurd to suggest that a person in such circumstances is detained in a constitutional sense and therefore entitled to be advised of his or her right to counsel. The second type of border search is the strip or skin search of the nature of that to which the present appellant was subjected, conducted in a private room, after a secondary examination and with the permission of a customs officer in authority. The third and most highly intrusive type of search is that sometimes referred to as the body cavity search, in which customs officers have recourse to medical doctors, to X-rays, to emetics, and to other highly invasive means.
>
> I wish to make it clear that each of the different types of search raises different issues. We are here concerned with searches of the second type and what I have to say relates only to that type of search. Searches of the third or bodily cavity type may raise entirely different constitutional issues for it is obvious that the greater the intrusion, the greater must be the justification and the greater the degree of constitutional protection. I turn now to a consideration of the appellant's specific *Charter* claims.

Dickson C.J. concluded that the standard of "reasonable cause to suppose" in s. 143 of the prior Act authorized border searches in both the first and second categories. No determination was made as to the degree of constitutional scrutiny required for the third category of intrusive border searches, nor is it necessary at this time to decide whether s. 98 of the current Act authorizes customs officers to adopt invasive techniques such as X-rays, emetics or the intervention of medical doctors. I conclude that the actions of the customs officers in detaining the respondent in a "drug loo facility" and conducting what could be characterized as a "bedpan vigil" amounted to a search within the second category.

The respondent has urged the Court to find that compelling a traveller who is suspected of swallowing narcotics to provide a urine sample or a bowel movement under supervision is not simply a passive vigil but constitutes state interference with a person's bodily integrity by seizing or otherwise making use of bodily samples. The respondent relied for support on the decision of the Court in *Stillman* [(1997), 113 C.C.C. (3d) 321 (S.C.C.)], in which Cory J. held for the majority that both probable cause and a warrant are the minimum constitutional standards for the seizure of bodily samples or the use of the body under s. 8 of the *Charter*. As s. 98 of the *Customs Act* does not require either probable cause or a warrant prior to conducting a border search, the respondent therefore contends that this provision cannot be used to authorize the seizure of body samples which occurred in the circumstances of this appeal. The respondent submits that the collection of bodily waste is sufficient to place a "bedpan vigil" within the category of "most highly intrusive" border searches on the basis that the search interferes with the right to bodily integrity.

The respondent's reliance on the Court's decision in *Stillman*, however, is misplaced. Detaining the respondent at the border in order to monitor his bowel movements and ascertain the presence of concealed narcotics is not analogous to the factual circumstances in *Stillman*, wherein the respondent was arrested for murder and refused consent to provide bodily samples for the purposes of DNA testing. The police, upon threat of force, nonetheless obtained bodily samples from the respondent while he was in custody, including strands of hair, dental imprints, saliva samples and buccal swabs. At one point, the police also retrieved a tissue that the respondent had used to blow his nose and had discarded in a wastebasket. At issue was whether the taking of the samples by the police was authorized by the common law search power incidental to an arrest. Cory J. concluded that the taking of bodily samples is a highly intrusive action which goes far beyond the typical frisk search that usually accompanies an arrest. Accordingly, he held that the respondent's rights under s. 8 had been violated.

The most significant distinction between the circumstances of this appeal and the situation of the Respondent in *Stillman* is that border crossings represent a unique factual circumstance for the purposes of a s. 8 analysis.

.....

Accordingly, decisions of this Court relating to the reasonableness of a search for the purposes of s. 8 in general are not necessarily relevant in assessing the constitutionality of a search conducted by customs officers at Canada's border.

A second important distinction between the circumstances of this appeal and those present in *Stillman* is that the customs officers, in detaining the respondent in this case and subjecting him to a passive "bedpan vigil", were not attempting to collect bodily samples containing personal information relating to the respondent. Cory J. in *Stillman* expressed particular concern that the actions of the police in gathering DNA evidence violated the respondent's expectations of privacy in using his body to obtain personal information. He relied in part on La Forest J.'s observation in *R. v. Dyment*, [1988] 2 S.C.R. 417 at pp. 431-32, 45 C.C.C. (3d) 244, 55 D.L.R. (4th) 503, that "the use of a person's body without his consent to obtain information about him, invades an area of personal privacy essential to the maintenance of his human dignity". Thus the right of privacy protected by s. 8 of the *Charter* ensures that individuals are able to maintain bodily integrity and autonomy in the face of potential state interference. Cory J. summarized the connection between privacy and bodily integrity as follows, at [p. 355]:

> Canadians think of their bodies as the outward manifestation of themselves. It is considered to be uniquely important and uniquely theirs. Any invasion of the body is an invasion of the particular person. Indeed, it is the ultimate invasion of personal dignity and privacy.

Heroin pellets contained in expelled faecal matter cannot be considered as an "outward manifestation" of the respondent's identity. An individual's privacy interest in the protection of bodily fluids does not extend to contraband which is intermingled with bodily waste and which is expelled from the body in the process of allowing nature to take its course. It is not necessary for determination of the issue in this appeal to address the question of whether, if the customs officers had adopted a more invasive form of collection, such as surgery or inducing a bowel movement, the result would necessarily be the same.

As to my determination that the passive "bedpan vigil" conducted by the customs officers is properly classified as a search within the second category, a review of the representative border searches provided by Dickson C.J. in his analytical framework reveals that the principal distinction between searches in the second and third categories is that all of the examples listed in the third category involve, to a greater or lesser degree, the intentional application of force. Search techniques such as the insertion of a probe into a body cavity or the administration of an emetic could all be characterized in the absence of lawful authority as an assault. Consequently, the potential degree of state interference with an individual's bodily integrity for searches in the third category requires a high threshold of constitutional justification.

.....

Thus the determination of this appeal revolves around the central question of whether a "bedpan vigil" can properly be characterized as an "invasive" procedure on a par with body searches involving the intentional application of force. In my opinion, it cannot. There is no doubt that Canadians expect treatment that recognizes a strong sense of modesty concerning bodily functions. A traveller who is detained in a "drug loo facility" and compelled to produce either urine or a bowel movement under supervision is subject to an embarrassing process. In my view, however, a passive "bedpan vigil" is not as invasive as a body cavity search or medical procedures such as the administration of emetics. In this sense, the right to bodily integrity is not to be confused with feelings of modesty, notwithstanding their legitimacy. Accordingly, a passive "bedpan vigil" is more appropriately analogous to a category two strip search on the basis that a suspect is detained and placed in an embarrassing situation, but is not subjected to an intentional application of force against his or her will.

While I conclude that the compelled production of a urine sample or a bowel movement is an embarrassing process, it does not interfere with a person's bodily integrity, either in terms of an interference with the "outward manifestation" of an individual's identity, as was the central concern in *Stillman*, or in relation to the intentional application of force, as was relevant in *Simmons*. As is the case with other investigation techniques in the second category such as a strip search, subjecting travellers crossing the Canadian border to potential embarrassment is the price to be paid in order to achieve the necessary balance between an individual's privacy interest and the compelling countervailing state interest in protecting the integrity of Canada's borders from the flow of dangerous contraband materials. Accordingly, I find that the border search conducted by the customs officers in the circumstances of this appeal was reasonable for the purposes of s. 8 of the *Charter*.

3. Did the customs officers have a reasonable suspicion that the respondent had narcotics secreted on or about his person?

The reasons of the majority in the Court of Appeal overturned the trial judge's ruling on the *voir dire* that Inspector Roberts had reasonable grounds *to believe* that the respondent had ingested narcotics prior to his arrival at Pearson International Airport, and was attempting to smuggle these narcotics across the Canadian border. The majority held instead that Inspector Roberts had only a reasonable *suspicion*. Having determined, however, that the search conducted by the customs officers was constitutionally permissible pursuant to s. 98 of the *Customs Act* on the basis of reasonable grounds to suspect, which can be viewed as a lesser but included standard in the threshold of reasonable and probable grounds to believe, I see no reason to interfere with the implicit factual finding at trial, confirmed on appeal, that Inspector Roberts had at the very least reasonable grounds to *suspect* that the respondent had ingested narcotics.

.....

VII. Conclusion and Disposition

I conclude that the actions of the customs officers were authorized by s. 98 of the *Customs Act* on the basis that: (a) s. 98 of the Act permits customs officers who have a reasonable suspicion that a traveller has ingested narcotics to detain the traveller for such a period of time as is necessary either to confirm or discredit this suspicion by means of a passive "bedpan vigil"; and (b) the customs officers in the circumstances of this appeal did have reasonable grounds to suspect that the respondent had indeed ingested narcotics. Accordingly, I would allow the appeal, set aside the judgment of the Ontario Court of Appeal, and restore the conviction entered at trial.

For the purposes of the *Hunter v. Southam* test, reasonable grounds are synonymous with reasonable and probable grounds, and import a standard of credibly based probability. See *R. v. Baron* (1993), 78 C.C.C. (3d) 510 (S.C.C.).

In *R. v. Collins* (1987), 33 C.C.C. (3d) 1 (S.C.C.), substantially reproduced at p. 410, Lamer C.J.C. stated that a search will be reasonable if:

(a) it is authorized by law,
(b) the law itself is reasonable, and
(c) the manner in which the search is carried out is reasonable.

Expanding upon these three broad principles, a *Charter*-based attack can be made upon a search or seizure on various grounds such as:

Where the search was done with prior judicial authorization (*i.e.*, a warrant):

(a) the search was conducted pursuant to a statute which is inconsistent with the minimum requirements of the *Charter* (for example, it permits a warrant to be issued relating to a criminal investigation based upon mere suspicion, absent exigent circumstances.) Therefore, the search is deemed to be warrantless. Similarly, the search was conducted pursuant to a statute which must be "read down" to survive *Charter* scrutiny. The statute, as read down, does not authorize the actual search conducted.

(b) the warrant, on its face, fails to meet the statutory preconditions or minimum requirements of the *Charter*.

(c) the supporting affidavit (the information), on its face, fails to meet the statutory preconditions or minimum requirements of the *Charter*.

(d) the supporting affidavit is subfacially invalid (for example, it contains misleading disclosure or material non-disclosure).

(e) the facts contained in the supporting affidavit were themselves obtained by a *Charter* violation; the untainted facts would not support the issuance of the warrant.

(f) the process involved in the issuance of the warrant failed to comply with the statute or the minimum requirements of the *Charter* (for example, the issuing judicial officer considered unsworn, unrecorded evidence).

(g) the actual search or seizure exceeded its authorized scope (and was not otherwise authorized by statute or at common law).

(h) the actual search or seizure was carried out in an unreasonable manner (for example, with gratuitous destruction of property).

(i) the actual search or seizure was accompanied by violations of the *Charter* other than under s. 8 (for example, a person's s. 10(*b*) rights were also violated during the search).

Where the search was done without prior judicial authorization:

(a) the search or seizure was done pursuant to a statute which is inconsistent with the minimum requirements of the *Charter*.

(b) the search or seizure failed to meet the statutory preconditions or minimum requirements of the *Charter*.

(c) the search or seizure was purportedly done pursuant to common law, which must be interpreted in a manner consistent with the *Charter*; so interpreted, the search was not authorized at common law.

(d) the facts which would otherwise justify the search or seizure were themselves obtained by *Charter* violations; the untainted facts would not have justified the search or seizure.

(e) **the same conditions in (g), (h) and (i) above which apply to a search done with prior judicial authorization.**

A search or seizure may be implicated by one or all of these violations. Of course, it does not necessarily follow under s. 24(2) of the *Charter* that a *Charter* violation will mandate exclusion. (See Chapter 8).

3. Breadth of Section 8 of the Charter

As earlier noted, following *Hunter v. Southam Inc.* (1984), 14 C.C.C. (3d) 97 (S.C.C.), s. 8 has been interpreted as extending not only to conventional searches or seizures but to a wide range of activities which raise privacy issues, including the installation and monitoring of tracking devices, the interception of private communications, and video surveillance.

In the following important case, the Supreme Court split 5-4 on whether the police conduct constituted a seizure within the meaning of s. 8.

R. v. COLARUSSO

(1994), 87 C.C.C. (3d) 193 (S.C.C.)

[The accused was involved in two serious motor vehicle collisions killing and injuring others. When the police arrived, the accused, who had been unconscious, smelled of alcohol and was cut. He was arrested for impaired driving and taken to hospital. While awaiting treatment, he asked to use the bathroom. With the assistance of a police officer, he urinated into a jug which the officer delivered to a nurse. A urine sample was retained for medical purposes, as were blood samples which were sent to the medical lab. The coroner arrived and requested samples of the urine and blood already taken to assist in determining the cause of death. Together with the officer who assisted in obtaining the urine sample, the coroner visited the lab technician, who released two vials of blood and the urine sample. The coroner signed for the samples and left his note with the lab as his warrant. He gave the samples to the officer for analysis at the Centre for Forensic Sciences. At trial, the analyst was subpoenaed to testify.]

[The majority judgment (5-4) of the Court was delivered by:]

La Forest J. [L'Heureux-Dubé, Sopinka, Gonthier and Iacobucci JJ. concurring]: — This appeal revisits the constitutionality of seizing blood or urine samples initially taken for medical purposes and using these samples as evidence against a defendant in a criminal prosecution. More specifically, the appeal requires this Court to determine whether a blood or urine sample initially seized and analyzed by a coroner acting pursuant to statutory authority and later appropriated by the state, without obtaining independent authorization, for the purpose of incriminating a defendant in an impaired driving trial violates the privacy rights inherent in s. 8 of the *Canadian Charter of Rights and Freedoms*, which guarantees everyone the right to be secure against unreasonable search or seizure.

.....

In the courts below, the appellant sought to impugn the introduction of the blood sample analysis in two ways. First, he argued that the sequence of events through which the police ultimately obtained the results of the blood sample analysis constitutes an unreasonable seizure by the police officers themselves. Secondly, he contended that the statutory provision enabling the coroner to seize the blood and urine samples, s. 16(2) of the *Coroners Act*, is unconstitutional on the basis that it is *ultra vires* the province of Ontario or, alternatively, that it violates s. 8 of the *Charter* by failing to incorporate sufficient procedural safeguards. I propose to deal with both these issues, although, as will appear, I do not find it necessary to rule definitively upon the constitutionality of s. 16(2) of the *Coroners Act*. I begin, then, by examining whether there was an unreasonable seizure on the assumption that s. 16(2) is constitutionally valid.

Was there an unreasonable seizure?

Hunter v. Southam Inc. (1984), 14 C.C.C. (3d) 97, 11 D.L.R. (4th) 641, [1984] 2 S.C.R. 145, teaches us that s. 8, like other *Charter* rights, must be broadly and liberally construed to effect its purpose. And that purpose, it identified, is to secure the citizen's right to a reasonable expectation of privacy against governmental encroachments. The need for privacy can vary with the nature of the matter sought to be protected, the circumstances in which and the place where state intrusion occurs, and the purposes of the intrusion. That physical integrity, including bodily fluids, ranks high among the matters receiving constitutional protection, there is no doubt; see *R. v. Pohoretsky*, [1987] 1 S.C.R. 945; *R. v. Dyment*, [1988] 2 S.C.R. 417. Moreover, hospitals have been identified as specific areas of concern in the protection of privacy, given the vulnerability of individuals seeking medical treatment. The requirement for seizing items for the purpose of criminal law enforcement has also been set at a high level; not surprisingly — it involves the freedom of the individual. Absent exigent circumstances, there is a requirement of prior authorization by a judicial officer as a precondition to a valid seizure for the criminal law purposes; see *Hunter, supra*. And the minimum requirement for such authorization is that the judicial officer be satisfied that there are reasonable and probable grounds that an offence has been committed and that the search will afford evidence of that offence. This high threshold, together with the general approach set forth in *Hunter*, at p. 105 C.C.C., p. 649 D.L.R., that the function of the *Charter* "is to provide ... for the unremitting protection of individual rights and liberties" sought to be protected, is the proper perspective from which the situation in the present case must be assessed.

It is beyond dispute that if the police had attempted to seize physically the blood sample directly from the hospital, the seizure would be subject to s. 8 scrutiny; see *Pohoretsky*. And *Dyment* establishes that even if a doctor or analyst had voluntarily given the sample to the police in a situation such as the present where the sample was taken solely for medical purposes, the sample would also fall within the protection of that provision.

The Court of Appeal obviously did not see the present case as falling within the ambit of the principles set forth in *Dyment*. It narrowly focused on the actions of the coroner in physically taking the blood and urine samples. After reviewing the chain of events leading up to the seizure of the samples by the coroner, the court concluded, at [(1991), 44 O.A.C. 241, p. 243], that, given that the evidence was seized by the coroner and turned over to the police for safekeeping and transportation to the laboratory, it is "apparent that the police did not seize any blood and urine samples from the appellant at any time."

In proceeding in this way, it seems to me, the actions of the police, the nature of the coroner's possession of the blood sample and other surrounding circumstances are completely obscured. Assuming for the moment that the seizure by the coroner pursuant to s. 16(2) of the *Coroners Act* is constitutionally valid, such an approach is still, in my opinion, inappropriate. It is obvious from *Dyment* that all the surrounding circumstances must be assessed to determine whether there has been a search by law enforcement officers, and I have no doubt the same is true in assessing the reasonableness of a search (a matter to which I shall return). Two statements in *Dyment* bear this out. In assessing the manner in which the police obtained the blood sample there, the Court at p. 257 C.C.C., p. 516 D.L.R. observed:

> As I see it, the essence of a seizure under s. 8 is the taking of a thing from a person by a public authority without that person's consent. That is what occurred in *Pohoretsky, supra*. The focus of the enquiry in that case was on the actual taking of the blood sample. But one must bear in mind why that was so. In *Pohoretsky*, the blood sample was taken at the request of the police officer. The taking of the blood sample, therefore, immediately triggered s. 8 scrutiny. Section 8 was designed to protect against actions by the state and its agents. Here too *the focus of enquiry must be on the circumstances in which the police officer obtained the sample. However, the circumstances under which it was obtained by the doctor are by no means irrelevant.*

(Emphasis added.) Again, at p. 258 C.C.C., p. 517 D.L.R., it is stated:

> ... I cannot conceive that the doctor here had any right to take Mr. Dyment's blood and give it to a stranger for purposes other than medical purposes unless the law otherwise required, and any such law, too, would be subject to *Charter* scrutiny. Specifically, I think the protection of the *Charter* extends to prevent a police officer, an agent of the state, from taking a substance as intimately personal as a person's blood from a person who holds it subject to a duty to respect the dignity and privacy of that person.

These excerpts make it clear that when a bodily fluid sample ends up being used by the police in a criminal prosecution, even when (as in *Dyment*) the sample was initially extracted for medical purposes in the absence of the police, the court must focus on the actions of the police because s. 8 guarantees protection against the actions *of the state or state actors*, a protection that is particularly strict in relation to law enforcement activities. As discussed in *Dyment* the actions of the doctor are relevant and important. Though he or she may have obtained the sample under lawful circumstances, the limited purpose for which it was obtained cannot be ignored. Equally, the lawful possession of the sample by another cannot be allowed to detract from the review of the police actions which must remain a primary focus for the court. The same is true in the present case. The police cannot rely on the actions of the coroner to shift the court's focus away from their actions. The fact that the sample in this case may have initially been properly seized by the coroner is relevant, but this does not necessarily preclude a finding that the police may also have seized the sample or that the subsequent appropriation of the evidence for use in a criminal prosecution may make the seizure unreasonable.

Consequently, in dealing with a situation in which a bodily sample is seized by a party other than the police, but ultimately winds up being used against the individual by the criminal law enforcement arm of the state, it is essential that the court go beyond the initial non-police seizure and determine whether the actions of the police (or other agent of the criminal law enforcement arm of the state) constitute a seizure by the state in and of themselves or make the initially valid seizure by the coroner unreasonable. That being so, the actions of the agents of the criminal law enforcement arm of the state will be subject to scrutiny under s. 8 of the *Charter* even if, absent the intervention of the police, the initial non-police seizure would not run afoul of the *Charter*.

In the present situation, we are aware of the following relevant facts: (1) the police charged the appellant at the accident scene *before* taking him to the hospital; (2) at the hospital, a police officer assisted the appellant in urinating into a bottle for subsequent analysis *for medical purposes*; (3) after seizing the blood and urine samples, the coroner turned the samples over to the police to transport them to the Centre for Forensic Sciences *for analysis for the purpose of determining the cause of death as required by the Coroners Act*; and (4) the Crown subpoenaed the analyst from the Centre to testify at the appellant's trial, *an analyst also used by the police on previous occasions*.

With these facts in mind, I will turn to a scrutiny of the two stages of police involvement, the first being the stage before the coroner was implicated, and the other following the seizure of the sample by the coroner.

I shall begin by briefly discussing the effect of the police officer's assistance in helping the appellant urinate into the bottle. According to the trial judge, the police officer was merely assisting the hospital in its medical analysis and had no ulterior motives respecting the sample. In other words, he was acting merely as an agent of the hospital and not in his capacity as a police officer, possessing no knowledge that the sample might ultimately be used for a purpose contrary to the interests of the appellant (which, as I discuss later, is a prerequisite to a s. 8 seizure). Since there was evidence to enable the trial judge to so conclude, I do not interfere with this finding of fact.

[However, La Forest J. then expresses his concern that such police involvement raises issues of unwelcome complicity between the police and the hospital.]

.....

I turn now to the activities of the police after the arrival of the coroner at the hospital. These can be viewed in two different ways: (1) as amounting to a seizure by the police independent of the prior seizure by the coroner, and (2) as making the originally valid seizure by the coroner unreasonable because that seizure was not confined to the limited statutory purpose for which it was obtained, but was ultimately used for law enforcement purposes. I shall examine each of these approaches in turn.

Were the samples unreasonably seized by the police?

In *Dyment*, at p. 257 C.C.C., p. 516 D.L.R., I observed that the essence of a seizure under s. 8 of the *Charter* is the taking of something from a person by a public authority without that person's consent. In my opinion, it is clear that the "taking" of a bodily fluid sample need not be directly from the person whose rights are affected (and from whom the sample originated), or even (as in *Dyment*) from the medical staff who extracted the sample, in order to constitute a seizure sufficient to invoke the protection of s. 8. The protection of s. 8 necessarily extends to a state seizure where the "taking" is from the immediate possession of another person who is lawfully in possession of the bodily sample.

.....

At the time the coroner gave the samples to the police, the appellant had already been charged with several offences related to impaired driving. As such, the criminal investigation had already begun. Prior to the blood and urine samples, the only evidence that the appellant was impaired was the observation of the police officer at the accident scene who smelled alcohol on the appellant's breath and noted that he was "disoriented". It is apparent that this evidence would be insufficient to sustain a conviction for the impaired driving offences, as disorientation is consistent with any number of injuries that may be sustained in an automobile accident, and the smell of alcohol on the appellant's breath does not indicate that the appellant's blood alcohol level was over the legal limit. Indeed, the trial judge expressly stated that this evidence was inadequate to support a conviction.

Evidently, the police were also aware that further evidence of intoxication was required and, consequently, formally demanded a breathalyzer sample at the accident scene. It is well established that a breathalyzer sample must be obtained within a short time of the alleged infraction to be of evidentiary value. Yet, after the coroner gave the blood and urine samples to the police officers for the purpose of transporting it to the laboratory, no further attempt was made to obtain a breathalyzer sample. Furthermore, the police did not request a blood sample from the appellant or even attempt to obtain a warrant to seize the original blood sample.

There is only one logical explanation for the strategy employed by the police: when the coroner gave possession of the blood and urine samples to the police officers for transportation to the centre for forensic science, the police knew that they could use the results of the analysis as evidence against the appellant. Indeed, the police may have regarded the blood sample as the best available evidence. Not only was it obtained within an hour of the accident, but the analysis was to be undertaken by the same analysts at the centre for forensic sciences who worked for the police on a regular basis. As a result, the police saw no need to obtain further evidence of intoxication through the various means available to them. In my opinion, there can be no question that the police took possession of the samples and transferred them to the centre for forensic sciences with the full knowledge that they might incriminate the appellant and with the intention of appropriating the results of the analysis for use in the criminal prosecution of the appellant. Given the effective control by the police over the samples held by another agent of the state, I would conclude that the police seized the blood sample from the appellant independently of the coroner's seizure (although the police seizure was obviously facilitated by the actions of the coroner).

At all events, they seized information involving the bodily integrity of the individual that could only be obtained originally with his consent or later pursuant to a statute for the limited purposes intended by the statute. This really goes to the underlying reason for the protection afforded by s. 8; one must not overemphasize the purely physical aspects of the seizure. In both *Hunter* and *Dyment*, the court emphasized that what is protected by s. 8 is people, not places or things. The principal right protected by s. 8 is individual privacy, and the provision must be purposively applied to that end. The following statement from *Dyment*, at pp. 255-6 C.C.C., pp. 515 D.L.R., is relevant here:

> *Finally, there is privacy in relation to information.* This too is based on the notion of the dignity and integrity of the individual. As the Task Force put it (p. 13): "This notion of privacy derives from the assumption that all information about a person is in a fundamental way his own, for him to communicate or retain for himself as he sees fit." *In modern society, especially, retention of information about oneself is extremely important. We may, for one reason or another, wish or be compelled to reveal such information, but situations abound where the reasonable expectations of the individual that the information shall remain confidential to the persons to whom, and restricted to the purposes for which it is divulged, must be protected.* Governments at all levels have in recent years recognized this and have devised rules and regulations to restrict the uses of information collected by them to those for which it was obtained; see, for example, the Privacy Act, S.C. 1980-81-82-83, c. 111.

(Emphasis added.)

Given the conclusion that the police seized the blood and urine samples from the appellant, does the police seizure violate s. 8 of the *Charter*? In my opinion, it is readily apparent that the actions of the police violated the right of the appellant to be secure against unreasonable seizures. As earlier discussed, this court has outlined the extent of s. 8 protection in *Hunter* and the privacy rights inherent in samples of one's own bodily fluids in *Dyment*. I can see no basis for holding that, at least in relation to the use of evidence for criminal law purposes, the reasonable expectation of privacy in one's own bodily fluids guaranteed by s. 8 of the *Charter* is diminished merely because a coroner chooses to exercise his or her power to seize evidence under s. 16(2) of the *Coroners Act*. As such, the intervention by the coroner does not alter the fact that the police must comply with the *Hunter* requirement of prior judicial authorization before seizing a bodily fluid sample which was initially taken from an impaired driving suspect for medical purposes.

In this case, the police obtained no such warrant prior to seizing the blood and urine samples. The note written by the coroner to obtain the release of the samples from the hospital staff is wholly insufficient under *Hunter*, since the coroner is not an independent judicial officer and the standard with which the coroner must comply is only the good faith belief that the evidence is necessary for the purposes of his or her non-criminal investigation. So far as the subpoena obtained to bring the analyst to trial is concerned, it is inadequate, whatever might otherwise be the case, because it was not obtained until after the seizure by the police occurred. The evidence obtained by means of the subpoena was the fruit of the invalid procedure.

In the result, I would conclude that the actions of the police officers amount to a warrantless seizure of bodily fluids for use in a criminal prosecution and so violate the guarantee against unreasonable search and seizure in s. 8 of the *Charter*.

Did the actions of the police make the coroner's seizure unreasonable?

As earlier mentioned, there is another way to establish an unreasonable seizure by the state in the present circumstances. Assuming once again that s. 16(2) of the *Coroners Act* is constitutionally valid, the confiscation of evidence by the coroner in furtherance of his or her investigation is certainly a "seizure" within the meaning of s. 8 of the *Charter*. But it must be kept in mind that a coroner is also a state actor, albeit one who is intended to be separated from the criminal law enforcement arm of the state. If the coroner's power to seize under s. 16(2) of the *Coroners Act* is constitutionally valid, it must be on the basis that the coroner's seizure is "reasonable". The arguments advanced by the Crown seeking to establish the reasonableness of warrantless seizures by a coroner rely on the underlying premise that the coroner fulfils an essential non-criminal role. The state cannot, however, have it both ways; it cannot be argued that the coroner's seizure is reasonable because it is independent of the criminal law enforcement arm of the state while the state is at the same time attempting to introduce into criminal proceedings the very evidence seized by the coroner. It follows logically, in my opinion, that a seizure by a coroner will only be reasonable while the evidence is used for the purpose for which it was seized, namely, for determining whether an inquest into the death of the individual is warranted. Once the evidence has been appropriated by the criminal law enforcement arm of the state for use in criminal proceedings, there is no foundation on which to argue that the coroner's seizure continues to be reasonable.

In considering this position, it must be understood that the protection against unreasonable seizure is not addressed to the mere fact of taking. Indeed, in many cases, this is the lesser evil. Protection aimed solely at the physical act of taking would undoubtedly protect things, but would play a limited role in protecting the privacy of the individual which is what s. 8 is aimed at, and that provision, *Hunter* tells us, must be liberally and purposively interpreted to accomplish that end. The matter seized thus remains under the protective mantle of s. 8 so long as the seizure continues.

Consequently, so long as the evidence (or the information derived from the evidence) is in the possession of the state (*i.e.*, the coroner or the criminal law enforcement branch), the following would hold true: (1) while the evidence is being used by the coroner for valid non-criminal purposes within the scope of the *Coroners Act*, the seizure is reasonable and not caught by s. 8 of the *Charter*, and (2) when the evidence, or the information derived from the evidence, is appropriated by the criminal law enforcement arm of the state for use against the person from whom it was seized, the seizure will become unreasonable and will run afoul of s. 8 of the *Char-*

ter. In other words, the criminal law enforcement arm of the state cannot rely on the seizure by the coroner to circumvent the guarantees of *Hunter*, *supra*, as any seizure by the coroner pursuant to s. 16(2) is valid for non-criminal purposes only.

The real nature of the investigative procedures in this case

Whichever of the foregoing approaches is taken, one arrives at the same conclusion: the seizure of the appellant's blood sample was unreasonable. It seems clear that what is involved in the circumstances of this case is a too convenient way of getting around the requirements set forth in *Hunter* and in *Dyment* for seizing property for purposes of law enforcement. What occurs is that property is seized by one state agent for a purpose for which the prerequisites for search may not be as demanding, and another state agent, one forming part of the law enforcement apparatus of the state, is permitted to claim the fruits of the search (the resulting information) for use for law enforcement purposes without regard to the rightly stringent prerequisites of searches for those purposes.

[La Forest J. went on to raise serious concerns as to whether the interaction between the police and the coroner under the *Coroners Act*, R.S.O. 1990, c. C.37, infringes upon the exclusive jurisdiction of Parliament to legislate in the sphere of criminal law. It was unnecessary to decide this issue. He also concluded that the evidence ought not to be excluded under s. 24(2) of the *Charter* in the particular circumstances of this case.]

R. v. EVANS

(1996), 104 C.C.C. (3d) 23 (S.C.C.)

[Motivated by an anonymous tip and an unproductive investigation, plain-clothes officers knocked on the suspects' door, intending to sniff for marijuana. The door was opened. Officers smelled marijuana, arrested both accused, and secured the premises, including several marijuana plants. They then obtained and executed a search warrant. All seven justices would have admitted the evidence. In a 4-3 split decision, the court held that the "knock and sniff" was an unreasonable search, within the meaning of s. 8 of the *Charter*.]

[The majority judgment of Sopinka, Cory and Iacobucci JJ. was delivered by:]

Sopinka J. [Cory and Iacobucci JJ. concurring]: — Four issues are raised in this appeal. First, the court must determine whether or not the conduct of the police in "sniffing" for marijuana at the door to the appellants' home constituted a "search" within the meaning of s. 8 of the *Canadian Charter of Rights and Freedoms*. Second, if the court concludes that the conduct in question was a search for constitutional purposes, the court must move on to decide whether or not that search was "reasonable" within the meaning of s. 8. Third, the court must consider whether the second search of the Evans' home, conducted after a warrant had been obtained, violated s. 8 of the *Charter*. Finally, the court must determine whether or not any evidence obtained in violation of s. 8 in the instant case must be excluded pursuant to s. 24(2).

I. Was the police conduct a "search"?

The first issue raised in this appeal is whether or not the conduct of the police in the instant case constituted a "search" within the meaning of s. 8. The conduct in question consisted of approaching the door to the Evans' home and knocking, with the intent of "sniffing for marijuana" when the occupant opened the door. According to my colleague Justice Major, the conduct in question was not a search. With respect, I disagree.

I agree with Major J. that not every investigatory technique used by the police is a "search" within the meaning of s. 8. In particular, I agree with Major J.'s view that the court must inquire into the purposes of s. 8 in determining whether or not a particular form of police conduct constitutes a "search" for constitutional purposes.

What then is the purpose of s. 8 of the *Charter*? Previous decisions of this Court make it clear that the fundamental objective of s. 8 is to preserve the privacy interests of individuals.

.....

...If the conduct in question did intrude upon the appellants' "reasonable expectations of privacy", then the conduct is a search within the meaning of s. 8, and is subject to the requirements of that section. In assessing the appellants' expectation of privacy, I agree with my colleague Major J. that it is necessary to consider the "invitation to knock" that individuals are deemed to extend to members of the public, including police. If the conduct of the police in approaching the Evans' home and sniffing for marijuana is a form of activity contemplated by the invitation to knock, then no violation of any privacy interest can be made out. Clearly, an individual's expectations of privacy cannot be infringed by conduct that has been authorized by the individual in question.

I agree with Major J. that the common law has long recognized an implied licence for all members of the public, including police, to approach the door of a residence and knock. As the Ontario Court of Appeal recently stated in *R. v. Tricker* (1995), 96 C.C.C. (3d) 198 at p. 203, 8 M.V.R. (3d) 47, 21 O.R. (3d) 575:

> The law is clear that the occupier of a dwelling gives implied licence to any member of the public, including a police officer, on legitimate business to come on to the property. The implied licence ends at the door of the dwelling. This proposition was laid down by the English Court of Appeal in *Robson v. Hallett*, [1967] 2 All E.R. 407, [1967] 2 Q.B. 939.

As a result, the occupier of a residential dwelling is deemed to grant the public permission to approach the door and knock. Where the police act in accordance with this implied invitation, they cannot be said to intrude upon the privacy of the occupant. The implied invitation, unless rebutted by a clear expression of intent, effectively waives the privacy interest that an individual might otherwise have in the approach to the door of his or her dwelling.

If one views the invitation to knock as a *waiver* of the occupier's expectation of privacy in the approach to his or her home, it becomes necessary to determine the terms of that waiver. Clearly, under the "implied licence to knock", the occupier of a home may be taken to authorize certain persons to approach his or her home for certain purposes. However, this does not imply that all persons are welcome to approach the home regardless of the purpose of their visit. For example, it would be ludicrous to argue that the invitation to knock invites a burglar to approach the door in order to "case" the house. The waiver of privacy interests that is entailed by the invitation to knock cannot be taken to go that far.

In determining the scope of activities that are authorized by the implied invitation to knock, it is important to bear in mind the purpose of the implied invitation. According to the British Columbia Court of Appeal in *R. v. Bushman*, [1968] 4 C.C.C. 17, 4 C.R.N.S. 13, 63 W.W.R. 346, the purpose of the implied invitation is to facilitate communication between the public and the occupant. As the Court in *Bushman* stated, at p. 24:

> The purpose of the implied leave and licence to proceed from the street to the door of a house possessed by a police officer who has lawful business with the occupant of the house is to enable the police officer to reach a point in relation to the house where he can conveniently and in a normal manner communicate with the occupant.

I agree with this statement of the law. In my view, the implied invitation to knock extends no further than is required to permit convenient communication with the occupant of the dwelling. The "waiver" of privacy rights embodied in the implied invitation extends no further than is required to effect this purpose. As a result, only those activities that are reasonably associated with the purpose of communicating with the occupant are authorized by the "implied licence to knock". Where the conduct of the police (or any member of the public) goes beyond that which is permitted by the implied licence to knock, the implied "conditions" of that licence have effectively been breached, and the person carrying out the unauthorized activity approaches the dwelling as an intruder.

In the present case, I am of the view that the actions of the police went beyond the forms of conduct permitted by the implied licence to knock. Although I accept that one objective of the police in approaching the Evans' door was to communicate with the occupants of the dwelling in accordance with the implied licence to knock, the evidence makes it clear that a subsidiary purpose of approaching the Evans' door was to attempt to "get a whif [*sic*] or a smell" of marijuana. As a result, the police approached the Evans' home not merely out of a desire to communicate with the occupants, but also in the hope of securing evidence against them. Clearly, occupiers of a dwelling cannot be presumed to invite the police (or anyone else) to approach their home for the purpose of substantiating a criminal charge against them. Any "waiver" of privacy rights that can be implied through the "invitation to knock" simply fails to extend that far. As a result, where the agents of the state approach a dwelling with the intention of gathering evidence against the occupant, the police have exceeded any authority that is implied by the invitation to knock.

As noted above, my colleague Major J. would hold that the conduct of the police in the present case did not constitute a search within the meaning of s. 8 of the *Charter*. In his view, the police were merely acting on the implied invitation to knock when approaching the Evans' door for the purpose of seeking evidence against the appellants. In Major J.'s opinion, the fact that the police intended to "sniff" for marijuana once the Evans' door was opened does not affect the validity of the officers' conduct. Simply put, Major J. would hold that the underlying purpose or intent of the police in approaching the Evans' door "does not affect the right to knock on the door".

Despite the difficulties involved in proving police "intention" when they approach a person's home, I disagree with Major J. that the intention of the police is irrelevant in assessing the legality of their actions. As stated above, the implied licence to knock extends only to activities for the purpose of facilitating communication with the occupant. Anything beyond this "licensed purpose" is not authorized by the implied invitation. In my view, an analogy can be drawn between the present case and the decisions of this court in *R. v. Duarte* (1990), 53 C.C.C. (3d) 1, 65 D.L.R. (4th) 240, [1990] 1 S.C.R. 30, and *R. v. Wiggins* (1990), 53 C.C.C. (3d) 476, [1990] 1 S.C.R. 62, 74 C.R. (3d) 311. In those cases, it was held that "participant surveillance" through the electronic recording of a private conversation constitutes a "search" within the meaning of s. 8. According to the majority in *Duarte* (at p. 12 C.C.C., p. 252 D.L.R.), "privacy may be defined as the right of the individual to determine for himself when, how, and to what extent he will release personal information about himself". Thus, while an individual may explicitly "invite" another to engage in private conversation, the invitation *cannot* be extended to authorize an activity with a different purpose, namely, the surreptitious recording of what is said. Where the person purporting to act on the "invitation to converse" exceeds the bounds of that invitation, the activity in question may constitute a "search" for constitutional purposes. Similarly, where the police, as here, purport to rely on the invitation to knock and approach a dwelling for the purpose, *inter alia*, of securing evidence against the occupant, they have exceeded the bounds of any implied invitation and are engaging in a *search* of the occupant's home. Since the implied invitation is for a specific purpose, the invitee's purpose is all-important in determining whether his or her activity is authorized by the invitation.

.....

In my view, there are sound policy reasons for holding that the intention of the police in approaching an individual's dwelling is relevant in determining whether or not the activity in question is a "search" within the meaning of s. 8. If the position of my colleague is accepted and intention is not a relevant factor, the police would then be authorized to rely on the "implied licence to knock" for the purpose of randomly checking homes for evidence of criminal activity. The police could enter a neighbourhood with a high incidence of crime and conduct surprise "spot-checks" of the private homes of unsuspecting citizens, surreptitiously relying on the implied licence to approach the door and knock. Clearly, this Orwellian vision of police authority is beyond the pale of any "implied invitation". As a result, I would hold that in cases such as this one, where evidence clearly establishes that the police have specifically adverted to the possibility of securing evidence against the accused through "knocking on the door", the police have exceeded the authority conferred by the implied licence to knock.

For these reasons, I conclude that individuals in the position of the Evans have a reasonable expectation of privacy in the approach to their home, an expectation that is waived for the purpose of facilitating communication with the public. Where members of the public (including police) exceed the terms of this waiver, and approach the door for some unauthorized purpose, they exceed the implied invitation and approach the door as intruders. As a result, where the police, as here, approach a residential dwelling for the purpose of securing evidence against the occupant, the police are engaged in a "search" of the occupant's home. The constitutional permissibility of such a "search" will accordingly depend on whether or not the search is "reasonable" within the meaning of s. 8.

II. Reasonableness

.....

When the police approached the Evans' home to knock on the door and sniff for marijuana, they were doing so without prior authorization. According to this court in *Hunter v. Southam Inc.*, *supra*, a warrantless search is *prima facie* unreasonable.

[Sopinka J. then addressed the "reasonableness" criteria outlined in *Collins* (1987), 33 C.C.C. (3d) 1 (S.C.C.).]

.....

In the instant case, the manner in which the police conducted their search was clearly reasonable. The police attended the Evans' home based on reasonable suspicions and did nothing more than "sniff" for marijuana. Despite the reasonableness of the officers' actions, however, I must nonetheless hold that the presumption of unreasonableness has not been rebutted. Clearly, the actions of the police in approaching the Evans' home and searching for marijuana were not "authorized by law" within the meaning of this Court's decision in *Collins*. By virtue of ss. 10 and 12 of the *Narcotic Control Act*, R.S.C., 1985, c. N-1, a search warrant is required in order to search a dwelling in connection with an investigation of an alleged offence under that Act. These provisions would take precedence over any common law right to search based on the "knock on" principles. But even if the statutory provisions in ss. 10 and 12 of the *Narcotic Control Act* were subject to the "knock on" principles, the implied invitation at common law would not extend to authorize an olfactory search.

As a result, the first and second prerequisites to rebut the presumption of unreasonableness, namely (1) that the search was authorized by law, and (2) that the law in question was reasonable, are not satisfied in this case. The inquiry into "reasonableness" ends there.

.....

III. The warrant

Following their initial search of the Evans' home, the police obtained a warrant based in part on the odour of marijuana that was detected when Mr. Evans opened his door. Some of the evidence supporting this warrant (i.e., the odour of marijuana) would not have been obtained had the police abided by the constitutional restrictions on their powers of search and seizure. As this court pointed out in *R. v. Kokesch* (1990), 61 C.C.C. (3d) 207, [1990] 3 S.C.R. 3, 1 C.R. (4th) 62, warrants based *solely* on information gleaned in violation of the *Charter* are invalid. However, where the warrant was issued only partially on the strength of tainted evidence, and partially on evidence that was properly obtained, the court must "consider whether the warrant would have been issued had the improperly obtained facts been excised from the information sworn to obtain the warrant": *R. v. Grant*...

.....

In the case at bar, the only untainted "evidence" supporting the warrant was an unconfirmed tip provided by an anonymous "Crime Stoppers" informant. ... As a result, I would hold that the warrant on which the officers relied in the second search of the Evans' home was invalid, and that the search conducted thereunder was accordingly unreasonable within the meaning of s. 8 of the *Charter*.

Having determined that all of the evidence gathered through the searches of the Evans' home was obtained in a manner that violated the *Charter*, it becomes necessary to consider whether or not that evidence must be excluded pursuant to s. 24(2). If the evidence is excluded, the Crown has no basis upon which to proceed against the appellants.

[Sopinka J. concluded that the evidence should not be excluded.]

[La Forest J. delivered reasons in substantial agreement with Sopinka J.]

Major J. [Gonthier J. concurring]: — This appeal addresses the scope of police investigative powers. The issue is whether the police were conducting a search within the meaning of s. 8 of the *Canadian Charter of Rights and Freedoms* by knocking on the door of a dwelling house in order to make an enquiry, and while in the course of that activity making observations of the party who answered the door and other observations arising normally from the door's being opened. It is my conclusion that they were not.

.....

The police conduct in this case did not constitute a search within the meaning of s. 8 of the *Charter*. In approaching the front door of the residence in broad daylight and knocking at the door, the police officers were exercising an implied licence at common law. When the door was opened, the observations made by the police officers from this position were simply that: observations of what was in plain view. The appellants could not have any reasonable expectation that no one, including police officers, would ever lawfully approach their home and observe what was plainly discernible from a position where police officers and others were lawfully entitled to be.

[L'Heureux-Dubé J. delivered reasons in substantial agreement with Major J.]

QUESTIONS

1. **What if the circumstances in *Evans* occurred in the context of a rented locker at a bus depot? What if security personnel at the depot smelled marijuana in a rented locker, contacted the police and opened the locker for the police, who seized the drugs inside without a warrant? Consider, in this regard, *R. v. Buhay*, [2003] S.C.J. No. 30.**

2. **Canadian Customs and Revenue Agency (formerly Revenue Canada) auditors have broad powers to inspect taxpayer documents and question taxpayers without the necessity of a warrant. Why are these audit powers not violative of the *Charter*? When can the fruits of an audit be used to further a criminal investigation? Put another way, at what point can it be said that auditors misuse their powers? Consider, in this regard, *R. v. Jarvis* (2002), 169 C.C.C. (3d) 1 (S.C.C.).**

3. **Does a vice-principal at a high school who searches a student engage s. 8 of the *Charter*? Does it matter if the search is conducted in the presence of a police officer? Consider, in this regard, *R. v. M.(M.R.)* (1998), 129 C.C.C. (3d) 361 (S.C.C.).**

4. **The police acting on an unproven source that the accused was growing and trafficking marijuana at his residence decide to conduct flights over his residence and take infrared photos. Is this considered a search within the ambit of s. 8 of the *Charter*? Does the accused have an expectation of privacy in this respect? Consider, in this regard, *R. v. Tessling* (2003), 171 C.C.C. (3d) 361 (Ont. C.A.); leave to appeal to S.C.C. granted (2003), 105 C.R.R. (2d) 376*n*.**

---

4. THE APPLICATION FOR A SEARCH WARRANT

(a) Overview

Section 487 of the *Criminal Code* outlines the statutory preconditions for the issuance of a conventional search warrant. Section 487 complies with s. 8 of the *Charter*. Though a s. 487 warrant is most often used to investigate *Criminal Code* violations, it may be used to investigate violations of any other federal statute, even where the other statute has its own search and seizure provisions.

QUESTION

5. **The police are investigating alleged violations of the *Controlled Drugs and Substances Act*, S.C. 1996, c. 19. They wish to apply for a warrant to search various commercial and residential premises, and they approach you, as Crown counsel, for advice as to whether to apply under *Criminal Code*, s. 487 or under *Controlled Drugs and Substances Act*, s. 11 for a warrant. What advice do you give?**

An informant (generally a police officer) attends personally[1] before a justice of the peace or a provincial court judge and swears to the truth of the contents of a supporting affidavit, known as the information. This is not to be confused with the document charging the accused, also known as the information.

The judicial officer must be satisfied, based upon the information under oath, that there are reasonable grounds to believe that there is in the building, receptacle or place to be searched, anything as outlined in s. 487(1)(*a*), (*b*), (*c*) or (*c*.1). Accordingly, to enable the judicial officer to be so satisfied, the information must state the evidentiary support or grounds for the informant's belief, not merely the conclusion. These grounds may include evidence known to the informant personally through investigation, and, reliable hearsay derived from other sources and communicated to the informant. Special procedures may be employed if the source relied upon is a confidential informer. These procedures are addressed later at p. 115. The information should not contain misleading facts or material non-disclosure of relevant facts.

The information must contain an adequate description of the offence(s) investigated.

QUESTIONS

6. A search warrant describes the offence as follows: between January 1, 1971, and August 12, 1976, in the cities of Calgary, Edmonton and elsewhere in the Province of Alberta, and in the City of Vancouver and elsewhere in the Province of British Columbia [certain named persons] did conspire each with the other together in whole or in part to defraud [certain named institutions] and other financial institutions contrary to the *Criminal Code*. Is the offence adequately described? Consider, in this regard, *Re PSI Mind Development Institute Ltd. et al. and The Queen* (1977), 37 C.C.C. (2d) 263 (Ont. H.C.J.)

7. Consider the scenario of overseas bank accounts. What if the Canadian authorities issued a letter of request to a foreign government to search and seize documents related to a Canadian accused who held bank accounts overseas? What if there was no judicial authorization prior to the issuance of the letter of request in Canada? Do the conditions of prior judicial authorization have to be met before the issuance of the letter? Consider *Schreiber v. Canada (Attorney General)* (1998), 124 C.C.C. (3d) 129 (S.C.C.).

8. Consider the additional powers conferred by s. 487.01 of the *Criminal Code*. What devices, techniques or procedures might be authorized by s. 487.01 which would otherwise be unavailable to the authorities?

9. The police learn that a bank robbery was committed by a person who has a Tweety Pie tattoo on his left buttock. He exposed himself as he left the bank. The police have reasonable grounds to believe that Fred Sylvester is

---

1 Sections 487.1, 487.01(7), 487.05(3) and 487.092(4) of the *Criminal Code* describe procedures available to obtain a telewarrant where it would be impracticable to appear personally before the judicial officer. See also s. 13(1) of the *Controlled Drugs and Substances Act*, S.C. 1996, c. 19.

the culprit but appreciate that the presence or absence of the tattoo is of critical importance. How, if at all, can the police resolve this issue?

The information must accurately specify the location to be searched. Section 487(2) of the *Criminal Code* addresses the procedure to be employed where the building, receptacle or place is in another territorial division. See *R. v. Haley* (1986), 27 C.C.C. (3d) 454 (Ont. C.A.). See also Section 487.03 of the *Criminal Code*.

(b) Access to the Information and the Confidential Informer

The following case addresses the extent to which the public has the right to access a search warrant and supporting information.

ATTORNEY-GENERAL OF NOVA SCOTIA ET AL. v. MACINTYRE

(1982), 65 C.C.C. (2d) 129 (S.C.C.)

[MacIntyre, a journalist, sought access to certain search warrants and informations. Access was denied by the issuing court. The matter made its way up the appellate ladder. The Nova Scotia Supreme Court, Appellate Division, held that the public could not only access the materials, but could be present when the warrants were applied for and issued! The Supreme Court of Canada split 5-4 on whether the public could even access the materials.]

Dickson J. [for the majority]: —

.....

III

The *Criminal Code* gives little guidance on the question of accessibility to the general public of search warrants and the underlying informations. And there is little authority on the point.

.....

It does seem clear that an individual who is "directly interested" in the warrant can inspect the information and the warrant after the warrant has been executed. The reasoning here is that an interested party has a right to apply to set aside or quash a search warrant based on a defective information (*R. v. Solloway Mills & Co.* (1930), 53 C.C.C. 261, [1930] 3 D.L.R. 293, [1930] 1 W.W.R. 779 (Alta. S.C.)). This right can only be exercised if the applicant is entitled to inspect the warrant and the information immediately after it has been executed.

.....

By reason of the relatively few judicial decisions it is difficult, and probably unwise, to attempt any comprehensive definition of the right of access to judicial records or delineation of the factors to be taken into account in determining whether access is to be permitted. The question before us is limited to search warrants and informations. The response to that question, it seems to me, should be guided by several broad policy considerations, namely, respect for the privacy of the individual, protection of the administration of justice, implementation of the will of Parliament that a search warrant be an effective aid in the investigation of crime, and finally, a strong public policy in favour of "openness" in respect of judicial acts.

.....

In my view, curtailment of public accessibility can only be justified where there is present the need to protect social values of superordinate importance. One of these is the protection of the innocent.

Many search warrants are issued and executed, and nothing is found. In these circumstances, does the interest served by giving access to the public outweigh that served in protecting those persons whose premises have been searched and nothing has been found? Must they endure the stigmatization to name and reputation which would follow publication of the search? Protection of the innocent from unnecessary harm is a valid and important policy consideration. In my view that consideration overrides the public access interest in those cases where a search is made and nothing is found. The public right to know must yield to the protection of the innocent. If the warrant is executed and something is seized, other considerations come to bear.

VI

That brings me to the second argument raised by the appellant. The point taken here is that the effective administration of justice would be frustrated if individuals were permitted to be present when the warrants were issued. Therefore, the proceeding must be conducted *in camera*, as an exception to the open court principle. I agree. The effective administration of justice does justify the exclusion of the public from the proceedings attending the actual issuance of the warrant.

.....

It appeared clear during argument that the act of issuing the search warrant is, in practice, rarely, if ever, performed in open court. Search warrants are issued in private at all hours of the day or night, in the chambers of the justice by day or in his home by night. Section 443(1) [now s. 487(1)] of the *Code* seems to recognize the possibility of exigent situations in stating that a justice may "at any time" issue a warrant.

Although the rule is that of "open court" the rule admits of the exception referred to in Halsbury, namely, that in exceptional cases, where the administration of justice would be rendered impracticable by the presence of the public, the court may sit *in camera*. The issuance of a search warrant is such a case.

In my opinion, however, the force of the "administration of justice" argument abates once the warrant has been executed, *i.e.*, after entry and search. There is thereafter a "diminished interest in confidentiality" as the purposes of the policy of secrecy are largely, if not entirely, accomplished.

.....

The "administration of justice" argument is based on the fear that certain persons will destroy evidence and thus deprive the police of the fruits of their search. Yet the appellant agrees these very individuals (*i.e.*, those "directly interested") have a right to see the warrant, and the material upon which it is based, once it has been executed. The appellants do not argue for blanket confidentiality with respect to warrants. Logically, if those directly interested can see the warrant, a third party who has no interest in the case at all is not a threat to the administration of justice. By definition, he has no evidence that he can destroy. Concern for preserving evidence and for the effective administration of justice cannot justify excluding him.

Undoubtedly every court has a supervisory and protecting power over its own records. Access can be denied when the ends of justice would be subverted by disclosure or the judicial documents might be used for an improper purpose. The presumption, however, is in favour of public access and the burden of contrary proof lies upon the person who would deny the exercise of the right.

.....

I conclude that the administration of justice argument does justify an *in camera* proceeding at the time of issuance of the warrant but, once the warrant has been executed, exclusion thereafter of members of the public cannot normally be countenanced. The general rule of public access must prevail, save in respect of those whom I have referred to as innocent persons.

In *Re Jany and The Queen* (1983), 9 C.C.C. (3d) 349 (B.C.S.C.), it was held that the accused, as an interested party, is entitled to full access to the information supporting the warrant, subject to the protection of the informer's identity, notwithstanding the fact that no seizure was made pursuant to the warrant. The latter fact is relevant only where a member of the public is seeking access.

Section 487.3(1) of the *Code* allows a judge or justice to issue an order denying access to information used to obtain any warrant. The reasons outlined in s. 487.3(2) for denying access are: compromising the identity of informants or the nature and extent of an ongoing investigation; endangering a person engaged in intelligence-gathering techniques and thereby prejudicing future investigations in which similar techniques would be used; prejudicing the interest of an innocent person; or any other sufficient reason.

Section 487.3(4) of the *Code* allows an application to the Court to terminate or vary an order made under s. 487.3(1).

Confidential informers raise special issues, as shown in the following case.

R. v. HUNTER

(1987), 34 C.C.C. (3d) 14 (Ont. C.A.)

The judgment of the court was delivered by

Cory J.A.: — The issue raised on this appeal requires an answer to a question which sets in opposition two competing principles of law. On one hand, it has long been a principle of the common law that the identity of informers should not be disclosed. On the other hand, the common law has also recognized that a person is entitled to make full answer and defence to the charges confronting him. As an essential element of making full answer and defence, an accused whose premises have been searched may need to have access to the information upon which the issuance of the warrant was based in order to attack it if the information discloses that it was improperly issued. What should be the result if the disclosure of the information would result in the identification of the informer?

.....

At the outset of the trial a *voir dire* was conducted with respect to two motions brought before the trial judge on behalf of the respondent. One motion was for the disclosure of the sealed information used when the search warrant was obtained. The other sought the exclusion of the evidence obtained as a result of the search of the premises of the respondent. On the *voir dire* Sergeant Hughes testified that about 1:00 p.m. on March 29, 1983, he obtained a search warrant under the *Narcotic Control Act*, R.S.C. 1970, c. N-1, for the premises of the respondent, penthouse 23 at 77 Huntley Street. He subsequently executed the warrant at 8:00 p.m. on the same day. The information in support of the warrant was provided by an informer, who spoke to Sergeant Hughes about 12:30 p.m. on March 29th. The informer had advised that cocaine was actually on the premises. Sergeant Hughes conceded that the informer had never been used before by the police as a basis for obtaining a search warrant, nor had his information ever been relied upon to make an arrest. However, the informer had given unspecified information on two earlier occasions and, although the police had not acted upon this information, it had proven to be reliable. It was also conceded that the informer had never again been used by the police subsequent to the search made in this case. It was the opinion of Sergeant Hughes that disclosure of the information sworn in support of the search warrant application would lead to the informer being identified by the respondent, Hunter.

.....

[At trial a] ruling was made that disclosure of the information would reveal the identity of the informer. In light of this the trial judge determined that counsel for Hunter should not be permitted access to the information. The trial judge then concluded that as a result of this decision Hunter was prevented from making a full answer to the charge and the evidence obtained from the search could not be admitted.

.....

The Crown elected to call no further evidence, and the accused was found not guilty of the charge. The Crown appeals that finding.

The conflicting principles

The trial judge recognized that a conflict existed between the two principles that are applicable to this case. On one hand there is the recognized obligation to protect the identity of the informer. On the other is the right, enshrined in the *Charter*, of everyone to be secure against unreasonable search. It is, of course, difficult for a citizen to determine if he has been the victim of an unreasonable search if he does not have access to the information that was the basis for issuing the search warrant. Without that information it is impossible for the accused to make full answer and defence, as he cannot attack the validity of the search warrant and thus the validity of the search.

It may be helpful to begin with a review of the principles underlying the protection of the identity of informers. Certainly great importance has been attached to that principle in this country and other jurisdictions. It may also be appropriate to consider the extent of the right of everyone whose premises have been searched to review the information upon which the search warrant was issued in order to be satisfied that it was issued upon reasonable and probable grounds. Lastly, an attempt should be made to resolve the conflict between the competing principles.

The common law principle that information which might identify an informer need not be disclosed, and its importance in the detection of crime

The rule against the non-disclosure of information which might identify an informer is one of long standing. It developed from an acceptance of the importance of the role of informers in the solution of crimes and the apprehension of criminals. It was recognized that citizens have a duty to divulge to the police any information that they may have pertaining to the commission of a crime. It was also obvious to the courts from very early times that the identity of an informer would have to be concealed, both for his or her own protection and to encourage others to divulge to the authorities any information pertaining to crimes. It was in order to achieve these goals that the rule was developed.

The principle admits but one exception, namely, where the disclosure of the identity of the informer could help to show that the accused was innocent of the offence. It has been said that only in such a case does the balance of interests require disclosure. The principle has been recognized in the Supreme Court of Canada in *Solicitor General of Canada et al. v. Royal Com'n. of Inquiry into Confidentiality of Health Records in Ontario et al.* (1981), 62 C.C.C. (2d) 193, 128 D.L.R. (3d) 193, [1981] 2 S.C.R. 494.

.....

There can be no doubt that the long-recognized common law principle that information that might tend to identify informers is privileged and ought not to be disclosed is of great importance to society in the detection of crime and criminals. It is particularly important in the prosecution of drug offences. Clearly it is a principle that should not be lightly set aside.

What effect, if any, do provisions of s. 8 of the Charter of Rights have upon the common law principle protecting the identity of informers?

Prior to the enactment of the Charter it is questionable whether an accused would have had access to the information upon which a search warrant was based if that information disclosed the identity of the informer. It is now necessary to reassess this position.

[Cory J.A. then reviews *Attorney-General of Nova Scotia et al. v. MacIntyre*, substantially reproduced at p. 112, as well as ss. 8 and 11(*d*) of the *Charter* and their American counterparts.]

What then should be done about the disclosure of information used to obtain a search warrant at the time of trial? I recognize the importance of the protection of informers. I recognize as well that a successful attack on a search warrant on the grounds that there were not reasonable and probable grounds for its issuance may well result in the suppression of the truth, as the evidence discovered during an illegal search may not be admissible.

Nevertheless, the right to search premises, particularly a home, is a powerful and potentially oppressive tool of the state. It should be exercised only on proper grounds. It is in the interest of all citizens that an accused should know the basis upon which the warrant was issued. The actions of the state taken against the least worthy of its citizens will eventually determine the pattern of its actions towards all its citizens. There should be reasonable disclosure made of the information which was used to obtain the search warrant, if it is needed and requested, despite the fact that it may disclose the identity of an informer. Yet the method by which the disclosure is made should take into account the importance of informers to society and strike a balance between the competing principles.

Upon receipt of such a request the trial judge should review the information with the object of deleting all references to the identity of the informer. The information so edited should then be made available to the accused. However, if at the conclusion of the editing procedure the Crown should still be of the opinion that the informer would become known to the accused upon production of the information, then a decision would have to be made by the Crown. The informer might by this time be willing to consent to being identified. Alternatively, the informer's identity might have become so notorious in the community or have become so well known to the accused that his or her identification would no longer be a significant issue.

It must be remembered that the object of the procedure is to make available to an accused enough information to enable the court to determine whether reasonable and probable grounds for the issuance of the warrant have been demonstrated. Most informations should lend themselves to careful editing. It would always be preferable to have the validity of the warrant determined on its merits.

This procedure should protect the rights both of the accused and of the informer, and ensure that in most cases the issue is determined on its merits. If the Crown is of the view that to produce the informant would be prejudicial to the administration of justice, the Crown may elect not to proceed or to proceed on the basis of a warrantless search. In those circumstances the trial judge will have to consider s. 24(2) of the *Charter* and determine whether the admission of the evidence would bring the administration of justice into disrepute. There is no way of knowing whether that situation will ever arise in this case, consequently nothing should be said about the possible result.

It is to be remembered that this case is not concerned with the propriety of a court order sealing an information used to obtain a search warrant, but only with the appropriate response of a trial court to a request for this information. There may well be other considerations to be taken into account in the former situation that need not be addressed in this case.

It was argued by the respondent that the search warrant should be declared invalid on the grounds that the justice of the peace who issued it should have made certain that the identity of the informer was not disclosed in the information. It was said that since the editing process had not been carried out at this stage the warrant should be declared invalid. This position goes too far.

It must be remembered that the search warrant is an important investigative tool. The affidavits used in support of an application for a warrant are often prepared in a hurry, frequently by persons who have little or no legal training. Detailed perfection should not be required at this stage of the investigative process.

Disposition

In this case the trial judge appears to have correctly taken the first step, and reviewed the information. An attempt should then have been made to edit it so that the identity of the informer was not disclosed. It is not absolutely clear whether this was done. When that process had been completed the edited information should have been returned to the Crown with the indication that an edited copy of the information would have to be given to the accused should the prosecution proceed. The Crown would then have been in a position to determine whether the edited version would identify the informer. Only if it did so would the Crown have to decide whether it was necessary to preserve the privilege which belongs exclusively to the informer to remain anonymous or whether, in the circumstances of this particular case, the Crown could proceed with the prosecution.

The decision to proceed could be based upon the consent of the informer to reveal his or her identity or the fact that the informer's identity had become known to the accused or become notorious within the community. In the absence of any of these circumstances, if the Crown still sought to adduce the evidence of the results of the search, then the trial judge would have to consider s. 24(2) of the *Charter* and determine whether the admission of the evidence would bring the administration of justice into disrepute.

The appeal must therefore be allowed and a new trial directed in order that this procedure may be followed.

It should be noted that Part VI of the *Criminal Code* empowers peace officers to intercept private communications, usually only after an application to the court under s. 184(2) for an authorization to do so, based

again upon a supporting affidavit. The procedures which regulate these interceptions are dealt with at p. 172. However, at this stage, it should be noted that s. 187 mandates that all documents relating to an application made pursuant to Part VI are confidential and shall be placed by the judge to whom the application is made in a sealed packet kept in the custody of the court and shall only be dealt with pursuant to further court order. Section 187 provides for a comprehensive procedure for opening the packet and removing, copying, examining and disclosing all or parts of its contents.

QUESTION

10. How do these procedures differ from the judicially made rules articulated in *R. v. Hunter* (1987), 34 C.C.C. (3d) 14 (Ont. C.A.)? Consider, in this regard, s. 187 of the *Criminal Code, R. v. Garofoli* (1990), 60 C.C.C. (3d) 161 (S.C.C.), substantially reproduced at p. 174 of this text, and *R. v. Dersch* (1990), 60 C.C.C. (3d) 132 (S.C.C.).

How can the police demonstrate the reliability of the supporting information when a confidential informer is involved? The following cases address this issue.

R. v. DEBOT

(1986), 30 C.C.C. (3d) 207 (Ont. C.A.); affd (1989), 52 C.C.C. (3d) 193 (S.C.C.)

Martin J.A.: —

.....

Unquestionably, information supplied by a reliable informer, even though it is hearsay, may in some circumstances provide the necessary "reasonable ground to believe" to justify the granting of a search warrant: see, for example, *R. v. Nepp*, (1927), 48 C.C.C. 275 at 276-7, [1927] 3 W.W.R. 353, 37 Man. R. 5 (Man. C.A.); *Illinois. v. Gates*, 462 U.S. 213 (1983). Such information may also provide the necessary reasonable and probable grounds to justify an arrest without warrant: see *Draper v. U.S.* (1959), 358 U.S. 307. It would seem to be entirely logical and reasonable that such information can also provide the necessary "reasonable ground to believe" to justify a warrantless search where a warrantless search is authorized by law. On an application for a search warrant, the informant must set out in the information the grounds for his or her belief in order that the justice may satisfy himself or herself that there are reasonable grounds for believing what is alleged: see *R. v. Noble* [(1984), 16 C.C.C. (3d) 146 (Ont. C.A.)] at p. 161 Consequently, a mere statement by the informant that he or she was told by a reliable informer that a certain person is carrying on a criminal activity or that drugs would be found at a certain place would be an insufficient basis for the granting of the warrant. The underlying circumstances disclosed by the informer for his or her conclusion must be set out, thus enabling the justice to satisfy himself or herself that there are reasonable grounds for believing what is alleged. I am of the view that such a mere conclusory statement made by an informer to a police officer would not constitute reasonable grounds for conducting a warrantless search or for making an arrest without warrant. Highly relevant to whether information supplied by an informer constitutes reasonable grounds to justify a warrantless search or an arrest without warrant are whether the informer's "tip" contains sufficient detail to ensure that it is based on more than mere rumour or gossip, whether the informer discloses his or her source or means of knowledge and whether there are any *indicia* of his or her reliability, such as the supplying of reliable information in the past or confirmation of part of his or her story by police surveillance. I do not intend to imply that each of these relevant criteria must be present in every case, provided that the totality of the circumstances meets the standard of the necessary reasonable grounds for relief.

.....

I am, with deference to the learned trial judge, of the view that Constable Birs, on the totality of the circumstances, had reasonable grounds to believe that the respondent was in possession of a prohibited drug. The information supplied by the informer to Constable Gutteridge was not a mere conclusory statement that the respondent was engaging in criminal activity with respect to drugs. Rather, the informer disclosed the underlying circumstances of the expected drug transaction, including the location where it was to take place. The informer told Gutteridge that the respondent was going to Carpenter's house to complete his part in the drug transaction. The police investigation confirmed that the respondent's car arrived at Carpenter's house and that one of the occupants, at least, entered the house. Two men and two women came out of the house shortly thereafter, got into the respondent's car and drove away. Furthermore, the informer had proved to be reliable with respect to information that he had given the police on previous occasions.

Constable Gutteridge had relayed to Constable Birs the information that he had received from the informer. The fact that information supplied by a fellow officer is hearsay does not exclude it from establishing probable cause: *Eccles v. Bourque et al.*, (1974), 19 C.C.C. (2d) 129 at p. 133, 50 D.L.R. (3d) 753, [1975] 2 S.C.R. 739 (S.C.C.). In addition, Constable Birs was informed by Sergeant Briscoe that DeBot's Ford Bronco was leaving Carpenter's residence and that it bore licence No. KP 7409.

One of the bases, among others, that Constable Birs mentioned as providing reasonable grounds for searching the respondent was that the respondent was reputed to be a drug user and drug trafficker. Obviously, the fact that a person is reputed to be a drug user and a drug trafficker would not by itself constitute reasonable grounds for believing that that person was in possession of a prohibited drug. That is not to say, however, that a suspect's reputation as a drug user and trafficker may not be a relevant factor constituting part of the total circumstances that induce a reasonable belief that the suspect has upon his person a prohibited drug. I have been unable to discover any Canadian case dealing with the relevance of a suspect's reputation in police circles on the issue of whether a police officer has reasonable grounds for searching the suspect. In *Spinelli v. U.S.* (1969),

393 U.S. 410, the Supreme Court of the United States, by a majority, held that an assertion by an F.B.I. agent in his affidavit in support of an application for a search warrant that Spinelli was known to the F.B.I. and others as a gambler and an associate of gamblers could not be used to give additional weight to allegations that would otherwise be insufficient to establish probable cause. There is, however, subsequent and weighty authority in the United States for the view that a police officer's knowledge of a suspect's reputation may at least properly be used in assessing the reliability of an informer's tip. Furthermore, it would seem that even the majority view in *Spinelli* does not preclude resort to prior convictions for similar offences or evidence of specific relevant prior misconduct on the issue of probable cause: see *Search and Seizure* by Wayne R. La Fave, vol. 1, (1978), pp. 468-75.

The respondent had one prior conviction for a narcotics offence, albeit a comparatively minor one, and Carpenter had a significant record for narcotics offences. I am of the view that the respondent's reputation in police circles as a drug user and trafficker was an item that Constable Birs could properly take into account, along with the other information he had, in deciding that there were reasonable grounds to believe that the respondent was in possession of a prohibited drug.

Evidence of bad character or prior criminal misconduct by an accused is excluded at his or her trial on a criminal charge, not on the ground that the evidence has no probative value, but on policy grounds, because the prejudicial effect of such evidence outweighs its probative value. The policy rule that, in general, excludes such evidence at an accused's trial has no application in determining whether reasonable and probable grounds exist for an arrest or a search.

R. v. HOSIE

(1996), 107 C.C.C. (3d) 385 (Ont. C.A.)

[The accused was charged with cultivating marijuana. The Crown's case depended entirely on evidence seized following the execution of a search warrant at the accused's home. In the information to obtain the search warrant, the police officer stated that an informant had supplied information that the accused was cultivating marijuana in a hydroponic laboratory located in his residence, and that a check with the utilities commission confirmed that the accused resided at the particular address, that he and a third party had been paying the hydro bill for several months, and that the accused's hydro bills appeared to be significantly larger than normal. The information to obtain the search warrant also stated that another source, who was believed reliable, had advised that the accused had recently moved to that address and had established a marijuana-growing operation. It was stated that information supplied by this source, while it had not led to previous arrests, had been found to be reliable in the past. It was also stated that the accused had a criminal record, which included a charge for possession of a narcotic eight years previously. In the police officer's testimony on the *voir dire*, held to determine the admissibility of the evidence obtained through execution of the warrant, it was revealed that the second source referred to in the information to obtain the search warrant had not supplied reliable information in the past and was, in fact, unproven.]

The judgment of the court was delivered by

Rosenberg J.A.: —

.....

The information to obtain the warrant

The grounds for obtaining the warrant were set out in app. "A" to the information, as follows. I have numbered the paragraphs for ease of reference.

> [1.] On September 8, 1993 Cst. A. Doucette received information from Cpl. GIBERON [*sic*] of the Royal Canadian Mounted Police which I investigated and found to be accurate and reliable.
>
> [2.] The information supplied by Cpl. Giberson is as follows: G. HOSIE who resides at 1498 Everts St. in Windsor, Ontario is cultivating marihuana in a hydroponic laboratory located in his residence.
>
> [3.] A check with Windsor Utilities Commission on September 8, 1993 confirms that George HOSIE resides at 1498 Everts St. and that he along with Mary SMITH have been paying the hydro bill since March 1993. HOSIE'S hydro bills appear to be significantly larger than normal.
>
> [4.] HOSIE has a criminal record dating back to 1971 for various offences, including a charge for possession of a narcotic in January 1985.
>
> [5.] I received information from Cpl. Campbell that a source believed reliable has advised that George HOSIE recently moved to Everts Ave, Windsor, Ontario and has established a very hightech hydroponic Marihuana growing operation. Cpl. Campbell further advised that information supplied by the source, while it has not lead to previous arrests, has been confirmed through other sources and otherwise investigated and found to be reliable.
>
> [6.] Based upon the above information the writer believes that George HOSIE is cultivating marihuana from a hydroponic laboratory in his residence.
>
> [7.] It is requested that a search warrant be granted as execution of warrant will afford evidence to support the charge of cultivation of cannabis marihuana contrary to Section 6 Subsection 1 of the Narcotic Control Act.

The evidence on the voir dire

Constable Doucette's testimony on the *voir dire* disclosed the following further information respecting these paragraphs.

Paragraph 2

Constable Doucette and Constable Rygerson drove out to 1498 Everts Ave. to "verify the residence", being the description of the house as a grey house, ranch style with a fence around the yard. Constable Doucette had no information as to the source of Corporal Giberson's information.

Paragraph 3

Constable Doucette called the Windsor Utilities Commission and was given the information about the apparently larger than normal utility bills. She testified that "[t]hey base it on the area of the house, the time of year as to compared to other paying customers of utilities who have the same size of house and in the same neighbourhood."

Paragraph 4

The appellant received an absolute discharge for the marihuana possession charge in 1985.

Paragraph 5

Corporal Campbell was in the office when Constable Doucette received the original telephone call from Corporal Giberson. Campbell then went to meet with a confidential informer and that source "also" told Campbell that he had information regarding the appellant and a hydroponic lab. Corporal Campbell's source had *not* supplied reliable information in the past. Constable Doucette testified that in para. 5 she meant to convey that Corporal Campbell's source had proved reliable because his information was verified by Corporal Giberson's source.

Constable Doucette was not asked directly whether Corporal Campbell and Corporal Giberson had two different sources. It seems unlikely that she could have answered the question since she did not know the identity of either and apparently made no inquiries.

.....

The validity of the warrant

In my view, the trial judge erred in holding that the information to obtain the search warrant in this case was sufficient to support the issuance of the warrant. As it was put by Dickson J. in *Hunter v. Southam Inc.* (1984), 14 C.C.C. (3d) 97 at p. 115, 11 D.L.R. (4th) 641, 2 C.P.R. (3d) 1 (S.C.C.), the state's interest in detecting crime prevails over the individual's interest in being left alone and a search warrant may issue where "credibly-based probability replaces suspicion". The material supplied by Constable Doucette in app. "A" as amplified by her evidence on the *voir dire* did not cross the threshold into *credibly based* probability.

Where, as in this case, the sufficiency of the information depends largely upon information supplied by a confidential source, the test to be applied by the reviewing court has been explained by Wilson J. in *R. v. Debot* (1989), 52 C.C.C. (3d) 193 at p. 215, [1989] 2 S.C.R. 1140, 73 C.R. (3d) 129. Although Wilson J. was there discussing the grounds to justify a warrantless search, the same principles apply in reviewing the sufficiency of a search warrant.

> In my view, there are at least three concerns to be addressed in weighing evidence relied on by the police to justify a warrantless search. First, was the information predicting the commission of a criminal offence compelling? Secondly, where that information was based on a "tip" originating from a

source outside the police, was that source credible? Finally, was the information corroborated by police investigation prior to making the decision to conduct the search? I do not suggest that each of these factors forms a separate test. Rather, I concur with Martin J.A.'s view that the "totality of the circumstances" must meet the standard of reasonableness. Weaknesses in one area may, to some extent, be compensated by strengths in the other two.

The sufficiency of the information in this case depends primarily upon the inferences to be drawn from paras. 2, 3 and 5 in light of the evidence supplied by Constable Doucette on the *voir dire*. As pointed out above, it is unclear both on the face of the information and from Constable Doucette's evidence whether Corporal Campbell and Corporal Giberson had two different sources. In any event, the information supplied by Giberson as set out in para. 2 is so devoid of detail as to the source and reliability of the information that it might be nothing more than rumour.

As to para. 5, in view of Constable Doucette's testimony, the words "believed reliable" and the entire second sentence must be deleted: see *R. v. Bisson* (1994), 94 C.C.C. (3d) 94 at pp. 95-6, [1994] 3 S.C.R. 1097, 65 Q.A.C. 241. As it is worded, para. 5 suggests that on previous occasions Campbell's source had proved reliable, albeit the information supplied by the source on these other occasions had not led to arrests. It is clear from the testimony of Constable Doucette on the *voir dire* that this is not correct.

Thus, what remains of para. 5 is information from an unproven source. Mr. O'Connell asked us to place substantial weight on the detail supplied in para. 5, namely, that the appellant had recently moved to Everts Ave. and that he had established a "very hightech hydroponic Marihuana growing operation". In my view, the information supplied is far from detailed and could not be described as compelling, in the sense referred to by Wilson J. in *Debot*. There is no indication as to the informer's source of knowledge or how current the information is. There is no way to know whether the informer has obtained this information through personal observation as opposed to rumour or second or third-hand information. The use of the phrase "very hightech" does not advance the case in any real sense. Had the informer provided information as to the type of equipment and similar details then the justice might have been able to infer that the informer had obtained the information first-hand. That kind of detail, however, is lacking.

As Wilson J. said in *Debot, supra*, at p. 218, "the level of verification required may be higher where the police rely on an informant whose credibility cannot be assessed or where fewer details are provided and the risk of innocent coincidence is greater". Since in this case the credibility of the informants cannot be assessed and few details were supplied, a relatively higher level of verification was required. The validity of the warrant thus depends upon the sufficiency of the police investigation to corroborate the informer's tip as set out in para. 3. For ease of reference I will repeat that crucial paragraph:

> A check with Windsor Utilities Commission on September 8, 1993 confirms that George HOSIE resides at 1498 Everts St. and that he along with Mary SMITH have been paying the hydro bill since March 1993. HOSIE'S hydro bills appear to be significantly larger than normal.

The fact that the appellant and Ms Smith had been paying the bills since March, 1993, confirms Campbell's information that the appellant "recently" moved to Everts Ave. Otherwise, the somewhat tentative opinion is not sufficiently detailed nor is its source sufficiently identified to be an opinion that supports the allegation that marihuana was being grown in the house. The justice of the peace could not have properly inferred from this paragraph the basis of the opinion, or that the opinion as to the size of the hydro bills was that of an informed person at the commission.

In concluding that the information in this case was sufficient the trial judge relied upon *R. v. Plant* [(1993), 84 C.C.C. (3d) 203 (S.C.C.)]. The *Plant* case bears some superficial resemblance to the case before us. The information to obtain the warrant in that case depended upon a tip from an unknown informer, an electricity records check, and observations made during a warrantless perimeter search. The Supreme Court held that the warrantless perimeter search was a violation of s. 8 of the *Charter* and thus the evidence gathered from that search and included in the information to obtain the warrant had to be eliminated in determining the sufficiency of the warrant. Thus, as in this case, the sufficiency of the information depended upon the anonymous tip and the information concerning electrical consumption.

While the full text of the information to obtain the warrant in *Plant* is not set out either in the report of the case in the Supreme Court or in the Alberta Court of Appeal (*R. v. Plant* (1991), 116 A.R. 1, 12 W.C.B. (2d) 640), the details of the information concerning electrical consumption are disclosed. The officer stated in the information that the electricity consumption was four times that of comparably sized homes on the same city block and that such electric consumption was "consistent with other hydroponic marihuana operations and the usage of high voltage grow lights" (116 A.R. at p. 3). In comparison to the statement in para. 3 of the warrant in the case before us, the material placed before the justice in *Plant* was sufficiently detailed to qualify as an informed opinion and thus could corroborate the anonymous tip. The additional piece of information in the case before us is the appellant's eight-year-old record for simple possession of narcotics. However, that dated record for a different offence does not render the information sufficient: see *R. v. Debot, supra,* at p. 216.

The test to be applied by a court when reviewing the sufficiency of a search warrant information has been laid down in *R. v. Garofoli* (1990), 60 C.C.C. (3d) 161 at p. 188, [1990] 2 S.C.R. 1421, 80 C.R. (3d) 317:

> The reviewing judge does not substitute his or her view for that of the authorizing judge. If, based on the record which was before the authorizing judge as amplified on the review, the reviewing judge concludes that the authorizing judge could have granted the authorization, then he or she should not interfere. In this process, the existence of fraud, non-disclosure, misleading evidence and new evidence are all relevant, but, rather than being a prerequisite to review, their sole impact is to determine whether there continues to be any basis for the decision of the authorizing judge.

In light of the decision of the Supreme Court in *R. v. Plant,* this is a close case, but considering the totality of circumstances, it is my view that when the misleading portions of para. 5 are deleted from the information, there is not sufficient material upon which the authorizing judge could have granted the search warrant. The search warrant was therefore invalid and the search of the appellant's home unreasonable.

[Rosenberg J.A. considered the seriousness of the violation and the long-term consequences on the repute of the administration of justice if the impugned evidence were admitted, and held that the evidence should be excluded pursuant to s. 24(2) of the *Charter*.]

Consider, also on this issue, *R. v. Garofoli* (1990), 60 C.C.C. (3d) 161 (S.C.C.), substantially reproduced at p. 174.

Counsel attacking a search founded upon a confidential informer should familiarize itself with the police force's internal rules and regulations about the handling of police informers. Failure to conform to these rules and regulations, designed, in part, to ensure their reliability, may assist in demonstrating a *Charter* violation (see *R. v. Eagle,* [1996] O.J. No. 2867 (Gen. Div.)).

(c) The Contents of the Warrant

Forms 5 and 5.1 contained in the *Criminal Code* provide guidance as to the contents of warrants issued under s. 487 and 487.1(6) of the *Criminal Code*. Sections 487(3) and 487.1(6) speak to the use of these forms. Not surprisingly, the minimum contents of the warrant track the minimum contents of the information. Put succinctly, the contents of the warrant are assessed to determine whether they adequately convey what is legitimately within the scope of the search and what is not. A warrant cannot effectively delegate the judicial determination of the scope of the search to the executing officers.

(d) The Duty of the Judicial Officer Considering the Application

CANADIAN BROADCASTING CORP. v. NEW BRUNSWICK (ATTORNEY GENERAL)

(1991), 67 C.C.C. (3d) 544 (S.C.C.)

[The C.B.C. filmed a fire, set during a demonstration. The police sought a warrant to seize the video cassettes. Cory J., for the majority of the Supreme Court, articulated a series of procedures applicable to searches and seizures at media offices.]

Cory J.: —

.....

Summary of factors to be considered on the issuance of a search warrant and review of a search warrant

It may be helpful to summarize the factors to be considered by a justice of the peace on an application to obtain a warrant to search the premises of a news media organization together with those factors which may be pertinent to a court reviewing the issuance of a search warrant.

(1) It is essential that all the requirements set out in s. 487(1)(*b*) of the *Criminal Code* for the issuance of a search warrant be met.
(2) Once the statutory conditions have been met, the justice of the peace should consider all of the circumstances in determining whether to exercise his or her discretion to issue a warrant.
(3) The justice of the peace should ensure that a balance is struck between the competing interests of the state in the investigation and prosecution of crimes and the right to privacy of the media in the course of their news gathering and news dissemination. It must be borne in mind that the media play a vital role in the functioning of a democratic society. Generally speaking, the news media will not be implicated in the crime under investigation. They are truly an innocent third party. This is a particularly important factor to be considered in attempting to strike an appropriate balance, including the consideration of imposing conditions on that warrant.
(4) The affidavit in support of the application must contain sufficient detail to enable the justice of the peace to properly exercise his or her discretion as to the issuance of a search warrant.
(5) Although it is not a constitutional requirement, the affidavit material should ordinarily disclose whether there are alternative sources from which the information may reasonably be obtained and, if there is an alternative source, that it has been investigated and all reasonable efforts to obtain the information have been exhausted.
(6) If the information sought has been disseminated by the media in whole or in part, this will be a factor which will favour the issuing of the search warrant.
(7) If a justice of the peace determines that a warrant should be issued for the search of media premises, consideration should then be given to the imposition of some conditions on its implementation so that the media organization will not be unduly impeded in the publishing or dissemination of the news.
(8) If, subsequent to the issuing of a search warrant, it comes to light the authorities failed to disclose pertinent information that could well have affected the decision to issue the warrant, this may result in a finding that the warrant was invalid.
(9) Similarly, if the search itself is unreasonably conducted, this may render the search invalid.

QUESTION

11. The police seek a warrant. They come to the justice of the peace with an information in draft form. The justice advises the police as to suitable wording and the information is changed accordingly. It is then sworn before the justice. Is this an acceptable procedure? Consider, in this regard, *R. v. Gray* (1993), 81 C.C.C. (3d) 174 (Man. C.A.). What if a justice receives the sworn information and questions the officer further about the investigation or the basis of the officer's belief? Can the justice rely upon that additional information? If so, should any special procedures be adopted?

(e) The Execution of the Warrant

Of course, a search warrant can be executed only at the location specified in the warrant.

QUESTIONS

12. The police are to search 345 Culprit Street, the residence of A. Bandit. On arrival, they note that 345 Culprit Street is a donut shop; the residence of A. Bandit is at 345A Culprit Street. Time is of the essence. What can they do? Consider, in this regard, *R. v. Hynds* (1982), 70 C.C.C. (2d) 186 (Alta. Q.B.).

13. Now assume the warrant correctly named 345A Culprit Street as Bandit's residence. Can the police search the garage? How about the car in the driveway? How about the car parked on the street in front of the residence? Would your answer to the last question be affected if the police checked the license plate of the car and noted it was registered to Mr. Bandit? What if the same car was parked immediately beside the residence in the donut shop's parking lot? Consider, in this regard, *R. v. Haley* (1986), 27 C.C.C. (3d) 454, 51 C.R. (3d) 363 (Ont. C.A.).

Section 488 provides that a s. 487 or 487.1 warrant shall be executed by day, unless otherwise authorized, based upon reasonable grounds to authorize a night search, contained in the supporting information.

Executing officers cannot search and seize in a manner that exceeds the authorized scope of the warrant. However, s. 489(1) of the *Criminal Code* provides:

> (1) Every person who executes a warrant may seize, in addition to the things mentioned in the warrant, anything that the person believes on reasonable grounds
>
> (*a*) has been obtained by [or]
> (*b*) has been used in the commission of an offence against this or any other Act of Parliament, or
> (*c*) will afford evidence in respect of an offence against this or any other Act of Parliament.

Similar powers are conferred upon officers who are lawfully present in a place pursuant to a warrant or otherwise in the execution of duties and who do not have a warrant.

QUESTIONS

14. Police enter A. Bandit's residence with a *Criminal Code* warrant, looking for documents relating to a bank fraud. In plain view, on the kitchen table, are 120 identical Versace raincoats. Mr. Bandit is known not to be in the clothing business. Indeed, he doesn't even dress nicely. Can the police seize the raincoats if they suspect they are stolen? Do they need any additional information? Now assume that the raincoats were only found when the police emptied out Mr. Bandit's dresser drawers. Would your answer be the same?

15. **Police execute a warrant under the *Controlled Drugs and Substances Act* looking for cocaine. They find a debt list secreted in the floor boards which obviously records drug transactions with customers. They also find records of frequent trips to and from Colombia. Can they seize the debt list and/or the travel records which are unspecified in the warrant? Compare, in this regard, s. 11(6) of the *Controlled Drugs and Substances Act* to s. 489 of the *Criminal Code*. Would your answer be different if the debt list related to stolen watches and not to drugs? Consider s. 11(8) of the *Controlled Drugs and Substances Act*. Now assume that the police reasonably believe that someone on the premises has, on his person, the items unspecified in the warrant. Under what circumstances can that person be searched? Why does s. 11(5) of the *Controlled Drugs and Substances Act* not assist?**

Where a search and seizure occurs in a large-scale document case, it may be attacked on the basis that more documents were seized than were authorized by the warrant. Alternatively, the breadth of the seizure may prove not that the officers seized more than permitted, but that the warrant was defective because it permitted such a wholesale seizure. Apart from its permissible scope, the manner in which a search is executed may be impugned. Was unnecessary force used? Was excessive damage occasioned to the premises? How did the police effect entry? Were there s. 10(*b*) *Charter* violations accompanying the search? Should the occupants have been "frozen" pending its completion?[2] The common law procedures established for the execution of search warrants under the *Criminal Code* are outlined in *Wah Kie v. Cuddy*, [1914] 23 C.C.C. 383 (Alta. C.A.).

(f) Solicitor-Client Privilege

Of course, documents may be subject to solicitor-client privilege and for that reason, not disclosable to the authorities or to the courts. Accordingly, procedures have been adopted to protect against the examination of privileged documents. The issue may arise where a lawyer's office is the subject of a search warrant or where the client's office is to be searched and contains documents which may be privileged. Section 488.1 of the *Criminal Code* was enacted to outline the procedure to be adopted for documents in the possession of a lawyer where privilege may be asserted. Its constitutionality was addressed in the following case.

---

[2] **The Supreme Court has divided on whether a s. 10(*b*) violation in the course of search truly goes to the manner of the search. Consider, in this regard, *Strachan v. The Queen* (1988), 46 C.C.C. (3d) 479 (S.C.C.).**

LAVALLEE, RACKEL & HEINTZ v. CANADA (ATTORNEY GENERAL); WHITE, OTTENHEIMER & BAKER v. CANADA (ATTORNEY GENERAL); R. v. FINK

(2002), 167 C.C.C. (3d) 1 (S.C.C.)

[The issue was brought before the Court by way of three separate appeals from the provinces of Alberta (*Lavallee, Rackel & Heintz v. Canada (Attorney General)* (2000), 143 C.C.C. (3d) 187 (Alta. C.A.)), Newfoundland and Labrador (*White, Ottenheimer & Baker v. Canada (Attorney General)* (2000), 146 C.C.C. (3d) 28 (Nfld. C.A.)) and Ontario (*R. v. Fink* (2000), 149 C.C.C. (3d) 321 (Ont. C.A.)).]

Arbour J. [McLachlin C.J.C. and Iacobucci, Major, Bastarache and Binnie JJ. concurring]: —

.....

IV. Analysis

A. Law Office Searches

Before the 1970s, law office searches were seldom employed in the course of criminal investigations. But since that time, there has been an observable trend in Canada and the United States towards more aggressive investigatory methods which include the issuing of warrants to search law offices for evidence of crime.

......

In Canada, the enactment of s. 488.1 of the *Criminal Code* (originally s. 444.1) in 1985 was in fact the legislative response to a line of cases culminating in this Court's decision *Descôteaux v. Mierzwinski*, [1982] 1 S.C.R. 860, 70 C.C.C. (2d) 385, 141 D.L.R. (3d) 590, that set out guidelines for the issuing of search warrants for law offices. From the outset, Canadian courts expressed serious concerns about the dangers of law office searches in light of solicitor-client privilege, and urged Parliament to create protective measures akin to those found in the *Income Tax Act*. Section 488.1 was designed to address these concerns and, in the words of the Minister of Justice, "establish a sealing procedure with respect to seized documents that will ensure protection of solicitor-client privilege" (House of Commons, Standing Committee on Justice and Legal Affairs, *Minutes of the Proceedings and Evidence*, January 22, 1985, Issue No. 5, at 5:9). As it will be explained further in these reasons, s. 488.1 of the *Criminal Code* falls short of providing the protection it promised and, indeed, unconstitutionally jeopardizes solicitor-client privilege. Before turning to the shortcomings of s. 488.1, it is perhaps worthwhile to review the jurisprudence that lead to its enactment in order to better understand the concerns that s. 488.1 was meant to address.

.....

C. Descôteaux v. Mierzwinski

This case involved the search of a legal aid bureau for evidence that an applicant for legal aid had illegally reported a lower income in order to be eligible for such services. The search was conducted in the presence of the syndic of the Bar and the police officers agreed to receive the documents in sealed envelopes pending the judicial determination of solicitor-client privilege. The legal aid bureau and Mr. Descôteaux brought a motion before the Superior Court in Montreal to quash the warrant on the grounds that the documents were protected by solicitor-client privilege. The Superior Court dismissed the motion and held that the documents were not privileged since they had been prepared before the solicitor-client relationship came into existence, [1978] C.S. 792. The Quebec Court of Appeal dismissed the appeal, adopting the conclusions of the Superior Court and stating further that solicitor-client privilege could not apply if the communication was made in furtherance of a criminal act or to facilitate the commission of a crime: (1980), 16 C.R. (3d) 188.

Writing for the Court, Lamer J. (as he then was) dismissed the appeal. After briefly tracing the historical development of solicitor-client privilege as a rule of evidence, Lamer J. confirmed that solicitor-client privilege had evolved into a substantive principle, referring to this Court's decision in *Solosky* [(1979), 50 C.C.C. (2d) 495 (S.C.C.)]. He stated at p. 875:

> It is quite apparent that the Court in that case [*Solosky*] applied a standard that has nothing to do with the rule of evidence, the privilege, since there was never any question of testimony before a tribunal or court. The Court in fact, in my view, applied a substantive rule, without actually formulating it, and, consequently, recognized implicitly that the right to confidentiality, which had long ago given rise to a rule of evidence, had also since given rise to a substantive rule.

Lamer J. went on to formulate the elements of the substantive rule concisely in the following terms (at p. 875), elements which, in my view, largely govern the outcome of the appeals presently before the Court:

> It would, I think, be useful for us to formulate this substantive rule, as the judges formerly did with the rule of evidence; it could, in my view, be stated as follows:
>
> 1. The confidentiality of communications between solicitor and client may be raised in any circumstances where such communications are likely to be disclosed without the client's consent.
> 2. Unless the law provides otherwise, when and to the extent that the legitimate exercise of a right would interfere with another person's right to have his communications with his lawyer kept confidential, the resulting conflict should be resolved in favour of protecting the confidentiality.
> 3. When the law gives someone the authority to do something which, in the circumstances of the case, might interfere with that confidentiality, the decision to do so and the choice of means of exercising that authority should be determined with a view to not interfering with it except to the extent absolutely necessary in order to achieve the ends sought by the enabling legislation.

> 4. Acts providing otherwise in situations under paragraph 2 and enabling legislation referred to in paragraph 3 must be interpreted restrictively.

See also *Jones, supra*, at para. 49.

.....

Second, Lamer J. considered the interplay between the state's search power and the substantive rule of solicitor-client privilege. He stated, starting at p. 889:

> Searches are an exception to the oldest and most fundamental principles of the common law, and as such the power to search should be strictly controlled. ... [T]here are places for which authorization to search should generally be granted only with reticence and, where necessary, with more conditions attached than for other places. One does not enter a church in the same way as a lion's den, or a warehouse in the same way as a lawyer's office.

.....

... I think it important to emphasize, as did Lamer J. at p. 891, that even if the necessary conditions precedent are met, "the justice of the peace *must* set out procedures for the execution of the warrant that reconcile protection of the interests this right [solicitor-client privilege] is seeking to promote with protection of those the search power is seeking to promote, and limit the breach of this fundamental right to what is strictly inevitable" (emphasis in original). In other words, solicitor-client privilege must only be impaired if necessary and, even then, minimally.

.....

E. The Constitutional Failings of Section 488.1 Identified in the Proceedings Below

As stated above, the appellate courts of Alberta, British Columbia, Newfoundland, Nova Scotia and Ontario all held that the procedure set out in s. 488.1 unconstitutionally offended to the rights enshrined in s. 8 of the *Charter*. In coming to that conclusion, these courts identified several problems within the provisions of s. 488.1 which, either directly or indirectly, compromise the integrity of solicitor-client privilege.

(1) Absence or Inaction of Solicitor

The courts below all found that privilege may be lost through the absence or the inaction of the solicitor. Pursuant to s. 488.1(2), the sealing procedure is only engaged if "a lawyer ... *claims* that a named client of his has a solicitor-client privilege" (emphasis added) in respect of the documents. If the solicitor is not present at the time and place of the search, the officers conducting the search must give the lawyer a reasonable opportunity to make the claim of privilege, as directed by s. 488.1(8). If no claim is made, they may seize the documents and freely examine their contents, thus causing the privilege to be lost. Similarly, the privilege may also be lost if the solicitor is present but fails to claim the privilege for whatever reason (incompetence, sickness or out of sheer nervousness arising out of having his or her office searched). See *Lavallee, supra,* at paras. 28 and 37; *White, supra,* at para. 21; *Fink, supra,* at para. 34; and, *Festing* [(2001), 159 C.C.C. (3d) 97 (B.C.C.A.)], at para. 17.

(2) The Naming of Clients

Courts have also identified another offensive aspect of s. 488.1(2) in the requirement that the lawyer name the client whose privilege is being threatened in order to engage the sealing procedure with respect to that client's documents. The name of the client may very well be protected by solicitor-client privilege, although this is not always the case. See *Thorson v. Jones* (1973), 38 D.L.R. (3d) 312 (B.C.S.C.); R.D. Manes, M.P. Silver, *Solicitor-Client Privilege in Canadian Law* (1993), at p. 141. Where the name of the client is indeed privileged information, s. 488.1(2) compels the lawyer to choose between two different privileged items: the name of the client or the confidential documents targeted by the search. In these situations, s. 488.1(2) requires that one privilege be sacrificed so that the other may be salvaged. See *Lavallee, supra,* at para. 50; *White, supra,* at para. 21; *Fink, supra,* at para. 39; *Festing, supra,* at para. 17, and *Several Clients* [(2001), 86 C.R.R. (2d) 249 (N.S.S.C.)], at para. 38.

(3) No Notice Given to Client

The courts below also criticized the fact that s. 488.1 fails to ensure that all interested clients are notified when their documents are about to be turned over to the investigators. Indeed, the procedure does not provide for the mandatory notification of privilege holders. This absence of notice is particularly striking when, as described above, the solicitor is absent or fails to act, thus irremediably depriving the client of the opportunity to assert his or her solicitor-client privilege. The absence of notice is the first step in a series of consequences which can be fatal to maintaining the confidentiality of privileged documents. See *Lavallee, supra,* at paras. 28-39; *White, supra,* at para. 21; *Fink, supra,* at para. 42; *Festing, supra,* at para. 17, and *Several Clients, supra* at para. 38.

(4) Strict Time Limits

If the privilege is not asserted at the time of the search, for whatever reason, the seized documents may be examined by the investigating officers and prosecutors. Even if solicitor-client privilege is asserted at the time of the search, it may still be lost if the client or solicitor fails to move for "a place and day ... for the determination of the question whether the document should be disclosed" within fourteen days of the search and seizure, as provided by s. 488.1(3)(*a*)(i) of the *Criminal Code*. In *Lavallee*, Côté J.A. further observed at para. 41: "The looming '14-day time' limit under s. 488.1(3) is really only 10 to 11 days, because the subsection says that 2 days' notice must be given. In view of the *Interpretation Act*, R.S.C. 1985, c. I-21, s. 27(2), that will eat up at least 3 days. Since the lawyer needs authority to move in court, and since only the client owns the privilege and can move, the 10 or 14 days might well be missed." This time limit was held to be unreasonably strict and unworkable by the courts below. This procedural rigidity is exacerbated by the fact that no time extension can be granted without the consent of the Crown. See also *White, supra*, at para. 21; *Fink, supra*, at para. 34; *Festing, supra*, at para. 17, and *Several Clients, supra*, at para. 38.

(5) Absence of Discretion

Even in cases where the privilege has been asserted at the first opportunity, if the strict procedures outlined above are not followed, the *Code* provides that the court has no remedial discretion to relieve the privilege holder from his or her default and maintain the confidentiality of the information claimed to be privileged. This means that if an application is not made within 14 days of the search for a judicial determination of the validity of the claim of privilege, and if the consent of the Attorney General cannot be obtained for an extension of time, the judge has no discretion under the *Code* and must order that the documents seized and held under seal be turned over to the prosecution. Pursuant to s. 488.1(6), "the judge *shall* order" (emphasis added) that the documents be delivered to the prosecuting authorities. See *Lavallee, supra*, at para. 28; *White, supra*, at para. 21; *Fink, supra*, at para. 35. The courts in *Festing, supra*, and *Several Clients, supra*, also found this aspect to be particularly offensive.

(6) Access of the Attorney-General Prior to Judicial Determination

Finally, some appellate courts took issue with the fact that, pursuant to s. 488.1(4)(*b*), the Attorney General may be allowed to inspect the documents where the judge is of the opinion that it would materially assist the court in determining the question of privilege. Several courts held that this subsection effectively nullifies solicitor-client privilege before it is even determined that such privilege exists. The courts were of the view that the Crown does not need to inspect the documents in order to make meaningful submissions with regards to the seized documents and that the issue of privilege could be determined without allowing the Attorney General to access the seized documents. In the first instance of *Festing*, Romilly J. opined at para. 82: "I fail to see how disclosure to the prosecuting authority for the purposes of determining privilege is a practical necessity. I appreciate that eventually someone will have to see the documents in order to decide privilege. But surely that someone does not have to be the prosecuting authority" ((2000), 31 C.R. (5th) 203). See also *Fink, supra*, at para. 34; *Festing, supra*, at para. 19; *Several Clients, supra*, at para. 41.

.....

F. Section 488.1 Violates Section 8 of the Charter

The proper approach to the constitutional issues here is under s. 8 of the *Charter*, and there is no need to undertake an independent s. 7 analysis. This was properly explained in *Fink* by Goudge J.A., at para. 15:

> While a seizure undertaken by the state in the course of a criminal investigation can be said to implicate s. 7 and while solicitor-client privilege is encompassed within the principles of fundamental justice, I think s. 8 provides

a sufficient framework for analysis. If the procedure mandated by s. 488.1 results in a reasonable search and seizure of the documents in the possession of a lawyer, it surely accords with the principles of fundamental justice and vice versa.

If the procedure set out in s. 488.1 results in an unreasonable search and seizure contrary to s. 8 of the *Charter*, it follows that s. 488.1 cannot be said to comply with the principles of fundamental justice embodied in s. 7. See also *Re Motor Vehicle Act*, [1985] 2 S.C.R. 486, 23 C.C.C. (3d) 289, 24 D.L.R. (4th) 536. In *R. v. Edwards*, [1996] 1 S.C.R. 128, 104 C.C.C. (3d) 136, 132 D.L.R. (4th) 31, at para. 33, Cory J. stated that "[t]here are two distinct questions which must be answered in any s. 8 challenge. The first is whether the accused had a reasonable expectation of privacy. The second is whether the search was an unreasonable intrusion on that right to privacy". A client has a reasonable expectation of privacy in all documents in the possession of his or her lawyer, which constitute information that the lawyer is ethically required to keep confidential, and an expectation of privacy of the highest order when such documents are protected by the solicitor-client privilege. This is not at issue in this case. I will therefore proceed immediately to the second step of the s. 8 analysis, namely the reasonableness of the statutory intrusion on the privacy interests of solicitor's clients.

At this stage, the issue is whether the procedure set out by s. 488.1 results in a reasonable search and seizure of documents, including potentially privileged documents, in the possession of a lawyer. Indeed, s. 8 only protects against unreasonable searches and seizures: *Hunter v. Southam Inc.*, [1984] 2 S.C.R. 145, 14 C.C.C. (3d) 97, 11 D.L.R. (4th) 641.

.....

... Since *Hunter*, this Court has striven to strike an appropriate balance between privacy interests on the one hand and the exigencies of law enforcement on the other. See *R. v. Araujo*, [2000] 2 S.C.R. 992, 2000 SCC 65, 149 C.C.C. (3d) 449, 193 D.L.R. (4th) 440; *R. v. Golden*, 2001 SCC 83 [reported 159 C.C.C. (3d) 449, 207 D.L.R. (4th) 18]. Sometimes, however, the traditional balancing of interests involved in a s. 8 analysis is inappropriate. As it was stated in *R. v. Mills*, [1999] 3 S.C.R. 668, 139 C.C.C. (3d) 321, 180 D.L.R. (4th) 1, at para. 86, "the appropriateness of the balance is assessed according to the nature of the interests at stake in a particular context, and the place of these interests within our legal and political traditions". Where the interest at stake is solicitor-client privilege — a principle of fundamental justice and civil right of supreme importance in Canadian law — the usual balancing exercise referred to above is not particularly helpful. This is so because the privilege favours not only the privacy interests of a potential accused, but also the interests of a fair, just and efficient law enforcement process.

.....

Indeed, solicitor-client privilege must remain as close to absolute as possible if it is to retain relevance. Accordingly, this Court is compelled in my view to adopt stringent norms to ensure its protection. Such protection is ensured by labeling as unreasonable any legislative provision that interferes with solicitor-client privilege more than is absolutely necessary. In short, in the specific context of law office searches for documents that are potentially protected by solicitor-client privilege, the procedure set out in s. 488.1 will pass *Charter* scrutiny if it results in a "minimal impairment" of solicitor-client privilege.

.....

Does s. 488.1 more than minimally impair solicitor-client privilege? It is my conclusion that it does.

While I think it unnecessary to revisit the numerous statements of this Court on the nature and primacy of solicitor-client privilege in Canadian law, it bears repeating that the privilege belongs to the client and can only be asserted or waived by the client or through his or her informed consent (*Solosky*, *supra*; *Descôteaux*, *supra*; *Geffen* [[1991] 2 S.C.R. 353]; *Jones* [[1999] 1 S.C.R. 455]; *McClure* [(2001), 151 C.C.C. (3d) 321 (S.C.C.)]; *Benson* [(2002), 162 C.C.C. (3d) 257 (S.C.C.)]). In my view, the failings of s. 488.1 identified in numerous judicial decisions and described above all share one principal, fatal feature, namely, the potential breach of solicitor-client privilege without the client's knowledge, let alone consent. The fact that competent counsel will attempt to ascertain the whereabouts of their clients and will likely assert blanket privilege at the outset does not obviate the state's duty to ensure sufficient protection of the rights of the privilege holder. Privilege does not come into being by an assertion of a privilege claim; it exists independently. By the operation of s. 488.1, however, this constitutionally protected right can be violated by the mere failure of counsel to act, without instruction from or indeed communication with the client. Thus, s. 488.1 allows the solicitor-client confidentiality to be destroyed without the client's express and informed authorization, and even without the client's having an opportunity to be heard.

In that respect I note that s. 488.1(8), which requires the investigative officers to give reasonable opportunity for a claim of solicitor-client privilege to be made before examining, making copies or seizing any documents, is limited to a claim "to be made under subsection (2)". The claim under subs. (2) is of course the claim that the lawyer is required to make, at the time of the search, in order to trigger the further procedural protections provided for in s. 488.1. Therefore, under this statutory scheme, reasonable opportunity has to be provided to the privilege keeper, but not to the privilege holder, to ensure that the privileged information remains so. This positive obligation on counsel shifts the burden of guaranteeing the respect for *Charter* rights from the state to the lawyer. I stress here that I am making no adverse assumption about the competence, professionalism and integrity of lawyers. However, in the context of searches of law offices, it cannot simply be assumed that the lawyer is the *alter ego* of the client. The solicitor-client relationship may have been terminated long before the search. This of course does not displace the duty of loyalty owed by the solicitor to the client. But law office searches may place lawyers in a conflict of interest with their clients, or may place them in conflict regarding their ongoing duties to several present and former clients. I cannot see how s. 488.1(8), limited as it is, can raise this entire procedural scheme to a standard of constitutional reasonableness when it fails to address directly the entitlement that the privilege holder, the client, should have to ensure the adequate protection of his or her rights. Indeed, because of the complete lack of notification provisions within the s. 488.1 scheme, the client may not even be aware that his or her privilege is threatened.

In cases where it would not be feasible to notify the potential privilege holders that they need to assert their privilege in order to bar an intrusion by the state into these protected materials, at the very least independent legal intervention, for instance in the form of notification and involvement of the Law Society, would go a long way to afford the protection that is so lacking under the present regime. Indeed, this is done routinely as a matter of practice in Quebec, and occasionally elsewhere. For a detailed description of the practice in Quebec, see *Maranda v. Quebec (Judge of the Court of Quebec)* (2001), 161 C.C.C. (3d) 64 (Que. C.A.), at paras. 34 to 38, application for leave to appeal granted May 16, 2002 (No. 28964) [163 C.C.C. (3d) vi].

I stress here again that the enactment of s. 488.1 represents an attempt to respect the solicitor-client privilege. However, in order to respect the constitutional imperatives, the enactment must strive to ensure that the chances of the state's accessing, through a search warrant, privileged information to which the state has no right of access, are reduced to their reasonable minimum. In my view, since the right of the state to access this information is, in law, conditional on the consent of the privilege holder, all efforts to notify that person, or an appropriate surrogate such as the Law Society, must be put in place in order for the section to conform to s. 8 of the *Charter*.

Another fatal flaw in the current statutory scheme is, in my view, the absence of judicial discretion in the determination of the validity of an asserted claim of privilege. I am not unduly concerned with the apparently strict time limits imposed by the *Code* for this issue to be dealt with, as I believe that a proper interpretation of these provisions would permit a court to relieve a party from its default to comply with the statutory time line, for instance on consent, in the interest of justice. However, I cannot see how one can read a residual judicial discretion in s. 488.1(6) which confers an entitlement on the Crown to access the seized documents if an application has not been made, or has not been proceeded with, with the dispatch required by subss. (2) and (3). The language is clear, "the judge shall" order the documents released to the prosecution. Short of replacing the word "shall" with the word "may" by way of constitutional remedy, a point to which I will return below, I cannot see how, as a matter of sound statutory interpretation, one can interpret this provision as containing an element of judicial discretion. Again, measured against the constitutional standard of reasonableness in s. 8 of the *Charter*, this mandatory disclosure of potentially privileged information, in a case where the court has been alerted to the possibility of privilege by the fact that the documents were sealed at the point of search, cannot be said to minimally impair the privilege. It amounts to an unjustifiable vindication of form over substance, and it creates a real possibility that the state may obtain privileged information that a court could very well have recognized as such. In my view, reasonableness dictates that courts must retain a discretion to decide whether materials seized in a lawyer's office should remain inaccessible to the state as privileged information if and when, in the circumstances, it is in the interest of justice to do so.

.....

In short, in my opinion, s. 488.1 fails to ensure that clients are given a reasonable opportunity to exercise their constitutional prerogative to assert or waive their privilege. Far from upholding solicitor-client confidentiality, s. 488.1 permits the privilege to fall through the interstices of its inadequate procedure. The possible automatic loss of protection against unreasonable search and seizure through the normal operation of the law cannot be reasonable. Nor can the provision be infused with reasonableness in a constitutional sense on the basis of an assumption that the prosecution will behave honourably and, for instance, initiate a review under s. 488.1(3), if neither the client nor the lawyer has done so, or refrain from exercising the right to inspect the sealed documents, even though authorized to do so by the reviewing judge, as contemplated by s. 488.1(4)(*b*). As Cory J. observed in *R. v. Bain*, [1992] 1 S.C.R. 91 at pp. 103-4, 69 C.C.C. (3d) 481, 87 D.L.R. (4th) 449: "Unfortunately it would seem that whenever the Crown is granted statutory power that can be used abusively then, on occasion, it will indeed be used abusively. The protection of basic rights should not be dependent upon a reliance on the continuous exemplary conduct of the Crown, something that is impossible to monitor or control." Even more so, I would add that the constitutionality of a statutory provision cannot rest on an expectation that the Crown will refrain from doing what it is permitted to do.

For these reasons, I find that s. 488.1 more than minimally impairs solicitor-client privilege and thus amounts to an unreasonable search and seizure contrary to s. 8 of the *Charter*.

.....

V. REMEDY

.....

In the interim, I will articulate the general principles that govern the legality of searches of law offices as a matter of common law until Parliament, if it sees fit, re-enacts legislation on the issue. These general principles should also guide the legislative options that Parliament may want to address in that respect. Much like those formulated in *Descôteaux*, *supra*, the following guidelines are meant to reflect the present-day constitutional imperatives for the protection of solicitor-client privilege, and to govern both the search authorization process and the general manner in which the search must be carried out; in this connection, however, they are not intended to select any particular procedural method of meeting these standards. Finally, it bears repeating that, should Parliament once again decide to enact a procedural regime that is restricted in its application to the actual carrying out of law office searches, justices of the peace will accordingly remain charged with the obligation to protect solicitor-client privilege through application of the following principles that are related to the issuance of search warrants:

1. No search warrant can be issued with regards to documents that are known to be protected by solicitor-client privilege.
2. Before searching a law office, the investigative authorities must satisfy the issuing justice that there exists no other reasonable alternative to the search.
3. When allowing a law office to be searched, the issuing justice must be rigorously demanding so to afford maximum protection of solicitor-client confidentiality.
4. Except when the warrant specifically authorizes the immediate examination, copying and seizure of an identified document, all documents in possession of a lawyer must be sealed before being examined or removed from the lawyer's possession.
5. Every effort must be made to contact the lawyer and the client at the time of the execution of the search warrant. Where the lawyer or the client cannot be contacted, a representative of the Bar should be allowed to oversee the sealing and seizure of documents.
6. The investigative officer executing the warrant should report to the Justice of the Peace the efforts made to contact all potential privilege holders, who should then be given a reasonable opportunity to assert a claim of privilege and, if that claim is contested, to have the issue judicially decided.
7. If notification of potential privilege holders is not possible, the lawyer who had custody of the documents seized, or another lawyer appointed either by the Law Society or by the court, should examine the documents to determine whether a claim of privilege should be asserted, and should be given a reasonable opportunity to do so.
8. The Attorney General may make submissions on the issue of privilege, but should not be permitted to inspect the documents beforehand. The prosecuting authority can only inspect the documents if and when it is determined by a judge that the documents are not privileged.
9. Where sealed documents are found not to be privileged, they may be used in the normal course of the investigation.
10. Where documents are found to be privileged, they are to be returned immediately to the holder of the privilege, or to a person designated by the court.

Solicitor-client privilege is a rule of evidence, an important civil and legal right and a principle of fundamental justice in Canadian law. While the public has an interest in effective criminal investigation, it has no less an interest in maintaining the integrity of the solicitor-client relationship. Confidential communications to a lawyer represent an important exercise of the right to privacy, and they are central to the administration of justice in an adversarial system. Unjustified, or even accidental infringements of the privilege erode the public's confidence in the fairness of the criminal justice system. This is why all efforts must be made to protect such confidences.

[L'Heureux-Dubé, Gonthier and LeBel JJ. dissented.]

QUESTION

16. A client calls you to advise that a search is presently underway at his offices. His files contain correspondence between the two of you, and various memoranda prepared by your law student outlining the client's stated position on various issues and the strength of those positions. What do you do?

(g) Detention of Things Seized

Sections 487(1)(*e*), 489.1, 490, 490.1, 491, 491.1 and 492 of the *Criminal Code* regulate what must be done with things seized, whether pursuant to a warrant or otherwise, in execution of an officer's duties.[3] In essence, a peace officer is required to bring the seized things or report their seizure, as soon as it is practicable, to a justice of the peace who can order their continued detention or their return. Defence counsel need not be notified of this initial "return" hearing before the justice of the peace. Nothing shall be detained pursuant to an initial order of detention more than three months unless proceedings are commenced before the expiry of that period in which the seized things may be required or unless further detention orders, upon notice to the person from whom the things were seized, are made, or unless the lawful owner or person lawfully entitled to the things seized consents in writing to a further detention. An order which cumulatively causes the detention to exceed one year cannot be made by a justice or provincial court judge.

QUESTIONS

17. Review s. 490(15) of the *Criminal Code*. Can the Toronto Police Service show documents they seized to the Winnipeg Police Force if such documents appear to be relevant to their own investigation and also to criminal activity in Winnipeg, even if there is no application by the Winnipeg police for an order permitting them to examine the detained documents? Would your answer be the same or different if the F.B.I. were interested in the documents?

18. The accused is charged with an indictable offence. She is fingerprinted and photographed, as mandated by law. The charges are ultimately withdrawn. Can the police retain those fingerprints and photographs? If retained, can they be used against the accused in a later criminal trial? What section 8 *Charter* issue is engaged here? Consider, in this regard, *R. v. Dore* (2002), 166 C.C.C. (3d) 225 (Ont.C.A.).

---

[3] Where searches or seizures are effected pursuant to other legislation, or pursuant to a specific provision in the *Criminal Code*, there may be discrete statutory provisions that govern the detention, disposition, return or forfeiture of things seized. See, for example, s. 117.05 of the *Criminal Code* and ss. 13 to 29 of the *Controlled Drugs and Substance Act*. Counsel should also be familiar with Part XII.2 of the *Criminal Code*, which provides for the forfeiture of the proceeds of special offences, and special seizure and freezing orders which can be made in relation to those proceeds.

---

5. The Warrantless Search

As previously noted, warrantless searches are presumptively unreasonable. They may be authorized by statute or at common law. An attack upon a warrantless search may be predicated upon the invalidity of the law which purported to authorize it.

(a) Authorized by Statute

A statutory warrantless search power may not survive *Charter* scrutiny, or may be "read down" to survive such scrutiny. Sections 117.02(1), 117.03(1), 117.04(2), 199(2), 254(2),(3),(4), 339(3), 447(2) and 462(2) of the *Criminal Code* are examples of statutory warrantless search or seizure powers. Although the following case was decided under s. 10 of the *Narcotic Control Act* (replaced by the *Controlled Drugs and Substances Act*, S.C. 1996, c. 19), it remains instructive.

R. v. GRANT

(1993), 84 C.C.C. (3d) 173 (S.C.C.)

The judgment of the court was delivered by

Sopinka J.: — This narcotic search and seizure case concerns the constitutional legitimacy of the warrantless search of a place other than a dwelling-house and specifically whether s. 10 of the *Narcotic Control Act*, R.S.C. 1985, c. N-1 ("NCA") in so far as it authorizes warrantless searches of places other than dwelling-houses violates s. 8 of the *Canadian Charter of Rights and Freedoms*.

.....

(2) Constitutional limitations of s. 10

This issue is whether s. 10 authorizes unreasonable searches and seizures contrary to s. 8 of the *Charter* if it permits a warrantless search of private property absent exigent circumstances which would render it impracticable to obtain a warrant. As I have stated, the Attorney-General of Canada conceded that, to the extent that the section authorizes such a search in circumstances in which it is practicable to obtain a warrant, it should be read down. In my opinion, this was a proper concession on the part of the Crown. In this regard, I am in agreement with the conclusion reached by Martin J.A. in *R. v. Rao* (1984), 12 C.C.C. (3d) 97, 9 D.L.R. (4th) 542, 40 C.R. (3d) 1 (Ont. C.A.)...

.....

In *Hunter v. Southam Inc.* (1984), 14 C.C.C. (3d) 97, 11 D.L.R. (4th) 641, [1984] 2 S.C.R. 145, this court indicated that prior authorization was necessary to insure the broadest protection of s. 8 rights.

.....

Some exceptions have been developed with respect to the strict application of the requirement for prior authorization in *Hunter, supra*. In situations where an individual can be said to have a lower expectation of privacy, such as in passing through customs at border crossings (*R. v. Simmons* (1988), 45 C.C.C. (3d) 296, 55 D.L.R. (4th) 673, [1988] 2 S.C.R. 495), or where a search is conducted in connection with a known and ongoing regulatory scheme (*Thomson Newspapers Ltd. v. Canada (Director of Investigation and Research, Restrictive Trade Practices Commission)* (1990), 54 C.C.C. (3d) 417, 67 D.L.R. (4th) 161, [1990] 1 S.C.R. 425, and *R. v. McKinlay Transport Ltd.* (1990), 55 C.C.C. (3d) 530, 68 D.L.R. (4th) 568, [1990] 1 S.C.R. 627), this court has indicated that a less rigorous application of the pre-authorization criterion is appropriate. Nevertheless, this court remains vigilant with respect to searches conducted in relation to criminal investigations, given that the liberty of individuals is ultimately at stake: *Baron v. Canada* (1993), 78 C.C.C. (3d) 510, 99 D.L.R. (4th) 350, [1993] 1 S.C.R. 416. Furthermore, it was indicated in *Simmons, supra*, that exceptions to the general rule ought to remain "exceedingly rare" in the face of a strong common law rule against warrantless intrusions onto private property: *Eccles v. Bourque* (1974), 19 C.C.C. (2d) 129, 50 D.L.R. (3d) 753, [1975] 2 S.C.R. 739; *Colet v. The Queen* (1981), 57 C.C.C. (2d) 105, 119 D.L.R. (3d) 521, [1981] 1 S.C.R. 2.

The present searches arose in the context of criminal investigations and must be assessed in strict accordance with the approach set out in *Hunter, supra*, especially given the serious penal consequences which may flow from conviction for these offences pursuant to the *NCA* [*Narcotic Control Act*]. Cautious protection of the right against unreasonable search and seizure is also warranted in wake of the formidable search powers available to police pursuant to the *NCA*. Not only may police intrude into places where individuals may have very high expectations of privacy, officers may break down walls and doors, seize a wide variety of evidence and search the person of individuals found in the place searched: see ss. 10, 11 and 14 of the *NCA*.

.....

The second and third criteria identified in *Hunter*, namely, prior authorization by an independent and neutral arbiter and evidence on oath of the grounds for issuance of the warrant, are not a requirement under s. 10 and were clearly absent in the case at bar in relation to the perimeter searches.

This court has stated that in criminal proceedings, deviations from the *Hunter* standards will rarely be permitted. Nevertheless, warrantless searches of private property have on occasion been upheld by Canadian courts, including this court. In determining the extent of the constitutional validity of s. 10, it is necessary to balance two interests: the reasonable expectation of privacy of individuals with respect to the free enjoyment of property against the societal interest in effective law enforcement.

The common law has long demonstrated a respect for freedom from trespass on private property by state authorities, especially where the homes of individuals are involved. That respect for privacy in the home has been expanded by this court to include other areas in which individuals expect a high degree of privacy, including the office (*Hunter*, *supra*) and to a lesser degree even a motor vehicle in some cases: see *R. v. Wise* (1992), 70 C.C.C. (3d) 193, [1992] 1 S.C.R. 527, 11 C.R. (4th) 253, and *R. v. Mellenthin* (1992), 76 C.C.C. (3d) 481, [1992] 3 S.C.R. 615, 16 C.R. (4th) 273. Protection against unreasonable search and seizure is maximized by the requirement that entries by state authorities be pre-authorized by a judicial arbiter. On the other hand, this court must also consider the societal interest in law enforcement, especially with regard to the illicit drug trade. This pernicious scourge in our society permits sophisticated criminals to profit by inflicting suffering on others. In attempting to strike a balance between these two sets of interests, I have concluded that warrantless searches pursuant to s. 10 of the NCA must be limited to situations in which exigent circumstances render obtaining a warrant impracticable. Warrantless searches conducted under any other circumstances will be considered unreasonable and will necessarily violate s. 8 of the *Charter*. To the extent that s. 10 of the *NCA* authorizes a search in the absence of the limiting circumstances, it is invalid. In these circumstances, it is unnecessary to consider s. 1: see *Baron*, *supra*, at p. 535.

This exception to the general rule which proscribes warrantless searches must be narrowly construed. In general, the test will only be satisfied where there exists an imminent danger of the loss, removal, destruction or disappearance of the evidence sought in a narcotics investigation if the search or seizure is delayed in order to obtain a warrant: see *R. v. D. (I.D.)* (1987), 38 C.C.C. (3d) 289, 61 C.R. (3d) 292, 33 C.R.R. 348, *per* Sherstobitoff J.A.

Exigent circumstances will often be created by the presence of narcotics on a moving conveyance such as a motor vehicle, a water vessel or aircraft. However, I do not favour a blanket exception for this species of private property. Such an exception does exist under the American Constitution. In *Rao*, *supra*, Martin J.A. pointed out the justification for the American exception was that vehicles, vessels and aircraft may move away quickly and frustrate an investigation. While I accept this fact, I must also be mindful of the fact that this court has recognized the existence of an expectation of privacy in respect of motor vehicles, albeit on a lower scale than that which exists in relation to a dwelling or a private office. In *Wise*, *supra*, the installation of a tracking device in a motor vehicle was held to be an unreasonable search in circumstances in which it would have been practicable for the police to have obtained a search warrant. The capability of these conveyances to move rapidly away will not in all circumstances create a situation in which it is impracticable to obtain a warrant and in which the criteria I have set out above will be present...

.....

To sum up on this point, s. 10 may validly authorize a search or seizure without warrant in exigent circumstances which render it impracticable to obtain a warrant. Exigent circumstances will generally be held to exist if there is an imminent danger of the loss, removal, destruction or disappearance of the evidence if the search or seizure is delayed. While the fact that the evidence sought is believed to be present on a motor vehicle, water vessel, aircraft or other fast moving vehicle will often create exigent circumstances, no blanket exception exists for such conveyances.

To the extent that s. 10 purports to authorize searches and seizures on a wider basis, it is in breach of s. 8 of the *Charter* and inoperable. It is necessary to consider next what the appropriate remedy should be.

.....

(3) Remedy

In *Schachter v. Canada* (1992), 93 D.L.R. (4th) 1 at p. 11, [1992] 2 S.C.R. 679, 92 C.L.L.C. 14,036, Lamer C.J.C., for the court, set out the range of remedies and the basic approach to their selection:

> A court has flexibility in determining what course of action to take following a violation of the *Charter* which does not survive s. 1 scrutiny. Section 52 of the *Constitution Act, 1982* mandates the striking down of any law that is inconsistent with the provisions of the Constitution, but only "to the extent of the inconsistency". Depending upon the circumstances, a court may simply strike down, it may strike down and temporarily suspend the declaration of invalidity, or it may resort to the techniques of reading down or reading in... In choosing how to apply s. 52 ... a court will determine its course of action with reference to the nature of the violation and the context of the specific legislation under consideration.

The Crown has admitted that s. 10 of the *NCA* is unreasonable in so far as it authorizes warrantless searches of places other than a dwelling-house in circumstances in which it would be practicable to obtain a warrant. The Crown further suggested that the appropriate remedy in the circumstances would be to "read down" s. 10 so as not to authorize warrantless searches where it is feasible to obtain a warrant. I am satisfied that this remedy is the appropriate one considering that the concerns generally associated with "reading down" do not arise in the case at bar. In this regard, I find the reasoning of Martin J.A. in the following passage in *Rao*, *supra*, persuasive (at p. 125):

> I have, for the reasons which I have set forth, concluded that the search of an office without a warrant where the obtaining of a warrant is not impracticable, is unreasonable and, to that extent, s. 10(1)(*a*) [now s. 10] is of no force or effect. On the other hand, the search of an office without a warrant in circumstances where it is not practicable to obtain a warrant may be entirely reasonable. Further, a warrantless search of vehicles, vessels or aircraft, which may move quickly away, may be reasonable where there are reasonable grounds for believing that such contains a narcotic.
>
> Section 10(1)(*a*) does not, on its face, necessarily clash with s. 8 of the *Charter* although in some circumstances a warrantless search authorized by that subsection may, in fact, infringe the constitutional requirement of reasonableness secured by s. 8 of the *Charter*, depending upon the circumstances surrounding the particular search. The statute is inoperative to the extent that it authorizes an unreasonable search.

Appeal allowed; new trial ordered.

QUESTION

19. **Section 32(5) of the *Liquor Licence Act*, R.S.O. 1990, c. L.19, allows a police officer who, having reasonable grounds to believe liquor is being unlawfully kept in a vehicle, to search the vehicle and its occupants. Does this authorization give the officer *carte blanche* to search everything inside the vehicle? What if drugs are hidden in a cigarette package inside the vehicle? Does the *Liquor Licence Act* authorize searches of this nature? Consider *R. v. Annett* (1986), 17 C.C.C. (3d) 332 (Ont. C.A.), and *R. v. Bennett*, [2001] O.J. No. 436 (C.J.).**

(b) Authorized at Common Law

(i) Search Incidental to Lawful Arrest

The most significant common law power to search is the power to search incidental to a lawful arrest.

CLOUTIER v. LANGLOIS

(1990), 53 C.C.C. (3d) 257 (S.C.C.)

The judgment of the court was delivered by

L'Heureux-Dubé J.: — This appeal raises squarely, for the first time in this court the question of the existence and scope of the power of the police to search a person who has been lawfully arrested.

.....

In general, despite certain comments in scholarly discussion, it seems beyond question that the common law as recognized and developed in Canada holds that the police have a power to search a lawfully arrested person and to seize anything in his or her possession or immediate surroundings to guarantee the safety of the police and the accused, prevent the prisoner's escape or provide evidence against him. The common thread in this line of authority is the objective of guaranteeing safety and applying the law effectively. While the existence of the power is accepted, there seems to be some uncertainty as to its scope. While at common law the British courts did not impose reasonable grounds as a prerequisite to the power to search a person lawfully arrested, neither have they gone so far as to recognize a power to search as a simple corollary of arrest. The Canadian courts on the other hand do not seem to have hesitated in adopting this latter approach.

.....

As we have seen, the common law gave the police only such powers as were consistent with the protection of individual rights. The courts have always held that a proper balance between these two fundamental components is vital, as illustrated by the observations of Williams J. in 1853 in *Leigh v. Cole* [(1853), 6 Cox C.C. 329] (at pp. 330-1):

> On one hand, it is clear that the police ought to be fully protected in the discharge of an onerous, arduous, and difficult duty — a duty necessary for the comfort and security of the community. On the other hand, it is equally incumbent on every one engaged in the administration of justice, to take care that the powers necessarily entrusted to the police are not made an instrument of oppression or of tyranny towards even the meanest, most depraved, and basest subjects of the realm.

In this regard a "frisk" search is a relatively non-intrusive procedure: outside clothing is patted down to determine whether there is anything on the person of the arrested individual. Pockets may be examined but the clothing is not removed and no physical force is applied. The duration of the search is only a few seconds. Though the search, if conducted, is in addition to the arrest, which generally entails a considerably longer and more sustained loss of freedom and dignity, a brief search does not constitute, in view of the objectives sought, a disproportionate interference with the freedom of persons lawfully arrested. There exists no less intrusive means of attaining these objectives.

A "frisk" search incidental to a lawful arrest reconciles the public's interest in the effective and safe enforcement of the law on the one hand, and on the other its interest in ensuring the freedom and dignity of individuals. The minimal intrusion involved in the search is necessary to ensure that criminal justice is properly administered. I agree with the opinion of the Ontario Court of Appeal as stated in *R. v. Brezack* [(1949), 96 C.C.C. 97, [1950] 2 D.L.R. 265], *R. v. Morrison* [1987], 20 O.A.C. 230] and *R. v. Miller* [(1949), 96 C.C.C. 97] that the existence of reasonable and probable grounds is not a prerequisite to the existence of a police power to search. The exercise of this power is not, however, unlimited. Three propositions can be derived from the authorities and a consideration of the underlying interests.

1. This power does not impose a duty. The police have some discretion in conducting the search. Where they are satisfied that the law can be effectively and safely applied without a search, the police may see fit not to conduct a search. They must be in a position to assess the circumstances of each case so as to determine whether a search meets the underlying objectives.
2. The search must be for a valid objective in pursuit of the ends of criminal justice, such as the discovery of an object that may be a threat to the safety of the police, the accused or the public, or that may facilitate escape or act as evidence against the accused. The purpose of the search must not be unrelated to the objectives of the proper administration of justice, which would be the case, for example, if the purpose of the search was to intimidate, ridicule or pressure the accused in order to obtain admissions.
3. The search must not be conducted in an abusive fashion and, in particular, the use of physical or psychological constraint should be proportionate to the objectives sought and the other circumstances of the situation.

A search which does not meet these objectives could be characterized as unreasonable and unjustified at common law.

See also *R. v. Stillman* (1997), 144 D.L.R. (4th) 193 (S.C.C.), substantially reproduced at p. 438.

QUESTIONS

20. **Suppose an accused is arrested while in his car for possession and trafficking of marijuana. The car is impounded by the police. Pursuant to police policy, the arresting officers enter the car at the police pound to take inventory of the items found inside. This is intended to safeguard the owner's valuables and permit an accurate notation of the car's condition. While taking inventory, the officers find $1,400 in cash and individual packages of cocaine. Is this search an infringement of the accused's s. 8 *Charter* rights? Does it matter that the officer was not searching for evidence? Conversely, could this be said to be a search incidental to arrest? Consider *R. v. Caslake* (1998), 121 C.C.C. (3d) 97 (S.C.C.).**

21. **Based upon surveillance, the police believe on reasonable grounds that Joe Suspect is in possession of heroin. They approach him and search him. They find a debt list and a small plastic bag containing heroin. They arrest him for possession of heroin for the purpose of trafficking. Can the search be justified as incidental to arrest? Assuming it can be so justified, when do the police advise the accused of his right to counsel without delay, before or after the search? Consider, in this regard, *R. v. Debot* (1986), 30 C.C.C. (3d) 207 (Ont. C.A.); affd (1989), 52 C.C.C. (3d) 193 (S.C.C.), partially reproduced on another issue at p. 119.**

22. **The accused is arrested at the front door of his residence and charged with theft of multiple Canada Savings Bonds. Only some of the bonds have been recovered. Can the accused's person be searched incidental to arrest? Can his entire house be searched? Can his vehicle in the driveway be searched? Assume he was arrested at his mother's house. Can the police then go to his house and search it, incidental to the arrest? Consider, in this regard, *R. v. Caslake* (1998), 121 C.C.C. (3d) 97 (S.C.C.); *R. v. Charlton* (1992), 16 W.C.B. (2d) 423, 15 B.C.A.C. 272 (C.A.); *R. v. Ewart* (1995), 27 W.C.B. (2d) 7, 58 B.C.A.C. 70 (C.A.); *R. v. Paul* (1994), 95 C.C.C. (3d) 266 (N.B.C.A.); *R. v. Garcia* (1992), 72 C.C.C. (3d) 240 (Que. C.A.); *R. v. Smellie* (1994), 95 C.C.C. (3d) 9 (B.C.C.A.); leave to appeal to S.C.C. refused June 8, 1995.**

23. **The accused is arrested for break and enter. He is transported in custody to jail. The officer notes that the accused has a fresh, fairly clean bandage on his right wrist. The next day, the officer realizes that the bandage could provide evidence, since entry to the premises was gained through a broken window, beside which was a trail of blood, samples of which were taken. The accused is still in custody. How, if at all, can the officer obtain the bandage as evidence? Consider, in this regard, *R. v. Miller* (1987), 38 C.C.C. (3d) 252 (Ont. C.A.); *R. v. Tomaso* (1989), 70 C.R. (3d) 152 (Ont. C.A.); *R. v. Stillman* (1997), 144 D.L.R. (4th) 193 (S.C.C.).**

When are strip searches authorized as incidental to arrest? Consider the following case.

R. v. GOLDEN

(2001), 159 C.C.C. (3d) 449 (S.C.C.)

[One of the officers at an observation post in an unoccupied building across from a sandwich shop observed Golden, who was in the shop, conduct two transactions in which persons entered the shop and received a substance from Golden. The officer testified that given the place where this transaction occurred, the manner in which it took place and the colour of the substance, he believed the substance was cocaine and that Golden was trafficking in drugs, and he instructed the take-down officers to arrest Golden. During the arrests, the police found what they believed to be crack cocaine under the table where one of the suspects was arrested, and Golden was observed crushing what appeared to be crack cocaine between his fingers. Following the arrests, a police officer conducted a "pat down" search of Golden and did not find any weapons or narcotics. The officer then decided to conduct a visual inspection of Golden's underwear and buttocks on the landing at the top of the stairwell leading to a basement, where public washrooms were located. The officer undid Golden's pants and pulled them back along with Golden's long underwear. The officer saw a clear plastic wrap protruding from between Golden's buttocks, as well as a white substance within the wrap. The officer tried to retrieve the plastic wrap, but Golden "hip-checked" and scratched him. Golden was then escorted to a seating booth at the back of the shop. The officers forced him to bend over a table, and his pants were lowered to his knees, and his underwear was pulled down. The officers tried to seize the package from his buttocks, but were unsuccessful. Following these attempts, Golden accidentally defecated; however, the package did not dislodge. An officer then retrieved a pair of rubber dishwashing gloves and again tried to remove the package while Golden was face-down on the floor, with another officer holding down his feet. Finally, the officer was able to remove the package once Golden unclenched his muscles. It contained 10.1 grams of crack cocaine. Golden was placed under arrest for possession of a narcotic for the purpose of trafficking, and for assaulting police. Golden was again searched at the police station.]

Iacobucci and Arbour JJ. [Major, Binnie and LeBel JJ. concurring]: —

.....

The appellant submits that the term "strip search" is properly defined as follows: the removal or rearrangement of some or all of the clothing of a person so as to permit a visual inspection of a person's private areas, namely genitals, buttocks, breasts (in the case of a female), or undergarments.

.....

Applying this definition of strip search to the facts, the appellant was subjected to three strip searches in the present case. The first strip search occurred in the stairwell when Constable Ryan undid the appellant's trousers, pulled back the long underwear the appellant was wearing and looked down the long underwear at the appellant's buttocks. The second strip search occurred in the back of the restaurant at which point the appellant's pants and underwear were pulled down to his knees while the officers tried to seize the package from between the appellant's buttocks. This second strip search also involved the police officers using rubber dish gloves to forcibly remove the package containing the cocaine from between the appellant's buttocks. This physical contact with the appellant's buttocks in the course of the second strip search places this search farther along on the spectrum of intrusiveness than the first search, although on the evidence it falls short of being a body cavity search. The third strip search occurred at the police station.

.....

It is clear that the common law in Canada recognizes the power of police to search a lawfully arrested person for the purpose of seizing weapons or evidence that may be in his possession (*Cloutier* [(1990), 53 C.C.C. (3d) 257 (S.C.C.)], at pp. 180-81). What is not clear, however, and what must be decided in this case, is the scope of this power to search incident to arrest. Specifically, does the common law authorize strip searches and, if it does, are there any restrictions at common law on the power to conduct such searches? In considering whether the common law in Canada authorizes strip searches carried out as an incident to arrest and, if so, whether the common law is consistent with s. 8 of the *Charter*, it is helpful to review the law concerning warrantless personal searches in the United Kingdom and the United States as well as the case authorities in Canada both before and after the enactment of the *Charter*.

[Iacobucci and Arbour JJ. reviewed the relevant authorities.]

.....

(d) The Preconditions of a Lawful Strip Search Incident to Arrest at Common Law

The appellant's position is that, given the negative impact of a strip search on an individual's privacy interests and psychological well-being, s. 8 should demand that at least probable cause be required to authorize strip searches and, absent exigent circumstances, a warrant. The intervener African Canadian Legal Clinic (ACLC) agrees with the appellant that probable cause and a warrant requirement should be required for strip searches to be constitutional under s. 8 of the *Charter*. The ACLC says that given the negative stereotyping of African Canadians by police and the large number of African Canadians who are stopped and searched by police, a public process of obtaining a warrant is required to reduce the danger of racist stereotyping by individual police officers, who are more likely than a neutral arbiter to conclude that a strip search of a black person is appropriate. The intervener Aboriginal Legal Services of Toronto (ALST) also advocates a regime of prior authorization for strip searches and submits that the common law does not authorize warrantless strip searches except in the most exceptional circumstances, such as where there is an immediate threat to the safety of police and the public or a threat of immediate destruction of evidence. For its part, the intervener Canadian Civil Liberties Association proposes three limits on strip searches incident to arrest: (1) strip searches should be prohibited when less intrusive investigative steps are available; (2) police must have reasonable grounds to conduct strip searches, and (3) prior authorization in the form of a warrant should be required except in rare exigent circumstances.

The respondent's position is that the common law authorizes strip searches and is reasonable within the meaning of s. 8. The respondent says that the restrictions on searches outlined by this Court in *Cloutier, supra*, and *Stillman* [(1997), 113 C.C.C. (3d) 321 (S.C.C.)], are adequate to ensure that strip searches incident to arrest meet the requirements of s. 8. The interveners Attorney General for Ontario and the Canadian Association of Chiefs of Police both agree with the respondent that the common law authorizes strip searches and is reasonable.

While the respondent and the interveners for the Crown sought to downplay the intrusiveness of strip searches, in our view it is unquestionable that they represent a significant invasion of privacy and are often a humiliating, degrading and traumatic experience for individuals subject to them. Clearly, the negative effects of a strip search can be minimized by the way in which they are carried out, but even the most sensitively conducted strip search is highly intrusive. Furthermore, we believe it is important to note the submissions of the ACLC and the ALST that African Canadians and Aboriginal people are overrepresented in the criminal justice system and are therefore likely to represent a disproportionate number of those who are arrested by police and subjected to personal searches, including strip searches (*Report of the Aboriginal Justice Inquiry of Manitoba* (1991), Vol. 1 [The Justice System and Aboriginal People], at p. 107; The Cawsey Report, *Justice on Trial: Report of the Task Force on the Criminal Justice System and its Impact on the Indian and Metis People of Alberta* (1991), Vol. II [p. 7, recommendations] 2.48 to 2.50; Royal Commission on Aboriginal Peoples, *Bridging the Cultural Divide* (1996), at [pp.] 33-39; Commission on Systemic Racism in the Ontario Criminal Justice System, *Report of the Commission on Systemic Racism in the Ontario Criminal Justice System* (1995)). As a result, it is necessary to develop an appropriate framework governing strip searches in order to prevent unnecessary and unjustified strip searches before they occur.

.....

Strip searches are ... inherently humiliating and degrading for detainees regardless of the manner in which they are carried out and for this reason they cannot be carried out simply as a matter of routine policy. The adjectives used by individuals to describe their experience of being strip searched give some sense of how a strip search, even one that is carried out in a reasonable manner, can affect detainees: "humiliating", "degrading", "demeaning", "upsetting", and "devastating" (see *King* [[1999] O.J. No. 565 (Gen. Div)]; *R. v. Christopher*, [1994] O.J. No. 3120 (QL) (Gen. Div.); J. S. Lyons, Toronto Police Services Board Review, "The Search of Persons Policy — The Search of Persons — A Position Paper" (April 12, 1999)). Some commentators have gone as far as to describe strip searches as "visual rape" (Paul Shuldiner, "Visual Rape: A Look at the Dubious Legality of Strip Searches" (1979), 13 J. Marshall L. Rev. 273). Women and minorities in particular may have a real fear of strip searches and may experience such a search as equivalent to a sexual assault (*Lyons, supra*, at p. 4). The psychological effects of strip searches may also be particularly traumatic for individuals who have previously been subject to abuse (Commission of Inquiry into Certain Events at the Prison for Women in Kingston [*The Prison for Women in Kingston*] (1996), at pp. 86-89). Routine strip searches may also be distasteful and difficult for the police officers conducting them (*Lyons, supra*, at pp. 5-6).

In order for a strip search to be justified as an incident to arrest, it is of course necessary that the arrest itself be lawful. In the present case, there is no question that the arrest was lawful. While the appellant disputes the lawfulness of arrest, the trial judge and the Court of Appeal concluded that there were reasonable and probable grounds for making the arrest, and we see no reason to dispute this conclusion. Thus, the first requirement of a valid search incident to arrest was met in this case.

The second requirement before a strip search incident to arrest may be performed is that the search must be *incident* to the arrest. What this means is that the search must be related to the reasons for the arrest itself. As expressed by Lamer C.J. in *Caslake* [(1998) 121 C.C.C. (3d) 97 (S.C.C.)], at para. 17, a search "is only justifiable if the purpose of the search is related to the purpose of the arrest". In the present case, the strip search was related to the purpose of the arrest. The arrest was for drug trafficking and the purpose of the search was to discover illegal drugs secreted on the appellant's person. Had the appellant been arrested for a different reason, such as for a traffic violation, the common law would not have conferred on the police the authority to conduct a strip search for drugs, even if the police had knowledge of previous involvement in drug-related offences, since the reason for the search would have been unrelated to the purpose of the arrest. In the circumstances of the present case, we conclude that the search was conducted incident to the arrest.

The reasonableness of a search for evidence is governed by the need to preserve the evidence and to prevent its disposal by the arrestee. Where arresting officers suspect that evidence may have been secreted on areas of the body that can only be exposed by a strip search, the risk of disposal must be reasonably assessed in the circumstances. For instance, in the present case, it was suggested that the appellant might have dropped the drugs on the sidewalk or in the police cruiser on the way to the station and that it was therefore necessary to search him in the field. As we discuss below, however, the risk of his disposing of the evidence on the way to the police station was low and, had the evidence been dropped in the police cruiser on the way to the station, circumstantial evidence could easily link it back to the accused.

In addition to searching for evidence related to the reason for the arrest, the common law also authorizes police to search for weapons as an incident to arrest for the purpose of ensuring the safety of the police, the detainee and other persons. However, a "frisk" or "pat-down" search at the point of arrest will generally suffice for the purposes of determining if the accused has secreted weapons on his person. Only if the frisk search reveals a possible weapon secreted on the detainee's person or if the particular circumstances of the case raise the risk that a weapon is concealed on the detainee's person will a strip search be justified. Whether searching for evidence or for weapons, the mere possibility that an individual may be concealing evidence or weapons upon his person is not sufficient to justify a strip search.

The requirement that the strip search be for evidence related to the grounds for the arrest or for weapons reflects the twin rationales for the common law power of search incident to arrest. Strip searches cannot be carried out as a matter of routine police department policy applicable to all arrestees, whether they are arrested for impaired driving, public drunkenness, shoplifting or trafficking in narcotics. The fact that a strip search is conducted as a matter of routine policy and is carried out in a reasonable manner does not render the search reasonable within the meaning of s. 8 of the *Charter*. A strip search will always be unreasonable if it is carried out abusively or for the purpose of humiliating or punishing the arrestee. Yet a "routine" strip search carried out in good faith and without violence will also violate s. 8 where there is no compelling reason for performing a strip search in the circumstances of the arrest.

.....

The fact that the police have reasonable and probable grounds to carry out an arrest does not confer upon them the automatic authority to carry out a strip search, even where the strip search meets the definition of being "incident to lawful arrest" as discussed above. Rather, additional grounds pertaining to the purpose of the strip search are required. In *Cloutier, supra*, this Court concluded that a common law search incident to arrest does not require additional grounds beyond the reasonable and probable grounds necessary to justify the lawfulness of the arrest itself: *Cloutier, supra*, at pp. 185-86. However, this conclusion was reached in the context of a "frisk" search, which involved a minimal invasion of the detainee's privacy and personal integrity. In contrast, a strip search is a much more intrusive search and, accordingly, a higher degree of justification is required in order to support the higher degree of interference with individual freedom and dignity. In order to meet the constitutional standard of reasonableness that will justify a strip search, the police must establish that they have reasonable and probable grounds for concluding that a strip search is necessary in the particular circumstances of the arrest.

In light of the serious infringement of privacy and personal dignity that is an inevitable consequence of a strip search, such searches are only constitutionally valid at common law where they are conducted as an incident to a lawful arrest for the purpose of discovering weapons in the detainee's possession or evidence related to the reason for the arrest. In addition, the police must establish reasonable and probable grounds justifying the strip search in addition to reasonable and probable grounds justifying the arrest. Where these preconditions to conducting a strip search incident to arrest are met, it is also necessary that the strip search be conducted in a manner that does not infringe s. 8 of the *Charter*.

.....

In this connection, we find the guidelines contained in the English legislation, P.A.C.E. concerning the conduct of strip searches to be in accordance with the constitutional requirements of s. 8 of the *Charter*. The following questions, which draw upon the common law principles as well as the statutory requirements set out in the English legislation, provide a framework for the police in deciding how best to conduct a strip search incident to arrest in compliance with the *Charter*:

1. Can the strip search be conducted at the police station and, if not, why not?
2. Will the strip search be conducted in a manner that ensures the health and safety of all involved?
3. Will the strip search be authorized by a police officer acting in a supervisory capacity?
4. Has it been ensured that the police officer(s) carrying out the strip search are of the same gender as the individual being searched?
5. Will the number of police officers involved in the search be no more than is reasonably necessary in the circumstances?
6. What is the minimum of force necessary to conduct the strip search?
7. Will the strip search be carried out in a private area such that no one other than the individuals engaged in the search can observe the search?
8. Will the strip search be conducted as quickly as possible and in a way that ensures that the person is not completely undressed at any one time?
9. Will the strip search involve only a visual inspection of the arrestee's genital and anal areas without any physical contact?
10. If the visual inspection reveals the presence of a weapon or evidence in a body cavity (not including the mouth), will the detainee be given the option of removing the object himself or of having the object removed by a trained medical professional?
11. Will a proper record be kept of the reasons for and the manner in which the strip search was conducted?

Strip searches should generally only be conducted at the police station except where there are exigent circumstances requiring that the detainee be searched prior to being transported to the police station. Such exigent circumstances will only be established where the police have reasonable and probable grounds to believe that it is necessary to conduct the search in the field rather than at the police station. Strip searches conducted in the field could only be justified where there is a demonstrated necessity and urgency to search for weapons or objects that could be used to threaten the safety of the accused, the arresting officers or other individuals. The police would also have to show why it would have been unsafe to wait and conduct the strip search at the police station rather than in the field. Strip searches conducted in the field represent a much greater invasion of privacy and pose a greater threat to the detainee's bodily integrity and, for this reason, field strip searches can only be justified in exigent circumstances.

Having said all this, we believe that legislative intervention could be an important addition to the guidance set out in these reasons concerning the conduct of strip searches incident to arrest. Clear legislative prescription as to when and how strip searches should be conducted would be of assistance to the police and to the courts.

.....

In this appeal, the Crown has failed to prove that the strip search of the appellant was carried out in a reasonable manner. More specifically, the evidence adduced at trial fell far short of establishing that a situation of exigency existed so as to warrant a strip search outside of the police station.

[Iacobucci and Arbour JJ. explained how in the circumstances, the Crown's submissions on the exigency created by the potential loss of evidence were unpersuasive.]

.....

Other than Constable Ryan's personal experience, the arresting officers had no reasonable and probable basis for conducting the strip search in the restaurant. No information was given to them by Constable Theriault that the appellant had reached into his pants to remove any substances, nor had they ever witnessed such conduct themselves. There was no bulging or protrusion in the appellant's buttock area to suggest that he was concealing evidence. In the result, the decision to strip search was premised largely on a single officer's hunch, arising from a handful of personal experiences. These circumstances, coupled with the absence of exigency discussed above, compel us to conclude that the police officers' decision to strip search the appellant in the restaurant was unreasonable.

Having so concluded, we should note, however, that there was some evidence suggesting the possibility of concealment of narcotics. The appellant was arrested for trafficking after police observed him engage in two transactions involving what they believed was a narcotic substance. Further, the arresting officers found what they thought was crack cocaine under the table where another suspect was arrested. Constable Ryan also observed the appellant crushing a substance that looked like crack cocaine between his fingers during the arrest. Finally, Constable Ryan did have some experience, albeit in relatively few cases, with drug arrests involving suspects who secreted evidence in their groin or buttock areas.

Taken together, these circumstances would have been sufficient to create reasonable and probable grounds to conduct a strip search of the appellant at the police station. However, by deciding to carry out the strip search in a public restaurant rather than the nearby station house, without appropriate safeguards in place, the police failed to meet a condition essential to the validity of such an intrusive, warrantless search. There were no reasonable and probable grounds to believe that this strip search had to be conducted with such urgency.

In addition, the manner in which the strip search was conducted in the restaurant did not comply with the requirements of reasonableness contained in s. 8 of the *Charter*. The appellant was not given the opportunity to remove his own clothing, a measure that might have reduced the sense of panic he clearly experienced. Rather, Constable Ryan pulled back the appellant's pants and underwear during the initial part of the search in the stairwell. He and Constable Powell then lowered the appellant's pants and underwear after the appellant was brought back into the main area of the restaurant. Also, the strip search was conducted without notice to, or authorization from, a senior officer. The decision to search the appellant was made unilaterally by the arresting officers, in particular, by Constable Ryan. Finally, the search was carried out in a manner that may have jeopardized the appellant's health and safety.

Where the circumstances of a search require the seizure of material located in or near a body cavity, the individual being searched should be given the opportunity to remove the material himself or the advice and assistance of a trained medical professional should be sought to ensure that the material can be safely removed. In this case, the plastic wrap was located between the appellant's buttocks. The police had no way of knowing whether it was physically lodged inside him in such a way that it could not be safely retrieved without medical intervention. Nevertheless, the arresting officers undertook to remove the package themselves, through physical coercion and forceful probing and tugging at the package, and by instructing the appellant to "let it out" and to "relax". The risk this presented to the appellant's health was made more acute by the fact that after the appellant accidentally defecated, Constable Powell retrieved a pair of rubber gloves that had been used for cleaning the shop's washrooms and toilets to continue in his attempts at dislodging the package. The entire episode created as well unsanitary conditions in a public restaurant, which would have been avoided had the search been conducted in a less precipitous manner.

The relevance of the appellant's resistance to the search also merits comment. At the *voir dire* hearing, McNeely J. held that had the appellant "relaxed and not attempted to retain the substance", the search would have been shorter and less intrusive. The respondent endorsed McNeely J.'s reasoning, relying on the British Columbia Court of Appeal's decision in *R. v. Garcia-Guiterrez* (1991), 5 C.R. (4th) 1, 65 C.C.C. (3d) 15. In that case, police observed the accused reach into his mouth, remove something and give it to another person, who gave the accused money in return. After arresting the accused for possession of cocaine for the purpose of trafficking, an officer grabbed his throat to prevent him from swallowing and breathing, and instructed him to open his mouth. The accused refused and a second officer punched him in the stomach. A majority of the Court of Appeal held that the search was reasonable, as it was found necessary to preserve the evidence. In this regard, Macdonald J.A. held (at para. 17) that the accused was "in complete control" of the violence inflicted upon him, since, had he simply opened his mouth, the police would have ceased applying physical force.

We particularly disagree with the suggestion that an arrested person's non-cooperation and resistance necessarily entitles police to engage in behaviour that disregards or compromises his or her physical and psychological integrity and safety. If the general approach articulated in this case is not followed, such that the search is unreasonable, there is no requirement that anyone cooperate with the violation of his or her *Charter* rights. Any application of force or violence must be both necessary and proportional in the specific circumstances. In this case, the appellant's refusal to relinquish the evidence does not justify or mitigate the fact that he was strip searched in a public place, and in a manner that showed considerable disregard for his dignity and his physical integrity, despite the absence of reasonable and probable grounds or exigent circumstances.

In light of the foregoing reasons, we conclude that the manner in which the strip search in this case was conducted was unreasonable. It therefore amounted to a breach of the appellant's constitutional guarantees under s. 8 of the *Charter*.

[Bastarache J. dissented with McLachlin C.J.C., Gonthier and L'Heureux-Dubé JJ. concurring.]

QUESTION

24. **The accused are teenagers who have no prior criminal records. They turn themselves in at the police station in the company of their parents. The police strip search them upon arrest. Is a strip search always justified when an accused is placed in a cell with other inmates? If not, what remedy might be available, where the strip search yielded no evidence? Consider, in this regard, *R. v. F.(S.)*, [2003] O.J. No. 92 (C.J.).**

(ii) Consensual Search

R. v. BORDEN

(1994), 92 C.C.C. (3d) 404 (S.C.C.)

[The accused was arrested for the sexual assault of a dancer. There was no intercourse alleged. The dancer knew and could identify the accused. The police suspected that he had sexually assaulted an elderly woman two months earlier. This assault did involve sexual intercourse and semen samples had been taken from the scene and preserved. After being advised of his right to counsel and being given a standard police caution, the accused gave an exculpatory statement to the police about the sexual assault of the dancer. The police then sought a blood sample from him. They wanted to compare it with the semen sample using DNA profiling. The accused was not told this, though he signed a consent to the taking of a blood sample "for the purposes relating to their investigations." (note emphasis on plural) The results of the DNA testing implicated the accused who was convicted at trial. An acquittal was entered on appeal to the Nova Scotia Court of Appeal. A Crown appeal to the Supreme Court of Canada was dismissed.]

[The majority judgment of the court was delivered by:]

Iacobucci J. [La Forest, Sopinka, Gonthier and Major JJ. concurring]: —

.....

Section 8

I agree with the conclusion of the trial judge on the *voir dire* and of the majority of the Court of Appeal that the respondent's s. 8 right to be secure against unreasonable search and seizure was violated. The police do not possess the statutory authority to demand or take a blood sample from a person charged with the offence of sexual assault. For the taking of the blood of the respondent in this case to be valid, the police required his consent. The police did obtain a lawful and valid informed consent from the respondent in relation to the taking of his blood for use in the investigation of the motel offence, for which he had been arrested. This fact led

Freeman J.A., in dissent, to conclude that there was no s. 8 infringement in this case, and that the respondent had to prove a breach of another *Charter* section.

I disagree. While it is true that the infringement of s. 8 of the *Charter* alleged in this case comes from the same source as the alleged s. 10 infringements, that is, the failure of the police to inform the respondent of their predominant purpose in seeking the blood sample, I am of the view that the respondent has demonstrated an infringement of s. 8 which is independent from the s. 10(*a*) and (*b*) claims.

The jurisprudence of this court indicates that a seizure occurs whenever there is a non-consensual taking of an item by the state in respect of which the citizen has a reasonable expectation of privacy: *R. v. Dyment* (1988), 45 C.C.C. (3d) 244 at pp. 257-8 and 259-60, 55 D.L.R. (4th) 503, [1988] 2 S.C.R. 417. The words of La Forest J. at p. 257 of that decision, are apposite:

> There was no consent to the taking of the blood sample in this case; Mr. Dyment was unconscious at the time. But even if he had given his consent, I do not think it would have mattered if the consent was restricted to the use of the sample for medical purposes... As I have attempted to indicate earlier, the use of a person's body without his consent to obtain information about him, invades an area of personal privacy essential to the maintenance of his human dignity.

Obviously a person does not cease to have a reasonable expectation of privacy in his or her blood at any time while that blood is still inside his or her body. In this case the taking of the sample, with consent, for use in the investigation of the motel offence, was coincident with its taking for use in the investigation of the October sexual assault. The officers testified that they had every intention of using the sample for the investigation of both crimes, and that the October offence was their main focus. They sought advice on how to ensure that they could use the sample for both purposes, and deliberately used broad language on the consent form, including the word "investigations" in the plural. The seizure of the blood for use in the present appeal was effected simultaneously with its seizure for use in the motel offence.

Therefore, the relevant time for assessing whether there was a seizure in relation to this appeal was at the time the sample was first taken. At that time, the respondent had an expectation of privacy with respect to his bodily integrity and the informational content of his blood. It must, therefore, be shown that the taking of the sample in respect of this appeal was accompanied by his consent. In the absence of such consent, there was a seizure, and its reasonableness must be scrutinized to determine whether s. 8 of the *Charter* was violated.

As noted above, the consent for the taking of the sample in relation to the motel offence was, on its own, a valid one. The issue, then, is whether the respondent also consented to a seizure of his blood in relation to the October sexual assault offence. The argument of the appellant in this regard was twofold. First, relying on *R. v. Mellenthin* (1992), 76 C.C.C. (3d) 481, [1992] 3 S.C.R. 615, 16 C.R. (4th) 273, the appellant argued that the proper test for determining whether a person has consented to the taking of an item by the state was one of voluntariness, akin to the standard applied when the admissibility of a confession is in issue. Secondly, the appellant argued that, even if the test for the waiver by an accused of his or her s. 8 right is identical to that used to determine whether there has been a valid waiver of the rights found in s. 10 of the *Charter*, such that some awareness of the consequences of the waiver is required, this threshold is met on the facts of this case. I will consider each of these submissions in turn.

With regard to the test to be applied, I cannot find that the decision of this court in *Mellenthin, supra*, is of assistance to the appellant. While it is true that Cory J. in that case stated, at p. 487 that it was, "... incumbent upon the Crown to adduce evidence that the person detained has indeed made an informed consent to the search based upon an awareness of his rights to refuse to respond to the questions or to consent to the search", I cannot interpret this assertion as purporting to set out an exhaustive statement of the general test for the requirements for a valid consent to a police search.

On the facts of *Mellenthin*, it was not necessary to consider whether it was also a requirement for a valid consent that the accused be aware of the consequences of that consent. Obviously, the accused in *Mellenthin* was aware that, if the police found the drugs that he had in his bag, this could lead to potential charges. The real issue was whether the accused knew that he was not required to show the officer what was in his bag.

I agree with Doherty J.A., for the Ontario Court of Appeal in *R. v. Wills* (1992), 70 C.C.C. (3d) 529 at p. 541, 12 C.R. (4th) 58, 9 C.R.R. (2d) 360, that:

> When one consents to the police taking something that they otherwise have no right to take, one relinquishes one's right to be left alone by the state and removes the reasonableness barrier imposed by s. 8 of the *Charter*. The force of the consent given must be commensurate with the significant effect which it produces.

In order for a waiver of the right to be secure against an unreasonable seizure to be effective, the person purporting to consent must be possessed of the requisite informational foundation for a true relinquishment of the right. A right to choose requires not only the volition to prefer one option over another, but also sufficient available information to make the preference meaningful. This is equally true whether the individual is choosing to forego consultation with counsel or choosing to relinquish to the police something which they otherwise have no right to take.

Such an approach, in my view, is implicit in the statement of Lamer J. (as he then was) in *R. v. Debot* (1989), 52 C.C.C. (3d) 193, [1989] 2 S.C.R. 1140, 73 C.R. (3d) 129, that, while as a general rule a lawful search of the person did not have to be suspended pending exercise of the detainee's right to counsel, an exception existed in cases where the search required the detainee's consent. It is also implicit in the decisions of this court in *Dyment, supra*, and in *R. v. Colarusso* (1994), 87 C.C.C. (3d) 193 at p. 216, 110 D.L.R. (4th) 297, [1994] 1 S.C.R. 20, which recognize that a consent to the taking of blood can be limited to a taking for certain purposes only. This concept reveals a link between the scope of a valid consent and the scope of the accused's knowledge in relation to the consequences of that consent.

.....

The degree of awareness of the consequences of the waiver of the s. 8 right required of an accused in a given case will depend on its particular facts. Obviously, it will not be necessary for the accused to have a detailed comprehension of every possible outcome of his or her consent. However, his or her understanding should include the fact that the police are also planning to use the product of the seizure in a different investigation from the one for which he or she is detained. Such was not the case here. Therefore, I conclude that the police seized the respondent's blood in relation to the offence forming the subject-matter of this charge.

Compare: *R. v. Clement* (1996), 107 C.C.C. (3d) 52 (S.C.C.). Note that ss. 487.04 to 487.091 of the *Criminal Code* now provide an additional method for securing DNA samples.

R. v. WILLS

(1992), 70 C.C.C. (3d) 529 (Ont. C.A.)

[The accused was convicted of impaired driving causing death. The Crown's case rested almost exclusively upon the results of a breath sample provided by the accused and an expert's opinion based largely upon those results. Immediately after the accident which caused the death of the accused's passengers, the accused went to a nearby farmhouse for assistance. The police arrived and, after some discussion, demanded that the accused blow into the roadside breath device (the A.L.E.R.T.). He registered a "warn", indicating that his blood alcohol level was between .05 and .1. The police had no basis on which to arrest the accused and no grounds to demand a breathalyzer test. Nonetheless, they requested that he take a breathalyzer test, which, they told him, might work to his benefit in any civil lawsuit. The police did not then believe that alcohol-related charges would be laid but did think (though they did not communicate) that accurate breathalyzer readings would assist their investigation. The accused was ultimately persuaded by his father to take the test. He was then advised by the police that he was not required to do so and agreed to do so of his own free will. The accused registered .128 on the breathalyzer and it was later learned that the A.L.E.R.T. was defective. The accused was deliberately not told of the tragic consequences of the accident, out of concern that his emotional reaction would affect the accuracy of the test. On appeal from conviction, the Ontario Court of Appeal determined that there was a "seizure" of the accused's breath and went on to consider the effectiveness of his consent.]

The judgment of the court was delivered by

Doherty J.A.: —

.....

When one consents to the police taking something that they otherwise have no right to take, one relinquishes one's right to be left alone by the state and removes the reasonableness barrier imposed by s. 8 of the *Char-*

ter. The force of the consent given must be commensurate with the significant effect which it produces.

The Supreme Court of Canada has applied a stringent waiver test where the Crown contends that an accused has yielded a constitutional right in the course of a police investigation. According to that doctrine, the onus is on the Crown to demonstrate that the accused decided to relinquish his or her constitutional right with full knowledge of the existence of the right and an appreciation of the consequence of waiving that right: *R. v. Clarkson* (1986), 25 C.C.C. (3d) 207 at pp. 217-9, 26 D.L.R. (4th) 493, [1986] 1 S.C.R. 383; *R. v. Manninen* (1987), 34 C.C.C. (3d) 385 at p. 393, 41 D.L.R. (4th) 301, [1987] 1 S.C.R. 1233; *R. v. Turpin* [(1989), 48 C.C.C. (3d) 8 (S.C.C.)] at pp. 22-3; *R. v. Askov* (1990), 59 C.C.C. (3d) 449 at pp. 481-2, 74 D.L.R. (4th) 355, [1990] 2 S.C.R. 1199; *R. v. Hebert* (1990), 57 C.C.C. (3d) 1, [1990] 2 S.C.R. 151, 77 C.R. (3d) 145, *per* McLachlin J. at pp. 40-1, *per* Sopinka J. at pp. 16-8; *R. v. Smith* (1991), 63 C.C.C. (3d) 313 at pp. 320-5, [1991] 1 S.C.R. 714, 4 C.R. 125. None of these cases involved s. 8 of the *Charter*, although they did pertain to a number of different constitutional rights engaged during the criminal process (*e.g.*, ss. 7, 10(*b*), 11(*b*) and (*f*)).

The high waiver standard established in these cases is predicated on the need to ensure the fair treatment of individuals who come in contact with the police throughout the criminal process. That process includes the trial and the investigative stage. In fact, it is probably more important to insist on a high waiver standard in the investigative stage where there is no neutral judicial arbiter or structured setting to control the process, and sometimes no counsel to advise the individual of his or her rights.

The exercise of a right to choose presupposes a voluntary informed decision to pick one course of conduct over another. Knowledge of the various options and an appreciation of the potential consequences of the choice made are essential to the making of a valid and effective choice.

The waiver doctrine has been expressly applied by the Saskatchewan Court of Appeal in determining the constitutional validity of "consent" searches or seizures: *R. v. Nielsen* (1988), 43 C.C.C. (3d) 548 at pp. 561-4, 39 C.R.R. 147, [1988] 6 W.W.R. 1, and impliedly invoked in *R. v. Meyers* (1987), 58 C.R. (3d) 176 at pp. 186-8, [1987] 4 W.W.R. 624, 52 Alta. L.R. (2d) 156 (Q.B.), and *R. v. Lim*, Ont. H.C.J., April 10, 1990, an unreported judgment of Doherty J., at pp. 4-5 [since reported 1 C.R.R. (2d) 130]. It has also found favour with commentators: see Hutchison and Morton, *Search and Seizure Law in Canada* (1991), at p. 7-2.

In my opinion, the requirements established by the Supreme Court of Canada for a valid waiver of a constitutional right are applicable to the determination of whether an effective consent was given to an alleged seizure by the police. The fairness principle which has defined the requirements of a valid waiver as they relate to the right to a trial within a reasonable time, or the right to counsel, have equal application to the right protected by s. 8. In each instance the authorities seek an individual's permission to do something which, without that permission, they are not entitled to do. In such cases, fairness demands that the individual make a voluntary and informed decision to permit the intrusion of the investigative process upon his or her constitutionally protected rights.

.....

The decision in *R. v. Debot* (1989), 52 C.C.C. (3d) 193, [1989] 2 S.C.R. 1140, 73 C.R. (3d) 129, provides further assistance in defining the nature of the consent required to validate an otherwise unauthorized seizure.

In *Debot*, the majority held that while an accused had to be informed of his right to retain and instruct counsel upon detention, it was not necessary to suspend a lawful search of the person, conducted as an incident of that arrest, pending exercise of the right to counsel. Lamer J. recognized two exceptions to that general rule, the first being where the search depended on the detainee's consent. In that situation, the detained person was entitled to seek the assistance and advice of counsel before submitting to the search.

I stress that *Debot* does not stand for the proposition that all persons must be advised of their right to seek the assistance of counsel before being asked to consent to what would otherwise be an unauthorized seizure. The right to counsel is triggered by a detention or arrest. However, in holding that a consent search, where the consenting person was detained, should not proceed until the person had an opportunity to seek legal advice, Lamer J. was, impliedly at least, acknowledging that the decision to consent to a search had to be an informed one. Consequently, the detained person was entitled to the advice of counsel. This requirement is consistent with the application of the waiver standard to cases where the prosecution asserts that a seizure was consented to by an accused.

This survey of the case-law as it relates to the doctrine of waiver as applied in the constitutional setting, and the definition of "consent" in somewhat analogous circumstances, demonstrates that a "consent seizure" must be one which is not only voluntary but also informed. These two demands can only be met by the application and adaptation of established waiver principles to the circumstances in which the police seek an individual's consent to an otherwise unwarranted invasion of his or her privacy.

.....

In my opinion, the application of the waiver doctrine to situations where it is said that a person has consented to what would otherwise be an unauthorized search or seizure requires that the Crown establish on the balance of probabilities that:

- (i) there was a consent, express or implied;
- (ii) the giver of the consent had the authority to give the consent in question;
- (iii) the consent was voluntary in the sense that that word is used in *Goldman* [(1979), 51 C.C.C. (2d) 1 (S.C.C.)], and was not the product of police oppression, coercion or other external conduct which negated the freedom to choose whether or not to allow the police to pursue the course of conduct requested;
- (iv) the giver of the consent was aware of the nature of the police conduct to which he or she was being asked to consent;
- (v) the giver of the consent was aware of his or her right to refuse to permit the police to engage in the conduct requested, and

(vi) the giver of the consent was aware of the potential consequences of giving the consent.

The awareness of the consequences requirement needs further elaboration. In *Smith, supra*, at pp. 322-3, McLachlin J. considered the meaning of the awareness of the consequences requirement in the context of an alleged waiver of an accused's s. 10(*b*) rights. She held that the phrase required that the accused have a general understanding of the jeopardy in which he found himself, and an appreciation of the consequence of deciding for or against exercising his s. 10(*b*) rights.

A similar approach should be applied where s. 8 rights are at stake. The person asked for his or her consent must appreciate in a general way what his or her position is *vis-à-vis* the ongoing police investigation. Is that person an accused, a suspect, or a target of the investigation, or is he or she regarded merely as an "innocent bystander" whose help is requested by the police? If the person whose consent is requested is an accused, suspect or target, does that person understand in a general way the nature of the charge or potential charge which he or she may face?

In addition, at least in cases where the person is an accused, suspect or target of the investigation, the person whose consent is sought must understand that if the consent is given the police may use any material retrieved by them in a subsequent prosecution.

The consent provided by Mr. Wills met the first five criteria outlined above.

I am satisfied that the last criterion was not established. Mr. Wills did not have a sufficient awareness of the potential consequences of giving his consent. He was unaware of three potentially important facts:

(i) Constable Watkins was still undecided as to what charges, apart from alcohol-related charges, should be laid and he wanted the breathalyzer results as part of his "data base" to be used in making his decision;
(ii) one of the passengers in the Wills vehicle had died and another was seriously injured;
(iii) the A.L.E.R.T. reading did not accurately reflect Mr. Wills' blood-alcohol level because of a malfunction in the machine.

The first two facts were deliberately kept from Mr. Wills by the police, the last was unknown to both Mr. Wills and the police.

In my view, the cumulative effect of this non-disclosure and misinformation caused Mr. Wills, when he agreed to take the test, to fail to realize both his potential jeopardy and the potential consequences of taking the test. Mr. Wills did not know that the police wanted the breathalyzer results in part to assist in an ongoing investigation into a very serious car accident. Mr. Wills was in jeopardy of being charged with some non-alcohol-related offence and he was not told of that jeopardy when asked to consent to the breathalyzer. Instead, the taking of the test was presented to him exclusively as a potential source of information should he become involved in civil litigation. Mr. Wills was not told that the breathalyzer had some potential relevance to an ongoing police investigation of which he was the target.

Furthermore, because of the misinformation provided by the A.L.E.R.T. device, Mr. Wills (and everyone else) had no reason to believe that there could be any criminal consequences flowing directly from the taking of the breathalyzer test. He had no reason to suspect that he could be charged with some alcohol-related offence as a result of taking the test.

Mr. Wills was aware that if one took a breathalyzer test and "failed" one could face criminal charges. This kind of general knowledge may, in many cases, suffice to establish an adequate awareness of the potential consequences of taking the test. In this case, however, that general information was clearly overridden by the specific information Mr. Wills was given as to his blood-alcohol level. Based on the information provided to Mr. Wills, he foresaw no possibility of any immediate criminal consequences flowing from taking the test. The misinformation provided by the A.L.E.R.T. device completely misled Mr. Wills (and everyone else) as to the potential criminal consequences of taking the breathalyzer test. The erroneous information provided by the machine so significantly impaired Mr. Wills', understanding of the consequences of taking the test, that standing alone it would have negated the consent.

In my opinion, the consent given by Mr. Wills did not operate as a waiver of his right to be free of unreasonable search or seizure. The taking of the breath sample constituted a seizure.

[The court ultimately held that, although there had been a violation of s. 8 of the *Charter*, the evidence should not be excluded under s. 24(2).]

QUESTIONS

25. When, if at all, can the police use hair samples, obtained for an investigative purpose known at the time, to advance their investigation in a later case? Consider *R. v. Arp* (1998), 129 C.C.C. (3d) 321 (S.C.C.).

26. The police knock on the door of 112 Criminal Pathway, a rented apartment shared by A. Crook, a college student, and D. Cent, a fellow student. The police suspect that Crook is a drug trafficker but have insufficient grounds for a warrant to search. Assume that nobody is home. Can the landlord consent to a search of the premises? Consider *R. v. Mercer*; *R. v. Kenny* (1992), 70 C.C.C. (3d) 180 (Ont. C.A.); leave to appeal to S.C.C. refused 74 C.C.C. (3d) vi. Can Crook's girlfriend who lives elsewhere but who has been given a key to the apartment consent? Consider *R. v. Blinch* (1993), 83 C.C.C. (3d) 158 (B.C.C.A.). Now assume that D. Cent is home when the police arrive. Can he consent to the search? Can his consent extend to Crook's unshared bedroom?

(iii) Exigent Circumstances

R. v. SILVEIRA

(1995), 97 C.C.C. (3d) 450 (S.C.C.)

[The majority judgment was delivered by:]

Cory J. [Sopinka, Gonthier, Iacobucci and Major JJ. concurring]: — At issue on this appeal is whether the evidence, secured as a result of a search that was conceded to be unreasonable, should be excluded pursuant to the provisions of s. 24(2) of the *Canadian Charter of Rights and Freedoms*. As is so often the case, the factual background and the findings of the courts below will have a profound effect upon the result.

Factual background

On August 28, 1990, the members of a drug squad of the Metropolitan Toronto Police commenced an investigation into the sale of cocaine. On that same date, an officer, working undercover, purchased a gram of cocaine from Antonio Scinocco for $600. On September 10th, 14th and 18th, an undercover officer made further purchases of cocaine from Scinocco at a community centre in Trinity Park, Toronto. On each occasion, the amount purchased was an ounce and the sum paid in advance was $2,000. On each of these occasions, the police officers observed the following pattern of events. Scinocco would meet with the appellant, Antonio Silveira. Silveira would then be driven by another co-accused to his residence at 486 Dufferin St. The appellant would then go inside and leave after a short time to meet, once again, with Scinocco. Scinocco would then return to the undercover officer and to give him the approximately 1 oz or 25 g of cocaine in rock form. At about 7:10 p.m. on the 18th, shortly after the third sale was made, the appellant was arrested, as were two co-accused. All the arrests took place in the vicinity of the community centre which was close to the appellant's residence.

The police were concerned that the public nature of those arrests would lead to instructions being given to the residents of 486 Dufferin St. to destroy or remove any evidence that might be on the premises. The police believed that they had sufficient evidence from the purchases of cocaine and the observations of Silveira made on the 10th and 14th to obtain a search warrant for 486 Dufferin St. Yet, they did not want to be accused of failing to present up-to-date information to the justice of the peace. It was therefore determined that further information relating to the purchase of cocaine made on the 18th would be added to the affidavit to be presented on the application for the search warrant. The police were satisfied that they had such an abundance of evidence establishing the reasonable and probable grounds for searching the premises that they would have no difficulty obtaining a search warrant. To prevent the destruction or the removal of the evidence between the time of the arrest and the arrival of the search warrant, officers attended at 486 Dufferin St. They knocked on the door, identified themselves, and entered the premises without an invitation. Upon entering, they checked the premises for weapons and for the location of residents within the house. They then holstered their weapons and advised the occupants of the house to continue preparing dinner and watching the Blue Jays baseball game on television. They did not search the premises, but waited for the search warrant which they believed would arrive shortly.

The officers who secured the premises were convinced that 486 Dufferin St. was the supply base for the cocaine that was sold to the undercover officer. One of the officers had, on two previous dates, observed the appellant and others return to the address prior to the sales being made. Further, they were concerned that, in light of the public nature of the arrests made in three locations close to 486 Dufferin St., word would get back to the residents with the result that the evidence would be destroyed or removed. This, in the opinion of the officers, was not uncommon in the case of hard drugs. It is not without significance that a brother of the accused arrived at the premises while the police were waiting for the search warrant. Although there had been no apparent phone call to him, he was aware of the arrest of his brother before he arrived at the house.

It was only when the search warrant arrived, a little over one hour later, that the actual search of the premises was undertaken. In the course of the search, the police found a locked duffle bag in the appellant's bedroom on the second floor of the house. When the officers opened it, they found some 285.56 g (10 oz) of cocaine and $9,535 in cash. The cash included substantial amounts of the marked money used by the undercover police to buy cocaine on earlier occasions.

Decisions and factual findings of the courts below

(a) Trial judge

The appellant challenged the admissibility of the evidence seized in the search on three grounds, all of which were dismissed by the trial judge. First, the trial judge concluded that, although the entry by the police officers could not be authorized retrospectively by the subsequent issue of a search warrant, it was none the less justified on the basis of exigent circumstances. He found that the three public arrests made close to the house gave rise to a valid concern on the part of the police officers that the drugs would be destroyed if steps were not taken to preserve the evidence. He concluded that the police acted reasonably in the circumstances.

Second, the trial judge found that the police did not begin the search of the premises until the search warrant arrived. He concluded that, in the meantime, the police were entitled to enter each room to search for weapons and occupants in order to protect themselves and prevent the destruction of the evidence. He concluded that the momentary display of firearms by the police was justified in light of the connection he found existed in Toronto between hard drugs and guns. Further, he determined that the search was conducted by the police in a reasonable manner.

Third, the search warrant was alleged to be invalid because of the failure of the police to disclose material information to the justice of the peace. The trial judge found that the police officer did not intentionally mislead the justice of the peace by failing to advise that officers might be on the premises at the time the warrant was issued. Further, he found that even after deleting any reference to the appellant's statement that drugs were on the premises, which he found to be inadmissible, there was still ample evidence put forward which would justify the issuance of the search warrant.

Although he did not make a specific finding that there was good faith, the trial judge certainly made it clear that, in his view, there was no bad faith manifested by the police actions, and he therefore admitted the evidence discovered as a result of the search.

[The majority and minority views in the Ontario Court of Appeal were then outlined.]

Did the entry by the police constitute a search?

In my view, the respondent very properly conceded that the entry by the police, undertaken in order to secure the premises and prevent the destruction of evidence, was indeed a form of search not authorized by law. There is no place on earth where persons can have a greater expectation of privacy than within their "dwelling-house". No matter how good the intentions of the police may have been, their entry into the dwelling-house without a warrant infringed the appellant's rights guaranteed by s. 8 of the *Charter*. Moreover, there can be no artificial division between the entry into the home by the police and the subsequent search of the premises made pursuant to the warrant. The two actions are so intertwined in time and in their nature that it would be unreasonable to draw an artificial line between them in order to claim that, although the initial entry was improper, the subsequent search was valid. It follows, then, that the question to be resolved is whether or not the admission of the cocaine and the money discovered during the search could bring the administration of justice into disrepute.

Section 24(2) of the Charter

This case comes down to a consideration of the balance that must be struck between the right to privacy within the home and the necessity of the police to act in exigent circumstances. On the one hand, the police, in direct contravention of s. 10 of the *Narcotic Control Act*, entered into a dwelling-house without a search warrant or authorization. The *Narcotic Control Act* itself recognizes the age-old principle of the inviolability of the dwelling-house. It must be the final refuge and safe haven for all Canadians. It is there that the expectation of privacy is at its highest and where there should be freedom from external forces, particularly the actions of agents of the state, unless those actions are duly authorized. This principle is fundamental to a democratic society as Canadians understand that term. Thus, it can be argued that the unauthorized entry into a dwelling-house is so grave a breach of a *Charter* right that evidence secured as a result of such an unauthorized entry should always be excluded.

Yet, on the other hand, the police were investigating a very serious crime, specifically the sale of a hard drug. It is a crime that has devastating individual and social consequences. It is, as well, often and tragically coupled with the use of firearms. This crime is a blight on society and every effort must be undertaken to eradicate it. It is so serious and the destruction or removal of evidence is so easy that it can be argued that the police, while awaiting a search warrant, should always have the right to enter a dwelling-house without authority to preserve the evidence. Perhaps the solution lies somewhere between these extreme positions.

.....

[Cory J. then addressed the seriousness of the *Charter* breach in the following way:]

Nature of the breach

The police, without warrant or authority, entered a dwelling-house. This was not a simple perimeter search as in *R. v. Kokesch* [(1990), 61 C.C.C. (3d) 207 (S.C.C.)], but an entry into the dwelling itself. It is hard to imagine a more serious infringement of an individual's right to privacy. The home is the one place where persons can expect to talk freely, to dress as they wish and, within the bounds of the law, to live as they wish. The unauthorized presence of agents of the state in a home is the ultimate invasion of privacy. It is the denial of one of the fundamental rights of individuals living in a free and democratic society. To condone it without reservation would be to conjure up visions of the midnight entry into homes by agents of the state to arrest the occupants on nothing but the vaguest suspicion that they may be enemies of the state. This is why for centuries it has been recognized that a man's home is his castle. It is for this reason that the *Narcotic Control Act* prohibits entry into a private dwelling-house without a warrant and it is for this reason that a search warrant must be obtained from a judicial officer on the basis of reasonable and proper grounds. Despite the historical importance attached to the privacy interest of an individual in his or her home, and the significance attached to a dwelling-house by s. 10 of the *Narcotic Control Act*, the police entered the appellant's home without a warrant.

The entry onto the property by the police was thus a very serious breach of a *Charter* right. It remains to be seen if there are other factors which can mitigate the seriousness of the *Charter* violation.

(b) Was the violation committed in good faith and was it motivated by circumstances of urgency or necessity?

These critical factors can, I think, be considered together. It will be remembered that the trial judge found that there were exigent circumstances which required the police to enter the premises to protect the evidence. These included, particularly, the arrest of three co-accused all in public places which were close to the home of the appellant. The police believed that those arrests might trigger the removal of the evidence. The trial judge concluded that the police had a valid basis for their concern to preserve the evidence pending the arrival of the warrant. He observed that the search itself was conducted reasonably, as was the original entry of the police into the home. Lastly, he concluded that there was a sound basis for issuing the search warrant. These findings were all confirmed by the majority of the Court of Appeal. There are, therefore, concurrent findings in this regard. If there was no specific finding that the police had acted in good faith, there was certainly no indication that there was any evidence of bad faith on the part of the police. Further, the evidence reveals that the police considered that they had the right to enter the house to preserve the evidence and an able and experienced trial judge appeared to agree with that conclusion. The trial judge, like the police, may have been in error in reaching that conclusion for the police actions specifically breached the provisions of s. 10 of the *Narcotic Control Act*. None the less, the circumstances of the public arrests and the need to preserve the evidence were found to constitute exigent circumstances. In those circumstances, it cannot be said that the breach of the *Charter* rights by the police was committed in bad faith.

There was strong and persuasive evidence upon which the trial judge and majority of the Court of Appeal could properly find that there were exigent circumstances which justified the police entry into the home of the appellant. That is to say that there were other factors which mitigated the seriousness of the *Charter* violation. It is sufficient to dispose of this issue to state that the appellant has not demonstrated that the findings of the courts below were unreasonable or that there was some error made as to the applicable principles of law.

Police dilemma

Yet, the question remains, how should the police act in a situation where they have a serious and valid concern pertaining to the preservation of evidence while awaiting a search warrant. As a result of this case, police officers will be aware that to enter a dwelling-house without a warrant, even in exigent circumstances, constitutes such a serious breach of *Charter* rights that it will likely lead to a ruling that the evidence seized is inadmissible.

In the future, this problem may disappear as a result of legislation which might, for example, amend the provisions of s. 10 of the *Narcotic Control Act*. However, apart from legislation, let us consider the options that are open to the police and their consequences.

In this case, evidence existed upon which a search warrant could have been obtained before the arrests were made. It may be that it would have been preferable for the police to have obtained a search warrant based on the earlier transactions completed prior to that made on the day of the arrests. The police could have advised the justice of the peace that they expected to make the arrests and that there might be further information that would be available from those arrests which could be supplied immediately after the arrest, perhaps by telephone and subsequently confirmed by a deposition. At the time of trial, if the search warrant was attacked on the grounds that it was outdated, evidence could be adduced of the difficulty of providing up-to-date material in circumstances like these and that, in light of the necessity of protecting the evidence, the police found it necessary to obtain a warrant based on the earlier transactions and observations. In the absence of an unreasonable delay between the observations and the application, it would be difficult to imagine that the warrant could be successfully attacked on the grounds that it was stale-dated. That is the way the police should have proceeded.

Yet, that is not to say that the police forever should be prohibited from entering premises in order to secure and preserve the evidence. Situations may arise when it will be impossible for the police to proceed by means of a search warrant based on earlier observations. Undercover officers may have worked long and hard in situations of great personal danger to proceed with one very large purchase of drugs in circumstances where it is essential to preserve the evidence which the police believe on reasonable and probable grounds to be in a home. Yet, it will take time to obtain a search warrant. In those circumstances, courts will have to determine on a case-by-case basis whether or not there existed such a situation of emergency and importance that the evidence obtained may be admitted notwithstanding the warrantless search. However, I must emphasize again that after this case it will be rare that the existence of exigent circumstances alone will allow for the admission of evidence obtained in a clear violation of s. 10 of the *Narcotic Control Act* and s. 8 of the *Charter*. Otherwise, routinely permitting the evidence to be admitted under s. 24(2) of the *Charter* in cases where exigent circumstances exist would amount to a judicial amendment of s. 10 of the *Narcotic Control Act*. This was the position taken by counsel for the respondent. In his submissions, he very carefully stated that he was not seeking *carte blanche* for the police to enter a dwelling-house to preserve evidence. Rather, he maintained, quite correctly I believe, that the issue should be considered on a case-by-case basis.

[Cory J. then reviewed the American authorities.]

.....

Thus, it can be seen that the careful case-by-case approach undertaken in the United States has resulted in the courts' admitting evidence seized during a search after premises have been secured in order to preserve evidence, if the exigent circumstances required such a measure. Although s. 10 of the *Narcotic Control Act* does not permit such measures in case of a dwelling-house, a careful case-by-case approach under s. 24(2) should be taken in Canada. Notwithstanding the specific provisions in the *Narcotic Control Act* prohibiting entry into a dwelling-house, and the historical importance that has always been attached to a dwelling-house, it cannot be forgotten that there is an unfortunate connection between illicit trafficking in drugs and the use of firearms. Further, as indicated by the facts in this case, a communication network often exists which facilitates the destruction of vital evidence. Proceeding on a case-by-case basis will permit the courts to recognize and balance the fundamental importance of the right to privacy in a person's dwelling against the gravity of drug crimes and the need of the police in emergency circumstances to preserve vital evidence. In my view, such circumstances existed in this case. Further, the fact that the police entered to preserve the evidence rendered the breach less serious.

Yet, s. 24(2) of the *Charter* should not be used as a matter of course to excuse conduct which has in the past been found to be unlawful. This case has confirmed that to enter and search a dwelling-house without a warrant constitutes a very serious breach of the *Narcotic Control Act* and the historic inviolability of a dwelling-place. Therefore, in the future, even if such exigent circumstances exist, the evidence would likely be found inadmissible under s. 24(2). It is difficult to envisage how the admission of the evidence could not bring the administration of justice into disrepute since in subsequent cases, it will be very difficult for the police to claim that they acted in good faith if they entered the dwelling without prior judicial authorization. The police must now know that exigent circumstances do not provide an excuse for failing to obtain a warrant. It is up to Parliament to amend s. 10 if it wishes to provide for exceptions to the warrant requirement. Although I do not wish to foreclose the possibility that the evidence may still be admitted under s. 24(2), it will only occur in rare cases.

At the time of the unauthorized entry, the police could not reasonably have been expected to consider that there was another investigatory technique available to them that would not have infringed the *Charter*. As a result, no other aspect of the seriousness of the *Charter* violation need be considered.

(c) The effect of the exclusion of the evidence

The last major factor to be considered in the s. 24(2) analysis is the effect the exclusion of the evidence would have on the administration of justice. The outcome of this issue was not seriously contested by the appellant. The appellant was charged with possession for the purpose of trafficking and trafficking in a hard drug in significant quantities. These are offences that can have a catastrophic effect on society and that carry with them a provision for imprisonment for life. The evidence at issue here was vitally important if not crucial to the prosecution of the case. Indeed, the respondent concedes that without this evidence there would be no possibility of obtaining a conviction on the charge of possession of cocaine for the purpose of trafficking. As well, exclusion of the impugned evidence would substantially diminish the strength of the Crown's case on the trafficking charges.

[Cory J. weighed all factors and determined that the evidence was properly found to be admissible. L'Heureux-Dubé J. concurred in the result, finding no *Charter* violation. La Forest J. vigorously dissented, delivering extensive reasons. He found, *inter alia,* no exigent circumstances. Part of that judgment is reproduced below.]

La Forest J. (dissenting): —

.....

Exigent circumstances

The existence of exigent circumstances appears to have dominated the thinking of the courts below. It, therefore, becomes important to review briefly the relevant law as it has thus far developed. Simply stated it is this: absent clear statutory language authorizing such a course, the police have no power to enter a dwelling-house to conduct a search without a warrant. Section 10 of the *Narcotic Control Act* makes this clear. It follows that the search also violated s. 8 of the *Charter*. Urgent situations, it is true, may, along with other circumstances, be considered in assessing the seriousness of the *Charter* breach in the course of considering whether evidence gathered as a result of such breach should be admitted into evidence under s. 24(2) of the *Charter* (see *R. v. Collins* (1987), 33 C.C.C. (3d) 1, 38 D.L.R. (4th) 508, [1987] 1 S.C.R. 265), but an examination under that provision of course presupposes a *Charter* breach.

.....

Even if exigent circumstances could be used as a justification for police searches of a dwelling-house without a warrant, I do not think such circumstances existed in this case. The facts here were such that the police could have obtained a warrant before beginning their operation. The exigent circumstances here arose solely out of the manner in which the police chose to structure the operation, *i.e.*, they created their own exigent circumstances. In *R. v. Grant* [(1993), 84 C.C.C. (3d) 173 (S.C.C.)] Sopinka J. made it clear that exigent circumstances could only be relied on where obtaining a search warrant was impracticable. This point will come out more clearly in my discussion of the issue of urgency under s. 24(2), which (in view of my holding that exigent circumstances have no role to play in this case) is the appropriate context to consider it.

.....

In the present case, the police maintain that they entered the appellant's home because they feared the public arrests they had just made could prompt occupants of the house, or other interested parties, to get rid of incriminating evidence. While there was no evidence that such a fear was justified, one can empathize with this general type of plight the police may face. The problem in this appeal is that the very circumstances that led to their conclusion that an exigency existed were the direct result of the manner in which they chose to structure their operation. Abella J.A., in her dissent in the Court of Appeal, aptly summarized the sequencing of events by the police [at p. 80]: "[t]hey chose ... to arrest first, enter secondly, and obtain authority last."

The police testimony at trial conclusively shows there was no need to proceed in this way. The appellant and the co-accused had, without their knowledge, been closely monitored by the police for several days. A group take-down meeting of the main police surveillance squad and assisting team of police was held at 5:00 p.m. on September 18, 1990, some two hours before the public arrests were made. At that preparatory strategy session, one of the squad leaders, Officer Clifford, was assigned the task of acquiring the requisite search warrant. Clifford testified that, by that time, he had already largely completed the preparation of the information necessary to be presented to a judicial officer, whom Parliament alone, by s. 12 of the *Narcotic Control Act* has vested with the authority to grant or deny the police power to enter a dwelling-house. It is not contested, and it is clear from the record, that, at the time of that take-down meeting, the police had already gathered enough information concerning the drug trading activities of the appellant that a search warrant would inevitably have been granted had it been sought before the arrests. However, the police delayed obtaining a warrant and chose instead to make public arrests. Upon making the arrests, they suddenly became concerned that their actions might have been noticed. The police then, not surprisingly, found themselves facing the possibility that the occupants of the house might be notified to destroy the evidence before a search warrant could be acquired. It was this possibility that prompted the police to occupy the appellant's home and control its occupants for an hour and a quarter before the warrant arrived.

Note s. 11(7) of the *Controlled Drugs and Substances Act*. Note also, s. 487.11 of the *Criminal Code*. Both were enacted following the *Silveira* decision.

(iv) Things in Plain View

In *R. v. Ruiz* (1991), 68 C.C.C. (3d) 500 (N.B.C.A.), Hoyt J.A. stated at p. 509:

> The plain view doctrine permits, within strict limits, the introduction into evidence of items obtained without a search warrant. In a sense, it is an exception to the rule requiring a search warrant. This court, in *R. v. Belliveau* (1986), 30 C.C.C. (3d) 163, 54 C.R. (3d) 144, 75 N.B.R. (2d) 18, had occasion to consider the application of the doctrine. At p. 174, Stratton C.J. outlined three requirements that must be satisfied before the doctrine may be invoked:
>
>> First, the police officer must lawfully make an "initial intrusion" or otherwise properly be in a position from which he can view a particular area. Secondly, the officer must discover incriminating evidence "inadvertently", which is to say, he may not "know in advance the location of [certain] evidence and intend to seize it", relying on the plain view doctrine only as a pretext. Finally, it must be "immediately apparent" to the police that the items they observe may be evidence of a crime, contraband, or otherwise subject to seizure. These requirements having been met, when police officers lawfully engaged in an activity in a particular area perceive a suspicious object, they may seize it immediately.

6. Interception of Private Communications

The interception of private communications is regulated by Part VI of the *Criminal Code* (Invasion of Privacy). The governing statutory provisions are somewhat complex and require careful reading, along with the many cases which have interpreted them. It is beyond the scope of this book to detail all of the applicable provisions. However, the following represents an overview of the statutory scheme.

Part VI, ss. 183 to 196 of the *Criminal Code*, governs the interception of private communications, one form of electronic surveillance. Part VI does not apply to electronic video surveillance (see *R. v. Wong* (1990), 60 C.C.C. (3d) 460 (S.C.C.)). Section 487.01 authorizes the issuance of a warrant permitting a peace officer to use any device, investigative technique or procedure, including video surveillance, under the circumstances described in s. 487.01(1). Section 487.01(4) and (5) specifically pertain to electronic video surveillance and incorporate by reference many of the provisions contained in Part VI.

A number recorder, which can record or identify the telephone number or location of the telephone from which a call originates or at which it is received or intended to be received, but which does not record the contents of any call, does not intercept a communication and therefore is not governed by Part VI. Section 492.2 of the *Criminal Code* authorizes the issuance of a warrant to permit the installation, maintenance, monitoring, and removal of a number recorder.

Similarly, s. 492.1 of the *Criminal Code* authorizes the issuance of a warrant to permit the installation, maintenance, monitoring, and removal of a tracking device, which may be used to help ascertain, by electronic or other means, the location of any thing or person.

Section 184(1) of the *Criminal Code* provides that it is a crime to wilfully intercept a private communication "by means of any electro-magnetic, acoustic, mechanical or other device". See also s. 342.1(1)(*b*) of the *Criminal Code*, which criminalizes the fraudulent interception of any function of a computer system. Section 184(2)(*a*) provides that s. 184(1) does not apply, *inter alia,* to "*a person who has the consent to intercept ... of the originator of the private communication or of the person intended by the originator thereof to receive it*". (Emphasis added.) This makes a consent interception lawful, and, historically, provided the justification for police to bodypack or otherwise intercept the communications of undercover police officers or their civilian agent with a suspect. Then came *R. v. Duarte* (1990), 53 C.C.C. (3d) 1 (S.C.C.), which held that the interception of private communications by the state, albeit with a participant's consent but without prior judicial authorization, violates s. 8 of the *Charter*. So, such an interception remains lawful but is an unreasonable search or seizure under the *Charter* and is susceptible to possible exclusion at trial.

Section 184(2)(*b*) provides that s. 184(1) also does not apply to "*a person who intercepts a private communication in accordance with [a prior judicial] authorization or pursuant to section 184.4*". (Emphasis added.) Section 184.4 provides for exceptional interceptions without prior authorization.

QUESTIONS

27. **Your client asks you whether she can intercept her own telephone calls from a harrassing ex-boyfriend with a device she purchased recently. Does s. 184(2)(*a*) of the *Criminal Code* enable you to advise her that she can proceed? Consider, in this regard, s. 191 of the *Criminal Code*.**

28. **If an undercover police officer makes an unauthorized recording of a confession that he solicited in person, can this tape be admissible as evidence? What if he uses the transcript of the tape to "refresh" his memory and essentially reads in the entire transcript of the tape? Consider *R. v. Fliss* (2002), 161 C.C.C. (3d) 225 (S.C.C.).**

Judicial authorization to intercept private communications can be obtained under the following sections of the *Criminal Code*:

(a) **Sections 185 and 186: Conventional Authorizations and Renewals;**
(b) **Section 188: Emergency Authorizations;**
(c) **Section 184.2: Authorizations for Consent Interceptions; and**
(d) **Section 184.3: Authorizations for Consent Interceptions by means of Telecommunicated Applications.**

The interception of private communications by the state, without prior judicial authorization, is permitted only in limited circumstances under the *Criminal Code*, for example:

(a) Section 184.4: Unauthorized Interceptions in Exceptional Circumstances; and

(b) Section 184.1: Unauthorized Consent Interceptions to Prevent Bodily Harm.

Sections 185 and 186 are the most significant statutory provisions, since they outline the procedures and criteria for applying for and granting a judicial authorization to intercept private communications. They also outline the contents of the supporting affidavit and authorization. Section 187 provides for the manner in which the documents relating to such an application are to be kept confidential and the circumstances under which the "sealed packet" may be opened. Section 187(4) to (7) [am. 1993, c. 40, s. 7], enacted in 1993, are largely patterned upon procedures established in *R. v. Garofoli* (1990), 60 C.C.C. (3d) 161 (S.C.C.), and in *Dersch v. Canada (Attorney General)* (1990), 60 C.C.C. (3d) 132 (S.C.C.).

Though several aspects of *R. v. Garofoli* have been overborne by statutory change, the case continues to represent the most significant decision on the procedures relating to an attack upon judicially authorized interceptions.

R. v. GAROFOLI

(1990), 60 C.C.C. (3d) 161 (S.C.C.)

Sopinka J.: —

.....

1. What is the entitlement of an accused person to the sealed packet?

The trial judge refused to order access based on the restricted access cases. For the reasons that I gave in *Dersch* [(1990), 60 C.C.C. (3d) 132 (S.C.C.)] those cases no longer apply in view of ss. 7 and 8 of the *Charter*. The accused is entitled to have the packet opened and, subject to editing, to have its contents produced in order to enable him or her to make full answer and defence. The Court of Appeal was, therefore, right in opening the sealed packets. [Author's note: now see s. 187(4)-(7) of the *Criminal Code*, since enacted.]

2. Upon what grounds may an accused challenge an authorization for wiretap and before what court?

[Sopinka J. outlines the statutory conditions for issuing a conventional authorization as contained in s. 178.13 (now s. 186(1)) and the conformity of those conditions to *Charter* requirements. The result is that the statutory requirements are identical to the constitutional requirements, and an authorizing judge must, therefore, be satisfied on the basis of the affidavit evidence that these conditions have been met.]

.....

Challenging the authorization

The current state of the law with respect to testing the admissibility of wiretap evidence is a procedural quagmire. The various procedures that are available have come to be known by the names of the cases that initiated them.

First there is a "*Parsons voir dire*". named after *R. v. Parsons* (1977), 37 C.C.C. (2d) 497, 80 D.L.R. (3d) 430, 17 O.R. (2d) 465 (C.A.); affirmed 51 C.C.C. (2d) 350, 110 D.L.R. (3d) 71, [1980] 1 S.C.R. 785, *sub nom. Charette v. The Queen*. The function of this hearing before the trial judge is to determine such issues as whether the authorization is valid on its face, whether the police executed the interception within the terms of the authorization, and whether statutory requirements such as reasonable notice were complied with. The remedy is exclusion under s. 178.16. The second is the "*Wilson* application". This hearing takes place before the issuing court, to determine the substantive or subfacial validity of the affidavit. The remedy is the setting aside of the authorization. The third is a "*Garofoli* hearing". This is a hearing before the trial judge to determine the compliance of the authorization with s. 8 of the *Charter*. The remedy is a determination under s. 24(2) of the *Charter*. The fourth, and last, procedure is a "*Vanweenan* hearing", so-called after one of the appellants in *R. v. Chesson* (1988), 43 C.C.C. (3d) 353, [1988] 2 S.C.R. 148, 65 C.R. (3d) 193. This again is a *voir dire* before the trial judge, but with the object of determining whether the authorization names all "known" persons as required by ss. 178.12(1)(*e*) and 178.13(2)(*c*). The remedy again is exclusion under s. 178.16. [Author's note: the mandated exclusion under s. 178.16 has been repealed; now exclusion is regulated by ss. 8 and 24(2) of the *Charter*.]

Consolidation of the *Parsons*, *Garofoli* and *Vanweenan* hearings presents no difficulty, and is in keeping with the view of this court that all matters that relate to the conduct of the trial should be dealt with by the trial judge. A more difficult question arises with respect to the *Wilson* and *Garofoli* applications. It would be highly desirable if they could be dealt with by the trial judge so that all aspects of the admissibility of evidence obtained pursuant to an authorization could be dealt with at one time and at trial. Whether this can be done requires an examination of this court's judgment in *R. v. Wilson, supra*, and the effects of s. 8 of the *Charter* on its application.

[After reviewing *R. v. Wilson* (1983), 9 C.C.C. (3d) 97 (S.C.C.) and *R. v. Meltzer* (1989), 49 C.C.C. (3d) 453 (S.C.C.), Sopinka J. concluded that the statutory provisions, which were in need of amendment, only permit the issuing court to open the sealed packet. However, the trial court is the appropriate court to review the authorization and can do so in a less restrictive way than contemplated by *Wilson, supra.* Post *Garofoli*, s. 187(1.4) was enacted, now permitting the trial court to open the sealed packet as well.]

.....

Grounds for review

In *R. v. Collins* (1987), 33 C.C.C. (3d) 1 at p. 14, 38 D.L.R. (4th) 508, [1987] 1 S.C.R. 265, Lamer J. (as he then was) set out the basic test for determining the reasonableness of a search under s. 8 of the *Charter*. He stated: "A search will be reasonable if it is authorized by law, if the law itself is reasonable and if the manner in which the search was carried out is reasonable."

In *Hunter v. Southam Inc.*[(1984), 14 C.C.C. (3d) 97 (S.C.C.)], this court set out the basic requirements with respect to prior authorizations. In *Duarte* [(1990), 53 C.C.C. (3d) 1 (S.C.C.)] this court decided that s. 178.13(1)(*a*) complies with these standards, and that before granting an authorization, a judge must be satisfied by affidavit that there are reasonable and probable grounds to believe that:

(a) a specified crime has been or is being committed, and
(b) the interception of the private communication in question will afford evidence of the crime.

To arrive at the conclusion that the search is authorized by law, the reviewing judge must therefore conclude that these conditions were complied with. If he concludes that they were not, then the search is not authorized by law and is unlawful. Consequently, in order to discharge the duty cast upon the reviewing judge to determine whether there has been a breach of s. 8, he or she must determine whether the *Code* provisions have been satisfied. This is the inevitable result of the statutory conditions being identical to the requirements of s. 8. Whereas *Wilson* precluded a review of the authorizing judge's decision that the statutory conditions had been complied with, unless some ground such as fraud or new evidence was established, the application of s. 8 requires review as a step in determining the reasonableness of the search and seizure.

While a judge exercising this relatively new power need not comply with the *Wilson* criteria, he should not review the authorization *de novo*. The correct approach is set out in the reasons of Martin J.A. in this appeal. He states (at p. 119):

> If the *trial judge* concludes that, on the material before the authorizing judge, there was no basis upon which he could be satisfied that the preconditions for the granting of the authorization exist, then, it seems to me that the trial judge is required to find that the search or seizure contravened s. 8 of the *Charter*.

The reviewing judge does not substitute his or her view for that of the authorizing judge. If, based on the record which was before the authorizing judge as amplified on the review, the reviewing judge concludes that the authorizing judge could have granted the authorization, then he or she should not interfere. In this process, the existence of fraud, non-disclosure, misleading evidence and new evidence are all relevant, but, rather than being a prerequisite to review, their sole impact is to determine whether there continues to be any basis for the decision of the authorizing judge.

.....

4. *What special requirements apply when information from informants is relied on to obtain an authorization?*

The appellant submitted that in order to establish reasonable and probable grounds to justify a search, a detailed set of requirements was necessary in respect of the use of informants' information. He contends that in coming to the conclusion that the affidavits in this case were sufficient, the Court of Appeal must have applied the "totality of the circumstances" test set out in *Illinois v. Gates*, 462 U.S. 213 (1983). The pertinent passage from that judgment reads as follows (at p. 238):

> The task of the issuing magistrate is simply to make a practical, common-sense decision whether, given all the circumstances set forth in the affidavit before him, including the "veracity" and "basis of knowledge" of persons supplying hearsay information, there is a fair probability that contraband or evidence of crime will be found in a particular place.

The general requirement with which the authorizing judge must comply has already been referred to in these reasons. He or she must be satisfied that the statutory conditions have been established. The reviewing judge should not set aside this decision unless he or she is satisfied on the whole of the material presented that there was no basis for the authorization. While this is the general instruction that each judge should apply, special problems arise with respect to the use of information of informants. It is, therefore, desirable to examine what special requirements, if any, should be developed to enable judges to apply the general instruction in a way that strikes a just balance between the needs of law enforcement and the protection of the rights of privacy.

This issue has been addressed by this court in connection with the use of informant information to support a warrantless search.

[After analyzing Lamer J.'s judgment in *R. v. Greffe* (1990), 55 C.C.C. (3d) 161, and the Court's earlier judgment in *R. v. Debot* (1989), 52 C.C.C. (3d) 193 (S.C.C.); affg (1986), 30 C.C.C. (3d) 207 (Ont. C.A.), Sopinka J. continued.]

.....

Although *Greffe* concerns admissibility under s. 24(2), in my opinion the discussion has a bearing on the sort of information that must be put before a judge issuing an authorization for electronic surveillance. I see no difference between evidence of reliability of an informant tendered to establish reasonable and probable grounds to justify a warrantless search (the issue in the cases cited by Lamer J.) and evidence of reliability of an informant tendered to establish similar grounds in respect of a wiretap authorization. Moreover, I conclude that the following propositions can be regarded as having been accepted by this court in *Debot* and *Greffe*:

(i) Hearsay statements of an informant can provide reasonable and probable grounds to justify a search. However, evidence of a tip from an informer, by itself, is insufficient to establish reasonable and probable grounds.

(ii) The reliability of the tip is to be assessed by recourse to "the totality of the circumstances". There is no formulaic test as to what this entails. Rather, the court must look to a variety of factors including:

(a) the degree of detail of the "tip";
(b) the informer's source of knowledge;
(c) indicia of the informer's reliability such as past performance or confirmation from other investigative sources.

(iii) The results of the search cannot, *ex post facto*, provide evidence of reliability of the information.

.....

... I am in agreement with the result reached by [Martin J.A.] that the affidavits were sufficient on their face. He concludes his reasons as follows (at pp. 129-30):

> I am satisfied that the affidavits set out ample facts upon which the authorizing judges could be satisfied that there were reasonable grounds to believe that the specified offences were being or had been committed, that the interceptions sought would afford evidence of the offences, that other investigative procedures were unlikely to succeed and that it would be in the best interests of the administration of justice to grant the authorizations.

5. *What principles and procedures apply to the editing of the contents of the sealed packet?*

The appellant does not take issue with the exercise by the Court of Appeal of the power to edit the affidavit in order to preserve the identity of informants. His principal submission is that the appellant should be provided with judicially approved summaries of the edited words and phrases.

The power to edit clearly exists and derives from the supervisory and protecting power which a court possesses over its own records: *A.-G.N.S. v. MacIntyre* (1982), 65 C.C.C. (2d) 129 at p. 149, 132 D.L.R. (3d) 385, [1982] 1 S.C.R. 175.

In determining the procedure to be followed in editing the materials in the packet, regard must be had for the competing interests of law enforcement, and in particular the protection of the identity of informers and investigative techniques, on the one hand and the right of the accused to make full answer and defence on the other.

.....

... In determining what to edit, the judge will have regard for the rule against disclosure of police informants. The most recent expression of the rule by this court is in the case of *Bisaillon v. Keable* (1983), 7 C.C.C. (3d) 385 at pp. 411-2, 2 D.L.R. (4th) 193, [1983] 2 S.C.R. 60. Beetz J. stated:

> It follows from these reasons that at common law the secrecy rule regarding police informers' identity has chiefly taken the form of rules of evidence based on the public interest, which prohibit judicial disclosure of police informers' identity by peace officers who have learned the informers' identity in the course of their duties. A witness also may not be compelled to state whether he is himself a police informer. The rule was developed in criminal

proceedings, apparently in trials for high treason, but it also applies in civil matters, and in both cases it has been established for reasons which relate to the essential effectiveness of the criminal law. The rule is subject to only one exception, imposed by the need to demonstrate the innocence of an accused person. There are no exceptions in proceedings other than criminal. Its application does not depend on the judge's discretion, as it is a legal rule of public order by which the judge is bound.

The identity of informers is generally not relevant. When a trial judge is engaged in the editing process, he or she must consider the "innocence at stake" exception. In *Re Rideout and The Queen* (1986), 31 C.C.C. (3d) 211 at p. 220, 61 Nfld. & P.E.I.R. 160 (S.C.), Goodridge J. took the following view of the exception:

> The rule against the identification of police informants is only made possible because, in almost every case, it will not be relevant... Where it is relevant, it will be admitted for that was the one exception mentioned by Beetz J. in the passage set forth above — the situation where disclosure was needed to demonstrate the innocence of an accused person.

In *Roviaro v. United States*, 353 U.S. 53 at pp. 60-1 (1957) (7th Cir.), Justice Burton wrote:

> Where the disclosure of an informer's identity, or of the contents of his communication, is relevant and helpful to the defence of an accused, or is essential to a fair determination of a cause, the privilege must give way. In these situations the trial court may require disclosure and, if the Government withholds the information, dismiss the action.

In *R. v. Chambers* (1985), 20 C.C.C. (3d) 440 at p. 451, 14 W.C.B. 268 (Ont. C.A.), Martin J.A. pointed out that the exception was "more likely to apply where the informer is a witness to material facts".

The determination in each case will require the balancing of the relevance of the identity of the informer to the accused's case against the prejudice to the informer and to the public interest in law enforcement which disclosure would occasion. The issue does not arise in this appeal since it is not contended that the identity of the informer is relevant. It is undesirable, therefore, to delve further into the process of weighing these interests in determining whether an exception has been made out. Suffice it to say that it is very much a determination to be made by the trial judge.

The question remains as to the extent of editing and the procedure to be followed. Since there will be more than one method of striking a proper balance between the interests of law enforcement and of the right to make full answer and defence, I would not wish to place trial judges in a "strait-jacket" by laying down ironclad rules with respect to editing. In deciding what to edit, the following factors outlined by Watt J. in *R. v. Parmar* (1987), 34 C.C.C. (3d) 260 at pp. 281-2, 1 W.C.B. (2d) 335 (Ont. H.C.J.), commend themselves to me:

> (a) whether the identities of confidential police informants, and consequently their lives and safety, may be compromised, bearing in mind that such disclosure may occur as much by reference to the nature of the information supplied by the confidential source as by the publication of his or her name;
>
> (b) whether the nature and extent of ongoing law enforcement investigations would thereby be compromised;

(c) whether disclosure would reveal particular intelligence-gathering techniques thereby endangering those engaged therein and prejudicing future investigation of similar offences and the public interest in law enforcement and crime detection, and
(d) whether the disclosure would prejudice the interests of innocent persons.

I have examined the procedure followed in *Parmar*, approved in *R. v. Rowbotham* (1988), 41 C.C.C. (3d) 1, 63 C.R. (3d) 113, 35 C.R.R. 207. (Ont. C.A.), and the procedure followed by the Court of Appeal in this case. The following outline is the procedure which, in my view, should be followed. It is not intended to be exclusive or exhaustive.

1. Upon opening of the packet, if the Crown objects to disclosure of any of the material, an application should be made by the Crown suggesting the nature of the matters to be edited and the basis therefor. Only Crown counsel will have the affidavit at this point.
2. The trial judge should then edit the affidavit as proposed by Crown counsel and furnish a copy as edited to counsel for the accused. Submissions should then be entertained from counsel for the accused. If the trial judge is of the view that counsel for the accused will not be able to appreciate the nature of the deletions from the submissions of Crown counsel and the edited affidavit, a form of judicial summary as to the general nature of the deletions should be provided.
3. After hearing counsel for the accused and reply from the Crown, the trial judge should make a final determination as to editing, bearing in mind that editing is to be kept to a minimum and applying the factors listed above.
4. After the determination has been made in step 3, the packet material should be provided to the accused.
5. If the Crown can support the authorization on the basis of the material as edited, the authorization is confirmed.
6. If, however, the editing renders the authorization insupportable, then the Crown may apply to have the trial judge consider so much of the excised material as is necessary to support the authorization. The trial judge should accede to such a request only if satisfied that the accused is sufficiently aware of the nature of the excised material to challenge it in argument or by evidence. In this regard, a judicial summary of the excised material should be provided if it will fulfill that function. It goes without saying that if the Crown is dissatisfied with the extent of disclosure and is of the view that the public interest will be prejudiced, it can withdraw tender of the wiretap evidence.

In this case, the Court of Appeal was in substantial compliance with the procedures outlined above. The process stopped after step 5. No issue can be taken with respect to the procedure followed.

6. Is the accused entitled to cross-examination on the affidavit filed with the authorizing judge?

The appellant asserts a right to cross-examine the affiant on the affidavits filed in support of the authorization. Specifically, he seeks to attack the statement made by the affiant that he (the affiant) received information from an informer, who had proved reliable in the past and that in the month of December, 1982, Garofoli and Criminisi had approached ... (edited) with an offer to supply him with two kilograms of cocaine to sell for them. He filed two affidavits, his own and that of his former counsel. The substance of the affidavits is described in the reasons of Martin J.A. as follows (at p. 130):

> Garofoli's affidavit states that he lived in Florida from September, 1977 up to August, 1983, when he returned to Hamilton to live. He was charged in Hamilton with certain offences of fraud and conspiracy to defraud, and he states in his affidavit that the only occasions on which he was in Hamilton, or even in Ontario, until he returned to Hamilton to live in August, 1983, were in connection with court appearances on those charges. He states that the only occasions on which he was in Hamilton during the latter part of 1982 or the early part of 1983 were in connection with court appearances on November 3, 1982, January 14, 1983, and on certain dates in February, March, April and May, 1983. He states that the allegation contained in Officer Campbell's affidavit, sworn on September 29, 1983, that some person was approached by Garofoli and Criminisi in December, 1982, with a proposal that this individual sell cocaine for them, is totally false, that he was not in Hamilton in the month of December, 1982, nor did he see or meet with Criminisi during any of his visits to Hamilton in connection with court appearances. He further states that the officer in charge of the fraud and conspiracy case was well aware that he was living in Florida and travelled to Hamilton only in connection with his court appearances, and that if Officer Campbell had made any inquiries he would readily have been aware that he was living in Florida during December, 1982.

The Court of Appeal refused cross-examination on the ground that accepting these affidavits as true, they did not establish that the affiant Campbell had "made a false statement in his affidavit knowingly and intentionally or with reckless disregard for its truth".

These pre-conditions for cross-examination of the affiant are based largely on the American case of *Franks v. Delaware* [438 U.S. 154 (1978)]. They were adopted by the Court of Appeal in *R. v. Church of Scientology* (1987), 31 C.C.C. (3d) 449, 30 C.R.R. 238 (and in *Rowbotham, supra*). Most recently, they were upheld by Watt J. in *R. v. Parmar* (1987), 37 C.C.C. (3d) 300 at p. 344, 61 O.R. (2d) 132, 2 W.C.B. (2d) 355, where Watt J. stated them to be as follows:

> (i) there must be specific allegation(s) of deliberate falsehood or reckless disregard for the truth in respect of specific aspects of the supportive affidavit;
>
> (ii) there must be *prima facie* proof by the applicant in admissible form, of the substance of what is alleged to controvert the specific contents of the affidavit; and
>
> (iii) it must be made to appear that, if the material impugned as false or in reckless regard of the truth is set aside, that which remains is insufficient to sustain the issuance of the impugned order under s. 178.13(1) or 178.13(4), as the case may be.

In my opinion, these pre-conditions are subject to the same criticisms that were levelled at the pre-conditions for the sealed packet imposed by the restricted access cases. In *R. v. Playford* [(1987), 40 C.C.C. (3d) 142 (Ont. C.A.)], Goodman J.A. stated (at p. 178): "... he cannot gain access to the affidavit unless he can prove on a *prima facie* basis the grounds for such access and he cannot prove such grounds unless he has access." And in *Finlay* [(1985), 23 C.C.C. (3d) 48 (Ont. C.A.)], Martin J.A. stated (at p. 77):

> Counsel for the appellants stated that in consequence of the restriction placed on an accused's access to the sealed packet, the accused finds himself in an impossible situation. To ascertain whether there has been fraud or non-disclosure he requires access to the sealed packet, but he cannot gain access to the sealed packet unless he proves fraud or non-disclosure.

Applying that statement to this situation, the appellant cannot cross-examine unless he provides proof of deliberate falsehood or reckless disregard for the truth, and he cannot establish deliberate falsehood or reckless disregard for the truth unless he can cross-examine.

Furthermore, I question the utility of cross-examination if the accused can establish, even on a *prima facie* basis, deliberate falsehood or reckless disregard for truth. Except on television, most cross-examiners would consider a cross-examination to have succeeded marvelously if the result is a *prima facie* case that the affiant has been deliberately false or reckless. If this can be made out *ab extra*, there is no need to cross-examine.

.....

In my opinion, the pre-conditions in *Franks v. Delaware*, *supra*, are too restrictive. I believe that they are inconsistent with the approach which we have taken in Canada with respect to the right to cross-examine. Moreover, subject to the protection of the identity of informants and the concern with respect to the prolongation of proceedings, I see no reason for such a drastic curtailment of the right. I believe these concerns can be accommodated without imposing restrictions as inhibitive as those in *Franks v. Delaware.* With respect to informants, there is no right to cross-examine them. The informant is not a witness and cannot be identified unless the accused brings himself within the "innocence at stake" exception.

With respect to prolixity, I am in favour of placing reasonable limitations on the cross-examination. Leave must be obtained to cross-examine. The granting of leave must be left to the exercise of the discretion of the trial judge. Leave should be granted when the trial judge is satisfied that cross-examination is necessary to enable the accused to make full answer and defence. A basis must be shown by the accused for the view that the cross-examination will elicit testimony tending to discredit the existence of one of the pre-conditions to the authorization, as for example the existence of reasonable and probable grounds.

When permitted, the cross-examination should be limited by the trial judge to questions that are directed to establish that there was no basis upon which the authorization could have been granted. The discretion of the trial judge should not be interfered with on appeal except in cases in which it has not been judicially exercised. While leave to cross-examine is not the general rule, it is justified in these circumstances in order to prevent an abuse of what is essentially a ruling on the admissibility of evidence.

In my opinion, the appellant has shown a basis for the cross-examination here. In view of the degree of reliance by the police on the informant in this case, if the informant is discredited then the factual basis for the authorization is undermined. If it is shown that the informant lied, then it could raise the inference that the police knew or ought to have known that he lied. If the police were not warranted in their belief that the information was true, then the basis for belief that a crime was to be committed disappears. Accordingly, the appellant should have been permitted to cross-examine. Cross-examination having been denied, there must be a new trial.

B. INVESTIGATIVE DETENTION AND THE CHARTER

One of the most significant issues which arises daily is the extent to which police can detain, short of arrest. This is particularly so, given the liberal interpretation of "detention" articulated by the Supreme Court of Canada. See "The Meaning of Detention" at p. 202 of this text.

R. v. SIMPSON

(1993), 79 C.C.C. (3d) 482 (Ont. C.A.)

[A street contact told one officer that a particular residence was a suspected "crack house". Officer Wilkin read that officer's memo. He did not know the source or anything else about the residence. On the material date, Wilkin patrolled the area around the residence. He observed the accused and a woman leave the residence and drive away and he followed, intending to pull them over for investigative purposes to see who they were and what they would say. He did direct the vehicle to pull over, and had the nervous-looking woman sit in the police cruiser while he questioned the accused. In response to questions from Wilkin, the accused identified himself and indicated that he had previously been in trouble "for theft and a knife". The accused also said that he did not have a knife in his possession at that time. Wilkin noticed a bulge in the accused's front pant pocket. He reached out and felt a "hard lump" there. Wilkin asked the accused what was in his pocket. The accused replied "Nothing". Wilkin asked the accused to remove the object from his pocket "very carefully". The accused removed the object very quickly as if trying to throw something away. Wilkin grabbed the accused's hand and after a slight struggle, subdued the accused. The object was a baggie of cocaine. In cross-examination, Wilkin confirmed that he did not have reasonable and probable grounds to arrest the accused until he realized that Simpson was in possession of what appeared to be cocaine. Wilkin stated that he felt the accused's pocket, in part because the accused said that he had been in trouble involving a knife at some earlier time. He denied that he had formed the intention to search the accused for a weapon when he saw the bulge in his pant pocket. At issue was the admissibility of the cocaine at the accused's trial for possession for the purpose of trafficking.]

The judgment of the court was delivered by

Doherty J.A.: —

.....

A. Was the appellant arbitrarily detained?

.....

The appellant was clearly detained when the motor vehicle in which he was riding was pulled over by constable Wilkin: *R. v. Ladouceur* (1990), 56 C.C.C. (3d) 22 at pp. 36-7, [1990] 1 S.C.R. 1257, 77 C.R. (3d) 110; *R. v. Hufsky* (1988), 40 C.C.C. (3d) 398 at p. 406, [1988] 1 S.C.R. 621, 63 C.R. (3d) 14; *R. v. Wilson* (1990), 56 C.C.C. (3d) 142, [1990] 1 S.C.R. 1291, 77 C.R. (3d) 136.

Section 9 of the *Charter* limits the power of the police to detain individuals. It draws the line, subject to s. 1 of the *Charter*, at detentions which are arbitrary. The words "arbitrary" and "unlawful" are not synonymous. A lawful detention may be arbitrary (*Ladouceur, supra*; *Hufsky, supra*), and an unlawful detention is not necessarily arbitrary: *R. v. Duguay* (1985), 18 C.C.C. (3d) 289 at p. 296, 18 D.L.R. (4th) 32, 50 O.R. (2d) 375 (C.A.); affirmed without reference to this point by the majority 46 C.C.C. (3d) 1, 56 D.L.R. (4th) 46, [1989] 1 S.C.R. 93; *R. v. Cayer* (1988), 66 C.R. (3d) 30 at p. 43, 42 C.R.R. 353, 6 M.V.R. (2d) 1 (Ont. C.A.), leave to appeal refused [1989] 1 S.C.R. *vi*, C.R.R. *loc. cit.*, 99 N.R. 276*n* (S.C.C.). Although an assessment of the lawfulness of a detention is not dispositive of the s. 9 claim, it is appropriate to begin by addressing the lawfulness of the detention. If the detention is lawful, it is not arbitrary unless the law authorizing the detention is arbitrary. If the detention is found to be unlawful, that finding will play a central role in determining whether the detention is also arbitrary.

This detention was a direct result of the stopping of a motor vehicle. The lawfulness of the detention depends on the police officer's authority to stop the vehicle. The officer's purpose in effecting the stop is, in turn, relevant to the lawfulness of that stop. Constable Wilkin candidly acknowledged that his decision to stop the motor vehicle had nothing to do with the enforcement of laws relating to the operation of motor vehicles. Nor did Constable Wilkin rely on any specific statutory authority (for example, ss. 10 or 11 of the *Narcotic Control Act*, R.S.C. 1985, c. N-1) when he stopped the vehicle. Constable Wilkin stopped the car for two reasons. He was seeking confirmation of the report concerning the activities at the alleged "crack house" and he wanted the opportunity, by questioning the occupants of the vehicle and looking into the vehicle, to develop grounds to arrest either or both of the occupants for drug-related offences. As Constable Wilkin put it, the stop was made for purely "investigative purposes".

The respondent submits that constable Wilkin's power to stop the vehicle and detain its occupants for purposes relating to the investigation of possible criminal activity can be found in s. 216(1) of the *Highway Traffic Act*, R.S.O. 1990, c. H.8. That section reads:

> 216(1) *A police officer, in the lawful execution of his or her duties and responsibilities may require the driver of a motor vehicle to stop* and the driver of a motor vehicle, when signalled or requested to stop by a police officer who is readily identifiable as such, shall immediately come to a safe stop.

(Emphasis added.)

The respondent contends that the duties referred to in s. 216(1) include the general duty to prevent and investigate crime recognized at common law and given statutory force by the *Police Services Act*, R.S.O. 1990, c. P.15, s. 42. I agree: *R. v. Hisey* (1985), 24 C.C.C. (3d) 20 at p. 26, 40 M.V.R. 152 (Ont. C.A.); leave to appeal refused M.V.R. *loc. cit.*, 67 N.R. 160*n* (S.C.C.).

Counsel for the respondent goes on to argue that s. 216(1) empowers the officer to stop motor vehicles and of necessity detain the occupants of those vehicles where that stop occurs in the context of an investigation of possible criminal activity such as the possession of illicit narcotics. In making this submission, counsel relies on the decision of the Saskatchewan Court of Appeal in *R. v. Duncanson* (1991), 12 C.R. (4th) 86, 30 M.V.R. (2d) 17, 4 W.A.C. 193 (Sask. C.A.); affirmed without reference to this point [1992] 1 S.C.R. 836, 12 C.R. (4th) 98, 36 M.V.R. (2d) 125. In *Duncanson*, the Court of Appeal held that the Saskatchewan statutory equivalent of s. 216(1) of the *Highway Traffic Act* authorized vehicle stops in the course of the investigation of drug-related criminal activity. In so concluding, the court relied on the judgment of the Supreme Court of Canada in *R. v. Ladouceur, supra*.

Ladouceur is one of a series of judgments of the Supreme Court of Canada involving the constitutionality of various forms of police "check stops". In these cases, the police randomly stopped automobiles to investigate the mechanical fitness of the vehicles, to determine whether the drivers were impaired and to ensure that the drivers were licensed and in possession of the required documents. In doing so, the police were enforcing the laws relating to the operation of motor vehicles on public thoroughfares. None of these cases involved a stop for investigative purposes not related to the operation of the motor vehicle stopped.

In *Ladouceur, supra*, and the earlier case of *Hufsky, supra*, the Crown argued that the stops were authorized by s. 189a(1) of the *Highway Traffic Act*, R.S.O. 1980, c. 198, as amended, 1981, c. 72, s. 2. That was the predecessor section to the present s. 216(1) of the *Highway Traffic Act*. The language in the two sections is identical.

In *Hufsky, supra*, p. 406, Le Dain J. for the court, held:

> Section 189a(1) of the *Highway Traffic Act* empowers a police officer who is in the lawful execution of his duties and responsibilities to require the driver of a motor vehicle to stop. It does not specify that there must be some grounds or cause for stopping a particular driver but on its face leaves the choice of the drivers to be stopped to the discretion of the officer. In carrying out the purposes of the spot check procedure, including the observation of the condition or "sobriety" of the driver, the officer was clearly in the lawful execution of his duties and responsibilities.

Read in isolation, this passage might support the respondent's position. However, when the judgment is read in its entirety, particularly the passages referrable to s. 1 of the *Charter*, it is clear to me that Le Dain J. was addressing the scope of s. 189*a*(1) of the *Highway Traffic Act* only in connection with stops made to assist in the enforcement of laws relating to the operation of motor vehicles.

Similarly, in *Ladouceur*, the authority to stop provided under the *Highway Traffic Act* was addressed entirely in the context of a "routine check" of drivers and their vehicles for purposes referrable to the enforcement of motor vehicle-related laws. Cory J., for the majority, wrote at pp. 37-8:

> The power of a police officer to stop motor vehicles at random is derived from s. 189a(1) of the *Highway Traffic Act* and is thus prescribed by law: see *Hufsky, supra,* at p. 407. The authority also has been justified by this court in its decision in *Dedman* [59 C.C.C. (2d) 97, 122 D.L.R. (3d) 655, 32 O.R. (2d) 641; appeal dismissed for different reasons 20 C.C.C. (3d) 97, 20 D.L.R. (4th) 321, [1985] 2 S.C.R. 2], as a prescription of the common law.

Equating the statutory power to stop found in the *Highway Traffic Act* with the common law power to stop referred to in *R. v. Dedman* (1981), 59 C.C.C. (2d) 97, 122 D.L.R. (3d) 655, 23 C.R. (3d) 228 (Ont. C.A.); appeal dismissed for different reasons 20 C.C.C. (3d) 97, 20 D.L.R. (4th) 321, [1985] 2 S.C.R. 2, is particularly illuminating. In *Dedman, supra,* at pp. 119-22, the court held that the common law ancillary police power justified random stops of vehicles in the course of the enforcement of laws relating to the operation of those vehicles. This power to stop was, however, closely tied to the particular purpose of the stops, the dangers presented by the activity targeted by the stops, the qualified nature of the liberty interfered with by the stops, and the absence of other less intrusive means of effective enforcement of the relevant laws. The authority to stop described in *Dedman* was clearly not a general power to stop for all police purposes, but was limited to stops made in furtherance of the police duty to protect those who use the public roadways from those who use those roadways in a dangerous manner.

Mr. Justice Cory's analysis in *Ladouceur* of the applicability of s. 1 of the *Charter* also indicates that he was considering s. 189*a*(1) of the *Highway Traffic Act* only as an authority for stops made in the course of the enforcement of laws relating to the operation of motor vehicles. He described the purpose of the legislation as being to achieve safety on the highway and referred to random stops as the only means capable of providing adequate enforcement of laws designed to provide for that safety. In deciding whether the legislation impaired individual rights as little as possible, Cory J. referred to the serious hazards posed by impaired and incompetent drivers and to the close regulation of motor vehicles and their operation. The entire s. 1 analysis of Cory J. and all of the evidence put before him proceeded on the premise that the section authorized stops as part of a scheme for the enforcement of motor vehicle related laws. Had the court been considering the constitutionality of s. 189*a*(1) as authority for stops outside of the highway safety context, s. 1 of the *Charter* would have required a much broader approach.

At the conclusion of his s. 1 analysis, Cory J. again made it very clear that he was concerned only with vehicular stops made for particular purposes. He said at p. 44:

> Finally, it must be shown that the routine check does not so severely trench upon the s. 9 right so as to outweigh the legislative objective. The concern at this stage is the perceived potential for abuse of this power by law enforcement officials. In my opinion, these fears are unfounded. *There are mechanisms already in place which prevent abuse. Officers can stop persons only for legal reasons, in this case reasons related to driving a car such as checking the driver's licence and insurance, the sobriety of the driver and the mechanical fitness of the vehicle. Once stopped the only questions that may justifiably be asked are those related to driving offences.* Any further, more intrusive procedures could only be undertaken based upon reasonable and probable grounds. Where a stop is found

> to be unlawful, the evidence from the stop could well be excluded under s. 24(2) of the *Charter*.

(Emphasis added.)

The limited reach of *Ladouceur* and *Hufsky* was made clear in *R. v. Mellenthin* (1992), 76 C.C.C. (3d) 481, [1992] 3 S.C.R. 615, 16 C.R. (4th) 273 (S.C.C.). In *Mellenthin*, the police pulled the appellant's vehicle over at random to check his documentation and his physical condition. After asking the driver to produce the appropriate documentation, the officers questioned the driver concerning the contents of a bag on the seat of the car. Eventually they searched that bag and found narcotics.

As the initial detention in *Mellenthin* was for purposes related to the enforcement of motor vehicle related laws, it was a constitutional, although arbitrary, detention. The court, however, through Cory J., emphatically set the permissible limits for such stops (at pp. 487 and 490):

> Check-stop programs result in the arbitrary detention of motorists. The programs are justified as a means aimed at reducing the terrible toll of death and injury so often occasioned by impaired drivers or by dangerous vehicles. The primary aim of the program is thus to check for sobriety, licences, ownership, insurance and the mechanical fitness of cars. The police use of check stops should not be extended beyond these aims. Random stop programs must not be turned into a means of conducting either an unfounded general inquisition or an unreasonable search.
>
> As noted earlier, check stops infringe the *Charter* rights against arbitrary detention. They are permitted as means designed to meet the pressing need to prevent the needless death and injury resulting from the dangerous operation of motor vehicles. The rights granted to police to conduct check-stop programs or random stops of motorists should not be extended.

In my opinion, the "check-stop" cases decide only that stops made for the purposes of enforcing driving-related laws and promoting the safe use of motor vehicles are authorized by s. 216(1) of the *Highway Traffic Act*, even where those stops are random. These cases do not declare that all stops which assist the police in the performance of any of their duties are authorized by s. 216(1) of the *Highway Traffic Act*.

Once, as in this case, road safety concerns are removed as a basis for the stop, then powers associated with and predicated upon those particular concerns cannot be relied on to legitimize the stop. Where the stop and the detention are unrelated to the operation of the vehicle or other road safety matters, the fact that the target of the detention is in an automobile cannot enhance the police power to detain that individual.

Section 216(1) of the *Highway Traffic Act* refers to stops made in the "lawful execution" of the officer's duty. In my opinion, the scope of the officer's power to investigate crimes unrelated to the operation of motor vehicles is unaffected by s. 216(1) except that the section empowers the officer to stop a vehicle where the officer otherwise has the lawful authority to stop and detain one or more of the occupants of the vehicle. Constable Wilkin had the authority to stop the vehicle and detain the occupants only if at the time he did so he could lawfully have stopped or detained one or both of the occupants had he encountered them on the street. If he had no such authority, he was not acting in the "lawful execution" of his duty as required by s. 216.

The search for a legal authority for this stop and detention must go beyond s. 216(1) of the *Highway Traffic Act*.

The law imposes broad general duties on the police but it provides them with only limited powers to perform those duties. Police duties and their authority to act in the performance of those duties are not co-extensive. Police conduct is not rendered lawful merely because it assisted in the performance of the duties assigned to the police. Where police conduct interferes with the liberty or freedom of the individual, that conduct will be lawful only if it is authorized by law. That law may be a specific statutory power or it may be the common law. As I have rejected the only statutory authority put forward to support this detention (s. 216(1) of the *Highway Traffic Act*), I will now consider whether the common law authorized this detention.

Attempts to set the ambit of police common law powers fill many pages of the reports and law journals...

.....

As the authorities plainly show, judicial efforts to define the police common law power have generated considerable disagreement. The appellant submits that, whatever uncertainties may exist concerning the reach of police common law powers, this court has held that a detention for investigative purposes, absent proper grounds for an arrest, is an unauthorized and potentially arbitrary detention. In *Duguay*, *supra*, at p. 296, MacKinnon A.C.J.O. said:

> In my view, on the facts as found by the trial judge, the arrest or detention was arbitrary, being for quite an improper purpose — namely, to assist in the investigation.

The facts which precipitated this statement were, however, significantly different than those present in this case. In *Duguay*, the police formally arrested the suspects near the scene of the alleged crime, placed them in a police cruiser, transported them to the police station and held them in locked interview rooms for a considerable period of time during which the suspects were interrogated at some length. It was that prolonged and highly intrustive detention, premised only on a suspicion short of reasonable and probable grounds for an arrest, that was held to be arbitrary. In my view, it does not follow from *Duguay* that any and all detentions for investigative purposes constitute a violation of s. 9 of the *Charter*: Young, "All Along the Watch Tower", *ibid.*, at p. 367.

The appellant also relies on this court's judgment in *R. v. Dedman*, *supra*, where Martin J.A. for the court said:

> In carrying out their general duties, the police have limited powers, and they are entitled to interfere with the liberty and property of the citizen only where such interference is authorized by law. It is, of course, a constitutional principle that the citizen has a right not to be subjected to imprisonment, arrest or physical restraint that is not justified by law, and every invasion of the property of the citizen is a trespass unless legally justified... Although a police officer is entitled to question any person in order to obtain information with respect to a suspected offence, he has no lawful power to compel the person questioned to answer. *Moreover, a police officer has no right to detain a person for questioning or for further investigation. No one is entitled to impose any*

> *physical restraint upon the citizen except as authorized by law, and this principle applies as much to police officers as to anyone else.*

(Emphasis added.)

The appellant argues that this passage limits the police power to detain to those situations where there are reasonable and probable grounds to arrest the individual detained. There is certainly support for this contention: *Report of the Canadian Committee on Corrections, Towards Unity: Criminal Justice and Corrections*, pp. 56-7 (Ottawa: The Queen's Printer, 1969) (Chair, R. Ouimet); Hogg, *Constitutional Law of Canada*, 4th ed., p. 1072 (1992); *Dedman, supra, per* Dickson C.J.C. in dissent at p. 104.

I have no doubt that the passage from *Dedman, supra*, accurately states the law. It has been approved in numerous subsequent judgments ...

.....

I do not, however, read the words of Martin J.A. in *Dedman* as holding that the common law power of the police never extends to the power to detain an individual in the course of a criminal investigation unless the police have the power to arrest that individual. I understand the passage to state that the desire to question or otherwise investigate an individual does not, in and of itself, authorize the detention of that individual. In other words, there is no general power to detain whenever that detention will assist a police officer in the execution of his or her duty. To deny that general power is not, however, to deny the authority to detain short of arrest in all circumstances where the detention has an investigative purpose.

I come to my interpretation of the language of Martin J.A. in *Dedman, supra*, in part from an examination of the judgment of the majority of the Supreme Court of Canada in the same case. In *Dedman*, the police had established check-points where vehicles were stopped at random and drivers asked to produce their licence, insurance and ownership documents. The stops were part of an organized publicized programme designed to deter drinking and driving and apprehend those who were not deterred. There was no statutory authority for the stops. Motorists who were stopped were detained during the stops to permit the police to assess the driver's sobriety.

The majority (*per* Le Dain J.) and the dissent (*per* Dickson C.J.C.) agreed that police powers were limited to those provided by statute or existing at common law. Le Dain J. said at p. 116:

> In my opinion, police officers, when acting or purporting to act in their official capacity as agents of the State, only act lawfully if they act in the exercise of authority which is either conferred by statute or derived as a matter of common law from their duties.

There was, however, strong disagreement between the majority and dissent as to the limits of the acknowledged common law authority. I need refer to only the majority position. Le Dain J. adopted the "ancillary power doctrine" set down in *R. v. Waterfield*, [1963] 3 All E.R. 659, [1964] 1 Q.B. 164 (C.C.A.), and reflected in *R. v. Knowlton, supra*, and *R. v. Stenning*, [1970] 3 C.C.C. 145, 10 D.L.R. (3d) 224, [1970] S.C.R. 631. Quoting from Ashworth J. in *Waterfield*, Le Dain J. said at pp. 119-20:

> In the judgment of this court it would be difficult, and in the present case it is unnecessary, to reduce within specific limits the general terms in which

> the duties of police constables have been expressed. In most cases it is probably more convenient to consider what the police constable was actually doing and in particular whether such conduct was prima facie an unlawful interference with a person's liberty or property. If so, it is then relevant to consider whether (a) such conduct falls within the general scope of any duty imposed by statute or recognized at common law and (b) whether such conduct, albeit within the general scope of such a duty, involved an unjustifiable use of powers associated with the duty.

Le Dain J. applied the *Waterfield* test to the random stops and detentions effected by the R.I.D.E. programme and decided that they were a lawful manifestation of the common law powers of the police. His conclusion constitutes a recognition that the common law police power can, in appropriate circumstances, authorize some forms of detention for investigative purposes.

Dedman, supra, in this court pronounces against a general power at common law to detain for investigative purposes. *Dedman, supra,* in the Supreme Court of Canada does not detract from that pronouncement but acknowledges that detentions imposed in the execution of a police officer's duty will be lawful if they meet the *Waterfield* criteria although they are for investigative purposes and although there are no grounds for the arrest of the detainee.

.....

Further support for a common law power to detain short of arrest for investigative purposes can be found in *R. v. Elshaw* (1989), 70 C.R. (3d) 197, 45 C.R.R. 140, 7 W.C.B. (2d) 383 (B.C.C.A.); reversed 67 C.C.C. (3d) 97, [1991] 3 S.C.R. 24, 7 C.R. (4th) 333.

.....

Especially in light of the definition of "detention" adopted in *R. v. Therens* (1985), 18 C.C.C. (3d) 481, 18 D.L.R. (4th) 655, [1985] 1 S.C.R. 613, and *R. v. Thomsen* (1988), 40 C.C.C. (3d) 411, [1988] 1 S.C.R. 640, 63 C.R. (3d) 1, I have no doubt that the police detain individuals for investigative purposes when they have no basis to arrest them. In some situations the police would be regarded as derelict in their duties if they did not do so. I agree with Professor Young, "All Along the Watch Tower", *ibid.*, at p. 367 when he asserts:

> The courts must recognize the reality of investigatory detention and begin the process of regulating the practice so that street detentions do not end up being non-stationhouse incommunicado arrests.

Unless and until Parliament or the legislature acts, the common law and specifically the criteria formulated in *Waterfield, supra,* must provide the means whereby the courts regulate the police power to detain for investigatory purposes.

In deciding whether an interference with an individual's liberty is authorized under the common law, one must first decide whether the police were acting in the course of their duty when they effected that interference. In this case, Constable Wilkin indicated that he was investigating the possible commission of drug-related criminal offences at the suspected "crack house". While a police officer's stated purpose is not determinative when deciding whether the officer was acting in the course of his or her duty, there is no suggestion here that Constable Wilkin was not pursuing an investigation into the possible commission of drug-related crimes when he stopped and detained the appellant. The wide duties placed on police officers in relation to the prevention of crime and the enforcement of criminal laws encompass investigations to determine whether criminal activities are occurring at a particular location as well as efforts to substantiate police intelligence. I am satisfied that Constable Wilkin was engaged in the execution of his duty when he stopped and detained the appellant. The lawfulness of that conduct will depend on whether the stop and detention involved an unjustifiable use of the powers associated with Constable Wilkin's duty.

The reasons of Le Dain J. in *Dedman, supra*, at pp. 121-2, indicate that the justifiability of an officer's conduct depends on a number of factors including the duty being performed, the extent to which some interference with individual liberty is necessitated in order to perform that duty, the importance of the performance of that duty to the public good, the liberty interfered with, and the nature and extent of the interference. This "totality of the circumstances" approach is similar to that found in the American jurisprudence referable to the constitutionality of investigative stops (*United States v. Cortez*, 449 U.S. 411 at pp. 417-8, 101 S. Ct. 690 (1981); *Alabama v. White*, 110 S. Ct. 2412 at p. 2416 (1990)), and in the Canadian case-law relating to s. 8 of the *Charter*: *R. v. Garofoli* (1990), 60 C.C.C. (3d) 161 at pp. 189-90, [1990] 2 S.C.R. 1421, 80 C.R. (3d) 317.

In applying the analytical technique developed in *Dedman, supra*, it is apparent that many of the factors relied on there have no application to this case. The appellant's liberty interest interfered with in this case was not the qualified right to drive a motor vehicle but what Le Dain J. referred to at p. 121 as "the fundamental liberty" to move about in society without governmental interference. Further, there is no suggestion that detentions such as the one which occurred in this case are necessary to properly and effectively enforce laws proscribing drug-related criminal activity. Some bases other than the limited nature of the right interfered with and the necessity of the interference must be found before this detention can meet the justifiability requirement in *Waterfield*.

In addressing this requirement, it is also essential to keep in mind the context of the particular police-citizen confrontation. Constable Wilkin was investigating the appellant and the driver of the car. They were his targets. Constable Wilkin interfered with the appellant's liberty in the hope that he would acquire grounds to arrest him. He was not performing any service-related police function and the detention was not aimed at protecting or assisting the detainee. It was an adversarial and confrontational process intended to bring the force of the criminal justice process into operation against the appellant. The validity of the stop and the detention must be addressed with that purpose in mind. Different criteria may well govern detentions which occur in a non-adversarial setting not involving the exercise of the police crime prevention function.

In my opinion, where an individual is detained by the police in the course of efforts to determine whether that individual is involved in criminal activity being investigated by the police, that detention can only be justified if the detaining officer has some "articulable cause" for the detention.

The phrase "articulable cause" appears in American jurisprudence concerned with the constitutionality of investigative detentions.

.....

[The American] cases require a constellation of objectively discernible facts which give the detaining officer reasonable cause to suspect that the detainee is criminally implicated in the activity under investigation. The requirement that the facts must meet an objectively discernible standard is recognized in connection with the arrest power (*R. v. Storrey* (1990), 53 C.C.C. (3d) 316 at p. 324, [1990] 1 S.C.R. 241, 75 C.R. (3d) 1), and serves to avoid indiscriminate and discriminatory exercises of the police power. A "hunch" based entirely on intuition gained by experience cannot suffice, no matter how accurate that "hunch" might prove to be. Such subjectively based assessments can too easily mask discriminatory conduct based on such irrelevant factors as the detainee's sex, colour, age, ethnic origin or sexual orientation. Equally, without objective criteria detentions could be based on mere speculation. A guess which proves accurate becomes in hindsight a "hunch". In this regard, I must disagree with *R. v. Nelson* (1987), 35 C.C.C. (3d) 347 at p. 355, 29 C.R.R. 80, 46 M.V.R. 145 (Man. C.A.), where it is said that detention may be justified if the officer "intuitively senses that his intervention may be required in the public interest". Rather, I agree with Professor Young in "All Along the Watch Tower", *ibid.*, at p. 375:

> In order to avoid an attribution of arbitrary conduct, the state official must be operating under a set of criteria that at minimum, bears some relationship to a reasonable suspicion of crime but not necessarily to a credibly-based probability of crime.

.....

I should not be taken as holding that the presence of an articulable cause renders any detention for investigative purposes a justifiable exercise of a police officer's common law powers. The inquiry into the existence of an articulable cause is only the first step in the determination of whether the detention was justified in the totality of the circumstances and consequently a lawful exercise of the officer's common law powers as described in *Waterfield*, *supra*, and approved in *Dedman*, *supra*. Without articulable cause, no detention to investigate the detainee for possible criminal activity could be viewed as a proper exercise of the common law power. If articulable cause exists, the detention may or may not be justified. For example, a reasonably based suspicion that a person committed some property- related offence at a distant point in the past, while an articulable cause, would not, standing alone, justify the detention of that person on a public street to question him or her about that offence. On the other hand, a reasonable suspicion that a person had just committed a violent crime and was in flight from the scene of that crime could well justify some detention of that individual in an effort to quickly confirm or refute the suspicion. Similarly, the existence of an articulable cause that justified a brief detention, perhaps to ask the person detained for identification, would not necessarily justify a more intrusive detention complete with physical restraint and a more extensive interrogation.

In summary, I do not consider the articulable cause inquiry as providing the answer to the lawfulness of the police conduct but rather as the first step in the broader inquiry described in *Waterfield*, *supra*, and *Dedman*, *supra*.

Turning to this case, I can find no articulable cause justifying the detention. Constable Wilkin had information of unknown age that another police officer had been told that the residence was believed to be a "crack house". Constable Wilkin did not know the primary source of the information and he had no reason to believe that the source in general, or this particular piece of information, was reliable. It is doubtful that this information standing alone could provide a reasonable suspicion that the suspect residence was the scene of criminal activity.

Any glimmer of an articulable cause disappears, however, when one considers whether Constable Wilkin had reason to suspect that the appellant or the driver of the car was involved in criminal activity. He knew nothing about either person and he did not suggest that anything either had done, apart from being at the house, aroused his suspicion or suggested criminal activity. Attendance at a location believed to be the site of ongoing criminal activity is a factor which may contribute to the existence of "articulable cause". Where that is the sole factor, however, and the information concerning the location is itself of unknown age and reliability, no articulable cause exists. Were it otherwise, the police would have a general warrant to stop anyone who happened to attend at any place which the police had a reason to believe could be the site of ongoing criminal activity.

As Constable Wilkin had no articulable cause for the detention, the common law police power did not authorize his conduct. It was unlawful. Following *Duguay*, *supra*, it may be that a detention although unlawful would not be arbitrary if the officer erroneously believed on reasonable grounds that he had an articulable cause. I need not decide whether such a belief could avoid an infringement of s. 9 of the *Charter*. Constable Wilkin clearly had no belief that the facts, as he believed them to be, constituted an articulable cause as I have defined it. The detention was both unlawful and arbitrary as that word has been defined in the jurisprudence: *Duguay*, *supra*; *Cayer*, *supra*. As the detention was not authorized by law, s. 1 of the *Charter* has no application. The appellant's right not to be arbitrarily detained was infringed by Constable Wilkin.

Before I turn to s. 8 of the *Charter*, I should add that although the appellant was not advised of his right to counsel until after he was formally arrested, counsel has not alleged a violation of s. 10(*b*) of the *Charter* and I will not address the s. 10(*b*) implications raised by this case.

[Doherty J.A. then relates to s. 8 of the *Charter*.]

This evidence does not establish even a belief based on reasonable grounds that the appellant was in possession of a knife, much less a reasonable belief that he was in possession of a knife which was a prohibited or restricted weapon. Constable Wilkin did not advert to the powers provided by s. 101 of the *Criminal Code* when questioned concerning the reasons for his search of the appellant. I regard this argument as an after-the-fact attempt to justify the search. The evidence cannot support it.

The appellant's reliance on s. 101 of the *Criminal Code* also assumes that the search of the appellant began when Constable Wilkin felt the appellant's front pant pocket. The reasons in *Mellenthin, supra*, indicate that the search cannot be so limited but must be taken as having commenced when the appellant was initially questioned by the police officer. The search proceeded from that point until the cocaine was recovered. Once the questioning of the appellant is taken as part of the search, then s. 101 of the *Criminal Code* cannot provide any authority for the search.

The search of the appellant by Constable Wilkin was unreasonable and in violation of the appellant's right to be secure against unreasonable search or seizure.

C. The admissibility of the cocaine

.....

The circumstances presented here are exacerbated by the unconstitutionality of the initial detention. If, as Cory J. indicated, the fruits of an unreasonable search conducted following a lawful stop "should not be admitted", the case for the exclusion of such evidence where the stop is unconstitutional becomes even stronger. There can be no doubt that Constable Wilkin would not have discovered the narcotics in the possession of the appellant but for the double-barrelled infringement of the appellant's constitutional rights.

The seriousness of these constitutional violations is also clear. Constable Wilkin obviously considered that any and all individuals who attended at a residence that the police had any reason to believe might be the site of ongoing criminal activity were subject to detention and questioning by the police. This dangerous and erroneous perception of the reach of police powers must be emphatically rejected. Judicial acquiescence in such conduct by the reception of evidence obtained through that conduct would bring the administration of justice into disrepute.

The evidence should have been excluded.

R. v. SMITH

(1996), 105 C.C.C. (3d) 58 (Ont. C.A.)

[A police officer suspected that the accused had been drinking and pulled his vehicle over. The officer questioned the accused, noting an odour of alcohol on his breath. The accused said he didn't think he had too much to drink but admitted some consumption. The officer then had the accused perform a co-ordination test, which he performed relatively well. The officer had already concluded that he had grounds to make a roadside breath demand. A demand was then made, the accused failed and he was arrested.]

The judgment of the court was delivered by

Doherty J.A.: —

I

This is yet another case in which the court must determine whether measures enacted to assist the police in the apprehension of those who commit offences involving drinking and driving go beyond the limits allowed by s. 1 of the *Canadian Charter of Rights and Freedoms* (*Charter*) and constitute an unjustifiable limitation on an individual's constitutional rights.

.....

The first three grounds of appeal require a consideration of the interaction of the *Charter* provisions that give detainees certain rights, and s. 1 of the *Charter* which contemplates constitutionally permissible limits on those rights. The appellant submits that he was detained as soon as he pulled his vehicle over to the side of the road in response to Constable Stuckey's direction. The Crown agrees. The appellant further submits that as he was detained, his rights under s. 10(*b*) of the *Charter* were triggered. He acknowledges that the applicable statutory provisions place some legitimate limitation on his s. 10(*b*) rights. The appellant submits, however, that the limitation does not countenance the use of multiple investigative procedures before advising a detainee of his right to counsel. I take the reference to multiple investigative techniques to include the use of two or more techniques aimed at determining whether there are reasonable grounds to believe that the driver is impaired or over the allowed blood-alcohol level. In this case, the officer used four. He observed the appellant while talking to him, asked the appellant if he had been drinking, asked the appellant to perform a standing sobriety test, and required the appellant to provide a sample of his breath into the screening device.

The Crown acknowledges that the appellant was not given his s. 10(*b*) rights until after he was arrested and the breathalyzer demand was made. It is the position of the Crown that Constable Stuckey's conduct was authorized by law and that the law by necessary implication limited the appellant's s. 10(*b*) rights in a manner that is consistent with the criteria found in s. 1 of the *Charter*.

The appellant also contends that Constable Stuckey's questions concerning alcohol consumption constituted an infringement of the appellant's rights under s. 7 of the *Charter*. The appellant maintains that s. 7 requires that a detained person be permitted to make an informed decision as to whether to answer questions posed by the police: *R. v. Hebert* (1990), 57 C.C.C. (3d) 1, [1990] 2 S.C.R. 151, 77 C.R. (3d) 145. He submits that he was unable to make that informed decision as he was neither told of his right to seek the assistance of counsel, nor advised by Constable Stuckey that he was not obliged to answer the question. The Crown submits that the s. 7 argument is merely a reformulation of the s. 10(*b*) argument and in the circumstances of this case adds nothing of substance. The Crown contends that as with the violation of s. 10(*b*), any s. 7 violation is saved by s. 1 of the *Charter*.

.....

The tension between individual rights and broader societal concerns is nowhere more apparent than in legislative attempts to deal with the carnage caused by those who commit offences involving drinking and driving.

Protecting those who use the public roadways from the menace posed by drinking and driving is a pressing and substantial concern. Federal and provincial lawmakers have responded to that menace by equipping the police with special powers designed to deter drinking and driving and facilitate the timely apprehension of those who commit drinking and driving offences. Generally, these special provisions give the police extraordinary powers to stop motor vehicles and engage in investigative procedures at the roadside intended to assist the police in making a quick but informed determination of whether there are reasonable and probable grounds to believe that the driver is impaired or over the prescribed blood-alcohol level. These procedures inevitably involve some encroachment on individual rights, particularly the right to be free from arbitrary detention and the right to counsel upon detention. By and large, the statutory provisions considered to date have been found to impose constitutionally justified limits on those rights...The question in each case must be whether the legislation in issue goes beyond the limits of s. 1 in seeking to protect community interests at the expense of individual rights.

To bring Constable Stuckey's conduct within the confines of s. 1 of the *Charter*, the Crown must establish that he acted pursuant to some authority prescribed by law which either expressly or by necessary implication limits the *Charter* rights to which the appellant was otherwise entitled. The Crown must further establish on the balance of probabilities that the limit is a reasonable one that can be demonstrably justified in a free and democratic society: *Thomsen* [(1988), 40 C.C.C. (3d) 411 (S.C.C.)], at pp. 418-22; *R. v. Therens* (1985), 18 C.C.C. (3d) 481 at p. 506, 18 D.L.R. (4th) 655, [1985] 1 S.C.R. 613.

VI

Constable Stuckey had express statutory authority to stop the appellant's vehicle. Section 48(1) of the *Highway Traffic Act*, R.S.O. 1990, c. H.8 (H.T.A.) provides:

> 48(1) A police officer, readily identifiable as such, may require the driver of a motor vehicle to stop for the purpose of determining whether or not there is evidence to justify making a demand under section 254 of the *Criminal Code* (Canada).

The section expressly refers only to the power to stop motorists. In *Saunders* [(1988), 41 C.C.C. (3d) 532 (Ont. C.A.)], at pp. 539-40, Cory J. held that by inference the section also authorizes taking reasonable steps to determine whether there is evidence to justify making the demands referred to in s. 254 of the *Criminal Code*. I agree with this interpretation and do not understand the appellant to suggest otherwise. The battle is joined over the scope to be given to that inferred power.

Section 48 of the *H.T.A.* refers to s. 254 of the *Criminal Code*. That section sets out two distinct demands. Section 254(2) authorizes a demand for a breath sample for analysis in an approved screening device. I will refer to this as the A.L.E.R.T. demand. This demand may be made where the officer "reasonably suspects" that the driver has alcohol in his or her body. The screening device is an investigative tool intended to assist the officer in determining whether he has reasonable and probable grounds to believe that the driver has committed one of the offences set out in s. 253 (impaired driving, over .08). The results of the test do not give rise to criminal liability but may provide the basis for a further demand under s. 254(3): *R. v. Bernshaw* (1995), 95 C.C.C. (3d) 193, *per* Cory J. at pp. 205-7, *per* Sopinka J. at p. 216, [1995] 1 S.C.R. 254, 35 C.R. (4th) 201.

.....

An officer who stops a person he suspects may have been drinking is concerned with both the possibility that the driver is impaired and the possibility that the driver's blood-alcohol level is over the permissible limit. While the two conditions are closely related, they are not identical. Section 48 of the *H.T.A.* authorizes the officer to take reasonable steps to determine whether there is evidence of either condition. The investigative procedure may yield a reasonable suspicion that the driver has alcohol in his body in which case an A.L.E.R.T. demand may be made; or it may reveal reasonable and probable grounds to believe that the driver is impaired or over the allowable blood-alcohol limit, in which case a breathalyzer demand may be made; or it may not provide evidence of either condition, in which case no demand can be made. In my opinion, s. 48 of the *H.T.A.* authorizes the officer to take reasonable steps to determine whether there is evidence to support an A.L.E.R.T. or a breathalyzer demand.

The facts of this case provide a good example of the interaction of s. 48 of the *H.T.A.* and s. 254 of the *Criminal Code*. Constable Stuckey acting under the authority of s. 48 stopped the appellant's vehicle and took certain steps to determine whether he had grounds to make either of the demands in s. 254. He concluded that he had grounds for an A.L.E.R.T. demand and at some point between 12:42 a.m. and 12:45 a.m. told the appellant that he would be required to perform the A.L.E.R.T. test. In my opinion, even though Constable Stuckey had decided to make the A.L.E.R.T. demand he was still entitled under s. 48 of the *H.T.A.* to take reasonable steps to determine whether he had grounds to make a breathalyzer demand on the basis of possible impairment. In taking any additional steps, however, Constable Stuckey was constrained by the requirement that the A.L.E.R.T. test be administered "forthwith". Constable Stuckey took one additional step. He required the appellant to perform the standing sobriety test. The results of that test enured to the benefit of the appellant as they satisfied Constable Stuckey that he did not have reasonable and probable grounds to believe that the appellant was impaired. Constable Stuckey then proceeded to make the formal A.L.E.R.T. demand and take the sample. Having ruled out impairment through the standing sobriety test, Constable Stuckey would have sent the appellant on his way had he not failed the A.L.E.R.T. test. That failure gave Constable Stuckey reasonable and probable grounds to believe that the appellant was over the prescribed blood-alcohol level and provided the grounds to make the breathalyzer demand.

Some courts have favoured a more restrictive interpretation of s. 48 of the *H.T.A.* ... These cases hold that the investigative powers in s. 48 are alternative powers to those found in s. 254. On this view, once a police officer has stopped a motor vehicle and formed the reasonable suspicion that the driver has been drinking, the officer must choose either to make an A.L.E.R.T. demand or to proceed with some other investigative step authorized by s. 48 (*e.g.*, physical sobriety tests). He cannot do both. It is said that *Saunders, supra*, supports this position.

I cannot agree with this interpretation of s. 48 of the *H.T.A.* and align myself with those who have rejected it...The language of s. 48 indicates that the investigative powers granted by that section are to be used in conjunction with the demand powers in the *Criminal Code*. The section is designed to assist the officer in making an informed decision about the existence of grounds to make either or both of the demands provided for in s. 254. By its very terms, s. 48 of the *H.T.A.* anticipates that resort to that section will in some cases lead to the making of one or more of the s. 254 demands. Section 48 and s. 254 are symbiotic, not mutually exclusive.

.....

Section 48 does not set out the specific procedures that an officer may use under the authority of that section, and it does not place any numerical limit on the procedures that may be employed. Instead, as interpreted in *Saunders*, the section authorizes any procedure or procedures that are both reasonable and done for the purpose of determining whether the officer has grounds for making either or both of the demands referred to in s. 254 of the *Criminal Code*. It is impossible to provide an exhaustive list of procedures that will meet these criteria in all cases. It is, however, safe to say that a procedure cannot be reasonable within the meaning of s. 48 unless it can be performed at the site of the detention, with dispatch, with no danger to the safety of the detainee and with minimal inconvenience to the detainee. The request that the appellant perform a standing sobriety test met those requirements and was a reasonable step performed to determine whether the officer had reasonable and probable grounds to believe that the appellant was impaired and could be properly subjected to a breathalyzer demand. The standing sobriety test remained reasonable and within the purview of s. 48 of the *H.T.A.*, notwithstanding that Constable Stuckey had grounds to make an A.L.E.R.T. demand before asking the appellant to perform the test and that he fully intended to make the A.L.E.R.T. demand and administer the A.L.E.R.T. test regardless of the results of the standing sobriety test.

Constable Stuckey's questions concerning the appellant's alcohol consumption were also clearly asked for the purpose referred to in s. 48 of the *H.T.A.* Constable Stuckey was trying to determine whether he had grounds to make one of the demands provided for in s. 254. The questions were asked at the scene of the detention, took little time and in no way endangered or further inconvenienced the appellant. They meet the reasonableness criteria outlined above. It is contended, however, that the questioning of the appellant concerning his alcohol consumption introduced an added element of self-incrimination, which distinguishes that form of questioning from other investigative procedures such as a standing sobriety test.

The extent to which a particular investigative procedure intrudes upon a detainee's constitutional rights is a factor to be considered in determining whether that procedure is reasonable. I do not, however, accept the contention that questions like those asked in this case concerning alcohol consumption are so qualitatively different from other forms of investigation as to place such questions beyond the limits of s. 48 of the *H.T.A.* The investigative avenues available to the police officer at the roadside are limited. Any grounds the officer develops at the roadside for making one or both of the demands in s. 254 will in almost every case emanate from the driver. There is simply no other source of information available. I see little distinction in terms of self-incrimination between evidence that flows from a standing sobriety test performed by a driver and evidence in the form of a driver's answers to questions put to him by the police officer: *R. v. Ross* (1989), 46 C.C.C. (3d) 129 at pp. 138-40, [1989] 1 S.C.R. 3, 67 C.R. (3d) 209; *R. v. Bartle* (1994), 92 C.C.C. (3d) 289 at p. 317, 118 D.L.R. (4th) 83, [1994] 3 S.C.R. 173. I see even less distinction between a direct question concerning alcohol consumption and questions relating to other matters asked in part at least for the purpose of determining whether the driver's speech will provide evidence of impairment or alcohol consumption. All of these procedures are aimed at getting information from the driver concerning alcohol consumption. The direct questions have the benefit of making the officer's purpose clear to the driver and avoid the subjectivity and ambiguity associated with attempts to assess intoxication from the sound of a stranger's voice. Nor should the incriminatory potential of admissions made by a driver in response to such questions be overrated. Those admissions may be significant in the officer's determination of whether he has grounds to make a demand under s. 254. That determination does not impose criminal liability and apart from *Charter* arguments about the admissibility of breathalyzer evidence will have little relevance at trial. Drinking and driving cases seldom turn on the accused's roadside confession.

In my opinion, a statute authorizing reasonable steps to determine whether there are grounds for making one or both of the demands in s. 254 contemplates direct questions of the driver concerning his alcohol consumption. In the circumstances of a roadside stop where the officer must make a quick assessment of the need for further action by way of a demand while at the same time minimizing the detention and inconvenience to the motorist, simple straightforward questions like the two asked by Constable Stuckey are eminently reasonable.

.....

Constable Stuckey's questions concerning alcohol consumption were a reasonable investigative step taken to determine whether he had evidence to make a demand under either s. 254(2) or (3) of the *Criminal Code*. The questions were a proper exercise of the authority granted under s. 48 of the *H.T.A.* Nor was the officer's authority under that section exhausted by the questions concerning alcohol consumption. The appellant's answers did not resolve the officers concerns about possible impairment. He was entitled to take further reasonable investigative steps and did so when he requested that the appellant perform the standing sobriety test. Furthermore, Constable Stuckey acted under lawful authority in requiring that the appellant take the A.L.E.R.T. test. His authority to make that demand came from s. 254(2) of the *Criminal Code*. Resort to the constable's *Criminal Code* powers had no effect on the lawfulness of the investigative procedures that preceded the demand. The various investigative steps taken by Constable Stuckey were all prescribed by law.

VII

Lawful authority for Constable Stuckey's conduct only opens the door to the s. 1 exemption. The Crown must demonstrate that the law (s. 48 of the *H.T.A.*) imposes a reasonable limit on the appellant's constitutional rights that can be demonstrably justified in a free and democratic society.

.....

The roadside investigation contemplated by s. 48 of the *H.T.A.* cannot accommodate the exercise of the right to counsel. Like the A.L.E.R.T. demand provisions, the powers granted by s. 48 enable the officer to determine whether there are grounds to arrest the detainee and make a breathalyzer demand. Whether the officer takes one reasonable investigative step or more than one, the nature and quality of the s. 10(*b*) infringement will not change. In all cases, the detainee will be denied the right to counsel for that brief period during which the officer attempts through reasonable investigative techniques to determine whether there are grounds to arrest the appellant and make a breathalyzer demand. In *Thomsen, supra,* it was held that the period during which the detainee may be constitutionally denied the right to counsel extends through the administration of the A.L.E.R.T. test. I cannot see how s. 48 of the *H.T.A.*, which authorizes investigative steps that are no more intrusive than the A.L.E.R.T. test, does not meaningfully prolong the detention, and does not alter the potential consequences of the detention to the detainee, could be said to result in an unconstitutional denial of the right to counsel. The nature and scope of the s. 10(*b*) violation under s. 48 of the *H.T.A.* is no greater than that countenanced under the existing case law. The prior decisions of the Supreme Court of Canada and this court leave no doubt that the denial of counsel implicit in the proper exercise of the investigative powers granted under s. 48 of the *H.T.A.* is justified under s. 1 of the *Charter*.

I should specifically address one argument advanced before this court and apparently not made in the earlier cases. It was argued that the investigative procedures contemplated by s. 48 of the *H.T.A.* cannot amount to a justifiable limit on a constitutional right because the detainee may refuse to perform the sobriety tests and decline to answer the officer's questions without penal consequences. The appellant submits that since the powers granted to the police under s. 48 of the *H.T.A.* are not supported by provisions that make compliance mandatory, as are the demand provisions in the *Criminal Code*, the section cannot meet the requirements of s. 1.

I do not agree with this submission. The objective of the legislation, the deterrence and apprehension of those who commit drinking and driving offences, remains unaffected by the absence of penal consequences for non-compliance with an officer's requests. Similarly, the rational connection between legislation that gives the police enhanced powers to investigate and apprehend those who commit drinking and driving offences and the objective of the legislation remains intact even though the legislature did not choose to visit penal consequences on motorists who choose not to comply with the officer's requests. Finally, the absence of penal consequences for non-compliance reduces the adverse impact of the denial of the detainee's constitutional rights and supports the Crown's contention that the proportionality component of the s. 1 test is met by s. 48 of the

H.T.A. This argument does not cause me to doubt the correctness of the earlier jurisprudence.

.....

I turn next to the submissions that Constable Stuckey's questioning of the appellant concerning his alcohol consumption resulted in a denial of his right to silence and that this infringement of s. 7 of the *Charter* cannot be justified under s. 1.

A detained person has no absolute right to remain silent. The police are not absolutely prohibited from questioning a detained person and they need not advise the detainee that he has a right to remain silent: *R.* v. *Farrell* (1992), 76 C.C.C. (3d) 201, 11 C.R.R. (2d) 255, 46 M.V.R. (2d) 318 (P.E.I.C.A.); *R. v. Van Haarlem* (1991), 64 C.C.C. (3d) 543 at p. 553, 15 W.A.C. 133, 135 N.R. 379 (B.C.C.A.). The so-called right to remain silent found in s. 7 of the *Charter* is in fact the right of the detained person to make an informed choice as to whether to speak to the police: *Hebert, supra*, at pp. 34-5, 38-9 and 43.

.....

Where, as here, a statutory provision limits a detainee's right to counsel in a manner that accords with s. 1, then as long as the police remain within the ambit of that provision, the detainee has no right to counsel. The police cannot be obliged under s. 7 of the *Charter* to inform a detainee of a "right" that the detainee does not have. If there is no right to counsel under s. 10(*b*), there can be no right to be informed of the right to counsel under s. 7 of the *Charter*. The appellant's reliance on s. 7 is premised on the erroneous contention that s. 7 creates a free-standing right to be informed of the right to counsel. It does not. If the detainee has the right to counsel based on the operation of s. 10(*b*), then s. 7 (like s. 10(*b*)) requires that the detainee be informed of that right. Where s. 10(*b*) rights do not exist, then the s. 7 right to make an informed choice as to whether to speak to the police requires only that the police not engage in conduct that effectively and unfairly deprives the detainee of the right to choose whether to speak to the police.

[Compare: *R. v. Chabot* (1993), 86 C.C.C. (3d) 309 (N.S.C.A.)].

QUESTIONS

29. The above cases support the position that roadside questioning and sobriety tests directed to a detained person who is not legally required but feels compelled to perform them are incompatible with s. 10(*b*) rights and are justified under s. 1 of the *Charter*. However, unlike failing a roadside A.L.E.R.T., sobriety tests and answers to roadside questions may have evidentiary value in proving impairment. Apart from their use to establish a basis for a lawful breath demand, would their use as incriminating evidence to establish guilt be in violation of the *Charter*? Consider, in this regard, *R. v. Milne* (1996), 107 C.C.C. (3d) 118; leave to appeal to S.C.C. refused (1996), 110 C.C.C. (3d) vi; *R. v. Sundquist* (2000), 145 C.C.C. (3d) 145 (Sask. C.A.); *R. v. Roy* (1997), 117 C.C.C. (3d) 243 (Que. C.A.); *R. v. Oldham* (1996), 109 C.C.C. (3d) 392 (N.B.C.A.).

30. Does a police officer asking a detainee how much he had to drink infringe his right to silence? Consider, in this regard, *R. v. Housley* (1996), 105 C.C.C. (3d) 83 (Ont. C.A.); leave to appeal to S.C.C. refused (1996), 108 C.C.C. (3d) vi.

C. ARREST OR DETENTION AND SECTION 10(*a*) AND (*b*) OF THE CHARTER

Section 10 of the *Charter* states (in part):

> **10. Everyone has the right on arrest or detention**
>
> **(*a*) to be informed promptly of the reasons therefor;**
>
> **(*b*) to retain and instruct counsel without delay and to be informed of that right ...**

1. THE MEANING OF DETENTION

Above, the courts considered when it is permissible to detain someone, short of arrest. However, it is not always clear whether someone is indeed detained.

R. v. THERENS ET AL.

(1985), 18 C.C.C. (3d) 481 (S.C.C.)

[The Court considered whether a person to whom a demand is made to provide breathalyzer samples in accordance with s. 235(1) (now s. 254(3)) of the *Criminal Code* is detained and entitled to s. 10(*b*) rights. Though the members of the court wrote five different judgments, Le Dain J.'s judgment as to the meaning of detention (though not his proposed disposition of this case) ultimately prevailed. The majority of the court excluded the breathalyzer results under s. 24(2), notwithstanding the officer's reliance on the law as it was then understood.]

Le Dain J. (dissenting): —

.....

The purpose of s. 10 of the *Charter* is to ensure that in certain situations a person is made aware of the right to counsel and is permitted to retain and instruct counsel without delay. The situations specified by s. 10 — arrest and detention — are obviously not the only ones in which a person may reasonably require the assistance of counsel, but they are situations in which the restraint of liberty might otherwise effectively prevent access to counsel or induce a person to assume that he or she is unable to retain and instruct counsel. In its use of the word "detention", s. 10 of the *Charter* is directed to a restraint of liberty other than arrest in which a person may reasonably require the assistance of counsel but might be prevented or impeded from retaining and instructing counsel without delay but for the constitutional guarantee.

In addition to the case of deprivation of liberty by physical constraint, there is in my opinion a detention within s. 10 of the *Charter* when a police officer or other agent of the state assumes control over the movement of a person by a demand or direction which may have significant legal consequence and which pre- vents or impedes access to counsel.

In *Chromiak* [(1979), 49 C.C.C. (2d) 257 (S.C.C.)] this court held that detention connotes "some form of compulsory constraint" [p. 478]. There can be no doubt that there must be some form of compulsion or coercion to constitute an interference with liberty or freedom of action that amounts to a detention within the meaning of s. 10 of the *Charter*. The issue, as I see it, is whether that compulsion need be of a physical character, or whether it may also be a compulsion of a psychological or mental nature which inhibits the will as effectively as the application, or threat of application, of physical force. The issue is whether a person who is the subject of a demand or direction by a police officer or other agent of the state may reasonably regard himself or herself as free to refuse to comply.

.....

A refusal to comply with a s. 235(1) [now s. 254(3)] demand without reasonable excuse is, under s. 235(2) [now s. 254(5)], a criminal offence. It is not realistic to speak of a person who is liable to arrest and prosecution for refusal to comply with a demand which a peace officer is empowered by statute to make as being free to refuse to comply. The criminal liability for refusal to comply constitutes effective compulsion. This psychological compulsion or coercion effected by the consequence of a refusal to comply with a s. 235(1) demand appears to be what Laskin J. (as he then was) had in mind in *Hogan v. The Queen*, [1975] 2 S.C.R. 574 at 587, 26 C.R.N.S. 207, 18 C.C.C. (2d) 65, 48 D.L.R. (3d) 427, 9 N.S.R. (2d) 145, 2 N.R. 343, where he said:

> There is no doubt, therefore, that the accused was "detained" within the meaning of s. 2(c)(ii) of the *Canadian Bill of Rights*; he risked prosecution under s. 235(2) if, without reasonable excuse, he refused the demand which involved accompanying the peace officer to fulfil it.

Any criminal liability for failure to comply with a demand or direction of a police officer must be sufficient to make compliance involuntary. This would be true, for example, of compliance where refusal to comply would amount to a wilful obstruction of a police officer in the execution of his or her duty, contrary to s. 118 [now s. 129] of the *Criminal Code*.

Although it is not strictly necessary for purposes of this case, I would go further. In my opinion, it is not realistic, as a general rule, to regard compliance with a demand or direction by a police officer as truly voluntary, in the sense that the citizen feels that he or she has the choice to obey or not, even where there is in fact a lack of statutory or common law authority for the demand or direction and therefore an absence of criminal liability for failure to comply with it. Most citizens are not aware of the precise legal limits of police authority. Rather than risk the application of physical force or prosecution for wilful obstruction, the reasonable person is likely, to err on the side of caution, assume lawful authority and comply with the demand. The element of psychological compulsion, in the form of a reasonable perception of suspension of freedom of choice, is enough to make the restraint of liberty involuntary. Detention may be effected without the application or threat of application of physical restraint if the person concerned submits or acquiesces in the deprivation of liberty and reasonably believes that the choice to do otherwise does not exist.

For these reasons I am of the opinion that the s. 235(1) demand to accompany the police officer to a police station and to submit to a breathalyzer test resulted in the detention of the respondent within the meaning of s. 10 of the *Charter*.

R. v. THOMSEN

(1988), 40 C.C.C. (3d) 411 (S.C.C.)

[The accused was charged with failure or refusal to comply with a s. 254(2) demand for a roadside sample, contrary to what is now s. 254(5) of the *Criminal Code*. The Court determined that a person to whom a roadside demand is made is no less detained than a person to whom a breathalyzer demand is made. In *Therens,* the Court held that the latter detention entitles such a person to be informed of his right to counsel without delay. In *Thomsen,* the Court held that, unlike the breathalyzer demand, the requirement that a s. 254(2) *roadside demand* be made *forthwith* is incompatible with the right to counsel without delay. Thus, s. 254(2) is a limit on the right to counsel prescribed by law within the meaning of s. 1 of the *Charter*. After analyzing the evidence bearing upon the effectiveness of the roadside programme and the extent of the problem it addresses, the Court concluded that s. 254(2) is also a *reasonable limit demonstrably justified in a free and democratic society*. In his judgment, Le Dain J. summarizes the meaning of *detention* for the purposes of s. 10(*b*) of the *Charter*.]

The judgment of the court was delivered by

Le Dain J.: —

.....

The first issue in the appeal is whether the demand made by the police officer to the appellant, pursuant to s. 234.1(1) [now s. 254(2)] of the *Criminal Code*, to accompany the officer to his car and to provide a sample of breath for a roadside screening device resulted in a detention of the appellant within the meaning of s. 10 of the *Charter*.

[Le Dain J. then quotes from *Trask v. The Queen* (1985), 18 C.C.C. 514 (S.C.C.)]

> For the reasons given in the judgment of this Court in *R. v. Therens,* we hold that as a result of the s. 235(1) [now s. 254(3)(a)] demand the appellant was detained within the meaning of s. 10 of the *Canadian Charter of Rights and Freedoms* and that he was therefore denied the right to be informed of his right to retain and instruct counsel without delay.

I venture to restate what I perceive to be the essentials of those reasons, as they appear in my judgment in *Therens*, as follows:

1. In its use of the word "detention", s. 10 of the *Charter* is directed to a restraint of liberty other than arrest in which a person may

reasonably require the assistance of counsel but might be prevented or impeded from retaining and instructing counsel without delay but for the constitutional guarantee.

2. In addition to the case of deprivation of liberty by physical constraint, there is a detention within s. 10 of the *Charter*, when a police officer or other agent of the state assumes control over the movement of a person by a demand or direction which may have significant legal consequence and which prevents or impedes access to counsel.
3. The necessary element of compulsion or coercion to constitute a detention may arise from criminal liability for refusal to comply with a demand or direction, or from a reasonable belief that one does not have a choice as to whether or not to comply.
4. Section 10 of the *Charter* applies to a great variety of detentions of varying duration and is not confined to those of such duration as to make the effective use of *habeas corpus* possible.

In my opinion, the s. 234.1(1) [now s. 254(2)] demand by the police officer to the appellant to accompany him to his car and to provide a sample of breath into a roadside screening device fell within the above criteria. The demand by which the officer assumed control over the movement of the appellant was one which might have significant legal consequence because, although the evidence provided by the roadside screening device could not be introduced against the appellant, it might provide the basis for a s. 235(1) [now s. 254(3)] breathalyzer demand. For this reason, and given the criminal liability under s. 234.1(2) [now s. 254(5)] for refusal, without reasonable excuse, to comply with the demand, the situation was one in which a person might reasonably require the assistance of counsel. The criminal liability for refusal also constituted the necessary compulsion or coercion to make the restraint of liberty a detention. The difference in duration of the restraint of liberty resulting from a s. 234.1(1) demand and that resulting from a s. 235(1) demand is not such as to prevent the former from constituting a detention within the meaning of s. 10 of the *Charter*. For these reasons I am of the opinion that as a result of the s. 234.1(1) demand the appellant was detained within the meaning of s. 10 of the *Charter*.

Thus the appellant had the right, upon being detained by the s. 234.1(1) demand and before responding to that demand, to retain and instruct counsel without delay and to be informed of that right, and there was an infringement of it, unless the right is subject, in the case of a s. 234.1(1) demand, to a reasonable limit prescribed by law that is demonstrably justified in a free and democratic society, within the meaning of s. 1 of the *Charter*.

.....

The first issue arising with respect to the application of s. 1 is whether the right to retain counsel without delay is subject, in the case of a s. 234.1(1) demand, to a limit prescribed by law, within the meaning of s. 1. In *Therens*, where the court held that s. 235(1) of the *Code* did not preclude contact with counsel prior to the breathalyzer test, I had occasion to state what I understood to be a limit prescribed by law within the meaning of s. 1 as follows at p. 506 C.C.C., p. 680 D.L.R., p. 645 S.C.R.:

> The limit will be prescribed by law within the meaning of s. 1 if it is expressly provided for by statute or regulation, or results by necessary implication from the terms of a statute or regulation or from its operating requirements. The limit may also result from the application of a common law rule.

I remain of the view that a limit prescribed by law within the meaning of s. 1 may result by implication from the terms of a legislative provision or its operating requirements. It need not be an explicit limitation of a particular right or freedom.

.....

[He then quotes from Finlayson J.A. in *R. v. Talbourdet.*]

> The right to retain counsel is incompatible with the effective use of this [roadside] device on a random basis with the purpose of demonstrating a police presence so as to convince the driving public that there is a high probability of detection in the event that they drive after drinking.

These observations emphasize what, as a practical matter, is implied by the words "forthwith" and "roadside" in s. 234.1(1). That there is to be no opportunity for contact with counsel prior to compliance with a s. 234.1(1) demand is, in my opinion, an implication of the terms of s. 234.1(1) when viewed in the context of the breath testing provisions of the *Criminal Code* as a whole.

IV

The next issue in the appeal is whether the limit imposed on the right to retain and instruct counsel by s. 234.1(1) of the *Code* is a reasonable one demonstrably justified in a free and democratic society, within the meaning of s. 1 of the *Charter*. The test for determining that question was formulated in *R. v. Oakes* (1986), 24 C.C.C. (3d) 327, 26 D.L.R. (4th) 200, [1986] 1 S.C.R. 103, and restated by Dickson C.J.C. in *Edwards Books and Art Ltd. v. The Queen* (1986), 30 C.C.C. (3d) 385 at p. 425, 35 D.L.R. (4th) 1 at p. 41, [1986] 2 S.C.R. 713 at pp. 768-9, as follows:

> Two requirements must be satisfied to establish that a limit is reasonable and demonstrably justified in a free and democratic society. First, the legislative objective which the limitation is designed to promote must be of sufficient importance to warrant overriding a constitutional right. It must bear on a "pressing and substantial concern". Second, the means chosen to attain those objectives must be proportional or appropriate to the ends. The proportionality requirement, in turn, normally has three aspects: the limiting measures must be carefully designed, or rationally connected, to the objective; they must impair the right as little as possible; and their effects must not so severely trench on individual or group rights that the legislative objective, albeit important, is, nevertheless, outweighed by the abridgment of rights. The court stated that the nature of the proportionality test would vary depending on the circumstances. Both in articulating the standard of proof and in describing the criteria comprising the proportionality requirement the court has been careful to avoid rigid and inflexible standards.

[Le Dain J. then outlined the evidence which was successful is demonstrating s. 1 justification under the *Charter.*]

QUESTION

31. The police attend E.'s home investigating the use of stolen credit cards at the gas station where he is employed. They ask him questions about certain invoices. He admits that he made them out but denies that he forged the signatures of the various customers reflected on them. Several other questions are asked about the invoices. The officers inform E. that they do not believe him, arrest him and inform him of his right to counsel and his right to remain silent. The officers feel that they did not have reasonable grounds to arrest until E.'s admission that he made out the invoices. At E.'s trial for fraud and forgery, E. does not testify on the *voir dire* dealing with his initial statement to police. What *Charter* breach, if any, arises on the facts? Consider, in this regard, *R. v. Esposito* (1985), 24 C.C.C. (3d) 88 (Ont. C.A.); leave to appeal to S.C.C. refused, February 24, 1986.

R. v. MORAN

(1987), 36 C.C.C. (3d) 225 (Ont. C.A.)

[At issue was whether the accused was detained when he was interviewed by the police on two occasions at the police station, thereby bringing into play s. 10(*b*) of the *Charter.* The court upheld the trial judge's ruling that the accused was not detained. In doing so, some helpful criteria for determining detention were articulated.]

The judgment of the court was delivered by

Martin J.A.: —

.....

The application or threat of application of physical restraint is unnecessary to constitute detention within s. 10 of the *Charter*. Compliance with a demand or direction of a police officer by a person who reasonably believes that he has no choice to do otherwise constitutes a detention.

[Le Dain J.'s judgment in *R. v. Therens* (1985), 18 C.C.C. (3d) 481 (S.C.C.) is then considered.]

.....

As Mr. Justice Tarnopolsky pointed out in *R. v. Bazinet* (1986), 25 C.C.C. (3d) 273, 54 O.R. (2d) 129, 51 C.R. (3d) 139, acquiescence in a "demand" or "direction" is essential to constitute "psychological" detention. He said at pp. 283-4:

> In this vein it is important to note that Le Dain J.'s extension of "detention" to instances of "psychological" restraint or compulsion or coercion is predicated upon two requirements: (1) a "demand or direction", in response to which (2) "the person concerned submits or acquiesces in the deprivation of liberty and reasonably believes that the choice to do otherwise does not

> exist". As far as the first of these two requirements is concerned, it is instructive to compare the term "demand" with the term "request". The Shorter Oxford English Dictionary defines the former as: "An act of demanding or asking by virtue of right or authority; a peremptory request or claim;" while the latter is defined as: "The act, on the part of a specified person, of asking for some favour, service, etc.; the expression of one's desire or wish directly addressed to the person or persons able to gratify it." Similarly, Webster's New World Dictionary defines a "demand" as: "A strong or authoritative request; an urgent requirement or claim;" while a "request" is defined as: "The act of asking, or expressing a desire for something; solicitation or petition."

The word "direction" has connotations of authoritative command similar to the word "demand". Thus, the Oxford English Dictionary provides the following definition: "An instruction how to proceed, an order, a precept." Similarly, the relevant definition in Webster's is: "an authoritative order or command".

In *R. v. Bazinet, supra*, the police went to the appellant's home and informed him that they were investigating a homicide and that they would like to ask him some questions. The appellant asked the police to wait "just a minute" and said that he would get dressed and go with them. The appellant got dressed and was driven to the police station in a police cruiser. The appellant was not arrested and the senior police officer concerned testified that he did not believe that he had reasonable and probable grounds for doing so. He testified that if the appellant had refused to go with the police, he would have left without him. The initial questioning of the appellant at the police station was directed to ascertaining his movements the preceding evening. The appellant's answers were exculpatory. Subsequently, the nature of the questioning changed, with the police confronting the appellant with some of the evidence they had. The appellant's statement was reduced to writing and, as the appellant finished reading the last page of the statement, he blurted out that he had committed the homicide. A few questions were then directed by the officer to the appellant to clarify what he had said. The appellant was then informed that he was arrested for first degree murder and advised that he had the right to retain and instruct counsel without delay. Tarnopolsky J.A., speaking for this court, held that at the time of making the above statement the appellant was not detained within s. 10(*b*). He stated that in the case before him there was no "demand or direction" by the police. There was not even a request that the appellant accompany the officers to the police station (p. 284).

Although in the *Bazinet* case there was not even a request that the appellant accompany the police to the station, it is clear that not every request by the police to a citizen to come to a police station for an interview in connection with an investigation of a crime or possible crime constitutes a detention of the citizen who complies with the request. In *R. v. Smith* (1986), 25 C.C.C. (3d) 361, 26 D.L.R. (4th) 666, 49 C.R. (3d) 210 (Man. C.A.), the police had commenced an investigation into the death of the infant child of the woman with whom the appellant was living, after a post-mortem examination of the child disclosed that it had died of a skull fracture. The police went to the residence of the appellant and the child's mother and indicated that an investigation was under way because the child had died of a head injury. The accused and the child's mother were asked to come to police headquarters to "discuss the matter further". They agreed. The appellant's parents also came along in the police cruiser. The appellant and his parents were left in a waiting-room while the child's mother was interviewed. After the child's mother had been interviewed, the appellant entered the interview room. The door of the interview room was closed, but the appellant was not then under arrest "or under any restraint". The police officers knew that the appellant and the child's mother were the persons having the care of the child, but they were merely seeking information. There could have been an explanation for the injury consistent with the innocence of both the appellant and the child's mother.

The initial interview with the appellant lasted about half an hour, during which he suggested that the injury to the child might have been caused by an intruder. After the initial interview with the appellant, the police re-interviewed the child's mother in a different room, leaving the appellant in the interview room. By the time the police went back for a second interview with the appellant he had become "the prime suspect" in what the police considered to be criminal homicide. He was charged with murder, cautioned and advised of his right to retain and instruct counsel. In the second interview, the appellant made what purported to be a confession. The Manitoba Court of Appeal held that there was no detention of the appellant until the police reattended the interview room, after speaking to the child's mother for the second time. Huband J.A., speaking for the Manitoba Court of Appeal, said at p. 367:

> In my opinion, there was no detention until the police officers reattended the interview-room after having spoken with Donna Popiel for a second time. At that stage they had become convinced that the accused had lied to them, that a crime had been committed and that the accused was responsible. His rights under s. 10(*b*) of the *Charter* were extended to him immediately.

He further said at p. 368:

> In the present case there was no physical constraint. Nor was there any "demand or direction". There was a request that the accused attend the Public Safety Building, which the accused was free to refuse. There was a request that he co-operate in providing information as to the circumstances of the death of the child which, once again, he was free to refuse. There was no physical constraint, nor any demand or direction that he remain in the interview-room after the first interview had been completed. And, throughout the entire period, until the police officers had a second interview with Donna Popiel, the police officers had no reason to think that the accused was criminally involved in the death of the child.

However, language used by a police officer, although phrased in the form of a request, may, depending on the circumstances, be reasonably construed by the person to whom the request is made to be a direction or command. All the circumstances must be considered: see *R. v. Soares* (a judgment of this court, released March 27, 1987) [since reported 34 C.C.C. (3d) 403].

In determining whether a person, who subsequently becomes an accused, was detained at the time he was interviewed by the police, it is important to bear in mind that a police officer when endeavouring to discover whether or by whom an offence has been committed, is entitled to question any person, whether suspected or not, from whom he thinks useful information can be obtained. Although a police officer is entitled to question any person in order to obtain information with respect to a suspected offence, as a general rule, he has no power to compel the person questioned to answer. Moreover, he has no power to detain a person for questioning and if the person questioned declines to answer, the police officer must allow him to proceed on his way unless he arrests him on reasonable and probable grounds: see *R. v. Esposito* (1985), 24 C.C.C. (3d) 88 at p. 94, 53 O.R. (2d) 356, 49 C.R. (3d) 193 (Ont. C.A.); leave to appeal to the Supreme Court of Canada refused February 24, 1986, O.R. *loc. cit.*, 65 N.R. 244*n*.

I venture to suggest that in determining whether a person who subsequently is an accused was detained at the time he or she was questioned at a police station by the police, the following factors are relevant. I do not mean to imply, however, that they are an exhaustive list of the relevant factors nor that any one factor or combination of factors or their absence is necessarily determinative in a particular case. These factors are as follows:

1. The precise language used by the police officer in requesting the person who subsequently becomes an accused to come to the police station, and whether the accused was given a choice or expressed a preference that the interview be conducted at the police station, rather than at his or her home;
2. whether the accused was escorted to the police station by a police officer or came himself or herself in response to a police request;
3. whether the accused left at the conclusion of the interview or whether he or she was arrested;
4. the stage of the investigation, that is, whether the questioning was part of the general investigation of a crime or possible crime or whether the police had already decided that a crime had been committed and that the accused was the perpetrator or involved in its commission and the questioning was conducted for the purpose of obtaining incriminating statements from the accused;
5. whether the police had reasonable and probable grounds to believe that the accused had committed the crime being investigated;
6. the nature of the questions: whether they were questions of a general nature designed to obtain information or whether the accused was confronted with evidence pointing to his or her guilt;
7. the subjective belief by an accused that he or she is detained, although relevant, is not decisive, because the issue is whether he or she *reasonably* believed that he or she was detained. Personal circumstances relating to the accused, such as low intelligence, emotional disturbance, youth and lack of sophistication are circumstances to be considered in determining whether he had a subjective belief that he was detained.

QUESTIONS

32. As a result of a complaint, police contact Mr. Smith and request an interview, which could be conducted at his home, business or at the police station. Smith agrees to come down to the police station, where he is advised of the nature of the complaint and his right to remain silent. No right to counsel is imparted, since the officer is of the view that Smith is not detained. Smith makes a written statement, following which the officer indicates that he does not know whether charges will be laid; that decision will be based upon legal advice. Smith is later charged with sexual assault and states, at trial, that he did not think the allegations were serious or would be pursued. Was Smith detained? The first appellate court rules as follows:

    It is our respectful view that Smith was psychologically detained, despite the absence of a demand or direction by the police, physical constraint or even subjective feelings of compulsion on Smith's part. A person is detained where the police have narrowed their investigation to him alone and the interview is solely designed to ascertain his culpability and to elicit evidence to be used against him at his trial. It is significant that even the police felt constrained to advise Smith of his right to remain silent.

    Render your opinion on appeal from that ruling. Consider, in this regard, *R. v. Hawkins* (1993), 79 C.C.C. (3d) 576 (S.C.C.).

33. The police are investigating embezzlement at the Whiplash Legal Publishing Co. Ms. Covert is the suspect. Constable Surefire goes to the company and advises Covert that he will return at the end of her work day to see her. At the end of the day he takes her to the police station, where he advises her of her right to remain silent. He also tells her that she is free to go if she wishes. She believes that she will be arrested if she gets up to leave. A three-hour interview follows. Was Covert detained? Consider, in this regard, *R. v. Keats* (1987), 39 C.C.C. (3d) 358 (Nfld. C.A.).

2. SECTION 10(*a*) AND (*b*) OF THE CHARTER

There is an obvious interrelationship between the detainee's s. 10(*a*) and 10(*b*) rights. For example, informing the detainee of his or her right to counsel and permitting the exercise of that right may be meaningless if the detainee is misled as to the reasons for his or her detention.

Section 10(*b*) has an informational component (what the accused or detainee must be told about his or her rights) and an implementational component (what must be done to enable the exercise of those rights). Many cases have addressed the meaning of s. 10(*b*) and its application to particular fact situations. The following is an outline of some general principles established by the cases, usually followed by one example of a case in point.

(a) It is inadequate to simply inform a detainee of his or her right to retain counsel without delay.
(b) The detainee must both be informed of, and allowed to exercise the right to counsel without delay: *R. v. Evans* (1991), 63 C.C.C. (3d) 289 (S.C.C.).

(c) A detainee must be informed about access to Legal Aid, that is, free counsel, where the prescribed financial criteria are met: *R. v. Bartle* (1994), 92 C.C.C. (3d) 289 (S.C.C.).

(d) A detainee must also be informed about access to duty counsel who will provide immediate, temporary legal advice, regardless of financial status, where such services are indeed available in that jurisdiction: *R. v. Bartle* (1994), 92 C.C.C. (3d) 289 (S.C.C.).

(e) The information must be comprehensive, timely and comprehensible. For example, information about duty counsel should include any toll-free number, if available: *R. v. Pozniak* (1994), 92 C.C.C. (3d) 472 (S.C.C.).

(f) There is no constitutional provision that requires the authorities to determine whether the detainee understood his or her rights, unless there are positive indications that, indeed, the detainee did not understand them: *R. v. Evans* (1991), 63 C.C.C. (3d) 289 (S.C.C.).

(g) Where (and only where) a detainee indicates a desire to exercise the right to counsel in response to satisfaction of the informational component of s. 10(*b*), the detainee must be provided with a reasonable opportunity to exercise that right to counsel, which may compel the authorities to facilitate the detainee's communication with counsel: *R. v. Manninen* (1987), 34 C.C.C. (3d) 385 (S.C.C.).

(h) Until the reasonable opportunity to exercise the right to counsel has been provided, the authorities may not continue to question the detainee or otherwise elicit incriminating evidence from the detainee. They must "hold off": *R. v. Manninen* (1987), 34 C.C.C. (3d) 385 (S.C.C.).

(i) There is no constitutional requirement that a duty counsel system, however well advised, exists in every jurisdiction. However, where no such system exists, the meaning of a reasonable opportunity to consult counsel will be affected: *R. v. Prosper* (1994), 92 C.C.C. (3d) 353 (S.C.C.).

(j) The authorities need not hold off efforts to elicit evidence from the accused where there are compelling and urgent circumstances. However, investigative or evidentiary expediency (such as the passage of the two-hour statutory presumption period relating to breathalyzer tests) does not demonstrate the requisite compelling and urgent circumstances without more evidence: *R. v. Prosper* (1994), 92 C.C.C. (3d) 353 (S.C.C.).

(k) Where the accused is not reasonably diligent in exercising his or her right to counsel, the authorities' duty to provide a reasonable opportunity and to refrain from eliciting evidence from the detainee is suspended: *R. v. Tremblay* (1987), 37 C.C.C. (3d) 565 (S.C.C.).

(l) A detainee may waive his or her s. 10(*b*) rights. However, the standard for waiver is stringent. Waiver must be clear and unequivocal, free and voluntary, and made with full knowledge of the rights: *R. v. Smith* (1991), 63 C.C.C. (3d) 313 (S.C.C.).

(m) Where the detainee initially expresses his or her desire to exercise the right to counsel and then indicates a change of mind, the authorities must satisfy an additional informational component by advising the detainee of his or her right to a reasonable opportunity to consult counsel and the obligation of the police to hold off during that period: *R. v. Prosper* (1994), 92 C.C.C. (3d) 353 (S.C.C.).

(n) When the detainee exercises his or her right to counsel, it must be afforded in private. This is so, whether or not the detainee indicates a desire to communicate in private: *R. v. Playford* (1987), 40 C.C.C. (3d) 142 (Ont. C.A.). *Quare* whether the police are required to inform the detainee of the right to consult in private: *R. v. Butler* (1995), 104 C.C.C. (3d) 198 (B.C.C.A.).

(o) There is an interrelationship between the detainee's s. 10(*a*) and 10(*b*) rights. Accordingly, where there is a fundamental and discrete change in the purpose of the investigation, one involving an unrelated or more serious offence, the police must restate the accused's right to counsel: *R. v. Evans* (1991), 63 C.C.C. (3d) 289 (S.C.C.).

Many of these principles are reflected in the following cases.

R. v. BARTLE

(1994), 92 C.C.C. (3d) 289 (S.C.C.)

Lamer C.J.C.: —

.....

I. Facts

On June 22, 1991, at approximately 1:00 a.m., Constable Pray arrested the appellant for impaired driving after he failed the roadside A.L.E.R.T. test. The constable read the appellant his rights under the *Charter* from a preprinted caution card. Specifically, the constable advised the appellant that:

> You have the right to retain and instruct counsel without delay.
>
> You have the right to telephone any lawyer you wish.
>
> You also have the right to free advice from a Legal Aid lawyer.
>
> If you are charged with an offence, you may apply to the Ontario Legal Aid Plan for legal assistance.

Constable Pray then asked the appellant if he understood, and the appellant responded affirmatively. Constable Pray did not make any reference to the specific availability of immediate, preliminary legal advice by duty counsel, or to the existence of the 24-hour, toll-free Legal Aid number which was printed on his caution card. Further, Constable Pray did not ask the appellant if he wanted to call a lawyer "now", a question printed on his caution card, because there was no telephone at the roadside. Constable Pray then gave the appellant the standard secondary caution regarding admissions and read him the breath sample demand. At this point, the appellant stated that he had five or six beers after baseball that evening.

Upon arrival at the police station, Constable Pray again asked the appellant if he wished to call a lawyer, making it clear that he could do so "now". The appellant said no, and was turned over to breathalyzer technician, Constable Hildebrandt. Constable Hildebrandt also asked the appellant if he wanted to call a lawyer (again, no mention was made of the 1-800 number or of the availability of immediate, preliminary legal advice by duty counsel). The appellant declined to call a lawyer, and then agreed to take the two breathalyzer tests, both of which he failed by a significant margin. The appellant was charged with having care or control of a motor vehicle while his blood-alcohol level was in excess of 80 mg. of alcohol in 100 ml. of blood, contrary to s. 253(*b*) of the *Criminal Code*, R.S.C. 1985, c. C-46.

The appellant testified that he thought that the caution he received from Constable Pray meant that he could contact a lawyer "when one would be available like maybe Monday morning call one" (the arrest was on a Friday night). He explained that he had refused to call counsel because he did not know whom to call, and was at a loss as to whom he could get a hold of. The appellant further testified that he indicated to Constable Hildebrandt that he wanted to call a lawyer, but that he did not know whom he could call. In response to Constable Hildebrandt's question "Why?", the appellant indicated that he had said "well I can't think of anybody to call, it's too late". He said that Constable Hildebrandt had no response to that comment, and that there was no indication that Constable Hildebrandt had heard him. Constable Hildebrandt, on the other hand, testified that the appellant simply said "no" when asked whether he wanted to call a lawyer. The appellant testified that he had played baseball on the night in question and afterward had had some beers. He admitted at trial that he probably should not have been on the road that evening.

.....

IV. Analysis

.....

It is now well accepted that under s. 10(*b*) a person who is arrested or detained (the "detainee") must be promptly informed of his or her right to retain counsel without delay. Because s. 10(*b*) has already been extensively considered by this court, I propose to simply summarize some of the basic principles which have been developed with respect to the right to counsel under the *Charter*. This will provide the necessary framework in which to approach the disclosure-related issue raised by this case, *Pozniak* [(1994), 92 C.C.C. (3d) 472 (S.C.C.)] and *Harper* [(1994), 92 C.C.C. (3d) 423 (S.C.C.)].

(a) The purpose of s. 10(b)

The purpose of the right to counsel guaranteed by s. 10(*b*) of the *Charter* is to provide detainees with an opportunity to be informed of their rights and obligations under the law and, most importantly, to obtain advice on how to exercise those rights and fulfil those obligations: *R. v. Manninen* (1987), 34 C.C.C. (3d) 385 at pp. 391-3, 41 D.L.R. (4th) 301, [1987] 1 S.C.R. 1233. This opportunity is made available because, when an individual is detained by state authorities, he or she is put in a position of disadvantage relative to the state. Not only has this person suffered a deprivation of liberty, but also this person may be at risk of incriminating him or herself. Accordingly, a person who is "detained" within the meaning of s. 10 of the *Charter* is in immediate need of legal advice in order to protect his or her right against self-incrimination and to assist him or her in regaining his or her liberty: *Brydges* [(1990), 53 C.C.C. (3d) 330 (S.C.C.)] at p. 343; *R. v. Hebert* (1990), 57 C.C.C. (3d) 1 at pp. 35-6, [1990] 2 S.C.R. 151, 77 C.R. (3d) 145, and *Prosper* [(1994), 92 C.C.C. (3d) 353 (S.C.C.)]. Under s. 10(b), a detainee is entitled as of right to seek such legal advice "without delay" and upon request. As this court suggested in *R. v. Clarkson* (1986), 25 C.C.C. (3d) 207 at p. 217, 26 D.L.R. (4th) 493, [1986] 1 S.C.R. 383, the right to counsel protected by s. 10(*b*) is designed to ensure that persons who are arrested or detained are treated fairly in the criminal process.

(b) The duties under s. 10(b)

This court has said on numerous previous occasions that s. 10(*b*) of the *Charter* imposes the following duties on state authorities who arrest or detain a person:

(1) to inform the detainee of his or her right to retain and instruct counsel without delay and of the existence and availability of Legal Aid and duty counsel;
(2) if a detainee has indicated a desire to exercise this right, to provide the detainee with a reasonable opportunity to exercise the right (except in urgent and dangerous circumstances), and
(3) to refrain from eliciting evidence from the detainee until he or she has had that reasonable opportunity (again, except in cases of urgency or danger).

(See, for example, *Manninen*, at pp. 391-2; *R. v. Evans* (1991), 63 C.C.C. (3d) 289 at pp. 304-5, [1991] 1 S.C.R. 869, 4 C.R. (4th) 144, and *Brydges*, at pp. 340-1.) The first duty is an informational one which is directly in issue here. The second and third duties are more in the nature of implementation duties and are not triggered unless and until a detainee indicates a desire to exercise his or her right to counsel.

Importantly, the right to counsel under s. 10(*b*) is not absolute. Unless a detainee invokes the right and is reasonably diligent in exercising it, the correlative duty on the police to provide a reasonable opportunity and to refrain from eliciting evidence will either not arise in the first place or will be suspended: *R. v. Tremblay* (1987), 37 C.C.C. (3d) 565 at p. 568, 45 D.L.R. (4th) 445, [1987] 2 S.C.R. 435; *R. v. Black* (1989), 50 C.C.C. (3d) 1 at pp. 13-4, [1989] 2 S.C.R. 138, 70 C.R. (3d) 97. Furthermore, the rights guaranteed by s. 10(*b*) may be waived by the detainee, although the standard for waiver will be high, especially in circumstances where the alleged waiver has been implicit: *Clarkson*, at pp. 217-9; *Manninen*, at p. 393; *Black*, at pp. 14-5; *Brydges*, at p. 341, and *Evans*, at pp. 307-8.

Under these circumstances, it is critical that the information component of the right to counsel be comprehensive in scope and that it be presented by police authorities in a "timely and comprehensible" manner: *R. v. Dubois* (1990), 54 C.C.C. (3d) 166 at p. 190, 74 C.R. (3d) 216, [1990] R.J.Q. 681 (C.A.). Unless they are clearly and fully informed of their rights *at the outset*, detainees cannot be expected to make informed choices and decisions about whether or not to contact counsel and, in turn, whether to exercise other rights, such as their right to silence: *Hebert*. Moreover, in light of the rule that, absent special circumstances indicating that a detainee may not understand the s. 10(*b*) caution, such as language difficulties or a known or obvious mental disability, police are not required to assure themselves that a detainee fully understands the s. 10(*b*) caution, it is important that the standard caution given to detainees be as instructive and clear as possible: *R. v. Baig* (1987), 37 C.C.C. (3d) 181 at p. 183, 45 D.L.R. (4th) 106, [1987] 2 S.C.R. 537, and *Evans*, at p. 305.

Indeed, the pivotal function of the initial information component under s. 10(*b*) has already been recognized by this court. For instance, in *Evans*, McLachlin J., for the majority, stated, at p. 305 that a "person who does not understand his or her right cannot be expected to assert it". In that case, it was held that, in circumstances which suggest that a particular detainee may not understand the information being communicated to him or her by state authorities, a mere recitation of the right to counsel will not suffice. Authorities will have to take additional steps to ensure that the detainee comprehends his or her s. 10(*b*) rights. Likewise, this court has stressed on previous occasions that, before an accused can be said to have waived his or her right to counsel, he or she must be possessed of sufficient information to allow him or her to make an informed choice as regards exercising the right: *R. v. Smith* (1991), 63 C.C.C. (3d) 313 at pp. 320-4, [1991] 1 S.C.R. 714, 4 C.R. (4th) 125, and *Brydges*, at p. 342.

To conclude, because the purpose of the right to counsel under s. 10(*b*) is about providing detainees with meaningful choices, it follows that a detainee should be fully advised of available services before being expected to assert that right, particularly given that subsequent duties on the state are not triggered unless and until a detainee expresses a desire to contact counsel. In my opinion, the purpose of the right to counsel would be defeated if police were only required to advise detainees of the existence and availability of Legal Aid and duty counsel *after* some triggering assertion of the right by the detainee. Accordingly, I am unable to agree with the trial judge and the Court of Appeal below that information about duty counsel and how to access it need only be provided to detainees when they express some concern about affordability or availability of counsel. Indeed, in putting forward such a position, I can only conclude with respect that both the trial judge and the Court of Appeal erred in their interpretation and application of *Brydges*. It is, therefore, to a consideration of *Brydges* that I must now turn.

(c) Brydges

.....

... *Brydges* had the effect of adding two new elements to the information component of s. 10(*b*):

(1) information about access to counsel free of charge where an accused meets the prescribed financial criteria set by provincial Legal Aid plans ("Legal Aid"), and
(2) information about access to immediate, although temporary legal advice irrespective of financial status ("duty counsel").

At the same time, *Brydges* made it clear that the specific nature of the information provided to detainees would necessarily be contingent on the existence and availability of Legal Aid and duty counsel in the jurisdiction: *Prosper*.

.....

Brydges stands for the proposition that police authorities are required to inform detainees about Legal Aid and duty counsel services which are in existence and available in the jurisdiction at the time of detention. In case there is any doubt, I would add here that basic information about how to access available services which provide free, preliminary legal advice should be included in the standard s. 10(b) caution. This need consist of no more than telling a detainee in plain language that he or she will be provided with a phone number should he or she wish to contact a lawyer right away. Failure to provide such information is, in the absence of a valid waiver (which, as I explain infra, will be a rarity), a breach of s. 10(*b*) of the *Charter*. It follows, therefore, that where the informational obligations under s. 10(*b*) have not been properly complied with by police, questions about whether a particular detainee exercised his or her right to counsel with reasonable diligence and/or whether he or she waived his or her facilitation rights do not properly arise for consideration. Such questions are simply not relevant under s. 10(*b*) (although they may be when it comes to considering whether the evidence obtained in the course of the *Charter* violation should be excluded under s. 24(2) of the *Charter*). The breach of s. 10(*b*) is complete, except in cases of waiver or urgency, upon a failure by state authorities to properly inform a detainee of his or her right to counsel and until such time as that failure is corrected.

(d) The aftermath of Brydges

Brydges imposed a 30-day transition period so as to allow police forces across the country to give effect to the new s. 10(*b*) warnings mandated by this court's ruling. According to a comprehensive study of duty counsel systems in Canada commissioned and financed by the federal Department of Justice, *Brydges* has had at least two effects: Prairie Research Associates, *Duty Counsel Systems: Summary Report* (April, 1993), and Prairie Research Associates, *Duty Counsel Systems: Technical Report* (April, 1993) (the "*P.R.A. Reports*"). First, *Brydges* has served as the impetus for adding more specific wording to the *Charter* cautions routinely recited to all detainees. Secondly, *Brydges* has encouraged many provinces to comply with the spirit of *Brydges* by ensuring that free, preliminary legal advice is made available to detainees upon request, notwithstanding the absence of any additional funding by the federal government under shared-cost agreements for Legal Aid. In the *P.R.A.Technical Report*, for example, it is observed, at pp. 3-4, that:

> [t]he *Brydges* case prompted the creation of systems of "*Brydges* duty counsel" where lawyers provide telephone consultation. Some police departments maintain lists of such duty counsel lawyers and in some provinces (*e.g.*, Ontario, Saskatchewan and British Columbia) a toll-free (1-800) telephone number is used.

Unfortunately, not every provincial government and bar has responded as positively to *Brydges* as might be desired. The *P.R.A. Reports* make it clear, as do the accompanying cases of *Prosper* and *Matheson* [(1994), 92 C.C.C. (3d) 434 (S.C.C.)], that there is no system of "*Brydges* duty counsel" in Nova Scotia and Prince Edward Island.

On the other hand, in Ontario, the province from which this case and the related case of *Pozniak* arise, *Brydges* has had a definite impact. In "Police Implementation of Supreme Court of Canada Charter Decisions: An Empirical Study", 30 Osgoode Hall L.J. (1992), 547, Kathryn Moore explains, at pp. 564-7, that, prior to the release of *Brydges* in February, 1990, the Ontario Legal Aid Plan had established a 1-800 number in the Metropolitan Toronto area, giving persons detained at police stations in the greater Toronto area access to duty counsel 24 hours a day. In the aftermath of *Brydges*, this system was expanded to areas outside of Metropolitan Toronto. The author describes in some detail the process by which police cautions in Ontario were revised to comply with *Brydges*.

One of the clauses which was added to the standard caution in Ontario and which received the most publicity was: "You also have the right to free advice from a Legal Aid lawyer". In addition, the 24-hour, 1-800 Legal Aid number for duty counsel was printed on all police caution cards. Initially, however, it appears that police in Ontario were not providing, as a matter of routine, detainees with the 1-800 number printed on their caution cards. This is clear not only from the case at bar and from its companion case, *Pozniak*, but also from the set of six cases (which include this case and *Pozniak*) which were heard at the same time by the Ontario Court of Appeal, as well as from several lower court decisions in Ontario. According to Moore, at p. 566, in June, 1992, after two lower court decisions were released in which it was held that the caution developed in Ontario in response to *Brydges* was inadequate because it did not clearly convey to detainees that Legal Aid was free and could be accessed immediately, Ontario's Solicitor-General advised provincial police forces to change the standard caution to include the 1-800 Legal Aid number already printed on their caution cards. This was corroborated by counsel for the respondent Crown in this case and that of *Pozniak*.

It also appears that the more fully people are advised of their rights under s. 10(*b*), the more likely they are to exercise these rights. According to the *P.R.A. Summary Report*, at p. 35:

> [*Brydges*] has prompted an increase in the demand for duty counsel because of the police requirement to inform all accused of their right to counsel. Whether telephone consultation, evening or weekend service, *Brydges* has led to more accused requesting services immediately after arrest. Twenty-four hour lines which were set up prior to *Brydges* had significant increases in calls following the ruling.

This is confirmed by Moore as well, who cites statistics, at p. 565, obtained from the deputy director of Ontario's Legal Aid Plan showing that, prior to *Brydges* and the implementation of the province-wide duty counsel number, the 1-800 number in Toronto received an average of 300 calls per month. After the release of *Brydges*, the Toronto number apparently averaged 550 to 600 calls per month, while outside of Toronto, the 1-800 number averaged 700 to 800 calls per month.

(e) Summary of s. 10(b) principles

A detainee is entitled under the information component of s. 10(*b*) of the *Charter* to be advised of whatever system for free, preliminary legal advice exists in the jurisdiction and of how such advice can be accessed (*e.g.*, by calling a 1-800 number, or being provided with a list of telephone numbers for lawyers acting as duty counsel). What remains to be decided, then, is whether the caution given to the appellant by the police in this case complied with the informational requirements under s. 10(*b*), or whether the appellant waived his informational s. 10(*b*) rights. It is to this question that I now turn.

(f) Application

At the time when the appellant was arrested and detained, there was in place in Ontario a 24-hour duty counsel service accessible by dialling a toll-free number. This service was known to the police and, indeed, the 1-800 number was printed on their caution cards. Section 10(*b*) required that the existence and availability of this duty counsel system and how to access it be routinely communicated by police in a timely and comprehensible manner to detainees. In reviewing what was said to the appellant, both at the roadside where he was arrested and later, at the police station, I am of the opinion that the appellant was not properly informed of his rights under s. 10(*b*). As a result, he may have been misled about the nature and extent of his right to counsel, particularly given that he was detained during the early hours of a Saturday, a time when a person might reasonably expect that immediate legal assistance would not be available.

On its face, the caution extended to the appellant both at the roadside and at the police station did not advise him of the existence and availability of any "duty counsel" service, nor did it provide him with the toll-free telephone number by which the service could be accessed. However, what must be considered is whether, despite the absence of precise words to this effect, the essence of the appellant's right to immediate and temporary free legal advice was adequately communicated to him, or, alternatively, whether the appellant fully understood his rights and waived the right to be expressly informed of them by the authorities.

In my opinion, the s. 10(*b*) caution that the appellant received, both at the roadside and at the police station, failed to convey the necessary sense of immediacy and universal availability of legal assistance. First, when the appellant was arrested at the roadside, he was not told of the existence of the 1-800 number for duty counsel and that he would be allowed to call a lawyer as soon as he arrived at the police station where there were telephones. Although it was subsequently made clear upon arrival at the station that he could call "now", the appellant had, in the intervening period between detention at the roadside and arrival at the station, made a self-incriminating statement. Secondly, reference to Legal Aid was confusing in so far at it implied that free legal advice, while available, was contingent on applying for it once charged — a process which takes time and for which there are qualifying financial requirements. The caution he received failed to communicate the fact that, at the pre-charge stage, a detainee has the opportunity by virtue of the scheme for immediate legal assistance set up by Ontario to speak to duty counsel and to obtain preliminary legal advice *before* incriminating him or herself.

The 1-800 number, or at least the existence of a toll-free telephone number, should have been conveyed to the appellant upon his arrest at the roadside even though there were no telephones available. Indeed, the police should have explained to the appellant that, as soon as they reached the police station, he would be permitted to use a telephone for the purpose of calling a lawyer, including duty counsel which was available to give him immediate, free legal advice. It can hardly be described as an undue hardship on police to require them to provide detainees with this basic information, especially when the toll-free number is already printed on their caution cards. I am satisfied that the 1-800 number was part of the informational requirement under s. 10(b) of the *Charter*. I agree with counsel for the appellant that, in today's highly technological and computerized world, 1-800 numbers are simple and effective means of conveying the sense of immediacy and universal availability of legal assistance which the majority of this court in *Brydges* said must be conveyed as part of the standard s. 10(*b*) warning in jurisdictions where such a service exists.

Furthermore, the appellant did not waive his right to receive a caution that fully informed him of his right to counsel. Although detainees can waive their s. 10(*b*) rights, valid waivers of the informational component of s. 10(*b*) will, in my view, be rare. As I stated in *Korponey v. A.-G. Can.* (1982), 65 C.C.C. (2d) 65 at p. 74, 132 D.L.R. (3d) 354, [1982] 1 S.C.R. 41, the validity of a waiver of a procedural right "... is dependent upon it being clear and unequivocal that the person is waiving the procedural safeguard and is doing so with full knowledge of the rights the procedure was enacted to protect...". This standard applies equally to waivers of *Charter* rights, including the rights guaranteed by s. 10(*b*): *Evans, supra*, at pp. 307-8. In the case of s. 10(*b*)'s informational component, requiring that a person waiving the right have "full knowledge" of it means that he or she must already be fully apprised of the information that he or she has the right to receive. A person who waives the right to be informed of something without knowing what it was that he or she had the right be informed of can hardly be said to be possessed of "full knowledge" of his or her rights. For this reason, the fact that a detainee indicates that he or she does not wish to hear the information conveyed by the standard police "caution" mandated by s. 10(*b*) will not, by itself, be enough to constitute a valid waiver of s. 10(*b*)'s informational component.

As this court held in *Evans* (at p. 306), state authorities have a duty under s. 10(*b*) "to make a reasonable effort to explain to the accused his right to counsel". In most cases, reading the accused a caution that meets the criteria I have outlined above will satisfy this duty. If the circumstances reveal, however, that a particular detainee does not understand the standard caution, the authorities must take additional steps to ensure that the detainee comprehends the rights guaranteed by s. 10(*b*), and the means by which they can be exercised: *Evans*, at p. 306; *Baig*, at p. 183. Conversely, situations may occasionally arise in which the authorities' duty to make a reasonable effort to inform the detainee of his or her s. 10(*b*) rights will be satisfied even if certain elements of the standard caution are omitted. In my view, however, this will only be the case if the detainee *explicitly* waives his or her right to receive the standard caution (for example, by interrupting the police when they begin to read the caution and telling them that they do not have to continue) *and* if the circumstances reveal *a reasonable basis for believing* that the detainee in fact knows and has adverted to his rights, and is aware of the means by which these rights can be exercised. The fact that a detainee merely indicates that he knows his rights will not, by itself, provide a reasonable basis for believing that the detainee, in fact, understands their full extent or the means by which they can be implemented. For example, a detainee who states that she knows that she has the right to consult with counsel and who purports to waive her right to be informed of it, might in fact be unaware both that she has the right to do so without delay, or that "*Brydges* duty counsel" service is available to her. In such a case, the state authorities have an obligation to take reasonable steps to assure themselves that the detainee is aware of all of the information he or she has the right to receive (that is, the information contained in a constitutionally valid standard caution). In most cases, of course, the simplest way in which the authorities can discharge this duty will be simply to read the standard caution.

In some circumstances, however, there may be a reasonable basis for believing that a detainee who waives the informational component of s. 10(*b*) is, in fact, cognizant of some, or all, of the information contained in the standard caution. In this case, omitting this information from the standard caution may not result in a violation of s. 10(*b*). For example, consider the case of a detainee who is initially charged with one offence, who consults with counsel before being charged with an additional offence. As this court held in *Black*, a change in the nature of the detention of this sort will cause the state authorities' obligation to inform the detainee of his or her s. 10(*b*) rights to be triggered anew. Although it would thus be necessary, in this example, for the police to once again inform the detainee that he or she had the right to consult with counsel without delay, it might not be necessary for them to remind the detainee about the existence of duty counsel. If, for instance, the detainee had spoken to duty counsel a few hours earlier, it might be reasonable to assume that he or she remembers that duty counsel service was available. In this case, a waiver by the detainee of this component of his or her informational rights might be valid.

It must be emphasized, however, that the standard for waiver of the informational right will, as explained above, be high. In my view, any lesser standard than the one indicated would not accord with the purposive approach to s. 10(*b*) that this court has consistently endorsed: see *Brydges*, at p. 349; *Black*, at pp. 11-2; *Clarkson*, at p. 217). As I noted earlier, this court has recognized the pivotal function the informational component of s. 10(*b*) plays. In light of the component's importance in ensuring that the purposes of s. 10(*b*) are fully realized, the validity of waivers of the informational component should only be recognized in cases where it is clear that the detainee already fully understands his or her s. 10(*b*) rights, fully understands the means by which they can be exercised, and adverts to those rights. Requiring that these conditions be met ensures that any subsequent waiver of the right to counsel made following a waiver of the informational component will be a fully informed one. Since the informational obligations s. 10(*b*) imposes on state authorities are not onerous, it is not unreasonable, in my view, to insist that these authorities resolve any uncertainty that might exist regarding the detainee's knowledge of his or her rights, something they can do by simply reading the standard caution, as they are required to do in cases where the detainee does not clearly and unequivocally indicate the desire to waive the informational component.

On the facts of this case, there is no evidence that the appellant expressed any interest in waiving any of his informational rights, including his right to be informed of the existence of *Brydges* duty counsel services. Although it is not, therefore, necessary to consider whether the appellant was, in fact, aware of the existence of duty counsel, I note in passing that there the evidence on the record does not reasonably support the inference that he knew that such services were available. I conclude, therefore, that the appellant did not waive his s. 10(*b*) informational rights, and that the authorities' failure to properly inform him of the availability of duty counsel resulted in a s. 10(*b*) violation.

Since I have concluded that the appellant should have been advised from the outset of the existence and availability of duty counsel and of the 1-800 telephone number, there is no need for me to consider under s. 10(*b*) the conflicting evidence as to whether or not the appellant expressed a concern to police about being able to reach a lawyer at a late hour. In addition, because the appellant was not properly informed of his right to counsel, his conduct cannot amount to a waiver of his facilitation rights. The standard for waiver of a *Charter* right is high. It is a pre- condition of a valid waiver that a person know what he or she is waiving. In this case, because the appellant did not know that he had access to free and immediate preliminary legal advice over the telephone, he was not in a position to give an effective waiver. However, there may be situations where a detainee is so clear about not wanting to speak to any lawyer that, notwithstanding imperfect compliance by police with the informational requirements under s. 10(*b*), the detainee's conduct will be a factor militating in favour of admission of the evidence under s. 24(2) of the *Charter*.

Under the circumstances of this case where no urgency was involved and where there was no valid waiver of s. 10(*b*)'s informational component, the breach of the appellant's s. 10(*b*) rights was complete upon his not being advised of the existence and availability of Ontario's duty counsel service and of the toll-free number by which it could be accessed. I find, therefore, that the appellant's rights under s. 10(*b*) of the *Charter* were infringed by the police. Accordingly, it is necessary to decide whether the evidence obtained as a result of this violation should be excluded under s. 24(2) of the *Charter*.

(g) Exclusion of evidence

The evidence at issue here are the results of two failed breathalyzer tests and the appellant's incriminating statement to the police at the roadside that he had had five to six beers that night.

... There are two requirements for exclusion of evidence under s. 24(2): *Strachan* [(1988), 46 C.C.C. (3d) 479 (S.C.C.)], *per* Dickson C.J.C., at pp. 494-5, and *R. v. Therens* (1985), 18 C.C.C. (3d) 481 at p. 508, 18 D.L.R. (4th) 655, [1985] 1 S.C.R. 613, *per* Le Dain J. First, there has to have been a *Charter* violation in the course of obtaining the evidence. Secondly, it must be found that having regard to all the circumstances, admission of the evidence would bring the administration of justice into disrepute.

Under the first threshold requirement, there must be some connection or relationship between the infringement of the right or freedom in question and the obtaining of the evidence which is sought to be excluded. However, a strict causal link between the *Charter* infringement and the discovery of the evidence is not required: *Therens*, *per* Le Dain J., at p. 509; *Strachan*, *per* Dickson C.J.C., at pp. 494-9, and Lamer J. (as he then was), at p. 501, and *Brydges*, at pp. 345-6. Generally speaking, so long as it is not too remotely connected with the violation, all the evidence obtained as part of the "chain of events" involving the *Charter* breach will fall within the scope of s. 24(2): *Strachan*, *per* Dickson C.J.C., at p. 499, and Lamer J. at p. 501. This means that in the initial inquiry under s. 24(2) as to whether evidence has been "obtained in a manner that infringed or denied" *Charter* rights, courts should take a generous approach. However, it should be borne in mind that the presence and strength of the causal connection between the evidence and the *Charter* breach may be a factor for consideration under the second, more important, branch of s. 24(2): *Strachan*, *per* Dickson C.J.C., at p. 499; *R. v. I. (L.R.)* (1993), 86 C.C.C. (3d) 289 at p. 307, 109 D.L.R. (4th) 140, [1993] 4 S.C.R. 504, *per* Sopinka J.

In the case at bar, I am satisfied that the breathalyzer evidence as well as the self-incriminating statement were obtained in the context of the infringement of the appellant's right to counsel under s. 10(*b*) and, therefore, that they pass the first hurdle under s. 24(2).

The analysis must then proceed to the second stage of inquiry under s. 24(2), where it must be determined whether, in all of the circumstances, admission of the evidence would tend to bring the administration of justice into disrepute. In order to make this determination, a court must balance factors relating to the effect of admission on the fairness of the trial, the seriousness of the breach, and the effect of exclusion on the repute of the administration of justice: *R. v. Collins* (1987), 33 C.C.C. (3d) 1 at pp. 19-21, 38 D.L.R. (4th) 508, [1987] 1 S.C.R. 265. The overall burden of persuasion under s. 24(2) rests on the party seeking exclusion of the evidence: *Collins*, at p. 16; *R. v. Simmons* (1988), 45 C.C.C. (3d) 296 at p. 323, 55 D.L.R. (4th) 673, [1988] 2 S.C.R. 495, *per* Dickson C.J.C., and *R. v. Duarte* (1990), 53 C.C.C. (3d) 1 at pp. 22-3, 65 D.L.R. (4th) 240, [1990] 1 S.C.R. 30. That is, it is the applicant for exclusion under s. 24(2) who must ultimately satisfy the court on a balance of probabilities that admission of the evidence could bring the administration of justice into disrepute.

However, just because the applicant bears the ultimate burden of persuasion under s. 24(2) does not mean that he or she will bear this burden on every issue relevant to the inquiry. As a practical matter, the onus on any issue will tend to shift back and forth between the applicant and the Crown, depending on what the particular contested issue is, which party is seeking to rely on it and, of course, the nature of the *Charter* right which has been violated. As Sopinka, Lederman and Bryant state at p. 397 of their text, *The Law of Evidence in Canada*:

> The applicant's burden under s. 24(2) is quite unlike an ordinary civil burden to establish facts. Once the *Charter* violation and circumstances surrounding it are proved, the inquiry departs the realm of pure fact and becomes concerned with matters that are not susceptible of proof in the ordinary sense, such as the possible effect of admission on the fairness of the trial, the relative seriousness of the *Charter* violation, and the very concept of the reputation of the administration of justice. Furthermore, the true burden is in practice bound to drift towards the Crown, since many factors in the equation are within the peculiar knowledge of the Crown (e.g., good faith, urgency, availability of other investigative techniques); and, perhaps more important, it is the Crown that is functionally responsible for the maintenance of the administration of justice.

The validity of these comments is confirmed when one considers the case-law. For example, in cases involving a breach of s. 8 of the *Charter* where evidence has been obtained as a result of an unreasonable search and seizure, it is clear that, unless the Crown can show that the police had reasonable and probable grounds to act as they did, such as a well-founded belief at the time that an accused was in possession of drugs or that there were compelling and urgent circumstances, there is a presumption that the violation is a serious one under s. 24(2) which must be rebutted by the Crown: *e.g.*, *R. v. Greffe* (1990), 55 C.C.C. (3d) 161, [1990] 1 S.C.R. 755, 75 C.R. (3d) 257, *per* Lamer J. for the majority.

One of the issues that tends to arise in cases where there has been a breach of s. 10(*b*) of the *Charter* is whether the accused would have acted any differently had there been no violation of his or her right to counsel. In the case at bar, for instance, a question that arises is whether the appellant would have actually contacted a lawyer if he had been properly advised of his right to duty counsel and of the existence of the 1-800 number. This issue is related to the strength of the causal link that exists between the violation and the evidence obtained, a matter that was mentioned above in the context of the first branch of inquiry under s. 24(2). Inevitably, the causal connection issue intersects with the question of burden of proof. That is, on whom should the risk of non-persuasion in these circumstances fall? Framed positively, does the Crown bear the burden of proving that the accused would not have acted any differently had his or her s. 10(*b*) rights been respected (so that the evidence would have been obtained in any event), or does the s. 24(2) applicant bear the burden of proving that he or she would have exercised his or her right to counsel if the police had complied with their informational obligation?

In my view, the Crown should bear the legal burden (the burden of persuasion) of establishing, on the evidence, that the s. 24(2) applicant would not have acted any differently had his s. 10(*b*) rights been fully respected, and that, as a consequence, the evidence would have been obtained irrespective of the s. 10(*b*) breach.

.....

Section 24(2) applicants thus do not bear the burden of proving that they would have consulted counsel had their s. 10(*b*) rights not been infringed. Of course, once there is positive evidence supporting the inference that an accused person would *not* have acted any differently had his or her s. 10(*b*) rights been fully respected, a s. 24(2) applicant who fails to provide evidence that he or she would have acted differently (a matter clearly within his or her particular knowledge) runs the risk that the evidence on the record will be sufficient for the Crown to satisfy its legal burden (the burden of persuasion). Although at p. 563 of my reasons in *R. v. Schmautz* (1990), 53 C.C.C. (3d) 556, [1990] 1 S.C.R. 398, 75 C.R. (3d) 129, I implied that the burden of proof on this issue rested upon the accused, upon further reflection I have decided that the approach I have adopted here is to be preferred.

A review of past decisions by this court clearly demonstrates that exclusion of evidence, even self-incriminatory evidence, will not necessarily follow each and every breach of the right to counsel under s. 10(*b*): *e.g.*, see *Strachan, per* Dickson C.J.C., at pp. 500-1; *Tremblay* ; *Black ; Schmautz, per* Lamer C.J.C., at pp. 562-3, and *R. v. Mohl* (1989), 47 C.C.C. (3d) 575*n*, [1989] 1 S.C.R. 1389, 69 C.R. (3d) 399. If the party resisting admission of the evidence is unable to establish in an overall sense that its admission would bring the administration of justice into disrepute, the evidence should be admitted.

(i) Breathalyzer evidence and the issue of statutory compellability

In the case at bar, not only is the appellant's statement about having five to six beers clearly self-incriminatory, but so too are the results of the breathalyzer tests. The breath samples provided by the appellant emanated from his body and, unlike real evidence, could not have been obtained but for the appellant's participation in their construction: Ross, at p. 139. The conscriptive character of breathalyzer evidence in the impaired driving context warrants further discussion in light of a line of argument which seeks to downplay or even deny the self- incriminatory nature of breath samples. This line of argument not only appears to be gaining acceptance amongst courts of appeal (*e.g.*, see the Nova Scotia Court of Appeal's reasons in *Prosper*) [reported 75 C.C.C. (3d) 1, 38 M.V.R. (2d) 268, 113 N.S.R. (2d) 156], but is also urged upon us by the respondent Crown in this and the related case of *Pozniak*. The argument can be summarized as follows: because the breathalyzer evidence was statutorily compellable whether or not the appellant spoke to counsel, it could not have affected the fairness of the trial and, therefore, should be admitted under s. 24(2) of the *Charter*.

One of the leading authorities for this approach to breathalyzer evidence is *R. v. Jackson* (1993), 86 C.C.C. (3d) 233, 25 C.R. (4th) 265, 15 O.R. (3d) 709 (C.A.). In that case, a unanimous Court of Appeal found a breach of s. 10(*b*) of the *Charter* because of the failure of the police in the circumstances to explain to the accused that he had a right to privacy when contacting his lawyer. Under s. 24(2), the court acknowledged, at p. 243, that the breath samples were not in existence at the time of the breach and could, therefore, be characterized as evidence emanating from the accused. However, the court did not believe that admission of such evidence would render the trial unfair. Unlike with other types of evidence emanating from an accused person, in the case of breath samples there is a legal obligation to provide them under s. 254(3)(*a*) of the *Code*, provided the requirements of that subsection are met. Indeed, it constitutes an offence under s. 254(5) of the *Code* to fail or refuse to provide a sample without a reasonable excuse. The court in Jackson noted that the evidence on the *voir dire* established reasonable and probable grounds for the police having made the breath sample demand. It found on the facts that there was no evidence to indicate a reasonable excuse which would justify the accused failing or refusing to provide a sample, no matter what advice he received from counsel. Writing for the court, Goodman J.A. concluded, at p. 244:

> It seems to me that the admission of evidence of the results of a breathalyzer test taken after a breach of s. 10(b), which test the accused would have been lawfully required to take in the circumstances of the particular case, cannot be said to operate unfairly in the conduct of the trial.

With respect, I am unable to agree that breathalyzer evidence should be treated in this manner. It is true that under the *Code* there are a unique set of offences relating to impaired driving which limit the options available to a person who is the subject of a breathalyzer demand. That is, the person can either "blow" as requested and risk failing the breathalyzer test and being charged with the "over 80" offence under s. 253(*b*) of the *Code*, or the person can refuse and be charged with the offence of "refusal to blow" pursuant to s. 254(5) of the *Code*. As this court said in *Therens*, *per* Le Dain J., at p. 505, it rings false to suggest that, under such circumstances, a detainee is "free" to choose not to blow...It is for this reason that breathalyzer evidence is often characterized as "statutorily compellable".

What is singular about the refusal offence in the impaired driving context is that it punishes a person who refuses to incriminate him or herself. In this respect, it should be noted that the constitutionality of s. 254(5) of the *Code* has not been raised here. If one considers, for example, a person charged with murder, it is clear that that person cannot be statutorily compelled to comply with a breathalyzer demand which is made in order to counter a possible defence of drunkenness. The sole authority for making a breathalyzer demand is found in s. 254(3)(*a*) of the *Code*, which says that police must believe on reasonable and probable grounds that a person is committing, or at any time within the preceding two hours has committed, as a result of the consumption of alcohol, an offence under s. 253. Section 253, in turn, specifically relates only to the operation and care and control of a "motor vehicle, vessel aircraft or railway equipment".

In light of the restricted options available to a detainee who has received a demand to provide breath samples under s. 254(3)(*a*) of the *Code*, it follows that the advice of a lawyer in such circumstances will be correspondingly limited. That is, a lawyer can advise his or her client to blow (indeed, it would be improper to advise the client not to blow simply for the sake of refusing or for some oblique motive because to do so would be counselling a crime). Alternatively, in a situation where a lawyer believes that the client may have a defence to a refusal charge under s. 254(5), such as a lack of reasonable and probable grounds by the police to make the demand, the lawyer can advise his or her client to refuse to blow. This is to be contrasted with our hypothetical murder case where a lawyer would very likely counsel his or her client not to risk incriminating him or herself by providing breath samples.

Although the scope of available legal advice in the impaired driving context is necessarily limited, one must be mindful of the fact that this court has clearly stated in the past that, where the right to counsel has been infringed, it is improper to speculate about the nature of the advice that a detainee would have received and whether the evidence would have been obtained had the right not been infringed: *Strachan*, *per* Dickson C.J.C., at p. 496, and *Elshaw* [(1991), 67 C.C.C. (3d) 97 (S.C.C.)], at pp. 127-8.

In *Elshaw*, which involved charges of attempted sexual assault, Justice Iacobucci, writing for the majority, held that certain statements obtained from the accused in violation of his s. 10(*b*) rights should be excluded. In the course of his reasons, Iacobucci J. rejected the conclusion of the Court of Appeal for British Columbia that the admission of the evidence would not greatly prejudice the accused because self-incriminating evidence would probably have been obtained from him even if the police had complied with s. 10(*b*) of the *Charter*. In support of his position, Iacobucci J. cited Wilson J.'s statement in *Black*, at p. 12, that "it is improper for a court to speculate about the type of legal advice which would have been given had the accused actually succeeded in contacting counsel after the charge was changed". Iacobucci J. concluded, at p. 128:

> This reasoning applies equally well to the Court of Appeal's speculation that self-incriminating evidence would have been obtained in any event. No one can speculate what the appellant might have said or done at the time of his detention had he been advised of his right to counsel or even of his right to remain silent. To base admission on the ground that he *might* have confessed completely undermines the enshrinement of the right to counsel in the *Charter*.

(Emphasis in original.)

I am satisfied that there is sufficient scope for legal advice to a detainee who has received a breathalyzer demand pursuant to s. 254(3)(*a*) of the *Code* to say that courts must not speculate about the nature of that advice and whether it would have made any difference to the outcome of the case. In addition, I must respectfully disagree with the Ontario Court of Appeal which adopts an *ex post facto* approach to determining whether or not the defence of "no reasonable and probable grounds" was actually available to the accused on the facts. One of the purposes of s. 10(*b*) is to provide detainees with an opportunity to make *informed* choices about their legal rights and obligations. This opportunity is no less significant when breathalyzer charges are involved. I am, therefore, not prepared to hold, *ipso facto*, either that breathalyzer evidence in the impaired driving context does not qualify as self-incriminating evidence or, if it does, that its admission does not affect the fairness of a trial.

[Lamer C.J.C. ultimately concluded that the breathalyzer evidence and the incriminating statement should be excluded and an acquittal entered.]

[La Forest and McLachlin JJ. delivered concurring reasons.]

R. v. PROSPER

(1994), 92 C.C.C. (3d) 353 (S.C.C.)

Lamer C.J.C.: —

.....

In sum, then, I find that s. 10(*b*) does not impose a positive obligation on governments to ensure that free, preliminary legal advice is available on a 24-hour, on-call basis. However, s. 10(*b*) does require, in situations where a detainee has asserted his or her right to counsel and been duly diligent in exercising it, that the police hold off in order to provide the detainee with a reasonable opportunity to contact counsel. It must also be noted that, although there is no constitutional obligation on governments to provide duty counsel services, the non-existence or unavailability of such services could, in some circumstances which I need not speculate on, give rise to issues of fair trial. Thus, in those situations, the state runs the risk of having evidence excluded under s. 24(2) of the *Charter*.

In circumstances where a detainee has asserted his or her right to counsel and has been reasonably diligent in exercising it, yet has been unable to reach a lawyer because duty counsel is unavailable at the time of detention, courts must ensure that the *Charter*-protected right to counsel is not too easily waived. Indeed, I find that an additional informational obligation on police will be triggered once a detainee, who has previously asserted the right to counsel, indicates that he or she has changed his or her mind and no longer wants legal advice. At this point, police will be required to tell the detainee of his or her right to a reasonable opportunity to contact a lawyer and of the obligation on the part of the police during this time not to take any statements or require the detainee to participate in any potentially incriminating process until he or she has had that reasonable opportunity. This additional informational requirement on police ensures that a detainee who persists in wanting to waive the right to counsel will know what it is that he or she is actually giving up.

Given the importance of the right to counsel, I would also say with respect to waiver that once a detainee asserts the right there must be a clear indication that he or she has changed his or her mind, and the burden of establishing an unequivocal waiver will be on the Crown: *Ross* [(1989), 46 C.C.C. (3d) 129 (S.C.C.)], at pp. 135-6. Further, the waiver must be free and voluntary and it must not be the product of either direct or indirect compulsion. This court has indicated on numerous occasions that the standard required for an effective waiver of the right to counsel is very high: *R. v. Clarkson* (1986), 25 C.C.C. (3d) 207, 26 D.L.R. (4th) 493, [1986] 1 S.C.R. 383 (S.C.C.); Manninen, and *R. v. Evans* [(1991), 63 C.C.C. (3d) 289 (S.C.C.)]. As I said in *Bartle* [(1994), 92 C.C.C. (3d) 289 (S.C.C.)], at pp. 12-3 and 27 [*ante*, pp. 302 and 311-2], a person who waives a right must know what he or she is giving up if the waiver is to be valid. That being said, it stands to reason that the right to counsel guaranteed under s. 10(*b*) must not be turned into an *obligation* on detainees to seek the advice of a lawyer.

Finally, I wish to point out that there may be compelling and urgent circumstances in which, despite a detainee's being unable to contact a lawyer due to the unavailability of a "*Brydges* duty counsel" system, police will not be required under s. 10(*b*) to hold off. However, in the context of impaired driving cases, I am satisfied that the existence of the two-hour evidentiary presumption available to the Crown under s. 258(1)(*c*)(ii) of the *Code* does not, by itself, constitute such a compelling or urgent circumstance. "Urgency" of the kind referred to by this court in cases such as *Manninen* [(1987), 34 C.C.C. (3d) 385 (S.C.C.)] and *R. v. Strachan* (1988), 46 C.C.C. (3d) 479, 56 D.L.R. (4th) 673, [1988] 2 S.C.R. 980 (S.C.C.), is not created by mere investigatory and evidentiary expediency in circumstances where duty counsel is unavailable to detainees who have asserted their desire to contact a lawyer and been duly diligent in exercising their s. 10(*b*) rights. A detainee's *Charter*-guaranteed right to counsel must take precedence over the statutory right afforded to the Crown which allows it to rely on an evidentiary presumption about what a breathalyzer reading would have been at the time of care and control of a vehicle. Loss of the benefit of this presumption is simply one of the prices which has to be paid by governments which refuse to ensure that a system of "*Brydges* duty counsel" is available to give detainees free, preliminary legal advice on an on-call, 24-hour basis. In the circumstances presented in this case, it is neither necessary nor appropriate to consider s. 1 of the *Charter*. However, if, for example, a section of the *Criminal Code* was to be enacted which required a person to take a breathalyzer test within a fixed time whether or not a lawyer had been consulted, then a court might well be required to consider, depending on the time allotted amongst other factors, whether such a provision could be justified under s. 1 of the *Charter*.

I would also note as an aside that where the Crown is unable to rely on the presumption under s. 258(1)(*c*)(ii) of the *Code* due to the unavailability of duty counsel, the Crown can still try and prove the "over 80" breathalyzer charge by adducing expert evidence which seeks to relate later and lower test results back to the blood-alcohol level at the time of the offence: see, *e.g.*, *R. v. Burnison* (1979), 70 C.C.C. (2d) 38 (Ont. C.A.). As this court said clearly in *R. v. Deruelle* (1992), 75 C.C.C. (3d) 118, 94 D.L.R. (4th) 638, [1992] 2 S.C.R. 663 (S.C.C.), where it considered the breathalyzer scheme under the *Code*, evidence obtained more than two hours after the alleged offence is still admissible.

It may be that on some occasions a detainee's reasonable opportunity to contact counsel, and the corresponding holding-off period, will extend to the point at which it is no longer possible to obtain breathalyzer readings that can be accurately extrapolated backwards to provide information about the accused's blood-alcohol level at the time of the alleged offence. The question of whether or not the imminent loss of the chance to obtain *any* meaningful breathalyzer data might constitute an "urgent circumstance" sufficient to curtail the holding-off period does not arise on facts of this appeal. In the case at bar, breathalyzer readings were obtained roughly an hour after the appellant was detained, well before any sense of urgency connected to the loss of the opportunity to obtain useful breathalyzer data would have developed. It is, therefore, unnecessary to decide in this case whether, under different circumstances, the prospect of the loss of all opportunity to obtain breathalyzer data might justify abridging the holding-off period. Moreover, this question could not, in my view, be decided without considering the statutory provisions upon which the police's ability to obtain breathalyzer data rests. As I noted in *Bartle*, at p. 37 [*ante*, p. 318], breathalyzer evidence in impaired driving cases is often characterized as "statutorily compellable" by virtue of the fact that refusing to provide a breath sample in these circumstances is itself a criminal offence under s. 254(5) of the *Code*. The results of a breathalyzer test are self-incriminatory evidence (*Bartle* at pp. 35-6 [*ante*, pp. 317-8]), and were it not for s. 254(5), a detainee would be free to choose not to assist the state's investigation by providing a breath sample. In my view, any consideration of the question of whether the state's interest in obtaining breathalyzer readings was sufficiently pressing to constitute an "urgent circumstance" warranting the curtailment of a detainee's s. 10(*b*) rights would, by inference, require an examination of the constitutionality of s. 254(5), an issue that was not raised directly on this appeal. For these reasons, I prefer not to decide this question at this time.

I should note, however, that whether or not breathalyzer data is available, it is always open to the Crown to proceed with a straight impaired driving charge under s. 253(*a*), as was customary before the advent of breathalyzer machines and Parliament's introduction in the late 1960's of the "over 80" breathalyzer charge under s. 253(*b*) of the *Code*.

(d) Summary of principles

Section 10(*b*) of the *Charter* does not impose a substantive constitutional obligation on governments to ensure that duty counsel is available, or likewise, provide detainees with a guaranteed right to free and immediate preliminary legal advice upon request. However, in jurisdictions where a duty counsel service does exist but is unavailable at the precise time of detention, s. 10(*b*) does impose an obligation on state authorities to hold off from eliciting evidence from a detainee, provided that the detainee asserts his or her right to counsel and is reasonably diligent in exercising it. In other words, the police must provide the detainee with what, in the circumstances, is a reasonable opportunity to contact duty counsel. While this holding-off requirement does not apply in cases of urgency, the evidentiary presumption under s. 258(1)(*d*) of the *Code*, which provides that readings taken within two hours of an alleged offence are proof of the blood-alcohol level at the time of the offence, is not a sufficiently "urgent" factor to override a detainee's right to counsel under s. 10(*b*).

In addition, once a detainee asserts his or her right to counsel and is duly diligent in exercising it, thereby triggering the obligation on the police to hold off, the standard required to constitute effective waiver of this right will be high. Upon the detainee doing something which suggests he or she has changed his or her mind and no longer wishes to speak to a lawyer, police will be required to advise the detainee of his or her right to a reasonable opportunity to contact counsel and of their obligation during this time not to elicit incriminating evidence from the detainee.

With respect to the initial information component of s. 10(*b*), I would reiterate what I said in *Bartle* — namely, that a detainee is entitled under s. 10(*b*) to be advised of whatever system for free, preliminary legal advice exists in the jurisdiction at the time and of how such advice can be accessed (*e.g.*, by dialling a 1-800 (toll-free) number). Where no such duty counsel system exists, as was the case here and in *Matheson*, a detainee must nevertheless be advised upon detention of his or her right to apply for Legal Aid under the applicable provincial or territorial Legal Aid Plan.

QUESTIONS

34. The accused is arrested in California on an extradition warrant for murder in Canada. At the request of the Canadian police, the accused is interrogated by American police, who give him a *Miranda* warning in compliance with American law, but fail to advise him of his right to counsel without delay. He gives a statement which the Crown wants to tender at his Canadian trial. Is the *Charter* applicable? Consider, in this regard, *R. v. Terry* (1996), 106 C.C.C. (3d) 508 (S.C.C.).

35. The accused is advised of her right to counsel in unobjectionable terms and speaks to her counsel. She then advises the police that she has done so and, on the advice of counsel, has nothing to say. Notwithstanding her assertion, the police then question the accused and obtain inculpatory utterances. Have her *Charter* rights been violated?

36. The accused is arrested for sexual assault. He indicates he would like to speak to counsel. The accused speaks with his lawyer for ten minutes. After he does so, the police question him about the offence. The accused indicates he wants to wait until he has spoken with a legal aid lawyer. The police continue to question him and obtain a statement that he did not have sex with the complainant. Later the accused changes the story and he indicates that he had consensual sex with the complainant. The Crown impeaches the accused's testimony with the earlier inconsistent statement. Is the initial statement (denying that he had sex with the complainant) obtained in violation of the accused's s. 10(*b*) rights? Consider, in this regard, *R. v. Whitford* (1997), 115 C.C.C. (3d) 52 (Alta. C.A.); leave to appeal to S.C.C. refused, [1997] 3 S.C.R. xiii.

D. CONSTITUTIONAL RIGHT TO SILENCE: SECTION 7 OF THE CHARTER

R. v. HEBERT

(1990), 57 C.C.C. (3d) 1 (S.C.C.)

McLachlin J. [Sopinka, Gonthier and Cory JJ. concurring]: — This case raises the issue of whether a statement made by a detained person to an undercover police officer violates the rights of the accused under the *Canadian Charter of Rights and Freedoms*.

.....

The parties agree that s. 7 of the *Charter* accords a right to silence to a detained person. As Cory J.A. (as he then was) stated in *R. v. Woolley* (1988), 40 C.C.C. (3d) 531 at p. 539, 63 C.R. (3d) 333, 37 C.R.R. 126 (Ont. C.A.): "The right to remain silent is a well-settled principle that has for generations been part of the basic tenets of our law." The parties disagree, however, over the extent of the right to silence of a detained person accorded by s. 7 of the *Charter*.

The Crown submits that the right to silence is defined by the ambit of the confessions rule as it stood at the time the *Charter* was adopted. It would follow from this that statements obtained by tricks such as the one practised here would be admissible: *Rothman* [(1981), 59 C.C.C. (2d) 30 (S.C.C.)].

The accused submits that the right to silence guaranteed by s. 7 of the *Charter* is broader than the confessions rule as it stood in 1982, and that the use of tricks to obtain a confession after the suspect has chosen not to give a statement violates the *Charter*.

The parties also agree that s. 10(*b*) of the *Charter* creates a right to counsel. The disagreement, once again, is as to the extent of that right. Is it confined to s. 10(*b*)? Or is there a broader right to counsel under s. 7?

I see the issues of the right of a detained person to remain silent and the right to counsel as intertwined. The question, as I view it, is whether, bearing in mind the *Charter* guarantee of the right to counsel and other provisions of the *Charter*, the accused's right to remain silent has been infringed.

Analysis

I. Have the appellant's Charter rights been violated?

(a) General considerations

The appellant's liberty is at stake. Under s. 7 of the *Charter*, he can only be deprived of that liberty in accordance with the principles of fundamental justice. The question is whether the manner in which the police obtained a statement from him violates that right. The answer to this question lies in an exploration of the underlying legal principles of our system of justice relevant to a detained person's right to silence. As Lamer J. stated in *Reference re s. 94(2) of Motor Vehicle Act* (1985), 23 C.C.C. (3d) 289 at p. 302, 24 D.L.R. (4th) 536, [1985] 2 S.C.R. 486: "... the principles of fundamental justice are to be found in the basic tenets of our legal system."

How do we discover the "basic tenets of our legal system" in a case such as this? Initially, it must be by reference to the legal rules relating to the right which our legal system has adopted. As D.J. Galligan points out in "The Right to Silence Reconsidered", 41 C.L.P. 69 at pp. 76-7 (1988): "The right ... is general and abstract, concealing a bundle of more specific legal relationships. It is only by an analysis of the surrounding legal rules that those more precise elements of the right can be identified." Thus rules such as the common law confessions rule, the privilege against self-incrimination and the right to counsel may assist in determining the scope of a detained person's right to silence under s. 7.

At the same time, existing common law rules may not be conclusive. It would be wrong to assume that the fundamental rights guaranteed by the *Charter* are cast forever in the straight-jacket of the law as it stood in 1982. The reference in s. 7 of the *Charter* is broadly to "principles of fundamental justice", not to this rule or that.

.....

For this reason, a fundamental principle of justice under s. 7 of the *Charter* may be broader and more general than the particular rules which exemplify it.

A second reason why a fundamental principle of justice under s. 7 may be broader in scope than a particular legal rule, such as the confessions rule, is that it must be capable of embracing more than one rule and reconciling diverse but related principles. Thus the right of a detained person to silence should be philosophically compatible with related rights, such as the right against self-incrimination at trial and the right to counsel.

The final reason why a principle of fundamental justice under s. 7 may be broader than a particular rule exemplifying it lies in considerations relating to the philosophy of the *Charter* and the purpose of the fundamental right in question in that context. The *Charter* has fundamentally changed our legal landscape. A legal rule relevant to a fundamental right may be too narrow to be reconciled with the philosophy and approach of the *Charter* and the purpose of the *Charter* guarantee.

These considerations suggest that the task of defining the scope of the right of a detained person to silence under s. 7 of the *Charter* must focus initially on the related rules which our legal system has developed — in this case the confessions rule and the privilege against self-incrimination. However, that is not the end of the inquiry. The scope of a fundamental principle of justice will also depend on the general philosophy and purpose of the *Charter*, the purpose of the right in question, and the need to reconcile that right with others guaranteed by the *Charter*.

(b) The scope of the pre-trial right to silence suggested by related rules

A detained person's right to silence under s. 7 of the *Charter* is general and abstract, subsuming a bundle of more specific legal relationships. The first step in defining the ambit of the right to silence is to consider these specific relationships and the rules which arise from them, with a view to identifying a common substratum of principle.

The right to silence conferred by s. 7 of the *Charter* is rooted in two common law concepts. The first is the confessions rule, which makes a confession which the authorities improperly obtain from a detained person inadmissible in evidence. The second is the privilege against self-incrimination which precludes a person from being required to testify against himself at trial. While the exact scope of the confessions rule has been the subject of debate over the past century, a common theme can be said to unite these two quite separate rules — the idea that a person in the power of the state in the course of the criminal process has the right to choose whether to speak to the police or remain silent.

(i) The confessions rule

The exact nature and definition of the confessions rule has long bedeviled our courts. One can, however, discern two distinct approaches. Lord Reid identified them in *Commissioners of Customs & Excise v. Hartz*, [1967] 1 All E.R. 177 at p. 184 (H.L.):

> I do not think that it is possible to reconcile all the very numerous judicial statements on rejection of confessions, but two lines of thought appear to underlie them: first, that a statement made in response to a threat or promise may be untrue or at least untrustworthy; and secondly, that *nemo tenetur seipsum prodere*.

Both versions of the confessions rule focus on voluntariness as the basic requirement for the admission of a statement made to the authorities by a detained person. The requirement of voluntariness, in turn, comports the idea that the detained person is entitled to choose whether to make a statement to the authorities or not. The difference between the two approaches to the confessions rule lies in the way they define voluntariness and choice.

The traditional confessions rule set out in *Ibrahim v. The King*, [1914] A.C. 599, defines the choice negatively, in terms of the absence of threats or promises by the authorities inducing the statement, and objectively, in terms of the physical acts and words of the parties. The awareness of the detained person of his alternatives is irrelevant. He need not be told that he has the right to remain silent. He need not be told that he has the right to consult counsel to determine what his options are. The only right he has is a negative right — the right not to be tortured or coerced into making a statement by threats or promises held out by a person who is and whom he subjectively believes to be a person in authority. The act of choosing is viewed objectively, and the mental state of the suspect, apart from his belief that he is speaking to a person in authority, is irrelevant. Were it not for the insistence in the cases that the absence of threats and promises establishes the voluntariness of the statement and that voluntariness is the ultimate requirement for an admissible confession, one would be tempted to say that choice in the usual sense of deciding between alternatives plays little role in the traditional narrow formulation of the confessions rule.

Allied with this narrow concept of choice in the traditional confessions rule, is the view that the rationale for the rule is the rejection of unreliable statements. The questions of the suspect's actual state of mind and whether, given that state of mind, it is unfair to use the statement against him, do not arise.

The second approach to choice in the confessions rule is much broader. It starts from the proposition that choice involves not only an act, but a mental element. On this view, the act of choosing whether to remain silent or speak to the police necessarily comprehends the mental act of selecting one alternative over another. The absence of violence, threats and promises by the authorities does not necessarily mean that the resulting statement is voluntary, if the necessary mental element of deciding between alternatives is absent. On this view, the fact that the accused may not have realized he had a right to remain silent (*e.g.*, where he has not been given the standard warning), or has been tricked into making the statement, are relevant to the question of whether the statement is voluntary.

The modern Canadian confessions rule accepts some aspects of this approach. Thus a voluntary choice to confess presupposes an "operating mind": *Horvath v. The Queen* (1979), 44 C.C.C. (2d) 385, 93 D.L.R. (3d) 1, [1979] 2 S.C.R. 376, and *Ward v. The Queen* (1979), 44 C.C.C. (2d) 498, 94 D.L.R. (3d) 18, [1979] 2 S.C.R. 30. Beyond this basic requirement, however, the mainstream of contemporary Canadian confessions law has not, by and large, acknowledged the mental element involved in choice. Nevertheless, the second, broader concept of choice persists as part of our fundamental notion of procedural fairness. Older Canadian cases acknowledge it, as does the law in other jurisdictions. And it recurs like a leitmotif through the dissenting judgments of distinguished Canadian jurists and in the work of scholars.

Allied with this second, broader approach to voluntariness or choice under the confessions rule is the view that the rule's rationale goes beyond the exclusion of unreliable statements and extends to considerations of whether reception of the statement will be unfair or tend to bring the administration of justice into disrepute.

Until the case of *R. v. Wray*, [1970] 4 C.C.C. 1, 11 D.L.R. (3d) 673, [1971] S.C.R. 272, the confessions rule in Canada, as in England and elsewhere in the commonwealth, may be characterized as an uneasy and to some extent illogical amalgam of these two quite different views of choice. It was said that the test for admissibility was whether the confession was voluntary, which carries with it the idea of an active choice between alternatives. At the same time, voluntariness was said to be established objectively by the simple absence of threats and promises: *Ibrahim*.

The law in England went (and continues to go) some way toward the reconciliation of the notion of voluntariness with the narrow legal test, by recognizing a discretion in judges to refuse to admit a statement which meets the *Ibrahim* test, on the ground that admission of the statement would be unfair to the accused and bring the administration of justice into disrepute. Violation of the "Judges' Rules" — guidelines laid down by the judges for the conduct of interrogations — frequently results in rejection of statements which meet the "threat-promise" test. Statements made where the police have not advised the suspect of his right to remain silent (required by the Judges' Rules) may be rejected on this basis, as may statements obtained by tricks. The practical result is that judges may reject confessions obtained where the mental factor relevant to true voluntariness is absent. Moreover, this discretion, not being tied to the traditional confessions rule, may be exercised where, because of police deception, the accused is unaware of the fact he is speaking to the authorities.

In Canada we have never had Judges' Rules. Yet one can discern in some of the earlier cases a willingness to go beyond the strict confines of the Ibrahim rule and to accord to the trial judge a discretion as to the admission of a statement taken in circumstances the judge deems unfair. In *Gach v. The King* (1943), 79 C.C.C. 221, [1943] 2 D.L.R. 417, [1943] S.C.R. 250, it was suggested that failure to give the accused the standard warning might render a statement inadmissible. In *Boudreau v. The King* (1949), 94 C.C.C. 1, [1949] 3 D.L.R. 81, [1949] S.C.R. 262, this court, while stating that the absence of a warning would not necessarily render a statement involuntary, suggested that it might be considered with all the other circumstances in determining whether a confession was voluntary (*per* Kerwin J. at p. 3). In the same case, Rand J. suggested at pp. 8-9 that the decision was very much one for the trial judge:

> The underlying and controlling question then remains: is the statement freely and voluntarily made? Here the trial Judge found that it was. It would be a serious error to place the ordinary modes of investigation of crime in a strait jacket of artificial rules; and the true protection against improper in-

> terrogation or any kind of pressure or inducement is to leave the broad question to the court. Rigid formulas can be both meaningless to the weakling and absurd to the sophisticated or hardened criminal...

At the same time, other cases continued to emphasize the threat-promise formulation: see *R. v. Fitton* (1956), 116 C.C.C. 1, 6 D.L.R. (2d) 529, [1956] S.C.R. 958.

Nevertheless, until the decision in *Wray*, *supra*, it was generally thought to be open to judges in Canada to reject statements which met the *Ibrahim* test, but which had been obtained unfairly. As Kaufman J.A. puts it (F. Kaufman, *The Admissibility of Confessions*, 3rd ed. (1979), p. 236):"It was generally believed, and not without reason, that a judge was entitled to exercise his discretion in cases such as these, and that appellate courts would not lightly interfere." Examples are not difficult to find. Laskin J.A. (as he then was) took the view in delivering the judgment of the Ontario Court of Appeal in *R. v. McLeod* (1968), 5 C.R.N.S. 101 at p. 104 (Ont. C.A.), that confessions could be excluded where the stratagems of police put in doubt whether the ensuing statement had been properly elicited. Similarly, Gale J. (as he then was) stated in rejecting a confession in *R. v. McCorkell*, 7 Crim. L.Q. 395 at p. 397 (1964-65) [see *R. v. McCorkell* (1962), 27 C.R.N.S. 155 (Ont. H.C.J.)]:

> It is my opinion that once an accused person has retained counsel to the knowledge of the police or other persons in authority, the latter ought not to endeavour to interview and question that accused person without first seeking and obtaining the concurrence of his solicitor. So strong is my view in this respect that I am therefore exercising my discretion in the way I have indicated, perhaps wrongly, because, strictly speaking, the statement thus procured was probably admissible. I decline, however, to give any encouragement in the future to persons in authority to circumvent the position of an accused's solicitor by going directly to speak to the accused.

To this point, the law in Canada was not significantly different from that elsewhere in the commonwealth.

Wray changed this. The issue in that case was the admissibility, not of a confession but rather of real evidence obtained as a result of a statement. Nevertheless, the principle enunciated had a profound effect on the power of a trial judge to exclude a confession which was, strictly speaking, admissible on the *Ibrahim* test. The ruling was simple: a court did not have the power to exclude admissible and relevant evidence merely because its admission would bring the administration of justice into disrepute. This represented a divergence from the approach to confessions elsewhere in the commonwealth. Instead of a two-pronged approach to confessions — the basic rule supplemented by a residual discretion to exclude on grounds of unfairness or the repute of the administration of justice — Canada was left with the narrow *Ibrahim* rule. Reliability was the only concern. All statements were admissible unless induced by threats, promises or violence.

It was in this context that the majority of this court ruled in *Rothman* that a statement obtained by a trick after the accused had indicated his wish not to speak to the authorities was admissible. As Martland J., speaking for five of the nine judges, succinctly put it at p. 38: "It was not, in my opinion, a sufficient basis for the refusal of the trial Judge to receive the confession in evidence solely because he disapproved of the method by which it was obtained."

Not all judges found it easy to accept the strictures of *Wray* and the departure it represented from a more liberal jurisprudence elsewhere in the commonwealth. In *Rothman*, Lamer J., after an extensive review of the authorities, concluded that the rule governing the reception of confessions was twofold; such statements might be excluded either where the conduct of the persons in authority to whom they were made might have rendered them untrue, or where the conduct of the authorities in obtaining the statement would tend to bring the administration of justice into disrepute. Lamer J. (who agreed with the majority in the result) also affirmed that the suspect's right of silence — the right to choose whether to make a statement to the authorities or to remain silent — was fundamental to the confessions rule.

Estey J. dissenting (Laskin C.J.C. concurring), similarly emphasized the connection between the confessions rule and the fairness and repute of the judicial process, basing his dissent on his conclusion that the use of an undercover agent to obtain a statement would bring into disrepute the administration of justice.

The reasons of Estey and Lamer JJ. disclose an array of distinguished Canadian jurists who recognized the importance of the suspect's freedom to choose whether to give a statement to the police or not, and emphasized the fairness and repute of the administration of justice as an underlying rationale for the confessions rule, both before and after *Wray*. Among them is Chief Justice Freedman, "Admissions and Confessions", reproduced in R.E. Salhany and R.J. Carter (eds.), *Studies in Canadian Criminal Evidence* (1972), at p. 99, who emphasized the centrality to the confessions rule of individual freedom and the integrity of the judicial system:

> It is justice then that we seek, and within its broad framework we may find the true reasons for the rule excluding induced confessions. Undoubtedly ... the main reason for excluding them is the danger that they may be untrue. But there are other reasons, stoutly disclaimed by some judges, openly professed by others, and silently acknowledged by still others — the last perhaps being an instance of an "inarticulate major premise" playing its role in decision-making. These reasons, all of them, are rooted in history. They are touched with memories of torture and the rack, they are bound up with the cause of individual freedom, and they reflect a deep concern for the integrity of the judicial process.

Some judges put the matter in terms of the accused's subjective and informed decision to remain silent or to speak. Thus Beetz J. wrote in *Horvath, supra*, at p. 430:

> Apart from the untrustworthiness of confessions extorted by threats or promises, other policy reasons have also been advanced to explain the rejection of confessions improperly obtained. *But the basic reason is the accused's absolute right to remain silent either completely or partially and not to incriminate himself unless he wants to*. This is why it is important that the accused understand what is at stake in the procedure.

(Emphasis added.)

As Estey J. observed in *Rothman*, this court in the post-*Wray* cases of *Horvath* and *Ward* in fact departed from the objective threat-promise formulation and the exclusive concern with the reliability of the statement, when it affirmed that to be admissible a statement must be truly voluntary in the sense of being the product of the accused's operating mind. Where the accused, because of hypnosis in the one case and drunkenness in the other, was not possessed of the requisite mental capacity to make a voluntary decision about whether to speak to the authorities or not, his statement could not be considered voluntary and hence was inadmissible. These decisions clearly affirmed the relevance of the mental element in the choice at issue in the confessions rule, at least in the minimal sense that the suspect must possess the mental capacity to make an active choice.

This then was the situation when the *Charter* was introduced in 1982. Notwithstanding a strong and continuing undercurrent of dissent, the narrow *Wray* principle continued to prevent the courts from considering the nature of the suspect's choice and the conduct of the authorities apart from threats, promises and violence, causing one trial judge, on being required to admit statements which he considered to have been taken in shocking circumstances, to comment (R. *v. Clot* (1982), 69 C.C.C. (2d) 349 at p. 365, 27 C.R. (3d) 324 (Que. S.C.), *per* Landry J.) :

> As it was torture in times past that led the courts to establish rules for the admissibility of extra-judicial statements, it would appear that situations like those described here might constitute an invitation for the courts to control their proceedings by adopting any rules necessary for the protection of the integrity of the judicial system and the fundamental rights of the citizen.

At the same time, other judges were suggesting that the adoption of the *Charter* justified a broadening of the rule. As Kaufman J.A. put it (*The Admissibility of Confessions* (3rd Supp. (cumulative) to 3rd ed.) (1986), p. 119):

> The views of Estey and Lamer JJ. (in *Rothman*) show the trend. So does the judgment in Clot. Now, with the *Charter*, the scope has increased, and while the parameters will not be known for some time, the foundation are ready.

Lamer J. alluded to this possibility in *R. v. Collins* (1987), 33 C.C.C. (3d) 1 at p. 21, 38 D.L.R. (4th) 508, [1987] 1 S.C.R. 265, where he stated with reference to *Rothman*:

> I still am of the view that the resort to tricks that are not in the least unlawful *let alone in violation of the Charter* to obtain a statement should not result in the exclusion of a free and voluntary statement unless the trick resorted to is a dirty trick, one that shocks the community.

(Emphasis added.) I return to the question of what the confessions rule suggests as to the scope of the right to pre-trial silence under s. 7 of the *Charter*. The foregoing review suggests that one of the themes running through the jurisprudence on confessions is the idea that a person in the power of the state's criminal process has the right to freely choose whether or not to make a statement to the police. This idea is accompanied by a correlative concern with the repute and integrity of the judicial process. This theme has not always been ascendant. Yet, its importance cannot be denied. It persists, both in Canadian jurisprudence and in the rules governing the rights of suspects in other countries. The question is whether, as Kaufman J.A. suggests, it should prevail in the post-*Charter* era.

(ii) The privilege against self-incrimination

The second rule which is closely concerned with the right to silence of a person in jeopardy in the criminal process is the privilege against self-incrimination. It is distinct from the confessions rule, applying at trial rather than at the investigatorial phase of the criminal process: see *Marcoux and Solomon v. The Queen* (1975), 24 C.C.C. (2d) 1 at pp. 4-6, 60 D.L.R. (3d) 119, [1976] 1 S.C.R. 763. Yet it is related to the confessions rule, both philosophically and practically.

Philosophically, courts have frequently justified both the confessions rule and the privilege against self-incrimination by reference to the right of every person not to be required to produce evidence against himself — *nemo tenetur seipsum accusare*. The privilege against self-incrimination, like the confessions rule, is rooted in an abhorrence of the interrogation practised by the old ecclesiastical courts and the Star Chamber and the notion which grew out of that abhorrence that the citizen involved in the criminal process must be given procedural protections against the overweening power of the state. While the privilege against self-incrimination relies in part on a notion which does not find place in the confessions rule — the obligation of the Crown to prove its case — it shares with that rule the notion that an accused person has no obligation to give evidence against himself, that he or she has the right to choose. This, it may be postulated, is the shared conceptual core of the two rules fundamental to the more general right to silence.

From a practical point of view, the relationship between the privilege against self-incrimination and right to silence at the investigatorial phase is equally clear. The protection conferred by a legal system which grants the accused immunity from incriminating himself at trial but offers no protection with respect to pre-trial statements would be illusory. As Ratushny writes (*Self-Incrimination in the Canadian Criminal Process* (1979), p. 253):

> Furthermore, our system meticulously provides for a public trial only after a specific accusation and where the accused is protected by detailed procedures and strict evidentiary rules. Ordinarily he is represented by a lawyer to ensure that he in fact receives all of the protections to which he is entitled. The accused is under no legal or practical obligation to respond to the accusation until there is an evidentiary case to meet. There is a hypocrisy to a system which provides such protections but allows them all to be ignored at the pre-trial stage where interrogation frequently occurs in secret, after counsel has been denied, with no rules at all and often where the suspect or accused is deliberately misled about the evidence against him.

The privilege against self-incrimination clearly imports the right to choose whether to testify or to remain silent. The accused is usually advised by counsel. The presence of the presiding judge precludes undue pressure by the Crown. The consequences of testifying or not are clear. The philosophic and practical relationship between the privilege against self-incrimination and the right of the suspect to silence prior to trial suggests that the same right of choice should prevail at the earlier phase of the criminal process.

(iii) Summary of implications to be drawn from the rules relating to the right to silence

Despite their differences, the common law confessions rule and the privilege against self-incrimination share a common theme — the right of the individual to choose whether to make a statement to the authorities or to remain silent, coupled with concern with the repute and integrity of the judicial process. If the measure of a fundamental principle of justice under s. 7 is to be found, at least in part, in the underlying themes common to the various rules related to it, then the measure of the right to silence may be postulated to reside in the notion that a person whose liberty is placed in jeopardy by the criminal process cannot be required to give evidence against himself or herself, but rather has the right to choose whether to speak or to remain silent. This suggests that the scope of the right of a detained person to silence prior to trial under s. 7 of the *Charter* must extend beyond the narrow view of the confessions rule which formed the basis of the decision of the majority of this court in *Rothman*.

(c) The scope of the right of a detained person to silence suggested by other provisions of the Charter

The common law rules relating to the right to silence suggest that the essence of the right is the notion that the person whose freedom is placed in question by the judicial process must be given the choice of whether to speak to the authorities or not. The next question is whether this hypothesis is confirmed by consideration of the right to silence in the context of other *Charter* provisions.

The rights of a person involved in the criminal process are governed by ss. 7 to 14 of the *Charter*. They are interrelated: *Reference re s. 94(2) of Motor Vehicle Act, supra*. It must be assumed that the framers of the *Charter* intended that they should be interpreted in such a manner that they form a cohesive and internally consistent framework for a fair and effective criminal process. For this reason, the scope of a fundamental principle of justice under s. 7 cannot be defined without reference to the other rights enunciated in this portion of the *Charter* as well as the more general philosophical thrusts of the *Charter*.

(i) Related rights

The first *Charter* right of importance in defining the scope of the right to silence under s. 7 of the *Charter* at the pre-trial stage is the right to counsel under s. 10(*b*) of the *Charter*.

The scheme under the *Charter* to protect the accused's pre-trial right to silence may be described as follows. Section 7 confers on the detained person the right to choose whether to speak to the authorities or to remain silent. Section 10(*b*) requires that he be advised of his right to consult counsel and permitted to do so without delay.

The most important function of legal advice upon detention is to ensure that the accused understands his rights, chief among which is his right to silence. The detained suspect, potentially at a disadvantage in relation to the informed and sophisticated powers at the disposal of the state, is entitled to rectify the disadvantage by speaking to legal counsel at the outset, so that he is aware of his right not to speak to the police and obtains appropriate advice with respect to the choice he faces. Read together, ss. 7 and 10(*b*) confirm the right to silence in s. 7 and shed light on its nature.

The guarantee of the right to consult counsel confirms that the essence of the right is the accused's freedom to choose whether to make a statement or not. The state is not obliged to protect the suspect against making a statement; indeed it is open to the state to use legitimate means of persuasion to encourage the suspect to do so. The state is, however, obliged to allow the suspect to make an informed choice about whether or not he will speak to the authorities. To assist in that choice, the suspect is given the right to counsel.

This suggests that the drafters of the *Charter* viewed the ambit of the right to silence embodied in s. 7 as extending beyond the narrow formulation of the confessions rule, comprehending not only the negative right to be free of coercion induced by threats, promises or violence, but a positive right to make a free choice as to whether to remain silent or speak to the authorities.

I should not be taken as suggesting that the right to make an informed choice whether to speak to the authorities or to remain silent necessitates a particular state of knowledge on the suspect's part over and above the basic requirement that he possess an operating mind. The *Charter* does not place on the authorities and the courts the impossible task of subjectively gauging whether the suspect appreciates the situation and the alternatives. Rather, it seeks to ensure that the suspect is in a position to make an informed choice by giving him the right to counsel. The guarantee of the right to counsel in the *Charter* suggests that the suspect must have the right to choose whether to speak to the police or not, but it equally suggests that the test for whether that choice has been violated is essentially objective. Was the suspect accorded his or her right to consult counsel? By extension, was there other police conduct which effectively deprived the suspect of the right to choose to remain silent, thus negating the purpose of the right to counsel?

The second *Charter* right relevant to the ambit of the right to silence conferred by s. 7 is the privilege against self-incrimination. This right has been enshrined in s. 11(*c*) of the *Charter*, which provides that no one can be required to give evidence against himself, and echoed in s. 13 of the *Charter*, which prevents evidence given by a witness being used against the witness in a subsequent proceeding. I have earlier suggested that these rights may be diminished to the extent that a person may be compelled to make statements at the pre-trial stage. It follows that if the *Charter* guarantees against self-incrimination at trial are to be given their full effect, an effective right of choice as to whether to make a statement must exist at the pre-trial stage.

I conclude that the consideration of other rights under the *Charter* suggests that the right to silence of a detained person under s. 7 of the *Charter* must be broad enough to accord to the detained person a free choice on the matter of whether to speak to the authorities or to remain silent.

(ii) The philosophy of the Charter with respect to improperly obtained evidence

The narrow view of the confessions rule adopted in Canada in recent years stems primarily from the *Wray* approach which emphasized reliability of evidence and virtually removed the discretion of the courts to reject statements on the ground they had been obtained unfairly.

The *Charter* introduced a marked change in philosophy with respect to the reception of improperly or illegally obtained evidence. Section 24(2) stipulates that evidence obtained in violation of rights may be excluded if it would tend to bring the administration of justice into disrepute, regardless of how probative it may be. No longer is reliability determinative. The *Charter* has made the rights of the individual and the fairness and integrity of the judicial system paramount. The logic upon which *Wray* was based, and which led the majority in *Rothman* to conclude that a confession obtained by a police trick could not be excluded, finds no place in the *Charter*. To say there is no discretion to exclude a statement on grounds of unfairness to the suspect and the integrity of the judicial system, as did the majority in *Rothman*, runs counter to the fundamental philosophy of the *Charter*.

This suggests that the right of a detained person to silence under s. 7 of the *Charter* should be viewed as broader in scope than the confessions rule as it stood in Canada at the time of the adoption of the *Charter*. The right must reflect the *Charter*'s concerns with individual freedom and the integrity of the judicial process, and permit the exclusion of evidence which offends these values.

(iii) The purpose of the right to silence under the Charter

An investigation of the ambit of a right or principle of fundamental justice under the *Charter* necessarily involves consideration of the underlying value which the right was designed to protect. This is the "purposive approach" set out by Dickson J. (as he then was) in *Hunter v. Southam Inc.* (1984), 14 C.C.C. (3d) 97, 11 D.L.R. (4th) 641, [1984] 2 S.C.R. 145.

Section 7 and the more specific procedural guarantees which follow it are generally concerned with the proper balance between the respective rights of the individual and the state in judicial proceedings where the accused's life, liberty or security of person is at stake. It guarantees the individual's life, liberty and security of person. But it recognizes that these rights are not absolute. In certain circumstances, the state may properly deprive a person of these interests. But it must do so in conformity with the principles of fundamental justice.

In a broad sense, the purpose of ss. 7 to 14 is twofold to preserve the rights of the detained individual, and to maintain the repute and integrity of our system of justice. More particularly, it is to the control of the superior power of the state *vis-à-vis* the individual who has been detained by the state, and thus placed in its power, that s. 7 and the related provisions that follow are primarily directed. The state has the power to intrude on the individual's physical freedom by detaining him or her. The individual cannot walk away. This physical intrusion on the individual's mental liberty in turn may enable the state to infringe the individual's mental liberty by techniques made possible by its superior resources and power.

The *Charter* through s. 7 seeks to impose limits on the power of the state over the detained person. It thus seeks to effect a balance between the interests of the detained individual and those of the state. On the one hand s. 7 seeks to provide to a person involved in the judicial process protection against the unfair use by the state of its superior resources. On the other, it maintains to the state the power to deprive a person of life, liberty or security of person provided that it respects fundamental principles of justice. The balance is critical. Too much emphasis on either of these purposes may bring the administration of justice into disrepute — in the first case because the state has improperly used its superior power against the individual, in the second because the state's legitimate interest in law enforcement has been frustrated without proper justification.

The right to silence conferred by s. 7 reflects these values. The suspect, although placed in the superior power of the state upon detention, retains the right to choose whether or not he will make a statement to the police. To this end, the *Charter* requires that the suspect be informed of his or her right to counsel and be permitted to consult counsel without delay. If the suspect chooses to make a statement, the suspect may do so. But if the suspect chooses not to, the state is not entitled to use its superior power to override the suspect's will and negate his or her choice.

The scope of the right to silence must be defined broadly enough to preserve for the detained person the right to choose whether to speak to the authorities or to remain silent, notwithstanding the fact that he or she is in the superior power of the state. On this view, the scope of the right must extend to exclude tricks which would effectively deprive the suspect of this choice. To permit the authorities to trick the suspect into making a confession to them after he or she has exercised the right of conferring with counsel and declined to make a statement, is to permit the authorities to do indirectly what the *Charter* does not permit them to do directly. This cannot be in accordance with the purpose of the *Charter*.

(iv) Summary of implications to be drawn from related Charter provisions

Charter provisions related to the right to silence of a detained person under s. 7 suggest that the right must be interpreted in a manner which secures to the detained person the right to make a free and meaningful choice as to whether to speak to the authorities or to remain silent. A lesser protection would be inconsistent not only with the implications of the right to counsel and the right against self-incrimination affirmed by the *Charter*, but with the underlying philosophy and purpose of the procedural guarantees the *Charter* enshrines.

(d) Conclusion on the scope of the right to silence

The common law rules related to the right to silence suggest that the scope of the right in the pre-trial detention period must be based on the fundamental concept of the suspect's right to choose whether to speak to the authorities or remain silent. Any doubt on the question is resolved by consideration of related rights protected by the *Charter*, by the *Charter*'s approach to the question of improperly obtained evidence, and by the fundamental purpose of the right to silence and related procedural guarantees. In keeping with the approach inaugurated by the *Charter*, our courts must adopt an approach to pre-trial interrogation which emphasizes the right of the detained person to make a meaningful choice and permits the rejection of statements which have been obtained unfairly in circumstances that violate that right of choice.

The right to choose whether or not to speak to the authorities is defined objectively rather than subjectively. The basic requirement that the suspect possess an operating mind has a subjective element. But this established, the focus under the *Charter* shifts to the conduct of the authorities *vis-^-vis* the suspect. Was the suspect accorded the right to consult counsel? Was there other police conduct which effectively and unfairly deprived the suspect of the right to choose whether to speak to the authorities or not?

Such a change, while important, is far from radical. It retains the essentially objective approach of the traditional confessions rule, while increasing the range of police conduct which may be considered in determining the admissibility of a suspect's statement, and it conforms to current trends in the law. Even before the *Charter*, this court had taken a step away from the traditional "threat-promise" formula by recognizing that the decision to speak to the police must be the product of an operating mind. Moreover, experience in other jurisdictions — and in ours, I venture to suggest — has proven the traditional *Ibrahim* formulation of the confessions rule too narrow. The idea that judges can reject confessions on grounds of unfairness and concerns for the repute and integrity of the judicial process has long been accepted in other democratic countries without apparent adverse consequences. Thus in England, Australia and New Zealand the traditional confessions rule has been supplemented by judicial discretion. In the United States it has been abandoned. In Canada, its retention has been marked by continual tension between minority and majority viewpoints, between what trial judges feel they should do in justice and what they find they are compelled to do. To those tensions has now been added an evident tension with the philosophy underlying the *Charter*. The jurisprudence on the rights of detained persons can only benefit, in my view, from rejection of the narrow confessions formula and adoption of a rule which permits consideration of the accused's informed choice, as well as fairness to the accused and the repute of the administration of justice.

Finally, the change proposed arguably strikes a proper and justifiable balance between the interest of the state in law enforcement and the interest of the suspect. The alternative — the strict post-*Wray* application of the confessions rule — leaves courts powerless to correct abuses of power by the state against the individual, so long as the objective formalities of the "threat-promise" formula are filled and the statement is reliable. Drawing the balance where I have suggested the *Charter* draws it permits the courts to correct abuses of power against the individual, while allowing them to nevertheless admit evidence under s. 24(2) where, despite a *Charter* violation, the admission would not bring the administration of justice into disrepute.

This approach may be distinguished from an approach which assumes an absolute right to silence in the accused, capable of being discharged only by waiver. On that approach, all statements made by a suspect to the authorities after detention would be excluded unless the accused waived his right to silence. Waiver, as defined in *R. v. Clarkson* (1986), 25 C.C.C.

(3d) 207, 26 D.L.R. (4th) 493, [1986] 1 S.C.R. 383, is a subjective concept dependent, among other things, on the accused's knowing that he is speaking to the authorities. On this approach, all statements made by a person in detention which were not knowingly made to a police officer would be excluded because, absent knowledge that the suspect is speaking to a police officer, the Crown cannot establish waiver. This would include statements made to undercover agents (regardless of whether the officer is merely passive or has elicited the statement) as well as conversations with fellow prisoners overheard by the police and statements overheard through mechanical listening devices on the wall. There is nothing in the rules underpinning the s. 7 right to silence or other provisions of the *Charter* that suggests that the scope of the right to silence should be extended this far. By contrast, the approach I advocate retains the objective approach to confessions which has always prevailed in our law and would permit the rule to be subject to the following limits.

First, there is nothing in the rule to prohibit the police from questioning the accused in the absence of counsel after the accused has retained counsel. Presumably, counsel will inform the accused of the right to remain silent. If the police are not posing as undercover officers and the accused chooses to volunteer information, there will be no violation of the *Charter*. Police persuasion, short of denying the suspect the right to choose or depriving him of an operating mind, does not breach the right to silence.

Secondly, it applies only after detention. Undercover operations prior to detention do not raise the same considerations. The jurisprudence relating to the right to silence has never extended protection against police tricks to the pre-detention period. Nor does the *Charter* extend the right to counsel to pre-detention investigations. The two circumstances are quite different. In an undercover operation prior to detention, the individual from whom information is sought is not in the control of the state. There is no need to protect him from the greater power of the state. After detention, the situation is quite different; the state takes control and assumes the responsibility of ensuring that the detainee's rights are respected.

Thirdly, the right to silence predicated on the suspect's right to choose freely whether to speak to the police or to remain silent does not affect voluntary statements made to fellow cellmates. The violation of the suspect's rights occurs only when the Crown acts to subvert the suspect's constitutional right to choose not to make a statement to the authorities. This would be the case regardless of whether the agent used to subvert the accused's right was a cellmate, acting at the time as a police informant, or an undercover police officer.

Fourthly, a distinction must be made between the use of undercover agents to observe the suspect, and the use of undercover agents to actively elicit information in violation of the suspect's choice to remain silent. When the police use subterfuge to interrogate an accused after he has advised them that he does not wish to speak to them, they are improperly eliciting information that they were unable to obtain by respecting the suspect's constitutional right to silence: the suspect's rights are breached because he has been deprived of his choice. However, in the absence of eliciting behaviour on the part of the police, there is no violation of the accused's right to choose whether or not to speak to the police. If the suspect speaks, it is by his or her own choice, and he or she must be taken to have accepted the risk that the recipient may inform the police.

.....

Some Canadian police forces appear to already be following the rules implicit in this approach. Thus in *R. v. Logan* (1988), 46 C.C.C. (3d) 354 at p. 365, 57 D.L.R. (4th) 58, 67 O.R. (2d) 87 (C.A.), it is stated:

> In his evidence, P.C. Grant (testifying under the pseudonym used by him in the undercover operation) said:
>
> > "[P]art of my instructions entailed — and it was made quite clear to me that *I was not to initiate any conversation, if possible, with the accused persons* and in the event that we did or were able to get in conversations with these persons, that *we would not ask leading questions or lead them on to the area in which I was attempting to gather information for.*
> >
> > "[W]e were to act as normal as possible and of course from further instructions from the official we had a very good idea of what would be an acceptable line of conversation, what questions would [sic] be acceptable, what wouldn't be acceptable."
>
> (Emphasis added.)

Moreover, even where a violation of the detainee's rights is established the evidence may, where appropriate, be admitted. Only if the court is satisfied that its reception would be likely to bring the administration of justice into disrepute can the evidence be rejected: s. 24(2). Where the police have acted with due care for the accused's rights, it is unlikely that the statements they obtain will be held inadmissible.

(e) Application of the right to silence in this case

The essence of the right to silence is that the suspect be given a choice; the right is quite simply the freedom to choose — the freedom to speak to the authorities on the one hand, and the freedom to refuse to make a statement to them on the other. This right of choice comprehends the notion that the suspect has been accorded the right to consult counsel and thus to be informed of the alternatives and their consequences, and that the actions of the authorities have not unfairly frustrated his or her decision on the question of whether to make a statement to the authorities.

In this case, the accused exercised his choice not to speak to the police when he advised them that he did not wish to make a statement. When he later spoke to the undercover policeman, he was not reversing that decision and choosing to speak to the police. He was choosing to speak to a fellow prisoner, which is quite a different matter. The Crown, in using a trick to negate his decision not to speak, violated his rights.

II. Section 1 of the Charter

Having found a violation of s. 7, the question arises of whether s. 1 of the *Charter* has application. In my view, it does not, since the conduct here in question is not a limit "prescribed by law" within s. 1.

In *R. v. Thomsen* (1988), 40 C.C.C. (3d) 411 at p. 419, [1988] 1 S.C.R. 640, 63 C.R. (3d) 1, Le Dain J. stated for the court [quoting from *R. v. Therens, supra,* at p. 506]:

> The limit will be prescribed by law within the meaning of s. 1 if it is expressly provided for by statute or regulation, or results by necessary implication from the terms of a statute or regulation or from its operating requirements. The limit may also result from the application of a common law rule.

The police conduct here at issue does not meet this test. It was not done in execution of or by necessary implication from a statutory or regulatory duty, and it was not the result of application of a common law rule. In short, it was not "prescribed by law" within s. 1 of the *Charter*.

III. Section 24(2) of the Charter

.....

The threshold required to satisfy the requirement of bringing the administration of justice into disrepute under s. 24(2) of the *Charter* is lower than the "community shock" test proposed by Lamer J. in the context of the confessions rule in *Rothman*: *Collins, supra,* at p. 21. Thus the conclusion of Lamer J. in *Rothman* that a police trick similar to that involved here is not necessarily inconsistent with a conclusion that such a trick should result in exclusion under s. 24(2).

.....

I am of the view that the evidence sought to be adduced in this case would render the trial unfair. I should not be taken as suggesting that violation of an accused's right to silence under s. 7 automatically means that the evidence must be excluded under s. 24(2). I would not wish to rule out the possibility that there may be circumstances in which a statement might be received where the suspect has not been accorded a full choice in the sense of having decided, after full observance of all rights, to make a statement voluntarily. But where, as here, an accused is conscripted to give evidence against himself after clearly electing not to do so by use of an unfair trick practised by the authorities, and where the resultant statement is the only evidence against him, one must surely conclude that reception of the evidence would render the trial unfair. The accused would be deprived of his presumption of innocence and would be placed in the position of having to take the stand if he wished to counter the damaging effect of the confession. The accused's conviction, if obtained, would rest almost entirely on his own evidence against himself, obtained by a trick in violation of the *Charter*.

I am also satisfied that the *Charter* violation was a serious one. The conduct of the police was wilful and deliberate. They intentionally set out on a course to undermine the appellant's right to silence notwithstanding his express assertion of that right, by having the undercover police officer engage the appellant in conversation. It is said that the police acted in good faith, relying on *Rothman* as authority to proceed as they did. However, ignorance of the effect of the *Charter* does not preclude application of s. 24(2) of the *Charter* (*Therens, supra*), nor does it cure an unfair trial.

The effect of the exclusion in this case is serious. It would result in an acquittal, since virtually the only evidence against the accused was his statement to the undercover policeman.

Balancing these factors, I arrive at the conclusion that the test in s. 24(2) is met. As the authorities to which I earlier referred amply demonstrate, it has long been felt inappropriate that an accused should be required to betray himself. Where virtually the only evidence against him is such a betrayal, the effect is that the accused is required to secure his own conviction. That is contrary to the notions of justice fundamental to our system of law and calculated, in my opinion, to bring the administration of justice into disrepute.

Conclusion

I would allow the appeal and restore the acquittal.

[Wilson and Sopinka JJ. concurred in the result. Their judgments make interesting reading since, if applied, would effectively end the state practice of obtaining jailhouse confessions through deception.]

In the following case, the Supreme Court of Canada addressed the meaning of "state agent" and "elicitation".

R. v. BROYLES

(1991), 68 C.C.C.(3d) 308 (S.C.C.)

[The accused was arrested for his grandmother's murder and advised of his right to counsel. At the request of the police, a friend visited the accused, wearing a recording device and questioned the accused about the killing. The inculpatory response was admitted at trial.]

The judgment of the court was delivered by

Iacobucci J.: — This appeal raises important questions as to the admissibility of evidence of a taped conversation between an accused in custody and a friend who visited him at the behest of the police, who made arrangements for the visit including providing the friend with a body-pack recording device.

.....

(a) The threshold question

In every case where the right to silence is raised, the threshold question will be: was the person who allegedly subverted the right to silence an agent of the state? In answering this question one should remember that the purpose of the right to silence is to limit the use of the coercive power of the state to force an individual to incriminate himself or herself; it is not to prevent individuals from incriminating themselves *per se*. Accordingly, if the person to whom the impugned remarks is made is not an agent of the state, there will be no violation of the right to silence.

In some cases, it will be clear that the person to whom the statements were made was an agent of the state. For example, if the statements were made to a police officer or to a prison official, whether in uniform or in plain clothes, there could be no question that the statements were made to an agent of the state. In other cases, it will be less clear. Where the statements are made to an informer, as in the case at bar, it may be arguable whether or not the coercive power of the state was brought to bear on the suspect in obtaining the statement from him or her.

In determining whether or not the informer is a state agent, it is appropriate to focus on the effect of the relationship between the informer and the authorities on the particular exchange or contact with the accused. A relationship between the informer and the state is relevant for the purposes of s. 7 only if it affects the circumstances surrounding the making of the impugned statement. A relationship between the informer and the authorities which develops after the statement is made, or which in no way affects the exchange between the informer and the accused, will not make the informer a state agent for the purposes of the exchange in question. Only if the relationship between the informer and the state is such that the exchange between the informer and the accused is materially different from what it would have been had there been no such relationship should the informer be considered a state agent for the purposes of the exchange. I would, accordingly, adopt the following simple test: would the exchange between the accused and the informer have taken place, in the form and manner in which it did take place, but for the intervention of the state or its agents?

If this test is applied to a conversation between a police officer and a suspect in custody, it is clear that the conversation would not have taken place but for the intervention of the officer. If it is applied to a conversation with a cellmate who has no contact with the authorities until after the conversation is concluded, it is equally clear that the actions of the authorities had no effect on the conversation, and that there would be no violation of the s. 7 right to silence. If, however, the cellmate spoke with the authorities before the conversation took place, then the question will be whether the conversation would have occurred or would have taken the same course had the cellmate had no contact with the authorities.

I would add that there may be circumstances in which the authorities encourage informers to elicit statements without there being a pre-existing relationship between the authorities and individual informers. For example, the authorities may provide an incentive for the elicitation of incriminating statements by making it known that they will pay for such information or that they will charge the informer with a less serious offence. The question in such cases will be the same: would the exchange between the informer and the accused have taken place but for the inducements of the authorities?

(b) Elicitation

Even if the evidence in question was acquired by an agent of the state, it will only have been acquired in violation of s. 7 if the manner in which it was acquired infringed the suspect's right to choose to remain silent. In general, there will be no violation of the suspect's right to silence if the suspect volunteers the information, knowing he or she is talking to an agent of the state.

.....

In *Hebert* [(1990), 57 C.C.C. (3d) 1 (S.C.C.)], my colleague, McLachlin J., left open the possibility that there will be cases amounting to more than permissible police persuasion but less than deprivation of an operating mind which will infringe the suspect's right to choose to remain silent. I would agree that there may well be such cases, but it is unnecessary to decide that question in this case.

If, on the other hand, the suspect is ignorant of the fact that he is talking to an agent of the state, whether a suborned informer or an undercover police officer, somewhat different considerations will apply. It is clear from the majority reasons in *Hebert, supra,* that statements volunteered by the suspect to the agent of the state will not infringe the suspect's right to silence. There will be a violation of the s. 7 right to silence only if the statement is elicited by the agent of the state. As McLachlin J. expressed it in *Hebert, supra,* at p. 41, the state agent must "actively elicit" the information or statement. The focus will be on what constitutes "elicitation" in the context of the right to silence.

In developing a definition of elicitation, I have found it unnecessary to refer at length to the U.S. jurisprudence dealing with the Fifth and Sixth Amendments of the U.S. Constitution. In broad terms, the concern with Sixth Amendment right to counsel is, to quote the judgment of Brennan J. in *Maine* v. *Moulton*, 474 U.S. 159 (1985), at p. 176 to protect the right of an accused "to rely on counsel as a 'medium' between him and the State", and not specifically to protect the right of an accused to choose whether or not to make a statement. Although the Fifth Amendment privilege against self-incrimination is similar in form to the right to silence in s. 7 of the *Charter*, the Supreme Court of the United States has recently held, in *Illinois v. Perkins*, 110 S. Ct. 2394 (1990), that Fifth Amendment rights do not prohibit surreptitious jailhouse conversations of the kind which this court found to violate s. 7 in *Hebert*. This is not to say that the U.S. jurisprudence will not be useful in resolving particular problems that may arise in developing the contours of the right to silence as McLachlin J. did in *Hebert*. In general, however, Canadian courts should not be hesitant to develop a uniquely Canadian approach to the right to silence, in keeping with the over-all goals of the *Charter*.

In my view, it is difficult to give a short and precise meaning of elicitation but rather one should look to a series of factors to decide the issue. These factors test the relationship between the state agent and the accused so as to answer this question: considering all the circumstances of the exchange between the accused and the state agent, is there a causal link between the conduct of the state agent and the making of the statement by the accused? For convenience, I arrange these factors into two groups. This list of factors is not exhaustive, nor will the answer to any one question necessarily be dispositive.

The first set of factors concerns the nature of the exchange between the accused and the state agent. Did the state agent actively seek out information such that the exchange could be characterized as akin to an interrogation, or did he or she conduct his or her part of the conversation as someone in the role the accused believed the informer to be playing would ordinarily have done? The focus should not be on the form of the conversation, but rather on whether the relevant parts of the conversation were the functional equivalent of an interrogation.

The second set of factors concerns the nature of the relationship between the state agent and the accused. Did the state agent exploit any special characteristics of the relationship to extract the statement? Was there a relationship of trust between the state agent and the accused? Was the accused obligated or vulnerable to the state agent? Did the state agent manipulate the accused to bring about a mental state in which the accused was more likely to talk?

In considering whether the statement in question was elicited, evidence of the instructions given to the state agent for the conduct of the conversation may be important. As McLachlin J. noted in *Hebert, supra*, evidence that the agent was instructed not to initiate the conversation nor to ask leading questions will tend to refute the allegation that the resulting statement was obtained in violation of s. 7. I would add, however, that in my opinion evidence that the state agent was instructed not to elicit information will not end the inquiry. The authorities may not take the benefit of the actions of their agent which exceed his or her instructions. To hold otherwise would be to ignore the fact that the primary emphasis of the right to silence in s. 7 is on the use of the coercive power of the state against the suspect. The authorities ought not to be able to shield themselves behind the subtleties of their relationship with the informer. It is the authorities who are in a position to control the actions of their informer; if they fail to do so, they ought not to benefit from that failure at the expense of the accused: see *United States v. Henry*, 447 U.S. 264 at pp. 271-2 (1980).

[A s. 24(2) analysis then follows, resulting in the exclusion of the evidence and a new trial ordered.]

QUESTIONS

37. **The police have reasonable and probable grounds to arrest M. for murder but wish to continue their investigation to secure more convincing evidence. They have taken statements from M. and, indeed, have advised him of his right to counsel. Further, they are aware that he now has counsel. Nonetheless, the police ask his employer to have M. fill out work-related documents, not because they are needed for work, but because the police wish to compare his printing of block letters to a block-lettered message left in lipstick on a mirror beside the deceased. M. complies with his employer's instructions and the items he produces are later tendered at his trial. Have his s. 7 rights been violated? Consider, in this regard, *R. v. Miller* (1991), 68 C.C.C. (3d) 517 (Ont. C.A.).**

38. **An inmate has shared the same prison range with I.M. Evil, an accused charged with murder. The inmate is assisting the police on unrelated investigations. He asks the police if they are interested in the accused. The police tell the inmate that if he could get information from the accused that could be of assistance, the Crown would be advised. He is given no**

instructions. Several weeks later, the inmate again finds himself in the same range as the accused. He actively questions the accused and elicits a confession. Have the accused's s. 7 rights been violated? Would your answer be different if the police had arranged for the inmate to be returned to the same range? Consider, in this regard, *R. v. Gray* (1991), 66 C.C.C. (3d) 6 (Ont. C.A.).

R. v. WHITE

(1999), 135 C.C.C. (3d) 257 (S.C.C.)

[The accused was charged with failure to stop at the scene of an accident contrary to s. 252(1) of the *Criminal Code*. The charge arose out of a fatal accident that occurred shortly before midnight. A motorist who had been changing a tire on his vehicle at the side of the road was struck by a vehicle that did not remain at the scene. At about 9:00 a.m. the next morning the accused called the police and said that she wanted to report an accident that she had been involved in the previous evening. Subsequently, the accused provided three statements to the police which described three versions of events. At the trial, the judge held that all three statements were freely and voluntarily made and that there had been no violation of the accused's rights under s. 10(*b*) of the *Charter*. The trial judge held, however, that the accused had made the three statements pursuant to the statutory duty imposed upon her under s. 61(1) of the *Motor Vehicle Act*, R.S.B.C. 1979, c. 288, which compelled a driver involved in certain types of accidents to provide a report to the police.]

Iacobucci J. [Lamer C.J.C., Gonthier, McLachlin, Bastarache and Binnie JJ. concurring]: —

.....

The principal s. 7 issue in this appeal is whether the *admission into evidence* in a criminal trial of statements made under compulsion of s. 61 of the *Motor Vehicle Act* would violate the principle against self-incrimination. The respondent did not challenge the constitutional validity of s. 61 at trial, but rather sought a remedy under s. 24(1) of the *Charter*. The respondent's position and the finding in the courts below is that, while compelling a driver to report a motor vehicle accident accords with s. 7 of the *Charter*, the principle against self-incrimination as embodied in s. 7 requires at least that the driver be protected against the subsequent use of such a report in criminal proceedings.

.....

... Where a court is called upon to determine whether s. 7 has been infringed, the analysis consists of three main stages, in accordance with the structure of the provision. The first question to be resolved is whether there exists a real or imminent deprivation of life, liberty, security of the person, or a combination of these interests. The second stage involves identifying and defining the relevant principle or principles of fundamental justice. Finally, it must be determined whether the deprivation has occurred in accordance with the relevant principle or principles: see *R. v. S. (R.J.)*, [1995] 1 S.C.R. 451 at p. 479, 96 C.C.C. (3d) 1, 121 D.L.R. (4th) 589, *per* Iacobucci J. Where a deprivation of life, liberty, or security of the person has occurred or will imminently occur in a manner which does not accord with the principles of fundamental justice, a s. 7 infringement is made out.

In the present case, it is clear that the respondent's liberty interest is engaged by the potential admission into evidence of her three statements to police on October 7, 1994, because she faces the possibility of up to five years' imprisonment if convicted on indictment under s. 252(1)(*a*) of the *Code*. The pivotal question is whether the admission of the three statements would accord with the principles of fundamental justice.

.....

C. The Principle Against Self-Incrimination

(1) General Principles

It is now well-established that there exists, in Canadian law, a principle against self-incrimination that is a principle of fundamental justice under s. 7 of the *Charter*. The meaning of the principle, its underlying rationale, and its current status within Canadian law have been discussed in a series of decisions of this Court, notably *Thomson Newspapers, supra*; *R. v. Hebert*, [1990] 2 S.C.R. 151, 57 C.C.C. (3d) 1; *R. v. P. (M.B.)*, [1994] 1 S.C.R. 555, 89 C.C.C. (3d) 289, 113 D.L.R. (4th) 461, *per* Lamer C.J.; *R. v. Jones*, [1994] 2 S.C.R. 229, 89 C.C.C. (3d) 353, 114 D.L.R. (4th) 645, *per* Lamer C.J.; *S. (R.J.), supra*; *British Columbia Securities Commission v. Branch*, [1995] 2 S.C.R. 3, 97 C.C.C. (3d) 505, 123 D.L.R. (4th) 462; and *Fitzpatrick* [(1995), 102 C.C.C. (3d) 144 (S.C.C.)].

The principle against self-incrimination was described by Lamer C.J. in *Jones, supra*, at p. 249, as "a general organizing principle of criminal law". The principle is that an accused is not required to respond to an allegation of wrongdoing made by the state until the state has succeeded in making out a *prima facie* case against him or her. It is a basic tenet of our system of justice that the Crown must establish a "case to meet" before there can be any expectation that the accused should respond: *P. (M.B.), supra*, at pp. 577-79, *per* Lamer C.J., *S. (R.J.), supra*, at paras. 82 and 83, *per* Iacobucci J.

In *Jones, supra*, the principle against self-incrimination was defined as an assertion of the fundamental importance of individual freedom. As the Chief Justice stated, at pp. 248-49:

> The principle against self-incrimination, in its broadest form, can be expressed in the following manner:
>
> > "... the individual is sovereign and ... proper rules of battle between government and individual require that the individual ... not be conscripted by his opponent to defeat himself ..."
>
> (*Wigmore on Evidence*, vol. 8 (McNaughton rev. 1961), §2251, at p. 318.)

.....

> Any state action that coerces an individual to furnish evidence against him- or herself in a proceeding in which the individual and the state are adversaries violates the principle against self-incrimination. Coercion, it should be noted, means the denial of free and informed consent.

Similarly, in *S. (R.J.), supra*, at para. 81, is the reference to "the principle of sovereignty embodied in the idea that individuals should be left alone in the absence of justification, and not conscripted by the state to promote a self-defeating purpose".

The definition of the principle against self-incrimination as an assertion of human freedom is intimately connected to the principle's underlying rationale. As explained by the Chief Justice in *Jones, supra*, at pp. 250-51, the principle has at least two key purposes, namely to protect against unreliable confessions, and to protect against abuses of power by the state. There is both an individual and a societal interest in achieving both of these protections. Both protections are linked to the value placed by Canadian society upon individual privacy, personal autonomy and dignity: see, *e.g.*, *Thomson Newspapers* [(1990), 54 C.C.C. (3d) 417 (S.C.C.)], at p. 480, *per* Wilson J.; *Jones, supra*, at pp. 250-51, *per* Lamer C.J.; and *Fitzpatrick, supra*, at paras. 51-52, *per* La Forest J. A state which arbitrarily intrudes upon its citizens' personal sphere will inevitably cause more injustice than it cures.

The jurisprudence of this Court is clear that the principle against self-incrimination is an overarching principle within our criminal justice system, from which a number of specific common law and *Charter* rules emanate, such as the confessions rule, and the right to silence, among many others. The principle can also be the source of new rules in appropriate circumstances. Within the *Charter*, the principle against self-incrimination is embodied in several of the more specific procedural protections such as, for example, the right to counsel in s. 10(*b*), the right to non-compellability in s. 11(*c*), and the right to use immunity set out in s. 13. The *Charter* also provides residual protection to the principle through s. 7.

(2) The Importance of Context

That the principle against self-incrimination does have the status as an overarching principle does not imply that the principle provides absolute protection for an accused against all uses of information that has been compelled by statute or otherwise. The residual protections provided by the principle against self-incrimination as contained in s. 7 are specific, and contextually sensitive. This point was made in *Jones, supra*, at p. 257, *per* Lamer C.J., and in *S. (R.J.), supra*, at paras. 96-100, *per* Iacobucci J., where it was explained that the parameters of the right to liberty can be affected by the context in which the right is asserted. The principle against self-incrimination demands different things at different times, with the task in every case being to determine exactly what the principle demands, if anything, within the particular context at issue. See also *R. v. Lyons*, [1987] 2 S.C.R. 309 at p. 361, 37 C.C.C. (3d) 1, 44 D.L.R. (4th) 193 *per* La Forest J.

In *Fitzpatrick, supra*, at paras. 21-25, La Forest J., speaking on behalf of the full Court, confirmed that this Court has always expressly limited the application of the principle against self-incrimination to cover only the specific circumstances raised by a given case. He stressed, at para. 25, that a court must begin "on the ground", with a concrete and contextual analysis of the circumstances, in order to determine whether the principle against self-incrimination is actually engaged on the facts.

The contextual analysis that is mandated under s. 7 of the *Charter* is defined and guided by the requirement that a court determine whether a deprivation of life, liberty, or security of the person has occurred in accordance with the *principles* of fundamental justice. As this Court has stated, the s. 7 analysis involves a balance. Each principle of fundamental justice must be interpreted in light of those other individual and societal interests that are of sufficient importance that they may appropriately be characterized as principles of fundamental justice in Canadian society. This analytical approach was applied, for example, in *S. (R.J.), supra*, at paras. 107-108, *per* Iacobucci J., where it was stated:

> ... the principle against self-incrimination may mean different things at different times and in different contexts. The principle admits of many rules. What should the rule be in respect of testimonial compulsion?
>
> .....
>
> *I begin this inquiry by asserting that any rule demanded by the principle against self-incrimination which places a limit on compellability is in dynamic tension with an opposing principle of fundamental justice. That is the principle which suggests that, in a search for truth, relevant evidence should be available to the trier of fact.* ... Obviously, the *Charter* sanctions deviations from this positive general rule. Sections 11(*c*) and 13 stand as obvious examples. The question is whether we need another exemption, and if so, why? [Emphasis added.]

See similarly, e.g., *R. v. Seaboyer*, [1991] 2 S.C.R. 577 at p. 603, 66 C.C.C. (3d) 321, 83 D.L.R. (4th) 193, *per* McLachlin J., and *Rodriguez v. British Columbia (Attorney General)*, [1993] 3 S.C.R. 519 at pp. 590-91, 85 C.C.C. (3d) 15, 107 D.L.R. (4th) 342, *per* Sopinka J.

It is the balancing of principles that occurs under s. 7 of the *Charter* that lends significance to a given factual context in determining whether the principle against self-incrimination has been violated. In some contexts, the factors that favour the importance of the search for truth will outweigh the factors that favour protecting the individual against undue compulsion by the state. This was the case, for example, in *Fitzpatrick, supra*, where the Court emphasized the relative absence of true state coercion, and the necessity of acquiring statements in order to maintain the integrity of an entire regulatory regime. In other contexts, a reverse situation will arise, as was the case, for example, in *Thomson Newspapers, supra, S. (R.J.), supra*, and *Branch, supra*. In every case, the facts must be closely examined to determine whether the principle against self-incrimination has truly been brought into play by the production or use of the declarant's statement.

(3) The Present Case

In the present appeal, the Crown has argued that it would not violate the principle against self-incrimination to permit the respondent's three statements to police under the *Motor Vehicle Act* to be used against her in a criminal trial. In its view, a proper understanding of the context in which the statements were taken and of the interplay between the relevant principles of fundamental justice results in a finding that s. 7 is not violated. The Crown relies, in particular, upon the decision of this Court in *Fitzpatrick*, *supra*.

Fitzpatrick involved enforcement proceedings in the regulatory context of the commercial fishery in British Columbia. The regulatory aspect of the case provided an opportunity for the Court to elaborate in a more detailed fashion on the types of contextual factors that are legally relevant in determining the ambit of the residual protections against self-incrimination provided by s. 7. The accused had made oral hail reports of his daily catch by radio, and had recorded daily fishing logs of his estimated catch, as required by the applicable fishery regulations. He was charged with the provincial offence of over-fishing, and the hail reports and fishing logs were sought to be introduced as evidence at trial.

In finding that the admission of the accused's oral and written statements at his trial would not violate the principle against self-incrimination, La Forest J. carefully reviewed the purposes and concerns underlying the principle against self-incrimination, as expressed throughout the Court's jurisprudence on the topic, and concluded that none of these purposes or concerns was meaningfully brought into play in the circumstances. In particular, La Forest J. focussed upon four main factors: (1) the lack of real coercion by the state in obtaining the statements; (2) the lack of an adversarial relationship between the accused and the state at the time the statements were obtained; (3) the absence of an increased risk of unreliable confessions as a result of the statutory compulsion; and (4) the absence of an increased risk of abuses of power by the state as a result of the statutory compulsion.

In my view, the Crown's argument that the factual and legislative context of this case parallels that which was at issue in *Fitzpatrick* is incorrect. Several of the self-incrimination concerns which were absent in *Fitzpatrick* are acutely present here. It will be helpful to address these concerns individually.

D. Inadmissibility of a Statement Made Under s. 61 of the Motor Vehicle Act

(1) Existence of Coercion

In *Fitzpatrick*, La Forest J. emphasized that the obligations created by the provincial fisheries regulations at issue in that case were imposed upon the accused with his free and informed consent. The accused had a free choice whether or not to participate in the commercial fishery. When he did choose to participate in the fishery, he was informed of his reporting obligations, of the penalties for non-compliance with fisheries regulations, and of the possibility that any reports he might make could be used against him. He was properly deemed to be aware of this information. It could not be said that, by regulating the commercial fishery as it did, the state was coercing the accused to incriminate himself.

In this case, the Crown makes submissions to the same effect. Driving is a regulated activity. All drivers are required to obtain a licence to drive. In so doing, the Crown states, they give free and informed consent to all of the rules of the road, including the requirement to report a motor vehicle accident. In such a context, the Crown submits, it cannot be said that a driver is coerced to provide an accident report when the occasion to do so does arise. In support of this proposition, the Crown relies upon, *inter alia*, statements regarding the voluntary nature of driving contained in the decisions of this Court in *Dedman v. The Queen*, [1985] 2 S.C.R. 2, 20 C.C.C. (3d) 97, 20 D.L.R. (4th) 321, *Hundal* [(1993), 79 C.C.C. (3d) 97 (S.C.C.)], and *R. v. Finlay*, [1993] 3 S.C.R. 103, 83 C.C.C. (3d) 513, 105 D.L.R. (4th) 699.

I agree with the Crown that drivers are deemed to be aware of their responsibilities on the road, and that driving is properly understood as a voluntary activity in the sense described by this Court in the cases cited by the Crown. However, driving is not freely undertaken in precisely the same way as one is free to participate in a regulated industry such as the commercial fishery. Driving is often a necessity of life, particularly in rural areas such as that where the accident occurred in this case. When a person needs to drive in order to function meaningfully in society, the choice of whether to drive is not truly as free as the choice of whether to enter into an industry. While the state should not be perceived as being coercive in requiring drivers to report motor vehicle accidents, the concern with protecting human freedom which underlies the principle against self-incrimination cannot be considered entirely absent in this context. As I view the matter, the issue of free and informed consent must be considered a neutral factor in the determination of whether the principle against self-incrimination is infringed by s. 61 of the *Motor Vehicle Act*.

(2) Adversarial Relationship

A key factor in the Court's reasoning in *Fitzpatrick* was that the accused and the state were not in an adversarial relationship at the specific time that the self-incriminatory statements were made. The hail reports and fishing logs were made in a context that was entirely free of psychological or emotional pressure for the accused, at a time when the accused was not under investigation by fishing authorities. Moreover, the hail reports and fishing logs were required by the state for the useful purpose of calculating fish stocks in order to determine appropriate fishing quotas. As noted by La Forest J., the accused and the fishing authorities could properly be seen, in exchanging information about the quantity of harvest in this way, as partners in the greater collective endeavour of conserving fish stocks and correspondingly conserving the commercial fishery. La Forest J. emphasized that the hail reports and fishing logs were an essential component of this conservation scheme.

The situation is very different under the *Motor Vehicle Act*. It is true, as the Crown suggests, that drivers and the state do participate in a form of partnership aimed at securing safe roads for the benefit of all citizens. The reporting requirement in s. 61 of the Act has the valid purpose of permitting the compilation of road safety information and accident statistics: see, e.g., *Walker v. The King*, [1939] S.C.R. 214 at p. 220, 71 C.C.C. 305, [1939] 2 D.L.R. 353. Yet the driver who provides an accident report under s. 61 is not in the same situation as the commercial fisher who radios in or documents the quantity of the day's catch.

The provincial decision to vest the responsibility for taking accident reports in the police has the effect of transforming what might otherwise be a partnership relationship into one that is potentially adversarial. Very often, the police officer who is receiving the accident report is simultaneously investigating a possible crime, in relation to which the driver is a suspect. At the same time that the officer is required by s. 61(4) of the *Motor Vehicle Act* to obtain information about the accident from the driver, the officer may equally be required or inclined to inform the driver of possible criminal charges and of the driver's legal rights under the *Charter*, including the right to remain silent. The result is seemingly contradictory instructions from police. Importantly, also, the driver is generally in the officer's immediate physical presence. The result is, quite unlike the situation in *Fitzpatrick*, a context of pronounced psychological and emotional pressure.

The facts of this appeal provide a clear illustration of the problem. The police arrived at the respondent's home immediately after she phoned them, suggesting a sense of urgency. Upon hearing the news of the victim's death, the respondent was extremely upset and accordingly vulnerable. Although the police did not interrogate her in a rigorous fashion, the respondent knew that Sgt. Tait was attending at her home in anticipation of receiving information about the accident. She also felt that she was required to speak to him, a feeling that was reinforced by Sgt. Tait's having waited outside her home while she spoke to a lawyer, and by his statement to her after she spoke to a lawyer that she remained under an obligation to provide an accident report, notwithstanding her right to remain silent and the advice of her lawyer.

Another important distinction between this appeal and *Fitzpatrick*, in so far as the existence of a partnership relationship is concerned, is that there is no suggestion in this case that the use of accident reports in criminal proceedings is an essential component of the regulatory partnership created by the *Motor Vehicle Act*. Under the fisheries regulations that were at issue in *Fitzpatrick*, the use of reports of daily fish harvests in the prosecution of over-fishing was found to be essential to the integrity of the entire regulatory regime — a regime that was beneficial to both the state and the accused as a commercial fisher. In contrast, under the *Motor Vehicle Act*, it is clear that the province of British Columbia does not consider the use of accident reports in subsequent legal proceedings to be essential at all. The inclusion of s. 61(7), extending use immunity in relation to the contents of an accident report in subsequent proceedings against the driver, reveals an intention to use accident reports in order to gather information only for *non-litigious purposes*. In other words, the partnership between the individual driver and the state does not encompass the use of the compelled accident report to incriminate the driver. The fact that the statements in this case are sought to be introduced in criminal rather than regulatory proceedings simply serves to accentuate the fact that the Crown seeks to use the statement for a purpose that was never contemplated as being a component of the regulatory regime.

(3) Unreliable Confessions

In *Fitzpatrick*, the Court found that the hail reports and fishing logs could not properly be characterized as "confessions" for the purpose of the confessions rule. The Court also found that, even if these reports were confessions, the use of these oral and written reports as evidence in regulatory proceedings for over-fishing did not increase the likelihood of the reports' being falsified. La Forest J. noted that there was probably already an incentive to submit false hail reports and fishing logs — a danger which was combatted to some degree by the prosecution of those who submit such false statements. He also could not envision an alternative scheme which would permit more reliable statements while still achieving the objectives of the regulatory regime.

Under the *Motor Vehicle Act*, the prospect of unreliable confessions is very real. In particular, accident reports under the Act are frequently given directly to a police officer, i.e., to a person in authority whose authority and physical presence might cause the driver to produce a statement in circumstances where he or she is not truly willing to speak: see *R. v. Hodgson*, [1998] 2 S.C.R. 449, 127 C.C.C. (3d) 449, 163 D.L.R. (4th) 577, at para. 24, *per* Cory J. The driver who reasonably believes that he or she has a statutory duty to provide an accident report under the *Motor Vehicle Act* will likely experience a significant "fear of prejudice" if he or she does not speak. At the same time, there may be a strong incentive to provide a false statement, given the serious consequences which the driver may feel will flow from telling the truth, even if the truth does not in fact support a finding that a criminal offence was committed. It is reasonable to expect that this fear of prejudice and incentive to lie would be dissipated if the driver could be confident that the contents of the accident report could never be used to incriminate him or her in criminal proceedings. A rule which granted use immunity in criminal proceedings would thus serve to *enhance* rather than impair the effectiveness of the statutory reporting scheme, as was suggested by Esson J.A. in the Court of Appeal below. Indeed, it is possibly for precisely this purpose that the province originally enacted the use immunity set out in s. 61(7).

(4) Abuse of Power

The final major concern underlying the principle against self-incrimination that was addressed by the Court in *Fitzpatrick* was the concern that permitting the use of compelled statements in order to incriminate commercial fishers would increase the likelihood of abusive conduct by the state. La Forest J. found that it was not abusive for the state to prosecute overfishing on the basis of true reports that fishers were required to complete as a condition of their voluntary participation in the commercial fishery. He noted, as I mentioned above, that the alternative to compulsory self-reporting would be far more intrusive, since the state would be required to investigate overfishing by increasing patrols and vessel searches. La Forest J. also relied upon the fact that there is a minimal expectation of privacy in daily hail reports and fishing logs. He noted that using the information contained in these reports could not be seen as an affront to human dignity, since nothing in the reports divulged information of a personal or private nature.

In the present case, again, the possibility is real and serious that permitting the use of compelled accident reports within criminal proceedings might increase the likelihood of abusive conduct by the state. In taking accident reports from drivers, police would have a strong incentive or perhaps an unconscious inclination to overemphasize the extent of the statutory duty to report an accident under the Act, in order to obtain relevant information. The effect of such an overemphasis might be to circumvent or defeat a driver's s. 7 right to remain silent when under investigation for a criminal offence. One can easily imagine the situation of a driver who, confused by the apparent inconsistency between the duty to report and the right to remain silent, would provide a more extensive statement to police than legally required under the Act. Conversely, in a situation where all statements made by the driver under compulsion of the Act are subject to use immunity, police are more likely to conduct an independent investigation rather than to use the compulsory accident reporting system as a source of information.

The inability of police to rely upon statements made under the compulsion of s. 61 of the *Motor Vehicle Act* highlights the importance of questioning a driver separately for the purpose of engaging in a criminal investigation. Clearly, police are entitled to question a person who is suspected of a motor vehicle offence, and who is properly advised of and given the opportunity to exercise his or her *Charter* rights. The effect of s. 61 of the *Motor Vehicle Act* is thus to create a logistical difficulty for police. If police wish to use in criminal proceedings information acquired from the driver through questioning, the information must not be provided pursuant to the duty in s. 61. There are several ways in which police might organize their investigation in order to prevent any information acquired independently of s. 61 from becoming "tainted", as it were, by the accident report that is subject to use immunity. One possibility, which appears to be contemplated by s. 61(4) of the Act, is for police to inform the driver that they intend to secure the details of the accident report, not from the driver himself or herself, but "by other inquiries", thus terminating the driver's statutory duty to report the accident and permitting police to begin their investigation immediately.

Finally, it should be noted that an accident report is not at all analogous to the hail reports and fishing logs in *Fitzpatrick*, which La Forest J. compared to business records in so far as they were impersonal lists in which the declarant had little expectation of privacy. The spontaneous utterances of a driver, occurring very shortly after an accident, are exactly the type of communication that the principle against self-incrimination is designed to protect. They are a personal narrative of events, emotions, and decisions that are extremely revealing of the declarant's personality, opinions, thoughts, and state of mind. The dignity of the declarant is clearly affected by the use of this narrative to incriminate. I would note that, while it is well established that there is a reduced expectation of privacy in a vehicle generally, compared to the expectation of privacy in a dwelling, this fact is largely irrelevant to the analysis here. The question in this case involves the expectation of privacy that a declarant has in a confession. The fact that the confession has to do with a car is entirely incidental.

(5) Conclusion on Contextual Factors

In sum, then, the analogy which the Crown has endeavoured to draw between the context of this case and that in *Fitzpatrick* is inapt. The principle against self-incrimination is strongly brought into play by numerous aspects of the context surrounding the compulsion to make an accident report under s. 61 of the *Motor Vehicle Act*. A driver who makes a statement pursuant to the statutory duty set out in s. 61 is entitled, at least, to use immunity in criminal proceedings in relation to the contents of that statement.

.....

F. Establishing the Existence of Compulsion Under s. 61

I have stated that a statement made under compulsion of s. 61 of the *Motor Vehicle Act* cannot be used to incriminate the declarant in subsequent criminal proceedings. There remains the question of how it is to be determined that a statement was, in fact, made under compulsion of the statute.

(1) The Need for an Honest and Reasonably Held Belief

A declarant under s. 61 of the *Motor Vehicle Act* will be protected by use immunity under s. 7 of the *Charter* only to the extent that the relevant statements may properly be considered compelled. Accordingly, the driver has an interest in knowing with some certainty precisely when he or she is required to speak, and when he or she is permitted to exercise the right to remain silent in the face of police questioning. Conversely, the ability of the state to prosecute crime will be impaired to the extent of the reporting requirement under s. 61 of the *Motor Vehicle Act*. Thus the public, too, has a strong interest in identifying with some certainty the dividing line between the taking of an accident report under s. 61, on the one hand, and ordinary police investigation into possible crimes, on the other. When will a driver's answers to police questioning cease to be protected by the use immunity provided by s. 7 of the *Charter*?

The Court of Appeal below did not discuss this issue in detail. I would like to elaborate briefly on the legal definition of a compelled statement under s. 61. In my view, the test for compulsion under s. 61(1) of the *Motor Vehicle Act* is whether, at the time that the accident was reported by the driver, the driver gave the report on the basis of an honest and reasonably held belief that he or she was required by law to report the accident to the person to whom the report was given.

The requirement that the accident report be given on the basis of a *subjective* belief exists because compulsion, by definition, implies an absence of consent. If a declarant gives an accident report freely, without believing or being influenced by the fact that he or she is required by law to do so, then it cannot be said that the statute is the cause of the declarant's statements. The declarant would then be speaking to police on the basis of motivating factors other than s. 61 of the *Motor Vehicle Act*.

The requirement that the declarant's honest belief be *reasonably held* also relates to the meaning of compulsion. The principle against self-incrimination is concerned with preventing the abuse of state power. It is not concerned with preventing unreasonable perceptions that state power exists. There is no risk of true oppression of the individual where the state acts fairly and in accordance with the law, but the individual unreasonably perceives otherwise. It is true that the individual who unreasonably believes that he or she is compelled to speak may produce an unreliable confession, but this result will have flowed from concerns that are outside the scope of the principle against self-incrimination: see *Hodgson, supra*, at para. 34, *per* Cory J. The requirement that an honest belief be reasonably held is an essential component of the balancing that occurs under s. 7. The application of the principle against self-incrimination begins, and the societal interest in the effective investigation and prosecution of crime is subordinated, at the moment when a driver speaks on the basis of a reasonable and honest belief that he or she is required by law to do so.

I would note that the requirement that a driver's honest belief be reasonably held does not necessarily mean that the driver must have had, as a strict matter of law, a statutory duty to report the accident. This point was made by the trial judge, who found that it may be reasonable for a driver to believe that he or she is required to report an accident even where the damage caused by the accident is not sufficient to trigger the duty to report under s. 61 of the *Motor Vehicle Act*, or where the driver is unaware of the extent of damage caused. Clearly, the existence of a general statutory duty to report accidents is a critical factor in determining the reasonableness of a driver's belief that he or she was required to do so. However, I would not go so far as to say that a driver's belief in the duty to report will be unreasonable simply because, for example, the property damage caused by the accident appeared to total only $500 in value, while the trigger value for the duty to report under the *Motor Vehicle Act* is $1000 in the case of a motor vehicle other than a motorcycle. The nature and extent of the damage caused by the accident, and the driver's awareness of such damage, will simply be factors for the trial judge to consider in evaluating the reasonableness of the driver's belief.

Having emphasized the importance of a driver's honest belief in compulsion being reasonably held, I should also emphasize that I agree with the trial judge that the scope of the compulsion created by s. 61(1) of the *Motor Vehicle Act* is fairly broad.

Section 61(1) requires a driver involved in an accident to report the accident and, in very general terms, to "furnish the information respecting the accident required by the police officer or designated person". Section 61(4) requires the person receiving an accident report from a driver to "secure from the person making [the report] ... the particulars of the accident, the persons involved, the extent of the personal injury or property damage *and other information necessary* to complete a written report of the accident" (emphasis added). Thus the Act defines the statutory duty to report an accident to police in vague terms. At the same time, the discretion to determine what information is necessary to a written accident report is vested exclusively in the police officer taking the report. The driver is largely subject to the will of this officer with respect to determining what constitutes a compelled statement. Provided that the police have offered no indication to the driver that the statutory requirements for the reporting of an accident have been satisfied, it will likely be reasonable for a driver to assume that he or she continues to be subject to a statutory duty to speak to police. Accordingly, as a practical matter, it will be very important for the police officer who takes an accident report while simultaneously investigating a crime to delineate clearly for the declarant the start and end points of the accident report. For example, it may be useful for police to tell the driver that they will postpone the taking of an accident report until after they have questioned, or attempted to question, the driver. Alternatively, as discussed above, police may wish to tell the driver that they intend to secure the details of the accident report from sources other than the driver, thus terminating the statutory duty to report.

[Iacobucci J. then determined that the onus rested with the accused to prove that an impugned statement was compelled.]

.....

H. Application to the Facts

In the Court of Appeal below, all judges agreed that the respondent's first and second conversations with police were properly found by the trial judge to have been compelled by s. 61 of the *Motor Vehicle Act*. There was evidence on the basis of which the trial judge could reasonably have found that, at both of these times when the respondent spoke to police, she believed that she was required to report the accident to them. There was also evidence to support the finding that her honest belief in the requirement to report was reasonable in the circumstances. Such a finding was supported by the conduct of the police in actively seeking a description of the accident from the respondent, from the visible property damage to the respondent's vehicle, as well as from the respondent's knowledge of the victim's injuries (whether that knowledge was acquired at the time of the accident or, as the respondent testified at trial, the following morning through radio reports).

The point of division between the majority and the dissenting judge in the Court of Appeal concerned the respondent's third conversation with police, which occurred after the respondent had been advised of her *Charter* rights and after she had spoken to counsel. Southin J.A., dissenting, found that the timing of this third conversation meant that it should not be considered compelled. If I understand Southin J.A.'s reasons correctly, she considered that any harm caused to the respondent by the admission of this third statement into evidence was the result of the respondent's own free will in choosing to speak to police after having been advised of her right to silence and after having spoken to a lawyer about her obligation to speak.

With respect, I do not agree with Southin J.A.'s finding in relation to the respondent's third conversation with police. The logic of use immunity is precisely that the individual who is granted use immunity *remains subject* to the statutory compulsion to make the original compelled statement. In the context of s. 61 of the *Motor Vehicle Act*, the existence of the principle against self-incrimination in s. 7 of the *Charter* does not eliminate the statutory compulsion to report an accident. The accused who has consulted counsel does not become immune from the reporting requirement set out in the statute. Rather, as I have discussed in these reasons, s. 7 provides protection to the person who is required to report an accident. Thus, when the respondent returned from speaking to counsel, she was still required by law to answer Sgt. Tait's questions regarding the accident, provided those questions were made pursuant to s. 61 of the *Motor Vehicle Act*. Indeed, if the respondent's lawyer acted appropriately in advising her, as the Court should assume he did, he would have told the respondent that she was required by law to answer the officer's questions pursuant to the *Motor Vehicle Act*, notwithstanding her general right to silence.

In the circumstances of this case, there was evidence on the basis of which the trial judge could reasonably have found that the respondent's third statement to police was compelled by s. 61 of the Act. First, prior to speaking to counsel, the respondent honestly and reasonably believed she was required to report the accident. This fact supports the view that, all other things being equal, she likely continued to believe in the subsistence of the duty. Second, after speaking to counsel, who could not lawfully have advised the respondent not to make an accident report, the respondent continued to reply to Sgt. Tait's questions about the accident. Although she stated that she did not *wish* to speak to Sgt. Tait any further, she did answer his question once it was asked. Third, the respondent was, in fact, under a statutory duty to answer any of Sgt. Tait's questions made pursuant to s. 61. Fourth, Sgt. Tait informed the respondent after the respondent had spoken to counsel that she remained under a statutory compulsion to report the accident. Although Sgt. Tait's reminder in this regard occurred after the respondent had completed her third statement regarding the accident, the fact that Sgt. Tait issued such a reminder shows that he still believed he was taking a s. 61 accident report, and thus that the general atmosphere between Sgt. Tait and the respondent likely reflected this belief. Fifth, the respondent's third statement to police regarding the accident was made in response to a leading question posed by Sgt. Tait, which referred back to the substance of her second statement. Again, the fact that Tait was asking the respondent to confirm her previous statement would likely have caused her to believe that she was required to answer, since she had been required to make the second statement.

V. Conclusion and Disposition

In sum, I am of the view that the trial judge did not err in finding that all three of the respondent's conversations with police on October 7, 1994 were made on the basis of the respondent's honest and reasonably held belief that she was required to report the accident to police. The appeal is therefore dismissed.

[L'Heureux-Dube J. dissented, holding that the third statement made by the accused was admissible, as it was made after the accused had had an opportunity to consult with counsel and was not compelled by s. 61 of the British Columbia *Motor Vehicle Act*.]

CHAPTER 5

COMPELLING THE ACCUSED'S APPEARANCE AND JUDICIAL INTERIM RELEASE

A. OVERVIEW

Part XVI of the *Criminal Code*, R.S.C. 1985, c. C-46 is headed "Compelling Appearance of Accused Before a Justice and Interim Release". It contains a labyrinth of interrelated statutory provisions regulating the initiation of the criminal process, procedures on how an accused is to be brought to court and whether that accused will be in or out of custody at various stages of the process.

An accused may be brought before the court and proceedings may be commenced against him or her in a variety of ways:

- **Any person, whether or not a peace officer, may arrest without a warrant in the circumstances outlined in s. 494 of the *Criminal Code*. That person must forthwith deliver the accused to a peace officer.**

Section 494(1)(*a*) permits any person to arrest without warrant anyone whom he or she finds committing an *indictable* offence. The following case addresses the meaning of "finds committing", contained in both ss. 494(1)(*a*) and 495(1)(*b*) of the *Criminal Code*. Section 495(1)(*b*) of the *Criminal Code* permits a peace officer to arrest, without a warrant, anyone whom he or she finds committing a criminal offence (*i.e.*, indictable or summary).

R. v. BIRON

(1975), 23 C.C.C. (2d) 513 (S.C.C.)

[Biron was charged with causing a disturbance in a public place by shouting, which is a summary conviction offence. He resisted his arrest and was charged with resisting a peace officer. He was later acquitted of causing a disturbance. The issue then arose as to his guilt on the second charge.]

Martland J. [Judson, Ritchie and Pigeon JJ. concurring]: —

.....

The question in issue is as to whether the charge against Biron of resisting Dorion in the execution of his duty must fail because of his successful appeal from his conviction ... for causing a disturbance.

.....

It is submitted by the respondent that Maisonneuve did not find him committing a criminal offence because he was acquitted on the charge laid against him....

.....

Paragraph (*b*) applies in relation to any criminal offence and it deals with the situation in which the peace officer himself finds an offence being committed. His power to arrest is based upon his own observation. Because it is based on his own discovery of an offence actually being committed there is no reason to refer to a belief based upon reasonable and probable grounds.

.....

If the reasoning in the *Pritchard* case [(1961), 130 C.C.C. 61 (Sask. C.A.)] is sound, the validity of an arrest under s. 450(1)(*b*) [now s. 495(1)(*b*)] can only be determined after the trial of the person arrested and after the determination of any subsequent appeals. My view is that the validity of an arrest under this paragraph must be determined in relation to the circumstances which were apparent to the peace officer at the time the arrest was made.

This was the view of the Court of Appeal in England in *Wiltshire v. Barrett*, [1965] 2 All E.R. 271, when interpreting a provision of the *Road Traffic Act, 1960* (U.K.), c. 16. Section 6(1) of that Act made it an offence for a person who, when driving or attempting to drive a motor vehicle on a road or other public place, is unfit to drive through drink or drugs.

Subsection (4) of s. 6 provided:

> A police constable may arrest without warrant a person committing an offence under this section.

The case was a civil action for assault and wrongful arrest. The plaintiff's car had been overtaken and stopped by the police. A constable sought to arrest the plaintiff, who resisted by remaining in his car. He was removed after a struggle and taken to the police station. He was examined by the police doctor, who concluded that he was not unfit to drive. He was then released. No further action was taken against him. Subsequently he sued the police constable who had arrested him.

Lord Denning said, at p. 273:

> Counsel for the plaintiff submitted that this section only empowered a constable to arrest a person who was actually committing an offence under the section; and, accordingly, that the constable was only justified if he could prove that the person was in fact guilty; whereas counsel for the defendant submitted that a constable was entitled to arrest any person who was apparently committing an offence; and, accordingly, the constable was justified so long as it appeared to him that the man was unfit through drink, even though the man should afterwards be found to be not guilty. This question has to be answered by examining the contents of this particular statute; see *Barnard v. Gorman*, [1941] 3 All E.R. 45 at pp. 50, 51; [1941] A.C. 378 at p. 387. On examining this statute, I find it very similar to the statute considered by this court in *Trebeck v. Croudace*, [1916-17] All E.R. Rep. 441; [1918] 1 K.B. 158. Just as Lord Wright thought, [1941] 3 All E.R. at p. 55; [1941]

A.C. at p. 394, that, in that context, "drunk" meant "apparently drunk", so I think that, in this context, "committing an offence" means "apparently committing an offence". My reasons are these: this statute is concerned with the safety of all of Her Majesty's subjects who use the roads in this country. It is of the first importance that any person, who is unfit to drive through drink, should not be allowed to drive on the road; and that the police should have power to stop him from driving any further. The most effective way to do it is by arresting him then and there. The police have to act at once, on the facts as they appear on the spot; and they should be justified by the facts as they appear to them at the time and not on any *ex post facto* analysis of the situation. Their conduct should not be condemned as unlawful simply because a jury afterwards acquit the driver.

.....

My conclusion is that, on the true construction of s. 6(4), a constable is justified in arresting the driver of a motor car if the driver was apparently committing an offence under the section.

In my opinion, this reasoning can properly be applied to the interpretation of s. 450(1)(*b*). It is true that the *Wiltshire* case was a civil action for damages, but it necessitated the judicial interpretation of a statutory provision which is substantially the same. There being no English equivalent of s. 25 of the *Criminal Code* to provide the constable with protection from suit, he could only escape from civil liability for damages if he could establish that he was entitled to make the arrest. His power to arrest without warrant arose in respect of "a person committing an offence under this section". The Court held that he was justified in making the arrest if the person arrested was apparently committing the offence.

In the *Wiltshire* case the statutory provision involved the power to arrest without a warrant a person unfit to drive because of drink or drugs and the Court referred to the public importance of an arrest being promptly made in such circumstances. Paragraph (*b*) of s. 450(1) deals with the power to arrest without a warrant a person found committing any criminal offence. It is certainly of public importance that the peace officer should be able to exercise this power promptly.

If the words "committing a criminal offence" are to be construed in the manner indicated in the *Pritchard* case, para. (*b*) becomes impossible to apply. The power of arrest which that paragraph gives has to be exercised promptly, yet, strictly speaking, it is impossible to say that an offence is committed until the party arrested has been found guilty by the courts. If this is the way in which this provision is to be construed, no peace officer can ever decide, when making an arrest without a warrant, that the person arrested is "committing a criminal offence". In my opinion the wording used in para. (b), which is oversimplified, means that the power to arrest without a warrant is given where the peace officer himself finds a situation in which a person is apparently committing an offence.

[Laskin C.J. (Spence and Dickson JJ. concurring) dissented.]

A determination as to whether an arrest is or is not proper may be important for a variety of reasons: first, as was argued here, an accused charged with resisting a peace officer or a related offence may have a

complete defence if the officer exceeded his or her lawful powers, thereby justifying the accused's use of force to resist. Second, a peace officer may face charges founded upon the unauthorized use of force. Third, an unauthorized arrest or use of force to effect arrest may constitute a *Charter* violation (for example under s. 9) and result in *Charter* relief.

- **A peace officer can arrest without a warrant in the more extensive circumstances outlined in s. 495(1) of the *Criminal Code*.[1] For example, s. 495(1)(*a*) permits a peace officer to arrest, without a warrant, anyone who has committed an indictable offence, or who, *on reasonable grounds*, he or she believes has committed or is about to commit an indictable offence.**

The requirement of "reasonable grounds" (which are synonymous with reasonable and probable grounds) is addressed in the following case.

R. v. STORREY

(1990), 53 C.C.C. (3d) 316 (S.C.C.)

Cory J.: —

.....

... It is not sufficient for the police officer to personally believe that he or she has reasonable and probable grounds to make an arrest. Rather, it must be objectively established that those reasonable and probable grounds did in fact exist. That is to say a reasonable person, standing in the shoes of the police officer, would have believed that reasonable and probable grounds existed to make the arrest: see *R. v. Brown* (1987), 33 C.C.C. (3d) 54 at p. 66, 76 N.S.R. (2d) 64 (C.A.); *Liversidge v. Anderson*, [1942] A.C. 206 at p. 228 (H.L.).

In summary then, the *Criminal Code* requires that an arresting officer must subjectively have reasonable and probable grounds on which to base the arrest. Those grounds must, in addition, be justifiable from an objective point of view. That is to say, a reasonable person placed in the position of the officer must be able to conclude that there were indeed reasonable and probable grounds for the arrest. On the other hand, the police need not demonstrate anything more than reasonable and probable grounds. Specifically they are not required to establish a *prima facie* case for conviction before making the arrest.

Section 495(2) circumscribes s. 495(1) in that a peace officer is obligated not to arrest without a warrant for any *summary* conviction, *hybrid*, or indictable offence which is within the *absolute jurisdiction* of a provincial court judge (hereafter referred to as the *S.H.A.J. offences*) if he or she believes, on reasonable grounds, that the public interest may be sat-

---

[1] **A peace officer has additional statutory powers to arrest without a warrant; for example, under ss. 31(1) and 199(2) of the *Criminal Code*, as well as under various federal and provincial statutes.**

isfied without arrest and if there are no reasonable grounds to believe that the accused will fail to attend court as required.

QUESTION

1. E. Racer is stopping by the police for riding his bicycle through a red light. The officer asks him for identification. Racer refuses to provide it. He is arrested for obstructing the peace officer. Is the arrest lawful? Consider, in this regard, *R. v. Moore* (1978), 43 C.C.C. (2d) 83 (S.C.C.). Is *Moore* still good law?

- Where by virtue of s. 495(2), the peace officer does not arrest for a S.H.A.J. offence, he or she may issue an appearance notice (s. 496). The contents of an appearance notice are mandated by s. 501 of the *Criminal Code*.

- Where a peace officer has arrested without a warrant for a S.H.A.J. offence, he or she is obligated, as soon as practicable, to release the accused with the intention of either having him or her summonsed to attend court, or of issuing an appearance notice and thereupon releasing him or her, unless the officer believes, on reasonable grounds, that the public interest compels a different approach or the person will fail to attend court or the accused is arrested for an extra-provincial offence (s. 497(1), (1.1) and (2)).

- Where an accused has been arrested without a warrant for either a S.H.A.J. offence or any other offence punishable by five years or less (collectively to be referred to as *S.H.A.J. Plus Five Offences*), and not released by a peace officer pursuant to the powers already described above, and not yet taken before a justice of the peace, the officer in charge or another peace officer shall, as soon as practicable, do one of the following: (a) release the accused with the intention of having him or her summonsed; (b) release the accused based on his or her giving a promise to appear; (c) release the accused on his or her entering into a recognizance before an officer without sureties of up to $500, without deposit; or, (d) if the accused is not ordinarily a resident of the province in which he or she has been arrested, or if the place he or she is being held is not within 200 kilometres of the accused's residence, then the accused shall be released based on his or her entering into a recognizance before an officer without sureties of up to $500, with or without deposit; that is, unless the officer believes, on reasonable grounds, that the public interest compels a different approach, the person will fail to attend court, or the accused has been arrested for an extra-provincial offence (s. 498(1), (1.1) and (2)).

- Where the accused has been arrested with a warrant for any offence other than those within the exclusive jurisdiction of the superior court, and a justice of the peace has endorsed the warrant authorizing the accused's release pursuant to s. 507(6), then the officer in charge can release the accused on all the forms of release reflected in the previous paragraph, except that he or she cannot release with the intention of only summonsing the accused. But further, he or she can require the accused to enter into an additional undertaking to do one or more specified things, such as undertaking to remain within a specified territorial jurisdiction, to abstain from communicating with named persons or to abstain from consuming alcohol. The accused or the prosecutor can later apply to a justice of the peace prior to the first appearance to replace the undertaking in whole or in part (s. 499(1) to (4)). Prior to this provision, many more accused were kept in custody for bail hearings because the police were not empowered to impose conditions for release. So, for example, the accused may have been an obvious candidate for quick release but had to remain in custody so that a term prohibiting communication with the complainant could be imposed by a justice of the peace.

- Apart from the above conditions, any appearance notice, promise to appear or recognizance described above, relating to an indictable offence (including a hybrid offence), may require the accused to appear at a specified time and place for photographs and fingerprints, pursuant to the *Identification of Criminals Act*, R.S.C. 1985, c. I-1. Where the accused has been arrested, fingerprinting and photographs may be taken immediately (s. 501(3)). The accused may be arrested and charged for failure to comply with his or her release, including a failure to attend for photographs and fingerprints (s. 145 and 512(2)(*b*) of the *Criminal Code*).

- Where the accused has been arrested with or without a warrant, and not released as above, he or she is to be taken before a justice of the peace without unreasonable delay and within 24 hours of arrest by a peace officer, or within 24 hours of the accused's being delivered to a peace officer. In cases where a justice is unavailable within 24 hours, the accused must be taken before a justice of the peace as soon as possible. However, at any time before the expiration of these periods, the peace officer or officer in charge can release the accused on the same forms of release and with the same conditions as reflected in the paragraph above. Again, these release provisions have no application to offences within the exclusive jurisdiction of the superior court (s. 503(1) to (2.1) of the *Criminal Code*).

- Special procedures exist for persons arrested without warrant for an indictable offence alleged to have been committed outside the territorial division where the arrest took place (s. 503(3) and (3.1)). As well, s. 503(4) provides that if a peace officer or officer in charge arrests a person without a warrant as someone *about* to

commit an indictable offence, then that officer shall release that person unconditionally as soon as practicable, once satisfied that continued detention is not required to prevent an indictable offence from being committed. The power to arrest without a warrant in order to prevent the commission of an indictable offence is reflected in s. 495(1)(*a*) of the *Criminal Code*.

- **As reflected above, the process may start with the accused's release, an arrest then release, or with an arrest followed by continued custody, all before an information has been laid. On the other hand, the proceedings may commence with the laying of an information, followed by the possible issuance of an arrest warrant or summons by the justice of the peace (ss. 504 and 505 of the *Criminal Code*). In either case, an information must generally be laid in writing and under oath, in person, before the justice of the peace, based upon the informant's belief, on reasonable grounds, that the accused has committed an offence (s. 504 of the *Criminal Code*). The information may be in Form 2 (s. 506 of the *Criminal Code*). Section 508.1, permits a peace officer to lay an information by means of telecommunication.**

Under s. 504 of the *Criminal Code* the justice is obligated to receive the information. Where the accused has already been released by the peace officer or officer in charge pursuant to a promise to appear, an appearance notice or a recognizance, the information relating to the offence alleged must be laid before a justice of the peace as soon as practicable and, in any event, before the first court attendance date specified in the release documents (s. 505). The justice of the peace may do one of the following: confirm the forms of release and so endorse the information; cancel the forms of release and issue either a summons or an arrest warrant and endorse on the summons or warrant that the prior forms of release are cancelled; or, simply cancel the appearance notice, promise to appear or recognizance and cause the accused to be so notified (s. 508(1)(*b*) and (*c*) of the *Criminal Code*. The last alternative relieves the accused of any obligation to attend court. Similarly, under s. 507(1)(*b*), a justice who receives an information where no prior process has been issued may issue a summons or, if necessary in the public interest, an arrest warrant, or may decline to issue any process. The contents, manner of service and territorial effectiveness of a summons are dictated by ss. 509, 703.1 and 703.2 of the *Criminal Code*. The summons may require an accused charged with an indictable offence to attend for photographs and fingerprints pursuant to the *Identification of Criminals Act*. The accused may be arrested and charged with failure to comply with the terms of the summons (ss. 145(4), 510 and 512(2)(*a*) of the *Criminal Code*). The accused may also be arrested if the accused evades service of a summons (s. 512(2)(*c*) of the *Criminal Code*). The contents of an arrest warrant, its manner of execution and where it can be executed and by whom are dictated by ss. 29, 511, 513, 514 and 703 of the *Criminal*

Code.[2] A justice must hear and consider, _ex parte_, the allegations of the informant and, if desirable or necessary, the evidence of witnesses, to determine what process, if any, should be issued. In the vast majority of cases, this hearing involves a police officer as informant and is _pro forma_.

- **Where the accused remains in custody, notwithstanding all of the above provisions, a bail hearing must be held before a justice of the peace or a provincial court judge for any offence other than a s. 469 offence within the exclusive jurisdiction of the superior court.**

QUESTION

2. When can a civilian make an arrest? How much force can a civilian use in making an arrest? Consider, in this regard, _R. v. Asante-Mensah_ (2003), 174 C.C.C. (3d) 481; affg (2001), 157 C.C.C. (3d) 481 (Ont. C.A.).

B. ARREST ON PRIVATE PROPERTY

The right to enter a home to effect an arrest, other than in cases of fresh pursuit, was addressed by the Supreme Court of Canada in the following case.

R. v. FEENEY

(1997), 115 C.C.C. (3d) 129 (S.C.C.)

[The victim was found dead at his home after having suffered a fierce attack with an iron bar or similar object. Blood was spattered everywhere at the victim's residence, and Sportsman brand cigarettes were found at the scene. The victim's truck had been found in a ditch earlier in the morning and the appellant had been walking in an easterly direction along the road where the victim lived. The appellant was living on property which was rented out to his sister, Angela Feeney, and her common-law spouse, Dale Russell. Russell told the police that he assumed it was the appellant who had crashed the pickup truck because the skid marks and the location of the accident were in the same place as skid marks from another accident earlier that morning which had involved the appellant and a blue flatbed truck. Russell also said that the appellant had come home at 7:00 a.m. after a night of drinking and was now asleep in the trailer behind his residence. The officer in charge went to the windowless trailer and knocked on the door and said, "Police". Receiving no answer, he entered the trailer

---

[2] **Where feasible, a person arrested should be given notice of the process or warrant under which the arrest is made, or the reason for the arrest. Where feasible, any warrant should be available and produced when requested (s. 29 of the _Criminal Code_). Section 10(_a_) and (_b_) of the _Charter_ entrench additional rights available to a person arrested or detained. These rights are discussed in Chapter 4.**

with his gun drawn, and pointing downward, went to the appellant's bed, shook the appellant's leg and said, "I want to talk to you." The officer then asked the appellant to get out of bed and to move into the better light at the front of the trailer. The officer stated in evidence that he did so in order to inspect the appellant's clothes for bloodstains. The officer conceded that he may have touched the appellant in leading him to the door. The officer noticed blood spattered all over the front of the appellant and had another officer read the appellant his rights. Following a caution with respect to the right to counsel but not the right to immediate counsel, the police asked the appellant a couple of questions, which the appellant answered. The appellant's shirt was seized and he was taken to the police detachment where, before the appellant had consulted with counsel, further statements and the appellant's fingerprints were taken. The police seized cash, cigarettes and shoes under a warrant obtained on the basis of the initial search of the trailer. At issue here was whether the police had violated the appellant's *Charter* rights.]

Sopinka J. [La Forest, Cory, Iacobucci and Major JJ. concurring]: —

.....

Analysis

The Lawfulness of the Arrest

In arguing that the police conduct in the present case did not violate the *Charter*, the respondent relied heavily on the lawfulness of the arrest. Since the arrest was lawful, the argument runs, the search and seizures incidental to the arrest were lawful and complied with the *Charter* according to *Cloutier v. Langlois*, [1990] 1 S.C.R. 158, 53 C.C.C. (3d) 257. In what follows, I will consider first whether the arrest was lawful under the common law rules relating to arrests in a dwelling-house. Subsequently, I will consider whether the common law rules are no longer appropriate in light of the *Charter*. I conclude that the arrest was unlawful under either the rules of the common law or the *Charter*.

[Sopinka J. analyzed the common law rules related to arrests in a dwelling-house and specifically the factors of: (a) reasonable grounds to believe the appellant was in the trailer; (b) proper announcement; (c) subjective grounds; and (d) objective grounds. Sopinka J. held that the officer's testimony clearly fails the subjective grounds requirement and this was ultimately fatal to lawfulness of the arrest under common law.]

.....

The Post-Charter Law of Arrests in Dwelling-Houses

(a) Principles in the Common Law

As noted, *Landry* [(1986), 25 C.C.C. (3d) 1 (S.C.C.)] set out the law concerning warrantless arrests following forcible entry into a dwelling-house. While the case was decided in 1986, it arose before the *Charter* came into effect, as the majority took care to point out at p. 165. In my view, the *Charter* suggests that the *Landry* test for warrantless arrests no longer applies. Before addressing this issue, it is useful first to review extensively the principles underlying the reasons in *Landry* itself.

.....

... In Dickson C.J.C.'s view, the authorities supported the proposition that a warrantless arrest in a dwelling is legal so long as: the officer believes, on reasonable and probable grounds, the person to be the subject of the arrest to have committed an indictable offence; there are reasonable and probable grounds to believe the person sought is within the premises; and proper announcement is made prior to entry.

Dickson C.J.C. also concluded that there were sound policy reasons to retain the law as it was. One policy reason supporting warrantless arrests in dwelling-houses was stated to be the absence of alternative means of arresting a suspect who has taken refuge in a private dwelling-house. Dickson C.J.C. stated, at p. 160, that:

> The policy underlying the cases, older and more recent, on this issue, is clear and compelling: there should be no place which gives an offender sanctuary from arrest. While the *Criminal Code* empowers a justice to issue a warrant, on proper grounds being shown, authorizing a search for *things*, there is no power to issue a warrant to search for a *person*. If the police did not possess the power to arrest on private premises, then a criminal offender might find complete and permanent protection from the law in his or her own home or the home of another.

Dickson C.J.C. further held that there were compelling practical reasons not to require the police to obtain always a warrant for arrest prior to entering a private dwelling to make an arrest. He outlined various scenarios, such as where the police officer witnesses a crime or arrives on the scene shortly thereafter and does not know the name of the suspect whom he or she has seen take refuge in a dwelling-house, that illustrate the impracticality and undesirability of obtaining a warrant before making a forcible entry. In *Landry*, as in other cases on the subject, the issue boiled down to a balance between aiding the police in their protection of society on the one hand, and the privacy interests of individuals in their dwellings on the other. Dickson C.J.C. held at p. 161 that the requirements for warrantless arrest that the majority set out reached the appropriate balance:

> These serious limitations against effective police work and public protection must be balanced against the intrusiveness of arresting a person in a house or apartment. This intrusiveness is carefully delineated and restricted by the requirement of reasonable and probable grounds for the belief that the person sought is within the premises, and the requirements of notice of presence, notice of authority and notice of purpose. These requirements minimize the invasiveness of arrest in a dwelling and permit the offender to maintain his dignity and privacy by walking to the doorway and surrendering himself.

(b) The Charter

In my view, the conditions set out in *Landry* for warrantless arrests are overly expansive in the era of the *Charter*. As noted, *Landry* was largely based on a balance between privacy and the effectiveness of police protection, but in the *Charter* era, as I will presently seek to demonstrate, the emphasis on privacy in Canada has gained considerable importance. Consequently, the test in *Landry* must be adjusted to comport with *Charter* values.

There is no question that the common law has always placed a high value on the security and privacy of the home. This emphasis was illustrated as early as the seventeenth century, as evidenced by *Semayne's Case* (1604), 5 Co. Rep. 91a, 77 E.R. 194, and has been illustrated more recently by cases such as *Colet v. The Queen*, [1981] 1 S.C.R. 2, 57 C.C.C. (2d) 105, 119 D.L.R. (3d) 521, which held that the police entered Colet's home, a rudimentary shelter, illegally since they did not have explicit authority to search for weapons, but only to seize them. Indeed, the existing legal protection of the security of the home was the basis for the dissenting opinion of La Forest J. in *Landry, supra*, which contained an extensive analysis of doctrine that concluded warrantless arrests in dwelling-houses were illegal; see also Graham Parker, "Developments in Criminal Law: The 1985-86 Term" (1987), 9 Supreme Court L.R. 247. Notwithstanding its prior importance, however, the legal status of the privacy of the home was significantly increased in importance with the advent of the *Charter*. Section 8 prevents all unreasonable searches and seizures. In *Hunter v. Southam Inc.*, [1984] 2 S.C.R. 145, 14 C.C.C. (3d) 97, 11 D.L.R. (4th) 641, the seminal case on s. 8, Dickson J. (as he then was), writing for the Court, discussed the impact of the *Charter* on searches and seizure in these terms (at p. 158):

> In my view the interests protected by s. 8 are of a wider ambit than those enunciated in *Entick v. Carrington* [(1765), 19 St. Tr. 1029, 1 Wils. K.B. 275; a common law case on searches and trespass]. Section 8 is an entrenched constitutional provision. It is not therefore vulnerable to encroachment by legislative enactments in the same way as common law protections. There is, further, nothing in the language of the section to restrict it to the protection of property or to associate it with the law of trespass. It guarantees a broad and general right to be secure from unreasonable search and seizure.

The shift in emphasis in the law of searches from trespass and basic property rights to the reasonableness of the search had a significant effect on the disposition of *Hunter*. In that case, there were provisions in the *Combines Investigation Act*, R.S.C. 1970, c. C-23, which permitted searches and seizures on the authority of the Restrictive Trade Practices Commission. The Supreme Court held that searches and seizures may only be undertaken after authorization from an independent judicial body, which has considered the reasonableness of the proposed search and seizure, has been granted.

.....

In my view, *Hunter* is helpful in analyzing the case at bar. The analysis in *Landry* was based on a balance between the individual's privacy interest in the dwelling-house and society's interest in effective police protection. This Court held that the latter interest prevailed and warrantless arrests in dwelling-houses were permissible in certain circumstances. While such a conclusion was debatable at the time, in my view, the increased protection of the privacy of the home in the era of the *Charter* changes the analysis in favour of the former interest: in general, the privacy interest outweighs the interest of the police and warrantless arrests in dwelling-houses are prohibited.

Such a conclusion is consistent not only with the general treatment of privacy in *Hunter*, but also with the specific implications of the privacy interest found in that case. *Hunter* held that a search and seizure violated s. 8 unless there was prior authorization. The purpose of the *Charter* is to prevent unreasonable intrusions on privacy, not to sort them out from reasonable intrusions on an *ex post facto* analysis. If *Landry* were to be adopted in the post-*Charter* era, there would be the anomalous result that prior judicial authorization is required to intrude on an individual's privacy with respect to a search for things, but no authorization is required prior to an intrusion to make an arrest. The result becomes more anomalous when *Cloutier v. Langlois, supra*, is considered. *Cloutier* held that a search incidental to a lawful arrest does not violate s. 8. Putting this proposition together with the proposition that a warrantless arrest in a dwelling-house is legal may lead to the conclusion that a warrantless search of a dwelling-house is legal so long as it is accompanied by a lawful arrest. Such a conclusion is clearly at odds with *Hunter*, which held that warrantless searches are *prima facie* unreasonable. I conclude that generally a warrant is required to make an arrest in a dwelling-house.

I recognize that there are exceptions with respect to the unreasonableness of warrantless searches for things. A warrantless search will respect s. 8 if authorized by law, and both the law and the manner in which the search is conducted are reasonable. In *R. v. Grant*, [1993] 3 S.C.R. 223, 84 C.C.C. (3d) 173, for example, it was held that s. 10 of the *Narcotic Control Act*, R.S.C. 1985, c. N-1, which provided that a peace officer may search a place that is not a dwelling-house without a warrant so long as he believes on reasonable grounds that a narcotic offence had been committed, was consistent with s. 8 of the *Charter* if s. 10 were read down to permit warrantless searches only where there were exigent circumstances. In the present context of searches for persons, in my view, there are also exceptions to the *Charter* prohibition of warrantless arrests in dwelling-houses. Indeed, these exceptions answer Dickson C.J.C.'s policy argument about hampering the effectiveness of police investigations.

Dickson C.J.C. observed that police work might be greatly impeded by a warrant requirement. He provided the example of an officer's arriving on the scene shortly after an offender has slipped into a private dwelling. By the time the officer has discovered the suspect's name and has obtained a warrant, the criminal will have sought refuge elsewhere. In my view, in circumstances such as these there is an exception to the general rule that warrantless arrests in private dwellings are prohibited. In cases of hot pursuit, the privacy interest must give way to the interest of society in ensuring adequate police protection. This Court explicitly held this to be true in *R. v. Macooh*, [1993] 2 S.C.R. 802, 82 C.C.C. (3d) 481, 105 D.L.R. (4th) 96. In *Macooh*, a police officer was in hot pursuit of a person he had seen drive through several stop signs when the person sought refuge in a private apartment. The officer announced his presence and eventually entered the apartment without permission and arrested the person. There was a question whether *Landry* would apply in *Macooh* given that the suspect was sought pursuant to an offence that was not indictable, but this Court held that the officer was acting under the well-established common law power of the police to enter private premises to make an arrest in hot pursuit. The policy behind such a rule is captured by the following passage from the dissent of La Forest J. in *Landry*, at p. 179, cited with approval by this Court in *Macooh*:

> As has been seen the common law sets a high value on the security and privacy of the home. The situations where it permitted entry by police without the consent of the owner or occupier were all demonstrably compelling. For example, entry to prevent murder is obviously justified. So too is entry on hot pursuit. Apart from the obvious practicality of that approach, in the case of hot pursuit the police officer is himself cognizant of the facts justifying entry; he acts on the basis of personal knowledge.

In cases of hot pursuit, society's interest in effective law enforcement takes precedence over the privacy interest and the police may enter a dwelling to make an arrest without a warrant. However, the additional burden on the police to obtain a warrant before forcibly entering a private dwelling to arrest, while not justified in a case of hot pursuit, is, in general, well worth the additional protection to the privacy interest in dwelling-houses that it brings. I leave for another day the question of whether exigent circumstances other than hot pursuit may justify a warrantless entry in order to arrest. I do not agree with my colleague L'Heureux-Dubé J. that exigent circumstances generally *necessarily* justify a warrantless entry — in my view, it is an open question. As with other matters in her reasons, I note that in reaching her conclusion she cites at [paras. 153-54] a *dissenting* opinion: *R. v. Silveira*, [1995] 2 S.C.R. 297, 97 C.C.C. (3d) 450, 124 D.L.R. (4th) 198, *per* L'Heureux-Dubé J.

While I have decided that a warrant is required prior to entering a dwelling-house to make an arrest, I have not yet set out the type of warrant that is required. In my view, an arrest warrant alone is insufficient protection of the privacy rights of the suspect. I agree with Dickson C.J.C. when he stated in *Landry* at p. 162 that it was questionable whether an arrest warrant would be useful in safeguarding privacy:

> I am unable, in any event, to fathom how a warrant for arrest can be perceived as a solution to the question of police authority to trespass incidental to arrest. The warrant is a judicial authorization to arrest and contains no express power of trespass. The justice of the peace must be given evidence as to the reasonable and probable grounds for making an arrest, but hears no evidence as to the likelihood or otherwise that the offender can be found at any particular location. There is no good reason, therefore, why the presence or absence of a warrant of arrest should have any bearing on the right to make an arrest in one particular place or another.

Dickson C.J.C. concluded that since an arrest warrant would not be useful in safeguarding privacy, and since there was (and is) no provision in the *Code* authorizing a search for persons, warrantless arrests in dwelling-houses were permissible; otherwise suspects could take permanent refuge in a dwelling-house. While I agree that an arrest warrant fails to safeguard privacy adequately, I disagree that since the *Code* is silent on prior authorization of a search for persons, warrantless searches for persons are permissible. In my view, privacy rights under the *Charter* demand that the police, in general, obtain prior judicial authorization of entry into the dwelling-house in order to arrest the person. If the *Code* currently fails to provide specifically for a warrant containing such prior authorization, such a provision should be read in. While the absence of such a provision could have a profound influence on the common law power of arrest, its absence cannot defeat a constitutional right of the individual. Once a procedure to obtain such prior authorization is created, the concern that suspects may find permanent sanctuary in a dwelling-house disappears.

In my view, then, warrantless arrests in dwelling-houses are in general prohibited. Prior to such an arrest, it is incumbent on the police officer to obtain judicial authorization for the arrest by obtaining a warrant to enter the dwelling-house for the purpose of arrest. Such a warrant will only be authorized if there are reasonable grounds for the arrest, and reasonable grounds to believe that the person will be found at the address named, thus providing individuals' privacy interests in an arrest situation with the protection *Hunter* required with respect to searches and seizures. Requiring a warrant prior to arrest avoids the *ex post facto* analysis of the reasonableness of an intrusion that *Hunter* held should be avoided under the *Charter*; invasive arrests without a basis of reasonable and probable grounds are prevented, rather than remedied after the fact. Such a policy was reflected in the following recommendation of the Law Reform Commission of Canada (*Working Paper 41, Arrest* (1985), at p. 115):

> The sanctity of the family dwelling is such in our legal tradition that, as with search, there ought to be no forcible entry into a private dwelling unless such entry is authorized by judicial authority.

I would add that the protection of privacy does not end with a warrant; the other requirements in *Landry* for an arrest in a dwelling-house must be met along with the warrant requirement. Specifically, before forcibly entering a dwelling-house to make an arrest with a warrant for an indictable offence, proper announcement must be made. As Dickson C.J.C. stated in *Landry* at p. 161, these additional requirements "minimize the invasiveness of arrest in a dwelling and permit the offender to maintain his dignity and privacy by walking to the doorway and surrendering himself."

To summarize, in general, the following requirements must be met before an arrest for an indictable offence in a private dwelling is legal: a warrant must be obtained on the basis of reasonable and probable grounds to arrest and to believe the person sought is within the premises in question; and proper announcement must be made before entering. An exception to this rule occurs where there is a case of hot pursuit. Whether or not there is an exception for exigent circumstances generally has not been fully addressed by this Court, nor does it need to be decided in the present case given my view that exigent circumstances did not exist when the arrest was made. I will elaborate on this last point presently.

(c) *Application to the Case at Bar*

When the police entered the trailer where Feeney was sleeping, which constituted his dwelling-house (recall that *Colet, supra*, stated that a rudimentary shelter may constitute a dwelling-house), they did not have a warrant. Consequently, regardless of whether reasonable and probable grounds existed, or whether proper announcement was made, the arrest was illegal, unless there were exceptional circumstances. This clearly was not a case of hot pursuit, nor, in my view, did exigent circumstances exist. Lambert J.A., for a unanimous Court of Appeal, stated at p. 234 that, "[T]he police were facing a situation which could be classified as an emergency, or as exigent circumstances which would require immediate action, and that in addition they were facing circumstances where the possibility of the destruction of evidence, particularly evidence in relation to bloodstains, was a real one and had to be addressed". I do not agree with this characterization of the circumstances. According to James A. Fontana (*The Law of Search and Seizure in Canada*, 3rd ed. (Toronto: Butterworths, 1992), at pp. 786-89), exigent circumstances arise usually where immediate action is required for the safety of the police or to secure and protect evidence of a crime. With respect to safety concerns, in my view, it was not apparent that the safety of the police or the community was in such jeopardy that there were exigent circumstances in the present case. The situation was the same as in any case after a serious crime has been committed and the perpetrator has not been apprehended. In any event, even if they existed, safety concerns could not justify the warrantless entry into the trailer in the present case. A simple watch of the trailer in which the police were told the appellant was sleeping, not a warrantless entry, would have sufficiently addressed any safety concerns involving the appellant. With respect to concern about the potential destruction of evidence, at the time the police entered the trailer, they had no knowledge of evidence that might be destroyed; at best, they had a suspicion that the appellant was involved in the murder. Simply because the hunch may have turned out to be justified does not legitimize the actions of the police at the time they entered the trailer. As I stated in *R. v. Kokesch*, [1990] 3 S.C.R. 3, at p. 29, 61 C.C.C. (3d) 207, "[i]t should not be forgotten that *ex post facto* justification of searches by their results is precisely what the *Hunter* standards were designed to prevent".

The circumstances surrounding the police entry into the trailer were similar to those following any serious crime: a dangerous person is on the loose and there is a risk that he or she will attempt to destroy evidence linking him or her to the crime. To define these as exigent circumstances is to invite such a characterization of every period after a serious crime. In my view, exigent circumstances did not exist when the police entered the trailer. Consequently, even if there is an exception to the warrant requirement in exigent circumstances generally, rather than only in hot pursuit, which I refrain from deciding in the present case, the forcible entry in this case required a warrant. Given that the police had not obtained a warrant, the arrest was illegal.

[Having found the arrest illegal, Sopinka J. concluded the search which was incidental to the arrest was also violative of the appellant's s. 8 rights. The Court then considered the issue of the appellant's s. 10(*b*) rights to counsel and found that the statement taken in the trailer was taken in violation of the appellant's *Charter* rights. Sopinka J. also concluded that the subsequent search warrant was also illegal, as the initial entry into the trailer was in itself illegal.]

.....

[Sopinka J. considered the question of trial fairness and held that the statements in the trailer, at the detachment, and the fingerprints were conscriptive and therefore inadmissible as affecting the fairness of the trial.

The bloody shirt, the shoes, the cigarettes and the money were not conscriptive evidence, and this evidence, while its admission would not affect trial fairness, must be analyzed in light of the second (seriousness of the breach) and third branches (effect of exclusion on the repute of the administration of justice) of the *Collins* test, which may require its exclusion.]

.....

Seriousness of the Violation

The violations were, in my view, very serious in the present case. One of the *indicia* of seriousness is whether the violations were undertaken in good faith: see *Therens* [[1985] 1 S.C.R. 613], at p. 652; *Collins* [[1987] 1 S.C.R. 265], at p. 285. One indication of bad faith is that the *Charter* violation was undertaken without any lawful authority. In *R. v. Genest*, [1989] 1 S.C.R. 59, 45 C.C.C. (3d) 385, for example, the Court held that a search in violation of well-known common law principles was performed in bad faith. In the instant case, the police did not even have subjective belief in reasonable and probable grounds for the appellant's arrest prior to their warrantless, forced entry into his dwelling-house where he was sleeping. Aside from the impact of the *Charter* on the requirements for warrantless arrests in dwelling-houses, the absence of subjective belief in reasonable grounds indicated that the police could not have lawfully arrested the appellant under s. 495 of the *Code* even had he been in a public place. That they flagrantly disobeyed the law of warrantless arrests in dwelling-houses as set out in *Landry* certainly renders the more serious the violation which directly led to the taking of the bloody shirt, and indirectly led to the taking of the shoes, cigarettes and money.

The trial judge found that the breach in searching the trailer "was not deliberate, wilful or flagrant and that if it occurred, it was committed in good faith". In my view, the following passage from the majority in *Kokesch, supra*, at p. 32, is instructive in the present case:

> The police must be taken to be aware of this Court's judgments in *Eccles* and *Colet*, and the circumscription of police powers that those judgments represent.
>
> Either the police knew they were trespassing, or they ought to have known. Whichever is the case, they cannot be said to have proceeded in "good faith", as that term is understood in s. 24(2) jurisprudence.

In the present case, the police did not have subjective grounds to arrest, and thus the requirements for a warrantless arrest in a dwelling-house set out in *Landry* were not met. Indeed, the statutory requirements to make a warrantless arrest in *any* location were not met. In these circumstances, as in *Kokesch*, the police either knew they were trespassing, or they ought to have known. The police could not be held to have acted in good faith and the trial judge erred in this respect.

The respondent submits that the seriousness of the violation is mitigated by the fact that if the grounds for arrest fell short of reasonable and probable grounds, they did not fall far short. I disagree that this is a mitigating factor. As discussed above, Sgt. Madrigga himself did not believe that there were reasonable grounds to arrest the appellant. In my view, the absence of a subjective belief that a necessary element of a lawful entry and arrest was present is a strong suggestion of bad faith.

The respondent argued that the evidence of the bloody shirt would have been discovered in any event, stating in its factum: "The police could have waited outside the trailer until the appellant eventually came out. At that time they would have observed the blood stains on him, unless he had destroyed that evidence." The respondent assumes that the appellant would walk out in broad daylight with blood stains on his shirt. In my view, this suggestion is unrealistic. Moreover, the appellant need not have destroyed the evidence on the shirt in order to avoid displaying it in public, but simply could have stored the shirt in the trailer. In any event, the availability of alternative constitutional means to discover the shirt does not mitigate the seriousness of the violation even if such means did exist. As Lamer J. (as he then was) stated in *Collins, supra*, at p. 285, "the availability of other investigatory techniques and the fact that the evidence could have been obtained without the violation of the *Charter* tend to render the *Charter* violation more serious." If other techniques were indeed available, it is demonstrative of bad faith and is particularly serious that the police chose to violate the appellant's rights.

A conclusion that the violations were serious is reinforced by the fact that they involved the unconstitutional entry of the appellant's dwelling-house. The sanctity of the home has been recognized time and again by courts at least since *Semayne's Case, supra*. The police in the present case did not have sufficient grounds either to arrest the appellant, or to obtain a search warrant, yet they forcibly entered the sleeping appellant's one-room dwelling with guns drawn, shook him awake and began questioning him. Such behaviour is antithetical to the privacy interests protected by the *Charter* and cannot be condoned. I note that the respondent suggested that the police did not know the trailer was a dwelling-house, but this is clearly contradicted by the evidence that Spurn had told police that the appellant was living on land he owned and that Russell had told police that the appellant was sleeping in the trailer.

The respondent argued that the seriousness of the intrusion into the dwelling-house is mitigated by Sgt. Madrigga's belief that the owner of the trailer had given his tacit consent to enter the trailer. In my view, this submission is unacceptable. First, the owner of the trailer did not consent to the search, but rather did not object when the police stated that they were going to "check it out" at the trailer. An inference of consent to a warrantless, forcible entry from Russell's silence is dubious. However, even accepting that Russell had consented, this would not have justified the search nor should it mitigate the seriousness of the violation entailed by the search. *Hunter, supra*, was clear that an ownership interest is unnecessary in invoking s. 8; what is required is a reasonable expectation of privacy. It would be inconsistent with this emphasis on the expectation of privacy to mitigate the seriousness of the violation based on the consent of the owner of the premises rather than the person with the profound expectation of privacy associated with his dwelling-house.

The respondent also argued that there were exigent circumstances in this case, which, according to *Silveira, supra*, may be a relevant consideration in a s. 24(2) analysis. As discussed above, in my view exigent circumstances did not exist in this case any more than they would exist in any situation following a serious crime. After any crime is committed, the possibility that evidence might be destroyed is inevitably present. To tend to admit evidence because of the mitigating effect of such allegedly exigent circumstances would invite the admission of all evidence obtained soon after the commission of a crime. In my view, however, there were no exigent circumstances in this case that mitigated the seriousness of the *Charter* breach. This is not to say that there may not be exigent circumstances arising out of matters other than the recent commission of the offence that serve to mitigate the seriousness of the breach.

In summary, the violations in the instant case that were associated with the gathering of the shirt, shoes, cigarettes and money were serious. The police flagrantly disregarded the appellant's privacy rights and moreover showed little regard for his s. 10(*b*) rights. Indeed, while such misconduct was not directly responsible for the gathering of the shirt, shoes, cigarettes and money, the fact that the appellant did not speak with a lawyer for two days following his detention, yet the police did not cease in their efforts to gather evidence from him, indicates the lack of respect for the appellant's rights displayed by the police. In light of this pattern of disregard for the rights of the appellant, in my view the obtention of the shirt, shoes, cigarettes and money was associated with very serious *Charter* violations.

Effect of Exclusion on the Repute of the Administration of Justice

The admission of the conscriptive evidence, the statements and the fingerprints, would, as discussed above, impact on the fairness of the trial. Consequently, the repute of the administration of justice would be harmed by their admission and they are inadmissible. The other evidence, while not conscriptive, was obtained as the result of a very serious intrusion of the appellant's privacy rights. Moreover, the evidence was associated with serious violations of the appellant's s. 10(*b*) rights, indicating a pattern of disregard for the *Charter* by the police in the present case.

While the appellant stood accused of a very serious crime, in my view the following words of Iacobucci J. in *Burlingham* [[1995] 2 S.C.R. 206], at p. 242, apply to the present case:

> ... we should never lose sight of the fact that even a person accused of the most heinous crimes, and no matter the likelihood that he or she actually committed those crimes, is entitled to the full protection of the *Charter*. Short-cutting or short-circuiting those rights affects not only the accused, but also the entire reputation of the criminal justice system. It must be emphasized that the goals of preserving the integrity of the criminal justice system as well as promoting the decency of investigatory techniques are of fundamental importance in applying s. 24(2).

The serious disregard for the appellant's *Charter* rights in the case at bar suggests that the admission of the evidence would bring greater harm to the repute of the administration of justice than its exclusion. The shirt, shoes, cigarettes and money were inadmissible under s. 24(2), along with the statements and the fingerprints. If the exclusion of this evidence is likely to result in an acquittal of the accused as suggested by L'Heureux-Dubé J. in her reasons, then the Crown is deprived of a conviction based on illegally obtained evidence. Any price to society occasioned by the loss of such a conviction is fully justified in a free and democratic society which is governed by the rule of law.

[Lamer C.J.C., L'Heureux Dubé, Gonthier and McLachlin JJ. dissented]

In response to *Feeney*, Parliament passed *An Act to amend the Criminal Code and Interpretation Act (powers to arrest and enter dwellings)*, S.C. 1997, c. 39 (also known as Bill C-16). Bill C-16 created two classes of warrants in the *Code*: s. 529 (a free-standing entry warrant issued with a conventional arrest warrant); and s. 529.1 (a free-standing entry warrant where authority to arrest already exists). Bill C-16 also outlined the authority to enter a dwelling without a warrant under s. 529.3(1) of the *Code* and defined "exigent circumstances" for this purpose under s. 529.3(2).

QUESTIONS

3. **Consider the scenario when the police are dispatched to a 911 call that has been disconnected before the caller says anything. The police arrive at the house and ask if everything is alright inside. The person at the door indicates, "Sure, there is no problem." The officers then ask if they can come inside but the person indicates no and tries to close the door. The police then push their way in and discover evidence of an assault and arrest the individual. Is this arrest legal? Consider, in this regard, *R. v. Godoy* (1998), 131 C.C.C. (3d) 129 (S.C.C.).**

4. **In response to the September 11, 2001 terrorist attacks, the Parliament enacted the *Anti-Terrorism Act*, S.C. 2001, c. 41, s. 4. One of the new additions to the *Code* is s. 83.3(4)(*a*)(i), which allows the police to arrest individuals without prior judicial authorization on reasonable grounds that a terrorist activity will be carried out and where exigent circumstances make it impractical to lay an information under s. 83.3(2) (which requires consent of the Attorney General). How does this provision accord with *Feeney*?**

C. "SHOW CAUSE" OR "BAIL" HEARINGS FOR NON-SECTION 469 OFFENCES

1. Adjournments, Onus and Available Dispositions

Where the accused is brought before a justice of the peace charged with a non-s. 469 offence, the "show cause" or "bail" hearing under s. 515 of the *Criminal Code* may take place that day. However, the accused may adjourn the hearing for preparation of the case favouring release from custody. This would include, *inter alia*, inquiries by counsel as to the nature and strength of the Crown's case, the availability of sureties, the accused's employment, prospective residence, criminal record and outstanding charges. D. Garth Burrow Q.C.'s *Bail Hearings* (Toronto: Carswell, 1993) at 77-85, provides an indispensable outline of how defence and Crown should prepare for a bail hearing. He provides suggested checklists to be used to ensure complete preparation.

The Crown may also wish to adjourn the hearing in order to enable the police to further investigate the accused's background, any outstanding charges, his or her immigration status or to follow up on an incomplete criminal investigation. Under s. 516 of the *Criminal Code*, the adjournment cannot exceed three days without the accused's consent. A request for an adjournment can take place before or during a bail hearing.

Generally, the onus is on the Crown to "show cause" as to why the accused should be detained or, failing that, to "show cause" as to why a more restrictive release order (on a ladder of available release orders from least to most restrictive), should be imposed (s. 515(1), (2) and (3), as amended). These subsections of the *Criminal Code* favour release on the least onerous terms possible.

The available release orders are reproduced in s. 515(2)(*a*) to (*e*) of the *Criminal Code*. All of these options permit conditions to be imposed on the release. Section 515(4)(*a*) to (*e*) outlines specific conditions which may be imposed.[3] Section 515(4)(*f*) permits "such other reasonable conditions specified in the order as the justice considers desirable". As stated in s. 515(4.1) of the *Criminal Code*, for those offences related to violence, terrorism offences, certain weapons offences, criminal harassment, intimidation of a justice system participant and some offences under the *Controlled Drugs and Substances Act*, S.C. 1996, c. 19, or the *Security of Information Act*, R.S.C. 1985, c. O-5, a justice should presumptively impose conditions prohibiting the possession of firearms, ammunition or explosive substances and should have the accused surrender any firearms acquisition certificates, authorizations or licences. For offences related to violence, criminal harassment, intimidation of a justice system participant, terrorism offences and some offences under the *Security of Information Act* under s. 515(4.2) of the *Criminal Code*, a justice is mandated to consider whether it would be beneficial for a condition to be imposed which would prohibit the accused from communicating with named witnesses or persons, or from going to named places, or which would ensure the safety and security of those persons.

The following is a list of many frequently imposed conditions which may be recommended by the Crown or considered by the court.

An accused may be required to:

- keep the peace and be of good behaviour.
- report to a particular police station bi-weekly, weekly, bimonthly or monthly.
- report immediately upon release to a named bail program, and thereafter as required, and reside at a residence approved by the bail program.
- reside at a particular address with the surety or with another named person and to obey the rules of the household.

---

3 Note that s. 515(2)(*d*) of the *Criminal Code* requires prosecutorial consent. In essence, this contemplates that a deposit may be required in lieu of suitable sureties. Unlike American practice, professional bail bondsmen are prohibited. Any deposit requirement should not be so prohibitive so as to effectively amount to a detention order.

- notify the police 48 hours in advance, in writing, of any change of address.
- observe a curfew between certain hours except, for example, when in the company of the surety, or for the purposes of school or employment.
- have no contact or communication directly or indirectly with the complainant or named witnesses, except through counsel, for the purposes of preparing a defence.
- not attend at (or, for example, within 500 metres) of a particular location. In cases involving domestic assault, there may be an exception to permit the accused to remove personal possessions from the home, while accompanied by a named person.
- not associate with the co-accused or other named individuals or anyone known to him or her to have a criminal record, including a record under the *Youth Criminal Justice Act*, S.C. 2002, c. 1.
- abstain absolutely from the consumption, purchase, or possession of alcoholic beverages and non-prescription drugs or narcotics.
- not enter licensed premises or premises licensed primarily for the sale of alcoholic beverages.
- not be in the presence of any child under a certain age, except when accompanied by the surety or other named individuals.
- not own, control or possess any firearms, ammunition, explosive devices, or weapons.
- surrender or be restricted from applying for any Firearms Acquisition Certificate.
- seek and maintain employment or attend school full-time.
- carry a copy of the recognizance or undertaking at all times while not in residence.
- not operate a motor vehicle, except for certain specified activities.
- attend upon a family physician and seek counselling or treatment for anger management, alcohol or drug abuse, psychiatric or psychological problems, or continue counselling or treatment with named individuals or organizations, within seven days of release.
- deposit passport with the police and to not apply for any new or replacement passport.
- remain within or outside of a particular territorial jurisdiction.

Under s. 515(6)(*a*) to (*d*) of the *Criminal Code*, the onus is upon the accused to "show cause" why he or she should be released where the accused is charged with:

(a) an indictable non-s. 469 offence allegedly committed while the accused was at large, after being released respecting another indictable offence.[4]

---

[4] Section 515(6)(*a*) also extends to accused who are charged with criminal organization or terrorism offences, and certain offences under the *Security of Information Act*.

(b) an indictable non-s. 469 offence and the accused is not ordinarily resident in Canada.

(c) an offence under any of s. 145(2) to (5) which was allegedly committed while the accused was at large, after being released respecting another offence.

(d) having committed an offence punishable by imprisonment for life under s. 5(3), 6(3) or 7(2) of the *Controlled Drugs and Substances Act*, or the offence of conspiring to commit such an offence.

An accused cannot be released on an undertaking without conditions where a reverse onus applies.

QUESTION

5. The accused is charged with sexual assault. He was at large on a promise to appear when this offence allegedly occurred. The prior alleged offence was also sexual assault but the Crown had already elected to proceed summarily on that charge. Where does the onus lie?

The constitutionality of the reverse onus provisions has been considered in several cases.

R. v. PEARSON

(1992), 17 C.R. (4th) 1, 77 C.C.C. (3d) 124 (S.C.C.)

[The Supreme Court considered the reverse onus contained in s. 515(6)(*d*) of the *Criminal Code*. Of the six justices hearing the appeal, only McLachlin J. found the section unconstitutional.]

Lamer C.J.C. (Sopinka and Iacobucci JJ. concurring): — This appeal was argued along with *R. v. Morales* (November 19, 1992), Doc. 22404 (S.C.C.) [now reported at (1992), 17 C.R. (4th) 74, 77 C.C.C. (3d) 91 (S.C.C.)]. Both cases involve the constitutionality of the bail provisions of the *Criminal Code*, R.S.C. 1985, c. C-46, and for the first time require this court to examine the scope of the right to bail under s. 11(*e*) of the *Canadian Charter of Rights and Freedoms*.

.....

(2) Section 11(e)

(i) The scope of the right

This court has never before been called upon to define the scope of the right contained in s. 11(*e*). As a result, some preliminary remarks about s. 11(*e*) are in order.

Section 11(*e*) guarantees the right of any person charged with an offence "not to be denied reasonable bail without just cause." In my opinion, s.

11(*e*) contains two distinct elements, namely the right to "reasonable bail" and the right not to be denied bail without "just cause".

.....

"Reasonable bail" refers to the terms of bail. Thus the quantum of bail and the restrictions imposed on the accused's liberty while on bail must be "reasonable". "Just cause" refers to the right to obtain bail. Thus bail must not be denied unless there is "just cause" to do so. The "just cause" aspect of s. 11(*e*) imposes constitutional standards on the grounds under which bail is granted or denied.

.....

The dual aspect of s. 11(*e*) mandates a broad interpretation of the word "bail" in s. 11(*e*). If s. 11(*e*) guarantees the right to obtain "bail" on terms which are reasonable, then "bail" must refer to all forms of what is formally known under the *Criminal Code* as "judicial interim release". In common parlance, "bail" sometimes refers to the money or other valuable security which the accused is required to deposit with the court as a condition of release. Restricting "bail" to this meaning would render s. 11(*e*) nugatory because most accused are released on less onerous terms. In order to be an effective guarantee, the meaning of "bail" in s. 11(*e*) must include all forms of judicial interim release.

.....

Most of the current bail provisions in the *Criminal Code* were enacted in the *Bail Reform Act*, S.C. 1970-71-72, c. 37. *The Bail Reform Act* established a basic entitlement to bail. Bail must be granted unless pre-trial detention is justified by the prosecution. In *R. v. Bray* (1983), 32 C.R. (3d) 316, 2 C.C.C. (3d) 325, 40 O.R. (2d) 766, 144 D.L.R. (3d) 305, 4 C.R.R. 73 (C.A.), at p. 328 [C.C.C., p. 320 C.R.], Martin J.A. described the *Bail Reform Act* as "a liberal and enlightened system of pre-trial release". In my view, s. 11(*e*) transforms the basic entitlement of this liberal and enlightened system into a constitutional right. Section 11(*e*) creates a basic entitlement to be granted reasonable bail unless there is just cause to do otherwise.

.....

(ii) Whether section 515(6)(d) denies bail

In order to determine whether s. 515(6)(*d*) infringes s. 11(*e*), it is first necessary to determine whether s. 515(6)(*d*) even has the effect of denying bail. The appellant and the intervening Attorneys General submit that s. 515(6)(*d*) does not deny bail because it merely requires the accused to show that detention is not justified in the circumstances of the case. With respect, I cannot agree.

Section 515(6)(*d*) is an exception to the basic entitlement to bail contained in s. 11(*e*). Instead of requiring the prosecution to show that pre-trial detention is justified, it requires the accused to show that pre-trial detention is not justified. In my view, the mere fact that there is a departure from the basic entitlement to bail is sufficient to conclude that there is a denial of bail for the purposes of s. 11(*e*) and that this denial of bail must be with "just cause" in order to be constitutionally justified. Furthermore, the very wording of s. 515(6)(*d*) establishes that it has the effect of denying bail in certain circumstances. Section 515(6)(*d*) provides that under certain circumstances "the justice shall order that the accused be detained in custody". This wording mandates a denial of bail. Such wording makes it impossible to accept the submission that s. 515(6)(*d*) does not constitute a denial of bail.

Given that s. 515(6)(*d*) denies bail in certain circumstances, it becomes necessary to determine whether there is just cause for this denial.

(iii) Whether section 515(6)(d) provides just cause to deny bail

Although s. 515(6)(*d*) constitutes a denial of bail in certain circumstances, in my opinion there is just cause for this denial of bail. There are two reasons for my conclusion. First, bail is denied only in a narrow set of circumstances. Second, the denial of bail is necessary to promote the proper functioning of the bail system and is not undertaken for any purpose extraneous to the bail system. The effect of s. 515(6)(*d*) is to establish a set of special bail rules in circumstances where the normal bail process is incapable of functioning properly. In my view, there is just cause for these special rules.

The circumstances in which bail is denied under s. 515(6)(*d*) are very narrow. Section 515(6)(*d*) applies only to a very small number of offences, all of which involve the distribution of narcotics.[5] Furthermore, s. 515(6)(*d*) does not deny bail for all persons who are charged with these offences, but rather denies bail only when these persons are unable to demonstrate that detention is not justified having regard to the specified primary or secondary grounds. The narrow scope of the denial of bail under s. 515(6)(*d*) is essential to its validity under s. 11(*e*). The basic entitlement of s. 11(*e*) cannot be denied in a broad or sweeping exception.

The offences which are included under s. 515(6)(*d*) have specific characteristics which justify differential treatment in the bail process. These characteristics are noted by the Groupe de travail sur la lutte contre la drogue, *Rapport du groupe de travail sur la lutte contre la drogue* (Québec: Publications du Québec, 1990). It notes at pp. 18-19 that drug trafficking generally constitutes a form of organized crime ...

.....

... It also notes at p. 21 that the nature of drug trafficking is sometimes mistakenly viewed as less serious than more openly violent crimes ...

.....

... It notes at p. 24 that narcotics offences increase the general level of criminality ...

The unique characteristics of the offences subject to s. 515(6)(*d*) suggest that those offences are committed in a very different context than most

---

5 **Author's Note: The Supreme Court's reasoning would appear to be no less applicable to substitute offence sections under the *Controlled Drugs and Substances Act*.**

other crimes. Most offences are not committed systematically. By contrast, trafficking in narcotics occurs systematically, usually within a highly sophisticated commercial setting. It is often a business and a way of life. It is highly lucrative, creating huge incentives for an offender to continue criminal behaviour even after arrest and release on bail. In these circumstances, the normal process of arrest and bail will normally not be effective in bringing an end to criminal behaviour. Special bail rules are required in order to establish a bail system which maintains the accused's right to pre-trial release while discouraging continuing criminal activity.

Another specific feature of the offences subject to s. 515(6)(*d*) is that there is a marked danger that an accused charged with these offences will abscond rather than appear for trial. Ensuring the appearance of the accused at trial is the primary purpose of any system of pre-trial release, and the system must be structured to minimize the risk that an accused will abscond rather than face trial. For most offences, the risk that an accused will abscond rather than face trial is minimal. It is not an easy thing to abscond from justice. The accused must remain a fugitive from justice for the rest of his or her lifetime. The accused must flee to a country which does not have an extradition treaty with Canada (or whose extradition treaty does not cover the specific offence which the accused is alleged to have committed). Alternatively, the accused must remain in hiding. Either prospect is costly. Neither prospect is possible unless the accused is exceedingly wealthy or part of a sophisticated organization which can assist in the difficult task of absconding. Most alleged offenders are neither wealthy nor members of sophisticated organizations. Drug importers and traffickers, however, have access both to a large amount of funds and to sophisticated organizations which can assist in a flight from justice. These offenders accordingly pose a significant risk that they will abscond rather than face trial.

There appears to be no evidence about the risk of absconding by those charged with narcotics offences in Canada. However, there is evidence from both the United States and Australia which demonstrates that those charged with narcotics offences pose a particular danger of absconding while on bail.

.....

[Lamer C.J.C. then responds to the argument that the section is unconstitutional because it does not differentiate between the commercial trafficker and the distributor of a few marijuana joints.]

Section 515(6)(*d*) does not mandate denial of bail in all cases and therefore does allow differential treatment based on the seriousness of the offence. Moreover, the onus which it imposes is reasonable in the sense that it requires the accused to provide information which he or she is most capable of providing. If a person accused of trafficking or importing is "small fry" or a "generous smoker", then the accused is in the best position to demonstrate at a bail hearing that he or she is not part of a criminal organization engaged in distributing narcotics.

R. v. MORALES

(1992), 17 C.R. (4th) 74, 77 C.C.C. (3d) 91 (S.C.C.)

[The Supreme Court considered the reverse onus in s. 515(6)(*a*) of the *Criminal Code*.[6] It also considered the vagueness of the words "public interest" in s. 515(10)(*b*), as it then read. The Court unanimously found that s. 515(6)(*a*) was not in violation of the *Charter* and found, Gonthier and L'Heureux-Dubé JJ. dissenting, that the criterion of "public interest" in s. 515(10)(*b*) did violate the *Charter*. The offending words were struck down and severed from the rest of the section.]

Lamer C.J.C. (La Forest, Sopinka, McLachlin and Iacobucci JJ. concurring): —

.....

At issue in this appeal is the validity of ss. 515(6)(*a*) ... and 515(10)(*b*) of the *Criminal Code* ...

.....

As the appellant submits, the secondary ground [s. 515(10)] contains two separate components. Detention can be justified either in the "public interest" or for the "protection or safety of the public". In my view each of these components entails very different constitutional considerations. As a result, the following analysis considers the public interest and public safety components of s. 515(10)(*b*) separately.

(1) Public Interest

For the reasons which I gave in *Pearson*, I am of the view that the respondent's challenge to the grounds upon which bail may be denied, specifically the public interest and public safety criteria should be considered under the specific guarantees set out in s. 11(*e*) [of the *Charter*] rather than under s. 7. However, as will appear in what follows, the analysis under s. 11(*e*) will draw considerable support from the constitutional doctrine of vagueness which has been articulated as a principle of fundamental justice.

(i) Section 11(e)

In *Pearson*, I noted that, pursuant to *Charter* s.11(*e*), there will be just cause for denial of bail if the denial can occur only in a narrow set of circumstances and if the denial is necessary to promote the proper functioning of the bail system.

In my view, the criterion of "public interest" as a basis for pre-trial detention under s. 515(10)(*b*) violates s. 11(*e*) of the *Charter* because it authorizes detention in terms which are vague and imprecise. D. Kiselbach, "Pre-trial Criminal Procedure: Preventive Detention and the Presumption of Innocence" (1988-89) 31 Crim. L.Q. 168, at p. 186, describes "public interest" as "the most nebulous basis for detention". I agree with this char-

---

6 **When *Morales* was decided, s. 515(6)(*a*) did not extend to the offences listed in note 4.**

acterization of the public interest component of s. 515(10)(*b*) and view it as a fatal flaw in the provision.

.....

In my view, the doctrine of vagueness is applicable to s. 515(10)(*b*) because there cannot be just cause for denial of bail within the meaning of s. 11(*e*) if the statutory criteria for denying bail are vague and imprecise. [*Canada v. Pharmaceutical Society (Nova Scotia)*, [1992] 2 S.C.R. 606] at p. 632 identified two rationales for the doctrine of vagueness, namely fair notice to the citizen and limitation of law enforcement discretion. Fair notice is "an understanding that certain conduct is the subject of legal restrictions" (p. 635), a factor which is not relevant to a provision like s. 515(10)(*b*) which does not prohibit conduct. However, limitation of law enforcement discretion is still a relevant factor. In the [*Reference re Sections 193 and 195.1(1)(c) of the Criminal Code*, [1990] 1 S.C.R. 1123, 56 C.C.C. (3d) 65] at p. 1157 [S.C.R.], I explained this rationale in terms of a "standardless sweep": "is the statute so pervasively vague that it permits a 'standardless sweep' allowing law enforcement officials to pursue their personal predilections?" In my view the principles of fundamental justice preclude a standardless sweep in any provision which authorizes imprisonment. This is all the more so under a constitutional guarantee not to be denied bail without just cause as set out in s. 11(*e*). Since pre-trial detention is extraordinary in our system of criminal justice, vagueness in defining the terms of pre-trial detention may be even more invidious than is vagueness in defining an offence.

.....

... As currently defined by the courts, the term "public interest" is incapable of framing the legal debate in any meaningful manner or structuring discretion in any way.

Nor would it be possible in my view to give the term "public interest" a constant or settled meaning. The term gives the courts unrestricted latitude to define any circumstances as sufficient to justify pre-trial detention. The term creates no criteria to define these circumstances. No amount of judicial interpretation of the term "public interest" would be capable of rendering it a provision which gives any guidance for legal debate.

As a result, the public interest component of s. 515(10)(*b*) violates the s. 11(*e*) of the *Charter* because it authorizes a denial of bail without just cause.

(ii) Section 1

In my view, this violation is not justified under s. 1. The limit cannot be justified under the test in *R. v. Oakes*, [1986] 1 S.C.R. 103, 50 C.R. (3d) 1, 65 N.R. 87, 53 O.R. (2d) 719 (headnote only), 24 C.C.C. (3d) 321, 14 O.A.C. 335, 26 D.L.R. (4th) 200, 19 C.R.R. 308, and may be too vague even to constitute a limit which is "prescribed by law" under s. 1.

.....

(2) Public Safety

It remains to determine whether the public safety component of s. 515(10)(*b*) is constitutionally valid.

.....

(i) Section 11(e)

.....

The public safety component of s. 515(10)(*b*) provides that pre-trial detention is justified where it is necessary "for the protection or safety of the public, having regard to all the circumstances including any substantial likelihood that the accused will, if he is released from custody, commit a criminal offence or interfere with the administration of justice". The appellant concedes, quite properly in my opinion, that danger or likelihood that an individual will commit a criminal offence does not in itself provide just cause for detention. In general, our society does not countenance preventive detention of individuals simply because they have a proclivity to commit crime. The appellant accepts this proposition but submits that there is just cause for preventive detention where an individual who presents a danger of committing an offence is already awaiting trial for a criminal offence.

In *Pearson*, I identified two factors which in my view are vital to a determination that there is just cause under s. 11(*e*). First, the denial of bail must occur only in a narrow set of circumstances. Second, the denial of bail must be necessary to promote the proper functioning of the bail system and must not be undertaken for any purpose extraneous to the bail system. In my opinion, the public safety component of s. 515(10)(*b*) provides just cause to deny bail within these criteria.

I am satisfied that the scope of the public safety component of s. 515(10)(*b*) issufficiently narrow to satisfy the first requirement under s. 11(*e*). Bail is not denied for all individuals who pose a risk of committing an offence or interfering with the administration of justice while on bail. Bail is denied only for those who pose a "substantial likelihood" of committing an offence or interfering with the administration of justice, and only where this "substantial likelihood" endangers "the protection or safety of the public". Moreover, detention is justified only when it is "necessary" for public safety. It is not justified where detention would merely be convenient or advantageous. Such grounds are sufficiently narrow to fulfil the first requirement of just cause under s. 11(*e*).

I am also satisfied that the public safety component of s. 515(10)(*b*) is necessary to promote the proper functioning of the bail system and is not undertaken for any purpose extraneous to the bail system. In my view, the bail system does not function properly if an accused interferes with the administration of justice while on bail. The entire criminal justice system is subverted if an accused interferes with the administration of justice. If an accused is released on bail, it must be on condition that he or she will refrain from tampering with the administration of justice. If there is a substantial likelihood that the accused will not give this cooperation, it furthers the objectives of the bail system to deny bail.

In my view, the bail system also does not function properly if individuals commit crimes while on bail. One objective of the entire system of criminal justice is to stop criminal behaviour. The bail system releases individuals who have been accused but not convicted of criminal conduct, but in order to achieve the objective of stopping criminal behaviour, such release must be on condition that the accused will not engage in criminal activity pending trial. In *Pearson*, the reality that persons engaged in drug trafficking tend to continue their criminal behaviour even after an arrest was one basis for concluding that there is just cause to require persons charged with certain narcotics offences to justify bail. Similarly, if there is a substantial likelihood that the accused will engage in criminal activity pending trial, it furthers the objectives of the bail system to deny bail.

.....

B. Validity of s. 515(6)(a)

.....

I am satisfied that the scope of s. 515(6)(*a*) is sufficiently narrow to satisfy the first requirement of just cause under s. 11(*e*). Section 515(6)(*a*) applies only to indictable offences. The number of accused who are charged with an indictable offence while on bail for another indictable offence is, hopefully, rather small. Furthermore, s. 515(6)(*a*) does not deny bail for all persons who have been charged with an indictable offence while on bail for another indictable offence, but rather denies bail only when these persons do not show cause that detention is not justified. Such grounds are sufficiently narrow to fulfil the first requirement of just cause under s. 11(*e*).

I also find that the effect of s. 515(6)(*a*) satisfies the second requirement of just cause under s. 11(*e*). The effect of s. 515(6)(*a*) is very similar to the effect of s. 515(6)(*d*). Both provisions establish a set of special bail rules in circumstances where the normal bail system does not function properly. As I noted in my discussion of s. 515(10)(*b*), one of the objectives of the criminal justice system, including the bail system, is to stop criminal behaviour. As a result, bail is granted on condition that the accused will cease criminal behaviour. Section 515(6)(*a*) establishes a set of special bail rules where there are reasonable grounds to believe that the accused has already breached this condition. In other words, the special bail rules in s. 515(6)(*a*) apply where there are reasonable grounds to believe that one of the objectives of the bail system, namely stopping criminal behaviour, is not being achieved. By requiring the accused to justify bail, s. 515(6)(*a*) seeks to ensure that the objective of stopping criminal behaviour will be achieved.

QUESTION

6. The "public interest" is considered by the officer in charge and a peace officer under ss. 495(2)(*d*), 497(1.1)(*a*) and 498(1.1)(*a*) of the *Criminal Code*. Those sections do particularize some of the circumstances that in-

form the "public interest" consideration. Are these provisions susceptible to *Charter* attack? Consider, in this regard, *R. v. Fosseneuve* (1995), 101 C.C.C. (3d) 61 (Man. Q.B.).

---

2. Criteria for Release

In the aftermath of *Morales*, s. 515(10) was amended in 1997. It provides that:

> **... the detention of an accused in custody is justified only on one or more of the following grounds:**
>
> **(*a*) where the detention is necessary to ensure his or her attendance in court ...;**
>
> **(*b*) where the detention is necessary for the protection or safety of the public, including any victim of or witness to the offence, having regard to all the circumstances including any substantial likelihood that the accused will, if released from custody, commit a criminal offence or interfere with the administration of justice; and**
>
> **(*c*) on any other just cause being shown and, without limiting the generality of the foregoing, where the detention is necessary in order to maintain confidence in the administration of justice, having regard to all the circumstances, including the apparent strength of the prosecution's case, the gravity of the nature of the offence, the circumstances surrounding its commission and the potential for a lengthy term of imprisonment.**

The question of detention "on any other just cause being shown" was considered by the Supreme Court of Canada in the following case.

R. v. HALL

(2002), 167 C.C.C. (3d) 449 (S.C.C.)

[The appellant was charged with first degree murder. The assailant had inflicted 37 wounds on his female victim and had tried to cut off her head. The murder caused significant public concern and a general fear that a killer was at large. A judge denied bail under s. 515(10)(*c*) of the *Criminal Code* in order "to maintain confidence in the administration of justice" in view of the highly charged aftermath of the murder, the strong evidence implicating the accused and the other factors referred to in s. 515(10)(*c*). A superior court judge dismissed the accused's *habeas corpus* application challenging the constitutionality of s. 515(10)(*c*). The Court of Appeal affirmed the decision.]

McLachlin C.J.C. [L'Heureux-Dubé, Gonthier, Bastarache and Binnie JJ. concurring]: —

.....

II. ANALYSIS

.....

3. Constitutionality of Bail Denial for "Any Other Just Cause"

The first phrase of s. 515(10)(c) which permits denial of bail "on any other just cause being shown" is unconstitutional. Parliament cannot confer a broad discretion on judges to deny bail, but must lay out narrow and precise circumstances in which bail can be denied: *Pearson* [(1992), 77 C.C.C. (3d) 124 (S.C.C.)] *and Morales* [(1992), 77 C.C.C. (3d) 91 (S.C.C.)]. This phrase does not specify any particular basis upon which bail could be denied. The denial of bail "on any other just cause" violates the requirements enunciated in *Morales, supra*, and therefore is inconsistent with the presumption of innocence and s. 11(*e*) of the *Charter*. Even assuming a pressing and substantial legislative objective for the phrase "on any other just cause being shown", the generality of the phrase impels its failure on the proportionality branch of the *Oakes* test (*R. v. Oakes*, [1986] 1 S.C.R. 103, 24 C.C.C. (3d) 321, 26 D.L.R. (4th) 200). Section 52 of the *Constitution Act, 1982*, provides that a law is void to the extent it is inconsistent with the *Charter*. It follows that this phrase fails. The next phrase in the provision, "without limiting the generality of the foregoing", is also void, since it serves only to confirm the generality of the phrase permitting a judge to deny bail "on any other just cause".

However, this does not mean that all of s. 515(10)(*c*) is unconstitutional. The loss of the above phrases leaves intact the balance of s. 515(10)(*c*), which is capable of standing alone grammatically and in terms of Parliament's intention. Whatever the fate of the broad initial discretion para. (*c*) seems to convey, Parliament clearly intended to permit bail to be denied where necessary to maintain confidence in the administration of justice, having regard to the four specified factors. This leaves the question of whether this latter part of s. 515(10)(*c*), considered on its own, is unconstitutional.

4. Constitutionality of the Provision for Denying Bail Where Necessary to Maintain Confidence in the Administration of Justice

(a) The Function of this Provision

Underlying much of the accused's argument is the suggestion that the first two grounds for denying bail suffice and that a third ground serves only to permit the denial of bail for vague and unspecified reasons. Accepting this argument, Iacobucci J. concludes, at para. 86, that "the fear that a situation may arise where the bail judge is unable to provide for the protection of the public without relying on the residual ground is without reasonable foundation".

Yet it seems to me that the facts of this case, as well as the facts in such cases as *R. v. MacDougal* (1999), 138 C.C.C. (3d) 38, 178 D.L.R. (4th) 227 (B.C.C.A.), and the pre-*Morales* case of *R. v. Dakin*, [1989] O.J. No. 1348 (QL) (C.A.), offer convincing proof that in some circumstances it may be necessary to the proper functioning of the bail system and, more broadly of the justice system, to deny bail even where there is no risk the accused will not attend trial or may re-offend or interfere with the administration of justice. Bolan J., on strong and cogent evidence, concluded that bail could not be denied on either of these grounds. But he also found that detention was necessary to maintain confidence in the administration of justice. The crime was heinous and unexplained. The evidence tying the accused to the crime was very strong. People in the community were afraid. As Proulx J.A., speaking of a similarly inexplicable and brutal murder stated in *R. v. Rondeau* (1996), 108 C.C.C. (3d) 474 (Que. C.A.), at p. 480 [translation], "[t]he more a crime like the present one is unexplained and unexplainable, the more worrisome bail becomes for society". The provision at issue serves an important purpose — to maintain confidence in the administration of justice in circumstances such as these.

Therefore, Parliament provided for denial of bail where paras. (*a*) and (*b*) of s. 515(10) are not met but the judge, viewing the situation objectively through the lens of the four factors stipulated by Parliament, has decided that there is "just cause" for refusing bail. To allow an accused to be released into the community on bail in the face of a heinous crime and overwhelming evidence may erode the public's confidence in the administration of justice. Where justice is not seen to be done by the public, confidence in the bail system and, more generally, the entire justice system may falter. When the public's confidence has reasonably been called into question, dangers such as public unrest and vigilantism may emerge.

Public confidence is essential to the proper functioning of the bail system and the justice system as a whole: see *Valente v. The Queen*, [1985] 2 S.C.R. 673, at p. 689, 23 C.C.C. (3d) 193, 24 D.L.R. (4th) 161. Indeed, public confidence and the integrity of the rule of law are inextricably intertwined. As Hall J.A. stated in *MacDougal, supra*, at p. 48:

> To sustain the rule of law, a core value of our society, it is necessary to maintain public respect for the law and the courts. A law that is not broadly acceptable to most members of society will usually fall into desuetude: witness the unhappy prohibition experiment in the United States. *Courts must be careful not to pander to public opinion or to take account of only the overly excitable, but I believe that to fail to have regard to the provisions of s. 515(10)(c) in the relatively rare cases where it can properly be invoked would tend to work against maintaining broad public confidence in the way justice is administered in this country.* [Emphasis added.]

.....

I conclude that a provision that allows bail to be denied on the basis that the accused's detention is required to maintain confidence in the administration of justice is neither superfluous nor unjustified. It serves a very real need to permit a bail judge to detain an accused pending trial for the purpose of maintaining the public's confidence if the circumstances of the case so warrant. Without public confidence, the bail system and the justice system generally stand compromised. While the circumstances in which recourse to this ground for bail denial may not arise frequently, when they do it is essential that a means of denying bail be available.

(b) Is the Ground for Denying Bail Unconstitutionally Vague or Overbroad?

This brings us to the main issue — whether denying bail "to maintain confidence in the administration of justice" having regard to the factors set out in s. 515(10)(*c*), complies with s. 11(*e*) of the *Charter*, which provides that bail may be denied only for "just cause".

The appellant says that maintaining confidence in the administration of justice is vague and overbroad, and amounts to substituting a new phrase for the ground of "public interest" which the Court held unconstitutional in *Morales, supra*. However, the ground of maintaining confidence in the administration of justice as articulated in para. (*c*) is much narrower and more precise than the old public interest ground. The term "public interest" is imprecise and "has not been given a constant or settled meaning by the courts": *Morales, supra*, at p. 732. The articulated ground of maintaining confidence in the administration of justice, by contrast, relies on concepts held to be justiciable and offers considerable precision.

The test for impermissible vagueness is whether the law so lacks precision that it fails to give sufficient guidance for legal debate: *R. v. Nova Scotia Pharmaceutical Society*, [1992] 2 S.C.R. 606 at pp. 638-40, 74 C.C.C. (3d) 289, 93 D.L.R. (4th) 36. The test sets a high threshold: *Winko v. British Columbia (Forensic Psychiatric Institute)*, [1999] 2 S.C.R. 625, 135 C.C.C. (3d) 129, 175 D.L.R. (4th) 193, at para. 68. Laws are of necessity general statements that must cover a variety of situations. A degree of generality is therefore essential, and is not to be confused with vagueness, which occurs when the law is so imprecise that it does not permit legal debate about its meaning and application. As noted in *Morales, supra*, at p. 729: "To require absolute precision would be to create an impossible constitutional standard".

The phrase "proper administration of justice" was held to provide an intelligible standard and hence not overbroad in *Canadian Broadcasting Corp. v. New Brunswick (Attorney General)*, [1996] 3 S.C.R. 480, 110 C.C.C. (3d) 193, 139 D.L.R. (4th) 385, in the context of preserving openness in the administration of justice. In that case, La Forest J. defined the phrase as including a discretionary power of the courts to control their own process. At para. 59, he states:

> The phrase "administration of justice" appears throughout legislation in Canada, including the *Charter*. Thus, "proper administration of justice", which of necessity has been the subject of judicial interpretation, provides the judiciary with a workable standard.

If the phrase "administration of justice" is sufficiently precise, it must follow that the phrase "necessary to maintain confidence in the administration of justice", amplified by a direction to consider four specified factors, is not unconstitutionally vague. The inquiry is narrowed to the reasonable community perception of the necessity of denying bail to maintain confidence in the administration of justice, judicially determined through the objective lens of "all the circumstances, including the apparent strength of the prosecution's case, the gravity of the nature of the offence, the circumstances surrounding its commission and the potential for a lengthy term of imprisonment". Even where a standard viewed alone is impermissibly vague, such factors may save it: *Nova Scotia Pharmaceutical Society, supra*.

The appellant argues that the factors set out in s. 515(10)(*c*) cannot be sufficient because cases under the old "public interest" criterion had identified similar factors, which were insufficient to save the public interest grounds for the denial of bail in *Morales, supra*. However, reference to factors in cases cannot be equated to a legislative direction to consider specific factors. Moreover, "public interest" is a broader and vaguer ground than "maintain confidence in the administration of justice". The latter is but one aspect of the former.

The result is that the ground based on maintaining confidence in the administration of justice is more narrowly defined than the "public interest" standard in *Morales, supra*. The operative concept is identified and criteria delineate a basis for the exercise of the discretion. The direction to consider all the circumstances does not render a provision unconstitutionally vague. In my opinion, the phrase does not result in a "standardless sweep". Like the Court of Appeal of Ontario and the Court of Appeal of British Columbia in *MacDougal, supra*, I am satisfied that the stated standard meets the test of providing an intelligible standard for debate.

This leaves the argument that the ground for denial of bail is overbroad, or of whether the means chosen by the state go further than necessary to accomplish its objective: see *R. v. Heywood*, [1994] 3 S.C.R. 761, at pp. 792-93, 94 C.C.C. (3d) 481, 120 D.L.R. (4th) 348. The meaning of a law may be plain, yet the law may be overbroad: *Heywood, supra*, at pp. 792-93. It is important that a bail provision not trench more than required on the accused's liberty and the presumption of innocence. Denial of bail must be confined to a "narrow set of circumstances" related to the proper functioning of the bail system: *Pearson* and *Morales, supra*.

Section 515(10)(*c*) sets out specific factors which delineate a narrow set of circumstances under which bail can be denied on the basis of maintaining confidence in the administration of justice. As discussed earlier, situations may arise where, despite the fact the accused is not likely to abscond or commit further crimes while awaiting trial, his presence in the community will call into question the public's confidence in the administration of justice. Whether such a situation has arisen is judged by all the circumstances, but in particular the four factors that Parliament has set out in s. 515(10)(*c*) — the apparent strength of the prosecution's case, the gravity of the nature of the offence, the circumstances surrounding its commission and the potential for lengthy imprisonment. Where, as here, the crime is horrific, inexplicable, and strongly linked to the accused, a justice system that cannot detain the accused risks losing the public confidence upon which the bail system and the justice system as a whole repose.

This, then, is Parliament's purpose: to maintain public confidence in the bail system and the justice system as whole. The question is whether the means it has chosen go further than necessary to achieve that purpose. In my view, they do not. Parliament has hedged this provision for bail with important safeguards. The judge must be satisfied that detention is not only advisable but *necessary*. The judge must, moreover, be satisfied that detention is necessary not just to any goal, but *to maintain confidence in the administration of justice*. Most importantly, the judge makes this appraisal objectively through the lens of the four factors Parliament has specified.

The judge cannot conjure up his own reasons for denying bail; while the judge must look at all the circumstances, he must focus particularly on the factors Parliament has specified. At the end of the day, the judge can only deny bail if satisfied that in view of these factors and related circumstances, a reasonable member of the community would be satisfied that denial is necessary to maintain confidence in the administration of justice. In addition, as McEachern C.J.B.C. (in Chambers) noted in *R. v. Nguyen* (1997), 119 C.C.C. (3d) 269, the reasonable person making this assessment must be one properly informed about "the philosophy of the legislative provisions, *Charter* values and the actual circumstances of the case" (p. 274). For these reasons, the provision does not authorize a "standardless sweep" nor confer open-ended judicial discretion. Rather, it strikes an appropriate balance between the rights of the accused and the need to maintain justice in the community. In sum, it is not overbroad.

[The Chief Justice reviewed the application of s. 515(10)(*c*) by the bail judge and held that there was no error in reasoning by Bolan J.]

[Iacobucci, Major, Arbour and LeBel JJ. dissented.]

Gary Trotter, *The Law of Bail in Canada*, 2nd ed. (Scarborough, Ont.: Carswell, 1999) at p. 123 provides a thorough review of the factors that would be considered in determining whether there is "just cause for detention". These are summarized briefly below.

- **Section 515(10)(*a*) — Primary Ground**
    - **The nature of the offence and the potential penalty**
    - **Strength of the evidence against the accused**
    - **The ties the accused has to the community**
    - **The accused's record for compliance with court orders on previous occasions**
    - **The accused's behaviour prior to apprehension: evidence of flight**
- **Section 515(10)(*b*) — The Secondary Ground**
    - **Criminal record of the accused**
    - **Whether the accused is already on bail or on probation**
    - **The nature of the offence and the strength of the evidence**
    - **The stability of the accused person**
    - **Conduct of the accused with respect to the likelihood of interference with the administration of justice**
- **Section 515(10)(*c*) — The Tertiary Ground**
    - **The seriousness of the offence**
    - **The nature and quality of the accused's alleged conduct**
    - **The strength of the evidence against the accused**
    - **The nature of the community in which the offence took place**
    - **The character of the accused**
    - **Young offenders**

QUESTION

7. Under what circumstances should an accused charged with murder get bail, despite the gravity of the offence?

---

3. Evidence at Hearing

Section 518 of the *Criminal Code* regulates the type of evidence that can be admitted at the bail hearing. The justice may receive and base his or her decision on evidence considered credible or trustworthy. This permits hearsay evidence to be admitted, which would not be admissible at trial. Practice varies as to how the Crown presents the evidence it relies on at a bail hearing. In Ontario, the defence often consents to the reading in of the alleged facts by the Crown and will direct questions, through the court, to the Crown to clarify matters. For example, "If I might ask my friend, through Your Worship, whether any physical evidence whatsoever was discovered in the accused's possession when she was arrested." When consent is withheld or in special circumstances, the Crown may call the investigating officer or, indeed, its court officer to outline the alleged facts. The Crown is permitted to lead all relevant evidence, including prior convictions, outstanding charges and the circumstances of the alleged offence, particularly as they relate to the probability of conviction.

R. v. WOO

(1994), 90 C.C.C. (3d) 404 (B.C.S.C.)

Fraser J.: — This is an application by the accused under s. 520 of the *Criminal Code* for a review of an order made in the Provincial Court of British Columbia that he be detained in custody pending his trial on a charge of trafficking in cocaine.

The detention order was made on the strength of statements made by Crown counsel to the court. The Crown tendered no evidence, in the ordinary sense of that word: no witness was called, nor was any affidavit filed.

It is the contention of the accused that a justice acting under s. 515 of the *Criminal Code* — and a judge reviewing an order made under s. 515, as I am doing here — can only act on the basis of evidence in deciding whether to detain an accused, where the statements of counsel are not agreed to, as happened below.

A ruling which accepted the proposition advanced by the accused would not end matters. Because of the charge he is facing, the accused here has the burden of showing cause why his detention in custody is not justified (s. 515(6)(*d*)). I am asked to consider the evidence tendered on behalf of the accused, to vacate the order made by the court below and order that the accused be released.

Section 518(1) of the *Criminal Code* governs show cause applications under s. 515.

.....

This section was considered by the Ontario Court of Appeal in 1972, in *R. v. West* (1972), 9 C.C.C. (2d) 369, [1973] 1 O.R. 211, 20 C.R.N.S. 15 (Ont. C.A.). In that case, the only material presented by the Crown to the judge before whom the show cause hearing took place consisted of the "oral statements of counsel". The court held that, unless relevant matters were agreed on by the accused and the prosecutor under s. 518(1)(*d*), "it would seem reasonably clear that [the facts] should be the subject of sworn testimony" (at p. 372). The court grounded this conclusion on para. (*e*), which says that the justice may base his decision "on evidence considered credible or trustworthy". The court said "[T]he application cannot initially be supported properly in any other way" (at p. 372). The court went on to say (at p. 373):

> If the prosecutor presents no material to support his opposition to the application, it will undoubtedly be granted . . .
>
> On the other hand, if the prosecutor does wish to show cause for withholding release and to file material for such purpose, again, that material must take the form of evidence or agreement.

The court specifically held that facts stated by counsel, not agreed to, could not be considered and weighed by the judge (at p. 373).

With respect to para. (*a*), which says that the justice may "make such inquiries, on oath or otherwise, of and concerning the accused as he considers desirable", the court said (at p. 374):

> What of the effect of [s. 518(1)(*a*)]? That question does not call for an answer here because Mr. Justice Osler did not exercise the power conferred upon him by that subsection, unless it can be said that the statements of counsel in his presence were the result of the type of inquiry envisaged by that subsection. It is my impression that they could not be so described. Hence, I prefer to defer any comment upon the scope of the subsection until its provisions have been relied upon or complaint is made that they ought to have been invoked.

.....

[Ewaschuk J. of the Ontario High Court reached an opposite conclusion in *R. v. Kevork.*] Shortly afterward, Barr J., of the Ontario High Court, in *R. v. Hajdu* [(1984), 14 C.C.C. (3d) 563], disagreed with *Kevork* and held that the oral statements of Crown counsel at a bail hearing were insufficient, unless admitted by the accused.

Where "relevant matters" are not agreed to, as contemplated by para. (*d*), *Hajdu* holds (at p. 566):

> A justice of the peace must act judicially. He cannot act on conjecture, private information, gossip or what he reads in the papers. Provided he is satisfied that it is credible or trustworthy he may act on unsworn evidence, for example the evidence of the child who does not understand the nature of an oath. Subject to the same limitation he may act on hearsay evidence. But he must act on evidence. The statement of the Crown Attorney in this case was not evidence. The *Code* permits the Crown Attorney to lead certain kinds of evidence, not give it. It does not purport to abolish the rule that counsel may not give evidence.

In the concluding passage in the judgment, the following was said (at p. 572):

> We are dealing with the imprisonment of a man the law presumes to be innocent and he is entitled to be released on bail unless the case for detention is properly established. No doubt the procedure followed by the prosecutor in this case was convenient. This does not justify it. While bail hearings should proceed expeditiously and should be limited to determining the facts relevant to the detention of the accused or the granting of bail, the rights of an accused person must not be sacrificed on the altar of expediency.

.....

It is not and never has been the ordinary practice in British Columbia for the Crown to lead evidence at a bail hearing. Crown counsel gives an outline to the court of the evidence which it expects to lead at trial, together with other pertinent information about the accused. The same cannot be said when the shoe is on the other foot, that is, when the burden of justifying release is on the accused. In such situations, the accused sometimes presents sworn and unsworn evidence to the court (the unsworn evidence typically consisting of letters of reference). That is what was done before the court below in this case.

Early in the history of the present provisions of the *Criminal Code* concerning judicial interim release, a decision of this court described our local practice. In *R. v. Baker* (1973), 13 C.C.C. (2d) 340 (B.C.S.C.) Berger J., on a bail review, held as follows: "I am going on the allegations that were made by Crown counsel. That is all I have to go on. But that is evidence for purposes of the *Bail Reform Act* ...".

Berger J. does not seem to have been referred to *West*. The issue before me does not appear to have been before him. He, of course, was using the word "evidence" in an informal sense.

After the decision in *Hajdu*, the issue was raised in British Columbia. Unfortunately, the debate took place in apparent ignorance of the decision of the Ontario Court of Appeal in *West* and of the decisions from Nova Scotia [not reproduced herein] I have referred to.

The first of the recent cases from British Columbia is the 1986 decision *R. v. Dhindsa* (1986), 30 C.C.C. (3d) 368, 17 W.C.B. 28 (B.C.S.C.). In that case, Toy J. held (at p. 370):

> Since 1972 in this province the lower courts and the superior courts of criminal jurisdiction have consistently permitted both Crown counsel and defence counsel to make assertions as to what the evidence anticipated to be led will be. Where there is a controversy or contradiction, in my experience, affidavits have been tendered and relied upon. If affidavits will not suffice to resolve the conflict, then *viva voce* evidence could be called with attendant cross-examination. Happily, the situation has not had to go to that last step in any hearing that I have presided over, but I can see that such a situation could well arise.
>
> In *R. v. DiMatteo* (1981), 60 C.C.C. (2d) 262 at p. 263, Mr. Justice Craig, of our Court of Appeal, tacitly approved the practice of Crown counsel outlining the gist of the Crown's allegations without the necessity of calling any evidence. I remain unpersuaded that *R. v. Hajdu* should be adopted and followed in this province.

Despite the concluding sentence in this passage, I cannot identify a difference between *Dhindsa* and *Hajdu*. Toy J. contemplated evidence being tendered where there is a controversy or a contradiction, that is, to use the words of subclause (*d*), where there is no agreement on relevant matters.

With respect, I am unable to find in *R. v. DiMatteo* (1981), 60 C.C.C. (2d) 262 (B.C.C.A.), more than a simple recitation of what had occurred in the court below.

.....

[A further analysis of the case law follows.]

It is a curious truth that, although criminal law and criminal procedure are in the exclusive jurisdiction of the Government of Canada, the procedures actually followed in criminal cases vary from province to province, and even from place to place within a province. This is not necessarily a bad thing. Local circumstances can have an important impact, as is demonstrated in *R. v. O'Neill* [(1973), 11 C.C.C. (2d) 240 (N.B.S.C.)], in which the court took steps in response to the fact that no sittings of a court which could review bail were expected to take place until four months after the original show cause hearing, in which detention of the accused was ordered. However, I can see no local circumstances in this province which call for a different interpretation of s. 515 from that which prevails in other provinces.

I do not see any conflict among *West*, *Hajdu* and *Dhindsa*. They arrive at this result:

(1) Where Crown counsel and defence counsel agree as to matters of fact, those facts may be presented to the court by means of statements of counsel.

(2) Where counsel do not agree as to matters of fact (where, in the words of *Dhindsa*, there is "controversy or contradiction"), evidence must be tendered.

(3) If evidence is required, it sometimes may be presented in affidavit form and may include hearsay.

.....

... I find myself led to the conclusion that *West*, *Hajdu* and *Dhindsa*, as I have summarized them above, govern the practice to be followed in British Columbia on applications under s. 515 of the *Criminal Code*, whether the onus is on the Crown or the accused.

It is well understood that, in sentencing hearings, the Crown must prove any fact it alleges relevant to sentence which is disputed by the defence. I can see no reason why the standard should be lower when what is in issue is imprisonment before trial. The reality is that there can be frailties in the prosecution dossier of which Crown counsel may have no inkling at the time of the bail hearing. *Hajdu* itself illustrates that. By the same token, the Crown may well wish to take issue with the assertions of the defence.

The procedure I have endorsed was in fact that followed by Toy J. in *Dhindsa*, where he held that the judge in the court below was correct in "giving no weight" to Crown counsel's assertions that the four accused were members of a particular group, because they were disputed. He commented that the Crown had the option of calling evidence on the point (at p. 372). Where Toy J. did rely on the assertions of Crown counsel (as he clearly did), those assertions had not been disputed.

Of course, as is stated in *West*, where the situation requires Crown counsel or defence counsel to lead evidence, time must be afforded to counsel to assemble the evidence upon which it is proposed to rely (at p. 373). In fact, the vast majority of bail hearings in Ontario are determined on agreed facts, without evidence.

It is apparent from the transcript of the reasons given by the learned Provincial Court judge here that she relied upon the statements of Crown counsel in holding that the accused had not justified his release from detention. It follows that I find that she fell into error, given that the facts alleged by Crown counsel were not agreed to — they were expressly denied —by defence counsel. In the circumstances, I propose to review the evidence put forward by the accused and the statements of his counsel which the Crown does not dispute in considering the primary and secondary grounds.

[That review follows.]

QUESTION

8. What should the relationship be between the role of the Crown and the role of the police? More particularly, should the Crown resist judicial interim release when the police recommend it? What special approach should the defence take to a bail hearing when the police, but not the Crown, recommend release?

Section 518(1)(*a*) of the *Criminal Code* states that "the justice may ... make such inquiries, on oath or otherwise, of and concerning the accused as he [or she] considers desirable". However, s. 518(1)(*b*) states that "the accused shall not be examined by the justice or any other person except counsel for the accused respecting the offence ... charged", and the accused shall not be cross-examined respecting that offence unless the accused has already testified respecting that offence.

QUESTION

9. The accused's spouse testifies at his bail hearing in support of his release on a charge of armed robbery. She is extensively cross-examined by the Crown about the accused's whereabouts when the offence allegedly occurred and about other matters respecting the charges. Is the cross-examination permissible? Would your answer be the same or different if she had been cross-examined about her conversations with the accused regarding the alleged offence? Consider, in the latter regard, s. 4(3) of the *Canada Evidence Act*, R.S.C. 1985, c. C-5.

---

4. How to Conduct a Bail Hearing: Tactical Considerations

See Gary Trotter, *The Law of Bail in Canada*, 2nd ed. (Scarborough, Ont.: Carswell, 1999), at pp. 193-238 for a review of the tactical considerations that inform the conduct of a bail hearing.

5. Special Orders and Sureties

As previously noted, s. 515 outlines the types of release orders that can be made. Section 519(1) and (2) regulates the timing of any release order.

QUESTION

10. **The accused is arrested for an offence and held for a bail hearing. He is on an immigration "hold". When should his bail hearing be held? Similarly, the accused is serving a custodial sentence when arrested and held on another offence. When should his bail hearing be heard? Consider, in this regard, s. 519(1) of the *Criminal Code*.**

Section 515(12) permits the justice to order an accused who is detained in custody to refrain from communication with any witness or other named person, except under specified conditions, if at all.

QUESTION

11. **Under what circumstances should the Crown ask for such a non-communication direction?**

Section 517 regulates the non-publication of certain matters at a bail hearing. An order must be made if requested by the accused and may be made if requested by the Crown.

QUESTION

12. **Are there any circumstances under which the accused would not request a non-publication order? If there are, what should the Crown's position be? Does s. 517 confer the power to prohibit publication of the decision to grant or refuse release, as opposed to the reasons for such a decision? Consider, in this regard, *R. v. Forget* (1982), 65 C.C.C. (2d) 373 (Ont. C.A.).**

Where a recognizance involving sureties has been ordered, the court is empowered to name particular persons as sureties, rather than simply permitting one or more sufficient sureties in a specific amount (s. 515(2.1) of the *Criminal Code*).

QUESTION

13. **What is the purpose of s. 515(2.1) and how should it be used by defence counsel?**

The *Criminal Code* is silent with respect to the non-financial qualifications of sureties.

QUESTIONS

14. Who would and would not make a good surety? What considerations should prevail, apart from financial worth? Can a person who is already a surety for one accused act as surety for another accused? Can a proposed surety in Ontario demonstrate financial sufficiency through ownership of property in Quebec? Consider, in this regard, *R. v. Martin (No. 2)* (1980), 57 C.C.C. (2d) 31 (Ont. C.A.). What happens if a surety changes his or her mind about acting as a surety after the accused is released? What if the surety learns that the accused failed to attend court as required or otherwise failed to comply with his or her recognizance pending trial? What if the police learn these facts first and arrest the accused on new charges? What implications are there for the surety and for the accused's original bail? Finally, can the accused and the surety agree that the surety will be reimbursed for acting as a surety or for any financial losses that may be occasioned if the accused breaches his or her bail? Consider ss. 139(1), 524 and 762 to 773 of the *Criminal Code*.

15. The accused Jesse James fails to appear for trial. He had entered into a recognizance in the amount of $5,000 with one surety, Ma Barker. What should the Crown ask the presiding judge to do? Consider ss. 770 and 771 of the *Criminal Code* (this procedure is often known as noting the bail for estreat).

D. "SHOW CAUSE" OR "BAIL" HEARINGS FOR SECTION 469 OFFENCES

Section 522 governs bail hearings for offences listed in s. 469 of the *Criminal Code*. Release can be ordered only by a judge of the superior court of criminal jurisdiction upon the application of the accused. There is no automatic bail hearing. The onus is on the accused.

QUESTION

16. Does the reverse onus contained in s. 522(2) of the *Criminal Code* violate the *Charter*? Compare, in this regard, *R. v. Sanchez* (1999), 136 C.C.C. (3d) 31 (N.S.C.A.); *R. v. Pugsley* (1982), 2 C.C.C. (3d) 266 (N.S.S.C. App. Div.); and *R. v. Bray* (1983), 2 C.C.C. (3d) 325 (Ont. C.A.).

E. JUDICIAL REVIEWS OF RELEASE OR DETENTION ORDERS: SECTIONS 520, 521 AND 525

Section 520 of the *Criminal Code* provides for a review of an order made by a justice or provincial court judge upon application for such review by the accused. The order sought to be reviewed may be a detention order or the terms of a release order. The application is brought before a judge as defined by s. 493 of the *Criminal Code*, upon two clear days'

written notice or, if consented to, a shorter period (s. 520(2) of the *Criminal Code*). Each jurisdiction may supplement s. 520 by rules of the court. For example, in Ontario, Rules 20.03(1) and 20.05(1) of the Ontario Court of Justice Criminal Proceedings Rules, SI/92-99, outline the contents of the written notice and the supporting materials to be provided. These include a transcript of the proceedings under review, an affidavit of the accused and where practicable, the affidavits of employers and prospective sureties. Rule 20.05(2) outlines the required contents of the accused's affidavit in Ontario. It may provide useful guidance for the content of such affidavits in other jurisdictions. As well, *viva voce* evidence is often tendered at a review.

The accused need not be present at the review. Where the accused is in custody, s. 520(3) of the *Criminal Code* requires a judge's order to be secured in order for the accused to be brought to court. Practice varies among jurisdictions on securing the judge's order. For example, in Ontario, under Rule 20.03(2), if the notice seeking review reflects that the accused wishes to be present, and the supporting materials contain the requisite particulars (such as the place of custody and a draft order), the judge's order can be made, *ex parte*, without counsel's attendance.

Section 520(7) of the *Criminal Code* and Ontario Rule 20.05(3) allow the prosecutor to respond by adducing evidence *viva voce* or by affidavit.

Under s. 520(8) of the *Criminal Code*, no further application for review can be brought within 30 days of the order made on review, except with leave of a judge. See also *R. v. Saracino* (1989), 47 C.C.C. (3d) 185 (Ont. H.C.J.).

Section 521 of the *Criminal Code* provides for a review, upon application by the Crown, in very similar terms to s. 520.

It is clear that a change in circumstances (reflected in new evidence before the reviewing judge) may cause the original order to be vacated and a new order to be made.[7] As well, new evidence may be tendered by the respondent to justify the continuation of the original order. The cases have seriously conflicted on the test for a reviewing judge, in the absence of changed circumstances. In any event, the applicant bears the burden of showing cause why the initial order should be vacated.

R. v. CARRIER

(1979), 51 C.C.C. (2d) 307 (Man. C.A.)

[The Manitoba Court of Appeal considered the bail procedures under what are now s. 520(7) and (8) of the *Criminal Code*.]

Matas J.A. (in Chambers): —

---

7 **Author's Note: see ss. 520(7)(*c*) and 521(8)(*c*); *R. v. English* (1983), 8 C.C.C. (3d) 487 (Ont. Co. Ct.); *R. v. Saswirsky* (1984), 17 C.C.C. (3d) 341 (Ont. H.C.J.). It would also appear that new evidence will not be refused simply because it could have been tendered at the original hearing.**

.....

In *Re Powers and the Queen* (1972), 9 C.C.C. (2d) 533, 20 C.R.N.S. 23 (Ont. H.C.J.), Lerner, J., reviewed the provisions of the *Code* and commented on the informal practice which had developed in review applications. In order to settle the practice, the learned Judge said [at p. 536] that on the return of such applications there should be filed in addition to affidavit material:

(1) the order of detention; and
(2) the record, including:
 (i) a copy of the information,
 (ii) the *reasons* for the order of the Provincial Judge,
 (iii) a transcript of any *viva voce* evidence of the accused or witnesses called by the accused or the prosecution.

Included in the material before me were the following:

1. the Queen's Bench file which includes the notice of motion in that Court and an affidavit by the accused sworn September 28, 1979;
2. the notice of motion referred to at the beginning of these reasons, together with a request for "written reasons for judgment, concerning" the policy of the Court of Queen's Bench and County Court Judges Criminal Court pursuant to which the Judges thereof refuse to hear applications under s. 457.5 when transcripts of original hearings are unavailable;
3. affidavit of Mr. A.D. Bourgeois, a student in the office of counsel for the accused; that affidavit was sworn October 17, 1979, and dealt with the steps taken by the accused's counsel;
4. informations in respect of each of the charges;
5. police report (filed with the consent of Mr. Wilinofsky).

.....

In Scollin, *Pre-Trial Release* (1977), p. 64, the divergent judicial views on s. 457.5(7) [now s. 520(7)] (and s. 457.6(8) [now s. 520(8)]) are summarized in this way:

> Two lines of thought have developed in relation to the matter of "review". One line concludes that the procedure is essentially a new hearing in which the judge on review is entitled to decide anew the proper order to be made. The other takes the stand that, no matter what the judge on review might himself have decided, the existing order should stand unless error is demonstrated.

It has also been suggested that the review procedure may be similar to that of an appeal by way of trial *de novo* in summary conviction offences.

In my respectful opinion, the review should not be categorized as an ordinary appeal nor is it helpful to relate a review to summary conviction appeals. On the former point, I agree with the comment made by my colleague O'Sullivan, J.A., in *R. v. Crellin*, [1976] 6 W.W.R. 661 at p. 662 (in Chambers), where he rejected the suggestion that "the review of bail provided for by Parliament is in the nature of an appeal from the order being reviewed". I am satisfied that Parliament intended the review to be conducted with due consideration for the initial order but, depending on the circumstances, with an independent discretion to be exercised by the review Court.

In my opinion, a useful summary of the scope of a review, in accord with the intent of s. 457.5(7), was set out by Berger J., in *R. v. Hill*, [1973] 5 W.W.R. 382 at p. 383, where he said:

> Upon an application for review the onus lies on the accused. He must show cause to vacate the order made below: s. 457.5(7)(*e*). In my view that onus is discharged if it is shown that the circumstances have altered since the hearing below: see Hinkson J. in *Regina v. Orlovich* (1972), 8 C.C.C. (2d) 567 (B.C.). Or, if the judge below misconceived the facts or was guilty of an error in law, the onus would be discharged: Verchere J. in *Regina v. Horvat* (1972), 9 C.C.C. (2d) 1 (B.C.). Those are not the only grounds. A judge of this Court may, if cause is shown, substitute his own discretion for that of the judge below: Anderson J. in *Regina v. Thompson*, [1972] 3 W.W.R. 729, 18 C.R.N.S. 102, 7 C.C.C. (2d) 70.

This approach is in accord with the definition of review found in Blacks Law Dictionary 4th ed., which reads: "To re-examine judicially. A reconsideration; second view of examination; revision; consideration for purposes of correction" and in the Shorter Oxford English Dictionary, where review is defined as follows: "2. *Law*. Revision of a sentence, etc., by some other court or authority." Revision is defined as: "1. The action of revising; esp. critical or careful examination or perusal with a view to correcting or improving."

It is necessary for the Court conducting the review to establish rules of practice and to require certain material to be available to the reviewing Judge. But I do not understand the judgment of Lerner, J. in *Powers, supra*, to require a transcript in all cases, even though no witnesses were called at the original hearing. To impose an inflexible rule requiring transcripts in all cases might defeat the intent of the legislation to encourage expeditious disposition of these matters. Where the review is not in the nature of an appeal, the absence of a transcript may not be a crucial factor. And the absence of the Court Reporter in the case at bar made it impossible to obtain a transcript within a reasonable time.

No evidence having been called before the Provincial Court Judge, the transcript would have contained the submissions of counsel and the reasons of the Provincial Court Judge. Having a transcript of counsels' submissions would not have appreciably assisted the reviewing Court in view of the comment of Crown counsel on the nature of his submission. Mr. Schachter also said that, very often, because of the volume of cases heard in Provincial Court, the reasons for denial of order for release are brief and might only be a terse statement that the detention of the accused is justified. Although generally, reasons of the trial Judge given at the initial hearing are useful, there is nothing here to suggest that the reasons went beyond the minimum. In my respectful opinion, the imposition of the requirement for production of a transcript was not necessary in this case. As for the agreed statement of facts, it is my view that it was not necessary either in view of the material available to the reviewing Court.

[The court then proceeds to assess, and ultimately, dismiss the application.]

Section 525 of the *Criminal Code* also provides for an automatic right of review for an accused charged with a non-s. 469 offence, not otherwise detained in custody, where the trial has been delayed for specified time periods. For indictable offences, this is often referred to as a *90-day review*.

QUESTIONS

17. Does the accused have the automatic right to a s. 525 review 90 days after his first court appearance, even if a s. 520 review was unsuccessful only several weeks before? Consider, in this regard, s. 525(1)(*a*)(ii) of the *Criminal Code*.

18. The accused has been unable to meet the terms of a release order, due to the unanticipated lack of a satisfactory surety. Does the accused have the right to a 90-day review? Consider, in this regard, *Ex p. Srebot* (1975), 28 C.C.C. (2d) 160 (B.C.C.A.).

Pursuant to s. 680 of the *Criminal Code* the Court of Appeal on direction by the Chief Justice or acting Chief Justice, may review a s. 522 order made in relation to a s. 469 offence. This manner of review is not frequently successful.

F. BAIL VARIATIONS AND OTHER WAYS TO REVISIT THE ACCUSED'S RELEASE OR DETENTION

For non-s. 469 offences, s. 523(1)(*b*) of the *Criminal Code* states that where an accused is at large on a form of release, the release remains in effect until the trial is completed and, where the accused is found guilty, until sentence is imposed, *unless* the trial court orders that the accused be taken into custody pending sentence. For s. 469 offences, the release remains in effect only until the trial is completed (s. 523(1)(*a*)). Counsel must anticipate and prepare the client for the possibility, in certain kinds of cases, that, if convicted, the accused may be detained pending sentence.

QUESTION

19. Section 520 of the *Criminal Code* provides no review for circumstances where the accused is detained pending sentence. Is there any way to secure the accused's release pending sentence, and if so, is it advisable? Consider, in this regard, *R. v. Morris* (1985), 21 C.C.C. (3d) 242 (Ont. C.A.), *R. v. Bencardino and De Carlo* (1973), 11 C.C.C. (2d) 549 (Ont. C.A.); *R. v. Smale* (1979), 51 C.C.C. (2d) 126 (Ont. C.A.).

Section 523(2) of the *Criminal Code* provides for other instances where the accused's interim release or detention may be revisited. Upon cause being shown, an interim release or detention order may be vacated and a new order made:

(a) by the trial court at any time. (For example, it comes to the court's attention that there has been a material change in circumstances since the original order: the accused has attempted to influence Crown witnesses, or, conversely, it has become clear that the Crown's case is substantially weaker than originally anticipated.)[8]

(b) by the justice or provincial court judge, at the completion of the preliminary inquiry, for a non-s. 469 offence, in relation to an offence for which the accused is ordered to stand trial. There is a s. 520 or s. 521 review from such an order. There is no s. 520 or s. 521 review from any of the other orders referred to in s. 523.

(c) with the consent of both parties, for a non-s. 469 offence, by any justice or provincial court judge, or, by the court, judge or justice before which or whom the accused is to be tried. The latter extends to any judicial officer of the court which will try the accused, and not only to the actual trial judge.

(d) with the consent of both parties, for a s. 469 offence, by any superior court judge.

These provisions become important when counsel seeks to vary terms of release by securing the Crown's consent and avoiding the more formal review procedures outlined in s. 520 of the *Criminal Code*. In some jurisdictions, even for a variation made on consent, the accused must step into custody, since the release order is being vacated, and must remain in custody, sometimes for several hours, while the new release order is prepared. The better judicial practice is to order that the previous order remain in effect until the new order is executed. Thus, there is no need for the accused to step into custody.

Often, the Crown will substitute a newly-worded information charging the same offences or related offences, prior to, or at the commencement of the preliminary inquiry. Section 523(1.1) of the *Criminal Code* enables the previous form of release to apply to the new information, without the necessity of a re-arrest and/or bail hearing. Where the accused or the Crown does not wish the previous bail order to apply, the issue can be revisited before the courts as listed in (c) and (d) above, without the consent of the opposing party (s. 523(2)(*c*)). Consider as well, s. 515.1 of the *Criminal Code*.

G. THE ACCUSED'S MISCONDUCT: REVOCATION OR CANCELLATION OF BAIL

Section 524 of the *Criminal Code* addresses the procedures employed where the accused is alleged to have violated specific terms of release or committed other offences while released.

---

8 *R. v. Prete and Tuchiaro* (1990), 47 C.R.R. 307 (Ont. H.C.J.). Note also that s. 523(2) permits only a previous *order* to be vacated. Accordingly, the Crown cannot use this section to cause the trial judge to detain an accused previously released on a summons, promise to appear or recognizance by the police. The Crown must follow the procedures in s. 524 of the *Criminal Code*, discussed below.

A justice may issue a warrant for the accused's arrest if satisfied that there are reasonable grounds to believe that the accused contravened or is about to contravene a release order or has committed an indictable offence after being released. A peace officer may arrest without a warrant where he or she so believes, on reasonable grounds. Section 524 outlines the cancellation hearing which applies to both s. 469 and non-s. 469 releases.

QUESTIONS

20. In a notorious Ontario case, Jonathan Yeo killed himself after murdering two women, one in Burlington, Ontario and one in New Brunswick. At an inquest investigating his death, the facts revealed that Yeo had been released on a surety bail for sexual assault with a weapon. At the time of his release, there was no condition that he not possess a firearm, although a 10 p.m. curfew had been imposed. He was stopped by American border officials while attempting to cross into the United States to visit Florida. He had a lawfully-possessed firearm in the car, as well as some disturbing notes and photographic cutouts. The American border officials contacted the relevant Canadian police forces who indicated that they could do nothing to detain Yeo. The Americans refused to permit Yeo into the United States and were compelled to send him on his way. Shortly thereafter, he murdered the first of his victims. What should the Canadian authorities have done?

21. The accused is on a surety bail for sexual assault. His release on bail had been vigorously contested by the Crown. While on bail, he is re-arrested for break and enter. He immediately pleads guilty, instead of embarking upon a difficult bail hearing. Since the Crown cannot rely upon his outstanding charge of sexual assault on sentence and the accused has no criminal record, he receives 30 days imprisonment. Several weeks later, he goes home. What could the Crown have done differently?

22. A justice of the peace issues an arrest warrant for an accused in Ontario. Under what circumstances can the warrant be executed in British Columbia? Would your answer be the same or different if the arrest warrant had been issued by an Ontario judge of the Superior Court of Justice, after the accused absconded during trial? Consider, in this regard, ss. 514, 528 and 703 of the *Criminal Code*.

CHAPTER 6

DISCLOSURE AND THIRD PARTY PRODUCTION

A. DISCLOSURE

1. Overview

Sections 650(3) (referring to indictable offences, and 802(1) (referring to summary conviction offences) of the *Criminal Code*, R.S.C. 1985, c. C-46, provide that the accused or defendant is entitled to make full answer and defence. Further, the Supreme Court has held that the right to make full answer and defence is constitutionally entrenched in ss. 7 and 11(*d*) of the *Charter*. In *R. v. Stinchcombe* (1991), 68 C.C.C. (3d) 1 (S.C.C.), the Supreme Court of Canada constitutionally entrenched the right of an accused to disclosure as necessarily incidental to the right to make full answer and defence.

R. v. STINCHCOMBE

(1991), 68 C.C.C. (3d) 1 (S.C.C.)

The judgment of the court was delivered by

Sopinka J.: — This appeal raises the issue of the Crown's obligation to make disclosure to the defence. A witness who gave evidence at the preliminary inquiry favourable to the accused was subsequently interviewed by agents for the Crown. Crown counsel decided not to call the witness and would not produce the statements obtained at the interview. The trial judge refused an application by the defence for disclosure on the ground that there was no obligation on the Crown to disclose the statements. The Court of Appeal affirmed the judgment at trial and the case is here with leave of this court.

.....

Production and discovery were foreign to the adversary process of adjudication in its earlier history when the element of surprise was one of the accepted weapons in the arsenal of the adversaries. This applied to both criminal and civil proceedings. Significantly, in civil proceedings this aspect of the adversary process has long since disappeared, and full discovery of documents and oral examination of parties and even witnesses are familiar features of the practice. This change resulted from acceptance of the principle that justice was better served when the element of surprise was eliminated from the trial and the parties were prepared to address issues on the basis of complete information of the case to be met. Surprisingly, in criminal cases in which the liberty of the subject is usually at stake, this aspect of the adversary system has lingered on. While the prosecution bar has generally cooperated in making disclosure on a voluntary basis, there has been considerable resistance to the enactment of comprehensive rules which would make the practice mandatory. This may be attributed to the fact that proposals for reform in this regard do not provide for reciprocal disclosure by the defence; see 1974 Working Paper at pp. 29-31; 1984 Report at pp. 13-5; Marshall Commission Report, *infra*, vol. 2, at pp. 242-4).

It is difficult to justify the position which clings to the notion that the Crown has no legal duty to disclose all relevant information. The arguments against the existence of such a duty are groundless while those in favour, are, in my view, overwhelming. The suggestion that the duty should be reciprocal may deserve consideration by this court in the future but is not a valid reason for absolving the Crown of its duty. The contrary contention fails to take account of the fundamental difference in the respective roles of the prosecution and the defence.

.....

I would add that the fruits of the investigation which are in the possession of counsel for the Crown are not the property of the Crown for use in securing a conviction but the property of the public to be used to ensure that justice is done. In contrast, the defence has no obligation to assist the prosecution and is entitled to assume a purely adversarial role toward the prosecution. The absence of a duty to disclose can, therefore, be justified as being consistent with this role.

.....

Refusal [by the Crown] to disclose is also justified on the ground that the material will be used to enable the defence to tailor its evidence to conform with information in the Crown's possession. For example, a witness may change his or her testimony to conform with a previous statement given to the police or counsel for the Crown. I am not impressed with this submission. All forms of discovery are subject to this criticism. There is surely nothing wrong in a witness refreshing his or her memory from a previous statement or document. The witness may even change his or her evidence as a result. This may rob the cross-examiner of a substantial advantage but fairness to the witness may require that a trap not be laid by allowing the witness to testify without the benefit of seeing contradictory writings which the prosecutor holds close to the vest. The principle has been accepted that the search for truth is advanced rather than retarded by disclosure of all relevant material.

Finally, it is suggested that disclosure may put at risk the security and safety of persons who have provided the prosecution with information. No doubt measures must occasionally be taken to protect the identity of witnesses and informers. Protection of the identity of informers is covered by the rules relating to informer privilege and exceptions thereto (see *Marks v. Beyfus* (1890), 25 Q.B.D. 494 (C.A.); *R. v. Scott* (1990), 61 C.C.C. (3d) 300, [1990] 3 S.C.R. 979, 2 C.R. (4th) 153), and any rules with respect to disclosure would be subject to this and other rules of privilege. With respect to witnesses, persons who have information that may be evidence favourable to the accused will have to have their identity disclosed sooner or later. Even the identity of an informer is subject to this fact of life by virtue of the "innocence exception" to the informer privilege rule (*Marks v. Beyfus*, *supra*, at pp. 498-9; *R. v. Scott*, *supra*, at pp. 315-6; *Bisaillon v. Keable* (1983), 7 C.C.C. (3d) 385 at pp. 411-2, 2 D.L.R. (4th) 193, [1983] 2 S.C.R. 60; *Solicitor-General of Canada v. Royal Commission of Inquiry (Health Records in Ontario)* (1980), 62 C.C.C. (2d) 193, 128 D.L.R. (3d) 193, [1981] 2 S.C.R. 494). It will, therefore, be a matter of the timing of the disclosure rather than whether disclosure should be made at all. The prosecutor must retain a degree of discretion in respect of these matters. The discretion, which will be subject to review, should extend to such matters as excluding what is clearly irrelevant, withholding the identity of persons to protect them from harassment or injury, or to enforce the privilege relating to informers. The discretion would also extend to the timing of disclosure in order to complete an investigation. I shall return to this subject later in these reasons.

This review of the pros and cons with respect to disclosure by the Crown shows that there is no valid practical reason to support the position of the opponents of a broad duty of disclosure. Apart from the practical advantages to which I have referred, there is the overriding concern that failure to disclose impedes the ability of the accused to make full answer and defence. This common law right has acquired new vigour by virtue of its inclusion in s. 7 of the *Canadian Charter of Rights and Freedoms* as one of the principles of fundamental justice: see *Dersch v. Canada (Attorney-General)* (1990), 60 C.C.C. (3d) 132 at pp. 140-1, 77 D.L.R. (4th) 473, [1990] 2 S.C.R. 1505. The right to make full answer and defence is one of the pillars of criminal justice on which we heavily depend to ensure that the innocent are not convicted. Recent events have demonstrated that the erosion of this right due to non-disclosure was an important factor in the conviction and incarceration of an innocent person. In the Royal Commission on the Donald Marshall, Jr., Prosecution, vol. 1: Findings and Recommendations (1989) (the "Marshall Commission Report"), the commissioners found that prior inconsistent statements were not disclosed to the defence. This was an important contributing factor in the miscarriage of justice which occurred and led the commission to state that "anything less than complete disclosure by the Crown falls short of decency and fair play" (vol. 1 at p. 238).

.....

In *R. v. C. (M.H.)* (1989), 46 C.C.C. (3d) 142 at p. 155, 6 W.C.B. (2d) 300 (B.C.C.A.), McEachern C.J.B.C. after a review of the authorities stated what I respectfully accept as a correct statement of the law. He said that: "there is a general duty on the part of the Crown to disclose all material it proposes to use at trial and especially all evidence which may assist the accused even if the Crown does not propose to adduce it". This passage was cited with approval by McLachlin J. in her reasons on behalf of the court (*R. v. C. (M.H.)* (1991), 63 C.C.C. (3d) 385, 4 C.R. (4th) 1, 123 N.R. 63). She went on to add (at p. 394): "This court has previously stated that the Crown is under a duty at common law to disclose to the defence all material evidence whether favourable to the accused or not."

As indicated earlier, however, this obligation to disclose is not absolute. It is subject to the discretion of counsel for the Crown. This discretion extends both to the withholding of information and to the timing of disclosure. For example, counsel for the Crown has a duty to respect the rules of privilege. In the case of informers the Crown has a duty to protect their identity. In some cases serious prejudice or even harm may result to a person who has supplied evidence or information to the investigation. While it is a harsh reality of justice that ultimately any person with relevant evidence must appear to testify, the discretion extends to the timing and manner of disclosure in such circumstances. A discretion must also be exercised with respect to the relevance of information. While the Crown must err on the side of inclusion, it need not produce what is clearly irrelevant. The experience to be gained from the civil side of the practice is that counsel, as officers of the court and acting responsibly, can be relied upon not to withhold pertinent information. Transgressions with respect to this duty constitute a very serious breach of legal ethics. The initial obligation to separate "the wheat from the chaff" must, therefore, rest with Crown counsel. There may also be situations in which early disclosure may impede completion of an investigation. Delayed disclosure on this account is not to be encouraged and should be rare. Completion of the investigation before proceeding with the prosecution of a charge or charges is very much within the control of the Crown. Nevertheless, it is not always possible to predict events which may require an investigation to be re-opened and the Crown must have some discretion to delay disclosure in these circumstances.

The discretion of Crown counsel is, however, reviewable by the trial judge. Counsel for the defence can initiate a review when an issue arises with respect to the exercise of the Crown's discretion. On a review the Crown must justify its refusal to disclose. In as much as disclosure of all relevant information is the general rule, the Crown must bring itself within an exception to that rule.

The trial judge on a review should be guided by the general principle that information ought not to be withheld if there is a reasonable possibility that the withholding of information will impair the right of the accused to make full answer and defence, unless the non-disclosure is justified by the law of privilege. The trial judge might also, in certain circumstances, conclude that the recognition of an existing privilege does not constitute a reasonable limit on the constitutional right to make full answer and defence and, thus, require disclosure in spite of the law of privilege. The trial judge may also review the decision of the Crown to withhold or delay production of information by reason of concern for the security or safety of witnesses or persons who have supplied information to the investigation. In such circumstances, while much leeway must be accorded to the exercise of the discretion of the counsel for the Crown with respect to the manner and timing of the disclosure, the absolute withholding of information which is relevant to the defence can only be justified on the basis of the existence of a legal privilege which excludes the information from disclosure.

The trial judge may also review the Crown's exercise of discretion as to relevance and interference with the investigation to ensure that the right to make full answer and defence is not violated. I am confident that disputes over disclosure will arise infrequently when it is made clear that counsel for the Crown is under a general duty to disclose *all* relevant information. The tradition of Crown counsel in this country in carrying out their role as "ministers of justice" and not as adversaries has generally been very high. Given this fact, and the obligation on defence counsel as officers of the court to act responsibly, these matters will usually be resolved without the intervention of the trial judge. When they do arise, the trial judge must resolve them. This may require not only submissions but the inspection of statements and other documents and indeed, in some cases, *viva voce* evidence. A *voir dire* will frequently be the appropriate procedure in which to deal with these matters.

Counsel for the accused must bring to the attention of the trial judge at the earliest opportunity any failure of the Crown to comply with its duty to disclose of which counsel becomes aware. Observance of this rule will enable the trial judge to remedy any prejudice to the accused if possible and, thus, avoid a new trial: see *R. v. Caccamo* (1975), 21 C.C.C. (2d) 257, 54 D.L.R. (3d) 685, [1976] 1 S.C.R. 786. Failure to do so by counsel for the defence will be an important factor in determining on appeal whether a new trial should be ordered.

.....

The general principles referred to herein arise in the context of indictable offences. While it may be argued that the duty of disclosure extends to all offences, many of the factors which I have canvassed may not apply at all or may apply with less impact in summary conviction offences. Moreover, the content of the right to make full answer and defence entrenched in s. 7 of the *Charter* may be of a more limited nature. A decision as to the extent to which the general principles of disclosure extend to summary conviction offences should be left to a case in which the issue arises in such proceedings. In view of the number and variety of statutes which create such offences, consideration would have to be given as to where to draw the line. Pending a decision on that issue, the voluntary disclosure which has been taking place through the co-operation of Crown counsel will no doubt continue. Continuation and extension of this practice may eliminate the necessity for a decision on the issue by this court.

There are, however, two additional matters which require further elaboration of the general principles of disclosure outlined above. They are: (1) the timing of disclosure, and (2) what should be disclosed. Some detail with respect to these issues is essential if the duty to disclose is to be meaningful. Moreover, with respect to the second matter, resolution of the dispute over disclosure in this case requires a closer examination of the issue.

With respect to timing, I agree with the recommendation of the Law Reform Commission of Canada in both of its reports that initial disclosure should occur before the accused is called upon to elect the mode of trial or to plead. These are crucial steps which the accused must take which affect his or her rights in a fundamental way. It will be of great assistance to the accused to know what are the strengths and weaknesses of the Crown's case before committing on these issues. As I have pointed out above, the system will also profit from early disclosure as it will foster the resolution of many charges without trial, through increased numbers of withdrawals and pleas of guilty. The obligation to disclose will be triggered by a request by or on behalf of the accused. Such a request may be made at any time after the charge. Provided the request for disclosure has been timely, it should be complied with so as to enable the accused sufficient time before election or plea to consider the information. In the rare cases in which the accused is unrepresented, Crown counsel should advise the accused of the right to disclosure and a plea should not be taken unless the trial judge is satisfied that this has been done. At this stage, the Crown's brief will often not be complete and disclosure will be limited by this fact. Nevertheless, the obligation to disclose is a continuing one and disclosure must be completed when additional information is received.

With respect to what should be disclosed, the general principle to which I have referred is that all relevant information must be disclosed subject to the reviewable discretion of the Crown. The material must include not only that which the Crown intends to introduce into evidence but also that which it does not. No distinction should be made between inculpatory and exculpatory evidence. The attempt to make this distinction in connection with the confession rule proved to be unworkable and was eventually discarded by this court: see *Piché v. The Queen*, [1970] 4 C.C.C. 27 at p. 37, 11 D.L.R. (3d) 700, [1971] S.C.R. 23; *R. v. Rothman* (1981), 59 C.C.C. (2d) 30 at pp. 48-9, 121 D.L.R. (3d) 578, [1981] 1 S.C.R. 640. To re-introduce the distinction here would lead to interminable controversy at trial that should be avoided. The Crown must, therefore, disclose relevant material whether it is inculpatory or exculpatory.

A special problem arises in respect to witness statements and is specifically raised in this case. There is virtually no disagreement that statements in the possession of the Crown obtained from witnesses it proposes to call should be produced. In some cases the statement will simply be recorded in notes taken by an investigator, usually a police officer. The notes or copies should be produced. If notes do not exist then a "will say" statement, summarizing the anticipated evidence of the witness, should be produced based on the information in the Crown's possession. A more difficult issue is posed with respect to witnesses and other persons whom the Crown does not propose to call.

.....

I am of the opinion that, subject to the discretion to which I have referred above, all statements obtained from persons who have provided relevant information to the authorities should be produced notwithstanding that they are not proposed as Crown witnesses. Where statements are not in existence, other information such as notes should be produced, and, if there are no notes, then in addition to the name, address and occupation of the witness, all information in the possession of the prosecution relating to any relevant evidence that the person could give should be supplied.

QUESTION

1. **In *R. v. Hutter* (1993), 86 C.C.C. (3d) 81 (Ont. C.A.); leave to appeal to S.C.C. refused (1994), 87 C.C.C. (3d) vi, the accused was charged with various sexual offences. Prior to trial, the defence advised the Crown that it was considering calling character evidence but, before committing itself, required disclosure of any bad character evidence the Crown intended to rely upon. The Crown refused to disclose this evidence and the**

trial judge did not order it disclosed. Dubin C.J.O., speaking for the court, stated:

> Dubin C.J.O.: — The narrow issue on this appeal is whether the trial judge erred in failing to order a stay of the proceedings at the commencement of the trial because of the failure of Crown counsel, upon request, to disclose the details of evidence and/or information in the possession of the Crown relating to the character of the appellant.
>
> Judgment was withheld to await the release of the Report of the Attorney-General's Advisory Committee on Charge Screening, Disclosure, and Resolution Discussions, by the Hon. G. Arthur Martin, which has just been recently released. As will presently be seen, the committee considered the duty of the Crown to disclose on request information in its possession relating to the character of an accused.
>
> .....
>
> Notwithstanding the submissions of Crown counsel, I am now satisfied in light of what was stated in *Stinchcombe* [(1991), 68 C.C.C. (3d) 1 (S.C.C.)] and in *Egger* [(1993), 82 C.C.C. (3d) 193 (S.C.C.)] that the trial judge erred in failing to direct disclosure of the information requested.
>
> The information in the hands of the Crown with respect to the character of the appellant could "reasonably be used by the accused in advancing a defence in making a decision which could affect the conduct of the defence such as, for example, whether to call evidence".
>
> That also appears to be the conclusion arrived at by the Attorney-General's advisory committee in the report referred to at the outset of these reasons. At p. 206 of the report, the committee commented:
>
>> *Where the accused*, prior to trial, has disclosed his or her defence, for example, alibi, in sufficient detail to permit the alibi to be investigated, or *has stated to Crown counsel that he or she will be relying upon evidence of good character in support of the defence advanced, and the Crown* is in possession of evidence that rebuts or tends to rebut the defence advanced, or *has evidence that tends to rebut the evidence of good character, that evidence must be disclosed promptly to the defence.* Conversely, if the Crown is in possession of evidence that tends to confirm the defence advanced, or the evidence of good character, such evidence must likewise be disclosed promptly to the defence.
>
> (Emphasis added.)
>
> In my opinion, the trial judge was correct in refusing to direct a stay of proceedings, which was the subject matter of the motion before him, but should have directed Crown counsel to disclose the details of the information he had with respect to the character of the appellant when the motion to stay was brought before him, leaving it to the defence to weigh that information and to determine then whether to introduce evidence of good character or not.

Must the defence specifically request disclosure of bad character evidence or indicate that character will be in issue before the Crown's obligation to disclose bad character evidence is triggered?

Subsequent decisions have made it clear that *Stinchcombe* applies to summary conviction proceedings. See, for example, *R. v. Kutynec* (1992), 70 C.C.C. (3d) 289 (Ont. C.A.); *R. v. Romain* (1992), 75 C.C.C. (3d) 379 (Ont. Ct. (Gen. Div.)), substantially reproduced at p. 325 of this text.

It seems clear that the right to disclosure does not bring with it the right to oral discovery of the prosecution witnesses in advance of trial. Indeed, a direct indictment may be preferred against the accused, bypassing the preliminary inquiry, without violating s. 7 of the *Charter*, if full disclosure has been provided to the accused. In other words, though a preliminary inquiry is a vehicle permitting discovery or disclosure of the prosecution's case, it is not the only method of providing such disclosure and the accused has no constitutional right to a preliminary inquiry. See *R. v. Sterling* (1993), 84 C.C.C. (3d) 65 (Sask. C.A.); *Re Regina and Arviv* (1985), 51 O.R. (2d) 551 (C.A.).

2. Exception to Disclosure: Evidence Not in the Crown's Control

The prosecution need not disclose information which is not within its control; it has been said that the prosecution is not an investigative agency for the defence. However, the extent to which information is said to be within the Crown's control is often a contentious issue.

R. v. T.(L.A.)

(1993), 84 C.C.C. (3d) 90 (Ont. C.A.)

The judgment of the court was delivered by

Lacourcière J.A.: —

.....

The first ground of appeal is that the learned trial judge erred in not declaring a mistrial by reason of the failure of the Crown to disclose a statement given to the police by K.T., a sister of the complainant C.T. The statement only came to light at the conclusion of the defence case, when the Crown applied to call K.T. in reply. The failure of the Crown to make timely disclosure of the statement was inadvertent: the police had not produced said statement to the Crown prosecutor. The statement had been given to the police two days before the preliminary inquiry in March 1991 and before the defence request for disclosure. In it, the complainant allegedly told her sister, K.T., that "a guy that she really trusted and really cared a lot about" had followed her on her bicycle to the back of the school in K. and "forced her down with a chain and did things to her". The Crown did not intend to call K.T. as a witness as her evidence with respect to the statement would have been inadmissible hearsay.

Defence counsel indicated that, had he known of the statement suggesting that a stranger had assaulted the complainant, he might not have re-elected trial by judge alone and would have conducted his cross-examination of C.T. and of the expert differently. Defence counsel claimed that he had been "irrevocably prejudiced".

.....

Defence counsel applied first for a stay of proceedings, but alternatively for a mistrial. The application for a stay of proceedings was based on the contention that the appellant had been irrevocably prejudiced by the late disclosure because the defence had now disclosed its defence and, on any re-trial, the appellant could be cross-examined on his testimony. The appellant submitted that his ability to make full answer and defence had been impaired by the late disclosure of this witness's statement resulting in an unfair trial.

The learned trial judge dismissed the application for a stay of proceedings or a mistrial. He held that the failure to produce the statement was an oversight, and he offered to have C.T. and the expert recalled for cross-examination.

I agree with counsel for the appellant that the reason for the late disclosure was not relevant on the application for a mistrial. While the reason for the late disclosure may be relevant if it amounts to abuse of process leading to a proper application for a stay of proceedings, this was clearly not the present case. The defence had certainly not suggested that the prosecutor had been influenced by an *oblique motive*: see *Lemay v. R.* (1952), 102 C.C.C. 1, [1952] 1 S.C.R. 232, 14 C.R. 89. The proper test on an application for a mistrial is,of course, whether the appellant's ability to make full answer and defence has been impaired. Did the failure to disclose create such prejudice that it cannot be said with certainty that the appellant received a fair trial? In *R. v. C. (M.H.)* (1991), 63 C.C.C. (3d) 385 at p. 395, [1991] 1 S.C.R. 763 at p. 776, 4 C.R. (4th) 1 (S.C.C.), McLachlin J., delivering the judgment of the court, said:

> Had counsel for the appellant been aware of this statement, he might well have decided to use it in support of the defence that the evidence of the complainant was a fabrication. In my view, that evidence could conceivably have affected the jury's conclusions on the only real issue, the respective credibility of the complainant and the appellant.

The leading authority in this area is *R. v. Stinchcombe* (1991), 68 C.C.C. (3d) 1, [1991] 3 S.C.R. 326, 9 C.R. (4th) 277 (S.C.C.). There is a duty on the Crown to make full disclosure and accordingly the Crown has a duty to obtain from the police — and the police have a corresponding duty to provide for the Crown — all relevant information and material concerning the case. In *R. v. V. (W.J.)* (1992), 72 C.C.C. (3d) 97 at p. 109, 14 C.R. (4th) 311, 10 C.R.R. (2d) 360 (Nfld. C.A.), Goodridge C.J.N. states:

> The duty rests upon Crown counsel to obtain from the police all material that should be properly disclosed to defence counsel. It is not for the court to direct what should pass between the police and Crown counsel but both should be aware that, if Crown counsel is unable to make proper disclosure because he or she has not obtained from the police all such material, a new trial may be ordered. It is, once again, a matter of common sense.

.....

It is obviously not an imperative, in every case of untimely disclosure, to direct a new trial. In many cases it will be possible and desirable for the trial judge to fashion a remedy that is less drastic. However, in the present case, I am not satisfied that the prejudicial effect could be repaired in the manner suggested by the learned trial judge.

The remedy proposed by the learned trial judge, *i.e.*, to permit further cross-examination, was inadequate in the circumstances. In *Stinchcombe, supra*, at pp. 13-4, Sopinka J. said with respect to the timing for disclosure:

> ... that initial disclosure should occur before the accused is called upon to elect the mode of trial or to plead. These are crucial steps which the accused must take which affect his or her rights in a fundamental way. It will be of great assistance to the accused to know what are the strengths and weaknesses of the Crown's case before committing on these issues.

And further at p. 17, he said:

> What are the legal consequences flowing from the failure to disclose? In my opinion, when a court of appeal is called upon to view a failure to disclose, it must consider whether such failure impaired the right to make full answer and defence.

Ever since the Crown's duty to disclose has been elevated to a constitutional imperative, courts have been interpreting the duty in a very strict fashion. In *R. v. Fineline Circuits Ltd.* (1991), 10 C.R. (4th) 241 (Ont. Ct. (Prov. Div.)), for example, Cole Prov. Ct. J. noted that since Sopinka J. wrote in *Stinchcombe, supra*, p. 14, that "... the obligation to disclose is a continuing one and disclosure must be completed when additional information is received", it followed that (at p.256): "Neither an offer to recall witnesses nor an adjournment can cure a substantive breach of the right to receive timely and full disclosure."

In the present case, whether or not one agrees with the tactical decision of defence counsel not to avail himself of the offer to conduct further cross-examination of the complainant and experts, it cannot be said with certainty that the appellant was not prejudiced. The critical opportunity to attack the credibility of the complainant C.T. was considerably, and arguably, irredeemably reduced.

It is apparent from the court's statement in *Stinchcombe, supra*, at p. 14, previously quoted, that the disclosure of evidence by the Crown can affect the defence's election with respect to the mode of trial or to the plea. Defence counsel argued that the late disclosure by the Crown may have affected the accused's choice of forum and his decision to testify. While this argument would not necessarily succeed in every case, I would give effect to it in this case having regard, among other things, to the clear statement of defence counsel on the record. The late disclosure may also have affected the ability of defence counsel to attack the complainants' credibility, which was critical in this case.

.....

Accordingly, I would allow the appeal, quash all convictions and direct a new trial.

QUESTIONS

2. What if the Crown's failure to disclose was due to the destruction of the evidence by a third party? What is the proper remedy in this case? Consider, in this regard, *R. v. Carosella* (1997), 112 C.C.C. (3d) 289 (S.C.C.).

3. What if the evidence is inadvertently lost by the authorities? What is the proper procedure to follow? Consider, in this regard, *R. v. La* (1997), 116 C.C.C. (3d) 97 (S.C.C.).

4. What if the Crown has inadvertently failed to disclose statements by witnesses to the defence and disclosed only summaries of the statements? How does defence counsel's role in diligently pursuing disclosure affect the Crown's inadvertent failure to disclose? Consider, in this regard, *R. v. Dixon* (1998), 122 C.C.C. (3d) 1 (S.C.C.).

3. Exception to Disclosure: Privilege

Exceptions to disclosure may arise out of solicitor-client privilege, Crown privilege (otherwise known as public interest immunity, addressed in s. 37 of the *Canada Evidence Act*, R.S.C. 1985, c. C-5, and in various provincial statutes), or informer privilege. Even where the privilege *prima facie* exists, it may yield, in very limited circumstances, where necessary, to demonstrate innocence. See *R. v. McClure* (2001), 151 C.C.C. (3d) 321 (S.C.C.). As well, once material, which may otherwise be privileged, is provided to the prosecution, the privilege may be lost or deemed to have been waived, and disclosure to the accused may be compelled: see *R. v. O'Connor* (1995), 103 C.C.C. (3d) 1 (S.C.C.), substantially reproduced at p. 328. Compare s. 278.2(2) of the *Criminal Code*, proclaimed as part of the 1997 *Act to Amend the Criminal Code,* S.C. 1997, c. 30 (formerly Bill C-46) (production of records in sexual offence proceedings).

4. Reciprocal Disclosure

In Canada, there is no general obligation upon the defence to make disclosure to the prosecution. See *R. v. Chambers* (1990), 59 C.C.C. (3d) 321 (S.C.C.); *R. v. P.(M.B.)* (1994), 89 C.C.C. (3d) 289 (S.C.C.), substantially reproduced on another issue, at p. 584 of this text. A recently enacted exception to this general rule is found in s. 657.3(3)(*c*) of the *Criminal Code*, which requires, *inter alia*, the disclosure by the defence of its intended expert testimony not later than the close of the prosecution's case. In other jurisdictions there are often obligations for the defence to disclose. For indictable trials in England, the defence must supply within 14 days of primary disclosure by the Crown (generally known as initial disclosure in Canada) the general nature of the defence and the aspects of the prosecution case which the defence will dispute, giving reasons.[1] In the United States, the decision in *Williams v. Florida,* 399

---

[1] *Criminal Procedure and Investigations Act 1996* (U.K.), 1996, c. 25, s. 5(6).

US 78 (1970), opened the door for a regime of expanded defence disclosure obligations. In some states (*e.g.*, New Jersey and Michigan), a full reciprocal disclosure regime is enforced by way of rules of court.[2]

Recently, observers of the O.J. Simpson trial became familiar with the reciprocal disclosure requirements in California.

QUESTIONS

5. Why not compel the defence to make pre-trial disclosure to the prosecution of the evidence it may rely upon at trial? Would this requirement infringe an accused's *Charter* rights under s. 7 (right to silence)?

6. Consider what evidentiary implications flow from the accused's failure to disclose an alibi in a timely and adequate manner. When and how should an alibi defence be disclosed to the prosecution? Consider, in this regard, *R. v. Cleghorn* (1995), 100 C.C.C. (3d) 393 (S.C.C.), substantially reproduced at p. 609.

7. Can the defence be called upon to make an election as to mode of trial prior to receiving complete disclosure? What remedies are available to the defence to address an ongoing failure to disclose prior to a preliminary inquiry? Consider, in this regard, *R. v. Girimonte* (1997), 121 C.C.C. (3d) 33 (Ont. C.A.).

---

5. Remedies for Non-Disclosure or Late Disclosure

Where the defence is of the view that the disclosure provided is incomplete, case law has developed procedures by which to initiate a judicial review of the adequacy of the disclosure. Where non-disclosure or late disclosure has been demonstrated at trial, various remedies have been developed, largely as a function of the trial judge's jurisdiction pursuant to ss. 7 and 24 of the *Charter*, to address the issue. These remedies include:

(a) a judicial stay;
(b) an adjournment;
(c) a mistrial;
(d) exclusion of evidence;
(e) an order of costs;
(f) a right to re-elect an alternative mode of trial;
(g) the right to have witnesses re-called for examination or cross-examination; and
(h) an order for productions.

Non-disclosure first discovered after trial may feed a successful appeal against conviction: see, for example, *R. v. Court* (1995), 99 C.C.C. (3d) 237 (Ont. C.A.).

---

2 *New Jersey Rules Governing Criminal Practice*, R. 3:13 and *Michigan Court Rules*, R. 6.201 respectively.

Sections 7 and 11(*b*) of the *Charter* may interact to compel a judicial stay. See, for example: *R. v. Samad* (1995), 29 W.C.B. (2d) 282 (Ont. Gen. Div.).

The following case illustrates how the court evaluates the appropriateness of various remedies for non-disclosure.

R. v. ROMAIN

(1992), 75 C.C.C. (3d) 379 (Ont. Gen. Div.)

McCombs J.: — The appellant was found guilty and granted a conditional discharge on a charge of mischief to private property valued at less than $1,000. His appeal raises two issues:

(1) Did the Crown have a duty to disclose, prior to trial, an inconsistent statement made by a prospective witness?
(2) If the Crown had that duty, does its failure to make that disclosure entitle the Appellant to a new trial?

The facts

The appellant owned a unit in a condominium apartment complex. He was not happy with upkeep of the common areas of the building, particularly the mail room, and had frequently complained about the "junk" mail which was often allowed to accumulate there. On September 7, 1991, during a mail strike, Bell Canada left a number of telephone bills in the mail room for residents of the building. The Crown alleged that the appellant, frustrated by the mess, ripped the bills up and threw them in the garbage.

The case turned on the question of whether the appellant knew that the material he destroyed included the Bell Canada bills.

At trial, the appellant acknowledged that he had destroyed the bills but maintained that when he did so he believed that they were part of the junk mail which had accumulated in the mail room.

In addition to the appellant's testimony, the defence relied on the evidence of Mr. Perry. He testified that he had been with the appellant at the relevant time, along with a Mr. Talangbayan. He essentially corroborated the testimony of the appellant and acknowledged that he too had ripped some of the Bell Canada bills thinking that they were junk mail.

The final defence witness, Mr. Talangbayan, had originally been under subpoena by the Crown. He was the third person present when the bills were destroyed, and he confirmed the accuracy of the appellant's and Mr. Perry's story.

The non-disclosure

During cross-examination, Crown counsel forcefully questioned Mr. Talangbayan about an undisclosed statement allegedly made to a third person, Mr. Michael Wong. Part of this statement was potentially quite damaging to the credibility of Mr. Talangbayan. Although he denied it, he was alleged in cross-examination to have said: "Off the record, he ripped them, but if anyone asks me, I'll deny it."

Motions by the defence

When cross-examination was concluded, defence counsel immediately advised the court that the alleged statement by Mr. Talangbayan to Mr. Wong had not been disclosed. In the discussion that followed, the trial judge observed that non-disclosure of the Wong statement "would be pretty crucial to the case".

Following an adjournment to allow both counsel to consider their positions, defence counsel moved for a stay of proceedings, or alternatively, a mistrial. She submitted that she had believed she had full disclosure when she made her decision to call Mr. Talangbayan as a witness. She said that in the middle of the cross-examination of Mr. Talangbayan, she had been "sucker-punched" by the previously undisclosed evidence of the alleged prior inconsistent statement. She also informed the court that if she had known of the alleged statement, she would not have called the witness. She submitted that the defence case had been irreparably damaged as a result of the non-disclosure.

.....

Was there a duty to disclose?

The trial judge's conclusion that the Crown did not have a duty to disclose the Wong statement is consistent with the traditional view that no such duty exists unless the statement bears directly on the issue of the guilt or innocence of the accused.

.....

In my opinion, recent pronouncements of the Supreme Court of Canada have established that non-disclosure of impeachment evidence for use in cross-examination is no longer permissible.

In *Stinchcombe* [(1991), 68 C.C.C. (3d) 1], Sopinka J. observed that there are sound policy reasons for a rule requiring that the Crown make full disclosure of all relevant material. Two of his conclusions are particularly apt to the case at bar (at pp. 15, 17):

> I am of the opinion that, subject to the discretion to which I have referred above, all statements obtained from persons who have provided relevant information to the authorities should be produced *notwithstanding that they are not proposed as Crown witnesses*.

.....

> ... counsel for the defence is entitled to know whether the witness s/he is calling will give evidence that will assist the defence or whether the witness will be adverse and necessitate an application to cross-examine on the basis of a prior inconsistent statement ... *Most counsel faced with this prospect would likely opt not to call the witness, a matter which bears on the right to make full answer and defence.*

(Emphasis added.)

The foregoing passages make it clear that the Crown is under a continuing duty to disclose all relevant statements of prospective witnesses, whether or not the Crown intends to call them.

Even prior to *Stinchcombe*, the Supreme Court of Canada had ruled that if evidence could affect the credibility of a witness, it is relevant and must be disclosed. In *R. v. C.(M.H.)* (1991), 63 C.C.C. (3d) 385, [1991] 1 S.C.R. 763, 4 C.R. (4th) 1 (S.C.C.), McLachlin J. concluded that the Crown had a duty to disclose that the complainant in a sexual case had made a statement inconsistent with her evidence as to whether she had ever been asked if she had been sexually abused. McLachlin J. stated, at p. 395, that the withheld evidence: "... could conceivably have affected the jury's conclusions *on the only real issue, the respective credibility of the complainant and the appellant*" (Emphasis added).

In the case at bar, the evidence which was withheld was also relevant to the only real issue: the respective credibility of the Crown and defence witnesses. The trial judge was therefore in error when he held that the Crown had no duty to disclose the statement.

Does the failure to make disclosure entitle the appellant to a new trial?

The learned trial judge denied the Crown's request to call Mr. Wong as a reply witness, because of his conclusion that the evidence was collateral. He also concluded that, alternatively, if he was in error, the appellant could nevertheless receive a "full and fair trial" because refusing to permit reply evidence was a suitable remedy under s. 24(1) of the *Canadian Charter of Rights and Freedoms*.

The respondent argues that the learned trial judge did not improperly consider the evidence which had been withheld by the Crown and used to impeach the witness in cross-examination. A careful review of the evidence and the reasons for judgment, however, leads me to conclude that the impermissible cross-examination may have influenced his decision. Some of the reasons for that conclusion are set out below.

[McCombs J. then reviews the trial judge's reasons, concluding that his decision was possibly influenced by the withheld evidence. A new trial was ordered.]

QUESTION

8. **Johnny B. Goode is the owner of a car dealership and is charged with conspiracy to commit murder. It is alleged that he hired his co-accused, Otto Partz and Moe Bile, to kill a disgruntled ex-employee, Billy Buick. Buick told police that he overheard the three accused plotting to kill him while attending a charity Guns n' Turnips concert at a local geriatric centre. The key witness for the prosecution, Billy Buick, dies the night before trial in an accident (he is swallowed by an alligator at Marine World). There is no suggestion that the accused was involved in Buick's death. Seeing the Crown's dilemma, the police advise Crown counsel that, in the early stages of the investigation, they were told by an amateur vibraphone player, Lionel Hampster, that he was visiting his mother at the geriatric centre shortly after the concert and was told by her that she had overheard three men in the hallway talking about killing someone named Chrysler. The police did not speak to Hampster's mother, since Lionel seemed unreliable and publicity-seeking, and the description of the conspirators' voices (as conveyed by Hampster) did not seem to correspond**

to the known voices of the three suspects. Upon hearing this, Crown counsel asks the trial judge for a one-day adjournment to pursue a new lead (which is granted) and interviews Mother Hampster at the geriatric centre. She recalls the events vividly. Indeed, perhaps induced by the publicity which has been given this case, she now recalls that Buick, not Chrysler, was the name she overheard. Interestingly, she also recollects that she saw Billy Buick earlier that day talking about how much he would like to "get" Johnny B. Goode. Lionel Hampster has no independent recollection of what his mother told him but does recall that he took notes of the incident which he threw out several months ago. Crown counsel wants to call Mother Hampster at the trial and, further, wishes to read into evidence Billy Buick's evidence at the preliminary inquiry. (See s. 715 of the *Criminal Code*, addressed at p. 371.) What issues arise for you as defence counsel? What options are available to the trial judge to resolve these issues?

B. THIRD PARTY PRODUCTION

The following judgment of the Supreme Court of Canada articulated procedures necessary for obtaining the production of confidential records held by third parties. The Court addressed the implications of these records being turned over to the Crown by the police or by a third party.

R. v. O'CONNOR

(1995), 103 C.C.C. (3d) 1 (S.C.C.)

[In the *O'Connor* decision, Major J. dissenting (Lamer C.J.C. and Sopinka J. concurring), would have upheld a judicial stay of proceedings. The judgment of Lamer C.J.C. and Sopinka (Cory, Iacobucci and Major JJ. concurring), represents the majority view on the procedures for production of sexual assault counselling records in the possession of third parties. The judgment of L'Heureux-Dubé J. (McLachlin, Cory and Iacobucci JJ. concurring), represents the majority view that the stay should be set aside and a new trial ordered. However, L'Heureux-Dubé J. (only McLachlin J. concurring), articulated a minority view on the procedures for the production of a full range of privacy-related records. Only the judgment of Lamer C.J.C. and Sopinka J. is reproduced here.]

Lamer C.J.C. and Sopinka J.: —

I

INTRODUCTION

This case, along with the companion decision in *A. (L.L.) v. B. (A.)* [*post*, p. 92, 29 W.C.B. (2d) 154, *sub nom. R. v. Beharriell*], S.C.C., No. 24568, released concurrently, raises the issue of whether and under what circumstances an accused is entitled to obtain production of sexual assault counselling records in the possession of third parties. It also raises the issue of when a stay of proceedings is the appropriate remedy for non-disclosure by the Crown of information in its possession which is neither clearly irrelevant nor privileged. On the latter issue, we agree with the reasons of Justice Major.

As for the issue of the production of therapeutic records, we have had the benefit of reading the reasons of our colleague Justice L'Heureux-Dubé, and we are in general agreement with her reasons on the issues of privacy and privilege. We wish, however, to make the following comments regarding the procedure to be followed for the *disclosure* and *production* of therapeutic records.

II

ANALYSIS

1. Introduction

The issues raised in the present appeal relate primarily to the production of therapeutic records beyond the possession or the control of the Crown. Generally speaking, this issue concerns the manner in which the accused can obtain production of therapeutic records from the third party custodian of the documents in question. Although issues relating to the disclosure of private records in the possession of the Crown are not directly engaged in this appeal, we nevertheless feel that some preliminary comments on that issue would provide a useful background to a discussion of therapeutic records in the possession of third parties. As a result, we begin our analysis with a brief consideration of the disclosure obligations of the Crown where therapeutic counselling records are in the Crown's possession or control. From there, we will move on to consider the case where such records remain in the hands of third parties and the production of those records is sought by the accused.

2. Records in the possession of the Crown

(a) The application of Stinchcombe

The principles regarding the disclosure of information in the possession of the Crown were developed by this court in *R. v. Stinchcombe* (1991), 68 C.C.C. (3d) 1, [1991] 3 S.C.R. 326, 9 C.R. (4th) 277. In that case, it was determined that the Crown has an ethical and constitutional obligation to the defence to disclose all information in its possession or control, unless the information in question is clearly irrelevant or protected by a recognized form of privilege.

.....

... [I]t is important to consider whether therapeutic records of the kind at issue in this appeal should be subject to a different disclosure regime than other kinds of information in the possession of the Crown. In answering this question, the court must consider whether the Crown's disclosure obligations should be tempered by a balancing of the complainant's privacy interests in therapeutic records against the right of the accused to make full answer and defence. In our view, a balancing of these competing interests is unnecessary in the context of disclosure.

(b) Privacy and privilege

As our colleague L'Heureux-Dubé J. points out, sexual assault counselling records relate to intimate aspects of the life of the complainant. As a result, therapeutic records attract a stronger privacy interest than many other forms of information that may be in the Crown's possession. One could accordingly argue that the intensely private nature of therapeutic records affects the Crown's obligation to disclose such material to the defence, or that disclosure by the Crown is not required owing to some form of privilege that may attach to the information contained in the records. In our view, however, concerns relating to privacy or privilege disappear where the documents in question have fallen into the possession of the Crown. We are accordingly of the opinion that the Crown's well-established duty to disclose all information in its possession is not affected by the confidential nature of therapeutic records.

.....

In deciding that the complainant waives any potential claim of privilege where therapeutic records are provided to the Crown, we recognize that any such waiver must be "fully informed" in order to defeat an attempted claim of privilege. Clearly, one could make the argument that the complainant would not have turned the documents over to the Crown had he or she been aware that the accused could be given access to the records. However, this problem is easily solved by placing an onus upon the Crown to inform the complainant of the potential for disclosure. Where the Crown seeks to obtain the records in question for the purpose of proceeding against the accused, the Crown must explain to the complainant that the records, if relevant, will have to be disclosed to the defence. As a result, the complainant will be given the opportunity to decide whether or not to waive any potential claim of privilege prior to releasing the records in question to the agents of the state.

.....

(c) Relevance

... With respect, we agree with the proposition [advanced by L'Heureux-Dubé J.] that the mere existence of therapeutic records is insufficient to establish the relevance of those records to the defence. However, we are of the opinion that the relevance of such records must be presumed where the records are in the possession of the Crown. ... If indeed the Crown merely surveyed the records and found them to contain no relevant material, the Crown would retain the opportunity to prove the irrelevance of the records on a *Stinchcombe* application by the defence.

.....

(d) Conclusion

For each of the foregoing reasons, we are of the view that the Crown's disclosure obligations established in the *Stinchcombe* decision are unaffected by the confidential nature of therapeutic records. Where the Crown has possession or control of therapeutic records, there is simply no compelling reason to depart from the reasoning in *Stinchcombe*: unless the Crown can prove that the records in question are clearly irrelevant or subject to some form of public interest privilege, the therapeutic records must be disclosed to the defence.

Having concluded that the principles of *Stinchcombe* are applicable in the context of therapeutic records within the Crown's possession, it remains to be determined what procedures for production will apply where the counselling records in question are possessed by third parties. Our views as to the appropriate procedure in that situation are discussed below.

3. Records in the hands of third parties

(a) The application of Stinchcombe

.....

Stinchcombe and its progeny were decided in the context of disclosure, where the information in question was in the possession of the Crown or the police. In that context, we held that an accused was entitled to obtain all of the information in the possession of the Crown, unless the information in question was clearly irrelevant. However, *Stinchcombe recognized* that, even in the context of disclosure, there are limits on the right of an accused to access information. For example, when the Crown asserts that the information is privileged, the trial judge must then balance the competing claims at issue. In such cases, the information will only be disclosed where the trial judge concludes that the asserted privilege "does not constitute a reasonable limit on the constitutional right to make full answer and defence" (*Stinchcombe*, at p. 12).

In our opinion, the balancing approach we established in *Stinchcombe* can apply with equal force in the context of production, where the information sought is in the hands of a third party. Of course, the balancing process must be modified to fit the context in which it is applied. In cases involving production, for example, we are concerned with the competing claims of a constitutional right to privacy in the information on the one hand, and the right to full answer and defence on the other. We agree with L'Heureux-Dubé J. that a constitutional right to privacy extends to information contained in many forms of third party records.

In recognizing that all individuals have a right to privacy which should be protected as much as is reasonably possible, we should not lose sight of the possibility of occasioning a miscarriage of justice by establishing a procedure which unduly restricts an accused's ability to access information which may be necessary for meaningful full answer and defence. In *R. v. Seaboyer* (1991), 66 C.C.C. (3d) 321 at p. 391, 83 D.L.R. (4th) 193 at p. 263, [1991] 2 S.C.R. 577, we recognized that:

> Canadian courts ... have been extremely cautious in restricting the power of the accused to call evidence in his or her defence, a reluctance founded in the fundamental tenet of our judicial system that an innocent person must not be convicted.

Indeed, so important is the societal interest in preventing a miscarriage of justice that our law requires the state to disclose the identity of an informer in certain circumstances, despite the fact that the revelation may jeopardize the informer's safety.

(b) The first stage: establishing "likely relevance"

When the defence seeks information in the hands of a third party (as compared to the state), the following considerations operate so as to require a shifting of the onus and a higher threshold of relevance:

(1) the information is not part of the state's "case to meet" nor has the state been granted access to the information in preparing its case; and
(2) third parties have no obligation to assist the defence.

In light of these considerations, we agree with L'Heureux-Dubé J. that, at the first stage in the production procedure, the onus should be on the accused to satisfy a judge that the information is *likely to be relevant*. The onus we place on the accused should not be interpreted as an evidential burden requiring evidence and a *voir dire* in every case. It is simply an initial threshold to provide a basis for production which can be satisfied by oral submissions of counsel. It is important to recognize that the accused will be in a very poor position to call evidence given that he has never had access to the records. *Viva voce evidence* and a *voir dire* may, however, be required in situations in which the presiding judge cannot resolve the matter on the basis of the submissions of counsel: see *Chaplin* [(1995), 96 C.C.C. (3d) 225], at p. 236.

In order to initiate the production procedure, the accused must bring a formal written application supported by an affidavit setting out the specific grounds for production. However, the court should be able, in the interests of justice, to waive the need for a formal application in some cases. In either event, however, notice must be given to third parties in possession of the documents as well as to those persons who have a privacy interest in the records. The accused must also ensure that the custodian and the records are subpoenaed to ensure their attendance in the court. The initial application for disclosure should be made to the judge seized of the trial, but may be brought before the trial judge prior to the empanelling of the jury, at the same time that other motions are heard. In this way, disruption of the jury will be minimized and both the Crown and the defence will be provided with adequate time to prepare their cases based on any evidence that may be produced as a result of the application.

According to L'Heureux-Dubé J., once the accused meets the "likely relevance" threshold, he or she must then satisfy the judge that the salutary effects of ordering the documents produced to the court for inspection outweigh the deleterious effects of such production. We are of the view that this balancing should be undertaken at the second stage of the procedure. The "likely relevance" stage should be confined to a question of whether the right to make full answer and defence is implicated by information contained in the records. Moreover, a judge will only be in an informed position to engage in the required balancing analysis once he or she has had an opportunity to review the records in question.

(c) The meaning of "likely" relevance

In the disclosure context, the meaning of "relevance" is expressed in terms of whether the information may be useful to the defence: see *Egger*, [(1993), 82 C.C.C. (3d) 193 (S.C.C.)], at p. 204 C.C.C., p. 689 D.L.R., and *Chaplin*, *supra*, at p. 233. In the context of production, the test of relevance should be higher: the presiding judge must be satisfied that there is a reasonable possibility that the information is logically probative *to an issue at trial or the competence of a witness to testify*. When we speak of relevance to "an issue at trial", we are referring not only to evidence that may be probative to the material issues in the case (*i.e.*, the unfolding of events) but also to evidence relating to the credibility of witnesses and to the reliability of other evidence in the case: see *R. v. R. (L.)* (1995), 100 C.C.C. (3d) 329 at p. 339, 127 D.L.R. (4th) 170 at p. 180, 39 C.R. (4th) 390 (Ont. C.A.).

This higher threshold of relevance is appropriate because it reflects the context in which the information is being sought. Generally speaking, records in the hands of third parties find their way into court proceedings by one of two procedures. First, under s. 698(1) of the *Criminal Code*, R.S.C. 1985, c. C-46, a party may apply for a subpoena requiring a person to attend where that person is likely to give material evidence in a proceedings. Pursuant to s. 700(1) of the *Code*, the subpoena is only available for those records in the custodian's possession "relating to the subject-matter of the proceedings". The second method of obtaining production of documents is to apply for a search warrant pursuant to s. 487(1) of the *Code*. Under s. 487(1)(*b*) a search warrant will be issued where a justice is satisfied that there is in a building, receptacle or place "anything that there are reasonable grounds to believe will afford evidence with respect to the commission of an offence". Consequently, under either of these schemes the individual seeking access to third party records must satisfy a neutral arbiter that the records are relevant to the proceedings in question. We agree with L'Heureux-Dubé J. that the appropriate procedure to follow is *via* the *subpoena duces tecum* route.

While we agree that "likely relevance" is the appropriate threshold for the first stage of the two-step procedure, we wish to emphasize that, while this is a significant burden, it should not be interpreted as an onerous burden upon the accused. There are several reasons for holding that the onus upon the accused should be a low one. First, at this stage of the inquiry, the only issue is whether the information is "likely" relevant. We agree with L'Heureux-Dubé J. that considerations of privacy should not enter into the analysis at this stage. We should also not be concerned with whether the evidence would be admissible, for example, as a matter of policy, as that is a different query: *Morris v. The Queen* (1983), 7 C.C.C. (3d) 97, 1 D.L.R. (4th) 385, [1983] 2 S.C.R. 190. As the House of Lords recognized in *R. v. Preston*, [1993] 4 All E.R. 638 at p. 664:

> ... the fact that an item of information cannot be put in evidence by a party does not mean that it is worthless. Often, the train of inquiry which leads to the discovery of evidence which is admissible at a trial may include an item which is not admissible ...

A relevance threshold, at this stage, is simply a requirement to prevent the defence from engaging in "speculative, fanciful, disruptive, unmeritorious, obstructive and time-consuming" requests for production: see *Chaplin, supra*, at p. 236.

Second, by placing an onus on the accused to show "likely relevance", we put the accused in the difficult situation of having to make submissions to the judge without precisely knowing what is contained in the records. This court has recognized on a number of occasions the danger of placing the accused in a "Catch-22" situation as a condition of making full answer and defence: see, for example, *Dersch v. Canada (Attorney-General)* (1990), 60 C.C.C. (3d) 132 at pp. 139-40, 77 D.L.R. (4th) 473 at pp. 480-81, [1990] 2 S.C.R. 1505; *R. v. Garofoli* (1990), 60 C.C.C. (3d) 161 at pp. 196-7, [1990] 2 S.C.R. 1421, 80 C.R. (3d) 317; *Carey v. Ontario* (1986), 30 C.C.C. (3d) 498, 35 D.L.R. (4th) 161, [1986] 2 S.C.R. 637, and *R. v. Durette* (1994), 88 C.C.C. (3d) 1, [1994] 1 S.C.R. 469, 28 C.R. (4th) 1. In *Durette*, at p. 58, Sopinka J., for a majority of the court, held: "The appellants should not be required to demonstrate the specific use to which they might put information which they have not even seen." Similarly, La Forest J. in *Carey*, at p. 529 C.C.C., p. 192 D.L.R., held in commenting on the lower court's decision which denied the applicant access to Cabinet documents because his submissions, according to that court, were no more than "a bare unsupported assertion ... that something to help him may be found":

> What troubles me about this approach is that it puts on a plaintiff the burden of proving how the documents, which are admittedly relevant, can be of assistance. How can he do that? He has never seen them; they are confidential and so unavailable. To some extent, then, what the documents contain must be a matter of speculation.

We are of the view that the concern expressed in these cases applies with equal force in the case at bar, where the ultimate goal is the search for truth rather than the suppression of potentially relevant evidence.

L'Heureux-Dubé J. questions the "Catch-22" analogy in the context of production. In her view, there is no presumption of materiality because the records are not created nor sought by the state as part of its investigation. However, it should be remembered that in most cases, an accused will not be privy to the existence of third party records which are maintained under strict rules of confidentiality. Generally speaking, an accused will only become aware of the existence of records because of something which arises in the course of the criminal case. For example, the complainant's psychiatrist, therapist or social worker may come forward and reveal his or her concerns about the complainant (as occurred in *R. v. Ross* (1993), 79 C.C.C. (3d) 253, 18 C.R. (4th) 122, 119 N.S.R. (2d) 177 (N.S.C.A.); *R. v. Ross* (1993), 81 C.C.C. (3d) 234, 21 C.R. (4th) 254 *sub nom. R. v. R. (K.A.)*, 121 N.S.R. (2d) 242 (N.S.C.A.)). In other cases, the complainant may reveal at the preliminary inquiry or in his or her statement to the police that he or she decided to lay a criminal charge against the accused following a visit with a particular therapist. There is a possibility of materiality where there is a "reasonably close temporal connection between" the creation of the records and the date of the alleged commission of the offence (*R. v. Osolin* (1993), 86 C.C.C. (3d) 481 at p. 524, 109 D.L.R. (4th) 478 at p. 522, [1993] 4 S.C.R. 595) or in cases of historical events, as in this case, a close temporal connection between the creation of the records and the decision to bring charges against the accused.

In *R. v. Morin* (1988), 44 C.C.C. (3d) 193 at p. 218, [1988] 2 S.C.R. 345, 66 C.R. (3d) 1, we recognized that "[i]t is difficult and arguably undesirable to lay down stringent rules for the determination of the relevance of a particular category of evidence". Consequently, while we will not attempt to set out categories of relevance, we feel compelled to respond to some of the statements expressed by our colleague. L'Heureux-Dubé J. suggests in her reasons that "the assumption that private therapeutic or counselling records are relevant to full answer and defence is often highly questionable" and that "the vast majority of information noted during therapy sessions bears no relevance whatsoever or, at its highest, only an attenuated sense of relevance to the issues at trial". With respect, we disagree. L'Heureux-Dubé J.'s observation as to the likelihood of relevance belies the reality that in many criminal cases, trial judges have ordered the production of third party records often applying the same principles we have enunciated in this case. The sheer number of decisions in which such evidence has been produced supports the potential relevance of therapeutic records.

Moreover, in *Osolin, supra,* this court recognized the importance of ensuring access to the kind of information at issue in this appeal. In *Osolin,* we ordered a new trial where the accused had been denied an opportunity to cross-examine regarding the psychiatric records of the complainant. Those records contained the following entry (at p. 515 C.C.C., p. 513 D.L.R.):

> She is concerned that her attitude and behaviour may have influenced the man to some extent and is having second thoughts about the entire case.

Cory J., for the majority, held, at p. 525 C.C.C., p. 523 D.L.R., that:

> ... what the complainant said to her counsellor ... could well reflect a victim's unfortunate and unwarranted feelings of guilt and shame for actions and events that were in no way her fault. Feelings of guilt, shame and lowered self-esteem are often the result of the trauma of a sexual assault. If this is indeed the basis for her statement to the counsellor, then they could not in any way lend an air of reality to the accused's proposed defence of mistaken belief in the complainant's consent. However, in the absence of cross-examination it is impossible to know what the result might have been.

By way of illustration only, we are of the view that there are a number of ways in which information contained in third party records may be relevant, for example, in sexual assault cases:

(1) they may contain information concerning the unfolding of events underlying the criminal complaint: see *Osolin, supra,* and *R. v. S. (R.J.)* (1985), 19 C.C.C. (3d) 115, 45 C.R. (3d) 161, 14 W.C.B. 19 (Ont. C.A.).

(2) they may reveal the use of a therapy which influenced the complainant's memory of the alleged events. For example, in *R. v. L. (D.O.)* (1993), 85 C.C.C. (3d) 289 at p. 308, [1993] 4 S.C.R. 419, 25 C.R. (4th) 285, L'Heureux-Dubé J. recognized the problem of contamination when she stated, in the context of the sexual abuse of children, that "the fear of contaminating required testimony has forced the delay of needed therapy and

counselling". See too *R. v. Norman* (1993), 87 C.C.C. (3d) 153, 26 C.R. (4th) 256, 16 O.R. (3d) 295 (C.A.).

(3) they may contain information that bears on the complainant's "credibility, including testimonial factors such as the quality of their perception of events at the time of the offence, and their memory since". See *R. v. R. (L.), supra*, at p. 339 C.C.C., p. 180 D.L.R.; *R. v. Hedstrom* (1991), 63 C.C.C. (3d) 261, 12 W.C.B. (2d) 267 (B.C.C.A.); *R. v. Ross, supra*; *Toohey v. Metropolitan Police Commissioner*, [1965] 1 All. E.R. 506 (H.L.).

As a result, we disagree with L'Heureux-Dubé J.'s assertion that therapeutic records will only be relevant to the defence in rare cases.

(d) The role of the judge at the second stage: balancing full answer and defence and privacy

We agree with L'Heureux-Dubé J. that "upon their production to the court, the judge should examine the records to determine whether, and to what extent, they should be produced to the accused" ... We also agree that in making that determination, the judge must examine and weigh the salutary and deleterious effects of a production order and determine whether a non-production order would constitute a reasonable limit on the ability of the accused to make full answer and defence. In some cases, it may be possible for the presiding judge to provide a judicial summary of the records to counsel to enable them to assist in determining whether the material should be produced. This, of course, would depend on the specific facts of each particular case.

We also agree that, in balancing the competing rights in question, the following factors should be considered: (1) "the extent to which the record is necessary for the accused to make full answer and defence; (2) the probative value of the record in question; (3) the nature and extent of the reasonable expectation of privacy vested in that record; (4) whether production of the record would be premised upon any discriminatory belief or bias"; and (5) "the potential prejudice to the complainant's dignity, privacy or security of the person that would be occasioned by production of the record in question" ....

However, L'Heureux-Dubé J. also refers to two other factors that she believes must be considered. She suggests that the judge should take account of "the extent to which production of records of this nature would frustrate society's interest in encouraging the reporting of sexual offences and the acquisition of treatment by victims" as well as "the effect on the integrity of the trial process of producing, or failing to produce, the record, having in mind the need to maintain consideration in the outcome". This last factor is more appropriately dealt with at the admissibility stage and not in deciding whether the information should be produced. As for society's interest in the reporting of sexual crimes, we are of the opinion that there are other avenues available to the judge to ensure that production does not frustrate the societal interests that may be implicated by the production of the records to the defence. A number of these avenues are discussed by the Nova Scotia Court of Appeal in *R. v. Ryan* (1991), 69 C.C.C. (3d) 226 at p. 230, 107 N.S.R. (2d) 357, 14 W.C.B. (2d) 477:

> As the trials of these two charges proceed, there are a number of protective devices to allay the concerns of the caseworkers over the contents of their files. The trial judge has considerable discretion in these matters. It is for the trial judge to determine whether a ban shall be placed on publication. It is for the trial judge to decide whether spectators shall be barred when evidence is given on matters that the trial judge deems to be extremely sensitive and worth excluding from the information available to the public. High on the list is, of course, the matter of relevance. Unless the evidence sought from the witness meets the test of relevancy, it will be excluded. The trial judge is able to apply the well-established rules and tests to determine whether any given piece of evidence is relevant.

We are also of the view that these options are available to the judge to further protect the privacy interests of witnesses if the production of private records is ordered.

Consequently, the societal interest is not a paramount consideration in deciding whether the information should be provided. It is, however, a relevant factor which should be taken into account in weighing the competing interests.

In applying these factors, it is also appropriate to bear in mind that production of third party records is always available to the Crown provided it can obtain a search warrant. It can do so if it satisfies a justice that there is in a place, which includes a private dwelling, anything that there are reasonable grounds to believe will afford evidence of the commission of an offence. Fairness requires that the accused be treated on an equal footing.

III

Conclusion and Disposition

Although the parties have obviously failed to observe the above procedures for the production of third party records, it is unnecessary to determine whether or not a production order was warranted in this case. In our view, Major J. is correct in holding that the impropriety of the production order at issue in this appeal "does not excuse the conduct of the Crown after the order was made". ... As a result, whether or not production was warranted in this case, the conduct of the Crown in refusing to comply with the production order is inexcusable, and warrants a stay of the proceedings against the accused. We are therefore in complete agreement with the reasoning and conclusions of Major J., and would accordingly hold that this appeal should be allowed.

In the aftermath of the *O'Connor* decision, Bill C-46 was passed and proclaimed as *An Act to Amend the Criminal Code* (production of records in sexual offence proceedings), S.C. 1997, c. 30. The legislation applies only to named sexual offences. Record disclosure relating to other offences will continue to be regulated by *O'Connor*. It is important to note that these new procedures need to be followed regardless of whether the records are in the possession of the Crown unless the complainant or witness to whom the record relates has expressly waived the application of these statutory procedures. These new provisions of the *Criminal Code*, s. 278.1 *et seq.* should be carefully compared to the *O'Connor* framework. Their constitutionality was addressed in the following case.

R. v. MILLS

(1999), 139 C.C.C. (3d) 321 (S.C.C.)

McLachlin and Iacobucci JJ. [L'Heureux-Dubé, Gonthier, Major, Bastarache and Binnie JJ. concurring]: —

.....

II. Summary

This appeal presents an apparent conflict among the rights to full answer and defence, privacy, and equality, all of which are protected by the *Canadian Charter of Rights and Freedoms* (ss. 7 and 11(*d*), s. 8, and s. 15, respectively). The underlying issue is what is required by the "principles of fundamental justice" protected by s. 7. Bill C-46 reflects Parliament's effort at balancing these rights. Our task is to decide whether Parliament's balance is a constitutional one.

.....

VI. Analysis

.....

D. Analysis of Sections 278.1 to 278.91 of Bill C-46

In enacting Bill C-46, Parliament was concerned with preserving an accused's access to private records that may be relevant to an issue on trial, while protecting the right to privacy of complainants and witnesses to the greatest extent possible. Notwithstanding Parliament's good intentions, the respondent suggests that Bill C-46 violates the constitutional right of the accused to a fair trial and full defence on a number of grounds. We will consider each in turn.

(1) The Definition of Documents Subject to the Legislation: Sections 278.1 and 278.2(1)

An initial issue to address is the definition of documents subject to the legislation. Pursuant to s. 278.1 and s. 278.2(1), the Bill applies to all records of complainants and witnesses in sexual offence proceedings containing "personal information for which there is a reasonable expectation of privacy", including "medical, psychiatric, therapeutic, counselling, education, employment, child welfare, adoption and social services records, personal journals and diaries and records containing personal information the production or disclosure of which is protected by any other Act of Parliament or a provincial legislature".

Belzil J., for the court below, found that the definition of records under the Bill is "extremely broad" [para. 47] and that the Bill therefore accords legislative protection to records not contemplated under *O'Connor*. The broader scope of the legislation, he held, imposes a significant burden on accused persons by requiring them to proceed with an application, supported by affidavits, for each different type of record listed. Belzil J. considered the greater reach of the Bill to be one of five significant differences between the Bill and *O'Connor* which led him to conclude that the Bill as a whole was unconstitutional.

The response to these claims is to remember that the legislation applies only to records "in which there is a *reasonable* expectation of privacy" (s. 278.1 (emphasis added)). Only documents that truly raise a legally recognized privacy interest are caught and protected: see *R. v. Regan* (1998), 174 N.S.R. (2d) 230 (S.C.). The Bill is therefore carefully tailored to reflect the problem Parliament was addressing — how to preserve an accused's access to private records that may be relevant to an issue on trial while protecting, to the greatest extent possible, the privacy rights of the subjects of such records, including both complainants and witnesses. By limiting its coverage to records in which there is a reasonable expectation of privacy, the Bill is consistent with the definition of s. 8 privacy rights discussed above. Moreover, as will be discussed below, the mere fact that records are within the ambit of Bill C-46 will not, in itself, prevent the accused from obtaining access to them. Applied in this way, s. 278.1 and s. 278.2(1) will not catch more records than they should, and are not overly broad.

It must also be remembered that the definition of records in s. 278.1 and s. 278.2(1) simply establishes the starting point for the analysis proposed by the Bill. Documents falling within the ambit of these provisions, after being subject to the legislative regime, may or may not be ordered to be disclosed to the accused. It is therefore the procedures established by the Bill and not the spectrum of records subject to these procedures that will determine the fairness or constitutionality of the legislation. If the legislative regime fairly provides access to all constitutionally required documents, then the spectrum of records brought under the Bill, if in keeping with the Bill's objectives, cannot be challenged.

The broad scope of Bill C-46 has also been challenged as imposing an excessive burden on judicial resources. However, the Bill safeguards the efficiency and resources of the judicial system while furthering its objective of protecting, to the greatest extent possible, the rights of all those involved in sexual offence proceedings, by mandating that judges can only review the records in question once these records have been established as likely relevant and their production to the court has been established as necessary in the interests of justice. The balancing process required at the first stage ensures that records are not needlessly or casually produced to the court for review: see *O'Connor, supra,* at para. 152, *per* L'Heureux-Dubé J. Moreover, as many interveners have pointed out, production of records to the court had become almost routine in sexual assault cases. It is unlikely that Bill C-46's procedures will be substantially more onerous on judicial resources. Finally, Parliament, with the benefit of a full legislative inquiry, has ruled on such questions of administrative convenience. We see no reason to disturb its conclusion. If the system proves unworkable in practice, then Parliament, not this Court, is better positioned to fix it.

(2) Third Party Records in the Possession of the Crown: Sections 278.2(2) and (3)

The next provision at issue extends the application of the legislative regime for the production of private records to records "in the possession or control of any person", including the Crown: s. 278.2(2).

Where private records are in the possession or control of the Crown two important variations on the regime for production exist. First, the legislative regime does not apply if the complainant or witness has expressly waived the protections of the Bill (s. 278.2(2)). Second, s. 278.2(3) requires the prosecutor to notify the accused of any records in the Crown's possession.

The respondent objects to the fact that this provision prevents the automatic disclosure of all relevant and non-privileged information in the possession of the Crown. He submits that this is contrary to the constitutional obligation upon the Crown set out in *Stinchcombe* [(1999), 68 C.C.C. (3d) 1 (S.C.C.)], and is inconsistent with this Court's conclusion in *O'Connor, supra,* that "the Crown's disclosure obligations established in the *Stinchcombe* decision are unaffected by the confidential nature of therapeutic records" (at para. 13, *per* Lamer C.J. and Sopinka J.). The respondent also argues that s. 278.2(2) gives the Crown an unfair advantage in that only the accused is subject to the legislative regime. The Crown can obtain private records through the complainant directly or through the power of a search warrant. The Bill not only exempts the Crown from the obligation to comply with the legislation regime when seeking private records, but also allows the Crown to possess information that the defence does not have.

The first response to the respondent's argument is that it is premature. Section 278.2 simply defines the scope of the legislation. It does not by itself deny access to documents to which the defence is constitutionally entitled. If the procedures set out in the sections that follow fairly provide access to all constitutionally required documents, then the accused has no constitutional complaint.

Second, the argument that this provision contradicts *Stinchcombe* and *O'Connor* rests on an overstatement of the Crown obligation to disclose that was affirmed in those cases. It is true that *Stinchcombe* spoke of a duty on the Crown to disclose to the defence all relevant documents in the Crown's possession, subject to privilege. Privacy interests, however, were not at issue in *Stinchcombe*. In *O'Connor*, the Court considered the Crown's obligation to disclose private records in the context of sexual offence proceedings where the complainant has made an informed waiver of her privacy rights. The majority in *O'Connor* concluded that "the Crown's well-established duty to disclose all information in its possession is not affected by the confidential nature of therapeutic records": *O'Connor, supra,* at para. 7. This conclusion, however, was premised upon the assumption that the records in the Crown's possession have been freely and voluntarily surrendered by the complainant or witness: "[W]here the documents in question have been shared with an agent of the state (namely, the Crown), it is apparent that the complainant's privacy interest in those records has disappeared." *O'Connor, supra,* at para 8. Lamer C.J. and Sopinka J. further found that "fairness must require that if the complainant is *willing to release* this information in order to further the criminal prosecution, then the accused should be entitled to use the information in the preparation of his or her defence", *O'Connor, supra*, at para. 9 (emphasis added). Bill C-46 imposes the same waiver rule. Where a fully informed complainant expressly waives the protection of the legislation, by declaration or by voluntarily providing her records to the Crown, the Bill C-46 procedure does not apply and the records are producible as at common law: s. 278.2(2). Bill C-46 thus conforms to the constitutional standard of *O'Connor*.

The respondent argues, however, that *O'Connor* should not be read as requiring the disclosure of confidential records pursuant to *Stinchcombe only* in cases of an express waiver and that s. 278.2(2) is unconstitutional. He asserts that any reasonable expectation of privacy is lost once the records are in the possession of the Crown, regardless of how the records came into the Crown's possession. Once in the Crown's hands, the records become "the property of the public" to be used to ensure that justice is done and must be disclosed pursuant to the common law.

This argument erroneously equates Crown possession or control with a total loss of any reasonable expectation of privacy. Privacy is not an all or nothing right. It does not follow from the fact that the Crown has possession of the records that any reasonable expectation of privacy disappears. Privacy interests in modern society include the reasonable expectation that private information will remain confidential to the persons to whom and restricted to the purposes for which it was divulged, *Dyment* [(1988), 45 C.C.C. (3d) 244 (S.C.C.)], at p. 429. Where private information is disclosed to individuals outside of those to whom, or for purposes other than for which, it was originally divulged, the person to whom the information pertains may still hold a reasonable expectation of privacy in this information, *R. v. Boudreau*, [1998] O.J. No. 3526 (QL) (Gen. Div.), at para. 18 [reported at 56 C.R.R. (2d) 345]. Third party records may fall into the possession of the Crown without the knowledge, consent, or assistance of the complainant or witness. Where the complainant or witness has not expressly waived her privacy right, Parliament can legitimately take steps to protect those privacy rights. Such protection is to be found in the procedures for production set out in s. 278.5 and s. 278.7 of the Bill.

The *O'Connor* majority did not address what procedure was to be followed where third party records were in the possession of the Crown without the existence of an express waiver. It was therefore open to Parliament to fill this void legislatively. Viewed in this context, s. 278.2(2) ensures that the range of interests triggered by production will be balanced pursuant to the procedure set out in s. 278.5 and s. 278.7. The mere fact that this procedure differs from that set out in *Stinchcombe* does not, without more, establish a constitutional violation. As noted, *Stinchcombe* and *O'Connor* did not address the situation at issue here, namely, records in the Crown's possession in which a complainant or witness has a reasonable, and non-waived, expectation of privacy. We are thus returned to our starting point — that s. 278.2 in itself violates no rights and any violation can be determined only by examining its impact in conjunction with ss. 278.5 through 278.8.

When the arguments that s. 278.2 is inconsistent with *Stinchcombe, supra*, and *O'Connor, supra*, are cleared away, the respondent's fundamental objection to the section emerges — it unfairly favours the Crown. The Crown can obtain the complainant's private records through a search warrant or subpoena. Where the complainant or witness does not expressly waive the protection of the legislation, the accused can get these documents only by applying under the Bill C-46 regime. If the accused does not succeed, the Crown may possess documents that the accused does not have. This, it is argued, puts the Crown at an advantage.

All this is true. But it begs the real question — is the Crown's advantage unconstitutional? In other words, does it deprive the accused of his right to make full answer and defence? That will be so only if the legislation prevents the accused from getting access to all constitutionally required documents. There is no principle of fundamental justice that the Crown and defence must enjoy precisely the same privileges and procedures. See *Leipert* [(1997), 112 C.C.C. (3d) 385 (S.C.C.)]. The real question is whether the procedures that Parliament has enacted prevent the accused from making full answer and defence. This is the true meaning of the passage from *O'Connor, supra*, at para. 34, which states that "[f]airness requires that the accused be treated on an equal footing" with the Crown, which has access to search warrants. Obviously, the search warrant procedure involves a different array of factors from those that are relevant to production of third party records to the accused. All that was meant by this passage is that the accused must have a procedure for obtaining evidence that respects all the relevant constitutional rights at stake, just as the prosecution does through the warrant process. As we will explain below, Bill C-46 is just such a procedure.

In *Stinchcombe*, this Court acknowledged that the Crown, by virtue of its unique role as agent of the state, has greater access to certain types of information than the accused. The Court therefore imposed a duty on the Crown to disclose all relevant information to the defence. The goal behind imposing this duty upon the Crown was not, however, to ensure equivalency of treatment between the accused and the Crown. Rather, the duty to disclose was imposed to advance the overall fairness, justice, efficacy, and truth finding elements of criminal proceedings. Since the right to full answer and defence must be defined in light of other principles of fundamental justice, that right is not an absolute one. Thus, while acknowledging the disparity in access to certain types of information, Sopinka J. conditioned the Crown's duty to disclose by investing in the Crown a discretion to withhold information where necessary to respect the rules of privilege, to protect persons from harassment or injury, or where this information is clearly irrelevant, at pp. 336 and 339. Similarly, in *O'Connor, supra*, at para. 16, Lamer C.J. and Sopinka J. held:

> ... *Stinchcombe* recognized that, even in the context of disclosure, there are limits on the right of an accused to access information. For example, when the Crown asserts that the information is privileged, the trial judge must then balance the competing claims at issue. In such cases, the information will only be disclosed where the trial judge concludes that the asserted privilege "does not constitute a reasonable limit on the constitutional right to make full answer and defence" (*Stinchcombe*, at p. 340).

Stinchcombe and *O'Connor* accept that it is constitutionally permissible for the Crown to be subject to different treatment, to different procedures, or even to end up with documents that the accused has not seen, as long as the accused can make full answer and defence and the trial is fundamentally fair.

Furthermore, when addressing the disparity of treatment between defence counsel and the Crown, we must remember the specific problem Bill C-46 was enacted to address. Through Bill C-46, Parliament sought to preserve an accused's access to private records that may be relevant to the defence in a sexual offence proceeding while protecting, to the greatest extent possible, the privacy rights of complainants and witnesses. The context of the Bill is one in which defence counsel were routinely seeking access to the private records of complainants or witnesses in sexual offence proceedings (K. Kelly, "'You must be crazy if you think you were raped': Reflections on the Use of Complainants' Personal and Therapy Records in Sexual Assault Trials" (1997), 9 C.J.W.L. 178; K. Busby, "Third Party Records Cases Since *R. v. O'Connor*: A Preliminary Analysis" [a study funded by the Research and Statistics Section, Department of Justice Canada, July 1998.)]. As Heather Holmes aptly summarizes:

> The *O'Connor* issue arose from new defence intrusion into the rights and interests of third parties. Defence applications for access to third party records are quite properly motivated only by the accused's concern to make full answer and defence to the charge. The Crown, by contrast, is responsible for a larger set of interests including those of third parties and the general public as well as those of the accused. [Emphasis in original; "An Analysis of Bill C-46, Production of Records in Sexual Offence Proceedings" (1997), 2 Can. Crim. L.R. 71, at p. 86.]

The greater procedural burden placed on the accused under Bill C-46 reflects the fact that unlike the Crown, the accused bears no responsibility to protect the rights of others. To protect such rights, when they are threatened by the acts of the accused, greater procedural protections are required.

The defence concern that it will be unable to obtain records relevant to its defence will be considered in greater detail later. However, in relation to s. 278.2(2) it is worth pointing out that Parliament inserted two provisions to offset any unfairness that might flow from the Crown's being in possession of documents that the defence has not seen. As discussed above, the first is the provision that if the complainant or witness waives the protection of the legislation, the documents must be disclosed to the defence: s. 278.2(2). Waiver should not be read in a technical sense. Where the complainant or witness, with knowledge that the legislation protects her privacy interest in the records, indicates by words or conduct that she is relinquishing her privacy right, waiver may be found. Turning records over to the police or Crown, with knowledge of the law's protections and the consequences of waiving these protections, will constitute an express waiver pursuant to s. 278.2(2).

The second aid to the accused is the requirement in s. 278.2(3) that the prosecutor notify the accused of the private documents in his or her possession. While the contents are not to be disclosed at this stage, the notification requirement reveals the existence of the record to the accused and allows the accused to make an application for production. When notifying an accused, the Crown should ensure that information as to date and context are provided so that the documents can be sufficiently identified. This will help furnish the accused with a basis for arguing that the documents may be relevant to the defence under s. 278.5: see *Boudreau, supra, per* Ewaschuk J.

We conclude that the fact that s. 278.2 may result in the Crown holding documents that the accused does not possess does not of itself deprive the accused of the right to make full answer and defence. Parliament has balanced the inevitably advantageous documentary position the prosecution enjoys with safeguards to protect the accused's interest in getting those documents that may be relevant to the defence. Provided the remainder of Bill C-46 permits the accused to obtain the documents to which the defence is entitled, the fact that the Crown may possess documents that the accused does not, does not vitiate the process. Section 278.2 is constitutional in that it does not violate ss. 7 or 11(*d*) of the *Charter*.

(3) The "Insufficient Grounds" Section: Section 278.3(4)

Section 278.3(4) lists a series of "assertions" that cannot "on their own" establish that a record is likely relevant. The respondent submits that on a plain reading, this provision prevents the accused from relying on the listed factors when attempting to establish the likely relevance of the records. This, he argues, interferes with the right to make full answer and defence by restricting what the judge can consider in determining whether the records must be produced to the defence. The legislation raises the bar for production, he asserts, making it difficult if not impossible for the accused to meet the likely relevance test of ss. 278.5 and 278.7. The respondent contends that it is unconstitutional to exclude the assertions listed in s. 278.3(4) as irrelevant.

This submission forgets that when legislation is susceptible to more than one interpretation, we must always choose the constitutional reading. See *Slaight*, [1989] 1 S.C.R. 1038, at p. 1078. This mistake leads the respondent to overstate the purpose and effect of s. 278.3(4). As has frequently been held, its purpose is to prevent speculative and unmeritorious requests for production, *R. v. Hurrie* (1997), 12 C.R. (5th) 180 (B.C.S.C.) at paras. 16-17; *Boudreau, supra*, at para. 6; *Regan, supra*, at paras. 26-27; *R. v. Stromner* (1997), 205 A.R. 385 (Prov. Ct.) at paras. 39-42; *R. v. G. (J.F.)*, [1997] N.W.T.J. No. 47 (QL) (S.C.) at paras. 27-28. It does not entirely prevent an accused from relying on the factors listed, but simply prevents reliance on *bare "assertions"* of the listed matters, where there is no other evidence and they stand "on their own".

As has frequently been noted, speculative myths, stereotypes, and generalized assumptions about sexual assault victims and classes of records have too often in the past hindered the search for truth and imposed harsh and irrelevant burdens on complainants in prosecutions of sexual offences. See *Seaboyer* [[1991] 2 S.C.R. 577] at p. 634. The myths that a woman's testimony is unreliable unless she made a complaint shortly after the event (recent complaint), or if she has had previous sexual relations, are but two of the more notorious examples of the speculation that in the past has passed for truth in this difficult area of human behaviour and the law. The notion that consultation with a psychiatrist is, by itself, an indication of untrustworthiness is a more recent, but equally invidious, example of such a myth. The purpose of s. 278.3(4) is to prevent these and other myths from forming the entire basis of an otherwise unsubstantiated order for production of private records.

The purpose and wording of s. 278.3 do not prevent an accused from relying on the assertions set out in subsection 278.3(4) where there is an evidentiary or informational foundation to suggest that they may be related to likely relevance. (An exception is "recent complaint" which has been abolished by the jurisprudence and cannot be relied on in any event, quite apart from the section.) The section requires only that the accused be able to point to case-specific evidence or information to show that the record in issue is likely relevant to an issue at trial or the competence of a witness to testify, see *Leipert, supra*, at para. 21. Conversely, where an accused does provide evidence or information to support an assertion listed in s. 278.3(4), this does not mean that likely relevance is made out. Section 278.3(4) does not supplant the ultimate discretion of the trial judge. Where any one of the listed assertions is made and supported by the required evidentiary and informational foundation, the trial judge is the ultimate arbiter in deciding whether the likely relevance threshold set out in ss. 278.5 and 278.7 is met.

We conclude that s. 278.3(4) does not violate ss. 7 or 11(*d*) of the *Charter*.

(4) The First Stage — Production to the Judge: Sections 278.4 and 278.5

Bill C-46, as noted, contemplates a two-stage procedure for gaining access to documents. At the first stage, the issue is whether the document should be produced to the judge. If that stage is passed, the judge looks at the document to determine whether it should be produced to the accused. Section 278.5 establishes the procedure for production to the judge at the first stage.

Section 278.4 also deals with procedure. The judge holds the hearing *in camera*, and may hear witnesses and take submissions. Witnesses are not, however, compellable, though under s. 278.4(2) they "may appear and make submissions". None of the parties or interveners in this appeal directly challenged the non-compellability of witnesses under s. 278.4(2) (though this section falls within the stated constitutional questions, and was addressed by Belzil J.). We are therefore reluctant to assess its constitutionality. That said, and without deciding the issue, we would note that the fact that witnesses are not compellable must be viewed in light of the preliminary, investigatory nature of the process at this stage and the other sources upon which the judge can draw in assessing whether the documents may be relevant and whether their production is necessary to the interests of justice, discussed more fully below. While *Stinchcombe* affirmed the right of the defence to obtain documents in the possession of the Crown which may be relevant to the defence, it did not suggest that the defence should have the right to examine witnesses on what documents are relevant. The common law has never compelled witnesses to testify as to records at the investigatory stage, although many inquisitorial, civilian systems do so. The fact that witnesses are not compellable under s. 278.4(2) is consistent, at the very least, with the common law tradition and with *Stinchcombe*. Moreover, as we discuss more fully *infra*, trial judges retain a broad discretion under s. 278.5(1) to order production. We must presume that Parliament intended for trial judges to exercise that discretion in a manner consistent with the *Charter* principles discussed above.

Both the majority and minority of this Court in *O'Connor, supra,* held that records must be produced to the judge for inspection if the accused can demonstrate that the information is "likely to be relevant": *O'Connor, supra,* at para. 19, *per* Lamer C.J. and Sopinka J., and at para. 138, *per* L'Heureux-Dubé J. The Court defined the standard of likely relevance as "a reasonable possibility that the information is logically probative to *an issue at trial or the competence of a witness to testify*" (emphasis in original; para. 22). Although the majority recognized that complainants have a constitutional right to privacy (at para. 17), it held that no balancing of rights should be undertaken at the first stage (at para. 24). This conclusion was premised on the finding that: (1) to require the accused to meet more than the likely relevance stage would be to "put the accused in the difficult situation of having to make submissions to the judge without precisely knowing what is contained in the records" (para. 25); and (2) there is not enough information before a trial judge at this initial stage of production for an informed balancing procedure to take place (para. 21). To this end, the majority held that the analysis should be confined to determining "likely relevance" and "whether the right to make full answer and defence is implicated by information contained in the records" (para. 21). In contrast, the minority held that once the accused meets the "likely relevance" threshold, he must then satisfy the judge that the salutary effects of ordering the documents produced to the court for inspection outweigh the deleterious effects of such production, having regard to the accused's right to make full answer and defence, and the effect of such production on the privacy and equality rights of the subject of the records (at para. 150). L'Heureux-Dubé J. found that a sufficient evidentiary basis could be established at this stage through Crown disclosure, defence witnesses, the cross-examination of Crown witnesses at both the preliminary inquiry and the trial and, on some occasions, expert evidence (at para. 146).

Parliament, after studying the issue, concluded that the rights of both the complainant and the accused should be considered when deciding whether to order production to the judge. In coming to this conclusion, Parliament must be taken to have determined, as a result of lengthy consultations, and years of Parliamentary study and debate, that trial judges have sufficient evidence to engage in an informed balancing process at this stage. Parliament began consultations on the production of complainants' private records in sexual assault cases in June 1994. The *O'Connor* decision became a part of that discussion when it was released December 14, 1995, and was subsequently addressed in the consultations which continued until March 1997. In developing the Bill C-46 production regime, we must therefore remember that Parliament had the benefit of information not available to the Court when it penned *O'Connor*. Specifically, Parliament had the advantage of being able to assess how the *O'Connor* regime was operating. The record indicates that Parliament received many submissions that under the *O'Connor* regime, private records were routinely being produced to the court at the first stage, leading to the recurring violation of the privacy interests of complainants and witnesses. While it is true that little statistical data existed at the time of the drafting of Bill C-46 on the application of *O'Connor*, it was open to Parliament to give what weight it saw fit to the evidence presented at the consultations. As a result of the consultation process, Parliament decided to supplement the "likely relevant" standard for production to the judge proposed in *O'Connor* with the further requirement that production be "necessary in the interests of justice". The result was s. 278.5. This process is a notable example of the dialogue between the judicial and legislative branches discussed above. This Court acted in *O'Connor*, and the legislature responded with Bill C-46. As already mentioned, the mere fact that Bill C-46 does not mirror *O'Connor* does not render it unconstitutional.

Section 278.5(1) requires the accused at the stage of production to a judge to demonstrate not only that the information is "likely relevant" but, in addition, that the production of the record "is necessary in the interests of justice". The first requirement takes up the unanimous view in *O'Connor* that the accused, to get production to the judge, must show that the record is "likely relevant". The additional requirement that production to the judge be "necessary in the interests of justice" encompasses (but is not confined to) the concern of the minority in *O'Connor* that even where likely relevance is shown, there should be room for the court to consider the rights and interests of all those affected by disclosure before documents are ordered disclosed to the court.

Section 278.5(1) is followed by s. 278.5(2) which gives substance to the requirement that trial judges consider the broad range of rights and interests affected before ordering disclosure to the court. Under this section, a trial judge is required to consider the salutary and deleterious effects of production to the court on the accused's right to make full answer and defence and on the rights to privacy and equality of the complainant or witness and any other person to whom the record relates. The section directs the trial judge to "take into account" a series of factors in deciding whether the document should be produced to the court: (a) the extent to which the record is necessary for the accused to make full answer and defence; (b) the probative value of the record; (c) the nature and extent of the reasonable expectation of privacy with respect to the record; (d) whether production of the record is based on a discriminatory belief or bias; (e) the potential prejudice to the personal dignity and right to privacy of any person to whom the record relates; (f) society's interest in encouraging the reporting of sexual offences; (g) society's interest in encouraging the obtaining of treatment by complainants of sexual offences; and (h) the effect of the determination on the integrity of the trial process.

The respondent takes no issue with the requirement that the records be established as likely relevant before production to the judge is ordered. His objection is that the accused must also show that disclosure to the judge is "necessary in the interests of justice". He argues that this requires a weighing and balancing of interests that cannot properly be done without reviewing the documents in question. To this end, s. 278.5 calls upon the trial judge to do the impossible — to weigh competing rights in a vacuum. The respondent contends that likely relevance should be the only requirement at the stage of deciding whether the judge can see the document. In imposing the additional requirement that production be established as "necessary in the interests of justice", s. 278.5 risks depriving the accused of documents relevant to his defence and hence is unconstitutional.

The question comes down to this: once likely relevance is established, is it necessarily unconstitutional that a consideration of the rights and interests of those affected by production to the court might result in production not being ordered? The answer to this question depends on whether a consideration of the range of rights and interests affected, in addition to a finding of likely relevance, will ultimately prevent the accused from seeing documents that are necessary to enable him to defend himself — to raise all the defences that might be open to him at trial. The non-disclosure of third party records with a high privacy interest that may contain relevant evidence will not compromise trial fairness where such non-disclosure would not prejudice the accused's right to full answer and defence.

Section 278.5(1) is a very wide and flexible section. It accords the trial judge great latitude. Parliament must be taken to have intended that judges, within the broad scope of the powers conferred, would apply it in a constitutional manner — a way that would ultimately permit the accused access to all documents that may be constitutionally required. Indeed, a production regime that denied this would not be production "necessary in the interests of justice".

The requirement that production be "necessary in the interests of justice" at this stage refers to whether production *to the judge* is necessary in the interests of justice. That is a phrase capable of encompassing a great deal. It permits the judge to look at factors other than relevancy, like the privacy rights of complainants and witnesses, in deciding whether to order production to himself or herself. Where the privacy right in a record is strong and the record is of low probative value or relates to a peripheral issue, the judge might decide that non-disclosure will not prejudice the accused's right to full answer and defence and dismiss the application for production.

However, pursuant to the first factor of s. 278.5(2), the judge must consider the accused's right to make full answer and defence. If the judge concludes that it is necessary to examine the documents at issue in order to determine whether they should be produced to enable the accused to make full answer and defence, then production to the judge is "necessary in the interests of justice". This answers the argument that s. 278.5(1) may require the judge to decide against production to himself or herself of documents necessary to the defence, and hence foreclose production to the accused in an unconstitutional manner. If a record is established to be "likely relevant" and, after considering the various factors, the judge is left uncertain about whether its production is necessary to make full answer and defence, then the judge should rule in favour of inspecting the document. As L'Heureux-Dubé J. stated in *O'Connor, supra*, at para. 152, "[i]n borderline cases, the judge should err on the side of production to the court". The interests of justice require nothing less.

The criterion in s. 278.5 that production must be "necessary in the interests of justice" invests trial judges with the discretion to consider the full range of rights and interests at issue before ordering production, in a manner scrupulously respectful of the requirements of the *Charter*: see *Baron, supra*, at p. 442, *per* Sopinka J. The fact that the approach set out in s. 278.5 does not accord with *O'Connor's* pronouncement, at para. 24, that at the stage of production to the Court, "considerations of privacy should not enter into the analysis", does not render it unconstitutional. In *O'Connor*, the Court was operating in a legislative vacuum, and fashioned what it considered to be the preferred common law rule. While the rule from that case was of course informed by the *Charter*, it should not be read as a rigid constitutional template. As discussed above, the relationship between the courts and legislatures allows a range of constitutional options. While this Court may have considered it preferable not to consider privacy rights at the production stage, that does not preclude Parliament from coming to a different conclusion, so long as its conclusion is consistent with the *Charter* in its own right. As we have explained, the Bill's directive to consider what is "necessary in the interests of justice", read correctly, does include appropriate respect for the right to full answer and defence.

This leaves the argument that the judge cannot consider the factors listed in s. 278.5(2) without looking at the documents. However, s. 278.5(2) does not require that the judge engage in a conclusive and in-depth evaluation of each of the factors. It rather requires the judge to "take them into account" — to the extent possible at this early stage of proceedings — in deciding whether to order a particular record produced to himself or herself for inspection. Section 278.5(2) serves as a check-list of the various factors that may come into play in making the decision regarding production to the judge. Therefore, while the s. 278.5(2) factors are relevant, in the final analysis the judge is free to make whatever order is "necessary in the interests of justice" — a mandate that includes all of the applicable "principles of fundamental justice" at stake.

Furthermore, contrary to the respondent's submissions, there is a sufficient evidentiary basis to support such an analysis at this early stage. This basis can be established through Crown disclosure, defence witnesses, the cross-examination of Crown witnesses at both the preliminary inquiry and the trial, and expert evidence, see: *O'Connor, supra,* at para. 146, *per* L'Heureux-Dubé J. As noted by Taylor J. for the British Columbia Supreme Court, "the criminal process provides a reasonable process for the acquisition of the evidentiary basis", *Hurrie, supra,* at para. 39. To this end, as the Attorney of British Columbia submitted: "Laying the groundwork prior to trial, or comprehensive examination of witnesses at trial, will go a long way to establishing a meritorious application under this legislation."

The nature of the records in question will also often provide the trial judge with an important informational foundation. For example, with respect to the privacy interest in records, the expectation of privacy in adoption or counselling records may be very different from that in school attendance records, see for example, *R. v. P. (J.S.),* B.C.S.C., Vancouver Registry Nos. CC970130 & CC960237, May 15, 1997. Similarly, a consideration of the probative value of records can often be informed by the nature and purposes of a record, as well as the record taking practices used to create it. As noted above, many submissions were made regarding the different levels of reliability of certain records. Counselling or therapeutic records, for example, can be highly subjective documents which attempt merely to record an individual's emotions and psychological state. Often such records have not been checked for accuracy by the subject of the records, nor have they been recorded verbatim. All of these factors may help a trial judge when considering the probative value of a record being sought by an accused.

The evidentiary foundation of a case, and considerations such as the nature of the records sought and the manner in which these records were taken, will often provide trial judges with sufficient information to be able to "consider" and to "take into account" the factors listed in s. 278.5(2) and to fulfil the requirements of s. 278.5(1). As a final protection for the accused, the trial judge is always free to make whatever order is "necessary in the interests of justice". As discussed above in the context of defining the right to full answer and defence, courts must as a general matter ensure that the accused can obtain all pertinent evidence required to make full answer and defence, and must be wary of the danger of putting the accused in a Catch-22 situation in seeking to obtain such evidence. Where there is a danger that the accused's right to make full answer and defence will be violated, the trial judge should err on the side of production to the court.

We conclude that s. 278.5 is constitutional. The respondent's argument depends on reading the requirement in s. 278.5(1)(*c*), that production can only be ordered where "necessary in the interests of justice", as capable of blocking production even where the accused might constitutionally require access to the documents in question. A finding of unconstitutionality also hinges on reading s. 278.5(2) as consisting of a check-list of factors and rights to be conclusively assessed and weighed-off against one other. Such readings, however, cannot stand. It can never be in the interests of justice for an accused to be denied the right to make full answer and defence and, pursuant to s. 278.5(2) the trial judge is merely directed to "consider" and "take into account" the factors and rights listed. Where the record sought can be established as "likely relevant", the judge must consider the rights and interests of all those affected by production and decide whether it is necessary in the interests of justice that he or she take the next step of viewing the documents. If in doubt, the interests of justice require that the judge take that step.

(5) Stage Two — Production to the Accused, Section 278.7: The Consideration of Societal Interests, Sections 278.5(2)(f) and (g), and the Integrity of the Trial Process, Section 278.5(2)(h)

Once the first hurdle is passed and the records are produced to the judge, the judge must determine whether it is in the interests of justice that they be produced to the defence. Again the judge must be satisfied that the records are "likely relevant" and that production, this time to the accused, is necessary in the interests of justice. In making this decision, the judge must once again consider the factors set out in s. 278.5(2).

The respondent accepts that weighing competing interests is appropriate at this second stage of the analysis. However, the respondent contends that the requirement under s. 278.7(2), that the trial judge take the factors specified in s. 278.5(2)(*a*) to (*h*) into account, inappropriately alters the constitutional balance established in *O'Connor*. Specifically, the respondent contends that ss. 278.5(2)(*f*) and (*g*) elevate the societal interest in encouraging the reporting of sexual offences and encouraging of treatment of complainants of sexual offences, to a status equal to the accused's right to make full answer and defence. This, he suggests, alters the constitutional balance established in *O'Connor*, where the majority specifically determined these factors to be of secondary importance to defence interests in any balancing of competing interests and better taken into account through other avenues. The respondent also contends that s. 278.5(2)(*h*) unfairly requires trial judges to consider the effect of disclosure on the integrity of the trial process. The respondent submits that this is a question going to admissibility.

These concerns are largely answered by the analysis advanced under s. 278.5(2), discussed at greater length above. Trial judges are not required to rule conclusively on each of the factors nor are they required to determine whether factors relating to the privacy and equality of the complainant or witness "outweigh" factors relating to the accused's right to full answer and defence. To repeat, trial judges are only asked to "take into account" the factors listed in s. 278.5(2) when determining whether production of part or all of the impugned record to the accused is necessary in the interest of justice [(s. 278.7(1))].

The respondent argues that the inclusion of the societal interest factors in ss. 278.5(2)(*f*) and (*g*) alters the constitutional balance established by the *O'Connor* majority. With respect, this argument is unsound. Lamer C.J. and Sopinka J. explicitly held that such factors were relevant and ought to be "taken into account in weighing the competing interests" (para. 33). Their concern was solely that such factors not be given controlling weight. The interpretation of s. 278.5(2) advanced above respects this concern. Nonetheless, it is worth noting that when considering the factors set out in ss. 278.5(2)(*f*) and (*g*), trial judges should acknowledge that such factors will likely arise in every case and may be more readily supported by evidence, and take them into account accordingly.

This leaves the argument that s. 278.5(2)(*h*) goes to admissibility and that any consideration of it at the stage of production distorts the fairness of the trial. While the *O'Connor* majority held that this factor was "more appropriately dealt with at the admissibility stage", this conclusion does not amount to a finding that a consideration of this factor at the stage of production would result in unfairness to the accused, see *O'Connor*, at para. 32. As noted above, when preparing Bill C-46 Parliament had the advantage of being able to assess how the *O'Connor* regime was operating. From the information available to Parliament and the submissions it received during the consultation process, Parliament concluded that the effect of production on the integrity of the trial was a factor that should be included in the list of factors for trial judges to "take into account" at both stages of an application for production. Several interveners have interpreted this factor as requiring courts to consider, along with the other enumerated factors, whether the search for truth would be advanced by the production of the records in question; that is, the question is whether the material in question would introduce discriminatory biases and beliefs into the fact-finding process. We agree with this interpretation of the inquiry required by s. 278.5(2)(*h*) and believe it to be in keeping with the purposes set out in the preamble of the legislation.

By giving judges wide discretion to consider a variety of factors and requiring them to make whatever order is necessary in the interest of justice at both stages of an application for production, Parliament has created a scheme that permits judges not only to preserve the complainant's privacy and equality rights to the maximum extent possible, but also to ensure that the accused has access to the documents required to make full answer and defence.

(6) Timing

Concerns were raised as to how the legislation would work in practice. One concern was that the application must be made to the trial judge: s. 278.3(1). This suggests that it may be deferred to the eve of trial or at the trial itself, allowing the accused little time for consideration of whether and how the records may relate to the accused's defence. One way of avoiding this is through the early assignment of the trial judge, a common practice in prosecutions of serious criminal offences. The trial judge may canvas the possibility of applications for production well in advance of the trial, leaving time for follow-up applications if the first is unsuccessful.

VII. Conclusion and Disposition

In the result we would allow the appeal, set aside the judgments of Belzil J., and uphold the constitutionality of Bill C-46.

QUESTIONS

9. **At trial, a provincial court judge orders that third party records be produced for inspection by the defence. What, if any, remedy does the third party have to challenge that order before the records are produced? What if the production order is made by a superior court judge? Consider, in this regard, *R. v. Beharriell* (1995), 103 C.C.C. (3d) 92 (S.C.C.).**

10. **The complainant in a sexual assault case attends therapeutic counselling sessions after the alleged assault. Records are kept by the social workers of these sessions. As well, there are school records pertaining to the complainant, and medical records held by her family practitioner. Finally, the complainant has kept a diary of her life from the earlier years. What procedures apply to these records? Assume that the defence does not seek the production of these records but first seeks to cross-examine social workers, a doctor and the complainant about the contents of these records. What procedures apply? Now assume that the therapeutic records are highly relevant to the complainant's credibility but contain numerous references to others who attended with the complainant for group counselling. What procedures apply when production is sought?**

11. **The police obtain the complainant's Children's Aid Society records, mistakenly advising the complainant that there is no right to confidentiality attached to them. When the police officer starts to show them to the Crown, the Crown briefly examines them, determines that, although some of them are clearly irrelevant, others are arguably relevant, but marginally so. What should the police and the Crown do? Would your answer be different if the Crown had refused to look at the records and had returned them to the police?**

Even where production is ordered, the court may regulate the distribution or publication of the record's content. See, for example: *R. v. Coon* (1992), 74 C.C.C. (3d) 146 (Ont. Gen. Div.) and s. 278.7(3) to (6) of the *Criminal Code*.

It should be remembered that an order compelling production does not predetermine the admissibility of the records or cross-examination based upon them.

QUESTION

12. The defence believes that police records contain information about the complainant: particulars of his criminal record, the nature of any offences he committed, occurrence reports where he was regarded as a suspect, charges withdrawn against him, and so on. What procedures can the defence utilize to get these records? Further, how can the records be secured prior to the trial date? Does it make a difference if the complainant is a "young person" within the meaning of the *Youth Criminal Justice Act*?

CHAPTER 7

THE PRELIMINARY INQUIRY

A. OVERVIEW

As outlined in Chapter 1, a preliminary inquiry is available for an accused charged with an indictable offence within the exclusive jurisdiction of the superior court or an indictable offence which permits the accused to elect the mode of trial if a preliminary inquiry is requested by the accused or prosecutor. The procedures governing preliminary inquiries are outlined in Part XVIII of the *Criminal Code*, R.S.C. 1985, c. C-46. A provincial court judge or justice of the peace acting under this Part has no inherent powers but only the statutory powers conferred by the *Criminal Code* (see *Doyle v. The Queen* (1976), 29 C.C.C. (2d) 177 (S.C.C.)).

The party requesting a preliminary inquiry must provide the court with a written statement of the issues on which the requesting party wants evidence to be given and the witnesses that the requesting party wants to hear at the inquiry (s. 536.3 of the *Criminal Code* (not in force at time of writing)). The justice can also order that a hearing be held (on application of either party or on the justice's own motion) to assist the parties to identify the issues on which evidence will be given, the witnesses to be heard or to encourage them to consider any other matters that would promote a fair and expeditious inquiry (s. 536.4(1) of the *Criminal Code* (not in force at time of writing)).

A preliminary inquiry serves several functions. First, it compels the prosecution to adduce sufficient evidence to justify sending the matter to trial. Thus, it screens out some weak cases. However, the test for committal, as will be seen below, is so easily satisfied that few prosecution cases fail to survive the preliminary inquiry. Nonetheless, the weaknesses exposed at the preliminary inquiry, even where a committal has been obtained, often will promote more successful plea negotiations, and sometimes, will induce the exercise of prosecutorial discretion to withdraw some or all of the charges. Sometimes, the Crown will welcome a full and probing preliminary inquiry relating to a weak prosecution case as it may provide some support in discussions with a complainant or investigating officer as to why the charges should not proceed or why a plea negotiation should be undertaken. Similarly, a preliminary inquiry may educate a recalcitrant accused as to the inevitability of a conviction.

Second, a preliminary inquiry enables the defence to discover the prosecution's case and to pin down the prosecution witnesses. The defence can better assess the demeanour of those witnesses, the strengths and weaknesses of their positions and can utilize the transcript of the preliminary inquiry to cross-examine them or to refresh their memories at trial. The *Criminal Code* under s. 536.5 (not in force at time of writing) provides for a limited scope preliminary inquiry where committal is not at issue.

Third, a preliminary inquiry enables the parties, most particularly the prosecution, to preserve evidence for trial which might otherwise be lost. Each of these functions will be further developed in this chapter.

In assessing the desirability of a preliminary inquiry, defence counsel must be aware of its negative features as well. Full cross-examinations at the preliminary inquiry may serve to educate the prosecution and its witnesses about the defence that will come and may enable the prosecution to improve its case for trial. Or, a full preliminary inquiry may cause the presiding judge to commit the accused on new offences disclosed in the evidence, respecting the same transaction (see discussion of ss. 535 and 548, in Section B of this chapter). Crown counsel must also assess the impact of a preliminary inquiry in determining whether to elect to proceed by indictment for hybrid offences. For example, the prosecution may be more inclined to elect to proceed summarily for a sexual assault case in order to prevent a young or traumatized complainant from being cross-examined twice before the proceedings are concluded.

QUESTION

1. Is there still a role to be played by preliminary inquiries or should they be abolished? See D. Pomerant & G. Gilmour, *A Survey of the Preliminary Inquiry in Canada*, Working Document (Ottawa: Department of Justice, 1993).

B. NATURE AND SCOPE OF A PRELIMINARY INQUIRY

Section 535 of the *Criminal Code* requires that the presiding judge inquire into the indictable offence with which the accused is charged, and *any other indictable offence, in respect of the same transaction*, founded on the facts that are disclosed by the evidence taken at the preliminary inquiry. Section 548(1) provides that, once all the evidence has been taken, the presiding judge shall:

> (*a*) if in his [or her] opinion there is *sufficient* evidence to put the accused on trial for the offence charged or any other indictable offence *in respect of the same transaction*, order the accused to stand trial; or
> (*b*) discharge the accused, if in his [or her] opinion on the whole of the evidence no *sufficient* case is made out to put the accused on trial for the offence charged or any other indictable offence *in respect of the same transaction*.

(Emphasis added.)

1. Meaning of "Sufficient"

The test imposed upon the presiding judge under s. 548 of the *Criminal Code* has been held to be the same test which governs a trial judge in

assessing whether the defence should be granted a directed verdict or non-suit at the end of the prosecution's case at trial, and the same test which governs an extradition judge in assessing whether a sufficient case has been made out to order a fugitive's extradition from Canada. The following case is most often cited for the articulation of that test.

UNITED STATES OF AMERICA v. SHEPPARD
(*sub nom. United States of America v. Shephard*)

(1976), 30 C.C.C. (2d) 424 (S.C.C.)

Ritchie J. [speaking for the majority of the Court, said at p. 427]: —

I agree that the duty imposed upon a "justice" under s. 475(1) [now s. 548] is the same as that which governs a trial Judge sitting with a jury in deciding whether the evidence is "sufficient" to justify him in withdrawing the case from the jury and this is to be determined according to whether or not there is any evidence upon which a reasonable jury properly instructed could return a verdict of guilty. *The "justice", in accordance with this principle, is, in my opinion, required to commit an accused person for trial in any case in which there is admissible evidence which could, if it were believed, result in a conviction.* [Emphasis added.]

The following case examines the test for committal where the Crown's evidence is entirely circumstantial.

R. v. ARCURI

(2001), 157 C.C.C. (3d) 21 (S.C.C.)

The judgment of the court was delivered by

McLachlin C.J.C.: —

.....

The question to be asked by a preliminary inquiry judge under s. 548(1) of the *Criminal Code* is the same as that asked by a trial judge considering a defence motion for a directed verdict, namely, "whether or not there is any evidence upon which a reasonable jury properly instructed could return a verdict of guilty": *Shephard* [[1977] 2 S.C.R. 1067 (*sub nom. United States of America v. Sheppard*), 30 C.C.C. (2d) 424] at p. 1080; see also *R. v. Monteleone*, [1987] 2 S.C.R. 154 at p. 160. Under this test, a preliminary inquiry judge must commit the accused to trial "in any case in which there is admissible evidence which could, if it were believed, result in a conviction": *Shephard, supra*, at p. 1080.

The test is the same whether the evidence is direct or circumstantial: see *R. v. Mezzo*, [1986] 1 S.C.R. 802, at p. 842-43, 27 C.C.C. (3d) 97, 30 D.L.R. (4th) 161; *Monteleone, supra*, at p. 161. The nature of the judge's task, however, varies according to the type of evidence that the Crown has advanced.

Where the Crown's case is based entirely on direct evidence, the judge's task is straightforward. By definition, the only conclusion that needs to be reached in such a case is whether the evidence is true: see *Watt's Manual of Criminal Evidence* (1998), at §8.0 [("[d]irect evidence is evidence which, if believed, resolves a matter in issue")]; *McCormick on Evidence* (5th ed. 1999), at p. 641; J. Sopinka, S. N. Lederman and A. W. Bryant, *The Law of Evidence in Canada* (2nd ed. 1999), at §2.74 (direct evidence is witness testimony as to "the precise fact which is the subject of the issue on trial"). It is for the jury to say whether and how far the evidence is to be believed: see *Shephard, supra,* at pp. 1086-87. Thus if the judge determines that the Crown has presented direct evidence as to every element of the offence charged, the judge's task is complete. If there is direct evidence as to every element of the offence, the accused must be committed to trial.

The judge's task is somewhat more complicated where the Crown has not presented direct evidence as to every element of the offence. The question then becomes whether the remaining elements of the offence — that is, those elements as to which the Crown has not advanced direct evidence — may reasonably be inferred from the circumstantial evidence. Answering this question inevitably requires the judge to engage in a limited weighing of the evidence because, with circumstantial evidence, there is, by definition, an inferential gap between the evidence and the matter to be established — that is, an inferential gap *beyond* the question of whether the evidence should be believed: see *Watt's Manual of Criminal Evidence, supra,* at §9.01 (circumstantial evidence is "any item of evidence, testimonial or real, other than the testimony of an eyewitness to a material fact. It is any fact from the existence of which the trier of fact may infer the existence of a fact in issue"); *McCormick on Evidence, supra,* at pp. 641-42 ("circumstantial evidence ... may be testimonial, but even if the circumstances depicted are accepted as true, additional reasoning is required to reach the desired conclusion"). The judge must therefore weigh the evidence, in the sense of assessing whether it is reasonably capable of supporting the inferences that the Crown asks the jury to draw. This weighing, however, is limited. The judge does not ask whether she herself would conclude that the accused is guilty. Nor does the judge draw factual inferences or assess credibility. The judge asks only whether the evidence, *if believed,* could reasonably support an inference of guilt.

.....

In performing the task of limited weighing, the preliminary inquiry judge does not draw inferences from facts. Nor does she assess credibility. Rather, the judge's task is to determine whether, *if the Crown's evidence is believed,* it would be reasonable for a properly instructed jury to infer guilt. Thus, this task of "limited weighing" never requires consideration of the inherent reliability of the evidence itself. It should be regarded, instead, as an assessment of the reasonableness of the inferences to be drawn from the circumstantial evidence.

QUESTIONS

2. The case for the prosecution is based upon the evidence of Detective Furball. He testifies unequivocally at the preliminary inquiry that he observed the accused commit the crime with which he is charged. However, on cross-examination, he admits that he has three prior convictions for perjury (which were unknown to the police force that had recently hired him), has hated the accused for years and would dearly love to see the accused "rot in jail" for past grievances. As well, Furball admits that he previously told his fellow officers that he did not see anything. Two other Crown witnesses testify that Furball was not in a position to see anything. Crown counsel still believes Furball and asks for a committal, noting that Furball has maintained his position, despite the cross-examination, and that Furball's evidence, if believed, could result in conviction. Should the presiding judge commit for trial?

3. Assume that a young complainant testifies in chief unequivocally that the accused molested him. In cross-examination, the complainant is no longer sure that it happened. His final answer is, "I don't *think* he did anything to me at all." Should the presiding judge commit for trial?

2. MEANING OF "THE SAME TRANSACTION"

R. v. STEWART

(1988), 44 C.C.C. (3d) 109 (Ont. C.A.)

The judgment of the court was delivered by

Morden J.A.: — This is another case concerned with the meaning and scope of "or any other indictable offence in respect of the same transaction" in s. 475(1)(*a*) [now s. 548(1)(*a*)] of the *Criminal Code*, which was enacted by the *Criminal Law Amendment Act*, S.C. 1985, c. 19, s. 101(1). ...

.....

The following is an outline of the proceedings. The respondent was charged in an information containing three counts which alleged that:

(1) during the months of August and September, 1985, he lived wholly or in part on the avails of prostitution of one A (who, the evidence showed, was a 15-year-old girl) contrary to s. 195(1)(*j*) [now s. 212(1)(*j*)] of the *Criminal Code*;

(2) during the same period, for the purpose of gain, he exercised control, direction or influence over the movements of A in such a manner as to show that he was aiding, abetting or compelling her to engage in or carry on prostitution contrary to s. 195(1)(*h*) [now s. 212(1)(*h*)] of the *Criminal Code*, and

(3) during August, 1985, he did unlawfully assault A contrary to s. 245 [now s. 266] of the *Criminal Code*.

The Crown elected to proceed by way of indictment with respect to the third count.

During the course of the preliminary inquiry the prosecution, in addition to the evidence of A., also called the evidence of one V., who was also a 15-year-old girl. At the conclusion of the inquiry the Provincial Court judge committed the respondent for trial on the counts to which I have referred and, also, on three new counts in virtually identical terms except that they referred to V. instead of to A.

The respondent applied before a High Court judge to quash the committals for trial which related to V. [The committals for the first two charges relating to V. were quashed for unrelated reasons.] ...

With respect to the charge of assault there was evidence that around August 20, 1985, when the respondent, V., and A. were in a hotel room, the respondent, because he was angry with the amount of money V. had earned for him, assaulted V. A. then stepped in and the respondent and A. got into "a big punching match". The respondent hit her on the face.

The High Court judge also quashed the committal on the count relating to the assault on V. He said:

> In my view, whatever the outward or inward limits of the phrase "same transaction" may be, the assaulting of separate persons in succession (be it ever so close in time) is not within the phrase "same transaction" as set out in s. 475(1)(*a*) of the *Criminal Code*.

The Crown appeals from this order.

Some four months after the decision of the High Court judge on the application in this proceeding, this court (comprising Dubin A.C.J.O., Houlden and Robins JJ.A.) in *R. v. Goldstein*, released May 18, 1988 [since reported, 42 C.C.C. (3d) 548, 64 C.R. (3d) 360, 32 C.R.R. 320 (Ont. C.A.)], considered the meaning of "or any other indictable offence in respect of the same transaction" in s. 475(1)(*a*) of the *Criminal Code*.

The relevant facts in *Goldstein* are fully set out in the reasons of Houlden J.A. and it is not necessary to relate them in any detail. It is sufficient to note that each of the appellants had been charged in a count relating to conspiracy to traffic in cocaine with 11 other named persons, including one Juan Fenn-Cruz, "and with a person or persons unknown" over a period between August 23, 1985, and July 15, 1986. The appellants were discharged on this count but each of them was ordered to stand trial for another indictable offence "in respect of the same transaction", which was on charges — slightly different from each other with regard to their time-spans — of conspiracy to traffic in cocaine with Fenn-Cruz over shorter periods of time than that alleged in the original count.

This court dismissed the appeals of Goldstein and Caicedo from an order of a High Court judge dismissing their applications to quash their committals on the new counts. Houlden J.A., speaking for himself and Robins J.A. (who also concurred in reasons given by Dubin A.C.J.O. for dismissing the appeal), after considering the legislative history relating to s. 475(1) and case-law since 1985 relating to it and other provisions in the *Criminal Code* using the term "transaction", said at p. 15 [p. 557 C.C.C.]:

> The words "the same transaction", in my opinion, mean the series of connected acts extending over a period of time which, the Crown alleges, prove the commission of the offence charged in the information. The participation of the accused in this series of connected acts or activity may be sufficient to permit the justice to put the accused on trial for the offence

> charged, or it may not. In addition, it may be sufficient to permit the justice to put the accused on trial for some other indictable offence. If it is, the other offence will, of necessity, be closely interwoven with or related to the offence charged in the information.

He then applied this test to the evidence before the court and said at pp. 15-6 [pp. 557-8 C.C.C.]:

> In the present case, there was evidence before the Provincial Court judge of a general over-all conspiracy between the co-accused other than the two appellants and the accused Dewtie to distribute and sell cocaine. This conspiracy was of a continuing nature, having as its object the sale and distribution of cocaine to various purchasers and other traffickers. There was evidence, and has been noted, that the accused Fenn-Cruz was an active member of that conspiracy.
>
> In charging the appellants with the over-all general conspiracy in count 1 of the information, the Crown was relying substantially on the evidence linking the appellants to the accused Fenn-Cruz. The acts of Fenn-Cruz in selling cocaine to the appellants were consistent with the agreement between Fenn-Cruz and his co-conspirators to traffic in cocaine and with the role played by Fenn-Cruz in the over-all conspiracy, and they occurred in the time-period during which the over-all conspiracy was alleged to have operated. As the Crown said in its factum, the appellants' involvement with Fenn-Cruz was a component part of the same series of acts comprising an ongoing transaction involving the agreement among various parties to sell and distribute cocaine. Thus, the finding by the Provincial Court judge that there was insufficient evidence to commit the appellants on the initial charge does not thereby reduce the appellants' involvement in a component part of the "same transaction" which led to the original charge against the appellants.

The appellant and the respondent before us each rely upon the reasons of Houlden J.A. in support of their respective positions. In my respectful view, the respondent's position is the correct one. It cannot be said that the evidence relating to the assault on V., while it was closely related in time to that relating to the assault on A., formed part of a series of connected acts which the Crown alleged proved the commission of the offence charged in the information.

The appellant relies upon the sentence in the test formulated by Houlden J.A. which includes "... the other offence will, of necessity, be closely interwoven with or related to the offence charged in the information". Accepting that these words could cover the evidence relating to the assault on V., it must be noted that this part of the reasons does not set forth the whole of the test. It amounts to an observation relating to the application of the test — possibly embodying a necessary condition for the applicability of "in respect of the same transaction", but not in itself a sufficient condition.

As I have indicated, the evidence relating to the assault on V. does not relate to a series of connected acts which the Crown alleges proved the assault against A. even though, from a practical point of view, it relates to the narrative respecting the assault against A. The appellant's conduct respecting V. is not, to refer to a further term used by Houlden J.A. in applying the test, a "component part" of the transaction relating to the assault on A.

For these reasons I would dismiss this appeal.

3. Admissibility of Evidence

It seems clear that the credibility or lack of credibility of Crown witnesses has little or no relevance to the presiding judge's function under s. 548 of the *Criminal Code*. As well, such a judge is not a "court of competent jurisdiction" within the meaning of s. 24 of the *Charter*. Accordingly, that judge has no jurisdiction to exclude evidence under s. 24(2) of the *Charter*, or to grant a stay or other relief pursuant to s. 24(1) of the *Charter*. Can the presiding judge therefore prevent the accused's counsel from cross-examining on issues solely relevant to credibility or on *Charter* issues (in anticipation of trial) because they have no relevance to the presiding judge's function?

R. v. COVER

(1988), 44 C.C.C. (3d) 34 (Ont. H.C.J.)

Campbell J. (orally): — [Campbell J. considers whether the provincial court judge presiding at the preliminary inquiry lost jurisdiction by his legal rulings. Since there is no appeal from a committal at a preliminary inquiry, only jurisdictional error permits review by extraordinary remedy. Campbell J. rejects all of the complaints made, except for one.]

.....

The refusal to permit cross-examination of Constable Akin on the information he conveyed to Constable Matthews and on any other matters which the defence wished to raise that might be relevant at trial is, however, a different matter.

The particular point at which counsel was cut off was when he sought to cross-examine Constable Akin on the information that was used as a basis for the search warrant.

The accused does have a right to use a preliminary inquiry to test the Crown's case, to get discovery and disclosure, and to set up the evidentiary basis for challenges at trial to the admissibility of evidence tendered by the Crown at trial. The dicta in *Caccamo v. The Queen* (1975), 21 C.C.C. (2d) 257, 54 D.L.R. (3d) 685, [1976] 1 S.C.R. 786 (S.C.C.) and the judgments in *Forsythe v. The Queen* (1980), 53 C.C.C. (2d) 225, 112 D.L.R. (3d) 385, [1980] 2 S.C.R. 268 (S.C.C.) and *Re Skogman and the Queen* (1984), 13 C.C.C. (3d) 161, 11 D.L.R. (4th) 161, 41 C.R. (3d) 1 (S.C.C.), do not detract from the important statements to this effect set out in statements to this effect set out in material such as the article by G.A. Martin in the *1955 Special Lectures of the Law Society of Upper Canada* or in cases such as *R. v. Churchman and Durham* (1959), 110 C.C.C. 382, 20 C.R. 137, [1955] O.W.N. 90 (LeBel J.) (Ont. H.C.J.). Indeed these principles are explicitly affirmed in *Skogman, supra*, by Estey J. at 171-2 C.C.C. ...

.....

It is irrelevant that a *voir dire* was waived at the preliminary. Notwithstanding any waiver of a *voir dire* the accused still retains the right to test the Crown's case and pin down witnesses on areas that might be relevant at trial. Where an accused is deprived of his right to cross-examine on the matters on which Constable Akin was sought to be cross-examined, he is effectively deprived of his right to test the basis for the Crown's case and to set up a foundation for later submissions at trial relevant to his rights under s. 8 and s. 24(2) of the *Canadian Charter of Rights and Freedoms*.

The refusal to permit cross-examination of Constable Akin thus deprived the accused of vital rights, including his right at the subsequent trial to make full answer and defence. That refusal was of such a nature in the particular circumstances of this case that it went beyond a mere error in law and out to the jurisdiction of the Provincial judge as a denial of natural justice which requires correction. The refusal to permit further cross-examination of Constable Cowan, although perhaps not quite as serious as that with respect to Constable Akin, fits into the same category.

Although there is of course no agreement between counsel that there was any lack of jurisdiction they do agree that should a jurisdictional defect be found the court does have an inherent power, flowing from the power to quash, to remit the matter to the Provincial Court judge: see, for example, *Re Demarais and The Queen* (1978), 42 C.C.C. (2d) 287, 5 C.R. (3d) 229 (Ont. C.A.).

It is ordered that the committal be quashed. An order will go as in *Durette* [(1979), 47 C.C.C. (2d) 170 (Ont. H.C.J.)] remitting the matter to the learned Provincial judge to permit further cross-examination by the defence for Constable Akin and Constable Cowan. The usual order will go for the protection of the learned judge and all public officials acting directly or indirectly under the authority of the order.

It follows from this and from similar judgments that admissibility of evidence is not dependent upon how relevant the evidence is to the issue of committal, but rather, is often to be determined upon the same principles that would govern at trial. For example, at trial, the prosecution must establish, as a pre-condition to admissibility and beyond a reasonable doubt, that an accused's statement to a person in authority was voluntary. Similarly, the prosecution must establish voluntariness beyond a reasonable doubt in a *voir dire* at the preliminary inquiry (see *R. v. Pickett* (1975), 28 C.C.C. (2d) 297 (Ont. C.A.)), unless the *voir dire* is waived by the defence. Note, of course, that the defence may concede the admissibility of statements or other evidence to be contested at trial, such as similar act evidence, if committal is inevitable even without the disputed evidence and if the defence has an interest in discovering the disputed evidence in advance of trial.

Sometimes, the absence of *Charter* jurisdiction generates questionable distinctions. For example, the admissibility of an accused's statement may be attacked because it was induced by threats and because it was elicited in violation of the accused's s. 10(*b*) right to counsel. A judge presiding at the preliminary inquiry could find that the statement was indeed induced by threats and exclude it as involuntary, but could not exclude it based upon a denial of the accused's right to counsel. The judge would have to permit the parties to explore the latter issue without ruling upon it.

QUESTION

4. In the above case, the refusal by the preliminary inquiry justice to allow cross-examination was framed as a jurisdictional error. When would such a refusal not constitute jurisdictional error? Consider, in this regard, *R. v. Dawson* (1998), 123 C.C.C. (3d) 385 (Ont. C.A.); *R. v. George* (1991), 69 C.C.C. (3d) 148 (Ont. C.A.), substantially reproduced at p. 380.

4. THE TYPICAL PRELIMINARY INQUIRY

At the commencement of the preliminary inquiry, the information is read to the accused and the accused is put to his or her election in the words set out in s. 536(2) of the *Criminal Code*. (This practice is likely to disappear given recent amendments to the *Code* not yet in force at time of writing.) Where the election has been recorded prior to the commencement of the preliminary inquiry, the information is generally read to the accused and the prior election is acknowledged. Often, a request is then made for a ban on publication of the evidence to be taken at the preliminary inquiry pursuant to s. 539 of the *Criminal Code*. Prior to the commencement of the taking of evidence, the presiding judge *must*, on the application of the accused, and *may*, on the application of the Crown, make an order directing that the evidence not be published or broadcast prior to any discharge of the accused or, where the accused is ordered to stand trial, prior to the end of the trial. Section 542 of the *Criminal Code* automatically prohibits the publication or broadcast of a confession, admission or statement of the accused tendered at the preliminary inquiry until the accused has been discharged or, where committed for trial, until the trial has ended. As well, the presiding judge may make an order directing that the identity of the complainant or a witness and any information that could disclose the identity of the complainant or witness shall not be published or broadcast, when the accused is charged with an offence under certain enumerated sections (such as sexual assault).[1] This order, available at a preliminary inquiry and at a trial, shall be made upon application by the complainant, witness or prosecutor.

QUESTION

5. In rare circumstances, the defence does not seek an order at the preliminary inquiry banning publication or broadcast of the evidence to be taken. What compelling reason might prompt the defence not to seek such an order?

Generally, an order is sought by the defence, and granted as a matter of course, excluding witnesses from the courtroom until their evidence

1 Section 486(3) and (4) of the *Criminal Code*. See also s. 276.3, which regulates non-publication of matters relating to an application under s. 276.1 or a hearing under s. 276.2. Section 486(1) to (2.3) also provides for the exclusion of all or part of the public and for other protective measures for witnesses in certain circumstances. All of these provisions apply to trials and to preliminary inquiries.

is taken. Exemptions may be granted for certain persons from such an order, such as the investigating officer, or an expert who may rely upon the evidence given at the preliminary inquiry as the foundation for an opinion to be expressed. Where the investigating officer is so exempted, the defence may request that he or she be called first or, alternatively, be excluded from the courtroom during limited portions of the evidence directly relating to his or her anticipated testimony.

The prosecution then tenders its witnesses, occasionally preceded by an opening statement. Examination, cross-examination and re-examination follow the trial format. The presiding judge may adjourn the preliminary inquiry from time to time or otherwise regulate the course of the inquiry as outlined in s. 537 of the *Criminal Code*. For example, s. 537(1)(*h*) of the *Criminal Code* permits the court to exclude the public from the courtroom under very limited circumstances: *e.g.*, where a child witness is unable to testify in the presence of the public.

After the prosecution's witnesses are completed, the presiding justice will hear the witnesses called by the accused. This may be preceded by the caution set out in s. 541(2) of the *Criminal Code* (which is mandatory where the accused is unrepresented and is customary in many jurisdictions even where the accused is represented). Again, the trial format is followed for the witnesses called by the defence.

QUESTIONS

6. The Crown calls some of the witnesses it intends to rely upon at trial. The defence decides to call the balance of those witnesses at the preliminary inquiry. Some of those witnesses are certainly adverse to the interests of the defence, if not hostile. Should counsel for the accused be compelled to examine those witnesses in chief in a non-leading way or should she be entitled to put leading questions to the witnesses, as if it were cross-examination? What rules, if any, should constrain the Crown when it is the Crown's turn to question the witnesses?

7. It is relatively rare for the defence to call a witness at the preliminary inquiry that it intends to rely upon at trial. Why? Are there any circumstances where the defence may wish to call such a witness at the preliminary inquiry?

Once the testimony of witnesses called by the defence is completed, or after the defence indicates that it will call no witnesses, counsel is invited to make submissions on the issue of committal. The presiding judge may decide immediately or reserve judgment.

Section 540 of the *Criminal Code* states that a written record is to be kept of the proceedings and is to be available for use at trial. Most frequently, defence counsel seeks to impeach prosecution witnesses through cross-examination at trial based upon the preliminary inquiry transcript. Defence or Crown counsel may seek to use the transcript to refresh the witness's memory. Under s. 9 of the *Canada Evidence Act*, R.S.C. 1985, c. C-5, Crown counsel may use the transcript to seek leave to cross-examine a witness who has resiled from an earlier position.

Section 540 of the *Criminal Code* used to provide that the evidence of witnesses called at the preliminary inquiry had to be taken in the presence of the accused; the presiding justice had no power to permit the accused to be absent. However, s. 537(1)(*j*) of the *Code* allows the presiding justice, with the consent of the parties, to "permit the accused to appear by counsel or by closed-circuit television or any other means ... for any part of the inquiry other than a part in which the evidence of a witness is taken". More importantly, newly enacted s. 537(1)(*j*.1) of the *Code* (not in force at time of writing) allows the presiding justice to permit, on the accused's request, that the accused be out of court during the whole or any part of the inquiry, subject to appropriate conditions. Finally, s. 544 of the *Code* permits the preliminary inquiry to continue in the absence of an accused who has absconded.

Other recently enacted additions to s. 540 may or may not radically alter the traditional preliminary inquiry. Section 540(7) (not in force at time of writing) permits the presiding justice to "receive as evidence any information that would not otherwise be admissible but tht the justice considers credible or trustworthy in the circumstances of the case, including a statement that is made by a witness in writing or otherwise recorded". However, s. 540(9) (not in force at time of writing) provides that "[t]he justice shall, on application of a party, require any person whom the justice considers appropriate to appear for examination or cross-examination with respect to information intended to be tendered as evidence under subsection (7)". It remains to be seen whether these provisions will be interpreted so as to routinely permit the admission of otherwise inadmissible hearsay evidence (as frequently occurs in the United States). In light of s. 540(9) and the statutory right of the defence to call relevant witnesses under s. 541(5), it is well arguable that s. 540(7) will not have a dramatic impact on the traditional preliminary inquiry.

C. PREFERRING AN INDICTMENT AFTER, OR IN THE ABSENCE OF, A PRELIMINARY INQUIRY

Section 574 of the *Criminal Code* outlines what charges can be preferred in an indictment after the accused has been ordered to stand trial at a preliminary inquiry or where no preliminary inquiry has been requested.

QUESTION

8. (a) Compare the breadth of ss. 548 and 574 of the *Criminal Code*.
   (b) The accused is charged with assault with a weapon. Over the Crown's objection, the provincial court judge presiding at the preliminary inquiry commits the accused on the lesser and included offence of assault only. Can the Crown prefer an indictment for assault with a weapon pursuant to s. 574(1)(*b*)? Consider, in this regard, *Tapaquon v. The Queen* (1993), 87 C.C.C. (3d) 1 (S.C.C.).
   (c) What, if any remedy does the Crown have?

Section 577 of the *Criminal Code* outlines when an indictment can be preferred, even if the accused has not been given the opportunity to request a preliminary inquiry, a preliminary inquiry has been commenced but not concluded, or a preliminary inquiry has been held and the accused has been discharged. There may also be instances where the Crown may choose to prefer a direct indictment even after committal at the preliminary inquiry (see *R. v. Benji* (2002), 161 C.C.C. (3d) 479 (S.C.C.)). Note that s. 566(3), amended in 1997, now permits a direct indictment to be preferred under s. 577 for non-jury and jury trials.

R. v. STERLING

(1993), 84 C.C.C. (3d) 65 (Sask. C.A.)

Bayda C.J.S. and Cameron J.A.: — These cases are concerned with whether three pre-trial orders for disclosure made by a judge of the Court of Queen's Bench in the course of a criminal prosecution are properly before this court and, if so, whether they were properly made.

The orders were made following the direct indictment by the Deputy Attorney-General of Ronald, Lynda and Travis Sterling and each of Edward Revesz and James Elstad, charging them with the assault, sexual assault and confinement of several children in what has become known as the "Martensville case". The indictment was preferred while these accused were awaiting preliminary inquiry and, accordingly, they were deprived of the advantages of the inquiry. That, coupled with concerns that more lay beneath the charges than had been disclosed by the Crown, including a concern that the allegations of the children might have been inspired by suggestive investigative techniques, prompted the accused to apply by notice of motion to the Court of Queen's Bench for relief.

Three applications were launched, one by the Sterlings and one by each of Messrs. Revesz and Elstad. They were launched in advance of a judge of the Court of Queen's Bench having been assigned the conduct of the trial of the charges and so they were directed not to the trial judge, as such, but to "the presiding judge in chambers": to such judge of the court at large, it seems, as should be sitting in chambers on their return date.

The applications differed a bit, but shared common characteristics. Each was launched pursuant to the *Constitution Act, 1982*, Part I, the Canadian Charter of Rights and Freedoms, s. 24(1); contained an allegation that the constitutional rights of the applicants to make full answer and defence to the charges, rights guaranteed them by s. 7 of the Charter had been infringed or denied, and sought relief in the form, among others, of an order under s. 24(1) allowing the accused to examine on oath the potential witnesses named in the indictment.None of these persons, however, was served with notice of any of the applications.

.....

The presiding chambers judge assumed jurisdiction under s. 24(1), heard the applications, and seemingly decided that the s. 7 rights of the accused to make full answer and defence had been violated. Then, drawing further on s. 24(1), he made three orders, each in the same terms, requiring "the key Crown witnesses", excluding the children, to appear before a clerk of the court at a time and place to be designated by the registrar and to answer all questions put to them by defence counsel. He went on to direct that the witnesses were not to be sworn; that the examinations were to be recorded and, upon request, transcribed; that disputes, if any, concerning the meaning or application of the orders were to be referred to him for further directions; and that the costs associated with the matter were to be borne by the Crown.

At that the Crown appealed against each of the orders. It relied on s. 676(1)(*c*) of the *Criminal Code* for its right of appeal, and contended that the orders had been granted in error since the Crown had made disclosure in keeping with *R. v. Stinchcombe* and since the Deputy Attorney-General was therefore entitled to prefer a direct indictment in accordance with *R. v. Arviv* (1985), 19 C.C.C. (3d) 395, 20 D.L.R. (4th) 422, 45 C.R. (3d) 354 (Ont. C.A.). In consequence, it requested that the orders be set aside.

Mr. Elstad also appealed. Relying for his right of appeal on the general idea that if the Crown was entitled to appeal so was he, he appealed against the order made in response to his application, contending that the order was too narrow in scope, for it excluded the children. And so he requested that it be varied to include them.

In addition to that, Heather Brennerman, Ruth Ann Bell, *et al.*, being "key Crown witnesses" affected by one or more of the orders, applied to this court by notice of motion requesting a declaration pursuant to s. 24(1) declaring the orders null and void on the footings, generally speaking, that the applicants had not been served with notice of the applications; that there was no authority in the judge to have made such orders; and that the orders violated the constitutional and legal rights and freedoms of the applicants.

.....

Let us turn first to the specific foundations upon which the orders were made. Assuming the judge properly took jurisdiction under s. 24(1) even though he had not been designated the trial judge, and even though the persons the applicant accused wished to question had not been served, we think it clear that the judge had first to decide that the s. 7 rights of the applicants had been violated before being empowered to grant them a remedy.

While the judge seems to have decided that the s. 7 rights of the applicant accused had been violated, he did not identify any act or omission on the part of the Crown, or any governmental officer or agency, that was capable in law of constituting such a "violation". He did not take the decision of the Deputy Attorney-General to proceed by way of direct indictment, authorized by s. 577 of the *Criminal Code*, to have been contrary to law or in breach of the Charter, at least not in itself. Nor did he take s. 577 to have been inconsistent with the Charter and of no force or effect under s. 52 of the *Constitution Act, 1982*, Part VII. Indeed, these avenues to the grant of a remedy were foreclosed in light of *R. v. Arviv*, unless, of course, the Crown had failed to disclose the fruits of its investigation in keeping with *R. v. Stinchcombe*, in which event the first of them would have been open to him. But the Crown, having provided the accused with a mass of information, appears to have been taken by the judge to have made such disclosure.

And so his decision, such as it was, that the s. 7 rights of the accused had been violated was grounded in something else: in the idea, as he expressed it, that "while the Crown has given disclosure to the [accused] by means of disclosure of documents and tapes and statements of witnesses ... full disclosure cannot have been deemed to have been given unless the [accused] has the right to question key Crown witnesses".

.....

Having taken those as the bases for the making of the orders, we concluded they had been made in error.

The first point of error lies in the finding (or the lack of a finding, depending on how one views it) that the accused had made out a violation of their rights *by the Crown* or by any governmental officer or agency. What was the specific act or omission that constituted the "violation" on the part of the Crown? Was it a failure by the Crown to afford the accused a preliminary inquiry? In light of *R. v. Arviv*, the law is clear that the act of preferring a direct indictment where a preliminary inquiry has not been held does not constitute a violation if accompanied by disclosure in accordance with *R. v. Stinchcombe*. Was it a failure by the Crown to direct the witnesses listed on the indictment to make themselves available to defence counsel for the purposes of answering questions in advance of trial? The prosecutor, who had no property in these or any other potential witnesses, had no right in law to compel them to do so and no duty, even, to suggest they do so. It follows that neither failure could constitute a "violation" under the Charter. Indeed, apart from the "deemed" failure of the Crown to make "full disclosure" by making the witnesses available for questioning by the defence (if that is what was meant), did the judge identify any such act or omission in his reasons for making the orders. And, of course, that failure is no failure at all.

As matters now stand, none of the accused could point to any specific act or omission on the part of the Crown or any governmental officer or agency that was capable in law of constituting a "violation" of their s. 7 rights.

That being so, there was no basis for the grant of a remedy under s. 24(1).

The second point of error is this: Even if a "violation" had been made out, the remedy the judge granted was wholly unknown to the law and not available to him as one he could select from the arsenal of s. 24(1) remedies to redress violations. There is nothing in the common law, nothing in statute, and nothing in constitutional law that empowers a judge of the Court of Queen's Bench, or any other judge, to compel a potential witness in a criminal proceeding, in advance of the proceeding, to present himself or herself to counsel for the accused in a non-judicial setting and to answer such questions as counsel might choose to put to that person. There is simply no law upon which the judge could have founded such a remedy.

Moreover, by what authority the judge assumed jurisdiction in the absence of persons directly and materially affected by the applications, namely the persons whom the applicant accused wished to question under compulsion of an order of the court, was not mentioned. Although these persons had vital interests at stake, none had been served. Nor were any of them present. Nor it seems did they know anything about the matter. Nothing was said of this by the judge, and the issue was left unexplained here. Since we were offered nothing in justification of this and since the orders substantially and adversely affected the legal if not the constitutional rights and freedoms of these persons, we can only conclude the orders ought not to have been made in the absence of these persons.

It was for these reasons essentially that we concluded that the orders had been improperly made and could not be left to stand. Indeed the orders and their making were so fundamentally flawed we were inclined to view them as nullities.

[The court then considered its jurisdiction and power to entertain these proceedings and set aside the orders. Wakeling J.A. delivered separate reasons, concurring in the result.]

R. v. ERTEL

(1987), 35 C.C.C. (3d) 398 (Ont. C.A.)

[The court considered whether a direct indictment preferred pursuant to s. 507(3) [now s. 577] infringes any fundamental right guaranteed by ss. 7, 9 or 15 of the *Charter*. In upholding the section, the court articulated some of the justifiable reasons for a direct indictment.]

Lacourcière J.A.: —

.....

There are many reasons why direct indictments can be justified for the necessary protection of society. In Del Buono, *Criminal Procedure in Canada* (1982), p. 323, Bruce MacFarlane and Judith Webster give the following reasons as justification for direct indictments:

(1) circumstances may be such that the security of the Crown's witnesses or the preservation of the Crown's case requires that the matter be brought to trial forthwith; the alleged offence may be so controversial or notorious that, in the interests of the public, the matter must be heard and determined as soon as possible;
(2) the preferring of a direct indictment may be the only way to remedy an unconscionable delay in bringing the matter to trial, and
(3) the holding of a second preliminary inquiry (even if it was permissible) might cause unnecessary and unjustifiable delay and expense. For example, when a committal for trial is quashed on technical grounds not related to the evidence tendered at the preliminary inquiry; or where a defendant is extradited back to Canada following the committal for trial of a co-defendant.

In my view, the court can take judicial notice of the above reasons, which are not an exhaustive list of the reasons that may justify a direct indictment. In addition, as in the present case, new evidence may come to light implicating the accused after the preliminary inquiry. It certainly cannot be said in considering its constitutionality, that the direct indictment permitted by s. 507(3), in circumstances which may have been rationally contemplated by Parliament, is fundamentally unfair.

D. WAIVER OF THE EVIDENCE

Section 549 of the *Criminal Code* provides that the presiding judge may, at any stage of the preliminary inquiry, with the consent of the accused and the prosecutor, order the accused to stand trial in the court having criminal jurisdiction, without taking or recording any evidence or further evidence.

QUESTION

9. **Consider under what circumstances the defence would waive the hearing of evidence at a preliminary inquiry. Now consider under what limited circumstances the prosecution would refuse to consent to an order for committal without the taking of evidence. Consider, in this regard, s. 715 of the *Criminal Code*, addressed in Section E, below.**

E. PRESERVATION OF THE EVIDENCE FOR TRIAL

Section 715 of the *Criminal Code* provides, *inter alia*, that evidence taken at a preliminary inquiry may be admitted as evidence in the proceedings where the witness refuses to testify or is dead, insane, too ill to testify or travel, or is absent from Canada, unless the accused can prove that it did not have full opportunity to cross-examine the witness.

R. v. POTVIN

(1989), 47 C.C.C. (3d) 289 (S.C.C.)

[Potvin, T. and D. were jointly charged with second degree murder. The Crown proceeded against the appellant first with the intention of using the other two as witnesses. D. refused to testify at the appellant's trial. The Crown was permitted to introduce D.'s evidence that had been given at the preliminary inquiry at Potvin's trial pursuant to s. 643(1) [now s. 715(1)] of the *Criminal Code*. The appellant alleged that D. and T. were the killers. The appellant was convicted at trial.]

Wilson J. (Lamer and Sopinka JJ. concurring): — The main issue on this appeal ... is whether the admission at trial of previously taken evidence under s. 643(1) of the Criminal Code, R.S.C. 1970, c. C-34, as amended (now R.S.C. 1985, c. C-46, s. 715(1)), violates an accused's rights under ss. 7 or 11(*d*) of the Canadian Charter of Rights and Freedoms. Other issues raised on the appeal [include] ... whether, assuming no such Charter violation, the trial judge nevertheless erred in admitting such evidence ...

.....

I think the appellant's submission that s. 643(1) violates s. 7 must fail. This court held in the *B.C. Motor Vehicle Act*, [1985] 2 S.C.R. 486 at p. 503 ... that the principles of fundamental justice are to be found in the basic tenets of our justice system. Our justice system has, however, traditionally held evidence given under oath at a previous proceeding to be admissible at a criminal trial if the witness was unavailable at the trial for a reason such as death, provided the accused had an opportunity to cross-examine the witness when the evidence was originally given.

.....

To the extent that s. 7 guarantees the accused a fair trial, can the admission of the previously obtained testimony under s. 634(1) be said to be unfair to the accused? In the absence of circumstances which negated or minimized the accused's opportunity to cross-examine the witness when the previous testimony was given, I think not. In this regard, I would respectfully adopt the following statement of Vancise J.A. of the Saskatchewan Court of Appeal in *R. v. Rogers* (1987), 35 C.C.C. (3d) 50 at pp. 60-6, 155 Sask. R. 198 (Sask. C.A.):

> Does this procedure offend the basic tenets and principles on which the principles of fundamental justice are based? Put another way, are these procedural safeguards sufficient to make the taking of the evidence accord with the principles of fundamental justice which are founded upon a belief "in the dignity and worth of a human person and on the rule of law"? In my opinion, they are. The conditions under which the evidence is given, including the solemnity of the occasion, are such as to guarantee its trustworthiness and to protect the rights of an accused. The evidence is given in open court in the presence of the accused, taken on oath or solemn affirmation, and the person against whose interest it is sought to be introduced has reasonable opportunity to cross-examine. The evidence is certified as to correctness by the judge before whom it was given. This is not a mechanism for the introduction of evidence which is not admissible, but rather a system for the use of evidence which would otherwise be lost. Its use, or admissibility, is provided for in a way which accords full safety to the rights of an accused. Those safeguards, together with the limited circumstances in which the procedure can be resorted to, justify its acceptance into evidence. The procedure is one which accords with the principles of fundamental justice, and in my opinion, s. 7 of the Charter has not been offended.

.....

What rights then does an accused have under s. 7 of the Charter with respect to the admission of previous testimony? It is, in my view, basic to our system of justice that the accused have had a full opportunity to cross-examine the witness when the previous testimony was taken if a transcript of such testimony is to be introduced as evidence in a criminal trial for the purpose of convicting the accused. This is in accord with the traditional view that it is the opportunity to cross-examine and not the fact of cross-examination which is crucial if the accused is to be treated fairly. As Professor Delisle has noted: Annotation to *R. v. Sophonow* (1986), 50 C.R. (3d) 195 at p. 196: "If the opposing party has had an opportunity to fully cross-examine he ought not to be justified in any later complaint if he did not fully exercise that right." I would respectfully adopt the following observations of Martin J.A. of the Ontario Court of Appeal in *Davidson* [(1988), 42 C.C.C. (3d) 289 (Ont. C.A.)] at pp. 298-9:

> An accused is not necessarily deprived of his or her constitutional right to a fair trial, where the evidence taken at a preliminary hearing from a crucial witness who has since died is read as evidence at the trial. However, if in a particular case, an accused proves that he or she did not have "full opportunity" to cross-examine the witness at the preliminary hearing because, for example, he or she was deprived of the right to counsel or because of improper restrictions by the court on the cross-examination by counsel, then the conditions of s. 643 have not been met, and the evidence taken at the preliminary hearing is not admissible under the section. Furthermore, the accused's constitutional right to a fair trial guaranteed by s. 11(*d*) of the Charter would also require the exclusion of evidence where the accused did not have full opportunity to cross-examine the witness at the preliminary hearing.

I would respectfully agree with Martin J.A. that the accused would have a constitutional right to have the evidence of prior testimony obtained in the absence of a full opportunity to cross-examine the witness excluded. When the evidence is sought to be introduced in order to obtain a criminal conviction which could result in imprisonment, the accused is threatened with a deprivation of his or her liberty and security of the person and this can only be done in accordance with the principles of fundamental justice. It is, as I have said, a principle of fundamental justice that the accused have had a full opportunity to cross-examine the adverse witness.

.....

The appellant submits that the provision of a full opportunity to cross-examine at the preliminary inquiry does not necessarily ensure fairness. More specifically, he argues that (1) the trier of fact is deprived of the ability to assess the credibility of the witness through observing his or her demeanour; (2) when the evidence is taken at a preliminary inquiry the credibility of that evidence is not in issue, and (3) the accused at the preliminary inquiry may have strategic reasons for not testing the credibility, or even conducting any cross-examination, of a witness. Despite the fact that these observations may be sound and could operate to the detriment of the accused, I do not think they are of such magnitude and effect as to deprive the accused of the basics of a fair trial. I say this for the following reasons.

I note that although it is possible that an accused might suffer a detriment because of the trier of fact's inability to assess the credibility of a witness on a face to face basis, it is also true that this feature of s. 643(1) could work to an accused's benefit. In any event, because s. 643(1) can only be invoked when its stringent prerequisites are met by the party seeking to introduce the previous testimony, it is not a provision that the Crown can use at will to its advantage or as a device to protect Crown witnesses who may not prove to be credible before the trier of fact.

Although it is true that credibility is not specifically an issue to be determined at a preliminary inquiry (see *U.S. v. Shephard*, [1977] 2 S.C.R. 1067, ... (1976), 30 C.C.C. (2d) 424 ... 70 D.L.R. (3d) 136 (S.C.C.), *per* Ritchie J. at pp. 1080 and 1084; *Mezzo v. R.*, [1986] 1 S.C.R. 802, 52 C.R. (3d) 113, [1986] 4 W.W.R. 557, (1986), 27 C.C.C. (3d) 97, 30 D.L.R. (4th) 161

... *per* McIntyre J. at pp. 836-37), this does not mean that an accused is taken unawares or unfairly surprised by the admission of testimony taken at a preliminary inquiry if a witness subsequently becomes unavailable. If a judge presiding at a preliminary inquiry seeks to curtail cross-examination designed to test a witness's credibility and that witness's testimony is subsequently admitted at trial under s. 643(1), this may very well constitute an infringement of the accused's right under s. 7 of the Charter to have had a full opportunity to cross-examine the witness.

As for the detriment an accused might suffer from the tactical decision of his or her counsel not to press certain issues at the preliminary inquiry with a witness who may subsequently become unavailable at the trial, I am in complete agreement with the observation of Martin J.A. in *Davidson*, *supra*, at p. 298:

> In my view, an accused is not deprived of "full opportunity" to cross-examine a witness at the preliminary hearing merely because his counsel, for tactical reasons, has conducted the cross-examination of a witness differently than he would have conducted the cross-examination at the trial, provided that there has been no improper restriction of the cross-examination by the provincial judge holding the preliminary hearing.

In short, I find that s. 643(1) of the *Criminal Code*, in so far as it allows evidence given at a preliminary inquiry to be admitted at a criminal trial when a witness is unavailable or unwilling to testify, does not infringe s. 7 of the Charter because it provides that the evidence will only be admitted if the accused has had a full opportunity to cross-examine the witness at the time the evidence was given.

[Wilson J. then concludes that s. 643(1) of the *Criminal Code* does not infringe on s. 11(*d*) of the *Charter*, although the accused bears the burden of demonstrating that he or she was deprived of the opportunity to cross-examine at trial.]

(b) Section 643(1): is there a discretion?

.....

It is my view that the word "may" in s. 643(1) is directed not to the parties but to the trial judge. I believe it confers on him or her a discretion not to allow the previous testimony to be admitted in circumstances where its admission would operate unfairly to the accused. I hasten to add, however, that such circumstances will be relatively rare and that the discretion to prevent unfairness is not a blanket authority to undermine the object of s. 643(1) by excluding evidence of previous testimony as a matter of course.

.....

What then is the nature and purpose of the discretion conferred in s. 643(1) which enables the trial judge not to allow the evidence in at trial even in cases in which the requirements of the section have been met? In my view, there are two main types of mischief at which the discretion might be aimed. First, the discretion could be aimed at situations in which there has been unfairness in the manner in which the evidence was obtained.

Although Parliament has set out in the section specific conditions as to how the previous testimony has to have been obtained if it is to be admitted under s. 643(1) (the most important, of course, being that the accused was afforded full opportunity to cross-examine the witness), Parliament could have intended the judge to have a discretion in those rare cases in which compliance with the requirements of s. 643(1) gave no guarantee that the evidence was obtained in a manner fair to the accused. This would, of course, represent a departure from the traditional common law approach that the manner in which evidence is obtained, with a few well-established exceptions such as the confessions rule, is not relevant to the question of its admissibility but it would be consistent with the contemporary approach to the expanded requirements of adjudicative fairness. An example of unfairness in obtaining the testimony might be a case in which, although the witness was temporarily absent from Canada, the Crown could have obtained the witness's attendance at trial with a minimal degree of effort. Another example might be a case in which the Crown was aware at the time the evidence was initially taken that the witness would not be available to testify at the trial but did not inform the accused of this fact so that he could make best use of the opportunity to cross-examine the witness at the earlier proceeding. These kinds of circumstances related to the obtaining of the evidence on the earlier occasion might have been in the mind of the legislator as triggering the judge's discretion with respect to its admission at the trial.

A different concern at which the discretion might have been aimed is the effect of the admission of the previously taken evidence on the fairness of the trial itself. This concern flows from the principle of the law of evidence that evidence may be excluded if it is highly prejudicial to the accused and of only modest probative value: see *Noor Mohamed v. R.*, [1949] A.C. 182 at 192 ... (P.C.); *R. v. Wray, supra*, at p. 295 [S.C.R.]; *Morris v. R.*, [1983] 2 S.C.R. 190 at p. 201, 36 C.R. (3d) 1, ... 7 C.C.C. (3d) 97, 1 D.L.R. (4th) 385 ... (S.C.C.). How the evidence was obtained might be irrelevant under this principle.

In practice, the two types of situations at which the discretion may have been aimed are not as distinct as the above analysis might suggest. As has been recognized in the constitutional context of s. 24(2) of the Charter, unfairness in the manner in which evidence is obtained can have a significant effect on the fairness of the trial: see *R. v. Collins*, [1987] 1 S.C.R. 265 ... 33 C.C.C. (3d) 1, 38 D.L.R. (4th) 508, *R. v. Manninen*, [1987] 1 S.C.R. 1233, ... 34 C.C.C. (3d) 385, 41 D.L.R. (4th) 301. In my view, therefore, s. 643(1) of the *Code* should be construed as conferring a discretion on the trial judge broader than the traditional evidentiary principle that evidence should be excluded if its prejudicial effect exceeds its probative value. I would respectfully differ in this regard from Martin J.A. who, while not interpreting s. 643(1) as conferring a discretion on the judge, nevertheless held that the operation of the section was subject "to the limited discretion recognized in *The Queen v. Wray*": see Tretter, at p. 89.

In my view, once it is accepted that s. 643(1) gives the trial judge a statutory discretion to depart from the purely mechanical application of the section, the discretion should be construed as sufficiently broad to deal with both kinds of situations, namely where the testimony was obtained in a manner which was unfair to the accused or where, even although the manner of obtaining the evidence was fair to the accused, its admission at his or her trial would not be fair to the accused. I would stress that in both situations the discretion should only be exercised after weighing what I have referred to as the "two competing and frequently conflicting concerns" of fair treatment of the accused and society's interest in the admission of probative evidence in order to get at the truth of the matter in issue: see *Clarkson v. R.*, [1986] 1 S.C.R. 383, 25 C.C.C. (3d) 207, 26 D.L.R. (4th) 493. ... Having regard to the reservations that have been expressed over the restrictive formulation of the common law discretion in *Wray*, *supra* (see *Morris v. R.*, *supra*, at p. 202 [S.C.R.]; *Clarkson v. R.*, *supra*, at pp. 392-3 [S.C.R.], *Corbett*, *supra*, at pp. 738-9 [S.C.R.]), I believe there is no need or justification for importing a similar restriction into the statutorily conferred discretion in s. 643(1). The protection of the accused from unfairness rather than the admission of probative evidence "without too much regard for the fairness of the adjudicative process" (see *Clarkson*, at p. 393 [S.C.R.]) should be the focus of the trial judge's concern.

It will follow that I cannot accept the hard and fast rule approach to this issue taken by the Manitoba Court of Appeal in *Sophonow*, *supra*. That court seems to suggest that the very importance of the evidence requires it to be excluded. For example, Huband J.A. states categorically at p. 432 that s. 643(1) "was never intended to apply to a crucial witness whose evidence could work an injustice to the accused if the jury were deprived of seeing his demeanour and his reaction to cross-examination". I believe that this proposition is at odds with the purpose of s. 643(1) in ensuring that evidence, even important and highly probative evidence, is not lost because of the unavailability of a witness at trial. As Vancise J.A. stated in *Rogers*, *supra*, at p. 63, "There is nothing in the section which restricts the use of the section to evidence which is not crucial to proof of the Crown's case."

In the case at bar I am of the view that the trial judge did not instruct himself properly as to the nature and scope of his discretion under s. 643(1). He stressed the high probative value of the evidence of someone who had been in the victim's home at the time the events occurred but failed, in my view, to give adequate consideration to possible unfairness to the accused arising from either the manner in which the evidence was obtained or the effect of its admission on the fairness of the trial. The Court of Appeal proceeded on the basis that the trial judge had no discretion other than the restrictive common law formulation in *Wray*. Neither court applied its mind to the question whether in the circumstances of this case the trial judge should have exercised his statutory discretion in s. 643(1) to exclude the evidence.

There can be no doubt about the fact that the decision whether or not to exercise the statutory discretion in this case would not have been an easy one. In favour of the admission of the evidence is the absence of any allegation that the manner in which Deschenes' testimony was obtained was unfair to the appellant. Moreover, the appellant's counsel exercised his right to cross-examine Deschenes at the preliminary inquiry and there was some cross-examination. There was also a measure of corroboration of Deschenes' testimony (so far as it purported Potvin as the culprit) by the testimony of Thibault at trial. Also favouring admission of Deschenes' testimony was the factor emphasized by the trial judge, namely its high probative value. The testimony purported to be an eyewitness account of the appellant beating and killing the victim. On the other hand, given the appellant's defence that he was a passive observer and that it was Deschenes, the unavailable witness, who did the actual beating and killing, the issue of Deschenes' credibility was obviously critical to the trier of fact's decision whether to accept or reject Deschenes' version of the events. Yet the jury had no opportunity to observe Deschenes' demeanour as an aid in assessing that witness's credibility.

This is not, however, a matter for this court to decide but rather a matter to be referred back to a trial judge properly instructed as to the nature and scope of his or her statutory discretion under s. 643(1).

(c) The Warnings

The appellant submits that the trial judge erred in not warning the jury of the dangers of accepting evidence and attempting to assess credibility in the absence of live cross-examination and in not warning the jury of the dangers of accepting the evidence of an accomplice in the absence of live cross-examination at trial. I am of the view that it is highly desirable in all cases in which previous testimony is introduced at trial pursuant to s. 643(1) that the trial judge remind the jury that they have not had the benefit of observing the witness giving the testimony. This is not to say that failure to do so will constitute reversible error in every case, but a warning seems particularly desirable in a case such as this where the unavailability of the witness to testify at trial is not the result of some unforeseen contingency such as death or illness but the result rather of a deliberate decision by the witness not to give evidence under oath before the trier of fact. [Indeed, Wilson J. notes that the trial judge compounded the failure to warn with a positive misdirection on this evidence.]

.....

V. Disposition

I would allow the appeal and order a new trial because the trial judge misdirected himself as to the proper interpretation of s. 643(1) of the *Criminal Code* and because of the combined effect of the trial judge's failure to warn the jury concerning the use of s. 643(1) and his erroneous instruction that the transcript of testimony taken at the preliminary inquiry should be treated in the same manner as live testimony given at trial.

[La Forest J. (Dickson C.J.C. concurring) concurred in the result, though not the complete reasoning of Wilson J.]

QUESTION

10. Discuss how any of the following factors might impact upon the discretion conferred under s. 715 of the *Criminal Code*:

(a) The witness lives in New York and refuses to return to Canada for trial because his American criminal record for crimes of dishonesty were exposed by the defence at the preliminary inquiry and he does not want to be exposed further.

(b) Since the preliminary inquiry, the Crown has provided further disclosure to the defence, which could arguably impact negatively upon the witness who is now too ill to return to Canada.

(c) Since the preliminary inquiry, the defence has investigated the witness, drawing upon information he provided at the inquiry, and has obtained very damaging evidence against him.

(d) The witness is dead. The Crown knew that the witness was seriously ill but failed to advise the defence prior to the preliminary inquiry.

(e) The accused has changed counsel since the preliminary inquiry. New counsel seriously questions the skill demonstrated by the previous counsel, who chose to ask few questions at the preliminary inquiry.

(f) At the preliminary inquiry, during cross-examination of a Crown witness, certain questions are disallowed by the preliminary inquiry judge.

It should be noted that where it appears, prior to or at the preliminary inquiry, that the witness may not return to Canada for the trial, defence counsel may seek to extract an undertaking from the Crown that it will endeavour to bring the witness back and, if it cannot do so, the evidence will not be read in at trial. The Crown may be prepared to so undertake, in return for concessions by the defence as to how the preliminary inquiry will be conducted.

F. CHALLENGING AN ORDER FOR COMMITTAL OR DISCHARGE

There is no appeal available against an order committing or discharging the accused at the preliminary inquiry. However, the extraordinary remedy, by an order in the nature of *certiorari*, is available in very limited circumstances to quash the original order. Lack of jurisdiction is the only basis upon which a committal or discharge can be set aside on review. The following cases address the very limited circumstances under which the presiding judge loses jurisdiction because of the way the judge conducted the preliminary inquiry.

R. v. SKOGMAN

(1984), 13 C.C.C. (3d) 161 (S.C.C.)

[The accused was committed for trial on a charge of conspiracy. The Crown conceded that there was no evidence on one essential element of the charge but contended that the provincial court judge did not commit jurisdictional error.]

[The majority judgment of the Court was delivered by:]

Estey J.: —

.....

... The Ontario Court of Appeal in [*Re Martin, Simard and Desjardins and The Queen*; *Re Nichols and The Queen* (1977), 41 C.C.C. (2d) 308 (Ont. C.A.)], in examining a *certiorari* review of a preliminary hearing, stated ... :

> ... we conclude that the learned Provincial Court Judge here acted within his jurisdiction, unless it can be said that he committed these respondents on the counts specified without any evidence at all, in the sense of an entire absence of proper material as a basis for the formation of a judicial opinion that the evidence was sufficient to put the accused on trial. That is quite a different question from the question "whether in the opinion of the reviewing tribunal there was evidence upon which a properly instructed jury acting judicially could convict". It remained, therefore, to examine the excerpts of evidence, as placed before this Court from the lengthy transcript taken at the preliminary hearing, in order to determine whether there was any evidence at all on which the committing tribunal was able to base its opinion to commit, as required by the terms of the *Code* ...

The Court of Appeal of Ontario then concluded:

> ... in the case of each of the three respondents *there is sufficient evidence relating to the charges* and the counts in issue to call upon the learned Provincial Judge to form an opinion as to whether there was sufficient evidence to commit the accused for trial, pursuant to s. 475 [now s. 548] ... Having properly directed his mind to the evidence and to the question of whether there was "sufficient evidence" to commit, his decision is not subject to review.

(Emphasis added.) An appeal was dismissed by this Court, the Chief Justice concluding as follows, at p. 345 C.C.C. ... :

> ... the review on sufficiency must be a review to determine whether the committal was made arbitrarily or, at the most, whether there was some evidence upon which an opinion could be formed that an accused should go to trial.

More recently, this Court engaged the problem of review of the preliminary hearing process in *Forsythe v. The Queen* (1980), 53 C.C.C. (2d) 225 ... [S.C.C.]. Again it was Chief Justice Laskin, speaking for the Court, and in reference to *Patterson* [(1970), 2 C.C.C. (2d) 227 (S.C.C.)] who stated at pp. 228-9 C.C.C.:

> In speaking of lack of jurisdiction, this Court was not referring to lack of initial jurisdiction of a judge or a magistrate to enter upon a preliminary inquiry. This is hardly a likelihood. The concern rather was with the loss of this initial jurisdiction and, in my opinion, the situations in which there can be a loss of jurisdiction in the course of a preliminary inquiry are few indeed. However, jurisdiction will be lost by a magistrate who fails to observe a mandatory provision of the *Criminal Code*: see *Doyle v. The Queen*, [1977] 1 S.C.R. 597. Canadian law recognizes that a denial of natural justice goes to jurisdiction ...

.....

The courts of this country have, since the judgment in *Martin, supra*, generally adopted the rule that a committal of an accused at a preliminary, in the absence of evidence on an essential ingredient in a charge, is a reviewable jurisdictional error. See: *Re Guttman and The Queen* (1981), 64 C.C.C. (2d) 342 (Que. S.C.); *Re Poirier and The Queen* (1981), 62 C.C.C. (2d) 452 (Que. C.A.); *Re Leroux and The Queen* (1978), 43 C.C.C. (2d) 398 ... (Que. S.C.); *Re Robar and The Queen* (1978), 42 C.C.C. (2d) 133 ... (N.S.S.C.A.D.); leave to appeal to the Supreme Court of Canada refused, October 3, 1978, C.C.C. ..., *loc. cit. fnx*; *Re Mackie and The Queen* (1978), 43

C.C.C. (2d) 269 ... (Ont. H.C.J.); *Re Stillo and The Queen* [(1981), 60 C.C.C. (2d) 243 (Ont. C.A.)]. "No evidence" on an essential element of the charge against the accused cannot amount to "sufficient evidence" under s. 475. In my view, this is the state of the law in this country on this issue.

I return, therefore, to the essential characteristic of this proceeding, accepting for the moment the concession by the prosecutorial authority that there is no evidence whatever of the involvement of the accused in the allegedly conspiratorial agreement which underlies and sustains, if it be sustainable, the charge before the preliminary hearing tribunal. In my view, with all respect to those including the courts below who may hold the view to the contrary, a committal cannot survive in these circumstances. The purpose of a preliminary hearing is to protect the accused from a needless, and indeed, improper, exposure to public trial where the enforcement agency is not in possession of evidence to warrant the continuation of the process. In addition, in the course of its development in this country, the preliminary hearing has become a forum where the accused is afforded an opportunity to discover and to appreciate the case to be made against him at trial where the requisite evidence is found to be present.

.....

... In the course of a preliminary hearing, evidence may be adduced through witnesses, exhibits, or admissions. The purpose of adducing evidence is to enable the judge to exercise his jurisdiction by making determinations of fact, applying the law to those facts, and finally, to exercise his discretion to commit or discharge the accused. Where the record established in the preliminary hearing does not include evidence relating to each essential element of the charge brought against the accused, a committal of the accused to stand trial can be brought forward by way of a writ of *certiorari* to a superior court and can be quashed.

[The majority judgment goes on to conclude that the committal should be quashed, notwithstanding the fact that the Crown's concession that there was no evidence on an essential element of the offence charged was erroneous.]

R. v. GEORGE

(1991), 69 C.C.C. (3d) 148 (Ont. C.A.)

The judgment of the court was delivered by

Carthy J.A.: — The Crown appeals from an order of Moldaver J. allowing an application for an order in lieu of *certiorari* quashing the committal for trial of the respondents and remitting the case to the Provincial Court judge to permit further cross-examination of a witness. The issue is whether erroneous rulings concerning the right to cross-examine, made by the judge on the preliminary hearing, go to his jurisdiction or are legal errors from which there is no appeal.

The accused persons were charged on several counts of possession for the purpose of trafficking and cultivation of narcotics after a raid of their premises pursuant to a search warrant. The respondents conceded to the

Provincial Court judge that there should be a committal and it is apparent that their major interest was the validity of the search warrant. That would have to be decided at trial and was being pursued as discovery at the preliminary hearing to enable the two accused to know the case against them.

It is apparent from the transcript of the preliminary inquiry that the Provincial Court judge felt cross-examination on the basis for the search warrant was irrelevant because the information proved true when the search was conducted and, in any event, the issue was one for the trial judge. He was in error on both counts. Nonetheless, a copy of the information presented to the justice of the peace was produced with the name of the informant blacked out, indicating that the informant had proven reliable on previous occasions. After considerable argument the following exchange occurred:

> MR. CUGELMAN [for the accused]: Well, I only have a couple of questions and then I am finished, Your Honour. But the questions I was going to be putting to this officer in no way would release anybody's identity. I mean, obviously, the informer is out there and I am not asking information that is so specific.
>
> THE COURT: Well, let's hear the questions and we'll decide whether or not they should be answered.
>
> MR. CUGELMAN: All right.
>
> By MR. CUGELMAN:
>
> Q. In your information to the Justice of the Peace you indicated that this informant had proven reliable on previous occasions. I am simply asking you on how many previous occasions? And this can't possibly go to disclose his identity, Your Honour.

After further argument the issue was concluded with this exchange:

> THE COURT: We'll leave that up to the Trial Judge. I am satisfied that we have dealt with this matter as far as we need to.
>
> MR. CUGELMAN: Well, the *Cover* case clearly states that Defence Counsel has full latitude to explore that at a preliminary hearing and I would like to do that.
>
> THE COURT: I think we have done it.
>
> MR. CUGELMAN: Thank you.

The "*Cover* case" is *R. v. Cover* (1988), 44 C.C.C. (3d) 34, 40 C.R.R. 381, 5 W.C.B. (2d) 444 (Ont. H.C.J.). Moldaver J. found the facts almost identical in the two cases and, applying the reasoning of Campbell J. in *Cover*, set aside the committal for trial so that the accused persons could exercise their right to cross-examine and make full answer and defence at a subsequent trial. The determination of this issue in Cover is set out in the following excerpt from the reasons at pp. 36-7:

[The reasons of Campbell J. are then substantially reproduced.]

If these reasons are read as saying that an accused may not be substantially deprived of the right to cross-examine on a preliminary hearing then

I take no issue with them. If, on the other hand, they are read as a finding that an accused has a right to discovery of what he may face at trial and that any interference with that right goes to the jurisdiction of the Provincial Court judge, then I disagree.

The right of an accused to cross-examine witnesses is clearly stated in s. 540(1) of the *Criminal Code*. In *R. v. Forsythe* (1980), 53 C.C.C. (2d) 225 at p. 229, 112 D.L.R. (3d) 385, [1980] 2 S.C.R. 268, Laskin C.J.C. discusses this type of mandatory provision in the context of jurisdictional error:

> However, jurisdiction will be lost by a Magistrate who fails to observe a mandatory provision of the *Criminal Code*: see *Doyle v. The Queen* (1976), 29 C.C.C. (2d) 177, 68 D.L.R. (3d) 270, [1977] 1 S.C.R. 597. Canadian law recognizes that a denial of natural justice goes to jurisdiction: see *L'Alliance des Professeurs catholiques de Montreal v. Labour Relations Board of Quebec* (1953), 107 C.C.C. 183, [1953] 4 D.L.R. 161, [1953] 2 S.C.R. 140. In the case of a preliminary inquiry, I cannot conceive that this could arise otherwise than by a complete denial to the accused of a right to call witnesses or of a right to cross-examine prosecution witnesses. Mere disallowance of a question or questions on cross-examination or other rulings on proffered evidence would not, in my view, amount to a jurisdictional error. However, the Judge or Magistrate who presides at a preliminary inquiry has the obligation to obey the jurisdictional prescriptions of s. 475 [am. R.S.C. 1970, c. 2 (2nd Supp.), s. 8] of the *Criminal Code*.

It is unnecessary to look beyond the right to cross-examine to test the jurisdictional issue. ...

[Carthy J.A. then notes that Estey J. in *R. v. Skogman*, substantially reproduced at p. 378 of this text, acknowledged the discovery function of the preliminary inquiry.]

However, nowhere is it indicated that this "opportunity" has become an element of common law natural justice such as to suggest jurisdictional error if the opportunity for full discovery is incidentally curtailed. It is now recognized that an accused is entitled to cross-examine Crown witnesses at a preliminary hearing relating to such matters as Charter defences which are not of concern to the judge conducting the hearing. Yet, that opportunity for broad discovery remains best tested on judicial review on the basis of the extent to which the statutory right to cross-examine was restricted. It is difficult to tell from the reasons in *Cover*, *supra*, how extensively the restraint imposed on that right. I might have reached the same conclusion as Campbell J. upon full analysis of the transcript. I would not take from the reasons of Campbell J. that he considered the "right" to discovery to be to complete discovery without interference of any kind by the presiding judge. In this respect it should be remembered that there are other forms of discovery to supplement that on the preliminary hearing and it would be intolerable if an appeal in the form of judicial review was available from every unanswered question. See in this respect reasons of McLachlin J. in *R. v. Seaboyer*, S.C.C., at pp. 57-8, released August 22, 1991 [since reported 66 C.C.C. (3d) 321 at pp. 413-4, 83 D.L.R. (4th) 193, 7 C.R. (4th) 117]:

> Thus, while Charter review will normally take place at trial, it may be possible to seek earlier review in cases where there is no other remedy for a wrong.
>
> Having said this, I would associate myself with the view that appeals from rulings on preliminary inquiries are to be discouraged. While the law must afford a remedy where one is needed, the remedy should, in general,

be accorded within the normal procedural context in which an issue arises, namely, the trial. Such restraint will prevent a plethora of interlocutory appeals and the delays which inevitably flow from them. It will also permit a fuller view of the issue by the reviewing courts, which will have the benefit of a more complete picture of the evidence and the case.

In the present case I accept the respondent's submission that, given the incriminating evidence found on the premises searched, the only live issue may be the validity of the search warrant. If no questions had been permitted on this subject, and if the information sheet had not been produced, I would have concluded that there was a denial of the right to cross-examination and error going to jurisdiction. As matters progressed at the hearing, that was not the case and a fair reading of the transcript indicates that the only question not allowed to be pursued was the number of times the informant had proved reliable and any proper follow-up questions. That comprises, in my view, what Laskin C.J.C. characterized as "mere disallowance of a question or questions" in *Forsythe*, *supra*, and does not constitute jurisdictional error.

I would therefore set aside the order of Moldaver J. and dismiss the application for an order in lieu of *certiorari*. Appeal allowed.

The rules of the court may regulate when and in what manner an application may be brought to quash an order committing or discharging the accused. For example, Form 1 of the Ontario Court of Justice Criminal Proceedings Rules, SI/92-99, provides for notice of such an application to be given within 30 days of the order. Rules 6 and 43 govern the application and generally require the filing of an application record and factum.

This relief is barred once the indictment is preferred. In this context, the indictment is preferred when it is placed before a court which is ready to try the accused: *R. v. Chabot* (1980), 55 C.C.C. (2d) 385 (S.C.C.).

QUESTIONS

11. The accused's preliminary inquiry for tax evasion under the *Income Tax Act*, R.S.C. 1985, c. 1 (5th Supp.), is conducted. The evidence discloses *Criminal Code* fraud offences arising out of the same transactions. After submissions, the court commits the accused on the tax offences but refuses to commit on the fraud offences, since they pertain to a completely different statute. In any event, he has a reasonable doubt about whether those offences were indeed committed by the accused. What remedy, if any, does the Crown have? Consider, in this regard: *R. v. Cancor Software Corp.* (1989), 58 C.C.C. (3d) 53 (Ont. C.A.); *Dubois v. The Queen* (1986), 25 C.C.C. (3d) 221 (S.C.C.).

12. The accused applies to quash his committal for trial on a charge of sexual assault. The judge presiding at the preliminary inquiry refuses to permit his counsel to cross-examine the complainants on their prior inconsistent statements, holding that cross-examination going solely to issues of credibility is irrelevant. There is ample evidence to justify committal for trial; indeed, committal is not in issue. Should a *certiorari* application be successful here and if so, what order should the reviewing court make?

Consider, in this regard: *R. v. Shyan* (1989), 7 W.C.B. (2d) 194 (Ont. H.C.J.).

13. **Section 133 of the *Criminal Code* provides that "[n]o person shall be convicted of [s. 132 perjury] on the evidence of only one witness unless the evidence of that witness is corroborated in a material particular by evidence that implicates the accused". Assume that one witness testifies at the preliminary inquiry and there is no corroboration available at this time. Should the court commit for trial? If not, has jurisdictional error occurred? Consider, in this regard: *Re Stillo and The Queen* (1981), 60 C.C.C. (2d) 243 (Ont. C.A.).**

14. **A provincial court judge presiding at a preliminary inquiry or at earlier "set date" appearances has no jurisdiction to stay the proceedings due to *Charter* delay. Assume that the date for a preliminary inquiry was adjourned a number of times because the Crown was not ready to proceed. The case is now several years old and the court would be inclined to stay the proceedings if it had jurisdiction to do so. As defence counsel, what would you ask the court to do? Would your answer be the same or different if the adjournments were caused by the failure of the Crown to make complete disclosure?**

CHAPTER 8

THE TRIAL OF AN INDICTABLE OFFENCE

A. INTRODUCTION

Part XIX of the *Criminal Code* regulates the trial of indictable offences without a jury, whether before a provincial court judge or any other judge without a jury. As earlier indicated, under s. 566(1) of the *Code*, the trial of an accused for an indictable offence, other than a provincial court trial, shall be on an indictment, rather than an information. Other than this difference, the procedures governing all non-jury trials are virtually identical, regardless of the forum. Part XX regulates jury trials. Of course, it contains procedures unique to jury trials, for example, jury selection procedures. However, by and large, under ss. 557, 572, and 646, jury and non-jury trials of indictable offences are governed by the same procedures.

B. THE PRE-TRIAL CONFERENCE

Section 625.1 of the *Criminal Code* statutorily provides for a pre-trial conference involving Crown and defence counsel, which is presided over by a judge of the trial court; the conference is mandated for jury trials. The section provides that arrangements can be made for decisions on matters which would be better decided before the start of the proceedings. In Ontario, Rule 28 of the Ontario Court of Justice Criminal Proceedings Rules, SI/92-99, provides for the preparation of a pre-trial conference report, first filled in as a draft by counsel, and finalized by the judge. It also particularizes the contents of such a report.

QUESTIONS

1. In some jurisdictions, counsel fills out a pre-trial conference form, outlining the positions of the Crown and the defence, any admissions, any legal issues which will arise, the anticipated length of the trial, and so on. Consider the difficult issues which arise when the defence is asked to disclose its position on various issues, including potential defences.

2. At the pre-trial conference, the facts are outlined for the judge. The Crown intends to ask for 12 months imprisonment on a plea of guilt. Defence counsel indicates that her client would plead guilty if a non-custodial sentence were to be imposed. The judge indicates that she would be inclined to agree with the defence. Defence counsel asks the judge to hear the plea. Can the judge hear the plea?

3. At a pre-trial conference, the judge asks defence counsel whether he intends to proceed with a jury, the currently recorded election. The defence counsel says "it depends on the trial judge". Some judges refer to this as a "DOJ" election. The judge notes that there may be a re-election at trial. The practice varies among jurisdictions as to whether Crown counsel will withhold consent to a same-day re-election. For example, in Toronto, consent is rarely withheld; in other jurisdictions, consent is regularly withheld for certain kinds of cases. What steps should the defence take, commencing at the preliminary inquiry, to best preserve an option to re-elect depending upon the presiding judge?

C. PRE-TRIAL MOTIONS AND THE VOIR DIRE: GENERAL

Historically, jury trials often commenced with the selection of jurors who were then sent home while extended pre-trial motions were argued and considered. Section 645(5) of the *Criminal Code* permits the trial judge to consider such motions, where feasible, before prospective jurors are called. This approach is often well advised where the issues have crystallized prior to trial. Further, the Crown should not refer to inadmissible evidence in its opening statement. Accordingly, an early determination of key admissibility issues in favour of the Crown enables it to refer to such evidence, without fear, in its opening.

Where pre-trial motions relate to the admissibility of evidence at trial or other issues which are uniquely the function of the trial judge to decide, that judge is seized of the trial (see *R. v. Litchfield* (1993), 86 C.C.C. (3d) 97 (S.C.C.), substantially reproduced at p. 471 of this text). However, there are pre-trial motions, such as applications for a change of venue, which may be brought prior to the formal commencement of the trial and which will not seize that judge of the trial.

Pre-trial motions may take a variety of forms, some of which are:

(a) motions without supporting evidence: for example, an attack upon the facial validity of the indictment.

(b) motions, based on facts which have been previously agreed upon.

(c) motions, based on affidavit evidence which may be unchallenged or may be supplemented by *viva voce* evidence or cross-examination on the affidavits: for example, a s. 11(*b*) *Charter* motion for a stay due to unreasonable delay.

(d) motions, based on counsel's outline as to the nature of the prospective evidence (sometimes, counsel is prepared to base submissions upon a transcript of the relevant evidence at the preliminary inquiry. But see *R. v. Gruenke* (1991), 67 C.C.C. (3d) 289 (S.C.C.)). The courts have indicated (*R. v. Dietrich* (1970), 1 C.C.C. (2d) 49 (Ont. C.A.); *R. v. Carpenter (No. 2)*, (1982), 1 C.C.C. (3d) 149 (Ont. C.A.)), that this is preferable to a full hearing where the issue, usually admissibility of evidence, is not dependent upon the credibility of a witness but rather upon whether the evidence, if believed by the trier of fact, meets the preconditions for admissibility. For example, alleged similar act evidence is often ruled upon in this way.

The defence does not concede the credibility of the similar act witness: it recognizes that admissibility is not dependent upon credibility but presupposes the accuracy of the evidence. There are issues relating to similar act evidence that may necessitate a full hearing: for example, the precise parameters of the proposed evidence may be unclear, or, the defence may contend that credibility is relevant, under limited circumstances, to the admissibility of, and not just the weight to be given to, the evidence.

(e) full *voir dires*, that is, trials within trials, based upon *viva voce* evidence.

Of course, *voir dires* and other motions may arise during the course of the trial proper as well. Evidence called during the *voir dire*, if admissible, generally needs to be retendered before the jury. In a trial by judge alone, the evidence called during the *voir dire* does not become evidence at the trial proper unless both parties consent. Absent consent, the evidence must be retendered.

One example of an issue often resolved through a *voir dire* is the admissibility of a statement made by the accused to a person in authority. The Crown bears the burden of proving voluntariness beyond a reasonable doubt. Accordingly, the *voir dire* essentially assumes the form of a trial proper (*Erven v. The Queen* (1978), 44 C.C.C. (2d) 76 (S.C.C.)). The accused may waive the holding of a *voir dire* as to voluntariness but must expressly do so (*Park v. The Queen* (1981), 59 C.C.C. (2d) 385 (S.C.C.)).

QUESTIONS

4. During a jury trial, *voir dires* are generally held in the absence of the jury. However, there are exceptions. A *voir dire* into the expertise of a witness whose opinion evidence is sought may be conducted before the jury, as may a *voir dire* into the competency of a child witness to be sworn or to testify upon a promise to tell the truth. Why?

5. The accused is tried by judge without a jury. On the *voir dire* as to the admissibility of the accused's confession, should the trial judge hear the statement itself?

6. The accused testifies on a *voir dire* in the absence of the jury. The statement is ruled admissible. Can the accused's evidence on the *voir dire*, which contains inculpatory remarks, be tendered by the Crown at the trial proper? Alternatively, can the accused be cross-examined on what he said on the *voir dire* or on the differences between his *voir dire* and trial evidence? Would your answer be the same or different if the statement was ruled inadmissible? What limitations are generally placed on the use to which prior evidence given in a *voir dire* (or another proceeding for that matter) can be put? Consider, in this regard, *R. v. Noël* (2002), 168 C.C.C. (3d) 193 (S.C.C.).

D. THE CHARTER VOIR DIRE

In Chapters 4 and 6, the impact of the *Canadian Charter of Rights and Freedoms* on police and prosecutorial practices was addressed. At trial, practices which allegedly violate the *Charter* may support an application pursuant to s. 24(2) for exclusion of evidence, or pursuant to s. 24(1) for another appropriate and just remedy, such as a judicial stay of proceedings. Section 52 of the *Constitution Act, 1982* may be used to invalidate state conduct and further support a s. 24 remedy. Alternatively, s. 52 may independently be used to invalidate the very offence with which the accused is charged, or, more likely, cause it to be read in a manner consistent with the *Charter*. There has been, and continues to be some confusion about the timing, notice requirements and format of *Charter* applications.

1. TIMING OF APPLICATIONS

R. v. DESOUSA

(1992), 76 C.C.C. (3d) 124 (S.C.C.)

The judgment of the court was delivered by

Sopinka J.: — This appeal concerns a constitutional challenge to s. 269 (unlawfully causing bodily harm) of the *Criminal Code*, R.S.C. 1985, c. C-46 (formerly s. 245.3). The appellant was involved in a fight in which a bystander was injured when a bottle allegedly thrown by the appellant broke against a wall and a glass fragment from the bottle struck the bystander.

Prior to trial, the appellant brought a motion to have s. 269 declared of no force or effect as contrary to s. 7 of the *Canadian Charter of Rights and Freedoms*. The appellant argued that the offence of unlawfully causing bodily harm was contrary to fundamental justice as it put an accused at risk of imprisonment without the requirement of a blameworthy state of mind. Additionally, the appellant argued that the provision allows a conviction despite an accused's lack of intent to cause the consequence of bodily harm. The motion succeeded and the indictment under which the appellant stood charged was quashed. On appeal, the motion judgment was overturned and the order quashing the indictment was set aside: 62 C.C.C. (3d) 95, 1 O.R. (3d) 152, 42 O.A.C. 375.

.....

This appeal raises two issues. The first is the correct procedure to be followed by a judge in considering a pre-trial motion contesting the constitutionality of the provision under which an accused is charged. The second issue is whether s. 269 of the *Code* violates either or both of ss. 7 and 11(*d*) of the *Charter*. This latter issue has two branches: (i) the mental element required by s. 269 and whether this element is constitutionally sufficient, and (ii) whether s. 7 of the *Charter* requires as a constitutional minimum, foresight of each or any of the consequences that comprise the *actus reus* of an offence.

A. The pre-trial procedure

The respondent submits that the learned trial judge erred in ruling on the application by the appellant to declare that s. 269 of the *Criminal Code* was of no force or effect before hearing the evidence at trial. It is clear that as the liberty interest of the appellant is ultimately at risk in this appeal, the appellant has the right to question the constitutional validity of the provision under which he is charged. This is the case even though the unconstitutional effects may not be directed at the appellant per se: *R. v. Morgentaler* (1988), 37 C.C.C. (3d) 449 at p. 470, 44 D.L.R. (4th) 385, [1988] 1 S.C.R. 30. The appellant submits that this court has the power and the duty to review the elements of criminal offences and this is not disputed by the Crown. As the elements of the offence necessarily affect adjudication under it, an accused has standing to contest the elements of any provision under which he or she is charged. While it is incumbent on a court to consider such issues at some point in its deliberations, it is less clear in what circumstances this review must or should be done prior to hearing evidence.

The general rule with respect to attacking an indictment by reason of a defect in law is that a motion to quash the indictment for a defect apparent on the face thereof must be made before pleading. This rule is subsumed in the provisions of s. 601(1) of the *Code*, which requires the motion to be made before the plea, and thereafter only with leave of the court. The main purpose of the rule, and of s. 601(1) to the extent that it embodies the rule, is to ensure that defects curable by amendment are attacked before pleading, since, if not cured by amendment, they may be waived by a plea: see *R. v. Côté* (1977), 33 C.C.C. (2d) 353 at p. 359, 73 D.L.R. (3d) 752, [1978] 1 S.C.R. 8; *R. v. Villeneuve* (1984), 54 A.R. 265 at p. 267 (C.A.); *R. v. Cook* (1985), 20 C.C.C. (3d) 18 at pp. 30-1, 40, 46 C.R. (3d) 129, 14 W.C.B. 155 (B.C.C.A.); *R. v. C.(R.I.)* (1986), 32 C.C.C. (3d) 399 at p. 404, 17 O.A.C. 354, 17 W.C.B. 370 (C.A.); *R. v. Peremiczky* (1973), 13 C.P.R. (2d) 242 at p. 244, 25 C.R.N.S. 399, [1974] 2 W.W.R. 386 (B.C.S.C.); *R. v. Denton* (1990), 100 N.S.R. (2d) 174 at p. 176, 11 W.C.B. (2d) 418 (Co. Ct.).

The temporal requirement of moving before pleading has no application, however, to a motion to quash which questions the validity of the law under which the accused is charged. I expressly refrain from addressing the effect of a plea of guilty: see *R. v. Tennen* (1959), 122 C.C.C. 375 at pp. 381-2, 29 C.R. 379, [1959] O.R. 77 (C.A.); affirmed 125 C.C.C. 336, [1960] S.C.R. 302, 32 C.R. 301, and *R. v. Sarson* (1992), 73 C.C.C. (3d) 1, 16 W.C.B. (2d) 200 (Ont. Ct. (Gen. Div.)). Such a defect goes to the jurisdiction of the court to proceed with the charge and is not subject to the temporal restriction in s. 601(1). Such an application may be brought at any time. Indeed, where the trial court is a court of inferior jurisdiction, a motion may be brought before trial to prohibit the trial court from proceeding: see *Canadian Broadcasting Corp. v. Attorney-General for Ontario* (1959), 122 C.C.C. 305, 16 D.L.R. (2d) 609, [1959] S.C.R. 188; reversing 120 C.C.C. 84, 27 C.R. 165, [1958] O.R. 55 (C.A.); which affirmed 118 C.C.C. 200, [1957] O.R. 466, [1957] O.W.N. 358 (H.C.J.). There is no question, therefore, that the trial judge has jurisdiction to hear and dispose of a motion to quash the indictment on the grounds of constitutional invalidity. Whether he or she is bound to do so or whether as a matter of practice should do so is more problematic.

With rare exceptions that do not apply here a trial judge is empowered to reserve on any application until the end of the case. He or she is not obliged, therefore, to rule on a motion to quash for invalidity of the indictment until the end of the case after the evidence has been heard. The decision whether to rule on the application or reserve until the end of the case is a discretionary one to be exercised having regard to two policy considerations. The first is that criminal proceedings should not be fragmented by interlocutory proceedings which take on a life of their own. This policy is the basis of the rule against interlocutory appeals in criminal matters: see *R. v. Mills* (1986), 26 C.C.C. (3d) 481, 29 D.L.R. (4th) 161, [1986] 1 S.C.R. 863. The second, which relates to constitutional challenges, discourages adjudication of constitutional issues without a factual foundation: see, for instance, *Moysa v. Alberta (Labour Relations Board)* (1989), 60 D.L.R. (4th) 1, [1989] 1 S.C.R. 1572, 89 C.L.L.C. 14,028, and *Danson v. Ontario (Attorney General)* (1990), 73 D.L.R. (4th) 686, [1990] 2 S.C.R. 1086, 43 C.P.C. (2d) 165. Both these policies favour disposition of applications at the end of the case. In exercising the discretion to which I have referred, the trial judge should not depart from these policies unless there is a strong reason for so doing. In some cases the interests of justice necessitate an immediate decision. Examples of such necessitous circumstances include cases in which the trial court itself is implicated in a constitutional violation as in *R. v. Rahey* (1987), 33 C.C.C. (3d) 289, 39 D.L.R. (4th) 481, [1987] 1 S.C.R. 588, or where substantial ongoing constitutional violations require immediate attention as in *R. v. Gamble* (1988), 45 C.C.C. (3d) 204, [1988] 2 S.C.R. 595, 66 C.R. (3d) 193. Moreover, in some cases it will save time to decide constitutional questions before proceeding to trial on the evidence. An apparently meritorious *Charter* challenge of the law under which the accused is charged which is not dependent on facts to be elicited during the trial may come within this exception to the general rule: see *Metropolitan Stores (MTS) Ltd. v. Manitoba Food & Commercial Workers, Local 832* (1987), 38 D.L.R. (4th) 321 at p. 337, [1987] 1 S.C.R. 110, 87 C.L.L.C. 14,015. This applies with added force when the trial is expected to be of considerable duration: see, for example, *R. v. Nova Scotia Pharmaceutical Society*, S.C.C., No. 22473, July 9, 1992, unreported [since reported 74 C.C.C. (3d) 289, 93 D.L.R. (4th) 36, 43 C.P.R. (3d) 1].

In this case no objection was taken at trial to the procedure adopted by the trial judge. The *Charter* challenge was not without merit notwithstanding its fate in this court. I am satisfied that the evidence at trial would not have assisted in the resolution of the constitutional question given the nature of the appellant's submissions. The Court of Appeal stated (at p. 96) that it was "purely speculative at this stage whether the facts at trial will establish a mental element compatible with criminal and constitutional requirements of blameworthiness for a finding of guilt under this section". The fact that the appellant's conduct would attract criminal responsibility because the mental element conforms to constitutional requirements would not resolve the issue if the section in its other applications criminalized conduct that did not meet constitutional standards. We have not adopted the "constitutional as applied" approach that is prevalent in the United States: see *R. v. Smith* (1987), 34 C.C.C. (3d) 97 at pp. 143-4, 40 D.L.R. (4th) 435, [1987] 1 S.C.R. 1045, *per* Lamer J. (as he then was), and at p. 150, *per* Le Dain J. Accordingly, I conclude that the trial judge did not err in disposing of the appellant's motion before hearing evidence.

[Sopinka J. went on to address the constitutional argument raised.]

R. v. L.(W.K.)

(1991), 64 C.C.C. (3d) 321 (S.C.C.)

The judgment of the court was delivered by

Stevenson J.: — The appellant, accused, appeals, as of right, a decision of the British Columbia Court of Appeal setting aside a stay of charges against him. The issue we are to address is whether the judge had sufficient material before him to enable him to act upon the accused's argument that the charges were a violation of fundamental justice and a denial of the accused's right to a fair trial.

.....

The judge at first instance, who was to be the trial judge, entered the stay on a motion made just before the trial was to commence. It is common ground that the application was based on pre-charge delay alleged to violate the *Canadian Charter of Rights and Freedoms*. I note that, in this court, the appellant relied on ss. 7 and 11(*d*) of the *Charter* as providing the basis for a stay under s. 24.

The procedure employed was unusual and in the view of the Court of Appeal, flawed. They set aside the stay, noting that the trial judge could properly deal with the application as part of the trial process when *viva voce* evidence could be offered. I agree with their conclusion.

.....

The appellant was ordered to stand trial on May 13, 1987. On January 28, 1988, an 18-count indictment, in substantially the same form as the 17-count information, was filed. On May 4, 1988, the appellant filed a notice of motion requesting that the proceedings be stayed pursuant to s. 24(1) of the *Charter* on the basis that the charges were contrary to ss. 7 and 11(*a*) and (*b*). On June 7, 1988, counts 17 and 18, the two charges relating to the second daughter, were severed.

When the trial was scheduled to open (before the judge sitting without a jury), counsel for the accused brought on the motion for a stay. No supporting material was referred to in the motion which was described as being of a "non-contentious nature". Counsel stated he would be mainly relying on s. 7 of the *Charter*.

Counsel for the accused then made submissions which consisted of a mix of argument, allegations of fact and readings from some of the evidence given at the preliminary hearing. Crown counsel responded with a similar mix, although occasionally referring to the lack of evidence on some points. He suggested that the trial continue, at least to the close of the Crown's case, so that the judge could hear evidence. It is clear that the judge did not himself read the preliminary hearing transcript. Counsel for the accused's main submission was:

> ... that it is contrary to the principles of fundamental justice to bring a person to court up to thirty years after an alleged event on the uncorroborated

> evidence of one witness in each count, particularly when these complainants had every opportunity many years before.

Counsel also suggested that it was open to the trial judge to stay the proceedings based solely on the length of time that had passed since the first incident. The trial judge stayed the proceedings.

.....

The accused bore the burden of showing an infringement in invoking s. 24 of the *Charter: R. v. Collins* (1987), 33 C.C.C. (3d) 1 at p. 13, 38 D.L.R. (4th) 508, [1987] 1 S.C.R. 265. Here, counsel had particularized the grounds of his attack at the hearing of the motion. Much of what the judge said lay outside those particulars. The decision of the Court of Appeal was grounded on the judge's making finding of facts in the absence of an evidentiary base for the findings.

Although I agree with the result in the Court of Appeal for the reasons set out below, I first address whether it was open to the trial judge to base his decision on the delay that was apparent on the face of the indictment. If so, the evidentiary question may not arise. I consider this issue because the accused's counsel in his submissions to the trial court judge argued that mere delay alone could result in a breach of an individual's rights and it is arguable the trial judge's order is based solely on the delay.

.....

[Stevenson J. then determined that mere pre-trial delay could not justify the order made.]

I turn now to the factual base for the trial judge's conclusions. The question here is not to define a breach of fundamental justice or of the right to a fair trial, but the much narrower one of determining whether there was evidence to support the fact findings; I do not find it necessary to analyze all the fact findings, it is sufficient that critical ones be found to be flawed.

The trial judge considered the sexual offence charges first. He held that the appellant's rights under ss. 7 and 11(*d*) of the *Charter* had been infringed and that counts 1 through 13 should be stayed. To support that conclusion, the trial judge made two key findings of fact. First, he found that the explanation given for reporting the offences in 1986 was "ludicrous" and "specious". Secondly, he found that there was an unexplained delay in reporting the offences and that the failure to "protest years ago when they were beyond parental control... seems extraordinary".

The trial judge's rejection of the explanation for the eventual reporting was a finding of credibility. He not only rejected that explanation but, in characterizing it as specious, appears to have found an improper motive contributing to "oppression". It was not open to him to reject unchallenged testimony. If the trial judge agreed with the appellant that the explanation for the late reporting was relevant, and had doubts about the credibility of the complainants, he ought to have heard their *viva voce* testimony. The informal procedure employed was, in these circumstances, inadequate.

There was, in addition, no evidence before the trial judge that "the complainants made no protest years ago when they were beyond parental control". Counsel for the accused had read to the trial judge excerpts from the preliminary hearing transcript in which the stepdaughter reviewed the various individuals she had told about the abuse. The trial judge contradicted his own finding of fact later in his reasons when he stated that:

> I am also of the view in this case that the position of the prosecutorial authorities and the Ministry of Human Resources which accepted some assertion apparently of one of the complainants, become the executive together and are indivisible as was discussed in *R. v. Young* ...

The trial judge then considered the assault charges in counts 14, 15 and 16. He relied on the same findings of fact which I have found to be flawed. In addition, he stated that the "incidents, if they occurred at all, were matters of discipline over an unruly and defiant young person who it would appear was more startled than struck". There was no evidence that the complainant was "unruly and defiant" or that she was more "startled than struck".

I do not read the judgment of the Court of Appeal as saying that any particular procedure must always be employed in resolving applications under s. 24. It might, for example, be open to the parties to put forward an agreed statement of facts. The decision to continue to trial and argue the motion at the close of the Crown's case, to submit evidence by affidavit, or to agree to a statement of facts will depend on the extent to which the parties can agree and the nature of the facts which the parties seek to establish. I agree with the Court of Appeal that the informal procedure employed on this motion was inadequate since it did not produce the evidence required to support the submissions of the accused. I reiterate that neither this court nor the Court of Appeal addresses the question of defining the circumstances in which an accused may successfully invoke ss. 7 or 11(*d*) of the *Charter*.

[The appeal was accordingly dismissed.]

2. Notice of Applications

R. v. BLOM

(2002), 167 C.C.C. (3d) 332 (Ont. C.A.)

The judgment of the court was delivered by

Sharpe J.A.: —

.....

Before trial, the appellant gave notice of his intention to bring a *Charter* challenge to the admissibility of certain evidence. The Notice was in the following terms:

> TAKE NOTICE that an application will be brought at 9:30 a.m. on the 16th day of November, 2000, at Courtroom No. 1 at 491 Steeles Avenue East, Milton, for an order excluding the evidence of utterances made by the Applicant and any evidence derivative therefrom.

THE GROUNDS FOR THIS APPLICATION ARE:

1. That the Applicant's right to retain and instruct counsel as provided by section 10(*b*) of the *Charter of Rights and Freedoms* was infringed and/or denied.

2. Such further and other grounds as counsel may advise and this Honourable Court may permit.

IN SUPPORT OF THIS APPLICATION, THE APPLICANT RELIES UPON THE FOLLOWING:

1. On May 11, 2000 at approximately 1:33 a.m., the arresting police officer arrived at the scene of the arrest to find a motor vehicle on the east side of the road engulfed in flames and the Applicant standing on the west side of the road watching the fire.

2. The arresting police officer approached the Applicant and asked questions of the Applicant to which the Applicant replied.

3. At 1:45 a.m. the arresting police officer arrested the Applicant and then read to the Applicant his Rights to Counsel, caution and breath demand.

THE RELIEF SOUGHT IS:

1. An Order allowing the application and excluding the evidence of the Applicant's utterances and any evidence derived therefrom, including but not limited to the results of the Intoxilyzer tests.

The Crown filed a response objecting to the sufficiency of the Notice based on the appellant's failure to state the grounds to be argued and to provide the documentary, affidavit or other evidence to be used in support of the *Charter* application.

Trial Proceedings

At the opening of trial, Crown counsel indicated that a *voir dire* to determine the admissibility of the appellant's statement would be required, but he elected to call both Jackson's and P.C. Clayton's evidence first. After Jackson's evidence was heard, P.C. Clayton was called and examined by the Crown. When he got to the point where he was about [to] give evidence about the appellant's statement at the scene of the accident, a *voir dire* commenced. On the *voir dire*, Clayton described his encounter with the appellant at the scene, and testified that the appellant "told me he was the driver". Clayton described asking the appellant for his licence, observing signs of impairment, arresting the appellant and advising him of his right to counsel.

At that point, Crown counsel indicated that as this appeared to be a combined *voir dire*, dealing with both voluntariness and admissibility under the *Charter*, he wished to object, arguing that the appellant had failed to give adequate notice to raise the *Charter* point. The appellant's trial counsel (not Mr. Breen) indicated that the *Charter* argument concerned only the admissibility of the statement, not the breath samples, and that he was relying on s. 7 as well as s. 10(*b*). The trial judge stated that he did not wish to embark on argument while Officer Clayton was on the stand and directed counsel to complete their examination and cross-examination before making any submissions.

After P.C. Clayton completed his evidence, but before the appellant testified on the *voir dire*, the trial judge heard submissions on Crown counsel's objection to the sufficiency of the Notice. Crown counsel submitted that the Notice did not comply with rules 30.03(*c*) and (*d*) and 30.05. The Crown pointed to the appellant's failure to file an affidavit and his reliance on s. 7, despite the omission of any reference to it in the Notice. Crown counsel also submitted that he was prejudiced because he did not have adequate time to prepare a legal argument in response to the appellant.

The appellant's trial counsel explained that the s. 7 argument was based on *R. v. White* (1999), 135 C.C.C. (3d) 257 (S.C.C.), a decision of which he was unaware when he prepared the Notice. *White* dealt with the admissibility of a statement made by a driver after an accident because of his belief that he was required to make the statement pursuant to British Columbia's *Motor Vehicle Act*, R.S.B.C. 1979, c. 288, s. 61(1), which requires [a] driver to report an accident in certain circumstances. The Supreme Court of Canada held that while the statement satisfied the common law voluntariness test, its admission would violate the principle against self-incrimination protected by s. 7 of the *Charter*. The statement was excluded pursuant to s. 24(2).

The appellant's trial counsel argued that an affidavit was unnecessary as the application was to be considered in the context of the trial and was not a stand-alone pre-trial application. He submitted that the factual basis for the argument was evident from the Crown disclosure as it rested upon the encounter between P.C. Clayton and the appellant. He submitted that if the Notice was found to be deficient, this procedural irregularity should not defeat the rights of an accused, and that the appropriate remedy would be to grant the Crown an adjournment.

The trial judge ruled that the Notice was deficient and that the appellant was therefore precluded from advancing his s. 7 argument. The trial judge ruled that the notice did not meet the requirements of Rules 30.03 and 30.05, as an affidavit was required to complete the record and to allow the Crown to respond. The trial judge referred to this court's judgment on *R. v. Dumont* (2000), 149 C.C.C. (3d) 568 (Ont. C.A.), indicating that a trial judge has the discretion to permit a party to proceed despite non-compliance with Rule 30. The trial judge also referred to the objective stated in rule 1.04 that the rules "be liberally construed to secure simplicity in procedure, fairness in administration and the elimination of unjustifiable expense and delay". However, the trial judge refused to exercise his discretion in favour of the appellant. He noted the importance of notice to allow for proper preparation and observed that the Crown had warned the appellant that the Notice was inadequate. The matter had been before the court on a number of occasions, and set for trial some time ago. In these circumstances the trial judge was unwilling to countenance any further delay. He refused to grant an adjournment and ruled that the appropriate remedy was to preclude the appellant from arguing his *Charter* application.

.....

ANALYSIS

Issue 1: Did the summary conviction appeal judge err by upholding the trial judge's refusal to consider the appellant's Charter application on the ground of inadequate notice?

I agree with the respondent that the trial judge's ruling was a discretionary one entitled to deference from this court. However, it is also well established that the discretionary decisions of trial judges on such issues are subject to appellate review where there is an error in principle: see *R. v. Loveman* (1992), 71 C.C.C. (3d) 123 (Ont. C.A.). In my view, the appellant has demonstrated such an error requiring the intervention of this court.

Rule 30, requiring notice of *Charter* applications to exclude evidence, is a procedural rule. Its purpose is to facilitate the fair and expeditious determination of *Charter* issues by ensuring that neither party is taken by surprise at trial and that both parties have adequate notice of the factual and legal basis for the *Charter* application. As has been frequently observed, procedural rules are servants not masters. They are servants to the cause of the just and expeditious resolution of disputes. Procedural rules are important, but they are not to be rigidly applied without regard to their underlying purpose. This is made clear by the Rules themselves. Rule 1.04 requires that Rule 30 "be liberally construed to secure simplicity in procedure, fairness in administration and the elimination of unjustifiable expense and delay". Rule 2.01 provides that failure to comply with Rule 30 is a mere "irregularity" and that even where a rule has not been followed, to the extent possible, steps should be taken "to secure the just determination of the real matters in dispute".

These provisions establish that where a procedural rule such as Rule 30 is invoked to foreclose consideration of a *Charter* issue, non-compliance with the rule is not necessarily fatal to the *Charter* application. Rather, the trial judge is required to consider and weigh a variety of factors to determine what course of action is required by the purpose of the rule. See *R. v. Loveman, supra*; *R. v. Lavallata* (1999), 47 M.V.R. (3d) 236 (Ont. C.J.).

Where a party complains of inadequate notice, it is crucial for the trial judge to consider the issue of prejudice: does the failure to provide adequate notice put the opposite party at some unfair disadvantage in meeting the case that is being presented? If there is no real prejudice, inadequate notice should not prevent consideration of the *Charter* application. If the inadequate notice does put the opposing party at a disadvantage, the court must consider whether something less drastic than refusing to consider the *Charter* argument, but still consistent with the goal of achieving "fairness in administration and the elimination of unjustifiable expense and delay", can be done to alleviate that prejudice. If so, that course should be followed in preference to an order refusing to entertain the *Charter* application.

The appellant's Notice of *Charter* application was factually skeletal and it failed to indicate that the appellant would rely upon s. 7. However, the Notice should be considered in the light of the charges the appellant faced and the nature of the argument he sought to advance.

This was a routine prosecution for a routine offence. The appellant's *Charter* argument was not factually complex. It was based on the undisputed facts of the encounter between the police officer and the appellant at the scene of the accident, and on the appellant's reason for admitting to the officer that he was the driver of the vehicle. The *voir dire* involved little evidence that would not be heard on the trial proper. It was conducted during the course of the trial, and quite apart from the *Charter* application, a *voir dire* was required to determine [the] voluntariness of the appellant's statement to the police officer in any event. The *Charter* argument rested on precisely the same facts as the voluntariness issue.

Nor was the *Charter* argument novel from a legal perspective, and [it] did not require extensive legal research. The appellant's argument rested squarely on the application of a recent decision of the Supreme Court of Canada that would almost certainly be very familiar to a prosecutor appearing before a court dealing with drinking and driving offences.

In view of the factual and legal issues raised by the *Charter* application, it is difficult to see how the appellant's defective Notice caused any prejudice to the Crown. There is no suggestion that the Crown would have called additional evidence on the *Charter* point. Nor is there any suggestion that Crown counsel would have conducted the examination of witnesses any differently had the notice been more complete. As already mentioned, the legal issue was routine and one Crown counsel could reasonably be expected to address without extensive preparation. At best, the Crown might have required a brief adjournment to review the *White* decision. The situation is similar to that presented in *R. v. Loveman, supra*, at 127 where Doherty J.A. held:

> In my opinion, the trial judge did not properly balance the various interests. His ruling sacrificed entirely the appellant's right to advance a *Charter*-based argument. The other interests engaged did not require the order made by the trial judge. As Crown counsel suggested, there were other alternatives. The trial judge could have heard the entire case except the Crown's legal argument in reply to the *Charter* argument, and then, if necessary (and it may well not have been necessary), allowed Crown counsel a brief adjournment to prepare his response to the legal issues flowing from the *Charter* argument.

I am mindful of the difficult task confronting the judges of the very busy trial courts of this province. Trial judges are expected to run their courts efficiently and they are entitled to insist upon adherence to rules designed to ensure the proper administration of justice. I am also mindful of the discretionary latitude that should be accorded to trial judges, who are often required to balance competing factors and make difficult choices on the spot. Appellate courts should hesitate to interfere with these decisions. No doubt, the trial judge in the present case was only trying to apply the Rules fairly and to run an efficient court when he refused to consider the appellant's *Charter* application. However, in my respectful view, in the absence of any significant prejudice to the Crown arising from the defective notice, the trial judge erred in principle by foreclosing the appellant's *Charter* application. It follows that the summary conviction appeal judge also erred in his analysis of this issue.

.....

In my view, the appropriate order is to allow the appeal, set aside the conviction and order a new trial.

Various provincial statutes mandate that formal notice be given to the provincial and federal Attorneys General when the constitutionality of legislation is impugned. See, for example, the Alberta *Judicature Act*, R.S.A. 2000, c. J-2, and the Ontario *Courts of Justice Act*, R.S.O. 1990, c. 43. As well, s. 482 of the *Criminal Code* permits the creation of rules of the court. See for example, Rules 27.1 to 27.6 of the Ontario Court of Justice Criminal Proceedings Rules which must be consulted by counsel when a constitutional or *Charter* issue arises.

3. The Voir Dire Format

The burden of proof for *Charter* motions is different than that in the trial proper. For example, under s. 24(2) of the *Charter*, the accused must prove on a balance of probabilities that evidence was obtained in a manner that infringed or denied the accused's *Charter* rights, and that the admission of that evidence would bring the administration of justice into disrepute (*R. v. Collins* (1987), 33 C.C.C. (3d) 1 (S.C.C.), substantially reproduced at p. 410 of this text). Or, there may be a mixed burden. For example, where the accused satisfies his or her burden of demonstrating that legislation infringes a *Charter* right, the state bears the burden under s. 1 of the *Charter* of proving that the infringement is reasonable and demonstrably justified in a free and democratic society (*R. v. Oakes* (1986), 24 C.C.C. (3d) 321 (S.C.C.)). Similarly, a warrantless search is presumptively unreasonable. Accordingly, upon proof that the search was warrantless, the burden shifts to the state to demonstrate its reasonableness. It is not surprising that courts have wrestled with the procedural implications which follow.

The problem is particularly acute when the witnesses who are relied upon to establish the *Charter* violation are the allegedly offending police officers. Some courts compel the accused to call these witnesses and to examine them in chief in a non-leading way; other courts compel the accused to call the witnesses but permit cross-examination: see, for example, *R. v. Feldman* (1994), 91 C.C.C. (3d) 256 (B.C.C.A.); affd (1994), 93 C.C.C. (3d) 575 (S.C.C.):

> ... it may be that a trial judge conducting a *voir dire* into an alleged breach of the *Charter* would grant the defence more leeway than might otherwise be permitted if fairness and the right to make full answer and defence appear to require relaxation of the normal rules with respect to permitting cross-examination of one's own witness.

Many Crown counsel will oblige the defence by calling the police witnesses themselves, eliciting in examination-in-chief their *Charter*-related evidence and thereby permitting the defence to cross-examine.

Consider the common problem raised in the following question.

QUESTION

7. The accused is charged with attempted murder. He is alleged to have admitted his guilt to the police shortly after his arrest. It is the position of the defence that the statement was obtained in violation of s. 10(*b*) of the *Charter*. Furthermore, voluntariness is in dispute. The same witnesses are

relevant to both issues. Two different onuses apply. Should both issues be resolved in one *voir dire*? How might the accused benefit if only one *voir dire* is held? Now assume that the accused is prepared to testify on the *Charter* motion but his evidence would undermine the defence position on the issue of voluntariness, which the Crown has difficulty proving. What should the defence do?

E. CHARTER EXCLUSION UNDER SECTION 24(2)

Section 24 of the *Charter* reads:

> **(1) Anyone whose rights or freedoms, as guaranteed by this *Charter*, have been infringed or denied may apply to a court of competent jurisdiction to obtain such remedy as the court considers appropriate and just in the circumstances.**
>
> **(2) Where, in proceedings under subsection (1), a court concludes that evidence was obtained in a manner that infringed or denied any rights or freedoms guaranteed by this *Charter*, the evidence shall be excluded if it is established that, having regard to all the circumstances, the admission of it in the proceedings would bring the administration of justice into disrepute.**

Where the exclusion of evidence is sought under s. 24(2) of the *Charter*, the court of competent jurisdiction, which effectively is confined to the trial judge, must find that the accused's rights or freedoms, as guaranteed by the *Charter*, have been infringed or denied. This is often referred to as an issue of *standing*. However, it is a misnomer to describe this issue as one of standing. The evidence is being tendered against an accused who undoubtedly has standing to challenge its admissibility. However, an accused has no access to s. 24 *Charter* relief unless he or she can demonstrate a breach of his or her personal *Charter* rights: *R. v. Belnavis* (1997), 118 C.C.C. (3d) 405 (S.C.C.).

R. v. EDWARDS

(1996), 104 C.C.C. (3d) 136 (S.C.C.)

Cory J. (Lamer C.J.C., Sopinka, McLachlin, Iacobucci and Major JJ. concurring): — What rights does an accused person have to challenge the admission of evidence obtained as a result of a search of a third party's premises? That is the question that must be resolved on this appeal.

Factual background

As a result of receiving information that the appellant was a drug trafficker operating out of his car using a cellular phone and a pager, the police placed him under surveillance. They were told that he had drugs either on his person, at his residence or at the apartment occupied by his girlfriend, Shelly Evers.

.....

On the day of his arrest, the police observed the appellant drive Ms Evers' vehicle from a residence to her apartment. The appellant entered the apartment and stayed there for a brief period of time. Shortly after he left, he was stopped by the police. They knew his driver's licence was under suspension and that a person driving while his or her licence is under suspension may be arrested without a warrant (pursuant to the provisions of the *Highway Traffic Act*, R.S.O. 1990, c. H.8, s. 217(2)).

The police saw the appellant speaking on the cellular phone in the car. When they approached the vehicle, they saw the appellant swallow an object wrapped in cellophane about half the size of a golf ball. The car doors were locked, and the appellant did not unlock them until he had swallowed the object. He was arrested for driving while his licence was under suspension and taken into custody. Evers' car was then towed to the vehicle pound.

It was conceded that the usual practice upon arresting a person for driving while under suspension was to impound the car and give the individual a ticket. It was unusual to take someone into custody and it was acknowledged that this procedure was adopted in order to facilitate the drug investigation.

The police suspected that there might be crack cocaine in Ms Evers' apartment, but they did not consider that they had sufficient evidence to obtain a search warrant. After taking the appellant into custody, two police officers attended at the apartment. They made a number of statements to Evers, some of which were lies and others half-truths, in order to obtain her co-operation. They advised her: (1) that the appellant had told them there were drugs in the apartment; (2) that if she did not co-operate, a police officer would stay in her apartment until they were able to get a search warrant; (3) that it would be inconvenient for them to get a search warrant because of the paperwork involved; and (4) that one of the officers would be going on vacation the following day and regardless of what they found in her apartment, she along with the appellant would not be charged.

There is conflicting evidence as to whether these statements were made before or after the officers were admitted to the apartment. None the less, once inside, Ms Evers directed them to a couch in her living room where she thought she had seen the appellant replacing a cushion a few days earlier. The cushion was removed, revealing a plastic bag containing six baggies of crack cocaine with a value of between $11,000 and $23,000. These were seized by the police. Twenty minutes later, they returned and arrested Ms Evers. This they had been instructed to do by a superior officer after he had consulted a Crown attorney. At no time prior to being taken into custody was Ms Evers advised of her right to refuse entry to the police or of her right to counsel.

At the police station, Ms Evers was questioned and in response, she gave a statement naming the appellant as the person who placed the drugs under the cushion of the couch in her apartment. She and the appellant were jointly charged under s. 4(2) of the *Narcotic Control Act*, R.S.C. 1985, c. N-1, with possession of crack cocaine for the purpose of trafficking. Ms Evers was then released. Charges against her were eventually dropped on the morning her trial was scheduled to begin.

On the evening of the arrest, the police attended at the vehicle pound and without a search warrant seized the cellular phone and pager used by the appellant. Then for several hours, they intercepted a number of calls from people ordering small amounts of crack cocaine from the appellant.

At the conclusion of the trial, the appellant was found guilty as charged. His appeal from conviction was dismissed by the Court of Appeal of Ontario, with Abella J.A. dissenting on the issue of the appellant's standing to assert his rights under s. 8 of the *Canadian Charter of Rights and Freedoms* in relation to the search of his girlfriend's apartment. The appeal to this court is limited to that issue.

.....

In any determination of a s. 8 challenge, it is of fundamental importance to remember that the privacy right allegedly infringed must, as a general rule, be that of the accused person who makes the challenge. This has been stressed by the United States Supreme Court in several cases dealing with searches that allegedly violated the Fourth Amendment guarantee. In *Alderman v. United States*, 394 U.S. 165 (1969), for example, White J., delivering the judgment of the majority, stated at pp. 171-2 that:

> [the] suppression of the product of a Fourth Amendment violation can be successfully urged *only by those whose rights were violated by the search itself, not by those who are aggrieved solely by the introduction of damaging evidence.*

(Emphasis added.)

This principle was adopted and applied in *Rakas v. Illinois*, 439 U.S. 128 (1978) at p. 425, and *United States v. Salvucci*, 448 U.S. 83 (1980) at p. 86. The view expressed in these cases is persuasive and should be applied when s. 8 challenges are considered.

The intrusion on the privacy rights of a third party may, however, be relevant in the second stage of the s. 8 analysis, namely, whether the search was conducted in a reasonable manner. The reasons in *R. v. Thompson* (1990), 59 C.C.C. (3d) 225, 73 D.L.R. (4th) 596, [1990] 2 S.C.R. 1111, considered this question. At issue was a wire-tap authorization which allowed the police to eavesdrop on several public pay telephones that were often used by the appellant as well as other members of the public. The appellants argued that the failure of the authorizing judge to limit the intrusion on those third party users rendered the search unreasonable. Sopinka J. agreed ...

.....

In the case at bar, there is no need to consider the reasonableness of the search since the appellant has not established the requisite expectation of privacy. Even if it were necessary to consider the invasion of the privacy of Ms Evers, I would conclude that there was neither a potentially massive invasion of property nor a flagrant abuse of individual's right to privacy.

Like the parties, I agree that the clearly stated reasons of Finlayson J.A. in *Pugliese* [(1992), 71 C.C.C. (3d) 295 (Ont. C.A.)] are correct and applicable to this case. The only difference between the parties arises from their view as to how it should be applied. In *Pugliese, supra,* the police obtained a search warrant for an apartment in a building owned by the accused but rented to another person. Illegal drugs, hidden by the tenant for the accused, were found in the apartment. The accused sought to challenge the search warrant on the basis of his right to privacy which, he contended, arose either from his proprietary interest in the apartment or his possessory interest in the goods seized.

This argument was rejected by Finlayson J.A. He found that, while the building may have been owned by Pugliese, he had leased the apartment to the tenant with the result that his right of entry was restricted by the provincial landlord-and-tenant legislation. It was the tenant who had a legitimate right to privacy. He alone was in a position to grant or refuse permission to enter the premises. Pugliese, on the other hand, had no right or authority to overrule the tenant's wishes in this regard. Nor did he have any demonstrated possessory interest in the drugs seized, since he had expressly disavowed any connection with them.

Finlayson J.A. emphasized that the essence of the test under s. 8 was the existence of a *personal* privacy right. He noted, however, that a proprietary or possessory interest could properly be considered as evidence of that personal right. Since Pugliese was unable to advance any ground other than his proprietary interest in the building, Finlayson J.A. concluded that there was nothing in the record that established an expectation of privacy in the apartment or in the portion of it in which the drugs were seized.

.....

In the case at bar, one of the bases upon which the appellant asserted his right to privacy in Ms Evers' apartment was his interest in the drugs. It is possible, in certain circumstances, to establish an expectation of privacy in the goods that are seized. ... However, this contention cannot be raised in the circumstances of this case. At trial, the appellant denied that the drugs were his and Ms Evers testified that they might have belonged to someone else. The appellant maintained in the Court of Appeal that the drugs were not his. It was only in this court that he acknowledged for the first time that the drugs were his. He should not now be permitted to change his position with regard to a fundamentally important aspect of the evidence in order to put forward a fresh argument which could not be considered in the courts below. The result in this appeal must turn solely on the appellant's privacy interest in Ms Evers' apartment.

A review of the recent decisions of this court and those of the United States Supreme Court, which I find convincing and properly applicable to the situation presented in the case at bar, indicates that certain principles pertaining to the nature of the s. 8 right to be secure against unreasonable search or seizure can be derived. In my view, they may be summarized in the following manner:

1. A claim for relief under s. 24(2) can only be made by the person whose *Charter* rights have been infringed: see *R. v. Rahey* (1987), 33 C.C.C. (3d) 289 at p. 308, 39 D.L.R. (4th) 481 at p. 500, [1987] 1 S.C.R. 588.
2. Like all *Charter* rights, s. 8 is a personal right. It protects people and not places: see *Hunter v. Southam Inc.*,[(1984), 14 C.C.C. (3d) 97 (S.C.C.)].
3. The right to challenge the legality of a search depends upon the accused establishing that his personal rights to privacy have been violated: see *Pugliese*, *supra*.
4. As a general rule, two distinct inquiries must be made in relation to s. 8. First, has the accused a reasonable expectation of privacy? Second, if he has such an expectation, was the search

by the police conducted reasonably?: see [*Rawlings v. Kentucky*, 448 U.S. 98 (1980)].

5. A reasonable expectation of privacy is to be determined on the basis of the totality of the circumstances: see *Colarusso*, [(1994), 87 C.C.C. (3d) 193 (S.C.C.)] at pp. 215-16..., and *Wong* [(1990), 60 C.C.C. (3d) 460 (S.C.C.)], at p. 465.
6. The factors to be considered in assessing the totality of the circumstances may include, but are not restricted to, the following:
   (i) presence at the time of the search;
   (ii) possession or control of the property or place searched;
   (iii) ownership of the property or place;
   (iv) historical use of the property or item;
   (v) the ability to regulate access, including the right to admit or exclude others from the place;
   (vi) the existence of a subjective expectation of privacy; and
   (vii) the objective reasonableness of the expectation.

   See *United States v. Gomez*, 16 F.3d 254 (8th Cir. 1994) at p. 256.
7. If an accused person establishes a reasonable expectation of privacy, the inquiry must proceed to the second stage to determine whether the search was conducted in a reasonable manner.

Taking all the circumstances of this case into account, it is my view that the appellant has not demonstrated that he had an expectation of privacy in Ms Evers' apartment.

[La Forest J., though concurring in the result, vigorously differed as to the reasons therefor.]

QUESTION

8. The police have reasonable and probable grounds to believe that a bank employee has created a fictitious bank account, deposited other clients' moneys into that account and caused, with the assistance of her boyfriend, withdrawals to be made from it for their benefit. The boyfriend is arrested, and enticed to provide handwriting samples to the police. Later analysis of the samples demonstrates that this handwriting matches certain withdrawal slips. That is the only evidence that ties the boyfriend to the crime. At the trial of both accused, the Crown concedes that the samples were obtained in violation of the boyfriend's right to counsel and that the samples should be excluded as evidence against him. Accordingly, the Crown withdraws the charges against him, intending thereby to proceed against the bank employee alone and seeking to tender the handwriting samples at her trial to prove that the withdrawal slips were filled out by her boyfriend and therefore circumstantially prove that she must be the guilty insider. Can the accused prevent the admission of these samples? Consider, in this regard, *R. v. Paolitto* (1994), 91 C.C.C. (3d) 75 (Ont. C.A.).

When exclusion of evidence is sought under s. 24(2), the court must also find that the evidence sought to be excluded must have been ob-

tained in a manner that infringed or denied the accused's *Charter* rights or freedoms. This raises issues of *nexus*.

R. v. STRACHAN

(1988), 46 C.C.C. (3d) 479 (S.C.C.)

[The police obtained a *Narcotic Control Act* [R.S.C. 1985, c. N-1, repealed 1996, c. 19, s. 94] warrant to search the accused's home. When the police arrived, they arrested the accused for possession of marijuana and advised him of his right to retain and instruct counsel without delay. The accused attempted to contact counsel but was told he could not do so until the police had matters under control. An officer later testified that he did not allow the accused to telephone counsel because at that stage, there were two unidentified men in the residence and he knew that the accused had two firearms, albeit legal, somewhere there. The police officer asked the accused several questions and the police conducted the search. Though the other occupants were identified and left the residence and the firearms were recovered, the accused was not allowed to contact counsel at the residence. Dickson C.J.C. (Beetz, McIntyre, La Forest and L'Heureux-Dubé JJ. concurring) held that there was no s. 10(*b*) violation when the officer initially prevented the accused from contacting counsel but, once the police were in control, access should have been given. In considering whether the seized items should be excluded under s. 24(2) of the *Charter*, the Crown contended that there was no causal connection between the s. 10(*b*) violation and the discovery of the items seized. Hence, the evidence was not obtained in a manner that infringed the *Charter*.]

Dickson C.J.C.: —

.....

... In my view, reading the phrase "obtained in a manner" as imposing a causation requirement creates a host of difficulties. A strict causal nexus would place the courts in the position of having to speculate whether the evidence would have been discovered had the *Charter* violation not occurred. Speculation on what might have happened is a highly artificial task. Isolating the events that caused the evidence to be discovered from those that did not is an exercise in sophistry. Events are complex and dynamic. It will never be possible to state with certainty what would have taken place had a *Charter* violation not occurred. Speculation of this sort is not, in my view, an appropriate inquiry for the courts.

A causation requirement also leads to a narrow view of the relationship between a *Charter* violation and the discovery of evidence. Requiring a causal link will tend to distort the analysis of the conduct that led to the discovery of evidence. The inquiry will tend to focus narrowly on the actions most directly responsible for the discovery of evidence rather than on the entire course of events leading to its discovery. This will almost inevitably lead to an intellectual endeavour essentially amounting to "splitting hairs" between conduct that violated the *Charter* and that which did not.

.....

Imposing a causation requirement in s. 24(2) would generally have the effect of excluding from consideration under that section much of the real evidence obtained following a violation of the right to counsel. Violations of the right to counsel may frequently occur in the course of a valid arrest or, as in the present appeal, in the execution of a valid search power. In these situations, real evidence discovered on the person of the accused or in the course of the search will not, subject to one exception, have a direct causal relationship with the denial of the right to counsel. Derivative evidence, obtained as a direct result of a statement or other indication made by the accused, is the only type of real evidence that may be said to be causally connected to violations of the right to counsel in these situations. With the exception of derivative evidence, infringements of the right to counsel occurring in the course of arrest or execution of a search warrant, can only be causally connected to self-incriminating evidence. *R. v. Manninen* (1987), 34 C.C.C. (3d) 385, 41 D.L.R. (4th) 301, [1987] 1 S.C.R. 1233 (S.C.C.) is a case in point. A strict causal requirement would tend to preclude real evidence discovered after a violation of s. 10(*b*) from being considered under s. 24(2) of the *Charter*.

In situations other than valid arrest or reasonable execution of a search warrant, it may be possible to argue that the presence of counsel might have prevented the discovery of real evidence. This could be the case, for example, under the personal search provisions of the *Customs Act,* R.S.C. 1970, c. C-40, considered in *R. v. Simmons,* judgment rendered December 8, 1988 [since reported 45 C.C.C. (3d) 296, [1988] 2 S.C.R. 495], or under the provisions of the new *Customs Act,* S.C. 1986, c. 1. These provisions permit a person about to be searched to request a second authorization before the search is conducted. Persons who are not given the opportunity to consult counsel in this situation may be unaware of their right to request a second opinion and the search may proceed without further authorization. It would be possible to argue that had the person been informed of the right to counsel, counsel would have advised the person to demand a second opinion and this might have been that a search should not be conducted. Imposing a causal requirement would result in treating violations of s. 10(*b*) differently depending on the role counsel could have performed and would invite idle speculation on what might have happened if the accused had exercised the right to counsel.

In my view, it is not useful to create a requirement in the first stage of s. 24(2) that would separate violations of s. 10(*b*) into two categories based on the role of counsel. Nor is it fruitful to read into the first stage a condition that would limit the scope of s. 24(2) to self-incriminating or derivative evidence for certain s. 10(*b*) violations. Ordinarily only a few *Charter* rights, ss. 8, 9 and 10, will be relevant to the gathering of evidence and therefore to the remedy of exclusion under s. 24(2). So long as a violation of one of these rights precedes the discovery of evidence, for the purposes of the first stage of s. 24(2) it makes little sense to draw distinctions based on the circumstances surrounding the violation or the type of evidence recovered. A better approach, in my view, would be to consider all evidence gathered following a violation of a *Charter* right, including the right to counsel, as within the scope of s. 24(2).

In my view, all of the pitfalls of causation may be avoided by adopting an approach that focuses on the entire chain of events during which the *Charter* violation occurred and the evidence was obtained. Accordingly, the first inquiry under s. 24(2) would be to determine whether a *Charter* violation occurred in the course of obtaining the evidence. A temporal link between the infringement of the *Charter* and the discovery of the evidence figures prominently in this assessment, particularly where the *Charter* violation and the discovery of the evidence occur in the course of a single transaction. The presence of a temporal connection is not, however, determinative. Situations will arise where evidence, though obtained following the breach of a *Charter* right, will be too remote from the violation to be "obtained in a manner" that infringed the *Charter*. In my view, these situations should be dealt with on a case by case basis. There can be no hard and fast rule for determining when evidence obtained following the infringement of a *Charter* right becomes too remote.

If a *Charter* violation has occurred in the course of obtaining the evidence, the analysis will proceed to the second, and in my view the more important, branch of s. 24(2), whether the admission of the evidence would bring the administration of justice into disrepute. In *R. v. Collins* the court articulated a comprehensive test for the second branch of s. 24(2). Lamer J. for the majority, identified three groups of factors to be considered in the course of this inquiry. The first group concerns the fairness of the trial. The nature of the evidence, whether it is real evidence or self-incriminating evidence produced by the accused, will be relevant to this determination. The second group relates to the seriousness of the *Charter* violation. Consideration will focus on the relative seriousness of the violation, whether the violation was committed in good faith or was of a merely technical nature or whether it was willful, deliberate and flagrant, whether the violation was motivated by circumstances of urgency or necessity, and whether other investigatory techniques that would not have infringed the *Charter* were available. The final set of factors relates to the disrepute that would arise from exclusion of the evidence. In my view, the three groups of factors encompass aspects of the relationship between the *Charter* violation and the evidence at issue, thereby permitting some examination of the relationship in the course of the core inquiry under s. 24(2). The presence of a causal link will be a factor for consideration under the second branch of s. 24(2).

I conclude that the narcotics in this appeal were obtained in a manner that infringed the *Charter*. During the execution of a search of his apartment, the appellant was denied his right to consult counsel. Marijuana was discovered during the course of the search. In my view, this chain of events is sufficient to clear the first branch of s. 24(2). I therefore turn to consider the second branch, whether admission of the evidence would bring the administration of justice into disrepute.

[Dickson C.J.C. held that the evidence need not be excluded.]

R. v. GOLDHART

(1996), 107 C.C.C. (3d) 481 (S.C.C.)

[Several individuals, including the accused and one Gerald Mayer were charged with narcotics offences arising out of a search of certain premises. The warrant used to search the premises was obtained on the strength of unlawfully garnered evidence, without which, the warrant could not have issued. The search conducted under the warrant was therefore in violation of s. 8 of the *Charter*. At the preliminary inquiry, Mayer pleaded guilty. At the accused's trial, the evidence obtained as a result of the search was excluded. The Crown then determined that it would call Mayer to give *viva voce* evidence against the accused. His evidence was admitted at trial but, on appeal to the Ontario Court of Appeal, the majority allowed the appeal on the ground that Mayer's evidence should have been excluded under s. 24(2) of the *Charter*. The Crown appealed.]

Sopinka J. (Lamer C.J.C., L'Heureux-Dubé, Gonthier, Cory, McLachlin, Iacobucci and Major JJ. concurring): — This appeal concerns the question of when evidence can be said to have been obtained in a manner that infringes a right or freedom of the *Canadian Charter of Rights and Freedoms* so as to attract the provisions of s. 24(2) of the *Charter*. Specifically, the court must determine whether the *viva voce* evidence of a witness who was arrested following an illegal search is subject to a s. 24(2) analysis. I have determined that s. 24(2) has no application in that there is no temporal connection between the *viva voce* evidence and the breach of the *Charter* and that any causal connection is too remote.

.....

IV

ISSUES

1. Was the *viva voce* evidence of Mayer obtained "in a manner" that violated the *Charter* so as to attract the provisions of s. 24(2) thereof?

2. If the answer to question 1 is "yes", would admission of the evidence bring the administration of justice into disrepute?

.....

V

ANALYSIS

I conclude in these reasons that the answer to the question raised in the first issue should be in the negative. It is therefore unnecessary to deal with the second issue.

Section 24(2) of the *Charter* makes it clear that only evidence that was "obtained in a manner" that breached the *Charter* can be subject to exclusion under that section. In the Crown's submission, the evidence given by Mayer is not sufficiently connected to the breach of s. 8 to warrant the invocation of s. 24(2). In other words, the Crown contends that the evidence given by Mayer was not "obtained in a manner" that breached the *Charter*.

When can evidence be said to have been "obtained in a manner" that breached the *Charter*? The proper method of determining whether s. 24(2) of the *Charter* is engaged was developed by this court in *R. v. Therens* (1985), 18 C.C.C. (3d) 481, 18 D.L.R. (4th) 655, [1985] 1 S.C.R. 613, and *Strachan* [(1988), 46 C.C.C. (3d) 479 (S.C.C.)]. In both cases, the court rejected the strict application of the form of "causal analysis" relied on by the courts below in the instant case.

.....

In these judgments of our court, causation was rejected as the sole touchstone of the application of s. 24(2) of the *Charter* by reason of the pitfalls that are inherent in the concept. Its use in other areas of the law has been characterized by attempts to place limits on its reach. The happening of an event can be traced to a whole range of causes along a spectrum of diminishing connections to the event. The common law of torts has grappled with the problem of causation. In order to inject some degree of restraint on the potential reach of causation, the concepts of proximate cause and remoteness were developed. These concepts place limits on the extent of liability in order to implement the sound policy of the law that there exist a substantial connection between the tortious conduct and the injury for which compensation is claimed. On the other hand, causation need not be proved with scientific precision: see *Snell v. Farrell* (1990), 72 D.L.R. (4th) 289, [1990] 2 S.C.R. 311, 4 C.C.L.T. (2d) 229.

.....

Although *Therens* and *Strachan* warned against over-reliance on causation and advocated an examination of the entire relationship between the *Charter* breach and the impugned evidence, causation was not entirely discarded. Accordingly, while a temporal link will often suffice, it is not always determinative. It will not be determinative if the connection between the securing of the evidence and the breach is *remote*. I take remote to mean that the connection is tenuous. The concept of remoteness relates not only to the temporal connection but to the causal connection as well. It follows that the mere presence of a temporal link is not necessarily sufficient. In obedience to the instruction that the whole of the relationship between the breach and the evidence be examined, it is appropriate for the court to consider the strength of the causal relationship. If both the temporal connection and the causal connection are tenuous, the court may very well conclude that the evidence was not obtained in a manner that infringes a right or freedom under the *Charter*. On the other hand, the temporal connection may be so strong that the *Charter* breach is an integral part of a single transaction. In that case, a causal connection that is weak or even absent will be of no importance. Once the principles of law are defined, the strength of the connection between the evidence obtained and the *Charter* breach is a question of fact. Accordingly, the applicability of s. 24(2) will be decided on a case-by-case basis as suggested by Dickson C.J.C. in *Strachan*.

In concluding that s. 24(2) applied in this case, the trial judge relied exclusively on his finding that there was a causal connection between the *Charter* breach and the *viva voce* evidence of Mayer. For convenience, I repeat that finding:

> ... the applicants have satisfied me on the balance of probabilities that *there is a causal connection between the seizure of the marijuana plants in violation of the Charter and the evidence obtained from Mr. [Mayer]*. I am not able to say that Mr. [Mayer] would have come forward had he not been arrested. The arrest was causally connected with the *Charter* breach.

(Emphasis added.)

Applying the principles in *Church of Scientology*, [(1992), 74 C.C.C. (3d) 341 (Ont. Ct. (Gen. Div.))], the trial judge concluded that s. 24(2) applied. With respect, the learned trial judge erred in concluding that the existence of a causal connection was sufficient to attract the provisions of s. 24(2). By focusing on the causal connection the trial judge failed to examine the entire relationship between the evidence and the illegal search and seizure. In particular, he failed to consider whether there existed a temporal link. He also failed to evaluate the strength of the connection between the impugned evidence and the breach. To the extent that the *Church of Scientology* decision supports this approach, it should not be followed. I note, however, that in that case the trial judge expressly found that the illegally seized documents incriminated the witnesses and were a key factor in the decisions of the witnesses to come forward and testify. Here, the trial judge, although he found a causal connection, went on to make the further finding that the *viva voce* evidence of Mayer was an expression of his own free will, a product of detached reflection and a sincere desire to co-operate, largely brought about by his recent conversion as a born-again Christian. A proper evaluation of these findings in relation to the causal connection might well have led the trial judge to the conclusion that the causal connection was tenuous.

In order to assess properly the relationship between the breach and the impugned evidence, it is important to bear in mind that it is the *viva voce* evidence of Mayer that is said to have been obtained in a manner that breaches the *Charter*. A distinction must be made between discovery of a person who is arrested and charged with an offence and the evidence subsequently volunteered by that person. The discovery of the person cannot simply be equated with securing evidence from that person which is favourable to the Crown. The person charged has the right to remain silent and in practice will usually exercise it on the advice of counsel. The prosecution has no assurance, therefore, that the person will provide any information let alone sworn testimony that is favourable to the Crown. In this regard it has been rightly observed that testimony cannot be treated in the same manner as an inanimate object. As Brooke J.A. observed in his dissenting opinion, at p. 85:

> Testimony is the product of a person's mind and known only if and when that person discloses it. It cannot be obtained or discovered in any other way. Testimony which is heard for the first time some months after a search cannot be equated with or analogized to evidence of an inanimate thing found or seized when an illegal search is carried out.

Similarly, Rehnquist J., as he then was, in *United States v. Ceccolini*, 435 U.S. 268 (1978), explained the difference as follows, at pp. 276-7:

> Witnesses are not like guns or documents which remain hidden from view until one turns over a sofa or opens a filing cabinet. Witnesses can, and often do, come forward and offer evidence entirely of their own volition. And evaluated properly, the degree of free will necessary to dissipate the taint will very likely be found more often in the case of live-witness testimony than other kinds of evidence.

When the evidence is appropriately characterized as indicated above, the application of the relevant factors yields a different result from that reached by the trial judge and the majority of the Court of Appeal. In order to find a temporal link the pertinent event is the decision of Mayer to co-operate with the Crown and testify, and not his arrest. Indeed the existence of a temporal link between the illegal search and the arrest of Mayer is of virtually no consequence. Moreover, any temporal link between the illegal search and the testimony is greatly weakened by intervening events of Mayer's voluntary decision to co-operate with the police, to plead guilty and to testify. The application of the causal connection factor is to the same effect. The connection between the illegal search and the decision by Mayer to give evidence is extremely tenuous. Having regard, therefore, to the entire chain of events, I am of the opinion that the nexus between the impugned evidence and the *Charter* breach is remote. In this regard I agree with Brooke J.A. when he states, at pp. 85-6:

> Clearly, the testimony of Mayer cannot be said to be derivative of the breach as was the case of the testimony of Hall in *R. v. Burlingham* [(1995), 97 C.C.C. (3d) 385 (S.C.C.)].... There may be some link to the evidence of the finding of the marijuana, but this is surely not a basis on which to say the testimony was discovered or obtained by the breach of the appellant's rights. There must be a point at which a chain connecting the breach and the testimony is sufficiently weakened as to render the testimony untainted or too remote from the original breach. If this is not so, the ramifications may be far-reaching with respect to the exclusion of testimony of a co-accused where the Crown seeks to take advantage of it. In my opinion, the link between the breach and Mayer's testimony does not survive an analysis of remoteness or attenuation.

For the foregoing reasons, the relationship between the infringement of s. 8 of the *Charter* and the *viva voce* evidence of Mayer does not lead me to conclude that the latter was obtained in a manner that infringes or denies a *Charter* right or freedom. Section 24(2) of the *Charter* is, therefore, not engaged and is not available to exclude the evidence. The evidence is relevant and was properly admitted at trial. The majority of the Court of Appeal was in error in setting aside the convictions.

In the result the appeal is allowed, the judgment of the Court of Appeal is set aside and the convictions are restored.

[La Forest J. dissented.]

Where the exclusion of evidence is sought, the court must also decide, having regard to all the circumstances, whether the admission of the evidence would bring the administration of justice into disrepute.

R. v. COLLINS

(1987), 33 C.C.C. (3d) 1 (S.C.C.)

[The majority judgment of the court was delivered by:]

Lamer J.: — The appellant, Ruby Collins, was seated in a pub in the town of Gibsons when she was suddenly seized by the throat and pulled down to the floor by a man who said to her "police officer". The police officer, then noticing that she had her hand clenched around an object, instructed her to let go of the object. As it turned out, she had a green balloon containing heroin.

It is common knowledge that drug traffickers often keep their drugs in balloons or condoms in their mouths so that they may, when approached by the narcotics control agent, swallow the drugs without harm and recoup them subsequently. The "throat-hold" is used to prevent them from swallowing the drugs.

The issue is whether the evidence obtained under these circumstances is to be excluded under s. 24(2) of the *Charter*.

.....

Jurisdiction

The trial judge's decision to exclude or not to exclude under s. 24(2) of the *Charter* is a question of law from which an appeal will generally lie: see *R. v. Therens* (1985), 18 C.C.C. (3d) 481, 18 D.L.R. (4th) 655, [1985] 1 S.C.R. 613, *per* Le Dain J. at p. 513 C.C.C., p. 687 D.L.R., p. 653 S.C.R. However, where the trial judge's decision is based, for instance, on his assessment of the credibility of the witness, that assessment cannot be challenged by way of appeal: see *R. v. DeBot,* Ont. C.A. (October 8, 1986), unreported [since reported 30 C.C.C. (3d) 207, 54 C.R. (3d) 120]. The exclusion of the evidence in this case did not depend on any such assessment, and the Court of Appeal and this court had jurisdiction to hear the appeals.

The law

The appellant seeks the exclusion of evidence that she was in possession of heroin, alleging that the heroin was discovered pursuant to a search which was unreasonable under s. 8 of the *Charter*. This court in *Therens, supra,* held that evidence cannot be excluded as a remedy under s. 24(1) of the *Charter*, but must meet the test of exclusion under s. 24(2) ...

.....

The reasonableness of the search

The appellant, in my view, bears the burden of persuading the court that her *Charter* rights or freedoms have been infringed or denied. That appears from the wording of s. 24(1) and (2), and most courts which have considered the issue have come to that conclusion: see *R. v. Lundrigan* (1985), 19 C.C.C. (3d) 499, 33 Man. R. (2d) 286, 15 C.R.R. 256 (Man. C.A.), and the cases cited therein, and Gibson, *The Law of the Charter: General Principles* (1986), p. 278. The appellant also bears the initial burden of presenting evidence. The standard of persuasion required is only the civil standard of the balance of probabilities and, because of this, the allocation of the burden of persuasion means only that, in a case where the evidence does not establish whether or not the appellant's rights were infringed, the court must conclude that they were not.

.....

[Lamer J. then reflects, as *per Hunter et al. v. Southam Inc.* (1984), 14 C.C.C. (3d) 97 (S.C.C.), substantially reproduced at p. 75, that a warrantless search is presumptively unreasonable.]

This shifts the burden of persuasion from the appellant to the Crown. As a result, once the appellant has demonstrated that the search was a warrantless one, the Crown has the burden of showing that the search was, on a balance of probabilities, reasonable.

A search will be reasonable if it is authorized by law, if the law itself is reasonable and if the manner in which the search was carried out is reasonable. In this case, the Crown argued that the search was carried out under s. 10(1) of the *Narcotic Control Act*. As the appellant has not challenged the constitutionality of s. 10(1) of the Act, the issues that remain to be decided here are whether the search was unreasonable because the officer did not come within s. 10 of the Act, or whether, while being within s. 10, he carried out the search in a manner that made the search unreasonable.

For the search to be lawful under s. 10, the Crown must establish that the officer believed on reasonable grounds that there was a narcotic in the place where the person searched was found. The nature of the belief will also determine whether the manner in which the search was carried out was reasonable. For example, if a police officer is told by a reliable source that there are persons in possession of drugs in a certain place, the officer may, depending on the circumstances and the nature and precision of the information given by that source, search persons found in that place under s. 10, but surely, without very specific information, a seizure by the throat, as in this case, would be unreasonable. Of course, if he is lawfully searching a person whom he believes on reasonable grounds to be a "drug handler", then the "throat-hold" would not be unreasonable.

Because of the presumption of unreasonableness, the Crown in this case had to present evidence of the officer's belief and the reasonable grounds for that belief. It may be surmised that there were reasonable grounds based on information received from the local police. However, the Crown failed to establish such reasonable grounds in the examination-in-chief of Constable Woods, and, as set out earlier, when it attempted to do so on its re-examination, the appellant's counsel objected. As a result, the Crown never did establish the constable's reasonable grounds. Without such evidence, it is clear that the trial judge was correct in concluding that the search was unreasonable because it was unlawful and carried out with unnecessary violence.

However, the problem is that the objection raised by the appellant's counsel was groundless: this court has held that reasonable grounds can be based on information received from third parties without infringing the hearsay rule (*Eccles v. Bourque* [(1974), 19 C.C.C. (2d) 129 (S.C.C.)]), and the question put to the constable in this case was not outside the ambit of the ground covered in cross-examination. A further problem is that the record does not disclose why the question was not answered: it is not clear whether the trial judge maintained the objection or whether the Crown had reacted to the objection by withdrawing the question. It is worthy by mention that, because a conviction was entered, the Crown could not, in any event, appeal against the decision.

This court has two options. We could resolve the doubt against the Crown, which had the burden of persuasion, and simply proceed on the basis that there was no such evidence. Alternatively, we could order a new trial. I would order a new trial on the basis that the trial judge either made an incorrect ruling or failed to make a ruling, and, in any event, the appellant should not, in the particular circumstances of this case, be allowed to benefit from her counsel's unfounded objection.

However, before ordering a new trial, we must decide whether we agree with the trial judge and the Court of Appeal that the evidence of the heroin would be admissible regardless of the constable's grounds for the search, for there then would be no point in a new trial and we should dismiss the appeal. As a result, I must determine whether I would exclude the evidence under s. 24(2) on the assumption that Constable Woods testifies that he had not received any further information, thereby leaving matters in that regard as they stand at present on the record.

Bringing the administration of justice into disrepute

.....

At the outset, it should be noted that the use of the phrase "if it is established that" places the burden of persuasion on the applicant, for it is the position which he maintains which must be established. Again, the standard of persuasion required can only be the civil standard of the balance of probabilities. Thus, the applicant must make it more probable than not that the admission of the evidence would bring the administration of justice into disrepute.

It is whether the *admission of the evidence* would bring the administration of justice into disrepute that is the applicable test. Misconduct by the police in the investigatory process often has some effect on the repute of the administration of justice, but s. 24(2) is not a remedy for police misconduct, requiring the exclusion of the evidence if, because of this misconduct, the administration of justice was brought into disrepute. Section 24(2) could well have been drafted in that way, but it was not. Rather, the drafts of the *Charter* decided to focus on the admission of the evidence in the proceedings, and the purpose of s. 24(2) is to prevent having the administration of justice brought into *further disrepute* by the admission of the evidence in the proceedings. This further disrepute will result from the admission of evidence that would deprive the accused for a fair hearing, or from judicial condonation of unacceptable conduct by the investigatory and prosecutorial agencies. It will also be necessary to consider any disrepute that may result from the exclusion of the evidence. It would be inconsistent with the purpose of s. 24(2) to exclude evidence if its exclusion would bring the administration of justice into greater disrepute than would its admission. Finally, it must be emphasized that even though the inquiry under s. 24(2) will necessarily focus on the specific prosecution, it is the long-term consequences of regular admission or exclusion of this type of evidence on the repute of the administration of justice which must be considered: see on this point *Gibson, ibid*, p. 245.

The concept of disrepute necessarily involves some element of community views, and the determination of disrepute thus requires the judge to refer to what he conceives to be the views of the community at large. This does not mean that evidence of the public's perception of the repute of the administration of justice, which Professor Gibson suggested could be presented in the form of public opinion polls (*supra*, pp. 236-47), will be determinative of the issue: see *Therens, supra*, pp. 653-4. The position is different with respect to obscenity, for example, where the court must assess the level of tolerance of the community, whether or not it is reasonable, and may consider public opinion polls: *R. v. Prairie Schooner News Ltd. and Powers* (1970), 1 C.C.C. (2d) 251 at p. 266, 12 Crim. L.Q. 462 at p. 477, 75

W.W.R. 585 at p. 599 (Man. C.A.), cited in *Towne Cinema Theatres Ltd. v. The Queen* (1985), 18 C.C.C. (3d) 193 at pp. 208-9, 18 D.L.R. (4th) 1 at p. 17, 1 S.C.R. 494 at p. 513. It would be unwise, in my respectful view, to adopt a similar attitude with respect to the *Charter*. Members of the public generally become conscious of the importance of protecting the rights and freedoms of accused only when they are in some way brought closer to the system either personally or through the experience of friends or family. Professor Gibson recognized the danger of leaving the exclusion of evidence to uninformed members of the public when he stated at p. 246: "The ultimate determination must be with the courts, because they provide what is often the only effective shelter for individuals and unpopular minorities from the shifting winds of public passion." The *Charter* is designed to protect the accused from the majority, so the enforcement of the *Charter* must not be left to that majority.

The approach I adopt may be put figuratively in terms of the reasonable person test proposed by Professor Yves-Marie Morissette in his article "The Exclusion of Evidence under the *Canadian Charter of Rights and Freedoms*: What to Do and What Not to Do", 29 McGill L.J. 521 at p. 538 (1984). In applying s. 24(2), he suggested that the relevant question is: "Would the admission of the evidence bring the administration of justice into disrepute in the eyes of the reasonable man, dispassionate and fully apprised of the circumstances of the case?" The reasonable person is usually the average person in the community, but only when that community's current mood is reasonable.

The decision is thus not left to the untramelled discretion of the judge. In practice, as Professor Morissette wrote, the reasonable person test is there to require of judges that they "concentrate on what they do best: finding within themselves, with cautiousness and impartiality, a basis for their own decisions, articulating their reasons carefully and accepting review by a higher court where it occurs." It serves as a reminder to each individual judge that his discretion is grounded in community values, and, in particular, long-term community values. He should not render a decision that would be unacceptable to the community when that community is not being wrought with passion or otherwise under passing stress due to current events. In effect, the judge will have met this test if the judges of the Court of Appeal will decline to interfere with his decision, even though they might have decided the matter differently, using the well-known statement that they are of the view that the decision was not unreasonable.

In determining whether the admission of evidence would bring the administration of justice into disrepute, the judge is directed by s. 24(2) to consider "all the circumstances". The factors which are to be considered and balanced have been listed by many courts in the country (see in particular Anderson J.A. in *R. v. Cohen* (1983), 5 C.C.C. (3d) 156, 148 D.L.R. (3d) 78, 33 C.R. (3d) 151 (B.C.C.A.); Howland C.J.O. in *R. v. Simmons* (1984), 11 C.C.C. (3d) 193, 7 D.L.R. (4th) 719, 45 O.R. (2d) 609 (Ont. C.A.); Philp J.A. in *R. v. Pohoretsky* (1985), 18 C.C.C. (3d) 104, 17 D.L.R. (4th) 268, 45 C.R. (3d) 209 (Man. C.A.); MacDonald J. in *R. v. Dyment* (1986), 25 C.C.C. (3d) 120, 26 D.L.R. (4th) 399, 49 C.R. (3d) 338 (P.E.I. S.C.A.D.), and Lambert J.A. in *R. v. Gladstone* (1985), 22 C.C.C. (3d) 151, 47 C.R. (3d) 289, [1985] 6 W.W.R. 504 (B.C.C.A.), and by Seaton J.A. in this case. The factors that the courts have most frequently considered include:

- what kind of evidence was obtained?
- what *Charter* right was infringed?
- was the *Charter* violation serious or was it of a merely technical nature?
- was it deliberate, wilful or flagrant, or was it inadvertent or committed in good faith?
- did it occur in circumstances of urgency or necessity?
- were there other investigatory techniques available?
- would the evidence have been obtained in any event?
- is the offence serious?
- is the evidence essential to substantiate the charge?
- are other remedies available?

I do not wish to be seen as approving this as an exhaustive list of the relevant factors, and I would like to make some general comments as regards these factors.

As a matter of personal preference, I find it useful to group the factors according to the way in which they affect the repute of the administration of justice. Certain of the factors listed are relevant in determining the effect of the admission of the evidence on the fairness of the trial. The trial is a key part of the administration of justice, and the fairness of Canadian trials is a major source of the repute of the system and is now a right guaranteed by s. 11(*d*) of the *Charter*. If the admission of the evidence in some way affects the fairness of the trial, then the admission of the evidence would *tend* to bring the administration of justice into disrepute and, subject to a consideration of the other factors, the evidence gradually should be excluded.

It is clear to me, that the factors relevant to this determination will include the nature of the evidence obtained as a result of the violation and the nature of the right violated and not so much the manner in which the right was violated. Real evidence that was obtained in a manner that violated the *Charter* will rarely operate unfairly for that reason alone. The real evidence existed irrespective of the violation of the *Charter* and its use does not render the trial unfair. However, the situation is very different with respect to cases where, after a violation of the *Charter*, the accused is conscripted against himself through a confession or other evidence emanating from him. The use of such evidence would render the trial unfair, for it did not exist prior to the violation and it strikes at one of the fundamental tenets of a fair trial, the right against self-incrimination. Such evidence will generally arise in the context of an infringement of the right to counsel. Our decisions in *R. v. Therens* (1985), 18 C.C.C. (3d) 481, 18 D.L.R. (4th) 655, [1985] 1 S.C.R. 613, and *Clarkson v. The Queen* (1986), 25 C.C.C. (3d) 207, 26 D.L.R. (4th) 493, [1986] 1 S.C.R. 383, are illustrative of this. The use of self-incriminating evidence obtained following a denial of the right to counsel will, generally, go to the very fairness of the trial and should generally be excluded. Several Courts of Appeal have also emphasized this distinction between pre- existing real evidence and self-incriminatory evidence created following a breach of the *Charter*: see *R. v. Dumas* (1985), 23 C.C.C. (3d) 366, 41 Alta. L.R. (2d) 348, 66 A.R. 137 (Alta. C.A.); *R. v. Strachan* (1986), 24 C.C.C. (3d) 205, 25 D.L.R. (4th) 567, 49 C.R. (3d) 289 (B.C.C.A.), and *R. v. Dairy Supplies Ltd.*, Man. C.A. (January 13, 1987), unreported [since reported [1987] 2 W.W.R. 661, 44 Man. R. (2d) 275]. It may also be relevant, in certain circumstances, that the evidence would have been obtained in any event without the violation of the *Charter*.

There are other factors which are relevant to the seriousness of the *Charter* violation and thus to the disrepute that will result from judicial acceptance of evidence obtained through that violation. As Le Dain J. wrote in *Therens*, *supra*, at p. 512 C.C.C., p. 686 D.L.R., p. 652 S.C.R.:

> The relative seriousness of the constitutional violation has been assessed in the light of whether it was committed in good faith, or was inadvertent or of a merely technical nature, or whether it was deliberate, wilful or flagrant. Another relevant consideration is whether the action which constituted the constitutional violation was motivated by urgency or necessity to prevent the loss or destruction of the evidence.

I should add, that the availability of other investigatory techniques and the fact that the evidence could have been obtained without the violation of the *Charter* tend to render the *Charter* violation more serious. We are considering the actual conduct of the authorities and the evidence must not be admitted on the basis that they could have proceeded otherwise and obtained the evidence properly. In fact, their failure to proceed properly when that option was open to them tends to indicate a blatant disregard for the *Charter*, which is a factor supporting the exclusion of the evidence.

The final relevant group of factors consists of those that relate to the effect of excluding the evidence. The question under s. 24(2) is whether the system's repute will be better served by the admission or the exclusion of the evidence, and it is thus necessary to consider any disrepute that may result from the exclusion of the evidence. In my view, the administration of justice would be brought into disrepute by the exclusion of evidence essential to substantiate the charge, and thus the acquittal of the accused, because of a trivial breach of the *Charter*. Such disrepute would be greater if the offence was more serious. I would thus agree with Professor Morissette that evidence is more likely to be excluded if the offence is less serious (*supra*, pp. 529-31). I hasten to add, however, that if the admission of the evidence would result in an unfair trial, the seriousness of the offence could not render that evidence admissible. If any relevance is to be given to the seriousness of the offence in the context of the fairness of the trial, it operates in the opposite sense: the more serious the offence, the more damaging to the system's repute would be an unfair trial.

Finally, a factor which, in my view, is irrelevant is the availability of other remedies. Once it has been decided that the administration of justice would be brought into disrepute by the admission of the evidence, the disrepute will not be lessened by the existence of some ancillary remedy: see *Gibson*, *supra*, at p. 261.

I would agree with Howland C.J.O. in *Simmons*, *supra*, that we should not gloss over the words of s. 24(2) or attempt to substitute any other test for s. 24(2). At least at this early stage of the *Charter's* development, the guidelines set out are sufficient and the actual decision to admit or exclude is as important as the statement of any test. Indeed, the test will only take on concrete meaning through our disposition of cases. However, I should at this point add some comparative comment as regards the test I enunciated in *Rothman*, *supra*, a pre-*Charter* confession case dealing with the resort to "tricks", which was coined in the profession as the "community shock test". That test has been applied to s. 24(2) by many courts, including the lower courts in this case. I still am of the view, that the resort to tricks that are not in the least unlawful let alone in violation of the *Charter* to obtain a statement should not result in the exclusion of a free and voluntary statement unless the trick resorted to is a dirty trick, one that shocks the community. That is a very high threshold, higher, in my view, than that to be attained to bring the administration of justice into disrepute in the context of a violation of the *Charter*.

There are two reasons why the threshold for exclusion under s. 24(2) is lower. The first, an obvious one, is that, under s. 24(2), there will have been a violation of the most important law in the land, as opposed to the absence of any unlawful behaviour as a result of the resort to tricks in *Rothman v. The Queen* (1981), 59 C.C.C. (2d) 30, 121 D.L.R. (3d) 578, [1981] 1 S.C.R. 640.

The second reason is based on the language of s. 24(2). Indeed, while both the English text of s. 24(2) and *Rothman* use the words "*would* bring the administration of justice into disrepute", the French versions are very different. The French text of s. 24(2) provides "*est susceptible* de deconsiderer l'administration de la justice", which I would translate as "*could* bring the administration of justice into disrepute". This is supportive of a somewhat lower threshold than the English text. As Dickson J. (as he then was) wrote in *Hunter et al. v. Southam Inc.* (1984), 14 C.C.C. (3d) 97 at p. 106, 11 D.L.R. (4th) 641 at pp. 650-1, [1984] 2 S.C.R. 145 at p. 157:

> Since the proper approach to the interpretation of the *Canadian Charter of Rights and Freedoms* is a purposive one, before it is possible to assess the reasonableness or unreasonableness of the impact of a search or of a statute authorizing a search, it is first necessary to specify the purpose underlying s. 8: in other words, to delineate the nature of the interests it is meant to protect.

As one of the purposes of s. 24(2) is to protect the right to a fair trial, I would favour the interpretation of s. 24(2) which better protects that right, the less onerous French text. Most courts which have considered the issue have also come to this conclusion: see Gibson, *supra*, at pp. 63 and 234-5. Section 24(2) should thus be read as "the evidence shall be excluded if it is established that, having regard to all the circumstances, the admission of it in the proceedings *could* bring the administration of justice into disrepute". This is a less onerous test than *Rothman*, where the French translation of the test in our reports, "ternirait l'image de la justice", clearly indicates that the resort to the word "would" in the test "would bring the administration of justice into disrepute" means just that.

Conclusion

As discussed above, we must determine in this case whether the evidence should be excluded on the record as it stands at present.

The evidence obtained as a result of the search was real evidence, and, while prejudicial to the accused as evidence tendered by the Crown usually is, there is nothing to suggest that its use at the trial would render the trial unfair. In addition, it is true that the cost of excluding the evidence would be high: someone who was found guilty at trial of a relatively serious offence will evade conviction. Such a result could bring the administration of justice into disrepute. However, the administration of justice would be brought into greater disrepute, at least in my respectful view, if this court did not exclude the evidence and dissociate itself from the conduct of the police in this case which, always on the assumption that the officer merely had suspicions, was a flagrant and serious violation of the rights of an individual. Indeed, we cannot accept that police officers take flying tackles at people and seize them by the throat when they do not have reasonable and probable grounds to believe that those people are either dangerous or handlers of drugs. Of course, matters might well be clarified in this case if and when the police officer is offered at a new trial an opportunity to explain the grounds, if any, that he had for doing what he did. But if the police officer does not then disclose additional grounds for his behaviour, the evidence must be excluded.

I would allow the appeal and order a new trial.

The court wrestled with the conscriptive-real evidence dichotomy in the following case:

R. v. ROSS

(1989), 46 C.C.C. (3d) 129 (S.C.C.)

Lamer J. [Beetz, Wilson and La Forest JJ. concurring]: — The appellants were convicted by a jury in Sault Ste. Marie of breaking and entering and of theft. Their appeal to the Ontario Court of Appeal was dismissed....

.....

... The three boys, one aged 16 and two aged 17, were arrested and charged with break and enter.

All three were advised of their right to counsel. The appellants each tried to telephone their respective counsel but received no answer. It was now around 2:00 a.m. The appellant Leclair was asked if he wanted to call another lawyer and he said "no". He was placed in a police cell. The appellant Ross was also taken to the cells. The police officer's notes did not indicate that the appellant Ross was asked if he wanted to call other counsel.

In the middle of the night, the officers went to a nearby pinball arcade and found seven people, of similar age to the accused, who could participate in a line-up. The four young witnesses were then taken to the police station and the line-up was held at 3:00 a.m. Neither of the appellants were advised that they were under no obligation to participate.

.....

Having been informed of their right to counsel and having clearly indicated their desire to assert that right, both appellants were permitted to telephone lawyers of their choice but were unable to make contact with them. This is hardly surprising since the calls were made at approximately 2:00 a.m. In the circumstances, it was highly unlikely that they would be able to contact their counsel before normal office opening hours.

At this juncture, I would underline the fact that the appellant Leclair was asked if he wanted to call another lawyer and his answer was "no". The Crown's submission was that by giving this answer Leclair waived his right to counsel. I do not agree. Leclair had clearly indicated that he wished to contact *his* lawyer. The mere fact that he did not want to call *another* lawyer cannot fairly be viewed as a waiver of his right to retain counsel. Quite the contrary, he merely asserted his right to counsel and to counsel of his choice. Although an accused or detained person has the right to choose counsel, it must be noted that, as this court said in *R. v. Tremblay* (1987), 37 C.C.C. (3d) 565, 45 D.L.R. (4th) 445, [1987] 2 S.C.R. 435 (S.C.C.), a detainee must be reasonably diligent in the exercise of these rights and if he is not, the correlative duties imposed on the police and set out in *Manninen* [(1987), 34 C.C.C. (3d) 385 (S.C.C.)] are suspended. Reasonable diligence in the exercise of the right to choose one's counsel depends upon the context facing the accused or detained person. On being arrested, for example, the detained person is faced with an immediate need for legal advice and must exercise reasonable diligence accordingly. By contrast, when seeking the best lawyer to conduct a trial, the accused person faces no such immediacy. Nevertheless, accused or detained persons have a right to choose their counsel and it is only if the lawyer chosen cannot be available in a reasonable delay that the detainee or the accused should be expected to exercise the right to counsel by calling another lawyer.

Moreover, once the appellant asserted his right to instruct counsel, and absent a clear indication that he had changed his mind, it was unreasonable for the police to proceed as if Leclair had waived his right to counsel.

.....

Since the evidence reveals that Leclair asserted his right to counsel, the burden of establishing an unequivocal waiver is on the Crown. Here, the Crown has failed to discharge the onus.

In the case of the appellant Ross, there is no evidence that the police even asked whether he wanted to call another lawyer. Once Ross had tried and failed to reach his lawyer, it would appear that the police assumed their obligation to provide a reasonable opportunity to retain counsel was at an end. One can reasonably infer that they also misconstrued the nature of their obligation as concerned the appellant Leclair. Obviously, there was no urgency or other reason justifying that the police proceed forthwith and it cannot be said that the appellants had a real opportunity to retain and instruct counsel. This therefore leads us to consider the second duty.

The second duty: refraining from taking further steps

Having seen that the appellants got no answer to their telephone calls, the police officers placed them in police cells and a few minutes later, the appellants were told to participate in a line-up, which they did.

The police were mistaken to follow such a procedure. As this court held in *Maninnen*, the police have, at least, a duty to cease questioning or otherwise attempting to elicit evidence from the detainee until he has had a reasonable opportunity to retain and instruct counsel. In my view, the right to counsel also means that, once an accused or detained person has asserted that right, the police cannot, in any way, compel the detainee or accused person to make a decision or participate in a process which could ultimately have an adverse effect in the conduct of an eventual trial until that person has had a reasonable opportunity to exercise that right. In the case at bar, it cannot be said that the appellants had a real opportunity to retain and instruct counsel before the line-up was held. Nor can it be said that there was any urgency or other compelling reason which justified proceeding with the line-up so precipitously.

The Crown urged upon us that it was necessary to hold the line-up immediately, while the memories of the witnesses were fresh and undisturbed. I cannot accept this submission. While it may be desirable to hold a line-up as soon as possible, this concern must generally yield to the right of the suspect to retain counsel, which right must, of course, be exercised with reasonable diligence. Here, the line-up was held with utmost, indeed highly unusual dispatch. There is nothing to suggest that the line-up could not have been held a few hours later, after the appellants had again attempted to contact their lawyers during normal business hours.

The respondent also submitted that there was no violation of the right to counsel because the appellants did not have the right to have their lawyers present during the line-up. This submission is without merit. Even if the appellants could not have their lawyers present during the line-up, this does not imply that counsel is of no assistance to a suspect. Identification evidence obtained through a line-up is usually strong evidence susceptible of influencing trial deliberations. ... In the case at bar, had the appellants been allowed access to their lawyers, they could have been advised that they were under no statutory obligation to participate in the line-up, although failure to do so might have certain prejudicial consequences. They could have been advised, for example, not to participate unless they were given a photograph of the line-up, or not to participate if the others in the line-up were obviously older than themselves. In short, they could have been told how a well run line-up is conducted, even though there is no statutory framework governing the line-up process. It was this advice, not the presence of their lawyers at the line-up, of which the appellants were deprived.

Furthermore, that the accused did not refuse to participate in the line-up cannot by itself amount to a waiver of the right to counsel. The very purpose of the right to counsel is to ensure that those who are accused or detained be advised of their legal rights and how to exercise them when dealing with the authorities. It would contradict this purpose to conclude that a detained or accused person has waived the right to counsel simply by submitting, before being instructed by counsel, to precisely those attempts to secure the detainee's participation from which the police should refrain. Here, the appellant's were unable to make an informed decision about participating in the line-up because they were ignorant of their legal position, not having been advised by their lawyers. Nor did the police even give them the choice as to whether they should participate. In the circumstances, therefore, to conclude that the appellants had waived their rights by participating in the line-up would render the right to counsel nugatory.

2. The exclusion of evidence under s. 24(2)

This court recently decided in *R. v. Strachan*, No. 19749, December 15, 1988 (S.C.C.) [since reported [1989] 1 W.W.R. 385], that for the purposes of s. 24(2), evidence was "obtained in a manner that infringed or denied ... rights" guaranteed by the *Charter* if the violation of one of those rights precedes the discovery of evidence, and if that discovery of evidence was not too remote from the violation. In this case, the violation of the right to counsel was immediately prior to the discovery of evidence through the line-up. There is no question of remoteness; in fact, there was even a direct link between the violation of the right to counsel and the evidence obtained. As such, what remains to be determined is whether the line-up evidence should be excluded under s. 24(2) of the *Charter*.

[Lamer J. then reviews the *Collins* categories.]

.....

In this case, there can be no doubt as to the importance of the line-up evidence. As the majority of this court held in *Collins*, among the factors relevant to determining the effect of the admission of the evidence on the fairness of the trial is the nature of the evidence obtained as a result of the violation. Any evidence obtained, after a violation of the *Charter*, by conscripting the accused against himself through a confession or other evidence emanating from him would tend to render the trial process unfair. In *Collins* we used the expression "emanating from him" since we were concerned with a statement. But we did not limit the kind of evidence susceptible of rendering the trial process unfair to this kind of evidence. I am of the opinion that the use of any evidence that could not have been obtained but for the participation of the accused in the construction of the evidence for the purposes of the trial would tend to render the trial process unfair.

It is true that, as a general matter, the identity of the accused is not evidence emanating from the accused, nor is it evidence that cannot be obtained but for the participation of the accused. A person's identity is pre-existing "real evidence" inasmuch as a person's physical characteristics exist irrespective of any *Charter* violation or of any steps taken by the police.

However, the identification evidence obtained through a line-up is not simply pre-existing "real evidence" in this sense. The purpose of a line-up is twofold. First, a line-up is designed to identify the detainee as the author of the crime. But secondly, and most important to the discussion here, the procedure of a line-up is designed to reinforce the credibility of identification evidence. In this sense the object of the line-up is to construct evidence that the accused was picked out from among a similar group of people, by a witness who was not prompted in any way to make that choice, and to settle the memory of the witness for the purpose of the trial. When participating in a line-up, the accused is participating in the construction of credible inculpating evidence. Obviously, this piece of evidence could not be obtained without the accused's participation in its construction since the evidence of a line-up held without the presence of the accused is irrelevant to the Crown's case. Thus, while the accused does not participate in the creation of "real evidence" of identity, the accused does participate in the creation of credible line-up evidence. An accused who is told to participate in a line-up before having had a reasonable opportunity to communicate with counsel is conscripted against himself since he is used as a means for creating evidence for the purposes of the trial. Line-up evidence is evidence that could not have been obtained but for the participation of the accused in the construction of the evidence for the purposes of the trial. In my view, the use of such evidence goes to the fairness of the trial process.

The nature of the *Charter* violation is also relevant, given that we are confronted with a serious breach of rights. The appellants clearly asserted their right to counsel and there was no urgency of any kind to explain the behavior of the police. Nothing prevented them from holding the line-up later in the day. Nor is this a case of a good-faith error in police conduct resulting in an inadvertent denial of the right to counsel. The police cannot be excused for misconstruing and misinterpreting the scope of their duty to provide a reasonable opportunity to retain and instruct counsel. Nor is this a case, for example, in which a longstanding precedent favouring the police procedure in question has been overturned or in which a novel constitutional principle has first been introduced. The scope of the right to counsel in the circumstances of this case is clear and well settled.

Furthermore, in this case, the appellants were young, 16 and 17 years old, and we can reasonably presume that they were not aware of their rights. Nor did the police inform them that they were not obliged to participate in the line-up. While the police were under no duty to give this information, had they done so this would have been a relevant factor to be weighed under s. 24(2), though probably not a determinative one in this case.

I am therefore of the opinion that, having regard to all the circumstances, the appellants have established that the admission of the line-up evidence into the proceedings would bring the administration of justice into disrepute. Accordingly, the evidence should have been excluded and a new trial should be ordered.

I would, accordingly, allow the appeal and order a new trial.

.....

L'Heureux-Dubé J. [McIntyre J. concurring] (dissenting): —

.....

... I do not see how the admission of this evidence affected the fairness of the trial, particularly since I do not share my colleague Justice Lamer's view that this identification evidence "emanates" from the accused in the same way that a confession does. In *Collins, supra*, Justice Lamer explains that the admission of evidence "emanating" from the accused is made problematic because it "did not exist prior to the violation and strikes at one of the fundamental tenets of a fair trial, the right against self-incrimination" (p. 19 C.C.C., p. 284 S.C.C.). I do not see how this is the case with line-up evidence. The identity of the accused existed prior to the violation, as did the perceptions of the witnesses to the crime. In my view, such evidence comes into existence when an accused is seen committing the crime. The evidence cannot be considered as "emanating" from the accused simply because it may later be used to establish the credibility of identification evidence. Evidence that could not have been obtained but for the participation of the accused will not automatically render the trial process unfair. While this might be so in some cases, it will not necessarily be so in all cases.

R. v. BURLINGHAM

(1995), 97 C.C.C. (3d) 385 (S.C.C.)

[B. was charged separately with the murders of W. and H. He was convicted of H.'s murder. This appeal related to his conviction for W.'s murder. For several days, the police subjected B., already charged with H.'s murder, to an "intensive and often manipulative interrogation" despite his repeated statements that he would not speak unless he could consult a lawyer. The police suggested that he should tell them what he knew about W.'s murder, and that any delay would hurt his parents. The police made disparaging comments about defence counsel's integrity, loyalty, commitment, availability and legal fees, and suggested that they themselves were more trustworthy. They purported to offer B. a plea bargain. His own lawyer was then unavailable and B. was given a limited time frame within which to decide. He eventually acquiesced despite another lawyer's advice not to speak to police. In satisfaction of the bargain, he confessed, was brought to the murder site to locate the murder weapon and the following day, made inculpatory remarks to his girlfriend. Later that day, he was told that the deal did not exist in the manner in which he understood it. Crown counsel had authorized something less than had been communicated. The trial judge did find that the officers had been honestly mistaken. After the accused was charged with first degree murder, the Crown sought to introduce all of the above evidence obtained while the accused was under this misunderstanding. Defence counsel had never been consulted about the plea bargain. The Court had little difficulty finding a serious breach of s. 10(*b*) of the *Charter*. Iacobucci J., speaking for the majority, articulates the principles which inform the exclusion of derivative evidence under s. 24(2) of the *Charter*. L'Heureux-Dubé J., in a strongly worded judgment, sharply criticizes the aggressive exclusionary rule created by the court. Sopinka J. offers up rebuttal to her position on behalf of the majority. It makes unusual and most interesting reading.]

Iacobucci J.: —

.....

... In the case at bar, there were several ways in which the appellant's right to counsel was denied.

First, the police continually questioned him despite his repeated statements that he would say nothing absent consultation with his lawyer. Section 10(*b*) requires, barring urgent circumstances, that the police refrain from attempting to elicit incriminatory evidence once a detainee has asserted his or her right to counsel: *R. v. Prosper* (1994), 92 C.C.C. (3d) 353, 118 D.L.R. (4th) 154, [1994] 3 S.C.R. 236; *R. v. Matheson* (1994), 92 C.C.C. (3d) 434, 118 D.L.R. (4th) 323, [1994] 3 S.C.R. 328; *R. v. Brydges* (1990), 53 C.C.C. (3d) 330, [1990] 1 S.C.R. 190, 74 C.R. (3d) 129.

Second, s. 10(*b*) specifically prohibits the police, as they did in this case, from belittling an accused's lawyer with the express goal or effect of undermining the accused's confidence in and relationship with defence counsel. It makes no sense for s. 10(*b*) of the *Charter* to provide for the right to retain and instruct counsel if law enforcement authorities are able to undermine either an accused's confidence in his or her lawyer or the solicitor-client relationship.

Third, the improper conduct by the police regarding the plea bargain also amounted to an infringement of s. 10(*b*). On this issue, I would affirm the conclusion of Toy J. at trial and McEachern C.J.B.C. on appeal that s. 10(*b*) was violated when the officers pressured the appellant into accepting the "deal" without first having the opportunity to consult with his lawyer.

An argument could be made that, at the moment the plea bargain was offered, no s. 10(*b*) violation arose since the accused had an opportunity to call a lawyer, albeit not his particular lawyer, whom the police knew to be unavailable for the one night the offer was left open. However, I am not persuaded by such an argument. Allowing the appellant to call a random lawyer is, given the seriousness of the situation he faced and the circumstances of this case, insufficient for the officers to discharge their responsibilities under s. 10(*b*). This is especially so when the call to this unknown lawyer is placed within the context of the general trickery and subterfuge used by the police in arranging matters so that the appellant himself had to decide on the plea in the absence of his own counsel. Although it is clear that s. 10(*b*) does not guarantee an accused the right to the counsel of his or her choice at all times, in a situation such as the appellant's I believe that either the offer should have been made at a point in time when the accused's lawyer (who was entirely familiar with the facts of his case) was available or the police should have kept it open to a point in time when the accused's counsel would reasonably be considered to be available.

In this conclusion I agree with the following passage from McEachern C.J.B.C.'s dissent in the court below at pp. 367 and 368:

> The s. 10 *Charter* rights of detained persons who have elected to exercise their constitutional rights to retain and instruct counsel would be seriously compromised if police officers having complete control over such persons, should seek... directly or indirectly, to disregard or act contrary to the advice they have received.
>
> .....
>
> Even more serious, in my view, was the police insistence that the accused make a decision that very evening when the police knew the lawyer for the accused was not available. This is worse than the "unfair trick" described in *R. v. Hebert* (1990), 57 C.C.C. (3d) 1 at p. 21, [1990] 2 S.C.R. 151, 77 C.R. (3d) 145. There was no urgency, and the police could well have waited over the weekend when the matter could have been discussed with counsel for the accused. Their failure to do so constituted a clear denial of the accused's s. 10(*b*) *Charter* right to retain and instruct counsel.

When, at first, the appellant refused to accept the deal without consulting with a lawyer, the officers resumed their attempts to discourage the appellant from meeting with his lawyer by observing that the appellant's lawyer was taking the weekend off, by stressing that any delays in accepting the deal would prove painful for the appellant's family, and by underscoring that the deal was being offered for that night only. The end result of this badgering was that the accused did not understand the full content of his right to counsel. When it is evident that there is such a misunderstanding, the police cannot rely on a mechanical recitation of the right to counsel in order to discharge their responsibilities under s. 10(*b*): *R. v. Evans* (1991), 63 C.C.C. (3d) 289 at p. 305, [1991] 1 S.C.R. 869, 4 C.R. (4th) 144. They must take positive steps to facilitate that understanding. In the case at bar, not only did the police fail to take affirmative steps to clear up the appellant's confusion, but they also, in fact, created this confusion in the first place.

The following excerpt from the decision of Toy J. indicates the extent to which Burlingham did not understand the meaning of the right to counsel [at p. 361]:

> In his testimony the accused was asked why, in light of the two lawyers' advice not to speak to the police, he had done so and replied, "I was under the impression that if I co-operated with the police I'd face a lesser charge and I didn't need a lawyer." In my judgment, this impression is totally justifiable when one reads the transcript of the denigrating way the police officers referred to the accused's then lawyer.

It is thus apparent from the transcripts that the accused would not have made the deal with police if it were not for the concerted effort by the police to convince the appellant *not* to consult with his counsel.

I underscore that, in *R. v. Evans, supra,* at pp. 301-2, and 307, McLachlin J. held that the police have the duty to advise a suspect of the right to counsel where there is a fundamental and discrete change in the purpose of an investigation which involves a different and unrelated offence or a significantly more serious offence than that contemplated at the time of the original instruction of the right to counsel. Such a situation arose in the case at bar. The deal offered by the police involved a different offence and was of such material importance to the appellant that it constituted a fundamental change in the course of his prosecution. For the reasons discussed earlier, a genuine effort should have been made to contact the accused's own lawyer.

Furthermore, I conclude that s. 10(*b*) mandates the Crown or police, whenever offering a plea bargain, to tender that offer either to accused's counsel or to the accused while in the presence of his or her counsel, unless the accused has expressly waived the right to counsel. It is, consequently, a constitutional infringement to place such an offer directly to an accused, especially (as in the present appeal) when the police coercively leave it open only for the short period of time during which they know defence counsel to be unavailable. In the case at bar, the police should have negotiated the "deal" with the appellant's counsel or, at a minimum, with the appellant while accompanied by his lawyer.

I emphasize that, in the case at bar, there was no urgency to the matter. Mere expediency or efficiency is not sufficient to create enough "urgency" to permit a s. 10(*b*) breach: *R. v. Prosper, supra.* Neither the precipitous issuing of the plea bargain by the police nor their conscious undermining of the accused's relationship with his counsel can be justified on the basis that such conduct allegedly facilitated the investigatory process.

In closing, given the appellant's success on the other questions he raises, I need not deal with his submission that the breach by the Crown of the plea bargain deal also triggered constitutional violations. However, I should mention that, to the extent that the plea bargain is an integral element of the Canadian criminal process, the Crown and its officers engaged in the plea bargaining process must act honourably and forthrightly.

.....

Having found a serious *Charter* violation, I now turn to the question of the appropriate remedy. I see no reason to interfere with the lower courts' conclusion that it is inappropriate to stay these proceedings. Stays should only be limited to the "clearest of cases."... Therefore, given the inappropriateness of staying these proceedings on account of the s. 10(*b*) violation, the fundamental question that must be addressed is whether s. 24(2) of the *Charter* can operate to exclude any or all of the derivative evidence that had been admitted at trial.

.....

When the *Collins* test is applied to the facts at bar, I find, as did McEachern C.J.B.C. in dissent below, that all of the derivative evidence ought to be excluded.

.....

I find that, in jurisprudence subsequent to *R. v. Collins*, this court has consistently shied away from the differential treatment of real evidence. For example, in *R. v. Ross* (1989), 46 C.C.C. (3d) 129 at p. 139, [1989] 1 S.C.R. 3, 67 C.R. (3d) 209, Lamer J. emphasized that the admissibility of evidence under s. 24(2) depended ultimately not on its nature as real or testimonial, but on whether or not it would only have been found with the compelled assistance of the accused:

> ... the use of *any evidence* that could not have been obtained but for the participation of the accused in the construction of the evidence for the purposes of the trial would tend to render the trial process unfair.

(Emphasis added.) These comments are apposite to the case at bar. Further, I draw attention to the conclusions of La Forest J. in *R. v. Colarusso* (1994), 87 C.C.C. (3d) 193 at p. 230, 110 D.L.R. (4th) 297 at p. 335, [1994] 1 S.C.R. 20, where it was noted that the mere fact that impugned evidence is classified as either real or conscriptive should not in and of itself be determinative.

The exclusion of real evidence was specifically dealt with in the decision of this court in *R. v. Mellenthin* (1992), 76 C.C.C. (3d) 481, [1992] 3 S.C.R. 615, 16 C.R. (4th) 273. The *Mellenthin* case involved the exclusion of drugs found in a car at a random roadside breathalyzer check stop. Cory J. reiterated the distinction between "independently existing evidence that *could* have been found without compelled testimony" and "independently existing evidence that *would* have been found without compelled testimony" established by La Forest J. in *Thomson Newspapers Ltd. v. Canada (Director of Investigation and Research, Restrictive Trade Practices Commission)* (1990), 54 C.C.C. (3d) 417 at p. 514, 67 D.L.R. (4th) 161 at p. 257, [1990] 1 S.C.R. 425. The admission of evidence that simply "could have otherwise been found" will have a higher chance of affecting the fairness of the trial. In *R. v. Mellenthin*, the admission into evidence of the drugs — despite their status as real evidence — would have certainly affected the trial's fairness because they would not have been found without the improper conduct. The drugs were consequently deemed inadmissible.

I conclude my review of the pertinent jurisprudence with the recent decision of *R. v. S. (R.J.)* (1995), 96 C.C.C. (3d) 1, 121 D.L.R. (4th) 589, [1995] 1 S.C.R. 451. In that case, it was recognized that, despite the fact that theoretically the onus rests on the accused to show that the impugned evidence would not have been found but for the unconstitutional conduct, in practice the burden will often fall on the Crown as it possesses superior knowledge. It was held, at p. 75 C.C.C., p. 663 D.L.R., that the "but for" test will be met by the Crown when it satisfies the court on a balance of probabilities that the law enforcement authorities would have discovered the impugned derivative evidence regardless of the information arising from the unconstitutional conduct.

I now turn to the application of this jurisprudence to the case at bar. At the outset, I note that my colleague, Justice L'Heureux-Dubé, concludes that it is the Hall testimony that constitutes the crux of this appeal. My colleague first decides to determine the admissibility of Hall's testimony and, deeming it to be in fact admissible, then goes on to hold that the admission of the gun and the fact of finding the gun would not bring the administration of justice into disrepute. With respect, I find this approach to be inverted. It is the gun and the fact of finding it that stand at the heart of this appeal. This is the key derivative evidence. To this end, the application of s. 24(2) should first concern itself with the gun and its finding, then Biddlecome's and Lewis' identification of it at trial, and thereafter the Hall testimony.

I suggest that it is appropriate to commence the consideration of what evidence should or should not be excluded from the trial process with the evidence obtained most proximate to the *Charter* breach and then work towards evidence arising more remotely therefrom. Since the trial judge deemed Burlingham's confession to be inadmissible, the contested evidence most proximate to the breach is the finding of the gun. As shall become evident, this gun would never have been found were it not for the unconstitutional conduct by the police officers. In any event, in terms of formulating this analysis, it must be kept in mind that there may be times (as in this case) where more remote evidence might not be admitted if its admission would have the same effect as admitting the most proximate evidence.

As mentioned earlier, I find that the derivative real evidence, the gun, *would not* have been found but for the information improperly obtained through the s. 10(*b*) breach. The question is not even whether such evidence would, on a balance of probabilities, have otherwise been located. The gun was at the bottom of the frozen Kootenay River and the only person who knew of its location was the appellant. In this regard, this case can be sharply distinguished from *R. v. Black* (1989), 50 C.C.C. (3d) 1, [1989] 2 S.C.R. 138, 70 C.R. (3d) 97. In *R. v. Black*, after the occurrence of a s. 10(*b*) violation, an accused helped the police identify a particular knife as the murder weapon. Wilson J. admitted this piece of real evidence, noting, at p. 20, that she had "...little doubt that the police would have conducted a search of the appellant's apartment with or without her assistance and that such a search would have uncovered the knife". Consequently, the position that the trial judge's discretion should, in the preponderance of cases, be exercised in favour of exclusion with respect to derivative evidence which *would not have been obtained but for a witness's testimony* is, in fact, consonant with *R. v. Black*.

On a policy level, if the appellant's gestures and directions arising from the s. 10(*b*) violation are inadmissible, yet real, evidence obtained pursuant to these directions is admissible, this court might create an incentive for law enforcement agents to disregard accuseds' *Charter* rights since, even in the case of an infringement of *Charter* rights, the end result might be the admission of evidence that, ordinarily, the state would not be able to locate.

I also share McEachern C.J.B.C.'s view that the appellant's statement to Ms. Hall that he had directed the police to the location of the gun can be classified as derivative evidence. It is true, as Cumming J.A. points out in his concurring majority opinion below, that the appellant made this statement voluntarily and that Hall was not a person in authority. However, even though the statement may have not have been "caused" directly by the breach, it was certainly made as a result of that breach. The statements to Hall flowed from the appellant's understandably confused state of mind stemming from the s. 10(*b*) violations and the critical decisions he had made in the absence of counsel. The appellant was still under the erroneous impression that the "deal" was on. The statement was made the morning after the appellant had been unconstitutionally conscripted to provide evidence against himself. He had never been properly informed of his right to counsel and it cannot be said with any degree of conviction that he would have made the same statement to Hall had he been duly advised of his constitutional rights. In fact, he would have had nothing to say to Hall had he not been improperly conscripted to provide evidence against himself by the police in the first place. For this reason, the rights violation had much more than, as characterized by L'Heureux-Dubé J., simply an incidental effect on the making of the impugned statement.

I note that my colleague describes these statements as a "windfall" to the Crown. Such a description, in my view, overlooks the fact that the content of the appellant's conversation with Hall is inextricably connected to the conduct of the police, found to violate s. 10(*b*). These self-incriminatory statements amount to evidence that could not have been obtained but for the unconstitutional manner in which the accused was tricked into participating in the construction of the evidence for the purposes of his trial. Given that no satisfactory indication has been given that, on a balance of probabilities, this evidence would have been found regardless of the unconstitutionally obtained information, it is to be excluded under s. 24(2): *R. v. Ross, supra*; *R. v. S. (R.J.), supra*.

The rationale behind the exclusion of evidence lying in close proximity with the *Charter* breach stems from the fact that, in the case at bar, such evidence, if tendered at trial, detracts from the integrity of the trial and thereby infringes both the fairness principle and reliability principle evoked by L'Heureux-Dubé J. in her reasons in the instant appeal. There is an overlap between these two principles in so far as unconstitutionally obtained information may well constitute unreliable evidence, especially when the particular constitutional right that has been breached is the right to counsel. In any event, even if the improperly obtained evidence were reliable, considerations of reliability are no longer determinative, given that the *Charter* has made the rights of the individual and the fairness and integrity of the judicial system paramount: *R. v. Hebert, supra*, at p. 36.

It is now necessary to focus more directly on the issues of proximity and remoteness. In this regard, the decision of this court in *R. v. Strachan* (1988), 46 C.C.C. (3d) 479 at pp. 498-9, 56 D.L.R. (4th) 673 at pp. 692-3, [1988] 2 S.C.R. 980, is helpful to this analysis.

R. v. Strachan concerned the admissibility of evidence (marijuana) obtained as a result of a valid search during which the accused's right to counsel was violated. Dickson C.J.C. made it clear that a strict causal analysis is not necessary in a s. 24(2) analysis and that the presence of a temporal connection is not determinative....

Seen in light of Dickson C.J.C.'s comments in *R. v. Strachan*, it appears that the problem with Cumming J.A.'s reasoning with respect to the statement to Hall is that he fails to recognize the important connection between the content of the statement and the s. 10(*b*) violation. The fact is that the Crown sought to introduce the statement at trial precisely because it allowed it to do indirectly what the trial judge had ruled the Crown could not do directly: introduce evidence that the appellant knew where the gun was hidden. In this regard, the inclusion of the statement to Hall would directly affect the fairness of the trial, which is a key consideration in affecting the repute of the justice system, despite the fact that the statement was but remotely connected to the unconstitutional conduct. In effect, excluding the gun while including the statements effectively eviscerates the *Charter* of most of its protective value to the accused in this case; including both would totally eliminate any such value. At this point, it is important to recall the observation by Lamer C.J.C. in *R. v. Bartle* (1994), 92 C.C.C. (3d) 289 at p. 313, 118 D.L.R. (4th) 83 at p. 108, [1994] 3 S.C.R. 173, in which the opinion was expressed that:

> Generally speaking, so long as it is not too remotely connected with the violation, all the evidence obtained as part of the "chain of events" involving the *Charter* breach will fall within the scope of s. 24(2)...

See also *R. v. Grant* (1993), 84 C.C.C. (3d) 173, [1993] 3 S.C.R. 223, 24 C.R. (4th) 1, *per* Sopinka J.

Returning to the question of the self-incriminatory nature of the evidence and its effect on the fairness of the trial, I agree entirely with McEachern C.J.B.C.'s reasons when he states, at p. 377:

> In my view, however, this was highly damaging evidence because even if the circumstances of finding the gun, and the gun itself were admissible, the statement to Ms. Hall was the only evidence that fixed the accused with knowledge that the gun was in the river. This fact tended to connect the accused more closely with the crime and could give rise to an inference of consciousness of guilt on the part of the accused. If, as I believe, the finding of the gun and the gun itself was inadmissible, this statement was the only evidence that proved the gun was even in a river, and that would make an inference of consciousness of guilt even stronger.
>
> .....
>
> In this connection, it is significant that the accused did not know that his s. 10(*b*) *Charter* rights had been violated at the time he made his first statement to Ms. Hall, or that the Crown would be reneging on its agreement with him. More important is the fact that the statement was so closely related both in time and content to the breach.

Furthermore, I note that in two recent decisions this court has concluded that, in cases of including evidence flowing from a s. 10(*b*) violation, the onus lies upon the Crown to demonstrate on a balance of probabilities that, regarding the unfairness of the trial component of the test under s. 24(2), the accused would not have consulted counsel even if properly advised: *R. v. Bartle*, *supra*; *R. v. Pozniak* (1994), 92 C.C.C. (3d) 472, 118

D.L.R. (4th) 205, [1994] 3 S.C.R. 310. The Crown has clearly not met this burden, nor even the less onerous requirements stipulated in earlier jurisprudence.

Moreover, the serious nature of the *Charter* breach in this case also supports the conclusion that the administration of justice would be brought into disrepute by the admission of the evidence.

.....

In this case, it is clear that the violation was wilful and flagrant. It is also clear, as discussed earlier, that there was no element of urgency. Indeed, as McEachern C.J.B.C. notes, the police actually created an artificial situation of urgency in order to trick the accused into accepting the deal without first consulting a lawyer.

As to the third branch of the *Collins* test, I am satisfied that the effect of excluding the evidence on the reputation of the administration of justice will be incidental and far outweighed by the negative consequences that would follow were this unconstitutional evidence to be included. I realize that the appellant stands accused of a serious offence. However, as shall become evident in my disposition of this matter, the end result of allowing this appeal is not the issuance of a stay, but the ordering of a new trial in which the accused will have to meet the lawful evidence adduced against him. All that is required is the holding of the constitutionally mandated fair trial that should have occurred in the first place, and would have occurred were it not for the misconduct of the law enforcement agents.

.....

Consequently, a new trial should be ordered in which the impugned evidence will not be admitted, namely: (1) the Hall testimony regarding the appellant's recounting of the events of the night of January 4, 1985; (2) evidence that police divers had found the gun in the river; (3) the Biddlecome and Lewis testimony identifying the murder weapon at trial; and (4) the gun itself. I add that, as was found at trial, the appellant's confession as well as his gestures and directions to the police with regard to the location of the gun are equally inadmissible. The Crown, if it chooses, can properly introduce the rest of the evidence it has adduced against the accused, including, as noted by McEachern C.J.B.C., the evidence of Biddlecome and Lewis that the accused had possession of a sawed-off .410 shotgun shortly before the disappearance of Ms Worms, as well as Hall's testimony that the accused had told her he was actually present when Biddlecome had beaten and killed Ms Worms.

.....

L'Heureux-Dubé J. (dissenting in part): — I have read the reasons of my colleague Justice Iacobucci and I agree with him that the accused's rights under s. 10(*b*) of the *Canadian Charter of Rights and Freedoms* were clearly violated in the case at bar. I must respectfully disagree, however, with his proposed remedy under s. 24(2) of the *Charter*. In particular, I do not believe that the administration of justice would be brought into disrepute by the admission of the voluntary statements by the accused to his girlfriend nor, under these unusual circumstances, by the admission of the murder weapon.

.....

[L'Heureux-Dubé J. traces the Court's treatment of s. 24(2) from *Collins* reflecting that the Court "has fashioned an extremely aggressive exclusionary remedy".]

It becomes evident how far this court has deviated from its original approach to s. 24(2) when we transplant the "but for" standard employed in *R. v. Mellenthin* back to *R. v. Collins*. If, in *R. v. Collins*, Lamer J. had approached the problem in the manner suggested by Cory J. in *R. v. Mellenthin*, he should have concluded that "but for" the *Charter* violation, the officer would not have seized the heroin balloon from the suspect in the bar. There was no evidence to suggest that the officer could have seized the drugs in any other way. Yet, how is it that Lamer J. concluded for the majority in *R. v. Collins* that this evidence, though prejudicial in the ordinary sense, did not render the trial unfair, and therefore did not tend to the almost automatic exclusion of the evidence? Why have our notions of what constitutes a "fair trial", and thereby inevitably leads to exclusion, changed so profoundly in the space of the five years between *R. v. Collins* and *R. v. Mellenthin*?

With great respect, I suggest that we have lost sight of the original concerns that motivated the court to remark that the admission of evidence affecting the fairness of the hearing would generally tend to bring the administration of justice into disrepute.

.....

In my opinion, evidence is capable of affecting "*trial* fairness", as that term is employed in the first branch of *R. v. Collins*, where its admission could give rise to concerns analogous to, or falling within, the rubric of the Reliability Principle. ... Where, by contrast, the complaint about the impugned evidence is, for instance, that it would not have been obtained "but for" the rights violation, then this complaint relates more fundamentally to the Fairness Principle. The objection to the admission of the evidence is not that it has the potential to mislead a trier of fact or convict an innocent person, but rather that the manner in which the authorities obtained the evidence was fundamentally unfair, and erodes values that are fundamental to our society. I therefore believe that the fact that the evidence could not have been obtained "but for" the rights violation is more accurately viewed as a relevant consideration to the second branch of the *Collins* framework: the impact of the seriousness of the rights violation on the reputation of the justice system. I shall return to this matter shortly.

To summarize, given that this court uses "trial fairness" within s. 24(2) as a proxy for circumstances in which the administration of justice is almost inevitably brought into disrepute, and where any other mitigating considerations or circumstances are virtually irrelevant, I believe that it is most consistent with the purpose and spirit of s. 24(2) to define that category of factors narrowly. In my respectful view, it runs counter to the inherently discretionary nature of a s. 24(2) determination, which is to be made "having regard to all of the circumstances", to formulate rigid rules or presumptions for the exclusion or admission of different kinds of evidence. Thus, to the extent that this court decides to set down such a rule in regard to "trial fairness", I believe that it should take care not to define that concept so broadly as to allow the "trial fairness" tail to wag the s. 24(2) dog.

Classifying evidence as "self-incriminatory" or "real", or "discoverable" or "not discoverable" is not, nor should it be, an end in itself. For this reason, I have considerable sympathy for the following observations of Professor David M. Paciocco in "The Judicial Repeal of s. 24(2) and the Development of the Canadian Exclusionary Rule", *supra*, at pp. 353-4:

> *The whole historical development of s. 24(2) drives home the point that it was intended to be a compromise between what is typically but inaccurately characterized as the automatic exclusionary rule in the United States, and the traditional common law Canadian position whereby evidence is admissible if relevant and material, regardless of how it was obtained.* Out of distaste and distrust for the American regime the first public draft of the *Charter* had provided expressly that no exclusionary remedy could be developed to enforce the *Charter*. Strong submissions against this position were made by various public-interest groups who favoured an exclusionary rule. Ultimately, s. 24(2) was adopted as a compromise position. It promised to be a provision which answered the most common objection to having an exclusionary enforcement mechanism, that requiring the exclusion of unconstitutionally obtained evidence may provide disproportionate relief to accused persons; serious offenders may be acquitted because of constitutional violations which are not nearly as shocking or outrageous as the crime shown by the evidence to have been committed.
>
> *The rejection of the polar extremes has been drafted into the provision. The section requires courts to determine whether admission of the evidence in question could cause the relevant kind of disrepute, "having regard to all of the circumstances". The spirit of the provision, if not that very language, calls into question the legitimacy of developing even quasi-automatic principles for exclusion. Despite this, the court has produced just such a principle, and its implications are enormous.*

(Emphasis added.)

.....

Since writing these reasons, I have had the advantage of reading the reasons of Justice Sopinka. I take great exception to his implication that I am in any way advocating an approach to exclusion of evidence that is reminiscent of this court's judgment in *R. v. Wray*, [1970] 4 C.C.C. 1, 11 D.L.R. (3d) 673, [1971] S.C.R. 272. In fact, the approach I suggest, which looks both to reliability and to the integrity of the judicial system, finds its genesis in Lamer J.'s influential remarks in *R. v. Rothman*, its inspiration in the wording and historical context of s. 24(2) of the *Charter*, and its application in this court's approach in *R. v. Collins*. Although it bespeaks the obvious, I must emphasize that a court's inquiry into exclusion does not end when it finds that unconstitutionally obtained evidence is inherently reliable (and therefore not subject to virtually automatic exclusion). Analysis then passes on to a consideration of the damage to the integrity of the system that could be occasioned by the admission of the impugned evidence. This must be approached from the point of the long-term effects on the community of the admission of evidence obtained under similar circumstances. The likelihood of exclusion under this framework, therefore, goes far beyond anything that ever existed at common law, particularly since evidence will be excluded whenever its admission *could* bring the administration of justice into disrepute.

The thrust of my criticism of this court's recent jurisprudence on s. 24(2) is that we may be digging ourselves into a hole. If we are to create a test of absolute exclusion to further the purposes of s. 24(2), then I believe that we must not define that test so broadly as to risk frustrating the text of s. 24(2), which calls upon courts to evaluate "all of the circumstances" in preserving the reputation of the justice system. I therefore prefer to formulate any absolute exclusionary rules more narrowly than most of my colleagues.

In my view, it is most consistent both with our common law approach to exclusion and with the purposes of s. 24(2) of the *Charter* to confine an absolute exclusionary rule to circumstances in which the unconstitutional conduct of state authorities is responsible for evidence which may possibly be unreliable. I do not feel that the nature of the evidence (real v. self- incriminatory, or discoverable v. undiscoverable) should be determinative of absolute exclusion. For my part, I believe that a viable distinction can and must be drawn between evidence whose admission potentially touches upon the adjudicative fairness of the hearing and evidence which is obtained in a manner which does violence to the integrity of the judicial system. Whereas the former must almost inevitably be excluded, the latter must be evaluated "having regard to all of the circumstances".

My colleague Sopinka J. notes that Lamer J. did not specifically mention reliability in his discussion of trial fairness. I agree. For this, one must go back to *R. v. Rothman*, the grandfather of *R. v. Collins*. I do not believe that our concept of what constitutes a minimal standard of "trial fairness" has changed so dramatically since the *Charter*. The justice system was not suffering from widespread disrepute as a result of "unfair trials" when s. 24(2) came onto the scene.

Finally, Sopinka J. concludes by opining that the majority's approach to s. 24(2) is more consistent with *R. v. Collins* than the framework I propose. In answer, I repeat the following rhetorical question that I have already asked about *R. v. Collins*: Given that the heroin balloon could not have been recovered "but for" the unreasonable search by the officer, why did this court, none the less, conclude that, although the admission of the evidence would operate unfortunately for the accused, the "fairness of the trial" was in no way implicated? I find further support, moreover, in my rejection of using discoverability as a proxy for trial fairness in the following excerpt from John Sopinka, Sidney N. Lederman, and Alan W. Bryant, *The Law of Evidence in Canada* (Toronto: Butterworths, 1992), at p. 407:

> [The] disposition in [*R. v. Black*] leaves open the question whether real evidence obtained as a consequence of a s. 10(b) violation, but which would not have been discovered but for the violation, can be characterized as falling within the trial fairness rationale for exclusion... In light of the strong indications in *Collins* and *Ross*, it is difficult to see how real evidence, no matter how obtained, could be said to affect the fairness of the trial. *The better view seems to be that the admission of real evidence (i.e., tangible evidence not created by the accused as a consequence of a Charter violation) must stand or fall on the basis of the seriousness of the Charter violation by which it was obtained.*

(Emphasis added.) I rest my case.

.....

In closing, I would like to turn very briefly to the Crown's conduct in repudiating the "deal" reached between the police officers and the appellant. I agree with my colleague's conclusion that the conduct of the authorities, though certainly contemptible, did not amount to one of the "clearest of cases" of abuse of process, requiring a stay of proceedings. I am also mindful of the fact that the trial judge found the police to have made an honest mistake and not to have acted with *male fides* in breaking their bargain. Their misunderstanding of the Crown's offer may very well have been genuine. However, I firmly believe that the Crown acted in bad faith by charging the accused with first degree murder notwithstanding the fact that the Crown was aware that the police had misled the appellant who, in full reliance on the "deal" proffered by the police, had fulfilled his half of the bargain. Under the circumstances, and given that the Crown did not object to the police officers presenting the "deal" on the Crown's behalf, it seems highly unfair and unjust to allow the Crown to act in total disregard for its agents' undertakings, and to impose the consequences for such disregard upon the appellant. For this reason, I would find a violation of the principle of fundamental fairness under s. 7 of the *Charter*, as discussed in my reasons in *R. v. S. (R.J.)*. Under the circumstances, while I do not believe that this case is one of the "clearest of cases" calling for a stay of proceedings, I am of the opinion that it would be appropriate and just under s. 24(1) of the *Charter* to require the Crown to uphold its half of the "deal", and for this court to substitute a conviction for the lesser included offence of second degree murder for the present conviction of first degree murder.

.....

Sopinka J. (Cory, Iacobucci and Major JJ. concurring): — I agree with the reasons and conclusion of Justice Iacobucci but wish to address the point made by my colleague, Justice L'Heureux-Dubé, that the court has departed from the approach adopted in *R. v. Collins* (1987), 33 C.C.C. (3d) 1, 38 D.L.R. (4th) 508, [1987] 1 S.C.R. 265, in favour of a rule of automatic exclusion.

The criticism made by my colleague closely parallels the opinion of Professor Paciocco who advocates a more literal and restrictive interpretation of s. 24(2) of the *Canadian Charter of Rights and Freedoms*: see David M. Paciocco, "The Judicial Repeal of s. 24(2) and the Development of the Canadian Exclusionary Rule" (1989-90), 32 Crim. L.Q. 326. Not surprisingly, commentators no less than the public differ as to the appropriate approach to the exclusion of evidence associated with a violation of a *Charter* right: see, for example, Yves-Marie Morissette "The Exclusion of Evidence under the *Canadian Charter of Rights and Freedoms*: What to Do and What Not to Do" (1984), 29 McGill L.J. 521; R. J. Deslisle, "Collins: An Unjustified Distinction" (1987), 56 C.R. (3d) 216; Tom Quigley and Eric Colvin, "Developments in Criminal Law and Procedure: The 1988-89 Term" (1990), 1 Sup. Ct. L. Rev. (2d) 187; Steven M. Penney, "Unreal Distinctions: The Exclusion of Unfairly Obtained Evidence Under s. 24(2) of the *Charter*" (1994), 32 Alta. L. Rev. 782 at p. 800. While Professor Paciocco favours an approach that would be less exclusionary and, in his opinion, more in tune with the views of the average Canadian, Steven Penney, in his comprehensive article, at p. 810, argues that by focusing on trial fairness, as opposed to the criminal justice system as a whole, we "render individual Canadians more susceptible to invasions of their constitutional rights".

Both Professor Paciocco and my colleague are of the view that the approach we have taken is out of step with the public mood. Quite apart from the admonitions of Lamer J. (as he then was) in *Collins*, at pp. 16-17

C.C.C., pp. 523-4 D.L.R., that individual rights are not to be submitted to an adjudication by the majority, there is no accurate assessment of public opinion. Adjusting the approach to *Charter* rights based on public opinion surveys is fraught with difficulties. This can be illustrated by reference to the empirical study to which my colleague refers by Alan W. Bryant, Marc Gold, H. Michael Stevenson and David Northrup, "Public Attitudes Toward the Exclusion of Evidence: Section 24(2) of the *Canadian Charter of Rights and Freedoms*" (1990), 69 Can. Bar Rev. 1. It purported to show "a significant gap between public opinion and judicial opinion" regarding the application of the Collins factors. After publication of that study, a further study by the same authors, "Public Support for the Exclusion of Unconstitutionally Obtained Evidence" (1990), 1 Sup. Ct. L. Rev. (2d) 555, concluded, at p. 557, that "taking into account some of the ambiguity in the case law, the gap between public and judicial opinion may not be that substantial over a broad range of cases".

The study concluded with the following warning, at p. 587:

> Whatever one's views on the merits or rationale of the exclusionary rule, our study illustrates the multi-faceted and complex nature of the public's judgments about admissibility. Levels of support for the exclusion of evidence varied considerably depending upon a number of factors, some of which were case-specific while others were attitudinal and demographic. In this respect, *any argument for or against how judges apply section 24(2) that relies upon a supposedly monolithic "public opinion" clearly must be rejected.*

(Emphasis added.)

Had the court reacted to the first study and altered its approach, the validity of cases decided under the altered approach would have been called into question by the subsequent study. It is for this reason that the test with respect to what could bring the administration of justice into disrepute was stated in *Collins* to be grounded in longer term community values rather than the public passion of the moment. These long-term community values are to be assessed in terms of the views of the hypothetical, reasonable, well-informed and dispassionate person in the community.

.....

... Nowhere in *Collins* is the fairness of the trial equated with the reliability of the evidence. The description used in *Collins* as to the kind of evidence that could render a trial unfair was "a confession or other evidence emanating from him". Leaving aside the words "or other evidence emanating from him", even the admissibility of a "confession" is not determined solely on the basis of reliability. Prior to the *Charter* and at common law, reliability ceased to be the exclusive basis for excluding confessions: see *R. v. Rothman* (1981), 59 C.C.C. (2d) 30, 121 D.L.R. (3d) 578, [1981] 1 S.C.R. 640; *R. v. Hebert* (1990), 57 C.C.C. (3d) 1, [1990] 2 S.C.R. 151, 77 C.R. (3d) 145, especially at p. 20; *R. v. Whittle* (1994), 92 C.C.C. (3d) 11 at pp. 24-5, 116 D.L.R. (4th) 416 at p. 429-30, [1994] 2 S.C.R. 914; and *R. v. Sang*, [1980] A.C. 402 (H.L.). It could hardly be suggested that exclusion of involuntary confessions did not relate to the fairness of the trial. The reliability principle would, therefore, impose a more restrictive exclusionary rule than that which existed at common law. Its preoccupation with the probative value of the evidence would also appear to be a close relative of the rule in *R. v. Wray*, [1970] 4 C.C.C. 1, 11 D.L.R. (3d)

673, [1971] S.C.R. 272. At p. 17 C.C.C., pp. 689-90 D.L.R. ... *Wray* was widely criticized, has not been followed by this court and was not the basis for the exclusionary power adopted by the *Charter* in s. 24(2): see A. Anne McLellan and Bruce B. Elman, "The Enforcement of the *Canadian Charter of Rights and Freedoms*: An Analysis of Section 24" (1983), 21 Alta. L. Rev. 205 at p. 230; *Penney, supra*, at p. 794; *R. v. S. (R.J.)*, S.C.C., Court File No. 23581, February 2, 1995, *per* L'Heureux-Dubé J., at pp. 16-17 [now reported [1995] 1 S.C.R. 451 96 C.C.C. (3d) 1 at pp. 97-9, 121 D.L.R. (4th) 589 at pp. 685-7].

It is not accurate to characterize the first branch of the *Collins* test as an automatic rule of exclusion with respect to all self-incriminating evidence. While a finding that admission of illegally obtained evidence would render the trial unfair will result in exclusion, the court must first conclude that "in all the circumstances" the admission of the evidence would render the trial unfair.

R. v. Tremblay (1987), 37 C.C.C. (3d) 565, 45 D.L.R. (4th) 445, [1987] 2 S.C.R. 435, and *R. v. Mohl* (1989), 47 C.C.C. (3d) 575*n*, [1989] 1 S.C.R. 1389, 69 C.R. (3d) 399, illustrate the kinds of circumstances that can be taken into account to secure admission of the evidence even in the case of a breach of the right to counsel under s. 10(*b*) of the *Charter*.

Discoverability

The discoverability or "but for" test which my colleague criticizes can also be traced to *Collins*. At p. 20 C.C.C., p. 526 D.L.R., Lamer J. stated that, in relation to the factors relating to the fairness of the trial, "[i]t may also be relevant, in certain circumstances, that the evidence would have been obtained in any event without the violation of the *Charter*". In *R. v. Ross, supra*, in relation to evidence that could be classed as real evidence, he observed that the fairness of the trial would be affected by "the use of any evidence that *could not have been obtained but for* the participation of the accused" (emphasis added). In *R. v. Dersch* (1993), 85 C.C.C. (3d) 1 at p. 5, [1993] 3 S.C.R. 768, 25 C.R. (4th) 88, my colleague L'Heureux-Dubé J. states:

> Pursuant to *Collins, supra*, the admission of evidence that would have been unlikely to have been discovered, had the *Charter* violation not occurred, severely affects the fairness of the trial. On the other hand, if the evidence had been discoverable regardless of the *Charter* violation, the fairness of the trial will not be influenced.

While the court has not decided the extent to which discoverability is relevant in all aspects of the *Collins* test, it has been applied to admit evidence (*R. v. Black* (1989), 50 C.C.C. (3d) 1, [1989] 2 S.C.R. 138, 70 C.R. (3d) 97), as well as to exclude evidence (*R. v. Mellenthin* (1992), 76 C.C.C. (3d) 481, [1992] 3 S.C.R. 615, 16 C.R. (4th) 273).

The distinction that was made in Collins between real evidence and evidence emanating from the accused was based, at least in part, on the rationale that real evidence (or things) can be discovered without the participation of the accused. They pre-existed the state action which is called into question, and were there to be discovered by investigative means not involving the accused. In a situation such as *R. v. Ross* in which this distinction is blurred, discoverability has been used to place the evidence in one or other of these two categories. If the evidence was discoverable without the participation of the accused, then it has the attributes of real evidence. Conversely, evidence that clearly emanates from the accused such as statements has not been subjected to the discoverability analysis. While it can be argued that when an accused has been denied the right to counsel under s. 10(*b*), an inquiry could be made as to whether the accused would have acted differently had his *Charter* rights been observed, the court has generally refused to enter into such an inquiry: see *R. v. Strachan* (1988), 46 C.C.C. (3d) 479 at p. 496, 56 D.L.R. (4th) 673 at p. 690, [1988] 2 S.C.R. 980; *R. v. Elshaw* (1991), 67 C.C.C. (3d) 97 at pp. 127-8, [1991] 3 S.C.R. 24, 7 C.R. (4th) 333; *R. v. Bartle* (1994), 92 C.C.C. (3d) 289 at pp. 319-20, 118 D.L.R. (4th) 83 at pp. 114-15, [1994] 3 S.C.R. 173. Unless the right to counsel is waived by the accused, such a breach generally results in the exclusion of the evidence.

Various proposals have been made as to the future direction that this court should take with respect to s. 24(2). Some would favour an approach that is less exclusionary and others more exclusionary. It has been suggested that the distinction between real and other evidence be eliminated as well as any distinction between the nature of the *Charter* right that has been infringed: see *Deslisle, supra*. It has been proposed that the distinction based on participation of the accused be eliminated, and that discoverability be the main touchstone of admissibility (*R. v. Meddoui* (1990), 61 C.C.C. (3d) 345 at p. 364, 2 C.R. (4th) 316, 5 C.R.R. (2d) 294 (Alta. C.A.)): see *Quigley and Colvin, supra*.

While we have not rushed in to adopt every current theory on the application of s. 24(2), these are serious proposals that have been and should be taken into account in the incremental evolution of the jurisprudence in this area. Accordingly, as my colleague Iacobucci J. points out, the distinction between real and conscriptive evidence is not treated as determinative and greater emphasis has been placed on the discoverability or "but for" test: see *Mellenthin, supra*. In my opinion, we should proceed to develop the law relating to s. 24(2) on this basis rather than adopt the new approach advocated by my colleague L'Heureux-Dubé J. In my view, our approach to date is more consistent with Collins and, therefore, with *stare decisis*. Moreover, I believe it strikes the appropriate balance between a restrictive versus a liberal exclusionary rule, and therefore is more faithful to the values that the *Charter* protects.

Gonthier J.: — I have had the benefit of the reasons of Justices L'Heureux-Dubé, Sopinka and Iacobucci. I consider that those of L'Heureux-Dubé J., read together with the comments of Sopinka J., contribute to a proper understanding of the principles governing the exclusion of evidence under s. 24(2) of the *Canadian Charter of Rights and Freedoms*. I am in agreement with Iacobucci J. that the accused's statement to Ms. Hall is to be excluded as well as the gun and its location, the discovery of which could be made possible by this statement. The making of this statement which recounted the carrying out by the accused of his part of the deal made with the police officers was intimately connected to that deal which was obtained through the highly egregious conduct of the police officers in pressing the accused to confess and systematically undermining the role of defence counsel. This conduct was a *Charter* violation of the most serious kind, bringing into play both the Reliability and the Fairness

Principles referred to by L'Heureux-Dubé J. though other evidence served to allay concern as to reliability. The charge of first degree murder is, it is true, one of the most serious known to the criminal law. In the circumstances, however, it is my view that the admission of this evidence would tend to bring the administration of justice into disrepute in the eyes of a reasonable person, dispassionate and fully apprised of the circumstances. The evidence should therefore be excluded. The accused must be tried for his crime but without having to face evidence which is the product of egregious police misconduct.

At the same time, in agreement with the reasons of Iacobucci J., I am not prepared to apply the curative provision of s. 686(1)(*b*)(iii) of the *Criminal Code*, R.S.C. 1985, c. C-46. The extreme egregious conduct of the police in this case casts a pall on the perception of fairness of the whole trial process and constitutes a substantial wrong for which the proper remedy is a new trial. While miscarriage of justice in s. 686(1)(*b*)(iii) may focus on avoiding conviction of the innocent, substantial wrong (which, I note, does not appear in s. 686(1)(*a*)(iii)) may be more encompassing.

I therefore concur in the disposition of this appeal by Iacobucci J.

In the following case, the Supreme Court of Canada sought to resolve confusing jurisprudence on the conscriptive-real evidence dichotomy and its relationship to discoverability.

R. v. STILLMAN

(1997), 113 C.C.C. (3d) 321 (S.C.C.)

Cory J. (Lamer C.J.C., La Forest, Sopinka and Iacobucci JJ. concurring): — On this appeal there are two major issues which must be considered. First, what should be the scope and the appropriate limits of the common law power to search which is incidental to an arrest? Second, in what circumstances should evidence obtained as a result of a breach of a *Charter* right be ruled inadmissible on the grounds that its admission would render the trial unfair?

I. Factual Background

On the evening of April 12, 1991, a group of seven teenagers gathered in the Oromocto area, in New Brunswick. They walked to a camp in the woods where they drank beer and wine and shared some LSD. Between 8:00 p.m. and 8:30 p.m. the 17-year-old appellant, William Stillman, and the 14-year-old victim, Pamela Bischoff, left the group. When he arrived at his home between 11:45 p.m. and midnight, the appellant was obviously cold, shaken and wet from the upper thighs down. He was cut above one eye, and had mud and grass on his pants. The explanation he gave for his condition was that he had been in a fight with five Indians. This explanation, as well as his account of where he had last seen the victim, varied over time.

The victim's body was found six days later in the Oromocto River next to a bridge some 300 to 400 metres from where she had last been seen by the group. An expert placed the time of death between 10:30 and 11:30 p.m. on April 12, 1991. A motorist and his passenger saw Pamela on the bridge with a male companion around 10:15 p.m. Between 11:45 p.m. and midnight, another motorist positively identified the appellant, walking on a public road that led to the bridge. Mud was observed on the appellant's pants from above the knees down to his feet.

The autopsy revealed that the cause of death was not drowning but rather a wound or wounds to the head. Semen was found in the victim's vagina and a human bite mark had been left on her abdomen.

On April 19, 1991, the appellant was arrested for the murder of Pamela Bischoff. At the time of the arrest, the appellant retained counsel. He was transported to the RCMP headquarters in Fredericton where he was met by his lawyers. The police indicated that they wished to take hair samples and teeth impressions and to question the appellant. After spending over two hours with the appellant, the two lawyers gave a letter to the police which read as follows:

> This is to confirm that Bryan Whittaker and I are representing the above young person who we understand has been arrested for murder.
>
> This is to confirm that we have advised this young person that he is not to consent to provide any bodily samples whatsoever including hair and or teeth imprints to you or anybody else.
>
> This is also to confirm that he has been advised not to give any statements to you or anyone else concerning your investigation into the death of Pam Bischoff. He is not to talk to you at all without one of the undersigned being present.

Notwithstanding this statement of intention, once the lawyers left, the RCMP took bodily samples from the appellant, under threat of force. A sergeant took scalp hair samples by passing a gloved hand through the appellant's hair, as well as by combing, clipping and plucking hairs. The appellant was made to pull some of his own pubic hair. Plasticine teeth impressions were then taken.

Then, in the absence of the appellant's parents or his lawyers, a constable interviewed the appellant for an hour in an attempt to obtain a statement. Although the appellant did not say anything, he sobbed throughout the interview. The appellant asked to speak to his lawyer, at which point the interview ended and he was permitted to make the telephone call. While waiting for his lawyer to arrive, the appellant asked to use the washroom. Escorted by the constable, he did so. As the appellant was leaving the washroom, he used a tissue to blow his nose and threw the tissue in the waste bin. The tissue containing mucous was seized by the constable and subsequently used for DNA testing.

When the appellant's lawyer arrived at the headquarters he objected to the actions taken by the RCMP with respect to the appellant. Yet, after the lawyer left, the sergeant brought the appellant into an interview room and, once again, attempted to obtain a statement. The police thought that they had enough evidence to charge the appellant, but the Crown's office disagreed. Accordingly, five days after the arrest, the appellant was released without being charged.

Several months later, after they had received the DNA and odontology analysis, the RCMP again arrested the appellant. This action was taken in part in order to obtain better impressions of the appellant's teeth. A dentist attended at the RCMP detachment for that purpose and, without the appellant's consent, took impressions of his teeth, in a procedure which took two hours. More hair was taken from the appellant, as well as a saliva sample and buccal swabs.

In mid-February 1993 a *voir dire* was held to determine the admissibility of certain evidence: [1993] N.B.J. No. 625 (Q.B.). The trial judge found that the hair samples, teeth impressions and buccal swabs had been obtained in a manner which violated the appellant's *Charter* rights, but that the evidence should be admitted. He found that the tissue containing mucous had not been obtained in a manner which violated the appellant's *Charter* rights.

The appellant was convicted, by a jury, of first degree murder and sentenced to lifeimprisonment with no eligibility for parole for eight years. The majority of the Court of Appeal of New Brunswick dismissed the appeal but Rice J.A. dissenting, would have allowed the appeal and ordered a new trial, on the ground that the evidence should have been excluded pursuant to s. 24(2) of the *Charter*: (1995), 159 N.B.R. (2d) 321, 409 A.P.R. 321, 97 C.C.C. (3d) 164. The appellant now appeals as of right to this Court.

.....

V. Analysis

A. Was any of the Impugned Evidence Obtained in a Manner that Infringed or Denied the Appellant's Charter Rights?

(1) The Hair Samples, Teeth Impressions and Buccal Swabs

(a) Did the Taking of the Hair Samples, Teeth Impressions and Buccal Swabs Contravene Section 8 of the Charter?

There are three requirements which must be met if a search is to be found reasonable: (a) it must be authorized by law; (b) the law itself must be reasonable; and (c) the manner in which the search was carried out must be reasonable: see *Collins,*[1987] 1 S.C.R. 165, at p. 278. An appropriate starting point, therefore, is to determine whether there existed either a statutory or common law power that authorized the police to search and seize the appellant's scalp hairs and pubic hairs or to take dental impressions or buccal swabs.

At the time that this seizure occurred in 1991, the *Criminal Code* only provided a procedure for obtaining a warrant to search a "building, receptacle or place". It did not authorize the search of a person, nor the seizure of parts of the body. It is only with the recent addition of s. 487.05 that this limitation has been removed to the extent of its provisions. Therefore, the taking of hair and teeth samples was conducted without statutory authority. The respondent can justify these searches only by demonstrating that they were authorized by a common law power or that the appellant had no reasonable expectation of privacy in the things seized. To this end, the respondent asserts that the hair samples and teeth impressions were seized pursuant to the common law power of search incident to a lawful arrest.

(i) The Common Law Power of Search Incident to a Lawful Arrest

Three conditions must be satisfied in order for a search to be validly undertaken pursuant to the common law power of search incident to a lawful arrest. First, the arrest must be lawful. No search, no matter how reasonable, may be upheld under this common law power where the arrest which gave rise to it was arbitrary or otherwise unlawful. Second, the search must have been conducted as an "incident" to the lawful arrest. To these almost self-evident conditions must be added a third, which applies to all searches undertaken by police: the manner in which the search is carried out must be reasonable. Were all three criteria satisfied in this instance?

[Cory J. concludes that the arrest was indeed lawful.]

.....

Were the Seizures of the Hair Samples, Teeth Impressions and Buccal Swabs Made "Incidental" to the Arrest?

The Scope of the Common Law Power of Search Incident to Arrest

[Cory J. reviews the various cases addressing search incidental to arrest.]

.....

It is important to recognize that these cases, which purport to expand the common law power of search incidental to arrest, involve less intrusive searches of motor vehicles and the seizure of evidence found in them. This type of search is not in issue in this case and I need not express any opinion with regard to them. Obviously, completely different concerns arise where the search and seizure infringes upon a person's bodily integrity, which may constitute the ultimate affront to human dignity.

The question of whether or not the common law power of search incident to arrest can be extended to permit the seizure of bodily substances has recently been considered by provincial appellate courts, with conflicting results...

.....

... It has often been clearly and forcefully expressed that state interference with a person's bodily integrity is a breach of a person's privacy and an affront to human dignity. The invasive nature of body searches demands higher standards of justification. In *R. v. Pohoretsky*, [1987] 1 S.C.R. 945, at p. 949, Lamer J., as he then was, noted that, "a violation of the sanctity of a person's body is much more serious than that of his office or even of his home". In addition, La Forest J. observed in *R. v. Dyment*, [1988] 2 S.C.R. 417, at p. 431-32, "the use of a person's body without his consent to obtain information about him, invades an area of personal privacy essential to the maintenance of his human dignity". Finally, in *R. v. Simmons*, [1988] 2 S.C.R. 495, at p. 517, Dickson C.J. stated:

> The third and most highly intrusive type of search is that sometimes referred to as the body cavity search, in which customs officers have recourse to medical doctors, to X-rays, to emetics, and to other highly invasive means.

> Searches of the third or bodily cavity type may raise entirely different constitutional issues for it is obvious that the greater the intrusion, the greater must be the justification and the greater the degree of constitutional protection.

It is certainly significant that Parliament has recently amended the *Criminal Code*, through the addition of s. 487.05, so as to create a warrant procedure for the seizure of certain bodily substances for the purposes of DNA testing. This suggests that Parliament has recognized the intrusive nature of seizing bodily samples. The section requires that the police have reasonable and probable grounds, as well as authorization from a judicial officer, before they can make such seizures. If this type of invasive search and seizure came within the common law power of search incident to arrest, it would not have been necessary for the government to create a parallel procedure for the police to follow. In my view, it would be contrary to authority to say that this is no more than a codification of the common law.

(ii) Application to the Facts of this Case

While the appellant was not subjected to a body "cavity" search, the search conducted went far beyond the typical "frisk" search which usually accompanies an arrest. Sergeant Kennedy passed his gloved hand through the appellant's hair to remove some hair, combed some more out, and clipped and pulled out still more. The appellant was then made to pull hair from his own pubic area. A dentist was called in to take the appellant's teeth impressions and buccal swabs. All this was without the appellant's consent and despite his protests. The dental procedure involved the placing of several instruments and various substances into the appellant's mouth. As well, photographs and a video were taken of his mouth. The whole procedure took two hours.

.....

[T]he making of dental impressions ... is a lengthy and highly intrusive process. Further, the taking of the scalp and pubic hair samples involved the forceful removal of hair from the body over the specific objections of the accused. Significantly, in *R. v. Borden*, [1994] 3 S.C.R. 145, it was found that where there is no statutory authorization for the seizure of bodily samples, consent must be obtained if the seizure is to be lawful. Here the police knew they were dealing with a young offender. They were aware that the *Young Offenders Act* required that a parent or counsel should be present when a suspected young offender was being interviewed. Nonetheless, in the absence of any adult counsellor and contrary to the specific instruction of his lawyers, the police interviewed the appellant at length and by threat of force took bodily samples and dental impressions. This was the abusive exercise of raw physical authority by the police.

No matter what may be the pressing temptations to obtain evidence from a person the police believe to be guilty of a terrible crime, and no matter what the past frustrations to their investigations, the police authority to search as an incident to arrest should not be exceeded. Any other conclusion could all too easily lead to police abuses in the name of the good of society as perceived by the officers. When they are carrying out their duties as highly respected and admired agents of the state they must respect the dignity and bodily integrity of all who are arrested. The treatment meted out by agents of the state to even the least deserving individual will often indicate the treatment that all citizens of the state may ultimately expect. Appropriate limits to the power of search incidental to arrest must be accepted and respected.

The power to search and seize incidental to arrest was a pragmatic extension to the power of arrest. Obviously the police must be able to protect themselves from attack by the accused who has weapons concealed on his person or close at hand. The police must be able to collect and preserve evidence located at the site of the arrest or in a nearby motor vehicle. As Rice J.A. put it in his dissenting reasons (at p. 360 N.B.R.):

> The power to search and seize incidental to an arrest is predicated on pragmatic and exigent considerations inherent to the circumstances of an arrest.

The common law power cannot be so broad as to empower police officers to seize bodily samples. They are usually in no danger of disappearing. Here, there was no likelihood that the appellant's teeth impressions would change, nor that his hair follicles would present a different DNA profile with the passage of time. There was simply no possibility of the evidence sought being destroyed if it was not seized immediately. It should be remembered that one of the limitations to the common law power articulated in *Cloutier v. Langlois*, [1990] 1 S.C.R. 158 was the discretionary aspect of the power and that it should not be abusive. The common law power of search incidental to arrest cannot be so broad as to encompass the seizure without valid statutory authority of bodily samples in the face of a refusal to provide them. If it is, then the common law rule itself is unreasonable, since it is too broad and fails to properly balance the competing rights involved.

It is clear that the appellant's right to be free from unreasonable search and seizure was very seriously violated. Since the search and seizure of the bodily samples was not authorized by either statutory or common law it could not have been reasonable. It is thus unnecessary to consider either the reasonableness of the law or the manner in which the search was conducted.

[Cory J. also finds a contravention of s. 7 of the *Charter*.]

(2) The Discarded Tissue

(a) Did the Taking of the Discarded Tissue Contravene Section 8 of the Charter?

The appellant had advised the police, through the letter from his lawyers, that he refused to provide any bodily samples whatsoever. Despite this express refusal, the police seized a tissue, used by the appellant to blow his nose, from the garbage bin in the washroom of the RCMP headquarters. In other words, the police obtained surreptitiously that which the appellant had refused to provide them voluntarily; namely a sample from which his DNA profile could be obtained.

The majority of the Court of Appeal found that when the appellant discarded the unwanted tissue he abandoned it and in so doing, ceased to have a reasonable expectation of privacy in it. In *Dyment*, [1988] 2 S.C.R.

417 the concept of "abandoning" something in which one usually has a privacy expectation was considered. Reference was made to the case of *R. v. LeBlanc* (1981), 64 C.C.C. (2d) 31 (N.B.C.A.), by way of illustration. There, the police, after taking the accused to hospital, obtained a sample of his blood from the front seat of the vehicle. The court held that the police were "gathering" as opposed to seizing the evidence. The accused was said to have abandoned his blood and, in the result, ceased to have a reasonable expectation of privacy with regard to it.

That situation was contrasted with the facts presented in *Dyment* where the doctor who treated the appellant gave the police a sample of the appellant's blood, which he had taken for medical purposes, without the appellant's knowledge or consent. It was found that the appellant retained an expectation of privacy in the sample which continued past the time of its taking and therefore, in seizing the sample, the officer breached the appellant's privacy interests.

There have been a number of cases supporting the proposition that, where a suspect or an accused, while in the presence of the police, discards an item offering potentially valuable DNA evidence, the officers may "gather" that evidence and it will not be considered an unlawful seizure...

.....

In the instant case, counsel for the respondent argued that the mucous sample was obtained by "happenstance", that it was "purely an accidental happening and was not being sought by the police". Counsel for the respondent submitted further that:

> Not only is this *not* a case where the police engineered the taking it is not even a case where the police, by design, deliberately afforded themselves the opportunity to make such observations. What the police did was take advantage of an otherwise unforeseen occurrence. (Emphasis in original.)

The difficulty with this argument is that when an accused person is in custody, the production of bodily samples is not an unforeseen occurrence. It is simply the inevitable consequence of the normal functioning of the human body. The police are only able to profit from the production of the samples because the accused is continuously under their surveillance. For this reason it is somewhat misleading to speak of "abandonment" in the context of evidence obtained from an accused who is in custody.

The appellant had been arrested at the time the tissue was seized, and was being detained. He had exercised his right to refuse to provide the police with bodily samples for the purposes of DNA analysis. Without that consent, the police had no right to take these samples from him. However, in the course of his five-day detention, it is reasonable to presume that, among other things, the appellant would blow his nose, use the toilet, possibly cut himself and bleed, and eat from a spoon. In other words, through "happenstance" the police would be able to take advantage of the appellant's imprisonment to obtain all the samples they needed, but which they could not legally seize in the absence of a valid search warrant. In those circumstances, how can the appellant assert his right not to consent to the provision of bodily samples? He would be required to destroy every tissue he used, to hide every spoon he ate from, to keep cigarette butts, chewed gum or any other potentially incriminating evidence on his person at all times in order to prevent the police from "retrieving" this "potentially useful waste".

R. v. Mellenthin, [1992] 3 S.C.R. 615, at p. 624, set out the requirements for a consent to be considered valid in the context of a search and seizure. Specifically it is, "incumbent upon the Crown to adduce evidence that the person detained had indeed made an informed consent to the search based upon an awareness of his rights to *refuse to respond to the questions or to consent to the search*" (emphasis added). It follows that for consent to be validly given, the accused must have the ability to prevent the police from conducting a search or seizure by withholding his consent. Where the accused is in custody, his announced refusal to consent to providing bodily samples becomes meaningless if, because he is incarcerated, he cannot prevent those samples from being taken.

Obviously an accused person will have a lower expectation of privacy following his or her arrest and subsequent custody. That expectation of privacy will be even lower when serving a sentence after conviction. Therefore, it may well be that certain kinds of searches and seizures may validly be performed on a person in custody which could not validly be performed on persons who have not yet been arrested or convicted. Nevertheless, I am of the view that the appellant's expectation of privacy in this instance, although lower after his arrest, was not so low as to permit the seizure of the tissue. The privacy expectation should not be reduced to such an extent as to justify seizures of bodily samples without consent, particularly for those who are detained while they are still presumed to be innocent.

Thus, where an accused who is not in custody discards a kleenex or cigarette butt, the police may ordinarily collect and test these items without any concern about consent. A different situation is presented when an accused in custody discards items containing bodily fluids. Obviously an accused in custody cannot prevent the authorities from taking possession of these items. Whether the circumstances were such that the accused had abandoned the items and relinquished any privacy interest in them will have to be determined on the particular facts presented in each case.

However, in this case, the accused had announced through his lawyers that he would not consent to the taking of any samples of his bodily fluids. The police were aware of his decision. Despite this they took possession of the tissue discarded by the appellant while he was in custody. In these circumstances the seizure was unreasonable and violated the appellant's s. 8 *Charter* rights.

.....

It is now necessary to consider whether the lower courts were correct in admitting the evidence of the hair samples, dental impressions and tissue containing mucous pursuant to the provisions of s. 24(2) of the *Charter*.

B. Section 24(2) of the Charter

(1) <u>The Hair Samples, Dental Impressions and Buccal Swabs</u>

It is clear that the seizures of the hair samples, dental impressions and buccal swabs violated s. 8 of the *Charter*. In my view, they also breached s. 7 since they violated the right to security of the person in a manner not consistent with the principles of fundamental justice. The evidence was obtained as a result of the *Charter* violation and s. 24(2) is thereby triggered.

It has been held that appellate courts should only intervene with respect to a lower court's s. 24(2) analysis when that court has made "some apparent error as to the applicable principles or rules of law" or has made an unreasonable finding: *R. v. Duguay*, [1989] 1 S.C.R. 93; *Mellenthin, supra*. The majority of the Court of Appeal of New Brunswick found that, in admitting the impugned evidence, the trial judge considered the appropriate principles and performed a correct analysis of the factors outlined in *Collins, supra*. With respect, I cannot agree.

The factors outlined by this Court in the trail blazing decision of *Collins* can be divided into three groups based on their effect on the repute of the administration of justice. The first of these categories includes those factors which relate to the fairness of the trial; the second group pertains to the seriousness of the *Charter* violation; and the third group concerns the possibility that the administration of justice could be brought into disrepute by excluding the evidence even though it was obtained in violation of the *Charter*. In my view, the trial judge erred in his consideration of the first two factors.

In considering how the admission of the evidence would affect the fairness of the trial, the trial judge erred in concluding that the hair samples and dental impressions existed independently of any *Charter* breach and were thus admissible. Certainly the appellant's hair samples, dental patterns and saliva existed as "real" evidence. However, the trial judge failed to appreciate the significance of the inescapable conclusion that, in violation of his *Charter* rights, the appellant was conscripted or forced by the police to provide evidence from his body thus incriminating himself. I have used the term "conscripted" to describe the situation where the police have compelled the accused to participate in providing self-incriminating evidence in the form of a confession or providing bodily samples. It is a term that has been used in other decisions of the Court, including *Collins*, to describe self-incriminating evidence obtained as a result of a *Charter* breach. In the circumstances, it was unnecessary and inappropriate to consider the seriousness of the breach. However, when he did so, the trial judge focussed exclusively on the conduct of the police. While police conduct is certainly one factor to be considered under this heading, it is not the only consideration. Here it was essential that other factors be considered. It is thus apparent that the trial judge erred in his appreciation and application of the proper legal principles to be considered in applying s. 24(2), and that the admissibility of the impugned evidence must be reconsidered.

There can be no question that the *Collins* decision was the pathfinder that first charted the route that courts should follow when considering the application of s. 24(2). However, subsequent decisions of this Court and their interpretations by the courts below indicate that a further plotting of the course for courts to follow is required, while maintaining the basic principles outlined in *Collins*. For example, confusion has arisen as to what constitutes "real" evidence and in what circumstances its exclusion or admission would render the trial unfair. Perhaps the ensuing review of some decisions and proposed procedure for classifying evidence will be of some assistance.

(a) Fairness of the Trial

A consideration of trial fairness is of fundamental importance. If after careful consideration it is determined that the admission of evidence obtained in violation of a *Charter* right would render a trial unfair then the evidence must be excluded without consideration ofthe other *Collins* factors...

[An extended analysis follows.]

.....

Perhaps it would be helpful to set out a summary of the approach that should be taken when the trial fairness factor is being considered.

(iii) Trial Fairness Summary

A simple method by which trial judges may approach the trial fairness factor is to divide the analysis into two steps. First, the evidence must be classified as either "conscriptive" or "non-conscriptive." The classification will be based on the manner in which the evidence was obtained.

Classification

If the evidence, obtained in a manner which violates the *Charter*, involved the accused being compelled to incriminate himself either by a statement or the use as evidence of the body or of bodily substances it will be classified as conscriptive evidence. See *Manninen, supra*; *Ross* [[1989] 1 S.C.R. 3], and *Bartle*, [[1994] 3 S.C.R. 173]. On the other hand, if the evidence, obtained in a manner which violates the *Charter*, did not involve the accused being compelled to incriminate himself either by a statement or the use as evidence of the body or of bodily substances it will be classified as non-conscriptive evidence. See *R. v. Silveira*, [1995] 2 S.C.R. 297, and *Evans* [[1996] 1 S.C.R. 8].

Conscripted or self-incriminating evidence may lead to what has been termed derivative evidence. This phrase has been used to describe "real" evidence which has been "derived" from, that is to say found as a result of, the conscriptive evidence. The evidence discovered should be classified as conscriptive, since the accused's compelled statement was a necessary cause of its discovery. In those cases, the courts must carefully review the events leading up to the finding of the evidence rather than simply considering whether the ultimate piece of evidence which the Crown is seeking to introduce is "real" evidence. As an example of derivative evidence that was conscripted from the accused, see *Burlingham* [[1995] 2 S.C.R. 206].

Where evidence is determined to be non-conscriptive, its admission generally will not render the trial unfair and the court should proceed to consider the seriousness of the violation. However, where evidence is found to be of a conscriptive nature the court must proceed to the second step, which involves an assessment of whether the evidence would have been discovered in the absence of (but for) the *Charter* violation.

Discoverability

There are two bases upon which it may be demonstrated that the evidence would have been discovered absent a *Charter* violation: (a) if the evidence would have been obtained, in any event, from an *independent source*; in other words, there were alternative non-conscriptive means by which the police could have seized the evidence and the Crown has established, on a balance of probabilities, that the police would have availed themselves of those means (see, for example, *Colarusso* [[1994] 1 S.C.R. 20]); or (b) if the evidence would inevitably have been discovered. See, for example, *Black* [[1989] 2 S.C.R. 138], and *R. v. Harper*, [1994] 3 S.C.R. 343. In both circumstances, even though it is conscriptive evidence, the probability of its discovery means that its admission will not render the trial unfair. However, in determining the admissibility of the evidence that would have been discovered by the alternative means, the court will have to consider the seriousness of the *Charter* breach and the effect of exclusion on the repute of the administration of justice.

On the other hand, there will be cases where the evidence would not have been discovered in the absence of the conscription of the accused in violation of the *Charter*. In those situations it will be apparent that the police could not have obtained the evidence in the absence of the unlawful conscription of the accused. See as examples, *Burlingham, supra*, and *Borden, supra*.

Therefore, where the conscriptive evidence would not have been discovered in the absence of the unlawful conscription of the accused, its admission would generally tend to render the trial unfair. In those circumstances it is not necessary to consider the seriousness of the violation, or the repute of the administration of justice, as a finding that the admission of the evidence would render the trial unfair means that the administration of justice would necessarily be brought into disrepute if the evidence were not excluded under s. 24(2): *R. v. Hebert*, [1990] 2 S.C.R. 151; *Mellenthin, supra*.

The summary itself can be reduced to this short form:

1. Classify the evidence as conscriptive or non-conscriptive based upon the manner in which the evidence was obtained. If the evidence is non-conscriptive, its admission will not render the trial unfair and the court will proceed to consider the seriousness of the breach and the effect of exclusion on the repute of the administration of justice.

2. If the evidence is conscriptive and the Crown fails to demonstrate on a balance of probabilities that the evidence would have been discovered by alternative non-conscriptive means, then its admission will render the trial unfair. The Court, as a general rule, will exclude the evidence without considering the seriousness of the breach or the effect of exclusion on the repute of the administration of justice. This must be the result since an unfair trial would necessarily bring the administration of justice into disrepute.

3. If the evidence is found to be conscriptive and the Crown demonstrates on abalance of probabilities that it would have been discovered by alternative non-conscriptive means, then its admission will generally not render the trial unfair. However, the seriousness of the *Charter* breach and the effect of exclusion on the repute of the administration of justice will have to be considered.

(iv) Application of the Principles Discussed to this Case

The Samples of Hair, the Dental Impression and Buccal Swabs: Was this Evidence Conscripted From the Appellant?

The police had no right to obtain the hair samples, teeth impressions or buccal swabs from the appellant without his informed consent. The appellant clearly expressed his refusal to provide bodily samples. Yet, by threat of force the police obtained the sample of scalp hair, buccal swabs and compelled the appellant to pluck his pubic hair to provide as a sample. They proceeded with the lengthy and intrusive process of taking impressions of his teeth. There can be no doubt that the police, by their words and actions, compelled the appellant to participate in providing the evidence. Equally there can be no doubt that the evidence of bodily samples constituted conscriptive evidence.

As Iacobucci J. noted in *R. v. S. (R.J.)*, [1995] 1 S.C.R. 451, "Physical objects, observations, and bodily fluids may exist prior to a *Charter* breach, but they do not exist *as evidence* unless the state has a means to acquire them for trial" (para. 138 (emphasis in original)).

Would the Evidence Have Been Discovered in the Absence of the Unlawful Conscription of the Accused?

It is apparent that the impugned evidence would not have been discovered had it not been for the conscription of the accused in violation of s. 7 and s. 8 of the *Charter*. The appellant was not obliged to provide the hair samples, teeth impressions or buccal swabs. His *Charter* guarantee of security of the person and the inviolability of his body meant that in the absence of statutory authority the Crown could not undertake the impugned procedure. Quite simply, the police could not, in the absence of valid statutory authority, lawfully obtain the samples without his consent. No independent source existed by which the police could have obtained the impugned evidence. Since the appellant expressly refused to consent to provide samples, the evidence was not discoverable by the state without the conscription of the accused in violation of the *Charter*. It follows that the admission of the evidence would render the trial unfair. This finding is sufficient to resolve the s. 24(2) issue as the evidence must be excluded: *Hebert, supra*. However, something should be said of the seriousness of the *Charter* violation which occurred in this case.

(b) Seriousness of the Charter Violation

The violations of ss. 7 and 8 of the *Charter*, pursuant to which this evidence was obtained, were of a very serious nature. The police acted with blatant disregard for the fundamental rights of the appellant. Notwithstanding the appellant's express refusal to provide bodily samples or to give a statement, the police purposely waited until the appellant's lawyers had left and then immediately proceeded, through the use of force, threats and coercion to take his bodily samples and to interrogate him in an effort to obtain a statement. They pulled and cut samples of the appellant's scalp hair and made him pull his own pubic hair. They forced a plasticine mold into his mouth in order to obtain dental impressions and later, had a dentist conduct a two hour procedure to take more accurate impressions.

Reprehensible as these actions were in themselves they become intolerable in these circumstances when the police were aware that the appellant was a young offender at the time, and that he was entitled to the special protection provided by the *Young Offenders Act*. The police knew the Act provides that a young person must be given a reasonable opportunity to have a lawyer, a parent, or a chosen adult present when the police seek to take a statement. All this was flagrantly disregarded.

The respondent argued that the police acted in good faith since they asked the Crown Attorney whether they had authority to seize bodily samples. I cannot accept this submission. The police were aware that, without the DNA evidence, they did not have enough to charge the appellant with murder. Under the circumstances, the comments of Sopinka J. in *R. v. Kokesch*, [1990] 3 S.C.R. 3, at p. 28, are apposite:

> ... the unavailability of other, constitutionally permissible, investigative techniques is neither an excuse nor a justification for constitutionally impermissible investigative techniques.

(c) The Administration of Justice

The *Charter* rights of the accused were infringed by the actions of the police. Those actions could be taken to be abusive. It is easy to understand the sense of frustration of the police officers. They were attempting to obtain evidence implicating the person they suspected had murdered a young girl. Yet *Charter* rights are the rights of all people in Canada. They cannot be simply suspended when the police are dealing with those suspected of committing serious crimes. Frustrating and aggravating as it may seem, the police as respected and admired agents of our country, must respect the *Charter* rights of all individuals, even those who appear to be the least worthy of respect. Anything less must be unacceptable to the courts. The words of Iacobucci J. in *Burlingham, supra*, at para. 30, bear repeating:

> ... we should never lose sight of the fact that even a person accused of the most heinous crimes, and no matter the likelihood that he or she actually committed those crimes, is entitled to the full protection of the *Charter*. Short-cutting or short-circuiting those rights affects not only the accused but also the entire reputation of the criminal justice system. It must be emphasized that the goals of preserving the integrity of the criminal justice system as well as promoting the decency of investigatory techniques are of fundamental importance in applying s. 24(2).

In this case, it would certainly shock the conscience of all fair minded members of the community that the police rode roughshod over a young offender's refusal to provide his bodily samples. As a result, the evidence of the hair samples, dental impressions and buccal swabs must be excluded.

(2) <u>The Tissue Containing Mucous</u>

In contrast to the hair samples, teeth impressions and buccal swabs, the police did not force, or even request, a mucous sample from the appellant. He blew his nose of his own accord. The police acted surreptitiously in disregard for the appellant's explicit refusal to provide them with bodily samples. However, the violation of the appellant's *Charter* rights with respect to the tissue was not serious. The seizure did not interfere with the appellant's bodily integrity, nor cause him any loss of dignity. In any event, the police could and would have obtained the discarded tissue. They would have had reasonable and probable grounds to believe that the tissue would provide evidence in their investigation and therefore would have sealed the garbage container and obtained a search warrant in order to recover its contents. Quite simply, it was discoverable. In my view, the administration of justice would not be brought into disrepute if the evidence obtained from the mucous sample were to be admitted.

.....

[Major J. agrees with Cory J.'s reasons excluding the conscripted evidence obtained from hair samples, buccal swabs, and dental impressions. He did not agree that the tissue containing the mucous sample taken from the waste basket was obtained in violation of s. 8 of the *Charter*.]

[L'Heureux-Dubé, Gonthier and McLachlin JJ. dissented.]

QUESTION

9. The accused confesses to a murder in Nova Scotia. Having confessed, she then tells the police where the murder weapon is. She takes the police to the weapon which is wedged into a glacier crevice near the North Pole. She then advises the police that she also admitted her guilt to a veterinarian she met at a bus stop in Red Deer, Alberta. That person is ultimately located by the police. He indicates that he would never have come forward on his own because he "doesn't like to get involved", but confirms that the accused did admit her guilt to him. It is clear that the confession was obtained in violation of the accused's s. 10(*b*) rights. Nonetheless, the Crown seeks to tender the murder weapon, the circumstances of its recovery, and the veterinarian's evidence. How does each piece of evidence fit into the conscriptive-real evidence dichotomy? What considerations should affect its admissibility?

Much attention has been directed to the conscriptive-real evidence characterization and the doctrine of discoverability since the Supreme Court has tied these issues so closely to trial fairness and thus, to exclusion. However, what has sometimes been overlooked is that the Supreme Court's pronouncements on the second group of *Collins* factors may arguably mandate exclusion in many cases where trial fairness is not implicated.

R. v. KOKESCH

(1990), 61 C.C.C. (3d) 207 (S.C.C.)

[The Court unanimously held that an officer trespassing onto the accused's property and peering into windows to confirm mere suspicions as to drug cultivating thereby conducted an unreasonable perimeter search. The Court was sharply divided on the application of s. 24(2) of the *Charter*. The majority judgment of Sopinka J. (Wilson, La Forest, and McLachlin JJ. concurring) provided an important interpretation of "good faith" and the significance of "the lack of availability of other investigative techniques", both relevant to the seriousness of the violation, the second group of *Collins* factors.]

Sopinka J.: — I have had the benefit of reading the reasons for judgment prepared in this appeal by Chief Justice Dickson, and I agree with him, for the reasons he gives, that the warrantless perimeter search conducted in this case was unlawful and therefore unreasonable within the meaning of s. 8 of the *Canadian Charter of Rights and Freedoms*. I agree also that this is a proper case for this court to consider *de novo* the question of the admissibility under s. 24(2) of the evidence obtained as a consequence of the search. I must, however, respectfully disagree with Chief Justice Dickson's conclusion that the evidence in this case ought not to be excluded.

.....

Upon considering the facts of the present case, I have concluded that the police conduct at issue represents an extremely serious *Charter* violation, from several perspectives. I should point out at the outset that I agree with Chief Justice Dickson that Judge Cashman may have placed too great an emphasis on the availability of other investigative techniques. I cannot, however, draw the same conclusion from that error that Chief Justice Dickson appears to draw. Chief Justice Dickson states: "it was the paucity of other investigative techniques that provoked the actions of the police and this fact does not necessarily militate against the admission of the evidence" (p. 17) [*ante*, p. 221]. Later in his reasons, Chief Justice Dickson cites this factor as support for the view that the *Charter* violation here was not serious: "The motivation behind the *Charter* infringement was to obtain evidence in a situation in which other avenues of investigation seemed to have been foreclosed" (p. 23) [*ante*, p. 224]. Of course, the reason why other investigative techniques were unavailable is that the police did not have the requisite grounds to obtain either a search warrant or an authorization to intercept private communications pursuant to the *Criminal Code*.

In my respectful view, the unavailability of other, constitutionally permissible, investigative techniques is neither an excuse nor a justification for constitutionally impermissible investigative techniques. In *R. v. Dyment* (1988), 45 C.C.C. (3d) 244, 55 D.L.R. (4th) 503, [1988] 2 S.C.R. 417, La Forest J. (Dickson C.J.C. concurring) reiterated the requirement in *Hunter v. Southam Inc.* (1984), 14 C.C.C. (3d) 97, 11 D.L.R. (4th) 641, [1984] 2 S.C.R. 145, that where feasible a warrant must be obtained, and stated, at p. 261:

> ... when the facts are scrutinized, the most probable reason why no warrant was obtained was because the officer *lacked* the requisite belief that the ac-

> cused had committed an offence and that the seizure was likely to yield evidence which was probative of that offence. Not only do the circumstances not reveal circumstances capable of justifying the failure to obtain a warrant, but the conduct of the police failed to comport with the minimal constitutional requirement that there be reasonable and probable grounds to believe that the search would yield evidence.

(Emphasis in original.)

Where the police have nothing but suspicion and no legal way to obtain other evidence, it follows that they must leave the suspect alone, not charge ahead and obtain evidence illegally and unconstitutionally. Where they take this latter course, the *Charter* violation is plainly more serious than it would be otherwise, not less. Any other conclusion leads to an indirect but substantial erosion of the *Hunter* standards: the Crown would happily concede s. 8 violations if they could routinely achieve admission under s. 24(2) with the claim that the police did not obtain a warrant *because* they did not have reasonable and probable grounds. The irony of this result is self-evident. It should not be forgotten that *ex post facto* justification of searches by their results is precisely what the *Hunter* standards were designed to prevent: see *Hunter, supra, per* Dickson J. (as he then was), at p. 109; and *Greffe, supra, per* Lamer J., at pp. 187-8 and 193-4.

From the point of view of individual privacy, which is the essential value protected by s. 8 of the *Charter*, this illegal intrusion onto private property must be seen as far from trivial or minimal. Even before the enactment of the *Charter*, individuals were entitled to expect that their environs would be free of prowling government officials unless and until the conditions for the exercise of legal authority are met: see *Eccles v. Bourque* (1974), 19 C.C.C. (2d) 129, 50 D.L.R. (3d) 753 [1975] 2 S.C.R. 739; and *Colet v. The Queen* (1981), 57 C.C.C. (2d) 105, 119 D.L.R. (3d) 521, [1981] 1 S.C.R. 2. The elevation of that protection to the constitutional level signifies its deep roots in our legal culture. La Forest J. put it this way in *Dyment, supra*, in words that commend themselves to me (at p. 254):

> Grounded in man's physical and moral autonomy, privacy is essential for the well-being of the individual. For this reason alone, it is worthy of constitutional protection, but it also has profound significance for the public order. The restraints imposed on government to pry into the lives of the citizen go to the essence of a democratic state.

An equally important aspect of the seriousness of the violation is the manner in which the police conducted themselves in deciding to execute this warrantless perimeter search. Was the s. 8 violation committed in "good faith", or was it "flagrant"? Both are terms of art in s. 24(2) cases. To decide whether either term is appropriate in the circumstances it is necessary to examine the evidence given at the preliminary hearing and read in on the s. 24(2) application at trial. The relevant portion of the cross-examination of Constable Povarchook reads as follows:

> Q: On November the fourth, when you went to the property and sniffed around, if I can say that, you didn't have a search warrant did you?
>
> A: No, I did not.

Q: At that time all you had was a suspicion that there was something going on in the house? You had no reasonable or probable grounds at that point did you?

A: Well, that fact is a matter of opinion.

Q: I'm asking your opinion. Did you have reasonable and probable grounds?

A: I did, Your Honour.

Q: Why didn't you go and get a search warrant?

A: *I don't believe I had enough to get a search warrant to enter the residence.*

Q: Did you believe on November 4, 1986 that you had reasonable and probable grounds to believe that an offense had been committed on the property under the Narcotic Control Act before you went to the property?

A: Your Honour, I believed —

Q: Can you just answer the question, please, Constable?

A: Can you re-ask the question?

Q: I'll have it read back, if you like.

(COURT REPORTER READS BACK AS REQUESTED)

Q: I note that you are taking your time. Do you have trouble understanding the question? Is your answer yes or no? Is that a yes or no?

A: No, with a qualification.

Q: It is a no with a qualification. You did not believe that you had reasonable and probable grounds before you went on November 4, 1986.

A: I did not have reasonable and probable grounds to believe that there was an offense being committed. I had a suspicion.

Q: Surely, you must have suspected something to go there?

A: *Well, I had more than just suspicion. I had solid grounds, but not enough for a search warrant.*

Q: Were you invited onto the property on November 4, 1986?

A: No, I was not, Your Honour.

Q: Did you have any authority to go onto the property on November 4, 1986?

A: Any authority?

Q: Any authority.

A: Well, I was in the execution of my duties. Whether or not that's authority or not, I'm not sure.

Q: That is the only authority you can think of?

A: Yes.

Q: You weren't chasing a felon? You weren't after someone who was in the process of — someone committing an indictable offense.

A: No, I was not.

Q: You didn't believe you had to go on to the property immediately on November fourth to preserve evidence did you?

A: No, I did not.

(Emphasis added.)

With respect to those who hold a contrary view, I cannot find that this state of affairs constitutes good faith capable of mitigating the seriousness of the s. 8 violation that occurred here. Judge Cashman, however, expressly found that there was good faith. He stated:

> From what I have heard in this case, I have no reason to doubt what Constable Povarchook did on November 4th at two o'clock in the morning he did in good faith, *albeit one may well view his procedure as somewhat of a short-cut in obtaining the evidence necessary to found a search warrant.*

(Emphasis added.)

This finding is vulnerable on two grounds. First, on its own terms, the finding of good faith is equivocal. The "shortcut" referred to in the emphasized passage was a search conducted in the knowledge that legal search powers were unavailable. The evidence clearly discloses that the police officers knew that they had insufficient grounds either to exercise the power to search without a warrant granted by s. 10(1)(*a*) of the *Narcotic Control Act*, or to obtain a search warrant pursuant to s. 10(2). The best answer provided to the question of any alternative source of lawful authority was a tentative "I'm not sure."

Secondly, even if Judge Cashman found that the constable honestly but mistakenly believed that he had the power to search, it is my view that in these circumstances the constable simply cannot be heard to say that he misapprehended the scope of his authority. As Chief Justice Dickson has amply demonstrated in his reasons in this appeal, "[t]his court consistently has held that the common law rights of the property holder to be free of police intrusion can be restricted only by powers granted in clear statutory language" (p. 13) [*ante*, p. 218]. The contrary contention is, in Chief Justice Dickson's words, "without foundation". The police must be taken to be aware of this court's judgments in *Eccles* and *Colet*, and the circumscription of police powers that those judgments represent.

Either the police knew they were trespassing, or they ought to have known. Whichever is the case, they cannot be said to have proceeded in "good faith", as that term is understood in s. 24(2) jurisprudence. I find support for this conclusion in *R. v. Genest*, (1989), 45 C.C.C. (3d) 385, [1989] 1 S.C.R. 59, 67 C.R. (3d) 224, in which Chief Justice Dickson, speaking for the court, held that the Crown could not argue that the police officers' failure to recognize obvious defects in a search warrant was inadvertent. Even in the absence of evidence of bad faith, the seriousness of the *Charter* violation in that case was enhanced, because "the defects in the search warrant were serious and the police officers *should have noticed them*"

(Emphasis added, p. 406); and later: "Well-established common law limitations on the powers of the police to search were ignored" (p. 409). In his reasons in this case, the Chief Justice points out that the error made by the police officer as to his authority to search was shared by a unanimous Court of Appeal. I do not agree. The Court of Appeal expressly found that the conduct of the police constituted a trespass but that in all the circumstances, this did not constitute an unreasonable search and seizure.

I do not wish to be understood as imposing upon the police a burden of instant interpretation of court decisions. The question of the length of time after a judgment that ought to be permitted to pass before knowledge of its content is attributed to the police for the purposes of assessing good faith is an interesting one, but it does not arise on these facts. The police here had the benefit of slightly more than 12 years to study *Eccles*, slightly less than six years to consider *Colet*, and slightly more than two years to digest the constitutional warrant requirement set out in *Hunter*. Any doubt they may have had about their ability to trespass in the absence of specific statutory authority to do so was manifestly unreasonable, and cannot, as a matter of law, be relied upon as good faith for the purposes of s. 24(2).

There is, in my opinion, a world of difference between the police conduct said to constitute good faith in this case and the police conduct endorsed by this court in *R. v. Sieben* (1987), 32 C.C.C. (3d) 574, 38 D.L.R. (4th) 427, [1987] 1 S.C.R. 295; *R. v. Hamill* (1987), 33 C.C.C. (3d) 110, 38 D.L.R. (4th) 611, [1987] 1 S.C.R. 301; *R. v. Duarte* (1990), 53 C.C.C. (3d) 1, 65 D.L.R. (4th) 240, [1990] 1 S.C.R. 30; and *R. v. Wiggins* (1990), 53 C.C.C. (3d) 476, [1990] 1 S.C.R. 62, 74 C.R. (3d) 311. In each of those cases, the police acted pursuant to express statutory authority that rendered the particular search lawful. The police are entitled, indeed they have a duty, to assume that the search powers granted to them by Parliament are constitutionally valid, and to act accordingly. The police cannot be expected to predict the outcome of *Charter* challenges to their statutory search powers, and the success of a challenge to such a power does not vitiate the good faith of police officers who conducted a search pursuant to the power. Where, however, police powers are already constrained by statute or judicial decisions, it is not open to a police officer to test the limits by ignoring the constraint and claiming later to have been "in the execution of my duties". This excuse has been obsolete since, at least, the decision of this court in *Colet* (see Ritchie J., at p. 111).

In conclusion on this point, the *Charter* violation at issue was very serious, and was in no sense mitigated by good faith on the part of the investigating officers.

Effect of exclusion on the reputation of the administration of justice

The final category of factors to be considered under s. 24(2) concerns the effect that judicial exclusion of relevant and probative evidence could have on the reputation of the administration of justice. If exclusion would occasion greater disrepute than admission, then the impugned evidence ought to be admitted: see *Collins, supra*, at pp. 20-1.

The offences with which the appellant is charged are serious offences, though narcotics offences involving marijuana are generally regarded as less serious than those involving "hard" drugs such as cocaine and heroin. The appellant would seem to be plainly guilty, and the impugned evidence is required for a conviction. It cannot be denied that the administration of justice could suffer some degree of disrepute from the exclusion of this evidence.

However, I have concluded, not without reluctance, that the administration of justice would suffer far greater disrepute from the admission of this evidence than from its exclusion. This court must not be seen to condone deliberate unlawful conduct designed to subvert both the legal and constitutional limits of police power to intrude on individual privacy. As Chief Justice Dickson stated in *Genest, supra*, at p. 410: "...the breach was not merely technical or minor". The violation of s. 8 of the *Charter* that occurred in this case must be regarded as flagrant, and the disrepute to the justice system that would necessarily result from the admission of the impugned evidence cannot be counterbalanced by speculation about the disrepute that might flow from its exclusion.

Conclusion

In view of the foregoing, the evidence must be excluded pursuant to s. 24(2) of the *Charter*. I would, therefore, allow the appeal and restore the acquittal.

[Dickson C.J.C. (L'Heureux-Dubé and Cory JJ. concurring) dissented.]

R. v. SILVEIRA

(1995), 97 C.C.C. (3d) 450 (S.C.C.)

[The Supreme Court of Canada's decision in *R. v. Silveira* was substantially reproduced in Chapter 4, at p. 163. One portion of Cory J.'s majority judgment, further constraining any finding of "good faith" should be revisited here.]

Cory J.: —

.....

Yet, s. 24(2) of the *Charter* should not be used as a matter of course to excuse conduct which has in the past been found to be unlawful. This case has confirmed that to enter and search a dwelling-house without a warrant constitutes a very serious breach of the *Narcotic Control Act* and the historic inviolability of a dwelling-place. Therefore, in the future, even if such exigent circumstances exist, the evidence would likely be found inadmissible under s. 24(2). It is difficult to envisage how the admission of the evidence could not bring the administration of justice into disrepute since in subsequent cases, it will be very difficult for the police to claim that they acted in good faith if they entered the dwelling without prior judicial authorization. The police must now know that exigent circumstances do not provide an excuse for failing to obtain a warrant. It is up to Parliament to amend s. 10 if it wishes to provide for exceptions to the warrant requirement. Although I do not wish to foreclose the possibility that the evidence may still be admitted under s. 24(2), it will only occur in rare cases.

In *R. v. Burton*, substantially reproduced at p. 799, the trial judge found that one officer's explanation of his conduct given on the *Charter* motion was a concoction. The Ontario Court of Appeal held that the trial judge was entitled to consider the conduct of the officers at the arrest and thereafter, *including the manner of their testimony before him when reflecting upon the public's perception of their conduct.*

F. ADJOURNMENT OF TRIAL

Section 571 (non-jury trials) and s. 645(1)-(3) (jury trials) confer discretion upon the presiding judge as to whether to adjourn a trial or a continuation thereof.

QUESTION

10. What are the factors that a trial judge must consider when deciding whether to grant an adjournment when witnesses are absent? Consider, in this regard, *Darville v. The Queen* (1956), 166 C.C.C. 113 (S.C.C.).

G. PRESENCE OF THE ACCUSED AT TRIAL

For all indictable trials, the accused, other than a corporation, must be present for the entire trial, subject to these exceptions: under certain specified conditions, the accused may appear by counsel or by closed circuit television for parts of the trial where evidence is not being taken (s. 650(1.1) and (1.2) of the *Code*); the accused may be removed for certain misconduct (s. 650(2)(*a*)); the accused may be absent during a fitness hearing which might adversely affect the accused's mental condition (s. 650(2)(*c*)); or the accused may be permitted to be absent during any part of the trial on such conditions as may be imposed by the court (s. 650(*b*)). A corporation may appear by counsel or by an agent (ss. 556(1) and 620 of the *Criminal Code*).

A recent amendment to the *Criminal Code* now permits an accused to appoint counsel to represent the accused by filing a designation with the court. If a designation is filed, the accused may appear by the designated counsel without being present for any part of the proceedings, other than a part during which oral evidence is taken, jurors are selected, and an application for *habeas corpus*. An accused must also be present for a plea of guilty and the pronouncement of sentence, unless the court otherwise orders: s. 650.01 of the *Criminal Code*. The designation is unnecessary for summary conviction offences or hybrid offences where the Crown has elected summarily. For summary conviction offences, a defendant may appear throughout, unless otherwise ordered, by counsel or agent: s. 800(2) of the *Criminal Code*.

QUESTIONS

11. The accused's jury trial before Justice Ogre commences. Justice Ogre rules on 17 consecutive motions in favour of the Crown. As well, the ac-

cused's defence counsel is conducting his first jury trial and responds to damaging evidence by whistling the overture to The Magic Flute. On the fifth day of trial, the accused does not attend. Calls to his landlord determine that his apartment has been emptied of its contents except for a travel brochure for Guam. What procedures follow? Now assume that the accused was also president of the co-accused company. What procedures obtain respecting the company's charges? Consider, in this regard, ss. 475, 556(2), 598 and 622 of the *Criminal Code*; *R. v. Lee* (1989), 52 C.C.C. (3d) 289 (S.C.C.); *R. v. Harris* (1991), 66 C.C.C. (3d) 536 (Ont. C.A.).

12. Prior to trial, many courts will issue a bench warrant with discretion or a bench warrant returnable on a future date. When will these be employed? Note in this regard, ss. 511(3)-(4) and 597(4)-(5).

13. Can a designation of counsel include agents and law students? Consider, in this regard, *R. v. Golyanik* (2003), 63 O.R. (3d) 276 (S.C.J.).

H. THE WITHDRAWAL OF CHARGES AND STAYS OF PROCEEDINGS

Frequently, the Crown chooses not to proceed on a charge against an accused. This may reflect, *inter alia*, the exercise of discretion based upon the absence of a reasonable prospect of conviction, the unavailability of a crucial witness, the Crown's decision to alter the accused's status from accused to witness, the culmination of a plea negotiation where pleas of guilt will be entered to other charges, or an agreement that the accused's charge will be "diverted", or dealt with by way of a "peace bond" rather than through criminal prosecution.

Generally, the Crown is permitted to withdraw as of right prior to plea and thereafter, with leave of the court.

QUESTION

14. Sometimes the defence will attempt to prevail upon the Crown to exercise its discretion to have the accused arraigned, plead not guilty and, thereafter, to lead no evidence and thereby cause the court to acquit the accused, rather than simply withdrawing the charge. Why? In some jurisdictions, the court will agree, upon application of the defence, to this procedure, even over the Crown's objection. Is there jurisdiction for the court to do so?

Sometimes, private citizens will swear informations before a justice of the peace, in circumstances where the police have declined to lay a charge. The Crown may exercise its discretion to intervene and prosecute the charge or withdraw the charge.

QUESTION

15. Can the Crown decline to intervene where the offence is indictable? Can a private citizen prosecute an indictable offence? How does this compare to a summary conviction proceeding? See Chapter 9, *infra*.

For indictable offences, the Attorney General, or counsel instructed by him or her for that purpose, may direct the clerk to stay the proceedings against the accused (s. 579 of the *Criminal Code*). This should not be confused with a judicial stay of proceedings, which is imposed by the court, almost invariably over the Crown's objection.

QUESTION

16. How is a s. 579 stay different than a withdrawal of charges?

Sometimes, a motion for a judicial stay is based upon an alleged undertaking by the Crown or upon conduct by the police or complainants indicating an intention not to proceed against the accused. When is the Crown bound not to proceed against the accused? When will the court preclude the Crown from proceeding? The following case reviews some of the law on these issues.

R. v. D.(E.)

(1990), 57 C.C.C. (3d) 151 (Ont. C.A.)

[The accused was alleged to have committed sexual offences against the 11- and 12-year-old daughters of his then common law wife, between 1978 and 1983. Their mother learned of the allegations in 1984 and informed the police, who met with a lawyer retained by her. In their meetings, it was agreed that the police would not proceed with charges if the mother assured the police that the complainants would have no contact with the accused, that the family other than the accused would continue counselling and that the police would be advised if the accused bothered the family. The officer then spoke to the accused on a "non-cautioned, no-charge basis", intending to place him on the sexual abuse register. The accused made some admissions referable to the older complainant only. He was told there would be no charges and to stay away from the complainants. He complied thereafter. After counselling, the older complainant decided that she wanted to press charges and four years later, charges were laid. Though the facts were not presented to the trial judge in the most appropriate way, he acted upon the above noted facts and directed a stay of proceedings.]

The judgment of the court was delivered by

Arbour J.A.: —

.....

Ultimately, the trial judge ordered the charges stayed on the basis that to proceed against the accused in the circumstances would constitute an abuse of process.

[Arbour J.A. finds that the trial judge was correct in holding that s.11(*b*) of the *Charter* was not violated due to the pre-charge delay and further, that s. 11(*d*) had not been shown to obtain at this stage of the proceedings.]

However, in my view, the learned trial judge erred in his conclusion that to proceed against the accused in the circumstances would constitute an abuse of process.

After some years of uncertainty, the guiding principles respecting abuse of process have now been clearly stated. They were articulated recently by the Supreme Court of Canada in *R. v. Keyowski* (1988), 40 C.C.C. (3d) 481, [1988] 1 S.C.R. 657, 62 C.R. (3d) 349, where Wilson J., for the court said [at p. 482]:

> The availability of a stay of proceedings to remedy an abuse of process was confirmed by this court in *R. v. Jewitt* (1985), 21 C.C.C. (3d) 7, 10 D.L.R. (4th) 651, [1985] 2 S.C.R. 128. On that occasion the court stated that the test for abuse of process was that initially formulated by the Ontario Court of Appeal in *R. v. Young* (1984), 13 C.C.C. (3d) 1, 46 O.R. (2d) 520, 40 C.R. (3d) 289. A stay should be granted where "compelling an accused to stand trial would violate those fundamental principles of justice which underlie the community's sense of fair play and decency", or where the proceedings are "oppressive or vexatious" (21 C.C.C. (3d) 7 at p. 14, 20 D.L.R. (4th) 651 at p. 658, [1985] 2 S.C.R. 128 at pp. 136-7). The court in *Jewitt* also adopted "the caveat added by the Court in *Young* that this is a power which can be exercised only in the 'clearest of cases'" (p. 14 C.C.C., p. 659 D.L.R., p. 137 S.C.R.).

.....

In *Keyowski*, the alleged abuse consisted of the Crown proceeding with a third trial of the accused, after the jury had been unable to agree in the first two trials. The court rejected the submission that prosecutorial misconduct was an essential element of the doctrine of abuse of process and decided rather that prosecutorial misconduct and improper motivation were but two of the many factors to consider in determining whether there has been an abuse of process. The Supreme Court concluded that the case before it was not one of those "clearest of cases" which would justify a stay.

Here, as in many recent cases, the parties proceeded on the understanding that the common law doctrine of abuse of process was now subsumed in s. 7 of the *Charter*, without any modification that would affect the outcome of this case: see *Keyowski, supra*; *R. v. Young* (1984), 13 C.C.C. (3d) 1, 46 O.R. (2d) 520, 40 C.R (3d) 289; *R. v. Miles of Music Ltd.* (1989), 48 C.C.C. (3d) 96, 24 C.P.R. (3d) 301, 69 C.R. (3d) 361 (Ont. C.A.).

.....

In *Keyowski*, Wilson J. stressed that many factors must be considered when a court is called upon to consider whether prosecutorial action constitutes an abuse of process. She said at p. 483:

> Prosecutorial conduct and improper motivation are but two of many factors to be taken into account when a court is called upon to consider whether or not in a particular case the Crown's exercise of its discretion to re-lay the indictment amounts to an abuse of process.

.....

> The appellant has, in my view, failed to demonstrate that this is one of those "clearest of cases" which would justify a stay. The charge is a serious one. The proceedings have not occupied an undue amount of time. The accused has not been held in custody, and while he has undoubtedly suffered substantial trauma and stigma from the proceedings and the attendant publicity, he is probably not distinguishable in this respect from the vast majority of accused. A third trial may, indeed, stretch the limits of the community's sense of fair play but does not of itself exceed them. In these circumstances, and having regard to the seriousness of the charge, I think that the administration of justice is best served by allowing the Crown to proceed with the new trial.

The relevant factors vary within the wide range of prosecutorial action which may give rise to a finding of abuse of process. The factors which are significant in the case at bar have been thoroughly canvassed by Dubin J.A. in *Young*, *supra*. In *Young*, the accused was charged some six years after the facts had been investigated and after the authorities had decided not to take action against him.

However, the facts in *Young* are significantly different from the facts here. The accused, a lawyer, had sworn an affidavit pursuant to the *Land Speculation Tax Act*, S.O. 1974, c. 17. The matter was investigated by the Ministry of Revenue in 1977; the accused's good faith was never in issue and the matter was resolved by the Ministry indicating that it intended merely to reassess the amount of tax, which it never did. No further action was taken at that time. In 1983, the same matter was brought to the attention of a Crown Attorney. The six-year limitation period for the offence of swearing a false affidavit contrary to the *Land Speculation Tax Act,* 1974, had expired and charges were laid under the *Criminal Code* for fraud and swearing a false affidavit. The Court of Appeal upheld the decision of a trial judge to stay these charges for abuse of process. It is noteworthy that in *Young*, in support of his application for a stay, the accused deposed as to the particulars of the prejudice caused to him by the delayed prosecution. He stated that in the initial investigation, the allegations against him had been communicated to his professional association, thereby placing him under a cloud of suspicion, which he since succeeded in dispelling.

Moreover, all the government officials involved in *Young* appeared to have concluded in 1977 that proceedings were not warranted. Six years later, the accused faced far more serious charges than he would have, and the limitation period under the provincial statute not expired. Under those circumstances, the court concluded that the fraud and perjury trial would put Mr. Young's liberty a trisk in a manner contrary to the fundamental principles of criminal justice. However, Dubin J.A. indicated that delay in laying criminal charges *per se* is not a basis for a stay. He said, at pp. 31-2:

> ... absent any finding that the delay in the institution of the proceedings was for the ulterior purpose of depriving an accused of the opportunity of making full answer and defence, delay in itself, even delay resulting in the impairment of the ability to make full answer and defence, is not a basis for a stay of process.

In the case at bar, the learned trial judge considered the allegations of prejudice made by counsel for the accused. He said:

> The assertions by counsel for the accused as to the nature and content of the evidence of the deceased witnesses and the consequential prejudicial effect of the delay herein on the ability of the accused to present full answer and

> defence fails to meet the requisite standard of proof even at the lowest degree of probability. Notwithstanding the evidential problem that might be involved during a jury trial, it is clear from *R. v. F.* [*R. v. F. (G.A.), supra*] that if it appears during the trial that the accused has been prejudiced by delay, the question of his fair trial can then be considered.

No other form of prejudice was alleged by the accused. In contrast to *Young*, the trial judge in this case found an abuse of process on the basis of what he perceived to be the unilateral breach of an agreement between the complainants, their mother and the police on the one hand, and the accused on the other.

In my view, the police decision not to lay charges against the accused in 1984, considering the complainants' reluctance to proceed, cannot be faulted. The alternative was to proceed against the wishes of the then 13 and 18-year-old complainants, by compelling them to testify and having them declared adverse or hostile witnesses if necessary. This is both unrealistic and repugnant to society's sense of decency, towards both the accused and the complainants. A further alternative was to say nothing to the accused about the allegations made against him, so as to not jeopardize the possibility of subsequent prosecution should the complainants change their minds. It was both in the interests of the accused and the protection of society that the police warn the accused about these accusations.

The conduct of the complainants may also be a factor in determining whether to stay the proceedings. In *R. v. Miles of Music Ltd., supra*, members of the court disagreed about whether the alleged unfairness must be attributable to either the Crown or the police, rather than to a private party, before the doctrine of abuse of process can be successfully invoked by the accused. It is unnecessary to address this issue here since in my view the conduct of the complainants cannot be faulted.

The first incident which gave rise to these charges is said to have occurred in 1978, when R. was 11. The police were first involved in the spring of 1984, when she was 18. Her reluctance to testify at 18 is consistent with her silence from age 11. Absent prejudice to the accused or other circumstances leading to unfairness, her willingness to lay charges at 22 offends neither common sense nor fair play. To hold otherwise would require young victims of sexual abuse to speak up immediately or never be heard.

.....

The trial judge viewed as oppressive and unfair the fact that "the accused now faces the very charges he was told in 1984 would not be pursued provided he left his family alone". The trial judge then added, at p. 209:

> Although not expressly stated as a fact, there is a manifest threat of charges being laid if the warning was not heeded. The accused has scrupulously heeded this warning.

Several courts have found it to be an abuse of process for the Crown to renege on an agreement with the accused. Typically though, these cases involved "deals" in which the accused had genuinely compromised his or her position and made a real concession in anticipation of some reward, such as the abandonment of prosecution. Moreover, and largely because of that, they were all cases where the accused had been prejudiced by the Crown reneging on the deal. In *R. v. MacDonald* (1990), 54 C.C.C. (3d) 97,

75 C.R. (3d) 238, 38 O.A.C. 9, this court upheld the decision of the trial judge not to stay proceedings for abuse of process. This was a case where the Crown agreed not to charge the accused with murder if he gave a complete and truthful statement to the police; instead, he would be charged only with being an accessory after the fact to murder. MacDonald would also be required to give evidence against the person charged with murder. The Crown subsequently charged him with first degree murder, having come to the conclusion that the statement he gave to the police was not truthful. In *MacDonald*, the accused had purported to provide something in exchange for lenient treatment by the Crown. The court found that he did not deliver on his promise. In considering the applicable factors that led him to conclude that no abuse of process had taken place, Zuber J.A., for the court, said at p. 106:

> Finally, although this is a case where the Crown extracted some benefit from the appellant (*i.e.*, his testimony at the preliminary hearing of Gray) and the appellant forfeited his right to silence, in fact, the appellant suffered no prejudice.

In *Re Smith and The Queen* (1974), 22 C.C.C. (2d) 268, 30 C.R.N.S. 383, [1975] 3 W.W.R. 454 (B.C.S.C.), the accused was charged with possession of marijuana. He informed the Crown that he had another quantity of the drug in his possession. The Crown Attorney made it clear to him that if he decided to turn over this other marijuana, no charges would be laid with respect to it. The accused did so and the Crown charged him with conspiracy to possess and conspiracy to traffic on the basis of the drug and of his conversation with the Crown when he turned it in. The court held that to proceed with these charges would be an abuse of process. Berger J. wrote at p. 272:

> ... I do not think that the result in this case should be conditioned by any nice distinctions based on what Mr. Lavallee [the Crown] said. The promise given by Lavallee should be interpreted in the way that any ordinary man would interpret such a promise, that is, as one encompassing any charge based on the admissions made and the evidence obtained as the result of the deal made.
>
> .....
>
> The ordinary man, having made such a deal with Crown counsel, would feel that he could walk in safety thereafter. He would be astounded and amazed if charges of conspiracy could be proceeded with. I think what occurred in this case constitutes oppression. The ordinary man is entitled to expect that the Crown will keep its word.

In *R. v. Crneck, Bradley and Shelley* (1980), 55 C.C.C. (2d) 1, 116 D.L.R. (3d) 675, 30 O.R. (2d) 1 (H.C.J.), three persons were charged with manslaughter. An agreement was reached between the Crown and counsel for Patricia Bradley that she would provide a formal statement to the police. In exchange, the Crown undertook that the statement would not be used against her, and, if it was consistent with the known facts, she would not be tried but would be called as a witness. After reviewing Bradley's statement, counsel for the Crown decided to proceed only against Crneck and conveyed this information to Shelley as well. A second Crown counsel took over the case, reneged on the deal, and informed the parties that he would proceed against all three. Bradley and Shelley moved for a stay on the basis of abuse of process.

Krever J. expressed the view that for the Crown to renege on an agreement to extend immunity in exchange for co-operation may in itself be an abuse of process which would justify a stay of proceedings. However, he found in the case of Bradley that the stay should be entered because she had suffered serious prejudice as a result of the conduct of the Crown in that her previous dealings with the Crown might undermine her credibility at trial if she were to testify. Krever J. found that there had been no abuse of process towards Shelley as he had not been the subject of an agreement but merely the beneficiary of a unilateral decision by the Crown not to proceed.

In *R. v. Metro News Ltd.* (1986), 29 C.C.C. (3d) 35, 32 D.L.R. (4th) 321, 56 O.R. (2d) 321 (C.A.) (leave to appeal to the Supreme Court of Canada refused, November 6, 1986, C.C.C. & D.L.R. *loc. cit.*, 57 O.R. (2d) 638*n*) the accused was charged with distributing an obscene publication consisting of an edition of Penthouse magazine. The magazine had been approved for import by Canadian customs and had also been approved by a committee established by the periodical distributors industry with the approval of the Attorney-General. The accused had an arrangement with the police that if they disagreed with the decision of the committee, he would withdraw the publication. The Court of Appeal found no abuse of process in the trial of the accused. On that point, Martin J.A. said, for the court, at p. 75:

> Further I do not think that the general arrangement which the appellant had with the policy of notifying them of the approval of the advisory council and the police, in turn, notifying the appellant of their disagreement with the opinion of the committee as to a particular publication, permitting the appellant to withdraw the publication from circulation, resulted in prejudice to the appellant which rendered a prosecution of the appellant unfair in respect of the particular publication which was the subject of the charge.

In *R. v. Agozzino*, [1970] 1 C.C.C. (2d) 380, [1970] 1 O.R. 480, 6 C.R.N.C. 147 (C.A.), the accused pleaded guilty to possession of counterfeit money following an undertaking by the Crown that he would not ask for a term of imprisonment. The Crown appealed the suspended sentence and the fine imposed by the trial judge. Without discussing the doctrine of abuse of process, Gale C.J.O. dismissed the appeal and said:

> We believe it would now be quite unfair, not only to the Magistrate but to the accused, for the Crown, by means of this appeal, to change its position by asking for a substantial term of imprisonment. In effect the appeal repudiates the position taken by Crown counsel at the trial and we do not care to give effect to that repudiation.

In *Re Abitibi Paper Co. Ltd. and The Queen* (1979), 47 C.C.C. (2d) 487, 99 D.L.R. (3d) 333, 24 O.R. (2d) 742 (C.A.), the doctrine of abuse of process was used to stay a provincial prosecution under pollution legislation. The court characterized the matter as being essentially civil rather than criminal. The accused had voluntarily embarked on a programme of abatement of water pollution and a senior official at the Ministry of the Environment had agreed not to prosecute him if the programme was completed by a certain date. Prior to the completion date, the Crown laid charges under the *Environmental Protection Act*, S.O. 1971, c. 86, and the *Ontario Water*

Resources Act, R.S.O. 1970, c. 332. The court held that this was one of the "exceptional circumstances" in which the Crown's conduct amounted to an abuse of process: see also *R. v. Betesh* (1976), 30 C.C.C. (2d) 233, 35 C.R.N.S. 238 (Ont. Sess. Ct.); *Re Delaney* (1977), 17 N.B.R. (2d) 224 (Q.B.).

In the case at bar, the facts are unclear as to whether the respondent made a "deal" with the police, under which he agreed to leave the complainants alone in exchange for the charges not being laid, or whether he was merely informed that the complainants were unwilling to testify and warned that he should stay away from them. The burden is on the accused to establish the facts that support his claim of abuse of process. If the conversation between Sergeant Babiak and the respondent can properly be characterized as an agreement, the respondent did not make a real concession, turn over evidence or in any way compromise his position. It appears that Sergeant Babiak was hoping to have the respondent's name placed on a sexual abuse registry. There is no evidence as to whether this was discussed with the respondent, let alone that he ever agreed to anything of the sort.

The respondent gave no formal statement to the police and Crown counsel informed the trial judge that Sergeant Babiak discussed the allegations with the respondent on an entirely "non-caution, no-charge basis". The respondent merely agreed not to contact the complainants or their mother, from whom he was already separated. Undoubtedly, the respondent obtained psychological comfort and peace of mind from being told by the authorities that charges would not be laid. This may only give rise to a proper claim of abuse of process if the prosecution *unfairly* reneges on expectations it has generated in the accused: see *Conway*, *supra*, *per* L'Heureux-Dubé J., at p. 304.

The respondent is not facing more serious charges now than he would have faced in 1984. There is no evidence that his life was disrupted, that his reputation had to be restored or that his working life was interfered with in the intervening period. There is no evidence of trickery, improper motives or malice on the part of the police or the complainants. The potential prejudice to the respondent in making full answer and defence can be resolved at trial. Without minimizing the importance of his personal sense of security and his peace of mind, it cannot be said that he suffered the degree of prejudice required to find an abuse of process, particularly in view of the nature and seriousness of the offences.

.....

Considering all the factors which must be weighed by the trial judge before exercising his or her discretion to stay proceedings on the basis of abuse of process, I am of the view that the absence of prejudice to the accused combined with the seriousness of the charges are fatal to the claim that the proceedings should be stayed...

I. MOTIONS RELATING TO THE FORM AND SUBSTANCE OF INFORMATIONS AND INDICTMENTS

The requisite content of an indictment (which, in this context, includes an information or a count therein: s. 2 of the *Criminal Code* is governed by ss. 581 to 586 of the *Criminal Code*. These provisions apply to indictable and summary conviction offences (s. 795). Excessive

deference to formalities in the past (arising in part from the availability of the death penalty for trivial crimes in England) has been replaced with more pragmatic rules intended to ensure, wherever possible, a trial on the merits and the imparting of sufficient information to enable full answer and defence. That having been said, the rules are often misunderstood and the jurisprudence correspondingly uneven.

A count is, simply put, a charge. An indictment may contain multiple counts, subject to the rules of joinder and severance of counts, later reviewed. The following is a list of the rules that govern the content of a count contained in an indictment:

(a) Each count shall generally apply only to a single transaction (s. 581(1)); *R. v. Cook* (1985), 20 C.C.C. (3d) 18 (B.C.C.A.); *R. v. Cotroni; Papalia v. The Queen* (1979), 45 C.C.C. (2d) 1 (S.C.C.).

(b) Each count "shall contain in substance a statement that the accused or defendant committed an offence therein specified" (s. 581(1)). In essence, this means that the count must charge an offence known to law. The statement can be in popular, non-technical language, without non-essential allegations, in the words of the offence section or in words that are sufficient to give the accused notice of the offence charged. The count can, and generally does, specifically refer to the offence section, or part thereof creating the offence charged, which may assist in ensuring sufficiency (s. 581(2) and (5)); *R. v. Petersen* (1980), 8 M.V.R. 139 (Sask. C.A.); revd on other grounds (1982), 30 C.R. (3d) 165 (S.C.C.).

(c) Each count shall contain sufficient detail of the circumstances of the alleged offence to give the accused reasonable information respecting the act or omission to be proven against him or her, and to identify the transaction referred to. Otherwise the absence or insufficiency of details does not vitiate the count (s. 581(3)); *R. v. Wis Developments Corp. Ltd.* (1984), 12 C.C.C. (3d) 129 (S.C.C.); *R. v. Côté* (1977), 33 C.C.C. (2d) 353 (S.C.C.).

This requirement is raised, most frequently, in connection with the date or time frame specified in the indictment, particularly where it is alleged that sexual offences occurred over an extended period of time: *Re Regina and R.I.C.* (1986), 32 C.C.C. (3d) 399 (Ont. C.A.).

(d) Where a count does fulfill the requirements of s. 581 of the *Criminal Code*, it is not insufficient by reason only that it omits the kinds of details specified in s. 583 of the *Criminal Code*, such as the name of the person injured or intended or attempted to be injured or the person who owns or has a special property or interest in the property mentioned in the count. If the owner of the alleged stolen property cannot be proven by the prosecution, that *may* result in an acquittal, not

because of any omission in the count but because the Crown has failed to prove its case. Under some circumstances, the Crown may be able to prove a theft, notwithstanding its failure to prove the identity of the owner.

QUESTION

17. The indictment alleges that the accused stole the property of Swamp Lands Properties Limited. The evidence establishes that the owner of the property is actually Artie Sneer carrying on business as Swamp Lands Properties. The trial judge dismisses the charge for that reason. Is he correct in doing so? Consider, in this regard, *Little and Wolski v. The Queen* (1974), 19 C.C.C. (2d) 385 (S.C.C.).

(e) A single count shall not charge two separate offences. This is a common law rule, often known as the rule against duplicity. If a count were to charge the accused with dangerous driving and impaired driving, this would be an obvious violation of this rule. These two offences should be charged in separate counts. However, it is sometimes very difficult to assess duplicity where the accused is charged in the words of the offence section: does the offence section itself create a number of offences or simply articulate different means of committing the same offence? See *R. v. Sault Ste. Marie (City)* (1978), 40 C.C.C. (2d) 353 (S.C.C.).

(f) Special pleading rules are set out in the *Criminal Code* for treason and other rare offences against the public order, libel, perjury and fraud (ss. 581(4), 584-586).

Pursuant to s. 587 of the *Criminal Code*, the court can order the Crown to furnish particulars relating to a count in the indictment, where necessary, for a fair trial. Particulars are ordered to supplement the count which, though sufficient within the meaning of s. 581, is not terribly informative. Particulars may be sought from the Crown in advance of trial and, if not voluntarily given, the subject of a motion to the court prior to trial but, most frequently, after arraignment and before plea. Particulars, when furnished, are said to "bind" the Crown, that is, the Crown's case fails if the particulars are unproven. However, if the particulars relate to non-essential matters ("mere surplusage"), and if the defence has not been prejudiced by relying upon them, the failure to prove particulars may not be fatal to the Crown's case. As well, as will be noted below, there is power to permit the Crown to amend the indictment, and the particulars relating thereto during the trial to conform to the evidence, again where the accused is not thereby irreparably prejudiced. There is no power to order particulars at a preliminary inquiry.

Sections 590 and 601 of the *Criminal Code* outline the remedies available to address alleged defects in the indictment. Where the defect is apparent on the face of the indictment, objection must be taken before plea and thereafter only with leave of the court. Generally, such objec-

tions take place immediately after arraignment and are made orally, in the absence of the jury panel. On a motion to quash, the court may indeed quash the count as unrectifiable by amendment or particulars, dismiss the motion outright, refuse to quash but amend the count to comply with statutory and common law requirements, or refuse to quash but order particulars to be provided to supplement a technically sufficient count. The Crown may seek an amendment, on its own initiative, usually at the outset of the trial, for example, to rectify an incorrect spelling of the complainant's name or a *Criminal Code* reference, or to fill in an essential element (also known as an "essential averment") of the offence. The court may also divide a count. During the trial, almost invariably at the Crown's initiative, the court may amend the count or the particulars previously provided to conform to the evidence. It is relatively infrequent that a count will be quashed. An order for particulars has already been addressed. The other remedies are further discussed below.

1. Dividing the Count

Where the count applies to more than one transaction, the court may divide the count into two or more separate counts (s. 590).

Where the count is duplicitous (that is, charges more than one offence or, more specifically, charges in the alternative different matters, acts or omissions that are stated in the alternative in the offence section), the court may divide the count into two or more separate counts (s. 590).

2. Amending the Count

Where the count contains certain specified defects or is in any way defective in substance and the matters in the proposed amendment are disclosed by the evidence taken on the preliminary inquiry or trial (s. 601(3)(*a*) and (*b*)), or where the count is defective in form (s. 601(3)(*c*)), the court *shall*, at any stage of the proceedings, amend the court as may be necessary.

Where there is a variation between the evidence tendered and the count as preferred, or as previously amended, or as if it had been amended in conformity with prior particulars, the court *may* amend the count or the particulars to conform to the evidence (s. 601(2)).

Section 601(4) of the *Criminal Code* addresses the considerations that inform the decision whether or not to make an amendment: *R. v. Moore* (1988), 41 C.C.C. (3d) 289 (S.C.C.). Section 601(5) also permits an adjournment and allows costs to rectify any prejudice to, or misleading of the defence.

Section 601(4.1) reflects that a variance between the evidence and a count is immaterial (a) as to the time when the offence is alleged to have been committed, if the charges were commenced within any applicable limitation period, and (b) as to the place where the proceedings' subject-matter allegedly arose, if it arose within the court's territorial jurisdiction.

But consider *R. v. P.(M.B.)* (1994), 89 C.C.C. (3d) 289 (S.C.C.), substantially reproduced at p. 584.

J. EXCLUSION OF WITNESSES

Generally, on the application of the Crown or the defence, an order is made excluding prospective witnesses, other than the accused, from the courtroom. Certain witnesses such as experts or the investigating officer may be exempted from the order.

QUESTIONS

18. What if a witness, deliberately or through inadvertence, comes into the courtroom and listens to other testimony? Consider, in this regard, *Dobberthien v. The Queen* (1975), 18 C.C.C. (2d) 449 (S.C.C.).

19. In order to prepare testimony, can counsel speak to a prospective witness who has been excluded? Assume that a previous witness has raised a new issue that counsel wishes to canvass with this prospective witness. How should counsel proceed? Can the court prohibit communication between counsel and a prospective witness? Consider, in this regard, *Re O'Callaghan and The Queen* (1982), 65 C.C.C. (2d) 459 (Ont. H.C.J.).[1]

20. Are witnesses excluded until the trial is completed or until their evidence is completed? What if there is a possibility that the witness may be recalled in reply?

K. APPLICATIONS RELATING TO JOINDER AND SEVERANCE

Section 591 of the *Criminal Code* provides in part that:

> (1) Subject to s. 589 [which prohibits joinder of a murder count with a non-murder count unless the counts arise out of the same transaction or unless the accused consents], any number of counts for any number of offences may be joined in the same indictment...
>
> .....
>
> (3) The court may, where it is satisfied that the interests of justice so require, order:
>
> (*a*) that the accused be tried separately on one or more of the counts; [severance of counts] and
>
> (*b*) where there is more than one accused or defendant, that one or more of them be tried separately on one or more of the counts [severance of accused].
>
> .....

---

1 Note that communication with a witness about his or her evidence, once that witness's evidence has commenced, raises very different issues. For example, the Law Society of Upper Canada's Rules of Professional Conduct provide that counsel is not permitted to discuss his or her witness's evidence out of court once that witness's evidence has commenced, except that, during examination in chief, counsel can continue to discuss areas not yet the subject of testimony: Rule 4.04(*a*).

Section 591(4) to (6) provides that an order under subsection (3) may be made before or during trial. If severance is granted during a jury trial, the jury is discharged from giving a verdict respecting the severed counts or the severed accused. The severed counts and or accused may be tried separately as if the relevant counts were contained in a separate indictment.

R. v. LITCHFIELD

(1993), 86 C.C.C. (3d) 97 (S.C.C.)

Iacobucci J. (La Forest, L'Heureux-Dubé, Sopinka, Gonthier and Cory JJ. concurring): —

.....

The respondent was a family physician practising in Edmonton. The respondent was charged with 14 counts of sexual assault involving seven complainants who were his patients at all relevant times. The assaults were alleged to have occurred while the complainants attended at the respondent's office for medical treatment and diagnosis. Each of the complainants consented to being touched in intimate areas of her body but that consent was predicated upon the touching being carried out for valid medical purposes.

Prior to trial, the respondent applied for an order that each of the counts alleged against him be tried separately. He requested in the alternative that the counts be severed by complainant. McDonald J., who was not the trial judge, heard the application. He did not order a separate trial for each count, but instead ordered that three different trials be held depending on the part of the complainant's body that was involved in the assault. McDonald J. ordered one trial for allegations involving the complainants' genitalia, a second trial for allegations concerning the complainants' breasts, and a third trial for any other matters. This resulted in an order that not only severed but also divided counts, such that separate trials were to be held for events that occurred within one visit to the respondent's office by the same complainant.

The respondent elected to be tried by judge alone. The Crown proceeded to trial first on those counts relating to vaginal examinations (nine counts in total), and sought to have the admissibility of the evidence relating to the severed counts determined at a *voir dire* at the outset of the trial. Hope J., the trial judge, refused to hold a *voir dire* and ruled that the Crown could proceed by calling all of the evidence relating to the severed counts, subject to a subsequent ruling on admissibility. ...The trial judge subsequently ruled all the evidence relating to the severed counts inadmissible as irrelevant or, even if relevant, too prejudicial.

At the close of the Crown's case, the respondent brought a motion for a nonsuit. The trial judge granted the application and the respondent was acquitted. The Crown's appeal was dismissed by the Court of Appeal, 8 W.A.C. 391, 15 W.C.B. (2d) 201, 120 A.R. 391, and this court granted leave to appeal.

.....

Before directly discussing the issues raised in this appeal, I think it is important to keep in mind the nature of the offence of sexual assault as well as the specific manifestation of the alleged sexual assaults in a doctor-patient relationship.

.....

The test to be applied in determining whether an accused's conduct had the requisite nature to constitute a sexual assault is therefore an objective one. As this court indicated in *Chase* [(1987), 37 C.C.C. (3d) 97 (S.C.C.)], all the circumstances surrounding the conduct in question will be relevant to the question of whether the touching was of a sexual nature and violated the complainant's sexual integrity. It is, therefore, important in individual cases that courts not create unnecessary barriers to considering all the circumstances surrounding conduct which is alleged to constitute a sexual assault. This is particularly true where the complainant has consented to some touching but not to touching of a sexual nature: in such a case, the court must have at its disposal as much relevant information as possible in order to determine whether the conduct was of a nature to which the complainant did not consent.

The importance of looking to all the circumstances surrounding an accused's impugned conduct is thrown into relief by a case such as that under consideration in this appeal, where a doctor-patient relationship is concerned. Certainly, medical evidence will be important to assessing the nature of an accused physician's conduct. However, when determining whether a complainant in fact consented to that which occurred, courts must also ensure that they neither ignore the testimony of a patient who complains of sexual assault nor underestimate the position of vulnerability in which a patient often finds herself when she is in the care of a professional medical doctor.

.....

With these considerations in mind, I now turn to the issues in this case.

.....

[Iacobucci J. then addresses the Court's appellate jurisdiction, arising from the order not having been made by the trial judge. He concludes that there is jurisdiction to review the order and proceeds to do so.]

The division and severance order is anomalous in that severance orders are usually made by the trial judge, in which case the order would be appealable as part of the verdict. Indeed, for the reasons that follow, I am of the opinion that no one but the trial judge has jurisdiction to issue a severance order.

Logically, an accused cannot bring a motion to quash an indictment, or to divide or sever counts in an indictment, until the indictment has been preferred. Until the indictment has been preferred, it does not exist as against the accused, it is not legally effectual, and therefore is not subject to being altered or quashed.

.....

The next question to ask is when is an indictment preferred against an accused. In *Chabot* [(1980), 55 C.C.C.(2d) 385 (S.C.C.)], this court held that an indictment is preferred only when it is lodged with the trial court properly constituted and ready to proceed, at the opening of the accused's trial. Dickson J. (as he then was) held for the court as follows at p. 396:

> ... I would hold that an indictment based upon a committal for trial without the intervention of a Grand Jury is not "preferred" against an accused until it is lodged with the trial Court at the opening of the accused's trial, with a Court ready to proceed with the trial.

According to the *Chabot* test, the indictment against the respondent was not preferred until it was lodged with Hope J. at the opening of the respondent's trial. Therefore, McDonald J. had no jurisdiction to divide or sever the counts since the indictment had not been preferred against the respondent at the time of the application. A further conclusion is that no one except the trial judge ever has jurisdiction to divide or sever counts since an indictment is only preferred at the opening of an accused's trial.

This does not mean that an accused must wait until the actual trial date to bring an application to divide or sever counts. Once a trial judge has been assigned to the matter, the indictment can be preferred against the accused by lodging it with the trial judge. Since *Chabot*, the *Criminal Code* has been amended such that in jury trials the trial judge need not be ready to proceed with the trial to deal with matters such as the validity of the indictment. [s. 645(5) of the *Criminal Code*]...

Thus, under s. 645(5), the trial judge can deal with matters concerning the indictment prior to the selection and calling of a jury, in the case of a jury trial. It was always open to a trial judge in the case of a trial by judge alone to hear pre-trial motions before preparing to hear evidence. The judge hearing the application for severance of counts in an indictment would either have to have been assigned as the trial judge or else would be seized of the trial upon the preferring of the indictment and the subsequent hearing of the severance application.

The statement in s. 591(4) of the *Criminal Code* that a severance order may be made "*before* or during the trial" is not deprived of its meaning under this approach to jurisdiction. A severance application brought after the indictment is preferred but before the court is constituted to begin hearing evidence would be brought before the trial.

Moreover, as a matter of practice and policy, it is obviously preferable that the trial judge hear applications to divide and sever counts so that such orders are not immunized from review. Otherwise, procedure begins to govern substance. Indeed, it makes sense that the trial judge consider applications to divide and sever counts since an order for division or severance of counts will dictate the course of the trial itself. Courts have recognized that it is preferable that trial judges make division and severance orders: see, *e.g.*, *R. v. Watson* (1979), 12 C.R. (3d) 259 (B.C.S.C.), and *R. v. Auld* (1957), 26 C.R. 266, 22 W.W.R. 336 (B.C.C.A.). Not only are trial judges better situated to assess the impact of the requested severance on the conduct of the trial, but limiting severance orders to trial judges avoids the duplication of efforts to become familiar enough with the case to determine whether or not a severance order is in the interests of justice. It seems desirable, therefore, that in the future only trial judges can make orders for division or severance of counts in order to avoid injustices such as occurred in this case.

Even had McDonald J.'s order been solid on jurisdictional grounds, I would be inclined to set it aside. The criteria for when a count should be divided or a severance granted are contained in ss. 590(3) and 591(3) of the *Criminal Code*. These criteria are very broad: the court must be satisfied that the ends or interests of justice require the order in question. Therefore, in the absence of stricter guidelines, making an order for the division or severance of counts requires the exercise of a great deal of discretion on the part of the issuing judge. The decisions of provincial appellate courts have held, and I agree, that an appellate court should not interfere with the issuing judge's exercise of discretion unless it is shown that the issuing judge acted unjudicially or that the ruling resulted in an injustice.

.....

McDonald J.'s order for division and severance resulted in an injustice in this case when it divided and severed the counts based on the body parts of the complainants. This arbitrary distinction greatly amplified the difficulties in assessing the alleged sexual assaults in the context of all of the circumstances surrounding the conduct by creating an evidentiary problem which would not have existed but for the order. With respect, the order reveals a misapprehension about the nature of the offence of sexual assault and the considerations that go into assessing if a particular procedure alleged to be medically proper and necessary constitutes a sexual assault.

McDonald J. held that proof that the respondent had performed one act (such as a breast examination) on the complainant which was not for the purposes of treatment or diagnosis would have no probative value with regard to whether or not another act (such as a vaginal examination) performed by the respondent on the complainant was for the purposes of treatment or diagnosis. In so holding, McDonald J. was in error. As stated above, this court emphasized in *Chase* that the court must look to all the circumstances surrounding the conduct in determining the nature and quality of the act. For example, if the respondent acted improperly towards a complainant during one part of a physical examination, evidence of that improper conduct would be relevant to assessing the respondent's conduct at other times during the examination.

The practical effect of McDonald J.'s order for division and severance was to create an unnecessary evidentiary problem by rendering evidence about one part of one visit to the respondent potentially inadmissible as regards another part of the same visit to the respondent's office since different parts of the same visit to the respondent would be contained in separate counts. McDonald J.'s discussion of the irrelevance and lack of probative value of the evidence of one type of act (breast examinations) to another type of act (internal examinations) was referred to directly by Hope J. in his decision to declare the evidence going to the severed counts inadmissible. As I will discuss below, the decision to exclude the evidence going to the severed counts was in error and prejudiced the Crown in its ability to make out its case. The division and severance order worked an injustice towards the Crown, the complainants and the administration of justice in that it placed an artificial barrier to the trial judge's ability to consider the respondent's conduct in all the circumstances.

I do not wish to leave this matter without making one final comment on McDonald J.'s severance order. The order denies the reality of how the complainants experienced the conduct which they have alleged constituted sexual assaults. Each aspect of one complainant's contact with the respondent interlocks with all the other aspects to form the larger context within which that complainant felt that the respondent's actions were inappropriate. Further, the message that a division and severance order in a sexual assault case based on the complainant's body parts sends to women is that the complainant's physical attributes are more important than her experience as a whole person. The order severed the complainants as well as the counts. In my opinion, the message sent by the order, although not intended to have this effect and although not amounting to an error of law, is inappropriate.

Given these jurisdictional and substantive flaws in McDonald J.'s order for division and severance of the counts, and that it was an error for Hope J. to apply the order, it must be set aside.

In the following case, the Supreme Court commented on joinder and severance in a way that has provided little comfort to the defence. The case also addressed the evidentiary use that could be made of the accused's pre-trial silence.

R. v. CRAWFORD

(1995), 96 C.C.C. (3d) 481 (S.C.C.)

[Crawford and Creighton were jointly charged with murder. The Crown alleged that they pretended to befriend the impaired deceased, robbed him and then one or both beat him to death. Crawford made no statement to the police but testified at trial, 13 months after the murder, implicating Creighton and denying that he struck the deceased or was a party to the assault. Creighton's counsel cross-examined Crawford on Crawford's failure to make any statements to the police. Creighton did not testify at trial but had given a videotaped statement to the police on his arrest which implicated Crawford. Creighton's counsel made much of the fact that Crawford had declined to give a statement to the police on his arrest, contrasting unfavourably with Creighton's full statement to the police at the earliest opportunity. Conversely, Crawford's counsel, when addressing the jury, stated that "an innocent man sitting in Creighton's seat would have gotten into that witness box and sworn that he was not guilty". The Ontario Court of Appeal dismissed appeals by both accused. On Crawford's further appeal, the Supreme Court considered the propriety of the cross-examination of Crawford by Creighton's counsel, the appropriate use that could be made of pre-trial silence and the jury instructions on this issue.]

Sopinka J. (Lamer C.J.C., La Forest, L'Heureux-Dubé, Gonthier, Cory, Iacobucci and Major JJ. concurring): — This appeal concerns the right of one co-accused in a joint trial to introduce evidence of the pre-trial silence of another co-accused and, if such evidence is permitted, the use that may be made of such evidence.

.....

... [N]o Canadian court or court in a common law jurisdiction has addressed squarely the issue of the right of one co-accused to comment on or cross-examine another accused on the latter's pre-trial silence. The analysis must, therefore, proceed on the basis of principle and policy. Involved are the competing assertions of two accused that their respective rights, both of which are protected under s. 7 of the *Charter*, be respected. One accused asserts his right to silence and that its exercise not be used against him to his prejudice, while the other contends that he has the right to make full use of the pre-trial silence of his co-accused in order to make full answer and defence. As well, the prosecution asserts that it is in the interest of effective law enforcement to have a joint trial in respect of charges arising out of a common enterprise and, in particular, in circumstances in which the co-accused are engaging in mutual recriminations.

Three plausible solutions for resolution of the competing interests have been put forward in this case:

1. The accused's pre-trial silence trumps the co-accused's right to make use of it in furtherance of his defence. This is the appellant's position.
2. The co-accused's right to make full answer and defence trumps the accused's right to pre-trial silence. This is essentially the approach of the majority of the Court of Appeal.
3. A balance between the rights of the two co-accused must be struck, taking into account the interest of the state in joint trials. This is the position of the Crown, and of Weiler J.A. in dissent, in the Court of Appeal.

A fourth solution would be to sever the trial whenever the conflict occurs, but no one in this appeal advocates such a solution and it would run counter to a uniform stream of authority in this country in favour of joint trials. No application for severance was made at trial and the issue was not raised or commented on in the Court of Appeal.

I turn to consider each of the competing rights and interests in order to determine which of the solutions is appropriate. I conclude that the third option is the solution that best accords with the interests involved and respects the principles of fundamental justice as well as society's interest in effective law enforcement.

The right to pre-trial silence

The right to silence embraces a number of distinct rights which are included in s. 7 of the *Charter* as principles of fundamental justice. Two aspects of the right to silence are pertinent to the discussion of the issues in this appeal, that is, the right to pre-trial silence and silence at trial. The latter is specifically protected in s. 11(*c*) of the *Charter*: see *Thomson Newspapers Ltd. v. Canada (Director of Investigation and Research, Restrictive Trade Practices Commission)* (1990), 54 C.C.C. (3d) 417, 67 D.L.R. (4th) 161, [1990] 1 S.C.R. 425; *R. v. Hebert* (1990), 57 C.C.C. (3d) 1, [1990] 2 S.C.R. 151, 77 C.R. (3d) 145; *R. v. Broyles* (1991), 68 C.C.C. (3d) 308, [1991] 3 S.C.R. 595, 9 C.R. (4th) 1; *R. v. S. (R.J.)*, S.C.C., No. 23581, released February 2, 1995, [now reported 96 C.C.C. (3d) 1, 121 D.L.R. (4th) 589, 36 C.R. (4th) 1]; and others.

It is a corollary of the right to choose to remain silent during the pretrial investigation that, if exercised, this fact is not to be used against the accused at a subsequent trial on a charge arising out of the investigation, and no inference is to be drawn against an accused because he or she exercised the right: see *R. v. Chambers* (1990), 59 C.C.C. (3d) 321, [1990] 2 S.C.R. 1293, 80 C.R. (3d) 235. The same general rationale would apply to trial silence, but the matter has been complicated by the specific statutory provision in s. 4(6) of the *Canada Evidence Act* which forbids the trial judge and Crown counsel from commenting on the failure of the accused to testify. This encompasses both comment prejudicial to the accused, as well as a direction that the jury must not draw an unfavourable conclusion from the accused's failure to testify. As a result, as a practical matter in a jury trial, as Martland J. writing for the majority in *R. v. Vezeau* (1976), 28 C.C.C. (2d) 81 at p. 85, 66 D.L.R. (3d) 418, [1977] 2 S.C.R. 277, stated, "it is open to a jury to draw an inference from the failure of the accused to testify, and, particularly, in a case in which it is sought to establish an alibi".

The above principles were developed in relation to the use that may be made of the accused's silence by the Crown and comment on such silence by the trial judge, and not its use by a co-accused. The main issue in this appeal is whether these principles must be applied in their full vigour when it is a co-accused who seeks to make use of the silence of his co-accused.

With respect to silence at trial, it has been held by several courts of appeal in Canada that a co-accused can comment on the failure of his co-accused to testify: see *R. v. Naglik, supra*, reversed on another point, 83 C.C.C. (3d) 526, 105 D.L.R. (4th) 712, [1993] 3 S.C.R. 122, and *R. v. Cuff* (1989), 49 C.C.C. (3d) 65,75 Nfld. & P.E.I.R. 1, 7 W.C.B. (2d) 232 (C.A.); see also *R. v. Wickham* (1971), 55 Crim. App. R. 199 (C.A.). In *Naglik*, this court found it unnecessary to deal with the point as a new trial was directed and, in the circumstances, the issue would not arise at the new trial. As pointed out by the Chief Justice, in order to decide the point it may be necessary to consider whether the right to comment and the restriction imposed by s. 4(6) can stand together in so far as the subsection precludes a limiting instruction. L'Heureux-Dubé J., dissenting on other grounds, opined that such a comment is permitted.

It has been submitted that to the extent that the above line of authority establishes that the right to silence at trial must give way to the rights of a co-accused and, therefore, it is not an absolute right, a clear distinction exists between the right of silence at trial and pre-trial silence. Prior to or on arrest, the accused is in a much more vulnerable position against the coercive power of the state. The environment in the police station is different from that of the courtroom where procedural rules protect the accused. In the police station, the accused may not be represented and he may be overwhelmed by the whole experience. The police possess considerably greater power than the accused, and there are no disclosure obligations. The police can disclose some or misleading information or no information at all. Evidential use of silence forces the suspect to co-operate with his interrogators without a reciprocal exchange of information and without placing proper limits on the power of the police to demand co-operation. In contrast, in the courtroom, the accused is represented, he knows the case that he has to meet (due to disclosure) and there are rules regarding admissibility of evidence: see S.B. McNicol in *Law of Privilege* (Sydney: Law Book Co., 1992), at p. 286.

I accept that the distinctions referred to are apt, but none the less I am not prepared to accept that, therefore, the right to pre-trial silence is absolute. In *Hebert, supra*, at p. 37, McLachlin J. stated:

> [Section 7] guarantees the individual's life, liberty and security of person. But it recognizes that these rights are not absolute. In certain circumstances, the state may properly deprive a person of these interests. But it must do so in conformity with the principles of fundamental justice.

This principle applies, *a fortiori*, when there is a conflict between two rights, both protected by the *Charter*. In *Dagenais v. Canadian Broadcasting Corp.* (1994), 94 C.C.C. (3d) 289 at p. 316, 120 D.L.R. (4th) 12, [1994] 3 S.C.R. 835, the Chief Justice, in his majority reasons, pointed out that "[a] hierarchical approach to rights, which places some over others, must be avoided". In this regard, it is significant that, even in the absence of a competing *Charter* right, the right to pre-trial silence is not absolute. Accordingly, failure to make a timely disclosure of an alibi defence can be used by the Crown to attack the credibility of this defence: see *Chambers, supra, per* Cory J., at p. 343.

The right to full answer and defence

There is no doubt about the right of co-accused persons to cross-examine each other in making full answer and defence: see *R. v. McLaughlin* (1974), 15 C.C.C. (2d) 562, 25 C.R.N.S. 362, 2 O.R. (2d) 514 (C.A.), and *R. v. Ma, Ho and Lai* (1978), 44 C.C.C. (2d) 537, 6 C.R. (3d) 325 and S-45, [1979] 1 W.W.R. 436 *sub nom. R. v. Chung Man Ma* (B.C.C.A.). Moreover, restrictions that apply to the Crown may not apply to restrict this right of the co-accused. As pointedly observed by D. W. Elliott, "Cut Throat Tactics: The Freedom of an Accused to Prejudice a Co-Accused", [1991] Crim. L. R. 5 at p. 17, "[t]he notion of the Crown having one hand tied behind its back is familiar and accepted, but not the notion of a person standing trial being in that position"; see also *R. v. Jackson* (1991), 68 C.C.C. (3d) 385 at p. 434, 9 C.R. (4th) 57, 51 O.A.C. 92, *per* Doherty J.A.; affirmed on other grounds, 86 C.C.C. (3d) 385, 109 D.L.R. (4th) 318, [1993] 4 S.C.R. 573. Accordingly, a co-accused may adduce evidence of, or cross-examine on, the disposition or propensity of a co-accused to commit the offence, even though the co-accused has not put his character in issue, and may cross-examine a co-accused on a statement the voluntariness of which has not been established: see *R. v. Kendall* (1987), 35 C.C.C. (3d) 105, 57 C.R. (3d) 249,20 O.A.C. 134 (C.A.); *Lowery v. The Queen*, [1974] A.C. 85 (P.C.); *R. v. Pelletier* (1986), 29 C.C.C. (3d) 533, 17 W.C.B. 14; and *R. v. Jackson*. Exclusionary rules based on a policy of fairness to the accused would preclude the Crown resorting to this kind of evidence.

The right to make full answer and defence is protected under s. 7 of the *Charter*.... This right extends to prevent incursions on its exercise not only by the Crown but by the co-accused.... The right to full answer and defence, as is the case with other *Charter* rights, is not absolute. It must be applied and be subject to other rules that govern the conduct of a criminal trial.... When the right is asserted by accused persons in a joint trial, regard must be had for the effect of the public interest in joint trials with respect to charges arising out of a common enterprise. Can this interest in joint trials prevail against the assertion of one accused to make full answer and defence while at the same time protecting another accused against the blows to his or her right to pre-trial silence that the exercise of the right to make full answer and defence entails? In order to resolve this question, it is necessary to examine the principles relating to joint trials and severance.

Joint trials and severance

In *Kendall, supra,* Goodman J.A., after concluding that the exclusion of evidence as to disposition of the co-accused violated the appellant's right to make full answer and defence, went on to deal with the question of severance. At p. 127, after the passage quoted above, he stated:

> It is no doubt true that the evidence of Dakin would have been highly prejudicial to McKay.... It may be that if the evidence had been admitted that McKay could have complained that it was highly prejudicial to him and could not have been introduced against him by the prosecution if he had been tried alone. He may then have applied for a separate trial on the ground that the admission of such evidence on the joint trial might cause a miscarriage of justice in so far as he was concerned.

There exist, however, strong policy reasons for accused persons charged with offences arising out of the same event or series of events to be tried jointly. The policy reasons apply with equal or greater force when each accused blames the other or others, a situation which is graphically labelled a "cut-throat defence". Separate trials in these situations create a risk of inconsistent verdicts. The policy against separate trials is summarized by *Elliott, supra,* at p. 17, as follows:

> There is a dilemma here which could only be avoided by separate trials. But separate trials will not be countenanced because, quite apart from the extra cost and delay involved, it is undeniable that the full truth about an incident is much more likely to emerge if every alleged participant gives his account on one occasion. If each alleged participant is tried separately, there are obvious and severe difficulties in arranging for this to happen without granting one of them immunity. In view of this, in all but exceptional cases, joint trial will be resorted to, despite the double bind inevitably involved.

Although the trial judge has a discretion to order separate trials, that discretion must be exercised on the basis of principles of law which include the instruction that severance is not to be ordered unless it is established that a joint trial will work an injustice to the accused. The mere fact that a co-accused is waging a "cut-throat" defence is not in itself sufficient. In *Pelletier, supra,* a co-accused was permitted to cross-examine another accused on a statement to the police that had not been proved to be voluntary. On appeal of his conviction, he contended if he had been tried separately, the cross-examination would not have been permitted. On this basis, he claimed that the trials should have been severed. In dismissing this ground, Hinkson J.A., on behalf of the court, stated, at p. 539:

> On this point it is necessary to keep in mind that the trial judge has a discretion as to whether or not he will grant a severance. The general rule of severance is that persons engaged in a common enterprise should be jointly tried unless it can be demonstrated that a joint trial would work an injustice to a particular accused: *R. v. Black and six others,* [1970] 4 C.C.C. 251 at pp. 267-8, 10 C.R.N.S. 17 at pp. 35-6, 72 W.W.R. 407. In this case, the trial judge was not persuaded that it was appropriate to grant a severance. I do not conclude that he erred in the exercise of his discretion.

As I pointed out above, neither party to this appeal contended that the solution to the problem is to order separate trials whenever the full exercise of the right to make full answer and defence by one accused appears to collide with the protections ordinarily accorded to an accused when facing the Crown alone. This position is consistent with both principle and policy as outlined above. The general rule, therefore, is that the respective rights of the co-accused must be resolved on the basis that the trial will be a joint trial. This does not mean, however, that the trial judge has been stripped of his discretion to sever. That discretion remains, and can be exercised if it appears that the attempt to reconcile the respective rights of the co-accused results in an injustice to one of the accused.

Resolving competing Charter rights

The proper approach to the problem created by a conflict in the protected rights of individuals was outlined by the Chief Justice in *Dagenais, supra.* After stressing that *Charter* rights are of equal value, he continued as follows, at pp. 316-7:

> When the protected rights of two individuals come into conflict, as can occur in the case of publication bans, *Charter* principles require a balance to be achieved that fully respects the importance of both sets of rights.

I have gone to some length to stress that *Charter* rights are not absolute in the sense that they cannot be applied to their full extent regardless of the context. Application of *Charter* values must take into account other interests and, in particular, other *Charter* values which may conflict with their unrestricted and literal enforcement. This approach to *Charter* values is especially apt in this case, in that the conflicting rights are protected under the same section of the *Charter*.

Applying the foregoing to the question posed at the commencement of this analysis, the appropriate choice of the three solutions is readily apparent. The first option would allow the right to silence to trump the right to full answer and defence. This would apply one right fully, in complete disregard of another equal right. Similarly, the second option would allow the right to full answer and defence to trump the right to silence. This, again, is counter to the approach which was approved in *Dagenais, supra*, in that it applies one right in absolute terms to the detriment of another equal right. The third solution which strikes a balance between the two is the correct approach. It remains to determine how the two rights can be reconciled in order to give the fullest respect possible to the *Charter* values which underpin these rights.

An accused who testifies against a co-accused must accept that his credibility can be fully attacked by the latter. In *R. v. Kuldip* (1990), 61 C.C.C. (3d) 385 at p. 398, [1990] 3 S.C.R. 618, 1 C.R. (4th) 285, the Chief Justice stated:

> An accused has the right to remain silent during his or her trial. However, if an accused chooses to take the stand, that accused is implicitly vouching for his or her credibility. Such an accused, like any other witness, has therefore opened the door to having the trustworthiness of his/her evidence challenged.

The accused who has incriminated a co-accused by his testimony cannot, therefore, rely on the right to silence to deprive the accused who is implicated by his testimony of the right to challenge that testimony by a full attack on the credibility of the former, including reference to his pre-trial silence. This enables the co-accused to dispel the evidence which implicates him emanating from his co-accused. He cannot, however, go further and ask the trier of fact to consider the evidence of his co-accused's silence as positive evidence of guilt on which the Crown can rely to convict. This is not essential to enable him to defend himself against the imputations of his co-accused and would constitute an unwarranted intrusion on the right to silence of his co-accused.

The limited use to which the evidence can be put must, of course, be explained to the jury with some care. The distinction between the use of evidence limited to credibility and evidence that can be used to infer guilt is well understood by lawyers but may not be easily understood by a jury. It has been criticized as being artificial: see *R. v. Gilbert* (1977), 66 Cr. App. R. 237 (C.A.). While I recognize that the distinction is a subtle one, it is none the less a distinction that is firmly rooted in our law and is one that can be adequately explained to a jury. The distinction was recently reaffirmed by this court in *Kuldip, supra*. At p. 398, the Chief Justice stated:

> This seems an appropriate time at which to mention that I share Martin J.A.'s concern that it is sometimes difficult to draw a clear line between cross-examination on the accused's prior testimony for the purpose of incriminating him and such cross-examination for the purpose of impeaching his credibility. A trial judge will have to be very clear in his or her instructions to the jury when setting out the uses to which previous testimony can be put and the uses to which such testimony must not be put. While such a distinction may be somewhat troublesome to the jury, it is my view that with the benefit of clear instructions from the trial judge the jury will not be unduly burdened with this distinction. These instructions should, in many ways, be reminiscent of those which are routinely given with respect to the use to which an accused's criminal record may be put. A trial necessarily involves evidentiary questions which are sometimes complex in nature. While simplicity in these matters is generally preferable to complexity, the policy reasons underlying the need for a jury to have before it all the relevant information related to the charge (discussed by this court in *R. v. Corbett* (1988), 41 C.C.C. (3d) 385, [1988] 1 S.C.R. 670, 64 C.R. (3d) 1), clearly outweigh the benefits of simplicity in these circumstances.

It is also a distinction that is made with respect to the alibi defence in respect of which the accused's failure to make timely disclosure may be used to attack credibility: see *Chambers, supra*.

A proper balance with respect to the competing rights in issue can be achieved if the trial judge, when sitting alone, carefully applies the distinction to which I refer above. The evidence of pre-trial silence is not to be used as positive evidence to infer the guilt of the accused, either as tending to show consciousness of guilt or otherwise. In a trial before a jury, the trial judge must explain the respective rights involved, how they are to approach the use of the evidence of silence, and its limited purpose. In her dissenting reasons, Weiler J.A. has suggested four points that the charge should contain. The Crown, in its argument and factum, suggests a fifth. With the benefit of these suggestions and the submissions of counsel, I propose the following as a guideline that trial judges should follow in these circumstances. The jury should be told:

(1) that the co-accused, who has testified against the accused, had the right to pre-trial silence and not to have the exercise of that right used as evidence as to innocence or guilt;

(2) that the accused implicated by the evidence of the co-accused has the right to make full answer and defence, including the right to attack the credibility of the co-accused;

(3) that the accused, implicated by the evidence of the co-accused, had the right, therefore, to attack the credibility of the co-accused by reference to the latter's failure to disclose the evidence to the investigating authorities;

(4) that this evidence is not to be used as positive evidence on the issue of innocence or guilt to draw an inference of consciousness of guilt or otherwise;

(5) that the evidence could be used as one factor in determining whether the evidence of the co-accused is to be believed. The failure to make a statement prior to trial may reflect on the credibility of the accused or it may be due to other factors such as the effect of a caution or the advice of counsel. If the jury concluded that such failure was due to a factor that did not reflect on the credibility of the accused, then it must not be given any weight.

Application to this appeal

There is no question in this appeal that Creighton's right of full answer and defence was respected, and he was given full right of cross-examination on the appellant's pre-trial silence. The issue is whether the use of the appellant's pre-trial silence violated his *Charter* rights. There was nothing in the manner or form of the cross-examination that amounted to an improper use of this evidence. Ordinarily, the extent of the use to be made of the answers obtained in cross-examination will not be apparent from the questions and answers themselves, and any limitations on such use must be imposed in the instructions to the jury. For the reasons which I have expressed above, I decline to accede to the appellant's submission that counsel for the accused, Creighton, should not have been allowed to cross-examine on the appellant's silence or that the jury should have been instructed to disregard this evidence. Accordingly, if the charge to the jury had contained proper instructions limiting the use of the evidence to credibility, then the appeal would have failed. The Crown concedes that the charge does not entirely follow the model which it proposes, but submits that it is not so far removed from it that it constitutes a substantial wrong or miscarriage of justice. I agree with Weiler J.A. and for the reasons that she gives that the charge and recharge contain serious misdirections. The jury were clearly invited to consider the evidence of pre-trial silence on the issue of innocence or guilt and as consciousness of guilt. The references to the right to remain silent did not mitigate this misdirection. The recharge was not substantially different.

It would be difficult to justify the position that the distinction between the use of evidence for the purpose of credibility and as positive evidence of guilt is a meaningful one but that, on the other hand, failure to make it in this case did not have any significant effect on the result. I agree with

Weiler J.A. that the Crown has not satisfied its obligation under s. 686(1)(*b*)(iii) of the *Code* to show that if a proper direction had been given the verdict would necessarily have been the same.

Disposition

The appeal is allowed and a new trial ordered.

McLachlin J.: — I agree that the appeal must be allowed and a new trial ordered, but for different reasons than Justice Sopinka.

In my view, the dilemma ably described by my colleague is best dealt with by exclusion of evidence that a co-accused failed to give his version to the authorities at an early date. The co-accused has a constitutional right to silence. He, therefore, cannot be faulted for not giving his version to the police. If the right to silence is to be meaningful, no adverse inferences can be drawn from his failure to do so, either as to guilt or credibility. Pre-trial silence is either a right or it is not a right. If it is a right, the trier of fact should not be permitted to draw adverse inferences from its exercise. If adverse inferences are permitted, then the right to silence is effectively lost, for no accused who wishes to preserve the possibility of putting his story forth at trial can afford to exercise it. The right to silence, if it means anything, must mean that a suspect has the right to refuse to talk to the police and not be penalized for it. Further, since the accused has been informed by the police of the right not to speak, his exercise of it cannot logically found an inference as to his credibility when he later testifies. On this, I agree with the unanimous decision of the High Court of Australia: "the fact of insistence on the right [to remain silent] in the face of questioning does not, of itself and standing alone, have any probative force at all against an accused" (*Bruce v. The Queen* (1987), 61 Aust. L.J. Rep. 603 at p. 604); see also David M. Paciocco, *Charter Principles and Proof in Criminal Cases* (Toronto: Carswell, 1987), at pp. 554-6.

The same considerations govern the contention of the other accused in a joint trial, that he should be allowed to cross-examine on the failure of his co-accused to disclose his version to the police. Since no valid inference can be drawn from exercise of the right to silence, the evidence sought to be adduced should be excluded for lack of relevancy. Alternatively, even if slight probative value could be found, the evidence should be excluded on the ground that it has insufficient probative value to overcome the prejudicial effect on the trial process that arises from the danger that the jury will follow the path of forbidden reasoning and infer, not just lack of credibility, but guilt: *R. v. Seaboyer* (1991), 66 C.C.C. (3d) 321, 83 D.L.R. (4th) 193, [1991] 2 S.C.R. 577.

In summary, exclusion of evidence of failure to disclose to the police is proper, given the absence of probative value of such evidence. Because the evidence lacks probative value, it cannot be suggested that its exclusion denies the co-accused the right to full answer and defence. There is no "trumping" of rights; one of them is simply not attracted. Exclusion also has the practical merit of avoiding putting the accused to the task of justifying the exercise of his rights under the *Canadian Charter of Rights and Freedoms*, and the jury to the almost impossible task of deciding whether "failure to make a statement prior to trial ... reflect[s] on the credibility of the accused or ... [is] due to other factors such as the effect of a caution or the advice of counsel" (as required by the fifth part of Sopinka J.'s suggested charge to the jury).

Admission of evidence of a co-accused's silence leads to this further difficulty. The law of evidence precludes the admission of prior consistent statements to bolster the credibility of an accused. If pre-trial silence can lead to a negative inference as to credibility, the accused is placed in the anomalous situation of being obliged to make a prior consistent statement in order to avoid cross-examination on his silence, but being unable to tender that evidence in support of his own credibility.

It follows, in my view, that the evidence in question should have been excluded. I would allow the appeal and direct a new trial.

The following case addresses whether an accused can be tried on *separate* informations. However, it should be noted that, subject to applications for severance, there is no prohibition against the Crown jointly indicting any multiple accused who have been separately committed for trial or preferring an indictment containing multiple counts against an accused who was committed to stand trial on separate informations.

R. v. CLUNAS

(1992), 70 C.C.C. (3d) 115 (S.C.C.)

[The accused was charged with assault causing bodily harm after an attack on his former girlfriend. He was then charged with re-assaulting her two days later. The accused elected trial by provincial court judge on the first charge. It was then a purely indictable offence. It has since become a hybrid offence. The Crown elected to proceed summarily on the second charge. Though the charges were contained in separate informations, the same trial date was set for each and the accused requested that both charges be dealt with together. The Crown consented. The accused's conviction appeal on the first charge was dismissed by the Court of Appeal.]

The judgment of the court was delivered by

Lamer C.J.C.: — [first, the importance of addressing criminal procedure in the context of potential prejudice rather than in terms of technicalities, is articulated.]

.....

I share this approach to criminal procedure and therefore welcome the opportunity afforded us in this appeal to reconsider this court's decision in *R. v. Phillips* (1983), 8 C.C.C. (3d) 118, 3 D.L.R. (4th) 352, [1983] 2 S.C.R. 161, and *R. v. Khan* (1984), 12 C.C.C. (3d) 193, 10 D.L.R. (4th) 140, [1984] 2 S.C.R. 62.

.....

The issues

Given the approach I intend to take in this appeal, the issues that I will be addressing will be as follows:

1. Did the proceedings in this case constitute two separate trials with the evidence in one trial applying in the other trial?

2. Does a court have jurisdiction to try two separate informations in a single trial?

3. Is it proper to join counts of a summary conviction offence and an indictable offence and try them together?

4. Did the proceedings constitute a procedural irregularity? If so, can s.686(1)(*b*)(iv) of the *Criminal Code*, R.S.C. 1985, c. C-46, be applied to uphold a conviction?

Issue No. 1

[Lamer C.J.C. reviews the conduct of the trial in greater detail.]

... It is clear to me, with all due respect for contrary views, that we are here facing a situation where a trial was conducted simultaneously as regards two distinct informations. This was done at the suggestion of the defence and, therefore, with the accused's consent. That is also amply clear to me.

Issue No. 2

This, therefore, takes us to the second issue, which is whether a court has jurisdiction to do this....

.....

[Lamer C.J.C. then reviews prior judgments of the Court in *Khan* and *Phillips* which held that there was no jurisdiction, even on consent, to try matters on separate informations or indictments together. Having reviewed the reasons then offered up for those judgments, including a concern as to the compellability of the accused, Lamer C.J.C. rejects those reasons.]

While an elaborate procedure is provided under the *Criminal Code* for joint trials, all that has to be done is that to the extent possible the same procedure be followed when joining indictments. For joint trials, the same procedure could be followed when proceeding simultaneously on multiple informations.

I do not think, furthermore, that accused persons being dealt with in separate informations at the same time should be any more compellable against each other, especially in light of s. 11(*c*) of the *Canadian Charter of Rights and Freedoms*, than when tried on one single information or indictment. When two or more accused in different informations are charged with the same offence or with different offences, if they are proceeded against jointly they will not be compellable one against the other. When the Crown chooses to proceed at the same time, the Crown then waives the right to call one accused against the other, as is the case of proceeding against the two accused on the same document.

I, therefore, with respect for contrary views, do not think that the problem referred to in *Phillips* arises. As regards the concern for an accused who might wish to testify with respect to only one of the informations, I think that such a problem would not arise, as it is a case where consent by the accused to a joint trial should and would not be given, and when consent is withheld, under such circumstances it would be inappropriate for the judge to order a joint trial.

As regards the third and fourth concerns alluded to by the court, counsel for the respondent in her factum said the following:

> ... the Court raised the issue of interpretation of provisions in the *Code* referring only to a trial on the "Information" or "Indictment", always worded in the singular. Pursuant to the *Interpretation Act*, R.S.C. 1985, I-21, s. 33(2):
>
> 33(2) words in the singular include the plural, and words in the plural include the singular.
>
> Therefore, it is submitted that the provisions in the *Code* relating to trial can be interpreted as referring to the plural "Information" or "Indictment". The court's fourth concern related to the *Code*'s provision for only one type of joint trial...[I]t is submitted that the *Code* provisions as to joinder and severance are not exhaustive, and should not be interpreted so as to exclude a procedure of joint trials permitted by common law. In addition, it is noteworthy that there is no section in the *Code* prohibiting a joint trial of separate Informations.

I agree with the respondent's argument.

To conclude this portion of the judgment, I would say that when joinder of offences, or of accuseds for that matter, is being considered, the court should seek the consent of both the accused and the prosecution. If consent is withheld, the reasons should be explored. Whether the accused consents or not, joinder should only occur when, in the opinion of the court, it is in the interests of justice and the offences or accuseds could initially have been jointly charged.

I would adopt the American Federal Rules of Criminal Procedure formulation, which is as follows:

> The court may order two or more indictments or informations or both to be tried together if the offenses and the defendants, if there is more than one, could have been joined in a single indictment or information. The procedures shall be the same as if the prosecution were under such single indictment or information.

I would also add, quoting from the Law Reform Commission's Working Paper No. 55, the following:

> ... any particular aspects of the rule in favour of severance would have to be inapplicable in order for this judicial joinder to occur. This rule would thus reflect the rule for unsuccessful severance on a joint charge.

Issue No. 3

This now takes us to the next issue, which is whether, given the difference in procedure, this can be done between charges for summary convictions and charges for indictable offences.

Khan, *supra*, which was heard and decided in 1984, is a case where that issue arises. Indeed, two informations were jointly heard, one setting out an indictable offence and the other a summary conviction. *Khan*, it will be recalled, was decided on the basis of *Phillips*, which stood as a bar to holding joint trials of separate informations whether these informations contained a mix of indictable alone, summary alone, or a mix of summary and indictable.

Applying *Phillips*, there was no need to address the issue as regards the law as it stood in 1985. Indeed, former s. 520(1) of the *Criminal Code* (now s. 591(1)) permitted joinder of any number of indictable offences in an indictment. No mention was made as regards joining either summary conviction offences together or joining summary conviction offences with indictable offences.

This section was substantially amended in 1985 (*Criminal Law Amendment Act*, 1985, S.C. 1985, c. 19, s. 119), to the effect that any number of counts for any number of offences may be joined in the same indictment. I am of the view that the 1985 amendment took away any impediment that might have existed prior to 1985, as regards coupling summary convictions and indictable offences. Therefore, if one can include, in one indictment, summary conviction offences and indictable offences, one should for the reasons I have given previously, be able to proceed jointly when these offences are contained in two distinct informations. Also, it must be noted that s. 795 of the *Criminal Code* states that s. 591(1) is applicable to summary conviction proceedings. There is nothing wrong with so doing. We must, nevertheless, keep in mind the difference of the process as regards indictable offences and summary convictions. It is obvious that the fact that indictable offences must, on some occasions, and may in others, be tried by a judge and a jury, is an impediment to proceeding jointly when before that court with a summary conviction.

Secondly, the fact that preliminary inquiries are available for most indictable offences is another impediment for the joinder of trials. I would, therefore, adopting the suggestion of the Law Reform Commission in its working paper, state the following:

> ... summary conviction offences should be joined with indictable offences only where the accused has waived the right to be tried in a higher court (either with or without a jury) and has also foregone his right to a preliminary hearing. In other words, joinder may occur only where trial on the indictable offence is to take place before the provincial court.

This will occur only when on the indictable offence the accused either will have chosen a trial by Provincial Court judge under Part XIX or, having chosen a trial by judge under Part XIX, has waived his preliminary. As suggested by the Law Reform Commission, in the event of any conflict as to the applicable procedure, indictable offence procedures should apply and crimes triable by jury may be joined with those carrying no right to a jury trial (or preliminary inquiry) provided the accused has consented to the trial of both matters in a forum without a jury and without a preliminary inquiry.

I find support in taking this direction from a resolution passed by the Uniform Law Conference of Canada (which is composed of all Deputy Ministers of Justice or Deputy Attorneys-General, representatives of the Canadian Bar, and other parties appended to the justice system), in

August, 1988, in the course of their proceedings of the 70th annual meeting of that body. It was resolved that the *Criminal Code* be amended to allow for the joinder of summary convictions and indictable offences, with the indictable procedure to then apply.

There remains the problem of appeals. Of course, in cases where an issue common to both informations has gone to the summary conviction appeal court and the Court of Appeal, common sense would dictate that the summary conviction court of appeal should await decision by the higher court.

Issue No. 4

The final question is whether, in this case, proceeding jointly constituted a procedural irregularity. Obviously, no. There is no suggestion on the part of the appellant that there was, understandably so, since it was at the appellant's own suggestion that both informations were tried at the same time.

Disposition

For all of these reasons, I would dismiss the appeal.

Appeal dismissed.

QUESTION

21. Tweetledum and Tweetledee are jointly charged with robbery. Dum made allegedly inculpatory comments to his ex-girlfriend, Alice, suggesting that both he and Dee were involved. An eyewitness also implicates Dum, but not Dee. The Crown has a circumstantial (but far less compelling) case against Dee. However, Dee cannot testify since he has told his own lawyer that he indeed committed the robbery with the Cheshire Cat, not with Dum. Dum knows that Dee is taking this position. What submissions could be made on the issue of severance? If Dee's potential evidence is relevant to this issue, how can it be addressed? Consider in this regard, *R. v. Boulet* (1987), 40 C.C.C. (3d) 38 (Que. C.A.); *Guimond v. The Queen* (1979), 44 C.C.C. (2d) 481 (S.C.C.); *R. v. Zurlo* (1990), 57 C.C.C. (3d) 407 (Que. C.A.).

L. JURY SELECTION

1. Overview

The *Criminal Code*, in large measure, delegates to the provinces the qualifications for jurors to serve in criminal proceedings (s. 626). However, jury selection is governed by the *Criminal Code*.

The jury selection procedure starts when the sheriff or another officer randomly summons eligible people for jury duty. These people comprise the *jury panel*. Though rarely done, "the accused or the prosecutor may challenge the jury panel only on the ground of partiality, fraud or wilful misconduct on the part of the sheriff or officer by whom the panel was returned" (s. 629). This challenge to the panel or *array* is

decided by the trial judge (s. 630). See, for example, *Regina v. Kent, Sinclair and Gode* (1986), 27 C.C.C. (3d) 405 (Man. C.A.).

Where there has been no challenge to the array (or an unsuccessful one), the clerk of the court randomly draws cards, each card containing the name, address and panel number of a prospective juror. The clerk calls out the name, number and occupation of each person. (Counsel can obtain a panel list in advance of the trial, to facilitate jury selection.) The prospective jurors come forward from the body of the courtroom. The clerk initially calls out the number of persons sufficient, in the judge's opinion, to provide a full jury after allowing for orders to excuse, challenges and directions to stand by (s. 629). Each prospective juror is asked to look upon the accused and the accused is asked to look upon the juror. It is at this point that challenges to a prospective juror take place. The accused is initially called upon to declare whether the first prospective juror is challenged either for cause or peremptorily, and thereafter, the Crown and the accused are called on alternately to first make a declaration. Each party indicates "challenge for cause", "challenge" or "content". If both parties are content, the juror is sworn and is seated in the jury box. Once 12 jurors are selected, the process ends.[2] If the first group of persons drawn is exhausted before 12 jurors are selected, the initial procedure is repeated. Where multiple accused are tried together, all of the accused exercise their challenges in the order in which they are named in the indictment or in any other order they agree upon, all of them either before or after the Crown, as outlined earlier (s. 635). The trial judge is also empowered to excuse any person from jury service, whether or not that person has already been called out by the clerk or whether or not any challenge has been made respecting that juror, by reasons of: the person's personal interest in the matter to be tried, the person's relationship with the judge, the prosecutor, the accused, counsel for the accused or with a prospective witness, or the person's personal hardship, or any other cause the judge finds reasonable (s. 632). Section 633 states that: "The judge may direct a [prospective] juror whose name has been called out ... to stand by for reasons of personal hardship or other reasonable cause." Many trial judges will address the entire jury panel prior to calling upon the clerk to call out names and will excuse some prospective jurors at this time. For example, a prospective juror may disclose a close relationship with a witness when a witness list is read out to the jury panel at this stage.

QUESTION

22. A prospective juror comes forward. The clerk announces the name and number of the juror and her occupation as "retired" or as "manager" or as "student". This information is singularly unhelpful to counsel. What can counsel do?

---

[2] Subject to s. 631(2.1) of the *Code*, addressed later.

2. Challenges for Cause

Under s. 638 of the *Criminal Code*, the accused or the Crown may challenge any number of prospective jurors for cause. The *Criminal Code* outlines the grounds for such a challenge, the most significant one being that "a juror is not indifferent between the Queen and the accused" (s. 638(1)(*b*)). In essence, this is an allegation that the prospective juror is not impartial. This challenge is determined by the last two jurors sworn or, if two jurors have not yet been sworn, by two persons present who are appointed by the court (s. 640(2)-(4)).

It is rare that a prospective juror is challenged for cause because of that juror's known partiality. Historically, the challenge has been more commonly based upon the allegation that the pre-trial publicity associated with the case displaces the presumption that jurors are impartial. If the trial judge agrees that a foundation has been laid to permit each prospective juror to be challenged for cause and to be questioned on the issue, counsel will generally submit a list of proposed questions to be put to prospective jurors.

R. v. SHERRATT

(1991), 63 C.C.C. (3d) 193 (S.C.C.)

L'Heureux-Dubé J. (Sopinka, Gonthier and Cory JJ. concurring): — The sole issue raised by this case is the proper interpretation of the challenge for cause provisions found in the *Criminal Code*, R.S.C. 1970, c. C-34. More specifically, the question is whether the accused in this case was properly denied the ability to challenge each prospective juror for cause on the ground of partiality or, in the words of the section, non-indifference.

.....

The accused was charged and convicted in the killing of a pimp by the name of Tommy T....

The crime was committed in Winnipeg, Manitoba, but the accused was picked up for questioning in Dryden, Ontario. On this occasion, he informed the police that he had killed Tommy T. A more detailed statement was given by the accused upon questioning by the Winnipeg police authorities. ... According to the accused's statement to the Winnipeg police, he had disposed of the body in a commercial garbage bin. Unfortunately, by the time the accused was transported back to Manitoba, the bin in question had been emptied. As a result, the police searched the local land-fill site in hopes of locating the body. This search was the subject of some publicity by the media. The media raised questions about the location of the body and about the background and identity of the victim and his involvement in certain killings in the United States. The background of the accused was also apparently the subject of some media speculation. The reports in the media occurred approximately nine to ten months prior to the trial of the accused.

It is against this factual background that the legal question must be analyzed.

.....

At trial, in May, 1988, counsel for the accused informed the judge that he wished to challenge for cause each prospective juror on the ground that they were not "indifferent between the Queen and the Accused". The allegation of potential partiality was based upon the pre-trial publicity described above. Counsel for the accused had prepared a list of 11 questions which he desired to put to each member of the jury panel. He argued that the speculation in the media went to the background and character of the accused and, hence, could prove prejudicial absent individual questioning of the prospective jurors on the basis of the 11 questions.

The Crown responded that the pre-trial publicity could not form the basis for the accused's challenge as it had occurred some nine or 10 months prior to trial. Further, it was the Crown's contention that the media reports were not prejudicial as they failed to establish any connection between the search and discovery of the body of Tommy T. and the arrest of the accused.

The trial judge was not persuaded by the arguments of the accused and rejected the general challenge on the ground of partiality.

.....

[L'Heureux-Dubé J. went on to examine the existing jurisprudence on challenge for cause.]

In rationalizing these various judicial expressions, it is necessary to reflect on what was in fact said by the Ontario Court of Appeal in *Hubbert*, *supra*. While certain broad statements in that case may warrant comment, the court's discussion of the pre-screening procedure and the proper course for a trial judge to follow in an application for a challenge for cause due to alleged partiality, in the main, cannot be challenged. Generally, the court correctly states the law as it is understood in this country when dealing with an application for a challenge for cause based upon partiality. Certain comments may, however, be appropriate in light of the coming into force of the *Charter*. While it is no doubt true that trial judges have a wide discretion in these matters and that jurors will usually behave in accordance with their oaths, these two principles cannot supersede the right of every accused person to a fair trial, which necessarily includes the empanelling of an impartial jury: see The Law Reform Commission of Canada, *The Jury in Criminal Trials* (1980), Working Paper 27.

This, however, does not mean that an accused has the right to a favourable jury nor that the selection procedure can be used to thwart the representativeness that is essential to the proper functioning of a jury. While it may be, in some instances, that the peremptory challenges allocated to the accused and the Crown, and the Crown's additional right to stand aside, will be used by the parties to alter somewhat the degree to which the jury represents the community, peremptory challenges are justified on a number of grounds. The accused may, for example, not have sufficient information to challenge for cause a member of the panel he/she feels should be excluded. Peremptory challenges can also, in certain circumstances, produce a more representative jury depending upon both the nature of the community and the accused. Challenges of this nature also serve to heighten an accused's perception that he/she has had the benefit of a fairly selected tribunal.

As to challenges for cause, they are properly used to rid the jury of prospective members who are not indifferent or who otherwise fall within s. 567 (now s. 638), of the *Code*, but they stray into illegitimacy if used merely, without more, to over- or under-represent a certain class in society or as a "fishing expedition" in order to obtain personal information about the juror. As previously mentioned, information obtained on an ultimately unsuccessful challenge for cause may, however, lead the challenger to exercise the right to challenge peremptorily or to stand aside the particular juror. If the challenge process is used in a principled fashion, according to its underlying rationales, possible inconvenience to potential jurors or the possibility of slightly lengthening trials is not too great a price for society to pay in ensuring that accused persons in this country have, and appear to have, a fair trial before an impartial tribunal, in this case, the jury.

This being said, some words of caution are in order as to the nature of the pre-screening that can be legitimately engaged in by trial judges. If one harkens back to the actual words used by the Court of Appeal in *Hubbert, supra*, it becomes clear, in my opinion, that the procedure envisioned is inoffensive and falls outside of the warnings delivered in *Barrow, supra*, and *Guerin, supra*, as evidenced by the following, at pp. 292-3:

> Turning to the practical consideration of the methods by which the process should be carried out, we deal first with the kind of *obvious partiality* dealt with in the English practice direction. Some trial Judges make a practice of saying to the jury panel, before the selection process begins, something of this nature:
>
> "If there is anyone on this panel who is closely connected with a party to this case or with a witness who is to testify, will you please stand?"
>
> *To take obvious examples, if the juror is the uncle of the accused, or the wife of a witness, or the brother of the investigating police officer, he ought not to serve.*
>
> In our view, the trial Judge on his own should excuse that prospective juror from the case, without more ado... *We think the practice of excusing jurors of obvious partiality is a desirable one in all cases.*

(Emphasis added.)

I agree. And, as pointed out by the Ontario Court of Appeal, if the trial judge does not excuse a juror at this stage, that juror is still subject to challenge or to a direction to stand aside. Nothing said by the Court of Appeal relates to cases of disputed partiality. The initial procedure outlined by the Court of Appeal goes only to such clear-cut cases of partiality that, as said in *Guerin, supra*, and *Barrow, supra*, the consent of counsel is and can be presumed. Once out of obvious situations of non-indifference, as in *Guerin, supra*, and *Barrow, supra*, the procedure takes on a different colour: consent can no longer be presumed and the procedure must conform to that which is set out in the *Criminal Code*. There is absolutely no room for a trial judge to increase further his/her powers and take over the challenge process by deciding controversial questions of partiality. If there exist legitimate grounds for a challenge for cause, outside of the obvious cases addressed by the *Hubbert, supra*, procedure, it must proceed in accordance with the *Code* provisions — the threshold pre-screening mechanism is a poor, and more importantly, an illegal substitute in disputed areas of partiality: see Vidmar and Melnitzer, "Juror Prejudice: An Empirical Study of a Challenge for Cause", 22 Osgoode Hall L.J. 487 (1984). After this initial, narrowly drawn procedure is complete, the process as set out in the *Criminal Code* must be adhered to. I will refer again to the clear words of Dickson C.J.C. in *Barrow, supra*, at pp. 208-9, which, though addressing a somewhat different question, are apposite here:

> The *Code* sets out a detailed process for the selection of an impartial jury. It gives both parties substantial powers in the process and sets up a mechanism to try the partiality of a potential juror when challenged for cause. The trier of partiality is not the judge but a mini-jury of two potential or previously selected jurors ... Parliament has decided that the issue of partiality is a question of fact that must be decided by two of the jurors themselves, not by the judge ... any judge who attempts to participate in such decisions usurps the function of the jurors...

Perhaps more pertinent to the issue here is the question of what degree of pre-trial publicity or, more generally, non-indifference, is necessary to lead to the right to challenge for cause and thus have the trial of the issue proceed before the "mini-jury". The example of pre-trial publicity arises on the facts of this case and the existence of publicity prior to trial would appear to be the most frequent cause for a challenge based upon non-indifference.

A number of factors need to be addressed in answering this question. To begin with, s. 567 (now s. 638) of the *Criminal Code* places little, if any, burden on the challenger. On the other hand, a reasonable degree of control must be retained by the trial judge and, thus, some burden placed upon the challenger to ensure that the selection of the jury occurs in a manner that is in accordance with the principles I have previously articulated and also to ensure that sufficient information is imparted to the trial judge such that the trial of the truth of the challenge is contained within permissible bounds. Thus, while there must be an "air of reality" to the application, it need not be an "extreme" case, as were, for example, the cases of *Zundel, supra*, and *Guerin, supra*. The Ontario Court of Appeal in *Zundel, supra*, provided a useful guide in this regard, at p. 132:

> The real question is whether the particular publicity and notoriety of the accused could potentially have the effect of destroying the prospective juror's indifference between the Crown and the accused.

Postulating rigid guidelines is obviously an impossible task. Lawton J. in *R. v. Kray* (1969), 53 Cr. App. R. 412, draws a valuable distinction, in pre-trial publicity cases, between mere publication of the facts of a case and situations where the media misrepresents the evidence, dredges up and widely publicizes discreditable incidents from an accused's past or engages in speculation as to the accused's guilt or innocence. It may well be that the pre-trial publicity or other ground of alleged partiality will, in itself, provide sufficient reasons for a challenge for cause. The threshold question is not whether the ground of alleged partiality will create such partiality in a juror, but rather whether it could create that partiality which would prevent a juror from being indifferent as to the result.In the end, there must exist a realistic *potential* for the existence of partiality, on a ground sufficiently articulated in the application, before the challenger should be allowed to proceed.

Application to the facts of the case

Applying these principles to the facts of this case, given the whole of the circumstances, the procedure followed by the trial judge was correct. It is unfortunate, however, in my view, that the trial judge used the word "extraordinary" to describe the challenge for cause procedure. As I have hopefully made clear throughout these reasons, the right to challenge for cause is an important one designed to ensure a fair trial. It is of great assistance in the selection of a jury that can properly fulfill those duties accorded it. Further, the ability to challenge for cause rests upon a showing by the challenger of a realistic potential for partiality. The process is neither "extraordinary" nor "exceptional".

Notwithstanding his seeming misapprehension of the nature of the process, the trial judge was correct, in my view, in deciding that there was nothing before him in the present instance that satisfied the requirement set out above. The pre-trial publicity did not satisfy the query, "whether the particular publicity and notoriety of the accused could potentially have the effect of destroying the prospective juror's indifference". Based on the information given to the judge, there was no realistic potential for the existence of partiality on the basis of pre-trial publicity. The trial occurred a substantial period of time after the publicity in question and, more importantly, it appears that the media reports were concerned more with the search and subsequent discovery of the remains of the victim and the victim's reputation than with the accused or subsequent proceedings against him. As Huband J.A. said at p. 249, the pre-trial publicity here "was not of the type to occasion partiality towards an accused". In addition, Jewers J. did not close off the challenge procedure at this point but rather invited continued challenges based on more appropriate information. Such information was not forthcoming despite the representation by accused's counsel that he had material to substantiate his allegations.

Having so concluded, I am none the less of the view that the majority of the Court of Appeal interpreted *Hubbert, supra,* too broadly. I refer particularly to the comments of Huband J.A., at p. 250, regarding the prescreening of prospective jurors for partiality undertaken by the trial judge. This initial process, in my view, only applies, as is evidenced by the words used in *Hubbert, supra*, to consensual, uncontested matters of partiality and not where the challenge for cause is grounded on some pertinent allegation as in *Barrow, supra*, and *Guerin, supra*.

Disposition

As the challenge for cause on the basis of the pre-trial publicity was groundless in this case, I agree in the result with the majority of the Court of Appeal and I would therefore dismiss the appeal.

Stevenson J.: — I have had the advantage of reading the opinion of my colleague Justice L'Heureux-Dubé and agree with her disposition of the appeal and her reasons for disposing of the point raised in the dissent which gave rise to the appeal.

I prefer, however, to restrict my concurrence to that point lest I be thought to be passing upon the discussion of the collateral questions, notably that of the "representative" nature of the jury.

R. v. PARKS

(1993), 84 C.C.C. (3d) 353 (Ont. C.A.);
leave to appeal to S.C.C. refused (1994), 87 C.C.C. (3d) vi

[The appellant was tried for second degree murder and convicted of manslaughter by the jury. He was a drug dealer and the deceased was a cocaine user. The defences put forward included self-defence. The principal ground of appeal arose out of the trial judge's refusal to permit the defence to put certain questions to prospective jurors while challenging them for cause.]

The judgment of the court was delivered by[3]

Doherty J.A.: —

.....

At the outset of the jury selection, defence counsel indicated that he intended to challenge prospective jurors for cause. He had reduced to writing the two questions which he wished to put to each potential juror. They were:

> As the judge will tell you, in deciding whether or not the prosecution has proven the charge against an accused a juror must judge the evidence of the witnesses without bias, prejudice or partiality:
>
> (1) In spite of the judge's direction would your ability to judge witnesses without bias, prejudice or partiality be affected by the fact that there are people involved in cocaine and other drugs?
>
> (2) Would your ability to judge the evidence in the case without bias, prejudice or partiality be affected by the fact that the person charged is a black Jamaican immigrant and the deceased is a white man?

The trial judge refused to permit either question. On appeal, counsel for the appellant argued that both questions should have been allowed. I see no merit in the argument as it relates to the first question. The question implies that a witness's involvement in the drug trade and his or her personal use of illicit drugs should have no relevance in "judging witnesses". To the contrary, those factors could properly be considered by the jury in its assessment of the credibility and reliability of witnesses. I need say no more than to indicate my agreement with the trial judge's ruling on the first question posed by defence counsel.

The propriety of the second question does require detailed consideration.

The appellant is black and the deceased was white. There was, however, no suggestion that the homicide was racially motivated or that race-related matters had anything to do with the events to be placed before the jury. Further, while the question referred to the accused as "a black Jamaican immigrant", it does not appear that his nationality or immigration status were relevant, or would be made known to the jury. In this court (and in

---

[3] **Author's Note: the judgment is extensively footnoted. The footnotes and references thereto have not been reproduced herein.**

the trial judge's reasons) the question was approached on the basis that it referred to a black accused without regard to his country of origin or his status in Canada.

Counsel for the accused did not call any evidence in support of the proposed challenge. He argued that anti-black racism in Toronto was a "notorious fact" which could assert itself through one or more members of the jury drawn from that community who were charged with the responsibility of determining the fate of a black man charged with murdering a white man. Counsel contended that the extent of race-based prejudice in Metropolitan Toronto and the interracial nature of the homicide provided a sufficient foundation for the limited inquiry he proposed.

The trial judge disagreed. He relied on the "presumption" that duly chosen and sworn jurors can be relied on to do their duty and decide the case on the evidence without regard to personal biases and prejudices. The trial judge held there was nothing particular in this case which negated that "presumption".

The "presumption" relied on by the trial judge is well established, both as a fundamental premise of our system of trial by jury, and as an operative principle during the jury selection process: *R. v. Vermette* (1988), 41 C.C.C. (3d) 523 at p. 530, 50 D.L.R. (4th) 385, [1988] 1 S.C.R. 985; *R. v. Hubbert* (1975), 29 C.C.C. (2d) 279 at pp. 289-96, 31 C.R.N.S. 27, 11 O.R. (2d) 464; affirmed 33 C.C.C. (2d) 207*n*, [1977] 2 S.C.R. 267, 15 O.R. (2d) 324*n*. The trial judge's conclusion that the "presumption" could be relied on to overcome potential racial prejudice against a minority accused is consistent with rulings made by other trial judges in this province: *R. v. Racco (No. 2)* (1975), 23 C.C.C. (2d) 205 at p. 208, 29 C.R.N.S. 307 (Ont. Co. Ct.); *R. v. Crosby* (1979), 49 C.C.C. (2d) 255 (Ont. N.C.J.); *R. v. McCollin*, Ont. Ct. (Gen. Div.), Toronto, Dunnet J., December 7,1992 (unreported). Only one trial decision to the contrary has been brought to my attention. That was my decision in *R. v. Lim and Nola*, Ont. S.C., April 2, 1990 (unreported). In that case, however, I went no further than to hold that a trial judge had the discretion to allow a challenge based on alleged racial prejudice.

Before turning to the principles controlling the challenge for cause process, the nature and ambit of the proposed question must be clearly understood. Counsel did not seek to challenge for cause based on race. He did not suggest that a person could be successfully challenged on the basis of his or her colour, or that only persons of a particular race would be challenged for cause. The question as posed was race-neutral and did not assume that only non-blacks would be subject to the challenge. The question also did not seek to challenge prospective jurors based only on their opinions, beliefs or prejudices. The question went beyond that and was directed to the jurors' ability to set aside certain beliefs, opinions or prejudices when performing their duty as a juror. The appellant does not challenge the proscription against challenges based on race, or the beliefs, opinions or prejudices of potential jurors set down in *Hubbert, supra,* at pp. 289-90, and reiterated in *R. v. Zundel* (1987), 31 C.C.C. (3d) 97 at p. 133, 35 D.L.R. (4th) 338, 56 C.R. (3d) 1; leave to appeal to S.C.C. refused, [1987] 1 S.C.R. xii, 61 O.R. (2d) 588*n*, 80 N.R. 317*n*.

The question which counsel wanted to put to potential jurors cannot be criticized as either an effort to obtain a favourable jury or an attempt to indoctrinate prospective jurors with the position to be advanced by the defence at trial. A "no" answer to the question would hardly suggest that the potential juror would be more likely to side with the defence than the Crown. A "yes" answer to the question could be based on a racial bias in favour of the accused in which case, a defence-initiated challenge would result in the loss of a juror who was potentially favourable to the defence. Similarly, as race played no part in the defence to be advanced, it could not be said that counsel sought to use the challenge-for-cause process to fire the first volley in a race-based defence.

I would not characterize the question as a device designed by counsel to gain some insight into the personality of potential jurors so as to enable counsel to more effectively use his peremptory challenges. The proposed inquiry involved a single question focused on a specific issue. It asked only the potential juror's own evaluation of his or her ability to abide by the juror's oath despite the colour of the accused and the interracial nature of the homicide. Counsel did not seek to inquire into individual jurors' life-styles, antecedents, or personal experiences with a view to exposing underlying racial prejudices. He did not propose the kind of wide-ranging personalized disclosure involved in *voir dire* inquiries into potential racial prejudice permitted in some American jurisdictions: *e.g.*, see E. Krauss and B. Bonora, eds., *Jurywork: Systematic Techniques*, 2nd ed. (1985), New York: Clark Boardman, pp. 10-53 to 10-56. Canadian courts have resisted that approach to jury selection: *R. v. Hubbert*, *supra*, at pp. 289-90. Attempts to introduce that methodology in the context of challenges for cause based on racial prejudice raise very difficult problems, which need not be addressed here, given the single and very specific question counsel wished to ask potential jurors.

Nor do I agree with Crown counsel's submission that the question proposed could be counter-productive in that it would "inject racial ... overtones into a case where none existed previously". This submission is borrowed from the concurring opinion of Powell J. in *Turner v. Murray*, 476 U.S. 28 at p. 49 (1986); see also *People v. Mack*, 473 N.E. 2d 880 at pp. 892-3 (1985) (Ill. S. Ct.). The argument, however, only has validity if one assumes that none of the prospective jurors is racially biased. If one or more are biased, their presence in the array, and their potential role as jurors "injects" racial overtones into the proceeding. A question directed at revealing those whose bias renders them partial does not "inject" racism into the trial, but seeks to prevent that bias from destroying the impartiality of the jury's deliberations.

I also cannot agree with the Crown's submission that in a case like the present it is somehow fairer to a black accused to prohibit a challenge premised on race-based partiality. Where that accused wishes to make that inquiry, presumably because of a perceived danger of partiality based on race, I do not think it lies with the Crown to argue that the accused should be protected from himself or herself by denying the request in the interest of fairness to the accused.

I turn now to the principles applicable to the challenge-for-cause process. The accused's right to challenge for cause based on partiality is essential to both the constitutional right to a fair trial and the constitutional right, in cases where the accused is liable to five or more years' imprisonment, to trial by jury. An impartial jury is a crucial first step in the conduct of a fair trial: *R. v. Sherratt* (1991), 63 C.C.C. (3d) 193 at p. 204, [1991] 1 S.C.R. 509, 3 C.R. (4th) 129. The accused's statutory right to challenge potential jurors for cause based on partiality is the only direct means an accused has to secure an impartial jury. The significance of the challenge process to both the appearance of fairness, and fairness itself, must not be underestimated.

The *Criminal Code*, R.S.C. 1985, c. C-46, provides for: the right to challenge for cause based on partiality (s. 638(1)(*b*)); the form in which the challenge may be presented (s. 639), and the way in which the validity of the challenge is to be determined (s. 640). The rest of the controlling law is judge-made. Under the prevailing jurisprudence, the trial judge must supervise and control the challenge process so that it remains within the bounds of a legitimate inquiry into the impartiality of potential jurors. In exercising this supervisory function, the trial judge does not decide the ultimate validity of any challenge for cause based on partiality, but only whether the challenge should proceed: *R. v. Barrow* (1987), 38 C.C.C. (3d) 193 at p. 209, 45 D.L.R (4th) 487, [1987] 2 S.C.R. 694.

Trial judges often perform their supervisory function by vetting the questions counsel propose to ask prospective jurors. The questions must go to an issue which is relevant to the jurors' potential partiality, that is the answers to the question or questions must provide a rational basis upon which the triers may assess partiality. It is not, however, enough that the questions be relevant. The party seeking to put the questions must go further and establish grounds for legitimate concern with respect to the basis for the alleged partiality put forward.

.....

[Sherratt, supra, and Hubbert, supra, are discussed.]

I turn now to the relevance of the question posed by counsel for the accused. To determine relevancy, one must define partiality in the context of the challenge-for-cause process. Partiality has both an attitudinal and behaviourial component. It refers to one who has certain preconceived biases, and who will allow those biases to affect his or her verdict despite the trial safeguards designed to prevent reliance on those biases: J.E. Pfeifer, "Reviewing the Empirical Evidence on Jury Racism: Findings of Discrimination or Discriminatory Findings?", 69 Neb. L.R. 230 (1990). A partial juror is one who is biased and who will discriminate against one of the parties to the litigation based on that bias. To be relevant to partiality, a proposed line of questioning must address both attitudes and behaviour flowing from those attitudes.

Partiality cannot be equated with bias: S.L. Johnson, "Black Innocence and the White Jury", 83 Mich. L.R. 1611 (1985), at pp. 1649-51; D.L. Suggs and B.D. Sales, "Juror Self-Disclosure in the *Voir dire*: A Social Science Analysis", 56 Ind. L.J. 245 (1981), at p. 248. Questions which seek to do no more than establish that a potential juror has beliefs, opinions or biases which may operate for or against a particular party cannot establish partiality. A diversity of views and outlooks is part of the genius of the jury system and makes jury verdicts a reflection of the shared values of the community. It is inevitable that with diversity come views which can be described as biases or prejudices for or against a party to the litigation. Those biases will take various forms and be of varying degrees. Some biases, such as the presumption of innocence, are crucial to the rendering of a true verdict. Others, by their very nature, will be irrelevant to the case in point. Those biases which can be set aside when a person assumes his or her role as juror are also irrelevant to the partiality of the juror. A juror's biases will only render him or her partial if they will impact on the decision reached by that juror in a manner which is immiscible with the duty to render a verdict based only on the evidence and an application of the law as provided by the trial judge.

In this case, the issue to be determined on a challenge for cause was not whether a particular potential juror was biased against blacks, but whether if that prejudice existed, it would cause that juror to discriminate against the black accused in arriving at his or her verdict.

The question framed by counsel for the accused captured both components of the partiality requirement. It asked whether a prospective juror's ability to act in accordance with the trial judge's directions would be affected by the colour of the accused and the interracial nature of the violence alleged. Its relevance to a juror's partiality is obvious if one contemplates the position of a juror who answered "yes" to the question as framed by counsel for the accused. Surely the triers of impartiality would be virtually compelled to reject that juror: *Aldridge v. U.S.*, 283 U.S. 308 (1931), at p. 312, quoting with approval, *State v. McAfee*, 64 N.C. 339 (1870).

Having concluded that the question as put by counsel was relevant to the potential partiality of jurors, I must now determine whether the appellant satisfied the threshold test referred to in *Sherratt*. Was there a realistic possibility that one or more prospective jurors would, because of racial prejudice, not be impartial as between the Crown and the accused?

This question raises two discrete issues:

> Was there a realistic possibility that a potential juror would be biased against a black accused charged with murdering a white person?
>
> AND
>
> Was there a realistic possibility that a prospective juror would be influenced in the performance of his or her judicial duties by racial bias?

Both questions must be addressed. Just as the mere existence of prejudicial pre-trial publicity does not give an automatic right to challenge for cause, the existence of racial prejudice within the community from which jurors are drawn does not entitle an accused to challenge for cause. Counsel's right to challenge for cause on the basis put forward in this case is not resolved by accepting the self-evident proposition that there are people in Metropolitan Toronto who are racially biased. The inquiry must go further. The nature and extent of the bias, the dynamics of jury adjudication, and the effect of directions intended to counter any jury bias must all be considered. In other words, the presumption that jurors will perform their duty according to their oath must be balanced against the threat of a verdict tainted by racial bias.

The existence and the extent of racial bias are not issues which can be established in the manner normally associated with the proof of adjudicative facts. Unlike claims of partiality based on pre-trial publicity, the source of the alleged racial prejudice cannot be identified. There are no specific media reports to examine, and no circulation figures to consider. There is, however, an ever-growing body of studies and reports documenting the extent and intensity of racist beliefs in contemporary Canadian society. Many deal with racism in general, others with racism directed at black persons. Those materials lend support to counsel's submission that widespread anti-black racism is a grim reality in Canada and in particular in Metropolitan Toronto.

That racism is manifested in three ways. There are those who expressly espouse racist views as part of a personal credo. There are others who subconsciously hold negative attitudes towards black persons based on stereotypical assumptions concerning persons of colour. Finally, and perhaps most pervasively, racism exists within the interstices of our institutions. This systemic racism is a product of individual attitudes and beliefs concerning blacks and it fosters and legitimizes those assumptions and stereotypes.

.....

[Doherty J.A. then reviews various reports addressing systemic racism.]

I do not pretend to essay a detailed critical analysis of the studies underlying the various reports to which I have referred. Bearing that limitation in mind, however, I must accept the broad conclusions repeatedly expressed in these materials. Racism, and in particular anti-black racism, is a part of our community's psyche. A significant segment of our community holds overtly racist views. A much larger segment subconsciously operates on the basis of negative racial stereotypes. Furthermore, our institutions, including the criminal justice system, reflect and perpetuate those negative stereotypes. These elements combine to infect our society as a whole with the evil of racism. Blacks are among the primary victims of that evil.

In my opinion, there can be no doubt that there existed a realistic possibility that one or more potential jurors drawn from the Metropolitan Toronto community would, consciously or subconsciously, come to court possessed of negative stereotypical attitudes toward black persons.

The trial judge did not deal directly with the possibility that one or more potential jurors would harbour anti-black bias. I do not suggest that he was not alive to that possibility, although absent an opportunity to examine the relevant materials, he may not have appreciated the nature and extent of those biases within our community. The trial judge proceeded directly to the second issue raised by the proposed challenge. His reliance on the "presumption" referred to earlier indicates that he was satisfied that any concerns referable to anti-black bias could be effectively dealt with by the safeguards present in the post-jury selection phase of the trial. Many such safeguards exist. The juror's oath or affirmation no doubt binds the conscience of many who might otherwise be disposed to decide matters based on assumptions and preconceptions including racial biases. The seriousness of the jury's task and the solemnity of the occasion may have the same effect: Pfeifer, *ibid*, at p. 245. The "diffused impartiality" produced by the melding of 12 diverse and individual perspectives into a single decision-making body may also counter personal prejudices. Similarly, the dynamics of jury deliberations where minds are focused on the evidence, and individual opinions and conclusions must withstand the scrutiny of fellow jurors, offer protection against discriminatory behaviour.

Finally, the trial judge's warnings to the jury that they must not resort to preconceptions or biases, including racial biases, in arriving at their verdict will no doubt have a salutory effect. This safeguard is particularly significant in that it brings to the surface of the proceedings, at a crucial point, the danger of allowing racial biases to influence the verdict. In doing so, it alerts jurors to the need to closely examine their own assessments and conclusions to ensure that such bias has not seeped into their deliberations. This trial judge gave a strong warning against resort to prejudices or biases during the deliberation process.

There is a long-standing debate about the effectiveness of these trial safeguards. That debate is part of the wider dispute concerning the effectiveness of the jury system as an adjudicative process. Our system requires that I accept that the jury system is effective, and that the safeguards are effective, and generally produce verdicts based only on an application of the law as provided by the trial judge to the evidence adduced at trial. The availability of the right to challenge for cause based on partiality, however, demonstrates that in some situations these safeguards are seen to be insufficient, and must be supplemented by the challenge process.

In deciding whether the post-jury selection safeguards against partiality provide a reliable antidote to racial bias, the nature of that bias must be emphasized. For some people, anti-black biases rest on unstated and unchallenged assumptions learned over a lifetime. Those assumptions shape the daily behaviour of individuals, often without any conscious reference to them. In my opinion, attitudes which are engrained in an individual's subconscious, and reflected in both individual and institutional conduct within the community, will prove more resistant to judicial cleansing than will opinions based on yesterday's news and referable to a specific person or event. Johnson, *ibid.*, at p. 1679.

.....

The criminal trial milieu may also accentuate the role of racial bias in the decision-making process. Antiblack attitudes may connect blacks with crime and acts of violence. A juror with such attitudes who hears evidence describing a black accused as a drug dealer involved in an act of violence may regard his attitudes as having been validated by the evidence. That juror may then readily give effect to his or her preconceived negative attitudes towards blacks without regard to the evidence and legal principles essential to a determination of the specific accused's liability for the crime charged: Johnson, *ibid.*, at pp. 1644-7.

Extensive social science research in the United States gives further reason to believe that racially prejudiced attitudes translate into discriminatory verdicts within the jury room. The foundational work of Kalven and Zeisel reached no conclusion with respect to the impact of race on jury verdicts. The authors indicated that the "few scattered findings" available from their study provided no basis for any conclusion. They also observed that it was impossible based on their study to say anything about interracial crimes. Kalven and Zeisel did, however, observe that jury "sympathy" for a particular defendant, a major contributor to jury leniency, was less likely to be shown in the case of a black defendant than in the case of a white defendant. Black defendants were more likely to be viewed as "unattractive".

Subsequent empirical studies in the United States using mock juries suggest that juries are more inclined to convict defendants who are not of the same race as the juror. This is especially so where the evidence against the accused is not strong, or where the victim of the offence is of the same race as the juror. Archival studies based on the results of actual cases are said to support this view.

The validity of applying the conclusions drawn from mock jury studies to the performance of real juries has been subject to strong and cogent criticism. There are also persuasive arguments against reliance on the archival data as a basis for concluding that juries discriminate based on race.

Even accepting that these studies suffer from the inadequacies detailed by the critics, they clearly go at least so far as to indicate that there is a realistic possibility that jurors' verdicts are affected by the race of the accused where that accused is of a different race than the juror. This possibility is greater in crimes involving interracial violence where the victim is of the same race as the juror.

[The American case law is then analyzed.]

There are relatively little Canadian data relating to the impact of racial bias on jury verdicts. Section 649 of the *Criminal Code* effectively bars research into the effect of racial bias on actual jury deliberations. I have located only one Canadian mock jury study. That study attempted to determine whether white jurors discriminated against a West Indian black accused on the basis of colour. The authors reported...:

> It was found that (a) prejudicial attitudes were not replicated in this simulated legal setting; (b) there was an absence of prejudicial, subjective perceptions of the victim and the defendant; (c) the perception of the victim was not affecting the subject's perception of the defendant; and (d) guilt ratings and sentencing decisions were not prejudiced by the ethnic background of either the defendant or victim.

The authors did, however, refer to a second Canadian study (not available to this writer), which reached a contrary conclusion. The study concluded:

> We present this interpretation of the results with caution. Further investigation of prejudicial attitudes both within and outside of the legal context in Canada is necessary before any national comparison can be drawn with the United States.

Despite the lack of empirical data, Canadian commentators have no doubt that racist attitudes do impact on jury verdicts where the accused is a member of a racial minority. In 1984, Vidmar and Melnitzer referred to the "growing awareness that Canadian society is marked by racism and other prejudices that might jeopardize the right of an accused to a fair trial". More recently, Professor Petersen observed:

> The threshold test, as established by the Supreme Court of Canada, is whether or not there exists a realistic potential for partiality on the part of a prospective juror. It remains to be seen whether the judiciary will be willing, in future cases, to admit the realistic potential for racist partiality on the part of virtually any juror.
>
> To refuse to do so would demonstrate a regrettable lack of even rudimentary race awareness. People of colour experience racism in all aspects of their lives (*e.g.* employment, housing, public transit and education). It is unrealistic to assume that racism will not also be present in the jury room...

Mr. D. Pomerant, in a paper prepared for the Law Reform Commission of Canada, reviewed the current practices relating to challenges for cause based on partiality. He found that they failed to adequately address claims of partiality based on general racial biases. He recommended ...:

> The law should clearly provide that lack of partiality may be established by evidence that a prospective juror harbours either general or specific discriminatory attitudes, beliefs or prejudices that will affect his or her judgment in the case to be tried.

The ever-developing awareness of the nature and extent of racism, and in particular anti-black racism in Metropolitan Toronto, suggests that the insights provided by the American material, and the conclusions of Canadian commentators have at least some application to juries selected from among the residents of Metropolitan Toronto. I am satisfied that in at least some cases involving a black accused there is a realistic possibility that one or more jurors will discriminate against that accused because of his or her colour. In my view, a trial judge, in the proper exercise of his or her discretion, could permit counsel to put the question posed in this case, in any trial held in Metropolitan Toronto involving a black accused. I would go further and hold that it would be the better course to permit that question in all such cases where the accused requests the inquiry.

There will be circumstances in addition to the colour of the accused which will increase the possibility of racially prejudiced verdicts. It is impossible to provide an exhaustive catalogue of those circumstances. Where they exist, the trial judge must allow counsel to put the question suggested in this case.

In my opinion, the interracial nature of the violence involved in this case, and the fact that the alleged crime occurred in the course of the black accused's involvement in a criminal drug transaction, combined to provide circumstances in which it was essential to the conduct of a fair trial that counsel be permitted to put the question. With respect, I must conclude that the trial judge erred in refusing to allow counsel to ask the question.

In reaching my conclusion I have not relied on a costs/benefit analysis. Fairness cannot ultimately be measured on a balance sheet. That kind of analysis, however, supports my conclusion: *Ham v. South Carolina*, [409 U.S. 524 (1973)], at pp. 533-4, *per* Marshall J. (dissenting). The only "cost" is a small increase in the length of the trial. There is no "cost" to the prospective juror. He or she should not be embarrassed by the question; nor can the question realistically be seen as an intrusion into a juror's privacy.

There are at least three benefits to allowing the question. Some potential jurors who would discriminate against a black accused are eliminated. Prospective jurors who can arrive at an impartial verdict are sensitized from the outset of the proceedings to the need to confront potential racial bias and ensure that it does not impact on their verdict. In this regard, the challenge process would serve the same purpose as the trial judge's directions to the jury concerning the basis on which they must approach their task and reach their verdict. Lastly, permitting the question enhances the appearance of fairness in the mind of the accused. As indicated earlier, many blacks perceive the criminal justice system as inherently racist. A refusal to allow a black accused to even raise the possibility of racial discrimination with prospective jurors can only enhance that perception. By allowing the question, the court acknowledges that the accused's perception is worthy of consideration.

[A new trial was ordered on the manslaughter charge.]

R. v. WILLIAMS

(1998), 124 C.C.C. (3d) 481 (S.C.C.)

[The accused was a member of the aboriginal community. At his first trial, he applied to question potential jurors for racial bias under s. 638 of the *Code*. The trial judge ruled that the accused had met the threshold test and allowed potential jurors to be asked two questions: (1) Would your ability to judge the evidence in the case without bias, prejudice or partiality be affected by the fact that the person charged is an Indian? (2) Would your ability to judge the evidence in the case without bias, prejudice, or partiality be affected by the fact that the person charged is an Indian and the complainant is white? After jury selection the Crown successfully applied for a mistrial based on procedural error made by the court. The accused brought a motion for an order permitting him to challenge jurors for cause at the second trial. The second trial judge while accepting that aboriginals historically have been and continue to be the object of bias and prejudice, rejected the argument that the widespread bias against aboriginals created a reasonable possibility of partiality sufficient to support a challenge for cause. The Court of Appeal upheld this decision. The issue made its way to the Supreme Court of Canada.]

The judgment of the court was delivered by

McLachlin J.: —

.....

The Prevailing Canadian Approach to Jury Challenges for Lack of Indifference Between the Crown and the Accused

The prosecution and the defence are entitled to challenge potential jurors for cause on the ground that "a juror is not indifferent between the Queen and the accused". Lack of "indifference" may be translated as "partiality", the term used by the Courts below. "Lack of indifference" or "partiality", in turn, refer to the possibility that a juror's knowledge or beliefs may affect the way he or she discharges the jury function in a way that is improper or unfair to the accused. A juror who is partial or "not indifferent" is a juror who is inclined to a certain party or a certain conclusion.

.....

... Interest prejudice arises when jurors may have a direct stake in the trial due to their relationship to the defendant, the victim, witnesses or outcome. Specific prejudice involves attitudes and beliefs about the particular case that may render the juror incapable of deciding guilt or innocence with an impartial mind. These attitudes and beliefs may arise from personal knowledge of the case, publicity through mass media, or public discussion and rumour in the community. Generic prejudice, the class of prejudice at issue on this appeal, arises from stereotypical attitudes about the defendant, victims, witnesses or the nature of the crime itself. Bias against a racial or ethnic group or against persons charged with sex abuse are examples of generic prejudice. Finally, conformity prejudice arises when the case is of significant interest to the community causing a juror to perceive that there is strong community feeling about a case coupled with an expectation as to the outcome.

Knowledge or bias may affect the trial in different ways. It may incline a juror to believe that the accused is likely to have committed the crime alleged. It may incline a juror to reject or put less weight on the evidence of the accused. Or it may, in a general way, predispose the juror to the Crown, perceived as representative of the "white" majority against the minority-member accused, inclining the juror, for example, to resolve doubts about aspects of the Crown's case more readily: see Sheri Lynn Johnson, "Black Innocence and the White Jury" (1985), 83 Mich. L. Rev. 1611. When these things occur, a juror, however well intentioned, is not indifferent between the Crown and the accused. The juror's own deliberations and the deliberations of other jurors who may be influenced by the juror, risk a verdict that reflects, not the evidence and the law, but juror preconceptions and prejudices. The aim of s. 638 of the *Code* is to prevent effects like these from contaminating the jury's deliberations and hence the trial: see *R. v. Hubbert* (1975), 29 C.C.C. (2d) 279 (Ont. C.A.). The aim, to put it succinctly, is to ensure a fair trial.

The practical problem is how to ascertain when a potential juror may be partial or "not indifferent" between the Crown and the accused. There are two approaches to this problem. The first approach is that prevailing in the United States. On this approach, every jury panel is suspect. Every candidate for jury duty may be challenged and questioned as to preconceptions and prejudices on any sort of trial. As a result, lengthy trials of jurors before the trial of the accused are routine.

Canada has taken a different approach. In this country, candidates for jury duty are presumed to be indifferent or impartial. Before the Crown or the accused can challenge and question them, they must raise concerns which displace that presumption. Usually this is done by the party seeking the challenge calling evidence substantiating the basis of the concern. Alternatively, where the basis of the concern is "notorious" in the sense of being widely known and accepted, the law of evidence may permit a judge to take judicial notice of it. This might happen, for example, where the basis of the concern is widespread publicity of which the judge and everyone else in the community is aware. The judge has a wide discretion in controlling the challenge process, to prevent its abuse, to ensure it is fair to the prospective juror as well as the accused, and to prevent the trial from being unnecessarily delayed by unfounded challenges for cause: see *Hubbert, supra*.

Judicial discretion, however, must be distinguished from judicial whim. A judge exercising the discretion to permit or refuse challenges for cause must act on the evidence and in a way that fulfills the purpose of s. 638(1)(*b*) — to prevent persons who are not indifferent between the Crown and the accused from serving on the jury. Stated otherwise, a trial judge, in the exercise of the discretion, cannot "effectively curtail the statutory right to challenge for cause": see *R. v. Zundel (No. 1)* (1987), 31 C.C.C. (3d) 97, at p. 135 (leave to appeal refused [1987] 1 S.C.R. xii). To guide judges in the exercise of their discretion, this Court formulated a rule in *Sherratt*, [(1991), 63 C.C.C. (3d) 193 (S.C.C.)]: the judge should permit challenges for cause where there is a "realistic potential" of the existence of partiality. *Sherratt* was concerned with the possibility of partiality arising from pretrial publicity. However, as the courts in this case accepted, it applies to all requests for challenges based on bias, regardless of the origin of the apprehension of partiality.

Applying *Sherratt* to the case at bar, the enquiry becomes whether in this case, the evidence of widespread bias against aboriginal people in the community raises a realistic potential of partiality.

Identifying the Evidentiary Threshold

Esson C.J. and the Court of Appeal applied the test of "realistic potential" of partiality. However, they took a different view from that of Hutchison J. as to when the evidence establishes a realistic potential of partiality. The debate before us divided on the same lines.

The Crown argues that evidence of widespread racial bias against persons of the accused's race does not translate into a "realistic potential" for partiality. There is a presumption that jurors will act impartially, whatever their pre-existing views. Evidence of widespread bias does not rebut that presumption. More is required. The Crown does not detail what evidence might suffice. However, it emphasizes that the evidence must point to not only bias, but also partiality, or bias that may affect the outcome. What is required, in the Crown's submission, is concrete evidence showing prejudice that would not be capable of being set aside at trial. The Crown interprets *Parks* [(1993), 84 C.C.C. (3d) 353 (Ont. C.A.)], where challenges for cause for racial bias in the community were permitted, as being an exceptional case where the nature and extent of the racial bias was sufficiently extreme to establish a reasonable possibility of partiality.

The defence takes a different view. First, it argues that *Sherratt, supra*, establishes that the right to challenge for cause is not exceptional or extraordinary or extreme. Second, it suggests that evidence of widespread prejudice against aboriginals in the community suffices to raise a "realistic potential" for partiality, entitling the accused to question potential jurors as to their prejudices as to whether they will be able to set them aside in discharging their duty as jurors. In the defence submission, the evidentiary threshold proposed by the Crown, Esson C.J. and the Court of Appeal is too high.

In my respectful view, the positions of the Crown, Esson C.J. and the Court of Appeal reflect a number of errors that lead to the evidentiary threshold for challenges for cause being set too high. I will discuss each of these in turn.

(1) The Assumption that Prejudice Will be Judicially Cleansed

Underlying the Crown's submissions (as well as the judgments of Esson C.J. and the Court of Appeal) is the assumption that generally jurors will be able to identify and set aside racial prejudice. Only in exceptional cases is there a danger that racial prejudice will affect a juror's impartiality. In contrast, the defence says that jurors may not be able to set aside racial prejudices that fall short of extreme prejudice. Is it correct to assume that jurors who harbour racial prejudices falling short of extreme prejudice will set them aside when asked to serve on a jury? A consideration of the nature of racial prejudice and how it may affect the decision-making process suggests that it is not.

To suggest that all persons who possess racial prejudices will erase those prejudices from the mind when serving as jurors is to underestimate the insidious nature of racial prejudice and the stereotyping that underlies it. As *Vidmar* ["Pre-trial prejudice in Canada: a comparative perspective on the criminal jury" (1996), 79 Jud. 249], points out, racial prejudice interfering with jurors' impartiality is a form of discrimination. It involves making distinctions on the basis of class or category without regard to individual merit. It rests on preconceptions and unchallenged assumptions that unconsciously shape the daily behaviour of individuals. Buried deep in the human psyche, these preconceptions cannot be easily and effectively identified and set aside, even if one wishes to do so. For this reason, it cannot be assumed that judicial directions to act impartially will always effectively counter racial prejudice: see *Johnson* ["Black Innocence and the White Jury" (1985), 83 Mich. L. Rev. 1611].

.....

Racial prejudice and its effects are as invasive and elusive as they are corrosive. We should not assume that instructions from the judge or other safeguards will eliminate biases that may be deeply ingrained in the subconscious psyches of jurors. Rather, we should acknowledge the destructive potential of subconscious racial prejudice by recognizing that the post-jury selection safeguards may not suffice. Where doubts are raised, the better policy is to err on the side of caution and permit prejudices to be examined. Only then can we know with any certainty whether they exist and whether they can be set aside or not. It is better to risk allowing what are in fact unnecessary challenges, than to risk prohibiting challenges which are necessary: see *Aldridge v. United States*, 283 U.S. 308 (1931) at p. 314, and *Parks, supra*.

It follows that I respectfully disagree with the suggestion in *R. v. B. (A.)* (1997), 33 O.R. (3d) 321 at p. 343, 115 C.C.C. (3d) 421 *sub nom. R. v. Betker* (C.A.) that a motion to challenge for cause must be dismissed if there is "no concrete evidence" that any of the prospective jurors "could not set aside their biases". Where widespread racial bias is shown, it may well be reasonable for the trial judge to infer that some people will have difficulty identifying and eliminating their biases. It is therefore reasonable to permit challenges for cause. This is not to suggest that a prospective juror who on a challenge for cause admits to harbouring a relevant racial prejudice must necessarily be rejected. It is for the triers on the challenge for cause to determine: (1) whether a particular juror is racially prejudiced in a way that could affect his or her partiality; and (2) if so, whether the juror is capable of setting aside that prejudice.

Parliament itself has acknowledged that jurors may sometimes be unable to set aside their prejudices and act impartially between the Crown and the accused, despite our hope and expectation that they will do so. It is implicit in s. 638(2) that in Parliament's view, jurors may harbour knowledge and prejudices that may not be entirely offset by the trial judge's direction to decide the case impartially on the evidence. If judicial cleansing were a complete answer to the preconceptions and predispositions of jurors, there would be no need for s. 638(1)(*b*). Trial judges may conclude that some predispositions can be safely regarded as curable by judicial direction. However, s. 638(1)(*b*) reminds us that judicial cleansing is not always a complete answer. Where the predisposition is one as complex and insidious as racial prejudice, we should not assume without more that the judges' instructions will always neutralize it.

This Court rejected the argument that prejudice based on pre-trial publicity could be cured by the safeguards in the trial process in *Sherratt, supra,* at p. 532, *per* L'Heureux-Dubé J.:

> While it is no doubt true that trial judges have a wide discretion in these matters and that jurors will usually behave in accordance with their oaths, these two principles cannot supersede the right of every accused person to a fair trial, which necessarily includes the empanelling of an impartial jury.

The same may be said of many forms of prejudice based on racial stereotypes. The expectation that jurors usually behave in accordance with their oaths does not obviate the need to permit challenges for cause in circumstances such as the case at bar, where it is established that the community suffers from widespread prejudice against people of the accused's race.

(2) Insistence on the Necessity of a Link Between the Racist Attitude and the Potential for Juror Partiality

The Court of Appeal, *per* Macfarlane J.A., stated that the existence of a significant degree of racial bias in the community from which the panel is drawn is, by itself, not sufficient to allow a challenge for cause because bias cannot be equated with partiality. The court held that in order for the appellant to be successful, there must be some evidence of bias against aboriginal persons which is of a particular nature and extent; evidence which only displays a "general bias" against a racial group is insufficient to warrant a challenge for cause. The Crown goes even further, arguing that racial prejudice in the community must be linked to specific aspects of the trial in order to support a challenge for cause. More particularly, it asserts that where, as here, the defence was that another aboriginal committed the crime, race could have no relevance because the jury was obliged to decide between two aboriginals.

I cannot, with respect, accept this contention. In my view, it is unduly restrictive. Evidence of widespread racial prejudice may, depending on the nature of the evidence and the circumstances of the case, lead to the conclusion that there is a realistic potential for partiality. The potential for partiality is irrefutable where the prejudice can be linked to specific aspects of the trial, like a widespread belief that people of the accused's race are more likely to commit the crime charged. But it may be made out in the absence of such links.

Racial prejudice against the accused may be detrimental to an accused in a variety of ways. The link between prejudice and verdict is clearest where there is an "interracial element" to the crime or a perceived link between those of the accused's race and the particular crime. But racial prejudice may play a role in other, less obvious ways. Racist stereotypes may affect how jurors assess the credibility of the accused. Bias can shape the information received during the course of the trial to conform with the bias: see *Parks, supra,* at p. 372. Jurors harbouring racial prejudices may consider those of the accused's race less worthy or perceive a link between those of the accused's race and crime in general. In this manner, subconscious racism may make it easier to conclude that a black or aboriginal accused engaged in the crime regardless of the race of the complainant: see

Kent Roach, "Challenges for Cause and Racial Discrimination" (1995), 37 C.L.Q. 410 at p. 421.

Again, a prejudiced juror might see the Crown as non-aboriginal or non-black and hence to be favoured over an aboriginal or black accused. The contest at the trial is between the accused and the Crown. Only in a subsidiary sense is it between the accused and another aboriginal. A prejudiced juror might be inclined to favour non-aboriginal Crown witnesses against the aboriginal accused. Or a racially prejudiced juror might simply tend to side with the Crown because, consciously or unconsciously, the juror sees the Crown as a defender of majoritarian interests against the minority he or she fears or disfavours. Such feelings might incline the juror to resolve any doubts against the accused.

Ultimately, it is within the discretion of the trial judge to determine whether widespread racial prejudice in the community, absent specific "links" to the trial, is sufficient to give an "air of reality" to the challenge in the particular circumstances of each case.

.....

At the second stage of the actual challenge for cause, the issue of how any prejudice may play out in the context of the trial comes to the forefront. The triers may conclude that the connection between a prospective juror's prejudices and the trial are so small that they cannot realistically translate into partiality. Conversely, the triers might conclude that a prospective juror's beliefs that people of the accused's race are more likely than others to commit the type of crime alleged are highly indicative of partiality. Such considerations, while not essential to finding a right to challenge for cause, may be determinative on the challenge for cause itself.

(3) Confusion Between the Two Phases of the Challenge for Cause Process

Section 638(2) requires two inquiries and entails two different decisions with two different tests. The first stage is the inquiry before the judge to determine whether challenges for cause should be permitted. The test at this stage is whether there is a realistic potential or *possibility* for partiality. The question is whether there is reason to suppose that the jury pool *may* contain people who are prejudiced and whose prejudice *might not* be capable of being set aside on directions from the judge. The operative verbs at the first stage are "may" and "might". Since this is a preliminary inquiry which may affect the accused's *Charter* rights (see below), a reasonably generous approach is appropriate.

If the judge permits challenges for cause, a second inquiry occurs on the challenge itself. The defence may question potential jurors as to whether they harbour prejudices against people of the accused's race, and if so, whether they are able to set those prejudices aside and act as impartial jurors. The question at this stage is whether the candidate in question *will* be able to act impartially. To demand, at the preliminary stage of determining whether a challenge for cause should be permitted, proof that the jurors in the jury pool will not be able to set aside any prejudices they may harbour and act impartially, is to ask the question more appropriate for the second stage.

The Crown conflates the two stages of the process. Instead of asking whether there is a potential or possibility of partiality at the stage of determining the right to challenge for cause, it demands proof that widespread racism will result in a partial jury. The assumption is that absent such evidence, no challenge for cause should be permitted. This is not the appropriate question at the preliminary stage of determining the right to challenge for cause. The question at this stage is not whether anyone in the jury pool will in fact be unable to set aside his or her racial prejudices but whether there is a realistic *possibility* that this *could* happen.

(4) Impossibility of Proving That Racism in Society Will Lead to Juror Partiality

To require the accused to present evidence that jurors will in fact be unable to set aside their prejudices as a condition of challenge for cause is to set the accused an impossible task. It is extremely difficult to isolate the jury decision and attribute a particular portion of it to a given racial prejudice observed at the community level. Jury research based on the study of actual trials cannot control all the variables correlated to race. Studies of mock juries run into external validity problems because they cannot recreate an authentic trial experience: see Jeffrey E. Pfeiffer, "Reviewing the Empirical Evidence on Jury Racism: Findings of Discrimination or Discriminatory Findings?" (1990), 69 Nebr. L. Rev. 230. As recognized by Doherty J.A. in *Parks, supra*, at p. 366, "[t]he existence and extent of [matters such as] racial bias are not issues which can be established in the manner normally associated with the proof of adjudicative facts".

"Concrete" evidence as to whether potential jurors can or cannot set aside their racial prejudices can be obtained only by questioning a juror. If the Canadian system permitted jurors to be questioned after trials as to how and why they made the decisions they did, there might be a prospect of obtaining empirical information on whether racially prejudiced jurors can set aside their prejudices. But s. 649 of the *Code* forbids this. So, imperfect as it is, the only way we have to test whether racially prejudiced jurors will be able to set aside their prejudices and judge impartially between the Crown and the accused, is by questioning prospective jurors on challenges for cause. In many cases, we can infer from the nature of widespread racial prejudice, that some jurors at least may be influenced by those prejudices in their deliberations. Whether or not this risk will materialize must be left to the triers of impartiality on the challenge for cause. To make it a condition of the right to challenge to cause is to require the defence to prove the impossible and to accept that some jurors may be partial.

(5) Failure to Read s. 638(1)(b) Purposively

The object of s. 638(1)(*b*) must be to prevent persons who may not be able to act impartially from sitting as jurors. This object cannot be achieved if the evidentiary threshold for challenges for cause is set too high.

As discussed above, to ask an accused person to present evidence that some jurors will be unable to set their prejudices aside is to ask the impossible. We may infer in many cases, however, from the nature of racial prejudice, that some prospective jurors, in a community where prejudice against people of the accused's race is widespread, may be both prejudiced and unable to identify completely or free themselves from the effects of those prejudices. It follows that the requirement of concrete evidence that widespread racism will cause partiality would not fulfill the purpose of s. 638(1)(*b*).

Similarly, an evidentiary threshold of extreme prejudice would fail to fulfill the object of s. 638(1)(*b*). Extreme prejudice is not the only sort of prejudice that may render a juror partial. Ordinary "garden-variety" prejudice has the capacity to sway a juror and may be just as difficult to detect and eradicate as hatred. A threshold met only in exceptional cases would catch only the grossest forms of racial prejudice. Less extreme situations may raise a real risk of partiality. Yet there would be no screening of jurors in those situations. The aim of the section — to permit partial jurors to be identified and eliminated — would be only partially achieved. The exceptional nature of a situation is a poor indicator of whether there is a realistic danger or potential of partiality. Widespread racial prejudice is by definition not exceptional. Indeed, the very fact that it is not exceptional may add to a concern that some members of the jury pool may possess attitudes that may interfere with the impartial discharge of their obligations.

This raises the question of what evidentiary standard is appropriate on applications to challenge for cause based on racial prejudice. The appellant appears to accept the standard of widespread racial prejudice in the community. Interveners, however, urge a lower standard. One suggestion is that all aboriginal accused should have the right to challenge for cause. Another is that any accused who is a member of a disadvantaged group under s. 15 of the *Charter* should have the right to challenge for cause. Also possible is a rule which permits challenge for cause whenever there is bias against the accused's race in the community, even if that bias is not general or widespread.

A rule that accords an automatic right to challenge for cause on the basis that the accused is an aboriginal or member of a group that encounters discrimination conflicts from a methodological point of view with the approach in *Sherratt, supra*, that an accused may challenge for cause only upon establishing that there is a realistic potential for juror partiality. For example, it is difficult to see why women should have an automatic right to challenge for cause merely because they have been held to constitute a disadvantaged group under s. 15 of the *Charter*. Moreover, it is not correct to assume that membership in an aboriginal or minority group always implies a realistic potential for partiality. The relevant community for purposes of the rule is the community from which the jury pool is drawn. That community may or may not harbour prejudices against aboriginals. It likely would not, for example, in a community where aboriginals are in a majority position. That said, absent evidence to the contrary, where widespread prejudice against people of the accused's race is demonstrated at a national or provincial level, it will often be reasonable to infer that such prejudice is replicated at the community level.

On the understanding that the jury pool is representative, one may safely insist that the accused demonstrate widespread or general prejudice against his or her race in the community as a condition of bringing a challenge for cause. It is at this point that bigoted or prejudiced people have the capacity to affect the impartiality of the jury.

I add this. To say that widespread racial prejudice in the community can suffice to establish the right to challenge for cause in many cases is not to rule out the possibility that prejudice less than widespread might in some circumstances meet the *Sherratt* test. The ultimate question in each case is whether the *Sherratt* standard of a realistic potential for partiality is established.

(6) Failure to Interpret s. 638(1)(b) in Accordance with the Charter

Parliament's laws should be interpreted in a way that conforms to the constitutional requirements of the *Charter*: see *Slaight Communications Inc. v. Davidson*, [1989] 1 S.C.R. 1038, 59 D.L.R. (4th) 416. More particularly, where Parliament confers a discretion on a judge, it is presumed that Parliament intended the judge to exercise that discretion in accordance with the *Charter*: see *Slaight, supra*. This applies to the discretion conferred on trial judges by s. 638(2) of the *Code*.

The s. 11(*d*) of the *Charter* guarantees to all persons charged in Canada the right to be presumed innocent "until proven guilty according to law in a fair and public hearing *by an independent and impartial tribunal*". A *Charter* right is meaningless, unless the accused is able to enforce it. This means that the accused must be permitted to challenge potential jurors where there is a realistic potential or possibility that some among the jury pool may harbour prejudices that deprive them of their impartiality.

This Court in *Sherratt, supra*, at p. 525, *per* L'Heureux-Dubé J., asserted the need for guarantees, as opposed to presumptions, of impartiality if *Charter* rights are to be respected:

> The perceived importance of the jury and the *Charter* right to jury trial is meaningless without some guarantee that it will perform its duties impartially and represent, as far as is possible and appropriate in the circumstances, the larger community. Indeed, without the two characteristics of impartiality and representativeness, a jury would be unable to perform properly many of the functions that make its existence desirable in the first place.

Doherty J.A. in *Parks, supra*, at p. 362, similarly underlined the need for safeguards of the accused's s. 11(*d*) *Charter* rights:

> The accused's statutory right to challenge potential jurors for cause based on partiality is the only direct means an accused has to secure an impartial jury. The significance of the challenge process to both the appearance of fairness, and fairness itself, must not be underestimated.

The challenge for cause is an essential safeguard of the accused's s. 11(*d*) *Charter* right to a fair trial and an impartial jury. A representative jury pool and instructions from counsel and the trial judge are other safeguards. But the right to challenge for cause, in cases where it is shown that a realistic potential exists for partiality, remains an essential filament in the web of protections the law has woven to protect the constitutional right to have one's guilt or innocence determined by an impartial jury. If the *Charter* right is undercut by an interpretation of s. 638(1)(*b*) that sets too high a threshold for challenges for cause, it will be jeopardized.

The accused's right to be tried by an impartial jury under s. 11(*d*) of the *Charter* is a fair trial right. But it may also be seen as an anti-discrimination right. The application, intentional or unintentional, of racial stereotypes to the detriment of an accused person ranks among the most destructive forms of discrimination. The result of the discrimination may not be the loss of a benefit or a job or housing in the area of choice, but the loss of the accused's very liberty. The right must fall at the core of the guarantee in s. 15 of the *Charter* that "[e]very individual is equal before and under the law and has the right to the equal protection and equal benefit of the law without discrimination".

Section s. 638(1)(*b*) should be read in light of the fundamental rights to a fair trial by an impartial jury and to equality before and under the law. A principled exercise of discretion in accordance with *Charter* values is required: see *Sherratt, supra*.

Although allowing challenges for cause in the face of widespread racial prejudice in the community will not eliminate the possibility of jury verdicts being affected by racial prejudice, it will have important benefits. Jurors who are honest or transparent about their racist views will be removed. All remaining jurors will be sensitized from the outset of the proceedings regarding the need to confront racial prejudice and will help ensure that it does not impact on the jury verdict. Finally, allowing such challenges will enhance the appearance of trial fairness in the eyes of the accused and other members of minority groups facing discrimination: see *Parks, supra*.

(7) The Slippery Slope Argument

The Crown concedes that practical concerns cannot negate the right to a fair trial. The Court of Appeal also emphasized this. Yet behind the conservative approach some courts have taken, one detects a fear that to permit challenges for cause on the ground of widespread prejudice in the community would be to render our trial process more complex and more costly, and would represent an invasion of the privacy interests of prospective jurors without a commensurate increase in fairness. Some have openly expressed the fear that if challenges for cause are permitted on grounds of racial prejudice, the Canadian approach will quickly evolve into the approach in the United States of routine and sometimes lengthy challenges for cause of every juror in every case with attendant cost, delay and invasion of juror privacy.

In my view, the rule enunciated by this Court in *Sherratt, supra*, suffices to maintain the right to a fair and impartial trial, without adopting the United States model or a variant on it. *Sherratt* starts from the presumption that members of the jury pool are capable of serving as impartial jurors. This means that there can be no automatic right to challenge for cause. In order to establish such a right, the accused must show that there is a realistic potential that some members of the jury pool may be biased in a way that may impact negatively on the accused. A realistic potential of racial prejudice can often be demonstrated by establishing widespread prejudice in the community against people of the accused's race. As long as this requirement is in place, the Canadian rule will be much more restrictive than the rule in the United States.

In addition, procedures on challenges for cause can and should be tailored to protect the accused's right to a fair trial by an impartial jury, while also protecting the privacy interests of prospective jurors and avoiding lengthening trials or increasing their cost.

In the case at bar, the accused called witnesses and tendered studies to establish widespread prejudice in the community against aboriginal people. It may not be necessary to duplicate this investment in time and resources at the stage of establishing racial prejudice in the community in all subsequent cases. The law of evidence recognizes two ways in which facts can be established in the trial process. The first is by evidence. The second is by judicial notice. Tanovich, Paciocco and Skurka observe that because of the limitations on the traditional forms of proof in this context, "doctrines of judicial notice [will] play a significant role in determining whether a particular request for challenge for cause satisfies the threshold test": see *Jury Selection in Criminal Trials* (1997), at p. 138. Judicial notice is the acceptance of a fact without proof. It applies to two kinds of facts: (1) facts which are so notorious as not be the subject of dispute among reasonable persons; and (2) facts that are capable of immediate and accurate demonstration by resorting to readily accessible sources of indisputable accuracy: see Sopinka, Lederman and Bryant, *The Law of Evidence in Canada* (1992), at p. 976. The existence of racial prejudice in the community may be a notorious fact within the first branch of the rule. As Sopinka, Lederman and Bryant note, at p. 977, "[t]he character of a certain place or of the community of persons living in a certain locality has been judicially noticed". Widespread racial prejudice, as a characteristic of the community, may therefore sometimes be the subject of judicial notice. Moreover, once a finding of fact of widespread racial prejudice in the community is made on evidence, as here, judges in subsequent cases may be able to take judicial notice of the fact. "The fact that a certain fact or matter has been noted by a judge of the same court in a previous matter has precedential value and it is, therefore, useful for counsel and the court to examine the case law when attempting to determine whether any particular fact can be noted": see *Sopinka, Lederman and Bryant, supra*, at p. 977. It is also possible that events and documents of indisputable accuracy may permit judicial notice to be taken of widespread racism in the community under the second branch of the rule. For these reasons, it is unlikely that long inquiries into the existence of widespread racial prejudice in the community will become a regular feature of the criminal trial process. While these comments are not necessarily limited to challenges for cause, the question whether they are applicable to other phases of the criminal trial is not to be decided in the present case.

At the stage of the actual challenge for cause, the procedure is similarly likely to be summary. The trial judge has a wide discretion in controlling the process to prevent its abuse, to ensure that it is fair to the prospective juror as well as to the accused, and to avoid the trial's being unnecessarily prolonged by challenges for cause: see *Hubbert, supra*. In the case at bar, Hutchison J. at the first trial confined the challenge to two questions, subject to a few tightly controlled subsidiary questions. This is a practice to be emulated. The fear that trials will be lengthened and rendered more costly by upholding the right to challenge for cause where widespread racial prejudice is established is belied by the experience in Ontario since the ruling in *Parks, supra*. The Criminal Lawyers' Association (Ontario), an intervener, advised that in those cases where the matter arises, an average of 35-45 minutes is consumed. The Attorney General for Ontario did not contradict this statement and supports the appellant's position.

While cost-benefit analyses cannot ultimately be determinative, permitting challenges for cause on the basis of widespread prejudice against persons of the accused's race seems unlikely to lengthen or increase significantly the cost of criminal trials. Nor, properly managed, should it unduly impinge on the rights of jurors.

.....

Summary

There is a presumption that a jury pool is composed of persons who can serve impartially. However, where the accused establishes that there is a realistic potential for partiality, the accused should be permitted to challenge prospective jurors for cause under s. 638(1)(*b*) of the *Code*: see *Sherratt, supra*. Applying this rule to applications based on prejudice against persons of the accused's race, the judge should exercise his or her discretion to permit challenges for cause if the accused establishes widespread racial prejudice in the community.

Conclusion

Although they acknowledged the existence of widespread bias against aboriginals, both Esson C.J. and the British Columbia Court of Appeal held that the evidence did not demonstrate a reasonable possibility that prospective jurors would be partial. In my view, there was ample evidence that this widespread prejudice included elements that could have affected the impartiality of jurors. Racism against aboriginals includes stereotypes that relate to credibility, worthiness and criminal propensity. As the Canadian Bar Association stated in Locking up Natives in Canada: A Report of the Committee of the Canadian Bar Association on Imprisonment and Release (1988), at p. 5:

> Put at its baldest, there is an equation of being drunk, Indian and in prison. Like many stereotypes, this one has a dark underside. It reflects a view of native people as uncivilized and without a coherent social or moral order. The stereotype prevents us from seeing native people as equals.

There is evidence that this widespread racism has translated into systemic discrimination in the criminal justice system: see Royal Commission on Aboriginal Peoples, *Bridging the Cultural Divide: A Report on Aboriginal People and Criminal Justice in Canada*, at p. 33; Royal Commission on the Donald Marshall Jr., Prosecution, Volume 1: *Findings and Recommendations* (1989), at p. 162; *Report on the Cariboo-Chilcotin Justice Inquiry* (1993), at p. 11. Finally, as Esson C.J. noted, tensions between aboriginals and non-aboriginals have increased in recent years as a result of developments in such areas as land claims and fishing rights. These tensions increase the potential of racist jurors siding with the Crown as the perceived representative of the majority's interests.

In these circumstances, the trial judge should have allowed the accused to challenge prospective jurors for cause. Notwithstanding the accused's defence that another aboriginal person committed the robbery, juror prejudice could have affected the trial in many other ways. Consequently, there was a realistic potential that some of the jurors might not have been indifferent between the Crown and the accused. The potential for prejudice was increased by the failure of the trial judge to instruct the jury to set aside any racial prejudices that they might have against aboriginals. It cannot be said that the accused had the fair trial by an impartial jury to which he was entitled.

I would allow the appeal and direct a new trial.

There has been much controversy generated over offence-based challenges for cause: most particularly, challenges for cause alleging partiality arising from general attitudes and beliefs held by the community relating to sexual offences. Consider the following case.

R. v. FIND

(2001), 154 C.C.C. (3d) 97 (S.C.C.)

The judgment of the court was delivered by

McLachlin C.J.C.: —

.....

The appellant was tried on 21 counts of sexual assault involving three complainants, who ranged between the ages of 6 and 12 at the time of the alleged offences. Prior to jury selection, defence counsel applied to challenge potential jurors for cause. No evidence was led in support of this application; rather, defence counsel contended a realistic potential for juror partiality arose from the ages of the alleged victims, the high number of alleged assaults, and the alleged use of violence. Defence counsel proposed that the following questions be put to potential jurors:

> Do you have strong feelings about the issue of rape and violence on young children?
>
> If so, what are those feelings based on?
>
> Would those strong feelings concerning the rape and violence on young children prevent you from giving Mr. Find a fair trial based solely on the evidence given during the trial of this case?

The trial judge, in a brief oral ruling, dismissed the application on the basis that it simply "doesn't fall anywhere near the dicta of the Court of Appeal in *Regina v. Parks*" (in *R. v. Parks* (1993), 84 C.C.C. (3d) 353, the Ontario Court of Appeal held that the accused was entitled to challenge potential jurors for cause on the basis of racial prejudice).

.....

C. Were the Grounds for Challenge for Cause Present in this Case?

To challenge prospective jurors for cause, the appellant must displace the presumption of juror impartiality by showing a realistic potential for partiality. To do this, the appellant must demonstrate the existence of a widespread bias arising from the nature of the charges against him (the "attitudinal" component), that raises a realistic potential for partial juror behaviour despite the safeguards of the trial process (the "behavioural" component). I will discuss each of these requirements in turn as they apply to this case.

1. Widespread Bias

In this case, the appellant alleges that the nature and the circumstances of the offence with which he is charged give rise to a bias that could unfairly incline jurors against him or toward his conviction. He further alleges that this bias is widespread in the community. In support of this submission, the appellant relies on the following propositions from Moldaver J.A.'s dissent in *K. (A.)* [(1999), 137 C.C.C. (3d) 225 (Ont. C.A.)], at para. 166. The parties generally agree on these facts, but dispute the conclusions to be drawn from them:

- Studies and surveys conducted in Canada over the past two decades reveal that a large percentage of the population, both male and female, have been the victims of sexual abuse. From this, it is reasonable to infer that any given jury panel may contain victims of sexual abuse, perpetrators and people closely associated with them.
- The harmful effects of sexual abuse can prove devastating not only to those who have been victimized, but those closely related to them. Tragically, many victims remain traumatized and psychologically scarred for life. By the same token, for those few individuals who have been wrongfully accused of sexual abuse, the effects can also be devastating.
- Sexual assault tends to be committed along gender lines. As a rule, it is women and children who are victimized by men.
- Women and children have been subjected to systemic discrimination reflected in both individual and institutional conduct, including the criminal justice system. As a result of widespread media coverage and the earnest and effective efforts of lobby groups in the past decade, significant and long overdue changes have come about in the criminal justice system. For some, the changes have not gone far enough; for others, too far.
- Where challenges for cause have been permitted in cases involving allegations of sexual abuse, literally hundreds of prospective jurors have been found to be partial by the triers of fact. In those cases where trial judges have refused to permit the challenge, choosing instead to vet the panel at large for bias, the numbers are equally substantial.
- Unlike many crimes, there are a wide variety of stereotypical attitudes and beliefs surrounding the crime of sexual abuse.

While the parties agree on these basic facts, they disagree on whether they demonstrate widespread bias. The appellant called no evidence, expert or otherwise, on the incidence or likely effect of prejudice stemming from the nature of the offences with which he is charged. Instead, he asks the Court to take judicial notice of a widespread bias arising from allegations of the sexual assault of children. The Crown, by contrast, argues that the facts on which it agrees do not translate into bias, much less widespread bias.

The appellant relies on the following: (a) the incidence of victimization and its effect on members of the jury pool; (b) the strong views held by many about sexual assault and the treatment of this crime by the criminal justice system; (c) myths and stereotypes arising from widespread and deeply entrenched attitudes about sexual assault; (d) the incidence of intense emotional reactions to sexual assault, such as a strong aversion to the crime or undue empathy for its victims; (e) the experience of Ontario trial courts, where hundreds of potential jurors in such cases have been successfully challenged as partial; and (f) social science research indicating a "generic prejudice" against the accused in sexual assault cases. He argues that these factors permit the Court to take judicial notice of widespread bias arising from charges of sexual assault of children.

It is worth reminding ourselves that at this stage we are concerned solely with the nature and prevalence of the alleged biases (*i.e.*, the "attitudinal" component), and not their amenability to cleansing by the trial process, which is the focus of the "behavioural" component.

(a) Incidence of Victimization

The appellant argues that the prevalence and potentially devastating impact of sexual assault permit the Court to conclude that any given jury pool is likely to contain victims or those close to them who may harbour a prejudicial bias as a consequence of their experiences.

The Crown acknowledges both the widespread nature of abuse and its potentially traumatic impact. Neither of these facts is in issue. Nor is it unreasonable to conclude from these facts that victims of sexual assault, or those close to them, may turn up in a jury panel. What is disputed is whether this widespread victimization permits the Court to conclude, without proof, that the victims and those who share their experience are biased, in the sense that they may harbour prejudice against the accused or in favour of the Crown when trying sexual assault charges.

The only social science research before us on the issue of victim empathy is a study by R.L. Wiener, A.T. Feldman Wiener and T. Grisso, "Empathy and Biased Assimilation of Testimonies in Cases of Alleged Rape" (1989), 13 Law & Hum. Behav. 343. The appellant cites this study for the proposition that those participants acquainted in some way with a rape victim demonstrated a greater tendency, under the circumstances of the study, to find a defendant guilty. However, as the Crown notes, this study offers no evidence that victim status *in itself* impacts jury verdicts. In fact, the study found no correlation between degree of empathy for rape victims and tendency to convict, nor did it find higher degrees of victim empathy amongst those persons acquainted with rape victims. Further, the study was limited to a small sample of participants. It made no attempt to simulate an actual jury trial, and did not involve a deliberation process or an actual verdict. In the absence of expert testimony, tested under cross-examination, as to the conclusions properly supported by this study, I can only conclude that it provides little assistance in establishing the existence of widespread bias arising from the incidence of sexual assault in Canadian society.

Moldaver J.A. concluded that the prevalence of sexual assault in Canadian society and its traumatic and potentially lifelong effects, provided a realistic basis to believe that victims of this crime may harbor intense and deep-seated biases. In arriving at this conclusion, he expressly relied on an unpublished article by Professor David Paciocco, "Challenges for Cause in Jury Selection after *Regina v. Parks*: Practicalities and Limitations", Canadian Bar Association, Ontario, February 11, 1995, which he quoted at para. 176 for the proposition that "[o]ne cannot help but believe that these deep scars would, for some, prevent them from adjudicating sexual offence violations impartially".

This is, however, merely the statement of an assumption, offered without a supporting foundation of evidence or research. Courts must approach sweeping and untested "common sense" assumptions about the behaviour of abuse victims with caution: see *R. v. Seaboyer*, [1991] 2 S.C.R. 577, 66 C.C.C. (3d) 321, 83 D.L.R. (4th) 193 (*per* L'Heureux-Dubé J., dissenting in part); *R. v. Lavallee*, [1990] 1 S.C.R. 852 at pp. 870-72, 55 C.C.C. (3d) 97 (*per* Wilson J.). Certainly these assumptions are not established beyond reasonable dispute, or documented with indisputable accuracy, so as to permit the Court to take judicial notice of them.

I conclude that while widespread victimization may be a factor to be considered, standing alone it fails to establish widespread bias that might lead jurors to discharge their task in a prejudicial and unfair manner.

(b) Strongly Held Views Relating to Sexual Offences

The appellant submits that the politicized and gender-based nature of sexual offences gives rise to firmly held beliefs, opinions and attitudes that establish widespread bias in cases of sexual assault.

This argument found favour with Moldaver J.A. in *K. (A.)*. Moldaver J.A. judicially noticed the tendency of sexual assault to be committed along gender lines. He also took judicial notice of the systemic discrimination women and children have faced in the criminal justice system, and the fact that recent reforms have gone too far for some and not far enough for others. From this foundation of facts, he inferred that the gender-based and politicized nature of sexual offences leads to a realistic possibility that some members of the jury pool, as a result of their political beliefs, will harbour deep-seated and virulent biases that might prove resistant to judicial cleansing. Quoting from the work of Professor Paciocco, Moldaver J.A. emphasized that strong political convictions and impartiality are not necessarily incongruous, but that for some "feminists" "commitment gives way to zealotry and dogma". The conviction that the justice system and its rules are incapable of protecting women and children, it is argued, may lead some potential jurors to disregard trial directions and rules safeguarding the presumption of innocence. Little regard for judicial direction can be expected from "those who see the prosecution of sexual offenders as a battlefront in a gender based war" (para. 177).

The appellant supports this reasoning, adding that the polarized, politically charged nature of sexual offences results in two prevalent social attitudes: first, that the criminal justice system is incapable of dealing with an "epidemic" of abuse because of its male bias or the excessive protections it affords the accused; and second, that conviction rates in sexual offence cases are unacceptably low. These beliefs, he alleges, may jeopardize the accused's right to a fair trial. For example, jurors harbouring excessive political zeal may ignore trial directions and legal rules perceived as obstructing the "truth" of what occurred, or may simply "cast their lot" with the victim. All this, the appellant submits, amounts to widespread bias in the community incompatible with juror impartiality.

The appellant does not deny that jurors trying any serious offence may hold strong views about the relevant law. Nor does he suggest such views raise concerns about bias in the trial of most offences. Few rules of criminal law attract universal support, and many engender heated debate. The treatment of virtually all serious crimes attracts sharply divided opinion, fervent criticism, and advocacy for reform. General disagreement or criticism of the relevant law, however, does not mean a prospective juror is inclined to take the law into his or her own hands at the expense of an individual accused.

The appellant's submission reduces to this: while strong views on the law do not ordinarily indicate bias, an exception arises in the case of sexual assaults on children. The difficulty, however, is that there is nothing in the material that supports this contention, nor is it self-evident. There is no indication that jurors are more willing to cross the line from opinion to prejudice in relation to sexual assault than for any other serious crime. It is therefore far from clear that strongly held views about sexual assault translate into bias, in the required sense of a tendency to act in an unfair and prejudicial manner.

Moreover, assuming that the strong views people may hold about sexual assault raise the possibility of bias, how widespread such views are in Canadian society remains a matter of conjecture. The material before the Court offers no measure of the prevalence in Canadian society of the specific attitudes identified by the appellant as corrosive of juror impartiality. Some people may indeed believe that the justice system is faltering in the face of an epidemic of abuse and that perpetrators of this crime too often escape conviction; yet, it is far from clear that these beliefs are prevalent in our society, let alone that they translate into bias on a widespread scale.

(c) Myths and Stereotypes About Sexual Offences

The appellant suggests that the strong views that surround the crime of sexual assault may contribute to widespread myths and stereotypes that undermine juror impartiality. In any given jury pool, he argues, some people may reason from the prevalence of abuse to the conclusion that the accused is likely guilty; some may assume children never lie about abuse; and some may reason that the accused is more likely to be guilty because he is a man.

Again, however, the proof falls short. Although these stereotypical beliefs clearly amount to bias that might incline some people against the accused or toward conviction, it is neither notorious nor indisputable that they enjoy widespread acceptance in Canadian society. Myths and stereotypes do indeed pervade public perceptions of sexual assault. Some favour the accused, others the Crown. In the absence of evidence, however, it is difficult to conclude that these stereotypes translate into widespread bias.

(d) Emotional Nature of Sexual Assault Trials

The appellant asks the Court to take judicial notice of the emotional nature of sexual assault trials and to conclude that fear, empathy for the victim, and abhorrence of the crime establish widespread bias in the community. His concern is that jurors, faced with allegations of sexual assaults of children, may act on emotion rather than reason. This is particularly the case, he suggests, for past victims of abuse, for whom the moral repugnancy of the crime may be amplified. He emphasizes that the presumption of innocence in criminal trials demands the acquittal of the "probably" guilty. An intense aversion to sexual crimes, he argues, may incline some jurors to err on the side of conviction in such circumstances. Undue empathy for the victim, he adds, may also prompt a juror to "validate" the complaint with a guilty verdict, rather than determine guilt or innocence according to the law.

Crimes commonly arouse deep and strong emotions. They represent a fundamental breach of the perpetrator's compact with society. Crimes make victims, and jurors cannot help but sympathize with them. Yet these indisputable facts do not necessarily establish bias, in the sense of an attitude that could unfairly prejudice jurors against the accused or toward conviction. Many crimes routinely tried by jurors are abhorrent. Brutal murders, ruthless frauds and violent attacks are standard fare for jurors. Abhorred as they are, these crimes seldom provoke suggestions of bias incompatible with a fair verdict.

One cannot automatically equate strong emotions with an unfair and prejudicial bias against the accused. Jurors are not expected to be indifferent toward crimes. Nor are they expected to remain neutral toward those shown to have committed such offences. If this were the case, prospective jurors would be routinely and successfully challenged for cause as a preliminary stage in the trial of all serious criminal offences. Instead, we accept that jurors often abhor the crime alleged to have been committed — indeed there would be cause for alarm if representatives of a community did *not* deplore heinous criminal acts. It would be equally alarming if jurors did not feel empathy or compassion for persons shown to be victims of such acts. These facts alone do not establish bias. There is simply no indication that these attitudes, commendable in themselves, unfairly prejudice jurors against the accused or toward conviction. They are common to the trial of many serious offences and have never grounded a right to challenge for cause.

Recognizing this fact, the appellant and the intervener Criminal Lawyers' Association ("CLA") contend that allegations of sexual offences against children incite emotional reactions of an intensity *above and beyond* those invoked by other criminal acts. Such offences, they contend, stand alone in their capacity to inflame jurors and cloud reason. Moldaver J.A., dissenting in *K. (A.)*, distinguished sexual offences from most other despicable criminal acts, on the basis that "sexual assault trials tend to be emotionally charged, particularly in cases of child abuse, where the mere allegation can trigger feelings of hostility, resentment and disgust in the minds of jurors" (para. 188).

The proposition that sexual offences are generically different from other crimes in their ability to arouse strong passion is not beyond reasonable debate or capable of immediate and accurate demonstration. As such, it does not lend itself to judicial notice. Nor was evidence led on this issue. Some may well react to allegations of a sexual crime with emotions of the intensity described by the appellant. Yet how prevalent such emotions are in Canadian society remains a matter of conjecture. The Court simply cannot reach conclusions on these controversial matters in an evidentiary vacuum. As a result, the appellant has not established the existence of an identifiable bias arising from the emotionally charged nature of sexual crimes, or the prevalence of this bias should it in fact exist.

(e) The History of Challenges for Cause in Ontario

The appellant refers this Court to the experience of Ontario trial courts where judges have allowed defence counsel to challenge prospective jurors for cause in cases involving allegations of sexual assault: see *Vidmar, supra*, at p. 5; D.M. Tanovich, D.M. Paciocco, S. Skurka, *Jury Selection in Criminal Trials: Skills, Science, and the Law* (1997), at pp. 239-42. These sources, cataloguing 34 cases, indicate that hundreds of potential jurors have been successfully challenged for cause as not indifferent between the Crown and the accused. It is estimated that 36 percent of the prospective jurors challenged were disqualified.

The appellant argues that the fact that hundreds of prospective jurors have been found to be partial is in itself sufficient evidence of widespread bias arising from sexual assault trials. This is proof, he asserts, that the social realities surrounding sexual assault trials give rise to prejudicial beliefs, attitudes and emotions on a widespread scale in Canadian communities.

The Crown disagrees. It argues first, that the survey lacks validity because of methodological defects, and second, that even if the results are accepted, the successful challenges do not demonstrate a widespread bias, but instead may be attributed to other causes.

The first argument against the survey is that its methodology is unsound. The Crown raises a number of concerns: the survey is entirely anecdotal, not comprehensive or random; not all of the questions asked of prospective jurors are indicated; there is no way in which to assess the directions, if any, provided by the trial judge, especially in relation to the distinction between strong opinions or emotions and partiality; and no comparative statistics are provided contrasting these results with the experience in other criminal law contexts. The intervener CLA concedes that the survey falls short of scientific validity, but contends that it nevertheless documents a phenomena of considerable significance. Hundreds of prospective jurors disqualified on the grounds of bias by impartial triers of fact must, it is argued, displace the presumption of juror impartiality. Nonetheless, the lack of methodological rigour and the absence of expert evidence undermine the suggestion that the Ontario experience establishes widespread bias.

The second argument against the survey is that the questions asked were so general, and the information elicited so scarce, that no meaningful inference can be drawn from the responses given by challenged jurors or from the number of potential jurors disqualified. Charron J.A., for the majority in *K. (A.)*, observed that prospective jurors in that case received no meaningful instruction on the nature of jury duty or the meaning and importance of impartiality. Further, they often indicated confusion at the questions posed to them or asked that the questions be repeated. In the end, numerous prospective jurors were disqualified for offering little more than that they would find it difficult to hear a case of this nature, or that they held strong emotions about the sexual abuse of children.

The challenge for cause process rests to a considerable extent on self-assessment of impartiality by the challenged juror, and the response to questions on challenge often will be little more than an affirmation or denial of one's own ability to act impartially in the circumstances of the case. In the absence of guidance, prospective jurors may conflate disqualifying bias with a legitimate apprehension about sitting through a case involving allegations of sexual abuse of children, or the strong views or emotions they may hold on this subject.

Where potential jurors are challenged for racial bias, the risk of social disapprobation and stigma supports the veracity of admissions of potential partiality. No similar indicia of reliability attach to the frank and open admission of concern about one's ability to approach and decide a case of alleged child sexual abuse judiciously. While a prospective juror's admission of racial prejudice may suggest partiality, the same cannot be said of an admission of abhorrence or other emotional attitude toward the sexual abuse of children. We do not know whether the potential jurors who professed concerns about serving on juries for sexual assault charges were doing so because they were biased, or for other reasons. We do not know whether they were told that strong emotions and beliefs would not in themselves impair their duty of impartiality, or whether they were informed of the protections built into the trial process.

In fact, the number of prospective jurors disqualified, although relied on as support for judicial notice of widespread bias, is equally consistent with the conclusion that the challenge processes, despite the best intentions of the participants, disqualified prospective jurors for acknowledging the intense emotions, beliefs, experiences and misgivings anyone might experience when confronted with the prospect of sitting as a juror on a case involving charges of sexual assault of children. As discussed, the mere presence of strong emotions and opinions cannot be equated automatically with bias against the accused or toward conviction.

It follows that the survey of past challenge for cause cases involving charges of sexual assault does not without more establish widespread bias arising from these charges.

(f) Social Science Evidence of "Generic Prejudice"

The appellant argues that social science research, particularly that of Vidmar, supports the contention that social realities, such as the prevalence of sexual abuse and its politically charged nature, translate into a widespread bias in Canadian society.

In *Williams* [(1998), 124 C.C.C. (3d) 481 (S.C.C.)], the Court referred to Vidmar's research in concluding that the partiality targeted by s. 638(1)(*b*) was not limited to biases arising from a direct interest in the proceeding or pre-trial exposure to the case, but could arise from *any* of a variety of sources, including the "nature of the crime itself" (para. 10). However, recognition that the nature of an offence may give rise to "generic prejudice" does not obviate the need for proof. Labels do not govern the availability of challenges for cause. Regardless of how a case is classified, the ultimate issue is whether a realistic possibility exists that some potential jurors may try the case on the basis of prejudicial attitudes and beliefs, rather than the evidence offered at trial. The appellant relies on the work of Vidmar for the proposition that such a possibility does in fact arise from allegations of sexual assault.

Vidmar is known for the theory of a "generic prejudice" against accused persons in sexual assault trials and for the conclusion that the attitudes and beliefs of jurors are frequently reflected in the verdicts of juries on such trials. However, the conclusions of Vidmar do not assist in finding widespread bias. His theory that a "generic prejudice" exists against those charged with sexual assault, although in the nature of expert evidence, has not been proved. Nor can the Court take judicial notice of this contested proposition. With regard to the behaviour of potential jurors, the Court has no foundation in this case to draw an inference of partial juror conduct, as discussed in more detail below, under the behavioural stage of the partiality test.

Vidmar himself acknowledges the limitations of his research. He concedes that the notion of "generic prejudice" lacks scientific validity, and that none of the studies he relies on actually asked the questions typically asked of Canadian jurors, including whether they can impartially adjudicate guilt or innocence in a sexual assault trial: *Vidmar, supra*. Moreover, the authorities Vidmar relies on are almost exclusively "confined to examination of public attitudes towards certain criminal acts, especially child sexual abuse. Not surprisingly, it appears the public is quite disapproving of persons who have sexually abused children, and of such conduct itself": *R. v. Hillis*, [1996] O.J. No. 2739 (QL) (Gen. Div.), at para. 7. While judicial notice may be taken of the uncontested fact that sexual crimes are almost universally abhorred, this does not establish widespread bias arising from sexual assault trials.

The attempt of Vidmar and others to conduct scientific research on jury behaviour is commendable. Unfortunately, research into the effect of juror attitudes on deliberations and verdicts is constrained by the almost absolute prohibition in s. 649 of the *Criminal Code* against the disclosure by jury members of information relating to the jury's proceedings. More comprehensive and scientific assessment of this and other aspects of the criminal law and criminal process would be welcome. Should Parliament reconsider this prohibition, it may be that more helpful research into the Canadian experience would emerge. But for now, social science evidence appears to cast little light on the extent of any "generic prejudice" relating to charges of sexual assault, or its relationship to jury verdicts.

(g) Conclusions on the Existence of a Relevant, Widespread Bias

Do the factors cited by the appellant, taken together, establish widespread bias arising from charges relating to sexual abuse of children? In my view, they do not. The material presented by the appellant, considered in its totality, falls short of grounding judicial notice of widespread bias in Canadian society against the accused in such trials. At best, it establishes that the crime of sexual assault, like many serious crimes, frequently elicits strong attitudes and emotions.

However, the two branches of the test for partiality are not watertight compartments. Given the challenge of proving facts as elusive as the nature and scope of prejudicial attitudes, and the need to err on the side of caution, I prefer not to resolve this case entirely at the first, attitudinal stage. Out of an abundance of caution, I will proceed to consider the potential impact, if any, of the alleged biases on juror behaviour.

2. *Is it Reasonable to Infer that Some Jurors May Be Incapable of Setting Aside Their Biases Despite Trial Safeguards?*

The fact that members of the jury pool may harbour prejudicial attitudes, opinions or feelings is not, in itself, sufficient to support an entitlement to challenge for cause. There must also exist a realistic possibility that some jurors may be unable or unwilling to set aside these prejudices to render a decision in strict accordance with the law. This is referred to as the behavioural aspect of the test for partiality.

The applicant need not always adduce direct evidence establishing this link between the bias in issue and detrimental effects on the trial process. Even in the absence of such evidence, a trial judge may reasonably infer that some strains of bias by their very nature may prove difficult for jurors to identify and eliminate from their reasoning.

This inference, however, is not automatic. Its strength varies with the nature of the bias in issue, and its amenability to judicial cleansing. In *Williams*, the Court inferred a behavioural link between the pervasive racial prejudice established on the evidence and the possibility that some jurors, consciously or not, would decide the case based on prejudice and stereotype. Such a result, however, is not inevitable for every form of bias, prejudice or preconception. In some circumstances, the appropriate inference is that the "predispositions can be safely regarded as curable by judicial direction": *Williams, supra*, at para. 24.

Fundamental distinctions exist between the racial prejudice at issue in *Williams* and a more general bias relating to the nature of the offence itself. These differences relate both to the nature of these respective biases, and to their susceptibility (or resistance) to cleansing by the trial process. It may be useful to examine these differences before embarking on a more extensive consideration of the potential effects on the trial process, if any, of the biases alleged in the present case.

The first difference is that race may impact more directly on the jury's decision than bias stemming from the nature of the offence. As Moldaver J.A. stated in *R. v. Betker* [(1997), 115 C.C.C. (3d) 421 (Ont. C.A.)], at p. 441, "[r]acial prejudice is a form of bias directed against a particular class of accused by virtue of an identifiable immutable characteristic. There is a direct and logical connection between the prejudice asserted and the particular accused". By contrast, the aversion, fear, abhorrence, and beliefs alleged to surround sexual assault offences may lack this cogent and irresistible connection to the accused. Unlike racial prejudice, they do not point a finger at a particular accused.

Second, trial safeguards may be less successful in cleansing racial prejudice than other types of bias, as recognized in *Williams*. As Doherty J.A. observed in *Parks, supra*, at p. 371: "[i]n deciding whether the post-jury selection safeguards against partiality provide a reliable antidote to racial bias, the nature of that bias must be emphasized". The nature of racial prejudice — in particular its subtle, systemic and often unconscious operation — compelled the inference in *Williams* that some people might be incapable of effacing, or even identifying, its influence on their reasoning. In reaching this conclusion, the Court emphasized the "invasive and elusive" operation of racial prejudice and its foundation "on preconceptions and unchallenged assumptions that unconsciously shape the daily behaviour of individuals" (paras. 21-22).

The biases alleged in this case, by contrast, may be more susceptible to cleansing by the rigours of the trial process. They are more likely to be overt and acknowledged than is racial prejudice, and hence more easily removed. Jurors are more likely to recognize and counteract them. The trial judge is more likely to address these concerns in the course of directions to the jury, as are counsel in their addresses. Offence-based bias has concerned the trial process throughout its long evolution, and many of the safeguards the law has developed may be seen as a response to it.

Against this background, I turn to the question of whether the biases alleged to arise from the nature of sexual assault, if established, might lead jurors to decide the case in an unfair and prejudicial way, despite the cleansing effect of the trial process.

First, the appellant contends that some jurors, whether victims, friends of victims, or simply people holding strong views about sexual assault, may not be able to set aside strong beliefs about this crime — for example, that the justice system is biased against complainants, that there exists an epidemic of abuse that must be halted, or that conviction rates are too low — and decide the case solely on its merits. Some jurors, he says, may disregard rules of law that are perceived as obstructing the "truth" of what occurred. Others may simply "cast their lot" with groups that have been victimized. These possibilities, he contends, support a reasonable inference that strong opinions may translate into a realistic potential for partial juror conduct.

This argument cannot succeed. As discussed, strongly held political views do not necessarily suggest that jurors will act unfairly in an actual trial. Indeed, passionate advocacy for law reform may be an expression of the highest respect for the rule of law, not a sign that one is willing to subvert its operation at the expense of the accused. As Moldaver J.A. eloquently observed in *R. v. Betker, supra,* at p. 447, "the test for partiality is not whether one seeks to change the law but whether one is capable of upholding the law...".

In the absence of evidence that such beliefs and attitudes may affect jury behaviour in an unfair manner, it is difficult to conclude that they will not be cleansed by the trial process. Only speculation supports the proposition that jurors will act on general opinions and beliefs to the detriment of an individual accused, in disregard of their oath or affirmation, the presumption of innocence, and the directions of the trial judge.

The appellant also contends that myths and stereotypes attached to the crime of sexual assault may unfairly inform the deliberation of some jurors. However, strong, sometimes biased, assumptions about sexual behaviour are not new to sexual assault trials. Traditional myths and stereotypes have long tainted the assessment of the conduct and veracity of complainants in sexual assault cases — the belief that women of "unchaste" character are more likely to have consented or are less worthy of belief; that passivity or even resistance may in fact constitute consent; and that some women invite sexual assault by reason of their dress or behaviour, to name only a few. Based on overwhelming evidence from relevant social science literature, this Court has been willing to accept the prevailing existence of such myths and stereotypes: see, for example, *Seaboyer, supra*; *R. v. Osolin,* [1993] 4 S.C.R. 595 at pp. 669-71, 86 C.C.C. (3d) 481, 109 D.L.R. (4th) 478; *R. v. Ewanchuk,* [1999] 1 S.C.R. 330, 131 C.C.C. (3d) 481, 169 D.L.R. (4th) 193, at paras. 94-97.

Child complainants may similarly be subject to stereotypical assumptions, such as the belief that stories of abuse are probably fabricated if not reported immediately, or that the testimony of children is inherently unreliable: *R. v. W. (R.)*, [1992] 2 S.C.R. 122, 74 C.C.C. (3d) 134; *R. v. D. (D.)*, [2000] 2 S.C.R. 275, 2000 SCC 43, 148 C.C.C. (3d) 41, 191 D.L.R. (4th) 60; N. Bala, "Double Victims: Child Sexual Abuse and the Canadian Criminal Justice System", in W.S. Tarnopolsky, J. Whitman and M. Ouellette, eds., *Discrimination in the Law and the Administration of Justice* (1993).

These myths and stereotypes about child and adult complainants are particularly invidious because they comprise part of the fabric of social "common sense" in which we are daily immersed. Their pervasiveness, and the subtlety of their operation, create the risk that victims of abuse will be blamed or unjustly discredited in the minds of both judges and jurors.

Yet the prevalence of such attitudes has never been held to justify challenges for cause as of right by Crown prosecutors. Instead, we have traditionally trusted the trial process to ensure that such attitudes will not prevent jurors from acting impartially. We have relied on the rules of evidence, statutory protections, and guidance from the judge and counsel to clarify potential misconceptions and promote a reasoned verdict based solely on the merits of the case.

Absent evidence to the contrary, there is no reason to believe that stereotypical attitudes about accused persons are more elusive of these cleansing measures than stereotypical attitudes about complainants. It follows that the myths and stereotypes alleged by the appellant, even if widespread, provide little support for any inference of a behavioural link between these beliefs and the potential for juror partiality.

Finally, the appellant argues that the strong emotions evoked by allegations of sexual assault, especially in cases involving child complainants, may distort the reasoning of some jurors. He emphasizes that a strongly held aversion to the offence may incline some jurors to err on the side of conviction. Others may be swayed by "undue empathy" for the alleged victim, perceiving the case as a rejection or validation of the complainant's claim, rather than a determination of the accused's guilt or innocence according to law.

Again, absent evidence, it is highly speculative to suggest that the emotions surrounding sexual crimes will lead to prejudicial and unfair juror behaviour. As discussed, the safeguards of the trial process and the instructions of the trial judge are designed to replace emotional reactions with rational, dispassionate assessment. Our long experience in the context of the trial of other serious offences suggests that our faith in this cleansing process is not misplaced. The presumption of innocence, the oath or affirmation, the diffusive effects of collective deliberation, the requirement of jury unanimity, specific directions from the trial judge and counsel, a regime of evidentiary and statutory protections, the adversarial nature of the proceedings and their general solemnity, and numerous other precautions both subtle and manifest — all collaborate to keep the jury on the path to an impartial verdict despite offence-based prejudice. The appellant has not established that the offences with which he is charged give rise to a strain of bias that is uniquely capable of eluding the cleansing effect of these trial safeguards.

It follows that even if widespread bias were established, we cannot safely infer, on the record before the Court, that it would lead to unfair, prejudicial and partial juror behaviour. This is not to suggest that an accused can never be prejudiced by the mere fact of the nature and circumstances of the charges he or she faces; rather, the inference between social attitudes and jury behaviour is simply far less obvious and compelling in this context, and more may be required to satisfy a court that this inference may be reasonably drawn. The nature of offence-based bias, as discussed, suggests that the circumstances in which it is found to be both widespread in the community and resistant to the safeguards of trial may prove exceptional. Nonetheless, I would not foreclose the possibility that such circumstances may arise. If widespread bias arising from sexual assault were established in a future case, it would be for the court in that case to determine whether this bias gives rise to a realistic potential for partial juror conduct in the community from which the jury pool is drawn. I would only caution that in deciding whether to draw an inference of adverse effect on jury behaviour the court should take into account the nature of the bias and its susceptibility to cleansing by the trial process.

VI. Conclusion

The case for widespread bias arising from the nature of charges of sexual assault on children is tenuous. Moreover, even if the appellant had demonstrated widespread bias, its link to actual juror behaviour is speculative, leaving the presumption that it would be cleansed by the trial process firmly in place. Many criminal trials engage strongly held views and stir up powerful emotions — indeed, even revulsion and abhorrence. Such is the nature of the trial process. Absent proof, we cannot simply assume that strong beliefs and emotions translate into a realistic potential for partiality, grounding a right to challenge for cause. I agree with the majority of the Court of Appeal that the appellant has not established that the trial judge erred in refusing to permit him to challenge prospective jurors for cause.

I would dismiss the appeal and affirm the conviction.

QUESTION

23. The accused is charged with sexual assault. He is black, as is the complainant. Is he entitled to the procedural protection articulated in *Parks*? Consider, in this regard, *R. v. Koh* (1998), 131 C.C.C. (3d) 257 (Ont. C.A.); and *R. v. Williams* (1998), 124 C.C.C. (3d) 481 (S.C.C.).

---

3. Peremptory Challenges

Under s. 634(1) of the *Criminal Code*, "[a] juror may be challenged peremptorily whether or not the juror has been challenged for cause...". Section 634 prescribes the number of peremptory challenges which may be exercised by the Crown and each accused, depending upon the offence charged. Experienced counsel hold wildly divergent views as to the criteria for exercising peremptory challenges. Of course, the deci-

sion to challenge or not to challenge is based upon very little information. In Canada, we only know the prospective juror's name, address and occupation[4] and observe his or her appearance briefly before making an assessment.[5]

QUESTION

24. Each of two accused is charged with fraud over $5,000. Accused A. is also charged with municipal corruption on the same indictment. How many peremptory challenges does each accused have and how many does the Crown have? Both accused are alleged to have engaged in a fraud on various banks by a sophisticated scheme of cheque kiting. The case is a strong one although difficult for the Crown to explain to a jury. Accused B. allegedly used the money to obtain special cancer treatments for a terminally ill son. Accused A. allegedly used the money to influence a municipal building inspector into approving a shoddy building he owned. Prospective jurors include a bank teller, a teacher, a retired sales manager, a cook, a housewife, a nurse, a farmer, an accountant, a tax assessor, an unemployed labourer, a mechanic, a librarian, a plumber, a university student, a pharmacist and a steel worker. How might counsel approach the exercise of peremptory challenges?

Peremptory challenges are, by their very nature, exercisable without the necessity of justification or rationale. Should there be any restrictions imposed upon why they are exercised? Does the answer depend upon which side is exercising them? Consider the following cases.

R. v. PIZZACALLA

(1991), 69 C.C.C. (3d) 115 (Ont. C.A.)

[The accused was charged with various sexual assaults on female employees. At the time, the Crown was entitled to 48 "stand asides" which were the functional equivalent of peremptory challenges. The *Criminal Code* has since been amended. An appeal against conviction succeeded, based upon the way in which those stand-asides were exercised by the Crown.]

The judgment of the court was delivered orally by

Morden A.C.J.O.: —

.....

---

4 **Sometimes, the occupation read out is extremely vague: for example, "retired" or "manager". Most trial judges will ask the prospective juror, upon request of counsel, or on the judge's own initiative, to clarify the occupation retired from or the nature of the business managed.**

5 **One advantage of a challenge for cause is that it provides one more opportunity to observe and hear from a prospective juror. An unsuccessful challenge for cause may provide some useful information in the exercise of peremptory challenges.**

The ground of appeal from conviction is based on the manner in which the jury selection procedure was used. Crown counsel employed 23 stand-asides during the selection process, 20 of which he frankly admitted were used to exclude men from the jury. The result was that the jury which was selected and which tried the appellant was composed entirely of women. The jury selection process was conducted before a judge who was not the trial judge.

At the beginning of the trial, counsel for the appellant applied to the trial judge for an order that the prosecution be stayed on the basis of abuse of process or, alternatively, that a mistrial be declared. Crown counsel then put his position clearly on the record before the judge. In the course of his submissions he said:

> Yes, Your Honour, the selection process is obviously weighted in favour of the Crown, inasmuch as, if the Crown chooses to employ its stand-asides, it can outlast the number of challenges ... I will concede that most of the challenges I used were directed at keeping men from this jury, and preferring to have women try this particular case. I have tried, in my experience, probably 50 or 100 jury trials involving sexual assaults. I have never before used the option that I used in this case, of attempting to get a jury of all women. This is a case involving sexual harassment in the workplace. In my experience, I was of the view that I might encounter a man or more than one man who felt that, somehow, a person in the workplace has the right to fondle, touch, make passes at, or otherwise touch people in the workplace.

The trial judge dismissed the motion.

Counsel for the respondent before us agrees with the appellant's submission that the manner in which Crown counsel exercised the right to stand aside jurors gave "the appearance that the prosecutor secured a favourable jury, rather than simply an impartial one". Reference is made to *R. v. Hubbert* (1975), 29 C.C.C. (2d) 279 p. 290, 11 O.R. (2d) 464, 31 C.R.N.S. 27 (C.A.); affirmed 33 C.C.C. (2d) 207*n*, 15 O.R. (2d) 324*n*, 38 C.R.N.S. 381; *R. v. Stoddart* (1987), 37 C.C.C. (3d) 351 at p. 368, 59 C.R. (3d) 134 (Ont. C.A.); *R. v. Favel* (1987), 39 C.C.C. (3d) 378 at p. 381, 60 Sask. R. 176 (C.A.); *R. v. Butler* (1984), 63 C.C.C. (3d) 243 at p. 256, 3 C.R. (4th) 174 (B.C.C.A.), and *R. v. Valente* (1985), 23 C.C.C. (3d) 193 at p. 204, 24 D.L.R. (4th) 161, [1985] 2 S.C.R. 673. On the particular facts of this case, which include Crown counsel's candid statement of his purpose, we agree with this concession. In giving effect to the concession we are not, of course, saying that a jury composed entirely of women, or of men, cannot render an impartial verdict in a case involving an accused person of the opposite sex or in any other case. Our decision is based upon the way in which the jury selection process was used.

The appeal is allowed, the convictions set aside, and a new trial is directed.

QUESTION

25. Read *R. v. Biddle* (1993), 86 C.C.C. (3d) 269 (Ont. C.A.); leave to appeal to S.C.C. refused 86 C.C.C. (3d) vii, where the Crown's use of stand-asides to select an all female jury for a sexual assault trial did not invalidate the proceedings. How, if at all, can it be reconciled with *Pizzacalla*, as partially reproduced on p. 529? *Biddle* was reversed by the Supreme Court on

other grounds: (1995), 96 C.C.C. (3d) 321. Only three of the nine members of the court commented on this issue.

R. v. LINES

[1993] O.J. No. 3284 (Gen. Div.)

Hawkins J.: —

.....

The Peremptory Challenge Issue

Next, I deal with the peremptory challenge issue.

This is a motion by the Crown to limit the exercise by it and the accused of the peremptory challenges afforded by section 634 of the *Criminal Code*. More specifically, the restriction sought is that no peremptory challenge may be exercised on the basis of race.

By way of background, the accused, a white police officer, is charged with criminal negligence causing bodily harm, with unlawful discharge of a firearm with intent to wound, and with careless use of a firearm, all three charges arising out of the shooting by the accused of a young black man in the course of an attempted arrest by the accused of the victim. I use the term "victim" simply as a convenient designation for Royan Bagnaut.

As anyone who lives in the Metropolitan Toronto area well knows, there have been a number of incidents in recent years in which white police officers have shot usually young black males, which has caused understandable concern in Toronto's black community.

The desirability of "representativeness" on juries is too obvious to require further exposition.

The Crown's position is that the exercise of a peremptory challenge solely on the basis of race would offend the provision of section 15 of the *Charter* which provides:

> 15(1) Every individual is equal before and under the law and has the right to equal protection and equal benefit of the law without discrimination and, in particular, without discrimination based on race, national or ethnic origin, colour, religion, sex, age or mental or physical disability.

The Crown does not seek to strike down the whole peremptory challenge machinery as unconstitutional but rather seeks an interpretation of section 634 by which the Court would limit the exercise of the peremptory challenge.

I am told, and accept, that there is no Canadian case in which this issue has been raised and it is, therefore a matter of first impression.

The issue has been raised and decided in the United States. The development of the American jurisprudence is as follows:

In 1880, the U.S. Supreme Court decided that a West Virginia statute which disqualified all blacks from serving as jurors offended the provisions of the 14th Amendment (the Equal Protection Clause). See *Strauder v. West Virginia*, 100 U.S. 303.

In 1986, the [U.S. Supreme] Court decided by a 7/2 vote that the exercise by the prosecution of a peremptory challenge solely on the basis of race was unconstitutional. The U.S. Constitution, like our own *Charter*, controls state or governmental action. The Court found that a prosecutor acts as an arm of government and that, as a state actor, his actions are subject to 14th Amendment scrutiny. See *Batson v. Kentucky* (1986), 476 U.S. 79.

The final (or perhaps penultimate) decision was reached in 1992, when the Court decided 7/2 that a criminal defendant participating in the jury selection process was a state actor and could not, therefore, exercise his peremptory challenges on the grounds of race. It is clear, to me at any rate, that the Court drew no distinction between an misrepresented defendant and a represented defendant. The decision did not turn on any status of defence counsel as an "officer of the court". It was held that the defendant was a state actor for the purposes of exercising his peremptory challenges.

When I speculate that this decision may not be the final act in the drama, I refer to the reluctant concurring opinion of Justice Thomas where he says, at 112 S.C.T. 2348:

> I am certain that black criminal defendants will rue the day that this Court ventured down this road that inexorably will lead to the elimination of peremptory strikes.

See *Georgia v. McCollum* (1992), 112 S.C.R. 2348.

So much for the American jurisprudence. What have we in Canada to assist by analogy?

In *Regina v. Pizzacalla* (1991), 69 C.C.C. (3d) 115, the Ontario Court of Appeal, in what must be one of the shortest judgments in living memory, allowed the appeal by an accused convicted of sexual assault before an all-female jury, during the empanelment of which the Crown had deliberately used its stand asides to fashion an all-female jury. This, the Court held, gave "the appearance that the prosecutor secured a favourable jury, rather than simply an impartial one".

The most useful case, in my view, is *Regina v. Bain*, [1992] S.C.R. 91, 69 C.C.C. (3d) 481. That case, as we all know, in a 4/3 split struck down the Crown stand aside provisions of the *Code* as contrary to the accused's right to be tried before an independent and impartial tribunal as dictated by section 11(*d*) of the *Charter*. The peremptory challenge was not under review. The ratio of the majority judgment was clearly based on the imbalance between the Crown, on the one hand, with its 48 stand asides and 4 peremptory challenges, and the accused, on the other hand, with his — in most cases — 12 peremptory challenges.

Cory J., writing for the majority, says (S.C.R. 102, C.C.C. 511):

> ... a discrepancy of 4.25 to one in favour of the Crown seems to be so unbalanced that it gives an appearance of unfairness or bias against the accused.

And (at S.C.R. 103, C.C.C. 512):

> The overwhelming numerical superiority of choice granted to the Crown creates a pervasive air of unfairness in the jury selection procedure.

As I say, the peremptory challenge was not under review in *Bain*, and observations about it are *obiter*. They are, nonetheless, informative.

Gonthier J., in his dissent, says (S.C.R. 115, C.C.C. 494):

> The *Criminal Code* gives the accused a variable number of peremptory challenges, depending on the seriousness of the offence. These peremptory challenges allow the accused to exclude prospective jurors from the jury. The main rationale for these has already been outlined by Blackstone in his Commentaries on the Laws of England:
>
> > The peremptory challenge is granted on two reasons. 1. As every-one must be sensible what sudden impressions and unaccountable prejudices we are apt to conceive upon the bare looks and gestures of another, and how necessary it is that a prisoner (when put to defend his life) should have a good opinion of his jury the want of which might totally disconcert him, the law wills not that he should be tried by any one man against whom he has conceived a prejudice even without being able to assign a reason for such his dislike. 2. Because upon challenge for cause shown if the reason assigned proves insufficient to set aside the juror, perhaps the bare questioning his indifference may sometimes provoke a resentment, to prevent all ill consequences from which the prisoner is still at liberty, if he pleases, peremptorily to set him aside.

I said earlier in these reasons that "the U.S. Constitution, like our *Charter*, controls state or governmental action." If any authority need be cited for that proposition, refer to the judgment of LaForest J. writing for the majority in *McKinney v. Board of Governors of the University of Guelph* (1990), 76 D.L.R. (4th) 545 at 633:

> The application of the *Charter* is set forth in section 32(1) which reads:
>
> The *Charter* applies
>
> "(*a*) to the parliament and Government of Canada ... [balance omitted]"
>
> "(*b*) to the legislature and government of each province ... [balance omitted]"
>
> These words give a strong message that the *Charter* is confined to government action. This Court has repeatedly drawn attention to the fact that the *Charter* is essentially an instrument for checking the powers of government over the individual.

And at page 634:

> The exclusion of private activity from the *Charter* was not the result of happenstance. It was a deliberate choice which must be respected.

Mr. Lepofsky, in his very able argument for the Crown, sought to persuade me that it is unnecessary for me to decide whether the accused or his counsel is a state actor when exercising a peremptory challenge. His argument is that what I am being asked to do is not to strike down the peremptory challenge but to interpret the provisions of section 634 of the *Code* in a manner that is consistent with section 15 of the *Charter* by requiring both counsel to exercise their peremptory challenges in conformity therewith. A peremptory challenging that is exercised in conformity with section 15 is not one which is simply not exercised on the basis of race, but one which is not exercised on the basis of "race, national or ethnic origin, colour, religion, sex, age or mental or physical disability," with the possible addition of some unenumerated analogous grounds. To hedge a peremptory challenging ... with such restrictions would result in the creation of something which could no longer be called a peremptory challenge.

In my view, this motion cannot be determined without deciding whether the accused, or his counsel, in exercising a peremptory challenge, is acting as an agent [of the] state. In a criminal trial the accused is pitted against the state. In my opinion it is fanciful to suggest that in the selection of a jury he doffs his adversarial role and joins the Crown in some sort of joint and concerted effort to empanel an independent and impartial tribunal. If the adversary system is thought to be the best method of discovering the truth, why must it be abandoned at the threshold of the trial in the jury selection process?

Gonthier J. in his dissent in *Bain* realized the fundamental difference between the respective roles of Crown and defence when he said (S.C.R. 115, C.C.C. 494):

> The accused has a fairly clear and circumscribed role in the trial and in the jury selection process [emphasis mine] [*Author's Note*: "Emphasis added" references have not been noted in the reported judgment.] Nothing more is expected of him or her than thing to avoid conviction and punishment by asserting his or her rights according to law.

Also in *Bain*, Stevenson J. in his concurring judgment said (S.C.R. 159, C.C.C. 530):

> The peremptory challenge is not, itself, under attack. It may be used under partisan considerations, and so long as the right of exercise is proportionate neither the Crown nor the accused can be said to have an unconstitutional advantage.

For these reasons, the Crown motion to restrict the use of the peremptory challenge is dismissed. The Crown will be guided by its own conscience in its use of the peremptory challenge and so will the accused.

4. DISCHARGE OF A JUROR

Section 631(2.1) of the *Criminal Code* allows for the trial judge to permit one or two alternate jurors where he or she considers it advisable in the interests of justice.[6] However, in the course of a trial, a trial judge may discharge a juror for illness or another reasonable cause (s. 644(1) of the *Criminal Code*). If a juror dies or is discharged, the trial can still proceed and the jury can render a verdict, so long as the number of jurors is not reduced below ten (s. 644(2) of the *Criminal Code*).

QUESTION

26. A jury is selected for the trial of Nehemiah Tubbenfliegel. The accused's plea of not guilty is recorded before that jury and the trial judge makes her introductory remarks. The Crown then makes an opening address.

---

6 **See s. 642.1 of the *Code* as to when alternate jurors are substituted or excused.**

One of the jurors then remarks "Oh, *that* Nehemiah Tubbenfliegel!" In the absence of the other jurors, he indicates that Tubbenfliegel had once defrauded his sister. He did not make the connection until he heard the Crown's opening address. No evidence has yet been heard. Should the trial judge discharge the juror and continue with 11 jurors, declare a mistrial, or permit the selection of a replacement juror? Would your answer be different if the juror admitted that he had already mentioned what he knew to several other jurors? Consider, in this regard, *Basarabas and Spek v. The Queen* (1982), 2 C.C.C. (3d) 257 (S.C.C.), and s. 644(1.1) of the *Criminal Code*.

M. OPENING ADDRESSES

After the jury is sworn and the charges and plea are recorded for the jury, the trial judge will make some introductory remarks to the jury. In Ontario, the accused is arraigned and enters a plea before the entire jury panel. After the jury is selected, the charges and plea are re-read to the jury. The Crown is then permitted to open to the jury. This opening is designed to outline the evidence which the Crown expects to lead and the position of the Crown. Argument is not permitted. Reference should not be made to evidence which has been ruled inadmissible or the admissibility of which is contested and to be later determined by the trial judge. At the conclusion of this opening, the Crown generally calls its first witness. This differs from the practice in American jurisdictions which permit the defence to open to the jury immediately after the prosecution.

R. v. BARROW

(1989), 48 C.C.C. (3d) 308 (N.S.S.C.)

Nathanson J. (orally): — A. Irvine Barrow was charged with conspiracy to commit influence peddling so-called, contrary to ss. 423(1)(*d*) and 110(1)(*d*) of the *Criminal Code*. A preliminary inquiry was held before a judge of the Provincial Court who committed the accused for trial before a judge and jury. The trial resulted in a verdict of guilty. That verdict was appealed to the Appeal Division of this court and then to the Supreme Court of which ordered a new trial. The retrial is expected to last five to six weeks. Prior to selection of a jury at the retrial, counsel for the accused ...

.....

... seeks permission to make his opening statement to the jury immediately after Crown counsel makes his opening statement ...

.....

... rather than wait until completion of the examinations of all witnesses who will be called to testify on behalf of the Crown. It is pointed out that the only statutory provision dealing with the timing of defence counsel's opening speech is s. 651(2) of the *Code* (formerly s. 578(2)), which states:

Summing up by accused

651(2) Counsel for the accused or the accused, where he [or she] is not defended by counsel, is entitled, if he [or she] thinks fit, to open the case for the defence, and after the conclusion of that opening to examine such witnesses as he [or she] thinks fit, and when all the evidence is concluded to sum up the evidence.

Counsel for the accused indicates that he has been able to find only two relevant decided cases. The first is *R. v. Vitale* (1987), 40 C.C.C. (3d) 267 (Ont. Dist. Ct.). In it, Vannini D.C.J. notes that he is not aware of, and counsel for the accused has not found, any authority or case touching upon the timing of the opening statement of counsel for the accused. However, a footnote by the editors of the series of reports makes mention of the case of *R. v. Edwards* (1986), 31 C.R.R. 343 (Ont. H.C.).

In *Vitale*, Vannini D.C.J. interpreted s. 578(2) as clearly conferring upon counsel for an accused the right to make an opening statement, but only if he declared that he proposed to adduce evidence on behalf of the accused. He held that an accused would not be deprived of the right to make full answer and defence and to a fair trial if the right of the accused to make an opening statement was restricted to doing so only at the end of the case for the Crown and only after declaring that he intended to adduce evidence.

In *Edwards*, Barr J. reached much the same conclusion:

.....

An opening statement is not designed as an argument but as a review of the evidence that is proposed to be called. It follows, in my view, that if defence counsel seeks to avail themselves of the opportunity which my ruling has afforded, they will both have to undertake to call evidence ...

However, this ... conclusion appears to be at odds with views expressed earlier in the decision:

... defence counsel have asked for the right to make opening statements to the jury following the opening statement of Crown counsel and without waiting until the Crown evidence has been completed.

This is perhaps of more importance in this case than some because the trial in this case is estimated to take some two weeks.

.....

As a judge, I have sat a number of times listening to legal argument and wondering where it was going; wondering what ultimately I was going to be asked to decide. In being lectured on the subject of the writing of judgments, I have been advised to state the issue for consideration early in the reasons, so that people may read intelligently. And so as far as I am concerned, it is a matter of common experience at least for me, and I think for people generally to know what the argument is about before listening to the argument: and in my view it is much more helpful for the jury to know what it is they are listening for ...

So in my view it is eminently desirable, where defence counsel wish to make an opening statement following that of Crown counsel that they be permitted to do so unless that is prevented by the wording of the *Criminal Code*. Crown counsel says that the section is not so clear as to prohibit the course under discussion, but says that convention requires that the opening for the defence be deferred until after the Crown evidence has been com-

> pleted. And I read the wording of section 578 subsection (2), in paraphrase to say, counsel for the accused is entitled if he thinks fit to open the case for the defence, and after conclusion of that opening to examine such witnesses as he thinks fit. And, of course, two things; one, I would read that ordinarily as saying that immediately after making such opening, the defence shall call witnesses: but having said that I realize to make that meaning clear beyond peradventure, I have to add the word "immediately" to the subsection.
>
> I conclude therefore that I am not precluded by the provisions of section 578 subsection (2) from making the order sought by the defence. In my view it will be helpful for the jury to know, in listening to the Crown case and particularly cross-examination of the Crown witnesses, what it is that the defence is going to say, so that they may listen in a discriminating fashion to the evidence given on behalf of the Crown.

I do not agree with the reasoning or conclusion in *Vitale*. I also do not agree with the conclusion reached in *Edwards*, although I find much of value in the views that constitute Mr. Justice Barr's reasoning in the case.

The conclusion reached in *Edwards* is consistent with the interpretation given to s. 578(2) in *Vitale*. In my opinion, that interpretation is not the only interpretation of which the section is susceptible. The section states that counsel for the accused is entitled to examine such witnesses as he thinks fit after the conclusion of his opening speech to the jury. That does not imply that witnesses must be called on behalf of the defence. Rather, it simply means that counsel for the accused may or may not call witnesses; he may think fit to call witnesses or he may think fit not to call any witnesses at all. The provision also does not require the defence to call evidence as soon as the opening speech has been concluded. Rather, the words "after the conclusion of that opening" mean at any time during the course of the trial after the opening speech. In summary, s. 578(2) provides that counsel for the accused is entitled to present his opening statement to the jury and, at some point of time thereafter, he is entitled to examine as many witnesses as he sees fit.

It is not necessary to read the word, "immediately", into s. 578(2) in order to make the meaning of the section perfectly clear. The present wording is sufficient on which to base a finding that the court may permit counsel for an accused to present his opening statement immediately after counsel for the Crown presents his opening statement.

I agree with Mr. Justice Barr that an opening statement is not designed to be an argument, and I also agree that it is designed to be a review of the evidence proposed to be called. But I cannot see any reason why that review should be limited to the evidence to be called by the defence. If the defence does not intend to call evidence or if the defence is not then prepared to indicate its intentions with respect to calling evidence, I do not see any reason why it cannot be permitted to tell the jury what evidence it expects to elicit upon cross-examination from the witnesses that it knows will be called by the Crown.

In most cases, such a course of action might be dangerous. One potential danger is that, in opening to the jury, defence counsel might intentionally or unintentionally get into argument; but that would not be tolerated by the court. A second potential danger is that defence counsel may not be able to fulfill his implied undertaking to prove everything that he tells the jury he expects to elicit from the Crown witnesses; but counsel's failure in that regard would no doubt be reflected in the verdict returned by the jury.

In the present case, we are dealing with the relatively unusual situation of a retrial. There are in existence transcripts of the preliminary inquiry and of the original trial. The persons proposed to be called to give evidence at the retrial are the same or very similar to those called at the original trial. Both counsel know — within reasonable limits — what the witnesses are likely to say when they testify at the second trial. Therefore, when defence counsel presents his opening statement to the jury and says that he expects to elicit certain facts from witnesses who will be called by the Crown, we can be confident that his statements in preview are likely to be quite accurate.

I also agree with Mr. Justice Barr's comments that it will be helpful to a jury to know near the beginning of the case what evidence will be given both in direct examination and cross-examination by the Crown witnesses. Any conclusions to which members of the jury may have jumped after hearing the opening statement by Crown counsel can be offset in a timely manner by the opening statement made immediately thereafter by counsel for the accused.

I also agree with Mr. Justice Barr in believing that the ability of defence counsel to open to the jury following the opening statement of the Crown is probably more important in the case of a lengthy trial. In *Edwards*, the trial was estimated to take two weeks. In the present case, counsel estimate that it will take five to six weeks. Ordinarily, the jury is expected to sit and listen and not, perhaps, fully appreciate what the defence is likely to be. I think it would be helpful for the jury and, therefore, tend to yield a fairer trial and a fairer result if the jury knew in listening to the witnesses as they are called by the Crown what it is that the defence expected to elicit from them. In this case, the defence is not prepared to say at this point in time whether it is going to call evidence. I do not think that it should be forced to do so.

It has been submitted that granting the application will be prejudicial to the Crown. In my opinion, the amount of prejudice will be minimal to non-existent. The real issue is not potential prejudice to the Crown but, rather, whether the trial will be as fair as it can be. I am inclined to permit a change in procedure in this particular fact situation so as to help ensure the fairest possible trial.

I do not believe that the long-standing practice in criminal trials in this county should be changed; but there will be a few cases in which justice and the requirement of a fair trial demand an amended procedure. In my opinion, because it is a retrial and because it will be lengthy, this is one of those cases.

The ... application is granted.

Some judges refuse to permit the defence to open immediately after the Crown. Others only permit the defence to do so, if the defence undertakes to call defence evidence. Still others have adopted the *Barrow* approach. In judge-alone trials, it is far more common for the defence to advise the court at the outset of the case, without objection, what the position of the defence is.

QUESTION

27. **Is there any policy reason that should prevent the defence from opening for the jury immediately after the Crown, if the defence desires to do so? Some experienced defence counsel never want to open to the jury at this stage. What disadvantages could result from opening to the jury at the beginning of the trial? In what kinds of cases should the discretionary remedy obtained in *R. v. Barrow* be sought?**

N. TENDERING EVIDENCE

The Crown calls its witnesses first, examining each witness in-chief. Each witness first swears to tell the truth, affirms or, in limited circumstances, is permitted to testify upon simply promising to tell the truth (see ss. 14 and 16 of the *Canada Evidence Act*, R.S.C. 1985, c. C-5.)

The nature of the inquiry under s. 16(1)(*b*) of the said Act ("whether the person is able to communicate the evidence") is addressed in the following case.

R. v. MARQUARD

(1993), 85 C.C.C. (3d) 193 (S.C.C.)

[The Supreme Court considered a number of issues, allowing the conviction appeal on grounds which are not relevant here. The appellant was charged and convicted after trial before judge and jury of aggravated assault upon her three-and-one-half-year-old granddaughter. At trial, 17 months after the alleged event, the Crown contended that the appellant put the child's face against a hot stove door to discipline her. The child, unsworn, testified: "My nanna put me on the stove." McLachlin J. delivered the majority judgment of the court.]

McLachlin J.: —

.....

1. The inquiry under s. 16(1)(b) of the Canada Evidence Act

The appellant, Mrs. Marquard, submits that the trial judge erred in failing to conduct an adequate inquiry into whether the complainant could rationally communicate evidence about the injury. The trial judge questioned Debbie-Ann on her schooling and on her appreciation of the duty to tell the truth. Several times the child reiterated that "You have to tell the truth". Asked whether it was important or unimportant to tell the truth, she responded that it was important. At the end of the questioning, the judge asked defence counsel whether she had omitted any questions. He replied: "I can't say that there's anything I think Your Honour has omitted." In further questioning by Crown counsel, Debbie-Ann demonstrated that she knew the difference between the truth and a lie. The judge indicated that while she did not believe the child capable of understanding an oath, her unsworn evidence should be accepted. Some further questioning on remembering took place, and Debbie-Ann told the judge that yesterday

"I went down to the donut shop, and I got a drink and bubble gum". After promising to tell the truth, the child's evidence was taken.

The trial judge was proceeding under s. 16(1)(*b*) of the *Canada Evidence Act*, R.S.C. 1985, c. C-5; repealed and substituted R.S.C. 1985, c. 19 (3rd Supp.), s. 18, which provides:

> 16(1) Where a proposed witness is a person under fourteen years of age or a person whose mental capacity is challenged, the court shall, before permitting the person to give evidence, conduct an inquiry to determine
>
> .....
>
> (*b*) whether the person is able to communicate the evidence.

The appellant's argument turns on the meaning of the phrase "conduct an inquiry to determine ... whether the person is able to communicate the evidence". She contends that it is not enough to explore the child's ability to understand the truth and communicate. The judge must, in her submission, satisfy herself that the child is competent to testify about the events at issue in the trial. To this end, the trial judge must test the child's ability to perceive and interpret the events in question at the time they took place, as well as her ability to recollect accurately and communicate them at trial. All the latter, she submits, are embraced by the phrase "able to communicate the evidence" in s. 16 of the Act.

The Crown, on the other hand, takes the position that Parliament, in choosing the infinitive "to communicate", evinced the intention to exclude all other aspects of testimonial competence. The ability of the witness to perceive and interpret the events at the time they occurred and the ability of the witness to recollect them at the time of trial are not part of the test. The only requirement is that the child be able to "communicate" her evidence.

It seems to me that the proper interpretation of s. 16 lies between these two extremes. In the case of a child testifying under s. 16 of the *Canada Evidence Act* testimonial competence is not presumed. The child is placed in the same position as an adult whose competence has been challenged. At common law, such a challenge required the judge to inquire into the competence of the witness to testify.

Testimonial competence comprehends: (1) the capacity to observe (including interpretation); (2) the capacity to recollect, and (3) the capacity to communicate: *McCormick on Evidence*, 4th ed. (1992), vol. 1, pp. 242-8; *Wigmore on Evidence* (Chadbourn rev. 1979), vol. 2, pp. 636-8. The judge must satisfy himself or herself that the witness possesses these capacities. Is the witness capable of observing what was happening? Is he or she capable of remembering what he or she observes? Can he or she communicate what he or she remembers? The goal is not to ensure that the evidence is credible, but only to assure that it meets the minimum threshold of being receivable. The inquiry is into *capacity* to perceive, recollect and communicate, not whether the witness *actually* perceived, recollects and can communicate about the events in question. Generally speaking, the best gauge of capacity is the witness's performance at the time of trial. The procedure at common law has generally been to allow a witness who demonstrates capacity to testify at trial to testify. Defects in ability to perceive or recollect the particular events at issue are left to be explored in the course of giving the evidence, notably by cross-examination.

I see no indication in the wording of s. 16 that Parliament intended to revise this time-honoured process. The phrase "communicate the evidence" indicates more than mere verbal ability. The reference to "the evidence" indicates the ability to testify about the matters before the court. It is necessary to explore in a general way whether the witness is capable of perceiving events, remembering events and communicating events to the court. If satisfied that this is the case, the judge may then receive the child's evidence, upon the child's promising to tell the truth under s. 16(3). It is not necessary to determine in advance that the child perceived and recollects the very events at issue in the trial as a condition of ruling that her evidence be received. That is not required of adult witnesses, and should not be required for children.

My colleague, Justice L'Heureux-Dubé, contends that the standard I have outlined is one which is inconsistent with "the trend to do away with presumptions of unreliability and to expand the admissibility of children's evidence and may, in fact, subvert the purpose of legislative reform in this area". I disagree. The test I have expounded is not based on presumptions about the incompetency of children to be witnesses nor is it intended as a test which would make it difficult for children to testify. Rather, the test outlines the basic abilities that individuals need to possess if they are to testify. The threshold is not a high one. What is required is the basic ability to perceive, remember and communicate. This established, deficiencies of perception, recollection of the events at issue may be dealt with as matters going to the weight of the evidence.

The examination conducted in this case was sufficient to permit the trial judge to conclude that Debbie-Ann was capable of perceiving events, remembering events and recounting events to the court. This in turn permitted the trial judge to receive her evidence, upon Debbie-Ann's promise to tell the truth. What Debbie-Ann actually perceived and recollected of the events in question was a matter for the jury to determine after listening to her evidence in chief and in cross-examination.

I would add this. It has repeatedly been held that a large measure of deference is to be accorded to the trial judge's assessment of a child's capacity to testify. Meticulous second-guessing on appeal is to be eschewed. As Dickson J.(as he then was) put it in the oft-cited case of *R. v. Bannerman* (1966), 48 C.R. 110 at p. 135, 55 W.W.R. 257 (Man. C.A.); affirmed [1966] S.C.R. *v*, 50 C.R. 76n, 57 W.W.R. 736*n*, a trial judge's discretion in determining that a child is competent to testify "unless manifestly abused, should not be interfered with".

I conclude that the trial judge did not err in the inquiry she conducted under s. 16(1)(*b*) of the *Canada Evidence Act* or in receiving the evidence of the child.

QUESTION

28. An eight-year-old girl is a key Crown witness. What questions should the Crown discuss with her, in anticipation of a s. 16 inquiry? Who should question her during the s. 16 inquiry? Assume that she indicates that she does not believe in a deity. Under what circumstances, if any, can she still be sworn as a witness? Under what circumstances should she be permitted to testify, upon promising to tell the truth? Consider, in this regard, *R. v. G.(C.W.)* (1994), 88 C.C.C. (3d) 240 (B.C.C.A.); *R. v. Khan* (1990), 59 C.C.C.

(3d) 92 (S.C.C.); *R. v. McGovern* (1993), 82 C.C.C. (3d) 301 (Man. C.A.); leave to appeal to S.C.C. refused (1993), 84 C.C.C. (3d) vi.

Generally, the Crown is not permitted to lead its witness, except on non-contentious matters. The defence may then cross-examine the witness, using leading or suggestive questions. The Crown may then re-examine the witness on matters which arose on cross-examination. The trial judge may then choose to ask clarifying questions, permitting counsel to then ask questions arising out of his or her questions. However, there are limits upon the rights of a trial judge to so intervene.

BROUILLARD (A.K.A. CHATEL) v. THE QUEEN

(1985), 17 C.C.C. (3d) 193 (S.C.C.)

Lamer J.: — Appellant was charged with extortion and convicted by a judge of the Court of Sessions of the Peace. His appeal to the Quebec Court of Appeal was dismissed. He appealed to this Court with its leave. In my view, his appeal should be allowed and a new trial ordered.

Facts

Appellant and the complainant, Mrs. Madeleine Lebel, have known each other since May 1977. They did business together and were partners in two companies. On July 3, 1979, appellant visited the complainant at her home and demanded the sum of $6,000 from her. According to the complainant and one of her daughters, he threatened her. This led to a charge of extortion....

[Lamer J. then summarizes the reasons of the trial judge and reproduces the judgment of the Quebec Court of Appeal finding that interventions by the trial judge were not such as to compel a new trial.]

In the case at bar I am certainly not convinced that the judge was biased. On the contrary, I am inclined to believe that he meant to be impartial. I am thus of the view that the accused was not prevented from presenting his defence, calling all relevant witnesses and adducing all relevant evidence, although not without difficulty. However, I am obliged to conclude that, by his conduct, the trial judge allowed there to be some doubt on this subject, which only a new trial can erase.

.....

Before discussing the judge's conduct, we should mention certain rules arising out of the principle put forward by Lord Hewart, as well as their limits. This is not intended to be exhaustive. There are numerous decisions and substantial legal opinion on the subject.

.....

First of all, it is clear that judges are no longer required to be as passive as they once were; to be what I call sphinx judges. We now not only accept that a judge may intervene in the adversarial debate, but also believe that it is sometimes essential for him to do so for justice in fact to be done. Thus a judge may and sometimes must ask witnesses questions, interrupt them in their testimony and if necessary call them to order.

One of the decisions most often cited in support of this rule is *Jones v. National Coal Board*, [1957] 2 All E.R. 155 (C.A.). Lord Denning stated the following, at pp. 158-59:

> No one can doubt that the judge, in intervening as he did, was actuated by the best motives. He was anxious to understand the details of this complicated case, and asked questions to get them clear in his mind. He was anxious that the witnesses should not be harassed unduly in cross-examination, and intervened to protect them when he thought necessary. He was anxious to investigate all the various criticisms that had been made against the board, and to see whether they were well founded or not. Hence he took them up himself with the witnesses from time to time. He was anxious that the case should not be dragged on too long, and intimated clearly when he thought that a point had been sufficiently explored. All those are worthy motives on which judges daily intervene in the conduct of cases and have done for centuries.
>
> Nevertheless, we are quite clear that the interventions, taken together, were far more than they should have been. In the system of trial which we have evolved in this country, the judge sits to hear and determine the issues raised by the parties, not to conduct an investigation or examination on behalf of society at large, as happens, we believe, in some foreign countries. Even in England, however, a judge is not a mere umpire to answer the question "How's that?" His object above all is to find out the truth, and to do justice according to the law ...

More recently, in Canada, in *R. v. Torbiak and Campbell* (1974), 26 C.R.N.S. 108 at pp. 109-10, which involved a problem similar to the one in the case at bar, the Ontario Court of Appeal stated the following:

> The proper conduct of a trial judge is circumscribed by two considerations. On the one hand his position is one of great power and prestige which gives his every word an especial significance. The position of established neutrality requires that the trial judge should confine himself as much as possible to his own responsibilities and leave to counsel and members of the jury their respective functions. On the other hand his responsibility for the conduct of the trial may well require him to ask questions which ought to be asked and have not been asked on account of the failure of counsel, and so compel him to interject himself into the examination of witnesses to a degree which he might not otherwise choose.
>
> Since the limits of the allowable conduct are not absolute, but relative to the facts and circumstances of the particular trial within which they are to be observed, every alleged departure during a trial from the accepted standards of judicial conduct must be examined with respect to its effect on the fairness of the trial.

.....

Finally, I cite with approval the judgment to which the respondent Crown referred us in *R. v. Darlyn* (1946), 88 C.C.C. 269 at p. 277... where Bird J.A. wrote the following on behalf of the British Columbia Court of Appeal:

> The nature and extent of a Judge's participation in the examination of a witness is no doubt a matter within his discretion, a discretion which must be

> exercised judicially. I conceive it to be the function of the Judge to keep the scales of justice in even balance between the Crown and the accused. There can be no doubt in my opinion that a judge has not only the right, but also the duty to put questions to a witness in order to clarify an obscure answer or to resolve possible misunderstanding of any question by a witness, even to remedy an omission of counsel, by putting questions which the judge thinks ought to have been asked in order to bring out or explain relevant matters...

In short, everyone agrees that a judge has a right and, where necessary, a duty to ask questions, but also that there are certain definite limits on this right.

.....

Finally, prudence and the resulting judicial restraint must be all the greater where the accused is a witness. He must be allowed to proceed, within limits, of course, but always bearing in mind that at the end of the day he is the only one who may be leaving the court in handcuffs.

In conclusion, although the judge may and must intervene for justice to be done, he must nonetheless do so in such a way that justice *is seen to be done*. It is all a question of manner.

In the case at bar, the least that can be said is that the judge was aware of his right to intervene. He asked the witness Dominique Gauthier, the complainant's daughter and the accused's girlfriend and witness, some sixty questions, almost as many as the Crown, and interrupted her more than ten times during her testimony.

During the accused's testimony the judge asked many more questions than the two counsel. In fact during the examination-in-chief he interrupted the examination being conducted by counsel for the defence almost 20 times, and cross-examined the accused. As a result he asked the accused, still during the examination-in-chief, twice as many questions as his own lawyer asked. Since his questions were more in the nature of a cross-examination, he thus clearly gave the impression of assisting the Crown by doing precisely what he would have had to prevent the Crown from doing if necessary. The accused was interrupted by the judge a total of over 60 times in his answers in chief and in cross-examination. Both the accused and the witness Gauthier were the object of sarcastic remarks.

By way of illustrating the general situation, I quote (translation):

> The Court:
>
> Q. Tell the truth Miss, tell what happened in this case, that document, what was it for, tell me the truth?
>
> A. Well I've been telling the truth.
>
> Q. Stop beating around the bush.
>
> .....
>
> The witness:
>
> No, no, no but can I explain myself?
>
> The Court:
>
> Ah! explain yourself. You need, I need very good explanations.

.....

Explain that to me. You know, I understand, I'm not intelligent, I've never studied law, I've never done any civil or whatever but in any case.

The witness:

If I told you that on the first of August '79 ...

The Court:

Ah! tell me what you like but you need ...

The witness:

But you are asking me questions.

The Court:

... you need to have an explanation, and a good one this time.

The witness:

If I told you that on the first of August '79, I didn't owe the company that sum of money.

The Court:

Ah! why didn't you tell the company to go to hell?

The Crown:

Q. What did you owe the company?

A. Well at that . . .

The Court:

When I don't owe anything, and a guy is trying to collect from me, do you know what I do? I tell the guy: get three lawyers, ten lawyers, do what you like, but come and collect from me if you can.

The witness:

That's right.

The Court:

Eh. You're a president ...

The witness:

That's right.

The Court:

... of marketing, you're a specialist in marketing and you write a letter to an individual saying he's going to be arrested and then after that he'll pay. Come on. Do you take me for an idiot? I'm not Mrs. Lebel. Just a minute. Do you take me for an imbecile?

.....

[More illustrations follow.]

In my view it is clearly in the interests of justice that a new trial be held.

QUESTIONS

29. You are counsel at trial. The trial judge is intervening in the manner described in the case above. What should you do? Would your answer be the same or different if the case were being heard by a judge sitting with a jury?

30. The Crown's last witness is on the stand. Examination-in-chief is completed. The Crown has failed to prove a critical point. Defence counsel is ecstatic. Then Judge Cleanup turns to the witness and asks the very question Crown counsel has omitted. Does the defence have any legitimate grievance?

Sometimes, a party contradicts an *adverse* witness which that party has produced, or proves that such a witness previously made an inconsistent statement (s. 9(1) of the *Canada Evidence Act*). As well, sometimes a party producing a witness may be permitted to cross-examine the witness as to a prior inconsistent statement made in writing, reduced to writing or recorded, without proof that the witness is *adverse* (s. 9(2) of the *Canada Evidence Act*). The complicated interrelationship between s. 9(1) and s. 9(2) and the applicable procedures on a s. 9 *voir dire* are addressed in the following case.

R. v. CASSIBO

(1982), 70 C.C.C. (2d) 498 (Ont. C.A.)

[After trial by judge alone, the appellant was convicted on four counts of incest relating to his daughters R. and D. R. testified that when she was 12 years of age, R. and D. told their mother what was happening and thereafter they were never left alone and there was no further sexual misconduct. The testimony of D. was similar. Their mother was called as a Crown witness to establish certain dates and other matters. In cross-examination, defence counsel elicited from the witness that neither of her daughters had ever complained about "sexual advances" made by the appellant nor had she ever overheard them talking about such a thing. In re-examination, Crown counsel sought to question her on an alleged prior inconsistent statement made to the police, though not signed or acknowledged by her. One issue that the court addressed was whether the prior oral statement could be relied upon in a s. 9(1) *Canada Evidence Act voir dire* to support a finding of adversity.]

The judgment of the court was delivered by

Martin J.A.: —

.....

It is common ground that the police officer's notes of his interview with Mrs. Cassibo did not constitute a statement in writing or reduced to writing within s. 9(2) of the *Canada Evidence Act*: see *R. v. Handy* (1978), 45 C.C.C. (2d) 232, 5 C.R. (3d) 97, [1979] 1 W.W.R. 90 (B.C.C.A.).

Mr. Gold, for the appellant, contended before us that the trial judge erred in permitting Crown counsel to cross-examine Mrs. Cassibo on a prior oral statement alleged to be inconsistent with her testimony, and in permitting the police officers to give evidence of the making of the statement for the purpose of determining whether she was adverse. His argument, as I understood it, was this: When s. 9(2) of the *Canada Evidence Act*, was enacted by 1968-69 (Can.) c. 14, s. 2, the decisions were conflicting on the question whether on an application under s. 9(1) by a party producing a witness to have the witness declared adverse, the judge could, in determining whether the witness was adverse, take into account a prior inconsistent statement made by the witness. Parliament, by expressly providing in s. 9(2) that the court may grant leave to a party to cross-examine his own witness with respect to a prior inconsistent statement in writing or reduced to writing without proof that the witness is adverse, and by expressly providing that such cross-examination may be taken into account in deciding whether the witness is adverse, had by necessary implication ruled out the use of a prior inconsistent oral statement for the purpose of determining whether the witness is adverse.

Mr. Then for the Crown, on the other hand, contended that s. 9(2) does not restrict the application of s. 9(1) which applies to both oral and written statements, and an oral statement can be considered under s. 9(1) in determining whether a witness is adverse.

.....

It would appear that the current view in England is that a previous inconsistent statement may properly be considered on the preliminary issue of whether the witness is adverse....

.....

The view that the making of a prior inconsistent statement is relevant on the issue of adverseness is also in accord with the modern trend in the law of evidence of eliminating purely artificial restrictions, no longer having any rational basis, which are not justified on policy grounds, and which serve merely to impede the search for truth. *Cf.* the provisions of s. 114 of the proposed Uniform Evidence Act [Uniform Law Conference of Canada] and s. 62 of the proposed Evidence Code of the Law Reform Commission of Canada, Report on Evidence (1975). Dean Wigmore has observed in *Wigmore on Evidence*, 3rd ed. (1940), p. 420:

> The general rule itself [against impeaching one's own witness] is so fraught with irrationality that to apply it with rational deduction is almost impossible.

In any event, the decision of this Court in the *Wawanesa Mutual Ins. Co. v. Hanes*, [1963] 1 C.C.C. 176, holding that the trial judge may receive on a *voir dire* evidence of the making of a previous inconsistent statement, oral or written, by a party's own witness, on the preliminary issue of whether the witness is adverse, concludes the matter in this Court, unless s. 9(2) of the *Canada Evidence Act* has, as Mr. Gold contended, altered the law as stated in that case. Mr. Gold's argument depends upon the premise that s. 9(2) represents a compromise between two conflicting streams of authority and that Parliament struck a balance between the competing lines of authority by providing that previous inconsistent statements could be taken into account on an application under s. 9(1) in deciding whether the witness was adverse but restricting the kind of statements that could be so used to statements in writing or reduced to writing.

There would be considerable force in this argument if s. 9(2) were to be construed only as providing a procedure to be used in deciding whether a witness was adverse within s. 9(1). See R. J. Delisle, "Witnesses — Now and Later" (1976), 34 C.R.N.S. 1 at 7. This has not, however, been the construction placed upon s. 9(2). It is now well established that s. 9(2) provides an independent procedure under which the judge may permit a party to cross-examine his own witness as to a statement previously made in writing or reduced to writing without any necessity for a declaration that the witness is adverse. The party may never seek a declaration that the witness is adverse. He may be satisfied to impeach the credibility of the witness only on the point or points covered by the prior statement, and may otherwise be quite content with the witness's evidence. However, if the party seeks a declaration that the witness is adverse, the trial judge may consider such cross-examination in determining whether the witness is adverse. Somewhat strangely s-s. (2) makes no express provision for proving the inconsistent statement if the witness denies making it, but the judicial interpretation placed upon the subsection makes it clear that such proof can be made: see *R. v. Milgaard,* [1971] 2 W.W.R. 266, 2 C.C.C. (2d) 206, 14 C.R.N.S.34 (Sask. C.A.). (Leave to appeal to the Supreme Court of Canada refused (1971), 4 C.C.C. (2d) 566n [1971] S.C.R. x.)

In *R. v. Milgaard,* Culliton C.J.S., after setting out s. 9(2), stated at p. 220 C.C.C.:

> *This subsection provides an exception to the law as stated in s-s. (1).* Under this subsection, a Judge in the exercise of his judicial discretion, may permit counsel to cross-examine his own witness as to a statement previously made in writing, or reduced to writing, that is inconsistent with the evidence which the witness is giving. The learned trial Judge may grant such permission without declaring the witness hostile. When such permission has been granted, the right to cross-examine is a limited one; it is confined to a cross-examination relative to the inconsistencies as disclosed in the statement. Under the section, however, if a subsequent application is made to declare the witness hostile, the learned trial Judge may consider the cross-examination as to the inconsistent statement in determining whether the witness is hostile. If the witness is declared to be hostile, then the right to cross-examine is not restricted.

(Emphasis added.) He further said at p. 222 C.C.C.:

> The determination whether a witness is hostile is a matter solely for the learned trial Judge. It is when the learned trial Judge is of the opinion that the witness proves adverse that s-s. (1) of s. 9 comes into play. The declaration of hostility, as provided for in s-s. (1), is an entirely different matter from that of permitting cross-examination under s-s. (2). In my opinion, there is no conflict and s-s. (2) is a specific exception to the provisions of s-s. (1). In the present case the learned trial Judge had every right to declare the witness Nichol John hostile, and in so doing had the right to consider the cross-examination that had taken place in the presence of the jury on the permission granted under s-s. (2).

In *McInroy et al. v. The Queen,* [1979] 1 S.C.R. 588, 89 D.L.R. (3d) 609, 42 C.C.C. (2d) 481, Martland J., delivering the majority judgment of the Supreme Court of Canada, said at p. 494 C.C.C.:

> Section 9(2) is not concerned with the cross-examination of an adverse witness. That subsection confers a discretion on a trial Judge where the party producing a witness alleges that the witness has made, at another time, a written statement inconsistent with the evidence being given at the trial. The discretion is to permit, without proof that the witness is adverse, cross-examination as to the statement.

Estey J., in a separate judgment, expressly stated at p. 499 that he agreed that the analysis of s. 9(2) by Culliton C.J.S. in *R. v. Milgaard, supra*, was both correct in law and practical in its results.

Since s. 9(2) does not require a finding that the witness is adverse, it would seem to be entirely logical and reasonable to confine its application to statements in writing or reduced to writing because they are more readily capable of proof. The fact that s. 9(2) also provides that the cross-examination on the prior written statement may be used on an application to have the witness declared adverse under s. 9(1) does not, in my opinion, have the effect of limiting the Court, on an application under s. 9(1) to have the witness declared adverse, to the consideration only of written statements. In my view, s. 9(2) should not be construed as restricting the provisions of s. 9(1), as those provisions and their Commonwealth counterparts have generally been interpreted in modern times, unless the language of s. 9(2) clearly requires that construction; and I am of the opinion that it does not. As I have previously indicated, such a construction would be retrograde.

It is one thing to withhold an alleged previous inconsistent oral statement from the jury or trier of fact, in the absence of a finding by the trial judge that the witness is adverse. It is quite another thing to hold that the trial judge on a *voir dire* is not entitled to take into account the statement as a part of the material to be considered in deciding whether the witness is adverse. The *voir dire* acts as a screening device. The judge on the *voir dire* for the purpose of determining whether the witness is adverse must satisfy himself that the statement was made, although if he rules that the witness is adverse and permits evidence of the making of the statement to be given at the trial, it is for the trier of fact to decide whether the statement was, in fact, made. The judge, after hearing the evidence with respect to the making of the statement on the *voir dire*, may, in the proper exercise of his discretion, refuse to declare that the witness is adverse or may refuse to grant leave to prove the statement at the trial because the evidence with respect to the making of the statement is too conflicting or unsatisfactory, or the words alleged to have been spoken are ambiguous, giving rise to a multiplicity of issues which would be prejudicial to the fair trial of the accused. If, however, the judge is satisfied on the *voir dire* that the oral statement was made by the witness and is substantially inconsistent with the testimony of the witness, then as MacKay J.A. pointed out in *Wawanesa Mutual Ins. Co. v. Hanes, supra*, the statement is cogent evidence on the issue of adversity.

I am, for the above reasons, of the opinion that the trial judge did not err in considering the evidence adduced on the *voir dire* of the previous inconsistent statement of Mrs. Cassibo.

R. v. Milgaard **(1971), 2 C.C.C. (2d) 206 (Sask. C.A.); leave to appeal to S.C.C. refused (1971), 4 C.C.C. (2d) 566*n*, outlines the step-by-step procedure on a s. 9(2) application (at pp. 221-2):**

(1) Counsel should advise the Court that he [or she] desires to make [a s. 9(2) application].
(2) ... the Court should direct the jury to retire.
(3) [Once the jury has retired] counsel should advise the ... trial Judge of the particulars of the application and produce ... the alleged statement in writing or the writing to which the statement has been reduced.
(4) The trial Judge should read the statement, or writing, and determine whether ... there is an inconsistency between [it and the testimony]. [If there is not, the matter ends. If there is an inconsistency, the trial judge should call upon counsel to prove the statement].
(5) Counsel should then prove the statement or writing. This may be done by producing the statement or writing to the witness. If the witness admits the statement, or the statement reduced to writing, such proof would be sufficient. If the witness does not so admit, counsel then could provide the necessary proof by other evidence.
(6) If the witness admits making the statement, counsel for the opposing party should have the right to cross-examine as to the circumstances under which the statement was made. A similar right to cross-examine should be granted if the statement is proven by other witnesses. It may be that [counsel for the opposing party] will be able to establish that there were circumstances which would render it improper for the ... trial Judge to permit the cross-examination, notwithstanding the apparent inconsistencies. The opposing counsel, too, should have the right to call evidence as to factors relevant to obtaining the statement, for the purpose of attempting to show that cross-examination should not be permitted.
(7) The learned trial Judge should then decide whether or not [the cross-examination will be permitted]. If so, the jury should be recalled.

These steps may be preceded by an attempt to "refresh the witness's memory". This procedure is described in *Reference re R. v. Coffin* (1956), 114 C.C.C. 1 (S.C.C.).

Reference should also be made to *R. v. B.(K.G.)* (1993), 79 C.C.C. (3d) 257 (S.C.C.) as to when prior inconsistent statements can be admitted for their truth.

There are a variety of other issues that arise in the course of the trial that may necessitate a *voir dire*. The following questions provide some examples.

QUESTIONS

31. The accused is charged with sexual assault. The complainant testified that she did not consent to any sexual activity because she found the accused, and all others of his ethnic origin, physically repulsive. The defence position is that the sexual activity was consensual. The defence wishes to elicit evidence, through the complainant and through the accused, that they had had consensual sexual intercourse on several prior occasions. Or, the defence wishes to prove that the complainant had prior consensual sexual intercourse with other men of the same ethnic origin. What procedures should be employed to determine admissibility? Consider, in this regard, ss. 276, 276.1 to 276.5 and s. 277 of the *Criminal Code*.

32. **The accused is charged with dangerous driving. The Crown calls the accused's wife, A.B., as a witness. It is alleged that the accused, in an uncontrollable rage, was following his wife's vehicle at the time of the incident. The defence objects to A.B.'s competence to testify under s. 4(5) of the *Canada Evidence Act* [am. 1985, c. 19 (3rd Supp.), s. 17]. What procedures are to be employed to determine competence? Consider, in this regard, *R. v. Czipps* (1979), 48 C.C.C. (2d) 166 (Ont. C.A.).**

33. **Review s. 715.1 of the *Criminal Code*. The accused is charged with sexually assaulting a young child. A videotaped statement had been made of the child's account within a very short time of the alleged offence. In it, the child described the sexual assault as well as other assaultive conduct by the accused on her and others. A *voir dire* is held to determine if the child is in a position to adopt the videotaped statement. The child remembers some aspects of the sexual assault previously described on the videotape but does not have present recollection of other aspects of the sexual assault. What procedures should be employed by the trial judge? Would your answer be the same or different if the remembered parts of the tape are inextricably interwoven with the unremembered parts? Does s. 715.1 extend to her videotaped description of other assaultive conduct? Consider, in this regard, *R. v. F.(C.C.)* (1997), 120 C.C.C. (3d) 225 (S.C.C.); and *R. v. L.(D.O.)* (1993), 85 C.C.C. (3d) 289 (S.C.C.).**

Generally, the Crown's case consists of *viva voce* evidence, together with documentary and physical evidence (s. 652 also permits the jury to have a view of any place, thing or person). Formal admissions may be made by each party to dispense with proof (s. 655). The Crown may bring a *Khan* application to permit, for example, the out of court statement of a child to be received for its truth, without requiring the child to testify (see *R. v. Khan* (1990), 59 C.C.C. (3d) 92 (S.C.C.); *R. v. A.(S).* (1992), 76 C.C.C. (3d) 522 (Ont. C.A.); and *R. v. Starr* (2000), 147 C.C.C. (3d) 449 (S.C.C.) generally for approaches to hearsay exceptions).

At the conclusion of the Crown's case, the accused may move for a non-suit. Unlike civil proceedings, the trial judge cannot compel an accused to elect whether or not to call evidence before deciding the motion. The motion must be determined before the case proceeds further: *R. v. Boissonneault* (1986), 29 C.C.C. (3d) 345 (Ont. C.A.). Where the trial judge allows the motion during a jury trial, he or she should withdraw the case from the jury and enter a verdict of acquittal: *R. v. Rowbotham* (1994), 90 C.C.C. (3d) 449 (S.C.C.). As reflected earlier, the test on a non-suit application, whether in a trial before judge alone or judge and jury, is the same as that which governs committal for trial: *United States of America v. Sheppard* (1976), 30 C.C.C. (2d) 424 (S.C.C.).

Assuming there is no directed verdict of acquittal, the defence then opens to the jury (if it intends to call evidence and with the assumption that no application has been brought by the defence for an earlier opportunity to open: see *R. v. Barrow* (1989), 48 C.C.C. (3d) 308 (N.S.S.C.), substantially reproduced at p. 535) and then calls its witnesses, following the same procedure as reflected in the Crown's case. Of course, where there are multiple accused, each accused or counsel can cross-examine any witnesses tendered by another accused, including the other accused. If the defence calls no evidence, it so indicates in the presence of the jury.

Special issues arise in connection with an accused's testimony. For example, s. 13 of the *Charter* provides that any "witness who testifies in any proceedings has the right not to have any incriminating evidence so given used to incriminate that witness in any other proceedings, except in a prosecution for perjury or for the giving of contradictory evidence." In *R. v. Noël* (2002), 168 C.C.C. (3d) 193 (S.C.C.), the Court addressed the distinction made in earlier jurisprudence between cross-examination on prior testimony aiming to incriminate, which is prohibited, and cross-examination aiming at challenging credibility, which is not. When an accused testifies at trial, he or she cannot be cross-examined on the basis of prior testimony unless the trial judge is satisfied that there is no realistic danger that his or her prior testimony could be used to incriminate. Cross-examination is permitted when there is no possibility that the jury could use the content of the prior testimony to draw an inference of guilt. The danger of incrimination will vary with the nature of the prior evidence and the circumstances of the cases including the efficacy of an adequate instruction to the jury. When the prior evidence is highly incriminating, no limiting instruction to the jury could overcome the danger of incrimination and the cross-examination should not be permitted.

An accused may be compelled to testify against another accused separately charged, though he or she may be thereby forced to acknowledge guilt or make other damaging admissions. Section 13 would not adequately immunize that accused since it by itself, would not prevent the Crown from obtaining evidence derived from the compelled testimony to build a stronger case against that accused and would still permit that accused to be cross-examined at his or her trial on prior compelled testimony to impugn credibility. The Supreme Court has held that s. 7 of the *Charter* provides additional protection by excluding derivative evidence which could not have been obtained, or the significance of which could not have been appreciated, but for the compelled testimony of the witness (sometimes referred to as "derivative use immunity"). Generally, the witness remains compellable at the other accused's trial, despite his or her own status as accused.

QUESTIONS

34. Are there any circumstances where such a witness as described above cannot be compelled to testify at the instance of the Crown in a separate proceeding? What if the Crown caused separate informations to be laid against each accused for the sole purpose of compelling one to testify against the other? Or, assume that accused A. is subpoenaed to testify at accused B.'s preliminary inquiry. A.'s counsel believes that A.'s evidence is not really significant against B. but A. is being called to enable the Crown to discover A.'s defence. What position could A.'s counsel take? What if accused A. provides compelled testimony which includes the production of relevant documents? Would derivative use immunity extend to those documents when tendered against A. at his trial? Would your answer be affected by the fact that the documents were pre-existing documents? Consider, in this regard, *R. v. S.(R.J.)* (1995), 96 C.C.C. (3d) 1 (S.C.C.); *R. v. Primeau* (1995), 97 C.C.C. (3d) 1 (S.C.C.); *R. v. Jobin* (1995), 97 C.C.C. (3d) 97 (S.C.C.); *British Columbia Securities Commission v. Branch* (1995), 97 C.C.C. (3d) 505 (S.C.C.).

35. Section 5 of the *Canada Evidence Act,* together with analogous sections in provincial evidence acts, outlines a procedure to provide some immunity for a witness against the subsequent use of evidence. Does s. 5 continue to have any role, in light of s. 13 of the *Charter*? Consider *R. v. Noël* (2002), 168 C.C.C. (3d) 193 (S.C.C.).

36. The accused has a criminal record for sexual assault which is 12 years old. He has no other criminal record. He is charged with sexual assault. His defence is consent. The Crown undoubtedly will attempt to cross-examine him on the record pursuant to s. 12 of the *Canada Evidence Act* [am. 1992, c. 47, s. 66]. In *R. v. Corbett* (1988), 41 C.C.C. (3d) 385, the Supreme Court of Canada held that a judicial discretion exists to exclude cross-examination on the record, where a mechanical application of s. 12 would undermine the right to a fair trial. A defence motion to exclude such cross-examination is known as a *Corbett* application. The accused brings the application at the commencement of trial. The trial judge rules that it is premature, as she must assess the application in light of how the trial is conducted and the issues which arise. The complainant is later cross-examined. The thrust of the cross-examination is that the complainant's story is implausible; there is no suggestion that the complainant has a prior record or is a person of bad character. At the end of the Crown's case, the defence renews the application. This exchange occurs:

    > Defence counsel: The accused is unlikely to testify if I lose this motion since, in my respectful submission, the record is so prejudicial that the accused will be all finished with the jury. In any event, if I lose this motion, and the accused does choose to testify, I will put the record to him in examination-in-chief so the jury will not infer that he was hiding it. So, the defence seeks a ruling now.
    >
    > Crown counsel: With respect, do not decide now. The accused must first choose whether he intends to testify. I need to hear what he will say. The appellate courts frown on prospective rulings on issues that may not arise.

    How should the judge decide this aspect of the application? Was the judge correct in deferring judgment at the beginning of the case? Consider, in this regard, *R. v. Underwood* (1997), 121 C.C.C. (3d) 117 (S.C.C.). Compare *R. v. P.(G.F.)* (1994), 89 C.C.C. (3d) 176 (Ont. C.A.); *R. v. Riehm*, [1993] O.J. No. 3922 (C.A.); *R. v. Hoffman* (1994), 32 C.R. (4th) 396 (Alta. C.A.).

37. An accused's statement is excluded as violative of s. 10(*b*) of the *Charter*. The accused testifies that he was with the complainant the relevant night but did not sexually assault her. In the excluded statement, the accused denied that he was with the complainant that night. Can the Crown successfully contend that whereas the administration of justice would be brought into disrepute by admitting the statement as part of its case, it would bring the administration of justice into disrepute by precluding cross-examination on the statement, and permitting the jury to be misled? Consider, in this regard, *R. v. Calder* (1996), 105 C.C.C. (3d) 1 (S.C.C.).

Joint trials raise unique issues. For example, the accused may have antagonistic defences who want to attack their co-accused in a way which is not open to the Crown.

QUESTION

38. Revisit *R. v. Crawford*, substantially reproduced at p. 475. Can counsel for one accused comment on the failure of the other accused to make a statement to the police? Can counsel for the other accused counterattack by commenting on the other's failure to testify?

Joint trials may also raise conflicts of interest.

R. v. SILVINI

(1991), 68 C.C.C. (3d) 251 (Ont. C.A.)

The judgment of the court was delivered by

Lacourcière J.A.: — The principal question raised in this appeal is whether the right of an accused person to make full answer and defence to a criminal charge, which is constitutionally protected through s. 7 of the *Canadian Charter of Rights and Freedoms,* encompasses a right, in a joint trial, to the effective assistance of counsel unencumbered by a conflict of interest.

After a four and one-half day trial before judge and jury in the District Court of Ontario at Toronto, the appellant was convicted of conspiracy to traffic in heroin contrary to s. 423(1)(*d*) (now s. 465(1)(*c*)) of the *Criminal Code*. The appellant appeals against his conviction and, at the time of his release on bail pending appeal, was granted leave to appeal against his sentence of six years.

.....

The procedural background of defence counsel's alleged conflict of interest

After a series of adjournments, Frank Leo, with the consent of the Crown, re-elected trial by judge alone, entered a plea of guilty, and was sentenced to 12 months consecutive on February 11, 1986. On February 12, 1986, the trial of the appellant and Gino Mangiapane commenced and a verdict of guilty was returned against both Silvini and Mangiapane on February 20, 1986. Sentence was imposed on March 26, 1986. Mangiapane abandoned his appeal against conviction and sentence.

At the opening of the trial, counsel, who up to that time had been representing the appellant and his co-accused, informed the court that he had just been discharged by Mangiapane and requested an adjournment of one or two days to allow Mangiapane to retain other counsel. He advised the court that, although both the appellant and Mangiapane were apparently content that he continue to act for the appellant, it was possible that Mangiapane's new counsel might not agree. Crown counsel pointed out that the possibility of a conflict between the interests of the appellant and Mangiapane had been apparent as early as the preliminary hearing, and that he and defence counsel had discussed that issue one or two years earlier.

Crown counsel noted that the charge had arisen in 1982 and had been up for trial eight or nine times, but had not proceeded, in part because of adjournments related to Mangiapane's health problems. He observed that nothing regarding the possibility of a conflict of interest had been said on the previous day when the case had been called but not reached, and that the problem had arisen only when the case was finally ready to proceed. He submitted that Mangiapane would not likely be able to find other counsel who would be able to represent him on short notice, and that, if the trial were to be adjourned, it would not be reached for at least six more months. He, therefore, urged the learned trial judge to require Mangiapane to proceed without counsel. Defence counsel advised the court that, if Mangiapane were to be forced to proceed without counsel, it would be necessary for defence counsel to seek advice from senior counsel as to whether he would be permitted ethically to continue to act for the appellant. His instinctive reaction was that he could not so act.

Following a brief adjournment which the trial judge had permitted in order to allow Mangiapane to decide whether he would proceed without counsel or renew the retainer, defence counsel advised the court that he was once again representing both accused. The learned trial judge then inquired of defence counsel whether a conflict existed as between his two clients. He replied that, except for a 15-minute period earlier that morning, there had never appeared to him to have been a conflict and he did not then perceive there to be one.

The joint trial presented a problem, in that Mangiapane did not testify. At the hearing of the appeal, with the Crown's consent, fresh evidence regarding this matter was received and considered by the court. This evidence shows that, until the opening of trial, Mangiapane had planned to plead guilty and to testify in the appellant's defence that the appellant was not involved in the alleged conspiracy.The appellant had expected Mangiapane to testify and he claims that he did not learn, until after he, the appellant, had testified, that he could not call Mangiapane as a witness. Trial counsel's affidavit states that he had advised both co-accused that neither could compel the other to testify in a joint trial. Trial counsel did not apply for severance.

I. Effective assistance of counsel

The appellant's first ground of appeal is that he was deprived of his right to make full answer and defence to the charge, because his counsel was in a position of conflict as between him and his co-accused Mangiapane. He contends that this resulted in a miscarriage of justice and in a breach of his rights under ss. 7, 10(*b*) and 11(*d*) of the *Canadian Charter of Rights and Freedoms*. In addition, he claims that trial counsel failed to provide effective assistance at the trial and that this ineffectiveness, in all reasonable probability, affected the verdict of the jury.

.....

A. The conflict of interest

In order to ensure that the adversarial system produces a fair trial, an accused is entitled to receive the assistance of counsel in making full answer and defence. Speaking for this court in *R. v. Williams* (1985), 18 C.C.C.

(3d) 356 at p.371, 44 C.R. (3d) 351, 14 C.E.R. 251; leave to appeal to the Supreme Court of Canada refused April 4, 1985, C.C.C. *loc. cit.*, [1985] 1 S.C.R. *xiv*, C.R. *loc. cit.*, Martin J.A. recognized that the right to make full answer and defence is constitutionally protected as one of the established principles encompassed in the term "fundamental justice" secured by s. 7 of the *Charter*. Martin J.A., for this court, also assumed in a recent case, although the issue was not finally decided, that an accused has a constitutional right to the *effective* assistance of counsel: *R. v. Garofoli* (1988), 41 C.C.C. (3d) 97 at pp. 150-1, 64 C.R. (3d) 193, 43 C.R.R. 252 (Ont.C.A.); appeal to Supreme Court of Canada on other grounds allowed, 60 C.C.C. (3d) 161, [1990] 2 S.C.R. 1421, 80 C.R. (3d) 317.

It is generally recognized that a lawyer representing more than one accused in a joint criminal trial is potentially in a position of conflict. In general, joint representation may lead the jury to link the co-accused together. The interpretation of the Constitution of the United States by their Supreme Court provides a useful and persuasive guide in the area of effective assistance of counsel. In the United States, the general recognition of a potential conflict of interest is based on the Sixth Amendment right to the assistance of counsel, which has been interpreted to mean the effective assistance of counsel.

.....

... In a case of joint representation of conflicting interests, defence counsel's basic duty of undivided loyalty and effective assistance is jeopardized and his performance may be adversely affected. That is, he may refrain from doing certain things for one client by reason of his concern that his action might adversely affect his other client.

.....

In *R. v. McCaw* (1971), 5 C.C.C. (2d) 416, [1972] 1 O.R. 742, long before the *Charter*, this court recognized that an accused, jointly charged with other parties and represented by the same counsel in a joint trial, may well have been prejudiced in his defence and, as a consequence, deprived of the statutory and common law right to make full answer and defence. One of the court's reasons for this recognition was that, in joint proceedings, it was impossible for an accused to call his co-accused to testify. Accordingly, a new trial was directed.

In *R. v. Stork and Toews* (1975), 24 C.C.C. (2d) 210, 31 C.R.N.S. 395, [1975] W.W.R. 127, the British Columbia Court of Appeal allowed two appellants to withdraw their pleas of guilty to a charge of conspiracy to traffic in a narcotic and directed a new trial, because their trial lawyer was "in a position of hopeless conflict of interest". The lawyer representing both accused at trial also represented a third accused who had paid the lawyer a substantial fee to defend him and the other two accused. The Crown withdrew the charge against the third accused in exchange for a plea of guilty by the co-accused. Consequently, there was an appearance of unfairness in that the lawyer had influenced the other two to plead guilty.

In the present case, trial counsel should have recognized immediately that, as a result of Mangiapane's change of plea, a position of conflict had arisen which could undermine the appellant's right to a fair trial. I accept the appellant's submission that trial counsel's effectiveness was seriously impaired in the following way. The appellant was prevented from compelling Mangiapane to testify, and trial counsel was unable to advise Mangiapane whether or not to testify without potentially harming the interests of one of his two clients. In addition, trial counsel could not cross-examine Crown witnesses so as to show that the case against Mangiapane was much stronger than was that against the appellant, since to do so would compromise Mangiapane's position. Trial counsel was also precluded from arguing during his address to the jury that, whereas Mangiapane — in whose apartment the concealed heroin had been found — was clearly guilty, the appellant was merely a visitor who had arrived in order to go with Mangiapane to pick up food for the restaurant where the appellant worked as a bookkeeper and singer.

By reason of the conflict of interest, it is further submitted that trial counsel was precluded from arguing before the jury that, unlike the appellant who had testified and denied his guilt, the co-accused Mangiapane had not testified. Counsel submits that, accordingly, the jury could have drawn an adverse inference against Mangiapane and a positive inference regarding the appellant.

The law permits counsel for a co-accused to comment on the failure of the other accused to testify. Section 4(6) of the *Canada Evidence Act*, R.S.C. 1985, c. C-5, only prohibits a judge or counsel for the prosecution from making such a comment. Moreover, this type of comment by counsel does not violate the accused's constitutional right, under s. 11(c) of the *Charter*, not to be compelled to be a witness in proceedings against himself: see *R. v. Naglik* (1991), 65 C.C.C. (3d) 272 at pp. 283-4, 3 O.R. (3d) 385, 13 W.C.B. (2d) 112. However, trial counsel, by reason of his conflict of interest, was precluded from asking the jury to draw an adverse inference against one of the accused. The legitimate and often effective strategy of shifting the blame to one's co-defendant was not available to counsel in this common defence. While it is doubtful that the jury would have translated Mangiapane's guilt as tending to cast doubt on the appellant's guilt, it certainly was not open to counsel for the appellant, even if the appellant had been separately represented, to invite the jury to draw a positive inference by reason only of the appellant's decision to testify. In any event, the appellant's right to effective assistance of counsel entitled him to the competent advice of counsel unburdened by a conflict of interest.

I do not accept the Crown's submission that counsel's failure to apply for a severance was a tactical decision which accrued to the appellant's benefit, in as much as Mangiapane's evidence exculpating the appellant would have carried greater weight in a joint trial. However, defence counsel knew that he could not compel Mangiapane to testify, he had no knowledge of Mangiapane's intention in that respect, and he was unable to advise Mangiapane in the decision because of the conflict of interest.

.....

The Crown did not take the position that the appellant's consent to joint representation and his failure to move for severance constituted a valid waiver of his right to counsel of undivided loyalty. It is conceded that there was no intentional relinquishment or abandonment of this right. Since defence counsel did not recognize that he had a conflict of interest, it is difficult to see how a layman could have any appreciation of the potential conflict: see *Hoffman v. Leeke*, 903 F.2d 280 (4th Cir., 1990) at p. 288.

Accordingly, the appellant could not voluntarily, knowingly and intelligently have waived his right to independent, loyal counsel.

.....

Because of the difficulty of assessing the effect of the conflict of interest on the defence of the appellant, I am not prepared to apply the curative proviso of s. 686(1)(*b*)(iii) of the *Criminal Code*. The appellant has satisfied the burden of showing that the conflict of interest had an adverse effect on the performance of defence counsel at trial. The United States courts have consistently refused to apply the "harmless error" rule to conflict of interest cases. The reasoning is that conflict of interest affecting the adequacy of representation by counsel is a denial of the constitutional right to the effective assistance of counsel, and that, therefore, it is unnecessary to demonstrate prejudice: see *Cuyler v. Sullivan*, 100 S. Ct. 1708 (1980) at p. 1719; *Glasser v. United States*, 315 U.S. 60 (1942).

Upon the completion of the evidence tendered by the defence, the Crown has a limited right to call reply evidence. In rare circumstances, the trial judge may permit surrebuttal (*R. v. Ewart* (1989), 52 C.C.C. (3d) 280 (B.C.C.A.)).

R. v. BIDDLE

(1995), 96 C.C.C. (3d) 321 (S.C.C.)

Sopinka J. (Lamer C.J.C., La Forest, Cory, Iacobucci and Major JJ. concurring): —

.....

The appellant was convicted of two counts of assault causing bodily harm and two counts of choking with intent to commit an indictable offence. He was acquitted at trial of two other charges. The four charges arose out of two separate incidents relating to attacks on a female complainant (C.L.F.) in September, 1986, and on a second female complainant (M.S.F.) in October, 1986. Both victims were attacked immediately after leaving the underground parking area of their respective apartment buildings. Both women were beaten and choked and suffered bodily harm.

On September 25, 1986, C.L.F. returned to her apartment building at about 1:00 a.m. She parked her car in the underground garage and went to the elevator. While waiting, she heard footsteps from behind but did not turn around. At that moment, she was attacked from behind as a black object came in front of her face and was then pulled tightly around her neck. After seeing her attacker briefly, C.L.F. passed out as a result of the choking. When she awoke, she noticed that her purse was gone.

On October 28, 1986, M.S.F. returned to her apartment building between 10:00 p.m. and 10:30 p.m. After parking her car in the underground garage she ran to the stairway leading to the foyer. She was confronted by a man who pushed her against a wall, punched her and then beat her and stomped on her. M.S.F. yelled "fire" and her assailant got up, looked at her and walked out the door. M.S.F. then went for assistance and was taken to the hospital.

At trial, the appellant testified that, on the night of October 28, 1986, he was at a show from around 7:30 p.m. to 9:15 p.m. He claimed that, after leaving the show early, he then walked his dog and went to visit a friend who was not home. The appellant stated that he then drove to two bars and left his car at a parking garage around 11:25 p.m. Upon returning to his car, the appellant was arrested. This was approximately two and one-half hours after the attack on M.S.F.

In order to refute the alibi of the appellant, the Crown called the evidence of Ms Ruth Geurts in rebuttal. She testified that, at around 8:30 p.m. that evening, she had been followed by the appellant in his car, while driving to the garage of her apartment building. At the time this evidence was adduced, the Crown did not specify its purpose and no objection was taken to its admissibility. The appellant was permitted to call surrebuttal evidence in response.

The appellant was tried by an all-female jury and was convicted on the four counts relating to the attacks on C.L.F. and M.S.F.

.....

Identity was the only issue in dispute at trial ... [with respect to the reply evidence, the appellant] argued that the reply evidence of Ms Geurts was not properly admissible, claiming that the Crown split its case.

.....

The rationale behind the rule against allowing the Crown to split its case was stated by this court in *John v. The Queen* (1985), 23 C.C.C. (3d) 326, 24 D.L.R. (4th) 713, [1985] 2 S.C.R. 476. The judgment of a unanimous court was delivered by Estey J. and Lamer J. (as he then was) who wrote, at pp. 329-30:

> Clearly, this is the situation referred to in criminal practice as the prosecution splitting its case. The wrongs which flow from such a practice are manifold and the practice has been prohibited from the earliest days of our criminal law.
>
> .....
>
> These are the consequences that flow from a violation of one of the fundamental precepts of our criminal process, namely, the dividing of the prosecution's case so as to sandwich the defence. This is a particularly lethal tactic where the evidence in reply raises a new issue and attacks the accused's credibility for this is the last evidence which the members of the jury hear prior to their deliberations. It also raises the question as to the propriety of the Crown's conduct in the context of the accused's right to elect to remain silent or to elect to enter the witness-box in his own defence. He must be given the opportunity of making this decision in the full awareness of the Crown's complete case. This did not occur in these proceedings.

In *R. v. Krause* (1986), 29 C.C.C. (3d) 385, 33 D.L.R. (4th) 267, [1986] 2 S.C.R. 466, McIntyre J., for the court, explained under what circumstances the Crown may call evidence in rebuttal. At p. 390, he noted that the general rule is that the Crown cannot split its case. McIntyre J. added [at pp. 390-1]:

> The Crown or the plaintiff must produce and enter in its own case all the clearly relevant evidence it has, or that it intends to rely upon, to establish its case with respect to all the issues raised in the pleadings, in a criminal

> case, the indictment and any particulars ... This rule prevents unfair surprise, prejudice and confusion which could result if the Crown or the plaintiff were allowed to split its case, that is, to put in part of its evidence — as much as it deemed necessary at the outset — then to close the case and after the defence is complete to add further evidence to bolster the position originally advanced. *The underlying reason for this rule is that the defendant or the accused is entitled at the close of the Crown's case to have before it the full case for the Crown so that it is known from the outset what must be met in response.*
>
> The plaintiff or the Crown may be allowed to call evidence in rebuttal after completion of the defence case, *where the defence has raised some new matter or defence which the Crown has had no opportunity to deal with and which the Crown or the plaintiff could not reasonably have anticipated. But rebuttal will not be permitted regarding matters which merely confirm or reinforce earlier evidence adduced in the Crown's case which could have been brought before the defence was made.*

(Emphasis added.)

The following excerpt from *R. v. Campbell* (1977), 38 C.C.C. (2d) 6 at p. 26, 1 C.R. (3d) 309, 17 O.R. (2d) 673 (Ont. C.A.), is also relevant:

> The general rule with respect to the order of proof is that *the prosecution must introduce all the evidence in its possession upon which it relies as probative of guilt, before closing its case.* ... The rule prevents the accused being taken by surprise, and being deprived of an adequate opportunity to make a proper investigation with respect to the evidence adduced against him. The rule also provides a safeguard against the importance of a piece of evidence, by reason of its late introduction, being unduly emphasized or magnified in relation to the other evidence.
>
> *Rebuttal evidence by the prosecution is restricted to evidence to meet new facts introduced by the defence. The accused's mere denial of the prosecution's case in the witness-box does not permit the prosecution in reply to reiterate its case, or to adduce additional evidence in support of it.* In practice, however, it may often be difficult to distinguish between evidence, properly the subject of rebuttal, and evidence of facts relevant to prove guilt which should have been proved in the first instance by a full presentation of the prosecution's case. ...
>
> The Court has, however, a discretion to admit evidence in reply which has become relevant to the prosecution's case as a result of defence evidence *which the Crown could not reasonably be expected to anticipate.*

(Emphasis added.)

In the present case, in my view, the evidence tendered in rebuttal could potentially be relevant for two purposes. First, Ms Geurts' testimony was relevant to rebut the appellant's assertion regarding his whereabouts at around 8:30 p.m. on October 28, 1986. While the evidence did not directly refute the appellant's alibi, since the offence occurred between 10:00 p.m. and 10:30 p.m. that night, it impeached his credibility with respect to his whereabouts during the course of that evening. As the Crown noted in its factum, the fact that the appellant may have lied about his whereabouts at 8:30 p.m. would cast doubt on the credibility of the appellant's testimony in respect of other facts in issue.

Aside from attacking the appellant's credibility, the rebuttal evidence was also potentially admissible as similar fact evidence going to the identity of M.S.F.'s attacker. Given that identity was essentially the sole issue at trial, the significance of this evidence cannot be underestimated. The nature of the evidence of Ms Geurts was summed up in the trial judge's charge to the jury, as follows:

> Her evidence would appear to therefore put Biddle on Holly Street at about 8:30 p.m., or let us say 8:30 to 8:45 p.m., in that area of time. This was the time when Biddle said he was at the Reveen performance at Danforth and Broadview. *It also puts Biddle in the sinister role of following a car driven by a woman of about the same age and category of [C.L.F.] and [M.S.F.] — by "category" I mean young businesswomen driving cars.*

(Emphasis added.) The charge to the jury, therefore, made it quite evident that there was a dual purpose to the admission of the reply evidence.

In oral argument, the Crown conceded that if the reply evidence was tendered as similar fact evidence, then it ought to have been adduced in the case-in-chief. This was an appropriate concession since the probative value of the similar fact aspect of Ms Geurts' testimony related to the identity of the appellant. This was a key issue with respect to the innocence or guilt of the appellant.

Permitting the Crown to adduce the evidence of Ms Geurts in rebuttal, which was at least partly probative as similar fact evidence tending to prove identity, enabled the Crown to split its case improperly. It was clear that identity was the key issue at trial and the Crown had an obligation to introduce all relevant evidence to this issue in the case-in-chief. It cannot be said that the defence had raised some new matter or defence with which the Crown had no opportunity to deal and which the Crown could not reasonably have anticipated. The Crown was in possession of the evidence of Ms Geurts prior to the defence case and must have reasonably anticipated that the appellant would challenge the identification evidence presented. As the appellant noted at the hearing of this appeal, the Crown knew of his explanation of his whereabouts as he had given a statement to the police. Therefore, the rebuttal evidence ought not to have been admissible in reply. There was no reason that the Crown could not have adduced the evidence of Ms Geurts prior to the defence case. By splitting the Crown's case, the appellant was deprived of the opportunity of knowing the entire case to meet prior to deciding whether or not to testify. The opportunity to present evidence in surrebuttal cannot remove this prejudice.

The Crown also sought to justify the evidence on the ground that it impugned the appellant's testimony as to his whereabouts early in the evening and therefore was relevant to credibility. As the assault was alleged to have taken place between 10:00 and 10:30 p.m. and the evidence of Ms Geurts related to a period between 8:30 to 8:45 p.m., it did not directly tend to rebut the alibi. Its admission would, therefore, encounter the collateral fact rule. This rule is subject to enumerated exceptions and, although none of the recognized exceptions would appear to apply in this case, it has been suggested that this is not a closed list: see *Cross on Evidence*, 7th ed. (London: Butterworths, 1990) at p. 310; Stanley A. Schiff, *Evidence in the Litigation Process*, 3rd ed. (Toronto: Carswell, 1988) at pp. 534-5.

It is unnecessary and undesirable to resolve that question in this case because, even if admissible for the purpose of impeaching the appellant's credibility, its use was not limited to that purpose. The Crown did not specify the purpose for which it was being led. Although no objection was taken by the appellant at the time, this alone does not prevent raising the illegality of the rebuttal evidence on appeal: see *Latour v. The Queen* (1976), 33 C.C.C. (2d) 377 at p. 382, 74 D.L.R. (3d) 12, [1978] 1 S.C.R. 361. Furthermore, the trial judge did not instruct the jury on the limited use of the rebuttal evidence. In fact, as illustrated by the above passage quoted from the charge to the jury, the trial judge actually invited the jury to consider the reply evidence as similar fact evidence. In light of this instruction, a jury might well have accepted this evidence as highly relevant to the identity of the perpetrator of the assault on the complainant.

In the circumstances of the case, this constituted a serious misdirection to the jury. As outlined by Doherty J.A. [in the unanimous decision of the Ontario Court of Appeal dismissing the appeal, reported at 84 C.C.C. (3d) 430, 24 C.R. (4th) 65, 14 O.R. (3d) 756)], the evidence of identification was already tenuous. In my view, the error could reasonably have affected the verdict of the jury. It cannot be said that, absent the error of allowing the Crown to adduce the similar fact evidence in rebuttal, no jury acting reasonably and properly instructed could have acquitted the accused: see *R. v. Morin* (1988), 44 C.C.C. (3d) 193, [1988] 2 S.C.R. 345, 66 C.R. (3d) 1; *R. v. Leaney* (1989), 50 C.C.C. (3d) 289, [1989] 2 S.C.R. 393, 71 C.R. (3d) 325; *R. v. S. (P.L.)* (1991), 64 C.C.C. (3d) 193, [1991] 1 S.C.R. 909, 5 C.R. (4th) 351; *R. v. Bevan* (1993), 82 C.C.C. (3d) 310, 104 D.L.R. (4th) 180, [1993] 2 S.C.R. 599. In *John v. The Queen, supra*, at pp. 329-30, it was held that s. 686(1)(*b*)(iii) of the *Code* could not be invoked to cure an error of law where the Crown had improperly split its case and was wrongly permitted to lead reply evidence. An appellate court cannot retry the case "to assess the worth of the residual evidence after the improperly adduced evidence has been extracted from the record" (*John v. The Queen, supra*, at p. 330). Furthermore, I note that the Crown made no arguments to substantiate a claim that the improper admission of the evidence would not amount to a substantial wrong or miscarriage of justice. The Crown did, however, submit that by allowing surrebuttal evidence any prejudice to the appellant was cured. That submission is properly considered in relation to the application of s. 686(1)(*b*)(iii).

It cannot be said that the opportunity to present evidence in surrebuttal removes the prejudice suffered by the appellant. As was noted by McIntyre J. in *R. v. Krause, supra*, and by Estey and Lamer JJ. in *John v. The Queen, supra*, an underlying reason for the rule against splitting the case is that the accused is entitled to know the entire case of the Crown which must be met. It is only where the accused has full knowledge of the Crown's case that one is able to decide whether or not to testify.

Furthermore, in *John v. The Queen, supra*, at p. 329, this court held that to allow the Crown to split its case "is doubly wrong because the effect was to force the accused to return to the witness box". Merely requiring the appellant to enter the witness-box for a second time has an adverse effect as it creates the impression that he was caught in a lie. As well, the appellant is subjected to cross-examination for a second time. In effect, the Crown is given a second chance to attack the credibility of the appellant when it ought to have put its entire case in evidence at the outset.

In *R. v. Wood* (1986), 28 C.C.C. (3d) 65 (Ont. C.A.), it was held that the Crown impermissibly split its case. Although the accused did not call evidence in surrebuttal, Goodman J.A., for the court, stated at p. 83 that:

> The probable detrimental effect of the improper admission of the reply evidence is beyond question. It constituted a direct contradiction of the evidence given by the appellant with respect to his knowledge, posses-

> sion and ownership of the knife. If the reply evidence was believed by the jury, it would have the inevitable effect of destroying the credibility of the appellant and his defence of self-defence and to a lesser extent his defence of provocation. The reply evidence was the last evidence to be heard by the jury with the attendant risk to the appellant that it would carry more weight with the jury for that reason. *Even if defence counsel had sought leave for the appellant to give evidence in surrebuttal, it would have meant that the appellant would have been subjected to a second cross-examination. Wittingly or unwittingly, the prosecution, in proceeding in the manner which it did, created a trap for the appellant.*

(Emphasis added.)

It should also be recognized that the late introduction of evidence may have the effect of unduly magnifying its importance and increasing its weight. This would not otherwise occur but for the improper splitting of the Crown's case. I agree with the submission of the appellant that, in this case, the timing and sequence of the evidence as it unfolded before the jury added to the prejudicial impact of admitting the evidence in reply. In *R. v. Campbell, supra*, at p. 26, Martin J.A. also acknowledged this aspect of the rule against splitting the case:

> The rule also provides a safeguard against the importance of a piece of evidence, by reason of its late introduction, being unduly emphasized or magnified in relation to the other evidence.

Given the frailties in the identification evidence adduced at trial, the evidence of Ms Geurts may have been quite significant in convicting the appellant. Placing this evidence before the jury at the end of the trial, rather than in the Crown's case, prejudiced the appellant by inordinately elevating its weight.

.....

In the case at bar, I would conclude that the surrebuttal evidence did not adequately address the prejudice caused to the appellant. Not only was the evidence of Ms Geurts highlighted, but also the appellant was forced to take the witness stand a second time to answer the Crown's case. I cannot, therefore, accept the Crown's submission that any prejudice to the appellant was cured by allowing surrebuttal evidence.

The appellant is entitled to a new trial.

O. CLOSING ADDRESSES

Once all the evidence has been presented, the parties make their closing addresses to the jury. When the defence calls no evidence, it is entitled to address the jury last. Otherwise, the defence addresses the jury first and the Crown is entitled to address the jury last. Where there are multiple accused, all of them or their counsel must address the jury before the Crown, if any of them have called evidence. No party is entitled to a reply, though generally this is permitted in cases tried without a jury (s. 651 of the *Criminal Code*).

R. v. ROSE

(1998), 129 C.C.C. (3d) 449 (S.C.C.)

[On a charge of second degree murder, Crown counsel addressed members of the jury last, and asked them to draw damaging inferences from the failure of the appellant to deal in his testimony with the presence or absence of a blue "pallor" on the deceased's face. The appellant, who claimed to be taken by surprise by this aspect of the closing address, asked to respond to the Crown's attack. The trial judge declined to give him that opportunity. The accused was convicted. At issue was the constitutionality of s. 651(3) and (4) of the *Criminal Code*, which compels the defence to make its closing address first when defence evidence has been called. The issue of the absence of any right of reply was also before the Court.]

Cory, Iacobucci and Bastarache JJ. [Gonthier J. concurring]: —

.....

C. Full Answer and Defence

It will be useful to address the appellant's full answer and defence claim at the outset, as it affects his argument that s. 651(3) and (4) [sets] up an unfair requirement to choose between two constitutionally protected rights.

The right to make full answer and defence is protected under s. 7 of the *Charter*. It is one of the principles of fundamental justice. In *R. v. Stinchcombe*, [1991] 3 S.C.R. 326 at p. 336, 68 C.C.C. (3d) 1, Sopinka J., writing for the Court, described this right as "one of the pillars of criminal justice on which we heavily depend to ensure that the innocent are not convicted". The right to make full answer and defence manifests itself in several more specific rights and principles, such as the right to full and timely disclosure, the right to know the case to be met before opening one's defence, the principles governing the re-opening of the Crown's case, as well as various rights of cross-examination, among others. The right is integrally linked to other principles of fundamental justice, such as the presumption of innocence, the right to a fair trial, and the principle against self-incrimination.

As suggested by Sopinka J. for the majority of this Court in *Dersch v. Canada (Attorney General)*, [1990] 2 S.C.R. 1505, 60 C.C.C. (3d) 132, 77 D.L.R. (4th) 473, however, the right to make full answer and defence does not imply an entitlement to those rules and procedures most likely to result in a finding of innocence. Rather, the right entitles the accused to rules and procedures which are fair in the manner in which they enable the accused to defend against and answer the Crown's case. As stated by Sopinka J., at p. 1515:

> The right to full answer and defence does not imply that an accused can have, under the rubric of the *Charter*, an overhaul of the whole law of evidence such that a statement inadmissible under, for instance, the hearsay exclusion, would be admissible if it tended to prove his or her innocence.

The sentiment expressed by Sopinka J. in *Dersch* accords with the more general principle stated by La Forest J. for the majority of the Court in *R. v. Lyons*, [1987] 2 S.C.R. 309 at pp. 361-62, 37 C.C.C. (3d) 1, 44 D.L.R.

(4th) 193, that while "at a minimum, the requirements of fundamental justice embrace the requirements of procedural fairness", nevertheless the entitlement to procedural fairness does not entitle the accused to "the most favourable procedures that could possibly be imagined". Similar statements of this principle are found in *R. v. Harrer*, [1995] 3 S.C.R. 562 at p. 573, 101 C.C.C. (3d) 193, 128 D.L.R. (4th) 98, *per* La Forest J.; *R. v. Finta*, [1994] 1 S.C.R. 701 at p. 744, 88 C.C.C. (3d) 417, 112 D.L.R. (4th) 513, *per* La Forest J.; *R. v. Bartle*, [1994] 3 S.C.R. 173 at p. 225, 92 C.C.C. (3d) 289, 118 D.L.R. (4th) 83, *per* L'Heureux-Dubé J.; *Dehghani v. Canada (Minister of Employment and Immigration)*, [1993] 1 S.C.R. 1053 at p. 1077, 101 D.L.R. (4th) 654, *per* Iacobucci J.; and *Thomson Newspapers Ltd. v. Canada (Director of Investigation and Research, Restrictive Trade Practices Commission)*, [1990] 1 S.C.R. 425 at p. 540, 54 C.C.C. (3d) 417, 67 D.L.R. (4th) 161, *per* La Forest J.

In order for the appellant to demonstrate that s. 651(3) of the *Code* infringes his right to make full answer and defence, he must show that the inability to address the jury after the Crown has done so unfairly interferes with his ability to defend himself and to answer the Crown's case. The essential question is whether the order of jury addresses set out in the impugned legislative provision creates an unfairness. Unfairness would exist, for example, if addressing the jury last provided an advantage to the Crown which was therefore denied to the defence, or if addressing the jury first interfered with the accused's right not to incriminate himself. Although there may be better ways that Parliament could structure the determination of the order of jury addresses, the question of whether or not the appellant's *Charter* rights have been infringed is concerned only with whether the existing provisions are unfair.

.....

In our view, it is useful to distinguish here between two discrete aspects of the right to make full answer and defence. One aspect is the right of the accused to have before him or her the full "case to meet" before *answering* the Crown's case by adducing defence evidence. The right to know the case to meet is long settled, and it is satisfied once the Crown has called all of its evidence, because at that point all of the facts that are relied upon as probative of guilt are available to the accused in order that he or she may make a case in reply: see *R. v. Krause*, [1986] 2 S.C.R. 466 at p. 473, 29 C.C.C. (3d) 385, 33 D.L.R. (4th) 267, *per* McIntyre J.; John Sopinka, Sidney Lederman and Alan Bryant, *The Law of Evidence in Canada* (1992), at p. 880. This aspect of the right to make full answer and defence has links with the right to full disclosure and the right to engage in a full cross-examination of Crown witnesses, and is concerned with the right to *respond*, in a very direct and particularized form, to the Crown's evidence. Inherent in this aspect of the right to make full answer and defence is the requirement that the Crown act prior to the defence's response.

A second and broader aspect of the right to make full answer and defence, which might be understood as encompassing the first aspect, is the right of an accused person to defend himself or herself against all of the state's efforts to achieve a conviction. The Crown is not entitled to engage in activities aimed at convicting an accused unless that accused is permitted to defend against those state acts. However, it is not always the case that defending against the Crown's efforts to convict will necessarily imply answering words already spoken or deeds already engaged in by the Crown. In our view, the jury address is an example of a situation in which an accused is equally capable of defending himself or herself against the Crown regardless of whether the Crown acts first or last. The defence jury address is both a *response* to the Crown's evidence and a *defence* against the argument and persuasion to be contained in the Crown jury address. As we discuss below, there is no evidence that an accused who addresses the jury first is less able to defend against the persuasive aspects of the Crown jury address than an accused who goes last. As such, although the jury address does bring into play the right to make full answer and defence, that right is not infringed by the procedures prescribed in s. 651(3) of the *Code*.

The purpose of the jury address was accurately described by Robert White, Q.C., in *The Art of Trial* (1993), at p. 213, as being "to present a party's case clearly and in a way that is of help to the court in the performance of its duty". Generally speaking, counsel are "limited to reviewing and commenting on the evidence and to the making of submissions which may properly be supported by the evidence adduced": see *Gray v. Alanco Developments Ltd.*, [1967] 1 O.R. 597 at p. 601, 61 D.L.R. (2d) 652 (C.A.). Nonetheless, few would deny the powerful persuasive force which well-crafted and skilfully presented submissions may have in a jury trial. What is more debatable are the persuasive force and other advantages associated with addressing the jury either first or last.

.....

We do not agree that the order of jury addresses significantly affects the knowledge that the accused will have, at the time of the defence address, regarding the Crown's theory of the case and interpretation of the evidence. The accused who addresses the jury first may not know in precise detail the manner in which the Crown will articulate to the jury the reasons why it should find the accused guilty. However, the Crown will already have articulated its preliminary theory of the case at the opening of the trial, and will have made fairly clear any refinements or re-directions in this theory through the questions asked of witnesses and through the nature of the non-testimonial evidence adduced. There is no evidence which the Crown will be interpreting in its jury address of which the defence will not be aware. The defence will also know, as the result of events during the trial, the likely manner in which the Crown will present the evidence to the jury.

Moreover, the Crown's ability to take the defence by surprise is severely curtailed by the restrictions placed on the scope of the Crown's closing address to the jury. In presenting closing submissions to the jury, Crown counsel must be accurate and dispassionate. Counsel should not advert to any unproven facts and cannot put before the jury as facts to be considered for conviction assertions in relation to which there is no evidence or which come from counsel's personal observations or experiences. As noted by Lamer C.J. writing for the majority in *R. v. P. (M.B.)*, [1994] 1 S.C.R. 555 at p. 580, 89 C.C.C. (3d) 289, 113 D.L.R. (4th) 461, "[o]nce the defence starts to 'meet the case', thus revealing its own case, the Crown should, except in the narrowest of circumstances be 'locked into' the case which, upon closing, it has said the defence must answer. The Crown must not be allowed in any way to *change* that case". Although the comments of Lamer C.J. in *P. (M.B.)* were addressed to the issue of the ability of the Crown to re-open its case, they are also applicable to the content of the Crown jury address. Crown counsel is duty bound during its jury address to remain true to the evidence, and must limit his or her means of persuasion to facts found in the evidence presented to the jury: see, e.g., *Pisani v. The Queen*, [1971] S.C.R. 738, 1 C.C.C. (2d) 477, 15 D.L.R. (3d) 1; *R. v. Munroe* (1995), 96 C.C.C. (3d) 431 (Ont. C.A.), affirmed [1995] 4 S.C.R. 53, 102 C.C.C. (3d) 383; *R. v. Neverson* (1991), 69 C.C.C. (3d) 80 (Que. C.A.), affirmed [1992] 1 S.C.R. 1014, 72 C.C.C. (3d) 480; and *R. v. Charest* (1990), 57 C.C.C. (3d) 312 (Que. C.A.). As is discussed in more detail below, the discretion of the trial judge to deal with those situations in which Crown counsel's address oversteps the bounds of propriety is a sufficient safeguard against any potential unfairness to the accused.

For the parties to a jury trial, success in convincing the jury to find in their favour flows from three essential ingredients, namely, a sufficient evidentiary foundation to support the legal result sought to be reached, skilful advocacy in interpreting the evidence for the jury, and appropriate jury instructions by the trial judge. Skilful advocacy involves taking the information acquired as a result of the trial — the evidence, the other party's theory of the case, and various other, intangible factors — and weaving this information together with law, logic, and rhetoric into a persuasive argument. Although not all jury addresses are, in actuality, either logically or rhetorically persuasive, there can be no denying the role of a party's persuasive skill in influencing the result in some jury trials. In this respect, we find little if any evidence to support the proposition that addressing the jury last would provide the accused with a persuasive advantage.

The enterprise of defending oneself against a criminal charge does not intrinsically imply a temporal order of speaking, with the accused "answering" the Crown's jury address with a jury address in reply. What is being answered in the accused's jury address is the evidence and the Crown's theory of the case, both of which, as just discussed, the accused will know prior to addressing the jury at the close of the defence evidence. The accused's jury address is his or her opportunity to answer the Crown evidence and theory of the case with argument and persuasion. Persuasion is a subtle force, which cannot be easily linked with any strict procedural rule regarding the order in which the parties are entitled to attempt to persuade the jury. Some would argue, as the respondent has suggested, that the party who is given the opportunity to address the jury first has an advantage in being able to create in the jury's minds a vivid image and a story regarding what is alleged to have occurred, which will be difficult for the other party to replace. The result of the accused's addressing the jury first in a criminal trial may be to place the Crown on the defensive by undercutting in advance the argument sought to be made against the accused.

The view that addressing the jury first may be an advantage for some accused persons has been endorsed by more than one provincial court of appeal. In the Court of Appeal below, Dubin C.J. stated, at p. 613, that it is "well known that many learned and experienced defence counsel prefer to address a jury first.... Many defence counsel are of the opinion that there is an advantage in addressing the jury first, shortly after the evidence of the defence is tendered, when it is fresh in the jury's mind". Similarly, in its earlier decision in *Tzimopoulos* [(1986), 29 C.C.C. (3d) 304 (S.C.C.)], at p. 338, the Court of Appeal noted that, "[t]here are undoubtedly many circumstances in which defence counsel would prefer to go first". In *R. v. Hutchinson* (1995), 99 C.C.C. (3d) 88 at p. 95, the Nova Scotia Court of Appeal concluded as follows:

> There is also a body of opinion that counsel who first addresses the jury has the advantage. If the jury is persuaded by that counsel's argument it is difficult for the counsel who speaks last to move the jurors from an established view. On the other hand there are those who consider the right to speak to the jury last is of great value. It would not appear to be of great significance who speaks first or last.

See also *R. v. G. (F.)*, [1994] M.J. No. 732 (QL) (C.A.); and *R. v. Strebakowski* (1997), 93 B.C.A.C. 139 (C.A.).

The accuracy of these jurisprudential remarks is generally supported by the social science literature, much of which indicates that under conditions similar to those which exist in a courtroom, the address which is presented first will be more effective and influential than the address given last: see, *e.g.*, Robert G. Lawson, "The Law of Primacy in the Criminal Courtroom" (1969), 77 J. of Soc. Psychol. 121; D. P. Schultz, "Primacy-Recency Within a Sensory Variation Framework" (1963) 13 Psychol. Rec. 129; Robert E. Lana, "Familiarity and the Order of Presentation of Persuasive Communications" (1961) 62 Abn. & Soc. Psychol. 573; and Michael J. Saks and Reid Hastie, Social Psychology in Court (1978), at p. 103.

The appellant submits that the studies and judicial statements which contend that addressing the jury first is an advantage are "speculative" and without "factual underpinning". We agree that there are inherent frailties in studies which attempt to simulate courtroom conditions. Thus, the social science evidence is not in itself determinative of whether, in fact, it is an advantage to address the jury either first or last. However, the appellant has not referred us to social science evidence which suggests that there is a persuasive advantage to addressing the jury last. In our view, and with respect for those who hold a contrary opinion, the social science evidence and the observations of experienced appellate court judges support a finding that the right to address the jury last is not a fundamental advantage, as the appellant suggests. In these circumstances, we agree with the conclusion of Dubin C.J. in the court below that the divergence of opinion on this issue counsels against a finding that the *Charter* has been violated, because it is not unfair to require an accused person to engage in one of two equally advantageous jury address procedures. The impugned provisions of the *Code* therefore do not infringe upon the appellant's right to make full answer and defence under ss. 7 and 11(*d*) of the *Charter*.

In the present case, the appellant asserts that it is not primarily the persuasive advantage of addressing the jury last which has resulted in a denial of the right to make full answer and defence, but rather the fact that addressing the jury first has deprived the accused of the ability to respond to specific statements made by the Crown in its address with which the accused disagrees. The appellant refers in particular to the inferences which the Crown asked the jury to draw from the expert evidence that the deceased would have had a blue pallor to her face after death had she hanged herself, and the failure of the accused to advert to having seen such a pallor.

The "blue-face" evidence was elicited by the Crown in cross-examination of the defence expert, Dr. Jaffe. Dr. Jaffe testified that a ligature around the neck would cause a blue pallor above the ligature, and that this blue pallor would be noticeable to "a reasonably skilled observer". The appellant's submission with respect to the "blue-face" evidence relates primarily to the facts that (a) it was not clear from the expert's testimony who would qualify as a reasonably skilled observer, and (b) when the appellant had testified prior to Dr. Jaffe, he was not questioned about the colour of the victim's face. The appellant contends that, had he been given the opportunity to address the jury after the Crown, his counsel would have been able to relate these concerns about the evidence to the jury.

It was open to counsel for the accused to address this evidence in his closing address to the jury. It was also open to counsel to re-examine Dr. Jaffe in order to determine whether the appellant could be considered "a reasonably skilled observer", or to ask that the appellant be recalled in order to question him regarding the existence of the blue pallor. Counsel for the accused apparently did not consider the issue of the blue pallor to be significant enough to do any of these things. In our view, standing alone, the fact that the Crown adverted to the blue pallor in his jury address, while the accused did not do so in his, reveals not an unfairness in the jury address procedure but merely a tactical choice by each party as to what to emphasize in its submissions. The appellant's trial counsel was fully aware of the "blue face" evidence that had been adduced, and must have known from the nature of the Crown's cross-examination of Dr. Jaffe on this point that the Crown viewed the existence of the blue pallor as relevant to the question of the appellant's guilt. If, as occurred here, trial counsel for the accused chose not to answer this evidence in his jury address, this was a strategic decision and not an unfairness imposed upon the appellant by the *Code*.

Having said this, it is important to stress the following: the appellant's focus in this case has been not only upon the alleged unfairness which flows from not being able to reply to the Crown's submissions as a general matter, but also and perhaps most importantly upon the unfairness which flows from not being able to reply, in particular, to Crown submissions to the jury which are misleading or unsupported by the evidence. The right of an accused in the latter circumstance to a corrective instruction by the trial judge, or to a limited reply, is discussed in more detail below. In stating that s. 651(3) of the *Code* does not infringe as a general matter upon an accused person's right to make full answer and defence to the Crown's case under s. 7 of the *Charter*, we do not intend to derogate from the principles governing those exceptional cases in which an accused will have a right of reply or a right to a corrective instruction.

[The Court also dismisses arguments based upon the inconsistency between the *Criminal Code* and comparable provisions in other jurisdictions, and based upon the accused's right to procedural fairness as guaranteed by ss. 7 and 11(*d*) of the *Charter*].

.....

(2) The Inherent Jurisdiction of Superior Court Judges Provides a Basis For Granting a Limited Opportunity to Reply

The obligation of a trial judge to ensure that an accused's right to a fair trial is preserved has been enshrined in s. 11(*d*) of the *Charter*. However, the inherent jurisdiction of superior court judges to remedy procedural unfairness during the trial has always existed at common law. In *R. v. Osborn*, [1969] 1 O.R. 152, [1969] 4 C.C.C. 185, 1 D.L.R. (3d) 664, the Ontario Court of Appeal correctly observed that courts have from the earliest times invoked an inherent jurisdiction to prevent the abuse of trial process resulting from oppressive or vexatious proceedings. In *Selvey v. Director of Public Prosecutions*, [1968] 2 All E.R. 497 (H.L.) at p. 520, Lord Guest referred to the overriding duty of the trial judge to ensure that a trial is fair. He wrote that this duty: "springs from the inherent power of the judge to control the trial before him and to see that justice is done in fairness to the accused".

The appellant argued that the explicit language of s. 651 makes it impossible for a trial judge to allow a right of reply. However, this contention appears to confuse the exercise of discretion with the exercise of inherent jurisdiction. As I. H. Jacob noted in "The Inherent Jurisdiction of the Court" (1970), 23 Curr. Legal Probs. 23 at p. 25:

> The inherent jurisdiction of the court is a concept which must be distinguished from the exercise of judicial discretion. These two concepts resemble each other, particularly in their operation, and they often appear to overlap, and are therefore sometimes confused the one with the other. There is nevertheless a vital juridical distinction between jurisdiction and discretion, which must always be observed.

Discretion is usually conferred on a judge by the words of a statutory provision. For instance, the use of the words "may" or "can" provides a judge with the ability to make a choice between two or more alternatives. By contrast, a trial judge always possesses an inherent jurisdiction to ensure that the trial is conducted fairly. Inherent jurisdiction cannot be circumvented by narrow or confining statutory language. Jacob aptly described this fundamentally important residual power in this way, at pp. 27-28:

> For the essential character of a superior court of law necessarily involves that it should be invested with a power to maintain its authority and to prevent its process being obstructed and abused. Such a power is intrinsic in a superior court; it is its very life-blood, its very essence, its immanent attribute. Without such a power, the court would have form but would lack substance. The jurisdiction which is inherent in a superior court of law is that which enables it to fulfil itself as a court of law. The juridical basis of this jurisdiction is therefore the authority of the judiciary to uphold, to protect and to fulfil the judicial function of administering justice according to law in a regular, orderly and effective manner.

Similarly in *Amato v. The Queen*, [1982] 2 S.C.R. 418 at p. 449, 69 C.C.C. (2d) 31, 140 D.L.R. (3d) 405, Estey J. quoted with approval the words of Jessup J.A. in *Osborn, supra*, at p. 155: "... the Courts of this Province have from the earliest times invoked an inherent jurisdiction to prevent the abuse of their process through oppressive or vexatious proceedings". Estey J. continued, at p. 453:

> It follows therefore that the observations of Jessup J.A. in Osborn with reference to the origins and breadth of the trial court discretion to protect the processes of the courts from abuse remain substantially unimpaired by succeeding decisions in this Court.

See also *R. v. Young* (1984), 46 O.R. (2d) 520 at pp. 541 and 547, 13 C.C.C. (3d) 1 (C.A.).

It can be seen that the inherent jurisdiction of superior courts is a significant and effective basis for preventing abuse of the court's process and ensuring fairness in the trial process. This enduring and important jurisdiction of the court, if it is to be removed can only be accomplished by clear and precise statutory language. There is not that clear and precise language in s. 651 which removes or impairs the inherent jurisdiction of the court to achieve trial fairness by prohibiting the court from granting a right of reply to defence counsel when that is required.

It is the existence of this significant residual jurisdiction which enables a trial judge to permit defence counsel to reply to an improper Crown address.

Thus, if a trial judge concludes that the unfairness caused by an improper jury address cannot be remedied in the instructions to the jury, the inherent jurisdiction can be exercised to allow the prejudiced party an opportunity to reply. The position was clearly and correctly outlined in the reasons of Dubin C.J. in these words, at p. 614:

> There may be cases where, by reason of the Crown addressing the jury last, the only way a fair trial can be assured is by giving defence counsel a brief right of reply. That would be so when Crown counsel's jury address gives rise to an issue that is so serious that comment by the trial judge in his charge to the jury will not suffice to ensure a fair trial.

It must be emphasized that the reply must be confined to those issues improperly dealt with by Crown counsel. It cannot be used simply to restate the original position of the defence or to advance new arguments or theories.

It follows that, where the Crown is entitled to address the jury last pursuant to s. 651, the trial judge may grant defence counsel an opportunity to reply in those limited circumstances where the accused's ability to make a full answer and defence and his or her right to a fair trial have been prejudiced. The intervener the Attorney General for Alberta properly observed that just such prejudice may arise where the substantive legal theory of liability which the Crown has added or substituted in its closing has so dramatically changed that the accused could not reasonably have been expected to answer such an argument. It may also be appropriate to grant a reply where the accused is actually misled by the Crown as to the theory intended to be advanced. It is only in the clearest cases of unfairness that the trial judge should grant an opportunity to reply as an exercise of inherent jurisdiction.

Nonetheless, in light of the evidence presented in this case and the addresses of counsel, and taking into account the entire charge to the jury, we agree with the Court of Appeal that it was not incumbent upon the trial judge to grant Mr. Rose's counsel an opportunity to reply. Nor did any substantial miscarriage of justice result from his failure to refer specifically to and to correct the improper statements of Crown counsel in his charge to the jury.

6. Disposition

In the result, the appeal must be dismissed and the Order of Court of Appeal confirmed.

[L'Heureux-Dubé J. agreed that the impugned sections are constitutional, but did not agree that the trial court had the inherent jurisdiction to grant a right of reply.]

[Binnie J. dissented, Lamer C.J.C., McLachlin and Major JJ. concurring.]

The responsibilities of counsel in their closing addresses, and most particularly those of the Crown, have been articulated in various judgments. The following are illustrative.

PISANI v. THE QUEEN

(1970), 1 C.C.C. (2d) 477 (S.C.C.)

[The accused was charged with possession of counterfeit money. He testified, denying that he knew there was a package containing counterfeit notes in his car. The police found the notes wedged among the wires under the dashboard next to the steering column. In his jury address, Crown counsel advised the jury of matters unproven in the evidence which came from Crown counsel's personal experience or observations. The Court of Appeal affirmed the accused's conviction. The Supreme Court of Canada considered whether the jury address deprived the accused of a fair trial.]

Laskin J.: — This appeal, from the affirmation by the Court of Appeal of Ontario of the conviction of the accused on a charge of possession of counterfeit money, is here by leave on two questions of law that were formulated as follows:

1. Did the Court of Appeal err in failing to hold that the learned trial judge should have declared a mistrial on the motion of counsel for the accused by reason of the nature of Crown counsel's address to the jury?
2. Did the Court of Appeal err in not holding that the address to the jury by Crown counsel was of such a nature as to deprive the accused of a fair trial and hence resulted in a miscarriage of justice?

.....

The reasons for judgment given separately in *Boucher* [(1954), 110 C.C.C. 263] by Kerwin C.J., Rand, Locke and Cartwright JJ. amply point up the obligation of Crown counsel to be accurate, fair and dispassionate in conducting the prosecution and in addressing the jury. Over enthusiasm for the strength of the case of the prosecution, manifested in addressing the jury, may be forgivable, especially when tempered by a proper caution by the trial judge in his charge, where it is in relation to matters properly adduced in evidence. A different situation exists where that enthusiasm is coupled with or consists of putting before the jury, as facts to be considered for conviction, matters of which there is no evidence and which come from Crown counsel's personal experience or observations. That is the present case.

At the conclusion of Crown counsel's address in this case, counsel for the accused moved for a declaration of a mistrial. The trial judge did not act on the motion but proceeded to charge the jury. There was nothing in his charge that can be regarded as directed to the serious breaches of duty exhibited by Crown counsel. The charge was in the general pattern that is followed when there is no untoward situation that demands particular consideration and instruction to the jury. I do not consider that the familiar observation or reminder to the jury that they alone are judges of the facts and that they may disregard any comments, whether of the trial judge or of counsel, on the facts in evidence, can meet a situation where Crown counsel, who addresses the jury last, puts extraneous prejudicial matters to the jury as if such matters were part of the record of evidence.

Of course, there can be no unyielding general rule that an inflammatory or other improper address to the jury by Crown counsel is *per se* conclusive of the fact that there has been an unfair trial and that conviction there at cannot stand. The issues in a case and the evidence that is presented are highly relevant in this connection, as is the supervision exercised by the trial judge in relation to the addresses of counsel and in the course of his charge. In the present case, I am satisfied that what Crown counsel at the trial improperly said to the jury bore so directly on the central issue in the case, namely knowing possession, and was so prejudicial in respect of that issue and of the related question of credibility of the accused, of whose criminal record the jury were aware, as to deprive the accused of his right to a fair trial. I have already observed that the trial judge did nothing to erase the effect of Crown counsel's remarks, and I should add that nothing said by defence counsel in his preceding address can be regarded as justifying what Crown counsel intruded into the trial.

I wish to refer to some of the facts of the case and to portions of Crown counsel's address as reproduced in the transcript. The accused was a man with a record not related to any offence involving counterfeit money, and he gave evidence in denial of knowledge of the presence in his car of a package consisting of three tightly rolled up counterfeit notes. They were found by the police wedged among the wires under the dashboard next to the steering column. He had $700 in cash on his person in genuine notes. There was evidence that his wife and two relatives had access to his car. He denied police evidence that he said, when the counterfeit notes were found, "I don't know. It looks like funny money", but admitted that he said to the police, "I guess you've got me good. I want to see a lawyer."

The Crown's theory was that the accused was a "distributor" rather than a "pusher" of counterfeit bills; that is, that he was, so to speak, a wholesaler who showed samples to "pushers" who would buy from the samples and then "sell" to the public. In opening to the jury before any evidence was led Crown counsel spoke as follows:

> So the essence of the charge as you heard from the indictment is that he had it in his custody of possession. It was his car. He had the car for some time; apparently nobody had access to it — that he had placed this money in this hiding place, and he had it for some purpose. I will explain the purpose to you when I address you later.

No evidence was adduced as to any purpose, nor was there any evidence as to how counterfeit bills are distributed or marketed. There was no evidence as to any association of the accused with so-called distributors or pushers.

The transcript of Crown counsel's address to the jury includes the following passages:

> All right, so what happens. The officers found it, and he has all his notes. He is going underneath like that. Now, if a person knew, if somebody in fact

had put it there—I suggest he did—you would know where it is. You would be able to put your hand underneath, probably while you are still sitting there and pull it out notwithstanding that it was wedged in; you would know where it is, so you would measure it up and if you needed it—and I will explain why he needed it—you are not going to carry three ten dollar counterfeit bills on your person because in fact you may be stopped by the police. They stop people and they interview people and check people, and he is not going to carry the bills on him; that is for sure. He is not going to put it in his car. You heard the evidence about the $700 on his person at that time, and this comes to the reason why I had Corporal Dore explain what type and quality this money was, going from fair to good to fairly deceptive. He said they were at the top range, deceptive, the best at that time.

Now, I suggest to you that what in fact Pisani had these bills for, was for specimens, for samples, and he would go out, and he was a distributor. He would not carry any of this money on him. It was too dangerous. The police might stop him, so he hides it in this very unusual hiding place in the car; somewhere where he could get it out fast if he wanted to show somebody, but he wouldn't carry it on his person. He would try to find pushers. People with records don't push counterfeit money. They are distributors. They sell it to pushers. They sell it to people without records and they push it. Pisani wouldn't be caught dead pushing ten dollar bills. It is not worth it to him. He has got a record, so he goes, he finds his pusher, he brings it to wherever the pusher is and then calls them as he reaches underneath the dashboard where it is. He tries to persuade the pusher. He says, "Look, it is good quality ten dollar bills." Here is the sales pitch. He takes the three ten dollar bills, he goes in and he says to the man, and he will take one or two perhaps; he will say: all right, take a look at this. The person looks at it, and if he has another ten dollar bill he would look at it, and he would say: It looks pretty good. Then he would say, all right take a look at this, and then lo and behold they have the same serial number; they have got to be counterfeit. He looks at it says: This is pretty good; these are top-notch counterfeit, I probably could get rid of this. Maybe that person wouldn't do it, he pushes it through his girlfriend or an associate. He says: Take another look at this. This is another sample. This is another of the batch with a different serial number; have a look at it. That is pretty good too. So that is the sales pitch. He has one. He shows them to everyone. It has to be counterfeit, because it has the same serial number. So he has three samples, and they are top-notch quality and that would push them say: Yes, I could fool a person with them.

How many of you people know what a counterfeit looks like? My Dad owns a store. He doesn't know. I work in a store. I don't know what counterfeit is unless there is something drastically wrong with the bill. That is when he questions it.

I suggest to you that Pisani had secreted these three counterfeit ten dollar bills, and he wouldn't touch it. He probably figured the police aren't going to find it there. You will recall that it took the officer quite some time. He would put it there knowing that it was dangerous to have it on his person, on his physical person, and only at the last minute then he arrives where the pusher is, whether it be in a store or an apartment, and he would park, look around and make sure there are no police officers, out and would show the samples to the person who is doing the pushing. Then when he comes back he would hide it in the same place.

Later on in the address, Crown counsel after referring to Pisani's seven previous convictions and to the legal limitations that these convictions could only be used to assess his credibility, said this:

> He had $700 in his possession at that time made up of hundreds, fifties, twenties and tens. Is it possible that he got that as down payment from one of his pushers? He wouldn't bring money to the pusher. The pusher would have to go to somebody else, another person or party that has no record to get money. Pisani wouldn't be caught dead with the money. He would arrange for the pusher to get the money. He wouldn't be caught dead with large quantities of counterfeit money.

Again, in a succeeding portion of the address he spoke as follows:

> You heard the evidence that if you put the bills through the silver nitrate processing solution you would ruin the paper itself. It would turn to dark brown as we have heard, and they handle this money gingerly in Ottawa. You don't lift prints off counterfeit; that was known to Pisani. Pisani is, as I suggest to you he is not a pusher, but a distributor. He knows these technical things. He knows you can't lift a print, so I suggest to you that there is a matter of credibility. The story at the scene contrast. There is no one that he mentions. No person that he mentioned that would plant this money, and I suggest to you if that was so there would be a good quantity of money put there instead of three ten dollar bills.

There was no evidence that Pisani knew that fingerprints cannot be lifted from counterfeit money, and Crown counsel was also again repeating as facts matters not in evidence.

Two more passages of the address should be quoted:

> I would ask you then to disbelieve Pisani entirely when he says he didn't know who put it there. I suggest to you exactly that he put it there. He might have been on a selling jaunt at the time. He might have gotten a deposit to line up the place where the pusher would have got the money from a third party who had no record and he was coming back. He had a large quantity of money and unfortunately he was stopped and his car was searched.

> There is no direct evidence in this case that anyone saw Pisani put it there. There is no statement, and you don't expect statement from a person like this, do you really? A person, I suggest to you, that a person without a record may give a statement, not a person like this. There is no statement: Yes, I put it there. There is nothing like that, so I ask you — I am going to have to ask you to draw your conclusion that he put it there on the basis of circumstantial evidence.

The foregoing passages bear out the assessment I made of the effect of the address.

In my view, no case was made out for the application of s. 592(1)(*b*)(iii) [now s. 686] of the *Criminal Code*. In the result, I would allow the appeal, set aside the conviction and direct a new trial.

Taschereau J.'s description of the Crown's function in *Boucher v. The Queen* (1954), 110 C.C.C. 263 at p. 267 (S.C.C.) is often cited in this context:

> **(Translation) The position held by counsel for the Crown is not that of a lawyer in civil litigation. His functions are quasi-judicial. His duty is not so much to obtain a conviction as to assist the judge and the jury in ensuring that the fullest possible justice is done. His conduct before the court must always be characterized by moderation and impartiality. He will have properly performed his duty and will be beyond all reproach if, eschewing any appeal to passion, and employing a dignified manner**

suited to his function, he presents the evidence to the jury without going beyond what it discloses.

R. v. SWIETLINSKI

(1994), 92 C.C.C. (3d) 449 (S.C.C.)

[A person convicted of first degree murder receives a mandatory life sentence and is only eligible for parole after 25 years. Section 745 of the *Criminal Code* permits an application to be made to a jury after 15 years for a reduction in parole ineligibility. On Swietlinski's appeal to the Supreme Court, a new hearing was ordered, in part, due to the Crown's opening and closing addresses. Lamer C.J.C., spoke for the 5-4 majority on this issue.]

Lamer C.J.C.: —

.....

[quoting from the Crown's opening address.]

> Ladies and gentlemen of the jury, in 1976 this country, our government abolished capital punishment. Mr. Swietlinski was convicted of the worst crime known to our criminal justice system. You will hear shortly about the facts of this offence. In 1976, the same year, Mary Frances McKenna, someone that you won't hear very much about in this proceeding — this is an application brought by Mr. Swietlinski — but you won't hear much about a person by the name of Mary Frances McKenna, who was 37 years of age at the time.

He went on to add:

> ... please don't forget the victim in this case, Mary Frances McKenna. She doesn't have a chance to come before a group of people to ask for a second chance.

He concluded his opening statement by reminding the jurors that, "... Mr. Swietlinski, a few years earlier, would have been sentenced to death for this offence...". In his final submission to the jury he returned to the same themes:

> Mary Frances McKenna doesn't get a chance to come before a jury and ask to have her parole eligibility reduced. Mary Frances McKenna is gone.
>
> If we wanted revenge, we would have capital punishment. As I say, we don't. We have a compromise. It's a mandatory sentence, life with no eligibility for parole for 25 years, and that's the sentence that our society imposes for the taking of a human life in the manner that Mr. Swietlinski took it. To do otherwise, as Mr. Swietlinski suggested to you about the rules at Millhaven, would be anarchy.

Counsel also sought, in questioning certain witnesses, to draw attention to the fact that the victim could not obtain the second chance the appellant was seeking and to the fact that no assistance programs were available to the victim's family whereas the penitentiary system offered the appellant a vast range of services.

Counsel further sought to discredit the parole process in the following language:

> Normally, issues of parole, parole hearings, are held by, basically, a faceless group of people. They're held in secret, in private, and really all that the Parole Board hears from is the applicant and perhaps his counsel and the kind of people that you're about to hear from, the various corrections people.

Finally, in questioning certain witnesses counsel insinuated that the Beaver Creek Institution, where the appellant had spent the last two years, was too comfortable to be called a prison and that in fact some visitors confused the institution with a neighbouring campground. In his final submission, he suggested that the transfer to this institution was sufficient reward for the appellant's good conduct during his sentence.

The combined effect of these remarks was to imply that the s. 745 hearing was a proceeding unduly favourable to the applicant, even a subversion of Parliament's intent to impose a definite 25-year penalty on first degree murderers. The conclusion that emerged from these observations, and it was not a difficult one to draw, was that the jury should deal more severely with the appellant.

Nevertheless, s. 745 is as much a part of the *Code* as the provisions providing for no parole for 25 years in cases of first degree murder. The possible reduction of the ineligibility period after 15 years is a choice made by Parliament which the jury must accept. Clearly, the prosecution may not call this choice into question by suggesting to the jury that it is an abnormal procedure, excessively indulgent and contrary to what it argues was Parliament's intent. That amounts to urging the jurors not to make a decision in accordance with the law if they feel that it is bad law. It is clearly unacceptable for a lawyer to make such an observation to the jury: *R. v. Morgentaler* (1988), 37 C.C.C. (3d) 449 at pp. 481-3, 44 D.L.R. (4th) 385 at pp. 417-9, [1988] 1 S.C.R. 30 (S.C.C.); *R. v. Finta* (1994), 88 C.C.C. (3d) 417, 112 D.L.R. (4th) 513, [1994] 1 S.C.R. 701 (S.C.C.).

In the same way, counsel may not constantly repeat that imprisonment for 25 years is a substitute for the death penalty. That is an invitation to offset the alleged excessive clemency of Parliament by a severity not justified by the wording of s. 745. The jury does not have to decide whether the penalties imposed by Parliament are too severe or not severe enough. It must simply apply the *Code*. The *Code* no longer contains the death penalty: on the contrary, s. 745 gives the appellant the right to seek a reduction in his ineligibility period. No one can be permitted to undermine the fairness of the proceeding in which the appellant may obtain such a reduction by constant references to the death penalty.

Additionally, counsel for the Crown sought to draw the jury's attention to other cases of murderers who had used their parole to commit other murders. Thus, in questioning Antonio Jean, a psychologist employed by Correctional Service Canada, counsel put the following questions:

> Q. You also mentioned, during the course of your evidence this morning, you made mention of the Rygrock Inquest. That was an inquest in Ottawa?
>
> A. Yes, ma'am.
>
> Q. And that, in fact, was an inquest involving an inmate who had been released to a half-way house and had subsequently murdered an employee of that half-way house?
>
> A. Yes, ma'am.

Q. Okay. And, presumably, out of that inquest, Corrections Canada had reasons to look at some of its procedures, correct, in terms of the releasing of people? I'm not asking the details, but obviously they would review the procedures.

A. Very definitely.

Q. Okay. And, in fact, after the inquest and after the review was done, another inmate was released to a half-way house here in Toronto, Melvin Stanton. You're aware of him, aren't you?

A. Yes, ma'am.

Q. Okay. And, in fact, what followed from that was the murder, within a few hours of his release, of Tema Conter, correct?

A. Correct.

Q. So it seems that Corrections Canada does make mistakes, fair enough?

A. Your conclusion, ma'am.

Q. Could you agree with me, given those two inquests?

A. Do I have to?

Q. I'm just asking you to answer the question.

A. I suppose, like any other organization — I'm afraid to say what I have to say because it might be taken wrongly. Maybe the judicial system makes some mistakes too at times. It's human error.

Counsel broached the same subject in the examination of Allan Partington, a Correctional Service officer.

Similarly, in his opening statement he invited the jury to take into consideration cases of violence other than those of the appellant:

> We read the papers. We open the headlines today and we see concerns about violence in our society, and, in particular, we hear concerns about violence against women. I want you, when you listen to that evidence, to bear in mind that you are here representing the best interests of this community as it pertains not only to Mr. Swietlinski but the broader issues that an application, such as this, brings to bear.

In his final submission he added the following:

> Violence is, unfortunately, increasing in our community. Every time you turn on the news, read the headlines you hear either reports of or people worried about the issue of violence and, in particular, violence against women.
>
> A lot of times people come into contact or read in the paper and hear, read or see on T.V. something that shocks them, and the facts of this case no doubt shocked you. Well, they have concerns about things going on in our society, and they think to themselves, "Someone should do something about that," and always the someone is someone off in the distance. For the purpose of this case ... you are the they. Consider that when you retire to reach your determination.

It is completely improper to invite the jury to consider isolated cases in which prisoners committed murder after being paroled. Even though the rules applicable in the s. 745 hearing are not as strict as in a criminal trial, the fact remains that the jury must consider only the applicant's case. Although the temptation may sometimes be very strong, the jury must not try the cases of other inmates or determine whether the existing system of parole is doing its job. The appellant should not be punished for the weaknesses of the system.

Furthermore, the other observations I have just referred to may have suggested to the jury that its function was in some way to solve the problem of violence in society. It is true that deterrence is one of the functions of the penalty and that it is, therefore, legitimate for the jury to take this factor into account when hearing an application under s. 745. However, the approach taken by counsel for the Crown was unacceptable. The jury cannot simply be referred to headlines in newspapers, which generally concern themselves with the worst crimes. Such a course could produce a disproportionate reaction in the jury by making it believe it could solve the problem of crime at one stroke and by giving the appellant's case the odour of a general threat. Such a tactic smacks of the *in terrorem* arguments disapproved by the Quebec Court of Appeal in *R. v. Vallieres*, [1970] 4 C.C.C. 69, 9 C.R.N.S. 24 (Que. C.A.). In my view, it is possible to invite the jury to take the deterrent aspect of the penalty into account, but this should be done in the context of a general submission on the various functions performed by the penalty.

In a trial by jury it is usual for the judge to indicate to the jurors that they must base their decision solely on the evidence and that they should not read the newspapers while the trial is in progress. Sometimes drastic methods such as sequestering the jury or banning publication may be used to keep the jury free from undue influence by the media. That being the case, it is astonishing that counsel for the Crown could have invited the jury to do precisely what any good judge would tell it not to do. It is still more surprising that the trial judge did not react and rectify these remarks.

.....

VI. Judgment

The appellant did not get the fair hearing to which he was entitled. The appeal is, therefore, allowed and a rehearing ordered in accordance with these reasons.

R. v. MORGENTALER, SMOLING AND SCOTT

(1988), 37 C.C.C. (3d) 449 (S.C.C.)

[Dr. Morgentaler and others were acquitted under the abortion provisions of the *Criminal Code* after trial before a judge and jury. The Crown appealed, alleging *inter alia*, impropriety in the defence's closing address to the jury. A majority of the Supreme Court of Canada ultimately found the abortion provisions to be in violation of the *Charter*. However, the Court unanimously was of the view (though it did not affect the disposition of the appeal) that defence counsel's closing address was improper.]

Dickson C.J.C.: —

.....

In his concluding remarks to the jury at the trial of the appellants, defence counsel asserted:

> The judge will tell you what the law is. He will tell you about the ingredients of the offence, what the Crown has to prove, what the defences may be or may not be, and you must take the law from him. But I submit to you that it is up to you and you alone to apply the law to this evidence and you have a right to say it shouldn't be applied.

The burden of his argument was that the jury should not apply s. 251 if they thought that it was a bad law, and that, in refusing to apply the law, they could send a signal to Parliament that the law should be changed. Although my disposition of the appeal makes it unnecessary, strictly speaking, to review Mr. Manning's argument before the jury, I find the argument so troubling that I feel compelled to comment.

It has long been settled in Anglo-Canadian criminal law that in a trial before judge and jury, the judge's role is to state the law and the jury's role is to apply that law to the facts of the case. In *Joshua v. The Queen*, [1955] A.C. 121 at p. 130 (P.C.), Lord Oaksey enunciated the principle succinctly:

> It is a general principle of British law that on a trial by jury it is for the judge to direct the jury on the law and in so far as he thinks necessary on the facts, but the jury, whilst they must take the law from the judge, are the sole judges on the facts.

The jury is one of the great protectors of the citizen because it is composed of 12 persons who collectively express the common sense of the community. But the jury members are not expert in the law, and for that reason they must be guided by the judge on questions of law.

The contrary principle contended for by Mr. Manning, that a jury may be encouraged to ignore a law it does not like, could lead to gross inequities. One accused could be convicted by a jury who supported the existing law, while another person indicted for the same offence could be acquitted by a jury who, with reformist zeal, wished to express disapproval of the same law. Moreover, a jury could decide that although the law pointed to a conviction, the jury would simply refuse to apply the law to an accused for whom it had sympathy. Alternatively, a jury who feels antipathy towards an accused might convict despite a law which points to acquittal. To give a harsh but I think telling example, a jury fueled by the passions of racism could be told that they need not apply the law against murder to a white man who had killed a black man. Such a possibility need only be stated to reveal the potentially frightening implications of Mr. Manning's assertions. The dangerous argument that a jury may be encouraged to disregard the law was castigated as long ago as 1784 by Lord Mansfield in a criminal libel case, *R. v. Shipley* (1784), 4 Dougl. 73 at pp. 170-1, 99 E.R. 774 at p. 824:

> So the jury who usurp the judicature of law, though they happen to be right, are themselves wrong, because they are right by chance only, and have not taken the constitutional way of deciding the question. It is the duty of the Judge, in all cases of general justice, to tell the jury how to do right, though they have it in their power to do wrong, which is a matter entirely between God and their own consciences.
>
> To be free is to live under a government by law. ... Miserable is the condition of individuals, dangerous is the condition of the State, if there is no

certain law, or, which is the same thing, no certain administration of law, to protect individuals, or to guard the State.

.....

In opposition to this, what is contended for? — That the law shall be, in every particular cause, what any twelve men, who shall happen to be the jury, shall be inclined to think; liable to no review, and subject to no control, under all the prejudices of the popular cry of the day, and under all the bias of interest in this town, where thousands, more or less, are concerned in the publication of newspapers, paragraphs, and pamphlets. Under such an administration of law, no man could tell, no counsel could advise, whether a paper was or was not punishable.

I can only add my support to that eloquent statement of principle.

It is no doubt true that juries have a *de facto* power to disregard the law as stated to the jury by the judge. We cannot enter the jury room. The jury is never called upon to explain the reasons which lie behind a verdict. It may even be true that in some limited circumstances the private decision of a jury to refuse to apply the law will constitute, in the words of a Law Reform Commission of Canada working paper, "The citizen's ultimate protection against oppressive laws and the oppressive enforcement of the law" (Law Reform Commission of Canada, Working Paper 27, *The Jury in Criminal Trials* (1980)). But recognizing this reality is a far cry from suggesting that counsel may encourage a jury to ignore a law they do not support or to tell a jury that it has a *right* to do so. The difference between accepting the reality of *de facto* discretion in applying the law and elevating such discretion to the level of a right was stated clearly by the United States Court of Appeals, District of Columbia Circuit, in *U.S. v. Dougherty*, 473 F. 2d 1113 (1972), per Leventhal J., at p. 1134:

The jury system has worked out reasonably well overall, providing "play in the joints" that imparts flexibility and avoid[s] undue rigidity. An equilibrium has evolved — an often marvelous balance — with the jury acting as a "safety valve" for exceptional cases, without being a wildcat or runaway institution. There is reason to believe that the simultaneous achievement of modest jury equity and avoidance of intolerable caprice depends on formal instructions that do not expressly delineate a jury *Charter* to carve out its own rules of law.

To accept Mr. Manning's argument that defence counsel should be able to encourage juries to ignore the law would be to disturb the "marvelous balance" of our system of criminal trials before a judge and jury. Such a disturbance would be irresponsible. I agree with the trial judge and with the Court of Appeal that Mr. Manning was quite simply wrong to say to the jury that if they did not like the law they need not enforce it. He should not have done so.

R. v. GIESECKE

(1993), 82 C.C.C. (3d) 331 (Ont. C.A.);
leave to appeal to S.C.C. refused (1994), 86 C.C.C. (3d) vii

[The accused, Giesecke and her friend Lynch, were charged with the murder of Giesecke's husband. Giesecke testified that she was not involved in the murder but that her co-accused, Lynch, had admitted that he killed

Giesecke's husband. Lynch did not testify. Following the closing address of Giesecke's counsel, counsel for Lynch in his jury address compared Giesecke's character to the "she-bear" who is "more deadly than the male". He repeatedly told the jury that it was the defence position that Giesecke had committed the murder, that his client knew that, but that he, defence counsel, could not force him to testify. Lynch was acquitted. On appeal by Giesecke from her conviction, a new trial was ordered.]

By the Court: —

.....

The closing address, particularly since it went unchallenged by the trial judge in his jury charge, crossed the line from enthusiastic advocacy into inflammatory rhetoric. While counsel is not held to a standard of perfection in his or her address to the jury, there is a significant difference between remarks or observations one can characterize as inappropriate but contextually acceptable, and those made by counsel for the co-accused in this case which, by their hyperbole, mischaracterization or insinuation, impair the possibility of a fair trial. He compared the appellant's character to the "she-bear" in a Kipling poem who, as an "accosted ... monster ... rends the peasant tooth and nail, for the female species is more deadly than the male".

The co-accused, who was acquitted, did not testify. The appellant, who was convicted, did. As a result, counsel for the appellant addressed the jury before counsel for the co-accused and, not having anticipated the improprieties, was unable to respond to them. The following passages, taken from the address to the jury of counsel for the co-accused demonstrate unfairness to the appellant:

> I have conducted the defence as I saw fit to the extent of electing to call no evidence, and I have not. I have done the things that I thought should be done. If you have criticism about the way the case has been handled about the defence of Bruce Lynch, level it not at him, but at me, and that includes whether or not calling a defence.
>
> ... what you will no doubt conclude, because we have no direct evidence, is that he was killed as a result of a planned and deliberate act that stemmed from the heart of that woman right there. She did it. That's my position.
>
> What happened to Randy Giesecke? Who is responsible for his death? I say to you that it is not this man that I represent who, for whatever reason, chooses, when he speaks to the police and then in this courtroom not to tell you and not to indicate his co-accused, and I don't know why. I can't get him to do. It would only be a matter of speculation. We are not to wonder why. We are to decide this case upon the evidence.
>
> Would that I could drag him from the box and put him in the stand and force him to tell you all that he knows. I can't; you can't; no one can. Bruce Lynch, no doubt, has knowledge, but did nothing. Bruce Lynch knows that Harriet Giesecke is guilty, but says nothing. Bruce Lynch is a fool who, in his letters to his girlfriend, says: "Why do I hate myself so much that I am prepared to do 25 years?" and essentially to remain silent. He may be guilty of being a fool. He is not guilty of murder.

These are examples of how counsel for the co-accused told the jury what evidence his client would have given against the appellant had he followed his lawyer's, rather than his female co-accused's, advice and given evidence in the trial.

The entire remarks of counsel express personal views unsupported by the evidence, speculation, and an invitation to the jury to convert the co-accused's silence into a positive statement that if the co-accused had given evidence he would have told the jury that the appellant was guilty.

Towards the end of his charge to the jury, the learned trial judge gave a brief review of the position taken by defence counsel for the co-accused. The review included the following passage:

> He [the co-accused's counsel] suggested that Ms. Giesecke lied to her husband and to the police and to Joyce McLeod [the co-accused's ex-girlfriend] and to you, that she couldn't bring herself to sink Mr. Lynch entirely.
>
> He said Bruce Lynch did not kill Randall Giesecke. He said it is obvious that he chooses not to tell you who did, but he chooses obviously not to implicate his co-accused. He said maybe it is a Code of silence that he asked Ms. Giesecke about and maybe the Code of silence that is referred to in the letter. He refers to what Ms. Giesecke said when she was arrested ... and asking about finding the gun. He said Bruce Lynch had knowledge but did nothing. He knew what she had done, but did nothing himself. He said that Bruce Lynch knew that she was guilty, but that is not enough to convict him. Protecting her, he may be fool, but he is not guilty of murder, and that your verdict in relation to him should be not guilty.

In our opinion, the unnecessary repetition of the co-accused's position added to the prejudice caused to the appellant by the earlier inflammatory address. The trial judge specifically told the jury that the address of counsel did not constitute evidence. However, the repetition of the improper comments was not accompanied by a further caution. In the entire context, we are satisfied that the inappropriate, inflammatory and prejudicial comments of counsel resulted in a miscarriage of justice for the appellant. Counsel for the appellant failed to raise an objection or to request a mistrial. This does not, however, preclude the appellant from now relying on this point in the circumstances of this case.

He did, however, after the charge to the jury, express concern about the propriety of suggesting a "jail house" ethic that would keep the co-accused off the stand, in the absence of evidence. He also complained of counsel's statement to the jury that he should probably have dragged his client into the stand over his protestation. He suggested, however, that it was difficult to correct the last statement without infringing s. 4(6) of the *Canada Evidence Act*, R.S.C. 1985, c. C-5.

In response to the observations of the appellant's counsel, the trial judge ruled in the absence of the jury. He said:

> I am completely satisfied that the old line, that the jury may infer guilt from failure to testify, survives. Even if it does and even if there may have been some degree of error in favour of Mr. Lynch, I do not see how any such degree of error requires a re-charge in relation to the case against Ms. Giesecke. The fact that it may be that the silence of an accused may tell against him does not necessarily mean logically that his silence would necessarily tell in favour of a co-accused, having regard to the evidence and the issue that they had been joined in this case.

> In any event, it is clear that to attempt to say anything further to the jury about that matter would fly directly in the face of the strictures in the *Canada Evidence Act*. I, therefore, do not propose to re-charge the jury on that point.

All these remarks required a clear and unequivocal response and instruction from the trial judge without infringing s. 4. The predecessor of s. 4(6) of the *Canada Evidence Act* has been interpreted, in a purposive manner, i.e., to prevent the silence of accused persons to be presented to the jury in a way that suggests that the silence is being used as a cloak for guilt: *McConnell and Beer v. The Queen*, [1968] 4 C.C.C. 257 at pp. 263-4, 69 D.L.R. (2d) 149, [1968] S.C.R. 802. In this case an express statement by the trial judge to the jury, that the submission by counsel for the co-accused to the effect that the co-accused had knowledge of the appellant's guilt and could have given evidence to that effect must not be used to support a finding of the appellant's guilt, should have been given. Such a direction would not have amounted to a violation of the subsection. No such corrective steps were taken and, as a result, in the context of the joint trial we are unable to say that the trial was unaffected by the cumulative prejudice to the appellant.

QUESTION

39. The Crown states in its closing address that the accused "surely would have testified if he were innocent". Consider the appropriateness of this comment, in light of s. 4(6) of the *Canada Evidence Act*. Could the Crown expressly ask for an adverse inference to be drawn against the accused because of his failure to testify, if the trial were being conducted without a jury? Consider, in this regard, *R. v. Noble* (1997), 114 C.C.C. (3d) 385 (S.C.C.); *R. v. Francois* (1994), 91 C.C.C. (3d) 289 (S.C.C.).

P. REOPENING THE CASE

R. v. P.(M.B.)

(1994), 89 C.C.C. (3d) 289 (S.C.C.)

[The accused was charged with sexual offences against his niece, who was under 14 years of age. At trial, the complainant, then 16 years old, testified that the accused had resided at her parents' home in the summer of 1982 for one or two months and had sexually assaulted her over a weekend while her parents were away with their van club. She further testified that about one week before the "van club weekend", the accused had sexually assaulted her while her mother was asleep. The last assault allegedly took place a few months later, when the accused no longer stayed at her parents' house. In 1989, she first described these assaults as having occurred in 1980. The accused was then arrested based upon an information which alleged offences between January 1, 1980 and January 1, 1981. Upon arrest, the accused was informed that the alleged incidents occurred while he resided at the complainant's home. After the preliminary inquiry, the information was amended, on consent, to allege that the incidents had occurred between

January 1, 1982, and January 1, 1983. At trial, the complainant testified that, because she and her mother had gone through old photographs, she was able to determine that all incidents had occurred in 1982. The complainant's mother also testified that the accused had lived with the family in the summer of 1982, and that the accused babysat her daughter during a van trip that summer. The Crown closed its case and the trial was adjourned to accommodate the defence, which had not received certain disclosure. Prior to adjourning, defence counsel advised the court that he would be calling three witnesses, including an alibi witness, and the Crown indicated that the defence had undertaken to provide particulars of the alibi. When the trial resumed, the Crown applied to reopen its case and recall the complainant's mother with new evidence pertaining to the offence dates. Over the defence's objection, the Crown was permitted to do so. The mother testified that her earlier evidence had been mistaken and that the accused had stayed with their family in the summer of 1983, not 1982. The alibi evidence was to have demonstrated the accused's whereabouts for 1982. The Crown then successfully moved, over the defence's objection, to have the indictment amended to extend the time period to include 1983. The time frame described in the indictment became January 1, 1982, to January 1, 1984. The accused ultimately testified that he did live with the complainant in the summer of 1983. He was convicted at trial.]

[The majority judgment (5-4) was delivered by:]

Lamer C.J.C.: — This case raises the question of whether, in circumstances where the defence has started to answer the case against it by announcing that it will be calling evidence, it is an appropriate exercise of a trial judge's discretion to allow the Crown's case to be reopened in order to recall a witness so she can correct her earlier testimony.

.....

With respect to the Crown's subsequent application for amending the indictment, the trial judge relied on the principles established in *R. v. B. (G.)* (1990), 56 C.C.C. (3d) 200, [1990] 2 S.C.R. 30, 77 C.R. (3d) 347, and stated that "there is always difficulty pinpointing the exact date because of the age of these complainants in trying to remember the time", and that,

> ... the incidents are not changed, we are talking here of people trying to recall a certain date by certain events and the young complainant related it to the van trip. Somebody has made a mistake in the summer of the van trip. I do not believe that this will prejudice the accused in amending that date.

In finding the respondent guilty of the offences charged, the trial judge concluded that:

> Although the evidence of the complainant was confusing as to the actual dates, I find that her evidence related to the time and place that the accused lived there.
>
> I accept the complainant's evidence as to the time and place and I accept Mrs. P.'s evidence as to the time and place and her method of recalling it as she thought about it and found pictures and related to that time period.
>
> I further accept Constable Rollin's evidence that she related to the accused that the alleged offences took place at ... and during the time the accused lived there.

.....

Although the appeal before the Court of Appeal concerned only the trial judge's ruling permitting the Crown to amend the indictment, Finlayson J.A. also considered the propriety of allowing the Crown to reopen its case in the circumstances. He observed that it was only in view of the evidence of alibi that it became necessary for the Crown to reopen its case so that it could adduce fresh evidence which made the alibi irrelevant. He held that the Crown should not have been permitted to reopen its case. The trial judge should have heard the alibi evidence and decided the case as the Crown had defined it. Finlayson J.A. explained (at p. 130):

> I do not wish to place this opinion on too narrow a basis. My objections are to the reopening of the Crown's case and to the amendment of the indictment. My reasons in both cases relate to prejudice. I do not see how the Crown can be permitted to recast its case when faced with an alibi, the accuracy of which it was not prepared to dispute. The defence went into a trial where the Crown had originally alleged offences in the year 1980. The year was changed to 1982. The [respondent's] defence was a denial bolstered by an alibi which the defence could establish independently of the [respondent's] evidence. Consequently, once the time frame was changed to include the year 1983, an adjournment could not have assisted the [respondent]. He had lost the ability to put forward an independent assertion of his innocence to the charge as contained in the indictment. In charges of sexual assault against very young children, the accused is often reduced to his own denial as a defence. The loss of an independent alibi is, therefore, a very serious loss indeed.

On the amendment issue, Finlayson J.A. noted that prejudice to the accused is provided for in s. 529(4) (now s. 601(4)) of the *Criminal Code*. He stated that in *B. (G.)*, *supra*, the Supreme Court of Canada recognized that the availability of an alibi is a significant consideration in assessing prejudice to an accused. He relied on the conclusion in *B. (G.)* (at p. 218) that, "[i]f the time of the offence cannot be determined and time is an essential element of the offence or crucial to the defence, a conviction cannot be sustained", to find the year in which the offences were alleged to have occurred as being crucial to the defence. He stated (at p. 131) that:

> [t]he defence was positioned to respond to the case as pleaded and led by the Crown. Accordingly, in my opinion, the prejudice to the [respondent] arising from the amendment to the indictment was total, and the learned trial judge was in error in granting the amendment.

Finlayson J.A. was of the view that the respondent was denied a significant procedural safeguard in that the case against him was materially changed to an altogether different case after he had announced his defence and the Crown had closed its case. He suggested that amendments during a trial should not be encouraged because they usually work to the prejudice of the accused. He concluded that the conviction could not stand, and accordingly, allowed the appeal, quashed the conviction and entered an acquittal.

.....

This case is, fundamentally, about the reopening of the Crown's case and not about the amendment to the indictment. I am not convinced that the respondent suffered any irreparable prejudice by the mere fact of the amendment to the dates specified in the indictment. However, the respondent was prejudiced by the trial judge's decision to allow the Crown's case to be reopened after the respondent had begun to answer the case against him by revealing that he would be calling three witnesses. Therefore, I am satisfied that the trial judge committed a reversible error at the reopening stage, before the Crown moved to amend the indictment.

The reason it was not the amendment in itself but the reopening which created the injustice is that, on the facts as found by the trial judge, the respondent knew what was alleged against him from the outset. He had been made aware at the time of his arrest that the relevant period during which he was alleged to have sexually assaulted the complainant was when he was living at her parents' house. I am inclined to think that, up until the point when the Crown closed its case, the dates in the indictment could have been amended so as to make them conform with the period during which the respondent was living with the complainant's family. In this regard, I would simply note that courts, including this one, have accepted that, in cases involving offences and particularly sexual offences against young children, absolute precision with respect to the timing of an alleged offence will often be unrealistic and unnecessary: *B. (G.), supra*, at p. 218; also see *R. v. W. (R.)* (1992), 74 C.C.C. (3d) 134 at pp. 142-4, [1992] 2 S.C.R. 122, 13 C.R. (4th) 257, and *R. v. C. (R.I.)* (1986), 32 C.C.C. (3d) 399 at p. 403, 17 W.C.B. 370 (Ont. C.A.).

The fact that an accused may have an alibi for the period (or part of the period) described in an indictment does not necessarily or automatically "freeze" the dates specified in that indictment. That is to say, there is no vested right to a given alibi. Alibi evidence must respond to the case as presented by the Crown, and not the other way around. Section 601(4) of the *Criminal Code*, R.S.C. 1985, c. C-46 (formerly s. 529(4)), directs a trial judge to consider certain factors in deciding whether to allow an indictment to be amended, including whether an accused has been misled or prejudiced and whether an injustice might result...

Nowhere does s. 601(4) say that inability to rely on a particular defence is coextensive with irreparable "prejudice" or "injustice", and nor can this be inferred from the language of the provision. Rather, such matters are properly left to the trial judge to consider in the particular circumstances of a case.

In any event, this appeal can be disposed of on the basis that the reopening of the Crown's case was in error, without considering the issue of amendment. At the point when the Crown moved to reopen its case, there was no basis in the evidence for the Crown to apply for an amendment. The indictment conformed with the evidence which, up to that point, had been that the alleged sexual assaults had occurred in July, 1982. The reopening of the Crown's case to recall the complainant's mother and have her correct her earlier testimony as to dates was, therefore, a condition precedent to the amendment which the Crown subsequently sought. I have concluded that, given the advanced stage reached in the proceedings, the Crown should not have been allowed to reopen its case in order to justify the subsequent amendment to the indictment.

The principles governing reopening

The keystone principle in determining whether the Crown should be allowed to reopen its case has always been whether the accused will suffer prejudice in the legal sense — that is, will be prejudiced in his or her defence. A trial judge's exercise of discretion to permit the Crown's case to be reopened must be exercised judicially and should be based on ensuring that the interests of justice are served.

Traditionally, courts in Canada and in England have treated the stage reached in a proceeding as correlative to prejudice and injustice to the accused. That is, a court's discretion with respect to reopening will be exercised less readily as the trial proceeds. The point is illustrated by taking the following three stages in a trial:

(1) before the Crown closes its case,
(2) immediately after the Crown closes its case but before the defence elects whether or not to call evidence (most commonly, this is where the defence has moved for a directed verdict of acquittal for failure by the Crown to prove some essential ingredient of its case), and
(3) after the defence has started to answer the case against it by disclosing whether or not it will be calling evidence.

In the first phase, before the Crown has closed its case, a trial judge has considerable latitude in exercising his or her discretion to allow the Crown to recall a witness so that his or her earlier testimony can be corrected. Any prejudice to the accused can generally be cured at this early stage by an adjournment, cross-examination of the recalled witness and other Crown witnesses and/or a review by the trial judge of the record in order to determine whether certain portions should be struck.

Once the Crown actually closes its case and the second phase in the proceeding is reached, the trial judge's discretion to allow a reopening will narrow and the corresponding burden on the Crown to satisfy the court that there are no unfair consequences will heighten. The test to be applied by the trial judge is generally understood to be that reopening is to be permitted to correct some oversight or inadvertent omission by the Crown in the presentation of its case, provided of course that justice requires it and there will be no prejudice to the defence.

Lastly, in the third phase after the Crown has closed its case and the defence has started to answer the case against it (or, as in much of the caselaw, the defence has actually closed its case), a court's discretion is very restricted and is far less likely to be exercised in favour of the Crown. It will only be in the narrowest of circumstances that the Crown will be permitted to reopen its case. Traditionally, an *ex improviso* limitation was said to apply to this stage of the proceeding; that is, the Crown was only allowed to reopen if some matter arose which no human ingenuity could have foreseen. At this late stage, the question of what "justice" requires will be directed much more to protecting the interests of the accused than to serving the often wider societal interests represented by the Crown, the latter being a more pressing consideration at the first and, to a lesser extent, the second phase.

.....

... While the strict *ex improviso* limitation imposed on reopening after the defence had closed its case may, as such, no longer apply (see *Robillard v. The Queen* (1978), 41 C.C.C. (2d) 1, 85 D.L.R. (3d) 449, [1978] 2 S.C.R. 728), I view it to be self-evident that a court's discretion to permit the Crown's case to be reopened where an accused has started to meet the case against him or her must be severely curtailed.

While I do not propose to provide an exhaustive review of the jurisprudence in the area, I believe that the authorities on reopening show clearly that courts have always attached great significance to the stage reached in the proceeding, drawing a particularly sharp distinction between the point at which the Crown has closed its case and the defence has simply moved for a directed verdict (the second phase described above), and the point at which the defence has closed its case (the third phase).

Notwithstanding the importance which has historically attached to the stage reached in the trial proceeding and the fact that a court's discretion to permit the Crown's case to be reopened is highly restricted once the defence starts to answer the case against it, it is true that the strict *ex improviso* rule is no longer applied in Canada. However, the circumstances in which the Crown may be allowed to reopen at this stage are very narrow. The two most common examples are where:

(1) the conduct of the defence has either directly or indirectly contributed to the Crown's failure to adduce certain evidence before closing its case: *R. v. Champagne, Fahlman and MacManus*, [1970] 2 C.C.C. 273, 8 C.R.N.S. 245, 70 W.W.R. 438 (B.C.C.A.); *Crawford v. The Queen* (1984), 43 C.R. (3d) 80, 33 M.V.R. 45 (Ont. Co. Ct.), and

(2) the Crown's omission or mistake was over a non-controversial issue to do with purely formal procedural or technical matters, having nothing to do with the substance or merits of a case: *Kissick v. The King* (1952), 102 C.C.C. 129, [1952] 1 S.C.R. 343, 14 C.R. 1; *Robillard, supra*; *Champagne, supra*; *R. v. Huluszkiw* (1962), 133 C.C.C. 244, 36 D.L.R. (2d) 309, 37 C.R. 386 (Ont. C.A.); *R. v. Assu* (1981), 64 C.C.C. (2d) 94 (B.C.C.A.).

.....

While courts have often been at pains to distinguish between the reopening principles which should govern a trial judge's exercise of discretion in earlier versus later phases of a trial, clearly viewing reopening after the defence has made an election and/or closed its case as more prone to creating injustice than reopening at the earlier directed verdict stage, few have been explicit about the reasons for the difference.

.....

What is so objectionable about allowing the Crown's case to be reopened *after* the defence has started to meet that case is that it jeopardizes, indirectly, the principle that an accused not be conscripted against himself or herself. In *Dubois*, [(1985), 22 C.C.C. (3d) 513] this court interpreted the privilege against self-incrimination contained in s. 13 of the *Charter* as preventing the Crown from indirectly conscripting the accused to defeat himself by using his previous testimony against him — something which the Crown is directly prohibited from doing under s. 11(*c*) of the *Charter*. In my opinion, a similar danger is involved when the Crown seeks to reopen its case after the defence has begun to answer the case against it — that is, there is a real risk that the Crown will, based on what it has heard from the defence once it is compelled to "meet the case" against it, seek to fill in gaps or correct mistakes in the case which it had on closing and to which the defence has started to respond. To ensure that this does not in fact happen, the Crown should not, as a general rule, be permitted to reopen once the defence has started to answer the Crown's case.

In other words, I agree with respondent's counsel in this case that there comes a point when "enough is enough", and a mistake or omission by the Crown must necessarily become fatal. Once the defence starts to "meet the case", thus revealing its own case, the Crown should, except in the narrowest of circumstances, be "locked into" the case which, upon closing, it has said the defence must answer. The Crown must not be allowed in any way to *change* that case. To hold otherwise would be to undermine the guiding principle against self-incrimination.

It is for this very important reason that *Robillard, supra,* with its more generous approach to a trial judge's discretion over reopening, even after the defence has closed its case, must be narrowly construed as applying only to situations where the Crown is seeking to reopen in order to correct a matter of form, and not generally to all situations where the defence has started to answer the case against it. Importantly, the Crown in *Robillard* was merely seeking to introduce non-controversial evidence which it would reasonably have been expected to introduce in order to *support* its case, but which it had omitted as a result of inadvertence. It was not attempting in any way to *change* the case which it had upon closing. I would also note that *Robillard* was decided in a pre-*Charter* era. With the entrenchment of the principle against self-incrimination in the *Charter*, it becomes necessary to ensure that the rules governing reopening are consistent with constitutional imperatives. Accordingly, any departure from the basic principle that the Crown not be allowed to reopen once an accused starts to reveal his or her defence must be assessed keeping that in mind.

I have suggested that it will only be in special circumstances that a trial judge should entertain an application by the Crown to reopen after the defence has begun answering the case against it. Two examples of such circumstances have been provided: where conduct of the defence has contributed to an omission by the Crown, or where matters of form rather than substance are involved. There may be other exceptional circumstances in which reopening will be justified. In *R. v. Nelson*, [1993] O.J. No. 1899 (Ont. Ct. (Gen. Div.)) [summarized 20 W.C.B. (2d) 461], a case involving a charge of second degree murder, the Crown applied to reopen its case in order to have evidence by the only eyewitness to the murder given by commission. The Crown brought its application after the trial had been completed and at the point where the trial judge had reached a decision, but had not yet released his judgment. In dismissing the Crown's application to reopen, Goodearle J. stated as follows (at para. 31):

> An application, brought in these circumstances, at this late date by the Crown should never be allowed unless the effect of such evidence is of such apparent strength as to be likely to convince the trier of fact that the verdict it (or he) has reached, on the evidence originally adduced would be wrong and would result in a palpable injustice to the accused.

Clearly, where the interests of the accused warrant reopening the Crown's case, a trial judge should exercise his or her discretion accordingly, no matter how late in the proceeding it may be.

In summary, in order to preserve the principle against self- incrimination and ensure that accused persons are not compelled to assist in their own prosecution, the Crown should not be allowed, except in the narrowest or most exceptional of circumstances, to reopen its case once the defence has started to answer the case against it.

Application to the case at bar

In this case, the Crown had closed its case and the defence had been granted an adjournment to deal with non-disclosure by the Crown of certain inculpatory statements made by the police. Before recessing, the defence announced that it would be calling three witnesses, one of whom would be offering alibi evidence. Upon resumption of the trial approximately five weeks later, the Crown sought leave to reopen its case in order to recall the complainant's mother to allow her to correct her testimony as to the dates of the alleged sexual assaults. The trial judge permitted the Crown to reopen its case for the purpose of recalling the mother, and then, subsequently, ruled in favour of the Crown's application to amend the dates in the indictment to make them correspond with the mother's new evidence. The cumulative effect of the reopening and the amendment was, as respondent's counsel phrased it, to "obliterate" the respondent's alibi defence.

I am satisfied that this is an appropriate case in which to interfere with the trial judge's exercise of discretion to allow the Crown to reopen its case. Not only had the defence started to "meet" the Crown's case by declaring its intention to call evidence, but also the complainant's mother was recalled in order to justify amending the charge. The mother's fresh evidence had the effect of *changing* the case which the accused had, by announcing his intention to call evidence and particularly alibi evidence, committed himself to answering.

Reopening in this case was contrary to the interests of justice and prejudicial to the accused because it violated, indirectly, the fundamental tenet of our criminal justice system that an accused must not be conscripted against himself. To reach this conclusion, I find it neither necessary nor appropriate to interfere with the trial judge's findings of credibility as the Court of Appeal did. In addition, it is unnecessary to consider, as the Court of Appeal did, the second ground of appeal, which is the question of whether the trial judge erred in allowing the amendment to the indictment.

V. Disposition

Because the appropriate remedy in the circumstances would be to quash the conviction at trial and replace it with a verdict of acquittal, the appeal is dismissed on the ground that allowing the reopening of the Crown's case was an improper exercise of the trial judge's discretion.

QUESTION

40. In a trial by judge alone, does the judge have the power to permit the defence to re-open the case after a conviction has been entered and before sentencing? Does that judge have the power to permit the Crown to re-open the case after an acquittal? In a jury trial, does the trial judge have the power to set aside the jury's verdict? Consider, in this regard, *R. v. Hayward* (1993), 86 C.C.C. (3d) 193 (Ont. C.A.); *R. v. Lessard* (1976), 30 C.C.C. (2d) 70 (Ont. C.A.).

Q. CHARGE TO THE JURY

After the closing addresses are completed, the trial judge provides instructions to the jury, known as the *charge*. It is beyond the scope of this book to outline all matters which must be addressed in the charge to the jury. However, examples of mandatory topics are: the law relating to all criminal trials, including the burden of proof, presumption of innocence, and the requirement of unanimity; the approach to be taken concerning credibility issues; the law relating to the specific charges, including the elements of the charges, and any included offences; any defences which fairly arise on the evidence and their legal definitions; the positions of Crown and the defence and the principal evidence in support thereof; and, special instructions as to the limited use of certain evidence. Most appeals turn, to a great extent, upon the adequacy of the charge. Many judges use model charge books to deliver standard portions of the charge and to reduce the risk of reversible error. A trial judge may invite counsel to provide assistance as to the contents of the charge prior to its delivery (s. 650.1 of the *Criminal Code*).

R. JURY DELIBERATIONS

After the charge to the jury, the jurors retire to consider their verdict. At this point they are sequestered until they reach a verdict or until they record their inability to do so. In Canada, jurors are rarely sequestered during the trial itself[7] (one pundit has suggested that it is only in the United States that they lock up the jurors and let the accused go home!). Once the jury retires, counsel records any objections to the charge. If the trial judge agrees with any objection, the jury will be recalled and re-charged on the relevant point. The trial judge often declines to re-charge the jury on all or some of the objections raised. The failure to object may be considered by an appellate court in assessing how serious any alleged misdirection was. Accordingly, counsel should consider, in advance of the charge, the areas that should be covered in the charge and what should be said about them. In any event, where no objections are noted, counsel should refrain from complimenting the judge on how

7 Section 647 of the *Criminal Code* regulates the separation and sequestration of jurors. Where the jurors are not sequestered, it is an offence to publish information regarding portions of the trial for which the jurors are not present (*e.g.*, *voir dire* evidence) until they retire to consider their verdict (s. 648).

well-executed the charge was. Appellate counsel finds this even more difficult to overcome than a mere failure to object.

The jury takes with it all of the exhibits and the indictment. A "dummy" indictment is provided to the jury where the original indictment contains prejudicial, inadmissible matters, such as a count which has previously been withdrawn or severed, or an endorsment by the trial judge of the disposition respecting another accused who pleaded guilty on the same indictment.

QUESTION

41. A prosecution witness is cross-examined on his prior inconsistent statement to the police. Should that statement be marked as a full exhibit at the trial? If not so marked, should the jury receive it in the jury room? Consider, in this regard, *R. v Rowbotham* (1988), 41 C.C.C. (3d) 1 (Ont. C.A.).

The jurors are informed during the charge that they are entitled to ask questions. The following case articulates how questions are to be dealt with.

R. v. S.(W.D.)

(1994), 93 C.C.C. (3d) 1 (S.C.C.)

[After deliberating for several hours on a charge of sexual assault, the jury sent the judge a note, indicating that they were "hung up" and they would like an explanation as to their duty regarding evidence and reasonable doubt. In assessing the adequacy of the trial judge's response, the court outlined the procedures for responding to jury questions.]

[The majority judgment was delivered by:]

Cory J.: —

.....

Summary

The manner in which questions from the jury should be handled may be summarized in this way:

1. All questions received from the jury must be considered to be of significance and important.
2. Counsel must be advised of the question and their submissions heard as to the nature and content of the response.
3. The answer to the question must be correct and comprehensive. Even if the issue was covered in the original charge it must, in its essence, be repeated even if this seems to be repetitious.
4. No precise formula need be used but the response to the question must always be accurate and complete.

5. The longer the delay the more important it will be that the recharge be correct and comprehensive. As a general rule, an error in the recharge on the question presented will not be saved by a correct charge which was given earlier. The question indicates the concern or confusion of the jury. It is that concern or confusion which must be correctly addressed on the recharge.

[Cory J. concluded that the trial judge's response was in error and necessitated a new trial.]

The recommended charge to the jury on proof beyond a reasonable doubt is contained in *R. v. Lifchus* (1997), 118 C.C.C. (3d) 1 (S.C.C.). The recommended instruction to the jury on reasonable doubt and its relationship to credibility is contained in *R. v. W.(D.)* (1991), 63 C.C.C. (3d) 397 (S.C.C.).

Frequently, the jury requests assistance concerning the evidence.

QUESTION

42. What should a trial judge do in the following circumstances?

(a) the jurors request copies of the statutory provisions to which the judge referred. Consider, in this regard, *R. v. Vawryk and Appleyard* (1979), 46 C.C.C. (2d) 290 (Man. C.A.); *R. v. Schimanowsky* (1973), 15 C.C.C. (2d) 82 (Sask. C.A.); *R. v. Tuckey, Bayham and Walsh* (1985), 20 C.C.C. (3d) 502 (Ont. C.A.); *R. v. Stanford* (1975), 27 C.C.C. (2d) 520 (Que. C.A.).

(b) the jurors request permission to take notes during the trial. Consider, in this regard, *R. v. Bengert et al. No. 3* (1979), 48 C.C.C. (2d) 413 (B.C.S.C.); *R. v. Andrade* (1985), 18 C.C.C. (3d) 41 (Ont. C.A.).

(c) during the trial, a juror wants to ask a witness a question which (i) would be admissible if tendered (ii) would be inadmissible if tendered. Consider, in this regard, *R. v. Andrade* (1985), 18 C.C.C. (3d) 41 (Ont. C.A.).

(d) during deliberations, the jury requests the answer to a matter which is not in evidence.

(e) during deliberations, the jury requests the evidence of a witness's examination-in-chief only be read back to them. Consider, in this regard, *R. v. Olbey* (1979), 50 C.C.C. (2d) 257 (S.C.C.).

(f) during deliberations, the jury requests a copy of the judge's charge to the jury. Consider, in this regard, *R. v. Wong* (1978), 41 C.C.C. (2d) 196 (B.C.C.A.).

(g) during deliberations, the jury's questions make it clear that some jurors have a reasonable doubt as to whether the accused personally killed his wife. Some jurors have a reasonable doubt as to whether the accused hired someone to kill his wife. They are all satisfied beyond any doubt that the accused, one way or the other, caused the premeditated death of his wife. Consider, in this regard, *Thatcher v. The Queen* (1987), 32 C.C.C. (3d) 481 (S.C.C.).

(h) during the trial, a juror advises the court that the accused's brother approached her and (i) said hello or (ii) offered her a bribe because things were going so badly for the accused. Consider, in this regard, *R. v. Lessard* (1992), 74 C.C.C. (3d) 552 (Que. C.A.); *R. v. Horne* (1987), 35 C.C.C. (3d) 427 (Alta. C.A.); leave to appeal to S.C.C. refused, 36 C.C.C. (3d) *vi*.

Generally, the jury should not be permitted to deliberate into the early morning hours but should be advised that accommodation will be provided and they can resume in the morning: *R. v. Martin* (1980), 53 C.C.C. (2d) 250 (Ont. C.A.); *R. v. Owen* (1983), 4 C.C.C. (3d) 538 (N.S.S.C. (App. Div.)); *R. v. Mohamed* (1991), 64 C.C.C. (3d) 1 (B.C.C.A.).

When the trial judge is of the view that the jury is experiencing difficulty in arriving at a verdict (which may be indicated by a note from the jury or an inordinate period of deliberations) he or she may *exhort* the jury to reach a verdict. Many appellate decisions wrestle with the difficult issue as to whether the trial judge prematurely exhorted the jury and whether the exhortation exceeded its permissible limits.

R. v. SIMS

(1992), 75 C.C.C. (3d) 278 (S.C.C.)

The judgment of the court was delivered by

McLachlin J.: — This appeal raises the issue of whether a judge should give his or her opinion on matters of fact while exhorting a deadlocked jury to reach a verdict.

The facts

This appeal arises from the trial of Sims for the murder of an elderly person, Flora Nelson, in the course of a break and enter into her home in Victoria. By January, 1987, the police investigation led the police to conclude that Sims and one Norman Johnson had been present in the deceased's apartment on the day of the murder, and that one or both of them might have murdered her. In February, 1987, Sergeants Oakley and Ross travelled to Toronto to interview the appellant, who was being detained on other charges in Ontario. In the course of subsequent questioning, Sims made certain statements to the police.

Sims talked to the officers about the possibility of pleading guilty to the lesser charge of manslaughter. He stated that he was sick and needed help — that he "couldn't keep on hurting old people". He expressed a wish to be transferred to Victoria to "get Norm off", asking out loud: "if Norm wasn't actually involved in the hitting, it may affect his sentence?". The interviews led to a critical statement. In response to a remark as to the laudable loyalty of Sims' father, Sergeant Ross testified that the appellant stated: "All the grief I have been causing ... all the shit I have been doing, killing a 71-year-old woman, nice."

Sims was charged with murder. His statements to the police were found to be voluntary and were admitted into evidence. The appellant took the stand and denied committing the murder. He said what he had really said in the critical portion of his comments to Sergeant Ross was, "All the grief I have been causing... all the shit I have been doing, *now charged with* killing a 71-year-old woman, nice" (emphasis added). In his cross- examination, Sergeant Ross appears to have confirmed the appellant's version of the statement.

At the conclusion of the trial on January 20, 1988, the trial judge charged the jury completely and correctly. He emphasized that all matters of fact were for them to decide, and them alone. The jury deliberated throughout the following day and into the next day. They clearly did not find the case easy. They twice interrupted their deliberations to ask that evidence be re-read to them, first the evidence of an inmate and later the portions of Sergeant Ross' testimony as to the appellant's statements to him in Toronto. At 9:04 p.m. on January 22nd, the jury indicated to the court that they were deadlocked. The trial judge recalled the jury and delivered an exhortation, which read, in part:

> I must also emphasize that the minority do not have to agree with the majority. All I want to remind you is of the fact that you as reasonable people might reconsider your position again and decide whether or not in good conscience you can change your mind so that a verdict may be given in this trial of guilty or not guilty.
>
> On the other hand, if, consistent with your oath, you cannot honestly alter your view or views to conform with that of [the]majority, and you cannot bring the other jurors around to your own point of view, then it is your duty to differ and there will be no verdict.
>
> Now, it seems to me the issue in this case is whether Michael Sims was in the apartment of Flora Nelson at the time and place mentioned in the indictment. *While matters of evidence are entirely up to you, as I told you before, and I tell you now, I suggest if you accept the evidence of Sergeant Ross the Crown has a very powerful case.* If you have a reasonable doubt on the whole of the evidence then the accused should be found not guilty.
>
> The matter is entirely up to you. All that I can do is ask you to try once again and listen to the arguments of your fellow jurors.

(Emphasis added.)

The jury continued to deliberate for another hour before retiring. They reconvened January 23rd at 9 a.m. and delivered a verdict of guilty at 9:59 a.m.

.....

Issues

This appeal presents two basic issues:

(1) What rule governs the statement of a trial judge's opinion on the facts to a deadlocked jury in the course of an exhortation?
(2) Did the exhortation in this case violate that rule?

Discussion

(1) The rule governing statements of opinion on matters of fact to a deadlocked jury

I have concluded that the appropriate rule is the following: a trial judge ought not to offer his or her opinion on the facts to a deadlocked jury, in the course of an exhortation, except to the extent that the jury has indicated the need for assistance on some particular point. My reasons for this conclusion are as follows.

It is not disputed that the trial judge can offer opinions on matters of fact to the jury in the course of his or her address: *R. v. Boulet* (1976), 34 C.C.C. (2d) 397, 75 D.L.R. (3d) 223, [1978] 1 S.C.R. 332, and R.E. Salhany, *Canadian Criminal Procedure*, 5th ed. (1989), pp. 291-2. This raises a threshold issue: is an exhortation to a deadlocked jury to be viewed as a continuation of the charge or do different considerations apply?

In my view, an exhortation to a deadlocked jury is generically different from a charge to a jury. They are alike in that both are directed to assisting the jury in coming to a just verdict. But they differ in their more particular purpose. The purpose of an exhortation is to impress on the jury the need to listen to each other and consider each other's views in order to avoid disagreement based on fixed, inflexible perceptions of the evidence that one or other of them may have developed. The purpose of an exhortation is not to suggest to the jury that one view of the evidence may be preferable to another, or that this inference as opposed to that inference should be drawn from the evidence. To put it another way, the focus of the exhortation is the process of deliberation which is the genius of the jury system. An essential part of that process is listening to and considering the views of others. As a result of this process, individual views are modified, so that the verdict represents more than a mere vote; it represents the considered view of the jurors after having listened to and reflected upon each other's thoughts. It is on that process that the exhortation should focus. In this respect it differs from the charge, which is aimed primarily at offering guidance and assistance to the jury on the legal issues, and their relation to the facts over which the jury is the sole arbiter.

Not only is the purpose of the charge and the exhortation different; the time when each occurs gives a different dynamic to each. The charge comes before the jury begins its deliberations. It sets out the general parameters which the jury should have in mind in the deliberations to follow. Because such deliberations have not yet commenced, there is no danger of interfering with the course of the jury's deliberations. Things are quite different with an exhortation to a deadlocked jury. Discussions have been underway, usually for some time. Those discussions have produced different points of view. One may presume that those holding one point of view have sought to persuade those holding different views of the rightness of their point of view, and *vice versa*. The dynamic of deliberations requires that the jurors work their differences out among themselves. It is a delicate dynamic, which can be upset by interjection of a judicial opinion on a matter of fact. A trial judge's interjection is rendered more problematic by reason of the fact that his or her reasons are not divulged to the jurors, and thus are not subject to examination and challenge. In short, the judge's opinion becomes part of the deliberative process, but in a way which runs counter to the assumption of examination and discussion which underlies the jury verdict.

It is not surprising, in view of the different purpose and dynamic underlying the charge and the exhortation to a deadlocked jury, to find that courts which have considered the matter view an interjection of judicial opinion at the stage of the exhortation very seriously. The fact that no prior case like this one was referred to the court suggests that trial judges rarely if ever offer their opinions on the evidence to the jury in the course of an exhortation. Those judicial comments which are to be found on the proper bounds of an exhortation focus on whether the trial judge, coerces or interferes with the jury's right to deliberate in complete freedom, rather than whether the trial judge has improperly influenced the jury's view on a substantive matter one way or the other. Typically, an accused's fair trial interest has been found to have been prejudiced when the judge's remarks indicated to the jurors that they "should be" or "ought to be" unanimous or that minority members should conform to the opinion of the majority. Implicitly, however, the case-law underlines the great danger of comment to a jury on an exhortation as opposed to a charge.

In *R. v. Littlejohn and Tirabasso* (1978), 41 C.C.C. (2d) 161 at p. 168, Martin J.A., on behalf of the Ontario Court of Appeal, stated:

> It is well established that in exhorting a jury to endeavour to reach agreement, the trial Judge must avoid language which is coercive, and which constitutes an interference with the right of the jury to deliberate in complete freedom uninfluenced by extraneous pressures: see *R. v. McKenna* (1960), 44 Cr. App. R. 63. The trial Judge equally must avoid the use of language which is likely to convey to a juror that, despite his own doubts, genuinely entertained, he is, none the less, entitled to give way and agree with the majority of his colleagues in the interest of achieving unanimity: see *R. v. Davey* (1960), 45 Cr. App. R. 11.
>
> In deciding whether the line has been crossed between what is permissible as mere exhortation, and what is forbidden as coercive, the entire sequence of events leading up to the direction which is assailed, must be considered.

.....

I conclude that the dangers associated with a trial judge offering his or her opinion on issues of fact during an exhortation to a deadlocked jury are of such potential detriment to an accused's fair trial interest that judges as a general rule should refrain from offering such comments. An exception may arise in the case where the jury requests the judge's view or where it is apparent from the jury's questioning that the jury requires further clarification. Even then, the judge should be careful to offer the required opinion in a balanced and fair way which will not sway the process of decision-making in which the jury is involved to one side or the other.

(2) Application of the rule to this case

In exhorting the jury to reach a verdict, the trial judge offered his opinion that "if you accept the evidence of Sergeant Ross the Crown has a very powerful case". This constitutes a statement of opinion on the evidence, and a strong one.

It is argued that the statement is conditional ("if you accept the evidence..."), and does not direct the jury to accept or reject the evidence. But this argument misses the point. The danger of the statement lies not in the effect it might have on the jury's acceptance or rejection of the evidence, but in the inference it invites the jury to draw from the evidence. The record discloses no serious issues of credibility; Sergeant Ross in cross- examination agreed with the accused's version of the statements he had made to the police.

.....

In short, I am satisfied that the statement of opinion on the inference to be drawn from Sergeant Ross' evidence may well have affected the course of deliberations, and hence the verdict, to the prejudice of the accused.

This was all the more the case because the trial judge did not confine himself to neutral terms; the use of the phrase "very powerful case" had the potential of communicating to the jury that there was little doubt in the trial judge's mind what inference they should draw from the evidence. I agree with Lambert J.A. as to the appropriate standard in such a case and concur in his conclusion thereupon (at p. 410):

> The question is whether there is a possibility that what the trial judge said could have persuaded a juror to go along with the majority notwithstanding that he or she had not been persuaded that guilt had been proven beyond a reasonable doubt.
>
> I think that could have happened here.

[A new trial was ordered.]

There are doubts about whether expressions of opinion should be permitted even in the original charge to the jury. The following case addresses this issue and the presently permitted expression of judicial opinion.

R. v. LORENTZ-AFLALO

(1991), 69 C.C.C. (3d) 230 (Que. C.A.); leave to appeal to S.C.C. refused 71 C.C.C. (3d) vii

Proulx J.A. (translation): —

[Proulx J.A. reviews the case law concerning the extent to which a trial judge can express his or her opinions on the evidence to the jury. He concludes that a trial judge is entitled to express views as to the evidence, so long as the jurors are told that they are not bound by that opinion and so long as the judge's personal conviction as to the guilt of the accused is not expressed. He then considers not only the application of the case law to this case but the appropriateness of the case law.]

.....

1. It is unacceptable for a judge, in his charge to the jury, to express his personal conviction as to the guilt of the accused, even if he cautions the jury that they are not bound by his opinion.
2. A fundamental defect will result from this which will vitiate the process if, considering the whole of the charge, the opinions of the judge,

   (1) [*sic*] were formulated forcefully and thereby present a risk that the jury was influenced by these opinions, or
   (ii) were imposed on the jury or had a dominant effect in the context of the charge, or
   (iii) tilted the balance in favour of the prosecution and thereby discredited the theory of the defence.

B. Application in the present case

In the present case, I have come to the conclusion that the trial judge, in delivering to the jury his "thirteen findings of fact of which he was convinced", and whether or not one adds them into the opinions he expressed in his comments on the 25 elements of the addresses by counsel for the appellants, exceeded the limits and usurped the role of the jury.

.....

Epilogue: Is it appropriate to continue to tolerate that the judge give his opinion on the facts?

This is the question at the end of this study that I now ask myself. Is it useful or necessary for a jury to have the judge presiding over the trial inform them of his opinion as to the facts? As we previously saw, the courts consider it unacceptable that a judge give his opinion as to the guilt of the accused. In order to avoid this situation, would it be appropriate to simply abolish the rule which presently allows a judge to give his opinion on the facts?

Turgeon J.A. in *Post and Gelfand*, [Nos. 2557 and 2558, Feb. 24, 1972, Que. C.A.] posed, it seems to me, the problem in all its acuity when he said:

> When a judge has given his opinion as to the credibility of a witness and as to the credibility of an accused, the caution which he thereafter expresses to the effect that the jurors are not obliged to follow his opinion can never wipe out the effect that it has produced in their minds. *Why then give his opinion if the jury is not bound by what he said?*

(Emphasis added.)

Turgeon J.A. was there inspired by the reflections of O'Halloran J. in *R. v. Pavlukoff* (1953), 106 C.C.C. 249, 17 C.R. 215, 10 W.W.R. 26 (B.C.C.A.), where he wrote in this regard, at p. 266:

> With great deference and I hope with proper humility, in view of the eminence of some of the jurists who have given voice to *dicta* of apparently wide scope, I think it is appropriate to express a rationalized view that since the question of guilt is solely for the jury, a Judge under Canadian jurisprudence at least, who expresses his own opinions to a jury is doing nothing else than attempting to usurp the functions of the jury; the more so if strong and stubborn preconceptions are freely ventilated in the hearing of the jury prior to the conclusion of the defence case.
>
> If guilt is solely for the jury, and the Judge in law so instructs them, what occasion can there be for the Judge to express his own opinions as to factual matters of guilt.
>
> It seems an absurdity for a Judge after telling the jury the facts are for them and not for him, then to volunteer his opinions of facts followed then or later by another caution to the jury that his own opinion cannot govern them and ought not to influence them. If his opinion ought not to govern or influence the jury then why give his opinion to the jury.

At p. 267:

> There is every reason why the Judge should confine himself strictly to his own responsibilities and leave the members of the jury alone to carry out their responsibility. There may be a tendency among some Judges perhaps to feel constantly nervous whether a jury will bring in the verdict they may

> think the jury should bring in. But the law does not give the Judge such a superior position.

At p. 268:

> It is by no means to be assumed that a Judge's view of the facts is more sound than that of a jury with whose verdict the presiding Judge may disagree. A jury is not apt to reason in the abstract as if all men were alike, and attempt to force life into a plaster cast of law.

What could have been the historical reason for authorizing a judge to give his opinion on the facts? Was it that it was feared that a jury was so stupid and ignorant that it could not discern truth from untruth? This is what Rivard J.A. noted in a decision of our court where in conclusion to his observations on the comments of the judge in his charge, he wrote (*St-Pierre v. The Queen*, [1967] B.R. 695*n*):

> It is true that on several occasions in his summing up, the judge repeated to the jury that they were masters of the facts and they were entitled to have a different opinion than his own, but the whole of his charge meant the following to the jury: "You are entitled to not understand anything that I have told you, to act like complete imbeciles and to find the accused not guilty."

It has always appeared to me at the very least contradictory that on the one hand our system has confidence that a jury is capable of absorbing the most complex concepts of law in such a short time but that, on the other hand, it entertains doubts about it believing that a jury *alone* cannot decide what is a question of common sense (that is, the facts), by authorizing a judge to advance his own opinion.

Can one doubt for a single instant in our age, that a jury is not able to assess the credibility of witnesses and to decide on the facts the issue of a person's guilt or innocence?

The subject was recently discussed in England, where the author posed the following questions:

> ... whether criminal trial judges should comment on the facts at all when summing up to the jury. Is the practice consonant with the interests of justice in the adversarial process? Does it accord with the public's expectation of the proper confines of the judge's role? Indeed, should judges even recapitulate the facts? Do the benefits, if any, of so doing justify the time and expense involved?

(David Wolchover, "Should Judges Sum Up on the Facts", [1989] Crim. L.R. 780.)

It would be appropriate to also note that in the majority of American states, a judge is not permitted to give his opinion on the facts. (William W. Schwarzer, "Communicating with juries: problems and remedies", Cal. L. R. (1981), p. 731; Wolchover, *ibid*, p. 784ff.)

In a document prepared by the Law Reform Commission of Canada on "The jury in criminal law" (Law Reform Commission of Canada (L.R.C.), *The jury in criminal law* (1980)), reference was made to the contention that the jury is a better fact-finder than the judge (p. 6):

> Indeed, some commentators allege that the most compelling justification for retention of the jury is that it is a better fact-finder than the judge. For example, Lord du Parcq has asserted that "when questions of fact have to be

> decided, there is no tribunal equal to a jury". Lord Halsbury said: "As a rule, juries are in my opinion, more generally right than judges."
>
> .....
>
> Several characteristics of the jury account for its fact-finding ability. First, a jury brings to bear on its decision a diversity of experiences. The evaluation of practically every item of evidence involves making judgments about human behaviour: the likelihood that the witness could have perceived and remembered what he or she relates to the court, the likelihood that in the circumstances of the case the witness is being sincere, the possible motivations of the parties, their character, habits, and their responses to a wide range of circumstances. By and large, the trier of fact must make these judgments on the basis of his or her personal experiences. The collective experience of the jury, it can be argued, representing a spectrum of society, provides a much better basis for making these kinds of judgments than the experiences of a judge alone.
>
> Second because the jury deliberates as a group, it has the advantage of collective recall. Different items of evidence will have a different impact on each juror. What was insignificant and forgotten by one juror, will be significant to another, and will be remembered. Thus during the jury's deliberations it is likely that all relevant facts and their significance will be considered by the jury.
>
> Third, the jury's deliberative process contributes to better fact-finding because each detail is explored and subjected to conscious scrutiny by the group.

The constitutional right to a jury trial can only be given its true meaning if the verdict rendered is that of the 12 jurors and not that of the judge and jury. In the continental law system, such as in France, for example, the judge deliberates with the jurors and even has a vote; our system is based on a clear division of roles; the judge is the umpire but also the professor of law or legal counsel and the exclusive responsibility for assessing the evidence and determining liability by the final verdict is for the jury.

The reserve which is presently imposed on the judge to properly advise the jury that they are not bound by his opinion, has never appeared to me to be a sufficient guarantee. In this area, the issue is not whether the opinion of the judge influenced the jury, but rather whether, in the eyes of a reasonable person listening to the charge, it is probable that the jury was influenced.

.....

Conscience of the community, the citizen's ultimate protection against oppressive laws, role in legitimizing the criminal justice system (see report of the L.R.C., *ibid.*, pp. 8-16), these are the major attributes of the jury which remains in our society a pillar of our democratic life. I consider that it would be to render it its full value not to attempt to invade what is its exclusive jurisdiction, that is, to decide on the facts in evidence.

Ultimately, "[w]here the [trial] judge is satisfied that the jury is unable to agree on its verdict and that further [deliberations] would be useless, he [or she] may ... discharge that jury and direct a new jury to be empanelled" at that time, or may adjourn the trial (s. 653 of the *Criminal Code*). Sometimes, a hung jury causes the parties to revisit their respective positions. For example, the Crown may decide not to reproceed against the accused.

QUESTION

43. What should the trial judge do if the jury indicates that it has reached a verdict in relation to some accused on some counts but is unable to reach a verdict in relation to other accused on the same counts?

If the jury is able to reach a verdict, it is announced in open court. Some defence counsel routinely ask that the jury be polled when the verdict is adverse. The jury is not permitted to particularize the basis for its verdict. Where the accused has been found guilty, he or she may be remanded, with or without bail, to a date fixed for sentencing.

In Canada, jurors are prohibited from later revealing the content of their deliberations, subject to very limited exceptions (s. 649 of the *Criminal Code*).

QUESTION

44. Can the restriction from revealing deliberations continue to be justified in a free and democratic society and if so, on what basis?

S. SPECIAL PROCEDURAL ISSUES

1. ENTRAPMENT

R. v. MACK

(1988), 44 C.C.C. (3d) 513 (S.C.C.)

The judgment of the court was delivered by

Lamer J.: —

INTRODUCTION

The central issue in this appeal concerns the doctrine of entrapment. The parties, in essence, ask this court to outline its position on the conceptual basis for the application of the doctrine and the manner in which an entrapment claim should be dealt with by the courts.

.....

[Lamer J. extensively reviews the case law on entrapment and then summarizes.]

Summary

... As mentioned and explained earlier there is entrapment when,

(a) the authorities provide a person with an opportunity to commit an offence without acting on a reasonable suspicion that this person is already engaged in criminal activity or pursuant to a *bona fide* inquiry;
(b) although having such a reasonable suspicion or acting in the course of a *bona fide* inquiry, they go beyond providing an opportunity and induce the commission of an offence.

It is neither useful nor wise to state in the abstract what elements are necessary to prove an entrapment allegation. It is, however, essential that the factors relied on by a court relate to the underlying reasons for the recognition of the doctrine in the first place.

Since I am of the view that the doctrine of entrapment is not dependent upon culpability, the focus should not be on the effect of the police conduct on the accused's state of mind. Instead, it is my opinion that as far as possible an objective assessment of the conduct of the police and their agents is required.

.....

Procedural Issues

The resolution of the issues surrounding the manner in which an entrapment claim should be considered at trial is, in my view, entirely dependent upon the conceptual basis for the defence, outlined earlier. If I were of the opinion that there was a substantive or culpability-based defence of entrapment, I would readily come to the conclusion that the defence raised a question of fact, which should be decided by a jury when there is a sufficient evidentiary basis on which to raise the defence, and I would hold that the onus would rest on the Crown to disprove the existence of entrapment beyond a reasonable doubt. Having come to the opposite viewpoint on the rationale for recognizing the doctrine of entrapment, I am not persuaded that the adoption of rules which historically, and by virtue of the *Charter*, conform to most substantive defences is either necessary or correct. It seems to me, however, that this court must be clear on how an entrapment claim is to be handled, as a brief review of some lower court decisions suggests that there is, at present, and understandably so, a great deal of confusion on the matter.

A: Who decides: judge or jury?

Both the appellant and respondent agree that objective entrapment, involving police misconduct and not the accused's state of mind, is a question to be decided by the trial judge, and that the proper remedy is a stay of proceedings. I too am of this view. The question of unlawful involvement by the state in the instigation of criminal conduct is one of law, or mixed law and fact. ...

[What follows in the judgment is an extensive review of the case law and policy considerations relevant to that view.]

.....

Finally, I am of the view that before a judge considers whether a stay of proceedings lies because of entrapment, it must be absolutely clear that the Crown had discharged its burden of proving beyond a reasonable doubt that the accused had committed all the essential elements of the offence. If this is not clear and there is a jury, the guilt or innocence of the accused must be determined apart from evidence which is relevant only to the issue of entrapment. This protects the right of an accused to an acquittal where the circumstances so warrant. If the jury decides the accused has committed all of the elements of the crime, it is then open to the judge to stay the proceedings because of entrapment by refusing to register a conviction. It is not necessary nor advisable in this case to expand on the details of procedure. Because the guilt or innocence of the accused is not in issue at the time an entrapment claim is to be decided, the right of an accused to the benefit of a jury trial in s. 11(*f*) of the *Charter* is in no way infringed.

B: Who bears the burden of proof and on what standard?

[Another extensive review of the case law bearing upon this issue follows in the judgment.]

.....

I have come to the conclusion that it is not inconsistent with the requirement that the Crown prove the guilt of the accused beyond a reasonable doubt to place the onus on the accused to prove on a balance of probabilities that the conduct of the state is an abuse of process because of entrapment. I repeat: the guilt or innocence of the accused is not in issue. The accused has done nothing that entitles him or her to an acquittal; the Crown has engaged in conduct, however, that disentitles it to a conviction. ... It is obvious to me that requiring an accused to raise only a reasonable doubt is entirely inconsistent with a rule which permits a stay in only the "clearest of cases". More fundamentally, the claim of entrapment is a very serious allegation against the state. The state must be given substantial room to develop techniques which assist it in its fight against crime in society. It is only when the police and their agents engage in a conduct which offends basic values of the community that the doctrine of entrapment can apply. To place a lighter onus on the accused would have the result of unnecessarily hampering state action against crime. In my opinion, the best way to achieve a balance between the interests of the court as guardian of the administration of justice, and the interests of society in the prevention and detection of crime, is to require an accused to demonstrate by a preponderance of evidence that the prosecution is an abuse of process because of entrapment. I would also note that this is consistent with the rules governing s. 24(2) applications ...where the general issue is similar to that raised in entrapment cases: would the administration of justice be brought into disrepute?

.....

In conclusion, the onus lies on the accused to demonstrate that the police conduct has gone beyond permissible limits to the extent that allowing the prosecution or the entry of a conviction would amount to an abuse of the judicial process by the state. The question is one of mixed law and fact and should be resolved by the trial judge. A stay should be entered in the "clearest of cases" only.

R. v. MAXWELL

(1990), 61 C.C.C. (3d) 289 (Ont. C.A.)

The judgment of the court was delivered by

Brooke J.A.: — This is an appeal from conviction for trafficking in a narcotic (cocaine). The issue is whether the trial judge erred in dismissing the appellant's motion to stay the proceedings on the ground that the conduct of the police amounted to an abuse of process as entrapment. There is also an appeal from the sentence of 15 months to be followed by a period of probation.

The appeal from conviction arises in the following manner. On December 6, 1988, the appellant pleaded guilty to the offence. The Crown read an agreed statement of facts into the record. The trial judge found the appellant guilty and put the case over to January 6, 1989 for sentencing. He was told at the time the case was remanded that there would be a joint submission made by counsel that 18 months imprisonment would be a fit sentence. On December 15, 1988, the Supreme Court of Canada released its judgment in *R. v. Mack* (1988), 44 C.C.C. (3d) 513, [1988] 2 S.C.R. 903, 67 C.R. (3d) 1, in which the court set out the principles to be considered in cases where entrapment is raised as an issue. The case at bar was further adjourned from time to time and finally came on [*sic*] on June 6 and 7, 1989 when, having refused the Crown submission to proceed with sentencing, the trial judge heard the appellant's application for a stay of the proceedings, based on entrapment.

At the opening of this appeal, the court raised the question of whether or not, in the circumstances, the plea of guilty constituted an admission of all of the issues necessary to support a conviction, and a bar to raising the issue of entrapment.

.....

It was argued by the Crown before the trial judge that the *Mack* decision stood for the proposition that the defence of entrapment may be argued only where the accused has proceeded on a plea of not guilty. I think the learned trial judge was correct in rejecting this submission. It was the opinion of the trial judge that the appellant's position with respect to entrapment should be the same as if the matter had gone before a jury and the jury had returned a verdict of guilty, and that she should not at this point be precluded from calling the conduct of the police into question.

I agree with the trial judge. He had not finally disposed of the case by sentencing the appellant. In the circumstances, the plea of guilty while amounting to an admission of all of the issues necessary to support a conviction does not address the issue of entrapment which is quite distinct.

Nothing in the judgment in *Mack* suggests that the plea of guilty, which would resolve the first step of the two-step inquiry, could or would amount to a bar to the second step.

R. v. VIRGO

(1993), 67 O.A.C. 275 (C.A.)

[The judgment of the court was delivered by:]

Austin J.A.: — Virgo pleaded guilty to trafficking and possession, two out of five drug-related charges. Before he was sentenced, he moved for a stay alleging entrapment. The trial judge found that there was entrapment with respect to the trafficking charge but not with respect to the possession charge. Appeals are brought against both dispositions.

.....

The Crown argued a ground of appeal upon which it is desirable to make some comment. As indicated at the outset of these reasons, the hearing of this matter began with pleas of guilty. Accordingly, no testimony was presented by or on behalf of the prosecution. The matter was put over for sentencing and in the intervening period a motion was brought for a stay on the ground of entrapment. On the hearing of that motion, counsel for the defendant asked for the opportunity to cross-examine the prosecution witnesses. In the result, the trial judge permitted such cross-examination. Part of her ruling reads as follows:

> I am prepared to rule on the submission in the unique circumstances of this case where there was a guilty plea to two counts out of five and an adjournment for sentence and only just prior to the sentence date was the entrapment motion brought that the defence will be allowed to call and cross-examine the officer who would have been called in-chief by the Crown to prove the charges pleaded to. Although the accused has elected not to seek to strike the plea and have the trial proceed in the normal course, this does not preclude him from seeking to obtain a ruling as he has the right to proceed in the entrapment motion in this way.

It is common ground that the onus was on the defendant to establish entrapment. The position of the Crown is that before any motion to permit cross-examination was entertained, the defendant should have been required to establish to some degree that the proposed witness was either hostile or adverse.

The respondent relied upon *R. v. Maxwell* (1990), 61 C.C.C. (3d) 289 (Ont. C.A.), a case similar to the present one. The accused had pleaded guilty to trafficking in cocaine. The matter was put over for sentencing and in the interim the decision in *Mack* was handed down by the Supreme Court of Canada. Counsel for the accused then moved for a stay on the ground of entrapment. The evidence on the entrapment hearing consisted of the statement of facts read into the evidence on the plea of guilty and the testimony of Maxwell. The motion for a stay was dismissed. On the appeal, this court found that there was evidence which, if believed, would support a finding that the police had gone beyond providing an opportunity to commit the offence and had indeed induced the commission of the offence by Maxwell. The court had already noted that "unlike proceedings on a plea of not guilty, the appellant did not have the opportunity to cross-examine the police officers." In disposing of the matter, Brooke J.A. noted at p. 299e that "in the circumstances [of that case], while the onus or proof remained on the appellant, there was an evidentiary burden on the Crown." There is no suggestion in those reasons that Maxwell should have had an "automatic" right to cross-examine the police officers on the entrapment hearing. I see no reason why the normal rules respecting hostile and adverse witnesses should not apply to the entrapment proceedings.

The appeal by the Crown is allowed. The stay of proceedings with respect to count one, for trafficking, is set aside and the matter remitted to the trial judge for sentencing. The cross-appeal with respect to possession is dismissed.

2. No Criminal Responsibility Due to Mental Disorder

The accused has the option of whether to raise a s. 16 "defence" during the course of the trial or to await any adjudication of guilt. Further, the Crown cannot raise the accused's lack of criminal responsibility due to mental disorder over the accused's objection, *during the course of the trial*, but can do so after the trier of fact concludes that the accused is otherwise guilty of the offence. There is an exception where during the course of the trial, the defence's evidence raises an issue as to the accused's mental capacity to commit the offence. Under those circumstances, the Crown can lead evidence as to the accused's mental disorder: *R. v. Swain* (1991), 63 C.C.C. (3d) 481 (S.C.C.). Where a finding is made that the accused actually committed the act or made the omission that formed the basis of the offence charged, but was, at the time, suffering from mental disorder which exempted him or her from criminal responsibility by virtue of s. 16(1) of the *Criminal Code*, the verdict rendered by the judge or jury is that the accused committed the act or made the omission, but is not criminally responsible due to a mental disorder. There is no longer a verdict of not guilty by reason of insanity.

Part XX.1 of the *Criminal Code* addresses a number of procedural issues arising out of a claim of an accused's mental disorder: the effect of the above-noted verdict (672.35), the disposition hearings which follow such a verdict (672.45 *et seq.*); court ordered assessments (672.11 *et seq.*); and the determination of the accused's fitness to stand trial (672.22 *et seq.*).

Note that the meaning of "unfit to stand trial" is set out in s. 2 of the *Criminal Code*. Note also that Part XX.1, s. 672.1 defines an "accused" to include a defendant in summary conviction proceedings and a "court" to include a summary conviction court.

3. Alibi

R. v. CLEGHORN

(1995), 100 C.C.C. (3d) 393 (S.C.C.)

Iacobucci J. (Lamer C.J.C. and Gonthier J. concurring): — I have read the reasons of my colleague Justice Major and, with respect, I do not arrive at the same conclusion he does. In my view, the trial judge did not err in concluding that there was inadequate disclosure of an alibi. ...

.....

At issue in this appeal is whether the alibi defence raised by the accused at trial was properly disclosed to the Crown. As outlined by my colleague, proper disclosure of an alibi has two components: adequacy and timeliness. This principle was recently reiterated in *R. v. Letourneau* (1994), 87 C.C.C. (3d) 481 (B.C.C.A.), where Cumming J.A. wrote for a unanimous court at p. 532:

> It is settled law that disclosure of a defence of alibi should meet two requirements:
>
> (a) it should be given in sufficient time to permit the authorities to investigate: see *R. v. Mahoney* (1979), 50 C.C.C. (2d) 380 (Ont. C.A.) at p. 387; and *R. v. Dunbar and Logan* (1982), 68 C.C.C. (2d) 13 (Ont. C.A.) at pp. 62-3.
>
> (b) it should be given with sufficient particularity to enable the authorities to meaningfully investigate: see *R. v. Ford* (1993), 78 C.C.C. (3d) 481 at pp. 504-5 ... (B.C.C.A.).
>
> Failure to give notice of alibi does not vitiate the defence, although it may result in a lessening of the weight that the trier of fact will accord it ....

As stated above, the consequence of a failure to disclose properly an alibi is that the trier of fact may draw an adverse inference when weighing the alibi evidence heard at trial (*Russell v. The King* (1936), 67 C.C.C. 28 (S.C.C.), at p. 32). However, improper disclosure can only weaken alibi evidence; it cannot exclude the alibi. My colleague correctly notes that the rule governing disclosure of an alibi is a rule of expediency intended to guard against surprise alibis fabricated in the witness box which the prosecution is almost powerless to challenge. Again as noted by my colleague, the development of the rule since its formulation in *Russell* shows that the rule has been adapted to conform to *Charter* norms. As such, disclosure is proper when it allows the prosecution and police to investigate the alibi evidence before trial. The criteria of timeliness and adequacy are thus evaluated on the basis of whether a meaningful investigation could have been undertaken as a result of disclosure. The flexibility of the standard is demonstrated by the fact that neither disclosure at the earliest possible moment, nor disclosure by the accused him or herself is required in order for the criteria to be met. Third party disclosure is sufficient. Thus, the fact that Mrs. Foster allegedly made disclosure of the alibi instead of the accused is immaterial.

.....

Turning to the disclosure itself, I must immediately note that the timeliness of the disclosure is not at issue. Statements concerning potential alibis, made shortly after the arrest, are timely (*R. v. Hogan* (1982), 2 C.C.C. (3d) 557 (Ont. C.A.)). The main difficulty with Mrs. Foster's statement to the police is that it is unclear and confused. Was there sufficient detail and coherence in Mrs. Foster's statement to enable the police to undertake a meaningful investigation of the evidence supporting the alibi? With great respect for my colleague, I am of the view that the trial judge did not err in finding that the statement was so disjointed that he could not imagine how her statement could be considered as a disclosure of an alibi, let alone adequate disclosure of an alibi.

.....

[The dissenting reasons of Sopinka and Major JJ. were delivered by:]

Major J. (Sopinka J. concurring, dissenting): —

.....

Respect for the accused's right to silence in the investigation stage has mandated some changes to the rule on the disclosure of an alibi from its original formulation by this Court in *Russell v. The King*. As noted at the outset of this analysis, the appropriate requirement now is that the disclosure of the alibi is made sufficiently early to permit investigation by the police and not that it is made at the earliest possible moment nor that it is made in a particular way.

It is no longer permissible to draw a negative inference against alibi evidence on the grounds that the accused did not disclose that alibi immediately upon arrest, nor to draw an inference that an innocent person would have made such immediate disclosure.

.....

The disclosure of an alibi should be given with sufficient particularity to enable the authorities to meaningfully investigate: see *Ford*, [(1993), 78 C.C.C. (3d) 481 (B.C.C.A.)], at p. 505. In my opinion, three pieces of information are necessary for sufficient disclosure of an alibi defence: a statement that the accused was not present at location of the crime when it was committed, the whereabouts of the accused at that time and the names of any witnesses to the alibi: see *Mahoney, supra*, and also *R. v. Laverty* (1977), 35 C.C.C. (2d) 151 (Ont. C.A.). The appellant's mother gave the police all of this critical information: the appellant could not have been present at 2:30 p.m., the appellant was at home watching television with his mother at that time, and she was the witness. Therefore, in my opinion, the discussion which the appellant's mother had with the police officer constituted sufficient disclosure of an alibi defence under the circumstances.

.....

The more formal disclosure of an alibi defence either at the preliminary hearing or by a letter from defence counsel to the Crown as suggested in the lecture referred to by the trial judge is preferable where practicable. Nevertheless, each case must be evaluated on its own facts and in some cases a less formal manner of disclosure may suffice, particularly when appropriate consideration is given to the accused's right to silence. In this case, the charge was not sufficiently serious to warrant a preliminary hearing and the appellant was not represented by counsel at the bail hearing, which would have been another appropriate time for formal disclosure of the alibi defence.

[The dissent ultimately spun on a different assessment of the particular alibi disclosure in this case.]

T. REASONS FOR JUDGMENT

R. v. SHEPPARD

(2002), 162 C.C.C. (3d) 298 (S.C.C.)

The judgment of the court was delivered by

Binnie J.: — In this case, the Newfoundland Court of Appeal overturned the conviction of the respondent because the trial judge failed to deliver reasons in circumstances which "crie[d] out for some explanatory analysis". Put another way, the trial judge can be said to have erred in law in failing to provide an explanation of his decision that was sufficiently intelligible to permit appellate review. I agree with this conclusion and would therefore reject the Crown's appeal.

Twenty-four-year-old Colin Sheppard, an unemployed carpenter from Spaniard's Bay, Newfoundland and Labrador, was charged with possession of stolen property, being two casement windows with a value of $429. No stolen windows were ever found in his possession. The case against Mr. Sheppard rested entirely on an accusation by his estranged girlfriend who took her story to the police two days after the termination of their tempestuous relationship saying that "she would get him". He testified in his own defence. He was convicted by a provincial court judge after a summary trial and fined $1,000 and ordered to "repay" the cost of two windows to a local builder's supply yard. He still does not understand the basis of his conviction and neither do we. The sum total of the trial judge's reasons consists of the following statement:

Having considered all the testimony in this case, and reminding myself of the burden on the Crown and the credibility of witnesses, and how this is to be assessed, I find the defendant guilty as charged.

Defence counsel says that he was able to sum up his argument in two or three minutes (46 lines of transcript) and Crown counsel rather more succinctly (15 lines of transcript) and questions why less should be expected of a trial judge.

The appellant Crown contends that "[i]t has been a settled principle of Canadian law that a trial judge does *not* have to give reasons" (factum, at para. 13 (emphasis in original)). This proposition is so excessively broad as to be erroneous. It is true that there is no general duty, viewed in the abstract and divorced from the circumstances of the particular case, to provide reasons "when the finding is otherwise supportable on the evidence or where the basis of the finding is apparent from the circumstances" (*R. v. Barrett*, [1995] 1 S.C.R. 752 at p. 753, 96 C.C.C. (3d) 319). An appeal lies from the judgment, not the reasons for judgment. Nevertheless, reasons fulfill an important function in the trial process and, as will be seen, where that function goes unperformed, the judgment itself may be vulnerable to be reversed on appeal.

At the broadest level of accountability, the giving of reasoned judgments is central to the legitimacy of judicial institutions in the eyes of the public. Decisions on individual cases are neither submitted to nor blessed at the ballot box. The courts attract public support or criticism at least in part by the quality of their reasons. If unexpressed, the judged are prevented from judging the judges. The question before us is how this broad principle of governance translates into specific rules of appellate review.

.....

IV. ANALYSIS

Reasons for judgment are the primary mechanism by which judges account to the parties and to the public for the decisions they render. The courts frequently say that justice must not only be done but must be seen to be done, but critics respond that it is difficult to see how justice can be seen to be done if judges fail to articulate the reasons for their actions. Trial courts, where the essential findings of facts and drawing of inferences are done, can only be held properly to account if the reasons for their adjudication are transparent and accessible to the public and to the appellate courts.

.....

In Canadian administrative law, this Court held in *Baker v. Canada (Minister of Citizenship and Immigration)*, [1999] 2 S.C.R. 817, 174 D.L.R. (4th) 193, at para. 43, that:

> ... it is now appropriate to recognize that, in certain circumstances, the duty of procedural fairness will require the provision of a written explanation for a decision. The strong arguments demonstrating the advantages of written reasons suggest that, in cases such as this where the decision has important significance for the individual, when there is a statutory right of appeal, or in other circumstances, some form of reasons should be required.

There are, of course, significant differences between the criminal courts and administrative tribunals. Each adjudicative setting drives its own requirements. If the context is different, the rules may not necessarily be the same. These reasons are directed to the criminal justice context.

Even in the criminal law context, Parliament has intervened to require the giving of reasons in specific circumstances. Section 276.2(3) of the *Criminal Code* requires trial judges to give reasons for their determination of the admissibility of a complainant's prior sexual history. All the factors affecting the decision must be referred to as well as the manner in which the proposed evidence is considered to be relevant. In the same way, s. 278.8(1) states that trial judges shall provide reasons for ordering or refusing to order the production of certain records that contain personal private information. Section 726.2 provides that when imposing a sentence the court shall state the reasons for it. The only discernable purpose for these provisions is to facilitate appellate review of the correctness of the conviction or acquittal or sentence. It would be strange to impose a more rigorous standard of judicial articulation on an evidentiary ruling or sentence than on the conviction whose correctness is equally before the appellate court for review.

The task is not so much to extol the virtues of giving full reasons, which no one doubts, but to isolate those situations where deficiencies in the trial reasons will justify appellate intervention and either an acquittal or a new trial.

There is a general sense in which a duty to give reasons may be said to be owed to the public rather than to the parties to a specific proceeding. Through reasoned decisions, members of the general public become aware of rules of conduct applicable to their future activities. An awareness of the reasons for a rule often helps define its scope for those trying to comply with it. The development of the common law proceeds largely by reasoned analogy from established precedents to new situations. Few would argue, however, that failure to discharge this jurisprudential function necessarily gives rise to appellate intervention. New trials are ordered to address the potential need for correction of the outcome of a particular case. Poor reasons may coincide with a just result. Serious remedies such as a new trial require serious justification.

On a more specific level, within the confines of a particular case, it is widely recognized that having to give reasons itself concentrates the judicial mind on the difficulties that are presented (*R. v. G. (M.)* (1994), 93 C.C.C. (3d) 347 (Ont. C.A.) at p. 356; *R. v. N. (P.L.F.)* (1999), 138 C.C.C. (3d) 49 (Man. C.A.) at pp. 53-56 and 61-63; *R. v. Hache* (1999), 25 C.R. (5th) 127 at pp. 135-39, 136 C.C.C. (3d) 285 (N.S.C.A.); *R. v. Graves* (2000), 189 N.S.R. (2d) 281, 2000 NSCA 150, at paras. 19-23; *R. v. Gostick* (1999), 137 C.C.C. (3d) 53 (Ont. C.A.) at pp. 67-68). The absence of reasons, however, does not necessarily indicate an absence of such concentration. We are speaking here of the articulation of the reasons rather than of the reasoning process itself. The challenge for appellate courts is to ensure that the latter has occurred despite the absence, or inadequacy, of the former.

A) Functional Test

In my opinion, the requirement of reasons is tied to their purpose and the purpose varies with the context. At the trial level, the reasons justify and explain the result. The losing party knows why he or she has lost. Informed consideration can be given to grounds for appeal. Interested members of the public can satisfy themselves that justice has been done, or not, as the case may be.

The issue before us presupposes that the decision has been appealed. In that context the purpose, in my view, is to preserve and enhance meaningful appellate review of the correctness of the decision (which embraces both errors of law and palpable overriding errors of fact). If deficiencies in the reasons do not, in a particular case, foreclose meaningful appellate review, but allow for its full exercise, the deficiency will not justify intervention under s. 686 of the *Criminal Code*. That provision limits the power of the appellate court to intervene to situations where it is of the opinion that (i) the verdict is unreasonable, (ii) the judgment is vitiated by an error of law and it cannot be said that no substantial wrong or miscarriage of justice has occurred, or (iii) on any ground where there has been a miscarriage of justice.

The appellate court is not given the power to intervene simply because it thinks the trial court did a poor job of expressing itself.

Reasons for decision may be examined in other contexts for other purposes. The Canadian Judicial Council, for example, regularly reviews reasons for judgment in response to complaints. Its criteria will be apt for its purpose and will obviously differ from the criteria applicable in the appellate context: see, e.g., Canadian Judicial Council, Report to the Canadian Judicial Council of the Inquiry Committee [in the case of Donald Marshall Jr.] Established Pursuant to Subsection 63(1) of the *Judges Act* at the Request of the Attorney General of Nova Scotia (August 1990). My focus in this case, to reiterate, is appellate intervention in a criminal case.

It is neither necessary nor appropriate to limit circumstances in which an appellate court may consider itself unable to exercise appellate review in a meaningful way. The mandate of the appellate court is to determine the correctness of the trial decision, and a functional test requires that the trial judge's reasons be sufficient for that purpose. The appeal court itself is in the best position to make that determination. The threshold is clearly reached, as here, where the appeal court considers itself unable to determine whether the decision is vitiated by error. Relevant factors in this case are that (i) there are significant inconsistencies or conflicts in the evidence which are not addressed in the reasons for judgment, (ii) the confused and contradictory evidence relates to a key issue on the appeal, and (iii) the record does not otherwise explain the trial judge's decision in a satisfactory manner. Other cases, of course, will present different factors. The simple underlying rule is that if, in the opinion of the appeal court, the deficiencies in the reasons prevent meaningful appellate review of the correctness of the decision, then an error of law has been committed.

.....

If the trial judge provides some reasons, and therein demonstrates that he or she has failed to grasp an important point or has disregarded it, then as McLachlin J. (as she then was) pointed out in *R. v. Burns*, [1994] 1 S.C.R. 656, 89 C.C.C. (3d) 193, this may also lead "to the conclusion that the verdict was not one which the trier of fact could reasonably have reached" (p. 665).

The more problematic situation is where the trial judge renders a decision and gives either no reasons or, as in this case, "generic" reasons that could apply with equal facility to almost any criminal case. The complaint is not that the reasoning is defective but that it is unknown or unclear. In this respect, McLachlin J. stated as follows on behalf of the full Court in *Burns, supra*, at p. 664:

> Failure to indicate expressly that *all* relevant considerations have been taken into account in arriving at a verdict is not a basis for allowing an appeal under s. 686(1)(*a*). This accords with the *general* rule that a trial judge does not err *merely* because he or she does not give reasons for deciding one way or the other on problematic points [citations omitted]. The judge is not required to demonstrate that he or she knows the law and has considered *all*

> aspects of the evidence. Nor is the judge required to explain why he or she does not entertain a reasonable doubt as to the accused's guilt. Failure to do any of these things does not, in itself, permit a court of appeal to set aside the verdict.
>
> This rule makes good sense. To require trial judges charged with heavy caseloads of criminal cases to deal in their reasons with every aspect of *every* case would slow the system of justice immeasurably. Trial judges are presumed to know the law with which they work day in and day out. *If they state their conclusions in brief compass, and these conclusions are supported by the evidence, the verdict should not be overturned merely because they fail to discuss collateral aspects of the case.* [Emphasis added.]

The appellant relies on this statement as establishing a simple rule that trial judges are under no duty to give reasons, but it seems to me, on the contrary, that this Court did expect trial judges to state more than the result. McLachlin J. anticipated at least "their conclusions" on the main issues (though perhaps not "collateral" issues) at least "in brief compass". Further, as pointed out by O'Neill J.A. in the court below, the observations in *Burns* were substantially qualified by the use of the words "all", "general", "merely", "all aspects", "in itself", "every aspect", "in brief compass", and "collateral aspects". What was said in *Burns*, it seems to me, was that the effort to establish the absence or inadequacy of reasons as a freestanding ground of appeal should be rejected. A more contextual approach is required. The appellant must show not only that there is a deficiency in the reasons, but that this deficiency has occasioned prejudice to the exercise of his or her legal right to an appeal in a criminal case.

(i) Allegation of "Unreasonable Verdict" Cases

It is important to note that *Burns* was a case in which the accused alleged an unreasonable verdict under s. 686(1)(*a*)(i) of the *Criminal Code*. The door was not shut to consideration of the absence of reasons, in an appropriate case, as an error of law under s. 686(1)(*a*)(ii) or a miscarriage of justice under s. 686(1)(*a*)(iii). In an appeal founded on s. 686(1)(*a*)(i), the Court is engaged in a review of the facts: *R. v. S. (P.L.)*, [1991] 1 S.C.R. 909 at p. 915, 64 C.C.C. (3d) 193. The test for an "unreasonable verdict" is whether "the verdict is one that a properly instructed jury acting judicially, could reasonably have rendered": *Corbett v. The Queen*, [1975] 2 S.C.R. 275 at p. 282, 14 C.C.C. (2d) 385, 42 D.L.R. (3d) 142; *R. v. Yebes*, [1987] 2 S.C.R. 168 at p. 185, 36 C.C.C. (3d) 417, 43 D.L.R. (4th) 424; and *R. v. Biniaris*, [2000] 1 S.C.R. 381, 2000 SCC 15, 143 C.C.C. (3d) 1, 184 D.L.R. (4th) 193, at para. 36. The test is equally applicable to a judge sitting at trial without a jury: *Biniaris*, at para. 37. In such a case, while a "Court must re-examine and to some extent reweigh and consider the effect of the evidence" (*Yebes*, at p. 186), the verdict itself is the error complained of. The absence or inadequacy of reasons, while potentially supportive of a conclusion of unreasonable verdict, is not the mischief aimed at by the remedy.

Barrett, supra, confirmed the correctness of the view that the *dicta* in *Burns* was not intended as an appellate invitation to trial judges to insulate their decisions from judicial review by saying as little as possible about the reasons for their judgment. That case involved allegations of police brutality which led to a four-day *voir dire* to determine the admissibility of the statements made by the accused after his arrest. The accused had sustained physical injuries while in custody and there was no evidence of a fight with other inmates. The trial judge issued no reasons for admitting the statement other than letting it be known through his staff that his ruling was based on a finding of credibility. Arbour J.A., as she then was, ruled that:

> Reasons must be given for findings of facts made upon disputed and contradicted evidence, and upon which the outcome of the case is largely dependent. [*R. v. Barrett* (1993), 82 C.C.C. (3d) 266 (Ont. C.A.), at p. 287]

In brief oral reasons this Court reversed, stating at p. 753:

> While it is clearly preferable to give reasons and *although there may be some cases where reasons may be necessary*, by itself, the absence of reasons of a trial judge cannot be a ground for appellate review when the finding is otherwise supportable on the evidence or where the basis of the finding is apparent from the circumstances. [Emphasis added.]

This statement did not bless the absence of reasons. It said only that appellate review in such cases would not be available where the disputed finding is otherwise supportable on the evidence (*i.e.*, the verdict is not unreasonable), *or where the basis of the finding is apparent from the circumstances*. The Court concluded, on the facts of *Barrett*, that these conditions were met. On this basis it disagreed with the Ontario Court of Appeal.

It should be added that even where the allegation is unreasonable verdict, the absence of adequate reasons may, in some circumstances, contribute to appellate intervention. This is shown by *R. v. Burke*, [1996] 1 S.C.R. 474, 105 C.C.C. (3d) 205, which involved the conviction of a former Christian Brother at the Mount Cashel Orphanage in St. John's, Newfoundland and Labrador, on multiple counts of indecent assault and assault causing bodily harm. In respect of one count, the Crown relied on the evidence of the witness L., who identified the accused from a photograph, but was not asked to identify him during the trial. The Crown offered no explanation for this omission. Sopinka J. reviewed the weaknesses of the identification evidence and concluded at para. 53:

> The trial judge made no comment on the frailty of the identification evidence other than the general statement that she found L.'s evidence credible and accepted it. No reference is made to the fact that the appellant was not identified in court and that no explanation for failure to ask L. to do so was given. No reference is made to the erroneous identification made by T. using the photograph of the appellant. Given the unsatisfactory nature of L.'s evidence in general, this uncritical reliance on the unorthodox identification evidence renders the conviction unreasonable. Pursuant to s. 686(1)(a)(i), I would quash the conviction.

The absence of an explanation by the trial judge contributed to the Court's conclusion that "this is one of those rare instances where the trial court's assessments of credibility cannot be supported on any reasonable view of the evidence" (para. 7). Sopinka J. said that the power to overturn "unreasonable verdicts" was intended "as an additional and salutary safeguard against the conviction of the innocent" (para. 6). The omissions of the trial judge would not be permitted to preclude the making of that appellate determination. I fully agree with that proposition.

(ii) Allegation of "Error of Law" Cases

More recently, the Court has explored circumstances where, short of finding a verdict to be unreasonable, the trial judge's failure to articulate reasons in relation to a key issue in circumstances which require explanation could be characterized as an error of law, giving rise to a new trial (rather than, as is the case with an unreasonable verdict, an acquittal).

[Binnie J. reviews the cases which support the principle that a failure to give reasons, not involving an unreasonable verdict, may constitute an error of law.]

These cases make it clear, I think, that the duty to give reasons, where it exists, arises out of the circumstances of a particular case. Where it is plain from the record why an accused has been convicted or acquitted, and the absence or inadequacy of reasons provides no significant impediment to the exercise of the right of appeal, the appeal court will not on that account intervene. On the other hand, where the path taken by the trial judge through confused or conflicting evidence is not at all apparent, or there are difficult issues of law that need to be confronted but which the trial judge has circumnavigated without explanation, or where (as here) there are conflicting theories for why the trial judge might have decided as he or she did, at least some of which would clearly constitute reversible error, the appeal court may in some cases consider itself unable to give effect to the statutory right of appeal. In such a case, one or other of the parties may question the correctness of the result, but will wrongly have been deprived by the absence or inadequacy of reasons of the opportunity to have the trial verdict properly scrutinized on appeal. In such a case, even if the record discloses evidence that on one view could support a reasonable verdict, the deficiencies in the reasons may amount to an error of law and justify appellate intervention. It will be for the appeal court to determine whether, in a particular case, the deficiency in the reasons precludes it from properly carrying out its appellate function.

(iii) Miscarriage of Justice

I would certainly not foreclose the possibility that the absence or inadequacy of reasons could contribute to a miscarriage of justice within the meaning of s. 686(1)(*a*)(iii) of the *Criminal Code*. Inadequate trial reasons may cause or contribute to an appellate conclusion that the trial judge failed to appreciate important evidence, but the failure might not be based on a misapprehension of some legal principle, and the court therefore may hesitate to characterize it as an error of law: *R. v. Morin*, [1992] 3 S.C.R. 286 at p. 295, 76 C.C.C. (3d) 193. In such cases, resort may be had to s. 686(1)(*a*)(iii): *R. v. Khan*, 2001 SCC 86, at para. 17 [reported 160 C.C.C. (3d) 1, 207 D.L.R. (4th) 289]; *R. v. Fanjoy*, [1985] 2 S.C.R. 233, 21 C.C.C. (3d) 312, 21 D.L.R. (4th) 321; *R. v. Morrissey* (1995), 97 C.C.C. (3d) 193 (Ont. C.A.) at pp. 220-21; *R. v. G. (G.)* (1995), 97 C.C.C. (3d) 362 (Ont.

C.A.) at p. 380. The present case, in my view, is more properly dealt with as an error of law under s. 686(1)(*a*)(ii).

B) The Floodgate Argument

Lurking beneath the Crown's argument is perhaps the concern that already burdened trial judges will become overburdened, and appeal courts will be swamped with a wave of new cases based on allegations of non-existent or inadequate reasons. I do not think this is so.

Canada has the advantage of professional judges at all levels and for the most part they regard it as a mark of professionalism to give at least an adequate, and usually a more than adequate, explanation of their decisions.

It will be up to the appeal courts themselves to determine whether the deficiencies in the trial reasons, taken together with the trial record as a whole, preclude meaningful appellate review. If that is their conclusion, they should have the power to intervene. Section 686(1)(*a*)(ii), which may lead to a new trial, is a more proportionate response to such a situation than is an acquittal based on s. 686(1)(*a*)(i) ("unreasonable verdict") which addresses a situation where the verdict itself is the error. In the present case, the verdict itself was not necessarily an error, but the Court of Appeal felt unable to subject the correctness of the conviction to proper appellate scrutiny because of "boilerplate" reasons. This engaged its authority under s. 686(1)(*a*)(ii) of the *Criminal Code* ("error of law"). Given the high standards set by trial judges in this country, I would expect situations to be rare where the verdict is not unreasonable but the right of appeal is nevertheless frustrated by a poor or non-existent set of reasons.

Moreover, for those who fear overburdening already burdened trial judges, the presumption that judges know the law and deal properly with the facts presupposes that whatever time is required to adjudicate the issues has in fact been taken. While, as suggested above, the act of formulating reasons may further focus and concentrate the judge's mind, and demands an additional effort of self-expression, the requirement of reasons as such is directed only to having the trial judge articulate the thinking process that it is presumed has already occurred in a fashion sufficient to satisfy the demand of appellate review.

Where the factual basis of the decision is intelligible to the appellate court for purposes of reviewing its correctness, it would rarely if ever be open to an appellant to argue "intelligibility to the parties" as an independent ground for reversal. It will generally be sufficient for purposes of judicial accountability if the appellate court, having decided that it understands from the whole record (including the allegedly deficient reasons) the factual and legal basis for the trial decision, then communicates that understanding to the accused in its own reasons.

C) Proponents of a More Extensive Duty to Give Reasons

I have stressed the necessary connection in the appellate context between the failure to provide proper reasons and frustration of rights of appeal. Some judicial commentators have taken recent cases in this Court and elsewhere as authority for a more general duty to give reasons: see, *e.g.*, "Do Trial Judges Have a Duty to Give Reasons for Convicting?" (1999), 25

C.R. (5th) 150, by Justice Gerard Mitchell of the Prince Edward Island Court of Appeal, at p. 156; Judge Ian MacDonnell of the Ontario Provincial Court, "Reasons for Judgment and Fundamental Justice", in J. Cameron, ed., *The Charter's Impact on the Criminal Justice System* (1996), 151, at pp. 158-59; and R.J. Allen and G.T.G. Seniuk, "Two Puzzles of Juridical Proof" (1997), 76 Can. Bar Rev. 65, at pp. 69-80. See also: D. Stuart, *Charter Justice in Canadian Criminal Law* (3rd ed. 2001), at p. 187; and G. Cournoyer, Annotation to *R. v. Biniaris* (2000), 32 C.R. (5th) 1, at p. 6. To the extent these commentators are saying that giving reasons is part of the job of a professional judge and accountability for the exercise of judicial power demands no less, I agree with them. To the extent they go further and say that the inadequacy of reasons provides a free-standing right of appeal and in itself confers entitlement to appellate intervention, I part company. The requirement of reasons, in whatever context it is raised, should be given a functional and purposeful interpretation.

Other observers criticize the rationale for the present rules, including the presumption that "judges are presumed to know the law with which they work day in and day out" (*Burns, supra,* at p. 664). A review of some reported cases appears in D.M. Tanovich, "Testing the Presumption That Trial Judges Know the Law: The Case of *W.(D.)*" (2001), 43 C.R. (5th) 298. Such attacks, in my view, take insufficient account of the differences between presumptions of law (which this is) and presumptions of fact. The presumption here simply reflects the burden on the appellant to demonstrate errors in the trial decision or to show frustration of appellate review of the correctness of that decision. This is entirely consistent with the normal operation of the adversarial process on appeal. Nothing more is intended. The appellant is not required to "rebut" the presumption of general competence. A judge who knows the law may still make mistakes in a particular case.

D) A Proposed Approach

My reading of the cases suggests that the present state of the law on the duty of a trial judge to give reasons, viewed in the context of appellate intervention in a criminal case, can be summarized in the following propositions, which are intended to be helpful rather than exhaustive:

1. The delivery of reasoned decisions is inherent in the judge's role. It is part of his or her accountability for the discharge of the responsibilities of the office. In its most general sense, the obligation to provide reasons for a decision is owed to the public at large.
2. An accused person should not be left in doubt about why a conviction has been entered. Reasons for judgment may be important to clarify the basis for the conviction but, on the other hand, the basis may be clear from the record. The question is whether, in all the circumstances, the functional need to know has been met.
3. The lawyers for the parties may require reasons to assist them in considering and advising with respect to a potential appeal. On

the other hand, they may know all that is required to be known for that purpose on the basis of the rest of the record.

4. The statutory right of appeal, being directed to a conviction (or, in the case of the Crown, to a judgment or verdict of acquittal) rather than to the reasons for that result, not every failure or deficiency in the reasons provides a ground of appeal.
5. Reasons perform an important function in the appellate process. Where the functional needs are not satisfied, the appellate court may conclude that it is a case of unreasonable verdict, an error of law, or a miscarriage of justice within the scope of s. 686(1)(*a*) of the *Criminal Code*, depending on the circumstances of the case and the nature and importance of the trial decision being rendered.
6. Reasons acquire particular importance when a trial judge is called upon to address troublesome principles of unsettled law, or to resolve confused and contradictory evidence on a key issue, unless the basis of the trial judge's conclusion is apparent from the record, even without being articulated.
7. Regard will be had to the time constraints and general press of business in the criminal courts. The trial judge is not held to some abstract standard of perfection. It is neither expected nor required that the trial judge's reasons provide the equivalent of a jury instruction.
8. The trial judge's duty is satisfied by reasons which are sufficient to serve the purpose for which the duty is imposed, *i.e.*, a decision which, having regard to the particular circumstances of the case, is reasonably intelligible to the parties and provides the basis for meaningful appellate review of the correctness of the trial judge's decision.
9. While it is presumed that judges know the law with which they work day in and day out and deal competently with the issues of fact, the presumption is of limited relevance. Even learned judges can err in particular cases, and it is the correctness of the decision in a particular case that the parties are entitled to have reviewed by the appellate court.
10. Where the trial decision is deficient in explaining the result to the parties, but the appeal court considers itself able to do so, the appeal court's explanation in its own reasons is sufficient. There is no need in such a case for a new trial. The error of law, if it is so found, would be cured under the s. 686(1)(*b*)(iii) proviso.

E) Application of These Principles to the Facts

The majority judgments of the Newfoundland Court of Appeal found the trial decision unintelligible and therefore incapable of proper judicial scrutiny on appeal. I agree with this conclusion.

(i) Intelligibility to the Parties and Counsel

A distinction may be drawn for these purposes between a situation of no reasons and an allegation of inadequate reasons.

In the present case the trial judge stated his conclusion (guilt) essentially without reasons. In the companion appeal in *R. v. Braich*, 2002 SCC 27 ..., the trial judge gave 17 pages of oral reasons, but the accused individuals argued that the reasons overlooked important issues and should be considered inadequate. The two types of situation raise somewhat different problems.

In this case, the trial judge says he "reminded himself" of various things including the burden on the Crown and the credibility of witnesses, but we are no wiser as to how his reasoning proceeded from there. The respondent was convicted of possession of stolen goods. It was central to Ms. Noseworthy's evidence that the "stolen" windows were to be incorporated into the respondent's house, but there was no evidence that a search had been made of his premises. The allegedly stolen property was never found in his possession. The respondent flatly asserted his innocence.

The trial judge's reasons were so "generic" as to be no reasons at all. Speaking of the Crown's attempt to excuse the "boilerplate" reasons by the busy nature of Judge Barnable's courtroom, Green J.A. commented (at. pp. 269-70):

> Reasons also relate to the fairness of the trial process. Particularly in a difficult case where hard choices have to be made, they may provide a modicum of comfort, especially to the losing party, that the process operated fairly, in the sense that the judge properly considered the relevant issues, applied the appropriate principles and addressed the key points of evidence and argument submitted.
>
> .....
>
> It is cold comfort, I would suggest, to an accused seeking an explanation for being convicted in a case where there was a realistic chance of success, to be told he is not entitled to an explanation because judges are "too busy".

I agree, provided it is kept in mind that in the vast majority of criminal cases both the issues and the pathway taken by the trial judge to the result will likely be clear to all concerned. Accountability seeks basic fairness, not perfection, and does not justify an undue shift in focus from the correctness of the result to an esoteric dissection of the words used to express the reasoning process behind it.

Given the weaknesses of the Crown's evidence in this case, even the most basic notion of judicial accountability for the imposition of a criminal record would include accountability to the accused (respondent) as well as to an appellate court: *R. v. Gun Ying*, [1930] 3 D.L.R. 925, 53 C.C.C. 378 (Ont. S.C., App. Div.); *R. v. McCullough*, [1970] 1 C.C.C. 366 (Ont. C.A.).

The respondent's expressed bewilderment about the trial judge's pathway through the evidence to his decision is not contrived. The majority of the Newfoundland Court of Appeal shared the bewilderment, as do I.

The next question is whether this failure of clarity, transparency and accessibility to the legal reasoning prevented appellate review of the correctness of the decision.

(ii) Meaningful Appellate Review

The majority of the Newfoundland Court of Appeal found the absence of reasons prevented them from properly reviewing the correctness of the unknown pathway taken by the trial judge in reaching his conclusion, but which remained unexpressed.

Their problem, clearly, was their inability to assess whether the principles of *R. v. W. (D.)*, [1991] 1 S.C.R. 742 at p. 757, 63 C.C.C. (3d) 397, had been applied, namely, whether the trial judge had addressed his mind, as he was required to do, to the possibility that despite having rejected the evidence of the respondent, there might nevertheless, given the peculiar gaps in the Crown's evidence in this case, be a reasonable doubt as to the proof of guilt. The ultimate issue was not whether he believed Ms. Noseworthy or the respondent, or part or all of what they each had to say. The issue at the end of the trial was not credibility but reasonable doubt.

Where a party has a right of appeal, the law presupposes that the exercise of that right is to be meaningful. This obvious proposition is widely supported in the cases. In *R. v. Richardson* (1992), 74 C.C.C. (3d) 15 (Ont. C.A.), for example, the accused was convicted of two counts of sexual assault. On appeal, in an argument that to some extent anticipates the present case, the accused submitted that the trial judge had concentrated solely on the credibility of the complainant and ignored the totality of evidence, particularly the evidence of five other witnesses that corroborated his version of events. In allowing the appeal, Carthy J.A., with whom Finlayson J.A. concurred, stated at p. 23:

> There is no need that the reasons of a trial judge be as meticulous in attention to detail as a charge to a jury. In moving under pressure from case to case it is expected that oral judgments will contain much less than the complete line of reasoning leading to the result. Nevertheless, if an accused is to be afforded a right of appeal it must not be an illusory right. An appellant must be in a position to look to the record and point to what are arguably legal errors or palpable and overriding errors of fact. If nothing is said on issues that might otherwise have brought about an acquittal, then a reviewing court simply cannot make an assessment, and justice is not afforded to the appellant.

To the same effect, see *R. v. Dankyi* (1993), 86 C.C.C. (3d) 368 (Que. C.A.); *R. v. Anagnostopoulos* (1993), 20 C.R. (4th) 98 (Nfld. S.C., App. Div.); *R. v. Davis* (1995), 98 C.C.C. (3d) 98 (Alta. C.A.); and *Hache, supra*. In each of these cases, the lack of reasons prevented the reviewing court from effectively addressing important grounds of appeal.

V. CONCLUSION

Cameron J.A., in dissent, protested that "if Ms. Noseworthy's version of events is accepted by the trier of fact there is evidence upon which a trier of fact could reasonably convict" (para. 85). I agree that this case does not amount to an "unreasonable verdict" within the meaning of s. 686(1)(*a*)(i) of the *Criminal Code*. That conclusion, however, did not exhaust the powers of the Court of Appeal. In my opinion, the failure of the trial judge to deliver meaningful reasons for his decision in this case was an error of law within the meaning of s. 686(1)(*a*)(ii) of the *Criminal Code*. The Crown has not sought to save the conviction under the proviso in s. 686(1)(*b*)(iii), and rightly so.

VI. Disposition

The appeal is dismissed. Whether or not to hold a new trial is in the discretion of the Attorney General of Newfoundland and Labrador.

CHAPTER 9

SUMMARY CONVICTION PROCEEDINGS

A. OVERVIEW

Summary conviction proceedings are governed by Part XXVII of the *Criminal Code*, R.S.C. 1985, c. C-46. There are few differences between the conduct of a summary conviction trial before a provincial court judge and the conduct of an indictable trial (whether on an elective or absolute jurisdiction offence) before that same judge. Section 795 of the *Criminal Code* provides that "Parts XVI and XVIII with respect to compelling the appearance of an accused before a justice, and ... Parts XX and XX.1, in so far as they are not inconsistent with [Part XXVII], apply, with such modifications as the circumstances require, to [summary conviction proceedings]". So, for example, the Part XX rules of pleading, joinder and amendments (ss. 589 to 593 and 601), and pleas (ss. 606-610 and 613) apply. Section 794 of the *Criminal Code* does add that no exception, exemption, proviso, excuse or qualification prescribed by law need be set out or negatived in an information.

Failure by the defendant (ss. 800(2)-(3) and 803(2)) or by the prosecutor (ss. 799 and 803(4)) to appear are addressed. The former may result in an *ex parte* trial; the latter may result in dismissal of the charges.

QUESTIONS

1. Need the Crown prove that the defendant has absconded before proceeding to an *ex parte* summary conviction trial?

2. The defendant is charged with sexual assault. The Crown has elected to proceed summarily. The defendant attends on the day of trial with an agent, not a lawyer. Should the trial judge permit the trial to proceed with an agent? Consider, in this regard, *R. v. Romanowicz* (1999), 138 C.C.C. (3d) 225 (Ont. C.A.), and newly enacted section 802.1 of the *Criminal Code*.

There are six significant distinctions between summary conviction and indictable proceedings, and they are as follows:

- the range of sentencing options available (ss. 735(1)(*b*) and 787 of the *Criminal Code*) (see Chapter 11).
- limitation periods for summary conviction offences (s. 786(2) of the *Criminal Code*) (see Chapter 3). Other statutes may provide

for different limitation periods than as set out in the *Criminal Code*.
- the forum for appellate relief therefrom (see Chapter 13).
- the defendant can appear personally or by counsel or agent for a summary conviction proceeding, though the court may require the defendant to appear personally under certain circumstances. For example, where identity is in issue (*R. v. Fedoruk*, [1966] 3 C.C.C. 118 (Sask. C.A.)).
- costs may be awarded by a summary conviction court (s. 809 of the *Criminal Code*).
- the role of the private prosecutor.

B. THE ROLE OF THE PRIVATE PROSECUTOR

Consider s. 785 (defining "informant" and "prosecutor") and s. 802 of the *Criminal Code*. Also consider the differences between s. 507 of the *Criminal Code* (which contemplates the situation where a justice receives an information from a law enforcement official) and s. 507.1 (which contemplates the situation where a justice receives an information from a private party). Under s. 507, a justice will generally issue process compelling the attendance of the accused based upon the sworn allegation of a police officer that there are reasonable grounds to believe that the offences contained in the information have been committed. Witnesses are generally not required. However, under s. 507.1, a provincial court judge or designated justice may issue process compelling the attendance of the accused where a hearing has been held (known as a pre-enquete hearing) only where the allegations of the informant and the evidence of witnesses have been heard and considered. Counsel for the Attorney General must receive reasonable notice of the hearing and be given an opportunity to fully participate in it. Section 507.1 is designed to better screen out frivolous private complaints at an early stage.

QUESTIONS

3. Carey Granite, a television celebrity, charged by the police with assaulting I.M. Starstruck, a fan, comes to see his defence counsel. Granite claims that Starstruck actually assaulted him and he only responded in self-defence. The police do not believe him. Granite wants Starstruck countercharged. What should be taken into consideration in giving him advice? Assume that a countercharge is laid. How can the charge and countercharge be tried? As Crown counsel, what decisions must be made?

4. A private citizen attends before a justice of the peace and swears an information alleging that an accused committed a purely indictable offence which the police have been unwilling to proceed with. The justice issues process, compelling the accused to appear in court. What options are available to the Crown's office? Can the charge be prosecuted by the private citizen personally or through his counsel or agent?

C. PEACE BONDS

Section 810 of the *Criminal Code* also provides for a procedure to obtain an order requiring a person "to keep the peace and be of good behaviour", without a criminal prosecution. An information is laid before a justice by or on behalf of a person who fears, on reasonable grounds, that another person will cause personal injury to him or her, or to his or her spouse or child, or will damage his or her property. At a hearing before a justice or a summary conviction court, the justice or court may require a person to enter into a recognizance, with or without sureties, to keep the peace and to be of good behaviour for a period not exceeding twelve months, if satisfied that the informant has reasonable grounds for his or her fears. Section 810(3.1) to (4.1) provides for additional conditions which may be imposed. Section 810.1 of the *Criminal Code* provides for a similar procedure where there is a reasonable fear that a person will commit certain sexual offences involving persons under the age of 14. Section 810.1(3.1), proclaimed in 1997, enables the provincial court judge to imprison the defendant for 12 months, if he fails or refuses to enter into the recognizance ordered. Section 811 criminalizes a breach of a s. 83.3, 810, 810.01, 810.1 or 810.2 recognizance.

QUESTION

5. The accused is charged with common assault. The defence has persuaded the Crown that the charge should be withdrawn upon the defendant signing a peace bond. Must a s. 810 information be laid in order to implement this agreement?

CHAPTER 10

INCLUDED OFFENCES, PLEAS AND DOUBLE JEOPARDY

A. INCLUDED OFFENCES

Section 662 of the *Criminal Code*, R.S.C. 1985, c. C-46, outlines the general rules which govern included offences. Where an accused is charged with an offence which is not proven, he or she may be found guilty of any included offence or an attempt to commit any such included offence which is proven. This is so whether the included offence is an indictable offence or a summary conviction offence. In a jury trial, the judge is obligated to instruct the jury on any included offences that truly arise on the evidence.

There are three ways in which an offence becomes an included offence:

- **by the description in the enactment which creates the offence charged (s. 662(1));**
- **by the way in which the offence charged is described in the indictment or the information (s. 662(1)); and,**
- **by specific statutory enactment (s. 662(2) to (6)).**

R. v. LUCKETT

(1980), 50 C.C.C. (2d) 489 (S.C.C.)

The judgment of the court was delivered by

Chouinard J.: — Charged with robbery the appellant was found guilty of common assault. His conviction was upheld by a majority judgment of the Court of Appeal for British Columbia.

The question in issue is whether the offence of common assault is included in that of robbery as described in the enactment creating it in the *Criminal Code*.

"Included offences" are governed by s. 589 [now s. 662] of the *Code*, para. (1) of which reads as follows:

> 589 (1) A count in an indictment is divisible and where the commission of the offence charged, as described in the enactment creating it or as charged in the count, includes the commission of another offence, whether punishable by indictment or on summary conviction, the accused may he convicted

(*a*) of an offence so included that is proved, notwithstanding that the whole offence that is charged is not proved, or
(*b*) of an attempt to commit an offence so included.

As it appears, there are two circumstances under which an offence is included in another: it can be included in the offence "as described in the enactment creating it" or "as charged in the count".

We are concerned here only with the first of these circumstances. It is not in dispute that common assault is not included in the offence as charged in the count which reads:

> Indictment: William Eric Luckett stands charged:
>
> That, at the City of Vancouver, County of Vancouver, Province of British Columbia, on the 23rd day of July, 1977, he unlawfully did commit robbery of Walter Leibel, of a quantity of cigarettes and approximately $4.00 in cash contrary to the form of the statute in such case made and provided and against the peace of our Lady the Queen her Crown and dignity.

Robbery is defined by s. 302 [now s. 343] of the *Criminal Code* as follows:

> 302. Every one commits robbery who
>
> (*a*) steals, and for the purpose of extorting whatever is stolen or to prevent or overcome resistance to the stealing, uses violence or threats of violence to a person or property;
> (*b*) steals from any person and, as the time he steals or immediately before or immediately thereafter, wounds, beats, strikes or uses any personal violence to that person;
> (*c*) assaults any person with intent to steal from him; or
> (*d*) steals from any person while armed with an offensive weapon or imitation thereof.

It is the appellant's submission that to be considered as an included offence under s. 589(1) *Criminal Code*, the offence must be a necessary ingredient in the description of the offence charged. It is not a necessary ingredient in para. (*d*) of s. 302 *Criminal Code*, nor is it in para. (*a*) when the violence or threats of violence used are to property as opposed to a person. The appellant therefore concludes that common assault is not included when the charge is one of robbery without any specific reference to one or the other of the subsections of s. 302 *Criminal Code*.

.....

To hold however that the lesser offence must be included in every subsection of the section referred to would seem to me to impose a requirement beyond those of s. 589.

Robbery is one offence which can be committed in different ways and a reference to the relevant section is a reference to it in its entirety.

Section 302 was s. 288 of the *Criminal Code*, 1953-54 (Can.), c. 51, which replaced ss. 445 to 448 of the *Criminal Code*, 1927.

As put in A.E. Popple, *Crankshaw's Criminal Code of Canada*, 7th ed., (1959), at p. 431:

> ROBBERY. The law of robbery was revised in the new *Criminal Code* by combining together ss. 445, 446 and 448 into one comprehensive section 288 (*above*). It will be noted that s. 288 (above) contains four clauses (*a*), (*b*), (*c*)

> and (*d*). The offence of robbery is punishable under s. 289 which provides that "every one who commits robbery is guilty of an indictable offence and is liable to imprisonment for life and to be whipped." There is, therefore, one offence only "robbery" which may be committed in different ways. These ways of committing robbery are set out in s. 288 (*above*).

I would therefore conclude that the lesser offence must be included in the offence charged as described in the enactment, albeit not in all the subsections and that "it is sufficient if the other offence is included in the enactment creating it" as was held in this case by the Court of Appeal for British Columbia, following its own decision in *R. v. Brown* [(1959), 124 C.C.C. 127].

.....

The appellant further submitted:

> ... that the effect of the decision of the majority of the Court of Appeal in the present case will be to require an accused charged with robbery *simpliciter* to seek particulars from the Crown as to the particular method in which the offence is alleged to have been committed. It is submitted that the onus of describing the offence in particulars should rest with the Crown and not the accused.

This seems to me of little relevance if assault is included in a charge of robbery and as submitted by counsel for the respondent an accused charged with robbery will at the outset know that he is faced with a charge of robbery and a charge of assault as well as of theft.

To hold otherwise would in the respondent's submission cause the inclusion in the indictment of multiple counts of robbery and of the specific actions under one or more of the subsections of s. 302 of the *Criminal Code* as the case may be.

Furthermore, it was the respondent's submission that an accused acquitted of robbery would not be able to plead *autrefois acquit* ... and would be subject to further prosecution on one or more other charges. In this respect however it can be queried whether in the case of an offence punishable on summary conviction all this could be done within the limitation period of six months.

For these reasons I am of the opinion that the appeal should be dismissed.

QUESTION

1. **The accused is charged with the attempted murder of A. The indictment does not specify the means by which the offence was committed. Is assault causing bodily harm an included offence? Consider, in this regard, *R. v. Simpson* (1981), 20 C.R. (3d) 36 (Ont. C.A.).**

B. PLEAS AND DOUBLE JEOPARDY

1. Overview

Section 606(1) of the *Criminal Code* provides that an accused may plead guilty or not guilty, or may enter a special plea as allowed by Part XX of

the *Criminal Code*, and no others (s. 613 provides that any other available defences are subsumed under the general plea of not guilty). Section 606(1.1) provides that the court must conduct a plea comprehension inquiry before accepting an accused's plea.

Where an accused pleads not guilty of the offence he or she is charged with but guilty to any other offence which may arise out of the same transaction, whether or not it is an included offence, the court may, if the prosecution consents, accept that guilty plea, and find the accused not guilty of the offence charged but guilty of the offence to which the plea relates (s. 606(4) of the *Criminal Code*). Of course, the Crown must consent to such a plea, since it may be of the view that it can prove the offence charged and that a plea to an included or less serious offence is not appropriate. On a plea of guilt to a non-included offence, s. 606(4) obviates the necessity of laying a new charge. A most interesting issue arises where the trial judge does not agree with the disposition proposed, notwithstanding the Crown's consent.

R. v. NARAINDEEN

(1990), 80 C.R. (3d) 66 (Ont. C.A.)

[The accused was charged with assault with a weapon. Unrepresented at trial, he pleaded not guilty to the offence as charged but guilty to the charge of simple assault. The Crown accepted the plea and read in the facts. The trial judge stated that the facts, as read in, demonstrated the greater offence, and struck the plea. The trial judge offered to allow the accused to be tried by another judge, in light of what he had already heard, but the accused was content to proceed before that judge, who ultimately convicted the accused.]

The judgment of the court was delivered by

Morden A.C.J.O.: —

.....

The applicable statutory provision is s. 606(4) of the *Criminal Code*, and this ground of appeal turns on how it should be applied to the facts of this case.

.....

Mr. Duncan submitted that the discretion conferred by the provision relates solely to the trial judge's discretion to accept the plea of guilty Ð after satisfying himself or herself only that the admitted facts support the plea. The discretion does not extend to the consideration of whether the facts support a conviction of the offence charged. He submitted that the terms of the provision relating to "find[ing] the accused or defendant not guilty of the offence charged" do not mandate a determination by the judge of the merits of the prosecutor's decision, but rather recognize the necessity of making some final disposition of every charge before the court.

.....

... I accept that the prosecutor has primary responsibility for the enforcement of the criminal law: see *Skogman v. R.*, [1984] 2 S.C.R. 93, 41 C.R. (3d) 1, [1984] 5 W.W.R. 52, 9 Admin. L.R. 153, 13 C.C.C. (3d) 161 at 173-74, 11 D.L.R. (4th) 161, 54 N.R. 33 [B.C.]. This responsibility carries with it the power to decide whether or not to charge an accused and what charge or charges to lay. It includes the power to withdraw charges before the commencement of the trial. However, once the prosecutor has seen fit to bring the proceeding before a court, the accused has pleaded, and what is sought involves something more than merely not proceeding with a charge, but rather the acquittal of the accused on the charge that brought him or her before the court, the court has a legitimate role to play in the decision made.

The court is not gratuitously interfering with a prosecutorial decision. The prosecutor has ample and unfettered scope, short of asking the court to acquit on the charge before the court, to enforce the criminal law as he or she sees fit and to decide what charges will be prosecuted.

I appreciate that practical considerations relating to the work of a busy prosecutor, and possibly limitation period considerations, support the appellant's position, but they do not persuade me to adopt a different view of the nature of the court's power.

.....

For the foregoing reasons, I do not think that the trial judge erred, on the facts of this case, in following the course that he did. However, I think it should be said that trial judges in most cases do, and should, give great weight to the decision of counsel for the prosecution, as a representative of the public interest with heavy responsibilities, to accept a plea of guilty to an included or lesser offence. Although it is not necessary to decide the point, I would not wish to be taken as holding that a trial judge would be wrong in accepting a plea to an included or lesser offence even though the facts might indicate that the full offence was committed, where a case is made out that the result reflects a reasonable exercise of prosecutorial discretion having regard to the public interest in the effective administration of justice. That is, I recognize that s. 606(4) confers a discretion and I would not necessarily restrict the scope of the provision to that indicated by the purpose underlying its original enactment. I note that in the present case the trial judge was given no reason at all why the proposed course of action was reasonable or justifiable.

[The appeal was dismissed.]

QUESTION

2. **Your client is charged with first degree murder. He is alleged to have disposed of the deceased's body after the fact. However, the body has not been recovered. The Crown and the defence agree that he will be permitted to plead to manslaughter, if he provides a full statement to the police acknowledging responsibility and disclosing the location of the deceased's body. Based upon that agreement, the accused provides the**

statement as requested. When the matter is addressed before the trial judge, he indicates that he disapproves of the resolution, as the facts disclose first degree murder. Accordingly, he refuses to accept the plea. The Crown then indicates that it intends to proceed to trial on first degree murder. How might the defence have ensured that the trial judge was compelled, in law, to allow the plea as agreed upon?

---

2. Special Pleas

The only special pleas provided for are *autrefois acquit, autrefois convict,* pardon and, for the offence of defamatory libel, justification (s. 607(1) and (2) of the *Criminal Code*). For indictable offences, the accused enters the pleas of *autrefois acquit, autrefois convict* and pardon at the outset of the trial, and the pleas are disposed of by a judge without a jury (see *R. v. Riddle* (1979), 48 C.C.C. (2d) 365 (S.C.C.), substantially reproduced at p. 636, respecting the availability of *autrefois acquit* in summary conviction proceedings). If unsuccessful, the accused may then plead guilty or not guilty (s. 607(3) and (4)). In essence, *autrefois acquit* and *autrefois convict* apply where the accused has already been acquitted, convicted or found guilty, and discharged (under s. 730(1) of the *Criminal Code*) of the offence charged in the count to which the plea relates (s. 607(5)). Section 607(6) provides an exception. Section 609 of the *Criminal Code* generally outlines when there is a sufficient identity between the past and present charges to sustain these special pleas. Section 610 also bars a subsequent indictment charging substantially the same offence as that of which the accused was previously convicted or acquitted, but adding a statement of intention or circumstances of aggravation tending, if proven, to increase punishment. For example, where an accused is acquitted of sexual assault, the accused cannot be later indicted for aggravated sexual assault arising out of the same conduct. Section 610(2) to (4) outlines special rules for homicides. For example, a conviction or acquittal for manslaughter bars a subsequent indictment for murder for the same homicide (see also s. 11(*h*) of the *Charter*).

Chapter 3 reflected that there are conflicting decisions as to whether the withdrawal of an information on which the Crown elected summarily and the relaying of an information to proceed by indictment to avoid a limitation period constitutes an abuse of process. The following case considered whether *autrefois acquit* applies.

R. v. KARPINSKI

(1957), 117 C.C.C. 241 (S.C.C.)

[The defendant was charged with a hybrid offence. At trial, the Crown elected summarily and the accused pleaded not guilty. The defendant then moved for dismissal as the charge was out of time. The Crown was permitted to withdraw the information, over the defendant's objection, and a new information was laid, which the Crown elected to proceed with by way of indictment. The defendant was convicted.]

Kerwin C.J.C.: — The Crown had the right to change its election before the magistrate and also the right to withdraw the information. Assuming that the respondent raised the plea of *autrefois acquit* before His Honour Judge Forsyth, there had certainly not been a formal acquittal by the magistrate on January 24, 1956, and in my opinion what occurred at that time did not amount to an acquittal. The first trial must have been concluded by an adjudication, or what amounts thereto: *Regina v. Charlesworth* [(1861), 1 B. & S. 460, 121 E.R. 786.]; *Re Rex v. Ecker*; *Re Rex v. Fry* [64 O.L.R. 1, 51 C.C.C. 409, [1929] 3 D.L.R. 760.]. It has been held that where a trial had commenced and the jury had been discharged and a new one empanelled, the plea could not avail even if the discharge of the first jury had been improper or if a Court of Error or Appeal considered that under the circumstances the first jury should not have been discharged: *Regina v. Charlesworth, supra*; *Winsor v. The Queen* [(1866), L.R. 1 Q.B. 289, 390.]; *Rex v. Lewis* [(1909), 2 Cr. App. R. 180.].

The appeal should be allowed, the conviction restored and the case remitted to the Court of Appeal so that the respondent's application for leave to appeal from the sentence may be dealt with.

Taschereau J.: — I am of the opinion that the withdrawal by the Crown of the first information did not amount to an acquittal, giving rise to the plea of *autrefois acquit*, and that the Crown could consequently proceed by indictment as it did. The respondent was not in jeopardy.

I would allow the appeal and restore the conviction, and remit the case to the Court of Appeal so that the respondent's application for leave to appeal from the sentence may be dealt with.

[The judgment of Fauteux and Abbott JJ. was delivered by:]

Fauteux J.: — The circumstances giving rise to this appeal are fully stated in the reasons for judgment of my brother Cartwright and need not be related here to a similar extent.

.....

The submission of respondent, rejected by the trial judge but accepted in the Court of Appeal, is that, the Crown having no right to change its election and withdraw the information after the plea of not guilty, such withdrawal was therefore tantamount to a dismissal giving rise to a plea of *autrefois acquit*.

In my respectful view, it is unnecessary to deal with the merits of the conclusion of this proposition, for the premises upon which it rests are not established. In the circumstances of this case, there were no right for the Crown to elect to proceed by way of summary conviction and no jurisdiction for the magistrate to accept and act upon the election by receiving a plea. On the face of the information itself, it was manifest that more than six months had elapsed from the date when the subject matter of the proceedings had arisen; and of its nature the offence charged was not capable of being one having a continuing character. Non-compliance with the statutory requirement of s. 693(2) [now, see s. 786(2)] was fatal to the validity of the election and plea, both of which were void.

[Cartwright J. dissented.]

R. v. RIDDLE

(1979), 48 C.C.C. (2d) 365 (S.C.C.)

The judgment of the Court was delivered by

Dickson J.: — Two questions of considerable practical importance emerge in this appeal: Can an accused raise the special plea of *autrefois acquit* in a summary conviction court? If so, is the plea available when in the earlier proceeding the charge is dismissed following non-appearance of the informant and refusal of an adjournment? Judicial authority and textbook opinion have been divided on both issues. Thus far, the respondent Riddle has succeeded in three Courts in Alberta.

.....

The plea of autrefois acquit at common law

One of the fundamental rules of the criminal law is expressed in the maxim, *nemo debet bis vexari pro una et eadem causa*, no person shall be placed in jeopardy twice for the same matter. By the special plea of *autrefois acquit*, founded upon that maxim, the accused says simply that he has been previously acquitted of the offence with which he is now charged; that offence is *res judicata. i.e.* it has passed into a matter adjudged. A second prosecution is, therefore, not open. In the case at bar, the respondent says that the assault alleged in the first information has become converted into *res judicata* or judgment.

The classic statement of the principle is found in Hawkins' *Pleas of the Crown* (1726), Bk. II, c. 35, p. 368:

> That a Man shall not be brought into Danger of his Life for one and the same Offence more than once. From whence it is generally taken, by all the Books, as an undoubted Consequence, that where a Man is once found *Not Guilty* on an Indictment or Appeal free from Error, and well commenced before any Court which hath Jurisdiction of the Cause, he may by the Common Law in all Cases whatsoever plead such Acquittal in Bar of any subsequent Indictment or Appeal for the same Crime.

[Emphasis added.] In short, when a criminal charge has been once adjudicated by a court having jurisdiction, the adjudication is final and will be an answer to a later information founded on the same ground of complaint.

.....

With respect, it would seem that those finding *autrefois acquit* not available in summary conviction cases at common law give to that term its narrow and specialized meaning. Professor Friedland in his book, *Double Jeopardy* (1969), describes the special pleas at pp. 113-4, noting the need for a formal record of the former judgment, carefully engrossed on parchment. Supported by the older case of *Weymss v. Hopkins* (1875), 10 L.R. Q.B. 378, and the more recent case of *Flatman v. Light,* [1946] 1 K.B. 414 (C.C.A.), Friedland continues:

> The special pleas are not strictly appropriate for cases tried by courts of summary jurisdiction, but the same result is reached by giving effect to the maxim *Nemo debet bis vexari pro una et eadem causa*.

A technical approach was rejected by Lord Goddard in *Flatman* and such a narrow approach was dismissed by Blackburn J. in *Weymss* in these words (p. 381):

> I think the fact that the jurisdiction of the justices is created by statute makes no difference. Where the conviction is by a Court of competent jurisdiction, it matters not whether the conviction is by a summary proceeding before justices or by trial before a jury.

Further down the same page, Blackburn J. makes reference to the availability of a certificate "freeing [a person] from further proceedings, civil or criminal, for the same cause", which goes further than the common law, but states explicitly that "in this case we must rely upon the common law", and this is in relation to a summary conviction matter.

.....

... In *Tremeear's Annotated Criminal Code*, 6th ed. (1964), p. 1531, the author, on the authority of *Weymss v. Hopkins*, states:

> The general rule is that where a person has been convicted and punished for an offence by a court of competent jurisdiction, *transit in rem judicatam*, *i.e.* the conviction is a bar to all further proceedings for the same offence, and he must not be punished again for the same matter. This applies not only to indictable offences, but also to courts whose jurisdiction is entirely statutory: *Weymss v. Hopkins* (1875), L.R. 10 Q.B. 378 (C.A.).

and at p. 1532:

> It is doubtful if the plea of *autrefois* is applicable to proceedings before justices, because of the special rules as to raising such a plea. It is probably more correct to say that what a court of summary jurisdiction must do is to give effect to the maxim *nemo debet bis vexari pro una et eadem causa*: *Flatman v. Light*, [1946] K.B. 414, *per* Lord Goddard, C.J.; *cf. In re Deserted Wives' Maintenance Act*; In *re Wilson*, [1948] 1 W.W.R. 680 (B.C.); *Burns v. Gan* (1955), 112 C.C.C. 395 (Ont.).

Crankshaw's Criminal Code of Canada (7th ed., 1959) p. 748, is to the same effect.

The formal status of the plea of *autrefois acquit* and the pleading and procedural technicalities of an earlier day should not stand in the way of an accused raising as a defence the fact that he has been previously acquitted of the offence with which he now stands charged. The proper procedure in summary conviction matters is not to raise the special plea of *autrefois acquit*, but simply to enter a general plea of not guilty embracing the concept of *res judicata*. Technically, such a general plea is not one of *autrefois acquit* but, as Lord Goddard was moved to say in *Flatman v. Light*, *supra*, at p. 419, "... that does not matter". The court gives effect to the broad maxim, *nemo debet bis vexari pro una et eadem causa*. The charge has been dismissed by a court of competent jurisdiction and the accused shall not be charged again with the same matter.

.....

[Dickson J. then addressed the submission that the special pleas were inapplicable to summary conviction offences since they were only specified for indictable offences. This submission can no longer be made. See s. 795 of the *Criminal Code*. Dickson J. then rejects the further submission that the defendant is precluded from relying upon *autrefois acquit* because he failed to obtain a certificate of dismissal in accordance with s. 743 [now s. 808] of the *Criminal Code*.]

.....

On the Merits

In some circumstances, it may be difficult to say whether the defendant has, indeed, been "*bis vexatus*"; for example, where an information has been withdrawn or dismissed on technical grounds, or, the Crown contends, as in the case at bar, where there was no disposition "on the merits". It will be recalled that the second question upon which leave to appeal was granted raises the issue of whether the information was dealt with "on the merits".

I am not at all certain of what is meant by the term "on the merits", or indeed whether the terminology of "on the merits" furthers in any way our understanding of the effect of the dismissal of an information.

.....

The term "on the merits" does nothing to further the test for the application of the *bis vexari maxim*. There is no basis, in the *Code* or in the common law, for any super-added requirement that there must be a trial "on the merits". That phrase merely serves to emphasize the general requirement that the previous dismissal must have been made by a court of competent jurisdiction, whose proceedings were free from jurisdictional error and which rendered judgment on the charge.

Speaking generally, it is not readily apparent why the Crown should have the right to decline to adduce evidence in support of its charge and then assert the irrelevance of a dismissal consequent thereon, or why the Crown should be enabled to avoid the effect of refusal of an adjournment by declining to lead evidence and laying a fresh information following dismissal of the first charge. It is the intent of the *Code* that summary conviction matters be disposed of with despatch. No good purpose is served by introducing unwarranted complexities into what are, or should be, simple and straight-forward and expeditious procedures.

In the result, I would dismiss the appeal.

QUESTION

3. Can a person be convicted or punished under different federal statutes, where her conduct constitutes an offence under two different federal statutes? Consider, in this regard, s. 12 of the *Charter*.

C. RES JUDICATA

***Autrefois acquit* and *autrefois convict* represent two facets of what may broadly be described as the principle of double jeopardy. A third facet may be described as *res judicata,* the rule against multiple convictions or commonly, as the *Kienapple principle*, named after the Supreme Court of Canada's decision that addressed this facet (see *Kienapple v. The Queen* (1974), 15 C.C.C. (2d) 524 (S.C.C.)). It should be noted that *res judicata* is sometimes also used interchangeably with *autrefois acquit* or *autrefois convict*, or with the doctrine of *issue estoppel,* addressed below.**

R. v. PRINCE

(1986), 30 C.C.C. (3d) 35 (S.C.C.)

[The accused stabbed B.D., who was six months pregnant, in the abdomen. She was charged with attempted murder. Several days later, B.D. gave birth to a child who died within minutes, allegedly due to the stabbing. The accused was acquitted of attempted murder but convicted of the included offence of causing bodily harm. She was then charged with the manslaughter of the child. The Supreme Court revisited the proper scope of the *Kienapple* principle.]

The judgment of the court was delivered by

Dickson C.J.C.: — This appeal raises once again the scope of the principle enunciated in *Kienapple v. The Queen* (1974), 15 C.C.C. (2d) 524, 44 D.L.R. (3d) 351, [1975] 1 S.C.R. 729. A single act of the respondent, Sandra Prince, caused injury to one person and is alleged to have caused the death of another. Prince has been convicted of causing bodily harm in respect of the injured victim. The question is whether she may also be tried for manslaughter in respect of the deceased victim.

.....

III

The Kienapple Case

Since this court's decision in *Kienapple v. R., supra,* there has been considerable controversy about the nature and scope of the principle of res judicata articulated for the majority by Laskin J., as he then was [citations omitted].

.....

The variance of views within the judiciary and in the learned journals suggests that the time may well be ripe for a review of the jurisprudence in this area. The appropriate point of departure is, of course, the judgment of the majority in *Kienapple v. The Queen*, in which an accused was indicted on two counts in respect of a single act of non-consensual sexual intercourse with a13-year-old girl who was not his wife. The defendant, Kienapple, was charged with rape contrary to s. 143 and unlawful carnal knowledge of a female under 14 years of age contrary to s. 146(1) of the *Criminal Code*. At p. 744, Laskin J. said:

> It is plain, of course, that Parliament has defined two offences in ss. 143 and 146(1), but *there is an overlap in the sense that one embraces the other* when the the sexual intercourse has been with a girl under age fourteen without her consent. It is my view that in such a case, if the accused has been charged, first with rape and, secondly, with a s. 146(1) offence, and there is a verdict of guilty of rape, the second charge falls as an alternative charge and the jury should be so directed. Correlatively, however, the jury should also be directed that if they find the accused not guilty of rape they may still find him guilty under s. 146(1) where sexual intercourse with a girl under age fourteen has been proved.

(Emphasis added.)

In describing the rationale underlying his conclusion, Laskin J. referred to a principle that there ought not to be multiple convictions for the same "delict", "matter" or "cause". At pp. 538-9 C.C.C., p. 366 D.L.R., p. 750 S.C.R., he explained: "The relevant inquiry so far as *res judicata* is concerned is whether *the same cause or matter* (rather than the same offence) is comprehended by two or more offences." (Emphasis added.) And at p. 539 C.C.C., p. 367 D.L.R., p. 751 S.C.R.: "If there is a verdict of guilty on the first count and *the same or substantially the same elements* make up the offence charged in a second count, the situation invites application of a rule against multiple convictions ..." (Emphasis added.) The majority judgment at p. 540 C.C.C., p. 368 D.L.R., p. 753 S.C.R., however, recognized that Parliament could create two separate offences out of the same matter and could mandate multiple convictions if it made clear its intentions in this regard.

After considering the legislative history of the two offences in the *Kienapple* case, Laskin J. stated at p. 541 C.C.C., p. 368 D.L.R., pp. 753-4 S.C.R.:

> If any conclusion can be drawn from this short history, it is that carnal knowledge of a victim under age ten, and later under age fourteen, with its lesser punishment after 1877 (and until that for rape was changed), was regarded as *an alternative charge* to rape, unnecessary where there was no consent (since age was not and is not a necessary averment in rape) but available where proof of want of consent could not be made or was doubtful.

(Emphasis added.)

Professor Dennis R. Klinck in the following passage at p. 286 of his article "'*The Same Cause or Matter': The Legacy of Kienapple*" [26 C.L.Q. 280 (1983-84)] has in my view correctly identified the manner in which the two charges in "*Kienapple*" were "alternative" to each other: "Sexual intercourse with a female under 14 could be regarded as a kind of 'constructive rape'; it might be said that the statute deems a girl under 14 to be incapable of consenting." It is only in this fashion that it can properly be said that "the same or substantially the same elements" made up the offences of rape and carnal knowledge of a female under 14 years of age.

.....

IV

The scope of the Kienapple principle

(i) The factual nexus between the charges

It is elementary that *Kienapple* does not prohibit a multiplicity of convictions, each in respect of a different factual incident. Offenders have always been exposed to criminal liability for each occasion on which they have transgressed the law, and *Kienapple* does not purport to alter this perfectly sound principle. It is therefore a *sine qua non* for the operation of the rule against multiple convictions that the offences arise from the same transaction.

.....

In most cases, I believe, the factual nexus requirement will be satisfied by an affirmative answer to the question: Does the same act of the accused ground each of the charges? As *Côté* [(1974), 18 C.C.C. (2d) 321 (S.C.C.)] demonstrates, however, it will not always be easy to define when one act ends and another begins. Not only are there peculiar problems associated with continuing offences, but there exists the possibility of achieving different answers to this question according to the degree of generality at which an act is defined: see Dennis R. Klinck ["ÔThe Same Cause or Matter': The Legacy of Kienapple," 26 C.L.Q. 280 (1983-84)] at p. 292, H. Leonoff and D. Deutscher ["The Plea and Related Matters", in V. Del Buono (editor), *Criminal Procedure in Canada* (1982)] at p. 261, and A. F. Sheppard, ["Criminal Law - Rule Against Multiple Convictions" 54 Can. Bar Rev. 627 (1976)] at p. 638. Such difficulties will have to be resolved on an individual basis as cases arise, having regard to factors such as the remoteness or proximity of the events in time and place, the presence or absence of relevant intervening events (such as the robbery conviction in *Côté*), and whether the accused's actions were related to each other by a common objective. In the meantime, it would be a mistake to emphasize the difficulties. In many cases, including the present appeal, it will be clear whether or not the charges are founded upon the same act.

(ii) The nexus between the offences: need there be one?

The next question which must be addressed is whether the presence of a sufficient factual nexus is the only requirement which must be met in order to justify application of the *Kienapple* principle. Counsel for Sandra Prince refers in his factum to the *Kienapple* principle as one relating to multiple convictions for the same act. Similarly, Sheppard, in his early commentary on *Kienapple*, propounds a same transaction test for the rule against multiple convictions. Some courts, too, have referred to the "same act" or "same transaction" underlying two offences in terms which might suggest that that was sufficient to sustain the operation of the rule: see, for example, *R. v. Boyce* (1975), 23 C.C.C. (2d) 16 (Ont. C.A.), *R. v. Allison* (1983), 33 C.R. (3d) 333 (Ont. C.A.) and *Hagenlocher* [(1981), 65 C.C.C. (2d) 101; affd 70 C.C.C. (2d) 41*n*] (Man. C.A.).

In my opinion, the application of *Kienapple* is not so easily triggered. Once it has been established that there is a sufficient factual nexus between the charges, it remains to determine whether there is an adequate relationship between the offences themselves. The requirement of an adequate legal nexus is apparent from the use by the majority in *Kienapple* of the words "cause", "matter" or "delict" in lieu of "act" or "transaction" in defining the principle articulated in that case. More telling is the fact that Laskin J. went to considerable pains to discuss the legislative history of rape and carnal knowledge of a female under 14 years and to conclude that the offences were perceived as alternative charges when there was non-consensual intercourse with a female under 14. I am not prepared to regard Laskin J.'s analysis in this regard as unnecessary or irrelevant to the outcome in *Kienapple*, which it would of course be if the rule against multiple convictions applied whenever there was a sufficient factual nexus between the charges.

.....

(iii) Is it sufficient that the offences share a common element?

It has frequently been suggested that the presence of a common element in the offences charged will be sufficient to attract the *Kienapple* principle. E. G. Ewaschuk, ["The Rule Against Multiple Convictions and Abuse of Process", (1975), 28 C.R.N.S. 28] at p. 41 of his 1975 article on the rule against multiple convictions suggests: "If the offences stem from the same act and have a common element or elements, then *Kienapple* should apply." The common element test rests on the proposition or principle that an act which constitutes an element of an offence can only be used to sustain a single conviction. It is thereafter "used up" for the purposes of the criminal law. Alan W. Mewett ["Nemo bis Vexari", 16 C.L.Q. 382 (1973-74)] at pp. 383-84, explained the *Kienapple* case in this light:

> *Kienapple* is as good an illustration as any. The offence on count one embraces the actus reus of (i) sexual intercourse (ii) woman not his wife and (iii) no consent. On count two, it embraces (i) sexual intercourse (ii) woman not his wife and (iii) under fourteen. But two of the elements necessary under count two have become, as Laskin, J., stated, *res judicata*—they are used up, leaving, on count 2 only the third element dangling in the air. *The acts (nouns) of the accused caused by his acting can only be used once—either for count one or count two but not both.* Any acts not previously adjudicated remain, but, detached from the now adjudicated other acts, could not support a conviction.

(Emphasis added.)

This principle against the duplication of elements appears to underlie a number of judicial decisions: see, for example, *R. v. Taylor* (1979), 48 C.C.C. (2d) 523 (Nfld. C.A.), at pp. 537-38 and *R. v. Allison and Dinel*, [(1983), 5 C.C.C. (3d) 30 (Ont. C.A.)] at pp. 339-40. But, like the "same act" test, it fails to explain a number of cases which I believe were correctly decided, such as *McKinney* [(1979), 46 C.C.C. (2d) 566 (S.C.C.)] and *Logeman* [(1978), 5 C.R. (3d) 219 (S.C.C.)].

In any event, I observe that a common element test has already been considered and rejected by this Court. In *Côté v. The Queen*, *supra*, at p. 310, Fauteux C.J. wrote:

> The fact that [a thief's] possession is a common ingredient of both offences [*i.e.* theft and unlawful possession] is no reason to exclude or ignore what is actually the crucial factor distinguishing one from the other, and is of the essence of their respective nature.

The majority in *Côté* thus pointed in the direction of a test which focused not on the presence or absence of a common element, but on the presence or absence of *additional distinguishing elements*.

.....

Most recently, in *Krug v. The Queen* (1985), 21 C.C.C. (3d) 193, 21 D.L.R. (4th) 161, [1985] 2 S.C.R. 255, this Court unmistakably focused on the presence of distinguishing elements, rather than on the presence of shared elements, in assessing the applicability of *Kienapple*. *Krug* was charged with robbery under s. 302(*d*) and with various firearms offences including an offence under s. 83(1)(*a*). *Krug* submitted that the *Kienapple* principle at common law and as allegedly constitutionalized in ss. 7 and 11(*h*) of the *Canadian Charter of Rights and Freedoms* precluded convictions for the firearms offences. His arguments regarding the s. 83 conviction were rejected in a unanimous judgment, delivered by La Forest J.

.....

It has been a consistent theme in the jurisprudence from *Quon* through *Kienapple* and *Krug* that the rule against multiple convictions in respect of the same cause, matter or delict is subject to an expression of Parliamentary intent that more than one conviction be entered when offences overlap: see, in particular, *McGuigan v. The Queen*, [1982] 1 S.C.R. 284. In *Krug*, La Forest J. was careful to explain that the presence of additional, distinguishing elements was in itself an expression of such an intent. No element which Parliament has seen fit to incorporate into an offence and which has been proven beyond a reasonable doubt ought to be omitted from the offender's accounting to society, unless that element is substantially the same as, or adequately corresponds to, an element in the other offence for which he or she has been convicted.

I conclude, therefore, that the requirement of sufficient proximity between offences will only be satisfied if there is no additional and distinguishing element that goes to guilt contained in the offence for which a conviction is sought to be precluded by the *Kienapple* principle.

There is, however, a corollary to this conclusion. Where the offences are of unequal gravity, *Kienapple* may bar a conviction for a lesser offence, notwithstanding that there are additional elements in the greater offence for which a conviction has been registered, provided that there are no distinct additional elements in the lesser offence. For example, in *R. v. Loyer*, [1978] 2 S.C.R. 631, *Kienapple* was applied to bar convictions for possession of a weapon for the purpose of committing an offence when convictions were entered for the more serious offence of attempted armed robbery by use of a knife. Although the robbery charges contained the element of theft which distinguished them from the weapons charges, there were no elements in the weapons charges which were additional to or distinct from those in the robbery charges. Accordingly, it was appropriate for the Court to apply *Kienapple* to bar convictions on the lesser weapons charges rather than on the robbery charges.

(iv) When is an element of an offence not additional or distinct?

I now turn briefly to the question of when an element of an offence sufficiently corresponds to another element so that it cannot be regarded as additional or distinct. When can it be said that elements are "substantially the same" or "alternative" the one to the other? This is a question which defies precise answers. Differences of degree are often important and, as La Forest J. has pointed out, abstract logic must be supplemented by an awareness of practical considerations in ascertaining Parliament's intention in creating different offences: *Krug*, *supra*, p. 269. Without purporting to be exhaustive, I believe that there are at least three ways in which sufficient correspondence between elements can be found, each of which is subject always to the manifestation of a legislative intent to increase punishment in the event that two or more offences overlap.

First, an element may be a particularization of another element. In *Krug*, the Court was called upon to consider not only the relationship between s. 83(1)(*a*) and s. 302(*d*), as described above, but also the relationship between s. 83(1)(*a*) and s. 84. Section 84 made it an offence to point a firearm at a person. Section 83(1)(*a*), it will be recalled, made it an offence to use a firearm while committing an indictable offence. The trial judge had characterized the element of "pointing at a person" as an ingredient additional to "use". This Court disagreed, saying, "It is obvious that pointing a gun is a manner of using it" (p. 268). Accordingly, the Court referred to pointing as a particularization of use. Under the circumstances, it was difficult to believe that Parliament intended "automatically to make the same objectionable behaviour the subject of two separate offences" (p. 270).

In general, the particularization in one offence of an element of another offence should not be regarded as a distinguishing feature that renders *Kienapple* inapplicable. Parliament may create offences of varying degrees of generality, with the objective (vis-à-vis the more general offence) of ensuring that criminal conduct will not escape punishment because of a failure of the drafters to think of each individual circumstance in which the conduct might be committed, or with the objective (vis- à-vis the more specific offence) of addressing with certainty particular conduct in particular circumstances. In the absence of some indication of Parliamentary intent that there should be multiple convictions or added punishment in the event of an overlap, the particularization of an element ought not to be taken as a sufficient distinction to preclude the operation of the *Kienapple* principle.

A second way in which elements may correspond relates to there being more than one method, embodied in more than one offence, to prove a single delict. In *R. v. Gushue* (1976), 32 C.C.C. (2d) 189 (Ont. C.A.), affirmed on other grounds, [1980] 1 S.C.R. 798, the accused was charged under s. 124 with giving evidence in a judicial proceeding that was contrary to his own previous evidence. He was also charged with perjury contrary to s. 121. The Court reached the conclusion that convictions under both offences would have infringed the *Kienapple* principle. I agree. Although s. 121 and s. 124 have different elements, the difference is clearly not a reflection of any Parliamentary intent to add extra punishment when both offences can be proven. Section 124 is designed merely to facilitate proof of false evidence having been given, notwithstanding that no one particular statement can be proven false. Parliament has merely succumbed to the imperatives of logic: if two contradictory statements are given, one of them must be false and the delict of giving false evidence must have been committed on one of the two occasions.

The third situation in which there is sufficient correspondence between elements to sustain the *Kienapple* principle is somewhat similar. It arises when Parliament in effect deems a particular element to be satisfied by proof of a different nature, not necessarily because logic compels that conclusion, but because of social policy or inherent difficulties of proof. The *Kienapple* case itself affords one example. There, as we have seen, the element of the victim's age served as a substitute for the element of non-consent. A girl of less than fourteen years of age could not in Parliament's opinion meaningfully consent to sexual intercourse. Another example is provided by *Terlecki v. The Queen*, [1985] 2 S.C.R. 483. Although the case largely dealt with a procedural issue, the Court's decision was predicated on the applicability of *Kienapple* as between the offences of impaired driving contrary to s. 234 and "over 80" contrary to s. 236. Impairment is inherently difficult to prove, and Parliament has deemed a certain proportion of alcohol in one's blood to constitute an impairment of driving ability. The differences between the elements of these offences are explained by an attempt to facilitate the apprehension by the police or the conviction by the courts of persons who are guilty of essentially the same wrongful conduct: see *Leonoff and Deutscher, supra*, at p. 261. I believe that elements which serve only as an evidentiary proxy for another element cannot be regarded as distinct or additional elements for the purposes of the rule against multiple convictions.

I emphasize that in applying the above criteria it is important not to carry logic so far as to frustrate the intent of Parliament or as to lose sight of the overarching question whether the same cause, matter or delict underlies both charges. For example, there exist offences aimed at a particular evil which (in certain circumstances) contain as an element the commission of some other offence directed toward an entirely different wrong. Such was the relationship between the offences in *Lecky*, *Earle*, *Pinkerton* and *Pere Jean Gregoire*. In these cases, it could be argued, a substantive offence was subsumed by a greater, generic offence: *Klinck*, ["ÔThe Same Cause or Matter': The Legacy of Kienapple," 26 C.L.Q. 280 (1983-84)], at pp. 301-02. To illustrate, the offence of breach of probation contains as an element the non-compliance with a Probation order which, as a matter of law, requires the accused to keep the peace and be of good behaviour: s. 663(2). The fact that breach of probation is an offence punishable by summary conviction (s. 666(1)) is a clear indication that Parliament cannot have intended a conviction for that offence to operate as a bar to a conviction for the substantive offence (which might attract a far more severe penalty) merely because the substantive offence might be regarded as a particularization of a failure to keep the peace and be of good behaviour. Plainly, breach of probation is an offence designed to protect the effective operation of the criminal justice system, a societal interest which is entirely different from that protected by an offence such as assault. Accordingly, *Kienapple* had no application in those four cases.

V

Applicability of the Kienapple principle in the present case

As has been noted above, the respondent Sandra Prince has been convicted of causing bodily harm to Bernice Daniels. She has been charged with a second offence, namely, the manslaughter of Daniels' child, arising out of the same act of stabbing. I should, perhaps, explain that no question arises regarding the viability of a manslaughter charge founded on an act prior to the victim's birth. Section 206(2) [now s. 223(2)] reads as follows:

> 206(2) A person commits homicide when he causes injury to a child before or during its birth as a result of which the child dies after becoming a human being.

The only issue before the Court, therefore, is the applicability of *Kienapple*.

I have no hesitation in concluding that the requirement of a sufficient factual nexus is satisfied in the present appeal. A single act of the accused grounds both charges. It is true that the stabbing produced two separate consequences, the injury to Bernice Daniels and the death of the child. But such matters as the consequences of an act, the circumstances in which it was committed, or the status of the victim are most appropriately considered in the analysis of the legal nexus requirement. For it is only when consequences, circumstances, or status are incorporated into elements of an offence that they are relevant.

Is there sufficient correspondence between the elements of the two offences to sustain the operation of the rule against multiple convictions? One offence contains as an essential ingredient the causing of bodily harm to Bernice Daniels. The other offence requires proof of the death of Daniels' child. I cannot see how either of these elements can be subsumed into the other. There is no sense in which it can be said that one is a particularization of the other or is designed to facilitate proof of the other.

.....

Although the above analysis suffices to dispose of this appeal, I wish to underline that the conclusion I have reached reflects the importance which the drafters of the *Code* have attached to criminal conduct that results in bodily injury or death of the victim or victims. Many of the provisions of the *Criminal Code*, particularly those in respect of crimes of violence, contain an escalation of penalties for acts of the accused that result in graver consequences than otherwise identical conduct. Parliament's concern for the physical safety of the public would be frustrated by holding that either of the respective elements of bodily injury to Bernice Daniels or the death of the child were (to use the words of Laskin J. in *Kienapple*) "meaningless as a distinguishing feature".

It is, moreover, of some interest to the present case that the majority judgment in *Kienapple* at p. 750 referred to the death of a victim of violent crime as a "new relevant element". It is clear from this reference that the consequence of a wrongful act of an accused is an "element" which is capable of distinguishing two convictions in respect of a single unlawful act by an accused.

Also of particular relevance to the present appeal is a passage at pp. 744-45 in which Justice Laskin referred to his conclusion in *Kienapple* in the following terms:

> The rationale of my conclusion that the charges must be treated as alternative if there is a verdict of guilty of rape on the first count, that there should not be multiple convictions for the same delict *against the same girl*, has a long history in the common law.

(Emphasis added.) It would appear from this passage that, at least in so far as crimes of personal violence are concerned, the rule against multiple convictions is inapplicable when the convictions relate to different victims. Indeed, I believe it was never within the contemplation of the majority in *Kienapple* that the rule enunciated therein would preclude two convictions for offences respectively containing as elements the injury or death of two different persons.

Society, through the criminal law, requires Prince to answer for both the injury to Bernice Daniels and the death of the child, just as it would require a person who threw a bomb into a crowded space to answer for the multiple injuries and deaths that might result, and just as it compels a criminally negligent driver to answer for each person injured or killed as a result of his or her driving: see *R. v. Birmingham and Taylor* (1976), 34 C.C.C. (2d) 386 (Ont. C.A.).

.....

I would allow the appeal, reverse the decision of the Manitoba Court of Appeal granting a writ of certiorari and an order quashing the indictment, and remit the matter for trial on the manslaughter indictment.

QUESTIONS

4. **The accused is charged with the impaired operation of a vehicle causing bodily harm and criminal negligence causing bodily harm. The victim of both offences is the same. While highly intoxicated, and despite warnings not to drive, the accused drove erratically for about five miles, crossing the centre line and causing other vehicles to swerve out of the way. Then, she drove into the oncoming lane and seriously injured the other driver in a head-on collision. Can the accused be convicted of both offences? Consider, in this regard, *R. v. Andrew* (1990), 57 C.C.C. (3d) 301 (B.C.C.A.).**

5. **The accused is on probation for one offence. He is charged with further offences and is released on a recognizance. Both the probation order and recognizance provide that the accused keep the peace and be of good behaviour and the probation order adds after the words "good behaviour", "especially towards his former wife". He then repeatedly breaches both of these orders by driving by and bothering his former wife. Can the accused be convicted of breach of probation and breach of his recognizance? Consider, in this regard, *R. v. Furlong* (1992), 81 C.C.C. (3d) 449 (Nfld. C.A.).**

6. **A Canadian drug enforcement official is acquitted of soliciting and accepting bribes in exchange for information given to him by the American authorities. Can he then be convicted of breach of duty in Canada for the**

same facts and circumstances? Consider, in this regard, *R. v. Van Rassel* (1990), 53 C.C.C. (3d) 353 (S.C.C.).

D. ISSUE ESTOPPEL

GRDIC v. THE QUEEN

(1985), 19 C.C.C. (3d) 289 (S.C.C.)

[The accused was charged with several offences. The defence was alibi. The trial judge acquitted, though indicating that it was apparent that perjury had been committed. The accused was then charged with perjury. The Crown called the same evidence as at the original trial as well as some additional evidence. The trial judge found that issue estoppel was applicable and acquitted the accused of perjury. The British Columbia Court of Appeal directed a new trial. In a 5-4 decision, the Supreme Court restored the acquittal.]

Lamer J. (Estey, McIntyre, Le Dain and La Forest JJ. concurring): — This appeal addresses the question of the availability of the defence of issue estoppel *per rem judicatam* on a charge of perjury. It also affords an opportunity to examine the application of the doctrine of double jeopardy and see to what extent its effect with respect to a perjury prosecution is to introduce an exception to the general rule that "issue estoppel" cannot be founded on fraud.

.....

The meaning of an acquittal

In the case at bar the trial judge alluded to the commission of perjury. Respondent has not sought support from this but I feel I should nevertheless address the matter briefly as the Court of Appeal made some reference to the matter as follows:

> At that trial the respondent in due course gave evidence to support a defence of alibi. I think it is by no means conclusive, of course, but it is not without significance that in giving his reasons for judgment the trial judge who acquitted the respondent on those charges said: "It is quite apparent that perjury has been committed in this Court room. I think it is not up to me to solve that problem. I think that it is up to somebody else and I dismiss both counts."

There are not different kinds of acquittals and, on that point, I share the view that "as a matter of fundamental policy in the administration of the criminal law it must be accepted by the Crown in a subsequent criminal proceeding that an acquittal is the equivalent to a finding of innocence": see Martin L. Friedland, *Double Jeopardy*, (1969), Clarendon Press, Oxford, p. 129; also Chitty, i, 648; *R. v. Plummer*, [1902] 2 K.B. 339 at p. 349. To reach behind the acquittal, to qualify it, is in effect to introduce the verdict of "not proven", which is not, has never been, and should not be part of our law.

If the trial judge did not believe the accused, as he was entitled to, and his remarks might be construed as suggesting that he in fact did not believe the accused, he should have entered a conviction. Not having done so, Grdic is entitled to the full benefit of his acquittal.

However, this does not mean that, for the purpose of the application of the doctrine of *res judicata*, the Crown is estopped from relitigating all or any of the issues raised in the first trial. But it does mean that any issue, the resolution of which had to be in favour of the accused as a prerequisite to the acquittal, is irrevocably deemed to have been found conclusively in favour of the accused (see *R. v. Carlson* [1970] 3 O.R. 213; contra, *Villemaire v. The Queen*, (1962), 39 C.R. 297 at p. 300). This is so even though the judgment might well be the result of a reasonable doubt on that issue, and even when the judge has said so or expressed views that indicate clearly that his finding, though inuring to the benefit of the accused, had been arrived at with reluctance and the judge has suggested that it is not conclusively in favour of the accused.

The favourable finding

The accused, by his defence, is saying: the breathalyzer test taken that evening cannot be mine because I could not be there since I was at home.

The only avenue of acquittal open to the trial court, therefore, given that defence and the nature of the case, was a finding by the trial judge that there was reasonable doubt that the appellant was the person investigated at 6:30 p.m. That issue, subject to certain exceptions, cannot be relitigated, because, as a matter of law *for the purpose of the application of the doctrine of* res judicata, there has been made in his favour a finding that he was not driving his car at 6:30 p.m.

Issue estoppel and fraud

Issue estoppel cannot inure to a defendant if it be proven that the issue was determined in his favour as a result of fraud, subject to two limitations, one related to the principle of *res judicata*, the other the result of a policy consideration related to fairness to the accused and to the judicial process. De Grey C.J. speaking for the Court in *The Duchess of Kingston's Case* (1776), 2 Smith L.C. (13th ed.) 644, stated clearly the rule as it had already developed at the time, at p. 651:

> ... if it was a direct and decisive sentence upon the point, and, as it stands, to be admitted as conclusive evidence upon the Court, and not to be impeached from within; yet, like all other acts of the highest judicial authority, it is impeachable from without: although it is not permitted to show that the Court was mistaken, it may be shown that they were misled.
>
> Fraud is an extrinsic, collateral act; which vitiates the most solemn proceedings of Courts of Justice. Lord Coke says, it avoids all judicial acts, ecclesiastical or temporal.

Fraud may be set up against an accused so as to deny him the benefit of issue estoppel.

There are many forms of fraud that may be invoked, one of which, and I imagine the most common, is the allegation by the Crown of perjury committed by the defendant. Such an allegation is to the effect that the judge not only erred but erred because he was misled by the fraud, in this case, the perjury. If the allegation is successfully established, then the accused cannot estop the Crown from inviting the judge to relitigate the issue.

The first limitation

If to prove the allegation the Crown is merely tendering the same evidence as that tendered previously, then issue estoppel will survive the attack because the Crown's allegation is, in disguise, but a relitigation of the issue as litigated previously, or, to use the words of De Grey C.J., an attempt "to impeach from within".

Indeed another judge, or conceivably the same judge, hearing the subsequent perjury charge is invited to reconsider the same evidence and conclude differently. This can only be done through the appeal process finding reversible error resulting in the ordering of a new trial before a different judge. Therefore perjury may defeat issue estoppel but, as said De Grey C.J., only "from without", that is, only if there is additional evidence (I use here the expression "additional evidence" as including any evidence that was not put before the trier of fact in the previous proceeding, whether available or not at the time); it may defeat the estoppel, but not necessarily, and this leads into the second limitation.

Second Limitation

If the additional evidence was available to the Crown under the laws of evidence, using reasonable diligence at the time of the first trial (I am paraphrasing Lord Hailsham of St. Marylebone in *Director of Public Prosecutions v. Humphrys* [1977] A.C. 1, at p. 40), and the Crown failed to tender it, then it is estopped from so doing later on, not *per rem judicatam*, but for reasons of fairness to the accused who was in jeopardy of answering the full case had the Crown been diligent.

[Lamer J. went on to conclude that the additional evidence was available at the time of the original trial and could have been called to rebut the accused's defence. The appeal was therefore allowed, and the acquittal restored.]

***Res judicata* and issue estoppel are not referred to in the *Criminal Code* but are preserved by s. 8(3) of the *Criminal Code*, which provides for the continuation of common law justifications, excuses or defences, not inconsistent with or altered by the *Criminal Code* or other federal statutes.**

QUESTION

7. **The accused was charged with assaulting his co-worker. At trial, the Crown seeks to introduce his statement to the police which contains an admission that he had assaulted her and a second co-worker. The judge**

rules that the statement was not proven to be voluntary and excludes it from evidence. The Crown's witness cannot swear that it was the accused who attacked her, since the attack came from behind. The judge acquits. The police then interview the second co-worker and charge the accused with assault causing bodily harm upon her. Can the Crown seek to tender the statement originally provided to police? Would your answer be the same or different if the original charge had been withdrawn by the Crown, with leave of the court, after the decision on the *voir dire*?

CHAPTER 11

SENTENCING AND RELATED ISSUES

A. RESOLUTION DISCUSSIONS

"Resolution discussions"[1] are pre-trial discussions between the defence and the Crown, sometimes in the presence of a pre-trial judge. Though such discussions may address a variety of matters including the narrowing of trial issues and the adequacy of disclosure or any proposed re-election, their most controversial aspect is dialogue intended to bring about the resolution of cases through negotiated pleas of guilt and pre-determined positions on sentence. These discussions are often referred to as "plea bargaining".

R. v. MACDONALD

(1990), 54 C.C.C. (3d) 97 (Ont. C.A.);
leave to appeal to S.C.C. refused 61 C.C.C. (3d) vi

[In discussions between the Crown and defence counsel, the Crown agreed that the accused would only face a charge of being an accessory after the fact to murder, provided that the accused gave a complete and truthful statement to the police regarding the murder committed by his co-accused, G. However, during further investigation, the police found a witness who testified at the preliminary inquiry (held for G. and the accused) that the accused had planned the murder. At the end of the preliminary inquiry, the Crown was successful in requesting that the court commit the accused to stand trial for first degree murder. On appeal from his murder conviction, the accused alleged that the Crown's conduct constituted an abuse of process.]

The judgment of the court was delivered by

Zuber J.A.: —

.....

[Zuber J.A. reviews the doctrine of abuse of process.]

---

1 **See the (Ontario) *Report of the Attorney General's Advisory Committee on Charge Screening, Disclosure, and Resolution Discussions: Recommendations and Opinions* (Toronto: Ontario Ministry of Attorney General, 1993), hereinafter [*Martin Report*], Chapter IV, Resolution Discussions, pp. 275 *et seq.***

In this case, while it cannot be denied that the conduct of the Crown was perhaps abrupt and clearly caught counsel for the appellant off guard, the treatment of the appellant was not so unfair or oppressive, nor was the prosecution so vexatious that the administration of justice would be served best by staying these proceedings.

There are three factors which lead to this conclusion. First, this is a case where an accused person made a bargain with the Crown in which he secured lenient treatment with respect to this prosecution and other outstanding charges in exchange for a *complete and truthful* statement and for his testimony at the preliminary hearing of the co-accused, Gerald Gray. In fact, the appellant received lenient treatment with respect to the drug charges and the Crown secured the appellant's testimony at Gray's preliminary hearing. However, because the Crown did not get from the appellant the complete and truthful statement for which it had bargained, it was under no obligation to meet the final requirement of the agreement to charge the appellant with the lesser charge of accessory; rather, he was properly committed for trial on a charge of first degree murder.

Secondly, at the time the Crown entered into the agreement with the appellant, it had no reason to believe that he might be guilty of murder. Circumstances changed once the Crown became aware of the evidence of the witness Carter, but it remained uncertain whether to proceed against the appellant on a charge of first degree murder until it had a chance to assess Carter under oath. As stated by Dubin J.A. in *R. v. Young* (1984), 13 C.C.C. (3d) 1 at p. 32, 46 O.R. (2d) 520, 40 C.R. (3d) 289 (C.A.):

> ... to compel the police or Crown counsel to institute proceedings before they have reason to believe that they will be able to establish the accused's guilt beyond a reasonable doubt would ... have a deleterious effect both upon the rights of the accused and upon the ability of society to protect itself.

In *R. v. Conway* [(1989), 49 C.C.C. (3d) 289 (S.C.C.)], Madam Justice L'Heureux-Dubé speaks of a concern with proceedings which are so unfair and tainted that to allow them to proceed "would tarnish the integrity of the court" (at p. 302). The integrity of the court would equally be tarnished in a case such as this, were the Crown to be held to a deal which was struck at a time when the appellant was not a suspect for murder, but where later, facts revealed his involvement. To permit the agreement to stand would allow the appellant to benefit from his incomplete and untruthful statements and from the deal he had struck with the Crown before all the facts were known.

Finally, although this is a case where the Crown extracted some benefit from the appellant (*i.e.*, his testimony at the preliminary hearing of Gray) and the appellant forfeited his right to silence, in fact, the appellant suffered no prejudice. None of the statements that he gave to police were used at his trial. The only real detriment that he suffered was that, in failing to successfully manipulate the system, he ended up being charged with first degree murder instead of as an accessory after the fact.

In light of all of the above considerations, this is clearly not a case where there is an affront to fair play and decency that outweighs the societal interest in the effective prosecution of criminal cases. In the result, there is no basis upon which the abuse of process doctrine could be invoked in this case, and the trial judge was correct in declining to exercise his discretion to grant a stay of proceedings.

.....

Appeal dismissed.

QUESTIONS

1. **On the morning that a fraud trial is to commence, the investigating officer advises the Crown that he has been unable to locate the key Crown witness. Moments later, defence counsel approaches the Crown and advises that her client is prepared to plead guilty to three of the four charges before the court. This disposition would have been acceptable to the Crown, even if it had been in a position to prove its case. What are the Crown's obligations in this regard? If the witness's absence is disclosed to the accused, who still wishes to plead guilty, can the Crown accept the guilty plea? Consider, in this regard, the *Martin Report*, Chapter IV, "Resolution Discussions", at p. 291 *et seq*.**

2. **Junior Crown counsel negotiates a guilty plea to one count of armed robbery and a joint submission that the accused receive a suspended sentence and probation, based upon his seven months pre-trial custody or "time served". You are the Crown counsel who is in court when the matter comes up for sentencing. You believe that the proposed resolution falls far below the acceptable range of sentences for this offence. What should you do? Would it make a difference if the negotiated sentence would have been appropriate on the information available to the junior Crown but you have since discovered that the accused has a prior record for two additional robberies in another jurisdiction?**

3. **The accused is to be tried for second degree murder. It is the accused's position that his conduct only amounted to manslaughter. The Crown's murder case is relatively strong but not overwhelming. In the circumstances, the Crown is prepared to accept a plea of guilt to manslaughter, but based only upon a joint submission of ten years imprisonment. As defence counsel, you believe that the appropriate sentence for this manslaughter is six years but recognize that the Crown is extracting a premium to justify abandoning the murder allegation and appreciating that a plea would enable your client to avoid the risk of life imprisonment and lengthy parole ineligibility. Can you accept the negotiated settlement? Should the trial judge implement it?**

4. **You are Crown counsel prosecuting a charge of fraud over $5,000. The victims are widowers whose life savings were taken. The case is a weak one but would attract a lengthy jail sentence upon conviction. The defence is prepared to enter a plea of guilt and make restitution to the victims if the Crown agrees to a non-custodial disposition. What should you do? What role, if any, should the victims play in your decision? Consider, in this regard, the *Martin Report*, Recommendations 50 and 51, at pp. 300 and 305.**

The following case addresses the role that the trial judge should or should not play in plea negotiations.

R. v. RAJAEEFARD

(1996), 104 C.C.C. (3d) 225 (Ont. C.A.)

[On the defendant's trial date for charges of assaulting his wife, a student from a legal aid clinic attended for the purpose of asking for an adjournment. The trial judge told the student in the courthouse hallway, *inter alia,* that on a plea the accused could expect to receive a suspended sentence and probation with counselling, but if convicted after a trial, the judge would impose a sentence of ten to 15 days in jail. The trial judge also said that he would not grant an adjournment. The accused pleaded guilty. The summary conviction appeal brought by the defendant on the basis that his guilty plea was not voluntary was dismissed and the defendant further appealed to the Court of Appeal.]

Morden A.C.J.O. (Goodman J.A. concurring): —

.....

The appellant submits that he had intended to plead not guilty and that he changed his plea to guilty as a result of what the student told him respecting what the judge had said in the hallway. He submits that, in the circumstances, the plea was not voluntarily and freely made and that the vital appearance of fairness was lost.

The appellant has the onus of showing that the plea of guilty was invalid. To be a valid plea it must be voluntary and unequivocal. In *R. v. T. (R.)*, [(1992), 17 C.R. (4th) 247 (Ont. C.A.)], Doherty J.A. said for this court at p. 253:

> A voluntary plea refers to the conscious volitional decision of the accused to plead guilty for reasons which he or she regards as appropriate: *R. v. Rosen*, [1980] 1 S.C.R. 961, 13 C.R. (3d) 215, 51 C.C.C. (2d) 65, 30 N.R. 483, 108 D.L.R. (3d) 60, at p. 974 [S.C.R.], p. 75 [C.C.C., p. 227 C.R.]. A guilty plea entered in open court will be presumed to be voluntary unless the contrary is shown: Fitzgerald, *The Guilty Plea and Summary Justice*, *supra*, at p. 71.
>
> Several factors may affect the voluntariness of a guilty plea. None are present in this case. The appellant was not pressured in any way to enter guilty pleas. Quite the contrary, he was urged by duty counsel not to plead but to accept an adjournment. No person in authority coerced or oppressed the appellant. He was not offered a "plea bargain" or any other inducement.

.....

... In my respectful view, the most useful source of guidance is to be found in the Martin Report at pp. 275-385. This part of the report deals with the case law and extrajudicial literature on resolution discussions in various jurisdictions, analyzes competing policies and principles, and contains statements and recommendations of policies and principles which should be followed in this jurisdiction.

Recommendation 73 at p. 365 in the Martin Report bears very directly on the question before us. It reads:

> 73. *The Committee is of the opinion that a judge presiding at a pre-hearing conference should not be involved in plea bargaining in the sense of bartering to determine the sentence, or pressuring any counsel to change their position. The presiding judge may, however, assist in resolving the issue of sentence by expressing an opinion as to whether a proposed sentence is too high, too low, or within an appropriate range.*

.....

For the reasons which I shall give, I have concluded that, in the particular circumstances of this case, the trial judge's conduct improperly pressured the appellant to plead guilty and that his plea of guilty was not freely and voluntarily given. I shall set forth these circumstances but, before doing so, I shall deal with a submission of the respondent relating to the lack of a causal connection between the judge's conduct and the plea.

The respondent has submitted that even if the conduct of the judge amounted to improper pressure it has not been shown that the appellant's plea of guilty was a direct consequence of the trial judge's comments regarding possible penalties. I do not accept this submission. Although the appellant's affidavit indicates that there were other matters of concern to him — such as, that he was busy with his courses and had a class that afternoon and an exam the following week, and that he was concerned he could not properly defend himself by reason of his very basic English and poor understanding of the legal system — I am satisfied on the material before us that the plea of guilty was a direct consequence of the trial judge's comments. I base this conclusion on the inherent tendency of the comments and I view the other matters of concern to the appellant as part of the context in which these comments operated. In his first affidavit the appellant said that the inability of the student to represent him on a trial and the judge's comment that if he were found guilty "the judge would put me in jail for, I believe, 15-20 days ... made me very afraid. I had never been in jail except for the few hours after my July 28, 1993 arrest prior to getting bail."

.....

In Ferguson and Roberts, "Plea Bargaining: Directions for Canadian Reform" (1974), 52 Can. Bar Rev. 497 at p. 558, the following appears:

> As a final argument against express judicial plea bargaining, it could develop that an accused would find it too difficult to reject a judicially offered bargain out of an apprehension that if he did reject it the judge would be annoyed and would not conduct a fair trial or would mete out a harsher sentence. While this could well be a false concern, if it is conceivable that an accused person would react this way, it is an argument against judicial plea bargaining that cannot be ignored.

In "Sentencing Reform: A Canadian Approach", the report of the Canadian Sentencing Commission, 1987, at pp. 424-5 the following is said:

> The basic concern with active judicial participation in plea bargaining is the erosion of a judge's role as an objective, non-partisan arbitrator. One rationale for involving the judge in the negotiation process is that it would enhance the intelligence of the guilty plea by informing the defendant of the anticipated sentence prior to entry of the plea. However, as one study notes,

> the actual effect of such intervention could have the opposite effect. This research suggests that because the judge is an authoritative, dominating figure in the process (which is confirmed by the results of the inmate survey in British Columbia concerning inmate perception of the importance of the judge in sentencing), the court's intervention could effectively coerce the accused into accepting the agreement and pleading guilty.

(The cited source is "Plea Bargaining and the Transformation of the Criminal Process" (1977), 90 Harv. L. Rev. 585.)

.....

These circumstances, in my opinion, combined to place improper pressure on the appellant to plead guilty. I should say that I have relied upon all of these circumstances because they were all present in this case and are relevant to the issue. I note, however, that I am not holding that all of these circumstances would necessarily have to be present for a finding of improper pressure to be made. I would think that the most salient circumstance is that the process was initiated by the trial judge who returned to the court to try the matter, all without the real consent of the appellant: see Martin report at pp. 378-82. I also note that in arriving at this conclusion I have not lost sight of the principle that a plea of guilty is generally a mitigating factor with respect to sentence and that it is right that an accused person should know this. My conclusion is based on the particular circumstances I have set forth.

For these reasons, I would grant leave to appeal, set aside the plea of guilty and the judgments below, and order a new trial.

R. v. DJEKIC

(2000), 147 C.C.C. (3d) 572 (Ont. C.A.)

The judgment of the court was endorsed on the appeal record as follows:

By the Court: — The appellant pleaded guilty on November 24, 1998 to one count of welfare fraud over $5,000.00. She wishes to withdraw that plea on the basis that it was not made voluntarily but was made under pressure and in circumstances which vitiated the voluntariness of the plea.

On May 14, 1998 the case was set for a preliminary hearing on December 1, 1998. In October of that year, Officer Kerr obtained information that the appellant was tampering with the witness and intended to charge her with obstructing justice. Officer Kerr informed appellant's counsel of this in November and as a result, counsel had the case brought forward for a judicial pre-trial on November 23. The appellant was not in court on that date and the pre-trial was put over to the next day. At that time defence counsel, Crown counsel, the officer and the judge held the judicial pre-trial. The Crown suggested a sentence of two years on a guilty plea while the pre-trial judge proposed that on a plea of guilty, a one-year sentence would be appropriate and that in those circumstances, no obstruct justice charge should be laid.

After the pre-trial, the appellant, who had attended court with her infant, was told about the pre-trial discussion and the fact that the officer intended to arrest her that day, and charge her with obstruct justice and hold her in custody pending a show cause hearing. The officer called the Children's Aid Society to look after the infant and the appellant called her mother for the same purpose.

The appellant was upset and was under pressure to decide whether to plead guilty in accordance with the pre-trial discussion or to be arrested that day on the new charge. She had trouble deciding what to do but eventually agreed to plead guilty. However, while she was considering what to do, the case was called and the presiding judge said the following to the appellant in open court:

> THE COURT: Yes.
>
> Mr. Grummett, you're acting on this matter or not?
>
> MR. GRUMMETT: Well, I haven't been able to get any instructions, Your Honour.
>
> THE COURT: Well, Miss. Djekic, I understand that this matter is up today, I understand you have a preliminary hearing coming in just a few days and once that starts and there's a — and I am also given to understand there's another charge waiting for you, so what are you going to do with all this?
>
> MISS DJEKIC: I don't know, I'm just waiting for my mom to come.
>
> THE COURT: All right. And do you think you'll be in a better position to instruct counsel after you've talked to her and have someone to look after the child?
>
> MISS DJEKIC: Yeah.
>
> THE COURT: Do you want me to stand it down for a little while?
>
> MISS DJEKIC: Please.
>
> THE COURT: Will you wait Mr. Grummett?
>
> MR. GRUMMETT: Yes, I will.
>
> THE COURT: All right.
>
> Try — ma'am, I — I — I can see that you're upset, but I also — I — I have not only a responsibility to be fair to you and I'm going to try to do that as best I can, but I've also got a whole day of court time coming up and at the moment I don't know how to say this politely, we had a pre-trial, we discussed the issue with the Crown Attorney and your lawyer, who's very experienced, and we persuaded — your lawyer and the Crown lawyer with a little bit of help at the pre-trial persuaded an officer not to arrest you just yet in the hope that we could work out something, but there's a charge there that is going to have to be dealt with unless we can work it out, today. So, you have got to get yourself under control and give some hard thought ...

MISS DJEKIC: Well, I didn't know I was coming here today for this.

THE COURT: Well, you were lucky not to be coming in custody. So, I think you need to go and get under control and speak to your mother, get somebody to look after the child and give some really hard thought to this, today. All right? Thank you.

MR. GRUMMETT: Thank you, Your Honour.

Following the plea the case was put over for sentencing to the end of January, but the appellant was not sentenced until May as the judge was ill. However, the appellant advised both the pre-sentence reporter and her new counsel that she wished to withdraw her plea and to plead not guilty. Unfortunately, her second counsel, who was not the counsel on appeal, advised her to wait to raise the issue on appeal rather than before sentencing.

This Court set out the law with respect to withdrawal of a guilty plea in the case of *R. v. T. (R.)* (1992), 17 C.R. (4th) 247. To be valid, a guilty plea must be made voluntarily and unequivocally. On an appeal the appellant has the onus of showing that the plea was invalid. The plea will be presumed voluntary unless the contrary is shown. At p. 253 the Court set out some of the factors which may affect the voluntary nature of the plea:

> Several factors may affect the voluntariness of a guilty plea. None are present in this case. The appellant was not pressured in any way to enter guilty pleas. Quite the contrary, he was urged by duty counsel not to plead but to accept an adjournment. No person in authority coerced or oppressed the appellant. He was not offered a "plea bargain" or any other inducement. He was not under the effect of any drug. There is no evidence of any mental disorder which could have impaired his decision-making processes. He is not a person of limited intelligence.

The appellant had not given any instructions to her counsel to discuss a guilty plea on her outstanding charge and was confronted on her arrival on November 24 with a fait accompli arranged without any authorization by her and sanctioned by a judge. She now faced not only with [*sic*] the prospect of being arrested and held in custody on a new charge, but of having to make a decision about her pending charge, which she did not know was going to be dealt with at all on that day.

Our concern is that in those circumstances the pre-hearing judge, clearly a person in authority, spoke to the appellant in a way which put significant pressure on her to make a decision about her case on that day when she had to consider the immediate needs of her child, all the circumstances of the new charge she would be facing, as well as the considerations relating to the existing charge. Although he no doubt had the best interest of the appellant in mind, it was unfortunate and inappropriate for the presiding judge to speak to the appellant about those issues in the circumstances. It was the role of her counsel to do that and to advise her with respect to her choices and the timing of those choices.

Given the comments made by the presiding judge in this situation, we are satisfied the appellant's guilty plea was not made voluntarily. She was emotionally distraught, as the judge observed, she had to deal with her child, the issue of a potential penitentiary sentence if she did not accept a plea, as well as the fact that she had not attended court on that date prepared to consider the full disposition of her charge. In those circumstances she was told by the trial judge that she was "lucky not to be coming into custody". This would certainly put significant pressure on a person to follow the suggestion of the judge.

In our view, the guilty plea and sentence must be set aside in this case and a trial ordered.

The appeal is therefore allowed.

Appeal allowed; new trial ordered.

As noted in Chapter 10, s. 606(1.1) of the *Criminal Code* now requires that the court conduct a plea comprehension inquiry. Before the court may accept a guilty plea, it must be satisfied that the accused is making the plea voluntarily, and understands (i) that the plea is an admission of the essential elements of the offence, (ii) the nature and consequences of the plea, and (iii) that the court is not bound by any agreement between the accused and the prosecutor.

B. ALTERNATIVE MEASURES

Section 717 of the *Criminal Code* now recognizes that "alternative measures", or diversion, may be used to deal with persons alleged to have committed criminal offences, if not inconsistent with the protection of society and if specified conditions are met. Alternative measures may involve performance of tasks, such as, community service, restitution, completion of a program or course, an apology or some other suitable conduct. After successful completion of the measures imposed, the criminal charges may be dismissed, withdrawn or a s. 579 stay may be entered. Alternative measures are available at the discretion of the Crown and are, as a matter of Crown policy, generally offered for first time offenders of minor property offences and minor drug possession charges under the *Controlled Drug and Substances Act*, S.C. 1996, c. 19. The availability of diversion for young offenders, referred to as extrajudicial measures and extrajudicial sanctions, is separately addressed in Chapter 12.

QUESTION

5. The accused is charged with shoplifting. She is head of surgery at a large teaching hospital. She denies guilt but will lose everything she has worked for if a trial is held and the charge becomes known. Accordingly, she wishes to avail herself of s. 717 of the *Criminal Code*. Can she? Consider, in this regard, s. 717(2) of the *Criminal Code*. If s. 717 is not available, is there another approach which defence counsel can take to resolve the case? Would your answers be the same or different if the accused had been charged with assault when she slapped her neighbour, Mr. Rogers? Consider, in this regard, the availability of peace bonds, addressed in Chapter 9. Finally, what if she had been charged with false pretences involving a $300 N.S.F. cheque? Assume that her position is that she honestly believed that sufficient funds were in the account.

C. SENTENCING

1. Overview

Part XXIII of the *Criminal Code* (Sentencing) has codified and, in some ways altered, the principles of sentencing, the conduct of a sentencing hearing and the dispositions available on sentence. An accused may be sentenced after a guilty plea to the offence(s) charged, an included offence or other offences arising out of the same transaction. As well, sentencing may follow a trial in which the accused has contested guilt. Sentencing may take place immediately after a finding of guilt or at a later date. The trial judge may remand the accused in or out of custody pending sentence. Sentencing for young offenders is separately addressed in Chapter 12.

2. Timing of Sentencing Hearing

R. v. BROOKES

[1970] 4 C.C.C. 377 (Ont. C.A.)

The judgment of the Court was delivered orally by

Gale, C.J.O.: — The respondent pleaded guilty and was convicted on April 2, 1969, on two charges of possession of stolen property of a value exceeding $50 and on a charge that he broke and entered a dwelling-house and stole therein a quantity of liquor. Both offences are serious. Entry into the house was accomplished by the breaking of a basement window and while inside the house the respondent and others ransacked it. The possession of stolen goods occurred when the respondent and two others deliberately planned, and almost succeeded in carrying out, a very sophisticated theft of radio and television sets from Simpsons-Sears' warehouse. Following the convictions on April 2nd, the respondent was "remanded" out of custody and the matter was adjourned from time to time and eventually on September 8, 1969, the learned trial Judge imposed a suspended sentence on the accused in respect of all convictions.

We are unanimously of the opinion that the sentence imposed was quite wrong in the circumstances. In the first place the sentences were totally inadequate having regard to the offences which were committed, to the accused's previous record of six similar offences (and in this respect I am relying upon the record of offences which is filed as ex. 1 at the trial), and to the way in which the offences were carried out. It is a curious thing that although the accused had been theretofore convicted of six previous offences, he had received a suspended sentence on five of those occasions and has been committed to jail for only 15 days in total. This experience seems to us to be an abuse of the practice of awarding a suspended sentence in proper circumstances. Moreover, the offences relating to the possession of the goods of Simpson-Sears were committed while the respondent was on bail pending disposition of the other charge of breaking, entering and theft. That is a circumstance, of course, which must tell against the respondent.

In postponing the imposition of sentence from April 2nd to September 8th of last year, a matter of some five months, the learned trial Judge apparently acted upon the request of counsel for the respondent for such postponement in order to see how the respondent would conduct himself in the meantime. Also, as is made quite clear on p. 33 of the transcript, the Judge delayed the sentencing for the purpose of awaiting certain amendments to the *Criminal Code* that he felt at that time would undoubtedly be introduced. Again, in our opinion, the learned trial Judge erred and in that respect we adopt that which was said by Dickson, J.A., in *R. v. Fuller*, [1969] 3 C.C.C. 348 at p. 352, 2 D.L.R. (3d) 27, 5 C.R.N.S. 148. There, in somewhat similar circumstances, Dickson, J.A., speaking for the Court of Appeal of Manitoba, had this to say:

> This Court recognizes that it may be necessary to postpone sentencing for the purpose of obtaining a pre-sentence report or additional information concerning the offence or the offender. This Court is firmly of the opinion, however, that sentencing should not be postponed for a lengthy period simply for the purpose of determining whether an accused will behave himself during the period of postponement. No such course of conduct is authorized by any provision of the *Criminal Code*.

As well as adopting that view, we similarly are satisfied that sentencing should not be postponed for any length of time in belief that the *Criminal Code* will be amended in the meantime. Counsel for the respondent pointed out that his client has apparently behaved himself since his conviction, but one might expect that he would, having regard to the fact that he faced sentencing and, since sentence, an appeal has been confronting him. Accordingly, that single circumstance does not override the gravity of the offences which he committed, the fact that he has six previous convictions, and the fact that one offence was committed while he was on bail. We are strongly of the view that in this case the sentencing ought not to have been postponed as it was. The appeal will therefore be allowed, the sentence imposed set aside and in its place the respondent will be sentenced to one year definite and one year indeterminate[2] with respect to the conviction for breaking, entering and theft, and to one year definite and one year indeterminate on each of the two convictions for possession. Those latter two sentences are to run concurrently to each other, but are to be consecutive to the sentence for breaking, entering and theft. This will have the effect of sending the respondent to the penitentiary where we think he ought to be.

Appeal allowed.

QUESTIONS

6. **Assume that the offender was 18 years old with a previous young offender record. He was abused as a child and apprehended by the Children's Aid Society. On appeal from sentence, he seeks to introduce fresh evidence on systemic racism in Canada and that he has been the victim of racism in the past. Should the proposed fresh evidence be ad-**

---

[2] **This kind of sentence is no longer available to the court.**

mitted?. If admitted, would it impact on the sentence appeal? Consider *R. v. Borde* (2002), 172 C.C.C. (3d) 225 (Ont. C.A.) and *R. v. Spencer*, [2003] O.J. No. 1052 (S.C.J.).

7. **The accused is charged with possession of heroin for the purposes of trafficking. The evidence is overwhelming and a guilty plea is ultimately inevitable. The evidence is also clear that the accused sold small quantities of heroin to support his own addiction. Upon arrest, counsel arranges for in-patient addiction treatment for the accused. Several months pass. The accused is making excellent strides towards rehabilitation and has remained free from drugs. How should counsel approach the issue as to the best timing for sentencing? Now assume that an accused is charged with defrauding a widower of $40,000. It will take the accused at least a year to effect restitution. How should counsel approach the timing of any sentencing?**

---

3. FACTS RELIED UPON AT A SENTENCING HEARING

R. v. GARDINER

(1982), 68 C.C.C. (2d) 477 (S.C.C.)

[The respondent pleaded guilty to assault causing bodily harm upon his wife. However, his version of the assault was very different from the Crown's. The Supreme Court addressed the standard of proof to be applied for establishing aggravating facts and the evidentiary rules applicable at sentencing hearings.]

[The judgment of the court was delivered by:]

Dickson J. [Martland, Ritchie and Chouinard JJ. concurring]: — In the second edition of his text *Principles of Sentencing* (1979), Professor D. A. Thomas speaks of an "evolving body of principle designed to ensure that the version of the facts adopted for the purpose of sentence is supported by evidence and reached according to appropriate procedural standards" (at pp. 366-7). One of those evolving principles, lying at the heart of this appeal, concerns the standard of proof to be applied for establishing aggravating facts which, while not affecting guilt or innocence, do have a critical effect on the length of sentence.

Two issues are raised. The first preliminary question: does the Supreme Court of Canada have jurisdiction to entertain appeals arising out of sentencing proceedings for indictable offences? The second issue, only reached if the first question is answered affirmatively, is this: where, on a sentencing hearing following conviction, the Crown seeks to prove aggravating facts relating to the offence committed and those facts are controverted, is the burden on the Crown the traditional criminal onus of proof of beyond a reasonable doubt or the lesser onus of proof upon a balance of probabilities?

[The jurisdictional issue is then addressed.]

The question now to be addressed is this: what burden of proof must the Crown sustain in advancing contested aggravating facts in a sentencing proceeding, for the purpose of supporting a lengthier sentence; is the standard that of the criminal law, proof beyond a reasonable doubt, or that of the civil law, proof on a balance of probabilities.

.....

Sentencing is part of a fact finding, decision-making process of the criminal law. Sir James Fitzjames Stephen, writing in 1863 said that "the sentence is the gist of the proceeding. It is to the trial what the bullet is to the powder" (quoted in Olah, "Sentencing: The Last Frontier of the Criminal Law" (1980), 16 C.R. (3d) 97, at p. 98). The statement is equally true today.

One of the hardest tasks confronting a trial judge is sentencing. The stakes are high for society and for the individual. Sentencing is the critical stage of the criminal justice system, and it is manifest that the judge should not be denied an opportunity to obtain relevant information by the imposition of all the restrictive evidential rules common to a trial. Yet the obtaining and weighing of such evidence should be fair. A substantial liberty interest of the offender is involved and the information obtained should be accurate and reliable.

It is a commonplace that the strict rules which govern at trial do not apply at a sentencing hearing and it would be undesirable to have the formalities and technicalities characteristic of the normal adversary proceeding prevail. The hearsay rule does not govern the sentencing hearing. Hearsay evidence may be accepted where found to be credible and trustworthy. The judge traditionally has had wide latitude as to the sources and types of evidence upon which to base his sentence. He must have the fullest possible information concerning the background of the accused if he is to fit the sentence to the offender rather than to the crime.

It is well to recall in any discussion of sentencing procedures that the vast majority of offenders plead guilty. Canadian figures are not readily available but American statistics suggest that about 85 percent of the criminal defendants plead guilty or *nolo contendere*. The sentencing judge therefore must get his facts after plea. Sentencing is, in respect of most offenders, the only significant decision the criminal justice system is called upon to make.

It should also be recalled that a plea of guilty, in itself, carries with it an admission of the essential legal ingredients of the offence admitted by the plea, and no more. Beyond that any facts relied upon by the Crown in aggravation must be established by the Crown. If undisputed, the procedure can be very informal. If the facts are contested the issue should be resolved by ordinary legal principles governing criminal proceedings including resolving relevant doubt in favour of the offender.

To my mind, the facts which justify the sanction are no less important than the facts which justify the conviction; both should be subject to the same burden of proof. Crime and punishment are inextricably linked. "It would appear well established that the sentencing process is merely a phase of the trial process" (Olah, *supra*, at p. 107). Upon conviction the accused is not abruptly deprived of all procedural rights existing at trial: he has a right to counsel, a right to call evidence and cross-examine prosecution witnesses, a right to give evidence himself and to address the court.

In *S. v. Manchester City Recorder et al.*, [1969] 3 All E. R. 1230 the suggestion was made that a court might be *functus officio* in the use of its powers to convict or acquit, as distinct from its powers to sentence. Lord Reid found this proposition to be both novel and erroneous, adding at p. 1233:

> In my judgment magistrates have only one officium — to carry the case before them to a conclusion. There is no reason to divide up their functions and hold that at some stage in the proceedings one officium comes to an end and another begins.

In my view, both the informality of the sentencing procedure as to the admissibility of evidence and the wide discretion given to the trial judge in imposing sentence are factors militating in favour of the retention of the criminal standard of proof beyond a reasonable doubt at sentencing (Olah, *ibid*, at p. 121).

> [B]ecause the sentencing process poses the ultimate jeopardy to an individual enmeshed in the criminal process, it is just and reasonable that he be granted the protection of the reasonable doubt rule at this vital juncture of the process.

The *rationale* of the argument of the Crown for the acceptance of a lesser standard of proof is administrative efficiency. In my view, however, the administrative efficiency argument is not sufficient to overcome such a basic tenet suffusing our entire criminal justice system as the standard of proof beyond a reasonable doubt. I am by no means convinced that if the standard of proof were lowered, conservation of judicial resources would be enhanced. In the event of a serious dispute as to facts, it would be in the interests of the accused to plead not guilty in order to benefit at trial from the higher standard of reasonable doubt. This would not only be destructive of judicial economy but at the same time prejudicial to whatever mitigating effect might have come from a guilty plea, as evidence of remorse. There would seem in principle no good reason why the sentencing judge in deciding disputed facts should not observe the same evidentiary standards as we demand of juries. In *R. v. Proudlock,* [[1979] 1 S.C.R. 525] Pigeon J., dealing with an issue involving conviction, observed (at p. 550 S.C.R.):

> In my view, there are in our criminal law only three standards of evidence:
>
> 1. Proof beyond a reasonable doubt which is the standard to be met by the Crown against the accused;
> 2. Proof on a preponderance of the evidence or a balance of probabilities which is the burden of proof on the accused when he has to meet a presumption requiring him to establish or to prove a fact or an excuse;
> 3. Evidence raising a reasonable doubt which is what is required to overcome any other presumption of fact or of law.

The civil test only comes into play when the accused has to meet a presumption and it operates in favour of the accused.

I can see no good purpose served by the alternate Crown submission, namely, the adoption of a third standard of proof, "clear and convincing" evidence, in Canadian law. I agree with the remarks of Lord Tucker in *Dingwall v. J. Wharton (Shipping), Ltd.*, [1961] 2 Lloyd's Rep. 213 at p. 216:

> ... I am quite unable to accede to the proposition that there is some intermediate onus between that which is required in criminal cases and the balance of probability which is sufficient in timeous civil actions.

In conclusion, I see no justification for the introduction of the complexity and confusion which would inevitably follow upon the acceptance of standards of proof varying from trial to sentence.

I would dismiss the appeal.

[Appeal dismissed, Laskin C.J.C., Estey and McIntyre JJ. dissenting on the question of jurisdiction.]

Post-*Gardiner*, ss. 723, 724, 725 and 726.1 of the *Criminal Code* were enacted to address the presentation of facts, disputed and otherwise, at a sentencing hearing. Consider these provisions in answering the following questions.

QUESTIONS

8. **A jury found the accused guilty of sexual assault. The complainant testified that, during the period in the indictment, the accused touched her private parts and, on one occasion, had forcible intercourse with her. The jury were instructed that they need not find all of these events in order to convict. Recognizing that some of these events would attract harsher sentences than others, the trial judge asks counsel what facts should she take into account for the purposes of sentencing. What approach can each counsel take in response?**

9. **The accused is charged with murder. It is alleged that he killed his co-worker in a jealous rage over a mutual love interest. The defence alleges that there was no such dispute over a love interest. However, the accused concedes that he did kill the co-worker, albeit while significantly intoxicated by alcohol. Both parties are content that the matter proceed as a guilty plea to manslaughter. What facts should be presented to the trial judge?**

10. **The defence and the Crown agree to a plea of guilty to certain offences. The defence takes serious issue with many of the aggravating facts. However, the Crown and the defence have agreed upon a joint submission as to the appropriate sentence. Should the Crown accept the defence version of the facts for the purposes of sentencing? What facts should be read in by the Crown at the sentencing hearing? Consider, in this regard, the *Martin Report* at pp. 323-7.**

11. **The accused pleads guilty to five break, enter and thefts. He also faces three outstanding charges of break, enter and theft. The latter charges are not scheduled to be tried for several months. Under what circumstances can the sentencing judge consider the outstanding charges? Now assume that the accused will only plead guilty to three break, enter and thefts, though he does not deny his involvement in the others. The Crown is prepared to proceed on that basis. However, she wants to have the facts relating to the other break, enter and thefts before the court. Can this be done?**

12. The accused pleads guilty to impaired driving causing bodily harm. His counsel, Joey Slipshod tells the sentencing judge that the accused no longer consumes alcohol or abuses his family, that he now goes to church every Sunday and also does volunteer work. The Crown is skeptical. What can he do? Now assume that Mr. Slipshod advises the court that the accused was understandably depressed on the material day as a close friend had died. Further, although impairment was a significant factor in his poor driving and the resultant accident, a bee flew into the car at the material time and causally contributed to the accident. How should the Crown respond? On which party does the onus lie to prove contested, mitigating facts?

Section 721 of the *Criminal Code* provides that the court may order a probation officer to prepare a *presentence report* relating to the accused for the purpose of assisting the court in determining an appropriate sentence. The pre-sentence report will contain valuable information about the accused on matters such as character, attitude, willingness to make amends and the history of previous dispositions, findings of guilt or alternative measures. The court may require that the probation officer include information on any further matters, relevant to sentencing.

QUESTIONS

13. A presentence report has been filed with the court at the sentencing hearing. The defence disputes that portion of the report where the author states: "Mr. Smith still feels that violence is an appropriate way to resolve disputes." What should defence counsel do?

14. The accused pleads guilty to break and enter and theft over $5,000. The presentence report contains, *inter alia,* the following: "The accused unequivocably denies his guilt. He stated to me that he only pleaded guilty so that he could get out on bail." What should the court do?

15. Many experienced defence counsel never request a presentence report and indicate that it is unnecessary when inquiries are made by the trial judge. Why? Assuming that a presentence report is ordered, what steps can defence counsel appropriately take to ensure that the report is as favourable as possible? What advice can defence counsel give to the accused who is about to be interviewed by the author of the report if the accused denied his guilt at trial?

Section 722 of the *Criminal Code* provides for the consideration of a *victim impact statement* by the sentencing court. "Victim" is defined in s. 722(4) of the *Code*.

QUESTION

16. The accused has pleaded guilty to impaired driving causing bodily harm. The victim has suffered speech and thought disorder and cannot prepare a victim impact statement. Her mother prepares a victim impact statement, reflecting not only the physical and emotional devastation to the victim, but to herself. The mother notes, *inter alia,* that she was going to retire, to be cared for by the victim before the incident. Instead, she must now continue to work and care for her daughter. She notes that her husband (the victim's father) died several days before this crime was committed. She hopes that the accused "will experience the same physical and emotional pain that we are experiencing" and that he should remain in jail for a long, long time. She advises the Crown that she wishes to tell all this, and more, to the judge personally. What issues arise and how should the parties address them? Consider, in this regard, *R. v. Curtis* (1992), 69 C.C.C. (3d) 385 (N.B.C.A.).

Of course, the parties, and most particularly the accused, may tender evidence, *viva voce* or in writing, relating to the character of the accused and the circumstances of the offence or offender which may mitigate sentence.

QUESTION

17. Various individuals are prepared to attend court or to write character letters for the accused. What factors should influence counsel as to which witnesses to rely upon and whether they should give *viva voce* evidence or simply write a letter? What instructions, if any, should counsel give to a witness who intends to write a character letter? Now assume that counsel receives such a letter. It states, *inter alia:* "No way would Louie commit a sexual assault on anybody. He's not that kind of person." What should counsel do?

The Crown may prove the accused's prior convictions, if any.

QUESTION

18. How does the Crown prove prior convictions which are not admitted? Consider, in this regard, s. 667 of the *Criminal Code*. Is s. 667 exhaustive?

---

4. Joint Submissions as to Sentence

The defence and Crown may differ as to the appropriate sentence to be imposed upon the accused. Or, they may agree to jointly recommend a range of sentences, such as six to nine months imprisonment. Or, they may agree that the Crown will recommend no more than a certain sentence and that the defence can recommend whatever it wants or no less than a certain sentence. There are countless variations arising out of resolution discussions. Sometimes, these discussions result in an agreement that the Crown and defence will put forward a *joint submission* or joint recommendation to the court on sentencing.

R. v. RUBENSTEIN

(1987), 41 C.C.C. (3d) 91 (Ont. C.A.); leave to appeal to S.C.C. refused 41 C.C.C. (3d) vi

The judgment of the court was delivered by

Zuber J.A.: —

.....

On June 17, 1986, the appellant pleaded guilty to a charge of wash trading contrary to s. 340 [now s. 382] of the *Criminal Code* and two charges of fraud contrary to s. 338 [now s. 380] of the *Criminal Code* before Judge D. Draper in Toronto. On July 22nd, the appellant pleaded guilty to a further charge of fraud contrary to s. 338 of the *Code* which had been transferred from Vancouver to Toronto. On August 19, 1986, the appellant was sentenced to a total of five years' imprisonment. The appellant appeals against both the convictions and the sentence.

Appeal against conviction

The appeal against conviction is based on the assertion that Judge Draper wrongfully refused to allow the appellant to withdraw his pleas of guilty. An appreciation of this issue requires a brief recital of the facts.

On June 17th, the appellant who was represented by experienced counsel pleaded to the three Ontario charges and an Agreed Statement of Fact was filed with respect to those charges. The Agreed Statement of Fact amply demonstrated the appellant's guilt. Since time was required to have the Vancouver charge transferred, the matter was adjourned to July 22nd. On June 17th, counsel for the appellant told the court that a joint submission would be made with respect to sentence but no details were given.

On July 22nd, the appellant pleaded guilty to the Vancouver charge. Following the guilty plea the facts of that charge were read by the Crown Attorney and admitted by counsel for the appellant. The facts as read fully supported the plea of guilty. Following this guilty plea, Judge Draper was told of the joint submission of counsel for the appellant and counsel for the Crown. The joint submission was that the appellant should be given a suspended sentence and placed on probation for a period of three years. If such sentence were imposed the appellant would arrange restitution to two of the victims in a total sum of $85,000 and would consent to a compensation order for an additional amount. It was further submitted that the appellant who was the subject of an extradition order to the United States would withdraw legal proceedings contesting the extradition order so that he would be immediately extradited to face stock promotion charges in Oregon and California.

In the course of these submissions it became apparent that Judge Draper did not look favourably on the joint submissions and was unlikely to accede to them. The case was further adjourned to July 25th, when counsel for the Crown and the appellant made further submissions in support of the propriety of the joint submissions. When it became clear that the joint submissions would not be accepted by Judge Draper, counsel for the appellant sought to withdraw the pleas of guilty but this request was refused.

Judge Draper concluded his remarks in which he refused to allow the withdrawal of the guilty pleas as follows:

> I'm certainly not going to allow a procedure in which you make a ... in which defence counsel makes a proposal, and when the Judge indicates it's unacceptable wishes to withdraw the plea. That would result in Judge shopping in the worst reprehensible way. That application to withdraw the plea is denied.

The matter was further adjourned to August 19th, when counsel for the appellant made further submissions respecting the withdrawal of the guilty plea. The application was again refused and the appellant was sentenced to a total of five years' imprisonment.

It is not suggested or argued that the appellant did not fully understand the charges he faced or that his plea was equivocal. Nor is there any question but that the facts admitted amply demonstrated the guilt of the appellant. The appellant was fully aware of his legal rights and was represented by competent and experienced counsel.

It is not argued that the trial judge was in any way bound by the joint submission. He was obliged to give serious consideration to the joint submission and he did so, but in the end he plainly and strongly disagreed with the joint submission.

It is argued in this court that when a trial judge regards the joint submission with respect to sentence as unreasonable or in error he should so inform an accused and give that accused an opportunity to withdraw the plea. It is argued that to do otherwise would be fundamentally unfair since an accused in the position of an appellant offers the plea in the expectation that the joint submission will be followed. It was further argued that the joint submission was the *quid pro quo* for the pleas of guilty and therefore the failure of the trial judge to heed the joint submission entitled the accused to be restored to his original position, *i.e.*, he could force the Crown to prove its case against him in full.

I disagree with this proposition. The power of the trial judge to impose a sentence cannot be limited to a joint submission, and the joint submission cannot be the basis upon which to seek to escape the sentencing judge when it appears that he chooses to reject the joint submission. As Judge Draper observed, an accused who could thus withdraw his plea could simply keep doing so until he found a trial judge who would accept a joint submission. A plea of guilty in the same way as a finding of guilt after trial exposes an accused to a proper sentence to be determined by the trial judge. In the case on appeal the difference between the sentence sought by the joint submission and that imposed by the trial judge was stark but that does not affect the principle involved. To permit an accused to withdraw his plea when the sentence does not suit him puts the court in the unseemly position of bargaining with the accused.

While a judge has a discretion to allow the withdrawal of a plea of guilty, Judge Draper was right in refusing to allow the withdrawal of the pleas of guilty in this case. The appeal against conviction is dismissed.

Appeal against sentence

At the conclusion of oral argument when this matter was heard the court expressed the view that the sentence imposed was too severe and the appeal against sentence was allowed. The custodial term was reduced to a period of two years less a day and there was added to that sentence a fine of $25,000 and in default of that fine an additional term of six months' imprisonment.

Appeal against conviction dismissed; appeal against sentence allowed.

R. v. DORSEY

[1999] O.J. No. 2957 (C.A.)

The following judgment was delivered by

The Court: —

Overview

The appellant was charged with two counts of fraud over $5,000. He pled guilty to one count of fraud over and in respect of the second count to the lesser and included offence of fraud under $5,000. The Crown accepted his pleas. After the facts were read in His Honour Judge Khawley convicted the appellant of one count of fraud over and one count of fraud under. He sentenced the appellant to imprisonment for 20 months on his fraud over conviction and 6 months concurrent on his fraud under conviction. This sentence was in addition to 8 months of pre-trial custody. The trial judge also imposed a restitution order of $94,000 in respect of the fraud over conviction and $1,100 in respect of the fraud under conviction.

The appellant appeals his sentence. His principal ground of appeal is that the trial judge erred in not accepting a joint submission made to him by Crown and defence counsel. The joint submission was that the appellant be sentenced to imprisonment for 7 months. The joint submission made no provision for a restitution order.

The circumstances of the offences and the joint submission

With respect to count 1, in September 1997, an elderly Saskatchewan man received a telephone call from a male person who identified himself as

Daryl Thompson. The victim was told that he had won a prize of $947,382. Over the following months the victim was repeatedly contacted, by collect telephone calls, about the prize and told that in order to get his winnings he had to come up with funds to pay taxes, shipping, insurance and exchange rates. The telephone calls were verified by the victim's telephone records. In the end, the victim made numerous payments, ostensibly to cover these costs. The total loss to the victim was about $94,000. This represented his life savings and some money he borrowed in the hope of collecting his winnings.

The second victim was also an elderly man. He was telephoned and told that he had won $50,000 (U.S.) in a sweepstake. To collect his winnings he wired about $1,100 to the appellant and his associates in Toronto. He also paid for collect calls made to his residence.

The appellant was not the only person involved in this fraudulent scheme. The case against the appellant was largely circumstantial. The Crown only had direct evidence to prove that two of the money orders were picked up by the appellant. The Crown acknowledged that it had no evidence to establish that the appellant was the "mastermind" behind the scheme. However, the Crown also did not accept the converse proposition, that the appellant was a "minor player." In the result, the matter proceeded on the basis that the appellant was a middle management player in the two frauds.

In making the joint submission that the appellant be sentenced to imprisonment for 7 months, Crown counsel described the fraudulent scheme as "heinous." She noted that all of the money was gone and that there was no hope of restitution. We assume that this latter comment was intended to explain why the joint submission did not include a restitution order.

Upon being advised that there would be a joint submission, and before the appellant entered his pleas, the trial judge spoke directly to the appellant to confirm that he had been told that there would be a joint submission and to advise the appellant that he was not bound by it. The trial judge said:

> All right. Mr. Dorsey, I just want you to be clear about what you are doing. You have excellent counsel, but I just want you to be sure you understand that both your lawyer and the Crown came to see me in my office, as you know, but they may ... from what I understand they may have a joint submission. Is my understanding correct?
>
> Defence Counsel: That's correct, Your Honour.
>
> Crown Counsel: Yes.
>
> The joint submission will be put to me. I am not bound by it. In other words, I can either accept it or reject it. I can go lower or higher or I can simply accept that. Do you understand that, sir?
>
> Appellant: Yes, sir.
>
> It was at that point that the appellant was arraigned and entered his pleas.

The Sentencing

After hearing counsels' submissions and statements from the victims, the trial judge adjourned the sentencing for one day so that he could further consider the joint submission, a submission that obviously troubled him. As the trial judge put it:

> One of the reasons that I adjourned the Sentence to this morning was not only to research the cases on sentencing, but also because my initial impression was that this called for five years in the penitentiary. I felt it prudent, therefore, to adjourn the matter to give me time for reflection.

The next day, the Crown called the two victims and counsel made some further submissions. The trial judge then rejected the joint submission and, as we have said, sentenced the appellant to imprisonment for a total of 20 months. He also imposed a restitution order totalling $95,100.

It is well established that a trial judge is not bound by a joint submission. The trial judge must, of course, give serious consideration and respect to a joint submission. The submission should be departed from only where the trial judge considers the joint submission to be contrary to the public interest and a submission which, if accepted, would bring the administration of justice into disrepute.

The appellant has a significant criminal record. It includes convictions for narcotic offences, assault, aggravated assault, escaping lawful custody, theft, failing to comply, obstructing police and impersonating with intent. The longest sentence served by the appellant was a four year sentence consequent upon his conviction for a robbery in 1989. Most significantly, in 1996, the appellant pled guilty to a charge of fraud over $5,000 which involved the same fraudulent scheme that was used to defraud the two victims to whom we have referred. The appellant was sentenced to imprisonment for 14 months. In the 1996 fraud the victim lost $76,000.

It is obvious that the trial judge gave considerable weight to counsels' joint submission. He said:

> I also appreciate that this is a joint submission and that *the Court must accept it unless it offends the administration of justice*. I come to the unfortunate conclusion that my position yesterday has not changed all that much. When all is said and done a five year penitentiary sentence is justifiable.
>
> ... Either way, he is facing today either twenty-two months or twenty-eight months. That is a far, far different sentence than the five year sentence I feel is justified, which subtracting one year for the guilty plea, would bring it to a four year sentence.
>
> ... In sum, I am rejecting the joint submission because, *in my view*, based on the comments I have made *it would bring the administration of justice into disrepute*. However, I must still give it some weight because there is no question that at times the Crown arrives at a joint submission for reasons that I am not privy to.
>
> ... The fair and proper sentence, in my view, is still one of thirty-two months. However, mindful, as I said of the joint submission, the sentence will be as follows — mindful of eight months of pre-trial custody, twenty months in jail. [Emphasis added.]

When he rejected the joint submission, the trial judge emphasized the appellant's lengthy criminal record. He reviewed the more than 30 convictions recorded on the appellant's record since 1978. He was understandably troubled by the appellant's conviction on October 30, 1996 for fraud over $5,000. That fraud, as we have said, involved the same scheme as was brought into play in this case. In rejecting the joint submission the trial judge also turned his mind to the fact that the circumstantial nature of the case may have adversely affected the likelihood of the Crown securing a conviction. This was not, however, a case where there was a concession by the Crown that the Crown could not secure a conviction were the case to go to trial. Indeed, defence counsel conceded in the course of her submissions that, "there is circumstantial evidence clearly establishing his involvement."

We are of the view that it was open to the trial judge, in the particular circumstances, to reject the joint submission. The trial judge advised Crown counsel, defence counsel and the appellant of that prospect before the appellant entered his plea. Having received the joint submission, he adjourned the sentencing to consider the matter more thoroughly in light of his concern about the joint submission. He rejected the joint submission, in the final analysis, on appropriate grounds. He was entitled to conclude that the joint submission, if accepted, would be contrary to public interest and would bring the administration of justice into disrepute. He considered all of the applicable aggravating and mitigating factors. The sentence imposed was within an acceptable range and we see no basis upon which to interfere with it.

We would not interfere with the restitution order. In total, it represented the losses of the two elderly victims of the fraudulent activity in which the appellant played a role. The fact that the appellant is, as matters now stand, unable to pay the restitution order or any meaningful part of it, is not a determinative factor. It was open to the trial judge to impose a restitution order, even though the joint submission did not include such an order.

For these reasons, we would grant leave to appeal but would dismiss the appeal against sentence.

QUESTIONS

19. The accused pleaded guilty to aggravated sexual assault. At the time of the offence, he knew he was a carrier of the AIDS virus. The accused, with great brutality, sexually assaulted the complainant and endangered her life. Indeed, the assault caused significant permanent injuries. The accused had an extensive criminal record for violent offences, including sexual assault. He had received 17 previous custodial sentences. The Crown and defence put forward a joint submission of seven years imprisonment which was rejected by the sentencing judge as unconscionably low. A 12-year sentence was imposed (see *R. v. Winn* (1995), 43 C.R. (4th) 71 (Ont. Prov. Ct.)). Are there steps that could have been taken by counsel to better ensure that the joint submission was acceptable to the court? How can a pre-trial be used in this regard? What if a sentencing judge indicates that he or she is inclined to reject the joint submission? Can the plea of guilt be struck? Can counsel then appear before another judge to implement the joint submission? Now assume that the joint submission was accepted by the trial judge. The case came to the attention of the Attorney General who instructed the Crown's office to appeal against the sentence imposed. Can the Crown appeal a sentence imposed in accordance with a joint submission? Can the accused appeal such a sentence? Consider, in this regard, the *Martin Report*, *supra*, pp. 327-34; *R. v. Dubien* (1982), 67 C.C.C. (2d) 341; *R. v. Simoneau* (1978), 2 C.R. (3d) S-17;

R. v. Wood (1988), 43 C.C.C. (3d) 570 (Ont. C.A.); *R. v. Goodwin* (1981), 21 C.R. (3d) 263 (N.S.C.A.).

20. The accused is charged with aggravated assault. He alleges that he acted in self-defence. His counsel advises the Crown that he has no instructions to enter a plea of guilt but would be interested in ascertaining the Crown's position on sentence. The Crown indicates that the victim is reluctant to testify. Accordingly, he will agree to a non-custodial disposition on a plea to assault causing bodily harm. If convicted of aggravated assault, the accused is likely to be sentenced to a substantial term of imprisonment. The accused maintains that he acted in self-defence but instructs counsel to "take the deal". What should defence counsel do? Note that the late American vice-president Spiro Agnew once pleaded *nolo contendere* to criminal offences in the United States. Is such a plea available in Canada?

---

5. Purpose and Principles of Sentencing

Section 718 of the *Criminal Code* provides as follows:

> 718. The fundamental purpose of sentencing is to contribute, along with crime prevention initiatives, to respect for the law and the maintenance of a just, peaceful and safe society by imposing just sanctions that have one or more of the following objectives:
>
> (*a*) to denounce unlawful conduct;
> (*b*) to deter the offender [specific deterrence] and other persons [general deterrence] from committing offences;
> (*c*) to separate offenders from society, where necessary;
> (*d*) to assist in rehabilitating offenders;
> (*e*) to provide reparations for harm done to victims or to the community; and,
> (*f*) to promote a sense of responsibility in offenders, and acknowledgment of the harm done to victims and to the community.

It is a fundamental principle of sentencing that a sentence must be *proportionate* to the gravity of the offence and the extent of the offender's participation (s. 718.1 of the *Criminal Code*). A mandated sentence which is grossly disproportionate may attract s. 12 *Charter* scrutiny (*R. v. Smith* (1987), 34 C.C.C. (3d) 97 (S.C.C.)). Further, a sentence should be increased or reduced to account for relevant aggravating or mitigating factors relating to the offence or the offender. Evidence of hate-motivated crime, spousal or child abuse and breach of trust are statutory examples of aggravating circumstances (s. 718.2(*a*)). The following case addresses the characterization of factors as aggravating or mitigating.

R. v. M.(G.)

(1992), 77 C.C.C. (3d) 310 (Ont. C.A.)

The judgment of the court was delivered by

Abella J.A.: — This is an appeal by the Crown from a suspended sentence and one year's probation following a guilty plea by G.M., the respondent in this appeal, to 12 charges of indecently assaulting his two daughters. The charges relate to assaults which occurred from 1973 until 1979, starting when the girls were 11 or 12 years old. They stopped, as did the marriage, when the oldest daughter in 1980 disclosed the assaults to her mother. The incidents involved extensive touching, digital penetration and *cunnilingus*. The Crown submits that the trial judge, Misener J., erred in failing to apply principles of general deterrence and denunciation when he imposed a non-custodial sentence.

The trial judge characterized the conduct as "an extremely serious breach of trust"; "systematic", "gross", and "outrageous" misconduct, and a "serious ... and a continuing trauma" to the daughters.

The trial judge rejected the application of specific deterrence because the respondent needed no further personal deterrence, having acknowledged, apologized for, and medically treated his former behaviour, and having remarried in 1988. Nor, for the same reasons, was the principle of rehabilitation of any relevance to the respondent, there being no indication that the possibility of recidivism or antisocial conduct existed. The trial judge then considered whether the principle of general deterrence applied, and concluded that it did not.

.....

While I agree with the trial judge that there is no need to invoke the principle of specific deterrence in this case, in my view he erred in concluding that the principle of general deterrence is inapplicable to incidents of indecent assault between parent and child. On the contrary, it is a significant consideration in determining the appropriateness of a sentence.

The differing purposes of general and specific deterrence were set out in the 1987 report of the Canadian Sentencing Commission entitled *Sentencing Reform: A Canadian Approach* (1987), p. 135:

> Deterrence is either general or individual (specific). General deterrence aims to discourage potential offenders. It is defined by the Panel on Research on Deterrent and Incapacitative Effects (1978; 3) as "the inhibiting effect of sanctions on the criminal activity of people *other than* the sanctioned offender" (emphasis in text). Individual deterrence aims to discourage the sanctioned offender from re-offending.

The commission concluded at p. 138 that even though the efficacy of general deterrence theory is not scientifically measurable, none the less "it is plausible to argue that a general effect of deterrence stems from the mere fact that an array of sanctions are known to be imposed with some regularity".

Denunciation has also been recognized as an aspect of the sentencing process: *R. v. Ingram and Grimsdale* (1977), 35 C.C.C. (2d) 376 (Ont. C.A.), at p. 379, *per* Dubin J.A.; Law Reform Commission of Canada, *Report on Dispositions and Sentences in the Criminal Process: Guidelines* (1977), pp. 27, 37 and 65. The principle was defined as follows by the Canadian Sentencing Commission at p. 142 of its report: "Denunciation is essentially a communication process which uses the medium of language to express condemnation...".

The public can logically be expected to infer from the nature of the sentence the extent to which a court views as serious, certain conduct by a given individual. If the presence or absence of denunciation can be inferred from a sentence, then the debate over whether denunciation is a valid aspect — as opposed to a valid objective — of sentencing merges with the observation that one of the instructive messages the public is likely to take from a sentence it views as deterrent, is that it is also denunciatory. The converse proposition is equally true. Sentences which appear on their face to be exceptionally lenient in the circumstances can be presumed to generate neither deterrence nor denunciation.

.....

In the end, of course, the sentence must attempt to blend a particular accused with the gravity of his or her offence. Aggravating and mitigating circumstances are weighed, with the objective of arriving at a disposition which is, to the extent that such a thing is humanly achievable, let alone universally accepted as such, reasonable and just in all the circumstances.

Looking at the circumstances in the respondent's case, the trial judge, in my view, placed inappropriate reliance on several factors he characterized as mitigating.

He identified the following as mitigating factors:

(a) the respondent was 51 years of age;
(b) he was a well-respected, successful and accomplished businessman;
(c) the respondent had the respect of the community;
(d) there was a breakdown in intimacy and sexual relations between the respondent and his first wife which, in part, was a cause of the misconduct;
(e) there were no threats or violence involved;
(f) the respondent "fully disclosed" his misconduct to all concerned in 1980;
(g) he sought treatment after the initial disclosure and was successful in his rehabilitation, and
(h) the respondent "fully and generously" supported his wife and children until 1988.

While aspects of character are of varying relevance in sentencing depending on the offence (see *R. v. S.(R.J.)* (1985), 19 C.C.C. (3d) 115 at p. 127, 45 C.R. (3d) 161, 14 W.C.B. 19 (Ont. C.A.), *per* Lacourcière J.A.), I have difficulty seeing how someone who is accomplished and successful in business is entitled to any more consideration from a court for an offence of this kind, than someone with less business acumen or fewer resources.

Nor is it clear to me why the breakdown of "the sexual part" of the relationship between the respondent and his wife, for whatever reason, is in any way relevant to his having abused his daughters. It suggests either that the daughters were understandable substitutes in the same home, or that the wife was in some way morally culpable for the father assaulting their daughters, both completely untenable suggestions.

Nor do I accept that the absence of tangible violence makes the offence less worthy of censure, since in my view "the offence of sexual assault is an inherently violent crime": *R. v. Abdulla Khan*, a decision of the Ontario Court (General Division), released June 5, 1991, *per* Moldaver J., at p. 4. There is no doubt, however, that there are escalating degrees of violence and that these degrees are undoubtedly relevant as aggravating factors where they exist.

Nor, in my view, do threats have to be articulated for a situation such as this to be deemed threatening. The dimensional harm of this offence when it occurs between parent and child is in its exploitation of the trust the child is entitled to place in a person upon whom she is dependent. While the conduct may often be explained by reference either to personal or social pathologies, it cannot ever be, or be seen to be, excused. The child is always, by virtue of the power imbalance inherent in his or her status as a child, in a more vulnerable position than the parent. In *Norberg v. Wynrib*, a decision of the Supreme Court of Canada, released June 18, 1992 [since reported 92 D.L.R. (4th) 449, [1992] 2 S.C.R. 226, 12 C.C.L.T. (2d) 1], La Forest J. at p. 23 [p. 463 D.L.R.] cites with approval the observations of one writer who refers to relationships where there is the capacity to "dominate and influence" as "'power dependency'" relationships:

> Professor Coleman outlines a number of situations which she calls "power dependency" relationships: see Phyllis Coleman, "Sex in Power Dependency Relationships: Taking Unfair Advantage of the 'Fair' Sex", 53 Albany L. Rev. 95. Included in these relationships are *parent-child*, psychotherapist-patient, physician-patient, clergy-penitent, professor-student, attorney-client, and employer-employee. She asserts that "consent" to a sexual relationship in such relationships is inherently suspect.

(Emphasis added.) (See also the opinion in *Norberg* of McLachlin J., who discusses such power imbalances and the duty they create at pp. 6-8 [pp. 487-9 D.L.R.].)

If consent is inherently suspect in these relationships, then while degrees of violence or threats may undoubtedly be considered as more or less aggravating factors in sentencing, it does not necessarily follow that their absence operates to reduce the seriousness of the offence. The status of parent-child, the dependency and vulnerability which flow from that status, and the trust the child is entitled to presume, all underscore that the relationship between parents and their children is a fiduciary one. The trust is offended no less when exploited in what appears otherwise to be a warm relationship between father and daughter, where the love a child feels for her father may generate acquiescence on her part without his subjecting her to additional physical or verbal victimization. It may even be seen, as it was by these two victims, as a greater and more traumatic invasion of their trust when it comes from a loved parent whom they are anxious to please.

I agree that the respondent acknowledged and apologized for his assaults, but only after his older daughter disclosed them to her mother. His "fully and generously" complying with his legal obligation to pay financial support to his wife and children after the disclosure resulted in their separation is, it seems to me, a neutral factor, as is his age in this case.

But while a custodial term is clearly warranted in this case, there are some mitigating factors which should be considered. From the evidence, the trial judge correctly concluded that neither specific deterrence nor rehabilitation applied. The respondent, after acknowledging the assaults, immediately sought and successfully completed counselling and therapeutic psychiatric care when his daughters disclosed his behaviour. He has consistently shown genuine remorse for his conduct. He has, according to a medical report filed with the court at sentencing, completely rehabilitated himself. The high regard and respect he enjoyed in his community have undoubtedly been irrevocably and profoundly impaired. And finally, it has been well over a year between the suspension of the respondent's sentence in May, 1991, and the imposition of this custodial term on appeal.

The factors the trial judge accepted as aggravating are the following:

(a) exploitation of the vulnerability of children;
(b) "extremely serious" breach of parental trust or duty;
(c) two victims;
(d) number of offences, which the learned sentencing judge described as "gross or "outrageous" systematic misconduct;
(e) nature of the misconduct, and
(f) victim impact.

Having identified them, however, he none the less found them to be worthy of less consideration than the factors he identified as mitigating. In my view, his emphasis was misplaced.

In erroneously concluding that general deterrence has no application in cases of this kind, the trial judge relied exclusively on whether there was any value of imprisonment for the particular accused, rather than taking into account any potential impact on the public perception of a father indecently assaulting two daughters over a six-year period. This court rejected that approach in *R. v. Palmer* (1985), 7 O.A.C. 348 (C.A.), where MacKinnon, A.C.J.O. said, at p. 350:

> The learned trial judge seemed to have only the welfare and rehabilitation of the accused in mind when he imposed the sentence he did. While it is a consideration and an important consideration, it is obviously not the only consideration. The sexual abuse of a child by one in loco parentis is a very serious crime. It is a gross abuse of trust and power which society does not tolerate. It warrants, absent quite exceptional circumstances, a denunciatory sentence which reflects society's revulsion at this type of conduct and at the same time has regard to the possibility of rehabilitation of the offender. It is not unusual that such offenders have steady work; that it is their first brush with the criminal law; and that they express remorse when their activities are discovered. There is also an aspect of general deterrence to such a sentence which should not be ignored.

Counsel for the respondent conceded before this court that the principle of general deterrence is not only applicable but paramount in cases involving the parental sexual abuse of children. But he submits that the mitigating circumstances in this case are sufficiently exceptional that no custodial term is required. I disagree both with the proposition that the mitigating circumstances are exceptional and with the submission that a custodial term is not justified in this case. In *R. v. Clayton* (1982), 69 C.C.C. (2d) 81 (Ont. C.A.), at p. 83, Cory J.A. stated:

> Incest is a serious crime. Although performed without violence, it may well leave lasting scars. The crime is one which often has terrible consequences for the victim. It constitutes a breach of the greatest trust that can be bestowed on a man, the trust of his children ... *It is appropriate that in most*

> *cases of incest involving young children that a term of imprisonment should be imposed.*

(Emphasis added.)

More recently, this court confirmed that view in *R. v. Fraser* (1987), 20 O.A.C. 78 (C.A.). Lacourciere J.A., in language directly apposite to this case, stated at p. 80:

> We are, nonetheless, all of the view that the sentence imposed failed totally to reflect the gravity of the offence and society's abhorrence with the conduct of the respondent. This court has on many previous occasions set out the principles which should be applied in determining the sentence in these and similar cases. Those principles establish that, in the absence of exceptional circumstances, the imposition of a suspended sentence in such cases is inappropriate. Sexual abuse of children cannot be tolerated and must be denounced so that society will be made aware of the court's revulsion for such conduct which, in this case, involved a serious breach of trust.
>
> General deterrence was not referred to in the reasons for sentence and does not seem to have been considered. The trial judge emphasized the voluntary interruption of the sexual activity as well as the rehabilitation of the offender. In our view, however, the extremely serious nature of the offence which, in itself continued over a lengthy period of time, requires a substantial period of incarceration in a reformatory.

(See also *R. v. Gianfelice,* a judgment of the Ontario Court of Appeal, released February 28, 1992 [since reported 52 O.A.C. 243, 15 W.C.B. (2d) 375]; *R. v. J.(T.R.)* (1991), 50 O.A.C. 75, 13 W.C.B. (2d) 626 (C.A.); *R. v. W.(A.)* (1991), 3 O.R. (3d) 171, 45 O.A.C. 359, 13 W.C.B. (2d) 23 (C.A.); *R. v. E.(R.J.)* (1990), 42 O.A.C. 374, 11 W.C.B. (2d) 386 (C.A.); *R. v. L.(G.A.)* (1990), 41 O.A.C. 150 (C.A.); *R. v. B.(J.)* (1990), 36 O.A.C. 307, 9 W.C.B. (2d) 622 (C.A.); *R. v. Brouillette,* a judgment of the Quebec Court of Appeal, released February 26, 1988 [summarized 4 W.C.B. (2d) 370]).

In the circumstances, I would grant leave to appeal, allow the appeal, and vary the sentence to a term of 12 months. But for the mitigating factors, a heavier penalty would clearly have been justified. I can see no basis for ordering a term of probation.

Section 718.2(*b*) to (*e*) also articulates other sentencing principles:

- **(*b*) a sentence should be similar to sentences imposed on similar offenders for similar offences committed in similar circumstances [the principle of *avoiding disparity*.];**
- **(*c*) where consecutive sentences are imposed, the combined sentence should not be unduly long or harsh [the principle of *totality*];**
- **(*d*) an offender should not be deprived of liberty, if less restrictive sanctions may be appropriate in the circumstances; and**
- **(*e*) all available sanctions other than imprisonment that are reasonable in the circumstances should be considered for all offenders, with particular attention to the circumstances of aboriginal offenders.**

The consideration of non-custodial alternatives is particularly important in the case of first or youthful offenders (see *R. v. Stein* (1974), 15 C.C.C. (2d) 376 (Ont. C.A.)) and aboriginal offenders (see *R. v. Gladue* (1999), 133 C.C.C. (3d) 385), substantially reproduced below. Further, in

an appropriate case, the court may consider both the systemic and background factors that may have played a role in the commission of the offence (see *R. v. Borde* (2003), 172 C.C.C. (3d) 225 (Ont. C.A.)).

R. v. GLADUE

(1999), 133 C.C.C. (3d) 385 (S.C.C.)

[The appellant was a member of the aboriginal community and one of nine children. She was 19 years old and five months pregnant at the time of the offence. The appellant had suspicions that her common-law spouse was having an affair with her older sister. During her 19th birthday celebration, she had said to a friend "the next time he fools around on me, I'll kill him". Later that evening, the appellant located the victim and her sister. An argument ensued and the appellant stabbed the victim in the chest, the knife penetrating the victim's heart. At the time of the stabbing, the appellant had a blood-alcohol content of between 155 and 165 milligrams of alcohol in 100 millilitres of blood. The appellant was originally charged with second degree murder but pleaded guilty to manslaughter. The appellant was sentenced to three years' imprisonment and to a ten-year weapons prohibition. Her appeal of the sentence to the British Columbia Court of Appeal was dismissed.]

The judgment of the Court was delivered by

Cory and Iacobucci JJ.: — On September 3, 1996, the new Part XXIII of the *Criminal Code*, R.S.C., 1985, c. C-46, pertaining to sentencing came into force. These provisions codify for the first time the fundamental purpose and principles of sentencing. This appeal is particularly concerned with the new s. 718.2(*e*). It provides that all available sanctions other than imprisonment that are reasonable in the circumstances should be considered for all offenders, with particular attention to the circumstances of aboriginal offenders. This appeal must consider how this provision should be interpreted and applied.

.....

The issue in this appeal is the proper interpretation and application to be given to s. 718.2(*e*) of the *Criminal Code*. The provision reads as follows:

> 718.2 A court that imposes a sentence shall also take into consideration the following principles:
>
> .....
>
> (*e*) all available sanctions other than imprisonment that are reasonable in the circumstances should be considered for all offenders, with particular attention to the circumstances of aboriginal offenders.

The question to be resolved is whether the majority of the British Columbia Court of Appeal erred in finding that, in the circumstances of this case, the trial judge correctly applied s. 718.2(*e*) in imposing a sentence of three years' imprisonment. To answer this question, it will be necessary to determine the legislative purpose of s. 718.2(*e*), and, in particular, the words "with particular attention to the circumstances of aboriginal offenders". The appeal requires this Court to begin the process of articulating the rules and principles that should govern the practical application of s. 718.2(*e*) of the *Criminal Code* by a trial judge.

.....

[Section 718 is reproduced.]

Clearly, s. 718 is, in part, a restatement of the basic sentencing aims, which are listed in paras. (*a*) through (*d*). What are new, though, are paras. (*e*) and (*f*), which along with para. (*d*) focus upon the restorative goals of repairing the harms suffered by individual victims and by the community as a whole, promoting a sense of responsibility and an acknowledgment of the harm caused on the part of the offender, and attempting to rehabilitate or heal the offender. The concept of restorative justice which underpins paras. (*d*), (*e*), and (*f*) is briefly discussed below, but as a general matter restorative justice involves some form of restitution and reintegration into the community. The need for offenders to take responsibility for their actions is central to the sentencing process: D. Kwochka, "Aboriginal Injustice: Making Room for a Restorative Paradigm" (1996), 60 Sask. L. Rev. 153, at p. 165. Restorative sentencing goals do not usually correlate with the use of prison as a sanction. In our view, Parliament's choice to include (*e*) and (*f*) alongside the traditional sentencing goals must be understood as evidencing an intention to expand the parameters of the sentencing analysis for all offenders. The principle of restraint expressed in s. 718.2(*e*) will necessarily be informed by this re-orientation.

Just as the context of Part XXIII supports the view that s. 718.2(*e*) has a remedial purpose for all offenders, the scheme of Part XXIII also supports the view that s. 718.2(*e*) has a particular remedial role for aboriginal peoples. The respondent is correct to point out that there is jurisprudence which pre-dates the enactment of s. 718.2(*e*) in which aboriginal offenders have been sentenced differently in light of their unique circumstances. However, the existence of such jurisprudence is not, on its own, especially probative of the issue of whether s. 718.2(*e*) has a remedial role. There is also sentencing jurisprudence which holds, for example, that a court must consider the unique circumstances of offenders who are battered spouses, or who are mentally disabled. Although the validity of the principles expressed in this latter jurisprudence is unchallenged by the 1996 sentencing reforms, one does not find reference to these principles in Part XXIII. If Part XXIII were indeed a codification of principles regarding the appropriate method of sentencing different categories of offenders, one would expect to find such references. The wording of s. 718.2(*e*), viewed in light of the absence of similar stipulations in the remainder of Part XXIII, reveals that Parliament has chosen to single out aboriginal offenders for particular attention.

C. Legislative History

Support for the foregoing understanding of s. 718.2(*e*) as having the remedial purpose of restricting the use of prison for all offenders, and as having a particular remedial role with respect to aboriginal peoples, is provided by statements made by the Minister of Justice and others at the time that what was then Bill C-41 was before Parliament. Although these statements are clearly not decisive as to the meaning and purpose of s. 718.2(*e*), they are nonetheless helpful, particularly insofar as they corroborate and do not contradict the meaning and purpose to be derived upon a reading of the words of the provision in the context of Part XXIII as a whole: *Rizzo & Rizzo Shoes* [[1998] 1 S.C.R. 27] at paras. 31 and 35.

.....

[The Court reviews statements made during the House of Commons Debates.]

It can be seen, therefore, that the government position when Bill C-41 was under consideration was that the new Part XXIII was to be remedial in nature. The proposed enactment was directed, in particular, at reducing the use of prison as a sanction, at expanding the use of restorative justice principles in sentencing, and at engaging in both of these objectives with a sensitivity to aboriginal community justice initiatives when sentencing aboriginal offenders.

D. The Context of the Enactment of Section 718.2(e)

Further guidance as to the scope and content of Parliament's remedial purpose in enacting s. 718.2(*e*) may be derived from the social context surrounding the enactment of the provision …

The parties and interveners agree that the purpose of s. 718.2(*e*) is to respond to the problem of overincarceration in Canada, and to respond, in particular, to the more acute problem of the disproportionate incarceration of aboriginal peoples. They also agree that one of the roles of s. 718.2(*e*), and of various other provisions in Part XXIII, is to encourage sentencing judges to apply principles of restorative justice alongside or in the place of other, more traditional sentencing principles when making sentencing determinations. As the respondent states in its factum before this Court, s. 718.2(*e*) "provides the necessary flexibility and authority for sentencing judges to resort to the restorative model of justice in sentencing aboriginal offenders and to reduce the imposition of jail sentences where to do so would not sacrifice the traditional goals of sentencing".

The fact that the parties and interveners are in general agreement among themselves regarding the purpose of s. 718.2(*e*) is not determinative of the issue as a matter of statutory construction. However, as we have suggested, on the above points of agreement the parties and interveners are correct. A review of the problem of overincarceration in Canada, and of its peculiarly devastating impact upon Canada's aboriginal peoples, provides additional insight into the purpose and proper application of this new provision.

(1) The Problem of Overincarceration in Canada

Canada is a world leader in many fields, particularly in the areas of progressive social policy and human rights. Unfortunately, our country is also distinguished as being a world leader in putting people in prison. Although the United States has by far the highest rate of incarceration among industrialized democracies, at over 600 inmates per 100,000 population, Canada's rate of approximately 130 inmates per 100,000 population places it second or third highest: see First Report on Progress for Federal/Provincial/Territorial Ministers Responsible for Justice, *Corrections Population Growth* (1997), Annex B, at p. 1; Bulletin of U.S. Bureau of Justice Statistics, "Prison and Jail Inmates at Midyear 1998" (1999); The Sentencing Project, *Americans Behind Bars: U.S. and International Use of Incarceration, 1995* (1997), at p. 1. Moreover, the rate at which Canadian courts have been imprisoning offenders has risen sharply in recent years, although there has been a slight decline of late: see Statistics Canada, *Infomat: A Weekly Review* (February 27, 1998), at p. 5. This record of incarceration rates obviously cannot instil a sense of pride.

.....

Notwithstanding its idealistic origins, imprisonment quickly came to be condemned as harsh and ineffective, not only in relation to its purported rehabilitative goals, but also in relation to its broader public goals. [The Court then examines the literature regarding the ineffectiveness of imprisonment to achieve goals of sentencing.]

.....

Thus, it may be seen [from the literature] that although imprisonment is intended to serve the traditional sentencing goals of separation, deterrence, denunciation, and rehabilitation, there is widespread consensus that imprisonment has not been successful in achieving some of these goals. Overincarceration is a long-standing problem that has been many times publicly acknowledged but never addressed in a systematic manner by Parliament. In recent years, compared to other countries, sentences of imprisonment in Canada have increased at an alarming rate. The 1996 sentencing reforms embodied in Part XXIII, and s. 718.2(*e*) in particular, must be understood as a reaction to the overuse of prison as a sanction, and must accordingly be given appropriate force as remedial provisions.

(2) The Overrepresentation of Aboriginal Canadians in Penal Institutions

If overreliance upon incarceration is a problem with the general population, it is of much greater concern in the sentencing of aboriginal Canadians. In the mid-1980s, aboriginal people were about 2 percent of the population of Canada, yet they made up 10 percent of the penitentiary population. In Manitoba and Saskatchewan, aboriginal people constituted something between 6 and 7 percent of the population, yet in Manitoba they represented 46 percent of the provincial admissions and in Saskatchewan 60 percent: see M. Jackson, *Locking Up Natives in Canada* (1988-89), 23 U.B.C. L. Rev. 215 (article originally prepared as a report of the Canadian Bar Association Committee on Imprisonment and Release in June 1988), at pp. 215-16. The situation has not improved in recent years. By 1997, aboriginal peoples constituted closer to 3 percent of the population of Canada and amounted to 12 percent of all federal inmates: Solicitor General of Canada, Consolidated Report, *Towards a Just, Peaceful and Safe Society: The Corrections and Conditional Release Act — Five Years Later* (1998), at pp. 142-55. The situation continues to be particularly worrisome in Manitoba, where in 1995-96 they made up 55 percent of admissions to provincial correctional facilities, and in Saskatchewan, where they made up 72 percent of admissions. A similar, albeit less drastic situation prevails in Alberta and British Columbia: Canadian Centre for Justice Statistics, *Adult Correctional Services in Canada, 1995-96* (1997), at p. 30.

This serious problem of aboriginal overrepresentation in Canadian prisons is well documented. Like the general problem of overincarceration itself, the excessive incarceration of aboriginal peoples has received the attention of a large number of commissions and inquiries: see, by way of example only, Canadian Corrections Association, *Indians and the Law* (1967); Law Reform Commission of Canada, *The Native Offender and the Law* (1974), prepared by D. A. Schmeiser; Public Inquiry into the Administration of Justice and Aboriginal People, *Report of the Aboriginal Justice Inquiry of Manitoba*, vol. 1, *The Justice System and Aboriginal People* (1991); Royal Commission on Aboriginal Peoples, *Bridging the Cultural Divide* (1996).

.....

Not surprisingly, the excessive imprisonment of aboriginal people is only the tip of the iceberg insofar as the estrangement of the aboriginal peoples from the Canadian criminal justice system is concerned. Aboriginal people are overrepresented in virtually all aspects of the system. As this Court recently noted in *R. v. Williams*, [1998] 1 S.C.R. 1128, 124 C.C.C. (3d) 481, 159 D.L.R. (4th) 493, at para. 58, there is widespread bias against aboriginal people within Canada, and "[t]here is evidence that this widespread racism has translated into systemic discrimination in the criminal justice system".

Statements regarding the extent and severity of this problem are disturbingly common. In *Bridging the Cultural Divide*, *supra*, at p. 309, the Royal Commission on Aboriginal Peoples listed as its first "Major Findings and Conclusions" the following striking yet representative statement:

> The Canadian criminal justice system has failed the Aboriginal peoples of Canada — First Nations, Inuit and Métis people, on-reserve and off-reserve, urban and rural — in all territorial and governmental jurisdictions. The principal reason for this crushing failure is the fundamentally different world views of Aboriginal and non-Aboriginal people with respect to such elemental issues as the substantive content of justice and the process of achieving justice.

To the same effect, the Aboriginal Justice Inquiry of Manitoba described the justice system in Manitoba as having failed aboriginal people on a "massive scale", referring particularly to the substantially different cultural values and experiences of aboriginal people: *The Justice System and Aboriginal People*, *supra*, at pp. 1 and 86.

These findings cry out for recognition of the magnitude and gravity of the problem, and for responses to alleviate it. The figures are stark and reflect what may fairly be termed a crisis in the Canadian criminal justice system. The drastic overrepresentation of aboriginal peoples within both the Canadian prison population and the criminal justice system reveals a sad and pressing social problem. It is reasonable to assume that Parliament, in singling out aboriginal offenders for distinct sentencing treatment in s. 718.2(*e*), intended to attempt to redress this social problem to some degree. The provision may properly be seen as Parliament's direction to members of the judiciary to inquire into the causes of the problem and to endeavour to remedy it, to the extent that a remedy is possible through the sentencing process.

It is clear that sentencing innovation by itself cannot remove the causes of aboriginal offending and the greater problem of aboriginal alienation from the criminal justice system. The unbalanced ratio of imprisonment for aboriginal offenders flows from a number of sources, including poverty, substance abuse, lack of education, and the lack of employment opportunities for aboriginal people. It arises also from bias against aboriginal people and from an unfortunate institutional approach that is more inclined to refuse bail and to impose more and longer prison terms for aboriginal offenders. There are many aspects of this sad situation which cannot be addressed in these reasons. What can and must be addressed, though, is the limited role that sentencing judges will play in remedying injustice against aboriginal peoples in Canada. Sentencing judges are among those decision-makers who have the power to influence the treatment of aboriginal offenders in the justice system. They determine most directly whether an aboriginal offender will go to jail, or whether other sentencing options may be employed which will play perhaps a stronger role in restoring a sense of balance to the offender, victim, and community, and in preventing future crime.

E. A Framework of Analysis for the Sentencing Judge

(1) What Are the "Circumstances of Aboriginal Offenders"?

How are sentencing judges to play their remedial role? The words of s. 718.2(*e*) instruct the sentencing judge to pay particular attention to the circumstances of aboriginal offenders, with the implication that those circumstances are significantly different from those of non-aboriginal offenders. The background considerations regarding the distinct situation of aboriginal peoples in Canada encompass a wide range of unique circumstances, including, most particularly:

- (A) The unique systemic or background factors which may have played a part in bringing the particular aboriginal offender before the courts; and
- (B) The types of sentencing procedures and sanctions which may be appropriate in the circumstances for the offender because of his or her particular aboriginal heritage or connection.

(a) Systemic and Background Factors

The background factors which figure prominently in the causation of crime by aboriginal offenders are by now well known. Years of dislocation and economic development have translated, for many aboriginal peoples, into low incomes, high unemployment, lack of opportunities and options, lack or irrelevance of education, substance abuse, loneliness, and community fragmentation. These and other factors contribute to a higher incidence of crime and incarceration. A disturbing account of these factors is set out by Professor Tim Quigley, "Some Issues in Sentencing of Aboriginal Offenders", in *Continuing Poundmaker and Riel's Quest* (1994), at pp. 269-300. Quigley ably describes the process whereby these various factors produce an overincarceration of aboriginal offenders, noting (at pp. 275-76) that "[t]he unemployed, transients, the poorly educated are all better candidates for imprisonment. When the social, political and economic aspects of our society place Aboriginal people disproportionately within the ranks of the latter, our society literally sentences more of them to jail."

It is true that systemic and background factors explain in part the incidence of crime and recidivism for non-aboriginal offenders as well. However, it must be recognized that the circumstances of aboriginal offenders differ from those of the majority because many aboriginal people are victims of systemic and direct discrimination, many suffer the legacy of dislocation, and many are substantially affected by poor social and economic conditions. Moreover, as has been emphasized repeatedly in studies and commission reports, aboriginal offenders are, as a result of these unique systemic and background factors, more adversely affected by incarceration and less likely to be "rehabilitated" thereby, because the internment milieu is often culturally inappropriate and regrettably discrimination towards them is so often rampant in penal institutions.

In this case, of course, we are dealing with factors that must be considered by a judge sentencing an aboriginal offender. While background and systemic factors will also be of importance for a judge in sentencing a non-aboriginal offender, the judge who is called upon to sentence an aboriginal offender must give attention to the unique background and systemic factors which may have played a part in bringing the particular offender before the courts. In cases where such factors have played a significant role, it is incumbent upon the sentencing judge to consider these factors in evaluating whether imprisonment would actually serve to deter, or to denounce crime in a sense that would be meaningful to the community of which the offender is a member. In many instances, more restorative sentencing principles will gain primary relevance precisely because the prevention of crime as well as individual and social healing cannot occur through other means.

(b) Appropriate Sentencing Procedures and Sanctions

Closely related to the background and systemic factors which have contributed to an excessive aboriginal incarceration rate are the different conceptions of appropriate sentencing procedures and sanctions held by aboriginal people. A significant problem experienced by aboriginal people who come into contact with the criminal justice system is that the traditional sentencing ideals of deterrence, separation, and denunciation are often far removed from the understanding of sentencing held by these offenders and their community. The aims of restorative justice as now expressed in paras. (*d*), (*e*), and (*f*) of s. 718 of the *Criminal Code* apply to all offenders, and not only aboriginal offenders. However, most traditional aboriginal conceptions of sentencing place a *primary* emphasis upon the ideals of restorative justice. This tradition is extremely important to the analysis under s. 718.2(*e*).

The concept and principles of a restorative approach will necessarily have to be developed over time in the jurisprudence, as different issues and different conceptions of sentencing are addressed in their appropriate context. In general terms, restorative justice may be described as an approach to remedying crime in which it is understood that all things are interrelated and that crime disrupts the harmony which existed prior to its occurrence, or at least which it is felt should exist. The appropriateness of a particular sanction is largely determined by the needs of the victims, and the community, as well as the offender. The focus is on the human beings closely affected by the crime. See generally, *e.g.*, *Bridging the Cultural Divide*, *supra*, at pp. 12-25; *The Justice System and Aboriginal People*, *supra*, at pp. 17-46; Kwochka, *supra*; M. Jackson, "In Search of the Pathways to Justice: Alternative Dispute Resolution in Aboriginal Communities" (1992) U.B.C. L. Rev. (Special Edition) 147.

The existing overemphasis on incarceration in Canada may be partly due to the perception that a restorative approach is a more lenient approach to crime and that imprisonment constitutes the ultimate punishment. Yet in our view a sentence focussed on restorative justice is not necessarily a "lighter" punishment. Some proponents of restorative justice argue that when it is combined with probationary conditions it may in some circumstances impose a greater burden on the offender than a custodial sentence. …

In describing in general terms some of the basic tenets of traditional aboriginal sentencing approaches, we do not wish to imply that all aboriginal offenders, victims, and communities share an identical understanding of appropriate sentences for particular offences and offenders. Aboriginal communities stretch from coast to coast and from the border with the United States to the far north. Their customs and traditions and their concept of sentencing vary widely. What is important to recognize is that, for many if not most aboriginal offenders, the current concepts of sentencing are inappropriate because they have frequently not responded to the needs, experiences, and perspectives of aboriginal people or aboriginal communities.

It is unnecessary to engage here in an extensive discussion of the relatively recent evolution of innovative sentencing practices, such as healing and sentencing circles, and aboriginal community council projects, which are available especially to aboriginal offenders. What is important to note is that the different conceptions of sentencing held by many aboriginal people share a common underlying principle: that is, the importance of community-based sanctions. Sentencing judges should not conclude that the absence of alternatives specific to an aboriginal community eliminates their ability to impose a sanction that takes into account principles of restorative justice and the needs of the parties involved. Rather, the point is that one of the unique circumstances of aboriginal offenders is that community-based sanctions coincide with the aboriginal concept of sentencing and the needs of aboriginal people and communities. It is often the case that neither aboriginal offenders nor their communities are well served by incarcerating offenders, particularly for less serious or non-violent offences. Where these sanctions are reasonable in the circumstances, they should be implemented. In all instances, it is appropriate to attempt to craft the sentencing process and the sanctions imposed in accordance with the aboriginal perspective.

(2) The Search for a Fit Sentence

The role of the judge who sentences an aboriginal offender is, as for every offender, to determine a fit sentence taking into account all the circumstances of the offence, the offender, the victims, and the community. Nothing in Part XXIII of the *Criminal Code* alters this fundamental duty as a general matter. However, the effect of s. 718.2(*e*), viewed in the context of Part XXIII as a whole, is to alter the method of analysis which sentencing judges must use in determining a fit sentence for aboriginal offenders. Section 718.2(*e*) requires that sentencing determinations take into account the *unique circumstances* of aboriginal peoples.

In *R. v. M. (C.A.)*, [1996] 1 S.C.R. 500, at p. 567, 105 C.C.C. (3d) 327, Lamer C.J. restated the long-standing principle of Canadian sentencing law that the appropriateness of a sentence will depend on the particular circumstances of the offence, the offender, and the community in which the offence took place. Disparity of sentences for similar crimes is a natural consequence of this individualized focus. As he stated:

> It has been repeatedly stressed that there is no such thing as a uniform sentence for a particular crime ... Sentencing is an inherently individualized process, and the search for a single appropriate sentence for a similar offender and a similar crime will frequently be a fruitless exercise of academic abstraction. As well, sentences for a particular offence should be expected to vary to some degree across various communities and regions of this country, as the "just and appropriate" mix of accepted sentencing goals will depend on the needs and current conditions of and in the particular community where the crime occurred.

The comments of Lamer C.J. are particularly apt in the context of aboriginal offenders. As explained herein, the circumstances of aboriginal offenders are markedly different from those of other offenders, being characterized by unique systemic and background factors. Further, an aboriginal offender's community will frequently understand the nature of a just sanction in a manner significantly different from that of many non-aboriginal communities. In appropriate cases, some of the traditional sentencing objectives will be correspondingly less relevant in determining a sentence that is reasonable in the circumstances, and the goals of restorative justice will quite properly be given greater weight. Through its reform of the purpose of sentencing in s. 718, and through its specific directive to judges who sentence aboriginal offenders, Parliament has, more than ever before, empowered sentencing judges to craft sentences in a manner which is meaningful to aboriginal peoples.

In describing the effect of s. 718.2(*e*) in this way, we do not mean to suggest that, as a general practice, aboriginal offenders must always be sentenced in a manner which gives greatest weight to the principles of restorative justice, and less weight to goals such as deterrence, denunciation, and separation. It is unreasonable to assume that aboriginal peoples themselves do not believe in the importance of these latter goals, and even if they do not, that such goals must not predominate in appropriate cases. Clearly there are some serious offences and some offenders for which and for whom separation, denunciation, and deterrence are fundamentally relevant.

Yet, even where an offence is considered serious, the length of the term of imprisonment must be considered. In some circumstances the length of the sentence of an aboriginal offender may be less and in others the same as that of any other offender. Generally, the more violent and serious the offence the more likely it is as a practical reality that the terms of imprisonment for aboriginals and non-aboriginals will be close to each other or the same, even taking into account their different concepts of sentencing.

As with all sentencing decisions, the sentencing of aboriginal offenders must proceed on an individual (or a case-by-case) basis: For *this* offence, committed by *this* offender, harming *this* victim, in *this* community, what is the appropriate sanction under the *Criminal Code*? What understanding of criminal sanctions is held by the community? What is the nature of the relationship between the offender and his or her community? What combination of systemic or background factors contributed to this particular offender coming before the courts for this particular offence? How has the offender who is being sentenced been affected by, for example, substance abuse in the community, or poverty, or overt racism, or family or community breakdown? Would imprisonment effectively serve to deter or denounce crime in a sense that would be significant to the offender and community, or are crime prevention and other goals better achieved through healing? What sentencing options present themselves in these circumstances?

The analysis for sentencing aboriginal offenders, as for all offenders, must be holistic and designed to achieve a fit sentence in the circumstances. There is no single test that a judge can apply in order to determine the sentence. The sentencing judge is required to take into account all of the surrounding circumstances regarding the offence, the offender, the victims, and the community, including the unique circumstances of the offender as an aboriginal person. Sentencing must proceed with sensitivity to and understanding of the difficulties aboriginal people have faced with both the criminal justice system and society at large. When evaluating these circumstances in light of the aims and principles of sentencing as set out in Part XXIII of the *Criminal Code* and in the jurisprudence, the judge must strive to arrive at a sentence which is just and appropriate in the circumstances. By means of s. 718.2(*e*), sentencing judges have been provided with a degree of flexibility and discretion to consider in appropriate circumstances alternative sentences to incarceration which are appropriate for the aboriginal offender and community and yet comply with the mandated principles and purpose of sentencing. In this way, effect may be given to the aboriginal emphasis upon healing and restoration of both the victim and the offender.

(3) The Duty of the Sentencing Judge

The foregoing discussion of guidelines for the sentencing judge has spoken of that which a judge must do when sentencing an aboriginal offender. This element of duty is a critical component of s. 718.2(*e*). The provision expressly provides that a court that imposes a sentence *should* consider all available sanctions other than imprisonment that are reasonable in the circumstances, and *should* pay particular attention to the circumstances of aboriginal offenders. There is no discretion as to whether to consider the unique situation of the aboriginal offender; the only discretion concerns the determination of a just and appropriate sentence.

How then is the consideration of s. 718.2(*e*) to proceed in the daily functioning of the courts? The manner in which the sentencing judge will carry out his or her statutory duty may vary from case to case. In all instances it will be necessary for the judge to take judicial notice of the systemic or background factors and the approach to sentencing which is relevant to aboriginal offenders. However, for each particular offence and offender it may be that some evidence will be required in order to assist the sentencing judge in arriving at a fit sentence. Where a particular offender does not wish such evidence to be adduced, the right to have particular attention paid to his or her circumstances as an aboriginal offender may be waived. Where there is no such waiver, it will be extremely helpful to the sentencing judge for counsel on both sides to adduce relevant evidence. Indeed, it is to be expected that counsel will fulfil their role and assist the sentencing judge in this way.

However, even where counsel do not adduce this evidence, where for example the offender is unrepresented, it is incumbent upon the sentencing judge to attempt to acquire information regarding the circumstances of the offender as an aboriginal person. Whether the offender resides in a rural area, on a reserve or in an urban centre the sentencing judge must be made aware of alternatives to incarceration that exist whether inside or outside the aboriginal community of the particular offender. The alternatives existing in metropolitan areas must, as a matter of course, also be explored. Clearly the presence of an aboriginal offender will require special attention in pre-sentence reports. Beyond the use of the pre-sentence report, the sentencing judge may and should in appropriate circumstances and where practicable request that witnesses be called who may testify as to reasonable alternatives.

Similarly, where a sentencing judge at the trial level has not engaged in the duty imposed by s. 718.2(*e*) as fully as required, it is incumbent upon a court of appeal in considering an appeal against sentence on this basis to consider any fresh evidence which is relevant and admissible on sentencing. In the same vein, it should be noted that, although s. 718.2(*e*) does not impose a statutory duty upon the sentencing judge to provide reasons, it will be much easier for a reviewing court to determine whether and how attention was paid to the circumstances of the offender as an aboriginal person if at least brief reasons are given.

(4) The Issue of "Reverse Discrimination"

Something must also be said as to the manner in which s. 718.2(*e*) should not be interpreted. The appellant and the respondent diverged significantly in their interpretation of the appropriate role to be played by s. 718.2(*e*). While the respondent saw the provision largely as a restatement of existing sentencing principles, the appellant advanced the position that s. 718.2(*e*) functions as an affirmative action provision justified under s. 15(2) of the *Charter*. The respondent cautioned that, in his view, the appellant's understanding of the provision would result in "reverse discrimination" so as to favour aboriginal offenders over other offenders.

There is no constitutional challenge to s. 718.2(*e*) in these proceedings, and accordingly we do not address specifically the applicability of s. 15 of the *Charter*. We would note, though, that the aim of s. 718.2(*e*) is to reduce the tragic overrepresentation of aboriginal people in prisons. It seeks to ameliorate the present situation and to deal with the particular offence and offender and community. The fact that a court is called upon to take into consideration the unique circumstances surrounding these different parties is not unfair to non-aboriginal people. Rather, the fundamental purpose of s. 718.2(*e*) is to treat aboriginal offenders fairly by taking into account their difference.

But s. 718.2(*e*) should not be taken as requiring an automatic reduction of a sentence, or a remission of a warranted period of incarceration, simply because the offender is aboriginal. To the extent that the appellant's submission on affirmative action means that s. 718.2(*e*) requires an automatic reduction in sentence for an aboriginal offender, we reject that view. The provision is a direction to sentencing judges to consider certain unique circumstances pertaining to aboriginal offenders as a part of the task of weighing the multitude of factors which must be taken into account in striving to impose a fit sentence. It cannot be forgotten that s. 718.2(*e*) must be considered in the context of that section read as a whole and in the context of s. 718, s. 718.1, and the overall scheme of Part XXIII. It is one of the statutorily mandated considerations that a sentencing judge must take into account. It may not always mean a lower sentence for an aboriginal offender. The sentence imposed will depend upon all the factors which must be taken into account in each individual case. The weight to be given to these various factors will vary in each case. At the same time, it must in every case be recalled that the direction to consider these unique circumstances flows from the staggering injustice currently experienced by aboriginal peoples with the criminal justice system. The provision reflects the reality that many aboriginal people are alienated from this system which frequently does not reflect their needs or their understanding of an appropriate sentence.

(5) Who Comes Within the Purview of Section 718.2(e)?

The question of whether s. 718.2(*e*) applies to all aboriginal persons, or only to certain classes thereof, is raised by this appeal. ...

The class of aboriginal people who come within the purview of the specific reference to the circumstances of aboriginal offenders in s. 718.2(*e*) must be, at least, all who come within the scope of s. 25 of the *Charter* and s. 35 of the *Constitution Act, 1982*. The numbers involved are significant. National census figures from 1996 show that an estimated 799,010 people were identified as aboriginal in 1996. Of this number, 529,040 were Indians (registered or non-registered), 204,115 Metis and 40,220 Inuit.

Section 718.2(*e*) applies to all aboriginal offenders wherever they reside, whether on- or off-reserve, in a large city or a rural area. Indeed it has been observed that many aboriginals living in urban areas are closely attached to their culture. ...

Section 718.2(*e*) requires the sentencing judge to explore reasonable alternatives to incarceration in the case of all aboriginal offenders. Obviously, if an aboriginal community has a program or tradition of alternative sanctions, and support and supervision are available to the offender, it may be easier to find and impose an alternative sentence. However, even if community support is not available, every effort should be made in appropriate circumstances to find a sensitive and helpful alternative. For all purposes, the term "community" must be defined broadly so as to include any network of support and interaction that might be available in an urban centre. At the same time, the residence of the aboriginal offender in an urban centre that lacks any network of support does not relieve the sentencing judge of the obligation to try to find an alternative to imprisonment.

VI. Summary

Let us see if a general summary can be made of what has been discussed in these reasons.

1. Part XXIII of the *Criminal Code* codifies the fundamental purpose and principles of sentencing and the factors that should be considered by a judge in striving to determine a sentence that is fit for the offender and the offence.
2. Section 718.2(*e*) mandatorily requires sentencing judges to consider all available sanctions other than imprisonment and to pay particular attention to the circumstances of aboriginal offenders.
3. Section 718.2(*e*) is not simply a codification of existing jurisprudence. It is remedial in nature. Its purpose is to ameliorate the serious problem of overrepresentation of aboriginal people in prisons, and to encourage sentencing judges to have recourse to a restorative approach to sentencing. There is a judicial duty to give the provision's remedial purpose real force.
4. Section 718.2(*e*) must be read and considered in the context of the rest of the factors referred to in that section and in light of all of Part XXIII. All principles and factors set out in Part XXIII must be taken into consideration in determining the fit sentence. Attention should be paid to the fact that Part XXIII, through ss. 718, 718.2(*e*), and 742.1, among other provisions, has placed a new emphasis upon decreasing the use of incarceration.
5. Sentencing is an individual process and in each case the consideration must continue to be what is a fit sentence for this accused for this offence in this community. However, the effect of s. 718.2(*e*) is to alter the method of analysis which sentencing judges must use in determining a fit sentence for aboriginal offenders.
6. Section 718.2(*e*) directs sentencing judges to undertake the sentencing of aboriginal offenders individually, but also differently, because the circumstances of aboriginal people are unique. In sentencing an aboriginal offender, the judge must consider:

(A) The unique systemic or background factors which may have played a part in bringing the particular aboriginal offender before the courts; and

(B) The types of sentencing procedures and sanctions which may be appropriate in the circumstances for the offender because of his or her particular aboriginal heritage or connection.

7. In order to undertake these considerations the trial judge will require information pertaining to the accused. Judges may take judicial notice of the broad systemic and background factors affecting aboriginal people, and of the priority given in aboriginal cultures to a restorative approach to sentencing. In the usual course of events, additional case-specific information will come from counsel and from a pre-sentence report which takes into account the factors set out in #6, which in turn may come from representations of the relevant aboriginal community which will usually be that of the offender. The offender may waive the gathering of that information.
8. If there is no alternative to incarceration the length of the term must be carefully considered.
9. Section 718.2(*e*) is not to be taken as a means of automatically reducing the prison sentence of aboriginal offenders; nor should it be assumed that an offender is receiving a more lenient sentence simply because incarceration is not imposed.
10. The absence of alternative sentencing programs specific to an aboriginal community does not eliminate the ability of a sentencing judge to impose a sanction that takes into account principles of restorative justice and the needs of the parties involved.
11. Section 718.2(*e*) applies to all aboriginal persons wherever they reside, whether on- or off-reserve, in a large city or a rural area. In defining the relevant aboriginal community for the purpose of achieving an effective sentence, the term "community" must be defined broadly so as to include any network of support and interaction that might be available, including in an urban centre. At the same time, the residence of the aboriginal offender in an urban centre that lacks any network of support does not relieve the sentencing judge of the obligation to try to find an alternative to imprisonment.
12. Based on the foregoing, the jail term for an aboriginal offender may in some circumstances be less than the term imposed on a non-aboriginal offender for the same offence.
13. It is unreasonable to assume that aboriginal peoples do not believe in the importance of traditional sentencing goals such as deterrence, denunciation, and separation, where warranted. In this context, generally, the more serious and violent the crime, the more likely it will be as a practical matter that the terms of imprisonment will be the same for similar offences and offenders, whether the offender is aboriginal or non-aboriginal.

VII. WAS THERE AN ERROR MADE IN THIS CASE?

From the foregoing analysis it can be seen that the sentencing judge, who did not have the benefit of these reasons, fell into error. He may have erred in limiting the application of s. 718.2(*e*) to the circumstances of aboriginal offenders living in rural areas or on-reserve. Moreover, and perhaps as a consequence of the first error, he does not appear to have considered the systemic or background factors which may have influenced the appellant to engage in criminal conduct, or the possibly distinct conception of sentencing held by the appellant, by the victim Beaver's family, and by their community. However, it should be emphasized that the sentencing judge did take active steps to obtain at least some information regarding the appellant's aboriginal heritage. In this regard he received little if any assistance from counsel on this issue although they too were acting without the benefit of these reasons.

The majority of the Court of Appeal, in dismissing the appellant's appeal, also does not appear to have considered many of the factors referred to above. However, the dissenting reasons of Rowles J.A. discuss the relevant factors in some detail. The majority also appears to have dismissed the appellant's application to adduce fresh evidence. The majority of the Court of Appeal may or may not have erred in ultimately deciding to dismiss the fresh evidence application. The correctness of its ultimate decision depends largely upon the admissibility of the fresh evidence and its relevance to the weighing of the various sentencing goals. However, assuming admissibility and relevance, it was certainly incumbent upon the majority to consider the evidence, and especially so given the failure of the trial judge to do so. Moreover, if the fresh evidence before the Court of Appeal was itself insufficient to inform the court adequately regarding the circumstances of the appellant as an aboriginal offender, the proper remedy would have been to remit the matter to the trial judge with instructions to make all the reasonable inquiries necessary for the sentencing of this aboriginal offender.

In most cases, errors such as those in the courts below would be sufficient to justify sending the matter back for a new sentencing hearing. It is difficult for this Court to determine a fit sentence for the appellant according to the suggested guidelines set out herein on the basis of the very limited evidence before us regarding the appellant's aboriginal background. However, as both the trial judge and all members of the Court of Appeal acknowledged, the offence in question is a most serious one, properly described by Esson J.A. as a "near murder".... Moreover, the offence involved domestic violence and a breach of the trust inherent in a spousal relationship. That aggravating factor must be taken into account in the sentencing of the aboriginal appellant as it would be for any offender. For that offence by this offender a sentence of three years' imprisonment was not unreasonable.

More importantly, the appellant was granted day parole on August 13, 1997, after she had served six months in the Burnaby Correctional Centre for Women. She was directed to reside with her father, to take alcohol and substance abuse counselling and to comply with the requirements of the Electronic Monitoring Program. On February 25, 1998, the appellant was granted full parole with the same conditions as the ones applicable to her original release on day parole.

In this case, the results of the sentence with incarceration for six months and the subsequent controlled release were in the interests of both the appellant and society. In these circumstances, we do not consider that it would be in the interests of justice to order a new sentencing hearing in order to canvass the appellant's circumstances as an aboriginal offender.

In the result, the appeal is dismissed.

QUESTIONS

21. The accused is to be sentenced for the offence of armed robbery. His co-accused has already been sentenced by another judge to 15 months imprisonment. However, the sentencing judge is of the view that the co-accused's sentence was excessively lenient and is inclined to impose a sentence of three years imprisonment. Defence counsel suggests that disparity in sentencing is to be avoided and that the appearance of justice compels the imposition of a similar sentence. What should the judge do? Consider, in this regard, *R. v. Fait* (1982), 68 C.C.C. (2d) 367 (Alta. C.A.). Assume that the Court of Appeal is reviewing the sentence imposed by the trial judge. Should there be "tariffs" or "starting points" for certain kinds of offences? Compare *R. v. Sandercock* (1985), 22 C.C.C. (3d) 79 (Alta. C.A.) and *R. v. Glassford* (1988), 42 C.C.C. (3d) 259 (Ont. C.A.); see also *R. v. M.(C.A.)* (1996), 105 C.C.C. (3d) 327 (S.C.C.).

22. Consider how the following facts could affect any sentence imposed:

(a) the crime was planned in advance by the co-accused though the accused was only recruited the day before.

(b) the sexual assault extended over several years but was terminated by the accused 20 years ago.

(c) the accused was motivated to commit fraud by a gambling addiction.

(d) a theft was accompanied by gratuitous violence perpetrated by the co-accused.

(e) the robbery was perpetrated with a toy gun which looked real.

(f) the sexual assault was committed on the accused's daughter who has forgiven him and does not want to see him incarcerated.

(g) the accused is guilty of impaired driving causing death but is now in very poor health and could die in prison.

(h) a drug trafficker has, since arrest, rehabilitated himself and has been drug-free for 18 months.

(i) the accused has confidentially informed on his accomplices on the condition that he not be called as a witness against them.

(j) the accused is to be sentenced for fraud. She has a prior record for impaired driving last year and a ten-year-old record for false pretences.

(k) the accused was on bail while this offence was committed; however, the charge for which he was on bail was later withdrawn.

(l) the accused is suffering from a personality disorder that explains why he shoplifted.

(m) the accused is suffering from a personality disorder which explains why he feels alienated and inclined to set houses on fire.

(n) the accused robbed a drug trafficker of his cash.

(o) the accused pushed another man with his hands, however, the victim died from a heart attack induced by the stress.

(p) **the accused has served ten months in pre-trial custody (consider, in this regard, s. 719(3) of the *Criminal Code*).**

(q) **the accused entered a plea of guilt at the earliest opportunity; the evidence against her was overwhelming.**

(r) **the accused committed a sexual assault on a neighbour's child; he has an impeccable reputation for honesty and integrity.**

---

6. Available Sentences

Indictable offences under the *Criminal Code* generally specify a maximum term of imprisonment. In the absence of a specified maximum, the maximum term for an indictable offence is five years (s. 743). Some indictable offences carry mandatory sentences. For example, first degree murder carries a mandatory term of life imprisonment with parole ineligibility for 25 years. Most summary conviction offences do not specify a discrete term of imprisonment. Section 787 of the *Criminal Code* states that, unless the law otherwise provides "everyone who is convicted of [a summary conviction offence] is liable to a fine of not more than two thousand dollars or to imprisonment for six months or to both". Some hybrid offences, such as sexual assault, are punishable by up to 18 months imprisonment, when the Crown elects summarily. Some offences, indictable or summary conviction, carry minimum sentences, whether imprisonment or fines. Some minimum sentences are only applicable where the Crown has proven a prior related criminal record and the accused has been served with a notice that an increased sentence will be sought because of the prior record.

The *Criminal Code* provides for various sentencing options in ss. 730 *et seq.*

(a) Absolute and Conditional Discharges

An accused may be given an *absolute* or *conditional discharge,* where the offence has no minimum sentence, is not punishable by imprisonment for fourteen years or life and where the court believes it to be in the accused's best interests and not detrimental to the public interest (s. 730(1) of the *Criminal Code*). A finding of guilt, but not a conviction, is registered.

R. v. FALLOFIELD

(1973), 13 C.C.C. (2d) 450 (B.C.C.A.)

The Court: —

.....

From this review of the authorities and my own view of the meaning of s. 662.1 [now s. 730(1)], I draw the following conclusions, subject, of course, to what I have said above as to the exercise of discretion.

(1) The section may be used in respect of *any* offence other than an offence for which a minimum punishment is prescribed by law or the offence is punishable by imprisonment for 14 years or for life....

(2) The section contemplates the commission of an offence. There is nothing in the language that limits it to a technical or trivial violation.

(3) Of the two conditions precedent to the exercise of the jurisdiction, the first is that the Court must consider that it is in the best interests of the accused that he should be discharged either absolutely or upon condition. If it is not in the best interests of the accused, that, of course, is the end of the matter. If it is decided that it is in the best interests of the accused, then that brings the next consideration into operation.

(4) The second condition precedent is that the Court must consider that a grant of discharge is not contrary to the public interest.

(5) Generally, the first condition would presuppose that the accused is a person of good character, without previous conviction, that it is not necessary to enter a conviction against him in order to deter him from future offences or to rehabilitate him, and that the entry of a conviction against him may have significant adverse repercussions.

(6) In the context of the second condition the public interest in the deterrence of others, while it must be given due weight, does not preclude the judicious use of the discharge provisions.

(7) The powers given by s. 662.1 should not be exercised as an alternative to probation or suspended sentence.

(8) Section 662.1 should not be applied routinely to any particular offence. This may result in an apparent lack of uniformity in the application of the discharge provisions. This lack will be more apparent than real and will stem from the differences in the circumstances of cases.

QUESTION

23. A defendant is found guilty of driving "over 80". He is a recidivist, having been convicted of impaired driving twice before. However, he has now recognized his chronic alcoholism and wishes to be treated for the first time. His prognosis is cautiously optimistic. Should he be given a discharge? Consider, in this regard, s. 255(5) of the *Criminal Code*; *R. v. Beaulieu* (1980), 53 C.C.C. (2d) 342 (N.W.T.S.C.); *R. v. Storr* (1995), 174 A.R. 65 (C.A.); *R. v. Ashberry* (1989), 47 C.C.C. (3d) 138 (Ont. C.A.). Note that s. 255(5) has not been proclaimed in Ontario, Quebec, Newfoundland, and British Columbia. *Ashberry* was decided before the Ontario Court of Appeal held that selective proclamation of the section did not violate s. 15 of the *Charter*.

(b) Suspended Sentence

Where the offence is not one for which a minimum punishment is prescribed, the court may suspend the passing of sentence and order that the accused be placed on probation for a maximum of three years (ss. 731(1)(*a*) and 732.2(2)(*b*) of the *Code*).

QUESTION

24. The accused is convicted of break, enter and theft relating to a dwelling-house. The court suspends the passing of sentence and imposes a probation order for two years. During the second month of the probation order, the accused is charged with another break, enter and theft, again relating to a dwelling-house. What option is available to the Crown *vis-a-vis* the first break and enter conviction? Consider, in this regard, s. 732.2(5) of the *Criminal Code*.

(c) Probation

A term of probation must accompany a suspended sentence, a conditional discharge and an intermittent sentence. It may also accompany a fine or any term of imprisonment not exceeding two years. It may not accompany a single sentence which involves both a fine and imprisonment (s. 731(1)(*b*)). A probation order enables the court to supervise and monitor the rehabilitation of an offender while in the community. The *Criminal Code* provides compulsory and optional conditions for probation orders (s. 732.1(2) and (3)). See also 731.1. The maximum term of a single probation order is three years (s. 732.2(2)(*b*)). The failure or refusal to comply with a probation order is an offence under s. 733.1 of the *Criminal Code*. Its conditions and duration may be varied by the court (s. 732.2(3)).

QUESTIONS

25. The accused, an admitted alcoholic, is convicted of an assault *simpliciter* and threatening bodily harm in relation to his wife. As Crown counsel, what conditions would you seek in a probation order? Consider, in this regard, s. 732.1(3) of the *Criminal Code*.

26. The accused is convicted of assault. The sentencing judge places the accused on probation for two years and orders as a term of probation that the accused's driver's licence be suspended. Will this condition of probation withstand appellate scrutiny? Consider, in this regard, *R. v. Ziatis* (1973), 13 C.C.C. (2d) 287 (Ont. C.A.).

27. The accused was placed on probation with the statutory term requiring that he "keep the peace and be of good behaviour". He assaulted his girlfriend while vacationing in Cuba and was subsequently charged, in Canada, with failing to comply with his probation order. Does a Cana-

dian court have the jurisdiction to try the accused? See *R. v. Greco* (2001), 159 C.C.C. (3d) 146 (Ont. C.A.); leave to appeal to the S.C.C. filed.

(d) Fine

The court may order that an offender pay a fine (s. 734), provided the court is satisfied of the offender's ability to pay a fine (s. 734(2), but see s. 736) and the offence is not punishable by a minimum term of imprisonment. The sentencing court no longer determines, in its discretion, imprisonment in default of payment. Rather, a formula calculates the default time based on the minimum wage of the province (s. 734(5)). The *Criminal Code* provides for licence suspensions for non-payment of fines (s. 734.5) and the civil enforcement of fines (s. 734.6). Section 735 addresses fines imposed upon corporations.

In addition to any other sentence that may be imposed, a court will impose a "victim fine surcharge" on the offender in an amount calculated in accordance with s. 737 of the *Code*. The court will not impose the surcharge where it would cause undue hardship to the offender or the dependants of the offender.

QUESTION

28. An accused is convicted of impaired driving and the matter is up for sentencing. The accused was convicted of "over 80" a year earlier and the Crown files the Notice of Increased Penalty at the sentencing hearing. Can the sentencing court impose a fine in addition to the minimum 14 days jail? Consider, in this regard, s. 734(1) of the *Criminal Code*.

(e) Forfeiture of Weapons and Ammunition

Section 491 of the *Code* provides a procedure for the forfeiture of weapons and ammunition under certain circumstances.

(f) Restitution or Forfeiture of Property Obtained by Crime

A number of *Criminal Code* and other statutory provisions regulate the forfeiture of property relating to criminal offences or its return to a lawful owner. For example, s. 462.37 (forfeiture of the proceeds of an enterprise crime), and s. 491.1 (the disposition of property obtained by crime).

(g) Restitution

The court may order an offender to make restitution for damaged, lost or destroyed property, for pecuniary damages as a result of bodily

harm, and, in the case of bodily harm or a threat thereof to the offender's spouse, child or other household member, reasonable expenses for having to move out of the offender's household (s. 738(1)(*a*), (*b*) and (*c*) of the *Criminal Code*). Restitution may also be ordered to be paid to persons who acquired property which was obtained by crime although acting in good faith and without notice (s. 739). The amount of restitution must be readily ascertainable; a restitution order is not the appropriate mechanism to unravel involved commercial transactions. (See *R. v. Zelensky* (1978), 41 C.C.C. (2d) 97 (S.C.C.) and *R. v. Devgan* (1999), 136 C.C.C. (3d) 238 (Ont. C.A.)). Where restitution is not paid forthwith, the person to whom restitution is ordered to be paid may file the restitution order as a judgment in civil court (s. 741). Interestingly, s. 740 of the *Criminal Code* now directs the court to prioritize restitution orders over fines or forfeiture of the same property respecting which an order of restitution could be made. Restitution may also be made a condition of probation.

QUESTION

29. The accused stands convicted of assault causing bodily harm. She punched the victim in the mouth, causing her to lose several teeth. The victim impact statement reveals that it has cost the victim $3,000 in dental fees. When arrested, the accused was in possession of $2,500 cash which the police suspected were proceeds from drug dealing. Can the court order restitution? Can the court order that the money found on the accused be used towards a restitution order? Consider, in this regard, s. 740(2) of the *Criminal Code*.

(h) Prohibition Orders

Certain *Criminal Code* provisions provide for the imposition of prohibition orders after a finding of guilt in relation to certain offences. See, for example, ss. 109 and 110, which address both mandatory and discretionary prohibition orders respectively against the possession of firearms, ammunition or other explosive devices. Mandatory and discretionary driving prohibitions are addressed in s. 259.

QUESTION

30. The accused is convicted of assault causing bodily harm. He lives in the north and lawfully hunts for food with a firearm. Will the court impose a firearms prohibition in this case? Are there any representations the defence may make to avoid the imposition of the prohibition? Consider s. 110(1) of the *Criminal Code*.

(i) Conditional Sentences

Conditional sentence orders are the most innovative part of the Part XXIII amendments to the *Criminal Code*. Courts have wrestled, often inconsistently, with the intended availability of these sentences. The following case provides guidance on the nature of a conditional sentence and the difference between a conditional sentence and a probation order.

R. v. PROULX

(2000), 140 C.C.C. (3d) 449 (S.C.C.)

[The accused pleaded guilty to dangerous driving causing death and dangerous driving causing bodily harm. After consuming some alcohol, the accused decided to drive his friends home even though he knew that his vehicle was mechanically unsound. The accused was 18 years of age and had only seven weeks of driving experience. He drove erratically. As the accused tried to pass another vehicle, he collided with an oncoming car. The driver of that car was seriously injured and a passenger in the accused's car was killed. The accused also suffered serious injuries but eventually recovered. Although the trial judge found that the accused would not endanger the community and that a sentence of incarceration was not necessary to deter him from similar conduct or to rehabilitate him, the trial judge held that a conditional sentence would not be consistent with the objectives of denunciation and general deterrence and thus imposed a sentence of 18 months incarceration, as well as a driving prohibition for five years. The Court of Appeal allowed the accused's appeal and substituted a conditional sentence for the jail term.]

The judgment of the court was delivered by

Lamer C.J.C.: — By passing the *Act to amend the Criminal Code* (*sentencing*) and other Acts in consequence thereof, S.C. 1995, c. 22 ("Bill C-41"), Parliament has sent a clear message to all Canadian judges that too many people are being sent to prison. In an attempt to remedy the problem of overincarceration, Parliament has introduced a new form of sentence, the conditional sentence of imprisonment.

As a matter of established practice and sound policy, this Court rarely hears appeals relating to sentences: see *R. v. Gardiner*, [1982] 2 S.C.R. 368 at p. 404, 68 C.C.C. (2d) 477, 140 D.L.R. (3d) 612, *R. v. Chaisson*, [1995] 2 S.C.R. 1118 at p. 1123, 99 C.C.C. (3d) 289, and *R. v. M. (C.A.)*, [1996] 1 S.C.R. 500 at para. 33, 105 C.C.C. (3d) 327. However, we have decided to hear this case and four related cases because they afford the Court the opportunity to set out for the first time the principles that govern the new and innovative conditional sentencing regime. Given the inevitable length of these reasons, I have summarized the essentials at para. 127.

.....

V. Analysis

A. The 1996 Sentencing Reforms (Bill C-41)

In September 1996, Bill C-41 came into effect. It substantially reformed Part XXIII of the *Criminal Code,* and introduced, *inter alia,* an express statement of the purposes and principles of sentencing, provisions for alternative measures for adult offenders and a new type of sanction, the conditional sentence of imprisonment.

As my colleagues Cory and Iacobucci JJ. explained in *R. v. Gladue,* [1999] 1 S.C.R. 688 at para. 39, 133 C.C.C. (3d) 385, 171 D.L.R. (4th) 385, "[t]he enactment of the new Part XXIII was a watershed, marking the first codification and significant reform of sentencing principles in the history of Canadian criminal law". They noted two of Parliament's principal objectives in enacting this new legislation: (i) reducing the use of prison as a sanction, and (ii) expanding the use of restorative justice principles in sentencing (at para. 48).

(1) Reducing the Use of Prison as a Sanction

Bill C-41 is in large part a response to the problem of overincarceration in Canada. It was noted in *Gladue,* at para. 52, that Canada's incarceration rate of approximately 130 inmates per 100,000 population places it second or third highest among industrialized democracies. ...

Parliament has sought to give increased prominence to the principle of restraint in the use of prison as a sanction through the enactment of s. 718.2(*d*) and (*e*). Section 718.2(*d*) provides that "an offender should not be deprived of liberty, if less restrictive sanctions may be appropriate in the circumstances", while s. 718.2(*e*) provides that "all available sanctions other than imprisonment that are reasonable in the circumstances should be considered for all offenders, with particular attention to the circumstances of aboriginal offenders". Further evidence of Parliament's desire to lower the rate of incarceration comes from other provisions of Bill C-41: s. 718(*c*) qualifies the sentencing objective of separating offenders from society with the words "where necessary", thereby indicating that caution be exercised in sentencing offenders to prison; s. 734(2) imposes a duty on judges to undertake a means inquiry before imposing a fine, so as to decrease the number of offenders who are incarcerated for defaulting on payment of their fines; and of course, s. 742.1, which introduces the conditional sentence. In *Gladue,* at para. 40, the Court held that "the creation of the conditional sentence suggests, on its face, a desire to lessen the use of incarceration".

(2) Expanding the Use of Restorative Justice Principles in Sentencing

Restorative justice is concerned with the restoration of the parties that are affected by the commission of an offence. Crime generally affects at least three parties: the victim, the community, and the offender. A restorative justice approach seeks to remedy the adverse effects of crime in a manner that addresses the needs of all parties involved. This is accomplished, in part, through the rehabilitation of the offender, reparations to the victim and to the community, and the promotion of a sense of responsibility in the offender and acknowledgment of the harm done to victims and to the community.

Canadian sentencing jurisprudence has traditionally focused on the aims of denunciation, deterrence, separation, and rehabilitation, with rehabilitation a relative late-comer to the sentencing analysis: see *Gladue*, at para. 42. With the introduction of Bill C-41, however, Parliament has placed new emphasis upon the goals of restorative justice. Section 718 sets out the fundamental purpose of sentencing, as well as the various sentencing objectives that should be vindicated when sanctions are imposed. ...

Parliament has mandated that expanded use be made of restorative principles in sentencing as a result of the general failure of incarceration to rehabilitate offenders and reintegrate them into society. By placing a new emphasis on restorative principles, Parliament expects both to reduce the rate of incarceration and improve the effectiveness of sentencing. ...

B. The Nature of the Conditional Sentence

The conditional sentence was specifically enacted as a new sanction designed to achieve both of Parliament's objectives. The conditional sentence is a meaningful alternative to incarceration for less serious and non-dangerous offenders. The offenders who meet the criteria of s. 742.1 will serve a sentence under strict surveillance in the community instead of going to prison. These offenders' liberty will be constrained by conditions to be attached to the sentence, as set out in s. 742.3 of the *Criminal Code*. In case of breach of conditions, the offender will be brought back before a judge, pursuant to s. 742.6. If an offender cannot provide a reasonable excuse for breaching the conditions of his or her sentence, the judge may order him or her to serve the remainder of the sentence in jail, as it was intended by Parliament that there be a real threat of incarceration to increase compliance with the conditions of the sentence.

The conditional sentence incorporates some elements of non-custodial measures and some others of incarceration. Because it is served in the community, it will generally be more effective than incarceration at achieving the restorative objectives of rehabilitation, reparations to the victim and community, and the promotion of a sense of responsibility in the offender. However, *it is also a punitive sanction capable of achieving the objectives of denunciation and deterrence*. It is this punitive aspect that distinguishes the conditional sentence from probation, and it is to this issue that I now turn.

(1) Comparing Conditional Sentences with Probation

There has been some confusion among members of the judiciary and the public alike about the difference between a conditional sentence and a suspended sentence with probation. This confusion is understandable, as the statutory provisions regarding conditions to be attached to conditional sentences (s. 742.3) and probation orders (s. 732.1) are very similar. Notwithstanding these similarities, there is an important distinction between the two. While a suspended sentence with probation is primarily a rehabilitative sentencing tool, the evidence suggests that Parliament intended a conditional sentence to address both punitive and rehabilitative objectives.

(a) A Comparative Reading of the Provisions

A comparative reading of the provisions governing conditional sentences and probation orders reveals three differences. First, a probation order includes only three compulsory conditions — to keep the peace and be of good behaviour, appear before the court when required, and notify the court or probation officer of any change in employment or address — whereas there are five such conditions in the case of a conditional sentence. The two additional compulsory conditions of a conditional sentence — to report to a supervisor and remain within the jurisdiction unless permission is granted to leave — are listed as optional conditions under a probation order.

The second difference concerns the power of the judge to order the offender to undergo treatment. Under a conditional sentence, the sentencing judge can order the offender to attend a treatment program, regardless of whether the offender consents.

Under a probation order, the judge can only impose a treatment order with the consent of the offender (with the exception of drug or alcohol addiction programs since the 1999 amendment to s. 732.1 (S.C. 1999, c. 32, s. 6). In practice, however, this difference is not very significant, since it is unlikely that an offender faced with the choice between imprisonment and a suspended sentence with treatment as a condition of probation would refuse to consent to treatment.

The third difference is in the wording of the residual clauses of the provisions governing the imposition of optional conditions. In the case of a conditional sentence, s. 742.3(2)(*f*) provides that the court may order that the offender comply with such other reasonable conditions as the court considers desirable "for securing the good conduct of the offender and for preventing a repetition by the offender of the same offence or the commission of other offences". By contrast, s. 732.1(3)(*h*) provides that the court may impose such other reasonable conditions of probation "for protecting society and for facilitating the offender's successful reintegration into the community".

On their face, these three differences do not suggest that a conditional sentence is more punitive than a suspended sentence with probation. Moreover, the penalty for breach of probation is potentially more severe than that for breach of a conditional sentence. Pursuant to s. 733.1(1), breach of probation constitutes a new offence, punishable by up to two years' imprisonment, while a breach of condition does not constitute a new offence *per se*. The maximum penalties are also different. In the case of a breach of probation, the offender is subject to the revocation of the probation order and can be sentenced for the original offence (in cases where a suspended sentence was rendered): see s. 732.2(5). By contrast, in the case of breaches of conditional sentences, the maximum punishment available is incarceration for the time remaining of the original sentence

(s. 742.6(9)). Presumably, if a conditional sentence is more onerous than probation, the consequences of breaching a condition should be more onerous as well.

(b) Conditional Sentences Must Be More Punitive Than Probation

Despite the similarities between the provisions and the fact that the penalty for breach of probation is potentially more severe than for breach of a conditional sentence, there are strong indications that Parliament intended the conditional sentence to be more punitive than probation. It is a well-accepted principle of statutory interpretation that no legislative provision should be interpreted so as to render it mere surplusage. It would be absurd if Parliament intended conditional sentences to amount merely to probation under a different name. While this argument is clearly not dispositive, it suggests that Parliament intended there to be a meaningful distinction between the two sanctions. I will now consider more specific arguments in support of this position.

The conditional sentence is defined in the *Code* as a sentence of imprisonment. The heading of s. 742 reads "Conditional Sentence of Imprisonment". Furthermore, s. 742.1(*a*) requires the court to impose a sentence of imprisonment of less than two years before considering whether the sentence can be served in the community subject to the appropriate conditions. Parliament intended imprisonment, in the form of incarceration, to be more punitive than probation, as it is far more restrictive of the offender's liberty. Since a conditional sentence is, at least notionally, a sentence of imprisonment, it follows that it too should be interpreted as more punitive than probation.

On a related note, with the enactment of s. 742.1, Parliament has mandated that certain non-dangerous offenders who would otherwise have gone to jail for up to two years now serve their sentences in the community. If a conditional sentence is not distinguished from probation, then these offenders will receive what are effectively considerably less onerous probation orders instead of jail terms. Such lenient sentences would not provide sufficient denunciation and deterrence, nor would they be accepted by the public. Section 718 provides that the fundamental purpose of sentencing is "to contribute ... to respect for the law and the maintenance of a just, peaceful and safe society". Inadequate sanctions undermine respect for the law. Accordingly, it is important to distinguish a conditional sentence from probation by way of the use of punitive conditions.

Earlier I drew attention to a subtle difference between the residual clauses in the provisions governing the imposition of optional conditions of probation orders and conditional sentences.

While the difference between the two residual clauses is subtle, it is also significant. In order to appreciate this difference, it is necessary to consider the case law and practice that has developed with respect to probation.

Probation has traditionally been viewed as a rehabilitative sentencing tool. Recently, the rehabilitative nature of the probation order was explained by the Saskatchewan Court of Appeal in *R. v. Taylor* (1997), 122 C.C.C. (3d) 376. Bayda C.J.S. wrote, at p. 394:

> Apart from the wording of the provision, the innate character of a probation order is such that it seeks to influence the future behaviour of the offender.

> More specifically, it seeks to secure "the good conduct" of the offender and to deter him from committing other offences. *It does not particularly seek to reflect the seriousness of the offence or the offender's degree of culpability. Nor does it particularly seek to fill the need for denunciation of the offence or the general deterrence of others to commit the same or other offences. Depending upon the specific conditions of the order there may well be a punitive aspect to a probation order but punishment is not the dominant or an inherent purpose. It is perhaps not even a secondary purpose but is more in the nature of a consequence of an offender's compliance with one or more of the specific conditions with which he or she may find it hard to comply.* [Emphasis added.]

Many appellate courts have struck out conditions of probation that were imposed to punish rather than rehabilitate the offender: see *R. v. Ziatas* (1973), 13 C.C.C. (2d) 287 (Ont. C.A.) at p. 288; *R. v. Caja* (1977), 36 C.C.C. (2d) 401 (Ont. C.A.) at pp. 402-3; *R. v. Lavender* (1981), 59 C.C.C. (2d) 551 (B.C.C.A.) at pp. 552-53, and *R. v. L.* (1986), 50 C.R. (3d) 398 (Alta. C.A.) at pp. 399-400. The impugned terms of probation in these cases were imposed pursuant to a residual clause in force at the time whose wording was virtually identical to that presently used in s. 742.3(2)(*f*).

Despite the virtual identity in the wording of s. 742.3(2)(*f*) and the old residual clause applicable to probation orders, it would be a mistake to conclude that punitive conditions cannot now be imposed under s. 742.3(2)(*f*). Parliament amended the residual clause for probation, s. 732.1(3)(*h*), to read "for protecting society and for *facilitating the offender's successful reintegration into the community*" (emphasis added). It did so to make clear the rehabilitative purpose of probation and to distinguish s. 742.3(2)(*f*) from s. 732.1(3)(*h*). The wording used in s. 742.3(2)(*f*) does not focus principally on the rehabilitation and reintegration of the offender. If s. 742.3(2)(*f*) were interpreted as precluding punitive conditions, it would frustrate Parliament's intention in distinguishing the two forms of sentence. Parliament would not have distinguished them if it intended both clauses to serve the same purpose.

In light of the foregoing, it is clear that Parliament intended a conditional sentence to be more punitive than a suspended sentence with probation, notwithstanding the similarities between the two sanctions in respect of their rehabilitative purposes. I agree wholeheartedly with Vancise J.A., who, dissenting in *R. v. McDonald* (1997), 113 C.C.C. (3d) 418 (Sask. C.A.), stated, at p. 443, that conditional sentences were designed to "permit the accused to avoid imprisonment but not to avoid punishment".

Accordingly, conditional sentences should generally include punitive conditions that are restrictive of the offender's liberty. Conditions such as house arrest or strict curfews should be the norm, not the exception. ...

There must be a reason for failing to impose punitive conditions when a conditional sentence order is made. Sentencing judges should always be mindful of the fact that conditional sentences are only to be imposed on offenders who would otherwise have been sent to jail. If the judge is of the opinion that punitive conditions are unnecessary, then probation, rather than a conditional sentence, is most likely the appropriate disposition.

The punitive nature of the conditional sentence should also inform the treatment of breaches of conditions. As I have already discussed, the maximum penalty for breach of probation is potentially more severe than that for breach of a conditional sentence. In practice, however, breaches of conditional sentences may be punished more severely than breaches of probation. Without commenting on the constitutionality of these provisions, I note that breaches of conditional sentence need only be proved on a balance of probabilities, pursuant to s. 742.6(9), whereas breaches of probation must be proved beyond a reasonable doubt.

More importantly, where an offender breaches a condition without reasonable excuse, there should be a presumption that the offender serve the remainder of his or her sentence in jail. This constant threat of incarceration will help to ensure that the offender complies with the conditions imposed: see *R. v. Brady* (1998), 121 C.C.C. (3d) 504 (Alta. C.A.); J.V. Roberts, *Conditional Sentencing: Sword of Damocles or Pandora's Box?* (1997), 2 Can. Crim. L. Rev. 183. It also assists in distinguishing the conditional sentence from probation by making the consequences of a breach of condition more severe.

(2) Conditional Sentences and Incarceration

Although a conditional sentence is by statutory definition a sentence of imprisonment, this Court, in *R. v. Shropshire*, [1995] 4 S.C.R. 227 at para. 21, 102 C.C.C. (3d) 193, 129 D.L.R. (4th) 657, recognized that there "is a very significant difference between being behind bars and functioning within society while on conditional release". See also *Cunningham v. Canada*, [1993] 2 S.C.R. 143 at p. 150, 80 C.C.C. (3d) 492, *per* McLachlin J. These comments are equally applicable to the conditional sentence. Indeed, offenders serving a conditional sentence in the community are only partially deprived of their freedom. Even if their liberty is restricted by the conditions attached to their sentence, they are not confined to an institution and they can continue to attend to their normal employment or educational endeavours. They are not deprived of their private life to the same extent. Nor are they subject to a regimented schedule or an institutional diet.

This is not to say that the conditional sentence is a lenient punishment or that it does not provide significant denunciation and deterrence, or that a conditional sentence can never be as harsh as incarceration. As this Court stated in *Gladue, supra*, at para. 72,

> ... in our view a sentence focussed on restorative justice is not necessarily a "lighter" punishment. Some proponents of restorative justice argue that when it is combined with probationary conditions it may in some circumstances impose a greater burden on the offender than a custodial sentence.

A conditional sentence may be as onerous as, or perhaps even more onerous than, a jail term, particularly in circumstances where the offender is forced to take responsibility for his or her actions and make reparations to both the victim and the community, all the while living in the community under tight controls.

Moreover, the conditional sentence is not subject to reduction through parole. This would seem to follow from s. 112(1) of the *Corrections and Conditional Release Act*, S.C. 1992, c. 20, which gives the provincial parole board jurisdiction in respect of the parole of offenders "serving sentences of imprisonment in provincial correctional facilities" (*R. v. Wismayer* (1997), 115 C.C.C. (3d) 18 (Ont. C.A.) at p. 33).

I would add that the fact that a conditional sentence cannot be reduced through parole does not in itself lead to the conclusion that as a general matter a conditional sentence is as onerous as or even more onerous than a jail term of equivalent duration. There is no parole simply because the offender is never actually incarcerated and he or she does not need to be reintegrated into society. But even when an offender is released from custody on parole, the original sentence continues in force. As I stated in *M. (C.A.), supra*, at para. 62:

> In short, the history, structure and existing practice of the conditional release system collectively indicate that a grant of parole represents *a change in the conditions* under which a judicial sentence must be served, rather than a *reduction* of the judicial sentence itself ... But even though the conditions of incarceration are subject to change through a grant of parole to the offender's benefit, the offender's sentence continues in full effect. The offender remains under the strict control of the parole system, and the offender's liberty remains significantly curtailed for the full duration of the offender's numerical or life sentence. [Emphasis in original.]

The parolee has to serve the final portion of his or her sentence under conditions similar to those that can be imposed under a conditional sentence, perhaps even under stricter conditions, as the parolee can be assigned to a "community-based residential facility": see s. 133 of the *Corrections and Conditional Release Act*, and s. 161 of the *Corrections and Conditional Release Regulations*, SOR/92-620.

In light of these observations, a conditional sentence, even with stringent conditions, will usually be a more lenient sentence than a jail term of equivalent duration: see also *Gagnon v. La Reine*, [1998] R.J.Q. 2636 at p. 2645, 130 C.C.C. (3d) 194 (C.A.); *Brady, supra*, at paras. 36 and 48-50. The fact that incarceration is a threatened punishment for those who breach their conditions provides further support for this conclusion. In order for incarceration to serve as a punishment for breach of a conditional sentence, logically it must be more onerous than a conditional sentence.

C. Application of Section 742.1 of the Criminal Code

.....

This provision lists four criteria that a court must consider before deciding to impose a conditional sentence:

(1) the offender must be convicted of an offence that is not punishable by a minimum term of imprisonment;
(2) the court must impose a term of imprisonment of less than two years;
(3) the safety of the community would not be endangered by the offender serving the sentence in the community; and
(4) a conditional sentence would be consistent with the fundamental purpose and principles of sentencing set out in ss. 718 to 718.2.

In my view, the first three criteria are prerequisites to any conditional sentence. These prerequisites answer the question of whether or not a conditional sentence is possible in the circumstances. Once they are met, the next question is whether a conditional sentence is appropriate. This decision turns upon a consideration of the fundamental purpose and principles of sentencing set out in s. 718 to 718.2. I will discuss each of these elements in turn.

(1) *The Offender Must be Convicted of an Offence That Is Not Punishable by a Minimum Term of Imprisonment*

This prerequisite is straightforward. The offence for which the offender was convicted must not be punishable by a minimum term of imprisonment. Offences with a minimum term of imprisonment are the only statutory exclusions from the conditional sentencing regime.

(2) *The Court Must Impose a Term of Imprisonment of Less than Two Years*

Parliament intended that a conditional sentence be considered only for those offenders who would have otherwise received a sentence of imprisonment of less than two years. There is some controversy as to whether this means that the judge must actually impose a term of imprisonment of a *fixed* duration before considering the possibility of a conditional sentence. Far from addressing purely methodological concerns, this question carries implications as to the role of ss. 718 to 718.2 in the determination of the appropriate sentence, the duration of the sentence, its venue and other modalities.

A literal reading of s. 742.1(*a*) suggests that the decision to impose a conditional sentence should be made in two distinct stages. In the first stage, the judge would have to decide the appropriate sentence according to the general purposes and principles of sentencing (now set out in ss. 718 to 718.2). Having found that a term of imprisonment of less than two years is warranted, the judge would then, in a second stage, decide whether this same term should be served in the community pursuant to s. 742.1. At first sight, since Parliament said: "and the court (*a*) imposes a sentence of imprisonment of less than two years", it seems that the sentencing judge must first impose a term of imprisonment of a *fixed* duration before contemplating the possibility that this term be served in the community.

This two-step approach was endorsed by the Manitoba Court of Appeal in the present appeal. However, this literal reading of s. 742.1 and the two-step approach it implies introduce a rigidity which is both unworkable and undesirable in practice.

(a) *Duration and Venue Cannot Be Separated*

This two-step process does not correspond to the reality of sentencing. In practice, the determination of a term of imprisonment is necessarily intertwined with the decision of where the offender will serve the sentence. A judge does not impose a fixed sentence of "x months" in the abstract, without having in mind where that sentence will be served (see *Brady, supra*, at para. 86; *R. v. Pierce* (1997), 114 C.C.C. (3d) 23 (Ont. C.A.) at p. 39; *R. v. Ursel* (1997), 96 B.C.A.C. 241 at p. 284, 117 C.C.C. (3d) 289 (B.C.C.A.) (*per* Ryan J.A.) and pp. 291-92 (*per* Rowles J.A.)). Furthermore, when a conditional sentence is chosen, its duration will depend on the type of conditions imposed. Therefore, the duration of the sentence should not be determined separately from the determination of its venue.

(b) "Penalogical Paradox"

There is a contradiction embedded in this rigid two-step process. After having applied ss. 718 to 718.2 in the first stage to conclude that the appropriate sentence is a term of imprisonment of a fixed duration (in all cases less than two years), the judge would then have to decide if serving *the same sentence* in the community is still consistent with the fundamental purpose and principles of sentencing set out in ss. 718 to 718.2, as required by s. 742.1(*b*). It is unrealistic to believe that a judge would consider the objectives and principles twice or make a clear distinction in his or her mind between the application of ss. 718 to 718.2 in the first stage and in the second stage. Even if this could be done, it could lead to a "penalogical paradox", as described by J. Gemmell in, *The New Conditional Sentencing Regime* (1997), 39 C.L.Q. 334 at p. 337:

> ... the judge must first determine that imprisonment is the only reasonable sanction in the circumstances then decide whether the offender should nevertheless serve that sentence in the community. The decision to impose a conditional sentence is almost a kind of *reductio ad absurdum* of the original decision that called for imprisonment. [Footnote omitted.]

This second step of the analytical process would effectively compromise the principles of sentencing that led to the imposition of a sentence of imprisonment in the first place. For instance, the principle of proportionality, set out in s. 718.1 as the fundamental principle of sentencing, directs that all sentences must be proportional to the gravity of the offence and the degree of responsibility of the offender. When a judge — in the first stage — decides that a term of imprisonment of "x months" is appropriate, it means that *this* sentence is proportional. If the sentencing judge decides — in the second stage — that *the same term* can be served in the community, it is possible that the sentence is no longer proportional to the gravity of the offence and the responsibility of the offender, since a conditional sentence will generally be more lenient than a jail term of equivalent duration. Thus, such a two-step approach introduces a rigidity in the sentencing process that could lead to an unfit sentence.

(c) A Purposive Interpretation of Section 742.1(a)

These problems can be addressed by a purposive interpretation of s. 742.1. For the reasons discussed above, the requirement that the court "imposes a sentence of imprisonment of less than two years" could not have been intended to impose on judges a rigid two-step process. Rather, it was included to identify the type of offenders who could be entitled to a conditional sentence. At one end of the range, Parliament denied the possibility of a conditional sentence for offenders who should receive a penitentiary term. At the other end, Parliament intended to ensure that offenders who were entitled to a more lenient community measure — such as a suspended sentence with probation — did not receive a conditional sentence, a harsher sanction in this legislative scheme.

Section 742.1(*a*), when read in conjunction with ss. 718.2(*d*) and 718.2(*e*), cautions sentencing judges against "widening the net" of the conditional sentencing regime by imposing conditional sentences on offenders who would otherwise have received a non-custodial disposition (*Gagnon, supra*, at p. 2645; *McDonald, supra*, at pp. 437-39). As Rosenberg J.A. puts it in *Wismayer, supra*, at p. 42:

> Parliament's goal of reducing the prison population of non-violent offenders and increased use of community sanctions will be frustrated if the courts refuse to use the conditional sentence order for offences that normally attract a jail sentence and resort to the conditional sentence only for offences that previously would have attracted non-custodial dispositions.

Erroneously imposing conditional sentences could undermine Parliament's objective of reducing incarceration for less serious offenders.

These concerns are illustrated by the English experience with a similar sentence called a "suspended sentence". As Parker L.C.J. explained, writing for the Court of Appeal (Criminal Division) in *R. v. O'Keefe* (1968), 53 Cr. App. R. 91 at pp. 94-95:

> This Court would like to say as emphatically as they can that suspended sentences should not be given when, but for the power to give a suspended sentence, a probation order was the proper order to make. After all, a suspended sentence is a sentence of imprisonment.
>
> Therefore, it seems to the Court that before one gets to a suspended sentence at all, a court must go through the process of eliminating other possible courses such as absolute discharge, conditional discharge, probation order, fine, and then say to itself: this is a case for imprisonment, and the final question, it being a case for imprisonment: is immediate imprisonment required, or can I give a suspended sentence?

A similar approach should be used by Canadian courts. Hence, a purposive interpretation of s. 742.1(*a*) does not dictate a rigid two-step approach in which the judge would first have to impose a term of imprisonment of a *fixed* duration and then decide if that fixed term of imprisonment can be served in the community. In my view, the requirement that the court must impose a sentence of imprisonment of less than two years can be fulfilled by a preliminary determination of the appropriate range of available sentences. Thus, the approach I suggest still requires the judge to proceed in two stages. However, the judge need not impose a term of imprisonment of a *fixed* duration at the first stage of the analysis. Rather, at this stage, the judge simply has to exclude two possibilities: (a) probationary measures; and (b) a penitentiary term. If either of these sentences is appropriate, then a conditional sentence should not be imposed.

In making this preliminary determination, the judge need only consider the fundamental purpose and principles of sentencing set out in ss. 718 to 718.2 to the extent necessary to narrow the range of sentence for the offender. The submissions of the parties, although not binding, may prove helpful in this regard. For example, both parties may agree that the appropriate range of sentence is a term of imprisonment of less than two years.

Once that preliminary determination is made, and assuming the other statutory prerequisites are met, the judge should then proceed to the second stage of the analysis: determining whether a conditional sentence would be consistent with the fundamental purpose and principles of sentencing set out in ss. 718 to 718.2. Unlike the first stage, the principles of sentencing are now considered comprehensively. Further, it is at the second stage that the duration and venue of the sentence should be determined, and, if a conditional sentence, the conditions to be imposed.

This purposive interpretation of s. 742.1(*a*) avoids the pitfalls of the literal interpretation discussed above, while at all times taking into account the principles and objectives of sentencing. As I stressed in *M. (C.A.), supra*, at para. 82.

> In the final analysis, the overarching duty of a sentencing judge is to draw upon all the legitimate principles of sentencing to determine a "just and appropriate" sentence which reflects the gravity of the offence committed and the moral blameworthiness of the offender.

(3) The Safety of the Community Would Not Be Endangered by the Offender serving the Sentence in the Community

This criterion, set out in s. 742.1(*b*), has generated wide discussion in courts and among authors. I intend to discuss the following issues:

(a) Is safety of the community a prerequisite to any conditional sentence?
(b) Does "safety of the community" refer only to the threat posed by the specific offender?
(c) How should courts evaluate danger to the community?
(d) Is risk of economic prejudice to be considered in assessing danger to the community?

(a) A Prerequisite to Any Conditional Sentence

As a prerequisite to any conditional sentence, the sentencing judge must be satisfied that having the offender serve the sentence in the community would not endanger its safety: see *Brady, supra*, at para. 58; *R. v. Maheu*, [1997] R.J.Q. 410, 116 C.C.C. (3d) 361 at p. 368 (C.A.); *Gagnon, supra*, at p. 2641; *Pierce, supra*, at p. 39; *Ursel, supra*, at pp. 284-86 (*per* Ryan J.A.). *If the sentencing judge is not satisfied that the safety of the community can be preserved, a conditional sentence must never be imposed.*

...

... It is only once the judge is satisfied that the safety of the community would not be endangered, in the sense explained in paragraphs 66 to 76 below, that he or she can examine whether a conditional sentence "would be consistent with the fundamental purpose and principles of sentencing set out in sections 718 to 718.2". In other words, rather than being an overarching consideration in the process of determining whether a conditional sentence is appropriate, the criterion of safety of the community should be viewed as a condition precedent to the assessment of whether a conditional sentence would be a fit and proper sanction in the circumstances.

(b) "Safety of the Community" Refers to the Threat Posed by the Specific Offender

The issue here is whether "safety of the community" refers only to the threat posed by the specific offender or whether it also extends to the broader risk of undermining respect for the law. The proponents of the broader interpretation argue that, in certain cases where a conditional sentence could be imposed, it would be perceived that wrongdoers are receiving lenient sentences, thereby insufficiently deterring those who may be inclined to engage in similar acts of wrongdoing, and, in turn, endangering the safety of the community.

Leaving aside the fact that a properly crafted conditional sentence can also achieve the objectives of general deterrence and denunciation, I think the debate has been rendered largely academic in light of an amendment to s. 742.1(*b*) (S.C. 1997, c. 18, s. 107.1) which clarified that courts must take into consideration the fundamental purpose and principles of sentencing set out in ss. 718 to 718.2 in deciding whether to impose a conditional sentence. This ensures that objectives such as denunciation and deterrence will be dealt with in the decision to impose a conditional sentence. Since these factors will be taken into account later in the analysis, there is no need to include them in the consideration of the safety of the community.

In my view, the focus of the analysis at this point should clearly be on the risk posed by the individual offender while serving his sentence in the community. I would note that a majority of appellate courts have adopted an interpretation of the criterion referring only to the threat posed by the specific offender: see *Gagnon, supra*, at pp. 2640-41 (*per* Fish J.A.); *R. v. Parker* (1997), 116 C.C.C. (3d) 236 (N.S.C.A.) at pp. 247-48; *Ursel, supra*, at p. 260; *R. v. Horvath*, [1997] 8 W.W.R. 357 at p. 374, 117 C.C.C. (3d) 110 (Sask. C.A.); *Brady, supra*, at paras. 60-61; *Wismayer, supra*, at p. 44.

(c) How Should Courts Evaluate Danger to the Community?

In my opinion, to assess the danger to the community posed by the offender while serving his or her sentence in the community, two factors must be taken into account: (1) the risk of the offender re-offending; and (2) the gravity of the damage that could ensue in the event of re-offence. If the judge finds that there is a real risk of re-offence, incarceration should be imposed. Of course, there is always some risk that an offender may re-offend. If the judge thinks this risk is minimal, the gravity of the damage that could follow were the offender to re-offend should also be taken into consideration. In certain cases, the minimal risk of re-offending will be offset by the possibility of a great prejudice, thereby precluding a conditional sentence.

(i) Risk of Re-offence

A variety of factors will be relevant in assessing the risk of re-offence. In *Brady, supra*, at paras. 117-27, Fraser C.J.A. suggested that consideration be given to whether the offender has previously complied with court orders and, more generally, to whether the offender has a criminal record that suggests that the offender will not abide by the conditional sentence. Rousseau-Houle J.A. in *Maheu, supra,* at p. 374 C.C.C. enumerated additional factors which may be of relevance:

> [TRANSLATION] 1) the nature of the offence, 2) the relevant circumstances of the offence, which can put in issue prior and subsequent incidents, 3) the degree of participation of the accused, 4) the relationship of the accused with the victim, 5) the profile of the accused, that is, his [or her] occupation, lifestyle, criminal record, family situation, mental state, 6) his [or her] conduct following the commission of the offence, 7) the danger which the interim release of the accused represents for the community, notably that part of the community affected by the matter.

This list is instructive, but should not be considered exhaustive. The risk that a particular offender poses to the community must be assessed in each case, on its own facts. Moreover, the factors outlined above should not be applied mechanically. As Fraser C.J.A. held in *Brady, supra,* at para. 124:

> Forgetting a court date once ten years ago does not automatically bar an offender from any future conditional sentence. Nor does turning up for his trial guarantee an offender a conditional sentence. The sentencing judge must of course look at all aspects of these previous disobediences of courts. That includes frequency, age, maturity, recency, seriousness of disobedience and surrounding circumstances.

The risk of re-offence should also be assessed in light of the conditions attached to the sentence. Where an offender might pose some risk of endangering the safety of the community, it is possible that this risk be reduced to a minimal one by the imposition of appropriate conditions to the sentence: see *Wismayer, supra,* at p. 32; *Brady, supra,* at para. 62; *Maheu, supra,* at p. 374 C.C.C. Indeed, this is contemplated by s. 742.3(2)(*f*), which allows the court to include as optional conditions "such other reasonable conditions as the court considers desirable ... for securing the good conduct of the offender and for preventing a repetition by the offender of the same offence or the commission of other offences". For example, a judge may wish to impose a conditional sentence with a treatment order on an offender with a drug addiction, notwithstanding the fact that the offender has a lengthy criminal record linked to this addiction, provided the judge is confident that there is a good chance of rehabilitation and that the level of supervision will be sufficient to ensure that the offender complies with the sentence.

This last point concerning the level of supervision in the community must be underscored. As the Alberta Court of Appeal stressed in *Brady, supra,* at para. 135:

> A conditional sentence drafted in the abstract without knowledge of what actual supervision and institutions and programs are available and suitable for this offender is often worse than tokenism: it is a sham.

Hence, the judge must know or be made aware of the supervision available in the community by the supervision officer or by counsel. If the level of supervision available in the community is not sufficient to ensure safety of the community, the judge should impose a sentence of incarceration.

(ii) Gravity of the Damage in the Event of Re-offence

Once the judge finds that the risk of recidivism is minimal, the second factor to consider is the gravity of the potential damage in case of re-offence. Particularly in the case of violent offenders, a small risk of very harmful future crime may well warrant a conclusion that the prerequisite is not met: see *Brady, supra*, at para. 63.

(d) Risk of Economic Harm Can Be Taken Into Consideration

The meaning of the phrase "would not endanger the safety of the community" should not be restricted to a consideration of the danger to physical or psychological safety of persons. In my view, this part of s. 742.1(*b*) cannot be given this narrow meaning. As Finch J.A. stated in *Ursel, supra*, at p. 264 (dissenting in part but endorsed by the majority on this issue, at p. 287):

> I would not give to this phrase the restricted meaning for which the defence contends. Members of our community have a reasonable expectation of safety not only in respect of their persons, but in respect as well of their property and financial resources. When homes are broken into, motor vehicles are stolen, employers are defrauded of monies, or financial papers are forged, the safety of the community is, in my view endangered. We go to considerable lengths to protect and secure ourselves against the losses that may result from these sorts of crimes, and I think most ordinary citizens would regard themselves as threatened or endangered where their property or financial resources are exposed to the risk of loss.

I agree with this reasoning. The phrase "would not endanger the safety of the community" should be construed broadly, and include the risk of any criminal activity. Such a broad interpretation encompasses the risk of economic harm.

(4) Consistent with the Fundamental Purpose and Principles of Sentencing Set Out in Sections 718 to 718.2

Once the sentencing judge has found the offender guilty of an offence for which there is no minimum term of imprisonment, has rejected both a probationary sentence and a penitentiary term as inappropriate, and is satisfied that the offender would not endanger the community, the judge must then consider whether a conditional sentence would be consistent with the fundamental purpose and principles of sentencing set out in ss. 718 to 718.2.

A consideration of the principles set out in ss. 718 to 718.2 will determine whether the offender should serve his or her sentence in the community or in jail. The sentencing principles also inform the determination of the duration of these sentences and, if a conditional sentence, the nature of the conditions to be imposed.

(a) Offences Presumptively Excluded from the Conditional Sentencing Regime?

Section 742.1 does not exclude any offences from the conditional sentencing regime except those with a minimum term of imprisonment. Parliament could have easily excluded specific offences in addition to those with a mandatory minimum term of imprisonment but chose not to. As Rosenberg J.A. held in *Wismayer, supra*, at p. 31,

> ... Parliament clearly envisaged that a conditional sentence would be available even in cases of crimes of violence that are not punishable by a minimum term of imprisonment. Thus, s. 742.2 requires the court, before imposing a conditional sentence, to consider whether a firearms prohibition under s. 100 of the *Criminal Code* is applicable. Such orders may only be imposed for indictable offences having a maximum sentence of ten years or more "in the commission of which violence against a person is used, threatened, or attempted" (s. 100(1)) and for certain weapons and drug offences (s. 100(2)).

Thus, a conditional sentence is available in principle for all offences in which the statutory prerequisites are satisfied.

Several parties in the appeals before us argued that the fundamental purpose and principles of sentencing support a presumption against conditional sentences for certain offences. The Attorney General of Canada and the Attorney General for Ontario submitted that a conditional sentence would rarely be appropriate for offences such as: sexual offences against children; aggravated sexual assault; manslaughter; serious fraud or theft; serious morality offences; impaired or dangerous driving causing death or bodily harm; and trafficking or possession of certain narcotics. They submitted that this followed from the principle of proportionality as well as from a consideration of the objectives of denunciation and deterrence. A number of appellate court decisions support this position.

In my view, while the gravity of such offences is clearly relevant to determining whether a conditional sentence is appropriate in the circumstances, it would be both unwise and unnecessary to establish judicially created presumptions that conditional sentences are inappropriate for specific offences. Offence-specific presumptions introduce unwarranted rigidity in the determination of whether a conditional sentence is a just and appropriate sanction. Such presumptions do not accord with the principle of proportionality set out in s. 718.1 and the value of individualization in sentencing, nor are they necessary to achieve the important objectives of uniformity and consistency in the use of conditional sentences.

This Court has held on a number of occasions that sentencing is an individualized process, in which the trial judge has considerable discretion in fashioning a fit sentence. The rationale behind this approach stems from the principle of proportionality, the fundamental principle of sentencing, which provides that a sentence must be proportional to the gravity of the offence and the degree of responsibility of the offender. Proportionality requires an examination of the specific circumstances of both the offender and the offence so that the "punishment fits the crime". As a by-product of such an individualized approach, there will be inevitable variation in sentences imposed for particular crimes. ...

My difficulty with the suggestion that the proportionality principle presumptively excludes certain offences from the conditional sentencing regime is that such an approach focuses inordinately on the gravity of the offence and insufficiently on the moral blameworthiness of the offender. This fundamentally misconstrues the nature of the principle. Proportionality requires that *full consideration* be given to both factors. As s. 718.1 provides,

> 718.1. A sentence must be proportionate to the gravity of the offence *and* the degree of responsibility of the offender. [Emphasis added.]

Some appellate courts have held that once the statutory prerequisites are satisfied there ought to be a presumption in favour of a conditional sentence. In the instant appeal, Helper J.A. found at p. 112 that:

> Generally (though certainly not in all cases), it will be that, when a sentencing judge has attributed the appropriate weight to each of the relevant principles in determining that a fit sentence would be less than two years and has found that the offender would not be a danger to the community, a decision to allow the offender to serve his sentence in the community will be consistent with ss. 718 to 718.2.

It is possible to interpret these comments as implying that once the judge has found that the prerequisites to a conditional sentence are met, a conditional sentence would presumably be consistent with the fundamental purpose and principles of sentencing. Assuming that Helper J.A. intended to suggest that there ought to be a presumption in favour of a conditional sentence once the prerequisites are met, I respectfully disagree with her. For the same reasons that I rejected the use of presumptions against conditional sentences, I also reject presumptions in favour of them. The particular circumstances of the offender and the offence must be considered in each case.

(b) A Need for Starting Points?

An individualized sentencing regime will of necessity entail a certain degree of disparity in sentencing. I recognize that it is important for appellate courts to minimize, to the greatest extent possible, "the disparity of sentences imposed by sentencing judges for similar offenders and similar offences committed throughout Canada": *M. (C.A.), supra,* at para. 92. Towards this end, this Court held in *R. v. McDonnell,* [1997] 1 S.C.R. 948, 114 C.C.C. (3d) 436, 145 D.L.R. (4th) 577, that "starting point sentences" may be set out as guides to lower courts in order to achieve greater uniformity and consistency. I am also acutely aware of the need to provide guidance to lower courts regarding the use of the conditional sentence, as it is a new sanction which has created a considerable amount of controversy and confusion in its short life.

That said, I do not find it necessary to resort to starting points in respect of specific offences to provide guidance as to the proper use of conditional sentences. In my view, the risks posed by starting points, in the form of offence-specific presumptions in favour of incarceration, outweigh their benefits. Starting points are most useful in circumstances where there is the potential for a large disparity between sentences imposed for a particular crime because the range of sentence set out in the *Code* is particularly broad. In the case of conditional sentences, however, the statutory prerequisites of s. 742.1 considerably narrow the range of cases in which a conditional sentence may be imposed. A conditional sentence may only be imposed on non-dangerous offenders who would otherwise have received a jail sentence of less than two years. Accordingly, the potential disparity of sentence between those offenders who were candidates for a conditional sentence and received a jail term, and those who received a conditional sentence, is relatively small.

The minimal benefits of uniformity in these circumstances are exceeded by the costs of the associated loss of individualization in sentencing. By creating offence-specific starting points, there is a risk that these starting points will evolve into *de facto* minimum sentences of imprisonment. This would thwart Parliament's intention of not excluding particular categories of offence from the conditional sentencing regime. It could also result in the imposition of disproportionate sentences in some cases.

Given the narrow range of application for conditional sentences, I am of the opinion that a consideration of the principles of sentencing themselves, without offence-specific presumptions, can provide sufficient guidance as to whether a conditional sentence should be imposed. Some principles militate in favour of a conditional sentence, whereas others favour incarceration. It is the task of this Court to articulate, in general terms, which principles favour each sanction. Although it cannot ensure uniformity of result, the articulation of these principles can at least ensure uniformity in approach to the imposition of conditional sentences. It is to this task that I now turn.

(c) Principles Militating For and Against a Conditional Sentence

First, a consideration of ss. 718.2(*d*) and 718.2(*e*) leads me to the conclusion that *serious consideration* should be given to the imposition of a conditional sentence in all cases where the first three statutory prerequisites are satisfied. Sections 718.2(*d*) and 718.2(*e*) codify the important principle of restraint in sentencing and were specifically enacted, along with s. 742.1, to help reduce the rate of incarceration in Canada. Accordingly, it would be an error in principle not to consider the possibility of a conditional sentence seriously when the statutory prerequisites are met. Failure to advert to the possibility of a conditional sentence in reasons for sentence where there are reasonable grounds for finding that the first three statutory prerequisites have been met may well constitute reversible error.

I pause here to consider an interpretive difficulty posed by s. 718.2(*e*). By its terms, s. 718.2(*e*) requires judges to consider "all available sanctions *other than imprisonment* that are reasonable in the circumstances" (emphasis added.). A conditional sentence, however, is defined as a sentence of imprisonment. As a sentence of imprisonment, it cannot be an alternative to imprisonment. It would therefore appear as though s. 718.2(*e*) has no bearing on the sentencing judge's decision as to whether a conditional sentence or a jail term should be imposed. Indeed, if interpreted in the technical sense ascribed to imprisonment in Part XXIII of the *Criminal Code*, s. 718.2(*e*) would only be relevant to the judge's preliminary determination as to whether a sentence of imprisonment, as opposed to a probationary measure, should be imposed. Once the sentencing judge rejects a probationary sentence as inappropriate, the legislative force of s. 718.2(*e*) is arguably spent.

This interpretation seems to fly in the face of Parliament's intention in enacting s. 718.2(*e*) — reducing the rate of incarceration. As this Court held in *Gladue, supra*, at para. 40:

> The availability of the conditional sentence of imprisonment, in particular, alters the sentencing landscape in a manner which gives an entirely new meaning to the principle that imprisonment should be resorted to only where no other sentencing option is reasonable in the circumstances. *The creation of the conditional sentence suggests, on its face, a desire to lessen the use of incarceration. The general principle expressed in s. 718.2(e) must be construed and applied in this light.* [Emphasis added.]

Moreover, if this interpretation of s. 718.2(*e*) were adopted, it could lead to absurd results in relation to aboriginal offenders. The particular circumstances of aboriginal offenders would only be relevant in deciding whether to impose probationary sentences, and not in deciding whether a conditional sentence should be preferred to incarceration. This would greatly diminish the remedial purpose animating Parliament's enactment of this provision, which contemplates the greater use of conditional sentences and other alternatives to incarceration in cases of aboriginal offenders.

.....

In determining which principles favour of a conditional sentence and which favour incarceration, it is necessary to consider again the nature and purpose of the conditional sentence. Through an appreciation of Parliament's intention in enacting this new sanction and the mischief it seeks to redress, trial judges will be better able to make appropriate use of this innovative tool.

The conditional sentence, as I have already noted, was introduced in the amendments to Part XXIII of the *Code*. Two of the main objectives underlying the reform of Part XXIII were to reduce the use of incarceration as a sanction and to give greater prominence to the principles of restorative justice in sentencing — the objectives of rehabilitation, reparation to the victim and the community, and the promotion of a sense of responsibility in the offender.

The conditional sentence facilitates the achievement of both of Parliament's objectives. It affords the sentencing judge the opportunity to craft a sentence with appropriate conditions that can lead to the rehabilitation of the offender, reparations to the community, and the promotion of a sense of responsibility in ways that jail cannot. However, it is also a punitive sanction. Indeed, it is the punitive aspect of a conditional sentence that distinguishes it from probation. As discussed above, it was not Parliament's intention that offenders who would otherwise have gone to jail for up to two years less a day now be given probation or some equivalent thereof.

Thus, a conditional sentence can achieve both punitive and restorative objectives. To the extent that both punitive and restorative objectives can be achieved in a given case, a conditional sentence is likely a better sanction than incarceration. Where the need for punishment is particularly pressing, and there is little opportunity to achieve any restorative objectives, incarceration will likely be the more attractive sanction. However, even where restorative objectives cannot be readily satisfied, a conditional sentence will be preferable to incarceration in cases where a conditional sentence can achieve the objectives of denunciation and deterrence as effectively as incarceration. This follows from the principle of restraint in s. 718.2(*d*) and (*e*), which militates in favour of alternatives to incarceration where appropriate in the circumstances.

I turn now to the question of when a conditional sentence may be appropriate having regard to the six sentencing objectives set out in s. 718.

(i) Denunciation

Denunciation is the communication of society's condemnation of the offender's conduct. In *M. (C.A.), supra*, at para. 81, I wrote:

> In short, a sentence with a denunciatory element represents a symbolic, collective statement that the offender's conduct should be punished for encroaching on our society's basic code of values as enshrined within our substantive criminal law. As Lord Justice Lawton stated in *R. v. Sargeant* (1974), 60 Cr. App. R. 74, at p. 77: "society, through the courts, must show its abhorrence of particular types of crime, and the only way in which the courts can show this is by the sentence they pass".

Incarceration will usually provide more denunciation than a conditional sentence, as a conditional sentence is generally a more lenient sentence than a jail term of equivalent duration. That said, a conditional sentence can still provide a significant amount of denunciation. This is particularly so when onerous conditions are imposed and the duration of the conditional sentence is extended beyond the duration of the jail sentence that would ordinarily have been imposed in the circumstances. I will discuss each point in turn.

First, the conditions should have a punitive aspect. Indeed, the need for punitive conditions is the reason why a probationary sentence was rejected and a sentence of imprisonment of less than two years imposed. As stated above, conditions such as house arrest should be the norm, not the exception. This means that the offender should be confined to his or her home except when working, attending school, or fulfilling other conditions of his or her sentence, *e.g.* community service, meeting with the supervisor, or participating in treatment programs. Of course, there will need to be exceptions for medical emergencies, religious observance, and the like.

Second, although a literal reading of s. 742.1 suggests that a conditional sentence must be of equivalent duration to the jail term that would otherwise have been imposed, I have explained earlier why such a literal interpretation of s. 742.1 should be eschewed. Instead, the preferred approach is to have the judge reject a probationary sentence and a penitentiary term as inappropriate in the circumstances, and then consider whether a conditional sentence of less than two years would be consistent with the fundamental purpose and principles of sentencing, provided the statutory prerequisites are met. This approach does not require that there be any equivalence between the duration of the conditional sentence and the jail term that would otherwise have been imposed. The sole requirement is that the duration and conditions of a conditional sentence make for a just and appropriate sentence: see *Brady, supra*, at para. 111; *Ursel, supra*, at pp. 284-86 and 291-92; *Pierce, supra*, at p. 39; J.V. Roberts, *The Hunt for the Paper Tiger: Conditional Sentencing after Brady* (1999), 42 C.L.Q. 38 at pp. 47-52.

The stigma of a conditional sentence with house arrest should not be underestimated. Living in the community under strict conditions where fellow residents are well aware of the offender's criminal misconduct can provide ample denunciation in many cases. In certain circumstances, the shame of encountering members of the community may make it even more difficult for the offender to serve his or her sentence in the community than in prison.

The amount of denunciation provided by a conditional sentence will be heavily dependent on the circumstances of the offender, the nature of the conditions imposed, and the community in which the sentence is to be served. As a general matter, the more serious the offence and the greater the need for denunciation, the longer and more onerous the conditional sentence should be. However, there may be certain circumstances in which the need for denunciation is so pressing that incarceration will be the only suitable way in which to express society's condemnation of the offender's conduct.

(ii) Deterrence

Incarceration, which is ordinarily a harsher sanction, may provide more deterrence than a conditional sentence. Judges should be wary, however, of placing too much weight on deterrence when choosing between a conditional sentence and incarceration: see *Wismayer, supra*, at p. 36. The empirical evidence suggests that the deterrent effect of incarceration is uncertain: see generally *Sentencing Reform: A Canadian Approach: Report of the Canadian Sentencing Commission* (1987) at pp. 136-37. Moreover, a conditional sentence can provide significant deterrence if sufficiently punitive conditions are imposed and the public is made aware of the severity of these sentences. There is also the possibility of deterrence through the use of community service orders, including those in which the offender may be obliged to speak to members of the community about the evils of the particular criminal conduct in which he or she engaged, assuming the offender were amenable to such a condition. Nevertheless, there may be circumstances in which the need for deterrence will warrant incarceration. This will depend in part on whether the offence is one in which the effects of incarceration are likely to have a real deterrent effect, as well as on the circumstances of the community in which the offences were committed.

(iii) Separation

The objective of separation is not applicable in determining whether a conditional sentence would be consistent with the fundamental purpose and principles of sentencing because it is a prerequisite of a conditional sentence that the offender not pose a danger to the community. Accordingly, it is not necessary to completely separate the offender from society. To the extent that incarceration, which leads to the complete separation of offenders, is warranted in circumstances where the statutory prerequisites are met, it is as a result of the objectives of denunciation and deterrence, not the need for separation as such.

(iv) Restorative Objectives

While incarceration may provide for more denunciation and deterrence than a conditional sentence, a conditional sentence is generally better suited to achieving the restorative objectives of rehabilitation, reparations, and promotion of a sense of responsibility in the offender. As this Court held in *Gladue, supra*, at para. 43, "[r]estorative sentencing goals do not usually correlate with the use of prison as a sanction". The importance of these goals is not to be underestimated, as they are primarily responsible for lowering the rate of recidivism. Consequently, when the objectives of rehabilitation, reparation, and promotion of a sense of responsibility may realistically be achieved in the case of a particular offender, a conditional sentence will likely be the appropriate sanction, subject to the denunciation and deterrence considerations outlined above.

I will now consider examples of conditions that seek to vindicate these objectives. There are any number of conditions a judge may impose in order to rehabilitate an offender. Mandatory treatment orders may be imposed, such as psychological counseling and alcohol and drug rehabilitation. It is well known that sentencing an offender to a term of incarceration for an offence related to a drug addiction, without addressing the addiction, will probably not lead to the rehabilitation of the offender. *The Final Report of the Commission of Inquiry into the Non-Medical Use of Drugs* (1973) noted at p. 59 that

> These adverse effects of imprisonment are particularly reflected in the treatment of drug offenders. Our investigations suggest that there is considerable circulation of drugs within penal institutions, that offenders are reinforced in their attachment to the drug culture, and that in many cases they are introduced to certain kinds of drug use by prison contacts. Thus imprisonment does not cut off all contact with drugs or the drug subculture, nor does it cut off contact with individual drug users. Actually, it increases exposure to the influence of chronic, harmful drug users.

House arrest may also have a rehabilitative effect to a certain extent insofar as it prevents the offender from engaging in habitual anti-social associations and promotes pro-social behaviours such as attendance at work or educational institutions: see Roberts, *The Hunt for the Paper Tiger: Conditional Sentencing after Brady, supra*, at p. 65.

The objectives of reparations to the victim and the community, as well as the promotion of a sense of responsibility in offenders and acknowledgment of the harm done to victims and to the community may also be well served by a conditional sentence. For example, in some cases, restitution orders to compensate the victim may be made a condition. Furthermore, the imposition of a condition of community service can assist the offender in making reparations to the community and in promoting a sense of responsibility. An interesting possibility in this regard would be an order that the offender speak in public about the unfortunate consequences of his or her conduct, assuming the offender were amenable to such a condition. Not only could such an order promote a sense of responsibility and an acknowledgment of the harm done by the offender, it could also further the objective of deterrence, as I discussed above. In my view, the use of community service orders should be encouraged, provided that there are suitable programs available for the offender in the community. By increasing the use of community service orders, offenders will be seen by members of the public as paying back their debt to society. This will assist in contributing to public respect for the law.

(v) Summary

In sum, in determining whether a conditional sentence would be consistent with the fundamental purpose and principles of sentencing, sentencing judges should consider which sentencing objectives figure most prominently in the factual circumstances of the particular case before them. Where a combination of both punitive and restorative objectives may be achieved, a conditional sentence will likely be more appropriate than incarceration. In determining whether restorative objectives can be satisfied in a particular case, the judge should consider the offender's prospects of rehabilitation, including whether the offender has proposed a particular plan of rehabilitation; the availability of appropriate community service and treatment programs; whether the offender has acknowledged his or her wrongdoing and expresses remorse; as well as the victim's wishes as revealed by the victim impact statement (consideration of which is now mandatory pursuant to s. 722 of the *Code*). This list is not exhaustive.

Where punitive objectives such as denunciation and deterrence are particularly pressing, such as cases in which there are aggravating circumstances, incarceration will generally be the preferable sanction. This may be so notwithstanding the fact that restorative goals might be achieved by a conditional sentence. Conversely, a conditional sentence may provide sufficient denunciation and deterrence, even in cases in which restorative objectives are of diminished importance, depending on the nature of the conditions imposed, the duration of the conditional sentence, and the circumstances of the offender and the community in which the conditional sentence is to be served.

Finally, it bears pointing out that a conditional sentence may be imposed even in circumstances where there are aggravating circumstances relating to the offence or the offender. Aggravating circumstances will obviously increase the need for denunciation and deterrence. However, it would be a mistake to rule out the possibility of a conditional sentence *ab initio* simply because aggravating factors are present. I repeat that each case must be considered individually.

Sentencing judges will frequently be confronted with situations in which some objectives militate in favour of a conditional sentence, whereas others favour incarceration. In those cases, the trial judge will be called upon to weigh the various objectives in fashioning a fit sentence. As La Forest J. stated in *R. v. Lyons*, [1987] 2 S.C.R. 309 at p. 329, 37 C.C.C. (3d) 1, 44 D.L.R. (4th) 193, "[i]n a rational system of sentencing, the respective importance of prevention, deterrence, retribution and rehabilitation will vary according to the nature of the crime and the circumstances of the offender". There is no easy test or formula that the judge can apply in weighing these factors. Much will depend on the good judgment and wisdom of sentencing judges, whom Parliament vested with considerable discretion in making these determinations pursuant to s. 718.3.

(d) Appropriate Conditions

In the event that a judge chooses to impose a conditional sentence, there are five compulsory conditions listed in s. 742.3(1) that must be imposed. The judge also has considerable discretion in imposing optional conditions pursuant to s. 742.3(2). There are a number of principles that should guide the judge in exercising this discretion. First, the conditions must ensure the safety of the community. Second, conditions must be tailored to fit the particular circumstances of the offender and the offence. The type of conditions imposed will be a function of the sentencing judge's creativity. However, conditions will prove fruitless if the offender is incapable of abiding by them, and will increase the probability that the offender will be incarcerated as a result of breaching them. Third, punitive conditions such as house arrest should be the norm, not the exception. Fourth, the conditions must be realistically enforceable. This requires a consideration of the available resources in the community in which the sentence is to be served. I agree with Rosenberg J.A., who, in *Recent Developments in Sentencing*, a paper prepared for the National Judicial Institute's Supreme Court of Nova Scotia Education Seminar in Halifax, February 25-26, 1999, at p. 63, wrote that:

> the courts must be careful not to impose conditions that are purely cosmetic and are incapable of effective enforcement. For example, I would think that any condition that can only be effectively enforced through an intolerable intrusion into the privacy of innocent persons would be problematic. Conditions that impose an unacceptable burden on the supervisor might also be of dubious value. If the conditions that the court imposes are impractical, the justice system will be brought into disrepute.

D. Burden of Proof

.....

...The wording used in s. 742.1 does not attribute to either party the onus of establishing that the offender should or should not receive a conditional sentence. To inform his or her decision about the appropriate sentence, the judge can take into consideration all the evidence, no matter who adduces it (*Ursel*, *supra*, at pp. 264-65 and 287).

In matters of sentencing, while each party is expected to establish elements in support of its position as to the appropriate sentence that should be imposed, the ultimate decision as to what constitutes the best disposition is left to the discretion of the sentencing judge. This message is explicit in s. 718.3(1) and (2):

> 718.3(1) Where an enactment prescribes different degrees or kinds of punishment in respect of an offence, the punishment to be imposed is, subject to the limitations prescribed in the enactment, in the discretion of the court that convicts a person who commits the offence.
>
> (2) Where an enactment prescribes a punishment in respect of an offence, the punishment to be imposed is, subject to the limitations prescribed in the enactment, in the discretion of the court that convicts a person who commits the offence, but no punishment is a minimum punishment unless it is declared to be a minimum punishment.

The sentencing judge can take into account the submissions and evidence presented by counsel (s. 723), but is in no way bound by them in the decision as to the sentence. Having said this, in practice, it will generally be the offender who is best situated to convince the judge that a conditional sentence is indeed appropriate. Therefore, it would be in the offender's best interests to establish those elements militating in favour of a conditional sentence: see *Ursel, supra*, at pp. 264-65; *R. v. Fleet* (1997), 120 C.C.C. (3d) 457 (Ont. C.A.) at para. 26. For instance, the offender should inform the judge of his or her remorse, willingness to repair and acknowledgment of responsibility, and propose a plan of rehabilitation. The offender could also convince the judge that he or she would not endanger the safety of the community if appropriate conditions were imposed. It would be to the great benefit of the offender to make submissions in this regard. I would also note the importance of the role of the supervision officer in informing the judge on these issues.

E. Deference Owed to Sentencing Judges

In recent years, this Court has repeatedly stated that the sentence imposed by a trial court is entitled to considerable deference from appellate courts: see *Shropshire, supra*, at paras. 46-50; *M. (C.A.), supra*, at paras. 89-94; *McDonnell, supra*, at paras. 15-17 (majority); *R. v. W. (G.)*, S.C.C., No 26705, October 15, 1999, at paras. 18-19 [reported 138 C.C.C. (3d) 23, 178 D.L.R. (4th) 76]. In *M. (C.A.)*, at para. 90, I wrote:

> Put simply, absent an error in principle, failure to consider a relevant factor, or an overemphasis of the appropriate factors, a court of appeal should only intervene to vary a sentence imposed at trial if the sentence is demonstrably unfit. Parliament explicitly vested sentencing judges with a *discretion* to determine the appropriate degree and kind of punishment under the *Criminal Code*. [Emphasis in original.]

Several provisions of Part XXIII confirm that Parliament intended to confer a wide discretion upon the sentencing judge. As a general rule, ss. 718.3(1) and 718.3(2) provide that the degree and kind of punishment to be imposed is left to the discretion of the sentencing judge. Moreover, the opening words of s. 718 specify that the sentencing judge must seek to achieve the fundamental purpose of sentencing "by imposing just sanctions that have *one or more* of the following objectives" (emphasis added). In the context of the conditional sentence, s. 742.1 provides that the judge "may" impose a conditional sentence and enjoys a wide discretion in the drafting of the appropriate conditions, pursuant to s. 742.3(2).

Although an appellate court might entertain a different opinion as to what objectives should be pursued and the best way to do so, that difference will generally not constitute an error of law justifying interference. Further, minor errors in the sequence of application of s. 742.1 may not warrant intervention by appellate courts. Again, I stress that appellate courts should not second-guess sentencing judges unless the sentence imposed is demonstrably unfit.

.....

VI. SUMMARY

At this point, a short summary of what has been said in these reasons might be useful:

1. Bill C-41 in general and the conditional sentence in particular were enacted both to reduce reliance on incarceration as a sanction and to increase the use of principles of restorative justice in sentencing.
2. A conditional sentence should be distinguished from probationary measures. Probation is primarily a rehabilitative sentencing tool. By contrast, Parliament intended conditional sentences to include both punitive and rehabilitative aspects. Therefore, conditional sentences should generally include punitive conditions that are restrictive of the offender's liberty. Conditions such as house arrest should be the norm, not the exception.
3. No offences are excluded from the conditional sentencing regime except those with a minimum term of imprisonment, nor should there be presumptions in favour of or against a conditional sentence for specific offences.
4. The requirement in s. 742.1(*a*) that the judge impose a sentence of imprisonment of less than two years does not require the judge to first impose a sentence of imprisonment of a fixed duration before considering whether that sentence can be served in the community. Although this approach is suggested by the text of s. 742.1(*a*), it is unrealistic and could lead to unfit sentences in some cases. Instead, a purposive interpretation of s. 742.1(*a*) should be adopted. In a preliminary determination, the sentencing judge should reject a penitentiary term and probationary measures as inappropriate. Having determined that the appropriate range of sentence is a term of imprisonment of less than two years, the judge should then consider whether it is appropriate for the offender to serve his or her sentence in the community.
5. As a corollary of the purposive interpretation of s. 742.1(*a*), a conditional sentence need not be of equivalent duration to the sentence of incarceration that would otherwise have been imposed. The sole requirement is that the duration and conditions of a conditional sentence make for a just and appropriate sentence.
6. The requirement in s. 742.1(*b*) that the judge be satisfied that the safety of the community would not be endangered by the offender serving his or her sentence in the community is a condition precedent to the imposition of a conditional sentence, and not the primary consideration in determining whether a conditional sentence is appropriate. In making this determination, the judge should consider the risk posed by the specific offender, not the broader risk of whether the imposition of a conditional sentence would endanger the safety of the community by providing insufficient general deterrence or undermining general respect for the law. Two factors should be taken into

account: (1) the risk of the offender re-offending; and (2) the gravity of the damage that could ensue in the event of re-offence. A consideration of the risk posed by the offender should include the risk of any criminal activity, and not be limited solely to the risk of physical or psychological harm to individuals.

7. Once the prerequisites of s. 742.1 are satisfied, the judge should give serious consideration to the possibility of a conditional sentence in all cases by examining whether a conditional sentence is consistent with the fundamental purpose and principles of sentencing set out in ss. 718 to 718.2. This follows from Parliament's clear message to the judiciary to reduce the use of incarceration as a sanction.
8. A conditional sentence can provide significant denunciation and deterrence. As a general matter, the more serious the offence, the longer and more onerous the conditional sentence should be. There may be some circumstances, however, where the need for denunciation or deterrence is so pressing that incarceration will be the only suitable way in which to express society's condemnation of the offender's conduct or to deter similar conduct in the future.
9. Generally, a conditional sentence will be better than incarceration at achieving the restorative objectives of rehabilitation, reparations to the victim and the community, and promotion of a sense of responsibility in the offender and acknowledgment of the harm done to the victim and the community.
10. Where a combination of both punitive and restorative objectives may be achieved, a conditional sentence will likely be more appropriate than incarceration. Where objectives such as denunciation and deterrence are particularly pressing, incarceration will generally be the preferable sanction. This may be so notwithstanding the fact that restorative goals might be achieved. However, a conditional sentence may provide sufficient denunciation and deterrence, even in cases in which restorative objectives are of lesser importance, depending on the nature of the conditions imposed, the duration of the sentence, and the circumstances of both the offender and the community in which the conditional sentence is to be served.
11. A conditional sentence may be imposed even where there are aggravating circumstances, although the need for denunciation and deterrence will increase in these circumstances.
12. No party is under a burden of proof to establish that a conditional sentence is either appropriate or inappropriate in the circumstances. The judge should consider all relevant evidence, no matter by whom it is adduced. However, it would be in the offender's best interests to establish elements militating in favour of a conditional sentence.
13. Sentencing judges have a wide discretion in the choice of the appropriate sentence. They are entitled to considerable deference from appellate courts. As explained in *M. (C.A.), supra*, at para. 90: "Put simply, absent an error in principle, failure to

> consider a relevant factor, or an overemphasis of the appropriate factors, a court of appeal should only intervene to vary a sentence imposed at trial if the sentence is demonstrably unfit."

VII. APPLICATION TO THE CASE AT HAND

In the case at hand, Keyser J. considered that a term of imprisonment of 18 months was appropriate and declined to permit the respondent to serve his term in the community. She found that, while the respondent would not endanger the safety of the community by serving a conditional sentence, such a sentence would not be in conformity with the objectives of s. 718. In her view, even if incarceration was not necessary to deter the respondent from similar future conduct or necessary for his rehabilitation, incarceration was necessary to denounce the conduct of the respondent and to deter others from engaging in similar conduct.

While Keyser J. seems to have proceeded according to a rigid two-step process, in deviation from the approach I have set out, I am not convinced that an 18-month sentence of incarceration was demonstrably unfit for these offences and this offender. I point out that the offences here were very serious, and that they had resulted in a death and in severe bodily harm. Moreover, dangerous driving and impaired driving may be offences for which harsh sentences plausibly provide general deterrence. These crimes are often committed by otherwise law-abiding persons, with good employment records and families. Arguably, such persons are the ones most likely to be deterred by the threat of severe penalties: see *R. v. McVeigh* (1985), 22 C.C.C. (3d) 145 (Ont. C.A.) at p. 150; *R. v. Biancofiore*, (1997), 119 C.C.C. (3d) 344 at paras. 18-24; *R. v. Blakely* (1998), 40 O.R. (3d) 541 at pp. 542-43, 127 C.C.C. (3d) 271 (C.A.).

I hasten to add that these comments should not be taken as a directive that conditional sentences can never be imposed for offences such as dangerous driving or impaired driving. In fact, were I a trial judge, I might have found that a conditional sentence would have been appropriate in this case. The respondent is still very young; he had no prior record and no convictions since the accident; he seems completely rehabilitated; he wants to go back to school; he has already suffered a lot by causing the death of a friend and was himself in a coma for some time. To make sure that the objectives of denunciation and general deterrence would have been sufficiently addressed, I might have imposed conditions such as house arrest and a community service order requiring the offender to speak to designated groups about the consequences of dangerous driving, as was the case in *Parker, supra*, at p. 239, and *R. v. Hollinsky*, (1995) 103 C.C.C. (3d) 472 (Ont. C.A.).

However, trial judges are closer to their community and know better what would be acceptable to their community. Absent evidence that the sentence imposed by the trial judge was demonstrably unfit, the Court of Appeal should not have interfered to substitute its own opinion for that of the sentencing judge. The trial judge did not commit a reversible error in principle and she appropriately considered all the relevant factors. Although the Court of Appeal's decision is entitled to some deference (see the companion appeal *R. v. R.A.R.*, 2000 SCC 8, at paras. 20-21 ...), in my opinion it erred in holding that the sentencing judge had given undue weight to the objective of denunciation. I see no ground for the Court of Appeal's intervention.

VIII. DISPOSITION

I would allow the appeal. Accordingly, the 18-month sentence of incarceration imposed by the trial judge should be restored. However, given that the respondent has already served the conditional sentence imposed by the Court of Appeal in its entirety, and that the Crown stated in oral argument that it was not seeking any further punishment, I would stay the service of the sentence of incarceration.

QUESTIONS

31. **The accused was convicted of sexually assaulting his daughter by kissing, fondling, simulating intercourse and having her masturbate him. The accused was remorseful. The complainant suffered emotionally. Is a conditional sentence appropriate? See, in this regard, *R. v. S.(M.)* (2003), 173 C.C.C. (3d) 526 (Sask. C.A.); and *R. v. S.(R.N.)* (2000), 140 C.C.C. (3d) 553 (S.C.C.).**

32. **The accused pleaded guilty to defrauding his employer of $100,000. The accused was given a 12-month conditional sentence with restitution; however, the conditional sentence order contained no terms restricting the accused's liberty. Is this an error which is subject to appellate review? See *R. v. Proulx* (2000), 140 C.C.C. (3d) 449 (S.C.C.); *R. v. Smith* [1999] O.J. 2694 (C.A.); and *R. v. Hirnschall*, [2003] O.J. No. 2296 (C.A.).**

33. **The accused doctor pleaded guilty to defrauding the hospital where he worked of $900,000. He acted in concert with his son and his son's friends. The doctor has made partial restitution of $150,000. Is a conditional sentence appropriate for this large breach of trust fraud? If so, under what circumstances? Consider, in this regard, *R. v. Wilson* (2003), 174 C.C.C. (3d) 255 (Ont. C.A.); *R. v. Bogart* (2002), 167 C.C.C. (3d) 390 (Ont. C.A.); leave to appeal to S.C.C. refused 171 C.C.C. (3d) vi.**

(j) Intermittent Sentences

The sentencing court may order that a term of imprisonment be served intermittently if the sentence does not exceed 90 days (s. 732 of the *Code*). An intermittent sentence enables an offender to maintain his or her employment. The court will order, for example, that the offender serve a sentence from 6:00 p.m. on Fridays until 6:00 a.m. on Mondays. Section 732(1)(*c*) of the *Code* states that an intermittent sentence must be accompanied by a probation order.

R. v. PARISIAN

(1993), 81 C.C.C. (3d) 351 (Man. C.A.)

The judgment of the court was delivered orally by

Twaddle J.A.: — The accused appeals from a sentence of three months' imprisonment imposed on her in Provincial Court for the offence of possessing *cannabis* resin for the purpose of trafficking. She asks only that she be permitted to serve her sentence intermittently.

Ordinarily, the decision to allow or not to allow a convicted person to serve time intermittently is one to be made by the sentencing judge. This court will only interfere if the decision is made on a wrong principle or is clearly wrong.

In the present case, the offence involved a relatively small quantity of the narcotic; the accused was a small player; the sales which the accused intended to make was to persons who frequent a beverage room. Her circumstances are such that a sentence of three months if not served intermittently will cause some hardship because she has two children whom it would be difficult to place for care if she serves her sentence other than intermittently. Additionally, she has the opportunity to take a course of education to upgrade herself if she is free to take it from Monday to Friday. The accused has no prior record.

The learned sentencing judge imposed a sentence which is within the range for this particular offence and this offender, but we think she was wrong to characterize it as one at the lower end of that range. Additionally, she placed undue emphasis on the fact that the accused was unemployed and did not need an intermittent sentence to save her job. The need for the accused to educate herself and make arrangements for her children are equally valid reasons for an intermittent sentence.

In the circumstances, we are of the view that the judge's decision not to allow the sentence to be served intermittently was clearly wrong. Accordingly, we allow the appeal, set aside the sentence of three months' imprisonment and substitute one of 90 days to be served intermittently.

Appeal allowed.

(k) Imprisonment

An offender who is sentenced to a term of imprisonment for two years or more will serve time in a federal penitentiary (s. 731(1)). If the sentence imposed is less than two years, the sentence is served in a provincial facility. A court may direct that custodial sentences for different offences be served concurrently or consecutively (s. 718.3(4)).

QUESTIONS

34. **The accused pleads guilty to numerous counts of sexual assault, incest, assault with a weapon and lesser offences, arising from a pattern of sexual, physical and emotional abuse inflicted upon his children over many years. None of the offences carry a term of life imprisonment. The trial judge finds the offences to be the most egregious he has ever dealt with.**

He tentatively indicates that he would like to impose a total sentence of 28 years imprisonment and asks you, the Crown, whether he has jurisdiction to do so. What is your answer? Consider, in this regard, *R. v. M.(C.A.)* (1996), 105 C.C.C. (3d) 327 (S.C.C.).

35. **The accused has a record for numerous sexual offences involving the stalking and sexual assault of young children. Intensive psychotherapy and drug treatment have been unsuccessful in curbing his sexual impulses. The accused is convicted of yet another sexual assault involving a young child. Under what circumstances should the Crown bring a dangerous offender or long-term offender application? Consider, in this regard, Part XXIV of the *Criminal Code*.**

---

7. Parole Ineligibility

Section 743.6 of the *Criminal Code* provides that the sentencing court may order that an offender who receives a sentence of two years or more may only be released on full parole after the lesser of one-half the sentence or ten years.

R. v. CHAISSON

(1995), 102 C.C.C. (3d) 564 (N.B.C.A.)

[The accused was charged with offences arising out of an incident where he and two others forcibly confined and assaulted three residents of a rooming house and uttered death threats against the owner. The accused pleaded guilty and was sentenced to three years and nine months imprisonment. Pursuant to what is now s. 743.6 of the *Criminal Code*, the accused was ordered to serve one-half of his sentence before being eligible for parole. The accused appealed the sentence and the parole ineligibility order.]

The judgment of the court was delivered by

Hoyt C.J.N.B.: —

.....

Mr. Chaisson, who was 45 years old at the time of the incident, has a lengthy criminal record consisting of 28 offences dating from 1963 to 1986. His longest imprisonment was for four years imposed in 1973 for three break, enter and thefts. Although the majority of Mr. Chaisson's convictions are for property-related crimes, three convictions since 1980 involved violence. His most recent previous sentence was in July of 1986, when he was sentenced to two years less a day for robbery. Taking into account Mr. Chaisson's incarceration for that sentence, there would have been approximately a five-year gap in his criminal activities until this incident. There was an earlier five-year gap in Mr. Chaisson's criminal record from 1975 to 1980.

The judge aptly described the crimes as bizarre, horrible and serious and noted that violence was used. He felt that there should be an element of both individual and general deterrence. He also said that the sentence should reflect society's "reaction, revulsion and abhorrence of these kinds of crimes".

The sentencing judge also enumerated several mitigating factors. He said that Mr. Chaisson "had nothing on [his] record since 1986 and I take note of that". He also noted that Mr. Chaisson had spent six months in custody from February 6, 1993, until he was sentenced on August 4th. He considered that alcohol was involved and that Mr. Chaisson had a history of alcoholism. He also took into account Mr. Chaisson's plea of guilty and his expression of remorse.

By any yardstick, the offences, particularly when taken together, are serious. They were violent in nature. They were degrading and entirely unprovoked. Although Mr. Chaisson does not appear to have been the leader, he was certainly a willing participant throughout. The maximum consecutive imprisonment for these offences is 42 years, while the maximum sentence for the most serious offence is 10 years. Taking into account Mr. Chaisson's previous criminal record and making some little allowance for the somewhat short gap since his last offence, the time that Mr. Chaisson spent in custody, his pleas of guilty, his expression of remorse and that these events occurred on the fifth day of what Mr. Chaisson's counsel described as a "five-day alcoholic binge", I do not feel that the sentencing judge imposed unfit sentences. When viewed in their totality or separately, they are well within any range that can be suggested for these offences. Indeed, they are, in my opinion, towards the lower end of any range. For the above reasons, I would dismiss the appeal against sentences.

Mr. Chaisson has also appealed the order made pursuant to s. 741.2 [now s. 743.6] of the *Criminal Code* whereby he is ineligible for parole until he served one-half of his sentence.

.....

The judge, on his own motion, imposed parole ineligibility. He said:

> And, likewise on these offences pursuant to section 741.2, the power of the court to delay the parole, I will order that before the offender may be released on full parole that one half of the sentence ... must be served.

The Crown did not request the imposition of a s. 741.2 order. Its failure to ask for such an order is not, in my view, in itself sufficient to permit a successful appeal of such an order. Before considering the imposition of such an order, however, it is desirable that an accused person be advised that such an order is being contemplated so that he or she may respond. The question of whether parole ineligibility should be imposed was fully canvassed before us.

The Crown has raised the threshold consideration of whether the appeal is moot because Mr. Chaisson has already served over one-half of his sentence. I prefer, however, Mr. Chaisson's submission that because such a prohibition will remain on his record, likely to his detriment should he reoffend, the question is not moot. For that reason, Mr. Chaisson's appeal against the order imposing parole ineligibility should be considered on its merits.

Section 741.2 requires the court, before imposing such parole ineligibility, to be satisfied of certain matters, namely, the circumstances of the commission of the offence, the character and circumstances of the offender and that either the expression of society's denunciation of the offences or the objective of specific or general deterrence requires such an order to be made. As noted by Fish J.A. in *R. v. Dankyi* (1993), 86 C.C.C. (3d) 368, 25 C.R. (4th) 395, [1993] R.J.Q. 2767 (Que. C.A.), and Griffiths J.A. in *R. v. Goulet* (1995), 97 C.C.C. (3d) 61, 37 C.R. (4th) 373, 22 O.R. (3d) 118 (C.A.), these factors are also taken into account when sentence is fixed. The judge, although he dealt with these factors thoroughly while sentencing Mr. Chaisson, did not relate them to the s. 741.2 order. In both *Dankyi* and *Goulet,* the s. 741.2 order was set aside because the sentencing judge did not give reasons for its imposition. In both cases, however, the sentencing judge's reasons for sentence, as well as counsel's representations, were brief. Such is not the case here. McKee Prov. Ct. J., following very lengthy representations from both Crown counsel and Mr. Chaisson's counsel, gave clear and full reasons for the sentence he imposed — if not for the s. 741.2 order. In my view, failure to give reasons for imposing a s. 741.2 order should not automatically result in the order being set aside. The failure to give reasons may be a factor for an appellate court to consider in cases where the reasons for the length of sentence are inadequate. It is, however, for us to consider the fitness of the sentence, including the s. 741.2 order.

Before us and in a subsequent written submission, Mr. Chaisson's counsel submitted that the use of s. 741.2 should be restricted to the most serious situation, somewhat approximating the worst case, worst offender scenario. I cannot accept that submission. While an order for parole ineligibility will likely be made more often in serious cases, I would not restrict its application to cases that only fall within that category. I would not deny its application when, for example, as here, modest sentences are imposed for a number of offences. A s. 741.2 order must not become routine, but be reserved for exceptional circumstances. In *Goulet,* Griffiths J.A. pointed out the difficulty in applying the section and illustrated situations when, in his view, the section had application. He said at p. 67:

> The sentencing judge should first determine what is a fit sentence having regard to the accepted principles relating to sentencing which will, of course, include the possible rehabilitation of the accused. It is only after the sentencing judge has arrived at an appropriate sentence that he or she should then consider whether the particular circumstances of the offence, or the character and circumstances of the offender, require that the normal statutory powers of the Parole Board be circumscribed by a s. 741.2 order.
>
> In my view, s. 741.2 should only be invoked as an exceptional measure where the Crown has satisfied the court on clear evidence that an increase in the period of parole ineligibility is "required". There should be articulable reasons for invoking s. 741.2 and, as suggested in *R. v. Dankyi, supra,* the trial judge should give clear and specific reasons for the increase in parole ineligibility.
>
> The circumstances of the offence will rarely provide much additional assistance under s. 741.2 where those circumstances have formed the primary basis for fixing the appropriate period of incarceration. If the offence is one of unusual violence, brutality or degradation, then the need to strongly express society's denunciation of the offence may make a s. 741.2 order appropriate. The section should not be invoked on the basis of more general concerns which are not specific to the particular offence such as the frequency of the commission of that type of offence in the community.
>
> The distinguishing characteristics of the offender may provide more fruitful grounds for invoking s. 741.2 as an exceptional measure. Where the Crown has adduced clear evidence that the offender will not be deterred or

rehabilitated within the normal period of parole ineligibility, an order under s. 741.2 will be appropriate. A history of prior parole violations, or violations of other forms of conditional release, or evidence that significant prior custodial sentences have had little impact would be appropriate factors to consider in applying s. 741.2.

.....

In my view, the circumstances here call for the imposition of parole ineligibility. The vicious, repulsive and degrading actions call for an expression of society's denunciation. The criminal activities occurred over a lengthy period during which Mr. Chaisson did not make any effort to leave. His actions, which were not casual or spontaneous, were the result of many separate decisions and show a basic character defect. Mr. Chaisson's previous criminal record, even making allowance for a relatively short gap in that record and his apparent inability to break a cycle of dependency upon alcohol, also place him within the ambit of s. 741.2. For the above reasons, it is my opinion that the sentences attract the application of s. 741.2. I say that with one caveat. Two of the offences committed by Mr. Chaisson, namely, theft (s. 334(*b*)) and uttering a death threat (s. 264.1(1)(*a*)), are not listed in Schedules I and II of the *Corrections and Conditional Release Act*, S.C. 1992, c. 20, and thus cannot be included in the s. 741.2 order.

For the above reasons, I would allow the appeal, but only with respect to the imposition of the s. 741.2 order to the two last mentioned sentences; otherwise, the application of the order made pursuant to s. 741.2 of the *Criminal Code* applies to the remaining four sentences.

Appeal allowed in part.

Note that parole ineligibility for first and second degree murder are addressed in ss. 745 to 746.1 of the *Criminal Code*. Section 745.6 is the "faint hope" provision that permits revisitation of the 25-year parole ineligibility for first degree murder after 15 years. See *R. v. Swietlinski* (1994), 92 C.C.C. (3d) 449 (S.C.C.), partially reproduced at p. 576.

8. Forensic DNA Analysis

Where an offender is convicted or discharged of a primary or secondary designated offence (as defined in s. 487.04), the court may order an offender to provide samples of his or her DNA to a national data bank in the circumstances set out in s. 487.051. The order is made at the sentencing stage of the trial. Section 487.051(1)(*a*) provides that a judge "shall" make an order in respect of a primary designated offence unless the accused has the ability to show under s. 487.051(2) that it should not be made because of its impact on his or her privacy. Section 487.051(1)(*b*) provides that a judge "may" make an order in respect of a secondary designated offence if the court is satisfied that it is in the best interest of the administration of justice to do so. Section 487.051(3) permits a judge to consider many factors when considering whether such an order under s. 487.051(1)(*b*) should be made, including, the accused's criminal record, the nature of the offence, the circumstances surrounding its commission and the impact of the order on the person's security and privacy. See *R. v. Briggs* (2000), 157 C.C.C. (3d) 38 (Ont. C.A).

CHAPTER 12

YOUTH CRIMINAL JUSTICE

A. THE POLICY OF THE YOUTH CRIMINAL JUSTICE ACT

The *Youth Criminal Justice Act*, S.C. 2002, c. 1 (the "YCJA") received royal assent on February 19, 2002 and was proclaimed in force on April 1, 2003. The YCJA replaces the *Young Offenders Act*, R.S.C. 1985, c. Y-1 (the "YOA"), which had been the law in Canada in relation to young persons since its passage in 1984. The YCJA emphasizes that jail is to be reserved for the most serious cases of violence.

Section 3(1) of the YCJA provides a "declaration of principle", which governs the interpretation and application of the law in respect of young persons. Its equivalent section in the YOA has been held to have the weight of substantive law (see *R. v. T.(V.)*, reproduced immediately below). Section 3(1) sets out four interconnected and, arguably, ranked statements of principle that attempt to balance the competing and often irreconcilable interests in the youth justice system. In contrast to the sentencing principles applicable to adults, the long-term protection of the public is not achieved through denunciation, deterrence or incarceration; rather, pursuant to the declaration of principle, it is achieved through rehabilitation of young persons. Further, the reference to "timely intervention" in s. 3(1)(*b*) of the YCJA incorporates case law that recognizes, in general, that youth criminal matters should be brought to trial expeditiously. (See, for example, *R. v. M.(G.C.)* (1991), 65 C.C.C. (3d) 232 (Ont. C.A.).)

R. v. T.(V.)

(1992), 71 C.C.C. (3d) 32 (S.C.C.)

[The 14-year-old young person had been involved in an incident at the group home where she lived which prompted the police to lay charges of mischief, assault and uttering threats. The appeal from the British Columbia Court of Appeal to the Supreme Court of Canada raised the issue of whether a youth court judge could decline to make a finding of guilt despite proof of the offence, where the judge was of the view that charges ought not to have been laid in the first place.]

The judgment of the court was delivered by

L'Heureux-Dubé J.: —

.....

There is no doubt that the Crown acting through the Attorney-General, and in turn through his or her prosecutors, has a wide amount of discretion in the carriage of criminal cases. Our own court has recognized the principle numerous times and I would cite, as an example, the words of Fauteux C.J.C. in *Smythe v. The Queen* (1971), 3 C.C.C. (2d) 366 at p. 370, 19 D.L.R. (3d) 480, [1971] S.C.R. 680:

> Obviously, the manner in which the Attorney-General of the day exercises his statutory discretion may be questioned or censured by the legislative body to which he is answerable, but that again is foreign to the determination of the question now under consideration. Enforcement of the law and especially of the criminal law would be impossible unless someone in authority be vested with some measure of discretionary power. The following statements made in [*R. v. Court of the Sessions of the Peace et al., Ex p. Lafleur,* [1967] 3 C.C.C. 244] at p. 248, by Montgomery, J., with the concurrence of Tremblay, C.J.Q. and Pratte, J., are to the point and I adopt them.
>
> > I cannot conceive of a system of enforcing the law where someone in authority is not called upon to decide whether or not a person should be prosecuted for an alleged offence. Inevitably there will be cases where one man is prosecuted while another man, perhaps equally guilty, goes free. A single act, or series of acts, may render a person liable to prosecution in more than one charge, and someone must decide what charges are to be laid.

.....

Later, in the context of the *Canadian Charter of Rights and Freedoms,* this court had occasion to consider whether such discretion constituted an affront to the principles of fundamental justice. In *R. v. Beare* (1988), 45 C.C.C. (3d) 57 at p. 76, 55 D.L.R. (4th) 481, [1988] 2 S.C.R. 387, La Forest J., speaking for the court, states:

> The existence of the discretion conferred by the statutory provisions does not, in my view, offend principles of fundamental justice. Discretion is an essential feature of the criminal justice system. A system that attempted to eliminate discretion would be unworkably complex and rigid. Police necessarily exercise discretion in deciding when to lay charges, to arrest and to conduct incidental searches, as prosecutors do in deciding whether or not to withdraw a charge, enter a stay, consent to an adjournment, proceed by way of indictment or summary conviction, launch an appeal and so on.

.....

It is important to understand the rationale for this judicial deference to the prosecutor's discretion. In this regard, the reasons of Viscount Dilhorne in *Director of Public Prosecutions v. Humphrys,* [1976] 2 All E.R. 497 at p. 511 (H.L.), are instructive:

> A judge must keep out of the arena. He should not have or appear to have any responsibility for the institution of a prosecution. The functions of prosecutors and of judges must not be blurred. *If a judge has power to decline to hear a case because he does not think it should be brought, then it soon may be thought that the cases he allows to proceed are cases brought with his consent or approval.*

(Emphasis added.)

.....

I wish to be clear, however, that while the principle of prosecutorial discretion is an important precept in our criminal law, and exists for good reason, it is by no means absolute in its operation. It is now apparent, for example, that a stay of proceedings is available to prevent violations of the principles of fundamental justice and abuse of the court's process. In *R. v. Jewitt* (1985), 21 C.C.C. (3d) 7, 20 D.L.R. (4th) 651, [1985] 2 S.C.R. 128, our own court relied heavily on the comments of the House of Lords in *Humphrys, supra,* at pp. 509-11, when it examined the question of whether or not the remedy was known in Canada:

> Where an indictment has been properly preferred...has a judge power to quash it and to decline to allow the trial to proceed merely because he thinks that a prosecution of the accused for that offence should not have been instituted? *I think there is no such general power* and that to recognise the existence of such a degree of omnipotence is, as my noble and learned friend Lord Edmund-Davies, has said, unacceptable in any country acknowledging the rule of law. *But saying this does not mean that there is not a general power to control the procedure of a court so as to avoid unfairness.* If at the time of *Connelly* it had been possible to try the murder and robbery charges together, then it might well have been held unfair, oppressive and an abuse of process for them to be tried separately, each charge being based on the same evidence. But that is very different from saying that a judge has power to stop a prosecution for perjury just because he thinks it should not have been brought and that it will show that the verdict at the trial at which it is alleged the perjury was committed should have been guilty.

.....

(Emphasis added.)

.....

From the preceding discussion it should be apparent that, while not absolute, the principle of prosecutorial discretion is an important and useful part of our criminal law. Hence, ... the interpretation of the Act which is urged upon us by the respondent and which was accepted by the Court of Appeal would represent a marked departure from the law as it currently exists.

.....

Consequently, subject to such exceptions as the doctrine of abuse of process (which was not argued before us), while it is open to Parliament to confer discretion upon youth court judges to dismiss charges on the basis that those charges ought not to have been laid, indeed, subject to overarching constitutional norms, it is open to Parliament to change the law in whatever way it sees fit, the legislation in which it chooses to make these alterations known must be drafted in such a way that its intention is no way in doubt. The question for the purposes of this case becomes, therefore, whether Parliament has drafted the *Young Offenders Act* in such a way so as to make this intention manifest.

The type of clarity necessary to effect such a change cannot, in my opinion, be found in s. 19(2) alone. The wording of that section is not explicit enough to reflect an intent on the part of Parliament to confer on youth court judges the discretion to dismiss charges whenever it strikes their fancy. The respondent recognizes this and submits that Parliament's expression lies rather in the combined operation of ss. 19(2) and 3(1). Section 19(2), she points out, provides that a youth court may dismiss a charge. The court may do so, the argument continues, where the prosecutor has not acted in conformity with the principles underlying the Act. Those principles are contained in s. 3(1). The respondent relies particularly on s. 3(1)(*d*) which contemplates the taking of "measures other than judicial proceedings" or "no measures" where doing to would "not be inconsistent with the protection of society".

.....

I am unable to accede to the submission of the appellant that s. 3(1) is merely a "preamble" and does not carry the same force one would normally attribute to substantive provisions, especially since Parliament has chosen to include the section in the body of the Act. Yet, I am equally unable to attribute to that section the clarity necessary to accept the respondent's interpretation. Section 3(1)(*d*) admittedly advocates the taking of no measures in certain circumstances. However, this subsection must be read in conjunction with the rest of s. 3 which states, *inter alia,* that "young persons who commit offences should nonetheless bear responsibility for their contraventions" (3(1)(*a*)), and that "society must ... be afforded the necessary protection from illegal behaviour" (3(1)(*b*)). These statements, on their face, would both militate against the action advocated by the Court of Appeal just as much as 3(1)(*d*) is said to militate in favour of it.

Some commentators have been relatively critical of the drafting of the Declaration of Principle as it appears in s. 3(1). Platt, in *Young Offenders Law in Canada* (1989), at 2.18, has said:

> In many respects, the policies are an articulation of the principles of criminal law in the context of young persons. The difficulty is that they are not coherent and, in some instances, are positively inconsistent. It is because of this that s. 3(1) is such a fertile ground for both the defence and the prosecution in searching out Parliament's legislative intention.

However, while I am not unmindful of the apparent inconsistencies of the stated goals of the Act as contained in s. 3(1), in my opinion the better view is that advocated by Bala and Kirvan in ch. 4 of *The Young Offenders Act: A Revolution in Canadian Juvenile Justice* (1991), at pp. 80-1:

.....

> While it may not be inaccurate to suggest that the Declaration of Principle reflects a certain societal ambivalence about young offenders, it is also important to appreciate that it represents an honest attempt to achieve an appropriate balance for dealing with a very complex social problem. The YOA does not have a single, simple underlying philosophy, for there is no single, simple philosophy that can deal with all situations in which young persons violate the criminal law. While the declaration as a whole defines the parameters for juvenile justice in Canada, each principle is not necessarily relevant to every situation. The weight to be attached to a particular principle will be determined in large measure by the nature of the decision being made and the specific provisions of the YOA that govern the situation. There are situations in which there is a need to balance competing princi-

ples, but this is a challenge in cases in the adult as well as the juvenile system.

.....

... I have come to the conclusion that the argument advanced by the respondent is not at all consonant with recent pronouncements of this court on the nature of s. 3(1). In *R. v. S.(S.)* (1990), 57 C.C.C. (3d) 115, [1990] 2 S.C.R. 254, 77 C.R. (3d) 273, the accused, a young person, had been charged with possession of stolen goods but before entering a plea brought a motion alleging that the failure of the Ontario Government to designate an alternative measures program constituted a violation of his s. 15 rights as guaranteed by the *Canadian Charter of Rights and Freedoms*. He relied on s. 3(1)(*d*) and (*f*), arguing that in conjunction with s. 4, they showed the government to be under a positive duty to initiate such programs. The trial judge accepted this argument as did the Court of Appeal. This court reversed. Speaking through Dickson C.J.C., the court held that no such mandatory duty could be inferred from the language Parliament had chosen in drafting the legislation. At p. 129, Dickson C.J.C. states:

> ... the use of the term "should" in s. 3(1)(*d*) does not provide evidence of a mandatory duty. While I agree that s. 3(2) dictates that a liberal interpretation be given to the legislation, in my opinion that does not require the abandonment of the principles of statutory interpretation nor does it preclude resort to the ordinary meaning of words in interpreting a statute. In the context of s. 3(1)(*d*), I find that the word "should" denotes simply a "desire or request"... and not a legal obligation.

In the circumstances of this case I am of the view that this pronouncement significantly undermines the submission of the respondent since she is arguing, in effect, that pursuant to s. 3(1)(*d*) the prosecutor is under a positive obligation to consider the bringing of no charges where doing so would be consistent with the underlying philosophy of the Act and, if the prosecutor fails to abide by this obligation and brings charges where they are not warranted, the youth court has authority to dismiss those charges. As seen from the decision in *R. v. S.(S.)*, no such positive obligation may be gleaned from the wording of s. 3(1)(*d*) and, consequently, none may be imputed to the authorities.

.....

... I would note that where a youth court judge is under the impression, for whatever reason, that though the strict elements of the charge have been established, the charges ought not to have been laid, he or she has the express power under s. 20(1)(*a*) to grant an absolute discharge. At this point, presumably, evidence of the young person's history would be available. I make no comment on whether an absolute discharge would have been the appropriate course of action in this case, but I cannot help but think that this would have responded to the concerns expressed by the trial judge and by the Court of Appeal in a manner consistent with the Act.

.....

Appeal allowed; finding of guilt restored.

Pursuant to s. 42(2)(*a*) of the YCJA, a court that is of the view that charges ought not to have been laid in the first place has the option of giving the young person a "reprimand".

B. JURISDICTION OF THE YOUTH JUSTICE COURT AND AGE

Section 13(1) of the YCJA provides for the designation of a "youth justice court". For the purpose of carrying out the provisions of the YCJA, a youth justice court judge is a justice and a provincial court judge and has the jurisdiction and powers of a summary conviction court under the *Criminal Code* (s. 14(6) of the YCJA). Pursuant to s. 140 of the YCJA, except to the extent that it is inconsistent with or excluded by the YCJA, the provisions of the *Criminal Code* apply to offences alleged to have been committed by young persons, with any modifications that the circumstances require. Section 13(2) and (3) provides that other criminal courts, which would be adult criminal courts, are deemed to be youth justice courts for the purposes of hearing youth cases. The YCJA provides that under certain circumstances, a young person may be sentenced as an adult and, therefore, where applicable, a young person may elect the following modes of trial:

(a) trial before a youth justice court judge alone without a preliminary inquiry in the provincial court for any offence, including murder; or
(b) trial before a judge alone, with a preliminary inquiry, in the superior court of criminal jurisdiction in the province; or
(c) trial before a judge of the superior court of criminal jurisdiction with a jury, following a preliminary inquiry.

Federally appointed superior court judges, who have jurisdiction to try cases with or without a jury after a preliminary inquiry, are deemed to be sitting as youth justice court judges; however, they retain their powers as superior court judges (ss. 13(2), 13(3) and 14(7)).

Section 14(1) of the YCJA confers exclusive jurisdiction on the youth justice court in respect of any federal offence alleged to have been committed by a person while he or she was a "young person" except for offences under the *Contraventions Act*, S.C. 1992, c. 47, and the *National Defence Act*, R.S.C. 1985, c. N-5.

"Offence" is defined in s. 2(1) of the *YCJA* as "an offence created by an Act of Parliament or by any regulation, rule, order, by-law or ordinance made under an Act of Parliament..." Young persons charged with provincial offences are, therefore, not proceeded against under the YCJA, but rather in accordance with provincial offences legislation enacted by each province or territory. The YCJA also confers jurisdiction on the youth justice court to make preventative orders such as an order under s. 810 of the *Criminal Code* (a peace bond or recognizance) where a complainant fears, *inter alia,* injury or property damage (s. 14(2)). Justices of the peace may conduct peace bond proceedings in respect of young persons under s. 810 of the *Criminal Code* (s. 20(2)). Where a young person fails or refuses to enter into a recognizance pursuant to s. 810, the matter must be referred to a youth justice court (s. 20(2)), which may impose a youth sentence on the young person, except that any custody order cannot exceed thirty days (s. 14(2)).

The youth justice court has jurisdiction over a "young person" who is alleged to have committed an offence. "Young person" is defined in s. 2(1) of the YCJA as, "a person who is or, in the absence of evidence to the contrary, appears to be twelve years old or older, but less than eighteen years old and, if the context requires, includes any person who is charged under [the YCJA] with having committed an offence while he or she was a young person or who is found guilty of an offence under [the YCJA]".

Jurisdiction of the youth justice court is determined by the age of the young person at the time of the offence. An 11-year old child is not a "young person" under the YCJA and cannot be prosecuted. Children under the age of 12 who commit criminal offences must be dealt with, if at all, under provincial child welfare legislation. A 28-year-old man charged with sexual assault alleged to have been committed when he was 16 years of age is a "young person" within the meaning of the YCJA (s. 14(5)).

The youth justice court has jurisdiction in respect of an offence alleged to have been committed during a period that includes a person's 18th birthday (s. 16). Provided that the young person has been put to an election under s. 67 after the Crown has indicated that it may seek an adult sentence, then, upon finding the person guilty, and if it has been proven that the offence was committed after the person turned 18, the youth justice court may impose an adult sentence: s. 16(*b*).

QUESTIONS

1. A 26-year-old is charged with sexually assaulting his younger cousin over a number of years. The assaults commenced when the accused was 16 years old and continued until the accused was 24. Should the accused be charged as a young offender, as an adult, or both?

2. A.B. was placed on probation for two years when she was 17. She is now 18. One of the terms of the probation order required that she report to and be under the supervision of a probation officer. Since turning 18, she has refused to report stating flatly that she's "no longer a young offender and doesn't have to report". The probation officer wants to charge her with breaching the reporting term of the probation order. What offence should be charged and should that charge be on a young offender or an adult information?

A person arrested, subsequent to turning 18 years of age, for an offence alleged to have been committed when he or she was a "young person" does not necessarily retain all of the rights accorded by the YCJA. The words "if the context requires" in the definition of "young person" (s. 2(1) of the YCJA) enable the court to engage in an analysis of the applicability of the various special protections set out in the YCJA (see *R. v. Z.(D.A.)* (1992), 76 C.C.C. (3d) 97 (S.C.C.), substantially reproduced below). Some provisions of the YCJA specifically provide that they are inapplicable where the "young person" has reached a certain age; see, for example, s. 26(12), which provides that the notice to parent requirements under the YCJA do not apply in respect of a "young person" who is 20 years old on the date of his or her first appearance in court. Further, s. 146(2) of the YCJA provides that the special protections given to young persons who provide statements to the police apply only to those young persons less than 18 years old at the time the statement was made.

C. FIRST APPEARANCE PROCEDURE

Pursuant to s. 32(1) of the YCJA, on the first appearance of a young person before the youth justice court, the youth justice court judge or justice must cause the information to be read to the young person and must inform an unrepresented accused of his or her right to legal counsel. A young person's counsel may waive the requirement that the information be read to the young person (s. 32(2)), subject to the court's overriding discretion to have the charges read where there is a concern that there is a possible miscommunication between counsel and the young person or where it appears that the young person may fail to appreciate the seriousness of the charges or the solemnity of the court process: *R. v. A.(A.)* (2003), 170 C.C.C. (3d) 449 (Ont. C.A.). *Quaere* whether duty counsel may waive the requirement of reading the information.

Further, if the prosecutor is seeking an adult sentence, the young person must be informed that an adult sentence may be imposed upon a finding of guilt. Also, a young person who is charged with a presumptive offence, defined in s. 2(1) of the YCJA as first or second degree murder, attempt to commit murder, manslaughter, aggravated sexual assault or a third serious violent offence, and the young person is 14 years old or between 14 and 16 years of age, as fixed by the province, must be informed that an adult sentence will be imposed upon a finding of guilt unless the court orders that a youth sentence is to be imposed.

Many provisions of the YCJA seek to involve the parents in the criminal justice process. At the commencement of criminal proceedings, the police will prepare a "notice to parent", which contains basic information about the charges, arrest or release of the young person. Pursuant to s. 26(9) of the YCJA, failure to give notice does not generally affect the validity of proceedings; however, failure to give notice where a young person is not detained in custody renders invalid subsequent proceedings unless a parent attends court with the young person or the court orders that notice be given in a particular manner and to particular persons, or dispenses with the notice where the court considers that dispensing with the notice is appropriate (s. 26(10)). Where a young person is detained in custody, the court may adjourn the proceedings and order that notice be given (s. 26(11)). Further, if the youth justice court believes that the presence of a parent is necessary or in the best interests of the young person, the court may order the attendance of a parent at any stage of the proceedings (s. 27).

QUESTION

3. An accused is charged on a young offender information with break, enter and theft at a school, an incident which occurred when he was 17 years of age. The evidence linking the accused to the crime consists of fingerprints found at the scene. With cutbacks to staff, the police were unable to analyze the prints for 14 months. The accused is now 19 years of age and has married. Should the police serve a notice to parent on the accused's parents? Consider, in this regard, *R. v. Z.(D.A.)* (1992), 76 C.C.C. (3d) 97 (S.C.C.), and s. 26 of the YCJA.

D. EXTRAJUDICIAL MEASURES AND EXTRAJUDICIAL SANCTIONS

Extrajudicial measures and extrajudicial sanctions are the mechanisms by which young persons who commit minor criminal charges may be diverted out of the formal youth criminal justice system.

1. Extrajudicial Measures

Extrajudicial measures are measures used to deal with young persons and do not require the laying of a formal criminal charge, although the laying of a charge is not an impediment to the use of these measures (see ss. 4-9 of the YCJA). The police must consider the suitability of using extrajudicial measures before commencing judicial proceedings against a young person (s. 6(1)). Extrajudicial measures are presumed to be adequate to address offending behaviour where the young person has committed a non-violent offence and has not been previously found guilty of an offence, although the use of informal measures is not precluded where a young person has previously been dealt with by the use of extrajudicial measures or has previously been found guilty of an offence (s. 4(*c*) and (*d*)). Police warnings, police and Crown cautions and referrals to community programs are examples of extrajudicial measures (ss. 6-8).

2. Extrajudicial Sanctions

Extrajudicial sanctions are one type of extrajudicial measures. Extrajudicial sanctions may be used to divert a young person out of the formal criminal process after a formal charge has been laid where extrajudicial measures are inadequate to deal with the offending behaviour because of the seriousness of the offence, the nature and number of previous offences committed by the young person, or any other aggravating circumstances (s. 10).

In accordance with the current extrajudicial sanctions program in place in Ontario, *Criminal Code* offences are divided into three classes. Class I offences are relatively minor offences such as theft, possession, false pretences, false statement, fraud and mischief where the value of the property involved is less than $5,000. The Crown ordinarily refers a first offender charged with a Class I offence to the program. Class II offences consist of all *Criminal Code* offences not considered in either

Class I or Class III, and include property offences where the value of the subject property exceeds $5,000, as well as minor assaults. A first offender charged with a Class II offence may be referred to the program if the offence consists of minor criminal activity. Class III offences, which include any form of culpable homicide, assault causing bodily harm, aggravated assault, assault with a weapon, firearms offences, sexual assault and alcohol-related driving offences, cannot be considered for the program. Upon approval by the Crown for the program, the young person is referred to a probation officer or other agent of the provincial director, who determines personal suitability and the appropriate sanctions. Where the Crown approves a young person for the program, the Crown will ask the court to stay or dismiss the charges. In the event that a young person fails to complete the sanctions, the Crown may recommence the prosecution.

Preconditions to the use of extrajudicial sanctions are set out in s. 10(2) of the YCJA. For example, the young person must fully and freely consent to the extrajudicial sanctions; the young person must accept responsibility for the offending behaviour; and there must be, in the opinion of the Crown, sufficient evidence to justify proceeding with the prosecution (see s. 10(2)(*a*)-(*g*). A parent must be informed of the extrajudicial sanction (s. 11) and, on request, the victim of the offence must be informed of the identity of the young person and advised as to how the offence has been dealt with (s. 12). The YCJA does not set out the various extrajudicial sanctions that may be imposed. Current extrajudicial sanctions used in Ontario include essays; verbal and written apologies to the victim; compensation or restitution; charitable donations; educational or information sessions; community service; and peer mediation.

Extrajudicial sanctions are one form of extrajudicial measures; however, pursuant to s. 40(2)(*d*)(iv) of the YCJA, extrajudicial sanctions used to deal with the young person and his or her response to the sanctions under the YCJA and its counterpart under the YOA, alternative measures, must be included in a pre-sentence report.

QUESTIONS

4. A 16-year-old is charged with assault in connection with an incident at a high school where it is alleged that he punched another student about the head several times. The victim sustained no physical injuries but is clearly afraid of the accused. The accused appears in court and requests that the charge be dealt with informally by extrajudicial measures. Failing that, the defence will request that the charge be dealt with by extrajudicial sanctions. As defence counsel, what representations do you make to the Crown? As Crown counsel, what position do you take?

5. A group of 11-year-olds are out "trick or treating" on October 31. A 14-year-old approaches one of the youngsters and demands her bag of candy. When she refuses, the young person pushes the victim and grabs the bag and flees. The young person is subsequently charged with robbery. The young person has no record and has never participated in extrajudicial measures. Duty counsel advises the Crown that there has been a recent death in the family and that the young person is a B+ student. The police

report indicates that the young person appeared remorseful and insisted on writing a letter of apology to the victim. Should this young person be considered for extrajudicial measures or sanctions? Now assume that the Crown insists on proceeding with the prosecution. Can the court compel diversion? Consider, in this regard, *R. v. B.(G.)* (1994), 26 W.C.B. (2d) 49 (Y.T.S.C.).

E. YOUTH JUSTICE COMMITTEES

The YCJA provides for the creation of youth justice committees. Citizens sit on these committees and assist in the administration of the YCJA or in any programs or services for young persons (s. 18). There are youth justice committees functioning in several jurisdictions as a means of delivering extrajudicial measures under the YCJA. Members of the community meet with victims and young persons accused of minor, non-violent offences and their parents to negotiate an appropriate way for the young person to make amends for offending behaviour. The YCJA provides for an expanded role for youth justice committees. Provided that there is funding available, youth justice committees may take on the following roles under the YCJA (s. 18(2)(*a*)-(*f*)):

(a) giving advice on appropriate extrajudicial measures to be used in respect of a young person;
(b) providing support to victims by soliciting concerns and facilitating reconciliation of the victim and the young person;
(c) ensuring that community support services are available to the young person;
(d) helping to co-ordinate the youth criminal justice system with an applicable child protection agency or community group; and
(e) acting as a conference (see "Conferences", below).

F. CONFERENCES

A "conference" is defined in s. 2 of the YCJA as a group of persons convened to provide advice as set out in s. 19 of the YCJA. Conferences have been used for many years in Australia and New Zealand. They are an integral part of aboriginal restorative justice in Canada. In the area of youth criminal justice, it is anticipated that conferences will generally be informal *ad hoc* groups established to deal with a specific case. The YCJA provides that a conference may be convened by a youth justice court judge, the provincial director of youth services, a police officer or any other person responsible for making a decision under the YCJA (s. 19(1)). A conference may be convened for purposes of, *inter alia,* providing advice on appropriate extrajudicial measures; conditions for judicial interim release; sentences, including the review of sentences; and plans for reintegration of a young person into the community (s. 19(2)). Conferences may be used to conduct "family group conferencing", which informally brings together the young person, his or her family, the victim and the victim's supporters to discuss the offence and its impact on

the victim with a view to reaching a suitable resolution of the matter between the parties. Examples of a resolution include the offender making restitution, providing a letter of apology or performing community service.

G. PRE-TRIAL DETENTION

The *Criminal Code* provisions regarding arrest and judicial interim release for adults are applicable to young persons except to the extent that they may be inconsistent with the YCJA (s. 28). The YCJA contains additional principles governing the detention of young persons. For example, s. 29(2) of the YCJA provides that, in determining whether the detention of a young person is necessary for the protection or safety of the public under s. 515(10)(b) of the *Criminal Code* (substantial likelihood the young person will commit an offence or interfere with the administration of justice), there is a presumption that detention is unnecessary under that section if the young person could not, upon being found guilty, be committed to custody. Section 29(1) provides that a young person must not be detained in custody as a substitute for appropriate child protection, mental health or other social measures.

Section 31 of the YCJA provides that a young person who would otherwise be detained in custody under s. 515 of the *Criminal Code* may be placed in the care of a responsible person, with conditions, where the court is satisfied that there is a responsible person willing and able to take care of and exercise control over the young person, and the young person is willing to be placed in the care of that person.

Both justices of the peace and youth justice court judges have jurisdiction to hear young offender bail hearings. Section 33(8) of the YCJA states that only a youth justice court judge, and not a justice of the peace, has jurisdiction when the offence is one listed under s. 469 of the *Criminal Code*, such as murder.

Where a justice of the peace makes an order, either the prosecutor or the young person may apply to a youth justice court judge for detention or release. This is treated as an original application rather than a review of the justice's order (s. 33(1)). A judge of the superior court of criminal jurisdiction generally hears a bail review from the order of the youth justice court judge. The exception is reflected in s. 33(9) of the YCJA.

QUESTION

6. **A young person has been residing in a group home for emotionally challenged youths for the last five years. She is a habitual runaway. She has a series of outstanding charges and is currently charged with theft over $5,000 for stealing a car. The Crown is seeking the detention of the young person at her bail hearing on both the primary and secondary grounds. The youth worker at the group home believes that the young person has made excellent progress at group counselling sessions and would like to see her return to the group home. The young person's parents want nothing to do with their daughter. As defence counsel, what suggestions can you make to promote the release of the young person?**

The issue of fitness to stand trial may arise during the course of the bail hearing. Subject to certain exceptions, the *Criminal Code* provisions regarding mental disorder (s. 16 and Part XX.1) apply to young persons (s. 141 of the YCJA).

H. ADMISSIBILITY OF STATEMENTS

The provisions of s. 146 of the YCJA govern the admissibility of statements made by a young person to a peace officer or to a person in authority upon arrest or detention, or in circumstances where the peace officer or person in authority has reasonable grounds for believing that the young person has committed an offence. The rules governing admissibility of statements set out in s. 146 extend only to young persons who were under 18 years of age at the time the statement was made (s. 146(8)). Pursuant to s. 146(2) of the YCJA, in order for a statement to be ruled admissible, the prosecutor must prove that:

(*a*) the statement was voluntary;

(*b*) the person to whom the statement was made has, before the statement was made, clearly explained to the young person, in language appropriate to his or her age and understanding, that

- (i) the young person is under no obligation to make a statement,
- (ii) any statement made by the young person may be used as evidence in proceedings against him or her,
- (iii) the young person has the right to consult counsel and a parent or other person in accordance with paragraph (*c*), and
- (iv) any statement made by the young person is required to be made in the presence of counsel and any other person consulted in accordance with paragraph (*c*), if any, unless the young person desires otherwise;

(*c*) the young person has, before the statement was made, been given a reasonable opportunity to consult

- (i) with counsel, and
- (ii) with a parent or, in the absence of a parent, an adult relative or, in the absence of a parent and an adult relative, any other appropriate adult chosen by the young person, as long as that person is not a co-accused, or under investigation, in respect of the same offence; and

(*d*) if the young person consults a person in accordance with paragraph (*c*), the young person has been given a reasonable opportunity to make the statement in the presence of that person.

Failure to strictly comply with the requirements set out above does not preclude admissibility of a statement in the following circumstances:

(a) An oral statement has been made spontaneously by the young person before the requirements can be fulfilled (s. 146(3)).

(b) The young person waives the right to consult with counsel and gives the statement in the presence of counsel, a parent or other adult. The waiver must be audio- or videotaped (s. 146(4)).

(c) A waiver that is not properly recorded due to a technical irregularity may still be valid if the court is satisfied that the young person was informed of his or her rights and voluntarily waived them (s. 146(5)).

(d) There has been a technical irregularity in complying with any of the conditions for admissibility set out in s. 146(2)(*b*), (*c*) or (*d*), if the court is satisfied that the admission of the statement "would not bring into disrepute the principle that young persons are entitled to enhanced procedural protection to ensure that they are treated fairly and their rights are protected" (s. 146(6)).

The youth justice court has the discretion to rule inadmissible a statement that was made under duress imposed by any person who is not, in law, a person in authority (s. 146(7)).

The following cases consider s. 56 of the YOA, the predecessor section to s. 146 of the YCJA. It should be noted that, except where there was a waiver, or a spontaneous utterance, there were no exceptions to the mandatory provisions of s. 56 under the YOA.

R. v. T.(E.)
(*sub nom*. R. V. I.(L.R.))
(1993), 86 C.C.C. (3d) 289 (S.C.C.)

[The appellant, E.T., was found guilty in youth court of the second degree murder of a taxi driver. At the time, E.T. was 16 years of age and living with his great-aunt, whom he considered to be like a mother. At issue on appeal was the admissibility of two statements that E.T. made to the police after the murder.]

The judgment of the court was delivered by

Sopinka J.: — This appeal concerns the appropriate principles which are applicable to determine the admissibility of a confession which is preceded by a confession that is ruled inadmissible. These principles will be examined in connection with three bases on which the first confession may be inadmissible, namely, because:

(i) it was involuntary;
(ii) it was obtained without complying with the *Young Offenders Act* ("*YOA*");
(iii) it was obtained in breach of s. 10(*b*) of the *Canadian Charter of Rights and Freedoms* ("*Charter*").

Facts

.....

During the course of the trial, the Crown sought to have admitted as evidence two statements made by E.T. to the police after the killing. The trial judge excluded a first statement made the day of E.T.'s arrest, but admitted a second statement made the next day. The circumstances surrounding the making of the two statements were as follows. On the morning of October 12th (the murder of the cab driver having taken place in the very early hours of that morning), the appellant was arrested at his home, warned, and his clothes were seized. He asked that his great-aunt, C.T., whom he regarded as his mother, be allowed to come with him and the two were taken to the R.C.M.P. station. While *en route* to the station in the police car, C.T. began searching in her purse for her lawyer's card, and was advised by the police officers that "all of that" would be taken care of at the police station. When they arrived at the station, however, E.T. and his aunt were taken directly to an interview room, and Constable Logan commenced taking a statement from E.T. which lasted some four and a half hours. The statement was preceded by the following exchange which involved the filling out of the "Statement to Person in Authority" form required by s. 56 of the *Young Offenders Act*, R.S.C. 1985, c. Y-1:

.....

[Logan] ..., now here it says I have the right to give my statement in the presence ah, of and you circle your choice. You have the right to give in the presence of a lawyer, of a parent or of an adult relative or an adult of your own choosing. And you just circle the person that you would like in the room when you ah, when you give a statement.

E.T.: I guess one of my parents?

.....

After the statement was completed, E.T. and C.T. were driven back to their home where E.T. produced a knife and the keys to the driver's cab. C.T. was told that she was through, and that E.T. would remain in police custody. Constable Logan then took E.T. to visit the scene of the crime after which they returned to the police station. Following the appellant's request, he had an interview in person with his lawyer which lasted half an hour. The next morning, the appellant telephoned Constable Logan and said he remembered some things he had forgotten the day before and wished to add them to his statement. When the constable arrived at the police station, he found the appellant engaged in a telephone conversation with his lawyer which ended shortly thereafter. When Logan sat down with the appellant, they again went through the filling out of the "Statement to Person in Authority" form and E.T. indicated without prompting that he did not wish to speak to anyone other than Constable Logan or have anyone else present during his statement. Constable Logan also explained to E.T. that if anyone had offered him any hope of advantage or suggested any fear of prejudice with respect to giving this statement, that E.T. should forget about what they had said. The second statement was taken over a relatively short period, and after covering the topics which E.T. had apparently mentioned over the phone, reverted to a discussion of what the youths' plan with respect to the cab driver had been. The second statement included the following exchange:

Q. ... What was the complete plan?

A. [A.] was gonna sit behind the driver and stab him in the neck, I was supposed to sit in the passenger side in the front and just stab when ah ... [L.R.I.] and [Allen] were to hold the guns to his head.

The same statement also included the following question and answer:

Q. ... Was everyone aware and in agreement with the plan to kill a taxi driver?

A. [A.] and [L.] were, Mike and I were I don't know, wondering I guess.

As mentioned above, the trial judge excluded the first statement but admitted the second, and convicted E.T. of second degree murder. The appellant appealed his conviction to the Court of Appeal for British Columbia, seeking to have the second statement excluded, and if successful, he claimed that he would be entitled to an acquittal on the ground that the evidence established his innocence as a principal, and that there was no evidence to support his conviction as an aider or abettor under s. 21(1)(*b*) and (*c*) of the *Criminal Code*, R.S.C. 1970, c. C-34. The Court of Appeal for British Columbia dismissed the appeal.

.....

The issues

It should be noted that it is only the second of the two statements given by E.T. to the police which is at issue on this appeal. The first statement was excluded by the trial judge because he was of the view neither E.T. nor his great-aunt, C.T., understood the consequences of E.T.'s confession to the police or the full extent of the jeopardy in which he found himself. The Court of Appeal assumed that the first statement had been properly excluded (and indeed the Crown did not dispute its exclusion on appeal) but Goldie J.A. made it clear that this assumption did not mean that he agreed with the trial judge's reasons for excluding the statement. The Crown likewise did not seek to reopen the analysis of the first statement in this court. As did the Court of Appeal, I am prepared to assume the correctness of the finding of the trial judge that the first statement was inadmissible because it was involuntary. In view of the fact that the admissibility of the second statement depends on the reasons for the inadmissibility of the first statement, I will consider whether it was inadmissible, as well, by reason of non-compliance with the *Charter* and the *YOA*. I will then deal with the admissibility of the second statement.

Requirements of the Charter and the Young Offenders Act

Section 10(*b*) of the *Charter* provides that "[e]veryone has the right on arrest or detention ... (*b*) to retain and instruct counsel without delay and to be informed of that right". Likewise, s. 11 *YOA* requires that all young persons arrested or detained under the Act have "the right to retain and instruct counsel without delay at any stage of the proceedings against [them]" and that they shall be advised of this right "forthwith on [their] arrest or detention" and "be given an opportunity to obtain counsel". Section 56 then imposes further obligations upon the police in respect of taking statements from young persons, including the obligation to allow the young person to consult with a parent, adult relative or other adult or a lawyer and to have that person present when making the statement. Section 56 provides explicitly that if its requirements are not complied with, then the statement is inadmissible.

In this case, the officer purported to comply with the *Charter* and the *YOA* by advising the appellant that he had the right to a reasonable opportunity to speak to either a lawyer or a parent or, in the absence of a parent, another adult of his choosing. The trial judge accepted this as a compliance with both the *Charter* and the *YOA*. I disagree. While s. 56 appears to provide that a parent or other adult is an alternative to counsel, s. 11 does not. How is this apparent conflict resolved? In my view, s. 56 cannot be interpreted in a manner that derogates from the mandatory requirement in s. 11. If so interpreted, s. 56 would purport to reduce the constitutional right of an accused young person under s. 10(*b*) of the *Charter*. This it cannot do and s. 56 should therefore be interpreted in a manner that is consistent with s. 10(*b*) of the *Charter* and with s. 11 *YOA*. The only interpretation of s. 56 which is consistent with both s. 10(*b*) of the *Charter* and s. 11 *YOA* is that a parent is not an alternative to counsel unless the right to counsel is waived.

E.T. was not advised of his independent right to counsel and therefore it cannot be said that he waived the right. In any event, apart from this omission, it is my view waiver would not have been valid in the circumstances of this case. In this regard, I accept the submission of counsel for the appellant that if waiver is to be relied upon in these circumstances, the young person cannot be presumed to know the extent of his or her jeopardy and must be advised that an application may be made to have the case tried in adult court under s. 16 *YOA* and that the result of such an application is that the appellant would face up to life imprisonment rather than the three-year maximum under the *YOA*. Such an application was, in fact, made here and was successful at first instance but reversed on appeal.

The right of the accused to know the extent of his or her jeopardy in the context of the s. 10(*b*) right to counsel was discussed by this court in *R. v. Smith* (1991), 63 C.C.C. (3d) 313, [1991] 1 S.C.R. 714, 4 C.R. (4th) 125, a case in which the police had failed to advise the accused that his shooting victim had died. McLachlin J., for the court, summarized the law in this area as follows, at p. 322:

> In Canada, we have adopted a different approach [than that in the United States]. We take the view that the accused's understanding of his situation is relevant to whether he has made a valid and informed waiver. This approach is mandated by s. 10(*a*) of the *Charter*, which gives the detainee the right to be promptly advised of the reasons for his or her detention. It is exemplified by three related concepts: (1) the "tainting" of a warning as to the right to counsel by lack of information; (2) the idea that one is entitled to know "the extent of one's jeopardy", and (3) the concept of "awareness of the consequences" developed in the context of waiver.

McLachlin J. went on to conclude that in the circumstances of the case, the accused must have been aware that he had been involved in a most serious crime and, particularly, that his victim had likely died. Thus, he was possessed of sufficient information as to make a valid decision whether or not to exercise his right to counsel.

Applying these principles to the young offender context, it seems to me that the phenomenal difference in potential consequences faced by the young person in youth court as opposed to adult court mandates that a young person be aware of the possibility (where it exists) that he or she will be elevated to adult court, and the potential result of this in terms of stigma and penalty. In the present case, this means that E.T. should have been advised that the Crown might apply to have him tried in adult court and that the maximum penalty which he might face, given that a death was involved, is life imprisonment without parole for 25 years. As McLachlin J. noted in *Smith*, however, the determination of whether or not a young person validly waived his or her s. 10(*b*) right to counsel is not to be based simply on what the police told the young person, but upon the young person's actual awareness of the consequences of his or her actions. In the present case, the trial judge concluded after hearing the testimony that, with respect to the first statement, neither E.T. nor his great-aunt appreciated the consequences of his act of confession, despite the fact that E.T. had had previous dealings with the police.

This is not to say that in the normal course, it is necessary that the police advise an accused of the maximum penalty he or she might face. In my view, the particular characteristics of young offenders make extra precautions necessary in affording them the full protection of their *Charter* rights.

With respect to the first statement, of course, I have already said that E.T. was neither advised of nor given a reasonable opportunity to exercise his right to counsel either under the *Charter* or the *YOA*, and thus the issue of whether he validly waived that right does not arise. If waiver were in issue, however, I would have found that E.T. did not have sufficient information concerning the extent of his jeopardy to make an informed and valid decision as to whether or not to speak with a lawyer. Accordingly, s. 56 was not complied with and the first statement was inadmissible. It follows from what I have said that there was a failure to comply with s. 10(*b*) of the *Charter* in addition to non-compliance with s. 56 *YOA*. The result of the total failure to comply with s. 10(*b*) was that a confession was obtained from a young person who was conscripted against himself. Admission of the statement would have affected the fairness of the trial and its rejection was mandated on any view of the *Collins* factors: *R. v. Collins* (1987), 33 C.C.C. (3d) 1, 38 D.L.R. (4th) 508, [1987] 1 S.C.R. 265.

This takes me to the admissibility of the second statement. I will address this question from two aspects:

(1) Was it admissible when considered independently of the first statement and the circumstances surrounding it?

(2) Was it admissible when considered in conjunction with the first statement?

The second statement

(1) Admissibility independent of first statement

Prior to the making of the second statement, E.T. had a half-hour interview in person with his lawyer and also spoke with his lawyer on the telephone immediately before making the second statement. He had therefore exercised his right to counsel, and the provisions of s. 56 as interpreted above were complied with.

.....

[However, the issue arises] as to whether s. 56, either by its express language or by implication in incorporating the common law doctrine of voluntariness, makes it mandatory that a young person be advised that he or she may be transferred to adult court prior to the taking of a statement. If so, then clearly this obligation was not met in this case, and it would be necessary to consider whether this deficiency was rectified by E.T.'s consultation with counsel prior to making the second statement.

Section 56 sets out strict requirements which must be complied with in order to render a statement made by a young person to a "person in authority" admissible in proceedings against him or her. The rationale for this lies in Parliament's recognition that young persons generally have a lesser understanding of their legal rights than do adults and are less likely to assert and exercise fully those rights when confronted with an authority figure. The requirements in s. 56(2)(*b*) reflect this concern; a young person is given the right to consult with a parent or other adult as well as the right to counsel upon arrest or detention, and is entitled to have a lawyer or a parent or other adult present when making a statement. The young person must also be specifically told prior to the taking of any statement, in language appropriate to his or her level of understanding, that he or she is under no obligation to make a statement and that anything said may be used as evidence in proceedings against him or her.

There is no express requirement in s. 56(2)(*b*) that a young person over the age of 14 be warned of the possibility of being raised to adult court. The initial inference to be drawn from this omission is that Parliament did not feel that such a warning should be an absolute requirement in every case. However, there are a number of ways in which this requirement may be seen to have been incorporated into s. 56. First, the requirement in s. 56(2)(*b*)(ii) that the young person be advised that "any statement given by him may be used as evidence in proceedings against him" could be seen to require by inference that the young person be told what the "proceedings against him" may consist of, at least where there may be special proceedings such as a trial in adult court. Such an interpretation would somewhat strain the wording of s. 56(2)(*b*)(ii), however, since the purpose of this part of the caution, in conjunction with that in s. 56(2)(*b*)(i), appears to be simply to advise of the right to silence and that any statements made may be used against the young person.

More importantly, s. 56(2)(*a*) provides that, along with the requirement of the specific procedures in s. 56(2)(*b*), the statement must be voluntary. Further, s. 56(1) provides that subject to the specific requirements of the rest of the section, the law relating to the admissibility of statements made by persons accused of committing offences applies in respect of young persons. The effect of these two paragraphs is clearly to incorporate the common law relating to the voluntariness of statements made by accused persons, including any special requirements applicable in the case of young persons. An analysis of the common law with respect to advising a young person over age 14 of the possibility of being tried in adult court demonstrates that this was considered to be an important consideration in determining voluntariness where the statement was tendered in adult court following a successful transfer application...

In my view, though, a warning that a young person may be raised to adult court should not be interpreted as an absolute requirement of s. 56 in all cases in which the young person is over the age of 14. Parliament has set out with great precision in s. 56(2)(*b*) those procedures which it has determined must be complied with in every case in order that a statement made by a young person to a person in authority be admissible against the young person. Those necessary procedures do not include a warning as to the possibility of being raised to adult court. In my view, therefore, the presence or absence of such a warning is to be considered not as a specific requirement of s. 56(2)(*b*) but as an aspect of determining whether or not, apart from complying with s. 56(2)(*b*), the statement was voluntary.

I have already stated that a valid waiver of the right to counsel in s. 10(*b*) or s. 56 can only be made where a young person is aware of the consequences of his or her actions, including the possibility of being raised to adult court. Here, E.T. exercised his right to counsel and s. 56(2)(*b*) was complied with prior to the making of the second statement ... In the circumstances of this case, I would hesitate to hold that the statement was involuntary simply because of the absence of an express police warning that E.T. might be raised to adult court.

(2) Admissibility: considered in conjunction with first statement

The principles that govern the admissibility of the second statement when considered in conjunction with the first statement are directly influenced by the grounds for the exclusion of the first statement.

.....

Under the rules relating to confessions at common law, the admissibility of a confession which had been preceded by an involuntary confession involved a factual determination based on factors designed to ascertain the degree of connection between the two statements. These included the time-span between the statements, advertence to the previous statement during questioning, the discovery of additional incriminating evidence subsequent to the first statement, the presence of the same police officers at both interrogations and other similarities between the two circumstances ... No general rule excluded subsequent statements on the ground that they were tainted irrespective of the degree of connection to the initial admissible statement.

.....

In applying these factors, a subsequent confession would be involuntary if either the tainting features which disqualified the first confession continued to be present, or if the fact that the first statement was made was a substantial factor contributing to the making of the second statement.

.....

In these cases the fact that a caution or warning had been given or that the advice of counsel had been obtained between the two statements was a factor to be considered but it was by no means determinative. While such an occurrence went a long way to dissipate elements of compulsion or inducement resulting from the conduct of the interrogators, it might have little or no effect in circumstances in which the second statement is induced by the fact of the first.

.....

In view of the fact that s. 56 incorporates the common law of voluntariness, these principles apply to resolve the issue as to the admissibility of a confession which is made after a prior involuntary confession. But s. 56 does more than incorporate the common law. It imposes additional statutory requirements with respect to the right to consultation and the presence of counsel or an adult, to which I have referred above. There is no requirement that failure to comply with these provisions has any causative relationship to the making of the statement. The only relationship prescribed is a temporal one. Unless the requisite explanations are made before the statement is taken from the young person, it is inadmissible. This responds to the declaration in s. 3 *YOA* that young persons "have special guarantees of their rights and freedoms" (s. 3(1)(*e*)), and have the right "to be informed as to what those rights and freedoms are" (s. 3(1)(*g*))...

In my opinion, the purpose of the requirement that the explanation prescribed by s. 56 precede the making of the statement is to ensure that the young person does not relinquish the right to silence except in the exercise of free will in the context of a full understanding and appreciation of his or her rights. A previous statement may operate to compel a further statement notwithstanding explanations and advice belatedly proffered. If, therefore, the successor statement is simply a continuation of the first, or if the first statement is a substantial factor contributing to the making of the second, the condition envisaged by s. 56 has not been attained and the statement is inadmissible.

The final basis for exclusion of the second statement is breach of s. 10(*b*) of the *Charter*. If a statement is followed by a further statement which in and of itself involves no *Charter* breach, its admissibility will be resolved under s. 24(2) of the *Charter*. This provides that evidence "obtained in a manner that infringed or denied any rights or freedoms guaranteed" by the *Charter* is inadmissible if its admission would bring the administration of justice into disrepute. This language has been interpreted to apply irrespective of any causal relationship between the breach and the obtaining of the evidence provided that there is a sufficient temporal relationship between the evidence and the breach.

Application to this case

I have concluded that applying any of the above bases, the second statement must be excluded. Not only was there a close temporal relationship between the statements, but the second statement was a continuation of the first, and the first statement was a substantial factor leading to the making of the second. The statements were taken less than a day apart by the same officer. There is no evidence that the police in the interval between the two statements had gathered further evidence tending to incriminate E.T. to which E.T. might be asked to respond. There was also continuous advertence by the police officer throughout the second statement to information given in the first statement. For example, after E.T. had said what he wished to say regarding the blood on his clothing, Constable Logan told him to think back to the plan and proceeded to ask him further details about it. In essence, E.T., having started a statement, asked to complete it and did.

All of the evidence in this case leads to the conclusion that the second statement was causally connected to the first.

.....

In view of the finding that the existence of the first statement was a substantial factor in inducing the making of the second statement, the latter is inadmissible both on the basis of the common law test and the exclusionary language of s. 56. Moreover, had it been necessary, I would have also excluded it under s. 24(2).

.....

Disposition

The appeal is allowed, the conviction for second degree murder is quashed and an acquittal is entered.

QUESTIONS

7. **Police attend a local community centre in response to a complaint about a hockey player threatening another player with a knife. Several players identify a young person as the perpetrator. The police question the young person about the incident and he responds, "Yeah, I threatened him." The police ask him where the knife is and he points to his jacket pocket. A police officer removes the knife from the pocket indicated. At trial, defence counsel objects to the admission of both the inculpatory statement and the introduction of the knife as an exhibit. What arguments can you make as both defence and Crown?**

8. **Officers in a patrol car observe a youth late at night in an industrial neighbourhood. The officers approach and ask what he is up to and ask to look in his knapsack. The youth agrees and as he unzips the bag, the young person says, "there's a crowbar in there that I borrowed to take a dent out of my mother's car". The officers suspect the young person of breaking into business premises and subsequently confirm this suspicion when they find a set of fresh footprints in the snow leading from one window to another at a nearby building. The young person is arrested. At the trial the Crown seeks to introduce the statement as a spontaneous utterance. What arguments would you make on behalf of the Crown and defence? See *R. v. W.(J.)* (1996), 109 C.C.C. (3d) 506 (Ont. C.A.).**

R. v. Z.(D.A.)

(1992), 76 C.C.C. (3d) 97 (S.C.C.)

[The 18-year-old accused was charged with theft, alleged to have been committed when he was 17 years of age. Upon the accused's arrest, the police took a statement which did not comply with s. 56 of the YOA [am. 1985, c. 24 (2nd Supp.), s. 38; 1995, c. 19, s. 35]. The issue for the court was whether the special rules and procedures afforded to a "young person" by s. 56 of the YOA should be extended to include someone over the age of 18.]

[The judgment of the court was delivered by:]

Lamer C.J.C.: —

.....

Analysis

The specific question before this court is whether the [Alberta] Court of Appeal erred in holding that the written confession given by the appellant was admissible notwithstanding that some of the conditions set out in s. 56(2) had not been complied with. In answering this question, this appeal affords this court an opportunity to resolve the more general question of whether s. 56(2) applies to statements made by a person 18 years of age or older. It is not disputed that the appellant was 18 years old when he gave the statement. Nor is it disputed that the appellant was not advised of his right to have an adult person present when making the impugned statement. ...

Whether s. 56(2) extends to an adult accused is strictly a matter of statutory interpretation. In interpreting the relevant provisions of an Act, the express words used by Parliament must be interpreted not only in their ordinary sense but also in the context of the scheme and purpose of the legislation ... In my opinion, both the express words used by Parliament and the over-all scheme and purpose of the Act support the conclusion that Parliament did not intend s. 56(2) to apply to statements made by an adult accused.

Section 56(2) mandates that no oral or written statement given by a young person to a peace officer or other person in authority be held admissible unless the enumerated conditions set out therein have been fully met. As is evident from the express words of the provision, s. 56(2) only applies with respect to statements made by a "young person". The question then becomes whether a person over the age of 18, at the time the impugned statement is made, is a "young person". Young person is a statutorily defined term within the Act. Normally, this would end the need for any further inquiry. Unfortunately, this is not the case given the manner in which Parliament has chosen to define the term. [The definition of "young person" is reproduced.]

As is evident, the definition of "young person" has two components. The principal component of the definition defines a young person as a person who is or appears to be at least 12 years old but under 18 years of age. The definition is further extended to include any person charged under the Act with having committed an offence while between the ages of 12 and 18 or found guilty of an offence under the Act. This latter component reflects the fact that, by virtue of s. 5(1), a person who is over the age of 18 can nevertheless be charged under the Act for offences occurring while he or she was between the ages of 12 and 18. However, Parliament has made it clear that the term "young person" should be extended to include someone over the age of 18 only "where the context requires" that person be deemed to be in the same position as a youth between the ages of 12 and 18. As one would expect, most of the conflict over the applicability of s. 56(2) turns on what effect should be given to the words "where the context requires".

.....

... The argument that Parliament intended the term "young person" to include an accused over the age of 18 wherever that term appears in the Act ignores the reality that in various provisions of the Act "young person" can only be understood to mean a person between the ages of 12 and 18. One need go no further than the definition of "young person" itself to demonstrate this point. Reference to the term "young person" in the latter component of the definition clearly speaks only of a person at least 12 years of age but under 18. The same interpretation must be given to the term as it is used in s. 5(1) and (3). Therefore, it is evident that Parliament did not intend "young person" to always include an adult accused wherever that term appears in the Act.

Moreover, the interpretation proposed by the appellant would render "where the context requires" superfluous. If Parliament had intended to define "young person" in the manner suggested by the appellant, there would have been no need for Parliament to have inserted the words "where the context requires" to effect this result. "Where the context requires" clearly carries a broader connotation than that of a mere disjunctive. The interpretation proposed by the appellant would have this court essentially ignore the words "where the context requires" found in the definition of "young person".

It is trite to say that, in interpreting a statute, due regard must be given to the ordinary meaning of words used by Parliament; in this case the words "where the context requires". In defining "young person" in this manner, Parliament has expressly left it with the courts to consider whether the context in which the term "young person" is used requires that it be interpreted to include an accused over the age of 18. In this regard ... Parliament has indeed launched the courts on an "odyssey" through the various sections of the Act to determine their applicability to an alleged offender who is over 18 years of age. The ordinary meaning of the words "where the context requires" cannot be ignored and must be given due effect as words of limitation in this case.

.....

In my opinion, interpreting "where the context requires" in its ordinary sense, as words of limitation, accords with the very nature and purpose of the Act. To state the obvious, the Act was enacted specifically to provide for a system to deal with youths separate and distinct from that in place for adults. In so doing, the Act establishes a code of unique procedural and evidentiary requirements as well as substantive provisions providing for special dispositions different from the sentencing provisions under the

Criminal Code. In enacting s. 5(1) and (3), Parliament recognized the possibility that an accused might not be charged or tried until after reaching adulthood. By making the relevant point of reference the age of the accused at the time of the alleged offence, it has guarded against an accused being subjected to a different standard of accountability merely because of the time at which he or she was charged or ultimately tried. No doubt Parliament was concerned ... that if jurisdiction turned on the age of an accused on the date of being charged the substantive provisions of the Act pertaining to accountability could easily be evaded by deliberate delays in charging an accused. In this regard, Parliament has sought, through provisions such as s. 5(1) and (3), to ensure that systemic or deliberate delays in the charging or prosecution of youths do not undermine the principle that a person should not, in all instances, be held accountable in the same manner and suffer the same consequences as an adult for acts committed while still a youth. It would be unjust to subject a person to a higher standard of accountability merely because of his or her age at the time of the trial. The fact that an accused is now an adult cannot take away from the fact that he or she is being held accountable to society for the acts committed while still a youth. …

This concern over ensuring that all accused are similarly held accountable for the mistakes of their youth does not dictate that all of the special protections afforded under the Act apply regardless of the age of an accused. In enacting certain of the special protections set out in the Act, Parliament has sought to address concerns specific to the very fact that the accused being brought through our judicial system is a youth rather than an adult. As such, special rules and procedures were enacted to take into account the unique needs and problems associated with dealing with a youth. It would be illogical to extend the application of these rules and procedures to an adult accused. One need only think of the requirement in the Act that a young person be detained separate from any adult. It would be absurd to hold that this requirement applies to a 35-year-old accused who absconded while a youth. It is clear that the concerns underlying some of the special procedures and rules within the Act no longer arise once an accused reaches adulthood. Therefore, in my opinion, interpreting Parliament's use of the words "where the context requires" as imposing the need for reasoned consideration into the appropriateness of applying the Act's special evidentiary rules to an adult accused accords with the very nature of the Act.

… Certainly, various of the other special provisions in the Act going to procedural matters may also be found to remain applicable to an adult accused. An obvious example is the prohibition set out in s. 38 of the Act against the publication of information serving to identify a young person. The concern underlying this provision of minimizing the stigma associated with the mistakes of a person's youth continues to apply notwithstanding the accused is no longer under the age of 18.

Having accepted that "where the context requires" should be interpreted as words of limitation, I am left to consider whether the actual context of s. 56 requires the term "young person" in s. 56(2) to be held to apply to a person over the age of 18.

.....

The purpose of s. 56 has been noted by several commentators. For example, Nicholas Bala, in "The *Young Offenders Act*: A Legal Framework", in Hudson, Hornick and Burrows, eds., Justice and the Young Offender in Canada (1988), at p. 17, has characterized the objective of s. 56 in the following manner:

> Section 56 is based on the recognition that young persons may lack the sophistication and maturity to fully appreciate the legal consequences of making a statement, and so require special protection when being questioned by police. It is also premised on the notion that some youths are easily intimidated by adult authority figures, and may make statements that they believe those authority figures expect to hear, even if the statements are false. It is hoped that consultation with a parent or lawyer [or both] will preclude the making of such false statements.

This view was echoed by John C. Pearson, "Section 56(2) of the *Young Offenders Act*: Forever Young?", 76 C.R. (3d) 389 (1990), who states at pp. 390-1:

> In determining how broad a reach s. 56(2) of the *Y.O.A.* should have, it must be remembered that the subsection codifies principles articulated in a substantial body of pre-*Y.O.A.* case law dealing with the confessions of juveniles. This case law recognizes that most minors do not possess the capability to understand their rights as well as adults and have reduced capacity to protect themselves in contacts with authority figures. From this recognition sprang the requirements in s. 56(2) for enhanced explanations and expanded consultation opportunities. The rationale for these additional obligations disappears when the statement is taken from an adult.

In *R. v. J.(J.T.)* [(1990), 59 C.C.C. (3d) 1] this court expressly considered the purpose of s. 56. One of the issues in that case was whether statements made by a 17-year-old were admissible. At the time the statements were made, several of the requirements set out in s. 56(2) had not been complied with by the police. A majority of this court found s. 56(2) to mandate the exclusion of these statements from evidence. The majority decision emphasized that s. 56 exists to protect all young persons and that principles of fairness require that the section be applied uniformly without regard to the characteristics of the particular young person. However, it is important to realize that, in that case, this court was only concerned with the applicability of s. 56 to statements made by an accused under the age of 18 and did not consider whether this provision applied to an adult accused given the definition of "young person" in the Act.

Cory J., writing for the majority of this court, acknowledged that the aim of s. 56 is to protect adolescents who, by virtue of their lack of maturity, are not likely to fully appreciate their legal rights and the consequences of making a statement to the police. ...

.....

None of these concerns, however, arise with respect to an accused over the age of 18. No further protection beyond that already afforded under the *Charter* and the common law is necessary to ensure that any statement made by an adult accused is truly voluntary. It is evident from the absence of similar provisions in the *Criminal Code* that Parliament has not deemed it necessary to afford an adult accused the right to consult with an adult relative prior to being questioned by police nor the right to have that relative present during questioning. Persons over the age of 18 have long been deemed to possess sufficient maturity and control over the situation they may find themselves into no longer require the watchful eye of a parent or adult relative to ensure any statement made is voluntary and made with full knowledge of their legal rights. It would be absurd to say that a statement made by a 25-year-old accused, for example, cannot be deemed to be made by a person having sufficient maturity because it was in regard to an offence he or she allegedly committed at a time when the law deemed him or her not to possess such maturity. There is clearly nothing underlying the purpose of s. 56(2) requiring its application to an adult accused.

.....

Conclusion

In my opinion, the Court of Appeal in this case correctly found s. 56 not to apply to the appellant. The special protections afforded a young person under s. 56(2) bear no application to a person 18 years of age or older. The admissibility of any statement made by such a person should be determined according to the law governing statements made by adults and not by s. 56(2). Accordingly, I agree with the Court of Appeal that the trial judge erred in finding the impugned statement made by the appellant inadmissible by reason of s. 56(2) of the Act. The appeal is dismissed.

Note that s. 146(2) of the YCJA now provides that the requirements of s. 146 apply only to young persons who are less than 18 years old.

I. SENTENCING

1. Purpose and Principles of Sentencing

Section 50 of the YCJA provides that the *Criminal Code* provisions for sentencing an adult (Part XXIII) do not apply in respect of young persons except for certain exceptions. Notable exceptions include the sentencing principles applicable to aboriginal offenders (s. 718.2(*e*)); victim impact statements (s. 722); pardons and remissions (s. 748); and when the court has ordered that the young person be sentenced as an adult pursuant to s. 74 of the YCJA.

In addition to having regard to the general principles set out in s. 3 of the YCJA, which guide the interpretation of the provisions of the YCJA, the court must, in crafting an appropriate sentence for a young person, have regard to the purpose and principles of sentencing set out in s. 38 of the YCJA. Section 38(1) reads:

> **The purpose of sentencing under s. 42 (youth sentences) is to hold a young person accountable for an offence through the imposition of just sanctions that have meaningful consequences for the young person and that promote his or her rehabilitation and reintegration into society, thereby contributing to the long-term protection of the public.**

Section 38(2) sets out the following sentencing principles:

(a) the sentence must not result in a punishment that is greater than the appropriate punishment for an adult convicted of the same offence committed in similar circumstances;
(b) the sentence must be similar to sentences imposed in the region on similar young persons found guilty of the same offence in similar circumstances;
(c) the sentence must be proportionate to the seriousness of the offence and the degree of responsibility of the young person for that offence;
(d) all reasonable alternatives to custody must be considered, with particular attention given to the circumstances of aboriginal young persons;
(e) subject to (c), the sentence must:
  (i) be the least restrictive sentence that is capable of achieving the purpose of sentencing as set out in s. 38(1);
  (ii) be the sentence most likely to achieve rehabilitation of the young person and reintegration into society;
  (iii) promote a sense of responsibility in the young person, and an acknowledgement of the harm done to victims and the community.

Further, in determining the appropriate youth sentence, the youth justice court must take into account the following factors set out in s. 38(3):

(a) the degree of participation by the young person in the commission of the offence;
(b) the harm done to victims and whether it was intentional or reasonably foreseeable;
(c) any reparation made by the young person to the victim or the community;
(d) the time spent in pre-trial detention as a result of the offence;
(e) previous findings of guilt of the young person; and
(f) any other aggravating and mitigating circumstances relevant to the purpose and principles of sentencing set out in s. 38.

2. RESTRICTIONS ON COMMITTAL TO CUSTODY

The YCJA restricts the use of custody primarily for violent offenders and serious repeat offenders. Section 39(1) provides that a youth justice court cannot sentence a young person to custody unless:

(a) the young person has committed a violent offence;
(b) the young person has failed to comply with previous non-custodial sentences;
(c) the young person has been found guilty of an indictable offence for which an adult would be liable to imprisonment for two years or more and the young person has a history of convictions in the youth court; or
(d) in exceptional cases, where the young person has committed an indictable offence, and, having regard to the aggravating circumstances, imposition of a non-custodial sentence would

be inconsistent with the purpose and principles set out in s. 38.

A further limitation on the use of custody is set out in s. 39(2), which provides that the youth justice court must not impose a custodial sentence unless the court has considered all reasonable alternatives to custody and has determined that there is no reasonable alternative, or combination of alternatives, that is in accordance with the purpose and principles set out in s. 38. In this regard, the court must consider submissions relating to available alternatives to custody; the likelihood that the young person will comply with a non-custodial sentence; and the alternatives to custody which have been used for other young persons who have been sentenced for similar offences committed in similar circumstances (s. 39(3)). Further, the previous imposition of a particular non-custodial sentence would not preclude a youth justice court from imposing the same or any other non-custodial sentence for another offence (s. 39(4)). For example, the fact that a young person received probation for two previous offences would not compel the court to impose a custodial sentence. Moreover, the court cannot use custody as a substitute for appropriate child protection, mental health or other social measures (s. 39(5)).

In determining the appropriate length of a youth custodial sentence, the court is guided by the principles set out in s. 38 and must not take into consideration the fact that the young person might not serve the entire custodial portion of the sentence in custody (s. 39(8)). Finally, pursuant to s. 39(9), the youth justice court must give reasons why a non-custodial sentence would be inadequate for achieving the purposes of sentencing, including, if applicable, why the case is an exceptional case for custody under s. 38(1)(*d*).

J. YOUTH SENTENCES

Except where the court orders that the young person be given an adult sentence upon the court making a finding of guilt, the court will impose one or more of the sentences set out in s. 42(2). The court will consider a pre-sentence report, if any, that has been ordered pursuant to s. 40, and, if the court has referred the matter to a conference, the court will consider the sentencing recommendations of the conference, along with the representations of the defence and prosecution, the parents of the young person, and any other relevant information before the court, such as medical or psychological assessments ordered pursuant to s. 34 of the YCJA.

1. Sentencing Options

Pursuant to s. 42(2), the court may impose any one or more of the following youth sentences, provided they are not inconsistent with each other:

(a) a reprimand;
(b) an absolute discharge;

(c) a conditional discharge with reporting and supervision conditions;
(d) a maximum $1,000 fine;
(e) an order to pay specified types of damages to any person;
(f) an order for the restitution of property obtained as a result of the commission of the offence;
(g) an order to compensate an innocent purchaser of property in respect of which the court has made a restitution order;
(h) an order of compensation in kind or by way of personal services to an aggrieved party instead of the payment for any loss, damage or injury, where the aggrieved party agrees;
(i) an order to perform community service;
(j) an order of prohibition, seizure or forfeiture that may be imposed under federal legislation (except a prohibition order under s. 161 of the *Criminal Code*);
(k) placement of the young person on probation for a period not exceeding two years;
(l) subject to the agreement of the provincial director, an order for the young person to be placed into an intensive support and supervision program;
(m) an attendance order requiring that the young person attend a non-residential program approved by the provincial director for a maximum of 240 hours, over a period not exceeding six months;
(n) a custody and supervision order not exceeding three years, where the young person has been found guilty of an offence punishable by life imprisonment under the *Criminal Code*, or not exceeding two years, in all other cases, whereby the young person will spend two-thirds of the period in custody and one-third under supervision in the community;
(o) an order of custody for a specified period and supervision for not more than three years, where the young person is found guilty of certain presumptive offences (attempted murder, manslaughter or aggravated sexual assault);
(p) a deferred custody and supervision order (analogous to a conditional sentence for an adult) for a specified period not exceeding six months and subject to conditions;
(q) where the young person has been found guilty of first degree murder, an order that the young person serve a sentence not to exceed ten years comprised of a maximum of six years in custody from the date of committal and conditional supervision in the community for the remainder; where the young person has been found guilty of second degree murder, an order that the young person serve a sentence not to exceed seven years comprised of a maximum four years custody from the date of committal and conditional supervision in the community for the remainder;
(r) an order of intensive rehabilitative custody and supervision; or

(s) imposition of any other reasonable and ancillary conditions on the young person that the court considers advisable and in the best interests of the young person and the public.

There are restrictions on the imposition of many sentences, and regard should be had to the various sentencing provisions of the YCJA.

2. Determination of "Serious Violent Offence"

Section 42(9) provides that after a young person is found guilty of an offence, and on the application of the Attorney General, the court may make a judicial determination that the offence is a serious violent offence and may endorse the information or indictment accordingly. Section 2(1) of the YCJA defines "serious violent offence" as, "an offence in the commission of which a young person causes or attempts to cause serious bodily harm". A young person against whom there have been three "serious violent offence" determinations would be subject to an adult sentence, unless the court is satisfied that a youth sentence would be sufficient to hold him or her accountable (s. 72).

3. Consecutive Youth Sentences

The court may impose consecutive sentences where a young person is sentenced while under a sentence for an offence involving custody or where the young person is found guilty of more than one offence in respect of which the court imposed a term of custody (s. 42(13)).

4. Duration of Youth Sentences

Generally, the total duration of a youth sentence in respect of any single offence is two years (s. 42(14)). Where a young person is found guilty of more than one offence, the combined duration of the youth sentences is limited to three years, except in the case of first and second degree murder, where the combined duration of youth sentences is ten and seven years respectively (s. 42(15)). If a youth sentence is imposed in respect of an offence committed after the commencement but before the completion of a youth sentence, the new sentence may be consecutive and the combined duration of all sentences may exceed three years, or ten years for first degree murder or seven years for second degree murder (s. 42(16)).

5. Weapons Prohibitions

Pursuant to s. 51 of the YCJA, when a young person is found guilty of an offence listed in s. 109(1)(*a*) to (*d*) of the *Criminal Code*, the youth justice court must impose an order prohibiting the young person from possessing any firearm, cross-bow, prohibited weapon, restricted weapon, prohibited device, ammunition, prohibited ammunition or explosive substances. The weapons prohibition is discretionary when the young person is found guilty of an offence listed in s. 110(1)(*a*) and (*b*) of the

Criminal Code. Weapons prohibitions are imposed in addition to any other youth sentence imposed under s. 42 (s. 51(3)). A mandatory prohibition order must be imposed for a minimum of two years (s. 51(2)) and a discretionary prohibition order may be imposed for a maximum of two years (s. 51(4)). Pursuant to s. 52, the young person may bring an application for a review of a prohibition order.

6. Level of Custody

Each province must provide two levels of custody for young persons distinguished by their level of restraint (s. 85). Under the YOA, these levels were referred to as "open" and "secure" custody. The YCJA provides for an administrative procedure for determining the appropriate level of custody for a particular offender; however, the YCJA also gives each province the option of giving the youth justice court the power to determine the level of custody (s. 88). In Ontario, the lieutenant governor in council has given the youth justice court the power to make determinations of the level of custody for young persons and to review those determinations in accordance with the YOA (O.C. 791/2003; O.C. 793/2003). The open and secure custody classifications will therefore continue under the YCJA in Ontario.

7. Review of Youth Sentence

Defence counsel often overlook the provisions which permit a review of a youth justice court sentence. The sections of the YCJA dealing with review of sentences should always be considered when acting for a young person who has received a custodial sentence. Section 59 of the YCJA provides for the review of a non-custodial youth sentences and s. 94 provides for the review of youth sentences involving custody.

8. Forensic DNA Analysis

The forensic DNA analysis provisions of the *Criminal Code* also apply to young persons. These provisions make no distinction between young and adult offenders. However, all legislation dealing with young persons recognizes that young persons must be treated differently by the courts because of differences in vulnerability, maturity, experience and other factors related to their youth; therefore, in determining whether or not to make a DNA order, the sentencing judge must look at each of the relevant factors in accordance with the sentencing principles and the goals of the YCJA. The court cannot assume that, as with an adult offender, there will be minimal impact on a young person's privacy and security of the person. See *R. v. B.(K.)*, [2003] O.J. No. 3553 (C.A.).

QUESTIONS

9. A young person appears before the youth justice court for sentencing in connection with four residential break and enters and failure to comply with a probation order. He committed these offences with a co-accused

from a previous offence with whom he was prohibited from associating. His record includes three previous break and enter charges (for which he received one month open custody in total), as well as several entries for theft and possession of stolen property (for which he received probation and community service). Victim impact statements from the homeowners have been filed describing their anger and fear generated by the crimes and requesting thousands of dollars in compensation for damage and unrecovered property. What representations do you make to the youth court as both Crown and defence counsel at the sentencing hearing?

10. A 15-year-old pleads guilty to taking an automobile without the owner's consent. She has previously had two sets of similar charges resolved through extrajudicial sanctions. Defence counsel is urging the judge to grant a conditional discharge. Is this appropriate?

11. A young person is sentenced to a total of three years secure custody for the offences of criminal negligence causing death, theft over $5,000 (involving a car theft and a police chase) and unrelated charges of impaired driving cause bodily harm and theft over $5,000. Within the first week of incarceration, the young person escapes custody, steals a car and engages police in a pursuit which results in serious injuries to passengers in an oncoming vehicle. What is the maximum combined duration this young person may be sentenced to after a guilty plea to charges of dangerous driving causing bodily harm (two counts), engaging police in pursuit, and theft over $5,000? Consider, in this regard, *R. v. B.(D.W.)* (1991), 64 C.C.C. (3d) 164 (Ont. C.A.); *R. v. R.(D.J.)* (1992), 76 C.C.C. (3d) 88 (Man. C.A.). See *contra*: *R. v. C.(W.J.)* (1988), 42 C.C.C. (3d) 253 (N.S.C.A.).

12. A young person is found guilty of dangerous driving causing death. He was sentenced to 18 months' probation and was prohibited from driving for seven years. Is the driving prohibition consistent with the provisions of the YCJA? See *R. v. T.(J.D.)* (2002), 163 C.C.C. (3d) 123 (B.C.C.A.).

K. ADULT SENTENCE AND ELECTION

Pursuant to the YOA, under certain circumstances, young persons could be transferred to adult court and tried and sentenced as adults. Under the YCJA, the transfer process is eliminated. Instead, the Crown will indicate early in the proceedings that it is seeking an adult sentence in the case of young persons 14 years of age (or 15 or 16 years, where the province has designated this age) charged with an offence for which an adult would be liable to imprisonment for more than two years (s. 64). Where a young person is at least 14 years of age (or 15 or 16 years, where the province has designated this age) and charged with murder, attempted murder, manslaughter or aggravated sexual assault, or where there is a pattern of serious violent offences (the "presumptive offences" as defined in s. 2(1)), it is presumed that the young person will be sentenced as an adult, and the young person may apply for an order that he or she is not liable to an adult sentence but rather may be sentenced as a youth. Each category of eligible offence has a separate set of procedural preconditions to the determination of whether the young person should be sentenced as a youth or an adult. Young persons who are at risk of being sentenced as adults will be put to their election as to mode of trial

(see s. 67). Before an adult sentence may be imposed, the court must determine whether a youth sentence would be sufficiently long to hold the young person accountable for the offence. The accountability of the young person must be consistent with the greater dependency of the young person and the reduced level of maturity. If a youth sentence would be of sufficient length to hold the young person accountable, the court must impose a youth sentence. The detailed provisions of sections 62-81 of the YCJA govern the procedure for determining whether a young person should be given an adult or youth sentence.

CHAPTER 13

APPEALS AND EXTRAORDINARY REMEDIES

A. INDICTABLE APPEALS

1. RIGHTS OF APPEAL

Part XXI of the *Criminal Code*, R.S.C. 1985, c. C-46, governs appeals from dispositions made at trials for indictable offences, whether the trials were held before a judge alone, before judge and jury on an indictment, or before a provincial court judge on an information. Further, appellate rights and procedures are governed by the indictable nature of the trial proceedings, not by the nature of the conviction which results. So, for example, where the accused is acquitted of an indictable offence but found guilty of a lesser included summary conviction offence, the appeal against conviction is still governed by Part XXI (see *R. v. Yaworski* (1959), 124 C.C.C. 151 (Man. C.A.)). Sections 675(1.1) and 676(1.1) regulate appeals respecting both summary conviction and indictable offences which were tried together.

Sections 675 and 676 of the *Criminal Code* outline the rights of appeal to the court of appeal conferred upon the accused and the Crown[1] from the dispositions made in indictable proceedings. For indictable appeals, the "court of appeal" means, in Prince Edward Island, the Appeal Division of the Supreme Court, and elsewhere, the Court of Appeal (ss. 2 and 673 of the *Code*). So, for example, three judges (and for special cases, perhaps five judges) of the Manitoba Court of Appeal would hear appeals from indictable trials held in Manitoba. A single judge of that court would hear applications for bail pending appeal.

QUESTION

1. Review ss. 675 and 676 of the *Criminal Code*. Consider the distinctions between Crown and defence appeals. In many foreign jurisdictions, the Crown is not entitled to appeal an acquittal. Should the Crown be similarly constrained in Canada?

---

[1] In proceedings conducted by the federal Crown, such as controlled drugs and substances or customs prosecutions, the Attorney General of Canada and his or her counsel have the same rights of appeal as their provincial or territorial counterparts (s. 696 of the *Criminal Code*).

The practice differs between jurisdictions as to whether the issue of leave to appeal need be separately addressed in advance of the appeal itself. For example, in Ontario, grounds of appeal against conviction, which technically require leave to appeal, are simply argued as part of the appeal itself. Similarly, though a sentence can only be appealed with leave of the Court of Appeal or a judge thereof, no separate application is brought for leave to appeal sentence in advance of the sentence appeal itself. There is an exception. Where the appeal is against sentence only, and bail pending appeal is sought, s. 679(1)(*b*) of the *Criminal Code* requires that leave to appeal be granted before bail pending appeal may be granted. Accordingly, the application for bail pending appeal is joined with an application for leave to appeal sentence.

Under s. 673 of the *Code*, for the purposes of appellate proceedings, "sentence" is not confined to imprisonment and or monetary fines but includes a full range of other dispositions imposed upon an accused found guilty, including firearm prohibition orders, forfeiture orders, restitution and compensation orders, and probation orders. Other dispositions besides these are listed. The definition is not exhaustive.

Sections 691 to 693 of the *Criminal Code* govern further appeals to the Supreme Court of Canada by the accused and by the Crown in indictable proceedings. Such appeals are restricted to questions of law. Where the accused's appeal against conviction has been dismissed by the court of appeal, an appeal may proceed to the Supreme Court of Canada on any question of law on which a court of appeal judge dissented and otherwise, on any question of law with leave of the Supreme Court. Where the court of appeal has set aside an acquittal, other than by reason of a verdict based upon s. 16 of the *Criminal Code*, an appeal as of right is available (as of 1997) only on any question of law on which a court of appeal judge dissented or if the court of appeal entered a verdict of guilty and otherwise, on any question of law, with leave of the Supreme Court. Where the Crown's appeal against acquittal has been dismissed by the court of appeal, or the court of appeal has set aside the accused's conviction, the Crown may appeal to the Supreme Court of Canada as of right on any question of law on which a court of appeal judge dissented and otherwise, on any question of law with leave of the Supreme Court. Bail pending an application for leave to appeal or an appeal to the Supreme Court of Canada may be addressed by a judge of the court of appeal (s. 679(1)(*c*)).

Though this chapter primarily addresses appeals against conviction, acquittal or sentence, various sections provide for appeals of other dispositions to the court of appeal.

NATURE OF DISPOSITION	APPELLANT	SECTION
Order of the trial court staying proceedings on an indictment or quashing an indictment.	Crown	*Criminal Code*, s. 676(1)(*c*).

Order of the superior court quashing an indictment or refusing or failing to exercise jurisdiction on an indictment.	**Crown**	***Criminal Code*, s. 676(1)(*b*).**
Parole ineligibility over ten years for second degree murder.	**Accused**	***Criminal Code*, s. 675(2).**
Parole ineligibility under 25 years for second degree murder.	**Crown**	***Criminal Code*, s. 676(4).**
Parole ineligibility in excess of the minimum for person under 18 convicted of murder.	**Accused**	***Criminal Code*, s. 675(2.2).**
The decision to make a s. 743.6 parole ineligibility order.	**Accused**	***Criminal Code*, s. 675(2.1).**
The decision not to make a s. 743.6 parole ineligibility order.	**Crown**	***Criminal Code*, s. 676(5).**
Not criminally responsible or unfit to stand trial.	**Accused**	***Criminal Code*, s. 675(3).**
Not criminally responsible or unfit to stand trial.	**Crown**	***Criminal Code*, s. 676(1)(*a*) and 676(3).**
Disposition or Placement Decision made by a court or review board pursuant to Part XX.1.	**Any party as defined in *Criminal Code*, s. 672.1**	***Criminal Code*, s. 672.72 to s. 672.8.**
Indeterminate sentence for dangerous offender.	**Accused**	***Criminal Code*, s. 759(1).**
Dismissal of application for dangerous offender order.	**Crown**	***Criminal Code*, s. 759(2).**
Granting or refusal of Prerogative relief.	**Accused/Crown**	***Criminal Code*, s. 784.**
Young offender dispositions respecting indictable offences.	**Young person/ Crown**	***Youth Criminal Justice Act*, s. 37(1).**

Order to pay costs.	Party so ordered	*Criminal Code*, s. 676.1.

See also ss. 691 to 695 of the *Criminal Code*, s. 37(10) of the *Youth Criminal Justice Act,* S.C. 2002, c. 1, and ss. 40 and 41 of the *Supreme Court Act,* R.S.C. 1985, c. S-26, respecting further appeals to the Supreme Court of Canada.

2. Procedure on Appeals

Section 482 of the *Criminal Code* provides that each court of appeal is entitled to enact rules of court to govern the procedure on appeals. Though the rules of court vary between jurisdictions, they share many common features. This chapter draws upon the Ontario Court of Appeal Criminal Appeal Rules, SI/93-169, formulated by the Ontario Court of Appeal. The rules and practices of the various courts of appeal should be consulted to determine the extent to which the practices deviate.

An appeal commences with a notice of appeal. Three copies are to be served in accordance with the rules within 30 days of the imposition of sentence. This is so, even when the appeal is against conviction only. The rules contemplate that counsel may wish to await the sentence before determining whether an appeal will be launched and, if so, on what grounds. Generally, a court reporter's certificate must be filed with the notice of appeal, reflecting that the transcript has been ordered. One exception relates to appeals which may be funded by Legal Aid: counsel is provided with a provisional legal aid certificate permitting him or her to file a notice of appeal, and apply for bail pending appeal, but not necessarily to order the transcript until an opinion letter as to the merits of the appeal has been provided to Legal Aid and funding for the appeal has been authorized. If necessary, a motion can be brought to extend the 30-day time limit. Generally, affidavit material should demonstrate that there was a *bona fide* intention to appeal within the 30 days. Extensions are not easily given.

Where the accused is sentenced to a term of imprisonment, counsel may apply for bail pending appeal before a single judge of the court. A notice of motion, together with the notice of appeal, affidavits from the accused, from trial counsel (as to the merits of the appeal), from proposed sureties and from the accused's employer, along with other evidence, is often filed in support of the application. A transcript of the charge to the jury, or the reasons for judgment may also be helpful. As noted earlier, where the appeal is against sentence only, leave to appeal must be obtained before bail can be granted. The criteria which govern bail applications are contained in s. 679(3) and (4) of the *Criminal Code.* The applicant bears the burden of persuasion. When release is ordered, it is generally a condition of release that the accused personally surrender into custody by 6 p.m. the day prior to the hearing of the appeal.

QUESTION

2. **One of the criteria for release on bail pending appeal is that the applicant's detention is not necessary in the public interest. How is consideration of the "public interest" affected by the decision of the Supreme Court of Canada in *R. v. Morales* (1992), 77 C.C.C. (3d) 91 (S.C.C.), substantially reproduced at p. 290. Consider, in this regard, *R. v. Daniel* (1997), 119 C.C.C. (3d) 413 (Ont. C.A.); *R. v. Farinacci* (1993), 86 C.C.C. (3d) 32 (Ont. C.A.).**

If bail is granted, the order, once formally entered, must be taken to the jail. Any sureties must also attend at the jail to secure the accused's release. A justice of the peace attends at the jail during predetermined hours or upon pre-arrangement to direct the accused's release, once the paperwork is completed. Where bail is denied, the court may direct that the appeal be heard on an expedited basis.

QUESTIONS

3. **Where the court of appeal ultimately allows an appeal against conviction and orders a new trial, a judge of the court of appeal has jurisdiction to entertain an application for bail pending the new trial. Which party bears the onus? Consider, in this regard, s. 679(7.1) of the *Criminal Code*.**

4. **Where an appeal is taken by the accused only against the sentence imposed, counsel may choose strategically not to apply for bail pending appeal. Why?**

The next step in the appellate process is that the appellant requests the original papers and exhibits from the trial court and files a copy of this requisition with the court. With the consent of the opposing counsel, the court will release the original papers and exhibits to counsel to enable an appeal book to be prepared, reproducing the notice of appeal, any bail or other preliminary orders, and exhibits capable of reproduction which could be of assistance on the hearing of the appeal.

The rules state which portions of the transcript are to be prepared by the court reporter. For example, closing addresses of counsel are generally not prepared. The rules also provide procedures for obtaining a court order to direct the preparation of additional transcripts, where required. Once the transcript is received, the appellant's counsel is to perfect the appeal within certain time periods by serving and filing those transcripts which were not provided directly to the opposing party or to the court by the court reporter, as well as the requisite copies of the appellant's factum and appeal book, together with a certificate of perfection. Once the appeal is perfected, a date for the hearing of the appeal and the service and filing of the respondent's factum is determined. Casebooks containing the relevant authorities are to be filed shortly before the appeal is to be heard.

There may be applications for bail variations before a single judge of the court, pending the hearing of the appeal. Frequently, these relate to the "sunset clause" contained in the original bail order. This is a condition placed in almost all bail orders requiring the accused to surrender into custody either on a specified date or on the date to be set for the hearing of the appeal, whichever is earlier. This is intended to act as an incentive to the appellant's counsel to be diligent in perfecting the appeal. When a bail variation is on consent, counsel need not attend in person.

Appeals generally commence at 10:30 a.m. Where the appellant was sentenced to imprisonment at trial and granted bail pending appeal, his or her appeal will not generally be heard unless the court has been officially advised by the correctional institution that the accused did personally surrender into custody on the previous day.

On appeal, the appellant's counsel generally makes oral submissions first, unless the court directs otherwise. The respondent's counsel then makes submissions, and the appellant's counsel is permitted to reply. Sometimes, it is unnecessary for the court to hear from the respondent. The court may also reserve judgment and is empowered to grant bail, pending its disposition of the appeal. Time limitations may be placed upon oral argument. In each jurisdiction, counsel must consult not only the applicable rules but also practice directions issued by the court.

Sometimes, the appellant seeks to introduce fresh evidence on appeal (s. 683(1)(*d*) of the *Criminal Code*; *Palmer and Palmer v. The Queen* (1979), 50 C.C.C. (2d) 193 (S.C.C.)).

3. Powers of the Court of Appeal

Section 686 of the *Criminal Code* outlines the most significant powers of the court on appeal.

R. v. BINIARIS

(2000), 143 C.C.C. (3d) 1 (S.C.C.)

[The accused was charged with second degree murder. The accused and S., a young offender, participated in a senseless and violent beating which left a man dead. S. threw the deceased against a plate glass window, then propelled him to the ground, causing the deceased to strike the back of his head on the pavement. Once the deceased was on the ground, S. straddled the deceased's thighs and began to punch the deceased in the stomach. The accused entered into the fray, ran up to the deceased and stomped on his forehead a number of times with sufficient force to leave tread marks from his shoes on the deceased's forehead. The Crown's expert testified that the fatal injuries to the deceased's brain resulted from the accused's actions. The defence expert was of the opinion that the deceased had sustained lethal brain injuries when S. caused him to strike his head on the pavement, fracturing the thickest bone in the skull. During the course of the trial, after consulting with the defence expert and another expert, the Crown's expert also came to share the view that the fatal injuries were attributable to the actions of S. The Crown's expert was recalled and testified to this effect. In its closing submissions to the jury, the Crown maintained its original theory and invited the jury to rely on its common sense and to convict the accused of second degree murder as the perpetrator of the fatal injuries, notwithstanding the medical evidence to the contrary. The Crown also suggested to the jury that it could find the accused guilty of second degree murder as S.'s co-perpetrator or accomplice. The trial judge charged the jury that it should proceed carefully before rejecting the ultimately unanimous expert evidence regarding causation. The accused was convicted of second degree murder. The majority of the Court of Appeal dismissed the accused's appeal but substituted a conviction for manslaughter on the basis that the jury's verdict was unreasonable and unsupported by the evidence. The dissenting judge concluded that it was not unreasonable for the jury to convict the accused of second degree murder.]

The judgment of the Supreme Court of Canada was delivered by

Arbour J.: —

I. Introduction

This appeal was heard together with *R. v. Molodowic*, 2000 SCC 16, and *R. v. A.G.*, 2000 SCC 17. In this trilogy, the Court was asked to reconsider its decision in *R. v. Yebes*, [1987] 2 S.C.R. 168, 36 C.C.C. (3d) 417, 43 D.L.R. (4th) 424, and, in particular, to decide two issues of general application. First, whether the reasonableness of a verdict involves a question of law, within the meaning of ss. 691 and 693 of the *Criminal Code*, R.S.C., 1985, c. C-46, so as to permit a further appeal to this Court from a decision by a provincial appellate court, and, second, what standard of review must be applied by the reviewing court in examining the reasonableness of a verdict. Each case involved, of course, an application of that standard to the facts of that case.

.....

V. Analysis

.....

B. Whether the Reasonableness of a Verdict Is a Question of Law

This Court, in *Yebes, supra*, decided unequivocally that the reasonableness of a verdict, within the meaning of s. 686(1)(*a*)(i) of the *Criminal Code*, involves a decision on a question of law, and as such gives rise to a further appeal to this Court. McIntyre J., speaking for a unanimous six-member panel of the Court, indicated that although the respondent Crown had raised that jurisdictional issue, it was not "strongly pressed" at the hearing of the appeal. McIntyre J. recognized that although the proper qualification of the issue as either one of law, fact, or mixed fact and law was far from self-evident, there was no reason to treat it differently from the similar issue of whether a substantial wrong or miscarriage of justice has occurred, within the meaning of s. 686(1)(*b*)(iii). That having been interpreted as a question of law in *Mahoney v. The Queen*, [1982] 1 S.C.R. 834, 67 C.C.C. (2d) 197, 136 D.L.R. (3d) 608, McIntyre J. concluded that whether a verdict was unreasonable or not supportable by the evidence also amounted to a question of law.

The revisiting of this issue in the current trilogy is based, in part, on an argument that the decision in *Yebes* was an unjustified departure from the previous state of the law, and that it has not been consistently followed by this Court since.

The terminology "question of fact", "question of law", "question of mixed fact and law", "question of law alone", as used in the *Criminal Code* and in the case law in relation to rights of appeal has created serious difficulties of interpretation that are best resolved by a broad, purposive interpretative approach, adopted by Iacobucci J. in *Rizzo & Rizzo Shoes Ltd. (Re)*, [1998] 1 S.C.R. 27 at para. 21, 154 D.L.R. (4th) 193 (quoting E. Driedger, *Construction of Statutes* (2nd ed. 1983), at p. 87):

> "Today there is only one principle or approach [to statutory interpretation], namely, the words of an Act are to be read in their entire context and in their grammatical and ordinary sense harmoniously with the scheme of the Act, the object of the Act, and the intention of Parliament."

The sole purpose of the exercise here, in identifying the reasonableness of a verdict as a question of fact, law or both, is to determine access to appellate review. One can plausibly maintain, on close scrutiny of any decision under review, that the conclusion that a verdict was unreasonable was reached sometimes mostly as a matter of law, in other cases predominantly as a matter of factual assessment. But when that exercise is undertaken as a jurisdictional threshold exercise, little is gained by embarking on such a case-by-case analysis. Rather, it is vastly preferable to look at the overall nature of these kinds of decisions, and of their implications. Ideally, threshold jurisdictional issues should be as straightforward and free of ambiguity as possible. Otherwise, as these and many similar cases illustrate, courts spend an inordinate amount of time and effort attempting to ascertain their jurisdiction, while their resources would be better employed dealing with the issues on their merits.

Whether a conviction can be said to be unreasonable, or not supported by the evidence, imports in every case the application of a legal standard. The process by which this standard is applied inevitably entails a review of the facts of the case. I will say more about the review process below. As a jurisdictional issue of appellate access, the application of that legal standard is enough to make the question a question of law. It is of no import to suggest that it is not a "pure question of law", or that it is not a "question of law alone".

Triers of fact, whether juries or judges, have considerable leeway in their appreciation of the evidence and the proper inferences to be drawn therefrom, in their assessment of the credibility of witnesses, and in their ultimate assessment of whether the Crown's case is made out, overall, beyond a reasonable doubt. Any judicial system must tolerate reasonable differences of opinion on factual issues. Consequently, all factual findings are open to the trier of fact, except unreasonable ones embodied in a legally binding conviction. Although reasonable people may disagree about their appreciation of the facts, a conviction, which conveys legality, authority and finality, is not something about which reasonable people may disagree. A conviction cannot be unreasonable, except as a matter of law, in which case it must be overturned.

Very little additional insight is gained by elaborate exercises in statutory interpretation. The intention of Parliament is better ascertained in broad terms than by microscopic examination of the relevant provisions of the *Criminal Code*. Although the cases before us today come as of right, on the basis of a dissent in the Court of Appeal, I think that the fact that they are appeals as of right obscures the true nature of the debate on the question of reviewability of alleged unreasonable convictions. Access to the Supreme Court is generally reserved for important cases that have legal significance. Inevitably, not all appeals as of right have great legal importance, although the assumption is that, as a category, they do. As with all other questions of law, not all dissents in an appeal court on the issue of unreasonable verdict rest on a question of great importance. However, if the reasonableness of a conviction is not a question of law, no right of appeal will exist from a decision on that issue, not even with leave of the Court. This result would, in my view, be incompatible with the intention of Parliament expressed, overall, in the totality of the scheme for appellate review.

Criminal appeals on questions of law are based in part on the desire to ensure that criminal convictions are the product of error-free trials. Error-free trials are desirable as such, but even more so as a safeguard against wrongful convictions. It is inconceivable that Parliament would have permitted access, by leave or as of right, to this Court, in the case of trials or appeals affected by legal error, but would have granted no access whatsoever in the case of possibly the gravest error of all: an unreasonable conviction, or one that cannot be supported by the evidence.

The conclusion that a finding by an appeal court that a verdict is unreasonable or cannot be supported by the evidence raises a question of law is in harmony with the overall intent and spirit of the two-tier criminal appeal structure in the *Criminal Code*, even if there are some statutory constructions that may lend support to a different conclusion. Several of these constructions were advanced, none of which, in my view, is conclusive.

(i) Sections 686(1)(a)(i) and 686(1)(a)(ii)

For instance, the contrast between s. 686(1)(*a*)(i) and s. 686(1)(*a*)(ii) has been relied upon to suggest that the opinion of a court of appeal that the verdict is unreasonable is merely an opinion on a question of fact. For convenience, I will set these subsections out again:

> 686.(1) On the hearing of an appeal against a conviction or against a verdict that the appellant is unfit to stand trial or not criminally responsible on account of mental disorder, the court of appeal
>
> (*a*) may allow the appeal where it is of the opinion that
>
> (i) the verdict should be set aside on the ground that it is unreasonable or cannot be supported by the evidence,
>
> (ii) the judgment of the trial court should be set aside on the ground of a wrong decision on a question of law ... .

The reasoning is that if it were a question of law, there would be no need for both s. 686(1)(*a*)(i) and s. 686(1)(*a*)(ii). See *Sunbeam Corporation (Can.) Ltd. v. The Queen*, [1969] S.C.R. 221 at pp. 237-38, [1969] 2 C.C.C. 189, 1 D.L.R. (3d) 161; *R. v. Lampard*, [1969] S.C.R. 373 at pp. 380-81, [1969] 3 C.C.C. 249, 4 D.L.R. (3d) 98. This inference from the wording of the two subsections is far from inescapable. True, the remedial power contained in s. 686(1)(*a*)(i) may be linked to the jurisdiction of the court of appeal to entertain, with leave, questions of mixed fact and law or indeed questions of fact (see s. 675(1)(*a*)(ii)). However, it may also be viewed as a question of law that needed to be specifically identified as a basis for appellate intervention, since it would not fit well under the terminology used in s. 686(1)(a)(ii): an unreasonable verdict is not a "wrong decision on a question of law". It is also arguable that the two subsections may coexist without creating a redundancy or in any way doing violence to the idea that an unreasonable verdict is a question of law, by contrasting the word "verdict" in s. 686(1)(*a*)(i) with the phrase "judgment of the trial court" in s. 686(1)(*a*)(ii). The "verdict" could be seen as referring to the wrong legal conclusion of the trial judge or the jury on the ultimate issue of guilt or innocence, as opposed to the wrong legal conclusions of the trial judge on a myriad of issues of substantive law, procedure and evidence.

(ii) "Question of Law Alone" and Unreasonable Acquittals

Various arguments have been advanced, based on the implications that should flow from the use of the expression "question of law alone" in s. 676(1)(*a*), which provides for appeals by the Crown to the court of appeal. These arguments are of little assistance or consequence in determining the scope of access to this Court under ss. 691 or 693. The use of that expression can be taken to mean either that the Crown has a right of appeal from an acquittal only on a question of law, or that there is such a thing as a "question of law alone", which is distinct from a "question of law". I think it means the former. It is used in contrast to the right of the accused to appeal both on questions of law, questions of fact, and questions of mixed fact and law (see s. 675(1)(*a*)(i) and (ii)), and it is of no assistance in further defining the scope of the expression "question of law" in ss. 691 and 693.

The fact that a "question of law alone" is nothing different than a "question of law", and that the reasonableness of a verdict is a "question of law" within the meaning of s. 686(1)(*a*)(i), raises the question of whether the Crown will have a right of appeal against an "unreasonable acquittal". Although this question does not squarely arise on the facts of any of the three cases before us, it arises unavoidably since the interpretation given to "question of law" in s. 693(1) must equally apply to the phrase "question of law alone" in ss. 675(1) and 676(1). The conclusion that the reasonableness of a verdict always raises a question of law has a single, inevitable, consequence for these two sections: an accused person does not require leave to appeal under s. 675(1) where he or she challenges the reasonableness of the verdict. On the other hand, it will not affect the Crown's rights of appeal from an acquittal in any way.

In their written submissions, both the Attorney General for Ontario and the Attorney General of Manitoba (who participated in the companion cases) recognized that the law, as it stood at the time of the appeal, is clear that the Crown has no right of appeal from an acquittal on the ground that it was unreasonable, because the reasonableness of a verdict is a question of fact (or one of mixed fact and law). See, *e.g.*, *Sunbeam, supra*, at p. 233; *Lampard, supra*, at pp. 380-81; *Ciglen v. The Queen*, [1970] S.C.R. 804 at pp. 814-15, [1970] 4 C.C.C. 83, 11 D.L.R. (3d) 1, *per* Cartwright C.J., dissenting; *R. v. B. (G.)*, [1990] 2 S.C.R. 57 at pp. 70-71, 56 C.C.C. (3d) 181; *R. v. H. (D.S.)*, [1994] 2 S.C.R. 392, 90 C.C.C. (3d) 564, reversing (1993), 90 C.C.C. (3d) at p. 565 (B.C.C.A.); *R. v. Blundon* (1993), 84 C.C.C. (3d) 249 (Nfld. C.A.) at pp. 279-80. There can be no suggestion that the Crown's right of appeal at first instance is being enlarged or expanded to include "unreasonable acquittals" as a result of the determination that the reasonableness of a verdict is a "question of law" as well as a "question of law alone". As before, the Crown is barred from appealing an acquittal on the sole basis that it is unreasonable, without asserting any other error of law leading to it.

There is no anomaly in this result. The powers of the court of appeal in the case of Crown appeals on a question of law are contained in s. 686(4) of the *Code*. There is no reference in that section to an unreasonable verdict. This is consistent with the limited rights of appeal conferred on the Crown by s. 676(1). The absence of language granting a remedial power corresponding to s. 686(1)(*a*)(i), suggests that Parliament did not intend "unreasonable acquittals" to be appealable by the Crown at first instance. Further, and more importantly, as a matter of law, the concept of "unreasonable acquittal" is incompatible with the presumption of innocence and the burden which rests on the prosecution to prove its case beyond a reasonable doubt. See *Lampard, supra*, at pp. 380-81; *Schuldt v. The Queen*, [1985] 2 S.C.R. 592 at p. 610, 23 C.C.C. (3d) 225, 24 D.L.R. (4th) 453; *B. (G.), supra*, at pp. 70-71. Since, different policy considerations apply in providing the Crown with a right of appeal against acquittals, it seems to me that there is no principle of parity of appellate access in the criminal process that must inform our interpretation of this issue.

(iii) Redundancy

Finally, there is little merit in the argument, which is more one of policy than of statutory interpretation, that a second level of assessment of the reasonableness of a verdict is unnecessary since this Court is in no better position than courts of appeal to arrive at a correct answer, and that the exercise is merely repetitious. The review by the Supreme Court of a decision by a court of appeal that a verdict is unreasonable or cannot be supported by the evidence is in reality the first level of appellate review of that conclusion. The court of appeal, in examining the issue, obviously does not have the benefit of the analysis of the question by the trial court, as it would, or should, on legal issues such as the admissibility of evidence or the availability of a defence. The determination of the reasonableness of the verdict is therefore an original decision by the court of appeal, and there is no reason to bar the possibility of a review of that important decision.

In the end, there is no statutory interpretation principle that precludes the conclusion reached in *Yebes*, which is in accordance with the overriding principle expressed in *Rizzo Shoes, supra*. To the extent that decisions subsequent to *Yebes* may have suggested that the reasonableness of a verdict does not raise a question of law so as to give rise to a right of appeal, either as of right or by leave, under ss. 691 or 693 of the *Criminal Code*, these decisions in my view are in error, and *Yebes* must be reaffirmed. Three cases were brought to our attention which are said to cast doubt on whether the reasonableness of a verdict involves a question of law. In all three cases, two of which were appeals by the Crown and one by the defence, this Court quashed the appeal which was launched as of right on the basis of a dissent in the court of appeal on the question of whether the verdict was reasonable. See *R. v. Jensen* (1996), 106 C.C.C. (3d) 430 (Ont. C.A.), appeal quashed [1997] 1 S.C.R. 304, 112 C.C.C. (3d) 384; *R. v. Osvath* (1996), 87 O.A.C. 274 (C.A.), appeal quashed, [1997] 1 S.C.R. 7; *R. v. Hamilton*, [1997] Q.J. No. 67 (QL) (C.A.) [summarized 34 W.C.B. (2d) 405], appeal quashed June 2, 1997, [1997] S.C.C.A. No. 105 (QL). The quashing of these appeals, which implies an absence of jurisdiction rather than a disposition of the appeal on the merits, could be viewed as a proper application of *Yebes*. Arguably, *Yebes* left open the possibility that some dissents in appellate courts on the unreasonableness of a verdict may not amount to dissents on a question of law. After referring to the difficulty in drawing a clear line between a question of fact and one of law, and in response to the argument advanced by the Crown in that case that there was no point of law dividing the majority and the dissenting judge in the Court of Appeal, McIntyre J. said, at p. 181:

> Therefore, whether or not an appeal raises a question of law can only be determined after an examination of both the statements of law and the application of the law to the facts in the courts below.

This may be taken to suggest that some, but not all differences of opinion about the reasonableness of a verdict will give rise to a question of law. Others, presumably, would at best involve a mixed question of fact and law, or a simple disagreement on the facts. With respect, I do not agree that such a distinction was intended by *Yebes*. It is both unsound and undesirable. When a conviction is said to be unreasonable, or unsupported by the evidence, it is that conclusion itself that raises a question of law, not merely the process by which the conclusion was reached. Therefore, there is no need to determine whether that conclusion was arrived at by the application of the wrong legal test, or otherwise tainted by a legal irregularity, since even when it applies the right test, in an error-free process, the court of appeal must be right, as a matter of law, on the legal appreciation of the verdict as a reasonable one. This approach is also consistent with the need for clarity in jurisdictional matters. There certainly would be little judicial economy in embarking upon a characterization of the appellate exercise as one of fact, rather than law, as a threshold determination of jurisdiction. Rather than streamlining or reducing appeals, it would add to their litigiousness, but on the wrong question.

C. *Whether the Standard of Review Under Section 686(1)(a)(i) Should Be Modified*

The test for an appellate court determining whether the verdict of a jury or the judgment of a trial judge is unreasonable or cannot be supported by the evidence has been unequivocally expressed in *Yebes* as follows:

> [C]urial review is invited whenever a jury goes beyond a reasonable standard ... The test is "whether the verdict is one that a properly instructed jury acting judicially, could reasonably have rendered". [*Yebes, supra,* at p. 185 (quoting *R. v. Corbett,* [1975] 2 S.C.R. 275 at p. 282, 14 C.C.C. (2d) 385, 42 D.L.R. (3d) 142, *per* Pigeon J.).]

That formulation of the test imports both an objective assessment and, to some extent, a subjective one. It requires the appeal court to determine what verdict a reasonable jury, properly instructed, could judicially have arrived at, and, in doing so, to review, analyse and, within the limits of appellate disadvantage, weigh the evidence. This latter process is usually understood as referring to a subjective exercise, requiring the appeal court to examine the weight of the evidence, rather than its bare sufficiency. The test is therefore mixed, and it is more helpful to articulate what the application of that test entails, than to characterize it as either an objective or a subjective test.

The *Yebes* test is expressed in terms of a verdict reached by a jury. It is, however, equally applicable to the judgment of a judge sitting at trial without a jury. The review for unreasonableness on appeal is different, however, and somewhat easier when the judgment under attack is that of a single judge, at least when reasons for judgment of some substance are provided. In those cases, the reviewing appellate court may be able to identify a flaw in the evaluation of the evidence, or in the analysis, that will serve to explain the unreasonable conclusion reached, and justify the reversal. For example, in *R. v. Burke,* [1996] 1 S.C.R. 474, 105 C.C.C. (3d) 205, this Court was in a position to identify the deficiencies in the trial judge's analysis of the evidence which led to her unreasonable conclusions in respect of the three counts of indecent assault facing the accused. In that case, Sopinka J. found that the trial judge had ignored the possibility of collusion or corroboration between witnesses before accepting their "strikingly similar" evidence, had not been alive to circumstances (*i.e.*, the absence of physical traces of an alleged indecent assault which, if true, should have left observable marks) which caused great concern about the reliability of evidence adduced in support of allegations of a bizarre nature, and had relied uncritically on unorthodox identification evidence. Similarly, in *R. v. Reitsma,* [1998] 1 S.C.R. 769, 125 C.C.C. (3d) 1, reversing (1997), 97 B.C.A.C. 303, 125 C.C.C. (3d) at p. 2, this Court agreed with Rowles J.A., dissenting, that the trial judge had failed to advert to deficiencies in the pre-trial identification procedure and the shortcoming of "in-dock" identification. Finally, in *R. v. O'Connor* (1998), 123 C.C.C. (3d) 487 at pp. 492-93, 518-20, 159 D.L.R. (4th) 304 (B.C.C.A.), the trial judge accepted the accused's evidence that he was not present at the place where the offence was alleged to have been committed, and yet convicted the accused. This logical inconsistency was relied upon by the Court of Appeal to explain the unreasonableness of the verdict. These examples demonstrate that in trials by judge alone, the court of appeal often can and should identify the defects in the analysis that led the trier of fact to an unreasonable conclusion. The court of appeal will therefore be justified to intervene and set aside a verdict as unreasonable when the reasons of the trial judge reveal that he or she was not alive to an applicable legal principle, or entered a verdict inconsistent with the factual conclusions reached. These discernible defects are themselves sometimes akin to a separate error of law, and therefore easily sustain the conclusion that the unreasonable verdict which rests upon them also raises a question of law.

The exercise of appellate review is considerably more difficult when the court of appeal is required to determine the alleged unreasonableness of a verdict reached by a jury. If there are no errors in the charge, as must be assumed, there is no way of determining the basis upon which the jury reached its conclusion. But this does not dispense the reviewing court from the need to articulate the basis upon which it finds that the conclusion reached by the jury was unreasonable. It is insufficient for the court of appeal to refer to a vague unease, or a lingering or lurking doubt based on its own review of the evidence. This "lurking doubt" may be a powerful trigger for thorough appellate scrutiny of the evidence, but it is not, without further articulation of the basis for such doubt, a proper basis upon which to interfere with the findings of a jury. In other words, if, after reviewing the evidence at the end of an error-free trial which led to a conviction, the appeal court judge is left with a lurking doubt or feeling of unease, that doubt, which is not in itself sufficient to justify interfering with the conviction, may be a useful signal that the verdict was indeed reached in a non-judicial manner. In that case, the court of appeal must proceed further with its analysis.

When a jury which was admittedly properly instructed returns what the appeal court perceives to be an unreasonable conviction, the only rational inference, if the test in *Yebes* is followed, is that the jury, in arriving at that guilty verdict, was not acting judicially. This conclusion does not imply an impeachment of the integrity of the jury. It may be that the jury reached its verdict pursuant to an analytical flaw similar to the errors occasionally incurred in the analysis of trial judges and revealed in their reasons for judgment. Such error would of course not be apparent on the face of the verdict by a jury. But the unreasonableness itself of the verdict would be apparent to the legally trained reviewer when, in all the circumstances of a given case, judicial fact-finding precludes the conclusion reached by the jury. Judicial appreciation of the evidence is governed by rules that dictate the required content of the charge to the jury. These rules are sometimes expressed in terms of warnings, mandatory or discretionary sets of instructions by which a trial judge will convey the product of accumulated judicial experience to the jury, who, by definition, is new to the exercise. For instance, a judge may need to warn the jury about the frailties of eyewitness identification evidence. Similarly, years of judicial experience has revealed the possible need for special caution in evaluating the evidence of certain witnesses, such as accomplices, who may, to the uninitiated, seem particularly knowledgeable and therefore credible. Finally, judicial warnings may be required when the jury has heard about the criminal record of the accused, or about similar fact evidence. But these rules of caution cannot be exhaustive, they cannot capture every situation, and cannot be formulated in every case as a requirement of the charge. Rather, after the jury has been adequately charged as to the applicable law, and warned, if necessary, about drawing possibly unwarranted conclusions, it remains that in some cases, the totality of the evidence and the peculiar factual circumstances of a given case will lead an experienced jurist to conclude that the fact-finding exercise applied at trial was flawed in light of the unreasonable result that it produced.

When an appellate court arrives at that conclusion, it does not act as a "thirteenth juror", nor is it "usurping the function of the jury". In concluding that no properly instructed jury acting judicially could have convicted, the reviewing court inevitably is concluding that these particular jurors who convicted must not have been acting judicially. In that context, acting judicially means not only acting dispassionately, applying the law and adjudicating on the basis of the record and nothing else. It means, in addition, arriving at a conclusion that does not conflict with the bulk of judicial experience. This, in my view, is the assessment that must be made by the reviewing court. It requires not merely asking whether twelve properly instructed jurors, acting judicially, could reasonably have come to the same result, but doing so through the lens of judicial experience which serves as an additional protection against an unwarranted conviction.

It is not particularly significant to describe this judicial oversight as either objective or subjective. It is exercised by an appeal court and therefore it will invariably draw on a collection of judicial experiences. Because of its judicial character, and because it purports to identify features of a case that will give experienced jurists cause for concern, it is imperative that the reviewing court articulate as precisely as possible what features of the case suggest that the verdict reached by the jury was unreasonable, despite the fact that it was not tainted by any erroneous instructions as to the applicable law. In some cases, the articulation of the grounds upon which an appellate court concludes that a conviction was unreasonable may elucidate previously unidentified dangers in evidence and give rise to additional warnings to the jury in subsequent cases. Most of the time, it will simply point to a case that presented itself with several causes for concern, none of which, in isolation, might have required that the jury be warned in any particular way. There are many illustrations from the case law of verdicts having been found unreasonable essentially on the strength of accumulated judicial experience. Concerns about various aspects of the frailty of identification evidence have been a recurrent basis, by itself or together with other considerations, for overturning verdicts as unreasonable. See, *e.g.*, *Burke, supra*; *Reitsma, supra*; *R. v. Keeper* (1993), 88 Man. R. (2d) 156 (C.A.); *R. v. Malcolm* (1993), 81 C.C.C. (3d) 196 (Ont. C.A.); *R. v. Tat* (1997), 117 C.C.C. (3d) 481 (Ont. C.A.); *R. v. D. (N.)*, [1993] O.J. No. 2139 (QL) (C.A.) [summarized 20 W.C.B. (2d) 609]. Judicial experience has also been relied upon to question the reasonableness of verdicts in cases of sexual misconduct presenting troubling features such as allegations of sexual touching of a bizarre nature (see, *e.g.*, *Burke, supra*; *R. v. V. (C.)*, [1993] O.J. No. 1512 (QL) (C.A.) [summarized 20 W.C.B. (2d) 228]; *R. v. L. (J.H.H.P.)* (1992), 75 C.C.C. (3d) 165 (Man. C.A.)), or the possibility of collusion between witnesses (see, *e.g.*, *Burke, supra*). Finally, the experience of the courts has occasionally been brought to bear, although not always explicitly, on the assessment of verdicts rejecting a defence with respect to which there may be unjustified skepticism or even prejudice because those relying on such justifications or excuses may be viewed as simply trying to avoid responsibility for their actions. See, *e.g.*, *R. v. Vaillancourt* (1999), 136 C.C.C. (3d) 530 (Que. C.A.); *Molodowic, supra*.

It follows from the above that the test in *Yebes* continues to be the binding test that appellate courts must apply in determining whether the verdict of the jury is unreasonable or cannot be supported by the evidence. To the extent that it has a subjective component, it is the subjective assessment of an assessor with judicial training and experience that must be brought to bear on the exercise of reviewing the evidence upon which an allegedly unreasonable conviction rests. That, in turn, requires the reviewing judge to import his or her knowledge of the law and the expertise of the courts, gained through the judicial process over the years, not simply his or her own personal experience and insight. It also requires that the reviewing court articulate as explicitly and as precisely as possible the grounds for its intervention. I wish to stress the importance of explicitness in the articulation of the reasons that support a finding that a verdict is unreasonable or cannot be supported by the evidence. Particularly since this amounts to a question of law that may give rise to an appeal, either as of right or by leave, the judicial process requires clarity and transparency as well as accessibility to the legal reasoning of the court of appeal. When there is a dissent in the court of appeal on the issue of the reasonableness of the verdict, both the spirit and the letter of s. 677 of the *Criminal Code* should be complied with. This Court should be supplied with the grounds upon which the verdict was found to be, or not to be, unreasonable.

D. Application to this Appeal

The appellant raised three issues before this Court:

1. Did the majority of the British Columbia Court of Appeal err in law in failing to consider that the verdict was reasonable and supported by the evidence on the basis of co-perpetrator liability as outlined in *Regina v. McMaster*, [1996] 1 S.C.R. 740, 105 C.C.C. (3d) 193?

2. Did the majority of the British Columbia Court of Appeal err in law by applying the wrong test to determine whether the verdict was unreasonable or could not be supported by the evidence?

3. Did the majority of the British Columbia Court of Appeal err in law in failing to review, and to some extent re-examine and reweigh, all of the evidence in the instant case when it concluded that the verdict was unreasonable and unsupported by the evidence?

These three issues can conveniently be addressed together. At the outset of the respondent Biniaris' trial and until the change in Dr. Carlyle's opinion, the Crown's position was that Biniaris alone had caused the fatal injuries suffered by Niven and was guilty of second degree murder as a principal. The shift in Dr. Carlyle's evidence led Crown counsel, at the end of the trial, to advance a modified, three-part theory of liability — liability as a principal, liability as a co-perpetrator or liability as an aider or abettor. Boyd J. dealt adequately with the implications of the reversal of Dr. Carlyle's position and the Crown's modified theory in her charge to the jury. The trial judge explained the Crown's position that it was open to the jury to reject the medical evidence offered by Drs. Rice and Carlyle on the issue of causation in favour of their own common sense and, if they were satisfied beyond a reasonable doubt that Biniaris had acted with the requisite intent, to conclude that Biniaris was guilty of second degree murder as the perpetrator of Niven's fatal injuries. However, Boyd J. quite properly urged the jury to be very careful, characterizing the choice to ignore the unanimous expert evidence on causation as a "dangerous venture". The trial judge then explained the circumstances under which it was open to the jury, applying the relevant principles of party liability set out in s. 21(1) of the *Criminal Code*, to convict the accused of second degree murder:

> The matter now to consider is under what circumstances one or more persons can be responsible for the death of the deceased and one actus reus.
>
> .....
>
> [I]f you should find after a consideration of all of the evidence that it has been shown beyond a reasonable doubt that the accused, Mr. Biniaris, together with Mr. Stark, participated in a chain of events which were all interrelated and interconnected from the time the altercation began until they left the scene, then you will have concluded that the actus reus has been committed.
>
> Assuming ... that you conclude there was such a chain of events, if you should find beyond a reasonable doubt that Mr. Biniaris, during the course of that chain of events, struck Mr. Niven in the manner which has been described in the evidence, and if you find again beyond a reasonable doubt that these blows were delivered by Mr. Biniaris either with the intent to cause his death or with the intent to cause Mr. Niven bodily harm which he knew was likely to cause his death and was reckless whether death ensued or not, then he is guilty of second degree murder [as a co-perpetrator] no matter which of the blows during that series of events, including the initial fall to the ground, caused Mr. Niven's death.
>
> Assuming again that you conclude there was a chain of events, an interrelated chain of events constituting the *actus reus*, if you find it was Mr. Stark who intended to kill Mr. Niven and that Mr. Biniaris, knowing of Stark's intention to cause bodily harm to Niven that was likely to cause death, aided or abetted Stark by either encouraging Niven to fight or by actually participating in the beating in order to carry out that purpose, then you will have found that Mr. Biniaris was an accomplice and is a party to the offence of second degree murder and is equally guilty regardless of whether or not Mr. Biniaris' actions, the stomping, the kicking, regardless [of] whether any of that actually caused Mr. Niven's death.
>
> What I am really saying to you is there are two routes to a second degree murder conviction. One is if you find that Mr. Biniaris was the principal offender, and that other is if you find that Mr. Biniaris was a party [either as a co-perpetrator or as an accomplice] to a single transaction, an interrelated series of events that led to and ultimately resulted in Mr. Niven's death.

The unusual course of the respondent's trial caused grave concern to the majority of the Court of Appeal and ultimately, in my respectful view, led Hall J.A.'s reasonableness analysis astray. Despite the availability of two alternative routes to a second degree murder conviction, neither of which was dependent on proof that the respondent actually caused Niven's fatal injuries, Hall J.A.'s reasons for judgment indicate that he remained unduly concerned about causation. In light of the state of the medical evidence at the end of the trial, Hall J.A. correctly concluded that, "the only safe route for a conviction of the appellant Biniaris for murder lay through the application of s. 21 of the *Criminal Code*" (p. 71). This was also clearly the view of the trial judge who directed the jury accordingly. However, Hall J.A.'s analysis remained focused on the issue of causation, despite its minor significance to the respondent's liability as a party. He wrote (at pp. 71-73):

> At the outset, the jury had, in the Crown opening, been advised of the theory that the fatal injuries were caused by actions of the [accused] Biniaris. By the end of the case there had been a complete reversal of this theory. He was now said to be liable to be found culpable of murder on the ground of being a party to the activity of Stark. It must be observed that the activity of Stark causative of the injuries had terminated almost entirely by the time Biniaris became involved in the affray. Blows struck by Stark after Niven was on the pavement were to his abdomen area and if, as was less than clear from the evidence, Stark did, near the termination of the incident, direct a kick at the chin of Niven, that again seems unlikely to have had any causal relationship to the serious brain injury. Thus in this case, we have the situation that anything done by Biniaris, the [accused], by his stomping activity, while no doubt manifesting an intention to assist Stark in his general assault of Niven, seems most unlikely to have been causative of the fatal brain injuries suffered by Niven. The nature of the brain injuries testified to by the experts makes the temporal sequence of events important here. This [accused] came into the fray at a point in time when, as I interpret the medical testimony, the damage to the brain of the deceased was irreversible.
>
> .....
>
> If one analyzes the activities of the two assailants, it seems to me to be an inescapable conclusion that the assaultive activity attributed to the [accused] all occurred after the infliction of the fatal harm and in circumstances where Biniaris' intention to assist in a murder is unclear.

In my opinion, Hall J.A. properly identified *mens rea* as a critical issue but erred in interfering with the conclusion reached by the jury on that question, which was fully open to them on the evidence. He said (at pp. 72-73):

> In order to be found guilty of murder as a party, the jury would have to conclude that the [accused] had the same intent as the killer [i.e., the intent to cause death or the intention to cause bodily harm that he knew was likely to cause death, being reckless whether death ensued or not] and was carrying out these acts of stomping for the purpose of aiding and abetting in the murder of the deceased. The intention is probably less easy to attribute in the case of a sudden affray of this sort than might be the case where a deadly weapon is anticipated to be used.
>
> I see the position of the [accused] in this case as rather different from that of Stark. Stark, the initial aggressor outside the store, decided to attack

> Niven and carried out that attack with great violence and with disastrous results. Biniaris was by no means the prime mover in the event. …
>
> Nor, as I observed, is this a joint venture case of the sort where one or more of the parties may possess a deadly weapon like a gun or a knife.

Whether Stark was the initial aggressor, the degree and the intensity of the respondent's participation in the attack and his intention or foresight at the time of his participation in the attack were all matters raised by the evidence and commented upon by the parties and by the trial judge. Although a conviction for manslaughter was a given, as was conceded by the respondent before this Court, and although reasonable people may disagree about whether they would have found, on the evidence, that the respondent had the requisite intent for murder, there is nothing to qualify that conclusion, which is really the only one in issue in this case, as an unreasonable one.

On the evidence adduced by the Crown, it was reasonable for the jury to conclude that the respondent and Stark had aided and abetted one another in a joint attack on Niven. There was evidence on the basis of which the jury could reasonably find that the respondent was no less a "prime mover" or "initial aggressor" than Stark. The evidence establishes that Biniaris stood up and moved close to Niven soon after the initial exchange of words between Stark and Niven, suggesting, not unreasonably, that the respondent was readying himself for a fight. The evidence also suggests that the respondent, as Ryan J.A. noted, "was the first to verbally challenge Niven to a fight" (p. 75) and that he entered the fray moments after Stark began to punch Niven, at a point where Niven was trying to raise himself, holding onto Stark's jacket sleeves. Finally, the evidence establishes that the respondent and Stark fled the scene together. It was clearly reasonable for the jury to conclude that the respondent had, through words and actions which encouraged and assisted Stark, participated in an interrelated chain of events which ultimately led to Niven's death. The respondent does not dispute the reasonableness of this conclusion as is reflected in his submission that he was properly convicted of manslaughter.

Both Boyd J., in her instructions to the jury, and Hall J.A. recognized that intent, namely whether Biniaris intended to cause Niven's death or to cause bodily harm which he knew was likely to cause death and was reckless as to whether death ensued or not, was the "real question to be faced by the jury" (p. 72). However, Hall J.A.'s reasons do not contain a thorough review and re-examination of the evidence as it relates to intent. In light of the respondent's brief involvement in the sudden affray, Hall J.A. opined that the respondent's "intention to assist in a murder [was] unclear" (p. 73). In contrast, Boyd J. thoroughly canvassed all the evidence adduced on the issue of intent in her charge to the jury, including the evidence of Valin and Lehtonen in relation to the number and strength of the kicks and stomps allegedly administered by the respondent, the evidence of these same witnesses regarding the short duration of the attack on Niven and of the respondent's participation therein, the evidence of Dr. Rice which, defence counsel suggested, contradicted Kaven Valin's testimony that the stomps administered by the respondent involved a substantial amount of force, the evidence of Dr. Carlyle that the effects of "lividity" enhanced and emphasized the tread mark patterns and related bruising on Niven's forehead, and the testimony of the arresting officers concerning the respondent's surprised reaction upon being informed that he was being charged with second degree murder.

I agree with Ryan J.A.'s conclusion that "[a]ll of these facts were for the jury to assess" (p. 77). There is nothing in the compendium of accumulated judicial experience that should cause concern that the jury went astray in its review and assessment of the evidence. Even though it might have been reasonable for the jury to conclude otherwise, it was perfectly reasonable for the jury to be satisfied beyond a reasonable doubt that Biniaris had acted with the requisite intent for murder. There was evidence upon which the jury could reasonably find that the respondent had administered one or more kicks to Niven, including the glancing blow to the face; and to accept the Crown's contention that the respondent had "changed gears" when he moved from kicking to stomping and that, in so doing, he "obviously intended deadly harm". In the same way, it was not unreasonable for the jury to conclude that in deciding to stomp, not once but twice, on Niven's head, the respondent's purposive, deliberate and intentional conduct, which involved the repeated use of violence against a defenceless man, established that he intended to cause Niven bodily harm which he must have known was likely to cause death, being reckless as to whether or not death ensued. As indicated earlier, in light of his responsibility as a party, the fact that the specific blows inflicted by the respondent were not the ones which were the immediate cause of death was of no significance.

In overturning the verdict of the jury as unreasonable, Hall J.A. was troubled by the unusual course of the trial, resulting from Dr. Carlyle's abandonment of the opinion upon which the Crown's case had originally been cast. He viewed this as a "dramatic" change in the composition of the Crown's case and was concerned that "the nuances of all this might not have been that easy for a jury to appreciate" (p. 72). Moreover, Hall J.A. considered this case to have been "highly emotional by reason of these outrageous assaults" (p. 73). These concerns, in my respectful opinion, were insufficient to set aside the verdict of the jury as unreasonable. They were more than adequately addressed by the trial judge, whose charge to the jury was instructive and fair.

The determination of the intent or foresight of a person at the time of his participation in a homicide is often a difficult question of fact. It certainly was so in this case where a very young man was involved in a brief, senseless and violent beating which left an innocent man dead. Despite the unusual turn of events at trial, and the fact that many similar incidents in the past have led to convictions for manslaughter only, the law required this jury to answer this difficult question on the facts of this case, and it did. In my view, the verdict was one that this properly instructed jury, acting judicially, could reasonably have rendered, and it should be restored.

VI. Conclusion and Disposition

For these reasons, I would allow the appeal, set aside the judgment of the Court of Appeal and restore the conviction for second degree murder and the sentence imposed by Boyd J.

R. v. MORRISSEY

(1995), 97 C.C.C. (3d) 193 (Ont. C.A.)

[The accused, who was a Christian Brother, was convicted, by a judge sitting without a jury, of indecent assault, assault and related offences alleged to have been committed upon inmates of the St. John's Training School in Uxbridge, Ontario. Multiple grounds of appeal against conviction were advanced. The reproduced aspects of the judgment address the effect of a trial judge's misapprehension as to the evidence.]

The judgment of the court was delivered by

Doherty J.A.: —

.....

In my opinion, the trial judge misapprehended the evidence of B.G. in several respects. In fairness, I should add that the evidence of B.G. was lengthy and even with the assistance of a transcript and of the luxury of time for repeated readings of that evidence, it was not easy to distil the net effect of B.G.'s evidence on some points.

I will now address the effect of the trial judge's misapprehension of the evidence. Submissions premised on an alleged misapprehension of evidence are commonplace in cases tried by a judge sitting without a jury. A misapprehension of the evidence may refer to a failure to consider evidence relevant to a material issue, a mistake as to the substance of the evidence, or a failure to give proper effect to evidence. Where, as in the case of Crown appeals from acquittals (s. 676(1)(*a*) of the *Criminal Code*) and appeals to the Supreme Court of Canada pursuant to s. 691, the court's jurisdiction is predicated on the existence of an error of law alone, characterization of the nature of the error arising out of the misapprehension of evidence becomes crucial. The jurisprudence from the Supreme Court of Canada demonstrates the difficulty in distinguishing between misapprehensions of the evidence which constitute an error of law alone and those which do not: *R. v. Harper* (1982), 65 C.C.C. (2d) 193, 133 D.L.R. (3d) 546, [1982] 1 S.C.R. 2; *R. v. Schuldt* (1985), 23 C.C.C. (3d) 225, 24 D.L.R. (4th) 453, [1985] 2 S.C.R. 592; *R. v.Roman* (1989), 46 C.C.C. (3d) 321, [1989] 1 S.C.R. 230, 73 Nfld. & P.E.I.R. 148; *R. v. B. (G.)* (No. 3) (1990), 56 C.C.C. (3d) 181, [1990] 2 S.C.R. 57, 77 C.R. (3d) 370; *R. v. Morin* (1992), 76 C.C.C. (3d) 193, [1992] 3 S.C.R. 286, 16 C.R. (4th) 291. The recent trend in that court suggests that most errors which fall under the rubric of a misapprehension of evidence will not be regarded as involving a question of law: *R. v. Morin, supra*; J. Sopinka, M.A. Gelowitz, *The Conduct of an Appeal* (Toronto: Butterworths, 1993), pp. 85-9.

The need, for jurisdictional purposes, to classify a misapprehension of the evidence as an error of law, as opposed to an error of fact or mixed fact and law, does not arise in this court where the appeal is from conviction in proceedings by way of indictment. Section 675(1)(*a*) gives this court jurisdiction to consider grounds of appeal which allege any type of error in the trial proceedings. The wide sweep of s. 675(1)(*a*) manifests Parliament's intention to provide virtually unobstructed access to a first level of appellate review to those convicted of indictable offences. (Where the ground of appeal does not allege an error in law, the appellant must receive leave to appeal. In Ontario, at least, leave to appeal poses no bar. All grounds of appeal are considered on their merits in a single hearing.)

The scope of this court's power to quash convictions is commensurate with the broad jurisdiction given to it by s. 676(1)(*a*). Section 686(1)(*a*)provides that:

> 686(1) On the hearing of an appeal against a conviction or against a verdict that the appellant is unfit to stand trial or not criminally responsible on account of mental disorder, the court of appeal
>
> (*a*) may allow the appeal where it is of the opinion that
>
> (i) the verdict should be set aside on the ground that it is unreasonable or cannot be supported by the evidence,
> (ii) the judgment of the trial court should be set aside on the ground of a wrong decision on a question of law, or
> (iii) on any ground there was a miscarriage of justice;

The powers granted in that section are qualified to some extent by s. 686(1)(*b*)(iii) and (iv). For present purposes I need reproduce only s. 686(1)(*b*)(iii):

> 686(1)(*b*) [the Court of Appeal] may dismiss the appeal where
>
> .....
>
> (iii) notwithstanding that the court is of the opinion that on any ground mentioned in subparagraph (*a*)(ii) the appeal might be decided in favour of the appellant, it is of the opinion that no substantial wrong or miscarriage of justice has occurred...

While s. 686(1)(*a*) provides three distinct bases upon which this court may quash a conviction, each shares the same underlying rationale. A conviction which is the product of a miscarriage of justice cannot stand. Section 686(1)(*a*)(i) is concerned with the most obvious example of a miscarriage of justice, a conviction which no reasonable trier of fact properly instructed could have returned on the evidence adduced at trial. Section 686(1)(*a*)(ii) read along with s. 686(1)(*b*)(iii) presumes that an error in law produces a miscarriage of justice unless the Crown can demonstrate the contrary with the requisite degree of certainty. Section 686(1)(*a*)(iii) addresses all other miscarriages of justice not caught by the two preceding subsections. In so far as the operation of s. 686(1)(*a*) is concerned, the distinction between errors of law and all other types of error has only one significance. Where the error is one of law, the Crown bears the burden of demonstrating that the error did not result in a miscarriage of justice. Where the error is not one of law alone, the appellant bears that burden.

In my opinion, on appeals from convictions in indictable proceedings where misapprehension of the evidence is alleged, this court should first consider the reasonableness of the verdict (s. 686(1)(*a*)(i)). If the appellant succeeds on this ground an acquittal will be entered. If the verdict is not unreasonable, then the court should determine whether the misapprehension of evidence occasioned a miscarriage of justice (s. 686(1)(*a*)(iii)). If the appellant is able to show that the error resulted in a miscarriage of justice, then the conviction must be quashed and, in most cases, a new trial ordered. Finally, if the appellant cannot show that the verdict was unreasonable or that the error produced a miscarriage of justice, the court must consider the vexing question of whether the misapprehension of evidence amounted to an error in law (s. 686(1)(*a*)(ii)). If the error is one of law, the onus will shift to the Crown to demonstrate that it did not result in a miscarriage of justice (s. 686(1)(*b*)(iii)).

In considering the reasonableness of the verdict pursuant to s. 686(1)(*a*)(i), this court must conduct its own, albeit limited, review of the evidence adduced at trial: *R. v. Burns,* [(1994), 89 C.C.C. (3d) 193 (S.C.C.)] at pp. 198-9. This court's authority to declare a conviction unreasonable or unsupported by the evidence does not depend upon the demonstration of any errors in the proceedings below. The verdict is the error where s. 686(1)(*a*)(i) is properly invoked. A misapprehension of the evidence does not render a verdict unreasonable. Nor is a finding that the judge misapprehended the evidence a condition precedent to a finding that a verdict is unreasonable. In cases tried without juries, a finding that the trial judge did misapprehend the evidence can, however, figure prominently in an argument that the resulting verdict was unreasonable. An appellant will be in a much better position to demonstrate the unreasonableness of a verdict if the appellant can demonstrate that the trial judge misapprehended significant evidence: *R. v. Burns, supra,* at p. 200.

I need not pursue the relationship between a misapprehension of the evidence and an unreasonable verdict any further. On the evidence adduced in this case and bearing in mind the errors made by the trial judge in his appreciation of that evidence, I cannot say that the convictions of counts 1, 2, 3, and 6 were unreasonable.

I turn next to s. 686(1)(*a*)(iii). This subsection is not concerned with the characterization of an error as one of law, fact, mixed fact and law or something else, but rather with the impact of the error on the trial proceedings. It reaches all errors resulting in a miscarriage of justice and vindicates the wide jurisdiction vested in this court by s. 675(1). The long reach of s. 686(1)(*a*)(iii) was described by McIntyre J., for a unanimous court, in *R. v. Fanjoy* (1985), 21 C.C.C. (3d) 312 at pp. 317-18, 21 D.L.R. (4th) 321, [1985] 2 S.C.R. 233: "A person charged with the commission of a crime is entitled to a fair trial according to law. Any error which occurs at trial that deprives the accused of that entitlement is a miscarriage of justice."

Fanjoy, like most cases where s. 686(1)(*a*)(iii) has been invoked, involved prosecutorial or judicial misconduct in the course of the trial: *e.g.*, see it *R. v. Stewart* (1991), 62 C.C.C. (3d) 289, 43 O.A.C. 109, 12 W.C.B. (2d) 20 (C.A.); *R. v. R. (A.J.)* (1994), 94 C.C.C. (3d) 168, 20 O.R. (3d) 405, 74 O.A.C. 363 (C.A.). Such conduct obviously jeopardizes the fairness of a trial and fits comfortably within the concept of a miscarriage of justice. Nothing in the language of the section, however, suggests that it is limited to any particular type of error. In my view, any error, including one involving a misapprehension of the evidence by the trial judge must be assessed by reference to its impact on the fairness of the trial. If the error renders the trial unfair, then s. 686(1)(*a*)(iii) requires that the conviction be quashed.

When will a misapprehension of the evidence render a trial unfair and result in a miscarriage of justice? The nature and extent of the misapprehension and its significance to the trial judge's verdict must be considered in light of the fundamental requirement that a verdict must be based exclusively on the evidence adduced at trial. Where a trial judge is mistaken as to the substance of material parts of the evidence and those errors play an essential part in the reasoning process resulting in a conviction, then, in my view, the accused's conviction is not based exclusively on the evidence and is not a "true" verdict.Convictions resting on a misapprehension of the substance of the evidence adduced at trial sit on no firmer foundation than those based on information derived from sources extraneous to the trial. If an appellant can demonstrate that the conviction depends on a misapprehension of the evidence then, in my view, it must follow that the appellant has not received a fair trial, and was the victim of a miscarriage of justice. This is so even if the evidence, as actually adduced at trial, was capable of supporting a conviction.

I am satisfied that the trial judge's errors with respect to the content of the evidence of B.G. were significant and resulted in a miscarriage of justice. The trial judge treated the evidence of F.P. and B.G. as if it was consistent on all significant points relating to the events surrounding the assaults except for the year in which those assaults actually occurred. In fact, as indicated above, there were other inconsistencies between the evidence of the two complainants which went unnoticed by the trial judge as a result of his misapprehension of the substance of the evidence. Similarly, the trial judge regarded the complainants' evidence concerning their initial complaint about the appellant as consistent save for minor details such as the exact familial relationship between B.G. and the person first complained to by him. Here too, the trial judge's misapprehension of the content of the evidence obscured numerous differences in the versions of events described by the two complainants. The cumulative effect of these errors was significant in that it infected the very core of the reasoning process which culminated in the conviction of the appellant on the four counts involving F.P. and B.G. Without the finding of mutual confirmation, the trial judge may not have found either F.P. or B.G. to be credible and their evidence to be reliable. Those findings were essential to the verdicts rendered by the trial judge.

The observation of Laycraft J.A. in *Whitehouse v. Reimer* (1980), 116 D.L.R. (3d) 594, 14 Alta. L.R. (2d) 380, 34 A.R. 414 (C.A.), has application here. In that case, the trial judge was faced with two conflicting versions of the relevant event. He found in favour of the plaintiff but in doing so misstated the evidence on three significant factual issues. In ordering a new trial, Laycraft J.A., speaking for a unanimous court, said at p. 595:

> Where a principal issue on a trial is credibility of witnesses to the extent that the evidence of one party is accepted to the virtual exclusion of the evidence of the other, it is essential that the findings be based on a correct version of the actual evidence. Wrong findings on what the evidence is destroy the basis of findings of credibility.

The appellant has demonstrated significant errors in the trial judge's understanding of the substance of the evidence. He has further demonstrated that those errors figured prominently in the reasoning process which led to crucial findings of credibility and reliability, and then to crucial findings of fact. In these circumstances, the appellant has met the onus of showing that the convictions on the counts relating to F.P. and B.G. constitute a miscarriage of justice. Those convictions must be quashed and a new trial ordered.

As I have concluded that the misapprehension of the evidence by the trial judge produced a miscarriage of justice, it is not necessary for me to decide whether that error constituted an error in law. I will, however, address that issue. In my opinion, the trial judge's mistaken apprehension of the content of the evidence of a witness cannot be classified as an error in law. There is no suggestion that he did not consider all of the relevant evidence (*R. v. Harper, supra*) or that he misdirected himself on the applicable law and thereby misapprehended the evidence (*R. v. B. (G.), supra*). The trial judge addressed his mind to all of the evidence and as revealed by his reasons for judgment, was simply mistaken as to what was said by B.G. in his evidence. That error was made in his fact-finding capacity and is not, in my view, an error in law: *Telmosse v. The King, supra*, at pp. 138-9.

.....

III

CONCLUSION WITH RESPECT TO THE CONVICTION APPEAL

The convictions on counts 1, 2, 3, and 6 must be quashed and a new trial ordered. Neither the trial judge's mistakes as to the content of some of the evidence, nor his resort to speculative conclusions had any impact on the conviction on count 7. The appeal from that conviction should be dismissed.

R. v. M.(C.A.)

(1996), 105 C.C.C. (3d) 327 (S.C.C.)

[The accused was sentenced to a total of 25 years imprisonment on guilty pleas to a number of serious offences. The Supreme Court determined that there was no predetermined ceiling on a fixed-term sentence which could be imposed under the *Criminal Code*. The court also addressed appellate jurisdiction in considering the "fitness" of the sentence imposed.]

The judgment of the court was delivered by

Lamer C.J.C.: —

.....

In addition to relying on the sentencing principles it had developed in *Rooke* [(1990), 9 W.C.B. (2d) 608 (B.C.C.A.)] and *D. (G.W.)*, [(1990), 9 W.C.B. (2d) 557 (B.C.C.A.)] the Court of Appeal also justified its reduction of the respondent's sentence on the grounds of fitness. More specifically, the Court of Appeal concluded that the sentence of 25 years imposed by the sentencing judge ought to be reduced as it was "unfit" under the circumstances. Accordingly, the Court of Appeal exercised its power of review under s. 687(1) of the *Code* to vary the sentence of the respondent from 25 years to 18 and eight months, incorporating credit for time served in custody.

In *Shropshire* [(1995), 102 C.C.C. (3d) 193 (S.C.C.)], this court recently articulated the appropriate standard of review that a court of appeal should adopt in reviewing the fitness of sentence under s. 687(1). In the context of reviewing the fitness of an order of parole ineligibility, Iacobucci J. described the standard of review as follows, at para. 46:

> An appellate court should not be given free reign to modify a sentencing order simply because it feels that a different order ought to have been made. The formulation of a sentencing order is a profoundly subjective process; the trial judge has the advantage of having seen and heard all of the witnesses whereas the appellate court can only base itself upon a written record. A variation in the sentence should only be made if the court of appeal is convinced it is not fit. *That is to say, that it has found the sentence to be clearly unreasonable*.

(Emphasis added.) As my learned colleague noted, this standard of review traces part of its lineage to the jurisprudence of the British Columbia Court of Appeal. As Bull J.A. described the nature of a trial judge's sentencing discretion in *R. v. Gourgon* (1981), 58 C.C.C. (2d) 193 at p. 197, 21 C.R. (3d) 384:

> ... the matter is clearly one of discretion and unless patently wrong, or wrong principles applied, or correct principles applied erroneously, or proper factors ignored or overstressed, an appellate Court should be careful not to interfere with the exercise of that discretion of a trial Judge.

Put simply, absent an error in principle, failure to consider a relevant factor, or an overemphasis of the appropriate factors, a court of appeal should only intervene to vary a sentence imposed at trial if the sentence is demonstrably unfit. Parliament explicitly vested sentencing judges with a *discretion* to determine the appropriate degree and kind of punishment under the *Criminal Code*. As s. 717(1)[now s. 718.3(1)] reads:

> 717(1) Where an enactment prescribes different degrees or kinds of punishment in respect of an offence, the punishment to be imposed is, subject to the limitations prescribed in the enactment, in the *discretion* of the court that convicts the person who commits the offence.

(Emphasis added.)

This deferential standard of review has profound functional justifications. As Iacobucci J. explained in *Shropshire,* at para. 46, where the sentencing judge has had the benefit of presiding over the trial of the offender, he or she will have had the comparative advantage of having seen and heard the witnesses to the crime. But in the absence of a full trial, where the offender has pleaded guilty to an offence and the sentencing judge has only enjoyed the benefit of oral and written sentencing submissions (as was the case in both Shropshire and this instance), the argument in favour of deference remains compelling. A sentencing judge still enjoys a position of advantage over an appellate judge in being able to directly assess the sentencing submissions of both the Crown and the offender. A sentencing judge also possesses the unique qualifications of experience and judgment from having served on the front lines of our criminal justice system. Perhaps most importantly, the sentencing judge will normally preside near or within the community which has suffered the consequences of the offender's crime. As such, the sentencing judge will have a strong sense of the particular blend of sentencing goals that will be "just and appropriate" for the protection of that community. The determination of a just and appropriate sentence is a delicate art which attempts to balance carefully the societal goals of sentencing against the moral blameworthiness of the offender and the circumstances of the offence, while at all times taking into account the needs and current conditions of and in the community. The discretion of a sentencing judge should thus not be interfered with lightly.

Appellate courts, of course, serve an important function in reviewing and minimizing the disparity of sentences imposed by sentencing judges for similar offenders and similar offences committed throughout Canada: see, *e.g.*, *R. v. Knife* (1982), 16 Sask. R. 40 (C.A.) at p. 43; *R. v. Wood* (1979), 21 C.L.Q. 423 (Ont. C.A.) at p. 424; *R. v. Mellstrom* (1975), 22 C.C.C. (2d) 472 at p. 485, 29 C.R.N.S. 327, [1975] 3 W.W.R. 385 (Alta. C.A.); *R. v. Morrissette* (1970), 1 C.C.C. (2d) 307 at pp. 311-12, 12 C.R.N.S. 392, 75 W.W.R. 644 (Sask. C.A.); *R. v. Baldhead*, [1966] 4 C.C.C. 183 at p. 187, 48 C.R. 228, 55 W.W.R. 757 (Sask. C.A.). But in exercising this role, courts of appeal must still exercise a margin of deference before intervening in the specialized discretion that Parliament has explicitly vested in sentencing judges. It has been repeatedly stressed that there is no such thing as a uniform sentence for a particular crime: see *Mellstrom, Morrissette* and *Baldhead.* Sentencing is an inherently individualized process, and the search for a single appropriate sentence for a similar offender and a similar crime will frequently be a fruitless exercise of academic abstraction. As well, sentences for a particular offence should be expected to vary to some degree across various communities and regions in this country, as the "just and appropriate" mix of accepted sentencing goals will depend on the needs and current conditions of and in the particular community where the crime occurred. For these reasons, consistent with the general standard of review we articulated in *Shropshire*, I believe that a court of appeal should only intervene to minimize the disparity of sentences where the sentence imposed by the trial judge is in substantial and marked departure from the sentences customarily imposed for similar offenders committing similar crimes.

In the case at hand, the majority of the Court of Appeal reduced the sentence of the respondent primarily as a result of the framework of sentencing principles the court inherited from the previous cases of *Rooke* and *D. (G.W.), supra.* As I have argued previously, I believe that this framework was incorrect in law. But the Court of Appeal also justified its reduction of sentence with reference to a contextual application of the accepted principles of sentencing to this case. More specifically, the majority concluded that the goals of deterrence and denunciation do not support a sentence of 25 years in this case, because both of these sentencing goals experience sharply diminishing returns following 20 years. On the subject of deterrence, Wood J.A. pointed to the empirical studies he outlined in his concurring judgment in Sweeney, *supra*, which question the deterrent effect of criminal sanctions. The majority also concluded that the protection of society would not be advanced by such a sentence; as Wood J.A. argued, as a result of the parole eligibility rules, an increase of sentence of five years to 25 years is potentially limited to an additional four months of imprisonment.

With the greatest respect, I believe the Court of Appeal erred in this instance by engaging in an overly interventionist mode of appellate review of the "fitness" of sentence which transcended the standard of deference we articulated in *Shropshire*. Notwithstanding the existence of some empirical studies which question the *general* deterrent effect of sentencing, it was open for the sentencing judge to reasonably conclude that the particular blend of sentencing goals, ranging from specific *and* general deterrence, denunciation and rehabilitation to the protection of society, required a sentence of 25 years *in this instance*. Moreover, on the facts, the sentencing judge was entitled to find that an overall term of imprisonment of 25 years represented a "just sanction" for the crimes of the respondent.

[The original sentence imposed was restored.]

QUESTIONS

5. The accused's conviction, after a jury trial, for impaired driving causing bodily harm is set aside on appeal. The jury had also found the accused guilty of driving over 80 (which was on the same indictment and respecting which the Crown elected to proceed by indictment). The trial judge conditionally stayed that charge, applying the *Kienapple* principle. Why did the trial judge impose a conditional stay and what happens to that charge on appeal?

6. The accused was acquitted of assault causing bodily harm by a judge sitting without a jury. The judge found that the accused, without justification, intentionally assaulted the victim, causing bodily harm which anyone could foresee. However, he found that the accused did not intend to cause the bodily harm inflicted and accordingly acquitted. The court of appeal held that an intention to cause bodily harm is not an element of the offence charged. What order(s) should the court now make? Would your answer be the same or different if the judge had erroneously instructed a jury as to the elements of the offence charged? Consider, in this regard, s. 686(4)(*b*) of the *Criminal Code*. Now assume that the court of appeal ordered a new trial in the first mentioned scenario. Can the accused now be tried before a judge and jury? Alternatively, can the accused be tried by the same judge sitting without a jury? Consider, in this regard, s. 686(5)(*a*) and (5.1) of the *Criminal Code*.

7. The accused was convicted of sexual assault and was sentenced to 18 months imprisonment. His conviction appeal was allowed and a new trial was ordered. He was again convicted. The new trial judge thinks the offence warrants a sentence of two years less a day. (The accused served only a few days' imprisonment between the first conviction and bail pending appeal.) Consider, in this regard, *R. v. W.(R.S.)* (1992), 74 C.C.C. (3d) 1 (Man. C.A.).

B. SUMMARY CONVICTION APPEALS

1. RIGHTS OF APPEAL

Summary conviction appeals are governed by Part XXVII, ss. 812 to 839 of the *Criminal Code*. Such appeals are brought in Ontario before a single judge of the Superior Court of Justice, sitting in the region, district

or county, or group of counties where the adjudication was made. In Quebec, appeals are brought before a single judge of the Superior Court. In Nova Scotia, British Columbia, Prince Edward Island, Newfoundland, Yukon and Northwest Territories, they are brought before a single judge of the Supreme Court (also referred to in some of those jurisdictions as a judge of the Trial Division of the Supreme Court), and in New Brunswick, Manitoba, Saskatchewan and Alberta, before a single judge of the Court of Queen's Bench (s. 812 of the *Criminal Code*). See also s. 814, which addresses the location of the sittings for the western provinces and territories.

A defendant may appeal from a conviction or order made against him or her, or against a sentence passed on him or her, or against a verdict of unfit to stand trial or not criminally responsible on account of mental disorder. There is no restriction upon the grounds which may be raised and no leave is required for any grounds advanced (s. 813(*a*)). The Crown may appeal from an order staying proceedings on an information or dismissing an information, or against a sentence passed on a defendant, or against a verdict of not criminally responsible on account of mental disorder or unfit to stand trial. Again, there is no restriction upon the grounds which may be raised and no leave is required for any grounds advanced (s. 813(*b*)).

The following case addresses the scope of appellate review from an acquittal.

R. v. BURTON

(1993), 16 O.R. (3d) 660 (C.A.)

The judgment of the court was delivered orally by

Finlayson J.A.: — The appellant was tried and acquitted before His Honour Judge Maurice Charles of two counts of possession of a narcotic. On appeal to the summary conviction appeal court, the acquittals were set aside and a new trial ordered. The appellant applies for leave to appeal and appeals to this court.

The facts, very briefly, were that the appellant entered the Waverley Hotel in Toronto. There he made contact with a person who was known to the police as a drug dealer and was, at the time, subject to police surveillance. The appellant left the hotel and drove to a retail plaza some distance away where he parked his car. He injected himself with a hypodermic needle and then left his car momentarily. While he was away from the vehicle, it was approached and inspected by Detective Tymburski. Having observed evidence of narcotics, Tymburski notified other police officers by radio.

Tymburski and two other police officers arrested the appellant after he had returned to his car and had fastened his seat-belt. In the course of making the arrest, Detective Braund fired his revolver. The bullet entered the car, ricocheted off the interior and exited through the front window. The appellant was taken from the vehicle, his hands were cuffed behind his back, and he was subjected to a public body search, in the view of some 25 to 30 persons. The appellant was not wearing undergarments and his genitalia were exposed to public view.

It was conceded at trial that the police officers had reasonable and probable cause for effecting a warrantless search and seizure. There were only two issues. First, was the search and seizure effected in violation of s. 8 of the *Canadian Charter of Rights and Freedoms* (the "*Charter*")? Second, would the admission of the evidence obtained therefrom bring the administration of justice into disrepute? In finding for the appellant, the trial judge stated:

> I therefore hold that in this case, although the search and seizure could be justified under s. 10 of the *Narcotic Control Act*, R.S.C. 1985, c. N-1, the manner of the search was unreasonable because of the excessive use of force that was used when that gun was fired unnecessarily and the way in which the accused was also searched in the presence of the public when there was no emergency at the time for such a search. In the circumstances, I rule that under s. 24(2) of the *Charter*, as there has been a blatant breach of the right of the accused, the admission of this evidence which was obtained as a result of this unreasonable search and seizure would bring the administration of justice into disrepute and I therefore exclude the evidence. Consequently the accused is found not guilty and the charges are dismissed.

Earlier in his reasons, the trial judge engaged in a full review of the evidence surrounding the firing of the revolver by Braund and concluded that his use of the gun was contrary to police regulations and unjustified. He was also critical of the evidence of Braund and specifically rejected his justification for the use of the firearm. Braund had said that he fired his revolver because he thought the appellant was pointing a gun at him. What was at first thought to be a gun, said Braund, turned out to be a pop can. The trial judge rejected this explanation and held that the appellant never picked up a pop can and pointed it at Braund. As to the testimony of Braund, he stated that:

> I find that this empty pop can was introduced into this case to extricate Detective Braund from the difficulties in which he found himself.

As to the manner of the body search of the appellant, the trial judge summarized the evidence of Tymburski as follows:

> Detective Tymburski said he searched the accused, put his hands in his pockets to get the things which he had in his pockets, removed them, then lifted up the sweater he was wearing to see whether he had any drugs or any weapons and then unzipped or unbuttoned his pants in the presence of members of the public, pulled them down and looked into his pants to see whether he had any weapons or drugs.

On appeal, the summary conviction appeal court judge was restricted to reading the transcript of the proceedings below. She held that the trial judge had made "a number of findings of fact that are not supported by the evidence". The only examples she cited, however, were inconsequential to the trial judge's ruling on the admissibility of the fruits of the search and seizure and on the consequent acquittal. She held that there was no evidence that the appellant was held by *two* police officers, as opposed to one, when Braund discharged his revolver. She held that Tymburski had grabbed the appellant by the face, not by the throat and head. She also held that there was no evidence to support the finding that Tymburski had "unzipped or unbuttoned [the appellant's] pants, in the presence of members of the public, pulled them down and looked into his pants to see if he had any weapons or drugs". Tymburski testified in-chief that he "undid the front of [the appellant's] pants and opened them up so I could look down inside of his pants to see if there was anything inside his pants".

With great respect to the summary conviction appeal court judge, these reasons were not sufficient to justify setting aside the acquittal of the accused. On the facts of this appeal, the learned judge was obliged to do more than raise her limited concerns about the trial judge's findings of fact; her decision to set aside the acquittal would only have been justified if she was prepared to find that the trial judge's findings of fact were unsupported to the point that what remained rendered unsustainable his opinion that the discharge of the revolver was unjustified and that the public search of the appellant was unnecessary. Her criticisms of the trial judge's findings are of no legal effect unless she is prepared to set aside these conclusions on the appropriateness of the police conduct in effecting the search and seizure. She must, in other words, find a significant error: *R. v. Kirkness*, [1990] 3 S.C.R. 74 at p. 83, 60 C.C.C. (3d) 97. In my view it must be an error of a magnitude which warrants setting aside an acquittal.

After ruling that there must be a new trial, the learned judge on appeal stated that:

> It is clearly the law that s. 24(2) of the *Charter* is not to be used to punish the police and I conclude that in the circumstances of this case, even if the action of Sgt. Braund requires a finding that the search is unreasonable and a breach of s. 8 (and I am not saying that is the necessary result, but I leave that to the trial judge), it does not mean that the evidence should not be admitted.

With respect, the judge on appeal is not entitled to reverse the trial judge's acquittal of the appellant based upon such a superficial analysis of the facts and the law. The judgment under appeal was fact specific. Unless she was in a position to set aside the trial judge's findings of fact on the two pivotal issues, the justification for the firing of the gun and the reasonableness of the body search, she was not entitled to send the matter back for a second trial. In particular, she was not entitled to do so with the advice that the new trial judge could take a different view of the admissibility of the evidence, even accepting the unreasonableness of the search based on Braund's conduct, as if this was the only basis for the trial judge holding to the contrary. Leaving aside the body search, the discharge of the firearm was but part of the problem with Braund's behaviour. His testimony in explication of his conduct was a concoction and was properly rejected by the trial judge. The trial judge was entitled to consider the conduct of all of the officers at the arrest and thereafter. This included the manner of their testimony before him when reflecting upon the public's perception of their conduct. This he did in a full and thorough judgment.

There is a very heavy onus on the Crown in seeking to set aside a verdict of acquittal: see *R. v. Evans*, [1993] 2 S.C.R. 629 at pp. 645-47, 21 C.R. (4th) 321 at pp. 332-34. The Crown did not meet this onus before the summary conviction appeal court; it effectively asked the appeal court judge to substitute her opinion for that of the trial judge. Yet on this set of facts the trial judge was fully justified in deciding as he did.

Accordingly, I would grant leave to appeal, allow the appeal, and restore the acquittals of the appellant below.

Appeal allowed.

The *Criminal Code* also provides for two other kinds of summary conviction appeals: appeals confined to jurisdictional issues or pure questions of law (s. 830), which are rarely employed, since the grounds which can be advanced are narrowly drawn, and appeals by way of trial *de novo* (s. 822(4)) where, by reason of the condition of the trial record or for any other reason, the court is of the opinion that the interests of justice would be better served by hearing and determining the appeal by holding a new trial in the appeal court (rather than by an appeal based upon the transcript of the original trial). Trials *de novo* are not frequently granted.

An appeal to the court of appeal may be taken, "with leave of that court or a judge thereof, ... on any ground that involves a question of law alone" (s. 839). So, for example, the fitness of a sentence imposed is not a question of law which permits a further appeal to the court of appeal, though a misdirection on a question of law relating to sentence or the imposition of an illegal sentence does raise questions of law permitting the court of appeal to review sentence (*R. v. Culley* (1977), 36 C.C.C. (2d) 433 (Ont. C.A.); *R. v. Loughery* (1992), 73 C.C.C. (3d) 411 (Alta. C.A.); *R. v. Thomas* (*No. 2*) (1980), 53 C.C.C. (2d) 285 (B.C.C.A.); *R. v. Guida* (1989), 51 C.C.C. (3d) 305 (Que. C.A.)).

The *Criminal Code* does not provide for summary conviction appeals to the Supreme Court of Canada. However, s. 40(1) of the *Supreme Court Act*, R.S.C. 1985, c. S-26, does permit such appeals, with leave of the court, on questions of law.

2. Procedures on Appeal

Like indictable appeals, s. 482 of the *Criminal Code* contemplates that the court will make procedural rules governing summary conviction appeals. Indeed, various courts have done so. It is beyond the scope of this casebook to further articulate the rules which govern these appeals. However, many of these rules draw, by analogy, upon the procedures established for indictable appeals. Further, Part XXVII of the *Criminal Code* adopts, by reference, certain *Criminal Code* sections applicable to indictable appeals (see, for example, s. 822(1)). Bail pending appeal is provided for in s. 816 of the *Criminal Code*. See also Rules 40 and 42 of the Ontario Court of Justice Criminal Proceedings Rules, SI/92-99.

QUESTION

8. **The accused was convicted at trial of impaired driving. It was a first offence. The provincial Highway Traffic Act provides for a mandatory licence suspension of one year. The judge sentenced the accused to a $500 fine and six months' probation, during which he must perform 150 hours of community service work. As well, he prohibited the accused from driving anywhere in Canada for a period of three months, pursuant to s. 259**

of the *Criminal Code*. The accused wishes to appeal conviction and sentence since, at trial, he was primarily motivated to plead not guilty to avoid the loss of his ability to drive. Can he obtain a stay of the driving prohibition pending appeal? What should he do about the provincially imposed licence suspension? Can he obtain a stay of the probation order pending appeal? Consider, in this regard, ss. 261, 683(5) and 822(1) of the *Criminal Code*. Can the judge who hears the application to stay the driving prohibition order that the accused be allowed to drive only for the purposes of employment?

C. EXTRAORDINARY REMEDIES

The remedies of *certiorari*, *mandamus*, *habeas corpus*, prohibition and *procedendo* are governed by Part XXVI of the *Criminal Code* and the applicable rules of the court. The use of extraordinary remedies to attack jurisdictional error at the preliminary inquiry was addressed in Chapter 7.

QUESTIONS

9. Prior to the *Charter*, applications were more frequently brought by way of *certiorari* to quash a search warrant. This application can still be brought prior to trial, as can an application pursuant to s. 24(1) of the *Charter* for the return of any items seized. Why are these applications rarely brought?

10. Multiple accused, former members of a religious order, are charged with sexual and physical abuse of children in an orphanage they operated. Prior to trial, a dramatic program is about to be televised which provides a "fictional" account of the sexual and physical abuse of children in an orphanage by members of a religious order. On the application of the accused, the trial judge issues an order preventing the broadcast of the program anywhere in Canada. Can the publication ban be lifted upon the application of the aggrieved television network? To which court would such an application be brought? Consider, in this regard, *Dagenais v. Canadian Broadcasting Corp.* (1994), 94 C.C.C. (3d) 289 (S.C.C.).

INDEX

A

E

J

W